Douglas Cobb's
Paradox 3 Handbook
Second Edition

Douglas Cobb's
Paradox 3 Handbook
Second Edition

Douglas Cobb

with

Jeff Yocom
Brian J. Smith

and

Steven Cobb
Ken Richardson
Rosemary Harding

BANTAM BOOKS
NEW YORK · TORONTO · LONDON · SYDNEY · AUCKLAND

Douglas Cobb's Paradox 3 Handbook, Second Edition

A Bantam Book / April, 1989

Production by Beth Riggle, Maureen Pawley, and Tara Billinger
Editing by Linda Baughman and Jody Gilbert

ISBN 0-553-34699-7

Published simultaneously in the United States and Canada

Bantam Books are published by Bantam Books, a division of
Bantam Doubleday Dell Publishing Group, Inc. Its trademark,
consisting of the words "Bantam Books" and the portrayal of
a rooster, is Registered in U.S. Patent and Trademark Office
and in other countries. Marca Registrada, Bantam Books,
666 Fifth Avenue, New York, New York 10103

PRINTED IN THE UNITED STATES OF AMERICA

BH 098765432

Table of Contents

Dedication

To my mother, Ann Ford Cobb, who is always there–DFC

To the memory of my father, Arthur Daniel Yocom–JPY

To my wife, Cynthia–BJS

Acknowledgments

The authors wish to thank the following people, without whom this book would not have been possible: Tom Cottingham, for putting the deal together; Beth Riggle, Maureen Pawley, Tara Billinger, Linda Baughman, Jody Gilbert, Toni Bowers, Linda Watkins, and Clyde Zellers, for making it happen; Ben Rosen, for making the introductions; Steve Dow, Kris Olsen, Richard Schwartz, Robert Shostak, and Ken Einstein, for their help; Sam Moeller and Alan Zenreich, for their tips and offers of help; Russ Claybrook, for presenting us with some interesting questions.

Finally, to the rest of The Cobb Group—Doug Been, Julia Bennett, Grand Britt, Gena Cobb, Teresa Codey, Mark Crane, Rose Fairfax, Donald Fields, Luanne Flynn, Patty Flynn, Laura Heuser, Lori Houston, Lori Junkins, Tim Landgrave, Kathleen Lane, Becky Ledford, Allan McGuffey, Lisa Miller, Tracy Milliner, Elayne Noltemeyer, Joe Pierce, Jonathan Pyles, Raven Sexton, Patricia Shields, Julie Tirpak, Margaret Walz, Jeff Warner, Barbara Wells, Teri Whitelaw, Kellie Woods, and Peggy Zeillmann—thanks for sharing the experience.

Preface

Paradox is great software—perhaps the best database program ever to be introduced for a personal computer. From the first time we saw Paradox in the summer of 1985, we knew that it was going to be popular. We also knew that it was a product we wanted to write about.

Paradox is great because it brings together so many characteristics that have never before been found in one database manager. Like the old standards, dBASE II and dBASE III, Paradox is a robust database manager that can handle most any data management task. Paradox offers a full-featured applications language (the Paradox Applications Language) that allows you to write complex programs that tie together your table systems.

Like Lotus 1-2-3—and unlike any power database we know of—Paradox is visual, intuitive software. In Paradox, your data is displayed in a simple, understandable row-and-column format. When you're working with a table, for instance, your data is organized on the screen in either a table or a form. These characteristics help make Paradox extremely easy to learn and use—much more so than old-fashioned, nonvisual programs, such as dBASE.

Paradox 1 offered several data management capabilities before any other popular program. Paradox's table-querying system, query by example, made the process of asking questions of your data simpler than it had been in any other program. Instead of *telling* Paradox which data you want it to select, you *show* it which data to choose by defining intuitive examples.

With Release 2, Paradox became the first no-compromise multi-user database for networked personal computers. There is almost no difference between single-user and multi-user Paradox functions and commands. Two or more users on a network can view and update the same table at the same time. Paradox controls the interaction between users and will update each user's screen as changes are made.

Paradox 3 substantially improved the tools you use to enter, interpret, and present the data in your Paradox tables. With Release 3, you can easily enter data into two or more tables at the same time, or print a report based on information from several tables. Also, the enhanced query system can help you identify trends and relationships in your data that Releases 1 and 2 could not recognize.

Learning Paradox

The name *Paradox* is very appropriate for this program. While it is easy to learn, it is also very sophisticated and powerful. Although many users will be able to get started with Paradox with little or no help, the program is so extensive that you could use it for years without learning everything there is to know about it.

If you are like most Paradox users, you'll master the program in stages. First, you'll learn to create tables and enter and edit data. Then, you'll design basic queries and create simple forms and reports. Next, you'll discover how to write simple scripts and become more adventuresome in your use of queries. Once you reach that point, you'll be an accomplished Paradox user—but you will still have a great deal more to learn. For as long as you work with Paradox, you'll continue to learn new things about the program.

As you begin working with Paradox, don't start with complex queries and scripts. Take the time to comprehend the Paradox basics before you move on to more complex topics. That way, when you get to more difficult material, you will have a solid foundation of knowledge. Similarly, when you approach the more advanced topics, start simple and build up. Before long, you'll find yourself creating complex multitable queries and sophisticated PAL programs.

About This Book

We've written *Douglas Cobb's Paradox 3 Handbook* to help you learn Paradox in stages. This book is divided into 17 chapters, which are grouped into four sections: "Paradox Basics," "Using Paradox," "Presenting Data," and "PAL." In addition, the five appendices discuss some of Paradox's more advanced or specialized features, which may be of interest only to certain readers. We've attempted to present the various Paradox concepts in a logical order. Because so many of these interrelate, however, there are places where we present one concept while explaining another. If you come across a concept that isn't familiar, you can use the index to find out more about it in another part of the book.

Chapter 1, "Getting Started," covers several fundamental concepts. For instance, you'll learn how to load Paradox and configure it for your computer system. You'll also see how Paradox uses the computer's keyboard and screen. In addition, you'll learn terms that have special importance to Paradox and learn to make selections from menus and lists.

In Chapter 2, "Creating and Viewing Tables," you'll create data and enter it into Paradox tables. We also show you how to change the entries in a table and how to bring one or more tables into view on your screen. We explain more about data entry and editing in Chapter 3. This chapter teaches you how to adjust the appearance of your table images with the Image command, and how to protect your tables with validity checks. In addition, you'll learn to create and use keyed tables.

In Chapter 4, "Forms," you'll learn to use forms to view, edit, and enter data into your Paradox tables. This chapter begins with a discussion of the default form, then explains how to create and use custom forms. You'll also see how to design multitable forms, which let you enter data into several tables at the same time.

In Chapter 5, "Managing Tables," we show you how to use the commands on the Tools menu to copy, erase, empty, and rename tables and their associated forms and reports. This chapter also explains the [Menu] Modify Restructure command, which lets you change the structure of existing tables.

In Chapter 6, "Sorting Your Tables," you'll learn to sort your Paradox tables. This chapter explains how to define a sort form and execute a sort.

Chapter 7, "Queries," shows you how to create and use queries. For instance, you'll learn about the [Menu] Ask command, which allows you to create query forms. Moreover, we'll teach you to select fields, define selection conditions, and use special query operators like find, delete, and changeto. Chapter 8, "Query by Example," introduces the concept of examples. Among other things, you'll discover how to use examples to link two tables in a query and make complex calculations. You'll also learn how to use the powerful calc operator and compare one group of records to a defined set of records in a table.

Chapter 9, "Multitable Operations," covers several commands that affect more than one table. In this chapter, we explain the [Menu] Tools More Add and [Menu] Tools More Subtract commands, which let you combine tables with identical structures. You'll also learn another way to enter data into multiple tables through a single form with the [Menu] Modify MultiEntry command. In addition, you'll learn to use the related [Menu] Tools More MultiAdd command, as well as work with insert queries.

In Chapter 10, "Report Fundamentals," we show you how to create reports from your Paradox tables. First, we teach you how to use the Instant Report capability to create quick reports. Then, we show you how to create and use custom Tabular reports. Chapter 11, "Other Reporting Topics," builds on the concepts presented in Chapter 10. In this chapter, you'll learn to create free-form and multitable reports, group your reports, and use the Custom Configuration Program to change the default report settings.

Chapter 12, "Graphs," introduces the graphics capabilities added to Paradox in Release 3. In this chapter, we show you how to design, display, and print graphs based on data in Paradox tables. In addition, we show you how to use queries and cross tabulations to transform tables that do not lend themselves to graphic interpretation into tables Paradox can use to generate graphs that communicate useful information about your data.

Chapter 13, "Simple Scripts," is your introduction to the world of scripts and PAL programming. In this chapter, you'll learn what scripts are and how you can create them. You'll also be introduced to the Script Editor and the PAL Debugger.

Chapter 14, "PAL Basics," explains several fundamental PAL concepts. In this chapter, you'll learn about PAL commands, variables, and formulas. The last important building block—functions—is covered in Chapter 15, "PAL Functions."

If you use PAL, Chapter 16, "Fundamental PAL Techniques," is an especially important chapter for you. You'll learn how to use PAL to write information to the screen, and how to interact with the user of your scripts, create menus, design FOR and WHILE loops, print from within scripts, and much more. You'll be able to use the information in this chapter to build your own PAL programs.

Chapter 17, "Other PAL Features," covers the remaining PAL topics. In this chapter, you'll discover how to use the Value command to make quick calculations and the MiniScript command to create simple, one-line scripts. This chapter also covers the PAL Debugger, tilde variables, arrays, and procedures.

Five appendices supplement the information in *Douglas Cobb's Paradox 3 Handbook*. Appendix A1, "Importing and Exporting Files," covers the commands on Paradox's Export-Import menu. These commands allow you to import data from Quattro, 1-2-3, Symphony, dBASE II and III, PFS: File, Reflex, and VisiCalc into Paradox, and to export data in Paradox tables to these programs.

Appendix A2, "Multi-user Paradox," covers the multi-user features added in Release 2, explaining how Paradox lets two or more users on a network share tables, forms, and reports while maintaining data integrity. It also covers private and shared directories, locks and security, and the multi-user PAL commands and functions.

Appendix A3, "PAL Utilities," introduces the useful tools provided with Paradox to help you develop your own PAL applications. The Paradox Personal Programmer can be used by novices and advanced users alike to do such things as develop Paradox-like menus; extend the power of queries; and link scripts, forms, and reports into a complete application system. The Data Entry Toolkit is an advanced PAL feature that gives your application total control over the user's movements and entries.

Appendix A4, "Special Versions of Paradox," discusses Paradox 386 and Paradox OS/2. These versions of Paradox are specially designed to get the most out of the new generation of personal computers based on the Intel 80386 processor and Microsoft's new OS/2 operating system.

Appendix A5, "Memory Management," explains how Paradox manages memory. In this appendix, you'll also learn how Paradox 2 and Paradox 3 can benefit from expanded memory and how you can control Paradox's use of expanded memory.

Conventions

Throughout this book, we use certain conventions, which we hope will make the text easier to understand. To avoid confusion, we'd like to explain these conventions to you now.

Table names, file names, and function names always appear in capital letters, as in "the CUSTOMER table" and "the CMAX() function." Unless instructed to do so, you are not required to use uppercase letters.

The names of standard keys like [Esc], [Ctrl], and [Home] are enclosed in square brackets, as are the "nameless" keys on the IBM PC keyboard: [Spacebar], [Backspace], [Tab], and [Shift]. The names of Paradox function keys are also enclosed in brackets, as in [Help], [Do-It!], and [Menu]. In addition, the names of function keys are usually accompanied by a parenthetical reminder of the key location, for example, "press the [Do-It!] key ([F2])." Furthermore, the Return/Enter key is represented by the symbol ↵ and the four arrow keys by the symbols →, ←, ↓, and ↑. When two or more keys must be pressed simultaneously, those key names are separated by hyphens, as in "press [Ctrl]-[R]" or "press [Alt]-[F10]." You should not type the hyphen.

Command names are usually presented in full form—for instance, "the [Menu] Forms Design command." In addition, the names of the individual options in the command name are always capitalized. When you are instructed to issue a command, the first letter of each word in the command is boldfaced, as in the phrase "issue the [Menu] Forms Design command." This will serve as a reminder that you can issue a command by simply pressing the first letter of the command name.

Similarly, when you are instructed to press a key or type an entry, the characters you should type will be in boldface, as in "press [Esc]," "press [Do-It!]," and "type 100."

A Note about Versions

This book describes Release 3 of Paradox. Although it does include discussions of a few topics that are important to previous releases, most of the discussion assumes that you have purchased or upgraded to Release 3.

You should be able to use this book as an introduction to Releases 1.0, 1.1, and 2. However, Release 3 contains many new features, such as its multitable capabilities. Therefore, if you own Release 1.0, 1.1, or 2, you will occasionally find us describing a feature that doesn't work for you, a function key that just beeps, a menu option that is missing, or a command PAL will not recognize. If you would like to upgrade to Release 3, contact Borland International. Borland's Paradox support number is (415) 595-4851. The address is 1301 Shoreway Road, Suite 221, Belmont, CA 94002-4106.

Where to Begin

Exactly where you begin in *Douglas Cobb's Paradox 3 Handbook* depends on how much experience you have with Paradox. If you're just starting, you should begin with Chapter 1. If you have been working with the program for a while and feel comfortable with the basics, you might want to skip Chapter 1, skim Chapter 2, and begin in earnest with Chapter 3. If you are already an experienced Paradox user, you might want to concentrate on Chapters 13 through 17, which deal with PAL programming.

Chapter 1

Getting Started

In this chapter, we will show you how to start using Paradox. We will begin by discussing hardware requirements and showing you how to install the program on your system. Then, we will give you an overview of the Paradox program and discuss the Paradox keyboard. Finally, we'll conclude with a discussion of Paradox's context-sensitive help facility.

If you have already installed Paradox on your computer and have begun to work with the program, you may want to skip this chapter and start with Chapter 2. If you are new to Paradox, you'll want to read this chapter carefully.

Hardware Requirements

To use Paradox, you must have the proper computer hardware and peripherals. Paradox is designed to run on the IBM PC, PC/XT, PC/AT, and PS/2, and on 100 percent compatible systems, such as the Compaq Portable and DeskPro lines. If you are not sure whether your computer is 100 percent compatible, you might want to ask for a demonstration of Paradox on your machine before you buy the program.

Regardless of your computer configuration, you will need DOS 2.0 or higher to run the program. You also will need a monochrome or color monitor and the appropriate video controller card.

Memory

Paradox requires that your computer have at least 512K of Random Access Memory (RAM). Even with that much memory, however, some of Paradox's features will be severely limited. When you load Paradox into your computer, most of the available RAM space is consumed by the Paradox program code, which is entirely RAM-resident. As you use Paradox, it imports into RAM portions of the tables and other objects you are using. As Paradox needs different portions of those tables, it replaces the information in RAM with new information from the disk. The more memory you have, the more information Paradox can hold in memory at once, and the less it needs to go to disk. The result is much faster performance. If you have only 512K of RAM, Paradox will swap information from disk to memory frequently, thus slowing down performance.

In addition, if you have just 512K of RAM, there are some operations that Paradox may simply be unable to perform. When Paradox approaches its memory limit while performing a task, it will display a message telling you it does not have enough memory to perform the task. If Paradox actually runs out of room, it will display a message telling you that a resource limit (memory) has been exceeded. Then, it will automatically try to recover memory by clearing the workspace, cancelling your scripts—whatever it can do to keep your tables and data intact. Despite its recovery system, Paradox will return you to DOS in some instances. Although Paradox will save your work before it exits to DOS, a few of these quick exits will convince you that you need more memory. Paradox Releases 2 and 3 use memory far more efficiently than Release 1.1, which, in turn, is an improvement over Release 1.0.

For these reasons, we suggest that you install a full 640K of RAM in your computer if you will be using Paradox extensively. If you are using Paradox 2 or 3, you can make use of extended memory with enhanced memory adapters (e.g., Intel Above Board or AST Rampage Board). Only Release 3 and higher releases support the LIM 4.0 (Lotus-Intel-Microsoft) expanded memory standard. Most extended memory will result in faster performance and will decrease the chances of running out of memory.

Disk Drives

Paradox 3 requires a system with a hard drive, but earlier releases will also run on a system with two 360K floppy disk drives. Regardless of the Paradox release you own, if you plan to use Paradox seriously, there are a couple of important reasons why you'll want to get a hard disk.

First, when used on a computer with floppy drives, Paradox is very slow. As you work with Paradox, it is constantly interacting with the disk, loading portions of tables and other objects into memory, and saving to disk information that it no longer needs. This swapping can become quite an irritation when you are using Paradox with floppy drives. The speed of a hard disk considerably reduces the time required for swapping.

Second, as you work with Paradox, you will find that your tables and the family of associated objects (such as forms) will grow rapidly to the point where they will not fit on a floppy disk. Since the smallest hard disks offer more than ten times the storage capacity of a floppy disk, having a hard disk will free you from constant worry about running out of space.

Therefore, for maximum performance, your system should have one hard disk with at least 2 megabytes (2000K) of free space to install the program (1 megabyte for releases earlier than 3) and run the Paradox tutorial, and an additional 1 megabyte of free space to manage your database. Of course, your system must also have one floppy disk drive.

Monitor

Paradox 1.0, 1.1, and 2 are strictly character-based products, so you can use any black-and-white, monochrome, or color monitor with these releases. However, to display graphs produced in Paradox 3, you'll need a CGA, EGA, or VGA color monitor, or a monochrome monitor with a Hercules graphics card installed in your PC.

Printer

To take full advantage of Paradox, you will also need a printer. Although you can use Paradox without a printer, you will not be able to create hard-copy reports from your Paradox data. Paradox supports most printers, but if you want to print graphs produced by Paradox 3, you'll need a graphics printer or plotter.

Network Requirements

To use Paradox on a network, you will need a network configuration. Paradox runs on most major network products, such as the Novell Network (Version 2 or higher), 3Com 3Plus, and IBM Token Ring. Each workstation using Paradox on the network will need at least 640K of RAM and DOS 3.1 or higher.

Installing Paradox 3

The Paradox program comes on several disks. The actual number of disks depends on the release you own and the type of disk (either $5^1/_4$ inch or $3^1/_2$ inch) you use. It is not necessary to load or use all the disks, just the ones with the features you need. If you are a new user, you will need only the Installation/Sample Tables, Data Enry Toolkit, and System disks. You will use the programs on the Installation/Sample Tables Disk to install Paradox on your system. These installation programs set up a directory, as well as a CONFIG.SYS file that allows you to run the program on your system.

Release 1.0 of Paradox is copy-protected; however, a back-up copy of System Disk I is provided with the program, and you can make copies of the other program disks. Releases 1.1, 2, and 3 of Paradox are not copy-protected, and you will probably want to use the DOS DISKCOPY command to make a back-up copy of all the disks before you do anything else. After you do this, you should place the original disks in a safe place and use the copies as your working disks.

We will limit our discussion to the installation procedure for Paradox 3, which is substantially different from the installation procedure for earlier releases. If you own an earlier release or have additional questions about installing Paradox 3, you'll want to read Chapter 3 of the *Introduction to Paradox* manual.

If you will be using Paradox 2 or 3 on a network, the following installation instructions do not apply. To install Paradox on a network file server, please refer to the *Paradox Network Administrator's Guide*.

As we explained earlier, you must have at least a hard disk and one floppy disk drive in order for your system to run Paradox. Paradox 3 includes a comprehensive installation program that you can use to install the basic Paradox files, as well as utilities such as the Paradox Personal Programmer and the Data Entry Toolkit, on your hard drive. Before you begin the installation procedure, you should be at the DOS prompt of the drive on which you want to install Paradox (usually drive C). To get to this point, turn your system on, or reboot it by pressing **[Ctrl]-[Alt]-[Del]**. When the DOS prompt appears on your screen (the prompt will probably be *C>*), insert the Installation Disk in drive A, type **a:install**, and press ↵. After you do this, Paradox will run the INSTALL.EXE program (the installation program) on the Installation Disk.

First, the installation program will present an introductory screen telling you that the program will ask for your name, the name of your company, and the serial number from your copy of Paradox, if you have not already installed your program at least one time. At the bottom of the screen, the prompt *Press Enter to continue, Esc to exit* will appear. To continue the installation, press ↵.

Next, the installation program will present a menu of installation operations, as shown in Figure 1-1. To install the Paradox 3 program on your hard drive, type **1** at the prompt at the bottom of the screen, and press ↵. After you choose the Hard Disk Installation option, Paradox will prompt you for the source drive, presenting *A* as the default selection. Press ↵ to accept the default source drive if you inserted the Installation Disk in drive A. If you are using another drive as the source drive, press **[Backspace]** to erase the default source drive, type the letter representing the source drive you want to use, and press ↵. Next, Paradox will prompt you for the destination drive (your hard disk), presenting *C* as the default destination drive. Press ↵ to accept the default, or erase and replace the default if your hard drive is represented by another letter. Next, Paradox will ask for the directory in which you want to install Paradox, presenting *c:\paradox3* as the default directory. Press ↵ to accept this default directory, or erase the default, type the name of the directory you want to use, and press ↵.

After you have told the installation program where to find and where to copy the Paradox 3 files, the program will ask you to select one of five international format sets: (1) United States, (2) English International, (3) European, (4) Swedish/Finnish, or (5) Norwegian/ Danish. The format set that you choose will determine how Paradox displays numbers and dates and how Paradox sorts alphanumeric data. To select a format set, type the number of the format set you want to use, and press ↵.

After you choose a format set, the message *Copying Files...* will appear on the screen for a few moments. Then, the installation program will ask you to insert System Disk 1 in the source disk drive. At this point, you can continue the installation by removing the

Installation Disk, inserting System Disk 1, and pressing ↵. Or, you can press [Esc] to discontinue the installation procedure. (You can exit the installation program at any time by pressing [Esc].)

Figure 1-1 The Paradox Installation Menu

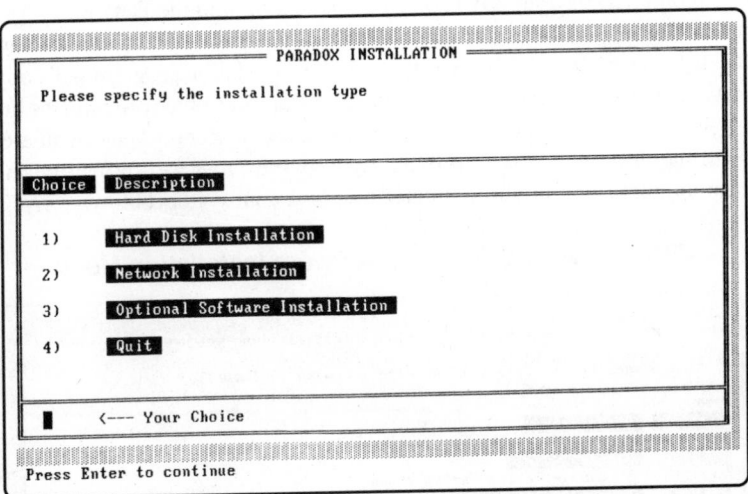

Next, the installation program will prompt you to enter personal signature information: your name, your company's name, and your Paradox serial number. Paradox will display this information every time you start the program. In addition to this information, the installation program will also ask you if you will need to access data on a network. After you have entered all your personal signature information, press [F2] to continue with the installation procedure.

During the rest of the installation procedure, you will need to insert and remove various program disks. Paradox will display instructions on the screen, prompting you for the disks it needs. Each time you insert a disk that the program has called for, press ↵ to continue with the installation procedure. During the installation procedure, the installation program will ask you to reinsert the Installation/Sample Tables and Data Entry Toolkit disks. Don't worry, the program is not copying any sample tables onto your hard disk; it is simply formatting the tables on these disks according to the international format set you have specified.

When you install Paradox on a hard disk, the installation program creates a directory called \paradox3, and copies the Paradox program files into that directory. In addition, the program sets up on the root directory of your hard disk a CONFIG.SYS file that contains two commands: Files=20 and Buffers=20. This configuration is essential to running the Paradox program. If you already have a CONFIG.SYS file on the root directory of your hard disk, Paradox will modify it as necessary. The program will not change any values in your original CONFIG.SYS file that are not relevant to Paradox and will save the original version of the file under the name CONFIG.PDX.

When the basic installation procedure is complete, the Optional Software Installation menu shown in Figure 1-2 will appear on your screen. Choice 1 installs sample tables that you can use to follow along with the Paradox tutorial in the *Introduction to Paradox*. Choice 2 installs a sample application designed to illustrate examples in the *PAL User's Guide*. Choices 3 through 5 install three software utilities that come with Paradox 3: the Paradox Personal Programmer, the Paradox Protection Generator, and the Data Entry Toolkit. To install any of these options, type the number for that option and press ↵. After asking you to enter the disk on which that software is stored, the installation program will copy the files for that software onto your hard disk. After installing any optional software, the installation program will return to the Optional Software Installation menu. When you are finished installing all the desired optional software, type **6** and press ↵. When the installation procedure is complete, you will be instructed to reboot your system before you run Paradox.

Figure 1-2 The Optional Software Installation Menu

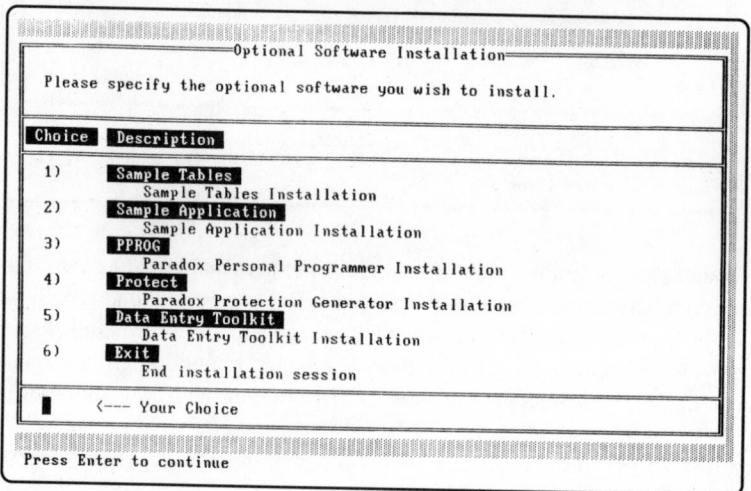

If the installation does not work properly at any point, Paradox will display a message that describes the problem briefly. You will need to correct the problem before you can continue with the installation. The most common problem you are likely to encounter is a lack of sufficient free space on your hard disk. If you encounter an installation problem that you cannot solve, you should call Borland Technical Support at the phone number listed in the *Introduction to Paradox* manual. For a detailed discussion of hard disk problems, you should refer to Chapter 3 of *Introduction to Paradox*.

Loading Paradox

After you have installed Paradox, you are ready to run the program. If you have a hard disk, you should press the **[Ctrl]-[Alt]-[Del]** keys simultaneously to reboot your system before you load the program for the first time. This will ensure that the values in the CONFIG.SYS file, which is set up during the installation procedure, will be in effect. Each time you boot your computer, from that point on, those values will take effect.

When the DOS prompt (usually *C>*) appears on the screen, type **cd\paradox3** to change the current directory (**cd\paradox2** for Release 2 or **cd\paradox** for Release 1.0 or 1.1). Then, type **paradox3** (**paradox2** for Release 2 or **paradox** for Release 1.0 or 1.1) and press ↵ to load the program. After a few moments, the Paradox title screen shown in Figure 1-3 will appear, followed by the screen shown in Figure 1-4.

Figure 1-3   The Title Screen

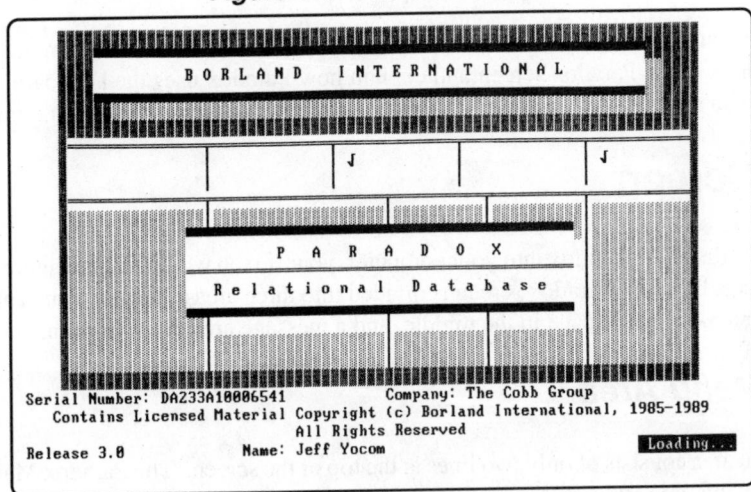

Figure 1-4   The Main Menu

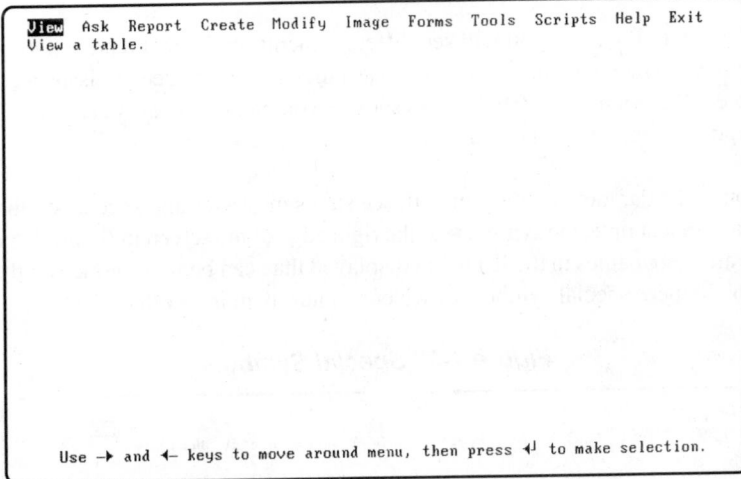

If you are running an earlier release of Paradox on a two-floppy drive system, insert your working copy of System Disk I into drive A and a Paradox data disk into drive B. Then, press **[Ctrl]-[Alt]-[Del]** to reboot your system. When the DOS prompt (usually *A>*) appears, type **paradox2** for Release 2 or **paradox** for Release 1.0 or 1.1 and press ↵. After a few moments, the title screen will appear, along with a message instructing you to insert System Disk II in drive A. When you see this message, remove System Disk I from drive A, insert System Disk II, and press any key. After a few moments, the Paradox Main menu will appear on the screen.

An Overview

Now that you know how to start Paradox, you're ready to take a brief tour. In this section, we will look at the Paradox screen and explain how Paradox uses the keyboard and how you issue commands. We will also introduce you to the concept of tables and images.

The Screen

When you first load Paradox into your computer, your screen will look like Figure 1-4. As you can see, the main Paradox screen is divided into three areas: the menu area at the top of the screen, the workspace in the middle, and a message area at the bottom.

The Menu Area

The menu area consists of only two lines at the top of the screen. The Paradox Main menu appears in this area after you load Paradox. The Main menu consists of 11 options, each of which allows you to perform a type of action. The second line in the menu area contains an explanation of the highlighted, or selected, option in the active menu.

As you work with Paradox, you will see different menus in the menu area. Occasionally, you will not see a menu at all. If you don't see a menu, and you need to issue a command, you can press the [Menu] key ([F10]). As soon as you press this key, Paradox will display the appropriate menu in the menu area.

In addition to the Paradox menus, you will see status messages and special symbols in the menu area. For example, the symbol ▶ at the right edge of the screen in Figure 1-5 indicates that there are more names in the list being displayed than can be seen at once on the screen. We'll explain these special symbols as we encounter them in our discussion.

Figure 1-5   Special Symbols

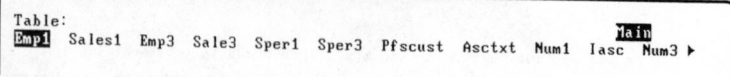

The Workspace

The workspace is the large area in the middle of the screen. This is the area that Paradox uses to display images, to design forms and reports, and to carry out queries. Most of the work you do with Paradox will be carried out in this area.

The Message Area

The message area consists of one line at the bottom of the screen. Paradox uses this area to display error messages, status messages, and instructions. When you first load Paradox, the message shown in Figure 1-6 will appear.

Figure 1-6   The Message Area

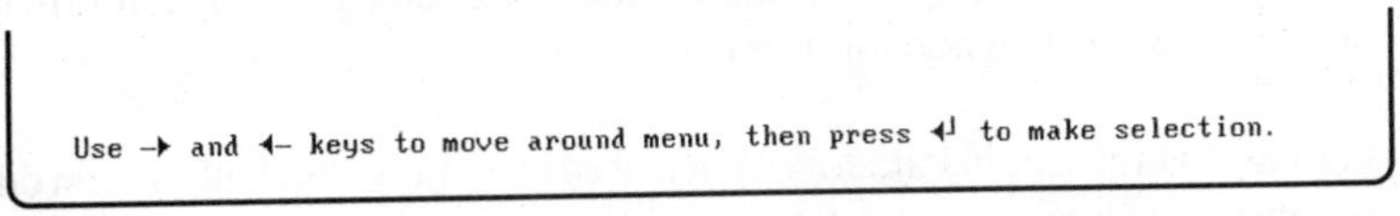

Use → and ← keys to move around menu, then press ↵ to make selection.

Many of the messages that appear in this area tell you that you have made an error or that something has gone wrong with Paradox. For instance, if you press [Do-It!] when there is nothing ready to be processed, Paradox will display the error message shown in Figure 1-7. For a complete list of Paradox error messages, see Appendix A of the *Paradox User's Guide*.

Figure 1-7   An Error Message

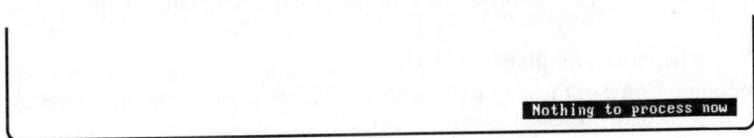

Nothing to process now

In addition to displaying error messages, Paradox will respond to certain keystrokes with a low-pitched or high-pitched beep. A low-pitched beep usually means that you have tried to move the cursor beyond the boundary of an image. A high-pitched beep usually means that you have pressed the wrong key. You may also occasionally hear a very high-pitched, short beep. This is your computer system's way of telling you that it cannot keep up with your typing; this is not unique to Paradox.

The Keyboard

Like most sophisticated programs, Paradox takes full advantage of the IBM PC keyboard. Although we will cover the purpose of each key in more detail later in this book, let's take a brief look at some of the more important keys before going on.

The Typewriter Keys

The middle portion of the IBM PC keyboard contains the keys found on standard typewriter keyboards. For the most part, you'll use the keys in this part of the keyboard to make entries into your Paradox tables, to type scripts, and so on. However, a few of these keys have special purposes in Paradox.

The [Esc] key is the all-purpose "back up" key. For example, you can use the [Esc] key to move from a submenu to the previous menu. This key also lets you back up if you select the wrong option from a menu so that you can make another selection.

The ↵ key has several functions in Paradox. You can use ↵ to select options from the menus. When you are viewing a table, you can use ↵ to move the cursor to the next field. It is also the key you press to tell Paradox you're finished supplying some requested information, like a table name. In the Report Generator, the ↵ key lets you insert a line.

The [Ctrl] key has several uses in Paradox. When used in conjunction with certain other keys, [Ctrl] lets you instantly copy the value from a field of the previous record into the same field of the next record, or change the order of the columns in a table image, among other things. Table 1-1 shows the various uses of the [Ctrl] key in Paradox.

In addition to the uses shown in Table 1-1, the [Ctrl] key can be used in conjunction with the arrow keys and the [Pg Up], [Pg Dn], [Home], and [End] keys to move the cursor around in table images and forms. When the [Ctrl] key is used in this way, the Paradox manual calls it the [Turbo] key. We'll cover these uses for the [Ctrl] key in later chapters.

The [Alt] key, when used simultaneously with certain other keys, can also be used to perform special functions. Some of these functions are used in network situations, but most apply to individual users as well. Table 1-2 shows various uses of the [Alt] key in Paradox.

The final key of interest in this section of the keyboard is [Backspace]. When you are working with a table in the Edit mode, pressing [Backspace] erases the character to the left of the cursor in the current field. Pressing [Ctrl]-[Backspace] in the Edit mode will erase the entire contents of the field.

Special Function Keys

Paradox uses function keys [F1] through [F10] on the IBM PC keyboard. Table 1-3 shows the name and function that Paradox gives to each of these keys. In addition to these ten special function keys, Paradox also supports several other function keys that combine the basic function keys with either the [Alt], [Ctrl], or [Shift] key. The names and functions of these keys are shown in Table 1-4 on page 12. Don't be concerned if the purpose of these keys doesn't make sense to you now. Throughout this book, we'll explain each of the function keys in detail.

Table 1-1 [Ctrl]-Key Combinations

Keys	Paradox Name	Function
[Ctrl]-[Break]		Cancels the current operation and returns to the main workspace
[Ctrl]-[D]	[Ditto]	In the Edit mode, copies the value in the field above the cursor to the current field
[Ctrl]-[F]		Same as [Field View] ([Alt]-[F5]): Enters field view
[Ctrl]-[O]	[DOS]	Suspends Paradox and returns to DOS
[Ctrl]-[R]	[Rotate]	Rotates fields to the right of the cursor (table view only)
[Ctrl]-[U]	[Undo]	In the Edit mode, undoes the last change made
[Ctrl]-[V]	[Vertical Ruler Toggle]	Shows or hides a vertical ruler in the Report Generator and Script Editor
[Ctrl]-[Y]	[Report Delete Line]	Deletes from the cursor to the end of the line in the Report Generator
[Ctrl]-[Z]	[Zoom]	Locates first occurrence of a given string in the current column

Table 1-2 [Alt]-Key Combinations

Keys	Paradox Name	Function
[Alt]-[C]	[Color Palette]	Toggles color palette during form design
[Alt]-[K]	[Key Viol]	Keys table violations
[Alt]-[L]	[Lock Toggle]	Locks record
[Alt]-[O]	[DOS Big]	Suspends Paradox and returns to DOS
[Alt]-[R]	[Refresh]	Updates current table
[Alt]-[X]	[CrossTab]	Cross tabulates current table
[Alt]-[Z]	[Zoom Next]	Locates next occurrence of given string

Table 1-3 Special Function Keys

Key	Paradox Name	Function
[F1]	[Help]	Displays a help screen
[F2]	[Do-It!]	Performs an operation
[F3]	[Up Image]	Moves the cursor up one image
[F4]	[Down Image]	Moves the cursor down one image
[F5]	[Example]	Enters an example in a query
[F6]	[Check]	Enters or removes a check mark in a query form
[F7]	[Form Toggle]	Switches between the table and form view
[F8]	[Clear Image]	Clears the current image from the workspace
[F9]	[Edit]	Enters the Edit mode
[F10]	[Menu]	Displays the current Paradox menu

Table 1-4 Function Key Combinations

Keys	Paradox Name	Function
[Alt]-[F3]	[Instant Script Record]	Begins or ends the recording of an instant script
[Alt]-[F4]	[Instant Script Play]	Plays an instant script
[Alt]-[F5]	[Field View]	Enters the field view
[Alt]-[F6]	[Check Plus]	Enters a check plus in a query form
[Alt]-[F7]	[Instant Report]	Prints an instant report for the current table
[Alt]-[F8]	[Clear All]	Clears all images from the workspace
[Alt]-[F9]	[Coedit]	Enters Coedit mode
[Alt]-[F10]	[PAL Menu]	Displays the PAL menu at the top of the screen
[Ctrl]-[F6]	[Check Descending]	Enters a Check Descending mark in a query form
[Ctrl]-[F7]	[Graph]	Generates a default graph
[Shift]-[F6]	[Group By]	Forces grouping in a set query without including field in ANSWER table

With your Paradox program, you should have received a special keyboard template that shows the Paradox name of each special function key. Because Paradox uses the special function keys so heavily, this template is a very important part of your Paradox program. If you lose your template, call Borland to get another one. You'll have a hard time remembering the purpose of all of the function keys without it.

The Numeric Keypad

As in most PC programs, Paradox uses the keys of the numeric keypad for two purposes. First, in the default condition, the keys in this part of the keyboard are used to move the cursor around the screen. Because the precise effect of these keys depends on where you are in Paradox, we'll save our discussion of them for later chapters.

If you press the [Num Lock] key, the keys on the keypad can be used to enter numbers into tables. While you are using these keys to enter numbers, you can't use them to move the cursor. When you are finished entering numbers and want to use these keys to move the cursor again, just press [Num Lock] again. On an enhanced keyboard, the directional keys next to the numeric keypad will always move the cursor.

There are a couple of other important keys in this part of the keyboard. When you are working in the Edit mode, the [Ins] key allows you to insert a new record into a table. When you are editing a table, you can use the [Del] key to delete a record. The [Ins] and [Del] keys also control the insertion and deletion of characters in reports, forms, and scripts.

Paradox Commands

Commands are the tools you'll use to create and work with your Paradox tables. They allow you to create tables, enter and edit data, change the structure of tables, create reports, and write and play PAL scripts.

Paradox commands are organized in a "top-to-bottom" system of menus that is similar in design to that first used by Lotus 1-2-3. The Main, or "top," menu looks like Figure 1-4.

When you see the Main menu on your screen, you will notice that the first option (View) is highlighted in reverse video. The highlight tells you that View is currently the active choice on the menu. If you press ↵ at this point, you will issue the View command.

Also notice the message on the second line of the screen, *View a table*. This message explains the purpose of the highlighted option. In this case, the message *View a table* explains that the View option allows you to view a table.

We will explain all of the Paradox commands in detail throughout this book. However, before we go on, we will show you how to select commands from menus, introduce you to the concept of submenus, and show you how to select files.

Issuing Commands

There are two ways to issue a command in Paradox. First, you can issue any command on the currently visible menu just by typing the first letter in the name of the command. For example, to issue the Report command, you could just press *R*.

Alternatively, you can select a menu option by highlighting it and pressing ↵. To highlight other menu options, press the → or ← keys. Each time you press →, the highlight will move one option to the right. Each time you press ←, it will move one option to the left. As you move the cursor across the screen, the message on the second line will change to tell you what each selection does. For example, if you press → twice, the menu will look like Figure 1-8. To issue the Report command at this point, you would just press ↵.

Figure 1-8 Highlighting Commands

```
View  Ask  Report  Create  Modify  Image  Forms  Tools  Scripts  Help  Exit
Output, design, or change a report specification.
```

If you press ← while the first option in the Main menu, View, is selected, the highlight will wrap around to the last option on the menu, Exit. Similarly, if you press → when the last option on the Main menu is selected, the highlight will scroll back to the View option. All Paradox menus have this wrap-around capability, which you can use to issue commands more quickly. For example, suppose the View option is selected, and you want to issue the Help command. Instead of pressing → nine times to move to the Help option, you can press ← twice.

In addition to using the arrow keys to move through a menu, you can move quickly to the first or last option by pressing the [Home] or [End] keys. If you select a menu option by mistake, you can press the [Esc] key to go to the original menu.

Selecting Tables

When you issue a command from the Main menu, Paradox will do one of several things. First, it may prompt you to enter a file or table name. For example, if you issue the View command, Paradox will prompt you to enter a table name, as shown in Figure 1-9.

Figure 1-9 A Paradox Prompt

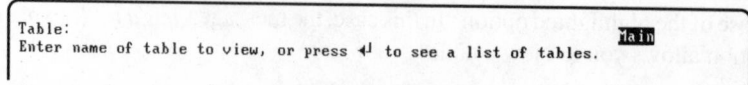

When you see this prompt, you should type the name of the table you want to view and press ↵. For example, to view a table named TEST, you would type **TEST** and press ↵. Immediately, Paradox would bring into view the table you selected. If the table you name is not in the active directory, Paradox will display the message *TABLENAME table not found*. If you see this message, you should press **[Backspace]** to erase the name you typed, then type another name.

If you are not sure of the name of the table you want to view (or if you are a terrible typist and don't want to type the name), you can press ↵ at the prompt to see a list of tables stored in the active directory. For example, suppose you have several tables on your data disk and you can't remember the exact name of the table you want to view. If you simply press ↵ at the prompt, Paradox will show you a list like the one in Figure 1-10.

Figure 1-10 A List of Tables

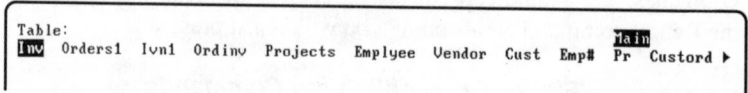

Notice that the first name in this list, *Inv*, is highlighted. Just as with menus, when you ask Paradox to display a list of table names, it will automatically highlight the first name in the list. You can select any name in the list just as you would select options from a menu: either by typing the first letter in the name of the table you want to select or by pointing to its name in the list and pressing ↵.

The symbol ▶ on the right side of the screen tells you that there are more table names than can be displayed on the screen at one time. To view the hidden table names, you can press → or ← to move the cursor one name at a time to the right or left. If you want to move more quickly, you can use the [Home] and [End] keys to move directly to the first or last name in the list, the ↑ or [Ctrl]-→ keys to scroll one screenful to the right, or the ↓ or [Ctrl]-← keys to scroll one screenful to the left. Once you locate the table you want, highlight it with the cursor and press ↵.

If you type the first letter in one of the names in the list, Paradox will immediately select the file that begins with that letter. If you type a letter, and there is more than one file in the list whose name begins with that letter, Paradox will narrow the list to include just those files whose names begin with that letter. Suppose you want to view a table whose name starts with the letter *C*. To find the table name, press **C** at the prompt. When you do, Paradox will display the names of all tables that start with the letter *C*, as shown in Figure 1-11.

Figure 1-11 Selecting a Table

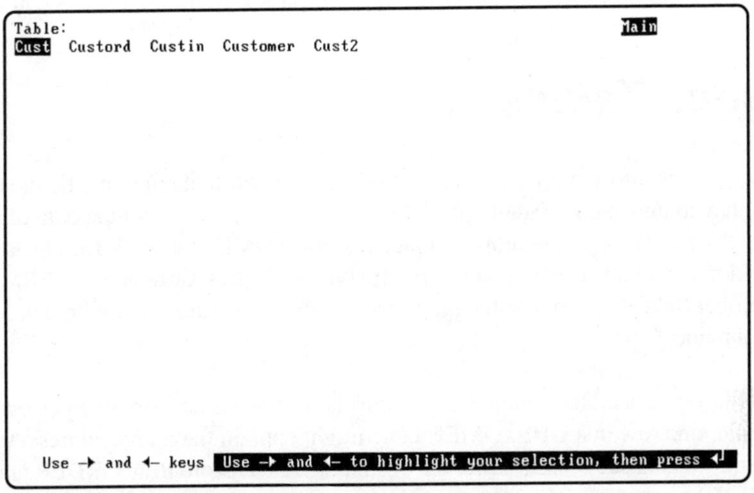

```
Table:                                                                   Main
Cust   Custord   Custin   Customer   Cust2




















  Use → and ← keys  Use → and ← to highlight your selection, then press ↵
```

When you look at the bottom of the screen shown in Figure 1-11, you will notice instructions for selecting the table you want. When you see these instructions, you should press the → or ← key to place the cursor on the table name you want, then press ↵. Paradox will then display the table you selected.

Although we used the View command to demonstrate the ways you can select a file, remember that you will be able to select files in this manner whenever Paradox prompts you to enter the name of an existing table.

Submenus

When you issue the Report, Modify, Image, Forms, Tools, or Exit commands, Paradox will display a submenu of additional commands (options). For example, if you issue the Report command, you will see the menu of options shown in Figure 1-12.

Figure 1-12 The Report Submenu

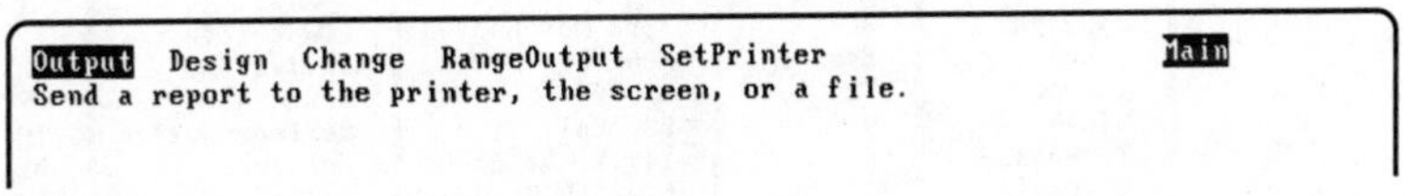

```
Output  Design  Change  RangeOutput  SetPrinter           Main
Send a report to the printer, the screen, or a file.
```

You select commands from a submenu in the same way that you select commands from the Main menu. After you choose a submenu option, Paradox may present another submenu or prompt you for a file name. By working your way down through layer upon layer of submenus, you will finally arrive at the specific command you wish to use.

If you select the wrong menu option, you can "back up" by pressing the [Esc] key. When you press [Esc], you will be returned to the previous submenu. You may continue to back up through the submenus in this manner until you arrive at the Main menu. In many cases, pressing [Esc] from the Main menu will make menus disappear altogether. You can press [F10] to make the Main menu reappear.

Paradox Tables

Paradox organizes information in tables. A table is a gridwork of columns (fields) and rows (records) that contain data. Each field (column) in a table contains all the data of a similar type for each record in the table. For example, in a CUSTOMER table, you might have a First Name field that contains the first names of all your customers; or in an ORDERS table, an Order Number field that contains the order number for each order. Every field in a Paradox table has a name.

Each record (row) in a table contains all the information about one particular person or thing. For example, one row in a CUSTOMER table might contain the name, address, telephone number, and balance due for one particular customer. Each record in an ORDER table might contain all of the information about one particular order. Each record in a table has a number.

For example, Figure 1-13 shows a table named CUSTOMER. Each row in this table is a complete record for one customer. The field names displayed across the top of the table—Cust Number, Last Name, First Name, Address, City, State, and Zip—identify the type of information contained in each field.

Figure 1-13 The CUSTOMER Table

CUSTOMER	Cust Number	Last Name	First Name	Address	City	State	Zip
1	1245	Priest	Stan	123 Hill St	Louisville	KY	40212
2	1690	Anderson	Harold	45 Mt. Rain	New Albany	IN	47130
3	1800	Jones	William	6610 Willow	Nashville	TN	61215
4	1132	Smith	David	Haven Drive	Louisville	KY	40208
5	1200	Doe	John	Milltown Rd	Louisville	KY	40215
6	1246	Doe	Jane	Crossbuck Dr	Louisville	KY	40215
7	1176	Robinson	Clifford	2323 Vane St	Jeffersonville	IN	47130
8	1509	Carson	Kit	45 Colt St	Clarksville	IN	47132
9	1286	Collins	Richard	1223 Fork Ave	Jeffersontown	KY	40209
10	1751	Ross	Melinda	Apt.12 Fox St	New Albany	IN	47130
11	2376	Baxter	John	# 5 Park Ave	New York	NY	20016
12	3726	Alda	Alan	4077 Mash	Hollywood	CA	90012
13	5171	Conner	Julie	Hopewell Dr	Clarksville	TN	61203
14	5421	Cambridge	Frank	552 B Hill St	Louisville	KY	40212
15	9610	Johnson	Joe	1000 Mob End Rd	Louisville	KY	40204
16	9051	Black	Emma	P.O. Box 397	Dallas	TX	87172
17	1500	Thomas	Tom	RFD 2	Goose Run	KY	40001
18	1136	Winder	Willie	896 Coil St	Jeffersonville	IN	47130
19	1202	Thompson	Zack	111 River Rd	New York	NY	20012
20	3626	O'Grady	Teddy	Limrick St # 3	Paris	KY	40002

A single Paradox table can contain up to 2 billion records and up to 255 fields. A single record can be up to 4,000 characters long. However, no one field of any record can contain more than 255 characters.

Every table in Paradox has a unique name. Due to the DOS file-name limitation of eight characters, table names can be no longer than eight characters. The name can contain letters, numbers, and special characters, like # and $, but it cannot contain blank spaces. As you will see in the next section, Paradox automatically assigns the extension .DB to every table you create.

You should not give a table a name that conflicts with the name of a subdirectory of the directory that contains the table. Also, you should avoid giving tables names that conflict with the names of special DOS device names, such as COM1, LPT1, and PRN.

Paradox Families and Objects

Every table you create can have a number of objects associated with it. For example, a single table can have up to 15 custom reports and forms. Each report or form is called an object and is associated with the table for which it was created. A collection of objects and its associated table are called a family.

In addition to custom forms and reports, a table's family can consist of specific image settings, validity checks, a primary index (also known as a key field), and several secondary indexes. Each object you create is automatically assigned the name of the table for which it was created, as well as an extension that identifies the type of object it is. The various objects and their extensions are listed in Table 1-5.

Table 1-5 Paradox Objects and File-name Extensions

Object	Extension
Table	.DB
Form	.F and .F1 through .F14
Report	.R and .R1 through .R14
Image Settings	.SET
Validity Checks	.VAL
Primary Index	.PX
Secondary Indexes	.Y01, .Y02, .Y03, and so on, and, .X01, .X02, .X03, and so on

Script files have the file-name extension .SC, and graph files have the file-name extension .G. Script and graph files are not objects associated with a family.

Temporary Tables

In performing the tasks you assign, Paradox creates up to 11 different temporary tables. These tables are named ANSWER, CHANGED, CROSSTAB, DELETED, ENTRY, FAMILY, INSERTED, KEYVIOL, LIST, PROBLEMS, and STRUCT. Each of these tables is created as a result of a specific operation to hold the information that is generated by that operation. For example, Paradox creates ANSWER tables to hold the results of queries. We'll explain each of these types of tables in more detail later in this book.

It is important for you to note that because Paradox reserves these names for its own use, you should not create permanent tables of your own using these names.

Images

When you are viewing or manipulating a table, Paradox displays an image of that table on the screen. Although the image looks like the actual table and contains all of the data that is in the table, technically, it is not the table. While you are viewing or editing an image on the screen, the actual table remains secure on the disk. Until you use the [Do-It!] key or the DO-IT! command to make your changes permanent, nothing you do will affect the actual table. If you make changes you don't want to keep, you can use the Cancel command, which is found on most Paradox menus.

The Table View

The default view in Paradox is the table view. When you look at a table in the table view, you see it as a columnar table, where each field is a column and each record is a row. For example, Figure 1-13 shows a table view image of the CUSTOMER table.

As you can see, the data contained in the table is displayed on the screen in columns and rows. If a table is quite large, the screen can display only a small part of that table at a time. You can think of your screen as a window through which you can view your tables. For example, if you were to cut a small square hole in a piece of cardboard and place it over this page, you would be able to read only what appears through the hole—you would need to move it around on the page in order to see the entire page. When you are viewing a Paradox table, you can move the window around so that you can see all of the data the table contains.

In addition, Paradox has a command called Image, which lets you change the way the image is displayed on the screen. Paradox also has a special key combination, [Ctrl]-[R], which lets you change the order of the fields in the image. We'll explain how to change the image on the screen in Chapter 3.

The Form View

If you wish, you can view, enter, or edit your tables through a form like the one shown in Figure 1-14. Paradox automatically will create a default form for any table. In addition, you can create custom forms for your tables.

Figure 1-14 The Form View

```
Viewing Customer table with form F: Record 1 of 20                  Main  =▼

                                                            Customer    #    1

         Cust Number:              1245
         Last Name:     Priest
         First Name:    Stan
         Address:       123 Hill St
         City:          Louisville
         State:         KY
         Zip:           40212
```

The main difference between the table view and the form view is the amount of information displayed on the screen at one time. In the table view, Paradox displays up to 22 records and as many fields as the screen-width will allow. In the form view, Paradox can display all the fields in a record, but can only display one record at a time.

Getting Help

Like the popular Lotus programs 1-2-3 and Symphony, Paradox has an on-line, context-sensitive help facility. To display a help screen at any time, you need only press [Help] ([F1]). For example, if you press [Help] immediately after you load Paradox, you'll see the help screen shown in Figure 1-15 on the following page.

Most help screens have their own submenus that allow you to get more information about a topic. For example, the menu at the top of the screen in Figure 1-15 includes the options Basics, GettingAround, Keys, MenuChoices, Index, and Scripts/PAL. If you select one of these options, Paradox will present a new help screen that contains more information about the selected topic. For instance, if you choose Basics from the main Help menu, Paradox will display the help screen shown in Figure 1-16. As you can see, this help screen offers its own menu, which allows you to dig even further into the selected topic. To move back to the previous menu after choosing an option in the help facility, just press [Esc].

Figure 1-15 The Main Help Screen

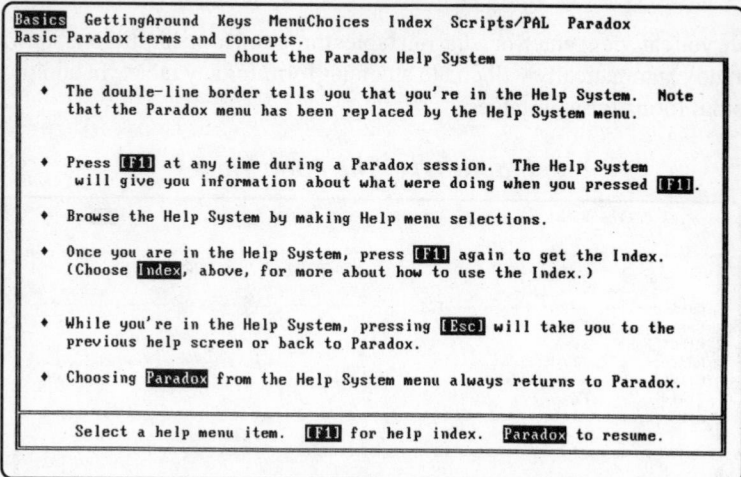

Figure 1-16 The Basics Help Screen

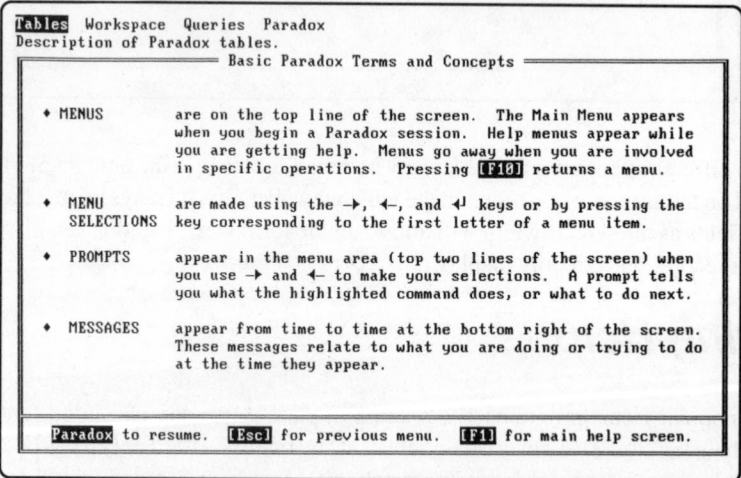

Because Paradox's help facility is context-sensitive, the screen that appears when you press the [Help] key will offer help that is relevant to what you are currently doing with Paradox. This means that much of the time you won't need to use the Help menus to find the answer to your question. For example, if you press [Help] while you are editing a table, you'll see the help screen shown in Figure 1-17. Notice that this screen offers instructions about editing a table.

If you want more help on the current subject, or you want information on a different subject, press [Help] a second time while in a help screen. This will display the Help Index shown in Figure 1-18. The Help Index is an alphabetical list of Paradox topics. Any listing that is preceded by a dot will have a help screen available. You can use the ↓, ↑, [Pg Up], and [Pg Dn] keys to scan through the list of topics, or use the [Zoom] ([Ctrl]-[Z]) and [Zoom Next] ([Alt]-[Z]) key combinations to quickly locate a desired topic. (A discussion of how to use [Zoom] and [Zoom Next] appears in Chapter 2.) Move through the Help Index until the topic you want is highlighted, then press ↵. Help on your selected topic will appear. You can return to the Help Index by pressing [Help], or you can return to what you were doing before entering Help by pressing [Esc].

Figure 1-17 The Edit Help Screen

```
FieldView Undo ValCheck Stuck? Paradox
Using the Field View key to edit within a field.
══════════════════════ Editing a Table ══════════════════════
  ♦ To change a record

      Use → and ← to move to the field to be changed.  Type to add
      characters, ◄─ to delete backwards, [Ctrl]◄─ to empty
      the field.

      [Ins] to insert a new record before the current one.

      [Del] to delete the current record.

  ♦ To add a new record at the end:

      [End] to go to the end of the table, then ↓ will add a new blank
      record to fill.

  ♦ Press [F2] or select DO-IT! when finished.  Undo or [Ctrl][U]
    will undo changes made, record-by-record, since the last DO-IT!.

  ──────────────────────────────────────────────────────────
  Paradox to resume.  [Esc] for previous menu.  [F1] for help index.
```

Figure 1-18 The Help Index

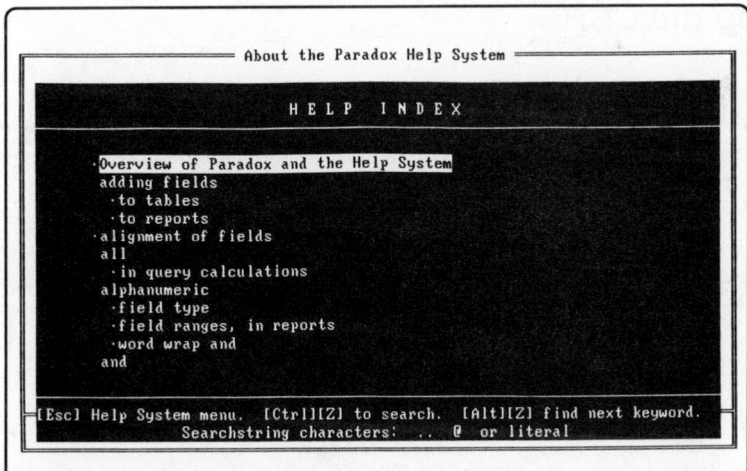

```
══════════════ About the Paradox Help System ══════════════

                  H E L P   I N D E X

    ·Overview of Paradox and the Help System
     adding fields
      ·to tables
      ·to reports
    ·alignment of fields
     all
      · in query calculations
     alphanumeric
      ·field type
      ·field ranges, in reports
      ·word wrap and
     and

  [Esc] Help System menu.  [Ctrl][Z] to search.  [Alt][Z] find next keyword.
           Searchstring characters:  ..  @  or literal
```

In addition to the [Help] key, most Paradox menus have a Help command. For example, notice the Help option in the Main menu in Figure 1-4 on page 7. If you are working with a menu that contains a Help option, you can display a help screen just by choosing the Help option. As with the [Help] key, the screen that appears when you issue a Help command usually will be relevant to what you are doing with Paradox.

To exit from the help facility and return to the program, you can either select **P**aradox from the Help menu, press **[Esc]**, or press **[Do-It!]** ([F2]). No matter which method you use, when you exit from Help, Paradox will return you to whatever you were doing before you accessed the help facility.

The CCP

Unlike many programs, Paradox does a good job of configuring itself automatically for the computer hardware you are using. Many users will never need to go through a configuration process before they start using Paradox. However, if you have a black-and-white monitor connected to a color/graphics card, or if you are using a portable computer, your screen may be hard to read when you first load Paradox. In addition, if you are using an IBM color/graphics adapter (CGA), you may see interference or "snow" on the screen.

If this is the case, you may need to run a special program, called the Custom Configuration Program (CCP), before you do anything else. The CCP allows you to customize Paradox to your computer system.

In this section, we'll explain how you can use the CCP to customize your screen and change some basic default settings. We'll save our main discussion of this tool for later when you've become more familiar with Paradox.

Loading the CCP

If you are using a hard disk system, the CCP files were copied to the \paradox, \paradox2, or \paradox3 directory when you installed the program. To run the CCP once you have loaded Paradox, issue the [**Menu**] **S**cripts **P**lay command. Paradox will display the prompt shown in Figure 1-19.

Figure 1-19 The Script Prompt

```
Script:                                            Main
Enter name of script to play, or press ↵ to see a list of scripts.
```

When you see this prompt, type **Custom** and press ↵. (You also can run the CCP directly from DOS by typing **paradox3 custom** at the DOS prompt. If you use this method, you won't need to issue the [Menu] Scripts Play command.)

If you are running an earlier Paradox release on a floppy disk system, the files for the CCP will be on the Installation Disk. To run the CCP, place the Installation Disk in drive B, then either run the Paradox program, issue the **[Menu]** Scripts Play command and run the Custom script, or run the program directly from the DOS prompt. If you run the program from the DOS prompt, be sure to insert System Disk I into drive A.

Next, Paradox will display the prompt shown in Figure 1-20. If you don't have a color/ graphics card in your computer, you won't see this question. Also, releases prior to Paradox 3 will ask you if you are using a color monitor.

Figure 1-20 The CCP Monitor Prompt

```
Are you using a B&W monitor right now?
       ( Y for yes, N for no )
```

If you are using a black-and-white monitor, you now should type **Y** (or **N** if you have an earlier Paradox release). This choice automatically corrects the problems with your screen. If you're not using a black-and-white monitor, you should type **N** (or **Y** if you have an earlier Paradox release). After you make this choice, Paradox will display the menu shown in Figure 1-21. The CCP menu will be slightly different if you own a release earlier than Paradox 3.

Figure 1-21 The CCP Menu

```
Video  Reports  Graphs  Defaults  Int'l  Net  PAL  Ascii  Help  Do-It!  Cancel
Monitor, Snow, Colors, NegativeColors, and FormPalette.
```

Making Changes

If the only reason you ran the CCP was to tell Paradox you are using a black-and-white monitor with a color/graphics card, you can issue the **DO-IT!** command at this point without making any additional changes. However, if you are using an IBM color/graphics adapter or a color monitor, you probably will want to make more changes in the video display before you leave the CCP. For example, you may want to set the colors for Paradox. To do this, issue the **V**ideo command. After you issue this command, you'll see a submenu that looks like Figure 1-22. If you are using a Paradox release earlier than 3, you will see the DisplayColor option instead of the Colors option, and the menu will not include the NegativeColors and FormPalette option.

Figure 1-22 The Video Menu

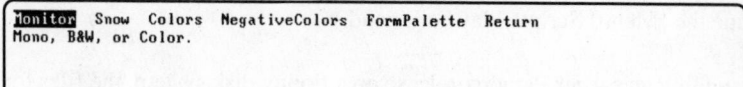

The Monitor command allows you to select either a monochrome, black-and-white, or color monitor as the default monitor. If you issue the Monitor command, you will see another menu, which looks like the one in Figure 1-23.

Figure 1-23 The Monitor Menu

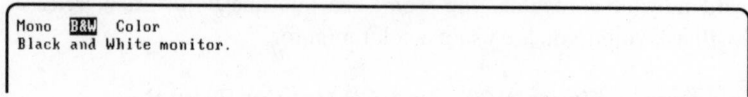

The current default monitor will be highlighted. For example, if you entered *Y* at the monitor prompt earlier, the B&W option would be highlighted now. To change the default monitor, use ← and → to point to the option you want, and press ↵. After you do this, the CCP Video menu will again appear on the screen.

The Snow command allows you to eliminate the interference (snow) you can get when you are using an IBM color/graphics adapter (CGA). If you issue the Snow command, you will see the menu shown in Figure 1-24.

Figure 1-24 The Snow Menu

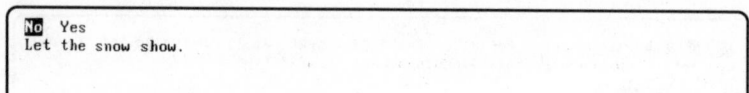

When you see this menu, the default (No) will be highlighted. To change the default, press the → key to place the cursor on Yes, and press ↵. After you do this, the CCP Video menu will appear on the screen.

The NegativeColors command lets you set Paradox to display negative number and dollar values in a different color from positive values. We'll explain this command in more detail in Chapter 2, when we discuss field types. The FormPalette command lets you determine whether Paradox will automatically display a color palette while you are designing forms to view the data in your Paradox tables. We'll explain this command in Chapter 4 when we discuss form design.

The Colors command lets you customize the text and background color of each element in Paradox's screen display. Only Paradox 3 provides this color customization feature.

Defining Color Settings

You'll probably want to work with Paradox a little to see how these screen elements interact before you start changing their colors. Improperly matched colors among screen elements that appear together can actually hinder the effectiveness of Paradox's design. For example, if an error message has the same background color as the Paradox workspace, the message will not stand out as obviously as it should.

If you do decide to change the colors of Paradox, you should select the Colors command from the Video menu. After you select the Colors command, the message *Loading color customization system...* will appear at the bottom of the screen briefly, then you will see the menu shown in Figure 1-25.

Figure 1-25 The Colors Menu

```
ExistingSettings  Modify  Help  Return
Select, rename or delete a color setting.
```

To change the colors used by Paradox 3, you must define a new, comprehensive color setting for the entire system of Paradox screens. Paradox comes with one defined color setting, named Default, which defines the colors Paradox uses when you install the software. After installing Paradox, you can modify the Default color setting, or another setting you have previously created, and assign a name to the new setting. Then, you can choose any one of the existing settings to define the colors used by Paradox.

To create a new color setting based on the current setting (the Default setting if you have just installed Paradox), select Modify from the Colors menu. At this point, you will see a large window showing a facsimile of a Paradox screen displaying a menu in Main mode. A menu of screen elements will appear above the window. Figure 1-26 on the following page shows the screen at this point.

To change the color of a particular element, you select that element from the menu at the top of the screen. For example, if you select the Top2Lines/Menu option, a color palette showing all the possible text and background color combinations will appear in the upper-right corner of the screen, as shown in Figure 1-27 on the next page. This palette consists of 128 squares, each of which contains a different combination of text and background colors. The square on the palette containing the current color combination for the top two lines of the screen (white text on a cyan background for the Default setting) will be blinking. Also, a description of the color combination will appear just above the color palette. To change the colors for the selected element, you use the cursor-movement keys (↓, ↑, →, and ←) to move to the desired color combination. As you move across the palette, the colors of the top two lines in the window will change to match the color combination currently selected on the palette. To select a color combination, press ↵ while that combination is blinking. The menu of screen elements will reappear at the top of the screen, and you can choose colors for another element.

Figure 1-26 Coloring Screen Elements

```
┌──────────────────────────────────────────────────────────────────────┐
│ Workspace  Top2Lines/Menu  CurrentSelection  Annotation                │
│ Color the workspace, PAL canvas and report generator literals and background. │
│ ┌───────────────────┤ The Paradox Main Menu ├────                     │
│ │ View  Ask  Report  Create  Modify  Image  Forms  Tools  Scri         │
│ │ View a table.                                                        │
│ │                                                                      │
│ │                                                                      │
│ │                                                                      │
│ │                                                                      │
│ │                                                                      │
│ │                                                                      │
│ │                                                                      │
│ │                                                     Press [F10] to   │
│ │                                                     Save or Cancel;  │
│ │  Use ← and → keys to move around menu, then press ↵ to ma│  [F1] - for Help. │
│ │ Screen-Paging:  [PgDn]=Next, [PgUp]=Prev., [Ctrl-Home]=First, [Ctrl-End]=Last. │
└──────────────────────────────────────────────────────────────────────┘
```

Figure 1-27 The Color Palette

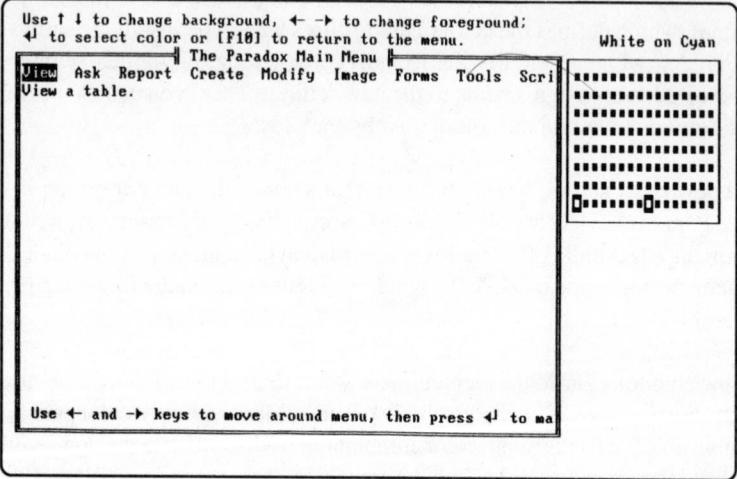

You can use the [Pg Dn] and [Pg Up] keys to page through a series of screens that show all the different screen elements that appear in Paradox. For example, if you press [Pg Dn], the image in the window will change to show the screen elements that appear when Paradox prompts you in response to a menu selection. Figure 1-28 shows the window that displays these elements. While viewing this window, you can change the color combination for any of the elements currently displayed.

Figure 1-28 A Different Set of Screen Elements

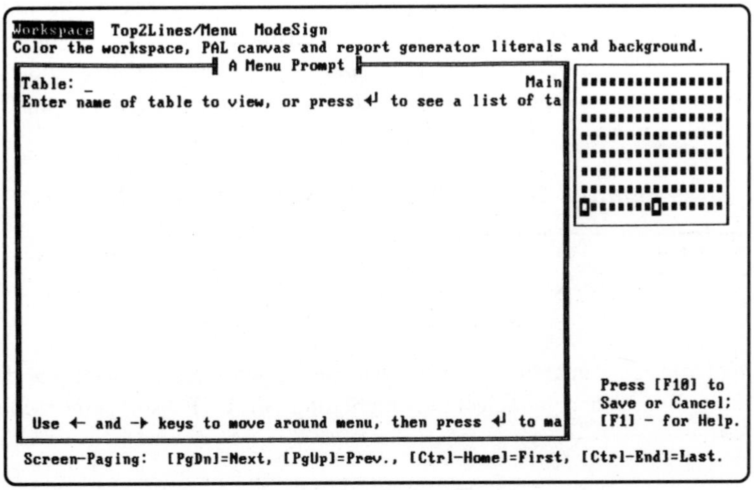

```
Workspace  Top2Lines/Menu  ModeSign
Color the workspace, PAL canvas and report generator literals and background.
                          ┤ A Menu Prompt ├
┌Table: _                                    Main│ ■■■■■■■■■■■■■■■
│Enter name of table to view, or press ↵ to see a list of ta│ ■■■■■■■■■■■■■■■
│                                                 │ ■■■■■■■■■■■■■■■
│                                                 │ ■■■■■■■■■■■■■■■
│                                                 │ ■■■■■■■■■■■■■■■
│                                                 │ ■■■■■■■■■■■■■■■
│                                                 │ ■■■■■■■■■■■■■■■
│                                                 │ ▯■■■■■■■▯■■■■■■■
│
│
│
│                                                   Press [F10] to
│                                                   Save or Cancel;
│                                                   [F1] - for Help.
│ Use ← and → keys to move around menu, then press ↵ to ma
└
  Screen-Paging:  [PgDn]=Next, [PgUp]=Prev., [Ctrl-Home]=First, [Ctrl-End]=Last.
```

You can move back to the first screen window by pressing [Ctrl]-[Home] at any time during the color selection process. You can also move to the last of the series of screens, which shows samples of all the screen elements, by pressing [Ctrl]-[End]. In all, there are 11 screens of elements that you can use to define color combinations. These screens include elements that appear in the Paradox workspace, as well as query forms, the Report and Form generators, and the PAL Script Editor. If you change the color of any element that is common to two or more screens, the CCP will automatically change the colors for each screen on which the element appears.

After you have finished making all the color changes you want, you can save the new color setting by pressing the [Menu] key. After you press [Menu], you will see a menu with two options: Save and Cancel. If you select Cancel, the CCP will return to the Colors menu without saving the new color setting. If you choose Save, the CCP will prompt you for the name of the new setting, as shown in Figure 1-29. You can give a color setting any name up to 21 characters long. For example, you could name the new setting MYCOLORS by typing this name at the *Color Setting Name:* prompt and pressing ↵.

Figure 1-29 The Color Setting Name Prompt

```
Color Setting Name:
Enter a name for the new color setting.
```

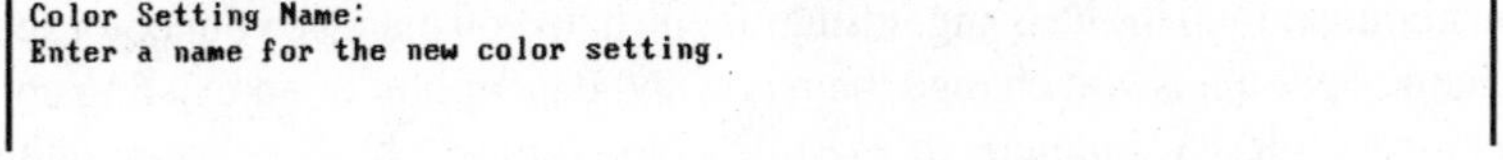

After you name the new color setting, the CCP will prompt you for a description of the setting, as shown in Figure 1-30. This description, which will appear below the menu from which you will select color settings, can be up to 80 characters long. For example, to give the new setting the description *My favorite color combinations,* you would type this description at the prompt and press ↵. After you enter the setting description, the CCP will return to the Colors menu.

Figure 1-30 The Setting Description Prompt

```
Description:
Describe the new color setting.
```

The ExistingSettings command of the Colors menu lets you select, rename, or delete an existing color setting. When you select ExistingSettings, the CCP displays the menu shown in Figure 1-31.

Figure 1-31 The ExistingSettings Menu

```
Select  ChangeName  Delete  Help  Return
Select an existing color setting to modify or implement in Paradox.
```

Selecting a Color Setting

The Select command lets you install one of the existing color settings. When you choose this command, the CCP presents a menu like the one in Figure 1-32, listing all the defined color settings. An asterisk appears next to the name of the currently installed setting. In Figure 1-32, the Default setting is the active color setting. To install the MYCOLORS setting, you would select MYCOLORS from the menu. After you make your selection, the CCP will return to the Colors menu. If you choose a new setting, the new setting will take effect the next time you load Paradox.

Figure 1-32 A Menu of Existing Settings

```
*Default  MYCOLORS
My favorite color combinations
```

The other commands on the ExistingSettings menu help you manage your color settings. The ChangeName option lets you change the name and description of an existing color setting; the Delete option lets you delete an existing color setting. If you choose either of these options, the CCP will ask you to choose a name from the menu of color settings. If you choose ChangeName, the CCP will ask you to specify a new name and description for the chosen setting. If you choose Delete, the CCP will display a Cancel/OK menu to verify your selection, deleting the setting if you choose OK. If you delete the current setting, the CCP will ask you to select a new setting from the list of existing settings. After you complete any operation on the ExistingSettings menu, the CCP will return to the ExistingSettings menu. From there, you can select Return to move back to the Video menu, then select Return again to return to the CCP main menu.

The Display Color Menu

As we mentioned earlier, Paradox 1.0, 1.1, and 2 feature the DisplayColor command rather than the Colors command. The DisplayColor command lets you choose the background color for Paradox. After you issue the DisplayColor command, you'll see the menu of options shown in Figure 1-33.

Figure 1-33 The DisplayColor Menu

```
DarkBlue  White  Green  Yellow  LightGrey  Cyan  Magenta  Brown
Display Paradox with white text on a dark blue background.
```

As you can see, there are eight color combinations from which to choose. If you select DarkBlue, for example, Paradox will display white text on a dark blue background. To select an option, place the cursor on that option and press ↵. After you do this, the CCP Video menu will appear on the screen. Note that Paradox does not change the screen color immediately. Your new color choice will take effect the next time you load Paradox. Select Return from the Video menu to return to the CCP main menu.

Changing Defaults

The Defaults option on the CCP menu lets you set several defaults that affect the way Paradox operates. When you issue the Defaults command, Paradox will display the menu shown in Figure 1-34. If you are using a release earlier than Paradox 3, these default commands will appear in other locations throughout the CCP menu system. For more information on the arrangement of commands in early CCP menu systems, see the "Advanced Topics" chapter of the *Paradox User's Guide*.

Figure 1-34 The Defaults Menu

```
SetDirectory  QueryOrder  Blank=Zero  EMS  AutoSave  DisableBreak  Return
Specify percentage of EMS to be allocated to the disk cache.
```

The SetDirectory command lets you set the default working directory for Paradox. When you issue this command, the CCP will prompt you for the name of a DOS directory. For example, if you issue this command and type *c:\data* at the *Directory:* prompt, the c:\data directory will be the current directory every time you load Paradox.

The QueryOrder command allows you to select the default field order for ANSWER tables produced by queries. We'll explain this command in Chapter 7, "Queries."

The Blank=Zero option lets you tell Paradox how to treat blank entries in numeric fields when performing numeric calculations. When you issue the Blank=Zero command, the CCP will present a menu with two options: No and Yes. Selecting No makes Paradox ignore blank entries in numeric operations. Selecting Yes makes Paradox treat blank entries as zeroes. The Blank=Zero setting affects the results of calculated fields in forms and reports, queries that do not involve counting field entries, and PAL calculations that do not involve counting field entries. The default Blank=Zero setting is No.

The EMS option lets you specify how much of the available extended memory Paradox should use as a disk cache to hold files accessed during a Paradox session. This command is useful only if you have an expanded memory board such as the Intel Above Board or the AST Rampage. For more information on Paradox's use of expanded memory, see Chapter 14 of the *Paradox User's Guide*.

The AutoSave command lets you set the frequency with which Paradox automatically saves your data to disk. By default, Paradox periodically saves to disk data you have entered or edited in order to prevent loss of the data due to a power failure or other accident. When you issue the AutoSave command, the CCP will display a No/Yes menu that you can use to turn off the automatic saving operation. Because Paradox performs autosaves by default, the default selection on this menu is Yes.

The DisableBreak command lets you disable the ability of the [Ctrl]-[Break] keystroke to interrupt the current Paradox operation. You may want to disable this keystroke because certain networks and European keyboard drivers can produce the effect of [Ctrl]-[Break] when you issue other keystrokes. When you issue this command, the CCP will present a menu with two options: Enable and Disable. The default option is Enable.

After you finish changing any default settings on the Defaults menu, the CCP will return to the Defaults menu. Then, you can issue the Return command to return to the CCP main menu. For more information on how these defaults affect Paradox's operation, see Chapter 14 of the *Paradox User's Guide*.

Leaving the CCP

When you have finished making any other desired changes, issue the **DO-IT!** command. After you do this, Paradox will ask you if you are using a floppy disk, hard disk, or network. (Paradox 3 will not include the floppy disk option.) If you select Network, Paradox will prompt you for your private directory name. Contact your network administrator if you have any problems. Selecting HardDisk will cause the changes made in the CCP to be saved to your hard disk. If you select TwoFloppy, Paradox will prompt you to insert System Disk I in drive B and will save the new settings to that disk. After saving your selections, Paradox will end its execution and return to the DOS prompt.

Command Line Configuration

If you do not want to change the default video settings with the CCP, you can use a command at the DOS prompt to tell Paradox what kind of monitor you are using. For example, suppose you are temporarily using a black-and-white monitor. To tell Paradox about your monitor, you can type **paradox3 -b&w** at the DOS prompt, and then press ↵. This will set up the proper configuration without going through the CCP. However, this command does not change the default settings. You will need to enter this command every time you load the program. Table 1-6 shows the command line configurations you can use.

Table 1-6 Command Line Configurations

Command	Result
paradox3 -b&w	Tells Paradox that you are using a black-and-white monitor with a color/graphics adapter
paradox3 -mono	Tells Paradox that you are using a monochrome monitor with a monochrome adapter
paradox3 -color	Tells Paradox that you are using a color monitor with a color/graphics adapter
paradox3 -snow	Tells Paradox to eliminate interference when using an IBM color/graphics adapter

You can combine commands. For example, to tell Paradox that you are using a color monitor with an IBM color/graphics adapter, type **paradox3 -color -snow**, at the DOS prompt, and then press ↵.

We will discuss the other options on the CCP menu in the chapters and appendices that deal with related topics, such as the Report Generator and the import/export commands. If you need more information at this point, refer to the index in this book or to Chapter 16 of the *Paradox User's Guide*.

Leaving Paradox

When you have finished a Paradox session, you should always issue the **[Menu] E**xit command to leave the program. When you issue this command, Paradox will present two options: No and Yes. If you do not want to leave Paradox, choose the **N**o option. If you want to exit, choose **Y**es. When you do this, Paradox automatically will close all the tables you have opened, save any changes you have made, and return to DOS.

You should never turn off your computer without first exiting from Paradox. If you turn off the computer while Paradox is still active, you can damage your tables, resulting in the loss of data. Always use [Menu] Exit Yes to exit from Paradox.

Conclusion

In this chapter, we have given you a broad overview of the Paradox program. We've explained some terminology, introduced you to the concepts of tables and families, and shown you how to issue commands and get help.

In the remainder of the book, we'll build on this basic knowledge as we show you how to use Paradox. We'll begin in the next chapter by showing you how to create a table.

Chapter **2**

Creating and Viewing Tables

In this chapter, we will show you how to create tables, enter data into tables, and edit the data in your tables. We will begin with the [Menu] Create command, which allows you to define the structure of tables. Then, we'll show you how to enter data into tables. After that, we'll talk about the [Menu] View command, which allows you to view your tables on the screen. Finally, we'll show you how to edit your tables.

We will discuss advanced techniques for editing and data entry in Chapter 3, and show you how to design and use forms in Chapter 4.

Creating Tables

Before you can do anything in Paradox, you must create one or more tables to hold your data. In this part of the chapter, we'll show you how to use the [Menu] Create command to create tables to store your information.

A Simple Example

Suppose you want to create the EMPLYEE table shown in Figure 2-1 on the following page. To begin, issue the **[Menu]** Create command. After you issue the command, Paradox will prompt you to enter a table name, as shown in Figure 2-2.

Figure 2-2 The Table Prompt

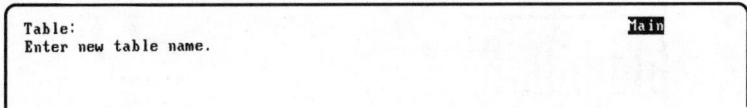

```
Table:                                                        Main
Enter new table name.
```

When you see this prompt, you should type the name you want Paradox to give to the new table you are creating. In this case, you should type **EMPLYEE** and press ↵.

Figure 2-1 The EMPLYEE Table

Emp Number	Last Name	First Name	SS Number	Address	City	State	Zip	Phone	Date of Birth	Date of Hire	Exemptions	Salary
1	Jones	Dave	414-76-3421	4000 St. James Ct.	St. Matthews	KY	40207	(502) 245-6618	10/06/42	1/14/87	3	70,000.00
2	Cameron	Herb	321-65-8765	2331 Elm St.	Louisville	KY	40205	(502) 451-8765	11/24/29	1/14/87	4	50,000.00
4	Roberts	Stewart	401-32-8721	4389 Oakbridge Rd.	Lyndon	KY	40222	(502) 452-1040	3/21/50	2/13/87	1	47,000.00
5	Jones	Darlene	417-43-7777	451 Lone Pine Dr.	Lagrange	KY	40012	(502) 897-3215	9/24/60	6/16/87	3	14,000.00
6	Williams	Jean	414-07-9123	4000 St. James Ct.	St. Matthews	KY	40207	(502) 245-6618	5/14/43	7/16/87	1	33,999.99
8	Myers	Brenda	401-55-1567	555 Court St.	Anchorage	KY	40223	(502) 894-9761	2/06/48	8/16/87	8	40,000.00
9	Link	Julie	314-30-9452	4512 Parkside Dr.	Louisville	KY	40206	(502) 454-5289	6/03/33	9/16/87	1	40,000.00
10	Jackson	Mary	345-75-1525	3215 Palm Ct.	Palo Alto	CA	94375	(400) 542-1940	8/12/56	11/14/87	4	32,000.00
12	Preston	Molly	424-13-7621	7821 Clark Ave.	Clarksville	IN	47130	(812) 288-6754	4/17/66	11/14/87	2	30,000.00
14	Masters	Ron	451-00-3426	321 Indian Hills Rd.	Louisville	KY	40205	(502) 456-3256	12/30/44	2/13/88	3	21,000.00
15	Triplett	Judy	317-65-4529	423 W. 72nd St.	New York	NY	10019	(212) 456-5478	8/12/58	2/13/88	1	14,750.00
13	Robertson	Kevin	616-10-6618	140 Ashby St.	Clarksville	IN	47130	(812) 288-3301	3/16/25	11/23/87	8	30,000.00
16	Garrison	Robert	415-24-6710	431 Bardstown Rd.	Elizabethtown	KY	40315	(502) 423-9823	5/09/45	2/27/88	2	15,750.00
17	Gunn	Barbara	312-90-1479	55 Wheeler St.	Boston	MA	25687	(617) 543-4124	5/18/58	5/15/88	1	37,000.00
19			321-97-0632	541 Kentucky St.	New Albany	IN	47132	(812) 325-4709		6/15/88	2	17,500.00

The STRUCT Table

Next, Paradox will display the STRUCT table shown in Figure 2-3. STRUCT is a special temporary table that you use to define the structure of permanent tables. By filling in the STRUCT table, you define the structure of the table you are creating.

Figure 2-3 The STRUCT Table

```
Creating new Employee table                                    Create
STRUCT┬───────────Field Name═══════════╥═Field Type╗
    1 ║                               ◄║          ║    ┌──── FIELD TYPES ────
                                                        A_: Alphanumeric (ex: A25)
                                                        Any combination of
                                                        characters and spaces
                                                        up to specified width.
                                                        Maximum width is 255

                                                        N: Numbers with or without
                                                         decimal digits.

                                                        $: Currency amounts.

                                                        D: Dates in the form
                                                        mm/dd/yy, dd-mon-yy,
                                                        or dd.mm.yy
                                                        ─────────────────────────
                                                        Use '*' after field type to
                                                        show a key field (ex: A4*).
```

The first column under the word *STRUCT* on the left side of the screen is the field number column. You will not enter anything in this column. As you add fields to the table, Paradox will automatically number them consecutively.

The next column is the Field Name column. This is where you will enter the names of the fields you want to include in the table you are creating. By typing the name of a field in this column, you are telling Paradox to include a field with that name.

The last column in the STRUCT table is the Field Type column. You will use this column to specify the field type for each field in the table. To do this, you enter a letter in this column that represents the field type: *A* for alphanumeric fields, *N* for number fields, *S* for short number fields, *$* for dollar fields, and *D* for date fields. When you designate a field as an alphanumeric field, you must also specify the size, or width, of the field. To specify the width of a field, you must enter a number between 1 and 255 after the letter *A* in the Field Type column.

When you look at Figure 2-3, you will notice that Paradox displays a reminder of the field types on the right side of the screen. This reminder is displayed only while you are creating or restructuring tables.

Defining the Table

Now, you are ready to create the EMPLYEE table. To begin, type **Emp Number** in the first and only row of the Field Name column. Next, press the ➡ key to move the cursor to the Field Type column and type **N** to designate this as a number field. After you do this, your screen will look like Figure 2-4.

Figure 2-4 Defining Fields

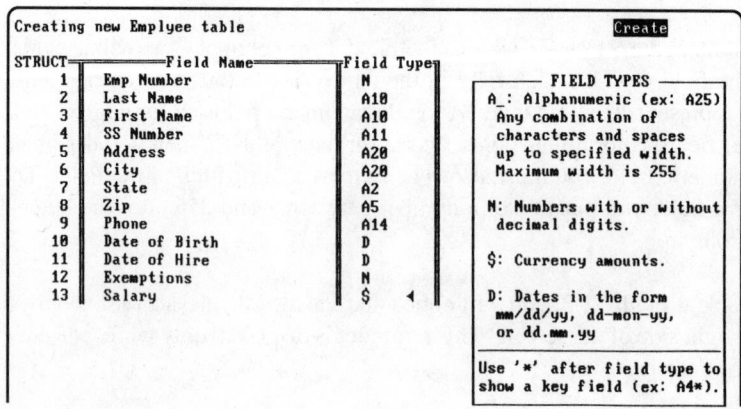

Now, press the ↵ key to move the cursor down one line, type **Last Name** in the Field Name column and **A10** in the Field Type column. The letter *A* defines this as an alphanumeric field and the number 10 in this entry specifies the width of the Last Name field. Next, press ↵ again to move to the third row of STRUCT, type the field name **First Name**, press ➡ to move to the Field Type column, and type **A10**. Continue entering field names and field types in this way until your screen looks like Figure 2-5.

Figure 2-5 The Completed STRUCT Table

```
Creating new Emplyee table                                          Create
STRUCT           Field Name        Field Type
        1   Emp Number            N                        ┌─── FIELD TYPES ───
        2   Last Name             A10                      A_: Alphanumeric (ex: A25)
        3   First Name            A10                       Any combination of
        4   SS Number             A11                       characters and spaces
        5   Address               A20                       up to specified width.
        6   City                  A20                       Maximum width is 255
        7   State                 A2
        8   Zip                   A5                       N: Numbers with or without
        9   Phone                 A14                       decimal digits.
       10   Date of Birth         D
       11   Date of Hire          D                        $: Currency amounts.
       12   Exemptions            N
       13   Salary                $    ◄                   D: Dates in the form
                                                            mm/dd/yy, dd-mon-yy,
                                                            or dd.mm.yy

                                                          Use '*' after field type to
                                                          show a key field (ex: A4*).
```

When you have filled in the STRUCT table, press [**Do-It!**] ([F2]), or issue the [**Menu**] DO-IT! command to save the new table. When you do this, Paradox will display the message *Creating Emplyee...* in the lower-right corner of the screen. After a few seconds, Paradox will return to the main workspace. The new empty table will be saved to disk under the name EMPLYEE.DB.

Notes

When Paradox prompts you for the name of the table you want to create, you should specify a name that does not already exist in the current directory. If you enter a name that is the same as the name of an existing table, Paradox will prompt you for confirmation, as shown in Figure 2-6. In addition, the message *TABLENAME table already exists* will appear at the bottom of the screen. If you select Cancel at this point, Paradox will return to the previous prompt so that you can erase the name you entered and enter another name. If you select Replace, Paradox will replace the old table with the new one you are creating. Be careful! All of the data in the old table will be lost if you choose Replace.

Figure 2-6 The Cancel/Replace Menu

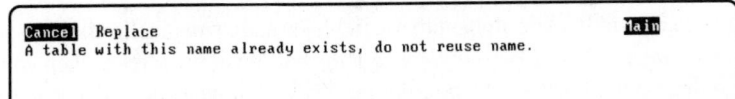

```
Cancel  Replace                                        Main
A table with this name already exists, do not reuse name.
```

Field Names

In Paradox, field names can be up to 25 characters long and can include any printable character except double quotes ("), brackets ([]), braces ({ }), and the combination ->. Field names can contain spaces, but cannot begin with a space.

You cannot use the same field name twice in the same table. If you attempt to do so, Paradox will display the message *Duplicate field name in the STRUCT table* when you press [Do-It!] to save the structure. Until you remove one of the duplicate field names, you won't be able to create the table.

You should select field names that describe the contents of the fields they name. For example, we chose the field name Emp Number in the EMPLYEE table to indicate that this field will contain the unique employee number assigned to each employee in the company. The name Salary tells you that the Salary field will contain the salary of each employee.

While your field names can be up to 25 characters long, we suggest that you try to use field names that are as short as possible. When you view a table, Paradox will display each field slightly wider than its field name. By using short field names, you can get more of your table on the screen at one time. One way to achieve short field names is to abbreviate long words. If you choose the abbreviations carefully, you can save space without losing the benefit of clarity. For example, notice that we have used the abbreviation Emp Number for the name of the field that will contain the employee number data, rather than Employee Number.

Field Types

Paradox recognizes five field types: alphanumeric, number, short number, dollar, and date. Let's look at each of these types in detail.

Alphanumeric (A) Fields

An alphanumeric field can contain entries that are made up of letters, numbers, and/or special characters. To define a field as an alphanumeric field, you should enter an *A* in the Field Type column of the STRUCT table next to that field's name. In addition, you must specify the width of the field by entering a number between 1 and 255 in this column after the letter *A*. The number you enter sets the maximum number of characters that can be entered into the field. For example, look at the Last Name row in the STRUCT table in Figure 2-5. The entry *A10* in the Field Type column tells Paradox that you want to create an alphanumeric field with a maximum width of ten characters.

If you do not enter a width for an alphanumeric field, Paradox will display the message *Enter length of alphanumeric field; for example A12* at the bottom of the screen when you attempt to move the cursor out of the Field Type column. You will not be allowed to leave the Field Type column until you have entered an acceptable width.

Alphanumeric fields are the only fields to which you must assign a width. Paradox will automatically set the width for number, short number, dollar, and date fields.

Since alphanumeric fields can contain numbers, letters, and special characters, you may wonder why you shouldn't make all of your fields alphanumeric. The reason is simple. While alphanumeric fields will accept any type of entry, Paradox does not allow you to perform math on the entries in alphanumeric fields. In general, you should use the alphanumeric field type for fields that contain letters only, or letters and numbers.

Number (N) Fields

To designate a field as a number field, enter an *N* in the Field Type column for that field in the STRUCT table. A number field can contain only numbers. Number fields can store positive and negative numbers with magnitudes as small as 10^{-307} and as large as 10^{308} with up to 15 significant digits. For example, you could enter the numbers 1234, .004356, and 123456789.012345 into a number field. Numbers with more than 15 significant digits are automatically rounded and stored in scientific notation. For example, the number 123456789123456789 would be stored as 1.23456789123457E+17 and displayed on the screen as a string of asterisks. To view the number, you would need to press [Field View] ([Alt]-[F5]) or use the [Menu] Image ColumnSize command to widen the column. We'll show you how to use [Field View], and we'll discuss the [Menu] Image ColumnSize command later in this chapter.

By default, Paradox displays number fields without commas and with up to two decimal places. For example, the number 1,234.00 would be displayed as 1234 in a number field. The number 1,234.56 would be displayed as 1234.56, and the number 1,234.50 would be displayed as 1234.5. Negative numbers are preceded by a minus sign (-) and appear in red.

Short Number (S) Fields

To designate a field as a short number field, type an *S* in the Field Type column of the STRUCT table. Short number fields are special number fields that can contain only whole numbers between -32,767 and 32,767. In addition, you cannot use any of Paradox's field formats (which you'll learn about in Chapter 3) in short number fields.

The principal advantage of using short number fields is that they require less disk space than regular number fields. In general, because of their limited range, we recommend that you use short number fields only in very large tables where conserving space is important. However, one excellent use of the short number field type is in fields that number the entries in a table. For example, we might have used the short number type for the Emp Number field in EMPLYEE. Since this type of field contains only integers and will not contain an entry greater than 32,767, the normal short number type limitations are not a problem.

Dollar ($) Fields

To designate a field as a dollar field, enter a dollar sign ($) in the Field Type column of that field in the STRUCT table. Like number and short number fields, dollar fields can contain only numbers.

Dollar fields are similar to number fields, with a couple of important differences. First, when numbers in dollar fields are displayed, they appear rounded to two decimal places, and large values are displayed with commas. For example, the number 1234.567 would be displayed as 1,234.57 in a dollar field. If the number does not have a decimal portion, Paradox will add two zeros to the right of the decimal for display purposes. For instance, the number 1234 would be displayed as 1,234.00 in a dollar field. In addition, negative numbers in dollar fields are displayed in parentheses instead of being preceded by a minus sign. For example, the value -1234.56 would be displayed as (1,234.56) in a dollar field.

It is important to understand that the formatting that occurs when you enter a number in a dollar field affects only the display of the number and not the number itself. In other words, although the number 1234.567 would be displayed as 1,234.57 in a dollar field, the actual value in the field would still be 1234.567. If you used this number in a calculation (we'll show you how to do that in a later chapter), Paradox would base the calculation on the full value, 1234.567, and not on the rounded value, 1,234.57.

Date (D) Fields

Date fields allow you to store dates in your Paradox tables. To designate a date field, you should enter a *D* in the Field Type column for that field in the STRUCT table. A date field can contain any valid date between January 1, 100, and December 31, 9999.

You can enter or display dates in several formats. The default date format is MM/DD/YY. To enter the date April 9, 1989, into a table in this form, you would type 4/09/89 or 4/9/89. Alternatively, you can enter dates in the form DD-Mon-YY, or DD.MM.YY. No matter how you enter the date, however, Paradox will display it in the form MM/DD/YY unless you use the [Menu] Image Format command to change the format. For instance, if you enter 24-Nov-89 in a date field, Paradox will display it as 11/24/89.

Just how you specify the year portion of a date depends on which century that date falls in. For dates between January 1, 1900, and December 31, 1999, you need only type the last two digits of the year. For dates before January 1, 1900, or after December 31, 1999, you must type all four digits. For example, to enter the date March 21, 2001, into a table, you would type 3/21/2001, 21-Mar-2001, or 21.3.2001.

Paradox automatically checks every date you enter to be sure that it is valid. A valid date is any date that appears on a calendar, including leap days. If you attempt to enter an invalid date into a date field, Paradox will display the message *No such date* in the lower-right corner of the screen.

Later in this book, we'll show you how to perform arithmetic using the entries in date fields and how to use date fields in queries to select records.

Moving around on the Screen

When you are creating a new table, you will use the cursor-movement keys (←, →, ↑, and ↓) and the ↵ key to move around in the STRUCT table. For the most part, the effect of pressing these keys should be clear. Later in this chapter, we will elaborate on how Paradox handles the cursor-movement keys.

Editing the STRUCT Table

From time to time, you will make errors as you are making entries in the STRUCT table. Fortunately, it is very easy to edit the contents of the STRUCT table. Let's look at a few examples of how you can do this.

Changing an Entry

If you make a typing error while making an entry in the STRUCT table, you can press [Backspace] to erase the error and then type the correct character or characters. For example, suppose that as you are defining the Emp Number field, you type *Emp Numbr* accidentally. Assuming that you haven't moved the cursor, you can press [Backspace] once to erase the *r* and then type *er*. If you have moved the cursor, just move it back to the Field Name column for the Emp Number field before you press [Backspace].

If the error is near the beginning of the entry or if the entire entry is an error, you can press [Ctrl]-[Backspace] to erase it completely and then start over from scratch. Suppose that when you are defining the Emp Number field, you absent-mindedly type *Cust Number*. Instead of pressing [Backspace] 11 times to erase the entry, you could press [Ctrl]-[Backspace] once to erase the entire entry and then type *Emp Number* in the empty column.

Inserting a Row

If you forget to define a field, you can use the [Ins] key to insert a blank row in the STRUCT table, then enter the missing field definition in that row. For example, suppose that while defining the EMPLYEE table, you left out the Address field. To add the Address field to the table definition, move the cursor to the City row of the STRUCT table and press [Ins] to insert a blank row. Figure 2-7 shows the screen at this point. Now, you can type *Address* in the Field Name column of the new row and *A20* in the Field Type column to define the Address field.

Figure 2-7 Inserting a Row

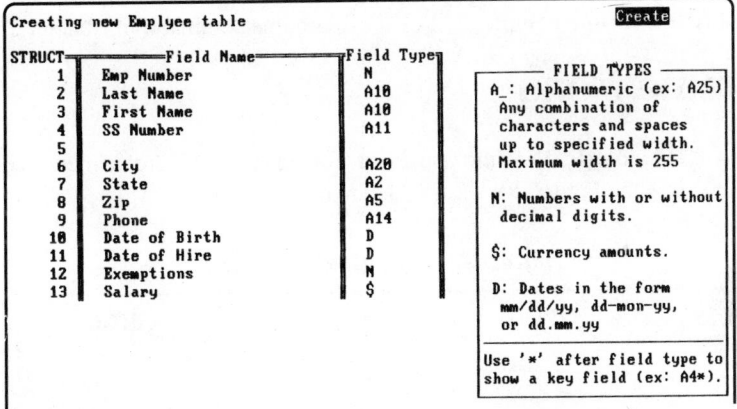

Deleting a Row

If you find you have entered a field in the STRUCT table by accident, you can delete that field by positioning the cursor on it and pressing [Del]. For example, suppose that in creating EMPLYEE, you accidentally included a field named MI (for middle initial) between the Last Name and First Name fields. Figure 2-8 shows this STRUCT table. To remove this unwanted field, just move the cursor to it and press [Del]. The finished STRUCT table will look just like Figure 2-5.

Figure 2-8 Deleting a Row

```
Creating new Emplyee table                                    Create
STRUCT          Field Name          Field Type
   1   | Emp Number              N*          ┌──── FIELD TYPES ────┐
   2   | Last Name               A18         A_: Alphanumeric (ex: A25)
   3   | MI                      A1          Any combination of
   4   | First Name              A18         characters and spaces
   5   | SS Number               A11         up to specified width.
   6   | Address                 A20         Maximum width is 255
   7   | City                    A20
   8   | State                   A2          N: Numbers with or without
   9   | Zip                     A5          decimal digits.
  10   | Phone                   A14
  11   | Date of Birth           D           $: Currency amounts.
  12   | Date of Hire            D
  13   | Exemptions              N           D: Dates in the form
  14   | Salary                  $           mm/dd/yy, dd-mon-yy,
                                             or dd.mm.yy

                                             Use '*' after field type to
                                             show a key field (ex: A4*).
```

Restructuring Tables

The techniques presented so far assume that you catch your mistakes before you press [Do-It!] to save the structure of your table. If you don't realize your mistake until after you have saved the structure, you can still correct the error. To do so, however, you must use the [Menu] Modify Restructure command. We'll explain this command in Chapter 5.

The Create Menu

When you press [Menu] ([F10]) while you are creating a table, the Create menu will appear at the top of the screen. Figure 2-9 shows the Create menu.

Figure 2-9 The Create Menu

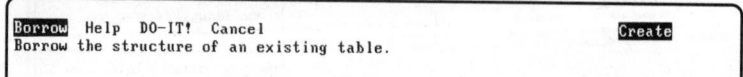

```
Borrow  Help  DO-IT!  Cancel                              Create
Borrow the structure of an existing table.
```

The Help Command

The Help command on this menu should already be familiar to you. As you learned in Chapter 1, most of Paradox's menus offer a Help option. The Help command allows you to access Paradox's context-sensitive help facility. You can also access help by pressing [Help] ([F1]).

The DO-IT! Command

The DO-IT! command appears on many Paradox menus. Although the precise effect of the DO-IT! command varies from menu to menu, its general purpose is to process whatever action you are taking. When you choose DO-IT! from the Create menu, Paradox creates the table you have defined in the STRUCT table and returns to the main workspace. Pressing the [Do-It!] key ([F2]) has the same effect as choosing the DO-IT! command.

The Cancel Command

The [Menu] Cancel command lets you leave the Create menu and return to the main workspace without saving your work. When you issue this command, Paradox "forgets" the entries you have made in the STRUCT table and returns to the main workspace without creating a table. Paradox does not prompt you for confirmation before it cancels the creation process. The message *Canceling table creation...* will appear in the lower-right corner of the screen. Pressing [Ctrl]-[Break] has the same effect as issuing the [Menu] Cancel command.

The Borrow Command

The [Menu] Borrow command allows you to borrow the structure of one or more existing tables to create a new table. Suppose you want to create a simple table named ADDRESS to store the names, addresses, and phone numbers of your business contacts. You want this table to include eight fields: Last Name, First Name, Spouse, Address, City, State, Zip, and Phone.

To create the ADDRESS table, issue the [**Menu**] Create command and type **ADDRESS** when Paradox asks you for the name of the new table. When the STRUCT table appears, you can do one of two things. First, you could begin defining the structure of ADDRESS in the same way you defined EMPLYEE: by typing the name of each field in the Field Name column of the STRUCT table and then entering the type for each field in the Field Type column. However, there is an easier way. You might have noticed that all of the fields you want to include in ADDRESS (except Spouse) are also defined in EMPLYEE. Instead of creating ADDRESS from scratch, you can create it by borrowing the structure of EMPLYEE.

To do this, issue the [**Menu**] Borrow command. After you issue the command, Paradox will prompt you to enter the name of the table whose structure you want to borrow. When you see this prompt, type **EMPLYEE** and press ↵. Paradox will then add the fields from the EMPLYEE table to the STRUCT table, as shown in Figure 2-10 on the following page.

Since ADDRESS and EMPLYEE do not have identical structures, you now need to do a bit of editing. First, press [**Del**] to delete the Emp Number column. Then, move the cursor to the SS number field and press [**Del**] to delete that Field. At this point, the cursor will be in the record of the STRUCT table that contains the field name Address. Press [**Ins**] to insert a new row. Then type **Spouse** in the Field Name column and **A10** in the Field Type column to add the Spouse field to the table. Next, move down to the Date of Birth field and press [**Del**] four times to delete the Date of Birth, Date of Hire, Exemptions, and Salary fields.

If you wish, you can also change the type of any field in the STRUCT table or change the length of any alphanumeric field. For example, to change the length of the Last Name field in the ADDRESS definition to 15 characters, just move the cursor to the Field Type column of the Last Name field in STRUCT, press [**Backspace**] once to erase the 0 in the length definition, type **5**, and press ↵. Figure 2-11 shows the completed STRUCT table.

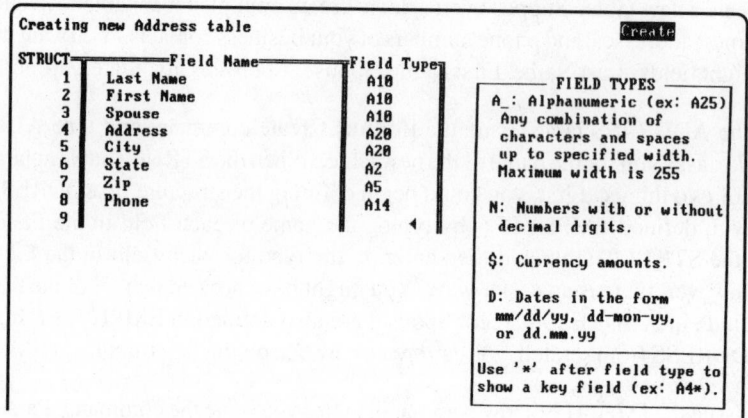

Figure 2-10 Borrowing the Structure of EMPLYEE

Figure 2-11 The Completed STRUCT Table

When you have made the changes you want, you should press [**Do-It!**] ([F2]) or issue the [**Menu**] DO-IT! command to save the table and return to the main workspace.

Entering Data

When you press [Do-It!] ([F2]) or issue the [Menu] DO-IT! command to save a newly created table, Paradox creates an empty table and returns to the main workspace. In order to enter data into the table, you must issue the [Menu] Modify DataEntry command. When you issue this command and specify the name of the table into which you want to enter data, Paradox will bring a special temporary table named ENTRY into view. You type the data you want to store in the main table into the fields of ENTRY. When you have entered your data into ENTRY, press [Do-It!]. When you press this key, Paradox copies the entries you've made in ENTRY into the permanent table, empties ENTRY, and returns you to the main workspace.

An Example

Suppose you want to enter the records shown in Figure 2-1 into the EMPLYEE table you just created. To do this, issue the [**Menu**] **M**odify **D**ataEntry command. After you issue the command, Paradox will prompt you to enter the name of the table into which you want to enter data. When you see this prompt, type **EMPLYEE** and press ↵. Paradox then will display the temporary ENTRY table shown in Figure 2-12.

Figure 2-12 The ENTRY Table

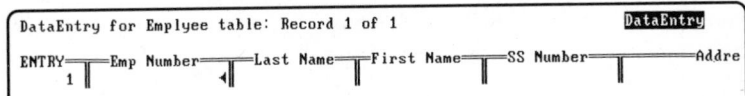

```
DataEntry for Emplyee table: Record 1 of 1                    DataEntry

ENTRY╤══Emp Number══╤══Last Name══╤══First Name══╤══SS Number══╤══════════Addre
  1 ║             ◄║
```

The ENTRY Table

When you use the [Menu] Modify DataEntry command to enter records into a table, you will first enter those records into a temporary table named ENTRY. Just as you use the STRUCT table to create permanent tables, you will use the ENTRY table to add records to permanent tables. The purpose of this process is to protect existing records in a permanent table while you are entering new records.

The structure of ENTRY always matches the structure of whatever table you are entering records into. When you look at Figure 2-12, you will notice that the names of the EMPLYEE table fields are displayed horizontally on the screen. You also will notice a current operation status message (*DataEntry for Emplyee table:*), a cursor location indicator (*Record 1 of 1*), and a mode indicator (*DataEntry*).

The leftmost column of the table (under the word *ENTRY*) is a record number column. Paradox will automatically number the records as you enter them—you do not need to enter anything in this column.

If you are using a multitable form to enter data into more than one table at the same time, then Paradox will hold information targeted for the master table in the ENTRY table and data for detail tables in additional ENTRY tables, each of which will be numbered. For example, if a multitable form includes a master table and two detail tables, Paradox will create three tables (ENTRY, ENTRY1, and ENTRY2) to hold the data being entered into the three permanent tables. We'll show you how to create multitable forms in Chapter 4. In Chapter 9, we'll discuss entering data with a multitable form.

Making Entries

When the ENTRY table first appears on the screen, the cursor will be in the first field of the table (in this case, the Emp Number field). To begin entering records, just start typing. For example, to enter the first record, type **1** and press the → key or the ↵ key. When you do this, Paradox will enter a 1 in the Emp Number column and move to the Last Name column. Now, type **Jones** and press ➜ or ↵ again. Paradox will add the name to the field and move the cursor to the next field. Figure 2-13 shows the screen at this point.

Figure 2-13 Adding Records to ENTRY

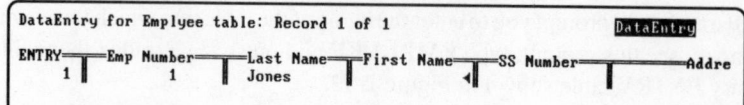

You should continue to enter information into each column until you have completed the first record. To do this, type **Dave** in the First Name field, press ↵ or ➜, type **414-76-3421** in the SS Number field, press ↵ or ➜ again, and so on.

Notice that as you move the cursor to the right through the fields of ENTRY, the leftmost fields disappear off the left side of the screen. This occurs because, like most tables you'll create, EMPLYEE and its ENTRY table are too wide to be viewed on the screen in their entirety. When you're viewing the leftmost fields of the ENTRY table, the rightmost fields, such as Salary, are out of view. When you press ➜ to move to the right, the leftmost fields disappear as the rightmost fields come into view.

After you type the information in the Salary column and press the ➜ key, Paradox will move the cursor down one line and back to the Emp Number field. Figure 2-14 shows how your screen will look at this point.

Figure 2-14 Adding Records to ENTRY

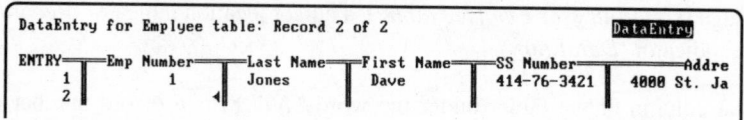

You now should enter all of the remaining records from Figure 2-1 into your new table, using the same technique you used to enter the record for Dave Jones.

Cursor Control

When you are entering data, you can use the cursor-movement keys to move around the ENTRY table. The main keys you will use and their functions are listed in Table 2-1. As you work with Paradox, you will discover that most of the keys have the same or very similar functions, regardless of what you are doing in the program. This consistency will help you learn the basics of the program very quickly.

If you use the cursor-movement keys to move beyond the edge of the table, Paradox will "wrap" the cursor onto the next line. For example, pressing the ➜, [Tab], or ↵ keys from the rightmost field of the table moves the cursor to the first field of the next record. Pressing ◄ from the leftmost field of the table will cause the cursor to move to the last field of the previous record (if you are already on the first record, Paradox will beep).

Table 2-1 Cursor-movement Keys

Key	Function
←	Moves the cursor left one field
→	Moves the cursor right one field
↑	Moves the cursor up one record
↓	Moves the cursor down one record
[Pg Up]	Moves the cursor up one screenful of records
[Pg Dn]	Moves the cursor down one screenful of records
[Home]	Moves the cursor to the first record of the current field
[End]	Moves the cursor to the last record of the current field
[Tab]	Moves the cursor right one field (same as →)
[Shift]-[Tab]	Moves the cursor left one field (same as ←)
↵	Moves the cursor right one field (same as →)
[Ctrl]-←	Moves the cursor left one full screen
[Ctrl]-→	Moves the cursor right one full screen
[Ctrl]-[Home]	Moves the cursor to the first field of the current record
[Ctrl]-[End]	Moves the cursor to the last field of the current record

If you attempt to move below the bottom of the table, such as by pressing the ↓ key from the last record, Paradox will add a new blank record to the end of the table and move the cursor to the first field in it.

Ending Data Entry

To end a data entry session, issue either the [Menu] DO-IT! command (or press [Do-It!]), the [Menu] Cancel Yes command, or the [Menu] KeepEntry command. Ending a session in any other way can endanger your data.

[Do-It!] and [Menu] DO-IT!

Pressing [Do-It!] or issuing the [Menu] DO-IT! command tells Paradox to end the data entry session, copy the records from the ENTRY table to the permanent table whose name you supplied at the beginning of the data entry session, empty the ENTRY table, then bring the permanent table into view on the screen. For example, when you have finished entering records into the ENTRY table, you should press **[Do-It!]** ([F2]) or issue the **[Menu]** DO-IT! command. When you do, Paradox will display the message *Adding records from Entry to Emplyee...* at the bottom of the screen. After a few moments, Paradox will display the EMPLYEE table in the workspace, as shown in Figure 2-15 on the following page.

The Cancel Command

The Cancel command throws away all of the records entered during the current data entry session and returns you to the main workspace. For example, suppose you are adding records to the EMPLYEE table and you discover a large number of errors. You could edit the records in the ENTRY table before adding them to EMPLYEE; however, you may find it easier to cancel the entire data entry operation and start over. To do this, issue the [Menu] Cancel command. After you issue the Cancel command, Paradox will prompt you for confirmation, as shown in Figure 2-16.

Figure 2-15 The EMPLYEE Table

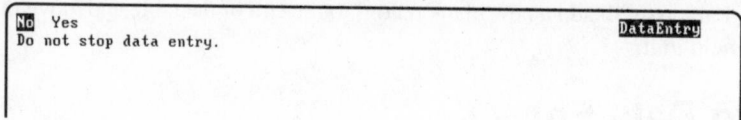

```
Viewing Employee table: Record 1 of 15                              Main

EMPLYEE┬─Emp Number─────┬─Last Name─┬─First Name─┬─SS Number──────┬──Addre
   1    │      1        │   Jones   │   Dave     │  414-76-3421   │ 4000 St. Ja
   2    │      2        │   Cameron │   Herb     │  321-65-8765   │ 2331 Elm St
   3    │      4        │   Jones   │   Stewart  │  401-32-8721   │ 4309 Oakbri
   4    │      5        │   Roberts │   Darlene  │  417-43-7777   │ 451 Lone Pi
   5    │      6        │   Jones   │   Jean     │  414-07-9123   │ 4000 St. Ja
   6    │      8        │   Williams│   Brenda   │  401-55-1567   │ 555 Court S
   7    │      9        │   Myers   │   Julie    │  314-38-9452   │ 4512 Parksi
   8    │     10        │   Link    │   Julie    │  345-75-1525   │ 3215 Palm C
   9    │     12        │   Jackson │   Mary     │  424-13-7621   │ 7821 Clark
  10    │     14        │   Preston │   Molly    │  451-00-3426   │ 321 Indian
  11    │     15        │   Masters │   Ron      │  317-65-4529   │ 423 W. 72nd
  12    │     13        │   Triplett│   Judy     │  616-10-6610   │ 14D Ashby S
  13    │     16        │   Robertson│  Kevin    │  415-24-6710   │ 431 Bardsto
  14    │     17        │   Garrison│   Robert   │  312-98-1479   │ 55 Wheeler
  15    │     19        │   Gunn    │   Barbara  │  321-97-8632   │ 541 Kentuck
```

Figure 2-16 Confirming the Cancel Command

```
No  Yes                                                        DataEntry
Do not stop data entry.
```

If you issue the No command at this point, Paradox will return to the DataEntry menu so that you can make another selection. If you issue the Yes command, Paradox will cancel all the changes you have made and return to the main workspace.

You can also cancel the operation by pressing [Ctrl]-[Break]. However, if you use this method, Paradox will not prompt you for confirmation. For this reason, we suggest that you always use the [Menu] Cancel command.

The KeepEntry Command

When you issue the KeepEntry command, Paradox ends the data entry session without adding the new records to the specified permanent table but preserves the ENTRY table (or ENTRY tables, if you are using a multitable form) containing the new data you have entered. You are most likely to use the KeepEntry command if you use Paradox on a network. Saving the ENTRY table is a useful ability if another user has a placed a lock on the table in which you want to enter the data when you try to transfer the data from ENTRY to the permanent table. After saving ENTRY, you can go about your business, then later try using the [Menu] Tools More Add command—or the [Menu] Tools More FormAdd command if you entered the data with a multitable form—to add the data in ENTRY to the permanent table. We will discuss the [Menu] Tools More Add command in Chapter 3 and the [Menu] Tools More FormAdd command in Chapter 9. For information on dealing with locks placed by other users, see Appendix A2.

Even if you do not use Paradox on a network, situations may arise in which you find the KeepEntry command useful. For example, suppose you have just spent an hour entering sales order information into a Paradox table, when a coworker tells you that your boss wants to postpone entering any new orders until later in the afternoon. In a case like this, you could use the KeepEntry command to save the new data that you have entered without actually adding it to the permanent table for which it is targeted. To save the ENTRY table, issue the [Menu] KeepEntry command. When you do, Paradox will display the message *Saving Entry table...* at the bottom of the screen. In a few moments, Paradox will display the ENTRY table on the Paradox workspace in the Main mode. Then, later in the afternoon, you could use the [Menu] Tools More Add command to add the new data to the permanent table for which it is targeted.

If you use the KeepEntry command in this manner, we suggest that you immediately use the [Menu] Tools Rename command to rename the ENTRY table. If you don't make ENTRY a permanent table by giving it a new name, Paradox will erase ENTRY along with any other temporary tables in the current directory as soon as you leave Paradox or change directories. After renaming the ENTRY table, you can add the renamed table to the permanent table, then erase the renamed table. We'll discuss the [Menu] Tools Rename command in Chapter 5.

Editing during Data Entry

It is inevitable that you will make errors as you enter records into your tables. As you might expect, Paradox offers several ways to edit these entries. In this section, we'll cover techniques you can use to edit entries while you're performing data entry. Later in the chapter, we'll show you how to edit records that you have already entered into a permanent table.

Table 2-2 shows the keys you will use to edit entries in a Paradox table. Let's consider a few examples of how these keys work.

Table 2-2 Editing Keys

Key	Function
[Ins]	Inserts a new record into the table
[Del]	Deletes a record from the table
[Backspace]	Erases a character in the current field
[Ctrl]-[Backspace]	Erases all of the characters in the current field
[Undo] ([Ctrl]-[U])	Undoes the last change made

Changing an Entry

If you make an error while you are typing an entry, you can press [Backspace] to erase the mistake. For example, suppose you are entering a record into EMPLYEE. As you make the Last Name field entry, you type *Johnsn* instead of *Johnson*, as shown in Figure 2-17. Provided that the cursor is still in the Last Name field, you can correct this error by pressing **[Backspace]** once to erase the letter *n*, and then typing **on**.

Figure 2-17 Changing an Entry

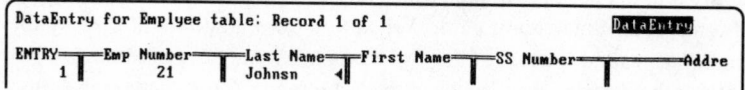

If the error is so great that you want to start from scratch, you can press [Ctrl]-[Backspace] to erase the entire entry, then type a new entry. For example, suppose that as you enter the Address field for the record in Figure 2-18, you type *2134 First St.* instead of *1234 First St.* To correct this error, you could press [Backspace] 14 times to erase the entire entry, then type the correct entry. An easier way, however, would be to press **[Ctrl]-[Backspace]** once to erase the entire contents of the field, as shown in Figure 2-19, and then type the correct entry.

Figure 2-18 Correcting Errors

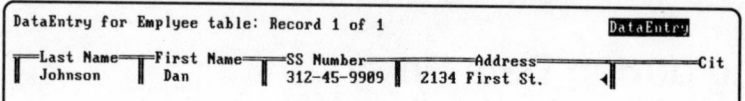

Figure 2-19 Using [Ctrl]-[Backspace]

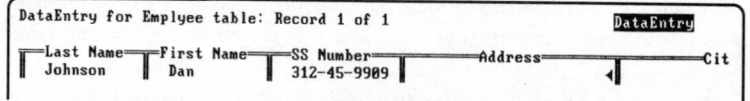

The Field View

If you make an error in the middle of an entry, but you don't want to erase the entry to make the correction, you can use the Paradox field view. The field view allows you to move around among the characters in the field, inserting new characters and deleting incorrect ones.

To enter the field view, position the cursor on the field you want to edit and press [**Field View**] ([Alt]-[F5]). Alternatively, you can press [Ctrl]-[F] to enter the field view. After you press [Field View], the cursor will change to a rectangular box. When you are using the field view, the effects of the cursor-movement keys change. For example, in the field view, the ➡ key moves the cursor one character to the right and the ← key moves the cursor one character to the left. The [Home] key moves the cursor to the first character in the field, while the [End] key moves the cursor to the last character. In fact, once you are in the field view, there is no way to move the cursor out of the current field until you press ↵ to leave the field view. Table 2-3 summarizes the effect of the cursor-movement keys in the field view.

Table 2-3 Cursor-movement Keys during the Field View

Key	Function
←	Moves the cursor left one character
→	Moves the cursor right one character
[Home]	Moves the cursor to the beginning of the current entry
[End]	Moves the cursor to the end of the current entry
[Ctrl]-←	Moves the cursor one word to the left
[Ctrl]-→	Moves the cursor one word to the right
[Ctrl]-[Home]	Same as [Home]
[Ctrl]-[End]	Same as [End]
↵	Ends the field view
[Ins]	Toggles between replace mode and insert mode
[Del]	Deletes the character at the cursor
[Backspace]	Deletes the character to the left of the cursor

The ↑, ↓, [Pg Up], and [Pg Dn] keys have no effect in the field view. For example, suppose that as you enter the City field for the record in Figure 2-19, you type *Phialdelphia* instead of *Philadelphia*. You could correct this error using the [Backspace] or [Ctrl]-[Backspace] techniques, but you might want to use the [Field View] key instead. To do this, first press the **[Field View]** key ([Alt]-[F5]) to enter the field view. Figure 2-20 shows the resulting screen. As you can see, the cursor has changed into a rectangular box.

Figure 2-20 The Field View

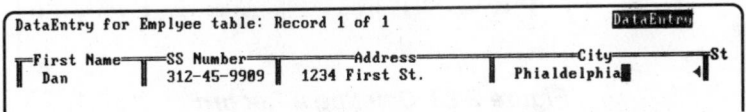

Now, press ← several times. You will notice that the cursor remains in the City field and moves to the left as you press this key. If you press →, the cursor will move to the right in the field, one character at a time. If you press [Home], the cursor will jump to the beginning of the entry in the field. If you press [End], it will jump to the end of the entry.

Using the cursor-movement keys, move the cursor to the first *a* in the entry you typed. Now, press **[Del]** twice to delete the letters *a* and *l*, and then type **la** to complete the entry. Figure 2-21 shows the screen at this point.

Figure 2-21 Correcting Errors in the Field View

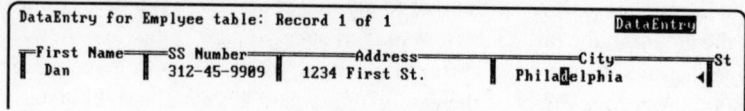

```
DataEntry for Emplyee table: Record 1 of 1                    DataEntry
┌First Name──┬─SS Number──────┬──────Address────┬──────City──────┬─St
│ Dan        │ 312-45-9909    │ 1234 First St.  │ Philadelphia   ◄
```

Now, press ↵ to leave the field view. Once you are out of the field view, you can resume
moving the cursor and making entries as you normally would.

There are times when you must use the field view to view or edit a field. For example, we
noted earlier that Paradox will display very large numbers as a string of asterisks. When it
does, you must use the field view to view or edit the data in the field. Alternatively, you can
issue the [Menu] Image ColumnSize command and make the column wider. We'll show you
how to do that later in this chapter.

Deleting a Record

If you make errors in several entries in a record—or if you enter a record that you did not mean
to enter—you can delete the entire record by positioning the cursor on any field of that record
and pressing [Del]. For example, suppose you have entered the records shown in Figure
2-22 into the ENTRY table for EMPLYEE, then discover that the second record should not
have been entered. To remove this record from the table, move the cursor to any field in the
second record and press **[Del]**. When you press this key, Paradox will remove the current
record from the ENTRY table. The resulting table will look like Figure 2-23.

Figure 2-22 The ENTRY Table

```
DataEntry for Emplyee table: Record 4 of 4                    DataEntry
ENTRY─┬─Emp Number──┬───Last Name─┬─First Name─┬─SS Number──────┬───────Addre
 1    │    21       │ Johnson     │ Dan        │ 312-45-9909    │ 1234 First
 2    │    22       │ Miller      │ Glen       │ 414-34-1234    │ 1776 Second
 3    │    23       │ Samuels     │ Sam        │ 401-12-5555    │ #12 Downing
 4    │    24       │ Diller      │ Mike       │ 401-00-7654    │ 666 Hall La
```

Figure 2-23 Deleting a Record

```
DataEntry for Emplyee table: Record 2 of 3                    DataEntry
ENTRY─┬─Emp Number──┬───Last Name─┬─First Name─┬─SS Number──────┬───────Addre
 1    │    21       │ Johnson     │ Dan        │ 312-45-9909    │ 1234 First
 2    │    23       │ Samuels     │ Sam        │ 401-12-5555    │ #12 Downing
 3    │    24       │ Diller      │ Mike       │ 401-00-7654    │ 666 Hall La
```

Inserting a New Record

If you need to add a record in the middle of the ENTRY table, you can use the [Ins] key to
insert a new blank record in the table. For example, suppose you need to enter a new record
between the first two records in Figure 2-23. To do this, move the cursor to any field in what

is currently the second record in ENTRY and press **[Ins]**. Immediately, Paradox will insert a blank record in the ENTRY table, as shown in Figure 2-24. Now, you can enter information into this blank record.

Figure 2-24 Inserting a Record

```
DataEntry for Emplyee table: Record 2 of 4                    DataEntry

ENTRY      Emp Number     Last Name    First Name    SS Number       Addre
  1            21         Johnson      Dan          312-45-9909   1234 First
  2
  3            23         Samuels      Sam          401-12-5555   #12 Downing
  4            24         Diller       Mike         401-00-7654   666 Hall La
```

Although it is perfectly acceptable to insert rows in the ENTRY table, there is no need to do so. Usually, the order of the records in ENTRY is not very important.

The Undo Command

Paradox offers a command, Undo, that allows you to undo changes you have made to the ENTRY table. The Undo command can be used to delete from a table entries you have made accidentally, to undo a change you made to an entry, or to recover a record you deleted by mistake. (Paradox 1.0 does not offer this capability.)

You can issue the Undo command by pressing [Menu] while performing data entry and choosing Undo from the DataEntry menu, or by pressing the [Undo] key ([Ctrl]-[U]). While you are entering data, issuing the Undo command will undo the last change you made to the ENTRY table. If the last change you made was to enter a new record, that new record will be deleted. If the last change you made was to edit a record in the table, the fields in that record will be restored to their previous value. If the last change was to insert or delete a record, then issuing the Undo command will remove the inserted record or restore the deleted record. Issuing the Undo command a second time will undo the second-most-recent change you made to the table. Issuing the command a third time will undo the third-most-recent change, and so on.

An Example

Suppose you are working in the ENTRY table shown in Figure 2-25 on the next page and you accidentally press [Del], thereby deleting a record. Figure 2-26, also on the next page, shows the new ENTRY table with the third record deleted. To restore the record to the table, press **[Undo]** ([Ctrl]-[U]). Immediately, Paradox will undo the deletion. The message area at the bottom of the screen will display the message *Record 3 reinserted*.

Notes

There are a couple of important things to keep in mind about Undo. First, you can't reverse Undo. Once you've used Undo, the only way to get back to your original record is to repeat the action. For example, suppose you use the [Undo] key to delete a record you think was entered erroneously. If you then discover that the record was indeed correct, there's only one way to get it back: by retyping it.

Figure 2-25 The ENTRY Table

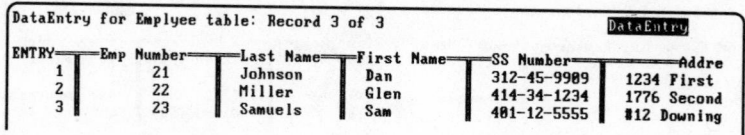

```
DataEntry for Emplyee table: Record 3 of 3                    DataEntry
ENTRY    Emp Number    Last Name    First Name    SS Number          Addre
  1          21         Johnson       Dan          312-45-9989    1234 First
  2          22         Miller        Glen         414-34-1234    1776 Second
  3          23         Samuels       Sam          401-12-5555    #12 Downing
```

Figure 2-26 Deleting a Record

```
DataEntry for Emplyee table: Record 2 of 2                    DataEntry
ENTRY    Emp Number    Last Name    First Name    SS Number          Addre
  1          21         Johnson       Dan          312-45-9989    1234 First
  2          22         Miller        Glen         414-34-1234    1776 Second
```

As you are performing data entry, Paradox maintains a transaction log of your actions. A "transaction" begins when you move the cursor into a new record and ends when you move the cursor out of that record. When you use the Undo command, Paradox simply reverses the effect of the last transaction.

Exactly how many transactions Paradox can record in its log depends on the amount of disk space on your computer. In most applications, you will never exceed the capacity of the log. However, in a few cases, it is possible that you will reach the limit. In that event, Paradox will warn you that you have reached a resource limit.

Advanced Data Entry Techniques

As you can see, entering records into a newly created table is extremely simple. However, as you become more experienced with Paradox, you will probably want to take advantage of its advanced data entry features. For example, you may want to change the way the table image is displayed on the screen, establish validity checks for certain fields, or enter data into more than one table by using a multitable form. We will discuss the Image command later in this chapter. Validity checks are covered in Chapter 3. We will explain how to design multitable forms in Chapter 4 and show you how to use them for entering data in Chapter 8.

The [Menu] View Command

The [Menu] View command allows you to view your tables on the screen. To view a table on the screen, you should issue the [Menu] View command and specify the table you want to view. When you press ↵ to lock in your choice, Paradox will bring the selected table into view on your screen.

For example, suppose you have created the EMPLYEE table discussed earlier, and you now want to view it. If the table is not already in view, you can bring it to the screen by issuing the [Menu] View command, typing the name of the table you want to view, **EMPLYEE**, and pressing ↵. Paradox then will bring the table onto the workspace, and your screen will look like Figure 2-27.

Figure 2-27 The Initial View of EMPLYEE

EMPLYEE	Emp Number	Last Name	First Name	SS Number	Addre
1	1	Jones	Dave	414-76-3421	4000 St. Ja
2	2	Cameron	Herb	321-65-8765	2331 Elm St
3	4	Jones	Stewart	401-32-8721	4389 Oakbri
4	5	Roberts	Darlene	417-43-7777	451 Lone Pi
5	6	Jones	Jean	414-07-9123	4000 St. Ja
6	8	Williams	Brenda	401-55-1567	555 Court S
7	9	Myers	Julie	314-38-9452	4512 Parksi
8	10	Link	Julie	345-75-1525	3215 Palm C
9	12	Jackson	Mary	424-13-7621	7821 Clark
10	14	Preston	Molly	451-00-3426	321 Indian
11	15	Masters	Ron	317-65-4529	423 W. 72nd
12	13	Triplett	Judy	616-10-6610	14D Ashby S
13	16	Robertson	Kevin	415-24-6710	431 Bardsto
14	17	Garrison	Robert	312-98-1479	55 Wheeler
15	19	Gunn	Barbara	321-97-8632	541 Kentuck

Viewing Emplyee table: Record 1 of 15   Main

When you bring a table into view, you are not looking at the actual table but at an image of the table. While you are viewing the image of the table on the screen, the actual table remains tucked away safely on your data disk. Keep this difference in mind as you work with Paradox: When you view a table, you are looking at an image of that table, not at the table itself. This difference is important because the changes you make in an image do not always affect the actual table.

As you will learn in Chapter 3, Paradox allows you to format the image of a table in a variety of ways. Since the image and the table are distinct, however, making changes to the appearance of the image has no effect on the actual table. Moreover, later in this chapter, you'll learn how to edit a table you are viewing. Since the changes you make are in the image of the table, not in the table itself, your data is safe from accidents. Paradox will not update the actual table with the changes you have made in the image until you press [Do-It!].

Selecting a Table

When you issue the View command, Paradox displays the prompt shown in Figure 2-28. When you see this prompt, you can type in the name of the table you want to view and then press ↵, or you can press ↵ to see a list of tables. If you press ↵ to see a list of tables, Paradox will display the names of the tables in the current directory, like the one shown in Figure 2-29 on the following page.

Figure 2-28 The Table Prompt

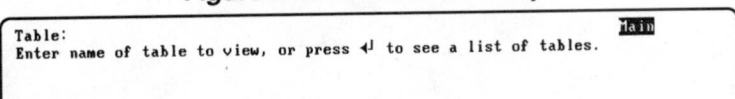

```
Table:
Enter name of table to view, or press ↵ to see a list of tables.    Main
```

Figure 2-29 A List of Tables

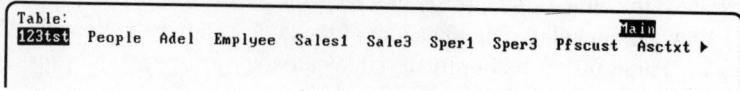

The symbol ▶ at the end of the line indicates that there are more tables than can be displayed on the screen at one time. To see the other table names, you can press the ← key or the → key to move the cursor from name to name. The [End] key will move the cursor to the last table name, while the [Home] key will move the cursor to the first table name. The ↑ key or the [Ctrl]-→ sequence will scroll one screen to the right, while the ↓ key or the [Ctrl]-← sequence will scroll one screen to the left.

To select a table to view from the list, just highlight its name with the cursor and press ↵. For example, to view the EMPLYEE table, you would point to its name in the list and press ↵.

You also can select a table by typing the first character of its name. For example, to select the EMPLYEE table, you can press **E** after you press ↵ at the *Table:* prompt.

If more than one table name on the current directory begins with the letter you type, Paradox will narrow the list to include just those tables whose names start with that letter. For example, suppose there are several tables in the current directory with names that begin with the letter *E*. When you type *E*, Paradox will narrow the list to display just the names of those tables, as shown in Figure 2-30. To select a table from this list, you must point to its name and press ↵.

Figure 2-30 Selecting a Table

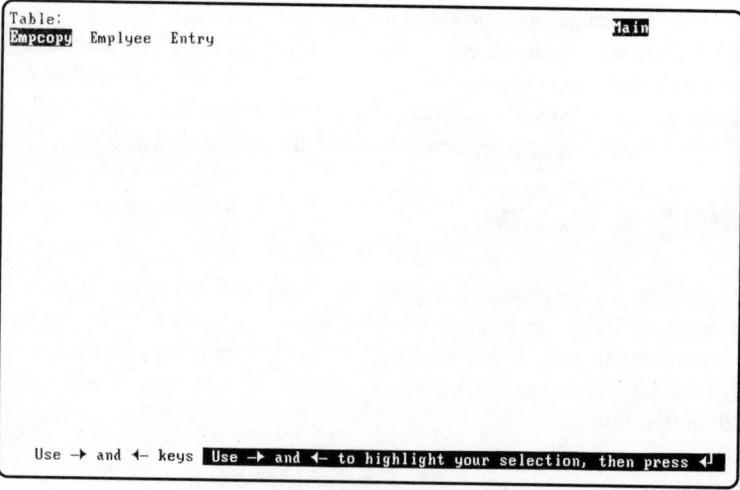

Moving around in an Image

When you are viewing a table, use the cursor-movement keys to move to the field or record you want to view. You can press the cursor-movement keys by themselves or in combination with other keys that enhance their action. The key combinations and their functions are the same as for data entry (see Table 2-1 on page 47).

Paradox will not create a new blank record if you attempt to move below the last record while viewing a table. For example, if the cursor is in the last column of the last record when you press ➡, you will hear a low-pitched beep. This is Paradox's way of letting you know that you have made an inappropriate selection—there is no field for the cursor to move to.

Viewing More of an Image

Like EMPLYEE, most tables are too large to be displayed in full on the screen. Whenever you use the [Menu] View command to bring a table into view, Paradox will position that table on the screen so that you see the upper-left corner of the table. In most cases, this means you'll see only the first few records and the leftmost fields in the table. For example, in Figure 2-27, you can see only the first four fields and part of the fifth field of EMPLYEE.

Viewing More Fields

Fortunately, it is easy to move the image around on the screen so that you can view the entire table. For example, to view more fields, press [Ctrl]-➡. After you do this, your screen will look like Figure 2-31.

Figure 2-31 Another View of EMPLYEE

```
Viewing Emplyee table: Record 1 of 15                          Main

      ═══Address═══         ═══City═══      ═State═ ═Zip═   ═══Phone═══
    4000 St. James Ct.    St. Matthews       KY     40207   (502) 245-6610
    2331 Elm St.          Louisville         KY     40205   (502) 451-8765
    4309 Oakbridge Rd.    Lyndon             KY     40222   (502) 452-1048
    451 Lone Pine Dr.     Lagrange           KY     40012   (502) 897-3215
    4000 St. James Ct.    St. Matthews       KY     40207   (502) 245-6610
    555 Court St.         Anchorage          KY     40223   (502) 894-9761
    4512 Parkside Dr.     Louisville         KY     40206   (502) 454-5209
    3215 Palm Ct.         Palo Alto          CA     94375   (408) 542-1948
    7821 Clark Ave.       Clarksville        IN     47130   (812) 288-6754
    321 Indian Hills Rd.  Louisville         KY     40205   (502) 456-3256
    423 W. 72nd St.       New York           NY     10019   (212) 276-5478
    14D Ashby St.         Clarksville        IN     47130   (812) 288-3301
    431 Bardstown Rd.     Elizabethtown      KY     40315   (502) 423-9823
    55 Wheeler St.        Boston             MA     25687   (617) 543-4124
    541 Kentucky St.      New Albany         IN     47132   (812) 325-4789
```

To view the remaining fields of the table, press [Ctrl]-➡ again. Now, your screen will look like Figure 2-32. As you can see, by moving the image around on the screen, you can easily view all of the records and fields in the table.

Figure 2-32 The Remaining Fields of EMPLYEE

```
Viewing Emplyee table: Record 1 of 15                              Main

     Phone        Date of Birth   Date of Hire   Exemptions       Salary
 (502) 245-6610    10/06/42         1/14/87           3          70,000.00
 (502) 451-8765    11/24/29         1/14/87           4          50,000.00
 (502) 452-1848    3/21/50          2/13/87           1          47,000.00
 (502) 897-3215    9/24/60          6/16/87           3          14,000.00
 (502) 245-6610    5/14/43          7/16/87           0          33,999.99
 (502) 894-9761    1/12/20          8/16/87           4          40,000.00
 (502) 454-5209    2/06/48          9/16/87           1          32,000.00
 (408) 542-1948    6/03/33         11/14/87           2          30,000.00
 (812) 288-6754    8/12/56         11/14/87           3          21,000.00
 (502) 456-3256    4/17/66          2/13/88           1          14,750.00
 (212) 276-5478   12/31/44          2/13/88           0          38,000.00
 (812) 288-3301    8/12/50         11/23/87           2          15,750.00
 (502) 423-9823    3/16/25          2/27/88           1          37,000.00
 (617) 543-4124    5/09/45          5/15/88           4          32,000.00
 (812) 325-4789    5/18/50          6/15/88           2          17,500.00
```

Viewing More Records

The EMPLYEE table contains a small number of records, so all of them are visible at once on the screen. In most cases, however, your tables will contain hundreds of records. The maximum number of records that can be displayed on the screen is 22. Fortunately, it is easy to bring other records into view. To move down through a table one record at a time, press ↓. To move down one screen at a time, press [Pg Dn]. To move directly to the last record in the table, press [End].

When you move down through the records in a large table, the first records in the table will scroll off the top of the screen as more records come into view at the bottom. If you want to view the top records again, you need only press ↑, [Pg Up], or [Home].

The [Menu] Image Zoom Command

The [Menu] Image Zoom command allows you to move the cursor instantly to a specific field, record, or value in the current table. (This command is known as [Menu] Image Goto in releases prior to Paradox 3.) When you issue this command, Paradox will display the Zoom menu, which is shown in Figure 2-33. As you can see, this menu offers three options: Field, Record, and Value.

Figure 2-33 The Zoom Menu

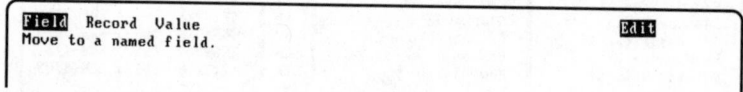

```
Field  Record  Value                                              Edit
Move to a named field.
```

The Field Option

When you issue the Field command, Paradox will display the field names for the current table, as shown in Figure 2-34. (You will recall that the ▶ symbol means that there are more options in the list that are not currently in view.) To select the field to which you want to go, either point to its name in the list and press ↵, or press the key corresponding to the first character of the field name. (If you have two or more field names that start with the same character, Paradox will prompt you to choose between them.) Once you select a field name, Paradox will move to that field instantly.

Figure 2-34 Selecting a Field for Zoom

```
Select a field to move to.                                      Main
Emp Number  Last Name  First Name  SS Number  Address  City  State  Zip  Phone ▶
```

For example, suppose you are viewing the EMPLYEE table and the cursor is in the Emp Number field. You want to move to the Exemptions field. To do this, issue the **[Menu]** I**mage** **Z**oom **F**ield command. When Paradox displays the field names for the current table, simply press **E** to select the Exemptions field. When you do this, Paradox will move the cursor to the Exemptions field, as shown in Figure 2-35.

Figure 2-35 Using the Image Zoom Command

```
Viewing Emplyee table: Record 1 of 15                           Main

     ┌Exemptions═══╗   ┌Salary═══╗
            3_           70,000.00
            4            50,000.00
            1            47,000.00
            3            14,000.00
            0            33,999.99
            4            40,000.00
            1            32,000.00
            2            30,000.00
            3            21,000.00
            1            14,750.00
            0            38,000.00
            2            15,750.00
            1            37,000.00
            4            32,125.00
            2            17,500.00
```

The Record Option

You also can use the Image Zoom command to move to a specific record in the current table. When you issue the [Menu] Image Zoom Record command, Paradox will display the prompt shown in Figure 2-36. You simply type the number of the record you want to move to and press ↵ to move the cursor to that record.

Figure 2-36 The Record Number Prompt

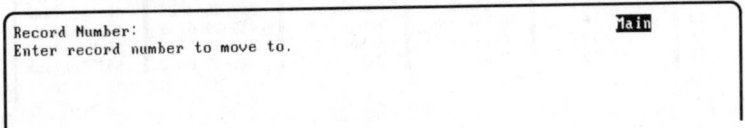

```
Record Number:                                                  Main
Enter record number to move to.
```

For example, suppose the cursor is in record 1 of EMPLYEE and you want to move it to record 15. To move to record 15, issue the **[Menu] I**mage **Z**oom **R**ecord command. When you see the prompt shown in Figure 2-36, type **15** and press ↵. When you do this, Paradox will move the cursor directly to record 15. The cursor will stay in the same field it was in when you issued the command.

The Value Option

You can use the [Menu] Image Zoom Value command to search for a particular entry in a field of a table. When you issue this command, Paradox will ask you to move the cursor to the field that contains the entry you want to find. After you have selected that field, Paradox will prompt you to specify the value you want to find. The search value can include numbers and/or letters. It can also include the Paradox wildcard operators .. and @. (See Chapter 7 for a discussion of wildcard operators.)

Once you've defined the search value, Paradox will search through the selected field for a matching entry. If it finds a match, Paradox will move the cursor to the record that contains the entry. If no match exists, Paradox will display the message *Match not found*, and the cursor will not move.

If you repeat the Image Zoom Value command while the cursor remains in the same field, Paradox will display the previous search value. You can press [Backspace] or [Ctrl]-[Backspace] to erase the old value and then type in a new value to search for.

For example, suppose you need to find information for employee Robertson. To find the record for this employee, first issue the [Menu] Image Zoom Value command. Then, move the cursor to the Last Name field and press ↵. Next, Paradox will prompt you to enter the value you want to search for. When you see this prompt, type **Robertson** and press ↵ . The cursor will move to record 13, which contains the first occurrence of the string *Robertson* in the Last Name field, and will momentarily highlight the field. Figure 2-37 shows the result.

Figure 2-37 The Image ZoomValue Command

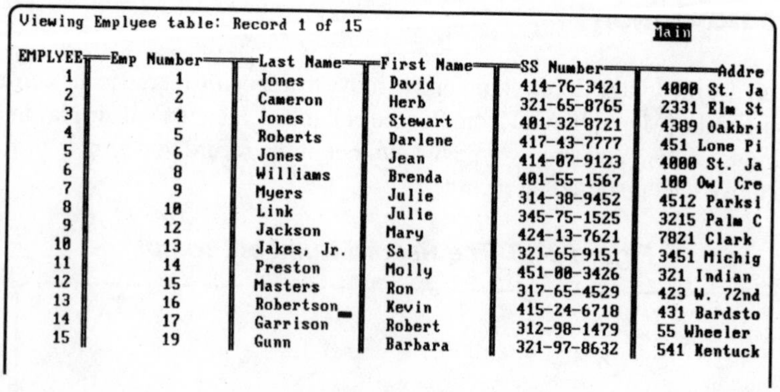

```
Viewing Emplyee table: Record 1 of 15                              Main

EMPLYEE──Emp Number──┬──Last Name──┬First Name──┬──SS Number──┬──────Addre
   1          1        Jones         David        414-76-3421    4000 St. Ja
   2          2        Cameron       Herb         321-65-8765    2331 Elm St
   3          4        Jones         Stewart      401-32-8721    4389 Oakbri
   4          5        Roberts       Darlene      417-43-7777    451 Lone Pi
   5          6        Jones         Jean         414-87-9123    4000 St. Ja
   6          8        Williams      Brenda       401-55-1567    100 Owl Cre
   7          9        Myers         Julie        314-38-9452    4512 Parksi
   8         10        Link          Julie        345-75-1525    3215 Palm C
   9         12        Jackson       Mary         424-13-7621    7821 Clark
  10         13        Jakes, Jr.    Sal          321-65-9151    3451 Michig
  11         14        Preston       Molly        451-08-3426    321 Indian
  12         15        Masters       Ron          317-65-4529    423 W. 72nd
  13         16        Robertson     Kevin        415-24-6718    431 Bardsto
  14         17        Garrison      Robert       312-98-1479    55 Wheeler
  15         19        Gunn          Barbara      321-97-8632    541 Kentuck
```

Paradox 2 and 3 include a special [Zoom] key ([Ctrl]-[Z]) that serves as a shortcut for the [Menu] Image Zoom Value command. When you press [Zoom], Paradox will immediately display a prompt asking you to specify a search value. All you have to do is type the search value you want to use and press ↵ to begin the search. Since [Zoom] does not give you a chance to select a field, you should be sure to move the cursor to the field you want to search before you press [Zoom]. If you have previously specified a search value for the current field, that value will appear next to the prompt. If you want to use that search value again, just press ↵ to begin the search. If you want to use a different search value, press [Backspace] or [Ctrl]-[Backspace] to erase the existing value, type a new one, and press ↵.

Once you've used the [Menu] Image Zoom Value command or the [Zoom] key to find the first occurrence of a search string in a field, you can use the [Zoom Next] key ([Alt]-[Z]) to search for the next occurrence. When you press [Zoom Next], Paradox will immediately begin searching at the location of the cursor in the table for the next occurrence of the search value. If there is another occurrence, Paradox will move the cursor to the record that contains the matching entry. After you have found the second occurrence, you can continue to press [Zoom Next] to find all entries in the table that match the search value. If no further match exists, Paradox will display the message *Match not found*.

Typing and Editing

You cannot make any changes to the data in a table you are viewing unless you first press the [Edit] key ([F9]) to enter the Edit mode. This feature of Paradox is designed to protect your data from being changed accidentally.

For instance, suppose you want to change the entry in the First Name field of the first record in the EMPLYEE table from *Dave* to *David*. You might try to move to that field and press [Ctrl]-[Backspace] to erase the current entry. When you do this, however, Paradox will display the message *Press the Edit key [F9] if you want to make changes* and will not erase the entry. If you want to change the entry, you must first press [Edit] to enter the Edit mode. We'll show you how to edit tables in the next section of this chapter.

Viewing More Than One Image

Paradox allows you to have more than one image on the screen at one time. In fact, you can have more than one image of a single table in view, or images of several different tables, or both. The number of images you can view at once is limited only by the memory capacity of your computer.

Viewing Two Images of the Same Table

If you want to view two parts of a single table at the same time, you can bring two images of that table into view simultaneously. For example, suppose you are viewing the EMPLYEE table as shown in Figure 2-27 on page 55, and you want to view more fields without changing the current image. To do this, issue the [**Menu**] View command again, type **EMPLYEE**, and press ↵. After you do this, your screen will look like Figure 2-38.

Figure 2-38 Two Views of EMPLYEE

```
Viewing Employee table: Record 1 of 15                          Main ▲═

EMPLYEE══Emp Number══════Last Name══First Name══SS Number══════════Addre
     12         13          Triplett   Judy        616-10-6610   14D Ashby S
     13         16          Robertson  Kevin       415-24-6710   431 Bardsto
     14         17          Garrison   Robert      312-98-1479   55 Wheeler
     15         19          Gunn       Barbara     321-97-8632   541 Kentuck


EMPLYEE══Emp Number══════Last Name══First Name══SS Number══════════Addre
      1          1          Jones      Dave        414-76-3421   4000 St. Ja
      2          2          Cameron    Herb        321-65-8765   2331 Elm St
      3          4          Jones      Stewart     401-32-8721   4389 Oakbri
      4          5          Roberts    Darlene     417-43-7777   451 Lone Pi
      5          6          Jones      Jean        414-07-9123   4000 St. Ja
      6          8          Williams   Brenda      401-55-1567   555 Court S
      7          9          Myers      Julie       314-38-9452   4512 Parksi
      8         10          Link       Julie       345-75-1525   3215 Palm C
      9         12          Jackson    Mary        424-13-7621   7821 Clark
     10         14          Preston    Molly       451-00-3426   321 Indian
     11         15          Masters    Ron         317-65-4529   423 W. 72nd
     12         13          Triplett   Judy        616-10-6610   14D Ashby S
     13         16          Robertson  Kevin       415-24-6710   431 Bardsto
     14         17          Garrison   Robert      312-98-1479   55 Wheeler
     15         19          Gunn       Barbara     321-97-8632   541 Kentuck
```

You now can adjust the two images to display the fields and records you want to view. For example, suppose you want to change the bottom image of EMPLYEE to display the rightmost fields in the table. To do this, press [**Ctrl**]-→ twice. After you do this, your screen will look like Figure 2-39.

Figure 2-39 Changing the Fields Displayed

```
Viewing Employee table: Record 1 of 15                          Main ▲═

EMPLYEE══Emp Number══════Last name══First Name══SS Number══════════Addre
     12         13          Triplett   Judy        616-10-6610   14D Ashby S
     13         16          Robertson  Kevin       415-24-6718   431 Bardsto
     14         17          Garrison   Robert      312-98-1479   55 Wheeler
     15         19          Gunn       Barbara     321-97-8632   541 Kentuck


    ══Phone══════Date of Birth══Date of Hire══Exemptions══════════Salary══
    (502) 245-6610   10/06/42     1/14/87          3          70,000.00
    (502) 451-8765   11/24/29     1/14/87          4          50,000.00
    (502) 452-1848   3/21/50      2/13/87          1          47,000.00
    (502) 897-3215   9/24/60      6/16/87          3          14,000.00
    (502) 245-6610   5/14/43      7/16/87          0          33,999.99
    (502) 894-9761   1/12/20      8/16/87          4          40,000.00
    (502) 454-5209   2/06/48      9/16/87          1          32,000.00
    (408) 542-1948   6/03/33     11/14/87          2          30,000.00
    (812) 288-6754   8/12/56     11/14/87          3          21,000.00
    (502) 456-3256   4/17/66      2/13/88          1          14,750.00
    (212) 276-5478  12/31/44      2/13/88          0          38,000.00
    (812) 288-3301   8/12/50     11/23/87          2          15,750.00
    (502) 423-9823   3/16/25      2/27/88          1          37,000.00
    (617) 543-4124   5/09/45      5/15/88          4          32,000.00
    (812) 325-4789   5/18/50      6/15/88          2          17,500.00
```

Notes

Notice that pressing [Ctrl]-→ while the cursor is in the lower image of EMPLYEE affects only that image. When you have more than one image displayed on the screen, the image containing the cursor is called the current image. All of your keystrokes refer to and affect the current image. For example, you have just seen that pressing [Ctrl]-→ when the cursor was in the bottom image affected that image, but not the top one.

The name of the table represented by the current image will always be the first in any list of names Paradox displays when you issue a command. For example, if you issue the [Menu] View command while the current image is an image of the EMPLYEE table, then press ↵ to see a list of table names, the name EMPLYEE will be the first name in the list. The same is true of the [Menu] Query command and any other command that offers a list of table names. Paradox 3 also sets off the current image on the screen by displaying the frame and column headings for that image in intense video. In earlier releases, all images appear in regular video.

Also notice that the second image of EMPLYEE came into view below the first image on the screen. The second table image you bring into view will always appear on the screen below the first, the third image will appear below the second, and so on.

In addition, notice that Paradox moved most of the first image of EMPLYEE out of view when you brought the second image into view. When you bring a second image to the screen, Paradox will display that image in full on the screen. If there are other images in view, Paradox will shift those images out of view off the top of the screen.

Whenever there is an image on the workspace that is not fully in view, Paradox will display a symbol in the upper-right corner of the screen. For example, notice the symbol ▲= at the top of the screen in Figure 2-39. This tells you that part of the upper image of EMPLYEE is not visible. Now, look at the symbol =▼ in the upper-right corner of Figure 2-40 on the next page. This tells you that a portion of the lower image of EMPLYEE is not in view. If there are images out of view at both the top and the bottom of the screen, Paradox will display the symbol ▲=▼.

Moving between Images

Of course, whenever there is more than one image on the screen, you will need a way to move between images. Moving between images is controlled by two keys: [Up Image] ([F3]) and [Down Image] ([F4]). [Up Image] moves the cursor from the current image to the image above. [Down Image] moves the cursor from the current image to the image below.

For example, suppose you want to move to the top image of the EMPLYEE table. To do this, press **[Up Image]**. After you do this, the screen will look like Figure 2-40.

Figure 2-40 Moving between Images

```
┌─────────────────────────────────────────────────────────────────────┐
│ Viewing Emplyee table: Record 1 of 15                    Main  ══▼    │
│                                                                       │
│ EMPLYEE┬─Emp Number─┬─Last name─┬─First Name─┬─SS Number─┬───────Addre │
│    1   │     1      │ Jones     │ Dave       │ 414-76-3421│ 4000 St. Ja│
│    2   │     2      │ Cameron   │ Herb       │ 321-65-8765│ 2331 Elm St│
│    3   │     4      │ Jones     │ Stewart    │ 401-32-8721│ 4389 Oakbri│
│    4   │     5      │ Roberts   │ Darlene    │ 417-43-7777│ 451 Lone Pi│
│    5   │     6      │ Jones     │ Jean       │ 414-07-9123│ 4000 St. Ja│
│    6   │     8      │ Williams  │ Brenda     │ 401-55-1567│ 100 Owl Cre│
│    7   │     9      │ Myers     │ Julie      │ 314-38-9452│ 4512 Parksi│
│    8   │    10      │ Link      │ Julie      │ 345-75-1525│ 3215 Palm C│
│    9   │    12      │ Jackson   │ Mary       │ 424-13-7621│ 7821 Clark │
│   10   │    14      │ Preston   │ Molly      │ 451-00-3426│ 321 Indian │
│   11   │    15      │ Masters   │ Ron        │ 317-65-4529│ 423 W. 72nd│
│   12   │    13      │ Triplett  │ Judy       │ 616-10-6610│ 14D Ashby S│
│   13   │    16      │ Robertson │ Kevin      │ 415-24-6718│ 431 Bardsto│
│   14   │    17      │ Garrison  │ Robert     │ 312-98-1479│ 55 Wheeler │
│   15   │    19      │ Gunn      │ Barbara    │ 321-97-8632│ 541 Kentuck│
│                                                                       │
│ ═══Phone═══┬═Date of Birth═┬═Date of Hire═┬═Exemptions═┬═══Salary═══   │
│ (502) 245-6610│  10/06/42   │   1/14/87    │     3      │ 70,000.00    │
│ (502) 451-8765│  11/24/29   │   1/14/87    │     4      │ 50,000.00    │
│ (502) 452-1048│   3/21/50   │   2/13/87    │     1      │ 47,000.00    │
│ (502) 897-3215│   9/24/60   │   6/16/87    │     3      │ 14,000.00    │
└─────────────────────────────────────────────────────────────────────┘
```

Paradox now displays the entire upper image because the cursor is in that image. Since the upper image is now the current image, all of your keystrokes will affect that image.

To move back to the lower image, press **[Down Image]**. When you press this key, Paradox will shift the upper image of EMPLYEE off the top of the screen, bringing the lower image into view again, as shown in Figure 2-39.

When you move the cursor back into a table, it will return to the field and record it occupied the last time it was in that table. For example, when you press [Down Image] to move the cursor back into the second EMPLYEE table, it will return to the position it was in before you moved it out of the table.

As you might expect, you cannot move beyond the top image on the workspace or down below the bottom image. If you press [Down Image] while the cursor is in the last image, Paradox will simply beep. The same thing will happen if you press [Up Image] while the cursor is in the top image.

Viewing Images of Several Tables

In addition to being able to view more than one image of a table, you can view more than one table at the same time. In fact, you are far more likely to have several images of different tables on the screen at once than you are to have multiple images of the same table in view.

For example, suppose you are viewing two images of the EMPLYEE table, and you want to bring the ADDRESS table into view. To do this, issue the **[Menu] V**iew command, type **ADDRESS** at the prompt, and press ↵. Figure 2-41 shows the resulting screen.

Figure 2-41 Viewing Three Images

```
┌─────────────────────────────────────────────────────────────────────────┐
│ Viewing Address table: Table is empty                          Main ▲═    │
│                                                                           │
│ EMPLYEE══Emp Number═══╤══Last name══╤═First Name══╤══SS Number══╤════Addre │
│                                                                           │
│      ══Phone══════╤Date of Birth═╤═Date of Hire═╤═Exemptions══╤══Salary══ │
│     (502) 245-6610 │ 10/06/42    │  1/14/87     │     3       │ 70,000.00 │
│     (502) 451-8765 │ 11/24/29    │  1/14/87     │     4       │ 50,000.00 │
│     (502) 452-1848 │  3/21/50    │  2/13/87     │     1       │ 47,000.00 │
│     (502) 897-3215 │  9/24/60    │  6/16/87     │     3       │ 14,000.00 │
│     (502) 245-6610 │  5/14/43    │  7/16/87     │     0       │ 33,999.99 │
│     (502) 894-9761 │  1/12/20    │  8/16/87     │     4       │ 40,000.00 │
│     (502) 454-5209 │  2/06/48    │  9/16/87     │     1       │ 32,000.00 │
│     (408) 542-1948 │  6/03/33    │ 11/14/87     │     2       │ 30,000.00 │
│     (812) 288-6754 │  8/12/56    │ 11/14/87     │     3       │ 21,000.00 │
│     (502) 456-3256 │  4/17/66    │  2/13/88     │     1       │ 14,750.00 │
│     (212) 276-5478 │ 12/31/44    │  2/13/88     │     0       │ 30,000.00 │
│     (812) 288-3301 │  8/12/50    │ 11/23/87     │     2       │ 15,750.00 │
│     (502) 423-9823 │  3/16/25    │  2/27/88     │     1       │ 37,000.00 │
│     (617) 543-4124 │  5/09/45    │  5/15/88     │     4       │ 32,000.00 │
│     (812) 325-4789 │  5/18/50    │  6/15/88     │     2       │ 17,500.00 │
│                                                                           │
│ ADDRESS══Emp Number═══╤══Last Name═══╤═First Name══╤══SS Number══╤═Spous  │
└─────────────────────────────────────────────────────────────────────────┘
```

Notice that in Figure 2-41, the top image of EMPLYEE has been shifted so much that none of its records are visible. Also notice the symbol ▲= in the top-right corner of the screen, which alerts you to this fact. The ADDRESS table appears as it does on the screen because it is an empty table. If it had contained any records, Paradox would have displayed as many of those records as possible when you brought the table into view.

To move between the images in Figure 2-41, you need only press [Up Image] and [Down Image]. For instance, to move from the ADDRESS image to the lower EMPLYEE image, you would press [Up Image] once. To move to the upper EMPLYEE image, you would press [Up Image] again. Figure 2-42 on the next page shows the screen as it would look if you moved the cursor into the upper image of EMPLYEE. Notice that the ADDRESS table has disappeared from view and that the symbol in the upper-right corner of the screen has changed to =▼.

This figure shows that, try as it might, Paradox is not always able to display even a small part of every table image that is in view. In fact, once you bring more than three or four tables to the screen, it is extremely unlikely that all of them will be visible at once. As you can imagine, the symbols in the upper-right corner of the screen are extremely important to help you remember what is where in the workspace.

The only limitation to the number of images you can bring into view at once is the memory of your computer. As you become more comfortable with Paradox, you are likely to encounter situations where you will have four, five, six, or more images in view at once. No matter how many images are in view, the same simple rules discussed in this section will apply.

Figure 2-42 Using [Up Image]

```
Viewing Emplyee table: Record 1 of 15                    Main  —▼

EMPLYEE┬─Emp Number──────Last name───┬First Name───┬──SS Number────┬────────Addre
   1   │     1           Jones         Dave          414-76-3421     4000 St. Ja
   2   │     2           Cameron       Herb          321-65-8765     2331 Elm St
   3   │     4           Jones         Stewart       401-32-8721     4389 Oakbri
   4   │     5           Roberts       Darlene       417-43-7777     451 Lone Pi
   5   │     6           Jones         Jean          414-07-9123     4000 St. Ja
   6   │     8           Williams      Brenda        401-55-1567     100 Owl Cre
   7   │     9           Myers         Julie         314-38-9452     4512 Parksi
   8   │    10           Link          Julie         345-75-1525     3215 Palm C
   9   │    12           Jackson       Mary          424-13-7621     7821 Clark
  10   │    14           Preston       Molly         451-00-3426     321 Indian
  11   │    15           Masters       Ron           317-65-4529     423 W. 72nd
  12   │    13           Triplett      Judy          616-10-6610     14D Ashby S
  13   │    16           Robertson     Kevin         415-24-6718     431 Bardsto
  14   │    17           Garrison      Robert        312-98-1479     55 Wheeler
  15   │    19           Gunn          Barbara       321-97-8632     541 Kentuck


 ══════Phone══════╤Date of Birth═╤═Date of Hire═╤═Exemptions═════╤═══════Salary═══
 (502) 245-6610   │ 10/06/42     │ 1/14/87      │      3         │  70,000.00
 (502) 451-8765   │ 11/24/29     │ 1/14/87      │      4         │  50,000.00
 (502) 452-1848   │ 3/21/50      │ 2/13/87      │      1         │  47,000.00
 (502) 897-3215   │ 9/24/60      │ 6/16/87      │      3         │  14,000.00
```

Removing Images from the Screen

To remove an image from the screen, move the cursor into that image and press [Clear Image] ([F8]). For example, suppose you want to remove the second EMPLYEE table image from the screen. To do this, use [Up Image] or [Down Image] to move the cursor into this image, then press **[Clear Image]**. Figure 2-43 shows the resulting screen.

Figure 2-43 Clearing an Image

```
Viewing Address table: Table is empty                    Main  ▲═

EMPLYEE┬─Emp Number───────Last Name───┬First Name───┬──SS Number────┬────────Addre
  12   │    13            Triplett      Judy          616-10-6610     14D Ashby S
  13   │    16            Robertson     Kevin         415-24-6718     431 Bardsto
  14   │    17            Garrison      Robert        312-98-1479     55 Wheeler
  15   │    19            Gunn          Barbara       321-97-8632     541 Kentuck

ADDRESS┬─Emp Number───────┬──Last Name────┬First Name──┬─SS Number─────┬──Spou
```

To remove all of the images from the workspace, press [Clear All] ([Alt]-[F8]). For example, suppose you have several images in the workspace, but you no longer need any of them to perform further operations. You should press **[Clear All]** to clear the workspace and return to the Main menu.

It is important to understand that clearing an image does not erase or delete the table with which that image is associated. Clearing an image simply removes the image from view. The table with which the image is associated remains on the disk, safe and sound.

Editing Entries

You have just seen how easy it is to create a table and then enter data into it. You have also seen how easy it is to make changes to the entries in the ENTRY table before you press [Do-It!] to add those entries to a permanent table. In this section, we'll show you how to edit the records that are already stored in a permanent table.

In fact, the techniques you use to edit the entries in a table are the same as the ones you use to edit the entries in the ENTRY and STRUCT tables. All you have to do to edit a table is enter the Edit or Coedit mode and use the editing keys in Table 2-2 on page 49 to edit the data in the table. While you are editing a table, you can change entries, insert and delete records, and even enter new records. When you have made the desired changes, save them by pressing [Do-It!]. If you want to cancel the edit, you can issue the [Menu] Cancel command.

Examples

Before you can edit a table, you must first enter the Edit mode. To enter the Edit mode, issue the [Menu] Modify Edit command and select the name of the table you want to edit. When you do this, Paradox will bring the table you specify into view and will enter the Edit mode.

For example, to edit the EMPLYEE table, issue the **[Menu] M**odify Edit command, type **EMPLYEE,** and press ←. You can also enter the Edit mode by pressing the [Edit] key while the table you want to edit is in view. We'll show you how to do this in a few pages.

Changing Entries

Suppose you want to change the First Name field entry of the first record in the EMPLYEE table from *Dave* to *David*. To make this change, first issue the **[Menu] M**odify Edit command, type **EMPLYEE**, and press ←. When the EMPLYEE table appears on the screen, move the cursor to the First Name field of the first record. When the cursor is in place, press **[Backspace]** once to erase the *e* in *Dave*, then type **id**, or press **[Ctrl]-[Backspace]** to erase the whole entry, then type **David**. Figure 2-44 shows the result of this correction.

Figure 2-44 Making Corrections

Editing Emplyee table: Record 1 of 15					Edit

EMPLYEE	Emp Number	Last Name	First Name	SS Number	Addre
1	1	Jones	David ◀	414-76-3421	4000 St. Ja
2	2	Cameron	Herb	321-65-8765	2331 Elm St
3	4	Jones	Stewart	401-32-8721	4309 Oakbri
4	5	Roberts	Darlene	417-43-7777	451 Lone Pi
5	6	Jones	Jean	414-07-9123	4000 St. Ja
6	8	Williams	Brenda	401-55-1567	555 Court S
7	9	Myers	Julie	314-38-9452	4512 Parksi
8	10	Link	Julie	345-75-1525	3215 Palm C
9	12	Jackson	Mary	424-13-7621	7821 Clark
10	14	Preston	Molly	451-00-3426	321 Indian
11	15	Masters	Ron	317-65-4529	423 W. 72nd
12	13	Triplett	Judy	616-10-6610	14D Ashby S
13	16	Robertson	Kevin	415-24-6710	431 Bardsto
14	17	Garrison	Robert	312-98-1479	55 Wheeler
15	19	Gunn	Barbara	321-97-8632	541 Kentuck

Field View

You can also use the field view to edit the entries in a table. To enter the field view, position the cursor on the field you want to edit and press [Field View] ([Alt]-[F5]). After you press [Field View], the cursor will change to a box, and you will be able to move around in that field to make changes.

As when you are editing records in the ENTRY table, entering the field view restricts the movement of the cursor to the one field you are editing. When you are in the field view, the cursor-movement keys move the cursor from character to character within the field you are editing, rather than moving it from field to field within the table. Table 2-3 on page 51 shows the effect of each of the cursor-movement keys in the field view.

Suppose you want to change the SS Number field entry for employee number 6, Jean Jones, from 414-07-9123 to 413-07-9123. To make this change, move the cursor to the SS Number field of record number 5 and press **[Field View]** to enter the field view. Now, press ← to move the field view cursor to the second 4 in the entry. Figure 2-45 shows the screen at this point. Now, press **[Del]** to delete the 4, and type **3**. Finally, press ↵ to exit from the field view.

Figure 2-45 Using the Field View

```
Editing Employee table: Record 5 of 15                          Edit

┌Emp Number══╤═Last Name══╤═First Name═╤═SS Number══╤════════Address═════
│     1      │ Jones      │ David      │ 414-76-3421 │ 4000 St. James Ct.
│     2      │ Cameron    │ Herb       │ 321-65-8765 │ 2331 Elm St.
│     4      │ Jones      │ Stewart    │ 401-32-8721 │ 4389 Oakbridge Rd.
│     5      │ Roberts    │ Darlene    │ 417-43-7777 │ 451 Lone Pine Dr.
│     6      │ Jones      │ Jean       │ 41█-07-91234│ 4000 St. James Ct.
│     8      │ Williams   │ Brenda     │ 401-55-1567 │ 100 Owl Creek Rd.
│     9      │ Myers      │ Julie      │ 314-38-9452 │ 4512 Parkside Dr.
│    10      │ Link       │ Julie      │ 345-75-1525 │ 3215 Palm Ct.
│    12      │ Jackson    │ Mary       │ 424-13-7621 │ 7821 Clark Ave.
│    14      │ Preston    │ Molly      │ 451-00-3426 │ 321 Indian Hills R
│    15      │ Masters    │ Ron        │ 317-65-4529 │ 423 W. 72nd St.
│    13      │ Triplett   │ Judy       │ 616-10-6610 │ 14D Ashby St.
│    16      │ Robertson  │ Kevin      │ 415-24-6710 │ 431 Bardstown Rd.
│    17      │ Garrison   │ Robert     │ 312-98-1479 │ 55 Wheeler St.
│    19      │ Gunn       │ Barbara    │ 321-97-8632 │ 541 Kentucky St.
```

Deleting a Record

If you want to delete a record, position the cursor in any field of the record you want to delete and press [Del]. For example, suppose you want to delete the record for Judy Triplett from the EMPLYEE table. To remove this record from the table, move the cursor to any field in the record and press **[Del]**. The resulting table will look like Figure 2-46.

Figure 2-46 Deleting a Record

```
Editing Employee table: Record 12 of 14                    Edit

 Emp Number      Last Name    First Name   SS Number          Address
        1        Jones        David        414-76-3421    4000 St. James Ct.
        2        Cameron      Herb         321-65-8765    2331 Elm St.
        4        Jones        Stewart      401-32-8721    4389 Oakbridge Rd.
        5        Roberts      Darlene      417-43-7777    451 Lone Pine Dr.
        6        Jones        Jean         413-07-9123    4000 St. James Ct.
        8        Williams     Brenda       401-55-1567    100 Owl Creek Rd.
        9        Myers        Julie        314-38-9452    4512 Parkside Dr.
       10        Link         Julie        345-75-1525    3215 Palm Ct.
       12        Jackson      Mary         424-13-7621    7821 Clark Ave.
       14        Preston      Molly        451-00-3426    321 Indian Hills R
       15        Masters      Ron          317-65-4529    423 W. 72nd St.
       16        Robertson    Kevin        415-24-6710◄   431 Bardstown Rd.
       17        Garrison     Robert       312-98-1479    55 Wheeler St.
       19        Gunn         Barbara      321-97-8632    541 Kentucky St.
```

Adding Records

You can also add new records to your tables using the Edit mode. You can either append the new records to the end of the table or use the [Ins] key to insert a new record in the middle of the table.

Appending Records

To append a new record to a table, you use the cursor-movement keys to move the cursor to the last record in the table, then press ↓ to add a new record. Once the new record is in place, you can fill it in just as you normally would.

For example, suppose you want to add a new record at the end of EMPLYEE. To add the record, press ↓ to move the cursor to the last record in the table, and then once more to add a new record. Now, enter the information for employee number 20 from Table 2-4 on the following page into the new record. Figure 2-47 shows the completed table.

Figure 2-47 Adding a Record

```
Editing Employee table: Record 15 of 15                    Edit

EMPLYEE  Emp Number      Last Name    First Name   SS Number         Addre
   1         1        Jones        David        414-76-3421    4000 St. Ja
   2         2        Cameron      Herb         321-65-8765    2331 Elm St
   3         4        Jones        Stewart      401-32-8721    4389 Oakbri
   4         5        Roberts      Darlene      417-43-7777    451 Lone Pi
   5         6        Jones        Jean         413-07-9123    4000 St. Ja
   6         8        Williams     Brenda       401-55-1567    100 Owl Cre
   7         9        Myers        Julie        314-38-9452    4512 Parksi
   8        10        Link         Julie        345-75-1525    3215 Palm C
   9        12        Jackson      Mary         424-13-7621    7821 Clark
  10        14        Preston      Molly        451-00-3426    321 Indian
  11        15        Masters      Ron          317-65-4529    423 W. 72nd
  12        16        Robertson    Kevin        415-24-6710    431 Bardsto
  13        17        Garrison     Robert       312-98-1479    55 Wheeler
  14        19        Gunn         Barbara      321-97-8632    541 Kentuck
  15        20    ◄   Emerson      Cheryl       401-65-1820    800 River R
```

You can use this technique to add as many records to a table as you want. However, we suggest that you use the [Menu] Modify DataEntry command if you are going to enter more than one or two records. Using this command will keep existing records safe from accidental alteration when you are entering records.

Table 2-4 Sample Data

Emp Number	20	13
Last Name	Emerson	Jakes, Jr.
First Name	Cheryl	Sal
SS Number	401-65-1820	321-65-9151
Address	800 River Rd.	3451 Michigan Ave.
City	Prospect	Dallas
State	KY	TX
Zip	40222	65987
Phone	(502) 896-5139	(214) 398-1987
Date of Birth	7/30/66	5/23/59
Date of Hire	1/01/86	5/01/85
Exemptions	2	6
Salary	12,000.00	34,000.00

Inserting a Record

You can also insert a record in the middle of a table in the Edit mode. All you have to do is move the cursor to the place in the table where you want the new record, press [Ins] to insert a new record above the cursor, and then fill that record with new data.

For example, suppose you want to add a new record between the records for employees 12 (Mary Jackson) and 14 (Molly Preston). To make this entry, move the cursor to any field in record 10 (Molly Preston) and press **[Ins]** to insert a new record. Now, enter the data for employee number 13 shown in Table 2-4 into the new record. Figure 2-48 shows the completed table.

Figure 2-48 Adding the Data

```
Editing Emplyee table: Record 11 of 16                          Edit

EMPLYEE──Emp Number──────Last Name──First Name──SS Number──────────Addre
   1         1          Jones       David       414-76-3421    4000 St. Ja
   2         2          Cameron     Herb        321-65-8765    2331 Elm St
   3         4          Jones       Stewart     401-32-8721    4389 Oakbri
   4         5          Roberts     Darlene     417-43-7777    451 Lone Pi
   5         6          Jones       Jean        413-87-9123    4000 St. Ja
   6         8          Williams    Brenda      401-55-1567    100 Owl Cre
   7         9          Myers       Julie       314-38-9452    4512 Parksi
   8        10          Link        Julie       345-75-1525    3215 Palm C
   9        12          Jackson     Mary        424-13-7621    7821 Clark
  10        13          Jakes, Jr.  Sal         321-65-9151    3451 Michig
  11        14          Preston     Molly       451-00-3426    321 Indian
  12        15          Masters     Ron         317-65-4529    423 W. 72nd
  13        16          Robertson   Kevin       415-24-6710    431 Bardsto
  14        17          Garrison    Robert      312-98-1479    55 Wheeler
  15        19          Gunn        Barbara     321-97-8632    541 Kentuck
  16        20          Emerson     Cheryl      401-65-1820    800 River R
```

The Undo Command

If you make a mistake while you are editing a table in Paradox, you can use the [Menu] Undo command or the [Undo] key ([Ctrl]-[U]) to reverse your error. As when you are entering records, the Undo command always undoes the last change you made to the table you are editing. If the last change you made was to edit a record in the table, the fields in that record will be restored to their previous values. If the last change was to delete a record, then issuing the Undo command will restore the record to the table. If you issue this command again, Paradox will undo your second-most-recent action, and so on.

For example, suppose you accidentally press the [Del] key while you are editing the EMPLYEE table, deleting the record for Molly Preston from the table. To recover from this error, you could press [Undo]. Immediately, Paradox will restore the deleted record to the table. In addition, the message *Record 11 reinserted* will appear at the bottom of the screen. (If you issue the [Menu] Undo command instead of pressing [Undo], Paradox will prompt you for confirmation before it restores the deleted record. You must choose Yes to bring the record back into the table.)

Leaving the Edit Mode

When you are finished editing, you can either press the [Do-It!] key or issue the [Menu] DO-IT! command to save the changes you have made. The message *Ending edit...* will appear briefly at the bottom of the screen, and Paradox will return to the main workspace.

If you don't want to save the changes you have made, you can issue the [Menu] Cancel command to end the editing session without saving your work. After you issue the Cancel command, Paradox will prompt you for confirmation. If you issue the No command at this point, Paradox will return to the Edit menu so that you can make another selection. If you issue the Yes command, Paradox will cancel all the changes you have made and return to the main workspace.

You can also cancel the operation by pressing [Ctrl]-[Break]. However, if you use this method, Paradox will not prompt you for confirmation. For this reason, we suggest that you always use the [Menu] Cancel command.

Using the [Edit] Key

In the previous example, we used the [Menu] Modify Edit command to enter the Edit mode. You can also enter the Edit mode, however, by bringing into view the table you want to edit and pressing the [Edit] key ([F9]). When you press [Edit] ([F9]) to enter the Edit mode, Paradox assumes that you want to edit a table in the workspace and does not prompt you for a table name.

Suppose you want to edit the EMPLYEE table. Rather than issuing the [Menu] Modify Edit command, you could issue the [Menu] View command to bring the EMPLYEE table into view, then press [Edit] to enter the Edit mode. Once you are in the Edit mode, everything works the same way. It doesn't matter whether you issue the [Menu] Modify Edit command or press [Edit] to invoke the Edit mode. After you have finished editing, you can press [Do-It!] or issue the [Menu] DO-IT! command to save the changes you have made, or issue the [Menu] Cancel command to cancel the changes and return to the View mode.

If there is more than one image in view when you press [Edit], you will be able to edit the records in all of the tables in view. For example, suppose both the EMPLYEE table and the ADDRESS table are in view, as shown in Figure 2-41 on page 65. If you press [Edit] at this point, you can edit the entries in either table. As always, you can use the [Up Image] and [Down Image] keys to move the cursor from table to table.

If there are two images of the same table in view when you press [Edit], one of the images will disappear. Paradox makes this change to avoid the problems that could arise from having two images of the same table—one that contains edited entries and one that doesn't.

The Coedit Mode

For multi-user Paradox, there is an alternative to Edit called Coedit. The Coedit mode allows two or more users on a network to modify the same table at the same time, while the Edit mode allows only one person to modify a table at a time. Coedit may also be used by a single user. For a single user, Coedit offers certain advantages and disadvantages. Coedit generally runs faster than Edit and handles duplicate keys in a more sophisticated manner. However, in Coedit you may undo only the last change made, while in the Edit mode you can undo an unlimited number of changes. These and other features of Coedit are discussed in detail in Appendix A2.

A Word about Designing Tables

Before you begin to create your own tables, you should take some time to consider the type of information you normally use and plan your tables accordingly. For example, consider the way you now use your paper filing (data storage) system. You probably have files on your employees, your customers, your company's products, and a host of other topics that you need for conducting your business. Your files most likely group similar types of information and provide easy accessibility. Your Paradox tables should be organized the same way.

For example, suppose you want to create a table to track the projects to which your employees are assigned. You may at first feel compelled to include every scrap of information you can think of in the table and create a table structured like the one shown in Figure 2-49. However, you will quickly discover it is better to create several smaller tables than to put everything into a "super table."

Figure 2-49 A Poorly Structured Table

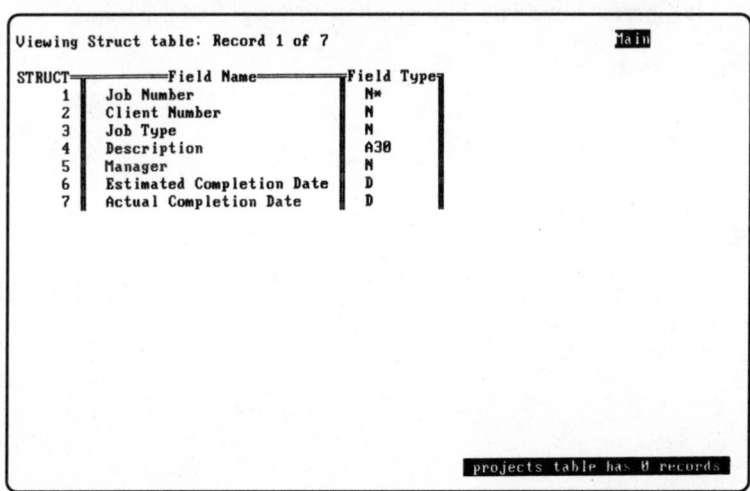

```
Creating new Projs table                                  Create
STRUCT═══════════Field Name══════════Field Type
     1    Emp Number                   N      ◄
     2    Last Name                    A18            ─── FIELD TYPES ───
     3    First Name                   A18        A_: Alphanumeric (ex: A25)
     4    SS Number                    A11        Any combination of
     5    Address                      A28        characters and spaces
     6    City                         A28        up to specified width.
     7    State                        A2         Maximum width is 255.
     8    Zip                          A5
     9    Phone                        A14        N: Numbers with or without
    18    Date of Birth                D             decimal digits.
    11    Date of Hire                 D
    12    Exemptions                   N          $: Dollar amounts.
    13    Salary                       $
    14    Job Number                   N          D: Dates in the form
    15    Client Number                N             mm/dd/yy or dd-mon-yy.
    16    Job Type                     N
    17    Description                  A38        ─────────────────────────
    18    Manager                      N          Use "*" after field type to
    19    Estimated Completion Date    D          show a key field (ex: A4*).
    28    Actual Completion Date       D
```

For example, you can break the large table PROJS into two smaller tables. Figure 2-5 on page 36 and Figure 2-50 show the structure of two tables—EMPLYEE (with which you are already familiar) and PROJECTS—that together contain every field from PROJS. The EMPLYEE table contains basic data about employees. The PROJECTS table tracks the various projects to which the employees are assigned.

Figure 2-50 The Structure of the PROJECTS Table

```
Viewing Struct table: Record 1 of 7                         Main
STRUCT═══════════Field Name══════════Field Type
     1    Job Number                   N*
     2    Client Number                N
     3    Job Type                     N
     4    Description                  A38
     5    Manager                      N
     6    Estimated Completion Date    D
     7    Actual Completion Date       D








                                       projects table has 8 records
```

By splitting one table into two, you make the database system more efficient and easier to use. As a general rule, you should strive to create small tables that contain the information you need, without duplicating information found in a related table.

When you break a large table like PROJS into several smaller tables, you need some way to link the tables so that you can recombine the information they contain. The linking fields do not need to have the same name, but they do need to contain the same kind of information. For example, the linking fields in EMPLYEE and PROJECTS are the Emp Number field in the EMPLYEE table and the Manager field in the PROJECTS table. Although these two fields do not have the same name, they contain the same information. The Manager field in the PROJECTS table contains the employee number (from the EMPLYEE table) of the employee assigned to manage each project. Because of this common field, the tables can be easily linked with a query. We'll show you how to do that in Chapter 8.

If you own Paradox 3, then you will probably want to take a slightly different approach to linking tables with common fields so that you can use a multitable form to enter or edit data in the linked tables. We'll show you how to organize tables for use with multitable forms in Chapter 4. However, before you move to that chapter, be sure to read the section on keyed tables in Chapter 3.

Conclusion

In this chapter, we have shown you how to create tables, enter data, and edit the data in your tables. In addition, we have shown you how to view tables.

In Chapter 3, we will show you how to change the appearance of images and how to set validity checks for your tables. We also will discuss advanced techniques for editing and entering data. In Chapter 4, we will show you how to design and use forms.

More on Data Entry and Editing

In the preceding chapter, we showed you how to create tables, enter data into tables, and edit the records in a table. In this chapter, you'll learn more about entering and editing data. First, you'll learn about key fields, and how to use the Image command to change the way Paradox displays the image on the screen. Then, we will discuss the ValCheck command, which allows you to define validity checks.

Keyed Tables

A keyed table is a table that has one or more key fields. A key field is a field that you designate as a primary index for a table. When you designate a key field, Paradox will arrange the records in the table so that the entries in the key field are in ascending order. In addition, Paradox will check every entry you make into the key field and will not allow you to make an entry that duplicates an existing entry. Designating key fields helps give your table order, builds a simple level of validity checking into your table, and makes queries work faster.

Key fields are strictly optional—you do not need to designate any field in any table as a key field. However, once you become familiar with Paradox, you'll find many uses for key fields.

Defining Key Fields

To designate a field as a key field, type an asterisk (*) after the field type in the Field Type column of the STRUCT table as you define the table. You can enter the asterisk by typing it or by pressing the [Spacebar] after you enter the field type.

The fields you use as key fields in a table must be the first fields in the structure. Paradox will not let you save the structure of a table that has a key field anywhere but the top of the table's structure.

An Example

For example, suppose you want to create the PROJECTS table with the structure shown in Figure 3-1. Notice that the Job Number field has been designated as a key field. To create this table, issue the [**Menu**] Create command, type **PROJECTS**, and press ↵. When the STRUCT table appears on the screen, type **Job Number** in the Field Name column. Then, to designate the Job Number field as a key field, move to the Field Type column, type **N**, and either type an asterisk (*) or press the [**Spacebar**]. Once you've defined this field, enter the remaining field names and types shown in Figure 3-1.

Figure 3-1 The PROJECTS Table

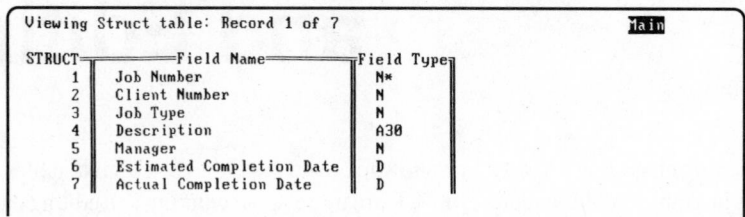

Now, press [**Do-It!**] to save the new table and return to the main workspace. As you can see, creating keyed tables is not very different from creating other tables; however, you will soon discover that there is a big difference in the way Paradox manages keyed tables.

Notes

You can designate any field type as a key field. If you designate an alphanumeric field as a key field, the records in the table will be sorted so that the key field entries are arranged alphabetically. If you designate a date field as a key field, the records will be sorted so that the entries in that field are in order from the earliest to the most recent date. If you designate a number, short number, or dollar field as a key field, the records will be sorted so that the entries in the key field are in ascending numeric order.

One disadvantage of using key fields is that they reduce the total number of characters you can enter per record. In non-keyed tables, you can enter up to 4,000 characters per record in the table, while keyed tables can contain no more than 1,350 characters per record.

Entering Records into Keyed Tables

Figure 3-2 shows the records we entered into the PROJECTS table. Notice that the records are arranged so that the entries in the key field, Job Number, are in ascending numeric order. Regardless of the order in which records are entered into this table, Paradox will always sort them into ascending order based on the entries in the Job Number field.

To enter the records from Figure 3-2 into your PROJECTS table, issue the [**Menu**] **M**odify **D**ataEntry command, type **PROJECTS**, and press ↵. When the ENTRY table for PROJECTS comes into view, simply type the records from Figure 3-2 into the table. When you are finished, press [**Do-It!**] ([F2]) or issue the [**Menu**] **D**O-IT! command to store the contents of ENTRY in PROJECTS.

Figure 3-2 A Keyed Table

Editing Projects table: Record 13 of 13

PROJECTS	Job Number	Client Number	Job Type	Description	Manager	Estimated Completion Date	Actual Completion Date
1	100	1001	1	Install PC AT/Paradox/1-2-3	1	3/01/88	4/11/88
2	101	1001	3	AT/Paradox/1-2-3 Intro	1	5/01/88	
3	102	1002	2	Paradox A/R Systems	1	6/01/88	
4	103	1003	1	Install Compaq Plus/Symphony	1	11/01/88	
5	104	1003	2	Symphony Intro Course	4	2/21/88	2/15/88
6	105	1003	4	Recommend AR System	4	3/21/88	
7	106	1004	2	Paradox Time Accounting System	1	9/01/87	9/01/87
8	107	1004	3	1988 Compilation/Review	8	3/15/87	
9	108	1005	3	1988 Compilation/Review	8	10/15/87	10/15/87
10	109	1006	3	1988 Compilation/Review	8	9/15/87	9/15/87
11	110	1007	5	Tax Consultation		11/15/87	11/15/87
12	111	1008	2	1988 Tax Return		12/15/87	12/22/87
13	112	1009	2	1988 Tax Return	16	1/15/88	

Key Violations

By now, you are probably wondering what is so different about keyed tables. Everything we've done so far has been pretty simple. However, suppose you now want to add the records shown in Table 3-1 to the PROJECTS table.

Table 3-1 Sample Data

Job Number	112	114	115
Client Number	1007	1013	1014
Job Type	1	2	1
Description	1988 Tax Return	1988 Tax Return	Install PC AT/Paradox/1-2-3
Manager	16	7	1
Estimated Completion Date	4/15/88	4/15/88	5/15/88

To do this, issue the [**Menu**] **M**odify **D**ataEntry command, type **PROJECTS**, and press ↵. When the ENTRY table appears on the screen, you should enter the new data from Table 3-1. Figure 3-3 shows the completed ENTRY table. Notice that the first Job Number field entry in this table conflicts with the last Job Number field entry in PROJECTS.

Figure 3-3 The Completed ENTRY Table

```
DataEntry for Projects table: Record 1 of 3                    DataEntry

ENTRY━━━━┳━Job Number━━━┳━Client Number━┳━Job Type━━┳━━━━━━━━━Descript
    1    ┃     112      ┃     1007      ┃     1     ┃ 1988 Tax Return
    2    ┃     114      ┃     1013      ┃     2     ┃ 1988 Tax Return
    3    ┃     115      ┃     1014      ┃     1     ┃ Install PC AT/Paradox
```

Now, press [**Do-It!**] ([F2]). After you do this, Paradox will add the records from ENTRY to PROJECTS as usual; however, the record in ENTRY to which you assigned the job number 112 will not be entered into PROJECTS. Instead, Paradox will copy this record to a temporary table named KEYVIOL. Figure 3-4 shows the screen at this point.

This happened because there already is a job number 112 in the PROJECTS table. Whenever you enter records in a keyed table, Paradox will check your entries to make sure that they do not duplicate an existing entry in the key field of the permanent table. If there is a conflict, a key violation will occur when Paradox attempts to copy the records from ENTRY into the permanent table. When a key violation occurs, Paradox will place the offending records into a KEYVIOL table for editing.

Editing the KEYVIOL Table

To add this record to the PROJECTS table, you first must edit the KEYVIOL table and change the Job Number entry for the record. To do this, press [**Edit**] ([F9]) to enter the Edit mode. Once you are in the Edit mode, position the cursor in the Job Number field of KEYVIOL, press

[Ctrl]-[Backspace] to erase the Job Number entry, and type a new entry, like **113**. Figure 3-5 shows the screen after you make this change. Next, press ↵ to lock in the new Job Number entry, then press **[Do-It!]** ([F2]) or issue the **[Menu]** DO-IT! command to leave the Edit mode and save the change.

Figure 3-4 The KEYVIOL Table

```
 Viewing Keyviol table: Record 1 of 1                      Main

 PROJECTS┬─Job Number─┬─Client Number─┬─Job Type─┬─────────────Descript
      1  │    100     │     1001      │    1     │ Install PC AT/Paradox
      2  │    101     │     1001      │    3     │ AT/Paradox/1-2-3 Intr
      3  │    102     │     1002      │    2     │ Paradox A/R Systems
      4  │    103     │     1003      │    1     │ Install Compaq Plus/S
      5  │    104     │     1003      │    2     │ Symphony Intro Course
      6  │    105     │     1003      │    4     │ Recommend AR System
      7  │    106     │     1004      │    2     │ Paradox Time Accounti
      8  │    107     │     1004      │    3     │ 1988 Compilation/Revi
      9  │    108     │     1005      │    3     │ 1988 Compilation/Revi
     10  │    109     │     1006      │    3     │ 1988 Compilation/Revi
     11  │    110     │     1007      │    5     │ Tax Consultation
     12  │    111     │     1008      │    2     │ 1988 Tax Return
     13  │    112     │     1009      │    2     │ 1988 Tax Return
     14  │    114     │     1013      │    2     │ 1988 Tax Return
     15  │    115     │     1014      │    1     │ Install PC AT/Paradox

 KEYVIOL┬─Job Number─┬─Client Number─┬─Job Type─┬─────────────Descripti
      1 │    112     │     1007      │    1     │ 1988 Tax Return
```

Figure 3-5 The Edited KEYVIOL Table

```
 Editing Keyviol table: Record 1 of 1                      Edit

 PROJECTS┬─Job Number─┬─Client Number─┬─Job Type─┬─────────────Descript
      1  │    100     │     1001      │    1     │ Install PC AT/Paradox
      2  │    101     │     1001      │    3     │ AT/Paradox/1-2-3 Intr
      3  │    102     │     1002      │    2     │ Paradox A/R Systems
      4  │    103     │     1003      │    1     │ Install Compaq Plus/S
      5  │    104     │     1003      │    2     │ Symphony Intro Course
      6  │    105     │     1003      │    4     │ Recommend AR System
      7  │    106     │     1004      │    2     │ Paradox Time Accounti
      8  │    107     │     1004      │    3     │ 1988 Compilation/Revi
      9  │    108     │     1005      │    3     │ 1988 Compilation/Revi
     10  │    109     │     1006      │    3     │ 1988 Compilation/Revi
     11  │    110     │     1007      │    5     │ Tax Consultation
     12  │    111     │     1008      │    2     │ 1988 Tax Return
     13  │    112     │     1009      │    2     │ 1988 Tax Return
     14  │    114     │     1013      │    2     │ 1988 Tax Return
     15  │    115     │     1014      │    1     │ Install PC AT/Paradox

 KEYVIOL┬─Job Number─┬─Client Number─┬─Job Type─┬─────────────Descripti
      1 │    113    ◀│     1007      │    1     │ 1988 Tax Return
```

Adding KEYVIOL to PROJECTS

Now, to add the record in the KEYVIOL table to the PROJECTS table, issue the **[Menu]** **T**ools **M**ore **A**dd command. This command allows you to add the records in one table (called the source table) to another table (the target table). Although we will discuss this command in detail in Chapter 9, we will explain enough about it here to let you recover from key violations.

After you issue this command, Paradox will prompt you to enter the name of the source table—the table that contains the records you want to add. When you see this prompt, type **KEYVIOL**, and press ↵. Paradox then will prompt you to enter the name of the table to which the records should be added—the target table. You now should type **PROJECTS** and press ↵. When you do, Paradox will display the menu shown in Figure 3-6.

Figure 3-6 The NewEntries/Update Menu

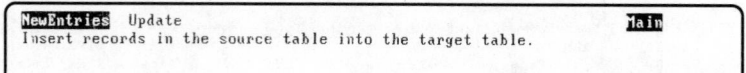

```
NewEntries  Update                                          Main
Insert records in the source table into the target table.
```

This menu tells Paradox how to treat the records you are adding to the table. The NewEntries option tells Paradox to append the records from the source table to the target table. The Update option tells Paradox to update the records in the target table, using the entries in the source table.

Since you want to add the records from the KEYVIOL table to those that are already in the PROJECTS table, you should issue the NewEntries command. Paradox then will add the records from the KEYVIOL table to the PROJECTS table and display the new PROJECTS table on the workspace, as shown in Figure 3-7.

Figure 3-7 The New PROJECTS Table

```
Viewing Projects table: Record 1 of 16                      Main

PROJECTS╤═Job Number═╤═Client Number═╤═Job Type═╤═════════════Descript
    1  ║     100     ║     1001      ║     1    ║  Install PC AT/Paradox
    2  ║     101     ║     1001      ║     3    ║  AT/Paradox/1-2-3 Intr
    3  ║     102     ║     1002      ║     2    ║  Paradox A/R Systems
    4  ║     103     ║     1003      ║     1    ║  Install Compaq Plus/S
    5  ║     104     ║     1003      ║     2    ║  Symphony Intro Course
    6  ║     105     ║     1003      ║     4    ║  Recommend AR System
    7  ║     106     ║     1004      ║     2    ║  Paradox Time Accounti
    8  ║     107     ║     1004      ║     3    ║  1988 Compilation/Revi
    9  ║     108     ║     1005      ║     3    ║  1988 Compilation/Revi
   10  ║     109     ║     1006      ║     3    ║  1988 Compilation/Revi
   11  ║     110     ║     1007      ║     5    ║  Tax Consultation
   12  ║     111     ║     1008      ║     2    ║  1988 Tax Return
   13  ║     112     ║     1009      ║     2    ║  1988 Tax Return
   14  ║     113     ║     1007      ║     1    ║  1988 Tax Return
   15  ║     114     ║     1013      ║     2    ║  1988 Tax Return
   16  ║     115     ║     1014      ║     1    ║  Install PC AT/Paradox


KEYVIOL╤═Job Number═╤═Client Number═╤═Job Type═╤═══════════Descripti
    1  ║     113     ║     1007      ║     1    ║  1988 Tax Return
```

Before you can use the NewEntries option to add records from a KEYVIOL table to a permanent table, you must correct the key violations in the KEYVIOL table. Paradox will not enter into the permanent table any record that still contains a key violation. Instead, Paradox will once again place the erroneous records into a KEYVIOL table.

Editing Keyed Tables

Editing keyed tables is a bit tricky. Because Paradox does not check for key violations during an edit, it is possible to overwrite records accidentally.

For example, suppose you are viewing the PROJECTS table, and you want to change the job number 112 to the job number 120. To do this, you would press [Edit] ([F9]), move to the Job Number field entry for record 13, press [Ctrl]-[Backspace] to erase the current entry, and type the new entry. However, suppose you type 102 instead of 120. When you press [Do-It!] to end the edit and save the change, Paradox will replace the original job number 102 with the renamed job number 112 without warning. Moreover, the replaced record will not be placed in any temporary table—it will be gone forever.

You can avoid this trap by using [Coedit] ([Alt]-[F9]) instead of [Edit]. When editing in Coedit mode, key violations are brought to your attention as soon as you attempt to move from the record with the duplicate key, or when you press [Do-It!]. Suppose you pressed [Coedit] instead of [Edit] when attempting to change job number 112 to 120. When you mistakenly type 102 instead of 120 and press [Do-It!], Paradox will display the message *Key exists — press [Alt][L] to confirm or [Alt][K] to see existing record.* Paradox will not let you finish editing or move to another record until you correct the key violation.

You can view the two records with the duplicate keys by pressing the [Key Viol] key ([Alt]-[K]). The first time you press [Key Viol], the original record will overwrite the new, or modified, record and the message *Viewing existing record with conflicting key* will appear at the top of the screen. The second time you press [Key Viol], the new record will reappear and the message *New key value conflicts with existing record* will appear at the top of the screen. Continuing to press [Key Viol] will cause the two records to appear alternately. After viewing the two records, you will need to do one of three things.

If the key violation is caused by a simple typing mistake, you can press [Key Viol] to display the record you want to modify, then move to the key field in question and use [Backspace] or [Ctrl]-[Backspace] to erase the mistake. Once you erase the mistake, simply type in the correct value. This type of correction may be made to either the original or the new record.

Another option is to remove the new record completely by pressing [Undo] ([Ctrl]-[U]). It does not matter if you are viewing the new record or the original record when you press [Undo]. Paradox will erase the new record and the original record will remain untouched.

The third option is to decide whether the new record should replace the original. To do this, press [Lock Toggle] ([Alt]-[L]) to overwrite the original record with the new one. When you press [Lock Toggle], Paradox will display the message *Posted change to record x* in the lower-right corner of the screen. You can now continue editing the table.

Another way to minimize any potential loss of data is to make a back-up copy of important tables. We'll show you how to do this with the [Menu] Tools Copy command in Chapter 5, "Managing Tables."

Except for the considerations we've just discussed, editing a keyed table is the same as editing any other table. Remember, though—use caution when editing the key fields in your keyed tables.

Tables with Two Key Fields

If you wish, you can designate more than one key field in a table. When you do this, Paradox will allow duplicate entries in each key field but will not allow any two records to have the same entries in all the key fields. For example, suppose you are using Paradox for order entry. You want to create a table named ORDLOG that records every order you write. Let's assume that each order you write may include three or four different lines, each of which represents the sale of a different product. For example, order 1001 may include three lines: an order for three widgets, an order for two wombats, and an order for one woofer. To track your orders accurately, you need to record two pieces of information about each item ordered: the order number and the line number. Figure 3-8 shows the structure of a table that will accomplish this task. You will notice that the first two fields in this table are Ord Num and Line.

Figure 3-8 The Structure of ORDLOG

```
Viewing Struct table: Record 1 of 4                          Main

STRUCT          Field Name        Field Type
      1    Ord Num                N*
      2    Line                   N*
      3    Description            A20
      4    Price                  $

                                        Ordlog table has 10 records
```

By designating both the Ord Num and Line fields as keys, you make it possible for both fields to contain duplicate entries, but impossible for any two records to have the same entry in both fields. In other words, while there might be several 1001 entries in the Ord Num field, and several 1 entries in the Line field, there could be only one record with the Ord Num field entry 1001 and the Line field entry 1. If you attempted to enter a second record with these entries, Paradox would copy that record into a KEYVIOL table.

Designating just one key field, in this case, won't work. You already know that each order may have several lines and thus will occupy several records in the table. For example, order 1001 would occupy three records: order 1001, line 1; order 1001, line 2; and order 1001, line 3. Since each of these records will have the same Ord Num field entry, you cannot make Ord Num alone a key field. Similarly, since every order will have at least one line 1, there will be many duplicate entries in the Line field.

If you designate more than one key field, you still must place the key fields at the top of the table. If the table has several key fields, then all of the key fields must be at the top of the table's structure, before any non-key fields.

When a table contains more than one key field, Paradox will arrange the table so that the entries in the primary (first) key field are in ascending order. If there are duplicate entries in the primary key field (as there will usually be), then Paradox uses the entries in the secondary key field to break the ties. For example, Figure 3-9 shows the ORDLOG table as it will look after records have been entered. Notice that the records are arranged in ascending Ord Num field order and that the records in each Ord Num group are arranged by the Line field entries.

Figure 3-9 The ORDLOG Table

```
Viewing Ordlog table: Record 1 of 10                          Main

ORDLOG======Ord Num=======   ====Line=====   ====Description====    ====Price====
     1  ║    1001               1             Widgets                    34.95
     2       1001               2             Wombats                    56.00
     3       1001               3             Woofer                     75.00
     4       1002               1             Woofer                     75.00
     5       1003               1             Wombats                    56.00
     6       1003               2             Wombats                    56.00
     7       1004               1             Wombats                    56.00
     8       1004               3             Widgets                    34.95
     9       1004               4             Wombats                    56.00
    10  ║    1005               1             Wombats                    56.00
```

Key Fields and Queries

In Chapter 7, we'll show you how to perform queries. Queries are special tools that allow you to select information from a table. One of the advantages of key fields is that they make your queries work faster. Although this may not make much sense to you right now, it will be very important later.

Changing the Image

The Image command allows you to change the way information is displayed on the screen, without affecting the actual table upon which the image is based. The Image command appears on three menus: Main, DataEntry, and Edit. Except the KeepSet option, which appears when you issue the Image command from the Main menu or the Edit menu, the Image commands on all three menus offer the same capabilities.

The Image Menu

Suppose you are viewing a table named EMPLYEE, and you want to change the way the image is displayed on the screen. To do this, issue the **[Menu] I**mage command. After you issue the command, Paradox will display the menu shown in Figure 3-10.

Figure 3-10 The Image Menu

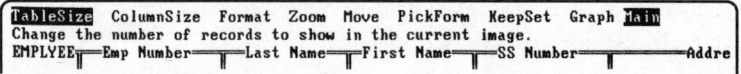

If you're viewing the table through a form, the menu will look like Figure 3-11. Notice that the TableSize, ColumnSize, and Move options are not available in the form view Image menu; however, the remaining options in the form view work the same as in the table view.

Figure 3-11 The Image Menu for Forms

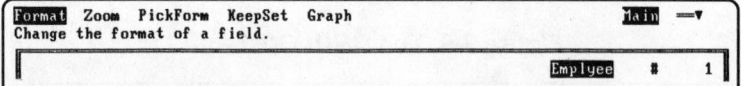

If you are using a release earlier than Paradox 3, you'll notice some differences in both Image menus. These menus will include the Goto command in place of Zoom, and the KeepSettings command instead of KeepSet. In addition, the Graph command will not appear on either of the Image menus. The Goto command performs the same function as Zoom, so when we tell you to press the [Menu] Image Zoom command in our examples, you can simply substitute the [Menu] Image Goto command. Similarly, the KeepSettings command performs the same function as KeepSet. The command was abbreviated to make room for the Graph command, which was added to the Image menu to accommodate the new graphing capabilities of Release 3.0. We will discuss the Graph command in Chapter 12, "Graphs."

Changing the Number of Records Showing

Normally, Paradox can display as many as 22 records of a table on the screen at one time. However, you can change the number of records displayed by issuing the [Menu] Image TableSize command.

For example, suppose you are viewing the EMPLYEE table. Since the EMPLYEE table contains just 16 records, its on-screen image is only 16 rows long. If you want to reduce the image to display only ten records at a time, issue the **[Menu] I**mage **T**ableSize command. After you issue this command, the cursor will change to a blinking box (sometimes referred to as the pointing cursor) in the last record of the table, and Paradox will display at the top of the screen the instructions shown in Figure 3-12.

At this point, you can press ↑, ↓, [Home], or [End] to change the size of the EMPLYEE image. Pressing the ↑ key reduces the number of records shown on the screen. Each time you press ↑, the size of the image shrinks by one row. You can reduce the number of records in the image to a minimum of two. If you want to shrink the image to the two-record minimum quickly, you can simply press [Home].

To increase the number of records displayed, press the ↓ key. You can press the [End] key to move quickly to the maximum allowable display (22 records) or the total number of records in the table, whichever is fewer.

Figure 3-12 The TableSize Instructions

```
┌──────────────────────────────────────────────────────────────────┐
│ Use ↑ to decrease the table by one row; ↓ to increase by one row...█Edit█ │
│ then press ◄┘ when finished.                                        │
│                                                                     │
└──────────────────────────────────────────────────────────────────
```

To reduce the size of the EMPLYEE image from 16 records to ten records, press ↑ six times, then press ↵ to lock in the change. Figure 3-13 shows the EMPLYEE table image as it will look after you make this change. Notice that only ten records are in view. When you've set the table size, you can view and manipulate the records as before. The only difference will be the number of records displayed on the screen at one time.

Figure 3-13 Changing the Number of Records Displayed

```
┌─────────────────────────────────────────────────────────────────┐
│ Viewing Emplyee table: Record 10 of 16                    █Main█  │
│                                                                    │
│ EMPLYEE╤═Emp Number═╤═Last Name═╤═First Name═╤═SS Number═╤═══Addre │
│   1    │     1      │ Jones     │ David      │ 414-76-3421│ 4000 St. Ja │
│   2    │     2      │ Cameron   │ Herb       │ 321-65-8765│ 2331 Elm St │
│   3    │     4      │ Jones     │ Stewart    │ 401-32-8721│ 4389 Oakbri │
│   4    │     5      │ Roberts   │ Darlene    │ 417-43-7777│ 451 Lone Pi │
│   5    │     6      │ Jones     │ Jean       │ 413-07-9123│ 4000 St. Ja │
│   6    │     8      │ Williams  │ Brenda     │ 401-55-1567│ 100 Owl Cre │
│   7    │     9      │ Myers     │ Julie      │ 314-38-9452│ 4512 Parksi │
│   8    │    10      │ Link      │ Julie      │ 345-75-1525│ 3215 Palm C │
│   9    │    12      │ Jackson   │ Mary       │ 424-13-7621│ 7821 Clark  │
│  10    │    13      │ Jakes, Jr.│ Sal        │ 321-65-9151│ 3451 Michig │
```

Changing the Column (Field) Size

You can use the ColumnSize option on the Image menu to increase or decrease the width of a column (field). One application of this command is to make the columns in the image narrower so that you can see more columns at once.

For example, when you look at Figure 3-13, you'll notice that the Address column is partially hidden. If you want to view the entire Address field, you can reduce the width of one or more of the columns to its left. To do this, issue the **[Menu] Image ColumnSize** command. After you issue this command, the cursor will change to a box, and Paradox will display the instructions shown in Figure 3-14 on the following page.

When you see these instructions, you should press the → and ← keys to position the pointing cursor in the Emp Number column, and press ↵. Paradox then will display the instructions for sizing the column, as shown in Figure 3-15.

Figure 3-14 The ColumnSize Prompt

```
Use → and ← to move to the column you want to resize...        Main
then press ↵ to select it...
EMPLYEE┬─Emp Number─┬──Last Name─┬─First Name─┬──SS Number─┬────────Addre
   1    │     1     │ Jones      │ David      │ 414-76-3421 │ 4000 St. Ja
   2    │     2     │ Cameron    │ Herb       │ 321-65-8765 │ 2331 Elm St
   3    │     4     │ Jones      │ Stewart    │ 401-32-8721 │ 4389 Oakbri
   4    │     5     │ Roberts    │ Darlene    │ 417-43-7777 │ 451 Lone Pi
   5    │     6     │ Jones      │ Jean       │ 413-07-9123 │ 4000 St. Ja
   6    │     8     │ Williams   │ Brenda     │ 401-55-1567 │ 100 Owl Cre
   7    │     9     │ Myers      │ Julie      │ 314-38-9452 │ 4512 Parksi
   8    │    10     │ Link       │ Julie      │ 345-75-1525 │ 3215 Palm C
   9    │    12     │ Jackson    │ Mary       │ 424-13-7621 │ 7821 Clark
  10    │    13     │ Jakes, Jr. │ Sal        │ 321-65-9151 │ 3451 Michig
```

Figure 3-15 Defining the Column Size

```
Now use → to increase column width, ← to decrease...        Main
press ↵ when finished.
```

At this point, you can press ← or → to narrow or widen the current column. Each time you press ←, the column width will decrease by one character. Pressing → will make the column wider, one character at a time. The minimum width of a column is one character. The maximum width of a column is equal to the width of the data in it or to the length of the column's field name, whichever is wider. If you want to reduce the width of a column to one character, just press [Home]. If you want to make it as wide as possible, press [End].

To reduce the size of the Emp Number field to one character, press the ← key several times or the [Home] key once. Notice that as you press ← or [Home] to decrease the width of Emp Number, the columns to its right are pulled to the left, and the entire Address field comes into view. When you have adjusted the column size, press ↵. Figure 3-16 shows the new image of the EMPLYEE table.

Figure 3-16 The New Image of EMPLYEE

```
Viewing Emplyee table: Record 10 of 16                      Main
EMPLYEE┬Emp┬──Last Name─┬─First Name─┬──SS Number─┬────────Address───────
   1   │ * │ Jones      │ David      │ 414-76-3421 │ 4000 St. James Ct.
   2   │ * │ Cameron    │ Herb       │ 321-65-8765 │ 2331 Elm St.
   3   │ * │ Jones      │ Stewart    │ 401-32-8721 │ 4389 Oakbridge Rd.
   4   │ * │ Roberts    │ Darlene    │ 417-43-7777 │ 451 Lone Pine Dr.
   5   │ * │ Jones      │ Jean       │ 413-07-9123 │ 4000 St. James Ct.
   6   │ * │ Williams   │ Brenda     │ 401-55-1567 │ 100 Owl Creek Rd.
   7   │ * │ Myers      │ Julie      │ 314-38-9452 │ 4512 Parkside Dr.
   8   │ * │ Link       │ Julie      │ 345-75-1525 │ 3215 Palm Ct.
   9   │ * │ Jackson    │ Mary       │ 424-13-7621 │ 7821 Clark Ave.
  10   │ * │ Jakes, Jr. │ Sal        │ 321-65-9151 │ 3451 Michigan Ave.
```

When you look at Figure 3-16, you will notice that the numerical values in the Emp Number field have been replaced with asterisks. This occurred because we made the column too small to display the values in it. If you use Lotus 1-2-3, this phenomenon may be familiar to you.

Whenever you reduce the width of a number, dollar, or short number field so much that Paradox cannot display in full the values in the field, it will display them as a series of asterisks. This does not mean that the values in your table now contain asterisks—only the image is affected. However, when you reduce the width of alphanumeric or date fields, Paradox simply displays as many characters as will fit in the narrow column.

Field View

If you want to view the entries in a narrow field, you can enter the field view. To do this, position the cursor on a record in the narrow column, and press **[Field View]** ([Alt]-[F5] or [Ctrl]-[F]). After you press [Field View], the cursor will change to a box, and the field value will be displayed. For example, Figure 3-17 shows the first record in the Emp Number field after we have entered the field view.

Figure 3-17   A Field View

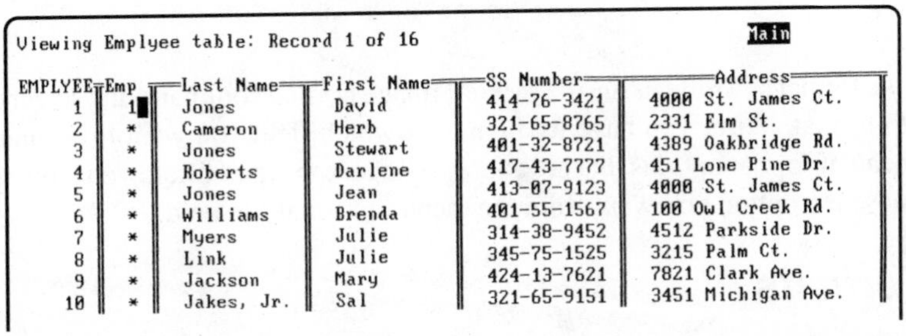

```
Viewing Emplyee table: Record 1 of 16                              Main

EMPLYEE Emp    Last Name   First Name   SS Number      Address
   1     1     Jones       David        414-76-3421    4000 St. James Ct.
   2     *     Cameron     Herb         321-65-8765    2331 Elm St.
   3     *     Jones       Stewart      401-32-8721    4389 Oakbridge Rd.
   4     *     Roberts     Darlene      417-43-7777    451 Lone Pine Dr.
   5     *     Jones       Jean         413-07-9123    4000 St. James Ct.
   6     *     Williams    Brenda       401-55-1567    100 Owl Creek Rd.
   7     *     Myers       Julie        314-38-9452    4512 Parkside Dr.
   8     *     Link        Julie        345-75-1525    3215 Palm Ct.
   9     *     Jackson     Mary         424-13-7621    7821 Clark Ave.
  10     *     Jakes, Jr.  Sal          321-65-9151    3451 Michigan Ave.
```

As you learned in Chapter 2, when you are in the field view, the functions of the cursor-movement keys change. For example, in the field view, the → and ← keys move the cursor one character to the right or left, respectively, within the current field. The [Home] key moves the cursor to the first character in the field, while the [End] key moves the cursor to the last character. You can use these keys to scroll through the entry in the narrow field. Although you can see only a few characters at a time (in the example, only one character at a time), by scrolling through the field, you can eventually see the entire entry.

Although you can use the field view to view the contents of fields in narrow columns, normally you will not want to leave any column in an image so narrow that you can't see at least most of the values it contains. For instance, you would probably not want to leave the width of the Emp Number field at one character. To widen this field to six characters (wide enough to view all of the entries the field contains), issue the **[Menu]** Image ColumnSize command, point to the Emp Number field, press ↵, press → five times, and press ↵ again. Figure 3-18 shows the EMPLYEE table at this point. Notice that all of the field values are now displayed, but the field name remains partially hidden.

Figure 3-18 The EMPLYEE Table

```
Viewing Emplyee table: Record 1 of 16                              Main

EMPLYEE Emp Numbe─Last Name──First Name──SS Number──────Address═══
   1      1       Jones       David       414-76-3421  4000 St. James Ct
   2      2       Cameron     Herb        321-65-8765  2331 Elm St.
   3      4       Jones       Stewart     401-32-8721  4389 Oakbridge Rd
   4      5       Roberts     Darlene     417-43-7777  451 Lone Pine Dr.
   5      6       Jones       Jean        413-87-9123  4000 St. James Ct
   6      8       Williams    Brenda      401-55-1567  100 Owl Creek Rd.
   7      9       Myers       Julie       314-38-9452  4512 Parkside Dr.
   8     10       Link        Julie       345-75-1525  3215 Palm Ct.
   9     12       Jackson     Mary        424-13-7621  7821 Clark Ave.
  10     13       Jakes, Jr.  Sal         321-65-9151  3451 Michigan Ave
```

Changing the Field Format

The Image menu also offers a command, Format, that allows you to change the display format of number, dollar, and date fields. Field formats in Paradox are very much like cell formats in Lotus 1-2-3.

To change the format of a field, issue the [Menu] Image Format command and select the field you want to format. After you have told Paradox which field you want to format, it will present a menu of format options that are appropriate for the type of field you have selected. Simply choose the option you want from the menu to format the field.

Date Formats

As you learned in Chapter 2, Paradox allows you to display dates in three different forms: MM/DD/YY, DD-Mon-YY, or DD.MM.YY. In the default state, Paradox will always display dates in the form MM/DD/YY. If you want to display the dates in a date field in DD-Mon-YY or DD.MM.YY form, you must format that field.

For example, suppose you want to change the format of the Date of Birth field in the sample EMPLYEE table. To do this, first issue the [**Menu**] **I**mage **F**ormat command. After you issue this command, the cursor will change to a box, and Paradox will instruct you to select the field you want to format. When you see this prompt, you should move the cursor to the Date of Birth field and press ↵. Paradox will recognize the field as a date field and will display the format options shown in Figure 3-19.

Figure 3-19 Format Options for Date Fields

```
MM/DD/YY  DD-Mon-YY  DD.MM.YY                            Main  ▲═══
All numeric month, day, year: e.g. 9/23/85.
```

The first option, MM/DD/YY, is the default display for date fields. The second option displays dates in the form DD-Mon-YY, so the date October 13, 1989, would be displayed as 13-Oct-89. The third option, DD.MM.YY, would display October 13, 1989, as 13.10.89.

You should select the format you prefer by highlighting it and pressing ↵. After you do this, Paradox will reformat all of the values in the column. For example, Figure 3-20 shows how the screen will look after you change the format for the Date of Birth field to the DD-Mon-YY format.

Figure 3-20 Changing the Default Date Format

```
Viewing Emplyee table: Record 1 of 16                              Main

        City         State  Zip          Phone       Date of Birth  Date o
    St. Matthews      KY    40207   (502) 245-6610     6-Oct-42       6/01
    Louisville        KY    40205   (502) 451-8765    24-Nov-29       6/01
    Lyndon            KY    40222   (502) 452-1848    21-Mar-50       7/01
    Lagrange          KY    40012   (502) 897-3215    24-Sep-60      11/01
    St. Matthews      KY    40207   (502) 245-6610    14-May-43      12/01
    Anchorage         KY    40223   (502) 894-9761    12-Jan-20       1/01
    Louisville        KY    40206   (502) 454-5289     6-Feb-48       2/01
    Palo Alto         CA    94375   (408) 542-1948     3-Jun-33       4/01
    Clarksville       IN    47130   (812) 288-6754    12-Aug-56       4/01
    Dallas            TX    65987   (214) 398-1987    23-May-59       5/01
```

Number and Dollar Fields

As you know, Paradox treats number and dollar fields in much the same way. In fact, the only difference between the two is their default display format. The default format for a number field is Paradox's General format; the default format for a dollar field is Comma. As you might expect, you can change the format of either dollar or number fields. In fact, the format options for these two types of fields are identical.

For example, suppose you want to reformat the Salary field in the EMPLYEE table. To do this, issue the [Menu] Image Format command, select the Salary field, and press ↵. Paradox will recognize the field as a dollar field and will display the menu shown in Figure 3-21. The current format for the field, Comma, will be highlighted. The other options are the available formats for number and dollar fields.

Figure 3-21 Format Options for Number and Dollar Fields

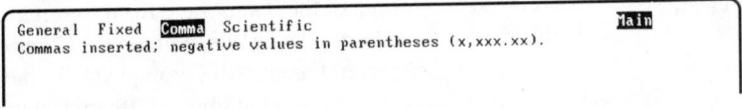

```
General  Fixed  Comma  Scientific                                  Main
Commas inserted; negative values in parentheses (x,xxx.xx).
```

The Format Options

The General format is the default format for number fields. In this format, numbers are displayed without commas and with up to two decimal places, if necessary. For example, the number 1,234.00 will be displayed as 1234; the number 1,234.56 will be displayed as 1234.56; the number 1,234.50 will be displayed as 1234.5; the number 1234.5678 will be displayed as 1234.57; and so on. In the General format, negative numbers are preceded with a minus sign (-). For example, the number -1,234.56 will be displayed as -1234.56. Large numbers are displayed as a series of asterisks. In the General format, numbers are aligned as though they have two decimal places, even if they have no decimals at all.

The Fixed format displays a set number of decimal places for the displayed values. For example, if you select Fixed and set the number of decimal places to 2, the number 1,234 will be displayed as 1234.00, and the number 1234.567 will be displayed as 1234.57. Negative numbers are preceded by a minus sign in the Fixed format.

You can specify from zero to 15 decimal places in the Fixed format. If you specify more decimal places than there are digits in the number being formatted, Paradox will append zeros to the number. For instance, the number 1234.5 would be displayed as 1234.50000 in the Fixed format with five decimal places. If the number of decimals you specify is less than the number of decimals in the number being formatted, Paradox will round the number for display purposes. For example, the number 1234.5678 would be displayed as 1235 in the Fixed format with zero decimal places. Be aware, however, that Paradox continues to store the extra digits in the table, even though it has rounded them in your image display.

The Comma format is the default format for dollar fields. In the Comma format, numbers are displayed with commas between the hundreds and thousands, thousands and millions, and so on. You can tell Paradox to include from 0 to 15 decimal places in the display. (The default is two decimal places.) Negative numbers are displayed in parentheses in the Comma format. For example, the value 33,999.99 will be displayed as 33,999.99 in the Comma format with two decimal places. The value -33,999.99 will be displayed as (33,999.99). The value 1234.567 will be displayed as 1,234.5670 in the Comma format with four decimal places and as 1,235 in the Comma format with zero decimal places.

The Scientific format displays values in exponential notation with up to 15 decimal places. For example, the number 70,000.00 will be displayed as 7.00E+04, and the number 1,234,567.89 will be displayed as 1.23E+06 in the Scientific format with two decimal places. Negative numbers are preceded by a minus sign in the Scientific format.

Changing the Format

To change the format of the selected field, select the format you prefer from the menu. For example, suppose you want to change the format of the Salary field from Comma with two decimal places to Comma with zero decimal places. To do this, point to the Comma option and press ↵. After you select the format you prefer, Paradox will prompt you for the number of decimal places. The default setting (2) is already filled in for you. If you want to accept this setting, just press ↵. To change this setting, press the [Backspace] key to erase the default setting, then type a number from 0 to 15. For instance, to change the setting to 0, press [Backspace], type 0, and then press ↵.

How Paradox Displays Formatted Numbers

As we have mentioned, it is important to understand that the number of decimals you specify when formatting a number or dollar field does not affect the actual values stored in that field. The format only changes the way the numbers appear in the image of the table. Even though the numbers are rounded for display purposes, the actual values remain unchanged.

Working with Formatted Fields

When you edit a rounded field value, the cursor will appear at the beginning of the field, rather than at the end, to remind you that the value has been rounded. In addition, an asterisk will appear at the end of the field, as shown in Figure 3-22. If you want to edit a rounded field value, you must use [Field View] or reformat the field.

Figure 3-22 Editing a Rounded Field

```
Editing Emplyee table: Record 5 of 16                            Edit

┌Date of Birth┬─Date of Hire─┬─Exemptions────┬─────Salary┐
    10/06/42       1/14/87          3                77000
    11/24/29       1/14/87          4                55000
     3/21/50       2/13/87          1                51700
     9/24/60       6/16/87          3                16940
     5/14/43       7/16/87          0        ─       37400*◄
     1/12/20       8/16/87          6                44000
     2/06/48       9/16/87          1                35200
     8/12/56      11/14/87          3                25410
     5/23/59      12/14/87          6                37400
     4/17/66       2/13/88          0                17847
```

Alphanumeric and Short Number Fields

You cannot change the format for alphanumeric or short number fields. If you try to format an alphanumeric or short number field, Paradox will display the message *Only N, $, and D fields may be formatted* at the bottom of the screen.

The Move Command

The Move command allows you to change the order of the fields in the image of a table without affecting the arrangement of the fields in the actual table structure. For example, suppose you want the State field to be the first field in the image of the EMPLYEE table. To make this change, issue the **[Menu]** Image Move command. After you issue the command, Paradox will display a list of the fields in the table and will prompt you to select a field to move, as shown in Figure 3-23.

Figure 3-23 Selecting a Field to Move

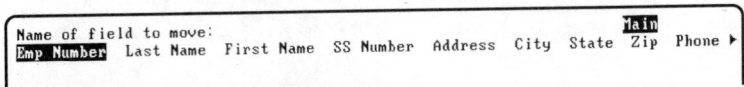

```
Name of field to move:                           Main
Emp Number  Last Name  First Name  SS Number  Address  City  State  Zip  Phone ▶
```

When you see this prompt, you should select the State field and press ↵. When you do, the cursor will change to a box, and Paradox will instruct you to point to the place where you want to insert the field. Exactly where you point depends on whether you are moving the column to the left or right of its original position. If you are moving a column to the left, it will be inserted to the left of the column in which you place the pointing cursor. If you are moving a column to the right, it will be inserted to the right of the column in which you place the pointing cursor.

Since you are moving the State field to the left of the Emp Number field, you should move the pointing cursor to the Emp Number field. When the cursor is in place, press ↵. After you do this, Paradox will move the column to its new location and shift all the other columns to the right. Figure 3-24 shows the screen after you move the column.

Figure 3-24 The New Field Order for EMPLYEE

```
Viewing Emplyee table: Record 1 of 16                      Main

EMPLYEE State Emp Number Last Name   First Name   SS Number      Addre
    1    KY      1       Jones       David        414-76-3421   4000 St. Ja
    2    KY      2       Cameron     Herb         321-65-8765   2331 Elm St
    3    KY      4       Jones       Stewart      401-32-8721   4389 Oakbri
    4    KY      5       Roberts     Darlene      417-43-7777   451 Lone Pi
    5    KY      6       Jones       Jean         413-07-9123   4000 St. Ja
    6    KY      8       Williams    Brenda       401-55-1567   100 Owl Cre
    7    KY      9       Myers       Julie        314-38-9452   4512 Parksi
    8    CA     10       Link        Julie        345-75-1525   3215 Palm C
    9    IN     12       Jackson     Mary         424-13-7621   7821 Clark
   10    TX     13       Jakes, Jr.  Sal          321-65-9151   3451 Michig
```

The [Rotate] Key [Ctrl]-[R]

You can also move columns by pressing [Rotate] ([Ctrl]-[R]). However, unlike the Move command, [Rotate] does not allow you to move a field to a specific location. Instead, [Rotate] always moves the current field all the way to the right end of the table so that it is the last field.

For example, suppose you now want to move the Emp Number field to the end of the table image. First, position the cursor in the Emp Number field, then press **[Rotate]** ([Ctrl]-[R]). Figure 3-25 shows the screen after you move the Emp Number column.

Figure 3-25 Using [Rotate]

```
Viewing Emplyee table: Record 1 of 16                      Main

EMPLYEE State Last Name   First Name   SS Number         Address
    1    KY    Jones       David        414-76-3421   4000 St. James Ct.
    2    KY    Cameron     Herb         321-65-8765   2331 Elm St.
    3    KY    Jones       Stewart      401-32-8721   4389 Oakbridge Rd.
    4    KY    Roberts     Darlene      417-43-7777   451 Lone Pine Dr.
    5    KY    Jones       Jean         413-07-9123   4000 St. James Ct.
    6    KY    Williams    Brenda       401-55-1567   100 Owl Creek Rd.
    7    KY    Myers       Julie        314-38-9452   4512 Parkside Dr.
    8    CA    Link        Julie        345-75-1525   3215 Palm Ct.
    9    IN    Jackson     Mary         424-13-7621   7821 Clark Ave.
   10    TX    Jakes, Jr.  Sal          321-65-9151   3451 Michigan Ave.
```

[Rotate] is useful when you want to scroll through the fields in a table but don't want to alter the image permanently. If you keep pressing [Rotate], the fields in the image will rotate toward the left edge of the image, enabling you to view each one without moving the cursor. If you press [Rotate] enough times, the original order of the columns will be restored.

The KeepSet Command

The KeepSet command tells Paradox to remember the image settings you have established for a particular table and to make them the default settings for viewing, entering data into, or editing that table in the future. Unless you issue this command, none of the changes made to the image will be permanent. Once you end the current session, the original settings will be restored.

For example, suppose you have used every command discussed in this chapter to define just the right image for your table. You certainly don't want to go through the same process every time you view the table. To avoid such frustration, you should issue the [Menu] Image KeepSet command. When you do, Paradox will save the image settings for the current table in a file with the extension .SET and will display the message *Settings recorded...* at the bottom of the screen. If you already have a .SET file associated with the table, Paradox will replace the existing file with the new one. The next time you view the table, enter data, or edit the records, the table image will be displayed with the image settings you saved.

You will recall that the Image command appears on the Main menu, the DataEntry menu, and the Edit menu. This command appears in three places so that you have the flexibility to change the image you are working with while you are viewing, editing, or entering records into a table. While these menus are nearly identical, there is no KeepSet option on the menu that appears when you issue the [Menu] Image command in the DataEntry mode. The commands on this menu allow you to change the image, but the changes you make cannot be saved.

You can delete the .SET file for a table with the [Menu] Tools Delete KeepSet command. For example, suppose you decide that you don't want to keep the settings you just saved for the EMPLYEE table. To delete the settings, issue the [Menu] Tools Delete KeepSet command. When Paradox prompts you to enter the name of the table whose settings you want to delete, type **EMPLYEE**, and press ↵. Paradox will delete the file and return to the main workspace. Once you delete the .SET file, Paradox will display the table with the default settings. (We'll discuss the Tools command in detail in Chapter 5, "Managing Tables.")

The ValCheck Command

The ValCheck command allows you to establish validity checks for your tables. As you know, Paradox does some validity checking automatically. For example, it won't let you enter letters into a number field or make an entry in an alphanumeric field that is longer than the field width. In addition, you've seen how key fields can be used to prevent duplicate entries in certain fields. However, ValCheck takes you one step further than these basic tests.

You will find the ValCheck command on both the DataEntry and Edit menus. When you issue the ValCheck command, Paradox will display the menu shown in Figure 3-26.

Figure 3-26 The ValCheck Menu

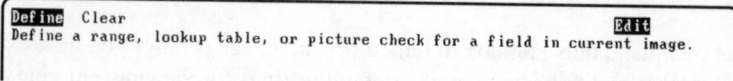

The ValCheck menu has two options: Define and Clear. The Define command lets you set the validity checks you want for the current image. The Clear command lets you clear validity checks for all fields in the current image or for individual fields. If you choose the Define command, the cursor will change to a small, blinking box, and Paradox will prompt you to select the field for which you want to establish a validity check. You should move the cursor to the appropriate field and press ↵. Paradox then will display the menu shown in Figure 3-27, which lists the types of validity checks you can establish. We will review each of these options in the examples that follow.

Figure 3-27 Validity Checks

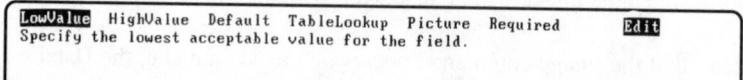

Setting a Low Value

The LowValue option allows you to set a minimum value for the entries in a field. Once you define a low value for a field, you will not be able to make an entry in the field that has a value lower than the low value.

For example, suppose you are viewing the EMPLYEE table, and you want to set a validity check for the Salary field that will not allow entries of less than $5,000.00. First, press **[Edit]** ([F9]) to enter the Edit mode, then issue the **[Menu]** ValCheck command. After you issue the ValCheck command, you will see the menu shown in Figure 3-26. Since you want to define a validity check, you should choose **Define**. When Paradox prompts you to specify the field to which you want to assign a validity check, move the cursor to the Salary field and press ↵. Paradox then will display the menu shown in Figure 3-27. To set a low value for the Salary field, choose the LowValue command.

Next, Paradox will prompt you to specify the low value for the field. When you see this prompt, type **5000** and press ↵. The message *Low value recorded* will appear in the lower-right corner of the screen. This message will disappear when you press any key.

From this point on, Paradox will check any value you enter in the Salary field to ensure that it is greater than or equal to 5000. If you try to enter a value that is less than 5000, Paradox will not accept the entry and will not let you move the cursor out of the field. For example, if you try to enter the value 4999 in the Salary field, your screen will look like Figure 3-28.

Figure 3-28 An Invalid Entry

```
Editing Emplyee table: Record 1 of 16                           Edit
┌─Date of Birth─┬─Date of Hire─┬─Exemptions─┬──────Salary──────
    10/06/42        1/14/87          3          4999           ◄
    11/24/29        1/14/87          4           55,000.00
     3/21/50        2/13/87          1           51,700.00
     9/24/60        6/16/87          3           16,940.00
     5/14/43        7/16/87          0           37,399.99
     1/12/20        8/16/87          6           44,000.00
     2/06/48        9/16/87          1           35,200.00
     8/12/56       11/14/87          3           25,410.00
     5/23/59       12/14/87          6           37,400.00
     4/17/66        2/13/88          0           17,847.50
    12/30/44        2/13/88          0           41,800.00
     3/16/25        2/27/88          1           40,700.00
     5/09/45        5/15/88          4           35,200.00
     5/18/50        6/15/88          2           21,175.00
     7/30/66        8/15/88          2           14,520.00
     6/03/33       11/14/87          2           33,000.00



                              Value no less than 5000.00 is expected
```

To correct the entry, press **[Ctrl]-[Backspace]** to clear the field, then type a number greater than or equal to 5000. Once you have made an appropriate response, you can leave the field and continue editing.

Although we used a dollar field to demonstrate the use of the LowValue command, you can also use the LowValue command in number, short number, and date fields. For example, suppose you want to make sure that no Date of Hire field entry is earlier than 6/1/84, the date your company was founded. To set this validity check, issue the **[Menu]** ValCheck **D**efine command and select the Date of Hire field at the prompt. Next, issue the LowValue command, type **6/1/84** at the prompt, and press ↵. Now, Paradox will not let you enter any date in that field earlier than 6/1/84.

You can even use LowValue in alphanumeric fields. If you define a low value for an alphanumeric field, Paradox will not allow any entry in that field that has an ASCII value lower than the ASCII value of the LowValue setting. For the most part, however, you will not find this particular validity check very useful for alphanumeric fields.

Setting a High Value

You can also establish an upper limit for the values entered in a field. For example, suppose you want to set a high value for the Exemptions field in EMPLYEE so that no number greater than 9 is entered. To do this, first issue the **[Menu] V**iew command, select the **EMPLYEE** table view (if it is not already in view), and press **[Edit]** to enter the Edit mode. Next, issue the **[Menu]** ValCheck **D**efine command. When Paradox prompts you to choose the field for which you want to set a validity check, select the Exemptions field. Next, issue the HighValue command.

Paradox will then prompt you for the high value. When you see this prompt, type **9** and press ↵. After you do this, the message *High value recorded* will appear at the bottom of the screen. The message will disappear when you press any key.

From this point on, if you enter a value greater than 9 in the Exemptions field, Paradox will display the message *Value no greater than 9 is expected* at the bottom of the screen and won't let you leave the field until you erase the erroneous value and enter an acceptable value.

Like the LowValue command, the HighValue command can be used with any type of field. When you set a high value for a date field, Paradox will not allow you to enter a date that is later than the high value date. If you set a high value for an alphanumeric field, Paradox will not let you enter a value in that field that has an ASCII value greater than the ASCII value of the high value you specify.

Setting a Default Value

The Default command on the ValCheck menu allows you to set a default value for a field. When you specify a default value for a field, Paradox will enter that value in that field of every record when you move through the field. If you want Paradox to enter the default value in the field, all you have to do is leave the field empty. This is an extremely useful feature that can save you a lot of typing.

For example, suppose that most of your employees live in Louisville. If you set *Louisville* as the default value for the City field, Paradox will automatically enter *Louisville* in the City field when you move through the field without typing anything into it.

To set *Louisville* as the default value for the City field in EMPLYEE, first bring EMPLYEE into view and enter the Edit mode. Next, issue the **[Menu]** ValCheck **D**efine command, and select the City field when Paradox prompts you for a field. Then, issue the **D**efault command, type **Louisville** at the prompt, and press ↵. When you do, the message *Default value recorded* will appear at the bottom of the screen. From this point on, if you leave the City field blank as you enter records, Paradox will automatically type in the value *Louisville* when you move the cursor out of the field.

Of course, you can set default values for date and number fields as well as for alphanumeric fields. For example, suppose you want to set the default for the Exemptions field at 1. To do this, issue the **[Menu]** ValCheck **D**efine command, select the Exemptions field, issue the **D**efault command, type **1**, and press ↵. Once you have set this default, Paradox will place a 1 into the Exemptions field automatically when you move the cursor through the field without filling it in.

For date fields, there is a special TODAY default you can use. For example, when entering new records into the EMPLYEE table, you can set up the TODAY default to automatically enter the current date into the Date of Hire field. To do this, issue the **[Menu]** ValCheck **D**efine command and select the Date of Hire field. Then, issue the **D**efault command, type

TODAY, and press ↵. Now, the current date will automatically be entered when you pass through the Date of Hire field. Keep in mind that Paradox gets the current date from your computer's system clock, so be sure it is set properly.

When you establish a default validity check, be sure to type the default value exactly as you want it entered. The value Paradox enters into your table will be identical to the default value you specify. If you mistype the default value, every entry Paradox makes for you also will be mistyped.

Also, please note that Paradox fills in the default only when you move the cursor through the field and leave the field blank. Thus, it is possible that the field might remain blank if you fill out the record in such a way that the cursor never enters the field. Suppose, in our previous example, that you create a new record in the EMPLYEE table, type in a few fields, but then press [Do-It!] before you get to the Exemptions field. In this case, Paradox will not enter a 1 into the Exemptions field because the cursor never entered that field.

The Picture Command

The Picture option on the ValCheck menu allows you to establish a "picture" or pattern for the entries in a field. Once you set a picture for a field, all subsequent entries in that field must conform to the picture.

Pictures can perform three basic functions. First, they can restrict the characters you may type into a field. Second, they can define the number of characters that a field may contain. Third, they can decrease typing by letting you tell Paradox to type in characters automatically.

Let's look at an example that exercises all three picture functions. In the EMPLYEE table, there is an SS Number field that will contain the employee's Social Security number. You want to restrict entries into that field to exactly 11 characters, such as 123-45-6789. Also, you want Paradox to type in the hyphens automatically in the fourth and seventh positions and allow only digits in the other nine places.

To set this picture, issue the **[Menu] V**alCheck **D**efine command and select the SS Number field. Next, issue the **P**icture command. When Paradox prompts you to supply the picture for this field, type **###-##-####** and press ↵. After you do this, Paradox will display the message *Picture specification recorded* at the bottom of the screen.

The picture ###-##-#### specifies an entry made up of nine digits separated by two hyphens. Once you assign this picture to the SS Number field, Paradox will allow in the SS Number field only entries that contain nine numbers. In addition, as you make entries in the SS Number field, Paradox will supply the hyphens between the digits for you. For example, suppose you want to enter the number 123-45-6789 in the SS Number field. When you type **123**, Paradox will display *123-*. After you type two more numbers, Paradox will insert the next hyphen, and the display will read *123-45-*. Now, all you need to do is enter the last four digits. Paradox will not let you move out of the field until you type all the digits; if you try, you will see the message *Incomplete field.*

There are several symbols you can use to define pictures. The basic building blocks for pictures are shown in Table 3-2. Each of these picture characters tells Paradox to accept a particular type of character. In addition to these simple symbols, there is another group of special symbols that you can use in pictures. We'll cover those symbols in the next part of this chapter.

Table 3-2 Picture Characters

Picture	Function
#	Accepts a number only
?	Accepts a letter only (uppercase or lowercase)
@	Accepts any character
&	Accepts only a letter and converts it to uppercase
!	Accepts any character and converts letters to uppercase

The # Character

The # character accepts only numbers. You can use this character to define pictures for alphanumeric fields that should contain only number entries—fields like Zip and SS Number. For example, suppose you want to be sure that every entry made in the Zip field of EMPLYEE will be entered in the form 12345. To do this, issue the **[Menu]** V**al**C**heck** D**efine** command. When Paradox prompts you to supply the field to which you want to assign the validity check, specify the **Z**ip field. Next, issue the **P**icture command. When you do, Paradox will prompt you to enter the picture for this field. To define the appropriate picture for this field, type ##### and press ↵. Paradox will then display the message *Picture specification recorded* at the bottom of the screen.

The picture ##### specifies an entry made up of five numbers. Once you assign this picture to the Zip field, Paradox will allow only entries in that field that match the picture. For one thing, this picture restricts the types of characters you can enter in the Zip field. If you try to enter a character other than a number in this field, Paradox will beep. This occurs because the symbol #, which you used throughout the picture, matches only numeric characters.

Second, this picture tells Paradox that Zip field entries must contain five characters. If you try to leave the field before you have typed five numbers, Paradox will display the message *Incomplete field* at the bottom of the screen. You will not be able to leave the field until you complete the entry.

The ? Character

The picture character ? tells Paradox to accept only letters, which may be either uppercase or lowercase. You might use this character in a picture in an alphanumeric field to restrict the field to letters. For example, suppose that you have a table named CLIENTS that contains a field named Code that, in turn, contains three-letter abbreviations of your clients' names.

Every Code field entry must be three characters long. You could use the picture *???* to force the user to enter three characters each time he or she makes an entry in the Code field. Since ? accepts only letters, the picture *???* would also prevent the user from entering a number in this field.

The @ Character

The @ character will accept any number or other character. Since Paradox will normally accept any character in an alphanumeric field, this symbol has the effect of requiring a character. For instance, the picture @@@ will accept any three-character entry. The difference between this picture and no picture is that the @@@ picture requires a three-character entry.

The & Character

The & symbol accepts only letters and converts any lowercase letter you type into uppercase. This picture character is very useful in fields that contain abbreviations in all uppercase, such as the State field in EMPLYEE. For example, suppose you want to define a picture for the State field of EMPLYEE that will accept only two letters and that will convert whatever you type into uppercase. To create this picture, issue the **[Menu]** **ValCheck** **Define** command, and specify the State field. Next, choose **Picture** from the ValCheck menu, and type **&&** when Paradox prompts you for the picture. When you press ↵, Paradox will assign this picture to the field and will display the message *Picture specification recorded* at the bottom of the screen.

Once you have defined this picture, Paradox will accept only two-letter entries in the State field. If you attempt to enter a number, a single letter, or more than two letters, Paradox will not accept the entry. You will have to correct the entry before going on.

If the letters you type are in lowercase, Paradox will convert them to uppercase. For instance, if you enter *ky* in the State field after you have defined this picture, Paradox will convert the entry to *KY* before storing it in the table.

The ! Character

The ! character is a hybrid of the & and @ characters. Like @, the ! character will accept any type of character. Like &, however, ! will convert any letter you type into uppercase. You might use this symbol in a field that contains both numbers and letters, and in which you want the letters to be capitalized. For instance, suppose you have a table named DRIVERS that includes a field called Tag. This field stores the license tag number for every driver listed in the table. In most states, tag numbers are made up of letters and numbers, as in NXX 478 and NYS 475. You could use a picture like *!!! !!!* to accept this type of entry. Since this picture will accept both numbers and letters, it will accept any six-character license number. Furthermore, since it will convert letters to uppercase, you don't have to press [Shift].

Literal Characters

You can also use literal characters in pictures. When you enter a literal character in a picture, Paradox will automatically type the literal characters for you. We showed you an example of this earlier when we defined the Social Security number picture ###-##-####. The hyphens, which fill in automatically as you type the Social Security number, are literal characters.

In addition to punctuation marks like -, you may include literal spaces, letters, and numbers in your pictures. For instance, the picture *!!! !!!*, which we used for the license tag number in our previous example, contains a literal space. If you use this picture, Paradox will automatically type a space for you after you type three characters.

Similarly, the picture *1989###-#* contains several literal characters. Even though this picture begins with a literal character, Paradox will not type the characters *1989* automatically as soon as you move the cursor into a field that is governed by this pattern. Instead, Paradox will wait for you either to type a 1 or press the [Spacebar]. If you do either of these things, Paradox will immediately type *1989*, then wait for you to type three digits. After you type these characters, Paradox will type a hyphen and then wait for you to type one more number. If you type a character that does not conform to the picture, Paradox will beep.

Other Picture Characters

In addition to the picture characters above, there are five characters that have special meanings when you are designing a picture: ;, *, [], { }, and ,. These symbols are modifiers; that is, they modify the function of the basic picture characters in your pictures.

The ; character tells Paradox to accept literally the picture character that follows it. For example, if you use the character # in a PAL picture, Paradox will accept only a number in that field. This can cause a problem if you want to include a number sign (#) in the actual entry in the field but still want to use a picture for that field. However, if you precede the # symbol with a semicolon (;), Paradox will include the literal character # in the field entry, rather than using the symbol # as a picture for a number. For example, suppose your company uses a three-digit code followed by a number sign for its inventory control number (for example, 123# or 999#). You could use the picture ###;# in that field. This picture tells Paradox to accept any three digits followed by the literal symbol #.

The * character tells Paradox to repeat a picture symbol a specified number of times. This symbol is followed by a number, which represents the number of times you want the picture symbol repeated, and by the symbol itself. For example, the picture *123*3#* tells Paradox to enter the characters *123*, then accept any three digits entered by the user. The characters **3#* tell Paradox to repeat the symbol # three times, making this the equivalent of the picture *123###*.

If you do not enter a number after the *, Paradox will accept any number of characters of the specified type, from zero to the maximum number of characters allowed in the field. For example, while the picture *2# tells Paradox to accept only two digits, the picture *# tells Paradox to accept as many digits as the user types.

As another example, the picture &*? could be used in the Last Name field. Paradox will capitalize the first letter of the name and allow any number of letters to follow. The picture *! allows an entry of any number characters and converts lowercase letters to uppercase.

The [ ] characters tell Paradox that the entry they enclose is optional. For example, suppose you want to define a picture for a phone number field that optionally allows for a three-digit extension. To do this, you could define a picture that looks like this: ###-####[x###]. This picture tells Paradox to accept at least seven digits, automatically placing a hyphen between the third and fourth digits. After the seventh digit, the user may optionally type an x followed by three more digits.

The characters { } are called the grouping operator. They can be used with other special characters to define a group. For example, the picture *2{#?}##, which is equivalent to #?#?##, tells Paradox to accept a number followed by a letter, then another number followed by another letter, and then two more numbers. The expression {#?} in this picture tells Paradox to treat the characters #? as a group.

The { } characters have another purpose. Earlier, we noted that when you include literal characters in your pictures, Paradox will automatically type those characters for you. For example, we said that the picture ###-##-#### will cause Paradox to type the hyphens between the sections of a Social Security number automatically. If you want, you can use the { } characters to suppress this automatic feature. For example, suppose you do not want Paradox to fill in the hyphens for you in the SS Number field. To suppress the automatic fill-in, place the hyphens inside curly braces, as in ###{-}##{-}####. Now, the hyphens will be filled in only if the user types them or presses the [Spacebar] after entering the digits.

The comma (,) is used in pictures to define a set of alternatives. For example, the picture Yes,No allows the entry of either the word Yes or the word No into a field, but nothing else. You could use the comma and the { } characters together to allow a given character in an entry to be any one of a group of characters. For example, the picture J{anuary,u{ne,ly}} forces the entry in a field to be one of the words January, June, or July. The user need only type the letters Ja, Jun, or Jul; at that point, Paradox will fill in the rest of the word.

A Note

Some picture characters are inappropriate for some fields. For example, you should not use the character ?, which accepts a letter, in a number field. Unfortunately, Paradox does not warn you when a picture is inappropriate for a given field. For example, suppose you define a picture like &### for a number field. This picture tells Paradox to accept only a letter for the first character, convert it to uppercase, and then accept three digits to complete the entry.

Paradox will let you define this picture for a number field. When you try to use the picture to enter data, however, Paradox won't allow you to enter anything in the field. If you try to enter a letter, Paradox will not accept it because of the field type. If you try to enter a number, Paradox will not accept it because of the picture.

Pictures can make data entry quicker and more accurate. The examples we've shown only scratch the surface of this powerful feature of Paradox. However, you should remember that creating and defining pictures can be tricky, especially when you move beyond the basics and begin to create pictures that are more flexible. You will want to take the time to practice with pictures before you begin relying on them in your important tables.

The Required Command

The Required command tells Paradox that a field must have a value—leaving it blank is not allowed. When you set a Required validity check on a field, you will not be able to move the cursor out of that field during data entry unless something has been typed into it.

For example, suppose you want to make sure that every employee has a value entered in the Salary field. To establish this requirement, issue the [Menu] ValCheck Define command and select the Salary field. Next, issue the Required command. After you issue the command, Paradox will prompt you for confirmation. You then should choose the Yes command. When you do, Paradox will display the message *Required status recorded* at the bottom of the screen. (If you do not want to put the Required status in effect, you should choose No.)

Once you use the Required command, Paradox will not let you leave the Salary field without entering a value. If you try to leave the field without entering a value, the message *A value must be provided in this field; press [F1] for help* will appear at the bottom of the screen. You must enter a value before you can leave the field. If an existing record has a blank in that field when you set the Required validity check, you can leave it blank. However, if you subsequently edit the field, Paradox will then insist that you enter a value.

TableLookup Validity Checks

The [Menu] ValCheck Define TableLookup command lets you create TableLookup validity checks for the fields in your tables. When you use this command to assign a TableLookup validity check to a field, Paradox will check the values you enter into that field against the values in a field of another table, called the lookup table. If an entry you make into the field that has the TableLookup validity check does not exist in the first field of the lookup table, Paradox will not accept the entry. TableLookup validity checks can be used to help with the accuracy of data entry as well as to speed up the data entry process. This feature can be used during data entry or while you are editing an existing table.

There are several options available when setting up the TableLookup validity check. First, you can specify a simple validity check that rejects any entries that do not appear in the first field of the lookup table. Second, you can ask Paradox to provide LookupHelp during the data entry process. If LookupHelp is on, you can view the lookup table during data entry just by placing the cursor in the field to which you've assigned the TableLookup validity check and pressing [Help] ([F1]). Third, if the table with the validity check has several fields in common with the lookup table, you can ask Paradox to fill in those common fields automatically each time you make an entry into the key field.

For example, suppose you have already entered records into a table named ADDRESS, assigning employee numbers to each employee. You are about to begin data entry for the EMPLYEE table, and you want to make sure the employee numbers correspond between the two tables. You can set up a TableLookup validity check on the Emp Number field of EMPLYEE that will check any entry in that field against the entries in the Emp Number field of the ADDRESS table.

To begin the process, issue the [Menu] Modify Edit command to bring EMPLYEE to the screen in the Edit mode. Next, issue the [Menu] ValCheck Define command and select the Emp Number field. When the ValCheck menu appears, issue the TableLookup command.

After you do this, Paradox will prompt you to enter the name of the table that contains the lookup values (the lookup table). You should type ADDRESS and press ↵. Next, Paradox will display the menu shown in Figure 3-29. At this point, you must decide if you want to verify only the value entered in the current field, or if you want to copy over as much data as possible from the lookup table.

Figure 3-29 TableLookup Submenu

```
JustCurrentField  AllCorrespondingFields                    Edit  ═▼
Check entered values in current field against stored values in lookup table.
```

The JustCurrentField Option

The first option on the TableLookup submenu, JustCurrentField, tells Paradox to verify only that any entry you make in the field matches an entry in the first field of the lookup table. For example, if you only want to make sure that each employee number you enter into EMPLYEE is accurate, you would select the JustCurrentField option.

If you select JustCurrentField, Paradox will display the submenu shown in Figure 3-30. The first option on this menu, PrivateLookup, tells Paradox that you do not want the user to be able to view the lookup table while entering data. For example, if there were confidential information in the ADDRESS table, you might want to use this option.

Suppose you enter data into the Emp Number field of the EMPLYEE table after selecting the PrivateLookup option. Paradox will check that entry against the values in the Emp Number column of the ADDRESS table. If no match is found, the error message *Not one of the possible values for this field* will appear at the bottom of the screen. You must either correct the entry or leave it blank before you can continue the data entry or editing session. If the entry is valid, you may continue without interruption.

Figure 3-30 JustCurrentField Submenu

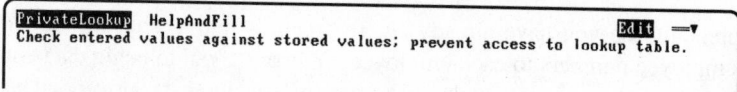

```
PrivateLookup HelpAndFill                                      Edit ═▼
Check entered values against stored values; prevent access to lookup table.
```

The HelpAndFill option tells Paradox that you want to allow the user to view the lookup table for assistance when making an entry into the field. If you choose this option, the user will be able to view the lookup table during data entry just by placing the cursor in the field to which you've assigned the TableLookup validity check and pressing [Help] ([F1]).

For example, suppose you have selected the HelpAndFill option for the Emp Number field of the EMPLYEE table. When you move the cursor into this field during data entry or editing, the message *Press [F1] for help with fill-in* will appear at the top of the screen. If you are not sure which employee number you want, press [**F1**] to view the lookup table ADDRESS, as shown in Figure 3-31. Then, use the cursor-movement keys or the [Zoom] ([Ctrl]-[Z]) key to move the cursor to the record you are looking for. When the cursor is in the correct record, press [**Do-It!**] ([F2]) to select that record. (The cursor can be in any field within the lookup table record.) Paradox will then return you to the EMPLYEE table and automatically fill in the Emp Number field with your choice.

Figure 3-31 The Lookup Table

```
Move to the record to be selected
Press [F2] to select the record; Esc to cancel; [F1] for help
ADDRESS══Emp Number═══╤═Last name═╤═First Name══╤═SS Number═══╤══Spouse══
   1  ║      1    ║ Jones     │ David      ║ 414-76-3421 ║ Jill
   2  ║      2    ║ Cameron   │ Herb       ║ 321-65-8765 ║ Denise
   3  ║      4    ║ Jones     │ Stewart    ║ 401-32-8721 ║
   4  ║      5    ║ Roberts   │ Darlene    ║ 417-43-7777 ║
   5  ║      6    ║ Jones     │ Jean       ║ 414-07-9123 ║ Robert
   6  ║      8    ║ Williams  │ Brenda     ║ 401-55-1567 ║ Dan
   7  ║      9    ║ Myers     │ Julie      ║ 314-30-9452 ║
   8  ║     10    ║ Link      │ Julie      ║ 345-75-1525 ║ Bryan
   9  ║     12    ║ Jackson   │ Mary       ║ 424-13-7621 ║
  10  ║     14    ║ Preston   │ Molly      ║ 451-00-3426 ║
  11  ║     15    ║ Masters   │ Ron        ║ 317-65-4529 ║ Betty
  12  ║     13    ║ Triplett  │ Judy       ║ 616-10-6610 ║ Brad
  13  ║     16    ║ Robertson │ Kevin      ║ 415-24-6718 ║
  14  ║     17    ║ Garrison  │ Robert     ║ 312-98-1479 ║ Urlene
  15  ║     19    ║ Gunn      │ Barbara    ║ 321-97-8632 ║
```

The *AllCorrespondingFields* Option

The AllCorrespondingFields option on the TableLookup submenu tells Paradox to verify each entry you make in the field and to fill in automatically any other fields that table has in common with the lookup table. For example, suppose you select the AllCorrespondingFields option while defining the validity check for the Emp Number field. Each time you enter an employee number, Paradox will copy the contents of all the fields in ADDRESS that have the same names as fields in EMPLYEE (Last Name, First Name, SS Number, Address, City, State, Zip, and Phone) to the new record in EMPLYEE.

If you select the AllCorrespondingFields option, Paradox will display the submenu shown in Figure 3-32. The first option on this menu, FillNoHelp, tells Paradox to prevent the user from viewing the lookup table during data entry.

Figure 3-32 *AllCorrespondingFields Submenu*

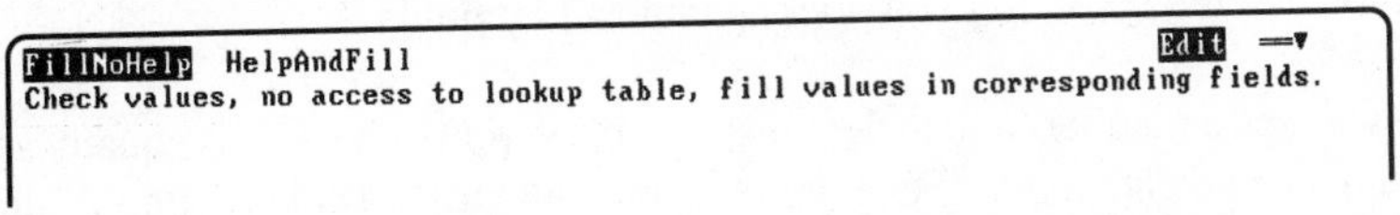

```
 FillNoHelp  HelpAndFill                                        Edit  ═▼
 Check values, no access to lookup table, fill values in corresponding fields.
```

For example, when you enter data into the Emp Number field of the EMPLYEE table after selecting the FillNoHelp option, Paradox will check that entry against the values in the Emp Number column of the ADDRESS table. If no match is found, the error message *Not one of the possible values for this field* will appear at the bottom of the screen. You must either correct the entry or leave it blank before you can continue the data entry or editing session. If the entry is valid, Paradox will automatically fill in all the fields of the EMPLYEE table that correspond to fields in the ADDRESS table. These fields may then be edited or left as is, and data entry may continue.

The HelpAndFill option tells Paradox to allow the user to view the lookup table for assistance when making an entry into the field. If you choose this option, the user will be able to view the lookup table during data entry just by placing the cursor in the field to which you've assigned the TableLookup validity check and pressing [Help] ([F1]).

For example, suppose you have selected the HelpAndFill option for the Emp Number field of the EMPLYEE table. When you move the cursor into this field during data entry or editing, the message *Press [F1] for help with fill-in* will appear at the top of the screen. If you are not sure which employee number you want, press **[F1]** to view the lookup table ADDRESS. Then, use the cursor-movement keys or [Zoom] ([Ctrl]-[Z]) to move the cursor to the record you are looking for. When the cursor is in the correct record, press **[Do-It!]** ([F2]) to select that record. (The cursor can be in any field within the lookup table record.) Paradox will then return you to the EMPLYEE table and automatically fill in the Emp Number field with your choice. Paradox will also automatically fill in all the fields of the EMPLYEE table that correspond to fields in the ADDRESS table.

Notes

There are a few things to keep in mind when setting up a lookup table. First, the validity check field in the lookup table must be the first field of that table. For example, Emp Number is the first field in ADDRESS. In fact, you will notice that Paradox does not even prompt you for the name of the field that contains the validity check values; it merely asks for the name of the table and looks in the first field of that table for the match values. (Of course, the field to which you assign the TableLookup validity check can be anywhere in the table.)

If you have set up validity checks for fields in the table being edited and have also used the AllCorrespondingFields option, Paradox will move the values "as is" from the lookup table, ignoring any validity checks there might be on those other fields.

Since Paradox must compare every entry you make with the values in the lookup table, the editing and data entry process will be slower. However, you can greatly speed up the validation by making the field in the lookup table a key field.

Although we used a number field to demonstrate this validity check, it is equally applicable to alphanumeric and date fields. For example, you could use a TableLookup validity check to verify the dates entered in a date field, or alphanumeric strings used as part numbers in an inventory table.

If the lookup table is not in the active directory, you must tell Paradox the directory in which the table is located. For example, suppose the EMPLYEE table is in a directory called c:\paradox3\people, and the ADDRESS table is in a directory called c:\paradox3\numbers. When Paradox prompts you to enter the name of the lookup table, you should type **c:\paradox3\numbers\address** and press ↵.

You should consider setting up validity checks on your tables as soon as possible. Since the ValCheck command is on the DataEntry menu, the ideal time to establish validity checks is when you issue the [Menu] Modify DataEntry command to enter your first set of records in a newly created table. By establishing validity checks early, you can minimize the potential for errors during data entry and editing. This is especially important if several people will be entering data or editing the records in your tables.

When you are setting up validity checks for a table, those checks will take effect immediately after you define them. Any existing records in the table will not be affected. For example, suppose you set the Required validity check for the SS Number field in the EMPLYEE table. Any pre-existing blanks in the field may be left blank; however, if you then decide to edit those records, Paradox will not let you leave the field until you have entered a value.

When you define validity checks for a table, Paradox creates a file with the same name as the table and the extension .VAL. This file holds the information Paradox needs to enforce your validity checks.

Prior to Release 2, Paradox offered only the TableLookup JustCurrentField FillNoHelp option. In Releases 1 and 1.1, the process of setting up the lookup table is the same as described above, but no submenus will appear.

Clearing Validity Checks

You can use the [Menu] ValCheck Clear command to clear any validity checks you have assigned to a table. This command allows you to clear the validity checks for a single field or for an entire table.

For example, suppose that after setting validity checks for the Salary field, you want to clear the checks for that field. To do this, issue the **[Menu]** **V**alCheck **C**lear Field command. Next, Paradox will prompt you to specify the field whose validity checks you want to clear. When you see this prompt, move the cursor to the Salary field and press ↵. Paradox then will remove the checks from the Salary field and display the message *Validity checks removed from field* at the bottom of the screen. Entries made in the field will not be checked except for the routine checking automatically performed by Paradox.

If you want to remove the validity checks from all of the fields in the table, issue the **[Menu]** ValCheck Clear All command. After you issue the command, Paradox will display the message *All validity checks removed* at the bottom of the screen. When you issue this command, Paradox will suspend all validity checks for the duration of the current data entry or edit session. When you press [Do-It!] or issue the [Menu] DO-IT! command to end the session, Paradox will delete the .VAL file from disk. From that point on, the default validity check settings will be in effect. If you issue the [Menu] Cancel command to end the data entry or edit session, however, Paradox will not delete the .VAL file.

Deleting a .VAL File

You can also delete a .VAL file with the [Menu] Tools Delete ValCheck command. For example, suppose you established and saved validity checks for the EMPLYEE table, and you now want to delete those validity checks. To do this, issue the **[Menu]** **T**ools **D**elete ValCheck command. After you issue the command, Paradox will prompt you to enter a table name. When you see this prompt, type **EMPLYEE** and press ↵. Paradox then will delete the .VAL file and return to the main workspace.

Special Tricks for Data Entry

By taking advantage of a few special tricks, you can reduce the amount of time you spend entering and editing data. We'll cover those topics next.

The Ditto Key ([Ctrl]-[D])

The [Ditto] key allows you to copy into the current field in one record the entry from that same field in the previous record. For example, suppose you are entering a few new records into the PROJECTS table, as shown in Figure 3-33. Now, suppose that the Client Number field entry for the second record is identical to the Client Number field entry for the first record. Instead of typing the Client Number entry for record 2, you could move the cursor to the Client Number field of the second record and press **[Ditto]** ([Ctrl]-[D]). Figure 3-34 shows the result. As you can see, Paradox has copied the entry from the Client Number field of record 1 into record 2.

Figure 3-33 The ENTRY Table for PROJECTS

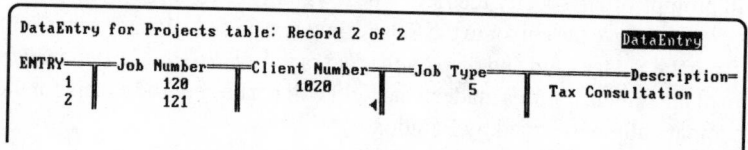

Figure 3-34 Using the [Ditto] Key

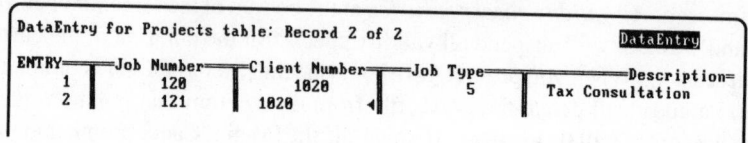

Whenever you have identical entries in a field in two or more consecutive records, you can use [Ditto] to copy the values from record to record. Using [Ditto] can save you a lot of time during data entry and editing.

Number and Dollar Fields

There are a couple of special data entry tricks that apply only to number and dollar fields. First, while you are entering a value into a number or dollar field, you can use commas to separate the hundreds from the thousands, the thousands from the millions, and so on. For example, you could enter the number 9123456 by typing **9,123,456**. You can use this trick to help keep things straight when you enter large numbers. (Of course, the final appearance of the value depends on the format you have assigned to the field.) If you use the commas incorrectly, Paradox will not accept the entry. For example, Paradox will reject the entry 91,234,56.

Paradox allows you to use the [Spacebar] to perform a wide variety of tasks during data entry and editing. For instance, when you are entering data into a number field, you can press the

[Spacebar], instead of typing a period, to enter a decimal point. For example, to enter the number 1234.56, you could type **1234[Spacebar]56**.

Normally, you'll enter a negative number by preceding it with a minus sign (-). However, you can also enter a negative number by enclosing it in parentheses. For example, you could enter the number -1234.56 as -1234.56 or (1234.56). Once again, the appearance of the final entry will depend on the format you've assigned to the field.

If you use parentheses to enter negative numbers, you can use the [Spacebar] to add the second parenthesis automatically. For instance, to enter the number -35 in a number or dollar field, type (**35**, then press the **[Spacebar]** to enter the closing parenthesis.

Paradox 3 automatically displays negative entries in number (N and S type) and dollar ($ type) fields in different text and background colors from those in which it displays other fields. You can use the Custom Configuration Program (CCP) to set Paradox to display positive and negative values in the same colors. For example, suppose you find the negative values in different colors annoying and decide that you want Paradox to display all fields with the same colors.

To play the CCP, first make sure that you are in the \paradox3 directory, then issue the [**Menu**] Scripts Play command. When Paradox asks you for the name of a script, type **paradox 3 \custom** and press ↵. After the CCP main menu appears on the screen, issue the Video NegativeColors command. After you issue this command, you will see the menu shown in Figure 3-35.

Figure 3-35 The NegativeColors Menu

```
┌──────────────────────────────────────────────────────────────────┐
│ BothDifferent  Numbers  Currency  Same                             │
│ Color negative number & currency field values differently than positive ones. │
```

The BothDifferent command sets Paradox to display negative entries in both number and dollar fields in different colors from other fields. This command is highlighted because it is the current setting. The Numbers command sets Paradox to display only negative entries in number fields in different colors. If you choose this command, Paradox will display negative entries in dollar fields in the same color as other fields. The Currency command sets Paradox to display only negative entries in dollar fields in different colors. If you choose this command, Paradox will display negative entries in number fields in the same color as other fields. The Same command displays negative entries in both number and dollar fields in the same colors that Paradox uses to display all other fields. Since you want all fields to appear in the same colors, select the Same command.

After you make your selection, the CCP will return to the Video menu, which is just above the NegativeColors menu. To return to the CCP main menu, issue the Return command from the

Video menu. When you see the CCP main menu, select **DO-IT!**. After you issue the DO-IT! command, the CCP will exit to DOS. The new color setting that you chose for negative fields will take effect the next time you load Paradox.

Date Fields

You will recall that there are three basic formats for date fields: MM/DD/YY, DD-Mon-YY, and DD.MM.YY. Paradox will let you enter dates in any of these formats and then convert the entry to the format set for the field.

In addition, Paradox will try to guess the date you want while you are entering a date. For example, suppose you want to enter the date 2/21/89. To do this, type **21-f**. Paradox will automatically recognize the date format you are using and capitalize the letter *F* for you. Now, press **[Spacebar]** and Paradox will supply the second letter in the month name, *e*. If you press [Spacebar] again, Paradox will complete the month name by typing a *b*.

In general, whenever you type the first letter of a month and then press the [Spacebar], Paradox will supply the next letter of the month's name. If the first letter you type is common to several months, Paradox will supply the second letter in the name of the earliest month of the year that begins with the first letter you typed. For example, suppose you want to enter the date May 5, 1989. You can type **5-M** and press the **[Spacebar]** to type the letter *a*. If you press the **[Spacebar]** again, however, Paradox will type an *r*—the third letter in *March*, the first month in the year that begins with the letters *Ma*. You can then press **[Backspace]** to erase the *r*, and type **y**.

When you are making entries in a date field, you can use the [Spacebar] to help you enter part of the date. If you press the [Spacebar] while you are entering a date, Paradox will define the current portion of the date as equal to that component of today's date. For example, suppose that today is March 1, 1989. If you press the [Spacebar] to begin a date field entry, Paradox will type *3*—the month portion of today's date. If you press the [Spacebar] three times, Paradox will enter the current date—3/01/89—into the field. To enter the date 3/23/89, you would type **[Spacebar]23[Spacebar]**.

If you omit the year portion of a date, Paradox will assume that the date is in the current year. For example, if the current year is 1989 and you type **12/25** and press ↵, Paradox will enter the date into your table as 12/25/89.

Conclusion

In this chapter, we have introduced you to several advanced data entry and editing concepts. First, we showed you how to create a keyed table and how to deal with key field violations. Then, we taught you how to change the appearance of your tables using the Image command. Finally, we showed you how to set up validity checks and offered a few tips that may help make your data entry faster and easier. As you work with Paradox, the editing shortcuts discussed in this chapter will become second nature to you.

Chapter 4

Forms

So far, we've discussed tables: how to create them, how to enter and edit records in them, and how to view them. In this chapter, we will show you how to design custom forms that you can use to enter, edit, or view data in your tables.

As you will see, Paradox's capacity to create forms gives you considerable flexibility for editing and viewing the records in your tables. For example, the default table view displays up to 22 records on the screen at one time, but a very limited number of fields. On the other hand, the form view displays one record at a time, but as many fields as will fit on the screen. The table view always shows the fields in columns and rows, while the form view can display fields any way you choose. In addition, the form view can contain calculated fields that aren't actually in the table.

The Default Form

Paradox automatically creates a default form for every table. To view a table through this default form, simply press [Form Toggle] ([F7]) while you are viewing the table. For example, to view EMPLYEE through its default form, you would issue the **[Menu]** View command to bring EMPLYEE into view, then press **[Form Toggle]** to enter the form view. Figure 4-1 on the following page shows this form on the screen.

Notice that the fields in the default form are placed vertically on the left side of the screen. Also, notice that Paradox automatically draws a double-line border around the screen. In the upper-right corner of the screen, Paradox displays the table name, EMPLYEE, in reverse video, as well as a record number field that tells you which record from the table you are viewing through the form. All default forms contain these same basic elements.

The message *Viewing Emplyee table with form F: Record 1 of 16,* which appears at the top of the screen, tells you which table you are viewing, which of that table's forms you are using, and which record is currently displayed in the form. A message like this one will always appear at the top of the screen while you are working in a form.

Figure 4-1 The Default Form for EMPLYEE

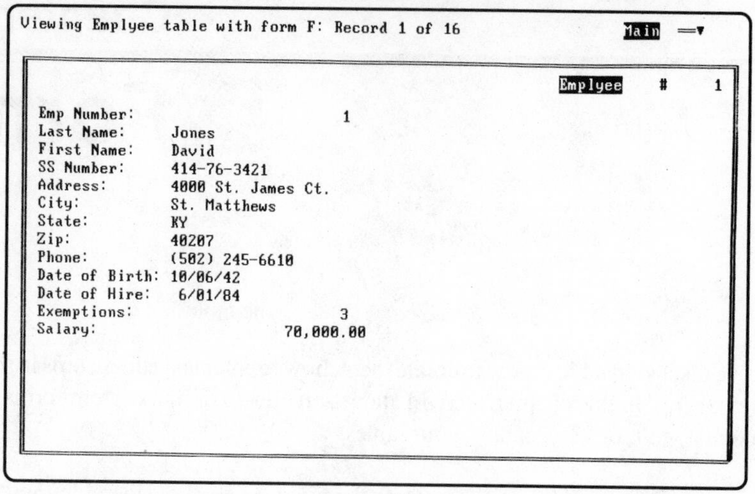

```
Viewing Emplyee table with form F: Record 1 of 16                Main  =▼

                                                    Emplyee    #    1
      Emp Number:                    1
      Last Name:     Jones
      First Name:    David
      SS Number:     414-76-3421
      Address:       4000 St. James Ct.
      City:          St. Matthews
      State:         KY
      Zip:           40207
      Phone:         (502) 245-6610
      Date of Birth: 10/06/42
      Date of Hire:   6/01/84
      Exemptions:                    3
      Salary:                 70,000.00

```

Also, notice the symbol =▼ in the upper-right corner of the screen. This symbol tells you that there are more records in the table following this record. If you were viewing a record in the middle of the table (instead of record 1), the symbol would be ▲=▼. This symbol tells you that there are records above and below the current record in the table. Similarly, if you were viewing the last record in the table (record 16, in this case), the symbol would be ▲=. This symbol tells you that there are more records in the table and that they are all above the record you are viewing.

Finally, Paradox automatically will create a multipage form for a table that has more than 19 fields. We'll cover multipage forms later in this chapter.

Using Forms

You can use forms to view, edit, or add to the records in a table. Using a form to perform these tasks is very similar to using the standard table view. The only difference is the way the records are displayed on the screen.

Moving Around in a Form

The cursor-movement keys work differently when you are using a form than they do when you are in the table view. However, you will find that, overall, using a form is not very different from using the default table view. Table 4-1 shows the effect of each of the cursor-movement keys in a form.

Table 4-1 Cursor Movement in Forms

Key(s)	Function
↑	Moves the cursor up one field in the current record or up to the last field of the previous record
→	Moves the cursor to the next field (right or down)
←	Moves the cursor to the previous field (left or up)
↓	Moves the cursor down one field in the current record or to the first field of the next record
↵	Same as →
[Home]	Moves the cursor to the first record of the table
[Ctrl]-[Home]	Moves the cursor to the first field of the current record
[End]	Moves the cursor to the last record in the table
[Ctrl]-[End]	Moves the cursor to the last field of the current record
[Pg Up]	Moves the cursor to the previous page in a multipage form or up to the previous record in a single-page form
[Pg Dn]	Moves the cursor to the next page in a multipage form or to the next record in a single-page form
[Ctrl]-[Pg Up]	Moves the cursor to the same field of the previous record
[Ctrl]-[Pg Dn]	Moves the cursor to the same field of the next record

Entering and Editing Records

Entering records through a form is similar to entering records through the table view. To enter records into a table through a form, first issue the [Menu] Modify DataEntry command and type the name of the table with which you want to work. When the ENTRY table for that table comes into view, press [Form Toggle] to switch to the form view. Immediately, the default form for the table will come into view.

Once the form is on the screen, you can make entries into it just as you would enter data through the table view. You can use the cursor-movement keys listed in Table 4-1 to move the cursor from record to record and from field to field. You can use [Field View] to enter the field view. When the entries are all in place, press [Do-It!] ([F2]) to copy the new data into the permanent table.

Editing an existing table through a form is essentially the same as entering records through a form. To edit a table through a form, first bring the table into the workspace in the Edit mode by issuing either the [Menu] Modify Edit command or the [Menu] View command, then press [Edit] ([F9]). Next, press [Form Toggle] to enter the form view.

Once you have the table in the Edit mode, you can make changes in the records by using the methods we described in Chapters 2 and 3. When you have finished editing the table, press [Do-It!] or issue the [Menu] DO-IT! command to save your changes, and return to the main workspace.

The DataEntry and Edit Menus

When you are editing records through a form, pressing [Menu] ([F10]) causes the Edit menu to appear at the top of the screen, as shown in Figure 4-2. (You will recall that the DataEntry menu includes these same options along with KeeepEntry.)

Figure 4-2 The Edit Menu

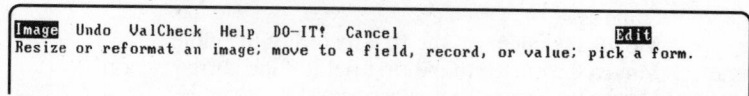

As you can see, this menu is the same as the one that appears when you're entering records through the default table view, which is explained in Chapters 2 and 3. In fact, the only difference involves the Image command. If you issue the Image command, you'll see the menu shown in Figure 4-3.

Figure 4-3 The Image Menu for Forms

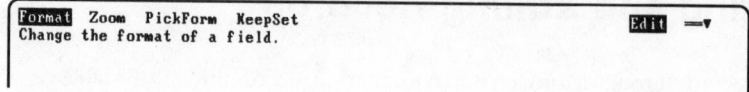

This menu contains only four commands: Format, Zoom, PickForm, and KeepSet. You may recall that when you are using the table view, the Image menu includes three additional commands: TableSize, ColumnSize, and Move.

The functions of the Format, Zoom, and KeepSet commands in a form are identical to their functions in the table view. The PickForm command, which we'll cover later in this chapter, lets you select a custom form. For more on the Image commands, see Chapter 3.

Creating Custom Forms

The default form may be perfectly adequate for most of your needs; however, there will be times when you will want to use a custom-designed form. For example, you may want to design a custom form for the EMPLYEE table that displays only the names and addresses of your employees. Alternatively, you might want to design a form that closely resembles a printed form or one that uses special calculated fields. Paradox allows you to design the form you want quickly and easily.

A Note to Users of Paradox 1.0 , 1.1, and 2

Between earlier versions of Paradox and Paradox 3, there have been quite a few changes to the form-design commands. The features are the same, but the menu choices you make to perform the functions have been changed. For example, in Paradox 1.0 and 1.1, the command to draw a border is [Menu] Place Border. In Paradox 2 and 3, the command is [Menu] Border Place. Paradox 3 also includes new commands that let you design multitable and multirecord forms. Throughout the chapter, we will use Release 3 commands.

An Example

Suppose you want to design a custom form for EMPLYEE like the one that is shown in Figure 4-4. This form displays only the names and addresses of the employees in the table.

Figure 4-4 A Custom Form

```
Viewing Emplyee table with form F1: Record 1 of 16          Main  ═▼
┌──────────────────────────────────────────────────────────────────┐
│                                                                    │
│                            ABC Company                             │
│                        Employee Address Form                       │
│                                                                    │
│                   Name: David      Jones                           │
│                                                                    │
│                   Address: 4000 St. James Ct.                      │
│                                                                    │
│                   City: St. Matthews                               │
│                                                                    │
│                   State: KY                                        │
│                                                                    │
│                   Zip: 40207                                       │
│                                                                    │
│                                                                    │
└──────────────────────────────────────────────────────────────────┘
```

To design this form, issue the **[Menu] F**orms command. The next menu you see will look like Figure 4-5. As you can see, this menu has two commands: Design and Change. The Design command allows you to design a new form for a table. The Change command allows you to revise an existing form.

Figure 4-5 The Design/Change Menu

```
Design  Change                                              Main
Design a new form for a table.
```

Since you want to design a form, you should issue the **Design** command. After you do, Paradox will prompt you to enter the name of the table for which you want to design a form. You should type **EMPLYEE** and press ↵.

Next, Paradox will prompt you to assign a number to the form, as shown in Figure 4-6. A table can have up to 15 different forms: the default form, *F*, and up to 14 custom forms that you design. Whenever you create a custom form for a table, you must assign that form the letter F or a number between 1 and 14. To assign a number to a form, just point to the form number you want to use, and press ↵. For example, to assign form number 1 to our sample form, you could point to the number 1 in the list, and press ↵.

Figure 4-6 The Form Number Prompt

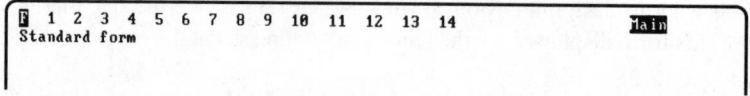

After you assign a number to the form, Paradox will prompt you to enter a form description. Every form you create should have a description. Paradox uses this description as the second-line prompt that appears whenever you point to the form's number in the Form Number menu. You should make sure the description defines the purpose of the form.

When you see this prompt, type **Employee Addresses**, and press ↵. After you do this, Paradox will display the form design screen shown in Figure 4-7.

Figure 4-7 The Form Design Screen

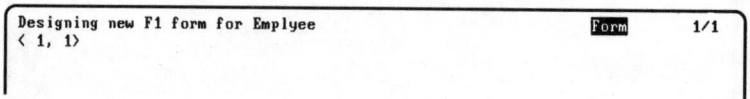

As you can see, the form design screen starts out completely empty. The only information displayed on the screen is the current operation reminder (*Designing new F1 form for Emplyee*), the menu reminder (*Form*), the cursor position indicator (*<1, 1>*), and the page indicator (*1/1*). The cursor position indicator tells you the current row and column of the cursor (*<row, column>*). The page indicator tells you which page of the form you are working on and the total number of pages in the form. For example, the page indicator in the example, *1/1*, tells you that you are working on the first page of a one-page form.

The actual work area of the form design screen is 23 lines long and 80 characters wide. You'll want to keep these numbers in mind as you design your form.

Adding a Border

To begin designing the sample form, issue the **[Menu]** Border command. After you issue this command, Paradox will display a menu with two options: Place and Erase. To create a border, you should select **P**lace from the menu. Paradox will then display a menu listing the types of borders you can create, as shown in Figure 4-8. We will discuss each of these options in detail later in this chapter.

Figure 4-8 The Border Menu

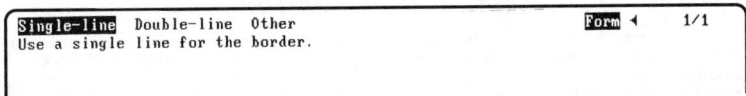

For now, you should issue the **D**ouble-line command. When you do, Paradox will prompt you to indicate where the border should begin. When you see this prompt, move the cursor to the upper-left corner of the screen, and press ↵. Paradox then will prompt you to indicate the diagonal (opposite) corner of the border. When it does, press the ↑ key, followed by the ← key to move the cursor to the lower-right corner of the screen. Now, press ↵ to place the border, as shown in Figure 4-9.

Figure 4-9 The Completed Border

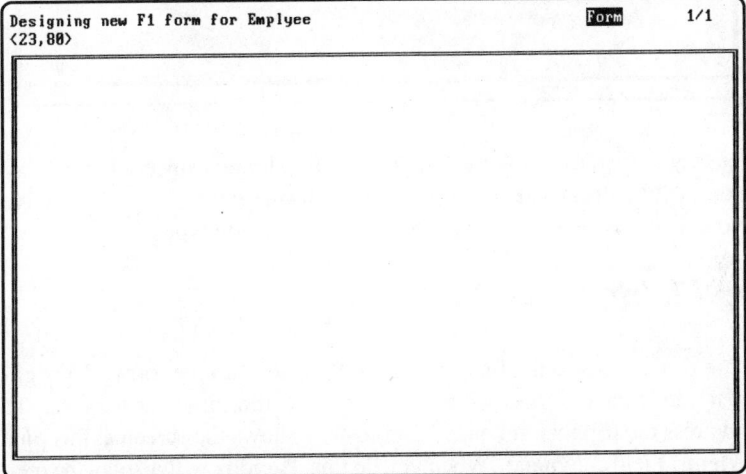

After you set the border, the cursor will be in the lower-right corner of the screen. Notice the cursor position indicator says *<23,80>*. To move the cursor to the upper-left corner of the screen, press **[Home]**, followed by **[Ctrl]-[Home]**.

Adding a Title

Now, you are ready to add a title to the form. To add the title shown in Figure 4-10, press ➡ several times to move the cursor to the center of the screen, followed by ⬇ to move the cursor down one line. Now, type **ABC Company**. Next, press the ↵ key to move the cursor down one line, then press the ➡ key repeatedly to move toward the center of the screen. Next, type **Employee Address Form**. (Don't worry if you didn't get the title exactly in the center of the screen; we'll show you how to make adjustments later.)

Figure 4-10 Adding a Title

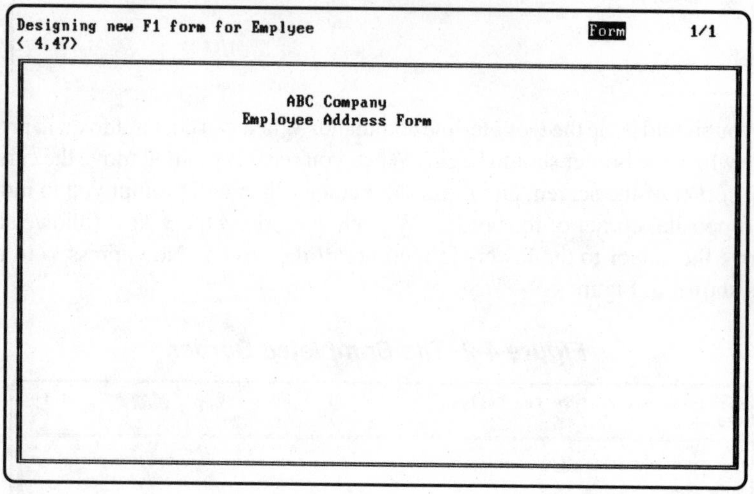

```
Designing new F1 form for Emplyee                          Form        1/1
< 4,47>

                              ABC Company
                          Employee Address Form
```

The characters you type from the keyboard are called literals since what you type on the screen is exactly (literally) what you will see on the form. If you want all capital letters, for example, you must use the [Shift] or [Caps Lock] key as you type.

Placing Fields

Now, you are ready to place the fields from EMPLYEE onto the form. To begin, use the arrow keys to move the cursor down two lines and position it under the title. Then, type **Name:**, and press the **[Spacebar]** once. Figure 4-11 shows the screen at this point. Next, issue the **[Menu] F**ield command. When you do this, Paradox will display the menu shown in Figure 4-12. These options let you place, erase, and format fields in a form. We will discuss each of these options later. For now, you should select **P**lace to tell Paradox that you want to place a new field in the form.

After you issue this command, Paradox will display a menu listing the types of fields you can put on the form, as shown in Figure 4-13. When you see this menu, issue the **R**egular command. Paradox then will display a list of the fields in EMPLYEE and prompt you to select one, as shown in Figure 4-14.

Figure 4-11 The Custom Form

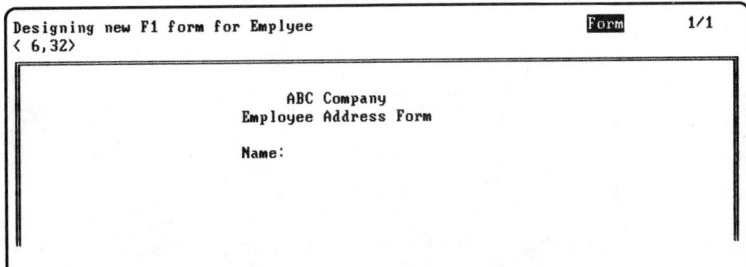

```
Designing new F1 form for Emplyee              Form    1/1
< 6,32>

                        ABC Company
                   Employee Address Form

                   Name:
```

Figure 4-12 The Field Menu

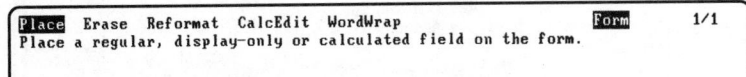

```
Place  Erase  Reformat  CalcEdit  WordWrap     Form    1/1
Place a regular, display-only or calculated field on the form.
```

Figure 4-13 The Place Menu

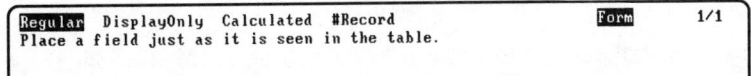

```
Regular  DisplayOnly  Calculated  #Record      Form    1/1
Place a field just as it is seen in the table.
```

Figure 4-14 Selecting a Regular Field

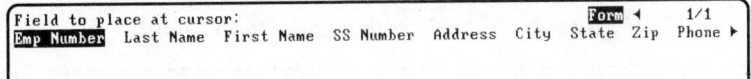

```
Field to place at cursor:                      Form ◄   1/1   ►
Emp Number  Last Name  First Name  SS Number  Address  City  State  Zip  Phone ►
```

When you see this prompt, press the ➔ key twice to position the cursor on the First Name field, and press ↵. After you do this, the cursor will change to a small box, and Paradox will prompt you to place the field. If you've been following this example, the cursor will already be positioned next to the word *Name:*. To place the First Name field on the form, all you need to do is press ↵. (If the cursor is not next to the word *Name:*, you should use the arrow keys to move it there, then press ↵.) At this point, a line of dashes representing the field will appear on the screen, as shown in Figure 4-15 on the following page.

Next, Paradox will prompt you to adjust the size of the field. To make the field the same size as its length in the table, just press ↵. After you do this, Paradox will place the field on the form, changing the field representation from a string of dashes to a series of underlines like the one shown in Figure 4-16.

Figure 4-15 A Newly Placed Field

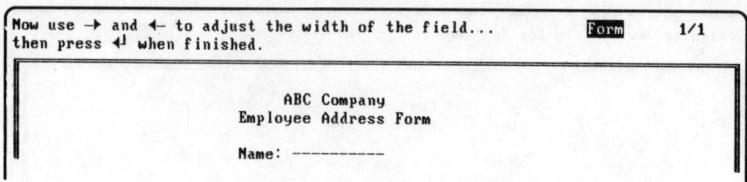

Figure 4-16 The First Name Field in Place

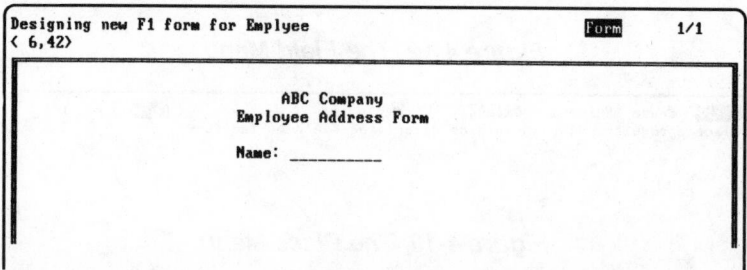

Now, press ➡ to move the cursor one space to the right. Issue the **[Menu]** **F**ield **P**lace **R**egular command again, and select the Last Name field from the list. Press ↵ to place it next to the First Name field, then press ↵ to accept the default length. Figure 4-17 shows the form with the Last Name field in place.

Figure 4-17 Adding the Last Name Field

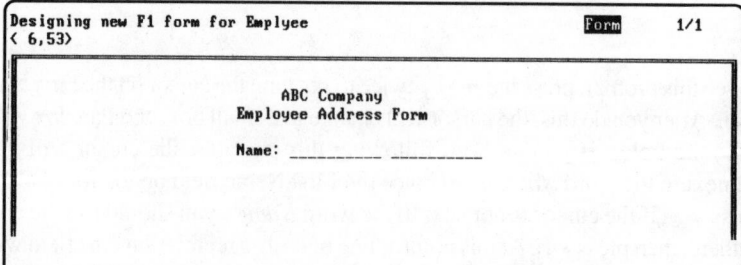

Notice that we have now placed two fields on the same line of the form. Although the default form (Figure 4-1) has only one field per line, you can enter two or more fields on the same line of a custom form. In fact, you can place as many fields on a line as will fit.

To put the Address field on the form, press ↵ twice to move the cursor down two lines, then move the cursor to the center of the screen, and type **Address:**, followed by a single space. Next, issue the **[Menu]** **F**ield **P**lace **R**egular command, select the Address field, and place it next to the word you just typed. You can continue in this way—positioning the cursor, typing the field name at the prompt, issuing the [Menu] Field Place Regular command to select the field name, and pressing ↵ to accept the default length—until your screen looks like the one shown in Figure 4-18.

Figure 4-18 The Completed Design Screen

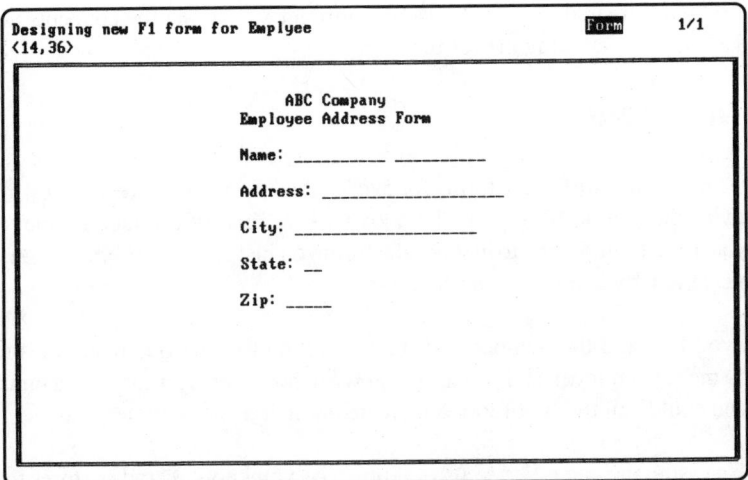

To save your new form, press **[Do-It!]** ([F2]) or issue the **[Menu]** DO-IT! command. Paradox then will save the form and return to the main workspace.

Using the PickForm Command

Once you create a form, you can use it immediately to enter, edit, or view records in the table. For example, to use the form you just created, first issue the **[Menu]** View command to bring the EMPLYEE table onto the workspace (if it is not already there). When the table appears on the workspace, issue the **[Menu]** Image PickForm command. After you issue this command, Paradox will display the Form Number menu, as shown in Figure 4-19.

Figure 4-19 The Form Number Menu

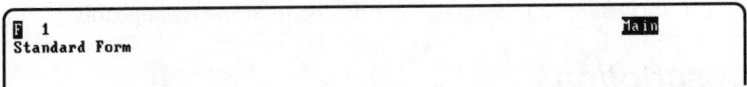

As you can see, this menu shows you the forms you have associated with the table. In this case, you have two forms: F, the default form, and 1, the form you just created. As you create more forms for the table, Paradox will add them to this menu.

To select your custom form, highlight it and press ↵, or press **1**. Then, Paradox will display the records in the table through the form. You now can use your form for entering, editing, or viewing data. Everything you learned about the default form applies to custom forms.

Form Creation Basics

Now that you have created your first custom form, let's examine the concepts we merely mentioned as we were creating the form.

Form Numbers

You can design up to 15 different forms for every table. When you create a new form, you must assign it a number or the letter F. Paradox will use this code to identify the form. For example, you used the number 1 to identify the form you just created. From now on, Paradox will use the name F1 when it refers to this form.

Normally, you'll assign the number 1 to the first custom form you create for a table, the number 2 to the second form, and so on. If you wish, however, you can skip a number. For instance, you could call the first form you create number 5.

You can also assign the name F to a custom form. As you know, Paradox stores the default form that it creates for each table under this name. If you do give a custom form the name F, that form will replace the standard default form. From that point on, you'll see your custom form, and not the Paradox default form, whenever you press [Form Toggle] while viewing the associated table.

You can also give a new custom form a number that has already been assigned to an existing form. For instance, suppose you are creating a new form for the EMPLYEE table. When Paradox presents the list shown in Figure 4-6, you choose number 1. Then, Paradox will display a Cancel/Replace menu and will display the message *F1 already exists* in the lower-right corner of the screen. If you issue the Cancel command, Paradox will return to the Form Number menu so that you can assign a different number to the form. If you issue the Replace command, however, Paradox will replace the existing form with the one you are creating.

The *Paradox User's Guide* and some Paradox menus refer to the form number as the form name. The terms *form name* and *form number* can be used interchangeably.

Form Descriptions

After you assign a number to the form, Paradox prompts you to enter a form description. The description you enter can be up to 40 characters long and should be specific so that you will be able to remember the purpose of the form. For example, *Employee Addresses* describes the form we created in the example. You can leave the form description blank if you want. To do this, simply press ↵ at the prompt.

The form description you specify will appear on the Form Number menu whenever the number for that form is highlighted. For example, if you issue the [Menu] Image PickForm command and point to option 1, Paradox will display the description *Employee Addresses* in the second line of the menu, as shown in Figure 4-20.

Figure 4-20 The Form Description

The Form Editor

The Form Editor is the tool you use to design forms. Although you've had some experience with the Form Editor already, there are several important characteristics of the Form Editor that you will need to understand before you begin designing your own forms. As you will learn, the concepts of creating and editing a form are closely related.

Moving Around on the Screen

Table 4-2 on the following page shows the function of the cursor-movement keys in the Form Editor. As you can see, these keys maintain their normal function, for the most part. About the only tricky part of moving the cursor in the Form Editor is the way it will "wrap around" whenever it reaches the edge of the workspace. For example, if the cursor is in the top line of the screen, pressing ↑ will move it to the bottom line of the same column on the workspace. Similarly, if the cursor is in the last (rightmost) column of the workspace, pressing → will move it to the first column of the same row.

You can use this characteristic of the Form Editor to your advantage. For example, when we created the custom form shown in Figure 4-18, we added a border around the entire form. To do this, we had to point to the upper-left corner of the screen, then press ↵ and point to the lower-right corner. Rather than pressing ↓ 21 times and → 79 times to point to the lower-right corner, we took advantage of the Form Editor's cursor wrap. To point to the lower-right corner of the screen, we pressed ↑ once, then ← once. Pressing ↑ moved the cursor to the bottom of the first column of the screen. Pressing ← then moved it to the last column in the last row.

Replace and Insert Modes

Like most text editors, the Paradox Form Editor offers two modes of operation: the insert mode and the replace (or overwrite) mode. When the form design screen first appears, it is in the replace mode. In the replace mode, characters you type from the keyboard will overwrite existing characters on the form. For example, suppose you are de..igning a new form for the EMPLYEE table, like the one shown in Figure 4-21 on the next page.

Table 4-2 Moving the Cursor in the Form Editor

Key(s)	Function
↑	Moves the cursor up one line. If the cursor is at the top of the screen, it will move to the last line in the same column.
→	Moves the cursor to the right. If the cursor is in the rightmost column on the screen, it will wrap around to the left on the same line.
←	Moves the cursor to the left. If the cursor is in the leftmost column of the screen, it will wrap around to the right on the same line.
↓	Moves the cursor down one line. If the cursor is at the bottom of the screen, it will move to the top in the same column.
[Home]	Moves the cursor to the top line of the screen.
[Ctrl]-[Home]	Moves the cursor to the beginning of a line.
[End]	Moves the cursor to the bottom line of the screen.
[Ctrl]-[End]	Moves the cursor to the end of a line.
[Pg Up]	Moves the cursor to the previous page in a multipage form.
[Pg Dn]	Moves the cursor to the next page in a multipage form.
↵	Moves the cursor down to the beginning of the next line.

Figure 4-21 A New Form

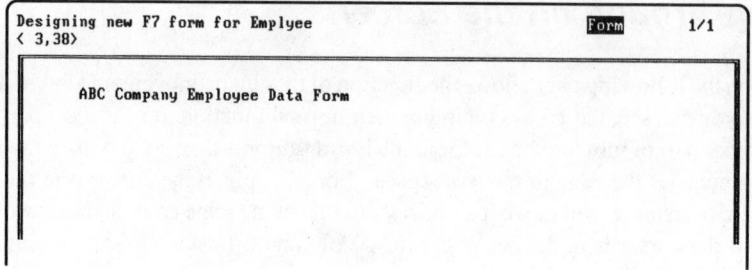

Suppose you want to change the word *Data* in the title in the figure above to the word *Information*. To do this, position the cursor on the *D* in *Data* and type **Information Form**. After you do this, your screen will look like Figure 4-22.

Figure 4-22 Changing a Form Title

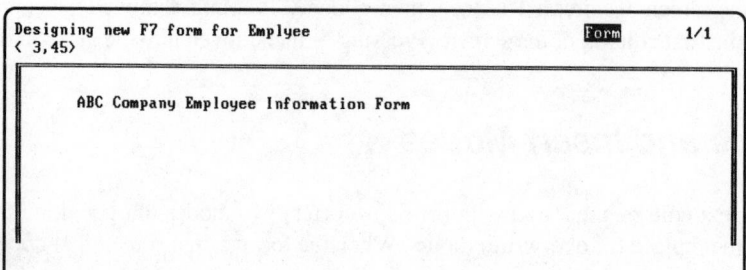

In the insert mode, the characters you type are inserted between existing characters, and the characters that follow the insertion are moved to the right. To switch to the insert mode, you simply press [Ins]. Since the [Ins] key is a toggle key, if you press it a second time, you will return to the replace mode. For example, suppose you want to add the word *Incorporated* after the company name in the title. To do this, position the cursor on the *E* in *Employee*, press **[Ins]**, and type **Incorporated.** As you type the word, Paradox will insert it and move the existing characters to the right, as shown in Figure 4-23.

Figure 4-23 Inserting a Word

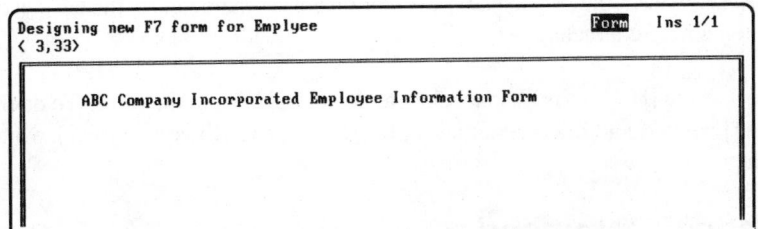

Notice the word *Ins* displayed in the upper-right corner of the screen. When you are working in the insert mode, the reminder *Ins* is displayed in the upper-right corner of the screen, next to the page indicator.

You can take advantage of the insert mode to center text on the screen. For example, to center the title in Figure 4-23, position the cursor on the letter *A* in *ABC* and, if the Form Editor is not already in the insert mode, press **[Ins]**. Now, press the **[Spacebar]** several times. Each time you press the [Spacebar], the title will move one space to the right. Figure 4-24 shows the title centered on the screen.

Figure 4-24 Centering the Title

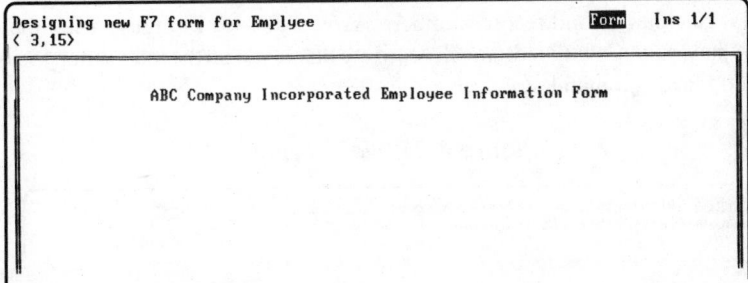

Deleting Characters

You can also delete characters from forms. For example, suppose you want to change the word *Incorporated* in the report title to *Inc*. To do this, position the cursor on the first *o* in *Incorporated*, and press [Del]. When you do this, Paradox will delete the character at the cursor and shift the remaining characters on the line one space to the left. You now can continue to press [Del] until all of the unwanted characters have been deleted.

You can also use the [Backspace] key to delete characters. For example, you could change the word *Incorporated* to *Inc* by placing the cursor on the space after the *d* in *Incorporated* and pressing the **[Backspace]** key nine times.

In the preceding examples, the Form Editor was in the insert mode. As you have seen, when you delete a character with the [Backspace] key while the Form Editor is in the insert mode, Paradox pulls any remaining characters on the same line to the left. When you are in the replace mode, however, the [Backspace] key merely erases characters to the left—it does not adjust the remaining characters.

You cannot use the [Del] or [Backspace] key to delete fields from the form. To do that, you must use the [Menu] Field Erase command or the [Menu] Area Erase command, which we'll describe later.

The Cancel Command

If you decide not to save a form you have begun to design, you can issue the [Menu] Cancel command. The Cancel command returns you to the main workspace without saving the form. After you issue this command, Paradox will prompt you for confirmation with a No/Yes menu. If you issue the No command, Paradox will return to the form design screen. Issuing the Yes command causes Paradox to return to the main workspace without saving your work. The message *Ending form design...* will appear at the bottom of the screen.

Placing Fields

To create the EMPLYEE custom form in Figure 4-4, you placed several of the fields from EMPLYEE into the form. There are four kinds of fields you can place on a form: regular, display-only, calculated, and record number. As you can see in Figure 4-25, the options Regular, DisplayOnly, Calculated, and #Record are displayed on the menu after you issue the [Menu] Field Place command.

Figure 4-25 Field Types

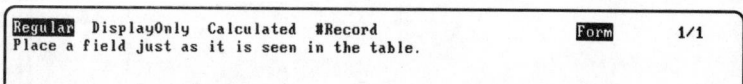

```
Regular  DisplayOnly  Calculated  #Record                    Form      1/1
Place a field just as it is seen in the table.
```

Let's suppose you want to create the form shown in Figure 4-26. This form includes five fields, identified by the literals: *Last Name* (a regular field), *Employee Number* (a regular field), *Salary* (a display-only field), *Hourly Rate* (a calculated field), and *Record Number* (a record number field). To create this form, first issue the **[Menu] Forms Design** command. When Paradox prompts you for a table name, type **EMPLYEE**, and press ↵. When Paradox prompts you to specify a number for the form, choose an unused number (we'll use **2**), then enter a description for the form (we'll use **Field Type Example**). When the form design screen is in view, you are ready to place fields.

Figure 4-26 A Sample Form

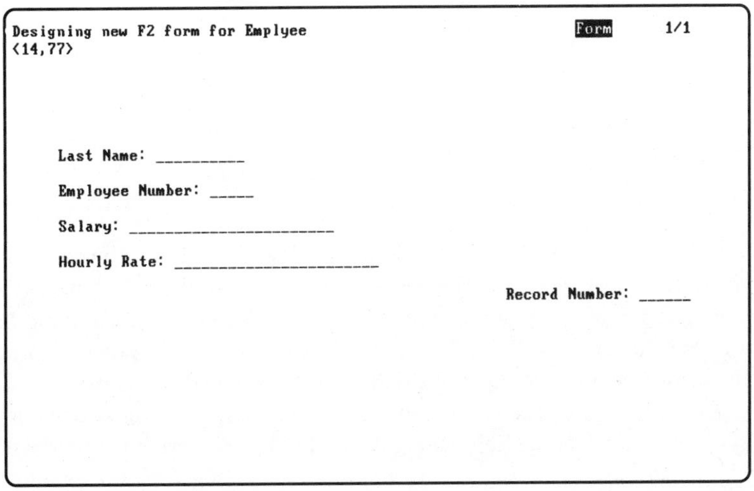

```
Designing new F2 form for Emplyee                    Form    1/1
<14,77>




    Last Name: _____

    Employee Number: _____

    Salary: _____

    Hourly Rate: _____

                                        Record Number: _____
```

Regular Fields

A regular field is any field that appears in the table on which you are working. The regular fields in the EMPLYEE table are Employee Number, Last Name, First Name, SS Number, Address, City, State, Zip, Phone, Date of Birth, Date of Hire, Exemptions, and Salary.

To place a regular field in a form, issue the [Menu] Field Place Regular command. After you issue this command, Paradox will display a list of field names and will prompt you to indicate the field you want to place. You can select a field in one of two ways: either by positioning the cursor on the field name and pressing ↵, or by pressing the key corresponding to the first character in the field name. If you have two or more fields that start with the same character, Paradox will prompt you to place the cursor on the field you want to place and select it by pressing ↵.

Placing an Alphanumeric Field

To create the form shown in Figure 4-26, you need to place the Last Name field in the form. To do this, first use the arrow keys to position the cursor, then type the literal **Last Name:** followed by a space. (This literal is not required, but it helps you remember which field it is.) Then, issue the **[Menu]** F**ield** P**lace** R**egular** command, point to the Last Name field in the list, and press ↵.

Once you select a field, the cursor will change to a small blinking box called the pointing cursor, and Paradox will prompt you to indicate where you want to place the field. You should point to the place in the form where you want the field to begin, and press ↵. You can place the field anywhere on the screen.

In the example, you should position the cursor next to the word *Name:*, and press ↵. After you do this, your screen will look like Figure 4-27.

Figure 4-27 Positioning the Field

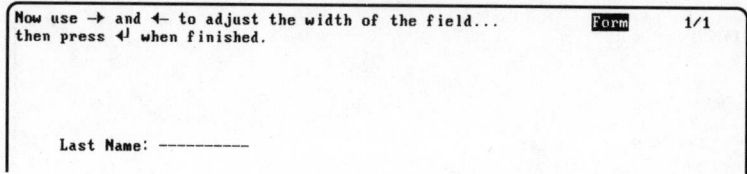

After you press ↵ to place the field, Paradox will display the field as a line of hyphens and will prompt you to adjust its width. The default length for the field is the same as the field's width in the table for which you are creating a form. Each dash you see on the screen represents one character in the field. You can reduce the width of the field by pressing the ← key at the field-width prompt. Once the field is the desired width, you can press ↵ to lock it in place. Alternatively, you can accept the default width by pressing ↵ without pressing ←. After you press ↵ to set the field width, the dashes that represent the field will change to a series of underlines.

You can reduce the size of a field to a minimum of one character. To do this, you can press the ← key several times to reach the minimum or press the [Home] key once. If you accidentally make the field too small, press the → key to increase its width or the [End] key to return it to the default width before you press ↵.

If you make a field too small, Paradox will display only part of the entry (if it's an alphanumeric field) or a series of asterisks (if it's a number field) when you view the records in the table. To view the entire entry, you must press [Field View] ([Alt]-[F5]).

You cannot increase the width of an alphanumeric field beyond its width in the table—the default width. Normally, you will not want to shorten an alphanumeric field, either. To accept the default width for the Last Name field in the example, then, you should press ↵. Figure 4-28 shows this field in place on the form.

Figure 4-28 Placing an Alphanumeric Field

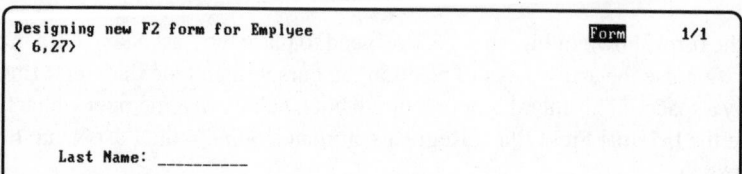

Placing a Number Field

Now, let's place the number field Emp Number on the form. First, move the cursor down two lines and type the literal text **Employee Number:**, then issue the **[Menu] F**ield **P**lace

Regular command and choose Emp Number from the list. When Paradox prompts you to define the position of the Emp Number field on the form, position the cursor after the word *Number:* , and press ↵. Figure 4-29 shows the screen at this point.

Figure 4-29 Placing a Number Field

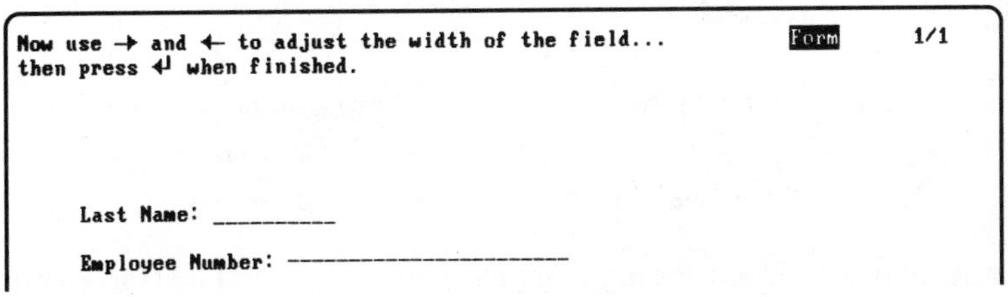

```
Now use → and ← to adjust the width of the field...        Form      1/1
then press ↵ when finished.




    Last Name: _____

    Employee Number: -----------------------
```

Now, Paradox will prompt you to define the length of the Emp Number field in the form. As before, you can use the ← and [Home] keys to narrow the field. Normally, you will want to change the width of the numeric fields (number, short number, or dollar fields) you place on a form. For example, notice how much space Paradox has allotted to the Emp Number field in the form even though this field contains only one- and two-digit numbers. Since you don't need all of this space, you will probably want to narrow the Emp Number field. To do this, press the ← key until the Emp Number field is just five characters wide, then press ↵. Your screen will now look like Figure 4-30. From now on when you use this form to work with the EMPLYEE table, the Emp Number field will display a maximum of five characters.

Figure 4-30 Reducing the Field Length

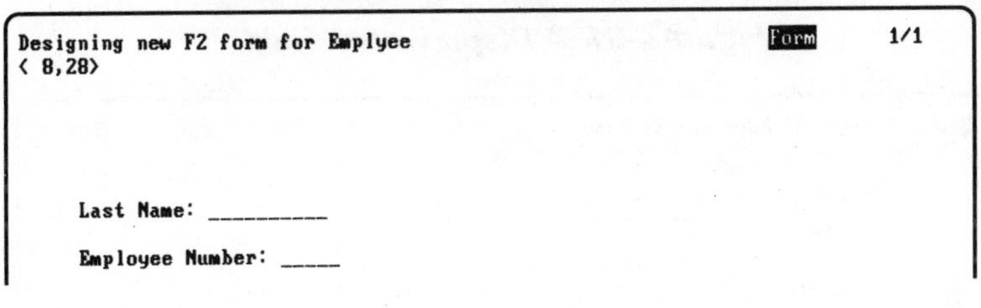

```
Designing new F2 form for Emplyee                          Form      1/1
< 8,28>




    Last Name: _____
    Employee Number: _____
```

Notes

You can place each regular field only once on the form. In fact, after you place a field, it is automatically removed from the list of fields that you see when you issue the [Menu] Field Place Regular command.

Once you place a field on the form, you can type a literal to its left or right; however, you can't type over it. If you try to type over a field, Paradox will display the message *Cannot place text on top of a field* at the bottom of the screen. If you're in the insert mode and you add literal text to the left of a field, the field will move to the right as you type. When the right edge of the field reaches the right edge of the form, Paradox will not allow you to continue typing.

You don't have to place every field in a table onto a form. When you are designing forms, you can place only those fields you want to see in the form. However, you must place at least one regular field on each page of the form. Paradox will not let you save a form unless it has at least one regular field on each page.

Display-only Fields

Display-only fields are like regular fields, except that they cannot be edited in any way; they are for display only. Unlike regular fields, which can only be placed once per form, display-only fields can be placed on a single form as many times as you want.

To place a display-only field on a form, you should issue the [Menu] Field Place DisplayOnly command. Paradox will prompt you to select a field, just as it does when you place a regular field on the form. After you select a field, Paradox will prompt you to place it and adjust its width as if you were placing a regular field.

For example, suppose you are designing the form shown in Figure 4-26 and you want to place the Salary field on the form as a display-only field. To do this, first move the cursor to the appropriate place and type the literal **Salary:**, then issue the **[Menu]** Field Place DisplayOnly command. After you issue this command, Paradox will prompt you to select a field, just as it does when you place a regular field on the form. When you see this prompt, select the Salary field. Next, Paradox will prompt you to place the field on the form. Position the pointing cursor next to the literal *Salary:*, and press ↵. Now, to accept the default width for the field, press ↵. Figure 4-31 shows the form at this point.

Figure 4-31 A Display-only Field

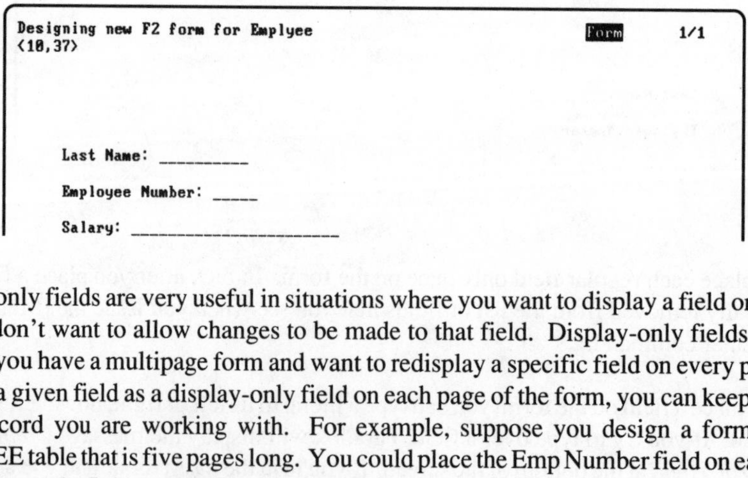

```
Designing new F2 form for Emplyee                        Form      1/1
<18,37>




      Last Name: _____

      Employee Number: _____

      Salary: _____
```

Display-only fields are very useful in situations where you want to display a field on a form, but you don't want to allow changes to be made to that field. Display-only fields are also useful if you have a multipage form and want to redisplay a specific field on every page. By entering a given field as a display-only field on each page of the form, you can keep track of which record you are working with. For example, suppose you design a form for the EMPLYEE table that is five pages long. You could place the Emp Number field on each page as a display-only field to help you keep track of the records.

Calculated Fields

A calculated field shows the result of mathematical calculations based on other fields in the table. For example, suppose you want to place the calculated field Hourly Rate on the form in Figure 4-31. This field will show the employee's hourly rate (calculated by dividing the Salary field entry by 40*52).

To place the Hourly Rate field in the form, first type the literal **Hourly Rate:** into the form at the appropriate place. Next, issue the **[Menu]** **F**ield **P**lace **C**alculated command. Paradox then will prompt you to enter a mathematical expression. When you see this prompt, type **[Salary]/(40*52)**, and press ↵. The expression *[Salary]* in this formula tells Paradox to use the Salary field entry of the current record as the dividend.

Next, Paradox will prompt you to place the field on the form. When it does, place the cursor next to the literal *Hourly Rate:*, and press ↵. When Paradox prompts you to adjust the width of the field, press ↵ to accept the default width. After you do this, your screen will look like Figure 4-32.

Figure 4-32 A Calculated Field

```
Designing new F2 form for Emplyee                    Form    1/1
<12,42>



     Last Name: _____

     Employee Number: _____

     Salary: _____

     Hourly Rate: _____
```

The expression you use in a calculated field can be up to 175 characters long. It can contain field names that are enclosed in brackets ([]), mathematical operators like +, -, *, /, and ( ), or constant values like .10, 30, and 1.5. You also can enter dates and literals as constant values. For example, the expression *7/1/88 + 30* would return the date *31-Jul-88*. The expression *"Employee " + [Last Name]* would display *Employee Jones*.

Whenever you include a field name in an expression, it must be enclosed in brackets. For example, to include the Salary field in the expression, you typed *[Salary]*, not *Salary*. If you do not include the brackets, Paradox will not recognize *Salary* as a field. Instead, it will be interpreted as a literal.

If the expression is more then 48 characters long, it will begin to scroll to the left as you enter additional characters. To view or edit any part of the expression while you are typing it, use [Field View] ([Alt]-[F5]). When you are finished entering the expression, press ↵.

Paradox automatically checks the validity of the expression you enter. If you enter an invalid expression, Paradox will display the message *Invalid expression* at the bottom of the screen. If you enter an expression incorrectly, Paradox will display the message *Syntax error in expression* at the bottom of the screen. When you see either of these messages, press [Backspace] or [Ctrl]-[Backspace] to erase the entry, and type in the correct expression. You also can edit the expression by using [Field View] ([Alt]-[F5]).

Note that calculated fields are record-oriented. For example, while you can include a reference to any field in the current record in a calculated field expression, you cannot place a calculated field that will compute the total number of hours worked by all employees or the total salary paid to all employees.

Record Number Fields

When Paradox creates a default form, it automatically puts a record number field in the upper-right corner of the form (see Figure 4-1). This field displays the number of the record you are viewing through the form. As you might expect, you can also include record number fields in your custom forms.

For example, suppose you are designing the form shown in Figure 4-32, and you want to display the record number for each record on the form. To do this, type the literal **Record Number:** into the form, then issue the [**Menu**] **F**ield **P**lace **#R**ecord command. After you issue this command, Paradox will prompt you to place the field, just as it does when you place a regular field. When you see this prompt, move the cursor to the lower-right corner of the screen, and press ↵. Then, when Paradox prompts you to adjust the width of the field, press ↵ to accept the default width. After you press ↵, Paradox will place the field on the form. Figure 4-26 on page 127 shows the completed form.

You can place a record number field anywhere you choose. You probably will want to place a record number field on each page of a multipage form to help you keep track of the records in your table. We'll show you how to do this later in this chapter.

Using the Form

When you have finished designing the form, press [**Do-It!**] to save your work and return to the main workspace. Now, let's edit the table through the form to see how each field type works. To do this, issue the [**Menu**] **M**odify **E**dit command, and type **EMPLYEE** to identify the table you want to edit. When the table comes into view, issue the [**Menu**] **I**mage **P**ickForm command, and select the form number assigned to the form you just created. (If you followed the example exactly, the new form will be form 2.)

Figure 4-33 shows the first record of EMPLYEE in the form. As you can see, the Last Name and Salary fields display the entries from those fields in the first record of EMPLYEE. The calculated field Hourly Rate shows the result of dividing the value in the Salary field of the current record by 40*52: 33.6538461538462. The record number field displays a 1, the current record number.

Figure 4-33 Using the Form

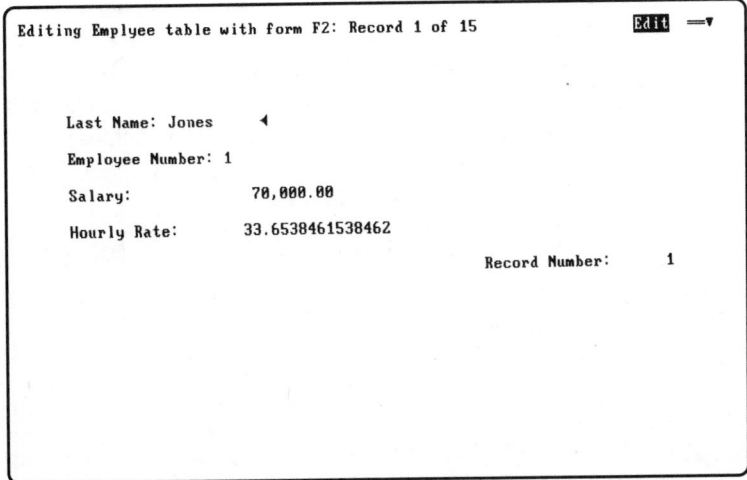

```
Editing Emplyee table with form F2: Record 1 of 15              Edit  —▼




     Last Name: Jones     ◄

     Employee Number: 1

     Salary:            70,000.00

     Hourly Rate:       33.6538461538462

                                            Record Number:      1
```

Paradox does not allow you to move the cursor into calculated, display-only, or record number fields. Since there are only two regular fields on this form, if you press ➡, ⬇, or ↩ twice, the cursor will jump past the Salary, Hourly Rate, and Record Number fields directly into the second record. As you view different records in the table, the fields will change to match the current record.

Reformatting Fields

The [Menu] Field Reformat command lets you change the format (the width) of any field in a form. This command comes in handy when you need to change the format of a field that you've already placed on a form.

To reformat a field on a form, issue the [Menu] Field Reformat command. Paradox will then prompt you to move to the field you want to reformat. You should point to the field you want to reformat, then press ↩. If the cursor is not on a field when you press ↩, the message *No field here* will appear. If you see this message, move the cursor onto a field, and press ↩.

When you press ↩, the cursor will automatically be placed at the end of the field, and you will be prompted to use the arrow keys to change the width of the field. You can press ➡ to increase the field's width or ⬅ to decrease it. When you press ↩, Paradox will accept the new width for the field.

For example, notice that the Hourly Rate field uses the default format for number fields (General), which allows up to 15 digits (including decimal places) to be displayed. Paradox always assigns the General format to calculated fields. In this case, it would probably be more meaningful to display just the first two or three decimal places instead of all 13.

To reformat the Hourly Rate field, issue the **[Menu] F**ield **R**eformat command. When Paradox asks you to move to the field you want to reformat, move the cursor so that it is on any part of the dashed line after *Rate:*, and press ↵. Next, press the ← key nine times to shorten the Hourly Rate field, and press ↵. Figure 4-34 shows the modified form. From now on, the Hourly Rate field will display fewer decimal places. The asterisk (*) at the end of the Hourly Rate value indicates that the number has been truncated for display purposes only.

Figure 4-34 The Modified Form

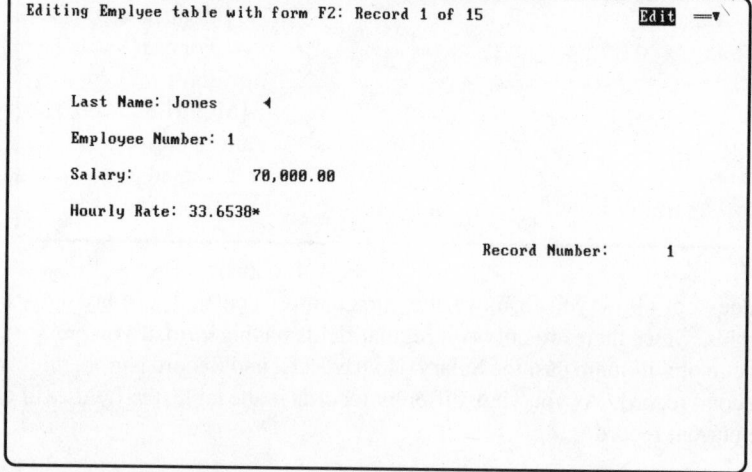

```
Editing Emplyee table with form F2: Record 1 of 15              Edit  ══▼

        Last Name: Jones      ◄

        Employee Number: 1

        Salary:              70,000.00

        Hourly Rate: 33.6538*

                                          Record Number:      1
```

Editing Calculated Fields

If you need to change the expression for a calculated field, you can use the [Menu] Field CalcEdit command. When you issue this command, Paradox will prompt you to move the cursor to the field you want to edit. You simply use the arrow keys to move to that field, and press ↵. If the cursor is not on a calculated field when you press ↵, the message *Cursor must be placed on a calculated field* will appear. If you see this message, move the cursor onto a calculated field, and press ↵.

Next, the expression for the calculated field you are editing will appear at the top of the screen. You can use the [Backspace] key to erase the formula, or [Field View] ([Alt]-[F5]) to edit it. When you press ↵, any changes you've made to the formula will be locked in.

For example, suppose you want to show the weekly rate instead of displaying the hourly rate for each employee in the form. To make this change, you should edit the expression that defines the calculated field Hourly Rate. To begin, issue the **[Menu] F**ield **C**alcEdit command, move the cursor to the Hourly Rate field, and press ↵.

At this point, the expression for Hourly Rate (*[Salary]/40*52*) will appear at the top of the screen. You must remove the term *40** from the formula. To do this, press **[Field View]** to enter the field view. Now, press ← to position the cursor over the 4, and then press **[Del]** three times. Finally, press ↵ to end the field view, and press ↵ a second time to set the expression. (By the way, don't forget to change the literal *Hourly Rate:* to *Weekly Rate:*.)

Erasing Fields

To erase a field after you have placed it on a form, issue the [Menu] Field Erase command. Position the cursor on the field you want to erase, and press ↵. For example, suppose you are designing the form shown in Figure 4-35, and you decide you don't want to include a record number field on the form. To erase this field, issue the **[Menu]** Field Erase command. Paradox then will prompt you to indicate the field you want to erase. When you see this prompt, position the cursor anywhere on the record number field, and press ↵. Paradox will remove the field from the form. Figure 4-36 on the following page shows the changed form.

Figure 4-35 A Custom Form

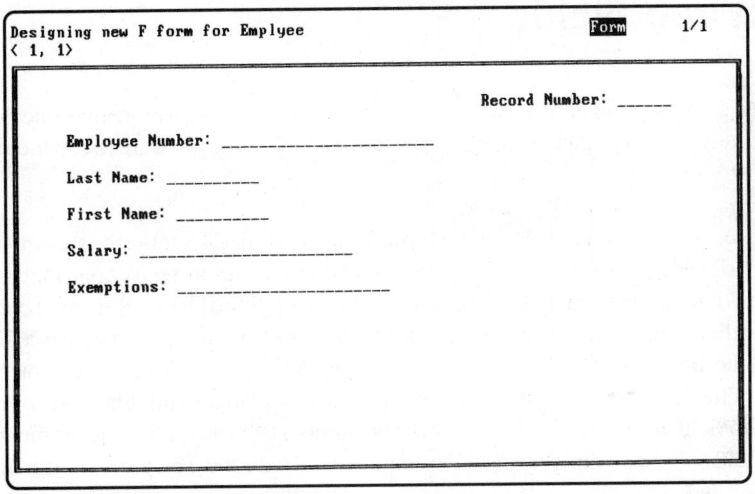

```
Designing new F form for Emplyee                         Form    1/1
< 1, 1>

                                          Record Number: _____

        Employee Number: _____

        Last Name: _____

        First Name: _____

        Salary: _____

        Exemptions: _____
```

Notice that the literal text *Record Number:* was not erased when you erased the record number field from the form. To erase the literal, press the **[Backspace]** key until the literal is erased, or position the cursor on the letter *R*, and press **[Del]** 14 times.

Figure 4-36 Erasing a Field

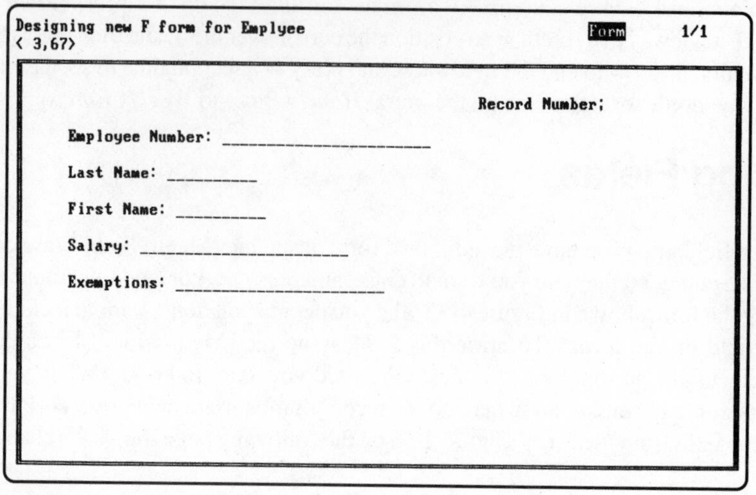

```
Designing new F form for Employee          Form    1/1
< 3,67>

                                     Record Number;

    Employee Number: _____

    Last Name: _____

    First Name: _____

    Salary: _____

    Exemptions: _____
```

WordWrap Fields

The WordWrap feature allows you to display alphanumeric fields on more than one line. This option is handy if you have a long memo-type field, or if you simply want to enhance the look of your custom form.

For example, suppose you are creating a form for the PROJECTS table, as shown in Figure 4-37. If you decide to display the Description field on two lines instead of one long one, first reduce the width of the field by ten characters using the **[Menu]** **F**ield **R**eformat command. Next, issue the **[Menu]** **F**ield **W**ordWrap command. Paradox will instruct you to position the cursor on the field you want to wrap. Use the arrow keys to move the cursor onto the Description field, and press ↵. Paradox will then ask you how many lines will be used for the wrapped field, as shown in Figure 4-38. The number 0 appears after the prompt because a normal field does not wrap over any additional lines. Erase the 0 by pressing **[Backspace]**, then press **2**, and ↵.

Figure 4-37 The PROJECTS Form

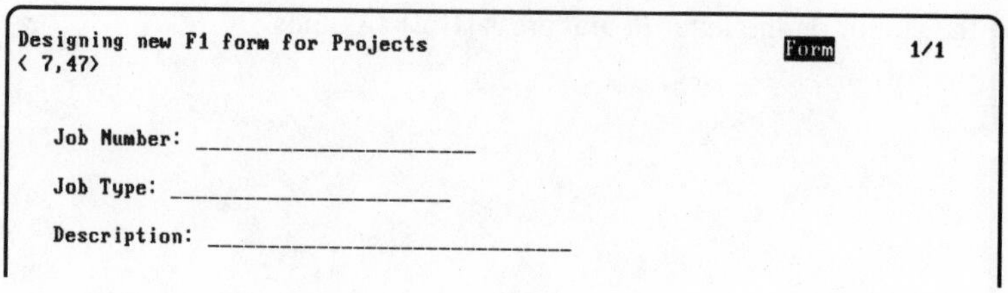

```
Designing new F1 form for Projects         Form    1/1
< 7,47>

    Job Number: _____

    Job Type: _____

    Description: _____
```

Figure 4-38 The WordWrap Prompt

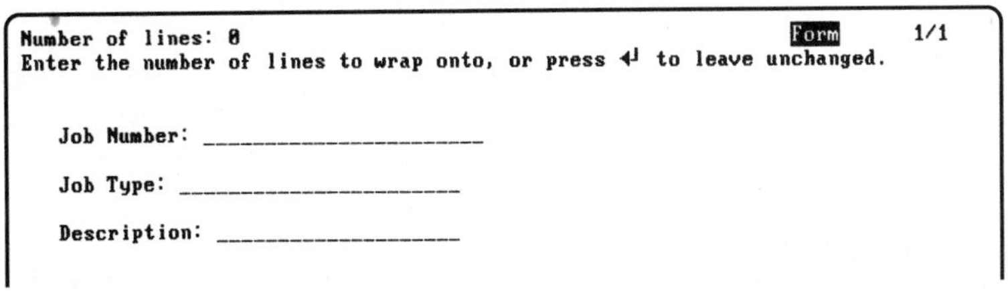

```
Number of lines: 0                                    Form    1/1
Enter the number of lines to wrap onto, or press ←┘ to leave unchanged.


   Job Number: _____

   Job Type: _____

   Description: _____
```

While nothing will appear on the form itself to show that Description is now a wrapped field, a message like the one shown in the upper-right corner of Figure 4-39 will appear whenever the cursor is on a wrapped field. The number 2 at the end of the message indicates that the field wraps onto a maximum of two additional lines, displaying the field over a total of three lines.

Figure 4-39 The WordWrap Indicator Message

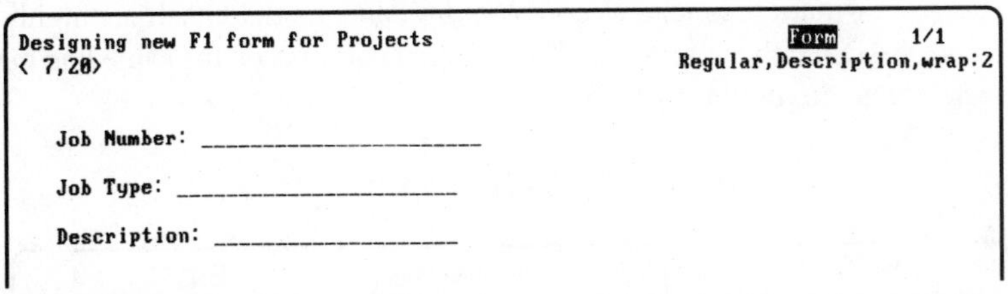

```
Designing new F1 form for Projects              Form    1/1
< 7,20>                                 Regular,Description,wrap:2


   Job Number: _____

   Job Type: _____

   Description: _____
```

When wrapping a field, Paradox always puts the additional lines directly under the displayed line. Therefore, the area under the displayed line must be completely blank. Otherwise, when you try to save the form, the error message *The area designated for wordwrap must be clear* will appear in the lower-right corner of the screen.

Paradox will try to break values displayed on a wrapped field at blanks or hyphens. If a particular word is too long to fit on one line, it will wrap onto the next line. Figure 4-40 shows what a wrapped field from the PROJECTS table will look like in the form view.

Figure 4-40 Viewing a Form with WordWrap

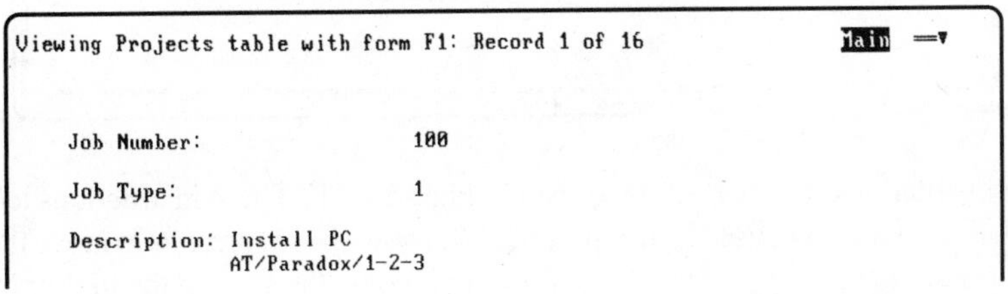

```
Viewing Projects table with form F1: Record 1 of 16    Main  ═▼


   Job Number:              100

   Job Type:                 1

   Description: Install PC
                AT/Paradox/1-2-3
```

Moving and Erasing Areas

The Form Editor offers two commands to alter entire regions of the form at once: [Menu] Area Move, to move a region from one part of the form to another, and [Menu] Area Erase, to erase an entire region.

Moving an Area

You can move a segment of your form from one place to another by using the [Menu] Area Move command. For example, suppose you want to move the record number field shown in Figure 4-35 from the upper-right corner of a form to the lower-right corner. You could erase it, then retype it on the form where you want it, but it's easier to move it. To do this, issue the **[Menu]** Area Move command. After you issue this command, Paradox will prompt you to indicate the area to be moved. When you see this prompt, position the cursor on the R in *Record*, and press ↵. Paradox then will prompt you to move to the diagonal corner of the area. When it does, press → until the literal *Record Number:* and the field itself are highlighted, as shown in Figure 4-41, and then press ↵. (The diagonal corner is on the same line in this case because the area you are moving is on one line.)

Figure 4-41 The Highlighted Area

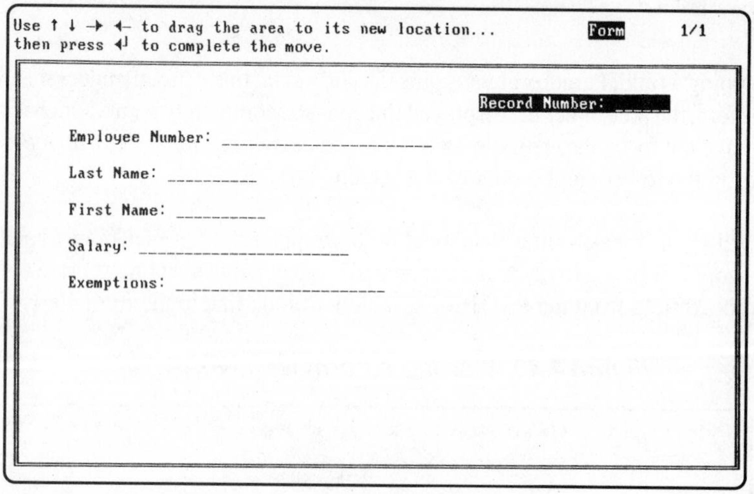

```
Use ↑ ↓ → ←  to drag the area to its new location...        Form     1/1
then press ↵  to complete the move.

                                          Record Number: _____


        Employee Number: _____

        Last Name: _____

        First Name: _____

        Salary: _____

        Exemptions: _____
```

Notice the instructions at the top of the screen in Figure 4-41. These instructions tell you to use the cursor-movement keys to move the area. You now should press ↓ to move the cursor to the bottom of the screen. As you move the cursor down the screen, the highlighted area "drags" to the new location. When you reach the desired location, press ↵. The area will be moved instantly, as shown in Figure 4-42.

Figure 4-42 Completing the Move

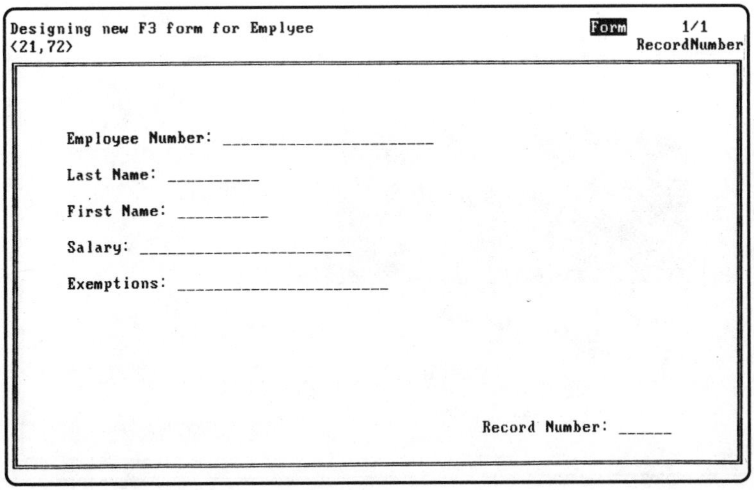

```
Designing new F3 form for Emplyee                      Form      1/1
<21,72>                                                        RecordNumber

    ┌──────────────────────────────────────────────────────────────┐
    │                                                                │
    │                                                                │
    │      Employee Number: _____             │
    │                                                                │
    │      Last Name: _____                                    │
    │                                                                │
    │      First Name: _____                                   │
    │                                                                │
    │      Salary: _____                        │
    │                                                                │
    │      Exemptions: _____                     │
    │                                                                │
    │                                                                │
    │                                                                │
    │                                      Record Number: _____     │
    │                                                                │
    │                                                                │
    └──────────────────────────────────────────────────────────────┘
```

Erasing an Area

You can use the [Menu] Area Erase command to erase all the fields and literals from any rectangular area of a form. For example, suppose you are designing the form shown in Figure 4-42, and you decide to redesign the entire form except the record number field at the bottom of the form. You could use the [Menu] Field Erase command to erase each field individually and then type blank spaces over all the literals, but it's easier to erase the entire area that you want to remove from the form.

To do this, issue the **[Menu]** Area Erase command. After you issue this command, Paradox will prompt you to place the cursor in one corner of the area that you want to erase. When you see this prompt, move the cursor to the character *E* at the beginning of the literal *Employee Number:*, and press ↵. Paradox will next prompt you to move the cursor to the diagonal corner of the area you want to erase. In response to this prompt, move the cursor to the line on which the Exemptions field appears and press → until the highlighted area completely covers every field displayed in that portion of the screen. Figure 4-43 shows the screen at this point. Finally, press ↵ to erase the area. After you do this, only the literal *Record Number:* and the record number field will remain on the form.

Figure 4-43 Defining the Area to Erase

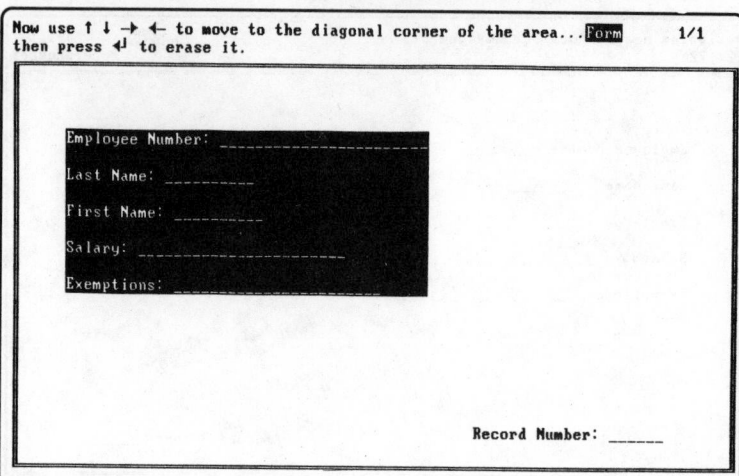

Borders

As you know, Paradox allows you to place borders around your forms. We've placed double-line borders around the forms we've designed so far. However, Paradox allows you to place several kinds of borders around and within your forms. In this section, we'll show you how to create different types of borders.

When you issue the [Menu] Border Place command, Paradox displays three options: Single-line, Double-line, and Other. The Single-line command lets you place a single-line border around your form. The Double-line command lets you place a double-line border around a form (the default form has a double-line border). The Other command lets you design your own border, using either keyboard characters or ASCII characters.

Single-line and Double-line Borders

Single-line and double-line borders come in handy when you want to frame a form with a border or when you want to set off a part of the form. For example, suppose you are designing the form shown in Figure 4-44 and you want to place a single-line border around it. To do this, issue the **[Menu] B**order **P**lace Single-line command. After you issue this command, Paradox will prompt you to point to one corner of the area around which you want to draw the border. When you see this prompt, move the cursor to the upper-left corner of the screen, and press ↵. Paradox then will prompt you to indicate the diagonal (opposite) corner of the border. When it does, press the ↑ key, followed by the ← key to move the cursor to the lower-right corner of the screen. Now, press ↵ to place the border, as shown in Figure 4-45.

Figure 4-44 A Sample Form

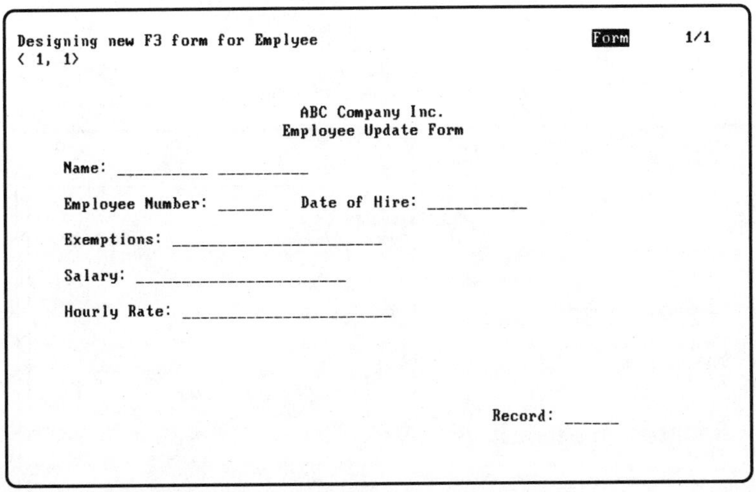

```
Designing new F3 form for Emplyee                    Form    1/1
< 1, 1>

                              ABC Company Inc.
                            Employee Update Form

      Name: _____ _____

      Employee Number: _____   Date of Hire: _____

      Exemptions: _____

      Salary: _____

      Hourly Rate: _____




                                        Record: _____
```

Figure 4-45 A Single-line Border

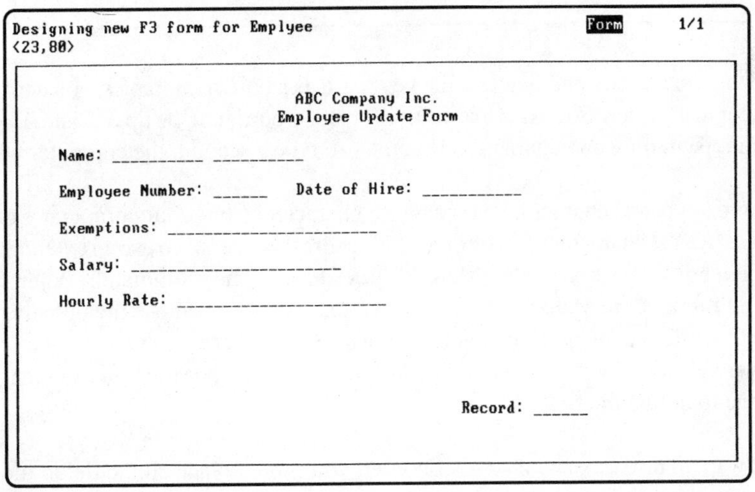

```
Designing new F3 form for Emplyee                    Form    1/1
<23,80>
  ┌──────────────────────────────────────────────────────┐
  │                         ABC Company Inc.               │
  │                       Employee Update Form             │
  │                                                        │
  │   Name: _____ _____                          │
  │                                                        │
  │   Employee Number: _____   Date of Hire: _____   │
  │                                                        │
  │   Exemptions: _____                     │
  │                                                        │
  │   Salary: _____                         │
  │                                                        │
  │   Hourly Rate: _____                    │
  │                                                        │
  │                                                        │
  │                                   Record: _____       │
  └──────────────────────────────────────────────────────┘
```

Special Character Borders

In addition to single-line and double-line borders, you can also create a border that is made up of any printable character. For example, suppose you want to place a border made up of dollar signs ($) around the Salary and Hourly Rate fields of the form shown in Figure 4-45. When you issue the **[Menu]** Border Place Other command, Paradox will prompt you to enter the character that you want to use for the border. When you see this prompt, type $, and press ↵. Paradox then will prompt you to define the border. Position the cursor on the line between

Exemptions: and *Salary:*, two columns to the left of the literals, and press ↵. Then, move the cursor one line below *Hourly Rate:* and to the right of the displayed fields, and press ↵ again to place the border. Figure 4-46 shows the new form.

Figure 4-46 A $ Border

```
┌─────────────────────────────────────────────────────────────────────┐
│Designing new F3 form for Emplyee                         Form    1/1  │
│<15,43>                                                                │
│                                                                       │
│    ┌──────────────────────────────────────────────────────────┐     │
│    │                     ABC Company Inc.                       │     │
│    │                  Employee Update Form                      │     │
│    │                                                            │     │
│    │   Name: _____ _____                              │     │
│    │                                                            │     │
│    │   Employee Number: _____    Date of Hire: _____      │     │
│    │                                                            │     │
│    │   Exemptions: _____                                   │     │
│    │ $$$$$$$$$$$$$$$$$$$$$$$$$$$$$$$$$$$$$$$$$$$$$$$$            │     │
│    │ $ Salary: _____         $                  │     │
│    │ $                                       $                  │     │
│    │ $ Hourly Rate: _____ $                  │     │
│    │ $$$$$$$$$$$$$$$$$$$$$$$$$$$$$$$$$$$$$$$$$$$$$$$$            │     │
│    │                                                            │     │
│    │                                                            │     │
│    │                            Record: _____                  │     │
│    │                                                            │     │
│    └──────────────────────────────────────────────────────────┘     │
└─────────────────────────────────────────────────────────────────────┘
```

Although you can use any character on the keyboard as a border character, you can use only one character in a border. For example, you can't place a border made up of $ and *A*. Paradox will let you type in only one character. If you try to type a second, the computer will beep.

In addition to keyboard characters, you can use characters from your computer's extended character set (ASCII characters 128 through 254) to draw borders. To use an extended ASCII character in a border, just issue the [Menu] Border Place Other command. When Paradox prompts you for the border character, hold down the [Alt] key and use the numeric keypad to type the three-digit code of the character you want to use. When you release the [Alt] key, the character specified by the three-digit code you typed will appear. You can then press ↵ and continue to define the border.

When you want to use a special character border, you should place all the fields and literals you want on the form before you add the border. If you don't, you may have trouble adjusting your fields and literals on the screen after you've added the border. Paradox creates special character borders by simply "typing" the special character around the area you define. If you try to insert characters on a line inside the border, the character along the right edge of the border on that line will shift one character to the right. For example, suppose you are designing the form in Figure 4-46. If you position the cursor just after the Salary field, press [Ins], and type the literal *(Annual)*, the screen will look like Figure 4-47. If you had typed the literal without pressing [Ins] first, then Paradox would have simply typed the literal over the top of the border.

Figure 4-47 Inserting within a Special Character Border

```
Designing new F3 form for Employee            Form  Ins 1/1
<12,47>
┌──────────────────────────────────────────────────────────┐
│                        ABC Company Inc.                    │
│                      Employee Update Form                  │
│                                                            │
│        Name:  _____  _____                       │
│                                                            │
│        Employee Number: _____   Date of Hire: _____  │
│                                                            │
│        Exemptions:_____                          │
│   $$$$$$$$$$$$$$$$$$$$$$$$$$$$$$$$$$$$$$$$$$$$$$            │
│   $ Salary: _____  (Annual)    $         │
│   $                                              $         │
│   $ Hourly Rate: _____      $         │
│   $$$$$$$$$$$$$$$$$$$$$$$$$$$$$$$$$$$$$$$$$$$$$$$            │
│                                                            │
│                                                            │
│                                Record: _____              │
│                                                            │
└──────────────────────────────────────────────────────────┘
```

Because Paradox treats border characters as independent literal characters, you cannot insert characters in an area enclosed by a special character border that runs along the right edge of the screen. If you try to insert a character anywhere in front of the border's edge, Paradox will display the message *Cannot move line further to the right* at the bottom of the screen. Paradox cannot move the line to the right because the character in the border is already at the right edge of the screen.

You can insert characters on a line enclosed by a special character border by deleting the right-edge border character on the line, typing in your insertion, and then replacing the border character. However, if you want to make insertions on several lines, it might be easier to erase the entire border, type the insertions, then replace the border when you are finished.

Erasing Borders

If you want to erase a border that you've placed on a form, use the [Menu] Border Erase command. For example, suppose you want to erase the special character border you just placed on the form in the previous example. To do this, issue the **[Menu] B**order **E**rase command. Paradox then will prompt you to position the cursor on a corner of the border you want to erase, just as it does when you place the border. After you've positioned the cursor, press ↵. Paradox then will prompt you to move the cursor to the diagonal corner. Move the cursor to the opposite corner, and press ↵. After you do this, Paradox will erase the border.

There are other ways to erase a border: You can type over it, or you can delete part of it with the [Del] key or the [Backspace] key. You also can erase a border (or a section of a border) by highlighting it as part of an area you erase with the [Menu] Area Erase command. Finally, whenever you place one border on top of another, the new border will replace the old one. If the new border partially overlaps the old border, only the portion of the old border that is under the new one will be replaced.

Multipage Forms

Throughout this chapter, we've used single-page forms to show you how to design forms. There may be times, however, when you want to design a multipage form. For example, if you have a large table with many fields that you want to place on the form, you may need to design a multipage form. In fact, if your table has more than 19 fields, its default form will be a multipage form.

Designing and using a multipage form is similar to designing and using a single-page form. You'll be able to use all of the techniques and commands you learned earlier in this chapter to design multipage forms.

A form can have up to 15 pages. A "page" in this case refers to the screen, not a printed page. When you design a multipage form, you must design each page individually. For example, if you want a double-line border around every page of the form, you must place the border on each page individually. Each page of the form must include at least one regular field, but the same field cannot appear on more than one page of the same form.

An Example

Suppose you are designing the form shown in Figure 4-18 on page 121, and you want to add a second page to the form. To do this, issue the **[Menu] P**age command. After you issue this command, Paradox will display a menu that offers two options: Insert and Delete. The Insert command allows you to insert a page in the form. The Delete command deletes the current page from the form.

When you see this menu, issue the **I**nsert command. Paradox then will ask you if you want the page inserted before or after the current page. If you choose the Before option, Paradox will add a blank page in front of the current page and move the cursor to it. If you choose the After option, Paradox will add a blank page to the form and make it the current page. In this example, you want to add the new page after the current page, so you should choose **A**fter. Paradox then will add the page and make it the current page.

Figure 4-48 shows the new, blank page on the screen. The only indication that you are on the second page of the form is the status message at the upper-right corner of the screen. It now reads: *2/2*, which means *Page 2 of 2*.

Figure 4-48 A Second Page

```
Designing new F9 form for Emplyee                        Form      2/2
< 1, 1>
```

At this point, designing the second page of the form is just like designing the first page. You can place a border around the screen, set the style, place fields, and add literals. You cannot, however, place on the second page a regular field that appears on the first page—you can place a regular field only once per form. Of course, you can always erase the field from the first page and then place it on the second page, or even use the [Menu] Area Move command to move it.

For example, suppose you want to place a double-line border around the second page of our sample form and then place the Salary, Exemptions, and Date of Hire fields on it. To do this, issue the **[Menu] B**order **P**lace **D**ouble-line command and place the border around the page. Then, use the **[Menu] F**ield **P**lace **R**egular command to place the Salary, Exemptions, and Date of Hire fields on the page and identify the fields with literals. Since the pages of a multipage form are not well identified, you might want to place a record number field on the page and add the literal *Page 2 of 2.* Your screen should now look like Figure 4-49 on the following page.

Instead of using a record number field to identify the second page, you could use a field from the form. For example, in the EMPLYEE table form, you might use the Emp Number field to help you remember which record you are looking at. Since you can place a regular field in a form only once, the occurrences of the field on the second and subsequent pages will have to be display-only fields.

Figure 4-49 Identifying the Page

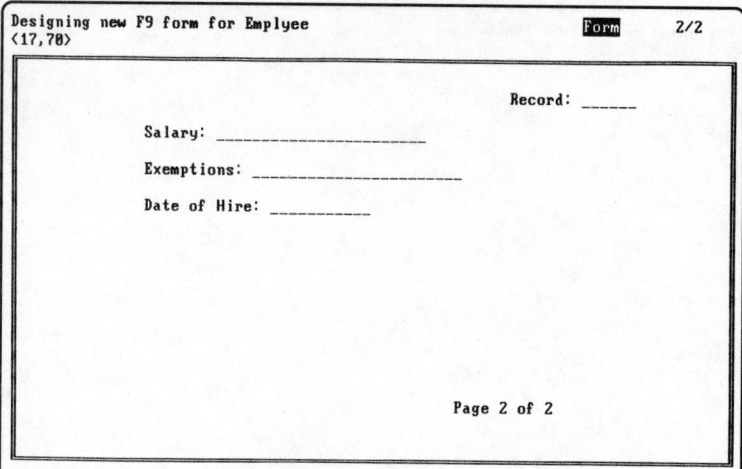

Moving between Pages

The [Pg Up] and [Pg Dn] keys let you move between the pages of a form. To move to the previous page, press [Pg Up]. Pressing [Pg Dn] moves you to the following page. For example, to move from page 1 of the sample form to page 2, press **[Pg Dn]**. To move back to the first page, press **[Pg Up]**.

As you move between pages, the page indicator at the top of the screen will change. For example, when the cursor is on page 1 of a two-page form, the indicator will read *1/2*. When you press [Pg Dn] to move to the next page, the indicator will read *2/2*.

Deleting Pages from a Form

You can use the [Menu] Forms Delete command to delete a page from a form. This command deletes the current page of the form (the page the cursor is on). You need to be sure that the cursor is on the page you want to delete before you issue this command.

The Delete command is very unforgiving. If you accidentally delete a page, the only thing you can do is insert a new page and start over. If you're working on page 1 of a single-page form and you issue the [Menu] Forms Delete command, Paradox will delete everything on the form and display an empty page 1.

Multitable Forms

Multitable forms let you use a single form to view, edit, or enter data into several tables. However, multitable forms do much more than simply display records from more than one table at the same time. Because you can link tables through a form based on values in certain fields, multitable forms are powerful tools for maintaining the integrity of data in normalized table systems.

A multitable form is actually a master form that contains one or more embedded forms. The master form displays fields from a master table, while the embedded forms display fields from "detail" tables. The records in these detail tables are usually linked to a record in the master table. For example, a master table might contain the names of your customers, while a detail table contains orders made by those customers. Records in both tables would contain a Customer Number field to link each order to the proper customer. The Customer Number field in the customer table would need to be a key field in order to ensure that each customer record had a unique customer number. You can use a multitable form to display on a single form information about a customer along with data pertaining to all of that customer's orders.

Designing a Multitable Form

There are several steps in creating a multitable form. First, you create an embedded form for each detail table that will appear on the form. Then, you design the master form that will display the embedded forms along with data from the master table. Finally, you place the embedded forms on the master form.

Let's walk through each of these steps as we design a multitable form. Suppose you have created a table called CLIENTS, which lists information about all of your company's regular clients. Figure 4-50 shows the structure of the CLIENTS table, and Figure 4-51 on the next page shows the table itself.

Figure 4-50 The Structure of CLIENTS

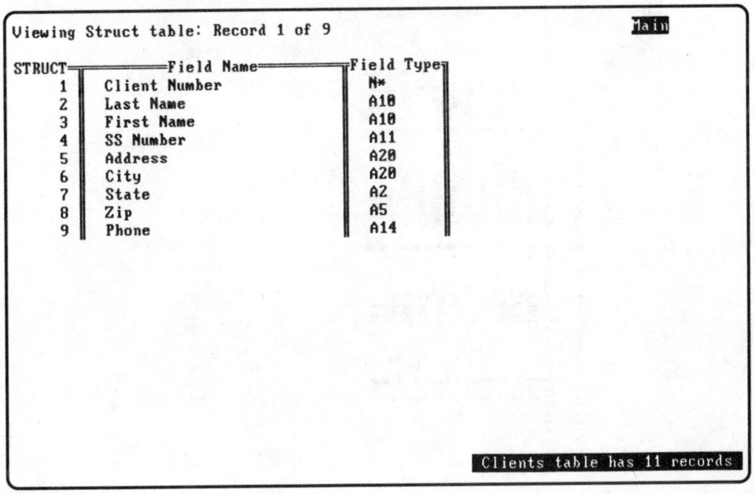
Viewing Struct table: Record 1 of 9 Main

STRUCT	Field Name	Field Type
1	Client Number	N*
2	Last Name	A10
3	First Name	A10
4	SS Number	A11
5	Address	A20
6	City	A20
7	State	A2
8	Zip	A5
9	Phone	A14

Clients table has 11 records

Figure 4-51 The CLIENTS Table

Viewing Clients table: Record 1 of 11

CLIENTS	Client Number	Last Name	First Name	SS Number	Address	City	State	Zip	Phone
1	1001	Smith	John	345-43-2232	2378 Maple Wood Dr.	Louisville	KY	40216	(502) 448-8989
2	1002	Zoeller	Greg	401-45-8098	456 Whipps Mill Rd.	Louisville	KY	40242	(502) 422-9856
3	1003	Klausing	Fred	457-98-8432	2394 Hazelwood Ave.	Louisville	KY	40214	(502) 369-9393
4	1004	Fritz	Jules	345-67-3454	2212 Elk St.	New Albany	IN	47158	(812) 223-7472
5	1005	Gies	Helen	289-98-4628	4583 Mary Catherine	Louisville	KY	40216	(502) 773-3234
6	1006	Payne	Ann	325-23-2323	1932 Hunter Ct.	Louisville	KY	40224	(502) 233-3344
7	1007	Wooley	Paul	367-98-1244	123 Clarks Lane	Louisville	KY	40213	(502) 634-1238
8	1008	Cooley	Dwayne	417-23-2938	3237 Henry St.	Louisville	KY	40283	(502) 897-1247
9	1009	Harris	Ralph	403-42-5775	Rt. 2, Box 123-D	Floyds Knobs	IN	47119	(812) 922-7876
10	1010	Crane	John	378-24-9476	1345 18th St.	Louisville	KY	40224	(502) 247-8919
11	1011	Jones	Thiora	319-21-8219	8924 Hallmark Rd.	New Albany	IN	47158	(502) 922-8492

In addition, you have also created a table called SALESORD, which lists sales orders placed by the people in the CLIENTS table. Figure 4-52 shows the structure of the SALESORD table, and Figure 4-53 shows the table.

Figure 4-52 The Structure of SALESORD

```
Viewing Struct table: Record 1 of 7                              Main

STRUCT            Field Name        Field Type
       1    Client Number              N*
       2    Date                       D*
       3    Product Number             A8*
       4    Product                    A20
       5    Price                      $
       6    Quantity                   N
       7    Sales Person               N




                                           Salesord table has 7 records
```

Figure 4-53 The SALESORD Table

```
Viewing Salesord table: Record 1 of 7                           Main

SALESORD  Client Number      Date        Product Number      Product
      1        1001         2/01/88           1           Paradox 3.0
      2        1001         2/01/88           2           Paradox 386
      3        1001         2/01/88           5           Lotus 1-2-3
      4        1002         3/23/89           2           Paradox 386
      5        1004        12/13/88           5           Lotus 1-2-3
      6        1004         1/12/89           2           Paradox 386
      7        1010         2/01/89           6           Excel
```

```
Viewing Salesord table: Record 1 of 7                           Main

       Product          Price        Quantity    Sales Person
   Paradox 3.0          399.99          1             1
   Paradox 386          599.99          1             1
   Lotus 1-2-3          495.00          1             1
   Paradox 386          599.99          1             1
   Lotus 1-2-3          495.00          2             1
   Paradox 386          599.99          1             1
   Excel                299.99          2            16
```

As you can see, the first field in both the CLIENTS and SALESORD tables is called Client Number. The Client Number field in both tables is a key field. However, the SALESORD table also has two other key fields: Date and Product Number. As a result, every Client Number entry in CLIENTS is unique, but several records in SALESORD can have the same Client Number entry. Our multitable form will display records in the CLIENTS table, along with records from SALESORD that have the same Client Number entry.

Creating an Embedded Form

First, let's design an embedded form for the SALESORD table. The size of the embedded form as it will appear on the master form depends on the location of fields, literals, and borders on the embedded form. The upper-left corner of the screen is always the upper-left corner of the embedded form. However, the right edge of the embedded form is defined by the location of the field, literal, or border that you place closest to the right edge of the form. The bottom edge of the embedded form depends on the location of the field, literal, or border that you place closest to the bottom of the form. To make an embedded form as compact as possible, you should always define the form in the upper-left corner of the screen.

For example, suppose you want the embedded SALESORD form to look like Figure 4-54. The bottom and right edges of the border that surrounds the form define the size of the form as it will appear on the master form. Placing borders around embedded forms is a good practice not only because it gives you an idea of the embedded form's size, but also because the border helps distinguish the embedded form on the master form.

Figure 4-54 Designing an Embedded Form

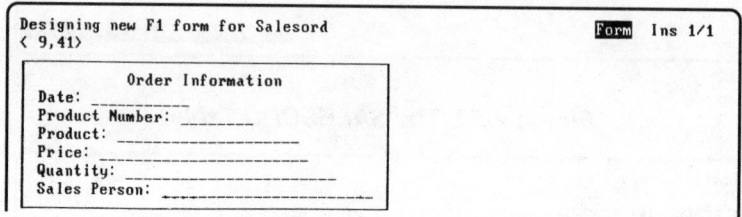

To design this embedded form, issue the **[Menu]** Forms Design command, type **SALES-ORD**, and press ↵. When Paradox asks you to select a report, press **1**. Then, type **Embedded Form** at the *Form description:* prompt and press ↵. First, type the literal **Order Information** on the second row of the form. Then, type all the literals that describe the fields and use the **[Menu]** Field Place Regular command to place the fields. After you've placed the fields on the form, use the **[Menu]** Border Place Single-line command to place a single-line border around all of the text and fields on the form. After you've finished designing the embedded form, press **[Do-It!]** to save the form.

As you may have noticed, the embedded SALESORD form does not include the Client Number field. An embedded form cannot include the field that links the form to its master form. Paradox allows linking fields to be displayed only on the master form in order to guarantee the referential integrity of the data in all linking fields. Since you can't change the entries in linking fields through an embedded form, the linking values in the detail table will always match the linking values in the master table. If you change an entry in a linking field of a record in a master table, Paradox automatically changes all the linking field entries in corresponding records in the detail table.

Creating a Master Form

Now, you are ready to design the master form for the CLIENTS table. Suppose you want your master form to look like the form in Figure 4-55.

Figure 4-55 The Master Form

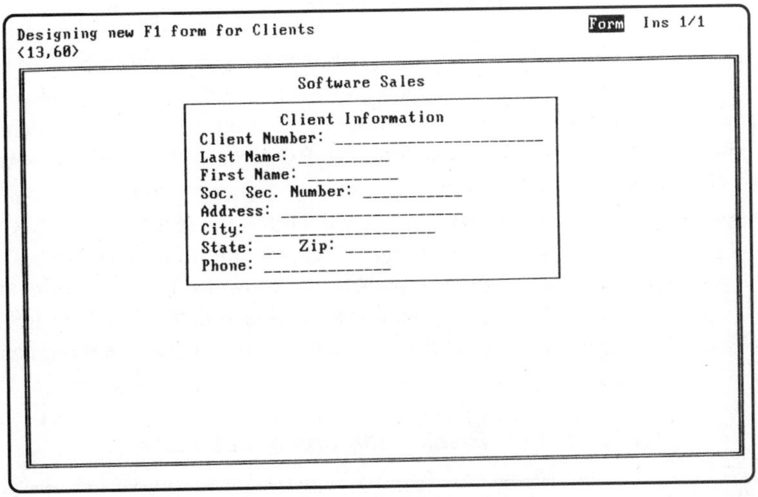

```
Designing new F1 form for Clients                    Form   Ins 1/1
<13,68>

                            Software Sales

                         Client Information
                Client Number: _____
                Last Name: _____
                First Name: _____
                Soc. Sec. Number: _____
                Address: _____
                City: _____
                State: __   Zip: _____
                Phone: _____
```

To design the master form, issue the **[Menu]** Forms Design command, type **CLIENTS**, and press ↵. Then, select form number **1**, type the form description **Master Form**, and press ↵. Now, type the form title **Software Sales** in the middle of the second line on the form. Then, type the subtitle **Client Information** in the middle of the fourth line. Next, type all the field descriptions and use the **[Menu]** Field Place Regular command to place all the fields. Finally, place a single-line border around the Client Information subtitle and fields, and a double-line border around the edge of the entire form. At this point, your screen should look like Figure 4-55.

To embed the form that you created for the SALESORDS table in the master form, issue the **[Menu]** Multi Tables Place command. After you issue this command, Paradox will present a menu with two options: Linked and Unlinked. The Linked option lets you place a form for a detail table that is linked to the master table in the master form. This link is based on the entries in one or more of the detail table's key fields. The Unlinked option lets you place a form for a table whose data is in no way linked to the data in the master table. Since we want to link the SALESORD table to the CLIENTS table based on entries in the Client Number fields in each table, you should choose Linked. After you select the Linked option, Paradox will prompt you for the name of the table for the form you want to place. When you see this prompt, type **SALESORD** and press ↵. Next, Paradox will ask you for the number of the form that you want to place, displaying a list of the defined forms for the SALESORD table. Select **1** to place the form that we designed earlier. After you select a form, Paradox will present the menu of the fields in the master table and ask you to pick a field to match the Client

Number field of SALESORD. Remember that Client Number is the first key field in the SALESORD table. Paradox asks you to choose a field to match Client Number because it is the only key field from SALESORD that is not placed on the form that you are embedding on the master form. If you had not placed the other SALESORD key fields (Date and Product Number) on the embedded form, Paradox would also ask you to select a matching field for these key fields. Select Client Number from the menu to link the Client Number field in CLIENTS to the Client Number field in SALESORD.

After you select a matching field, a reverse video box representing the embedded form will appear in the lower-right corner of the screen, as shown in Figure 4-56. Paradox will also display directions at the top of the screen telling you to use the cursor-movement keys to place the embedded form. To position the SALESORD form, press the ↑ and ← keys until the reverse video box is located directly under the client information on the master form, then press ← to embed the form. After you place the form, the reverse video box will dim slightly and you will see the message *External Salesord table with form F1, linked* in the upper-right corner of the screen. This message lets you know that the cursor is located in an embedded form for the SALESORD table and that the records in SALESORD are linked to records in CLIENTS. Figure 4-57 shows the screen at this point. To save the completed form, press [Do-It!].

Figure 4-56 Placing the Embedded Form

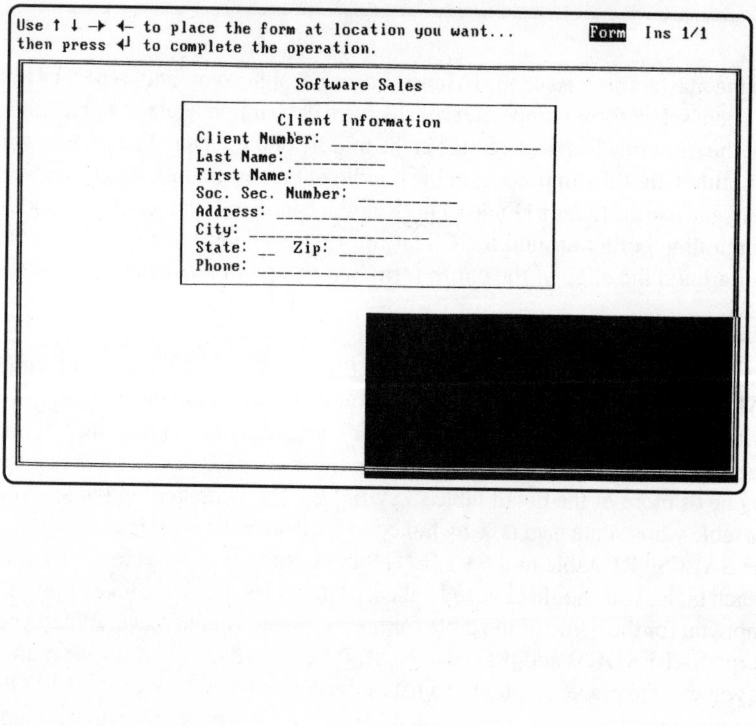

```
Use ↑ ↓ → ←  to place the form at location you want...      Form   Ins 1/1
then press ↵ to complete the operation.

                          Software Sales

                        Client Information
                  Client Number: _____
                  Last Name: _____
                  First Name: _____
                  Soc. Sec. Number: _____
                  Address: _____
                  City: _____
                  State: __  Zip: _____
                  Phone: _____
```

Figure 4-57 The Completed Form

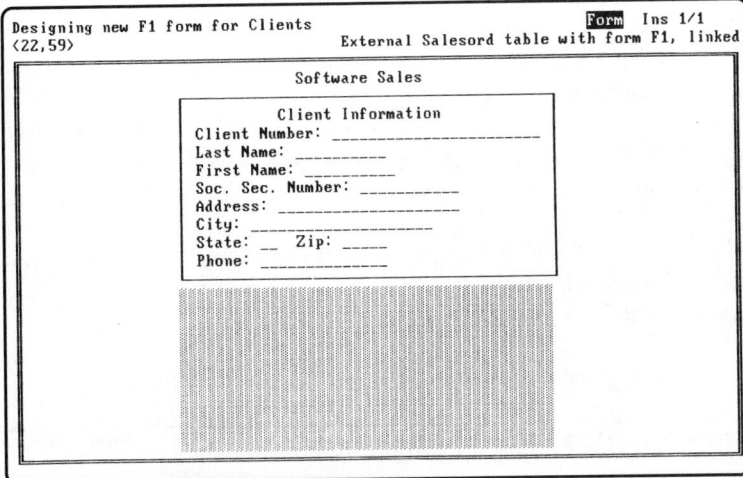

```
Designing new F1 form for Clients                    Form  Ins 1/1
<22,59>                          External Salesord table with form F1, linked

                              Software Sales

                            Client Information
                      Client Number: _____
                      Last Name: _____
                      First Name: _____
                      Soc. Sec. Number: _____
                      Address: _____
                      City: _____
                      State: __  Zip: _____
                      Phone: _____
```

Using a Multitable Form

To edit the CLIENTS and SALESORD tables with the new form, first issue the [**Menu**]
Modify Edit command and select the **CLIENTS** table. When the CLIENTS table appears
on the workspace, issue the [**Menu**] Image Pickform command and select form number **1**.
When Paradox displays the CLIENTS table in the form view, your screen will look like Figure
4-58. As you can see, the form displays data from both the CLIENTS and the SALESORD
tables. The SALESORD record that Paradox displays in the embedded form is linked to
the CLIENTS record displayed in the form by a common entry in the Client Number field of
each table.

Figure 4-58 Editing with a Multitable Form

```
Editing Clients table with form F1: Record 1 of 11           Edit  —▼

                              Software Sales

                            Client Information
                      Client Number:            1001      ◄
                      Last Name: Smith
                      First Name: John
                      Soc. Sec. Number: 345-43-2232
                      Address: 2378 Maple Wood Dr.
                      City: Louisville
                      State: KY  Zip: 40216
                      Phone: (502) 448-8989

                            Order Information
                      Date: 2/01/88
                      Product Number: 1
                      Product: Paradox 3.0
                      Price:            399.99
                      Quantity:            1
                      Sales Person:            1
```

While all the cursor-movement keys work the same in a multitable form as they do in a single-table form, the [Up Image] key ([F3]) and the [Down Image] key ([F4]) work differently. Paradox treats tables displayed on a multitable form as if each table occupies a separate image. As a result, you can move from the fields on the master form to fields in an embedded form by pressing either [Up Image] or [Down Image]. While you are using a multitable form, you cannot use the [Up Image] and [Down Image] keys to move to other images on the workspace. In order to move to these images, you must press [Form Toggle] first to return the current image to table view.

For example, to move from the fields of the CLIENTS table to the embedded SALESORD form, press **[Up Image]** (or **[Down Image]**). After you move the cursor to the embedded form, your screen will look like Figure 4-59.

Figure 4-59 Moving to an Embedded Form

```
Editing Salesord table with form F1: Record 1 of 3 (1-M Group)    Edit  =▼
┌──────────────────────────────────────────────────────────────────────┐
│ ┌────────────────────────────────────────────────────────────────┐   │
│ │                       Software Sales                             │   │
│ │        ┌───────────────────────────────────────────┐            │   │
│ │        │           Client Information               │            │   │
│ │        │ Client Number:              1001           │            │   │
│ │        │ Last Name: Smith                           │            │   │
│ │        │ First Name: John                           │            │   │
│ │        │ Soc. Sec. Number: 345-43-2232              │            │   │
│ │        │ Address: 2378 Maple Wood Dr.               │            │   │
│ │        │ City: Louisville                           │            │   │
│ │        │ State: KY  Zip: 40216                      │            │   │
│ │        │ Phone: (502) 448-8989                      │            │   │
│ │        └───────────────────────────────────────────┘            │   │
│ │        ┌───────────────────────────────────────────┐            │   │
│ │        │           Order Information                │            │   │
│ │        │ Date:  2/01/88   ◄                         │            │   │
│ │        │ Product Number: 1                          │            │   │
│ │        │ Product: Paradox 3.0                       │            │   │
│ │        │ Price:              399.99                 │            │   │
│ │        │ Quantity:               1                  │            │   │
│ │        │ Sales Person:             1                │            │   │
│ │        └───────────────────────────────────────────┘            │   │
│ └────────────────────────────────────────────────────────────────┘   │
└──────────────────────────────────────────────────────────────────────┘
```

If the master form includes only one embedded table, it doesn't matter which image-movement key you press to move to the embedded form. However, if there is more than one embedded form, the [Up Image] key will move you in one direction through the embedded forms, and the [Down Image] key will move you in the other direction.

When you move from the fields in the master table to the fields in an embedded form, the message at the top of the screen changes to reflect the move. For example, in Figure 4-59, the message has changed from *Editing Clients table with form F1: Record 1 of 11* to *Editing Salesord table with form F1: Record 1 of 3 (1-M Group)*. In addition to letting you know that you are now editing the SALESORD table, this new message tells you that there are three records in SALESORD linked to the current record in CLIENTS. In other words, there are three SALESORD records that have the same Client Number entry as the current CLIENTS record. If you press [Pg Dn] now, the *Record 1 of 3* portion of the message will change to *Record 2 of 3*, and the embedded form will display the second SALESORD record for customer number 1001. Because this new record is linked to the same CLIENTS record as the previous SALESORD record, the CLIENTS section of the form will remain the same.

Once you have entered an embedded form, you can move from any linked record in the detail table directly to the last linked record by pressing the [End] key. Conversely, you can move directly to the first linked record by pressing [Home].

The *(1-M Group)* designation that appears at the top of the screen in Figure 4-59 tells you something very important about the link between the records in the master table and records in the detail table. The *1-M Group* abbreviation stands for one-to-many. In a one-to-many link, many records in a detail table can be linked to one record in the master table. In this case, each record in the CLIENTS table is linked to many records in the SALESORD table because the link is based on the Client Number fields in both tables. Since Client Number is the only key field in the CLIENTS table, every Client Number entry in that table must be unique. However, the SALESORD table includes two additional key fields, so many records in SALESORD can have the same Client Number entry. As a result, each record in CLIENTS can be linked to several records in SALESORD. We'll talk about other types of links later in this chapter.

When the current record of the master table is not linked to any records in the detail table, an embedded form displays a blank record from the end of the detail table. For example, as you page through the CLIENTS records, you will come across some instances where the form displays client information on the master form but only blank fields on the embedded form. The embedded SALESORD form displays an empty record when there are no records in the SALESORD table linked to the current record in the CLIENTS table. When you enter data into this empty record, Paradox links it to the current record in the master table, copying the entries in the linking fields of the master record into the linking fields of the new detail record.

Linking Key Fields

When you issue the [Menu] Multi Tables Place Linked command and then select a detail table and an embedded form, Paradox will ask you to select a matching field for every key field of the detail table that is not included in the embedded form. You can link the detail table to the master table on one, several, or all of the key fields in the detail table. You need to decide which key fields you want to use in the link while you are designing the embedded form. If you want to include a key field in the link, be sure to leave it off the embedded form. In our example, the embedded form for the SALESORD table included two of the table's key fields (Date and Product Number), but not the first key field in the table (Client Number). As a result, Paradox asked you to choose a matching field for only the Client Number field.

In our example, we linked two fields that happened to have the same name. However, you can link any field in the master table to a key field in the detail table as long as the two fields are the same field type. For example, if the Client Number field in the SALESORD table were named Purchaser, you could still create a link between the Client Number field of CLIENTS and the Purchaser field of SALESORD. However, you cannot link fields that are not the same field types. For example, if the Client Number field in SALESORD were an alphanumeric field and the Client Number field in CLIENTS a number field, then you could not link the two tables on these two fields.

The first key field in the detail table must always be included in the link, so you should never place the first key field in a detail table on an embedded form. While you can base a link on any number of key fields in the detail table, Paradox requires that the linking fields be grouped at the top of the table. For example, suppose that you were designing an embedded form for a detail table that has three key fields. In this case, you could link the detail table to the master table based on the values in the first and second key fields by leaving these fields off the embedded form. When you placed the embedded form on the master form, Paradox would ask you to select matching fields from the master table for both the first and second key fields. Similarly, you could create a link based on all three key fields in the detail table by leaving all three fields off the embedded form. However, you could not create a link based on the first and third key fields of the detail table. If you left these fields off the embedded form but placed the second key field on the form, Paradox would not let you place the embedded form on the master form. After you issued the [Menu] Multi Tables Place Linked command and specified a detail table and embedded form, Paradox would display the message *Embedded form must have all non-linking key fields placed on it* at the bottom of the screen.

If you do not use a key field in the detail table in the link with the master table, then that key field must appear on the embedded form. As we've just explained, if you do not place a key field on the embedded form, then Paradox assumes that the key field is part of the link.

These rules governing the placement of linking fields protect the logical association between the records in the master and detail tables. Because linking fields appear only in the master form, you cannot change the linking field entries for a record in the detail table, thereby breaking its link with the record in the master table. The preservation of this link establishes the records in the detail table as logical extensions of records in the master table. In effect, each record in the detail table is "owned" by a record in the master table.

Types of Links

As we mentioned earlier, most of your master and embedded forms will probably share a one-to-many relationship. However, there are four types of relationships that can join records in a master table to records in a detail table: one-to-one, one-to-many, many-to-one, and many-to-many. The type of link that exists between the tables depends on the number of key fields in each table and the number of key fields that are involved in the link.

In a one-to-one link, each record in the master table can be linked to one record in the detail table, and each record in the detail table can be linked to only one record in the master table. For example, a one-to-one link results when you match the single key field in the master table to the single key field in the detail table. Since every record must contain a unique entry in its key field, each record in the master table can match only one record in the detail table, and vice versa. When a record in the master table appears on a multitable form, only the single, linked record in the detail table can appear on the form with it.

In a one-to-many link, each record in the master table can be linked to many records in the detail table. For example, a one-to-many link results when you match the first key field of a detail table with multiple key fields to the single key field in a master table. The link that we demonstrated earlier was a one-to-many link because it involved the only key field for the CLIENTS master table (the Client Number field) but only the first of three key fields for the SALESORD detail table. When a record in the master table appears on a multitable form, the form will display all of the linked records in the detail table.

In a many-to-one link, many records in the master table can be linked to a single record in the detail table. For example, a many-to-one link results when you link the single key field of a detail table to a field in the master table that contains duplicate values. This linking field in the master table can be any field except a single key field. Since the linking entries for the master table are not unique, but the linking entries for the detail table are, each record in the master table can be linked to only one record in the detail table. When a record in the master table appears on a multitable form, the form will display only the single linked record from the detail table. However, this record from the detail table may appear on the form with several records in the master table. In this case, there is no easy way to tell how many records in the master table are linked to a record in the detail table.

In a many-to-many link, records in the master table can be linked to many records in the detail table, and records in the detail table can be linked to many records in the master table. For example, a many-to-many link results when you match the first of several key fields in a detail table with a field in the master table that contains duplicate values. This linking field in the master table can be any field except a single key field. Since the entries on both ends of the link are not unique, records in both tables can be linked to several records in the other table. As a result, there is a pool of records in each table that is involved in each link, but there is no element of exclusivity at either end of the link. When a record in the master table appears on a multitable form, all of the linked records from the detail table will appear on the form with it. However, these detail records will also appear with any other master table records to which they are linked. As a result, you can see all of the detail records that are linked to a particular master record, but you cannot easily determine all of the master records that are linked to a particular detail record.

Paradox can guarantee referential integrity only for tables that are joined by one-to-one and one-to-many links. In these links, each record in the detail table is linked to only one record in the master table. Since the linking fields always appear only on the master form, you cannot change the entries in the linking fields without changing the linking entries for the master record and every other detail record linked to the master record. As a result, the master table and its family of detail tables cannot be split up. However, in many-to-one and many-to-many links, the records in the detail table may appear with several records in the master table. If you use the multitable form to change the linking fields for one record in the master table that is linked to a detail table, you may break that detail record's link to another master record. There is no way to guarantee that any relationship established in the link will remain intact.

Multitable Forms with Unlinked Tables

If you use the [Menu] Multi Tables Place Unlinked command to place an embedded form, Paradox will not link the detail and master tables with any logical association. Viewing a multitable form that contains unlinked tables is a lot like viewing two tables that happen to be on the workspace at the same time. However, if you are viewing or editing unlinked tables with the same form, you cannot use the [Up Image] and [Down Image] keys to move to other tables on the workspace. When you press these keys, Paradox will move among only those tables that appear on the multitable form. To move to other tables, you must first press [Form Toggle] to switch to the table view. Then, you can use the [Up Image] and [Down Image] keys to move among all the tables on the workspace. However, the tables in the embedded forms will be on the workspace if you used the [Menu] View command to place them on the workspace before you began using the multitable form.

Rules for Structuring Linked Detail Tables

The rules that govern links between master and detail tables can exert a profound influence on the design of tables that you want to use in multitable forms. This is especially true for detail tables. For example, you may have noticed that instead of using a single key field like the Client Number field in CLIENTS, we used three key fields for the SALESORD table. This multiple-key field structure is necessary because the first key field in a detail table must be involved in the link with the master table. Since we wanted to link the SALESORD table to the CLIENTS table based on entries in the Client Number fields of each table, the Client Number field had to be the first field in the SALESORD table. Because several records in the SALESORD table must include the same Client Number entry, we had to create a multiple-key field by making the Date and Product Number fields key fields. Although each record in SALESORD does not include a unique "Order Number" field to identify that record, each record does include a unique Client Number/Date/Product Number combination. It is this combination of field values that provides a unique key that you can use to identify the records in SALESORD.

You may have to rearrange the fields in some of your existing tables if you want to use them in multitable forms. For example, suppose you wanted to design a multitable form using CLIENTS as a master table and PROJECTS as a detail table. These tables both contain a number field called Client Number that relates the two tables, but you could not use them in a multitable form. If you look at the structure of the PROJECTS table, shown in Figure 4-60, you can see the reason.

Because the Client Number field in PROJECTS is not a key field, Paradox cannot use this field to establish a link for a multitable form. However, you could make such a link possible by restructuring the PROJECTS table. In the restructured table, Client Number should be the first field in the table and a key field. You can use the [Menu] Modify Restructure command to move the Client Number field and change it into a key field. The modified STRUCT table should look like Figure 4-61.

Figure 4-60 The Structure of PROJECTS

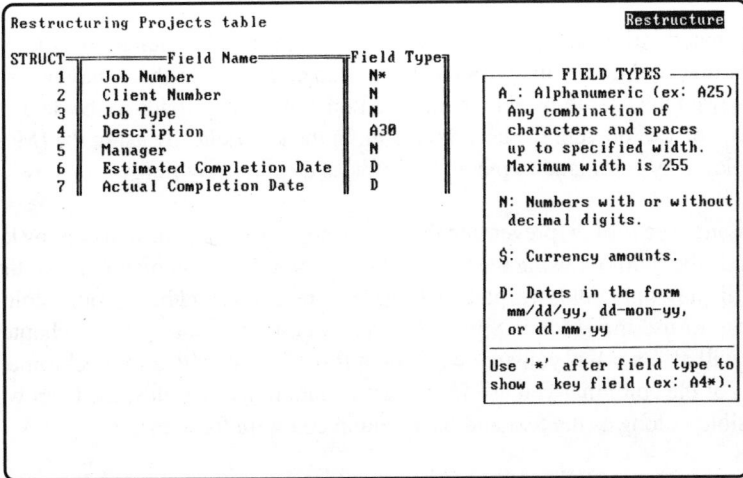

Figure 4-61 The New Structure for PROJECTS

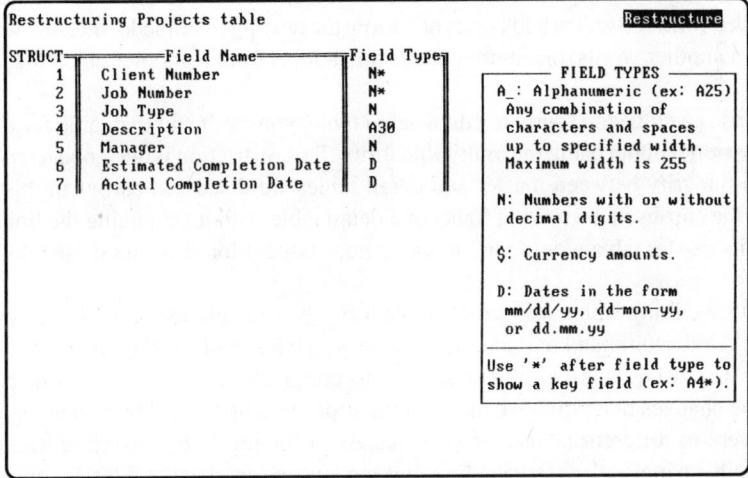

Now, you can create a PROJECTS form displaying every field in the table except Client Number and embed this form in a master form for the CLIENTS table.   To create this multitable form, follow the steps that we explained earlier, substituting the PROJECTS table for the SALESORD table. In the next section of this chapter, we'll use the restructured PROJECTS table to create a three-table form. However, in the rest of this book, we'll use the PROJECTS table in its original structure.

Hiding Linking Fields

As we mentioned earlier, an embedded form must display any key fields from the detail table that are not involved in the link with the master table. However, there may be times when you do not want the user to be able to edit the non-linking key fields in the detail table. In these cases, you can prevent the user from editing the key fields by using the [Menu] Field Place DisplayOnly command to place the fields as display-only fields.

You may want to go further, preventing the user from even seeing the non-linking key fields. You can hide the fields by using the [Menu] Style Color Area command to give the area on which the display-only fields are placed the same foreground and background color. (We'll explain how to use the [Menu] Style Color Area command later in this chapter.) This technique will also work if you are designing a form for use with a monochrome monitor. Regardless of the color that you use for the area containing the fields, the form will render them invisible as long as the text and background color are the same.

Notes

While you can use a multipage form as a master form, you cannot use a multipage form as an embedded form. Also, Paradox does not allow the nesting of embedded forms within one another. In another words, one embedded form cannot contain another embedded form.

After you use an embedded form to edit a detail table, you can't edit that table for the rest of the Edit session without using the multitable form. This restriction is designed to enforce the referential integrity between master and detail tables we discussed earlier in this section. Changing the entries in the linking fields of a detail table without changing the linking field entries in its master table would violate the logical association that join these tables.

While you are editing tables with a multitable form, you can use the [Ctrl]-[U] keystroke or the [Menu] Undo command to undo the changes you have made during the Edit session. If you press [Ctrl]-[U] or issue the [Menu] Undo command, Paradox will work backward through the changes that you have made in the order in which you made them, even if the changes were to different tables. If you changed a linking field entry in a master table, Paradox will change all corresponding linking entries in detail tables to preserve the referential integrity of the link.

If you use a multitable form in Coedit mode, you should be aware of certain limitations that apply to your ability to undo changes. As we mentioned in Chapter 2, Coedit mode is a special editing mode that allows two or more users on a network to edit a table at the same time. Usually, you can undo only the last change you made to the current table in Coedit mode. When you use a multitable form in Coedit mode, moving from the master record to a detail record takes away your ability to undo a change that you have made to the master record. Moving to other master records does not affect your ability to undo changes to a master record. If you make a change to a detail record, you can undo that change as long as you do not change the image displaying the master record to which the detail record is linked. Once you move to another master record or press [Form Toggle] to switch the master table to table view, you lose your ability to undo the change to the detail record. However, the cursor must be in the detail table image to undo the change. Appendix A2, "Multi-user Paradox," discusses the Coedit mode.

When you use the DataEntry command with a multitable form to enter data into several tables, Paradox creates a temporary ENTRY table for each table displayed on the form. Paradox names the temporary table that holds data targeted for the master table ENTRY and numbers each temporary table holding data for embedded tables. For example, Paradox would use temporary tables named ENTRY, ENTRY1, and ENTRY2 to hold data targeted for a master table and two detail tables on a multitable form. We'll discuss data entry with multitable forms in Chapter 9, "Multitable Operations."

Multiple Embedded Forms

Often, information associated with a master table is spread out over several detail tables. For example, both PROJECTS and SALESORD contain information that is associated with records in the CLIENTS table. Fortunately, Paradox allows you to place as many as five embedded forms on a single master form, linking each detail table to the master table.

While designing a form that includes several embedded forms, you need to keep in mind that all of the embedded forms must be small enough to fit on the same master form. Earlier in this chapter, we showed you how to specify the number of digits or characters displayed in a field when you place the field on the form. Using smaller field lengths is one way to make embedded forms smaller so that you can fit several of them on the same master form.

Figure 4-62 shows form 3 for SALESORD. To make this form smaller, we shortened the Quantity field when we placed it on the form, removing ten characters from its default length. We also shortened the Sales Person field by ten characters.

Figure 4-62 A Smaller SALESORD Form

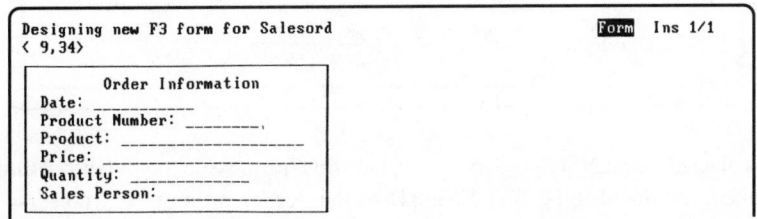

We'll take a different, much simpler approach to making the embedded form for the PROJECTS table as small as possible. Instead of shortening the fields on this form, we'll simply abbreviate the literals that describe the fields. Figure 4-63 shows form 3 for the

PROJECTS table. On this form, we've shortened the literal *Description:* to *Desc:*, the literal *Estimated Completion Date:* to *Est. Completion Date:*, and the literal *Actual Completion Date:* to *Act. Completion Date:*.

Now, let's place the embedded forms on a master form. Figure 4-64 shows the completed master form, which is form 3 for the CLIENTS table. This form has essentially the same design as the master forms that we used earlier in this chapter. To create this form, first place the fields from the CLIENTS table, with the literals that describe them, and the single-line border around the fields. Then, place the embedded forms on the master form.

Figure 4-63 A PROJECTS Form

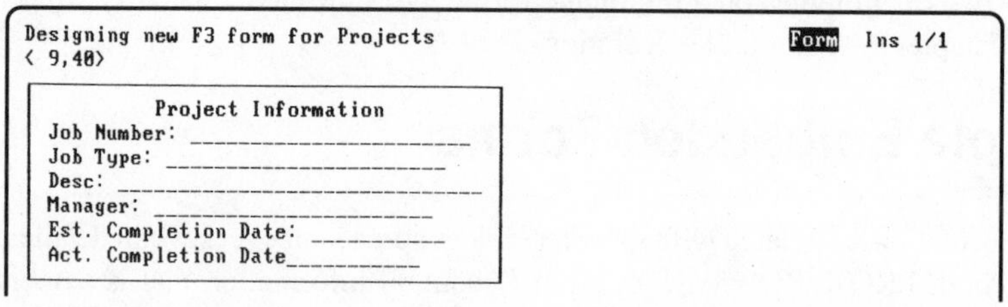

```
Designing new F3 form for Projects                    Form  Ins 1/1
< 9,48>

                Project Information
    Job Number: _____
    Job Type: _____
    Desc: _____
    Manager: _____
    Est. Completion Date: _____
    Act. Completion Date_____
```

Figure 4-64 A New Master Form

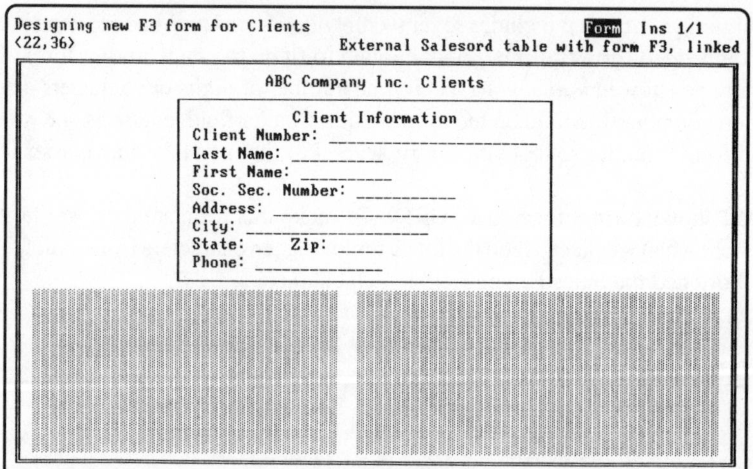

```
Designing new F3 form for Clients                     Form  Ins 1/1
<22,36>                      External Salesord table with form F3, linked

                      ABC Company Inc. Clients

                          Client Information
        Client Number: _____
        Last Name: _____
        First Name: _____
        Soc. Sec. Number: _____
        Address: _____
        City: _____
        State: __   Zip: _____
        Phone: _____
```

Now, let's place the SALESORD form. To place this form, issue the **[Menu]** **M**ulti **T**ables **P**lace **L**inked command, type **SALESORD** at the *Table:* prompt, and press ←. When Paradox asks you for a form number, choose **3**. When Paradox asks you which field should match the Client Number field in the SALESORD table, pick Client Number. Then, place the embedded form in the lower-left corner of the master form and press ←. To place the PROJECTS form, issue the **[Menu]** **M**ulti **T**ables **P**lace **L**inked command, type **PROJECTS** at the *Table:* prompt, and press ←. When Paradox asks you for a form number, choose **3**. When Paradox asks you which field should match the Client Number field in the SALESORD table, pick **Client Number**. Then, place the embedded form in the lower-right corner of the master form, and press ↵. After you have placed both embedded forms, the master form will look like Figure 4-64. Press **[Do-It!]** to save the form.

If you view the CLIENTS table with the new form, your screen will look like Figure 4-65. As you can see, the form displays the PROJECTS and SALESORD records that are linked to the current CLIENTS record. As we explained earlier, you can move through the three tables in the form by pressing the [Up Image] and [Down Image] keys. If you press [Up Image] while the cursor is in the CLIENTS area of the form, the cursor will move to the PROJECTS area. Then, if you press [Up Image] twice, the cursor will move to the SALESORD area, then back to the CLIENTS area. On the other hand, if you press [Down Image] three times while the cursor is in the CLIENTS area, the cursor will move first to the SALESORD area, then to the PROJECTS area, and then back to the CLIENTS area.

Figure 4-65 Viewing Three Tables at Once

```
Viewing Clients table with form F3: Record 1 of 11          Main  =▼

        ABC Company Inc. Clients

            Client Information
        Client Number:            1001
        Last Name: Smith
        First Name: John
        Soc. Sec. Number: 345-43-2232
        Address: 2378 Maple Wood Dr.
        City: Louisville
        State: KY  Zip: 40216
        Phone: (502) 448-8989


       Order Information            Project Information
   Date:  2/01/88             Job Number:            100
   Product Number: 1          Job Type:                1
   Product: Paradox 3.0       Desc.: Install PC AT/Paradox/1-2-3
   Price:          399.99     Manager:                 1
   Quantity:        1         Est. Completion Date: 10/13/88
   Sales Person:    1         Act. Completion Date: 11/23/88
```

Removing Embedded Forms

The [Menu] Multi Tables Remove command lets you remove an embedded form from a master form. For example, suppose you decide to remove the embedded SALESORD form from the master form shown in Figure 4-64. To remove the embedded form, issue the **[Menu] Multi Tables Remove** command. After you issue the command, Paradox will present the prompt shown in Figure 4-66, which tells you to move to the embedded form you want to remove. To remove the SALESORD form, position the cursor anywhere in that form and press ↵. Then, Paradox will present a Cancel/OK menu to verify that you want to remove the selected form. If you choose **OK**, Paradox will remove the embedded SALESORD form from the master form.

Figure 4-66 The Multi Tables Remove Prompt

```
Use ↑ ↓ → ← to point to the form to be removed...        Form      1/1
then press ↵ to confirm its removal.
```

Moving Embedded Forms

The [Menu] Multi Tables Move command lets you move an embedded form from one area of a master form to another. For example, suppose after removing the embedded SALES-ORD form from the master form, you decide to move the PROJECTS form into the middle of the master form. To move the embedded form, issue the **[Menu]** Multi Tables Move command. After you issue the command, Paradox will present the prompt shown in Figure 4-67, which tells you to point to the embedded form you want to move. When you see this prompt, position the cursor anywhere in the embedded form, and press ↵. Next, Paradox will present the prompt shown in Figure 4-68, asking you to reposition the form. After you move the embedded form to the middle of the master form, press ↵. At this point, the screen will look like Figure 4-69.

Figure 4-67 The Multi Tables Move Prompt

```
Use ↑ ↓ → ← to point to the form to be repositioned...   Form      1/1
then press ↵ to select it...
```

Figure 4-68 The Repositioning Prompt

```
Now use ↑ ↓ → ← to move the form to its new location...   Form      1/1
then press ↵ to confirm the move.
```

Figure 4-69 Completing the Move

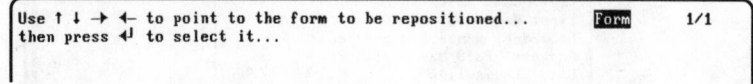

```
Designing new F3 form for Clients                        Form      1/1
<22,58>                      External Projects table with form F3, linked
┌──────────────────────────────────────────────────────────────┐
│                    ABC Company Inc. Clients                    │
│                                                                │
│               ┌────────────────────────────────┐              │
│               │        Client Information       │              │
│               │ Client Number: _____  │              │
│               │ Last Name: _____            │              │
│               │ First Name: _____           │              │
│               │ Soc. Sec. Number: _____     │              │
│               │ Address: _____       │              │
│               │ City: _____       │              │
│               │ State: __ Zip: _____             │              │
│               │ Phone: _____             │              │
│               └────────────────────────────────┘              │
│                                                                │
└──────────────────────────────────────────────────────────────┘
```

Defining Display-only Forms

As a rule, you can use multitable forms to view, edit, or perform data entry on your Paradox tables. However, sometimes you may want to design a form that allows a user to edit one table on the form but only view data in another table. You can use the [Menu] Multi Tables DisplayOnly command to make the master form or any embedded form on a multitable form display-only.

When you issue the [Menu] Multi Tables DisplayOnly command, Paradox will present a menu with two options: Master and Other. The Master command lets you specify the display status of the fields that appear on the master form. If you select the Master command, Paradox will present a Yes/No menu. If you choose Yes, Paradox will allow the master form to be used only for viewing data in the master table. If you choose No, Paradox will allow viewing, editing, and data entry with the master form. The display status of the master form has no effect on the display status of the individual embedded forms.

The Other command on the DisplayOnly menu lets you specify the display status for fields that appear on embedded forms. If you choose the Other command, Paradox will ask you to point to an embedded form and press ↵ to select that form. After you select a form, you will see a Yes/No menu. If you choose Yes, Paradox will allow the embedded form to be used only for viewing data in the master table. If you choose No, Paradox will allow viewing, editing, and data entry with the embedded form.

Multirecord Forms

Multirecord forms display several records from the same table at the same time. The records appear stacked on top of one another in the form, similar to the way Paradox stacks records in a table in the table view. Like the table view, multirecord forms let you see records as they are arranged sequentially in the table. However, there are some distinct differences between viewing records in the table view and viewing records with a multirecord form. While viewing a table with a multirecord form, you can't scroll horizontally off the screen as you can in the table view. All the fields that appear on a multirecord form must be placed within the confines of a single screen. In addition, multirecord forms cannot contain more than one page. However, fitting all of a table's fields on the same screen is no problem because you can stack fields from the same record on top of one another in a form. Another advantage that multirecord forms have over the regular table view is that you can place calculated fields on multirecord forms.

The real value of multirecord forms becomes apparent when you use one of them as an embedded form. A multitable form that contains an embedded multirecord form lets you view or edit several detail records linked to the current master record. We'll show you how to embed a multirecord form after we cover the basics of designing multirecord forms.

Creating a Multirecord Form

To design a multirecord form, you first lay out the format that you want to use to display each record on a form. The area that contains the literals and fields to be replicated for each record is called the multirecord region. After defining the multirecord region, you use the [Menu] Multi Records command to define the number of times that this area should be repeated on the form. For example, suppose that you have designed the form for the SALESORD table shown in Figure 4-70 and want to use this form to display three records simultaneously. This form includes all the regular fields from the SALESORD table, as well as a calculated field that computes the total price for each order. (The equation for this calculated field is *[Quantity]*[Price]*.) To repeat the record layout that you've defined on the form, issue the **[Menu] Multi Records Define** command. After you do this, Paradox will display the prompt shown in Figure 4-71.

Figure 4-70 A Custom Form

```
Designing new F4 form for Salesord                    Form      1/1
< 8,60>                                          Regular,Sales Person
  ┌─────────────────────────────────────────────────────────────┐
  │                  ABC Cmpany Inc. Sales Orders                 │
  │                                                               │
  │      Client Number: _____ Date: _____     │
  │      Product Number: _____ Product: _____     │
  │      Price: _____                              │
  │      X Quantity: _____    Sales                │
  │      = Total:    _____    Person: _____   │
  │                                                               │
  └─────────────────────────────────────────────────────────────┘
```

Figure 4-71 The Multi Records Define Prompt

```
Use ↑ ↓ → ←- to move to a corner of the region to define...  Form   1/1
then press ↵ to select it...
  ┌─────────────────────────────────────────────────────────────┐
  │                  ABC Cmpany Inc. Sales Orders                 │
  │                                                               │
  │      Client Number: _____ Date: _____     │
  │      Product Number: _____ Product: _____     │
  └─────────────────────────────────────────────────────────────┘
```

When you see this prompt, move to the *C* character at the beginning of the *Client Number:* literal and press ↵. Next, Paradox will prompt you to move to the diagonal corner of the multirecord region. As you move the cursor, the rectangular area that has the already-defined corner and the current cursor position as diagonal corners will appear in reverse video. Move the cursor to the last underline character in the Sales Person field, then press ↓. Including a blank line at the bottom of the multirecord region will force Paradox to place a blank line after each record on the form, making it easier to distinguish the individual records. At this point, your screen will look like Figure 4-72. Press ↵ to finish defining the multirecord region.

When you press ↵, Paradox will prompt you to use the ↓ and ↑ keys to add repeating rows to the multirecord region. Since you want the form to display three records, press ↓ twice to create two copies of the multirecord region under the original region. After you press ↵ to finish defining the multirecord region, your screen will look like Figure 4-73. Press **[Do-It!]** to save the form.

Figure 4-72 Defining the Multirecord Region

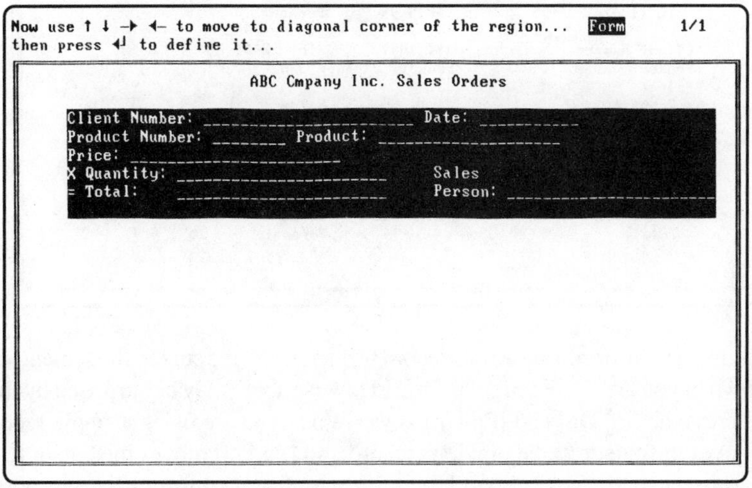

Figure 4-73 The Completed Form

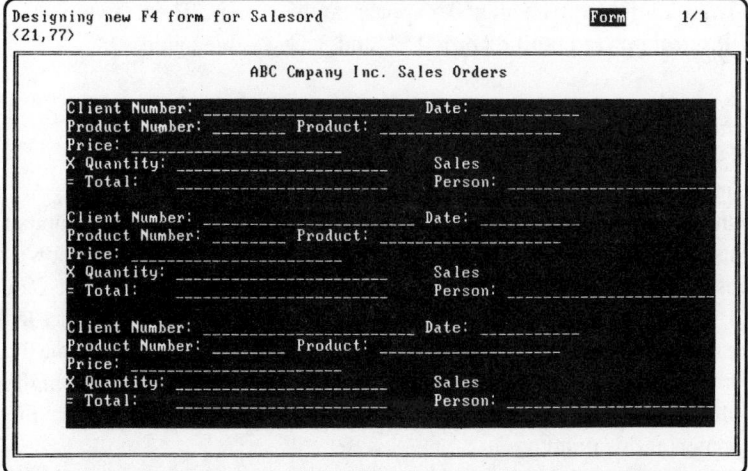

To use the form, first issue the **[Menu]** Modify Edit command and select the **SALESORD** table. With the SALESORD table on the Paradox workspace in Edit mode, issue the **[Menu]** Image **P**ickform command and select form **4**. After Paradox enters the form view, your screen will look like Figure 4-74.

Figure 4-74 Editing with a Multirecord Form

```
Editing Salesord table with form F4: Record 1 of 7              Edit  ═▼

                    ABC Cmpany Inc. Sales Orders
       Client Number:            1001   ◄Date:  2/01/88
       Product Number: 1      Product: Paradox 3.0
       Price:            399.99
       X Quantity:              1        Sales
       = Total:            399.99        Person:              1

       Client Number:            1001    Date:  2/01/88
       Product Number: 2      Product: Paradox 386
       Price:            599.99
       X Quantity:              1        Sales
       = Total:            599.99        Person:              1

       Client Number:            1001    Date:  2/01/88
       Product Number: 5      Product: Lotus 1-2-3
       Price:            495.00
       X Quantity:              1        Sales
       = Total:               495        Person:              1
```

While you are viewing or editing a multirecord form, most of the cursor-movement keys work as they do when you are using a regular form. However, you may be surprised by the results when you press the [Pg Dn] and [Pg Up] keys. When you are using a single-record form, [Pg Up] moves the cursor to the previous record and [Pg Dn] moves the cursor to the next record. However, when you are working with a multirecord form, these keys scroll the records vertically until only one record on the form remains on the screen. For example, if you press [Pg Dn] while editing records 1, 2, and 3 of the SALESORD table, Paradox will scroll downward until records 3, 4, and 5 appear on the screen. Then, if you press [Pg Up], Paradox will scroll upward until records 1, 2, and 3 are visible again.

Adjusting a Multirecord Region

After defining a multirecord region, you can use the [Menu] Multi Records Adjust command to change the material that is repeated in the multirecord region and the number of times that it repeats on a form. For example, after defining the multirecord region shown in Figure 4-74, suppose you decide that the records on the form are too close together. You want to include two, rather than three, records in the region and add two more blank lines to the space between the records. To make these adjustments to the multirecord region, issue the **[Menu]** Multi **R**ecords Adjust command. After you issue this command, Paradox will highlight your original multirecord region, asking you to adjust the current diagonal corner. Figure 4-75 shows the screen at this point.

Figure 4-75 The Adjust Prompt

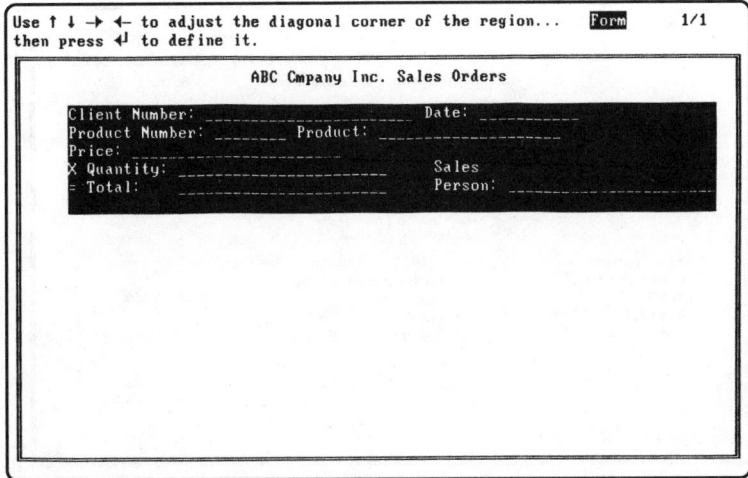

Since you want to add two more blank lines to the region, press ↓ twice, then press ↵. Next, Paradox will ask you to specify the number of repeating rows in the multirecord region. Press ↓ once to add a single repeating row to the region. At this point, the screen will look like Figure 4-76. Press ↵ to save the newly defined region, then press **[Do-It!]** to save the report. Figure 4-77 on the following page shows what the screen will look like if you edit the SALESORD table with the modified multirecord form.

Figure 4-76 The Adjusted Multirecord Region

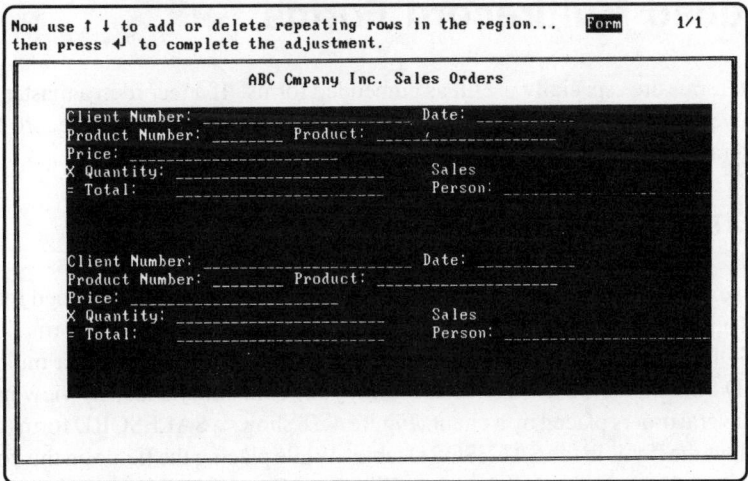

Figure 4-77 Editing with the Adjusted Form

```
Editing Salesord table with form F4: Record 1 of 7              Edit  =▼

                        ABC Cmpany Inc. Sales Orders

       Client Number:              1001     Date:  2/01/88
       Product Number: 1           Product: Paradox 3.0          ◄
       Price:              399.99
       X Quantity:              1          Sales
       = Total:            399.99          Person:                    1



       Client Number:              1001     Date:  2/01/88
       Product Number: 2           Product: Paradox 386
       Price:              599.99
       X Quantity:              1          Sales
       = Total:            599.99          Person:                    1
```

Deleting a Multirecord Region

You can use the [Menu] Multi Records Remove command to delete a multirecord region from
a form. For example, to remove the repeated records from the form in Figure 4-73, issue the
[Menu] Multi Records Remove command. After you issue this command, Paradox will
remove the multirecord region from the form, and the screen will look like Figure 4-70 again.

Embedded Multirecord Forms

Multirecord forms are especially useful as embedded forms. If a record in a master table is
linked to several records in a detail table, you can use an embedded multirecord form to
display several of the linked records at the same time.

An Example

Let's use an example to illustrate how well multirecord forms work as embedded forms. In
Figure 4-58 on page 153, we used a single-record embedded form to display information from
the SALESORD table on a form for the CLIENTS table. By embedding a multirecord
SALESORD form on the CLIENTS master form, you could simultaneously view information about several orders placed by a client. Figure 4-78 shows a SALESORD form (number
5) that displays the fields in the SALESORD table. While placing the fields on this form, we
adjusted the lengths of the Product Number, Price, and Quantity fields so that all the fields
would fit on a single line. Because all the fields fit on a single line, the literals that identify
the field need appear only once on the form, at the top of the column containing each field.
This columnar arrangement gives an appearance very similar to a table displayed in the table

view on the Paradox workspace. To make sure that the headings at the top of each column appear only once on the form, you should leave the headings out of the multirecord region when you define it.

Figure 4-78 A SALESORD Form

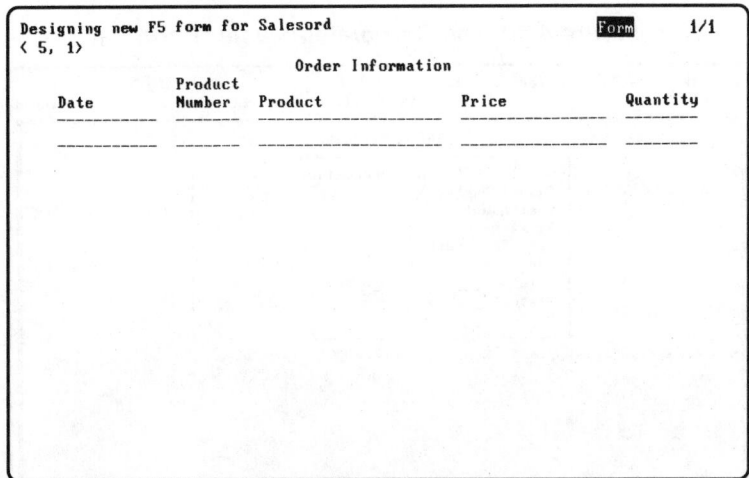

To define the multirecord region, issue the **[Menu] M**ulti **R**ecords **D**efine command. When Paradox prompts you to define a corner of the multirecord region, move the cursor to the first character in the Date field and press ↵. Then, when Paradox prompts you to move to the diagonal corner of the region, move the cursor to the last character in the Quantity field and press ↵. When Paradox prompts you to define the number of rows in the multirecord region, press ↓ four times to add four rows and press ↵. At this point, the screen should look like Figure 4-79. As you can see, the repeating rows in the multirecord region contain fields, but no literals. To finish defining the multirecord region, press ↵. Then, press **[Do-It!]** to save the form.

Figure 4-79   The Completed Form

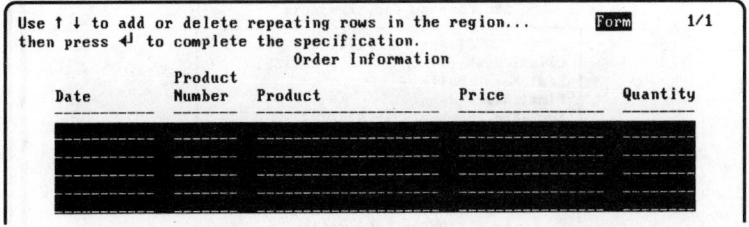

Figure 4-80 shows form 6 for the CLIENTS table, which includes form 5 for SALESORD as an embedded form. To create this form, first use the **[Menu] F**orms **D**esign command to create a new blank form. Next, place the CLIENTS fields, literals describing those fields, and the two borders on the form. To embed the multirecord form for SALESORD on the

CLIENTS form, issue the [**Menu**] **M**ulti **T**ables **L**inked command, type **SALESORD**, press
↵, and select form number **5**. Next, select Client Number as the field to match the Client
Number field in the SALESORD table. When Paradox prompts you to place the embedded
form, position the reverse video outline of the embedded form under the Client Information
area and press ↵.

Figure 4-80 The Completed Master Form

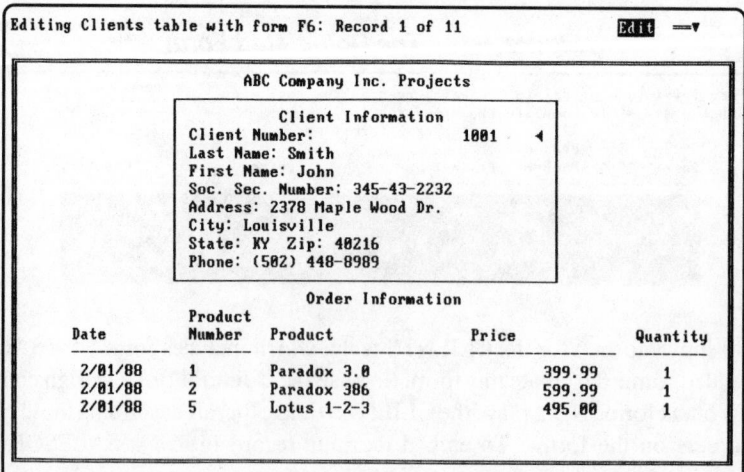

When you use the master form to edit the CLIENTS and SALESORD tables, your screen will
look like Figure 4-81 As you can see, the embedded form displays all the fields in the detail
table that are linked to the current record in the master table. If there are too many linked
records in the detail table to fit on the screen at one time, you can scroll through the linked
records, displaying five records at a time.

Figure 4-81 Editing with the Master Form

```
Editing Clients table with form F6: Record 1 of 11            Edit  —▼

┌─────────────────────────────────────────────────────────────────────┐
│                      ABC Company Inc. Projects                        │
│               ┌──────────────────────────────────────┐               │
│               │            Client Information         │               │
│               │  Client Number:           1001    ◄   │               │
│               │  Last Name: Smith                     │               │
│               │  First Name: John                     │               │
│               │  Soc. Sec. Number: 345-43-2232        │               │
│               │  Address: 2378 Maple Wood Dr.         │               │
│               │  City: Louisville                     │               │
│               │  State: KY  Zip: 40216                │               │
│               │  Phone: (502) 448-8989                │               │
│               └──────────────────────────────────────┘               │
│                                                                       │
│                          Order Information                            │
│                    Product                                            │
│          Date      Number   Product           Price       Quantity    │
│        --------   -------  ---------------    -------      --------    │
│        2/01/88      1      Paradox 3.0         399.99         1        │
│        2/01/88      2      Paradox 386         599.99         1        │
│        2/01/88      5      Lotus 1-2-3         495.00         1        │
└─────────────────────────────────────────────────────────────────────┘
```

A Note

While multirecord forms are often ideal as embedded forms, you cannot use a multirecord form as a master form. The only way to display multiple records from the same table on a multitable form is to display those records on an embedded form.

Setting the Style for Your Form

The [Menu] Style command allows you to control whether field names are displayed on a form, whether multirecord regions are highlighted, and how text and borders are displayed on the screen. For example, you can use this command to display the text in your forms in high intensity or reverse video, or to change the colors of text and borders.

When you issue the [Menu] Style command, Paradox will display the Style menu shown in Figure 4-82. As you can see, this menu has several commands for setting the style of your form. We will discuss each of these commands in the sections that follow.

Figure 4-82   The Style Menu

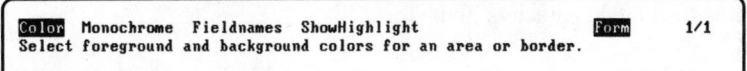

```
Color  Monochrome  Fieldnames  ShowHighlight              Form     1/1
Select foreground and background colors for an area or border.
```

Displaying Field Names

When you place a field on the forms design screen, the field name is not automatically shown. For example, Figure 4-83 shows a sample form without field names. To display the field names on the form, issue the [Menu] Style Fieldnames command. When you do, Paradox will display a menu that offers two options: Show and Hide. The Show command displays field names on the screen. The Hide command, the default, hides the field names. When you issue the Hide command, your screen will not change—it will look like Figure 4-83.

Figure 4-83   A Sample Form

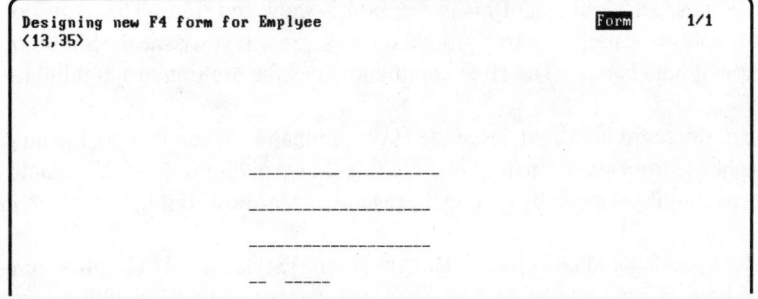

```
Designing new F4 form for Emplyee                         Form     1/1
<13,35>
```

To bring the field names into view, issue the Show command. When you do this, the underline characters that represent the fields on the form will be partially or completely replaced by the names of the fields they represent, as shown in Figure 4-84.

Figure 4-84 Displaying the Field Names

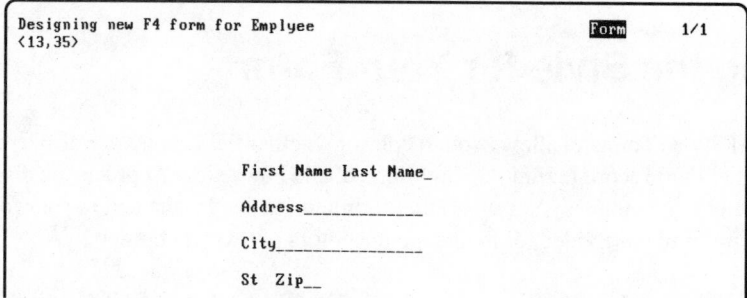

```
Designing new F4 form for Emplyee                        Form      1/1
<13,35>




                    First Name Last Name_

                    Address_____

                    City_____

                    St  Zip__
```

It is important to understand that the [Menu] Style Fieldnames Show command causes the field names to be displayed only when you are working in the Form Editor. The field names will not be displayed when you use this form to enter, edit, or view records. The only way to have the field names displayed when you are viewing records with the form is to include the field names as literal characters in the form.

The Show command displays the names of all the fields on the form. However, even when you are not using this feature, you can display the names of the fields one at a time. To do this, move the cursor so that it is positioned on the series of underlines representing a field. When you do this, the name of that field will appear in the upper-right corner of the screen. By moving the cursor to every field, you can view all the field names.

Hiding the Multirecord Highlight

As we demonstrated earlier in the section on multirecord forms, the Form Editor automatically highlights a multirecord region in reverse video. For example, Figure 4-85 shows a sample form that contains a multirecord region. To turn off the highlight that distinguishes the multirecord region, issue the [Menu] Style ShowHighlight command. When you do, Paradox will display a menu that offers two options: Show and Hide. The Show command, the default, displays the multirecord highlight on the screen. If you issue the Show command, your screen will not change. The Hide command hides the multirecord highlight.

To hide the multirecord highlight, issue the Hide command. When you do, the multirecord region will change from reverse to normal video, as shown in Figure 4-86. You could display the multirecord highlight again by issuing the [Menu] Style ShowHighlight Show command.

Like the [Menu] Style Fieldnames command, the [Menu] Style ShowHighlight command has no effect on how a form looks when you when you view or edit a table with the form. The multirecord highlight appears only while you are viewing the form in the Form Editor.

Figure 4-85   A Multirecord Form

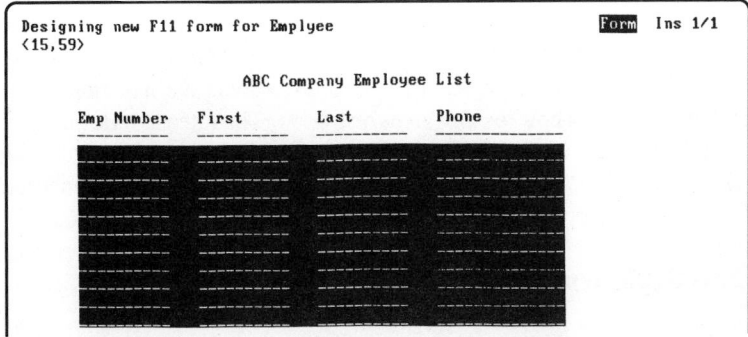

```
Designing new F11 form for Emplyee                    Form  Ins 1/1
<15,59>

                       ABC Company Employee List

     Emp Number    First        Last         Phone
     _____  _____  _____  _____
```

Figure 4-86   Hiding the Multirecord Highlight

```
Designing new F11 form for Emplyee                    Form  Ins 1/1
<15,59>

                       ABC Company Employee List

     Emp Number    First        Last         Phone
     _____  _____  _____  _____
     _____  _____  _____  _____
     _____  _____  _____  _____
     _____  _____  _____  _____
     _____  _____  _____  _____
     _____  _____  _____  _____
     _____  _____  _____  _____
     _____  _____  _____  _____
     _____  _____  _____  _____
     _____  _____  _____  _____
     _____  _____  _____  _____
```

Setting Styles and Colors

The Color and Monochrome options on the Style menu let you control the display of literal text and borders in your forms. If you have a color monitor, the Color option lets you set character and background colors for areas and borders on the form. The Monochrome option lets you set style attributes such as blinking, reverse , and intense video for areas and borders.

Setting Monochrome Styles

If you select the Monochrome command from the Style menu, Paradox will present a menu with two options: Area and Border. The Area command lets you select a style for a rectangular area on the form. This rectangular area can include all or part of a border. The Border command lets you select a style for a border without affecting any of the literal text within the border.

Paradox offers six display styles: Normal, Blink, Non-Blink, Intense, Reverse, and Intense-Reverse. Except for Blink, these styles are visible only on a monochrome monitor. The Normal style is the style that Paradox usually uses to display text and borders. The Blink style makes text and borders blink on and off. The Non-Blink style lets you turn off the Blink style without losing a color pattern that you have assigned to an area. We'll demonstrate the Non-Blink style when we explain how to color areas on a form. The Intense style displays text and borders in high intensity. The Reverse style displays text and borders in reverse video, and the Intense-Reverse style combines the Intense and Reverse styles. The monochrome styles affect all fields, text, and borders in the area that you define.

Setting the Style for an Area

Suppose you are designing the form shown in Figure 4-87, and you want to display the title at the top of the form in reverse video. First, issue the **[Menu]** Style Monochrome Area command. After you issue the command, Paradox will present a prompt at the top of the screen asking you to move the cursor to one corner of the area for which you want to define a style. When you see this prompt, move to the *A* character at the beginning of the *ABC Company Employee Address Form* literal and press ↵. Next, Paradox will prompt you to move to the diagonal corner of the area. When you see this prompt, move to the *m* character at the end of the literal and press ↵ again.

Figure 4-87 A Sample Form

```
Designing new F9 form for Emplyee                        Form   Ins 1/1
< 4,20>
┌────────────────────────────────────────────────────────────────────┐
│                                                                      │
│                                                                      │
│              ABC Company Employee Address Form                       │
│                                                                      │
│                                                                      │
│         Name: _____  _____                                 │
│                                                                      │
│         Address: _____                               │
│                                                                      │
│         City: _____                                    │
│                                                                      │
│         State: __  Zip: _____                                        │
│                                                                      │
│                                                                      │
│                                                                      │
│                                                                      │
│                                                                      │
└────────────────────────────────────────────────────────────────────┘
```

At this point, your screen will look like Figure 4-88. As you can see, the prompt at the top of the screen tells you to use the → and ← keys to select a style. The current style, *Normal*, appears in the upper-right corner of the screen. To change the style to Reverse, press → four times. Each time you press →, the style of the form title will change on the screen to match the current style selection. After you select the Reverse style, your screen will look like Figure 4-89. When you've selected the desired style, press ↵ to lock in your selection.

Figure 4-88 Changing the Style

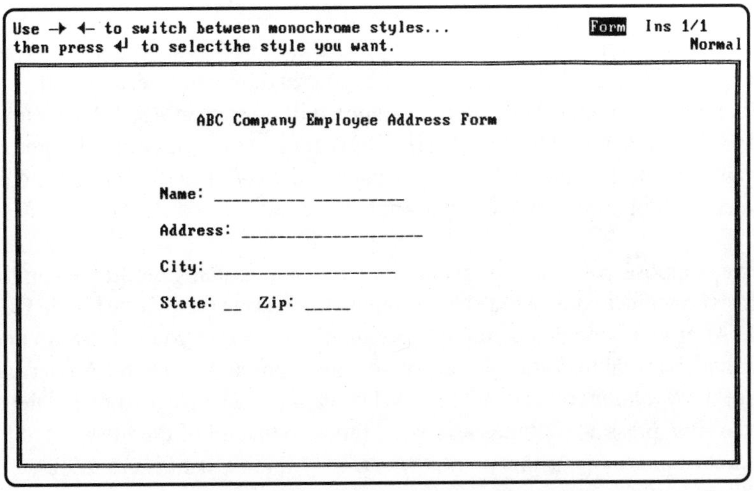

```
Use → ← to switch between monochrome styles...        Form  Ins 1/1
then press ↵ to selectthe style you want.                   Normal
┌────────────────────────────────────────────────────────┐
│                                                          │
│              ABC Company Employee Address Form           │
│                                                          │
│                                                          │
│          Name: _____ _____                       │
│                                                          │
│          Address: _____                     │
│                                                          │
│          City: _____                        │
│                                                          │
│          State: __  Zip: _____                           │
│                                                          │
│                                                          │
│                                                          │
│                                                          │
│                                                          │
└────────────────────────────────────────────────────────┘
```

Figure 4-89 The Reverse Style

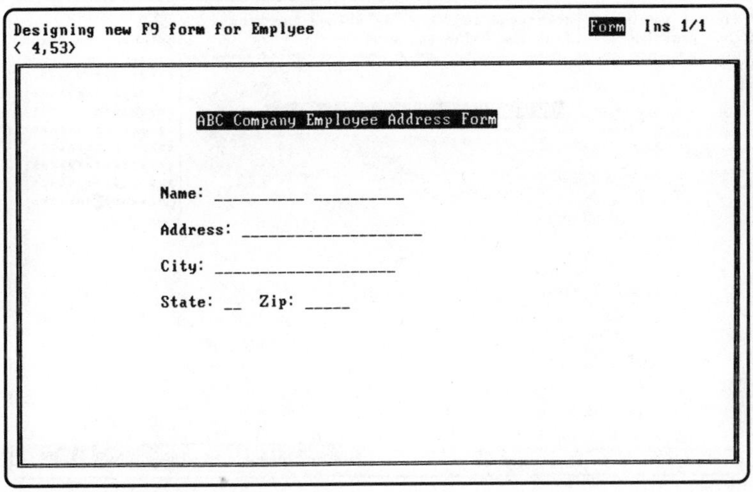

```
Designing new F9 form for Emplyee                     Form  Ins 1/1
< 4,53>
┌────────────────────────────────────────────────────────┐
│                                                          │
│              ABC Company Employee Address Form           │
│                                                          │
│          Name: _____ _____                       │
│                                                          │
│          Address: _____                     │
│                                                          │
│          City: _____                        │
│                                                          │
│          State: __  Zip: _____                           │
│                                                          │
│                                                          │
│                                                          │
└────────────────────────────────────────────────────────┘
```

Setting the Style for a Border

Now, let's change the style of the border around the form from Normal to Intense. First, issue the **[Menu]** Style Monochrome Border command. After you issue this command, Paradox will ask you to move to one corner of the border. When you see this prompt, use the cursor-movement keys to move to the upper-left corner of the border and press ↵. Next, Paradox will ask you to move to the diagonal corner of the border. Press ↑ and ← to move to the edge of the border at the lower-right corner of the screen and press ↵. Then, press → until the border changes to the Intense style and press ↵ again. After you finish, Paradox will display the border around the form in intense video.

Coloring Forms

If you use a color monitor, you can set foreground and background colors for areas and borders on a form in much the same manner that you set monochrome styles. If you choose the Color command from the Style menu, Paradox will present an Area/Border menu to let you specify whether you want to color an area or a border. After you define the area or border that you want to color, Paradox will present a palette displaying all the available colors, and you can select the color combination you want to use.

For example, suppose you want to display the area that contains the literals and fields in Figure 4-89 with white text on a blue background. First, issue the **[Menu] S**tyle **C**olor **A**rea command. After you issue this command, Paradox will prompt you to move to one corner of the area that you want to color. When you see this prompt, move to the *N* character at the beginning of the *Name:* literal and press ↵. When Paradox asks you to move to the diagonal corner of the area, press ↓ six times and → 30 times so that all of the literals and fields are highlighted, then press ↵. At this point, the screen will look like Figure 4-90.

Figure 4-90 Defining the Area to Color

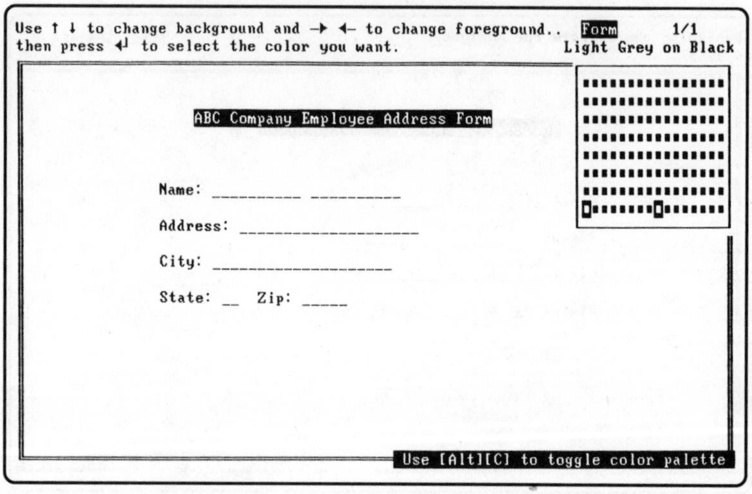

As you can see, the prompt at the top of the screen tells you to use the ↑ and ↓ keys to change the background color and the → and ← keys to change the foreground color. The current color (your default color for forms) appears in the upper-right corner of the screen above the color palette. In this case, our default color for forms is light grey on black.

The color palette includes every possible combination of eight background colors and 16 foreground colors. Each row on the palette displays the combinations for a different background color. Paradox distinguishes the current color combination by making the foreground color for that combination blink on and off. As you can see by the message at the bottom of the screen, you can toggle the palette display on and off by pressing [Alt]-[C]. You can select colors without the palette, but it is a handy tool because it lets you see which keys you need to press to change to a particular color combination.

To select the white foreground on blue background combination, use the ↑ and ↓ keys to move to the row that shows the blue background combinations. Then, use → and ← to move to the square that includes a white foreground. As you move through the different color combinations, the highlighted area on the form will change to display each color combination that you pass over. After moving to the white foreground and blue background selection, press ← to select that color combination. After you press ←, the area around the fields will be displayed in a white-on-blue color scheme.

You can color the border around the form as easily as you colored the area around the fields. Just issue the **[Menu]** Style Color **B**order command, point to two of the diagonal corners of the border, and then select a color combination.

Suppressing the Color Palette Display

If you find it annoying that the color palette covers part of the screen every time you color an area or border, you can use the Custom Configuration Program (CCP) to make Paradox suppress the palette display. To play the CCP, issue the **[Menu]** Scripts **P**lay command from the Main mode, type **\paradox3\custom** at the *Script:* prompt, and press ←. If the CCP asks you if you are using a black-and-white monitor, answer appropriately (*Y* or *N*). When you see the CCP menu, issue the **V**ideo FormPalette command. After you issue this command, Paradox will present a menu with two selections: On and Off. The Off selection tells Paradox not to display the color palette every time you issue the [Menu] Style Color command. On is the default setting. If you don't want Paradox to display the palette automatically, point to the **O**ff selection and press ←. Then, select the **R**eturn command from the next menu to move back to the CCP main menu. When you see the main menu, issue the **D**O_IT! command, then choose either **N**etwork or **H**ardDisk, depending on the type of system you are using. After you make this selection, the CCP will exit Paradox and return to DOS. The next time you load Paradox, the palette won't automatically appear when you color an area or border. However, you will still be able to see the color palette by pressing [Alt]-[C].

Using Monochrome Styles and Colors Together

Most of the time, placing a monochrome style over a colored area of a form simply changes the color scheme for the area. For example, suppose you used the [Menu] Style Monochrome Area command to change the white-on-blue area that we created in our last example to reverse video. Assuming that you are using Paradox's default color setting, the area would appear in a black-on-cyan color scheme after you changed the style. Paradox changes the colors because it uses different color combinations to depict monochrome styles on a color monitor. The colors that Paradox associates with different monochrome styles depend on the color settings that you have installed with the CCP. If you later used the form on a computer with a monochrome monitor, the area that you set for Reverse style would appear in reverse video.

The one exception to this rule is the Blink monochrome style. If you apply the Blink style to a colored area, then the text in the area will actually blink on and off. If you apply the Blink style to a colored border, the border will blink on and off. For example, suppose you want to make the text blink in the white-on-blue area of our example form. First, issue the **[Menu]** Style Monochrome command. When Paradox asks you to specify a corner of the area that you want to style, move to the upper-left corner of the white-on-blue area and press ↵. Then, move to the lower-right corner of the white-on-blue area and press ↵ again. When Paradox asks you to select a style, press → or ← until Blink is the selected style and the text in the highlighted area begins blinking. Then, press ↵. After you apply the Blink style, the area will display white, flashing text on a blue background. (If you want to make a colored area blink, make sure that you color the area first, then apply the Blink style. If you apply the Blink style first, then color the area, the new color will turn off the Blink style.)

To make a colored area stop blinking, apply the Non-Blink style to that area. For example, to turn off the Blink style in the white-on-blue area, issue the **[Menu]** Style Monochrome command and specify the diagonal corners of the area. When Paradox asks you to select a style, press → or ← until the style indicator in the upper-right corner of the screen says *Non-Blink*. After you press ↵ to select the Non-Blink style, the text in the area will stop blinking, but the white-on-blue color scheme will remain intact.

Changing Forms

After you have designed and saved a form, you can make changes to it by issuing the **[Menu]** Forms Change command. After you issue this command, Paradox will prompt you to specify the name of the table that is associated with the form you want to change. For example, to change a form that is associated with the EMPLYEE table, you would issue the **[Menu]** Forms Change command, type **EMPLYEE**, and press ↵.

Next, Paradox will display the Form Number menu. You should select the number of the form you want to change. Next, Paradox will display the form's description and allow you to change it. To change the description, you can press [Backspace] to erase it, then type a new one, or use [Field View] ([Alt]-[F5]) to edit it. To retain the current description, press ↵.

After you specify the description, Paradox will display the form on the screen. At this point, making changes in the form is exactly like designing a new form. You can erase, place, and move fields; add pages; design borders; and select different styles. After you have made the changes you want, you can press **[Do-It!]** or issue the **[Menu]** DO-IT! command to save the form and return to the main workspace. If you don't want to save your changes, issue the **[Menu]** Cancel Yes command.

Copying Forms

Designing forms can be a difficult and time-consuming task. Fortunately, you don't have to begin each new form from scratch. If you have already created a form that is similar to the new form you want to create, you can use the [Menu] Tools Copy Form SameTable command to make a copy of that form, then use the copy as the basis for your new form. If you want to use a form that you designed for one table as the basis for a form for another table that has the same structure, you can use the [Menu] Tools Copy Form DifferentTable command to copy the form between the two tables.

For example, suppose you designed the form shown in Figure 4-89 for the EMPLYEE table. (This is form 9, if you are following the examples.) Now, suppose you need a slightly different form. To create the second form, issue the **[Menu]** **T**ools **C**opy Form SameTable command. When Paradox prompts you to enter the name of the table with the form to be copied, type **EMPLYEE**, and press ↵. When Paradox displays the form numbers associated with EMPLYEE, select form number **9**.

Next, Paradox will prompt you to enter a form number for the copy. You can select any form number except the one being copied. For this example, select **8**. The message *Copying form F9 for Emplyee to form F8...* will appear at the bottom of the screen. When the copying process is complete, Paradox will return to the workspace. Now, you can issue the **[Menu]** **F**orms **C**hange command to edit the copied form.

Now, suppose you want to use form 9 for the EMPLYEE table to edit another table called OLDEMP. In order to do this, both tables must have the same structure. To make the copy, issue the **[Menu]** **T**ools **C**opy Form DifferentTable command. When Paradox asks you for the name of the table with the form to be copied, type **EMPLYEE**, and press ↵. When Paradox displays the form numbers associated with EMPLYEE, select form number **9**.

Next, Paradox will ask you for the name of the table to which you want to copy the form. At this prompt, type **OLDEMP**, and press ↵. When Paradox asks you to enter a form number for the copy, you can select any number. For this example, select form **1**. The message *Copying F9 form for Emplyee to F1 form for Oldemp...* will appear at the bottom of the screen, and Paradox will return to the workspace when the copying process is complete.

Whether you are copying a form within the family of the same table or from one table to another, if you select a form number for the copy that already has a form assigned to it, Paradox will prompt you to confirm your choice by presenting a Cancel/Replace menu. If you issue the Cancel command, Paradox will return to the Form Number menu so that you can select a different form number for the copy. If you issue the Replace command, Paradox will replace the existing form with the copy.

Deleting Forms

You can delete a form with the [Menu] Tools Delete Form command. For example, suppose you have a form for the EMPLYEE table that you no longer need. To delete the form, issue the **[Menu]** **T**ools **D**elete Form command. After you issue this command, Paradox will prompt you to enter the name of the table associated with the form you want to delete. When you see this prompt, type **EMPLYEE**, and press ↵. Paradox then will display the forms (by form number) associated with the table and will prompt you to select the one to be deleted.

You can now enter the number of the form you want to delete. For example, to delete form 1, select number **1**. As Paradox deletes the form, the message *Deleting F1 form for Emplyee...* will appear at the bottom of the screen. When the deletion is complete, Paradox will return to the main workspace.

You should exercise caution when you delete forms. Paradox does not present a Cancel/OK menu when it deletes forms. Once you specify the number of the form you want to delete, the form is irretrievable.

Changing Form Names

You can change the name (number) of a form by issuing the [Menu] Tools Rename Form command. For example, suppose you design a form for the EMPLYEE table and store it under the name 4. Then, suppose you decide to rename it F, making it the default form.

To do this, issue the **[Menu] T**ools **R**ename **F**orm command. Then, Paradox will prompt you to enter the name of the table associated with the form you want to rename. When you see this prompt, type **EMPLYEE**, and press ↵. Next, Paradox will display the form numbers associated with the table and prompt you to select the one to be renamed. You now should select form **4**. After you select the form to be renamed, Paradox will prompt you to assign a new name (number) to the form. When you see this prompt, type **F**.

If the number you select as the new name for the form does not already have a form stored under it, Paradox will simply rename the form. Since F already has a form assigned to it, however, Paradox will display a Cancel/Replace menu. To replace the current form F with the form whose name you are changing, select **R**eplace. After you do this, the message *Renaming F4 form for Emplyee to F...* will appear at the bottom of the screen. After a moment, Paradox will return to the main workspace.

If you do not want to replace the current default form, you can choose Cancel from the Cancel/Replace menu. When you do this, Paradox will return to the previous prompt so that you can select another number.

Conclusion

In this chapter, we showed you how to design and use forms. We began with a discussion of the default form, explaining how to enter and edit data. Then, we showed you how to design custom forms, including multitable and multirecord forms. Next, we covered the various options in the Forms menu. Finally, we showed you how to manage forms.

Chapter 5

Managing Tables

In Chapters 2, 3, and 4, we showed you how to create tables and enter data into tables. We also showed you how to edit the information in your tables, create validity checks, and change the appearance of table images on the screen.

In this chapter, we'll show you how to use several commands that affect tables as a whole. We'll begin with the [Menu] Tools commands, which allow you to rename, copy, erase, and empty tables and other objects. We'll also cover the ToDOS command, which lets you exit from Paradox to DOS, use DOS programs, then return to Paradox in the exact spot from which you left. Finally, we'll cover the [Menu] Modify Restructure command, which enables you to change the structure of your Paradox tables.

The Tools Menu

When you issue the [Menu] Tools command, Paradox will display the Tools menu shown in Figure 5-1 on the next page. This menu contains a number of useful "utility" commands, which you can use to perform certain housekeeping chores, such as renaming, copying, and emptying tables. In this chapter, we'll look at the Rename, Copy, Delete, Info, and More options. We'll cover the QuerySpeedup command in Chapter 7, the Net command in Chapter 17, and the ExportImport command in Appendix A1.

If you choose the More command from the Tools menu, Paradox will display the submenu shown in Figure 5-2 on the following page. We will discuss the Add, MultiAdd, FormAdd, and Subtract commands in detail in Chapter 9. We will limit our discussion here to the Empty, Protect, Directory, and ToDOS commands.

Many of the commands on the Tools menu offer options that allow you to operate on objects other than tables. For instance, the Copy command offers options that allow you to copy forms, scripts, and reports, as well as tables. We'll discuss how to use these commands with objects other than tables as we cover the various types of objects throughout this book.

Figure 5-1 The Tools Menu

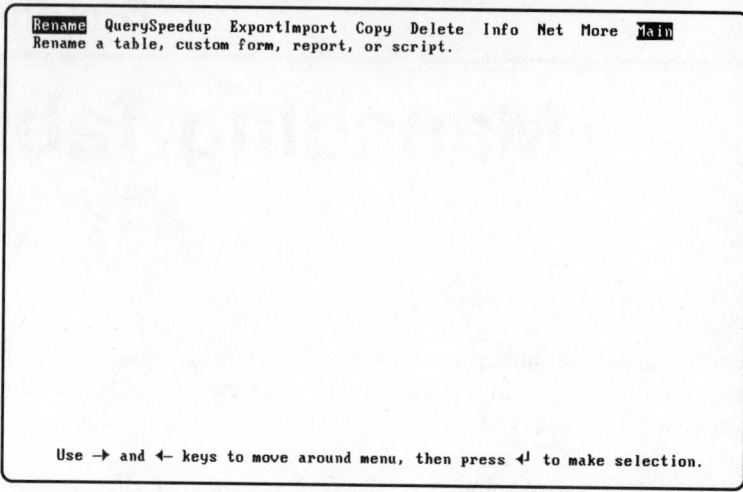

```
Rename QuerySpeedup ExportImport Copy Delete Info Net More Main
Rename a table, custom form, report, or script.
```

```
Use → and ← keys to move around menu, then press ↵ to make selection.
```

Figure 5-2 The Tools More Menu

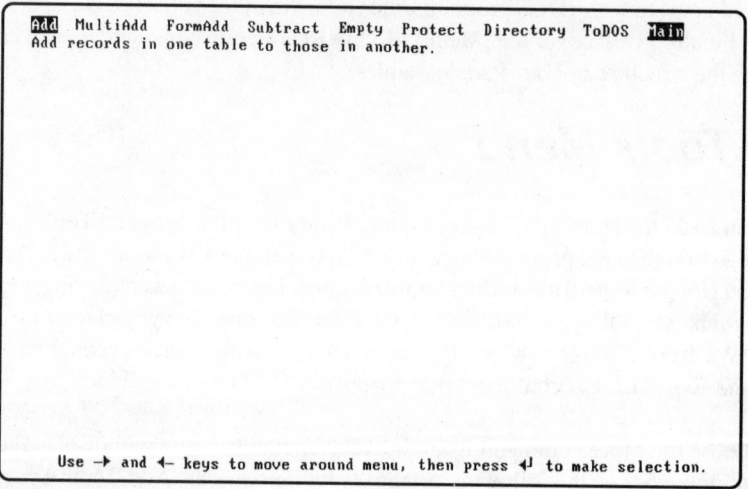

```
Add  MultiAdd  FormAdd  Subtract  Empty  Protect  Directory  ToDOS  Main
Add records in one table to those in another.
```

```
Use → and ← keys to move around menu, then press ↵ to make selection.
```

Renaming Tables

The [Menu] Tools Rename command can be used to rename Paradox tables, forms, reports, and scripts. When you issue this command, Paradox will display the menu shown in Figure 5-3, which lists the objects you can rename. To rename a table, choose the Table option from this menu, then specify the name of the table you want to rename and the new name for the table. When you press ↵, Paradox will rename the table as you have instructed.

Figure 5-3 The Tools Rename Menu

```
Table Form Report Script                           Main
Rename a table and its family of forms, reports, and indexes.
```

You will probably use the [Menu] Tools Rename Table command frequently to rename and save temporary tables, like the ANSWER table (discussed in Chapter 7) or the KEYVIOL table (covered in Chapter 3). Those chapters contain more examples of this command.

An Example

Suppose you want to change the name of the table TASKS to JOBS. To begin, issue the **[Menu]** Tools **R**ename command. Since you want to rename a table, you should choose **T**able when Paradox presents the menu in Figure 5-3. Next, Paradox will prompt you to enter the current name of the table you want to rename. At this point, type **TASKS** and press ↵. Alternatively, you can press ↵ to see a list of the tables in the current directory and select the name from this list. Once you've specified the name of the table you want to rename, Paradox will prompt you to enter the new name for the table. When you see this prompt, you should type in the new name for the table: **JOBS**. When you press ↵, Paradox will display the message *Renaming Tasks to Jobs...* in the lower-right corner of the screen.

Notes

When you rename a table, all of the objects associated with the table (reports, forms, indexes, validity checks, and image settings) will be transferred to the new name. This means that when you rename a table, you won't lose any of the forms or reports you created.

If you enter a new name that duplicates the name of an existing table, Paradox will prompt you for confirmation and display the message *TABLENAME table already exists* at the bottom of the screen. If you issue the Cancel command, Paradox will return to the previous prompt so that you can erase the entry with the [Backspace] key and enter another name for the table. If you choose Replace, Paradox will replace the existing table with the table you are renaming.

If you supply the name of a nonexistent table when Paradox asks you to specify the table you want to rename, Paradox will display the message *Cannot find TABLENAME table.*

Copying Tables

The [Menu] Tools Copy command allows you to make copies of existing Paradox objects, like tables, forms, and reports. When you issue the [Menu] Tools Copy command, Paradox will display the menu shown in Figure 5-4. This menu, which is similar to the one you see when you issue the Rename command, allows you to choose the type of object you want to copy. To copy a table, you should choose the Table option, then type the name of the table you want to copy, followed by the name under which you want to store the copy. When you press ↵, Paradox will copy the contents and structure of the table you specify and will create a new table with the name you selected. The original table will remain intact after the copy is completed.

Figure 5-4 The Copy Menu

```
Table  Form  Report  Script  JustFamily  Graph                    Main
Copy a table and its family of forms, reports, and indexes.
```

An Example

Suppose you want to make a copy of the table EMPLYEE. Also, suppose you want to save the copy under the name PEOPLE. To do this, issue the **[Menu] T**ools **C**opy command. When you see the menu in Figure 5-4, choose the **T**able option. Next, Paradox will prompt you to enter the name of the table you want to copy. You should type the name of the table to be copied, **EMPLYEE**, and press ↵. When you do this, Paradox will prompt you to enter a name for the copy of the table. You should type the new name, **PEOPLE**, and press ↵.

After you press ↵, Paradox will copy the structure and contents of the EMPLYEE table into a new table named PEOPLE. As it does this, the message *Copying from Emplyee to People* will appear at the bottom of the screen. After a few moments, Paradox will return you to the main workspace.

Notes

When you copy a table, all of the objects associated with the table will be copied with the data to the new table. This means that you won't need to recreate the forms or reports you have defined for the new table.

If the name you supply as the destination of the copy duplicates the name of an existing table, Paradox will prompt you for confirmation and will display the message *TABLENAME table already exists* at the bottom of the screen. If you issue the Cancel command, Paradox will return to the previous prompt so that you can erase the entry and enter another name for the table. If you choose Replace, Paradox will replace the existing table with the table you are copying.

If you specify the same table as the source and destination of the copy (in other words, if you ask Paradox to copy a table onto itself), Paradox will display the message *Can't copy a table to itself.* If you supply the name of a nonexistent table when Paradox asks you to specify the source for the copy, Paradox will display the message *TABLENAME table not found.*

Copying JustFamily

The [Menu] Tools Copy JustFamily command lets you copy a table's family of objects from one table to another without copying the table itself. When you issue this command, Paradox will prompt you to enter the name of the table whose family you want to copy, followed by the name of the destination table. Since copying JustFamily from one table to another will overwrite the existing family of the destination table, Paradox will prompt you to confirm the command. If you issue the Cancel command, Paradox will return to the previous prompt so that you can re-enter the name of the destination table. If you issue the Replace command, Paradox will copy the family to the destination table. The message *Copying family members from TABLENAME to TABLENAME...* will appear at the bottom of the screen. After a few moments, Paradox will return to the main workspace.

An Example

Suppose you have a table called CUSTOMER, which lists all of your customers, and you have spent considerable time creating various forms, reports, and validity checks for it. Now, suppose you have created a query that copies all of the information for customers who live in the state of Indiana to an ANSWER table, and you have used the [Menu] Tools Rename Table command to save the ANSWER table under the name INDIANA. (We'll discuss queries in detail in Chapters 7 and 8.)

As a result of these steps, you'll have a table, INDIANA, that contains just the records you requested from CUSTOMER. However, none of the "family members" of related objects from the CUSTOMER table will be associated with the new table. To copy the CUSTOMER table family to the new table INDIANA, issue the **[Menu]** Tools Copy JustFamily command. When Paradox prompts you for the table whose family you want to copy, type **CUSTOMER** and press ↵. At the next prompt, type the name of the destination table, **INDIANA**, and press ↵. When Paradox prompts you to confirm the command, you should select **R**eplace from the menu. After a few moments, all of the family members from the CUSTOMER table will be copied to the new table. Now, you can use the various objects you have created for both tables.

Notes

When you use the [Menu] Tools Copy JustFamily command, you must already have a destination table in place to receive the copied objects. If the destination table you specify does not exist, Paradox will display the message *Cannot find TABLENAME table*.

The source and destination tables must have identical structures. If they don't, Paradox will display the message *TABLENAME and TABLENAME have incompatible structures*.

Deleting Tables

The [Menu] Tools Delete command allows you to delete tables, reports, and other Paradox objects. When you issue the [Menu] Tools Delete command, Paradox will display the menu shown in Figure 5-5. This menu lists the various objects you can delete with this command. To delete a table and its related objects, choose the Table option. When you make this selection, Paradox will prompt you for the name of the table to delete.

Figure 5-5 The Tools Delete Menu

```
Table  Form  Report  Script  QuerySpeedup  KeepSet  ValCheck  Graph  Main
Delete a table and its family of forms, reports and indexes.
```

When you type the name and press ↵, Paradox will display a menu that prompts you to confirm the deletion. In addition, the message *If you select OK, TABLENAME and its family will be deleted* will appear at the bottom of the screen. If you choose Cancel, Paradox will return you to the previous prompt. If you want to delete a different table, you can erase the current entry and type a different name. If you want to cancel the command, just press [Esc] several times to return to the Main menu.

If you choose OK, Paradox will delete the table you have specified and its family. As it deletes the table, Paradox will display the message *Deleting TABLENAME and its associated family* at the bottom of the screen. After a few moments, Paradox will return to the main workspace.

For example, suppose you want to delete a table named JOBS and its family. To do this, issue the **[Menu] Tools Delete Table** command. When Paradox prompts you to enter a table name, type **JOBS**, and press ↵. Next, Paradox will prompt you for confirmation. If you've entered the correct table name, choose **OK**. When you do this, Paradox will delete the table and its family. If you have made a mistake (such as mistyping the table name or typing the name of the wrong table) or have decided you don't want to delete the table after all, choose **Cancel**.

Remember that the [Menu] Tools Delete command is very unforgiving. Once you have selected the OK option from the Confirmation menu, the table or other object you asked Paradox to delete is gone forever. Needless to say, you always should use this command with caution.

The [Menu] Tools Info Command

The [Menu] Tools Info command allows you to obtain some basic information about your database. For one thing, this command can be used to review the structure of a table. It can also be used to obtain an inventory of the tables, scripts, and other files in any directory, or a listing of the family of objects associated with a table.

When you issue the [Menu] Tools Info command, Paradox will display the menu shown in Figure 5-6. Notice that this menu offers five options: Structure, Inventory, Family, Who, and Lock. The Structure option allows you to review the structure of any table. The Inventory option allows you to obtain an inventory, or directory, of the tables, scripts, or files in a directory. The Family option allows you to obtain a listing of the objects associated with a particular table. The Who and Lock options apply to networks and will be discussed in Appendix A2.

Figure 5-6 The Info Menu

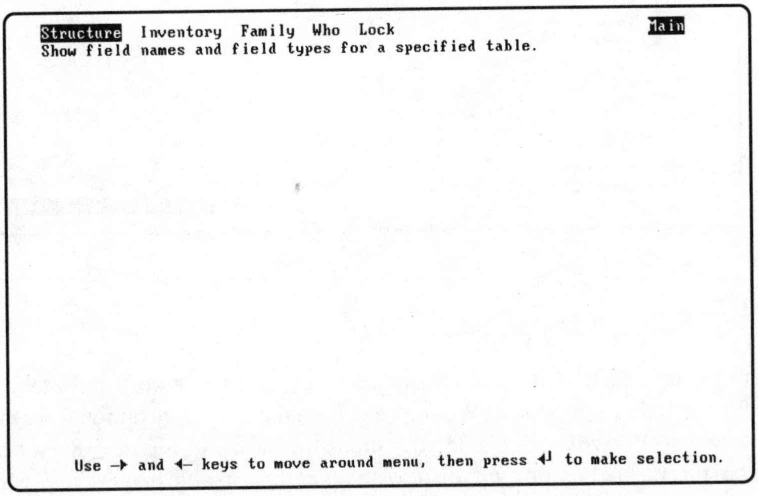

```
Structure  Inventory  Family  Who  Lock                          Main
Show field names and field types for a specified table.




                                  ↕




  Use → and ← keys to move around menu, then press ↵ to make selection.
```

Reviewing the Structure

Suppose you want to check the structure of the EMPLYEE table. To do this, issue the **[Menu]** Tools Info command and select the Structure option. Next, Paradox will prompt you to enter the name of the table whose structure you want to review. When you see this prompt, type **EMPLYEE** and press ↵. After a few moments, Paradox will display the structure of the table on the screen, as shown in Figure 5-7 on the following page.

Notice that the STRUCT table in Figure 5-7 is almost identical to the STRUCT table you use to create or restructure a table. (See Chapter 2 for more information on creating tables.) Unlike the Create and Modify Restructure commands, however, the [Menu] Tools Info Structure command only allows you to review the structure of the table; it won't let you make any changes to the table.

Since the STRUCT table is a temporary table, you may want to print a copy of it for future reference before you remove it from view. To do this, simply get your printer ready and, with the cursor on the table, press **[Instant Report]** ([Alt]-[F7]). (We'll cover reporting in detail in Chapters 10 and 11.)

Figure 5-7 The STRUCT Table

```
Viewing Struct table: Record 1 of 13                    Main
STRUCT            Field Name          Field Type
    1     Emp Number                  N
    2     Last Name                   A10
    3     First Name                  A10
    4     SS Number                   A11
    5     Address                     A28
    6     City                        A28
    7     State                       A2
    8     Zip                         A5
    9     Phone                       A14
   10     Date of Birth               D
   11     Date of Hire                D
   12     Exemptions                  N
   13     Salary                      $



                                      EMPLYEE table has 16 records
```

Inventory

The [Menu] Tools Info Inventory command lets you view an inventory of the tables, scripts, or other files stored in a directory. When you choose the Inventory option from the [Menu] Tools Info menu, Paradox will display the submenu shown in Figure 5-8. If you choose Tables from this menu, Paradox will display an inventory of table names only. Similarly, if you choose Scripts, Paradox will display a list of script files. Selecting Files tells Paradox to display a list of all files of all types.

Figure 5-8 The Inventory Menu

```
Tables  Scripts  Files                                  Main
List tables.
```

After you choose one of these three options, Paradox will prompt you to specify the name of the directory from which you want to obtain the inventory. When you see this prompt, you should type the name of the directory with which you want to work and press ↵. Alternatively, you could just press ↵ at the prompt to view an inventory of the files in the current directory. When you do either of these things, Paradox will present a temporary table named LIST, which contains the names and creation dates of all files of the specified type in the indicated directory.

An Example

Suppose you want to see a list of the tables that are stored in the current directory. To obtain this inventory, issue the [Menu] Tools Info Inventory command. When Paradox presents this menu, choose **Tables**. Next, when Paradox prompts you to specify the directory from which you want to obtain the inventory, press ↵ to select the current directory.

After you press ↵, Paradox will display a LIST table like the one shown in Figure 5-9. As you can see, the LIST table contains two fields: Name and Date. The Name field contains the names of the files of the type you've selected (in this case, tables) in the selected directory. The Date field contains the creation date of each file.

Figure 5-9 The LIST Table

```
Viewing List table: Record 1 of 34                                        Main
LIST                               Name                                  Date
     1  | Addhold                                                     |  9/15/88
     2  | Address                                                     |  7/21/88
     3  | Clients                                                     |  1/17/89
     4  | Customer                                                    |  8/02/88
     5  | Emp2                                                        |  9/14/88
     6  | Emphold                                                     | 11/14/88
     7  | Emplyee                                                     |  1/30/89
     8  | Emptmp                                                      |  9/15/88
     9  | Figback                                                     | 10/19/88
    10  | Figbak                                                      |  9/16/88
    11  | Figure                                                      |  9/16/88
    12  | Figure2                                                     |  8/18/88
    13  | Fixed                                                       |  6/20/88
    14  | Fonepros                                                    |  1/01/88
    15  | Holder                                                      | 11/16/88
    16  | Jjj                                                         |  9/14/88
    17  | Jobs                                                        |  9/15/88
    18  | List                                                        |  2/13/89
```

The Scripts Option

If you issue the [Menu] Tools Info Inventory Scripts command, Paradox will create a LIST table that contains the names of the script files (.SC files) in the specified directory. If you issue this command before creating any script files, Paradox will create an empty LIST table. After you have created scripts, use this command to obtain an inventory of those scripts.

The Files Option

The [Menu] Tools Info Inventory Files command produces a LIST table that contains the names of all the files in the specified directory, or just those files that conform to a pattern you define. After you issue this command, Paradox will display the prompt shown in Figure 5-10 on the next page. When you see this prompt, you should enter a directory and a DOS pattern, then press ↵. For example, if you want to obtain an inventory of the 1-2-3 worksheet files on the disk in drive A, type **a:*.wks**. If you want to obtain a list of the dBASE III files in the directory c:\dbase\data, type **c:\dbase\data*.dbf**.

After you supply the directory and DOS pattern, Paradox will create a LIST table that contains all the files in the selected directory that match the pattern you defined.

Figure 5-10 The Files Prompt

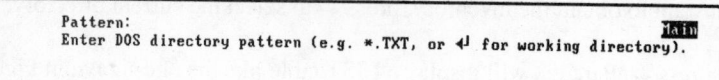

```
Pattern:                                                Main
Enter DOS directory pattern (e.g. *.TXT, or ↵ for working directory).
```

Notes

Like the STRUCT table, the LIST table you see when you issue the [Menu] Tools Info command is a temporary table. If you wish, you can rename it as a permanent table with the [Menu] Tools Rename command. If you want to obtain a printout of the inventory, you can press [Instant Report] ([Alt]-[F7]).

If there are no files of the specified type in the directory you designate, Paradox will create an empty LIST table. If you feel certain that there are files of the specified type in the directory, check to make sure that you selected the correct option (Tables, Scripts, or Files), that you specified the right directory, and, if you selected the Files option, that you defined the correct pattern.

The Family Option

The [Menu] Tools Info Family command allows you to view an inventory of the family of objects associated with a particular table. When you issue this command, Paradox will prompt you to enter the name of the table whose family you want to review. When you type a table name and press ↵, Paradox will display a temporary table named FAMILY, which displays the family associated with a Paradox table.

For example, suppose you want to review the family of objects associated with the table EMPLYEE. To review this list, issue the **[Menu]** Tools Info Family command, and type the name **EMPLYEE** when you see the *Table:* prompt. After a moment, Paradox will display the FAMILY table shown in Figure 5-11.

Figure 5-11 The EMPLYEE Family

```
Viewing Family table: Record 1 of 9                     Main
FAMILY┌──────────────────────Name──────────────────────┬────Date────┐
     1│ Emplyee                                         │  9/15/88   │
     2│ Form F                                          │  9/15/88   │
     3│ Form F1                                         │  9/15/88   │
     4│ Form F2                                         │  9/15/88   │
     5│ Form F3                                         │  9/15/88   │
     6│ Form F4                                         │  9/15/88   │
     7│ Form F7                                         │  1/29/89   │
     8│ Form F9                                         │  1/29/89   │
     9│ Form F11                                        │  9/15/88   │
```

Like the LIST table, the FAMILY table includes only two fields: Name and Date. As you can see, the FAMILY table for EMPLYEE contains the table itself and the forms we created in Chapter 4. If you did not delete the .SET and .VAL files created in Chapter 4, your FAMILY table will also show those files. Notice that the first record shows the name and creation date of the table whose family you are reviewing. The second record shows the name and creation date of the standard form for this table, F, and so on. As in this case, the name of the table you are investigating will always be the first record in the FAMILY table.

Also like the LIST table, the FAMILY table is a temporary table. If you wish, you can rename it as a permanent table with the [Menu] Tools Rename command. If you want to obtain a printout, you can press [Instant Report] ([Alt]-[F7]).

Emptying Tables

The [Menu] Tools More Empty command allows you to delete the records in a table without deleting the table itself. When you issue the [Menu] Tools More Empty command, Paradox will prompt you to enter the name of the table you want to empty. When you see this prompt, you should enter a table name and press ↵. Next, Paradox will display a Cancel/OK menu, which prompts you for confirmation. Also, the message *All records will be deleted from TABLENAME* will appear at the bottom of the screen.

If you issue the Cancel command at this point, Paradox will return to the previous prompt. You can either erase the current entry and type a different name or press [Esc] or [Ctrl]-[Break] to cancel the command. If you choose OK, Paradox will delete every record from the table, and the message *Emptying table...* will appear briefly in the lower-right corner of the screen. After a few moments, Paradox will return to the main workspace.

An Example

Suppose you have a table named STOCK that lists the stock numbers and descriptions of all the items in your inventory. Figure 5-12 shows this table on the screen. Now, suppose you have just reorganized your inventory and you want to change the SKU and Description entries in the table. You could edit the table and make the changes you want; however, you may find it easier to empty the table and start over.

Figure 5-12 The STOCK Table

```
Viewing Stock table: Record 1 of 5                              Main

STOCK======SKU========Description=======Price====Quantity=
      1 ║ 123A499  ║ Widget      ║       50.00 ║      10 ║
      2 ║ 234B066  ║ Wombat      ║       50.00 ║       4 ║
      3 ║ 311A473  ║ Woofer      ║      200.00 ║      17 ║
      4 ║ 345C111  ║ Zither      ║       75.00 ║     100 ║
      5 ║ 215W778  ║ Xylophone   ║      100.00 ║      54 ║
```

To empty the table, issue the **[Menu] Tools More Empty** command. When Paradox prompts you for the name of the table to be emptied, type **STOCK** and press ↵. Then, when Paradox presents the Confirmation menu, choose **OK**. Immediately, Paradox will display the *Emptying table...* message and will delete every record from STOCK.

Notes

Like the [Menu] Tools Delete command, the [Menu] Tools More Empty command can be very destructive. Once you choose OK to confirm the command, Paradox will immediately delete every record in the specified table. There is no way to restore the deleted records. Be careful!

However, there is one way to ensure against accidentally destroying a table with this command. You can use the [Menu] Tools Copy command to copy all of the records into a new table before you use the [Menu] Tools More Empty command. Then, if you discover that you've made an error, you can use the [Menu] Tools Add command to add the records back to the table that you just emptied.

Emptying a table has no effect on the objects associated with the table. Any object that existed before you emptied the table will exist after you empty the table.

Protecting Your Tables

The [Menu] Tools More Protect command allows you to establish a security system for the tables in your database. By using this command, you can assign one or more passwords to a table or script, or lock a table in its current form by write-protecting it. When you issue the [Menu] Tools More Protect command, Paradox presents the submenu shown in Figure 5-13.

Figure 5-13 The Protect Menu

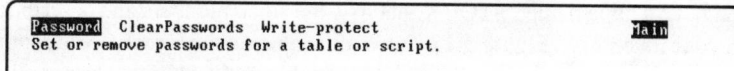

Password ClearPasswords Write-protect   Main
Set or remove passwords for a table or script.

Password Protection

The Password option allows you to assign a password to a table (or a script). After you have assigned a password to a table, anyone trying to view or edit the table will be prompted to supply the password. If the person does not supply the correct password, he or she will not be able to view or edit the table.

An Example

Suppose you want to assign the password *CESSNA* to the EMPLYEE table. To do this, issue the **[Menu] T**ools **M**ore **P**rotect command and choose the **P**assword option. When you do, Paradox will display the menu shown in Figure 5-14, which offers two options: Table and Script.

Figure 5-14 The Password Menu

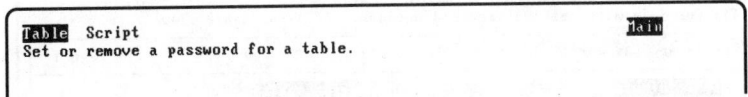

Since you want to protect a table, choose the **T**able option. Next, Paradox will prompt you to enter the name of the table you want to protect. You should type **EMPLYEE** and press ↵. Finally, Paradox will prompt you to specify the password you want to use to protect this table. You now should type the password **CESSNA** and press ↵. Notice that it does not appear on the screen as you type it. After you enter a password, Paradox will prompt you to confirm the password by typing it a second time. When you see this prompt, you should retype the password and press ↵. If you do not type the same password the second time, Paradox will display the error message *Password not same as originally entered.* If you see this message, type the correct password and press ↵. This step is included to prevent you from permanently locking a table with a mistyped password.

Auxiliary Passwords

When you have typed the same password twice, Paradox will accept your entry as the master password and then display the auxiliary password form shown in Figure 5-15 on the following page. In addition to the master password, you may define any number of auxiliary passwords, each with different access rights to the table. For example, you can assign to one user a password allowing only viewing of the table, and to another user a password permitting complete editing rights.

Unlike the master password, auxilary passwords appear on the screen as you type them at the *Auxiliary password:* prompt. Also, you have to type an auxiliary password only one time at the top of the Auxiliary Password form. You define the rights associated with an auxiliary password by filling in the three sections on the Auxiliary Password form. Each section controls a different type of rights for the protected table.

The Table Rights section lets you control the user's overall rights to data in the table. To select from the list of available rights displayed on the left side of this section, you press the first letter of the desired option. Selecting the All option gives a user unlimited ability to alter the table, including the rights to edit existing records, add or delete records, or change the table's structure. No other option grants the right to modify a table's structure. The InsDel option allows the user to change the data in the table in any way. The Entry option allows the user to add records and edit non-key fields, but does not grant the right to delete existing records or edit key fields in those records. The Update option allows the user to edit non-key fields, but does not give the user the ability to add or delete records, or to edit key fields. The ReadOnly option lets the user view the table without making any changes to it.

Figure 5-15 The Auxiliary Password Form

```
Defining auxiliary password 1 of Emplyee table          Password
[F1] for help with setting password options.  [F7] for table view

   Auxiliary password:                  ◀                    Page 1
   _____

   Table Rights                     Family Rights

   Enter one │ Rights conferred      Enter all that apply, ↵ for none

   All       │ all operations        (F)orm      │ change forms
   InsDel    │ change contents       (V)alCheck  │ change validity checks
   Entry     │ data entry and updates(R)eport    │ change reports
   Update    │ update nonkey fields  (S)ettings  │ change image settings
   ReadOnly  │ no modifications

   Field Rights  Enter ReadOnly or None for each field or leave blank for All.

   Emp Number                        Zip
   Last name                         Phone
   First Name                        Date of Birth
   SS Number                         Date of Hire
   Address                           Exemptions
   City                              Salary
   State
```

The Family Rights section allows you to specify the user's ability to create, modify, or delete the forms, validity checks, reports, and image settings associated with the table. To give the user the ability to work with one of these objects, you press the letter that corresponds to that object (*F*, *V*, *R*, or *S*) while the cursor is in the Family Rights section.

The Field Rights section at the bottom of the Auxiliary Password form lets you define rights for individual fields. These field-specific rights override the table rights specified in the Table Rights section. Every field in the table appears on this section of the form. If the table has more than 16 fields, you'll need to press [Pg Dn] to view the remaining fields.

You can choose one of two options when defining the field rights for a key field or one of three options for a non-key field. First, you can allow the user to have complete control over a field, or at least as much control as is allowed by the selection in the Table Rights section. To allow complete rights, leave blank the space next to the field's name in the Field Rights section. Second, you can limit the user to viewing, but not editing, a field. To do this, you move the cursor next to the field's name and press *R*. When you press *R*, the word *ReadOnly* will appear next to the field name. When specifying the field rights for a key field, you must choose one of these first two options. You can also choose to blank out a non-key field so that the user cannot even view it. To do this, press *N* while the cursor is next to the field name. When you use this third option, the word *None* will appear next to the field name. Note that when you use this option, the field name and column will still appear when the user views the table.

An Example

Suppose you want to set up the auxiliary password *MAULE*. After you type in *CESSNA* twice for the master password, Paradox will display the auxiliary password form shown in Figure 5-15. Type the word **MAULE** after the *Auxiliary password:* prompt and press ↵. The cursor will move to the Table Rights section.

To allow the user to modify some fields, but not add new records or delete existing records, type **U** for Update (Paradox will supply the rest of the word) and press ↵. When you do this, the cursor will move to the Family Rights section. Now, suppose you want the user to be able to change the image settings and create input forms. Type **FS** after the Family Rights prompt to specify Form and Settings, then press ↵. When you do this, the cursor will move to the Field Rights section.

If you want the user to be able to view the Emp Number field but not edit it, use the arrow keys to move the cursor to the right of Emp Number. Type **R** for ReadOnly (Paradox will fill in the rest of the word). You want the user to be able to modify the Name fields, so leave blank the space to the right of Last Name and First Name. This tells Paradox to let the user edit these fields.

Next, you decide the employee's Social Security number is confidential. To prevent the user from seeing this field, type **N** to the right of SS Number. (Paradox will fill in the rest of the word *None*.) Now, the user will not be able to view or modify this field.

The user may modify any of the remaining fields, so leave blank the area to the right of them. Your screen should now look like Figure 5-16. This is the completed form for the auxiliary password *MAULE*. If you want to create another auxiliary password, press [Pg Dn] to get a new auxiliary password form.

Figure 5-16 *The Completed Auxiliary Password Form*

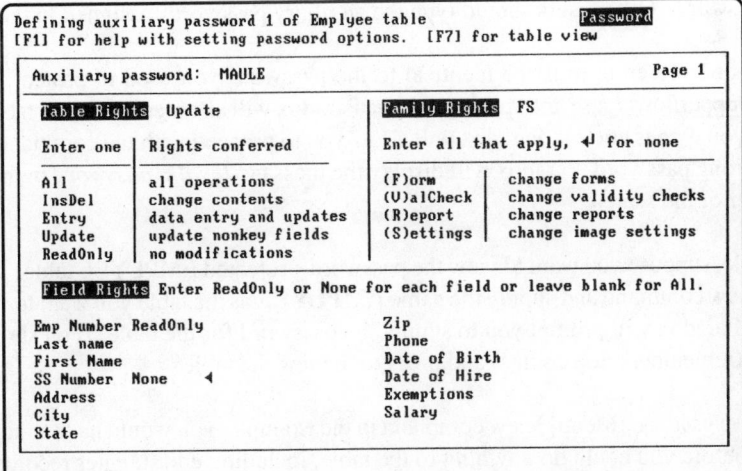

When you have set up all the auxiliary passwords you need, press **[Do-It!]** ([F2]). Paradox will display the message *Encrypting...* in the lower-right corner of the screen. Later, when the user tries to view or edit EMPLYEE, he or she will be asked to enter the password. If the user types MAULE, the EMPLYEE table will appear as shown in Figure 5-17.

Figure 5-17 The EMPLYEE Table

```
Viewing Emplyee table: Record 1 of 15                                   Main

EMPLYEE┬─Emp Number──┬─Last name──┬─First Name──┬─SS Number──┬──────Addre
   1   │      1      │  Jones     │  David      │            │   4000 St. Ja
   2   │      2      │  Cameron   │  Herb       │            │   2331 Elm St
   3   │      4      │  Jones     │  Stewart    │            │   4389 Oakbri
   4   │      5      │  Roberts   │  Darlene    │            │    451 Lone Pi
   5   │      6      │  Jones     │  Jean       │            │   4000 St. Ja
   6   │      8      │  Williams  │  Brenda     │            │    100 Owl Cre
   7   │      9      │  Myers     │  Julie      │            │   4512 Parksi
   8   │     10      │  Link      │  Julie      │            │   3215 Palm C
   9   │     12      │  Jackson   │  Mary       │            │   7821 Clark
  10   │     13      │  Jakes, Jr.│  Sal        │            │   3451 Michig
  11   │     14      │  Preston   │  Molly      │            │    321 Indian
  12   │     15      │  Masters   │  Ron        │            │    423 W. 72nd
  13   │     16      │  Robertson │  Kevin      │            │    431 Bardsto
  14   │     17      │  Garrison  │  Robert     │            │     55 Wheeler
  15   │     19      │  Gunn      │  Barbara    │            │    541 Kentuck
```

Notice that the SS Number field column is blank. If the user tries to edit either the SS Number field or the Emp Number field, the computer will beep and display the message *Insufficient password rights to modify field*. Furthermore, if the user tries to add a new record using [Menu] Modify DataEntry, Paradox will display the message *Access rights not sufficient— see "auxiliary passwords" in help index*.

Working with Passwords

Once you've assigned a password to a table, you'll be prompted to enter that password before you can do anything to, or with, the table. As soon as you issue a command and select the name of a protected table, Paradox will prompt you to enter the password. You then type the master password. Other users should type the auxiliary passwords assigned to them.

The password you enter must be identical to the password you used to protect the table (including upper/lowercase and spacing) before Paradox will allow access to the table. If the password you type is correct, Paradox will allow you to proceed with the command. If you type the wrong password, Paradox will display the message *Invalid password* in the lower-right corner of the screen.

For example, suppose you want to view the password-protected EMPLYEE table. Issue the **[Menu]** V**iew command and supply the name **EMPLYEE** as the table you want to view. At this point, Paradox will prompt you to supply the password for the table. You should type **CESSNA** (remember, case counts) and press ↵ to view the table.

Although we used the [Menu] View command in the example, you would have to supply the password before you could do anything to the table, including edit it, enter records into it, restructure it, or even view its structure. However, once you have supplied a proper password for a table, Paradox will remember it and not ask you for it again unless you issue the [Menu] Tools More Protect ClearPasswords command or end the current Paradox session and try to access the table during a subsequent session.

Notes

Your passwords can be up to 15 characters long and can include alphabetic characters, spaces, punctuation marks like !, numerals, and special symbols like @ and #. For example, *12345*, *ABCDE*, *10/6/57*, *Piper*, *PIPER*, *Beech2*, *!!!!!*, and @@@@@ are all acceptable passwords.

You cannot create an auxiliary password until you have assigned a master password. You can have as many auxiliary passwords as you want, or none at all.

You should try to choose passwords for your tables that are easy to remember. You might want to use technical terms, brand names related to a hobby, or any other distinct and memorable word or number as your password. In addition to choosing memorable words, always write your passwords and store them in a secure place. Remember: Once you assign a password to a table, there is no way to access the table without the password.

Removing or Changing a Password

The process of removing or changing a password is essentially the same as that for establishing a password for the first time. However, to remove or change a password, you must know the existing master password. For example, suppose the EMPLYEE table is password-protected and you want to remove the password. To do this, issue the **[Menu] Tools More Protect Password Table** command. When Paradox prompts you to enter a table name, type **EMPLYEE** and press ↵. After you do this, Paradox will prompt you to enter the password. You then should type the current password, **CESSNA**, and press ↵.

Paradox will ask you if you want to change the master and auxiliary passwords, or just the auxiliary password. To remove all passwords, select Master from the menu. Next, Paradox will prompt you to enter the new password for the table. If you just want to remove the existing password, all you need to do is press ↵. Paradox will remove all passwords for the table. If you want to change the password instead, type in the new password and press ↵. Paradox then will prompt you to confirm the new password. Once you confirm it, Paradox will allow you to modify existing auxiliary passwords or set up new ones. When you press **[Do-It!]** ([F2]), Paradox will encrypt the table.

Clearing Passwords during a Paradox Session

When you are working with tables or scripts that have passwords, you are required to enter each password only once. Paradox remembers the passwords you supply for the duration of the Paradox session. If you leave your computer without exiting from Paradox, however, anyone who comes along will have access to your protected tables and scripts. To avoid this problem, you can issue the [Menu] Tools More Protect ClearPasswords command. Paradox will then display the Cancel/OK menu. If you select OK, Paradox will clear the workspace. Now, to view or edit a protected table or script, the user will have to re-enter the password.

Write-protecting Your Tables

The [Menu] Tools More Protect Write-protect command allows you to protect a table from being overwritten, modified, or deleted. Write-protecting a table locks the table so that no changes can be made to its contents or structure.

When you issue this command, Paradox will prompt you for the name of the table you want to write-protect. When you type the name and press ↵, Paradox will display the menu shown in Figure 5-18. (If the table is password-protected, you will need to supply the password before you see this menu.) To write-protect the table, choose Set. If the table is already protected, you can unprotect it by choosing Clear.

Figure 5-18 The Write-protect Menu

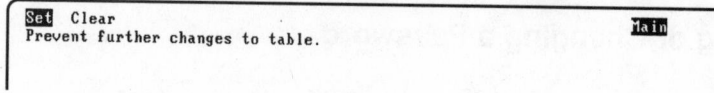

```
Set  Clear                                                        Main
Prevent further changes to table.
```

Since a write-protected table can be easily unprotected, it is not a foolproof form of protection. One of the greatest advantages of write-protecting important tables is that doing so prevents you from accidentally destroying the table or the data it contains. Because you would need to unlock the table to make any changes, there is no chance of mistakenly deleting or emptying the table.

The [Menu] Tools More Directory Command

The [Menu] Tools More Directory command allows you to change the current directory during a Paradox session. When you issue this command, Paradox will display a prompt that shows the current directory. To change the active directory, press [Backspace] to erase all or part of the existing setting, and then type in the name of the new directory, and press ↵.

Since changing the active directory clears the workspace and deletes all temporary tables, Paradox will display a Cancel/OK menu that prompts you to confirm the change. If you issue the Cancel command, Paradox will return to the previous prompt. If you issue the OK command, Paradox will clear the workspace and change the working directory.

An Example

Suppose you are using a hard disk system and your working directory is c:\paradox3\data. Now, suppose you want to work with a few tables that are stored on a floppy disk in drive A. To do this, issue the [Menu] Tools More Directory command. After you issue this command, Paradox will display the current directory and prompt you to change it, as shown in Figure 5-19.

Figure 5-19 The Directory Prompt

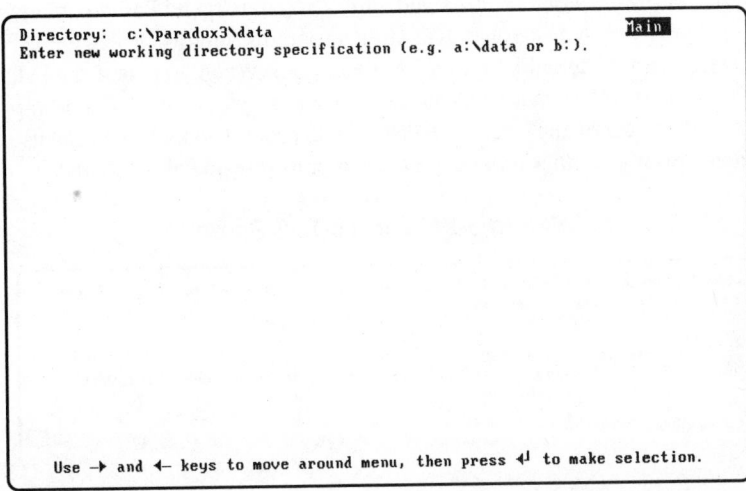

```
Directory:  c:\paradox3\data                                    Main
Enter new working directory specification (e.g. a:\data or b:).




                              .




    Use → and ← keys to move around menu, then press ◄┘ to make selection.
```

When you see this prompt, you should press [Ctrl]-[Backspace] to erase the current directory, then type a:, press ↵, and choose OK from the Confirmation menu. When you do this, Paradox will clear the workspace and change the working directory. In addition, the message *Working directory is now a:* will appear at the bottom of the screen. The message will disappear when you press any key.

Changing the Default Directory

If you wish, you can change the default working directory through the Custom Configuration Program (CCP). To do this, issue the [Menu] Scripts Play command, type **paradox3\custom**, and press ↵. If you are using an earlier version of Paradox on a floppy disk system, you will need to insert the Installation Disk in drive B before you issue the command. Then, Paradox will display the CCP main menu. Figure 5-20 shows this menu for Paradox 3.

Figure 5-20 The CCP Menu

```
Video  Reports  Graphs  Defaults  Int'l  Net  PAL  Ascii  Help  Do-It!  Cancel
Monitor, Snow, Colors, NegativeColors, and FormPalette.
```

When you see this menu, issue the **Defaults SetDirectory** command (or simply the SetDirectory command for earlier versions). Paradox then will display the working directory and prompt you to change it. To change the default directory, press the **[Ctrl]-[Backspace]** key to erase it, type the name of the new directory, and press ↵. After you do this, Paradox will return to the CCP main menu. When it does, issue the **DO-IT!** command to exit from the CCP and save the new default directory specification.

The [Menu] Tools More ToDOS Command

The [Menu] Tools More ToDOS command allows you to suspend Paradox temporarily and access DOS. In this way, you can use DOS utility programs, such as DISKCOPY, FORMAT, and CHKDSK, without actually exiting from Paradox. When you issue the [Menu] Tools More ToDOS command, Paradox will suspend its operation, and the DOS prompt shown in Figure 5-21 will appear on the screen. Once the DOS prompt appears, you can use any of the DOS utilities or run any other program (except memory-resident programs).

Figure 5-21 The ToDOS Screen

```
WARNING! Do not delete or edit Paradox objects, or load RAM-resident programs.
To return to Paradox, type exit.


The IBM Personal Computer DOS
Version 3.30 (C)Copyright International Business Machines Corp 1981, 1987
               (C)Copyright Microsoft Corp 1981, 1986

C:\PARADOX3\DATA>
```

When you're ready to return to Paradox, simply type **exit** and press ↵. When the Paradox screen reappears, everything will be just as you left it when you exited to DOS. Any tables that were in view before will be in view now, and any temporary tables that existed when you exited from Paradox will still exist.

Instead of issuing the [Menu] Tools More ToDOS command, you can simply press the [DOS] key ([Ctrl]-[O]). Pressing this key has the same effect as issuing the command.

When you use the ToDOS command, Paradox uses 420K of memory, leaving the rest of the memory for your DOS commands. If you don't think the remaining amount of memory will be enough, you can use the [DOS Big] key ([Alt]-[O]) to exit to DOS. When you use the [DOS Big] key, Paradox is suspended and takes up only 100K of memory. Other than the memory allocation difference, [DOS Big] works the same as [DOS].

An Example

Suppose you are working in Paradox and your screen currently looks like Figure 5-22. This screen shows a query form and ANSWER table based on the EMPLYEE table.

Figure 5-22 A Query Form and ANSWER Table

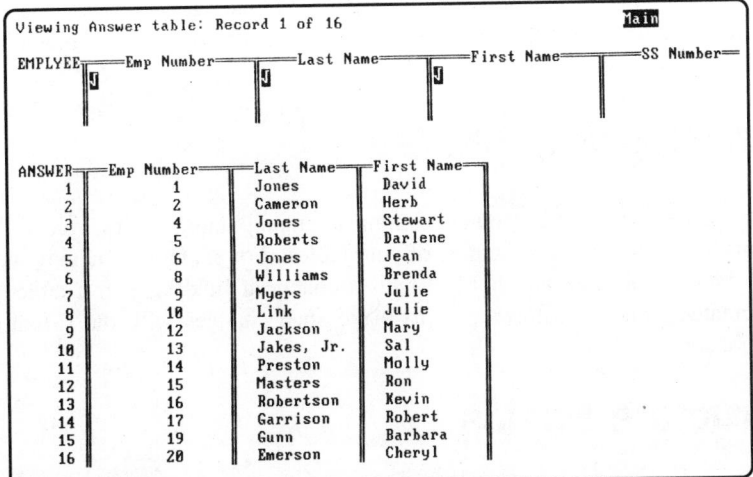

```
Viewing Answer table: Record 1 of 16                    Main

EMPLOYEE    Emp Number      Last Name       First Name      SS Number
            9               9               9


ANSWER      Emp Number      Last Name       First Name
   1        1               Jones           David
   2        2               Cameron         Herb
   3        4               Jones           Stewart
   4        5               Roberts         Darlene
   5        6               Jones           Jean
   6        8               Williams        Brenda
   7        9               Myers           Julie
   8        10              Link            Julie
   9        12              Jackson         Mary
  10        13              Jakes, Jr.      Sal
  11        14              Preston         Molly
  12        15              Masters         Ron
  13        16              Robertson       Kevin
  14        17              Garrison        Robert
  15        19              Gunn            Barbara
  16        20              Emerson         Cheryl
```

Now, suppose that you need to format a floppy disk during a Paradox session. To do this, issue the **[Menu] T**ools **M**ore **T**oDOS command, or press **[ToDOS]** ([Ctrl]-[O]). At the DOS prompt, type **format a:** and press ←. When DOS prompts you to place a new disk in drive A, insert the disk you want to format, and press ←.

After the disk is formatted, you can type **exit** and press ← to return to Paradox. When you return to the program, your screen will again look like Figure 5-22. The ANSWER table that was on the screen when you issued the ToDOS command will still be there when you return.

Notes

If you use an earlier release of Paradox on a system with two floppy disk drives, you'll need to remove the Paradox System Disk II from drive A and insert your DOS disk. When you type **exit** to return to Paradox, Paradox will prompt you to insert System Disk II in drive A.

Notice the message *WARNING! Do not delete or edit Paradox objects, or load RAM-resident programs* at the top of the screen in Figure 5-21. As we have said, Paradox makes full use of the memory in your computer. While you are using ToDOS, Paradox freezes the contents of its memory so that nothing is lost while you're at the DOS level. If you run any memory-resident program (such as Sidekick or Superkey), while you're at the DOS level, you could lose data.

When you are in DOS, the automatic mechanisms built into Paradox to prevent data loss cannot function. Therefore, you must exercise caution when you are using DOS. For example, never delete or edit Paradox objects while you are in DOS. If you change disks while in DOS, you must restore the original configuration before you return to Paradox. When you are ready to return to Paradox, type **exit** and press ←. Never turn off your computer or press [Ctrl]-[Alt]-[Del] to reboot while Paradox is suspended!

As a general rule, it is safer to issue the [Menu] Exit Yes command to exit from Paradox, then use DOS. The biggest advantage of using ToDOS is that it allows you to leave Paradox temporarily without losing all of your temporary tables. If you use the ToDOS command carefully, it can save you some time.

Restructuring Tables

As you become more experienced in designing and manipulating tables, you will probably want to make changes in the structures of your tables. For example, you may want to add or delete fields, designate key fields, or even change a field type in a table you have already created. Paradox allows you to make such changes with the [Menu] Modify Restructure command.

Restructure Basics

Although Paradox has some built-in features for protecting against data loss when you are restructuring a table, we recommend that you always use the [Menu] Tools Copy Table command to make a copy of the table you want to change before you begin restructuring. This ensures that you will not lose any data if you make an error.

Once you have made a copy of the table, issue the **[Menu]** **M**odify **R**estructure command. When you see the prompt, you should type the name of the table you want to restructure. When you press ↵, Paradox will display a STRUCT table for the table you are restructuring. If you type **EMPLYEE** when Paradox prompts you for the name of the table to restructure, Paradox will bring a STRUCT table for EMPLYEE to the screen, as shown in Figure 5-23. As you can see, this STRUCT table lists the name and type of every field in the table being restructured. This table is very similar to the STRUCT table you see when you use the [Menu] Create command to define a new table. In fact, the process of restructuring a table is fundamentally the same as creating a new table.

Figure 5-23 The STRUCT Table for EMPLYEE

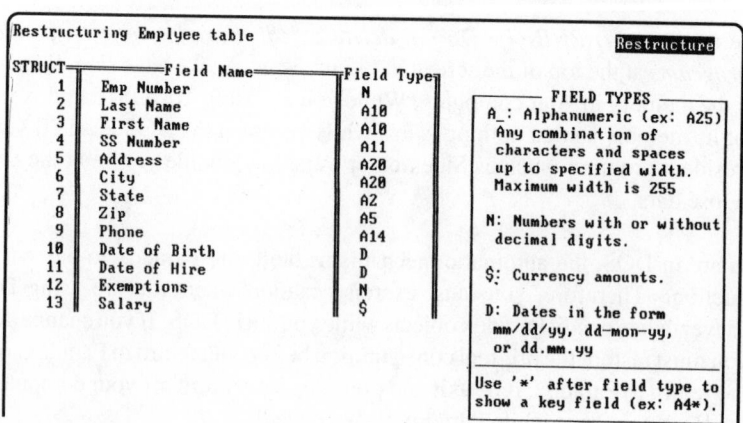

You can edit the STRUCT table using the techniques you learned in Chapters 2 and 3 for editing regular Paradox tables. For example, you can use the ↓ key to move to the bottom of STRUCT, add a new blank row, and enter a new field. Or, you can press [Ins] to insert a new row in STRUCT at the current cursor location and define a new field there. You can use the [Del] key to delete fields from the table. You can even move a field to a different location in the STRUCT table and change the name or the type of any field. Since most of the techniques you use to restructure a table are identical to the ones you use to edit a table's structure during its creation, we won't cover them here. We'll discuss only only a few techniques that are unique to restructuring.

When you have made the desired changes to the table, you can press [Do-It!] ([F2]) to make the changes permanent. If you make an error or decide not to make changes after all, you can issue the [Menu] Cancel command to stop the restructure.

Deleting Fields

When you are restructuring a table, you can delete a field in the same way you can while creating the table: by placing the cursor on that field and pressing [Del]. As soon as you press [Del], the field will be deleted from the image of STRUCT.

Since deleting a field from an existing table will usually result in the loss of data, Paradox will prompt you to confirm the deletion. When you press [Do-It!] ([F2]) or issue the [Menu] DO-IT! command to save the new table, Paradox will display a menu that offers two options: Delete and Oops!. If you choose the Delete command, Paradox will delete the field (and all of the information it contains) as it saves the restructured table and will return to the main workspace. If you choose Oops!, Paradox will return to the restructure screen so that you can restore the field to the table or select [Menu] Cancel.

If you delete more than one field from the table during one restructure operation, Paradox will prompt you to confirm the deletion of each field individually. If you choose the Oops! option for any deleted field, Paradox will return you to the restructure screen so that you can make any needed corrections.

Changing the Field Order

As you learned in Chapter 3, you can change the order of the fields in the image of a table and make that change permanent with the [Menu] Image KeepSet command. This technique affects only the order of the fields in the table's image; it has no effect on the underlying structure. The only way to change the order in the actual table is to restructure the table.

For example, the original order of the fields in the EMPLYEE table is: Emp Number, Last Name, First Name, SS Number, Address, City, State, Zip, Phone, Date of Birth, Date of Hire, Exemptions, and Salary. Suppose you want to rearrange the fields into the following order:

Emp Number, Last Name, First Name, Address, City, State, Zip, Phone, Date of Birth, SS Number, Date of Hire, Exemptions, and Salary.

To begin, issue the **[Menu] T**ools Copy command and copy the records in EMPLYEE into a table called **TEMP**. When the copy is complete, issue the **[Menu] M**odify **R**estructure command, type **EMPLYEE** to identify the table you want to restructure, and press ↵.

To begin changing the order of the fields, move the cursor down to the Date of Hire field, and press **[Ins]** to insert a blank line above it. Next, type **SS Number** in the Field Name column and press ↓ to move the cursor out of the new row. When you do this, Paradox will recognize that you want to move the SS Number field and will complete the move for you. You do not need to enter anything in the Field Type column or delete the SS Number field from its previous location. As Paradox makes the change, the message *Moving SS Number field...* will appear briefly in the lower-right corner of the screen. Figure 5-24 shows the STRUCT table after the change is made. Notice that the SS Number field is now between the Date of Birth and Date of Hire fields.

Figure 5-24 Moving a Field

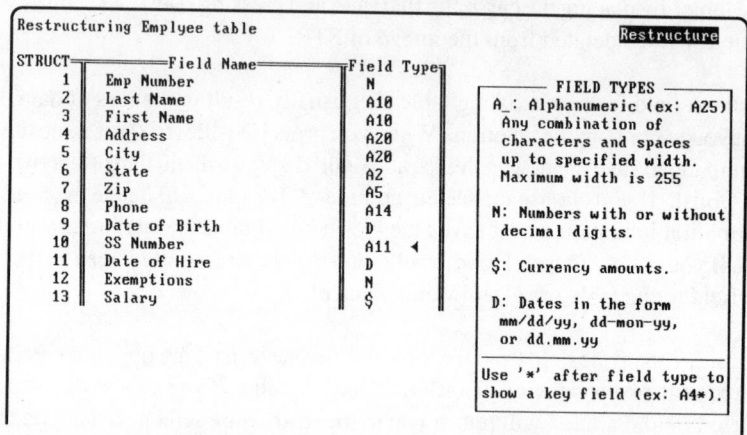

You must type the field name exactly as it appears in the table in order for Paradox to recognize it and move the field. If you do not duplicate an existing name exactly, Paradox will assume that you are adding a new field to the table.

When you are finished rearranging the table, press **[Do-It!]** ([F2]) or issue the **[Menu] DO-IT!** command to save the new table. After a few moments, Paradox will display the revised table, EMPLYEE, in the workspace.

Changing the Field Size

When you are restructuring a table, you can expand or contract the width of any alphanumeric field in the table. (The widths of number, dollar, and date fields are set by Paradox and cannot be changed.) To change the width of a field, first issue the [Menu] Modify Restructure command to bring the STRUCT table into view. Next, move to the Field Type column for the field you want to change, erase the current width setting, and type a new width. When you press [Do-It!] ([F2]), Paradox will make the change permanent.

An Example

Suppose you want to expand the size of the Last Name field in the EMPLYEE table from ten to 15 characters. To do this, issue the **[Menu]** Modify **R**estructure command, type **EMPLYEE**, and press ↵. When the STRUCT table for EMPLYEE appears, move the cursor to the Field Type column for the Last Name field, press the **[Backspace]** key once to erase the 0 in the existing entry, 10, and type **5**. After you do this, your screen will look like Figure 5-25. If you press [Do-It!] ([F2]) at this point, Paradox will permanently change the width of the Last Name field to 15 characters.

Figure 5-25 Increasing the Field Size

Shortening a Field

You can also reduce the width of an alphanumeric field. For example, suppose you decide to reduce the width of the First Name field in EMPLYEE from ten to five characters. To do this, issue the **[Menu]** Modify **R**estructure command, type **EMPLYEE**, and press ↵. When the STRUCT table for EMPLYEE appears, move the cursor to the Field Type column for the First Name field, press the **[Backspace]** key twice to erase the current width, and type **5**. Figure 5-26 shows the screen at this point.

Figure 5-26 Reducing the Field Size

```
Restructuring Emplyee table                                    Restructure
STRUCT           Field Name            Field Type
   1    Emp Number                      N                  ┌─── FIELD TYPES ───
   2    Last Name                       A15                A_: Alphanumeric (ex: A25)
   3    First Name                      A5   ◄             Any combination of
   4    Address                         A20               characters and spaces
   5    City                            A20               up to specified width.
   6    State                           A2                Maximum width is 255
   7    Zip                             A5
   8    Phone                           A14               N: Numbers with or without
   9    Date of Birth                   D                 decimal digits.
  10    SS Number                       A11
  11    Date of Hire                    D                 $: Currency amounts.
  12    Exemptions                      N
  13    Salary                          $                 D: Dates in the form
                                                          mm/dd/yy, dd-mon-yy,
                                                          or dd.mm.yy

                                                          Use '*' after field type to
                                                          show a key field (ex: A4*).
```

If any entry in the alphanumeric field exceeds the new length you have specified, you run the risk of losing data. Therefore, when you press [Do-It!] ([F2]) or issue the [Menu] DO-IT! command after shortening a field, Paradox displays the menu shown in Figure 5-27. In addition, the message *Possible data loss for the FIELDNAME field* will appear in the message area. If you issue the Oops! command, Paradox will return to the restructure screen so that you can adjust the field size. If you issue the [Menu] Cancel command after you choose Oops!, Paradox will disregard all of the changes you have made.

Figure 5-27 The Trimming/No-Trimming/Oops! Menu

```
Trimming  No-Trimming  Oops!                                   Restructure
Allow trimming First Name field values if necessary
```

Trimming

If you issue the Trimming command, Paradox will truncate the characters that don't fit within the new field size and save the new table. For example, Figure 5-28 shows the EMPLYEE table as it will look if you now choose the Trimming option and press ↵. Notice that some of the entries in the First Name field have been "trimmed" to fit in the new, shorter field.

No-Trimming

If you choose the No-Trimming option, Paradox will restructure the table according to your instructions, shortening the fields you have specified. Paradox will remove from the table any records that include entries that don't fit in the newly shortened fields and place them into a special table named PROBLEMS. The PROBLEMS table is a temporary table that has a structure identical to the original table. PROBLEMS temporarily preserves the records you might otherwise lose until you decide what to do with them. Choosing No-Trimming ensures that you, and not Paradox, will have control over the trimming process.

Figure 5-28 Shortened First Name Field

```
Viewing Emplyee table: Record 1 of 16                              Main
EMPLYEE┬─Emp Number─┬──Last Name─┬First Name┬─SS Number─┬──────Address═
    1  │     1      │  Jones     │ David    │414-76-3421│4000 St. James
    2  │     2      │  Cameron   │ Herb     │321-65-8765│2331 Elm St.
    3  │     4      │  Jones     │ Stewa    │401-32-8721│4389 Oakbridge
    4  │     5      │  Roberts   │ Darle    │417-43-7777│451 Lone Pine
    5  │     6      │  Jones     │ Jean     │413-07-9123│4000 St. James
    6  │     8      │  Williams  │ Brend    │401-55-1567│100 Owl Creek
    7  │     9      │  Myers     │ Julie    │314-38-9452│4512 Parkside
    8  │    10      │  Link      │ Julie    │345-75-1525│3215 Palm Ct.
    9  │    12      │  Jackson   │ Mary     │424-13-7621│7821 Clark Ave
   10  │    13      │  Jakes, Jr.│ Sal      │321-65-9151│3451 Michigan
   11  │    14      │  Preston   │ Molly    │451-00-3426│321 Indian Hil
   12  │    15      │  Masters   │ Ron      │317-65-4529│423 W. 72nd St
   13  │    16      │  Robertson │ Kevin    │415-24-6710│431 Bardstown
   14  │    17      │  Garrison  │ Rober    │312-98-1479│55 Wheeler St.
   15  │    19      │  Gunn      │ Barba    │321-97-8632│541 Kentucky S
   16  │    20      │  Emerson   │ Chery    │401-65-1898│800 River Rd.
```

For example, suppose you restructure EMPLYEE, shortening the First Name field from ten to five characters. There are six records in EMPLYEE with First Name field entries that will not fit in the new, five-character-wide First Name field: employee numbers 4, 5, 8, 17, 19, and 20. If you choose the No-Trimming option, Paradox will remove those records from EMPLYEE and enter them into a PROBLEMS table like the one shown in Figure 5-29. Notice that PROBLEMS has the same structure as EMPLYEE, but with the original ten-character-wide First Name field.

Figure 5-29 The PROBLEMS Table

```
Viewing Problems table: Record 1 of 6                             Main
EMPLYEE┬─Emp Number─┬──Last Name─┬First Name┬─SS Number─┬──────Address═
    1  │     1      │  Jones     │ David    │414-76-3421│4000 St. James
    2  │     2      │  Cameron   │ Herb     │321-65-8765│2331 Elm St.
    3  │     6      │  Jones     │ Jean     │413-07-9123│4000 St. James
    4  │     9      │  Myers     │ Julie    │314-38-9452│4512 Parkside
    5  │    10      │  Link      │ Julie    │345-75-1525│3215 Palm Ct.
    6  │    12      │  Jackson   │ Mary     │424-13-7621│7821 Clark Ave
    7  │    13      │  Jakes, Jr.│ Sal      │321-65-9151│3451 Michigan
    8  │    14      │  Preston   │ Molly    │451-00-3426│321 Indian Hil
    9  │    15      │  Masters   │ Ron      │317-65-4529│423 W. 72nd St
   10  │    16      │  Robertson │ Kevin    │415-24-6710│431 Bardstown

PROBLEMS┬─Emp Number─┬──Last Name─┬First Name┬─SS Number─┬────Addr
    1  │     4      │  Jones     │ Stewart  │401-32-8721│4389 Oakbr
    2  │     5      │  Roberts   │ Darlene  │417-43-7777│451 Lone P
    3  │     8      │  Williams  │ Brenda   │401-55-1567│100 Owl Cr
    4  │    17      │  Garrison  │ Robert   │312-98-1479│55 Wheeler
    5  │    19      │  Gunn      │ Barbara  │321-97-8632│541 Kentuc
    6  │    20      │  Emerson   │ Cheryl   │401-65-1898│800 River
```

To preserve the records in PROBLEMS, you can edit the PROBLEMS table to make the records fit the new field size, then add them to the restructured table. In this case, you must reduce the length of the entries in that field to no more than five characters, so they will fit in the new table. You might want to shorten the entry to an initial or abbreviate the entry in some other way. On the other hand, you might simply want to press [Backspace] to erase the excess characters.

Once all of the entries have been shortened sufficiently, you must add the edited records in the PROBLEMS table to the restructured EMPLYEE table. To do this, issue the **[Menu]** Tools More Add command. When Paradox prompts you to enter the name of the source table, type **PROBLEMS** and press ↵. Then, when Paradox prompts you for the name of the table to which the records should be added, type **EMPLYEE** and press ↵. After you do this, Paradox will display the message *Adding Problems to Emplyee...* at the bottom of the screen. After a few moments, Paradox will display the EMPLYEE table (with the records added at the end of the table) in the workspace. Figure 5-30 shows the completed EMPLYEE table.

Figure 5-30 Adding PROBLEMS to EMPLYEE

```
Viewing Emplyee table: Record 1 of 16                           Main

EMPLYEE══Emp Number════Last Name══First Name══SS Number══════════Address═
   1   ║    1      ║  Jones      David      414-76-3421   4000 St. James
   2   ║    2      ║  Cameron    Herb       321-65-8765   2331 Elm St.
   3   ║    6      ║  Jones      Jean       413-87-9123   4000 St. James
   4   ║    9      ║  Myers      Julie      314-38-9452   4512 Parkside
   5   ║   10      ║  Link       Julie      345-75-1525   3215 Palm Ct.
   6   ║   12      ║  Jackson    Mary       424-13-7621   7821 Clark Ave
   7   ║   13      ║  Jakes, Jr. Sal        321-65-9151   3451 Michigan
   8   ║   14      ║  Preston    Molly      451-80-3426   321 Indian Hil
   9   ║   15      ║  Masters    Ron        317-65-4529   423 W. 72nd St
  10   ║   16      ║  Robertson  Kevin      415-24-6710   431 Bardstown
  11   ║    4      ║  Jones      Stew       401-32-8721   4389 Oakbridge
  12   ║    5      ║  Roberts    D.         417-43-7777   451 Lone Pine
  13   ║    8      ║  Williams   Brnda      401-55-1567   100 Owl Creek
  14   ║   17      ║  Garrison   Robrt      312-98-1479   55 Wheeler St.
  15   ║   19      ║  Gunn       Barb       321-97-8632   541 Kentucky S
  16   ║   20      ║  Emerson    C.         401-65-1898   800 River Rd.
```

The [Menu] Tools More Add command will work only if the two tables have compatible field types in the same order. In the example, the only change we made in the structure of the EMPLYEE table was to reduce the size of a field. In this case, the [Menu] Tools More Add command worked just fine. However, if you make other changes in the structure of the table—such as adding a field or changing the type of the field—you may not be able to add records from the PROBLEMS table to the newly restructured table. Should you fall into this trap, you may be able to construct an insert query to insert the records from PROBLEMS into EMPLYEE. We will discuss insert queries and the [Menu] Tools More Add command in detail in Chapter 9, "Multitable Operations." Alternatively, you may rename the PROBLEMS table something else, such as TEMP, and restructure TEMP to be identical in structure to EMPLYEE. Then, you will be able to use [Menu] Tools More Add.

Since the PROBLEMS table is a temporary table, Paradox will warn you if you are about to perform an operation that could cause the data in PROBLEMS to be lost. For example, if a PROBLEMS table exists and you issue the [Menu] Modify Restructure command, Paradox will display a Cancel/OK prompt that asks you to confirm the loss of the PROBLEMS table. If you choose Cancel at this point, Paradox will cancel the restructure operation so that you can edit or rename the PROBLEMS table. If you choose OK, Paradox will continue with the restructure operation and will overwrite the PROBLEMS table if necessary.

Changing Field Types

You may encounter situations where you need to change a field type in a table. To change the type of a field, issue the [Menu] Modify Restructure command to bring into view the STRUCT table for the table you want to modify. Then, move to the Field Type entry for the field whose type you want to change, press [Backspace] or [Ctrl]-[Backspace] to erase the existing Field Type entry, and insert the new field type. Paradox will do its best to convert existing data from one type to another. It is always safe to convert from an N field to a $ field, or from $ to N. Most other attempted conversions will result in the Trimming/No-Trimming/Oops! menu, or a PROBLEMS table, or be totally disallowed. In general, except for number-to-number conversions, we recommend that you do not change the type of a field when restructuring unless you fully understand the consequences.

The Restructure Menu

When you are restructuring a table, pressing [Menu] ([F10]) causes the Restructure menu to appear at the top of the screen. Figure 5-31 shows this menu.

Figure 5-31 The Restructure Menu

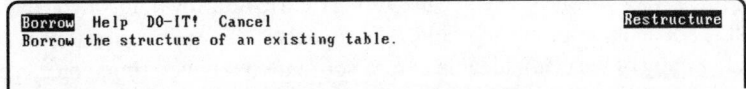

The Help command on this menu displays a Paradox help screen and is equivalent to pressing [Help] ([F1]). The [Menu] DO-IT! command saves the restructured table and returns you to the main workspace. Issuing the [Menu] DO-IT! command is the same as pressing [Do-It!] ([F2]). The Borrow command allows you to borrow the structure of one or more existing tables. This command works like the Borrow command on the Create menu.

The Cancel command cancels the restructuring process and returns you to the main workspace without saving any of the changes you've made. When you issue the [Menu] Cancel command, Paradox does not prompt you for confirmation. However, the message *Cancelling restructure...* will appear briefly in the lower-right corner of the screen. Issuing the Cancel command is equivalent to pressing [Ctrl]-[Break].

Other Paradox Objects

When you restructure a table, Paradox will update the forms and reports for that table. In many cases, Paradox removes the altered fields from forms and reports. Therefore, after you restructure a table, you should also modify any reports or forms that are part of the table's family. When you press [Do-It!] ([F2]) or issue the [Menu] DO-IT! command to complete the restructuring of a table, Paradox will display various messages at the bottom of the screen to remind you of the changes made in the objects associated with the table.

After you have restructured a table, you can use the [Menu] Report Change command (discussed in Chapters 10 and 11) to review and revise your reports and the [Menu] Forms Change command (discussed in Chapter 4) to review and revise your forms.

Restructuring Keyed Tables

You can restructure keyed tables just as easily as non-keyed tables. However, there are some important differences you should remember. For one thing, while you can rearrange and change the key fields in a table, you must place all key fields at the top of the STRUCT table. If you try to process a STRUCT table in which the key fields are not at the top, Paradox will display the error message *Non-consecutive key found for FIELDNAME*.

Second, you must be careful not to define a field that contains duplicate entries as a key field while you are restructuring a table. If you designate a field with duplicate entries as the primary key while you're restructuring a table, Paradox will place records with duplicate values into a KEYVIOL table. As you learned in Chapter 3, when you see a KEYVIOL table, you can edit the entries in that table to remove the key field conflict, then use the [Menu] Tools More Add command to add the contents of the KEYVIOL table to the main table.

Often, when you see a KEYVIOL table after you've restructured a table, it means you've made an error. Either you have selected the wrong field to be a key field, or you have selected a field that is not an appropriate key field. Fortunately, this type of error is easy to correct. If you made a copy of the original table before you started restructuring, you can erase both the restructured table and the KEYVIOL table and begin again. If you did not copy the original table, you should restructure the table again to remove the key field, then use the [Menu] Tools More Add command to add the data in KEYVIOL to that table.

Recovering Disk Space

When you delete a record from a table, the space occupied by that record is not automatically recovered on the disk and, therefore, becomes wasted space. To recover this space for future use, issue the [Menu] Modify Restructure command, type the table name, and press ↵. When the STRUCT table appears on the screen, press [Do-It!] ([F2]) or issue the [Menu] DO-IT! command without making any changes in the table's structure. After you do this, Paradox will "clean up" the table and reclaim the space that was occupied by the deleted records.

Conclusion

In this chapter, we've shown you how to copy, empty, rename, password-protect, and otherwise work with tables. (Throughout the remainder of this book, we'll show you specific instances where you should use a Tools command.) In addition, we have shown you how to change the structure of a table and have pointed out some of the traps you should avoid when restructuring a table. In the next chapter, we'll show you how to sort your tables.

Chapter 6

Sorting Your Tables

So far, we have shown you how to create tables and how to enter and edit data. This chapter begins the section of *Douglas Cobb's Paradox 3 Handbook* in which we'll tell you how to use the data in your tables. We'll begin this chapter with a discussion of the [Menu] Modify Sort command. In the next two chapters, we'll show you how to query, or ask questions of, your tables. In Chapter 9, we'll consider tools that will let you work on more than one table at a time.

The [Menu] Modify Sort command allows you to rearrange the records in your tables based on the entries in certain selected fields. You can sort a table on any type of field in ascending or descending order. You can choose to store the sorted records in a new table or have the sorted records overwrite the original, unsorted table. If you wish, you can sort a table on more than one field. In fact, Paradox is one of the few programs that allows you to sort a table on as many fields as there are in the table.

A Simple Example

The EMPLYEE table shown in Figure 6-1 on the following page contains no key fields and, therefore, stores records in the order in which they were entered. Suppose you want to sort the records in the table alphabetically by the entries in the Last Name field, then save the resulting sorted table under the name SORTEMP. To begin, issue the **[Menu]** Modify Sort command. After you issue this command, Paradox will prompt you to enter the name of the table you want to sort. When you see this prompt, you should type **EMPLYEE** and press ↵.

Specifying the Destination

When you supply the name of the table you want to sort and press ↵, Paradox will display the menu shown in Figure 6-2. This menu lets you choose where Paradox will store the result of the sort.

Figure 6-1 The EMPLYEE Table

```
Viewing Emplyee table: Record 15 of 16                              Main
EMPLYEE══Emp Number═══════Last Name══First Name═══SS Number═══════════Addre
    1  ║     1         Jones         David       414-76-3421 ║   4000 St. Ja
    2  ║     2         Cameron       Herb        321-65-8765 ║   2331 Elm St
    3  ║     4         Jones         Stewart     401-32-8721 ║   4389 Oakbri
    4  ║     5         Roberts       Darlene     417-43-7777 ║   451 Lone Pi
    5  ║     6         Jones         Jean        413-07-9123 ║   4000 St. Ja
    6  ║     8         Williams      Brenda      401-55-1567 ║   100 Owl Cre
    7  ║     9         Myers         Julie       314-38-9452 ║   4512 Parksi
    8  ║    10         Link          Julie       345-75-1525 ║   3215 Palm C
    9  ║    12         Jackson       Mary        424-13-7621 ║   7821 Clark
   10  ║    13         Jakes, Jr.    Sal         321-65-9151 ║   3451 Michig
   11  ║    14         Preston       Molly       451-00-3426 ║   321 Indian
   12  ║    15         Masters       Ron         317-65-4529 ║   423 W. 72nd
   13  ║    16         Robertson     Kevin       415-24-6710 ║   431 Bardsto
   14  ║    17         Garrison      Robert      312-98-1479 ║   55 Wheeler
   15  ║    19         Gunn          Barbara     321-97-8632 ║   541 Kentuck
   16  ║    20         Emerson       Cheryl      401-65-1898 ║   800 River R
```

Figure 6-2 Specifying the Sort Destination

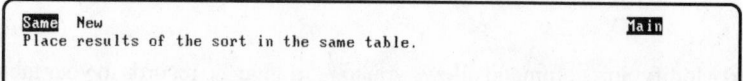

```
Same New                                                           Main
Place results of the sort in the same table.
```

If you choose the Same option, Paradox will overwrite the existing table with the sorted table as it performs the sort. As a result, the original order of the records will be lost. If you choose New, Paradox will place the sorted records into a new table. When you choose New, the records are sorted from the original table to a new table, and the original table remains intact after the sort is completed. Since, in this case, you want the sorted records to be placed into a new table, you should choose New. When you choose this option, Paradox will prompt you to enter a name for the new table. When you see this prompt, you should type **SORTEMP** and press ↵.

Defining the Sort

After you choose the destination, Paradox will display the sort form shown in Figure 6-3. The sort form lists the fields in the table and allows you to specify which fields you want to use to arrange the table. Notice that the first line on the screen contains the operation message *Sorting Emplyee table into new Sortemp table,* as well as the name of the current mode, *Sort*. The next few lines contain the instructions for defining the sort. Notice also that the names of the fields from the EMPLYEE table are displayed vertically on the left side of the screen.

To sort the table alphabetically by last name, you should press the ↓ key once to position the cursor on the Last Name field, then type the number **1**. This number tells Paradox to use the Last Name field as the primary (first) sort key field when it performs the sort. Figure 6-4 shows the screen at this point. Since you want to sort the table on only one field, and you want to sort in ascending order, you don't need to make any more entries in the sort form.

Figure 6-3 The Sort Form

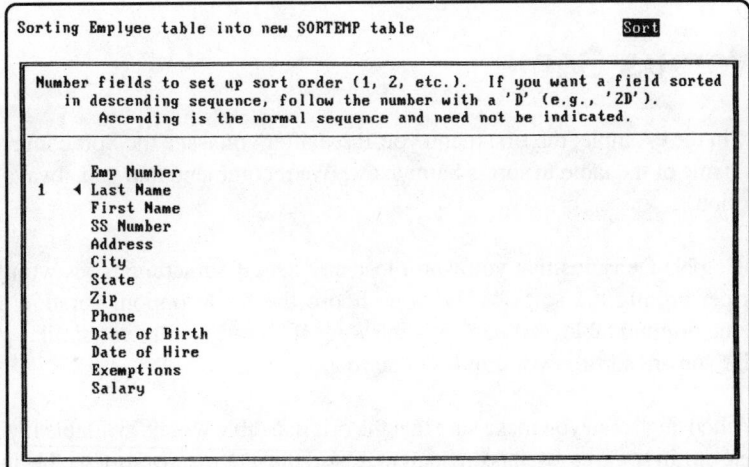

```
Sorting Emplyee table into new SORTEMP table                    Sort

 Number fields to set up sort order (1, 2, etc.).  If you want a field sorted
   in descending sequence, follow the number with a 'D' (e.g., '2D').
         Ascending is the normal sequence and need not be indicated.


      ◄ Emp Number
        Last Name
        First Name
        SS Number
        Address
        City
        State
        Zip
        Phone
        Date of Birth
        Date of Hire
        Exemptions
        Salary
```

Figure 6-4 Defining the Sort

```
Sorting Emplyee table into new SORTEMP table                    Sort

 Number fields to set up sort order (1, 2, etc.).  If you want a field sorted
   in descending sequence, follow the number with a 'D' (e.g., '2D').
         Ascending is the normal sequence and need not be indicated.

        Emp Number
    1 ◄ Last Name
        First Name
        SS Number
        Address
        City
        State
        Zip
        Phone
        Date of Birth
        Date of Hire
        Exemptions
        Salary
```

Sorting

Once you have defined the sort for the EMPLYEE table, you should either press **[Do-It!]** ([F2]) or issue the **[Menu]** DO-IT! command to sort the table. When you do either of these things, Paradox will sort the table according to the specifications you defined, store the result in the table SORTEMP, and bring that table to the screen. Figure 6-5 shows the SORTEMP table.

Figure 6-5 The SORTEMP Table

```
Viewing Sortemp table: Record 1 of 16                          Main

SORTEMP┬─Emp Number──┬──Last Name─┬─First Name┬──SS Number──┬──────Addre
   1   ┃     2       ┃ Cameron    ┃ Herb      ┃ 321-65-8765 ┃ 2331 Elm St
   2   ┃    20       ┃ Emerson    ┃ Cheryl    ┃ 401-65-1898 ┃ 800 River R
   3   ┃    17       ┃ Garrison   ┃ Robert    ┃ 312-98-1479 ┃ 55 Wheeler
   4   ┃    19       ┃ Gunn       ┃ Barbara   ┃ 321-97-8632 ┃ 541 Kentuck
   5   ┃    12       ┃ Jackson    ┃ Mary      ┃ 424-13-7621 ┃ 7821 Clark
   6   ┃    13       ┃ Jakes, Jr. ┃ Sal       ┃ 321-65-9151 ┃ 3451 Michig
   7   ┃     1       ┃ Jones      ┃ David     ┃ 414-76-3421 ┃ 4000 St. Ja
   8   ┃     4       ┃ Jones      ┃ Stewart   ┃ 401-32-8721 ┃ 4389 Oakbri
   9   ┃     6       ┃ Jones      ┃ Jean      ┃ 413-07-9123 ┃ 4000 St. Ja
  10   ┃    10       ┃ Link       ┃ Julie     ┃ 345-75-1525 ┃ 3215 Palm C
  11   ┃    15       ┃ Masters    ┃ Ron       ┃ 317-65-4529 ┃ 423 W. 72nd
  12   ┃     9       ┃ Myers      ┃ Julie     ┃ 314-38-9452 ┃ 4512 Parksi
  13   ┃    14       ┃ Preston    ┃ Molly     ┃ 451-00-3426 ┃ 321 Indian
  14   ┃     5       ┃ Roberts    ┃ Darlene   ┃ 417-43-7777 ┃ 451 Lone Pi
  15   ┃    16       ┃ Robertson  ┃ Kevin     ┃ 415-24-6710 ┃ 431 Bardsto
  16   ┃     8       ┃ Williams   ┃ Brenda    ┃ 401-55-1567 ┃ 100 Owl Cre
```

Sort Basics

Now that you have seen one example of a sort, let's go back and cover a few basics. After we cover these important points, we'll show you how to sort on more than one field and then how to sort a keyed table.

New Versus Same

As you saw in the example, the first menu you'll see after you issue the Sort command and specify the name of the table to sort is Same/New. We recommend that you always choose the New option.

First, choosing New ensures that you won't lose any data if something goes wrong while Paradox is performing the sort. When you choose the Same option, Paradox actually overwrites the original table as it performs the sort. If a power failure or similar problem occurs while you are sorting, you can lose your data.

Second, by choosing New, you make sure that the original table will be available if you need it for any reason. In some cases, it is difficult to re-sort the records in a sorted table into their original order. Unless you use the New option, you might find that you cannot recreate the original table when you need it. If you later decide you really don't need the original table, you can always delete it with the [Menu] Tools Delete Table command.

In the example, we selected the New option, and Paradox asked us to supply a name for the new, sorted table for the sort. If you choose Same, Paradox will display the sort specification screen immediately. Since the sorted records will be stored in the original table, you don't need to supply a name for the destination.

If you choose the New option and then supply the name of an existing table, Paradox will display the Cancel/Replace menu. If you choose Cancel from this menu, Paradox will back up to the previous prompt so that you can erase the table name with the [Backspace] key and type in a different name for the destination table. If you choose Replace, Paradox will replace the existing table that has the specified name with the sorted table.

Sort Order

By default, Paradox sorts into ascending order. This means that number and dollar fields are sorted into ascending numeric order, and date fields are sorted so that the earlier dates come before the later dates. Alphanumeric fields that contain only alphabetic characters (a, b, c, and so on) are sorted into alphabetical order. Alphanumeric fields that contain only numeric entries (such as zip codes) are sorted into ascending numeric order.

Alphanumeric fields that contain mixed entries (like *123 Main Street* or *#43A345*) are a bit trickier. In alphanumeric fields like this, Paradox will perform the sort based on the ASCII order of the characters. For example, *123 Main Street* comes before *426 Market Street*. Similarly, *#43A345* comes before *#77B555*, but after *!43A345*. If you are sorting an alphanumeric field in which the entries start with both uppercase and lowercase letters, Paradox will sort all of the uppercase letters first, then all of the lowercase letters.

You can also ask Paradox to sort tables in descending order. Descending order sorts number and dollar fields in descending numeric order (highest numbers first), and date fields so that the most recent dates appear before the earlier dates. Alphanumeric fields that contain only alphabetic characters are sorted in reverse alphabetical order (*z* before *y*, *b* before *a*). If the alphanumeric field contains mixed entries, it is sorted into descending order using the same rules Paradox follows in sorting into ascending order.

To change the sort order of a field from ascending to descending, you simply type a *D* (for *Descending*) next to the field name in the sort specification. For example, suppose you want to re-sort the EMPLYEE table into reverse alphabetical order on the Last Name field. To begin, issue the **[Menu]** Modify Sort command, type **EMPLYEE**, and press ↵. When Paradox displays the Same/New menu, choose New, and then specify **SORTEMP2** as the new table. After you press ↵, Paradox will display a fresh sort form. Paradox does not retain the previous sort definition when you issue the Modify Sort command.

To specify a descending sort on the Last Name field, move the cursor to that field in the sort form, and type **1D** next to the field name. As before, the *1* tells Paradox that you want to use the Last Name field as the primary key when you sort the table. The *D* tells Paradox to sort this field into descending order. Figure 6-6 on the following page shows the completed sort form.

Now press **[Do-It!]** to sort the table. When you press this key, Paradox will sort the table into descending order based on the Last Name field and store the result in the table SORTEMP2. Figure 6-7 shows the table that results from these instructions.

Figure 6-6 The Completed Sort Form

```
Sorting Emplyee table into new SORTEMP2 table                        Sort

 Number fields to set up sort order (1, 2, etc.).  If you want a field sorted
    in descending sequence, follow the number with a 'D' (e.g., '2D').
         Ascending is the normal sequence and need not be indicated.


        Emp Number
  1D  ◄ Last Name
        First Name
        SS Number
        Address
        City
        State
        Zip
        Phone
        Date of Birth
        Date of Hire
        Exemptions
        Salary
```

Figure 6-7 The SORTEMP2 Table

```
Viewing Sortemp2 table: Record 1 of 16                            Main

SORTEMP2─┬─Emp Number──┬──Last Name─┬─First Name─┬─SS Number──┬────────Addr
    1    │      8      │ Williams   │ Brenda     │ 401-55-1567│ 100 Owl Cr
    2    │     16      │ Robertson  │ Kevin      │ 415-24-6710│ 431 Bardst
    3    │      5      │ Roberts    │ Darlene    │ 417-43-7777│ 451 Lone P
    4    │     14      │ Preston    │ Molly      │ 451-80-3426│ 321 Indian
    5    │      9      │ Myers      │ Julie      │ 314-38-9452│ 4512 Parks
    6    │     15      │ Masters    │ Ron        │ 317-65-4529│ 423 W. 72n
    7    │     10      │ Link       │ Julie      │ 345-75-1525│ 3215 Palm
    8    │      1      │ Jones      │ David      │ 414-76-3421│ 4000 St. J
    9    │      4      │ Jones      │ Stewart    │ 401-32-8721│ 4389 Oakbr
   10    │      6      │ Jones      │ Jean       │ 413-07-9123│ 4000 St. J
   11    │     13      │ Jakes, Jr. │ Sal        │ 321-65-9151│ 3451 Michi
   12    │     12      │ Jackson    │ Mary       │ 424-13-7621│ 7821 Clark
   13    │     19      │ Gunn       │ Barbara    │ 321-97-8632│ 541 Kentuc
   14    │     17      │ Garrison   │ Robert     │ 312-98-1479│ 55 Wheeler
   15    │     20      │ Emerson    │ Cheryl     │ 401-65-1898│ 800 River
   16    │      2      │ Cameron    │ Herb       │ 321-65-8765│ 2331 Elm S
```

Sorting Over and Over

As shown in the previous example, you can sort your tables as many times and in as many different ways as you need. All you have to do each time you want to sort a table is issue the [Menu] Modify Sort command, define the correct sort specifications, and press [Do-It!].

There may be times when you'll define a complex or important sort specification and want to save that specification for future use. One way to save a sort specification is to record a script for it, as we will explain in Chapter 13. Then, you can replay the script any time you want to perform the sort. As an alternative, you may find it helpful to use your computer's print screen function [Shift]-[PrtSc] to produce a hard copy of the sort form screen.

Reversing a Sort

As long as you choose the New option from the Same/New menu, you don't need to worry about reversing a sort. Since Paradox will not change the original table as it performs the sort, the records in that table will remain in their original order.

If you choose the Same option, however, things can be a good deal more difficult. When you choose Same, the records are sorted back into the original table, and the original order of the records is lost. Unless the table has a field that identifies the original order of the records, it will be impossible to reverse the sort.

For example, the Emp Number field in the EMPLYEE table identifies the original order of the table and could be used to reverse a sort on any other field. As long as the table has a field of this type, you can reverse the sort easily just by re-sorting the table onto itself. For example, suppose you used the [Menu] Modify Sort Same command to sort the EMPLYEE table into ascending order by the entries in the Last Name field. Figure 6-5 shows the sorted table. Now, you want to restore the table to its original order. To begin, issue the **[Menu]** **M**odify Sort command, specify **EMPLYEE** as the table to sort, and choose the **S**ame option. When the sort specification screen appears, move to the Emp Number field and type **1**.

After the specification is completed, press **[Do-It!]** to process the sort. The re-sorted EMPLYEE table will appear on the screen, as shown in Figure 6-1.

The Sort Menu

If you press [Menu] ([F10]) while you are defining a sort specification, Paradox will display the Sort menu shown in Figure 6-8. As you can see, this menu has only three options. The Help command, which is equivalent to pressing [Help] ([F1]), displays Paradox's context-sensitive help screen. The DO-IT! command, which is equivalent to pressing [Do-It!] ([F2]), tells Paradox to perform the sort and display the sorted table in the workspace. The Cancel command tells Paradox to cancel the sort specification and return to the main workspace. When you issue the Cancel command, Paradox does not prompt you for confirmation. However, the message *Cancelling sort...* will appear in the lower-right corner of the screen. You can also cancel a sort by pressing [Ctrl]-[Break].

Figure 6-8 The Sort Menu

```
Help  DO-IT!  Cancel                                          Sort
Help with sorting a table.
```

Copying JustFamily

When you sort the records in a table into a new table, Paradox does not automatically copy the family (reports, forms, validity checks, etc.) of the original table to the new table. You can use the [Menu] Tools Copy JustFamily command to copy those objects after you complete the sort. This command copies a table's family without copying the table itself.

For example, suppose you want to copy the family of objects of EMPLYEE to the new table SORTEMP. To begin, issue the **[Menu]** Tools Copy JustFamily command. After you issue this command, Paradox will prompt you for the name of the original table. When you see this prompt, you should type **EMPLYEE** and press ↵. Next, Paradox will prompt you for the name of the target table. You should type the name of the sorted table, in this case **SORTEMP**, and press ↵. Since the objects you are copying will replace any existing objects associated with the target table, Paradox will prompt you for confirmation with the Cancel/ Replace menu.

If you issue the Cancel command at this point, Paradox will return to the previous prompt and wait for you to specify a different target file name. If you issue the Replace command, Paradox will copy the family from the original table to the target table. You will see the message *Copying family members from EMPLYEE to SORTEMP...* displayed at the bottom of the screen.

When you use the [Menu] Tools Copy JustFamily command, there must be a target table ready to receive the family. This means that you should sort first, then use the [Menu] Tools Copy JustFamily command to copy the related objects. In addition, both the source and target tables must have the same structure. If you used the [Menu] Modify Sort command to create the target table, you can be sure that both tables have the same structure.

If you want to copy only a single form to the sorted table, then you can use the [Menu] Tools Copy Form DifferentTable command, which we explained in detail in Chapter 4. If you want to copy only a single report specification to the sorted table, then you can use the [Menu] Tools Copy Report DifferentTable command, which we will discuss in Chapter 11.

Sorting on More Than One Field

In the examples we've considered so far, we've asked Paradox to sort tables on only a single field. You can, however, designate more than one field to sort on if you want. In fact, you can ask Paradox to sort on as many fields as there are in the table.

Why Sort on Multiple Fields?

The need for multiple-field sorts arises when there are identical records in a table's primary sort field. If there are duplicate entries in the primary sort field, then the records in the sorted table may still appear to be "out of order." For example, Figure 6-5, shows the sorted table SORTEMP, which we created by asking Paradox to sort the EMPLYEE table into ascending order based on the Last Name field. Notice the three records with the last name *Jones*. Although these records are in proper order in relation to the other records in the SORTEMP table, notice that the names in the First Name field are not in alphabetical order.

If you want both the First Name and Last Name fields to be sorted, you'll need to perform a two-field sort. When you perform a two-field sort, Paradox will first sort the table based on the entries in the field you designate as the primary sort field. Then, if there are duplicate entries in the primary sort field, Paradox will sort those records based on the entries in the secondary sort field. The secondary sort will serve as a "tie-breaker" for any duplicate entries in the primary field.

An Example

To sort the EMPLYEE table on two fields, first issue the **[Menu] M**odify Sort command, type **EMPLYEE** when Paradox asks for the name of the table to sort, choose **N**ew, and specify **SORTEMP3** as the name of the table to receive the sorted records. When the sort form appears, move to the Last Name field, and type the number **1**. This number tells Paradox that you want to use the Last Name field as the primary sort field for the table. Next, move the cursor to the First Name field, and type the number **2**. This entry tells Paradox to use First Name as the secondary sort field for EMPLYEE. Figure 6-9 shows the completed specification.

Figure 6-9 A Two-field Sort

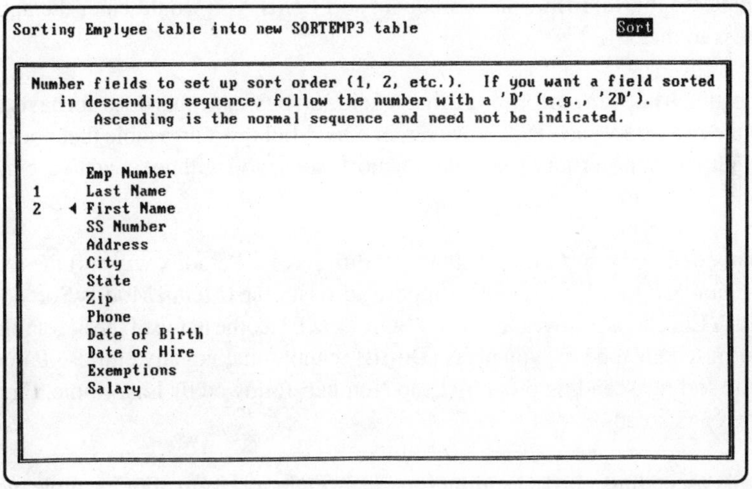

```
Sorting Emplyee table into new SORTEMP3 table                    Sort

  Number fields to set up sort order (1, 2, etc.).  If you want a field sorted
     in descending sequence, follow the number with a 'D' (e.g., '2D').
            Ascending is the normal sequence and need not be indicated.


          Emp Number
     1    Last Name
     2  ◄ First Name
          SS Number
          Address
          City
          State
          Zip
          Phone
          Date of Birth
          Date of Hire
          Exemptions
          Salary
```

When you press **[Do-It!]**, Paradox will sort the EMPLYEE table and store the results in the table SORTEMP3. Figure 6-10 shows this table. Notice that, as in the SORTEMP table, the records in SORTEMP3 are arranged in alphabetical order according to the entries in the Last Name field. However, notice that the three records with the last name *Jones* are now arranged in alphabetical order according to their first names. Since the First Name field was designated as the secondary sort field, Paradox used that field to decide which Jones should be placed first in the table.

Figure 6-10 The SORTEMP3 Table

```
Viewing Sortemp3 table: Record 1 of 16                              Main
SORTEMP3╤═Emp Number═══════╤═Last Name══╤═First Name══╤═SS Number═══╤═════════Addr
     1  ║      2           ║ Cameron    ║ Herb        ║ 321-65-8765 ║ 2331 Elm S
     2  ║     20           ║ Emerson    ║ Cheryl      ║ 401-65-1898 ║ 800 River
     3  ║     17           ║ Garrison   ║ Robert      ║ 312-98-1479 ║ 55 Wheeler
     4  ║     19           ║ Gunn       ║ Barbara     ║ 321-97-8632 ║ 541 Kentuc
     5  ║     12           ║ Jackson    ║ Mary        ║ 424-13-7621 ║ 7821 Clark
     6  ║     13           ║ Jakes, Jr. ║ Sal         ║ 321-65-9151 ║ 3451 Michi
     7  ║      1           ║ Jones      ║ David       ║ 414-76-3421 ║ 4000 St. J
     8  ║      6           ║ Jones      ║ Jean        ║ 413-07-9123 ║ 4000 St. J
     9  ║      4           ║ Jones      ║ Stewart     ║ 401-32-8721 ║ 4389 Oakbr
    10  ║     10           ║ Link       ║ Julie       ║ 345-75-1525 ║ 3215 Palm
    11  ║     15           ║ Masters    ║ Ron         ║ 317-65-4529 ║ 423 W. 72n
    12  ║      9           ║ Myers      ║ Julie       ║ 314-38-9452 ║ 4512 Parks
    13  ║     14           ║ Preston    ║ Molly       ║ 451-00-3426 ║ 321 Indian
    14  ║      5           ║ Roberts    ║ Darlene     ║ 417-43-7777 ║ 451 Lone P
    15  ║     16           ║ Robertson  ║ Kevin       ║ 415-24-6710 ║ 431 Bardst
    16  ║      8           ║ Williams   ║ Brenda      ║ 401-55-1567 ║ 100 Owl Cr
```

Notes

As we have said, Paradox does not limit you to only two-field sorts. You can continue to designate fields for the sort, up to the total number of fields in that table. To designate the third sort field, you would type a 3 in the sort specification next to that field on the sort form. To designate the fourth, fifth, and subsequent sort fields, you would enter the appropriate number next to them.

There is not much point in performing a three-field sort on a table that does not have duplicate entries in the secondary sort field, however, or a four-field sort on a table that does not have duplicate entries in the tertiary sort field. In most cases, you will not need to use more than two or three sort fields.

If you do not define the sort order on the sort form screen, Paradox will sort the records by field in ascending order. For example, suppose you issue the [Menu] Modify Sort command, type EMPLYEE, choose New, and specify SORTEMP4 as the name of the new table. When the sort form screen appears, you press [Do-It!] without making any entries. Paradox will perform the sort in ascending order by Emp Number, followed by Last Name, First Name, SS Number, and so on.

You can mix ascending and descending sorts in a single sort form. For example, you could ask Paradox to sort the EMPLYEE table into ascending order on the Last Name field by placing a 1 next to that field in the form, and then ask it to sort the First Name entries in each Last Name group into descending order by typing 2D next to that field.

If you do not define the sort in numeric order, Paradox will not perform the sort. Instead, it will display the message *Sortkey X is missing,* where *X* is the number you omitted. For example, notice that the number *2* is missing from the sort specification in Figure 6-11. If you try to process this sort, Paradox will display the message *Sortkey 2 is missing.*

Figure 6-11 A Sort Form Missing a SortKey

```
Sorting Emplyee table                                              Sort

  ┌────────────────────────────────────────────────────────────────┐
  │ Number fields to set up sort order (1, 2, etc.).  If you want a field sorted │
  │    in descending sequence, follow the number with a "D" (e.g., "2D"). │
  │          Ascending is the normal sequence and need not be indicated. │
  │ ──────────────────────────────────────────────────────────────── │
  │                                                                  │
  │            Emp Number                                            │
  │        1   Last Name                                             │
  │        3 ◄ First Name                                            │
  │            SS Number                                             │
  │            Address                                               │
  │            City                                                  │
  │            State                                                 │
  │            Zip                                                   │
  │            Phone                                                 │
  │            Date of Birth                                         │
  │            Date of Hire                                          │
  │            Exemptions                                            │
  │            Salary                                                │
  │                                                                  │
  └────────────────────────────────────────────────────────────────┘
```

If you enter a number next to a field in the sort specification by mistake, you can erase it just by pressing [Backspace]. For example, suppose you entered the number 3 next to the First Name field in the sort specification in Figure 6-11 by mistake. To erase the error, just move the cursor to the First Name field, and press [Backspace]. Once you have erased the mistake, you can type a new number or move to a different field.

Sorting Keyed Tables

You will recall from our previous discussion of key fields that designating a key field in a table automatically establishes a sort order for the records in that table. Since Paradox will not let you violate the sort order in a keyed table, you cannot sort a keyed table onto itself. If you are sorting a keyed table, therefore, you will not see the Same/New option. Instead, Paradox will prompt you to enter a name for the new table.

Suppose you want to sort the records in the PROJECTS table in descending order by client number. To begin, issue the **[Menu]** Modify Sort command, type **PROJECTS**, and press ↵. When you do this, Paradox will recognize the key field in the table and prompt you to supply the name of the new table. When you see this prompt, you should type a name for the new table (we called ours SORTPRJ) and press ↵. When the sort form appears, you should press the ↓ key to position the cursor on the Client Number field, then type **1D.** Next, press **[Do-It!]** ([F2]). After you do this, Paradox will perform the sort and display the new table in the workspace, as shown in Figure 6-12.

Figure 6-12 The Sorted PROJECTS Table

```
Viewing Sortprj table: Record 1 of 16                              Main
SORTPRJ┬─Job Number──┬─Client Number──┬─Job Type─┬─────────────Descripti
     1 │    115      │     1014        │    1     │ Install PC AT/Paradox/
     2 │    114      │     1013        │    2     │ 1988 Tax Return
     3 │    112      │     1009        │    2     │ 1988 Tax Return
     4 │    111      │     1008        │    2     │ 1988 Tax Return
     5 │    110      │     1007        │    5     │ Tax Consultation
     6 │    113      │     1007        │    1     │ 1988 Tax Return
     7 │    109      │     1006        │    3     │ 1988 Compilation/Revie
     8 │    108      │     1005        │    3     │ 1988 Compilation/Revie
     9 │    106      │     1004        │    2     │ Paradox Time Accountin
    10 │    107      │     1004        │    3     │ 1988 Compilation/Revie
    11 │    103      │     1003        │    1     │ Install Compaq Plus/Sy
    12 │    104      │     1003        │    2     │ Symphony Intro Course
    13 │    105      │     1003        │    4     │ Recommend AR System
    14 │    102      │     1002        │    2     │ Paradox A/R Systems
    15 │    100      │     1001        │    1     │ Install PC AT/Paradox/
    16 │    101      │     1001        │    3     │ AT/Paradox/1-2-3 Intro
```

Conclusion

In this chapter, we showed you how to sort your Paradox tables. We showed you how to choose the destination for the sorted records, how to define the fields on which you want to sort, and how to define the order of the sort. You'll find that sorting will be an important part of your work with Paradox. In the next chapter, "Queries," we will begin to show you how to query, or ask questions of, your Paradox tables.

Chapter 7

Queries

In the first chapters in this book, we showed you how to create Paradox tables, how to modify the structure of those tables, and how to enter data into tables. Yet, if all you could do with Paradox were create tables and type entries into those tables, the program would not be very useful. The real power of Paradox lies in its ability to locate, reorganize, and change your data.

In Paradox, the tools you use to locate information that is stored in a table are called queries. The word "query" means "to ask." You can use queries to ask Paradox to extract selected information from a table, to delete information from a table, to change selected data, or even to combine two tables into a single table.

In this chapter, we'll show you how to query your Paradox tables. We'll begin with some very simple examples and build up to more complex ones. Along the way, we'll offer notes, hints, and cautions that you can apply to your own queries.

A Simple Example

Suppose you have created the table named EMPLYEE, whose structure is shown in Figure 7-1, and have entered the information shown in Figure 7-2 on the next page into the table. Figure 7-3 on page 231 shows this table in view on the screen. Now, suppose you want to extract from this table all of the records that have the entry *KY* in the State field. To do this, you'll want to create a query on the EMPLYEE table.

Figure 7-1 The Structure of EMPLYEE

```
Viewing Struct table: Record 1 of 13                          Main

STRUCT            Field Name         Field Type
     1    Emp Number                 N
     2    Last Name                  A18
     3    First Name                 A18
     4    SS Number                  A11
     5    Address                    A20
     6    City                       A20
     7    State                      A2
     8    Zip                        A5
     9    Phone                      A14
    10    Date of Birth              D
    11    Date of Hire               D
    12    Exemptions                 N
    13    Salary                     $
```

Viewing Emplyee table: Record 1 of 16

EMPLYEE—Emp Number	Last name	First Name	SS Number	Address	City	State	Zip	Phone	Date of Birth	Date of Hire	Exemptions	Salary
1	Jones	David	414-76-3421	4000 St. James Ct.	St. Matthews	KY	40207	(502) 245-6618	10/06/42	1/14/87	3	70,000.00
2	Cameron	Hank	321-65-8765	2331 Elm St	Louisville	KY	40208	(502) 451-8765	11/24/29	1/14/87	4	58,000.00
4	Jones	Stewart	401-52-8721	4389 Oakbridge Rd.	Lyndon	KY	40222	(502) 452-1048	3/21/50	2/13/87	4	47,000.00
5	Roberts	Darlene	417-43-7777	451 Lone Pine Dr.	Lagrange	KY	40012	(502) 897-3215	9/24/60	7/16/87	3	14,000.00
6	Jones	Jean	414-87-9123	4000 St. James Ct.	St. Matthews	KY	40207	(502) 245-6618	5/14/43	7/16/87	5	33,999.99
8	Williams	Brenda	401-55-1567	100 Owl Creek Rd.	Louisville	KY	40223	(502) 894-9761	1/12/20	8/16/87	5	40,000.00
9	Myers	Julie	314-38-9452	4512 Parkside Dr.	Louisville	KY	40209	(502) 454-5289	2/06/40	9/16/87	1	32,000.00
10	Link	Julie	345-75-1525	3215 Palm Ct.	Palo Alto	CA	94375	(400) 542-1940	6/03/33	11/14/87	3	30,000.00
12	Jackson	Mary	424-13-7621	7021 Clark Ave.	Clarksville	IN	47138	(812) 288-6754	8/12/56	12/14/87	3	21,000.00
13	Jakes, Jr.	Sal	421-65-9151	3451 Michigan Ave.	Dallas	TX	65907	(214) 398-1907	5/23/59	2/13/88	6	34,000.00
14	Preston	Molly	451-08-9156	3251 Indian Hills Rd.	Louisville	KY	40208	(502) 456-3256	4/17/66	2/13/88	8	14,750.00
15	Masters	Ron	317-65-4529	423 W. 72nd ST.	New York	NY	10019	(212) 276-5478	12/30/44	2/13/88	8	30,000.00
16	Robertson	Kevin	415-24-6718	431 Bardstown Rd.	Elizabethtown	KY	10015	(212) 543-3723	3/16/25	2/27/88	4	37,000.00
17	Garrison	Robert	312-98-1479	55 Wheeler St.	Boston	MA	25687	(617) 543-4124	5/07/45	5/15/88	1	32,000.00
19	Gunn	Barbara	321-97-8632	541 Kentucky St.	New Albany	IN	47132	(818) 325-4789	5/18/58	6/15/88	2	17,500.00
20	Emerson	Cheryl	401-65-1828	800 River Rd.	Prospect	KY	40222	(502) 896-5139	7/30/66	8/15/88	2	12,000.00

Figure 7-2 The EMPLYEE Table

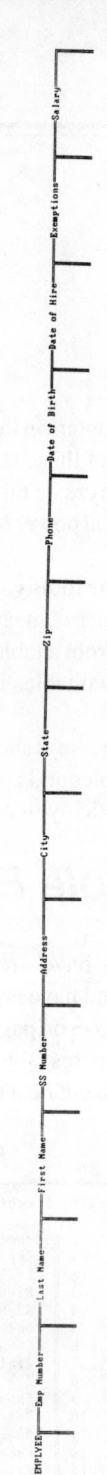

EMPLYEE—Emp Number—Last Name—First Name—SS Number—Address—City—State—Zip—Phone—Date of Birth—Date of Hire—Exemptions—Salary

Figure 7-4 A Query Form for EMPLYEE

Figure 7-3 The EMPLYEE Table

```
Viewing Emplyee table: Record 1 of 16                           Main

EMPLYEE┬═Emp Number═┬══════Last Name═╤═First Name═┬═SS Number═╤══════════Addre
   1  ║      1     ║  Jones         │  David     ║ 414-76-3421 ║ 4000 St. Ja
   2  ║      2     ║  Cameron       │  Herb      ║ 321-65-8765 ║ 2321 Elm St
   3  ║      4     ║  Jones         │  Stewart   ║ 401-32-8721 ║ 4389 Oakbri
   4  ║      5     ║  Roberts       │  Darlene   ║ 417-43-7777 ║ 451 Lone Pi
   5  ║      6     ║  Jones         │  Jean      ║ 413-07-9123 ║ 4000 St. Ja
   6  ║      8     ║  Williams      │  Brenda    ║ 401-55-1567 ║ 100 Owl Cre
   7  ║      9     ║  Myers         │  Julie     ║ 314-38-9452 ║ 4512 Parksi
   8  ║     10     ║  Link          │  Julie     ║ 345-75-1525 ║ 3215 Palm C
   9  ║     12     ║  Jackson       │  Mary      ║ 424-13-7621 ║ 7821 Clark
  10  ║     13     ║  Jakes, Jr.    │  Sal       ║ 321-65-9151 ║ 3451 Michig
  11  ║     14     ║  Preston       │  Molly     ║ 451-00-3426 ║ 321 Indian
  12  ║     15     ║  Masters       │  Ron       ║ 317-65-4529 ║ 423 W. 72nd
  13  ║     16     ║  Robertson     │  Kevin     ║ 415-24-6710 ║ 431 Bardsto
  14  ║     17     ║  Garrison      │  Robert    ║ 312-98-1479 ║ 55 Wheeler
  15  ║     19     ║  Gunn          │  Barbara   ║ 321-97-8632 ║ 541 Kentuck
  16  ║     20     ║  Emerson       │  Cheryl    ║ 404-14-1422 ║ 8100 River
```

Creating a Query Form

Before you can define a query for any table, you must create a query form for that table. To create a query form, issue the **[Menu]** **A**sk command and supply the name of the table that you want to query. In this case, when Paradox asks you for the name of the table you want to query, either type the table name **EMPLYEE** or press ↵ and point to the table name in the list that Paradox provides.

When you have specified the table you want to query, Paradox will present a new image, called a query form, for that table. Figure 7-4 shows a query form for the EMPLYEE table. Figure 7-5 shows this form on the screen. You'll use this query form to tell Paradox on which fields and records you want to operate.

Figure 7-5 A Query Form for EMPLYEE

```
√ [F6] to include a field in the ANSWER; [F5] to give an Example   Main

EMPLYEE┬═════Emp Number═══════┬═════Last Name═══════┬════First Name═══════┬═══SS Number═══
       │                      │                     │                     │
       │                      │                     │                     │
       │                      │                     │                     │
```

Filling in the Query Form

Once you have created a query form, you will usually make entries in that form that define the query you want Paradox to perform. At this stage, you can select the fields you want Paradox to include in the result of the query, and you can define selection conditions that select records based on the entries in those records.

In the example, we want to extract all of the information (that is, the data stored in each field) for all of the records that have the entry *KY* in the State field. To fill in this query form, press the **[Check Mark]** key ([F6]) while the cursor is still in the area under the query form name.

Pressing [Check Mark] causes Paradox to place a check mark in each field of the query, as shown in Figure 7-6. When you process this query, Paradox will include every selected field (that is, every field that includes a check mark) in the result.

Figure 7-6 Selecting Fields

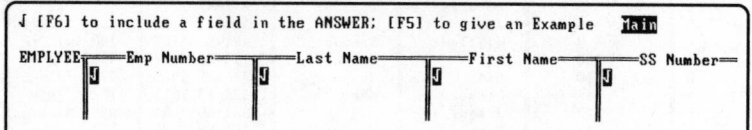

Now, you must enter a selection condition in the form that tells Paradox to select only those records that have the entry *KY* in the State field. To do this, press ➜ seven times to move the cursor to the State field of the query form. Now, type **KY**. Notice that you don't need to press [Edit] before you type. Figure 7-7 shows the screen at this point, and Figure 7-8 shows the entire completed query.

Figure 7-7 The Completed Query

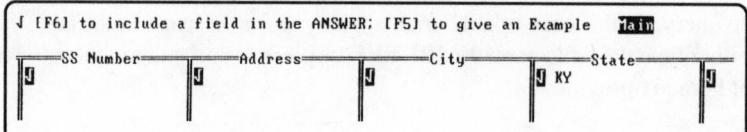

Processing the Query

To process the query, press **[Do-It!]** ([F2]). When you press this key, Paradox will display the message *Processing query...* in the lower-right corner of the screen. (If the query is improperly defined, Paradox will instead display one of a variety of error messages.)

Figure 7-9 on page 230 shows the screen as it will look after you process the query. As you can see, Paradox has created a new table, ANSWER, which includes only those records that have the entry *KY* in the State field. Figure 7-10 shows the entire ANSWER table. Because you selected every field in the query form, the ANSWER table includes every field from the EMPLYEE table. In other words, the ANSWER table contains the information that answers your query.

Of course, this is a very simple query. Paradox queries can be far more complex than this one. In the remainder of this chapter, we'll show you how to build more sophisticated queries in Paradox.

Figure 7-8 The Completed Query

EMPLOYEE	Emp Number	Last Name	First Name	SS Number	Address	City	State	KY	Zip	Phone	Date of Birth	Date of Hire	Exemptions	Salary

Figure 7-10 The ANSWER Table

Viewing Answer table: Record 1 of 18

Emp Number	Last name	First Name	SS Number	Address	City	State	Zip	Phone	Date of Birth	Date of Hire	Exemptions	Salary
1	Jones	David	414-76-3421	4000 St. James Ct.	St. Matthews	KY	40207	(502) 245-6618	10/06/42	1/14/87	3	70,000.00
2	Cameron	Herb	321-65-8765	2331 Elm St.	Louisville	KY	40208	(502) 451-8765	11/24/29	1/14/87	4	58,000.00
3	Jones	David	401-32-8721	4389 Oakbridge Rd.	Lyndon	KY	40222	(502) 452-1040	3/21/58	2/13/87	1	47,000.00
4	Roberts	Darlene	417-43-7777	451 Lone Pine Dr.	Largrange	KY	40012	(502) 897-2215	9/24/60	6/16/87	3	14,000.00
5	Jones	Jean	414-87-9123	4000 St. James Ct.	St. Matthews	KY	40207	(502) 245-6618	5/14/43	7/16/87	8	33,999.99
6	Williams	Brenda	401-55-1567	100 Owl Creek Rd.	Anchorage	KY	40223	(502) 894-9761	1/12/28	8/16/87	5	40,000.00
7	Myers	Julie	314-30-9452	4512 Parkside Dr.	Louisville	KY	40209	(502) 454-5209	2/06/40	9/16/87	1	32,000.00
11	Preston	Molly	451-80-3426	321 Indian Hills Rd.	Louisville	KY	40200	(502) 456-3256	4/17/66	2/13/88	0	14,750.00
13	Robertson	Kevin	415-24-6718	431 Bardstown Rd.	Elizabethtown	KY	40315	(502) 423-9823	3/16/25	2/27/88	1	37,000.00
16	Emerson	Cheryl	401-65-1828	800 River Rd.	Prospect	KY	40222	(502) 896-5139	7/30/66	8/15/88	2	12,000.00

Figure 7-9 The ANSWER Table

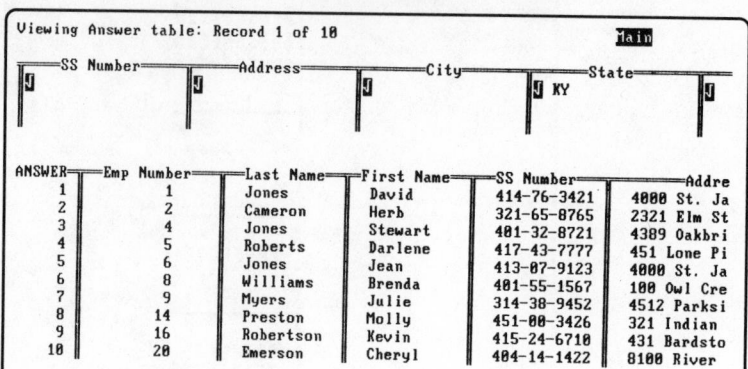

Query Basics

Now that you have seen an example of a query, we should go back and cover a few basics about queries. We'll start with some notes about query forms and then look in detail at ANSWER tables.

Query Form Notes

Before you can define a query for a table, you must create a query form for that table. This step is always required, since without a query form there can be no query. As you have seen, you create a query form for a table by issuing the [Menu] Ask command and specifying the name of the table.

The query form that Paradox creates for a table always has the same structure as that table. For example, the query form you created for EMPLYEE has the same structure as the EMPLYEE table. It includes all of the fields that are in EMPLYEE; furthermore, the fields in the query form are in the same order as the fields in the table. In fact, the query form even has the name EMPLYEE.

You will notice that the query form in Figure 7-9 appears at the top of the screen. Whenever you create a new query form, it will always appear at the top of the screen, above normal table images.

Notice that the EMPLYEE table was not in view when we created the query in Figure 7-7. Paradox does not require that you view a table in order to create a query form for that table. If you are viewing a table when you create a query form, the form will appear above the table image at the top of the screen. Similarly, the table you are querying does not need to be in view when you process the query. If the table is not in view when you press [Do-It!], Paradox will not bring it into view. If the table is in view, the ANSWER table will appear below it on the screen.

More than one query form can be active at once. In fact, some types of queries require you to create several different query forms. To create a second and third query form, you just repeat the [Menu] Ask command and specify the name of the table for which you want to create a form. If there are already other query forms on the screen when you create a new query form, the new form will appear below the existing forms on the screen, but it will appear above any normal table images.

Although there can be query forms for several different tables on the screen at once, you can only have one query form at a time for a given table. If there is already one query form for a table on the screen when you issue the [Menu] Ask command to create another form for that table, Paradox will move the cursor to the existing query form, rather than create a second query form for it.

Moving the Cursor

If there are other images on the screen with a query form, you can move the cursor from image to image with the [Up Image] ([F3]) and [Down Image] ([F4]) keys. For example, to move the cursor from the ANSWER table in Figure 7-9 to the EMPLYEE query form, press **[Up Image]** once.

You can move the cursor around within a query form the same way you move it around in a table image. The → and ← keys move the cursor right and left from field to field. If you move far enough to the right, the query form will shift so that new fields come into view at the right side of the screen, and other fields will disappear to the left.

Just as in a table image, the [Ctrl]-→ and [Ctrl]-← keys move the cursor one screen to the right or left. The [Ctrl]-[Home] combination will move the cursor to the far-left edge of the query form, and the [Ctrl]-[End] combination will move it to the far-right edge.

You can use the ↑ and ↓ keys to move the cursor from row to row in the query form. However, Paradox will not allow you to move the cursor to the second row of a query form until you have made some entry in the first row. If you press ↓ before you make an entry in the first row, Paradox will beep. We'll use these keys in a few pages when we talk about OR queries.

Making Entries

In the example, you made two kinds of entries in the query form. First, you used the [Check Mark] key to enter check marks in all the fields of the form. These check marks select the fields you want Paradox to include in the ANSWER table.

As a rule, you must select at least one field in a query form before you process a query. If you press [Do-It!] to process a query form in which no fields are check-marked, Paradox will deliver one of two messages. If the query is completely blank, Paradox will return the message *Nothing to process now*. If the query contains a selection condition, but no selected fields, Paradox will return the message *Query has no checked fields* when you press [Do-It!].

Second, in our example, we entered the letters *KY* in the State field of the form. This entry is an example of a selection condition. By entering these characters in the State field of the query form, we asked Paradox to select those records in EMPLYEE that have the State field entry *KY*.

As you saw, making an entry in a query form is as easy as moving the cursor to the field where you want the entry to be stored and typing the entry. The big difference between making an entry in a query form and making an entry in a table is that you don't need to press [Edit] or issue any commands before you make an entry in a query form.

Reusing Query Forms

You don't need to start from scratch each time you want to construct a query on a table. If you have previously queried the table, and the query form you used is still on the workspace, you can use that existing query form to perform the new query. All you need to do is change the form so that it defines the new query, then press [Do-It!].

For example, suppose you now want to select all of the records from the EMPLYEE table that have the entry *IN* in the State field. To do this, move the cursor to the query form, then move to the State field. When the cursor is in place, press **[Ctrl]-[Backspace]** to erase the existing entry, *KY*. Then, just type **IN**. Figure 7-11 shows the completed query form.

Figure 7-11 The Query Form: IN

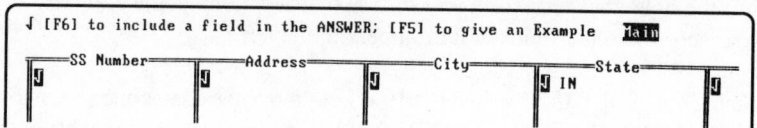

Now press **[Do-It!]** to process the query. Figure 7-12 shows the resulting ANSWER table. This table includes all of the fields from EMPLYEE, but only two records. The records in ANSWER are the only records in the table that meet the selection condition you described.

Figure 7-12 The ANSWER Table: IN

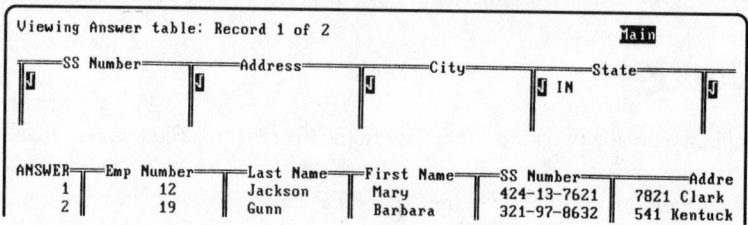

By the way, when you processed this query, Paradox replaced the original ANSWER table with the new ANSWER table. Unless you renamed the original ANSWER table, its contents are now lost. The only way to recreate the old ANSWER table would be to redefine and process the query shown in Figure 7-7.

Clearing a Query Form

You can clear a query form from the workspace the same way you clear any other image. To clear a query form, move the cursor to that form and press [Clear Image] ([F8]). For example, to clear the query form you created in the previous example, you would press [Up Image] to move the cursor into the form, and then press [Clear Image] to clear the query form from view. As you might expect, if you press [Clear All] ([Alt]-[F8]) while a query form is on the workspace, it will be cleared away along with all of the other images on the workspace.

Query forms are temporary. When you clear a query form from the screen, that query form ceases to exist. Any entries you have made in the query form are lost. If you want to reuse a query that you have cleared from the screen, you must recreate it from scratch with the [Menu] Ask command.

There is one exception to this rule. You can use the [Menu] Scripts QuerySave command to save your queries into special query scripts. We'll cover this command at the end of this chapter.

Creating a New Query Form

Suppose you want to define a new query on a table for which a query form already exists, but the new query you want to create is vastly different from the existing query. You might find it easier to clear the existing query and start from scratch than to edit the existing query. To create a new, blank query for a table, first use the **[Clear Image]** or **[Clear All]** key to clear the existing query form. Then, use the **[Menu]** Ask command to create a query form for the table. Another method is to press the [Del] key while the cursor is positioned in the query form. The [Del] key erases the entire contents of the line on the query form, while leaving the form itself intact.

Throughout this chapter, we'll ask you to begin an example by creating a new, blank query form for a table. When we ask you to do this, use one of these techniques to create the form.

The ANSWER Table

In general, when you perform a query, Paradox will copy the information you have requested from the table you are querying into a temporary table called ANSWER and will display that table on the screen. (In certain cases, Paradox may copy the information to other places as well, or may not create an ANSWER table.) In most situations, ANSWER is a perfectly normal Paradox table. However, there are a couple of things you need to know about the ANSWER table.

Note that in Figure 7-9, the cursor is in the ANSWER table. No matter where the cursor is when you process a query, it will be in the first field of the first record in ANSWER when the query is completed.

If the ANSWER table that results from a query is large, it may push the query form, and perhaps other images as well, off the top of the screen. The hidden images still exist; they're simply out of view. If you want to look at them, press the [Up Image] key.

Editing ANSWER

You can edit the contents of an ANSWER table just as you edit the contents of any other Paradox table. However, you must keep in mind that the ANSWER table that results from a query is completely independent from the table you queried to produce the ANSWER table. Changes you make to the data in an ANSWER table do not affect the entries in the original, permanent table.

Querying ANSWER

Because ANSWER tables are normal Paradox tables, they can be queried like any other table. For example, suppose you have created the ANSWER table shown in Figure 7-13. Remember that this table includes only those records from EMPLYEE that have the State field entry *IN*. Now, suppose you want to query the ANSWER table to locate those records with the City field entry *New Albany*.

To make this selection, first press **[Clear Image]** to clear the EMPLYEE query form, then use the **[Menu]** Ask command to create a new query form for the ANSWER table. Next, press **[Check Mark]** with the cursor in the space under the form name to select every field in the form. Then, move to the City field and type **New Albany**. Figure 7-13 shows the completed query.

Figure 7-13 Query Form on the ANSWER Table

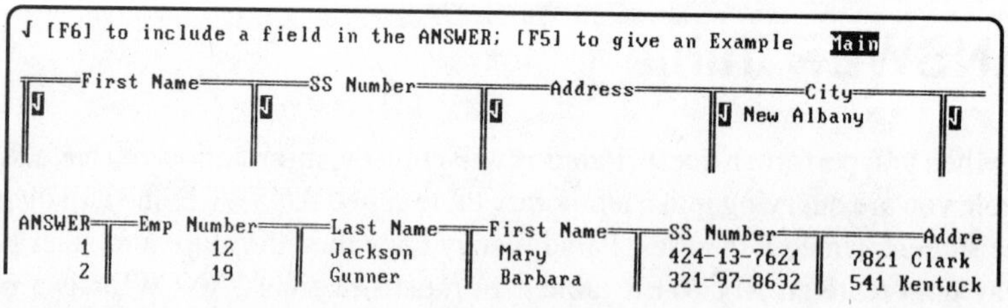

To process the query, press **[Do-It!]**. As before, pressing [Do-It!] will cause Paradox to select the requested records from the table you are querying (in this case, ANSWER) and write them into a table called ANSWER. Figure 7-14 shows the new ANSWER table. Notice that it includes only the one record from the original ANSWER table (shown in Figure 7-13) that has the City field entry *New Albany*.

Figure 7-14 The New ANSWER Table

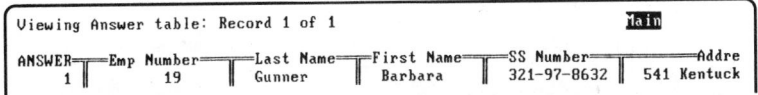

```
Viewing Answer table: Record 1 of 1                          Main

ANSWER┬─Emp Number─────┬──Last Name─┬─First Name─┬─SS Number──┬────Addre
    1 ║        19      ║  Gunner    ║  Barbara   ║ 321-97-8632 ║ 541 Kentuck
```

Since the table you are querying in this example is an ANSWER table, it will be overwritten by the new ANSWER table as the query is processed. In addition, Paradox will erase the query form for the original ANSWER table as you perform the query. This only makes sense—after all, how could a query form exist for a table that has been replaced with a new table? Whenever you perform a query on the ANSWER table, both the previous ANSWER table and the ANSWER query form will be erased when you press [Do-It!]. If you want to preserve the first ANSWER table, you should rename it before you create the second query.

Saving ANSWER

Only one ANSWER table can exist at any time. Whenever you perform a query, the ANSWER table created by that query will overwrite the existing ANSWER table, if there is one. Any information stored in the first ANSWER table will be lost. Furthermore, when you end your Paradox session using the [Menu] Exit command, Paradox will delete the ANSWER table, if there is one, before returning to DOS. When you start Paradox again, the ANSWER table from a previous session will be gone.

As a result, if you want to preserve the results of a query, you'll need to rename the ANSWER table that is produced by the query before you perform another query. You can rename an ANSWER table (or any other table, for that matter) by issuing the [Menu] Tools Rename Table command, supplying the name of the table to be renamed, and supplying the new name you want to give the table. For example, to change the name of the ANSWER table you just created to NEWALB, you would issue the **[Menu] T**ools **R**ename **T**able command, type **ANSWER**, press ↵, type **NEWALB**, and then press ↵ once again.

Selecting Fields

When you process a query, Paradox creates a special table, called ANSWER, that contains the information you requested. Although the structure of ANSWER will always be related to the structure of the table you are querying, ANSWER can include all or only some of the fields (and all or only some of the records) from the table you are querying. You indicate which fields to include in ANSWER by selecting fields in the query form.

You select fields in query forms by pressing either [Check Mark] or [Check Plus] while the cursor is in the appropriate place in the form. In the first few examples, you selected every field in the query form by pressing [Check Mark] while the cursor was in the space under the query form name. This action placed a check mark in every field of the form. When the form was processed, Paradox included every field from the query form in the ANSWER table.

You don't need to select every field in a query form, however. You can select just one field or several fields, depending on how you want the ANSWER table to look.

Selecting One Field

To select a field in a query form, use the arrow keys to move the cursor into that field, then press the [Check Mark] key ([F6]). For example, suppose you want to select the Last Name field in an EMPLYEE query form. To begin, press **[Clear All]** to clear the screen, then use the **[Menu]** Ask command to create a new query form for EMPLYEE. To select the Last Name field, press ➡ twice to move the cursor into that field of the query form, and then press **[Check Mark]** ([F6]). Figure 7-15 shows the completed query. As you can see, Paradox has marked the selected field in the query form with a check mark.

Figure 7-15 Selecting the Last Name Field

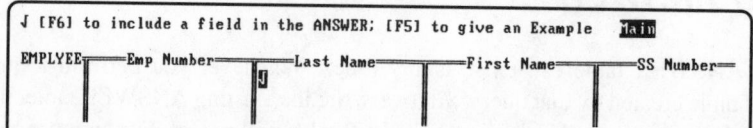

Once you have selected a field, you can deselect it by pressing the [Check Mark] key a second time. For example, to deselect the Last Name field, you would move the cursor to the Last Name field in the query form (it should already be there) and press [Check Mark] again. As soon as you press [Check Mark], Paradox will remove the check mark from the field, indicating that it has been deselected. If you then want to reselect the field, you need only press [Check Mark] again.

If you press [Do-It!] to process this query when only the Last Name field is selected, Paradox will create the ANSWER table shown in Figure 7-16. As always, this table includes the records in the table that answer the query you have defined. Since you selected only one field in the query form, the ANSWER table includes only one field. The records in this field are arranged in alphabetical order.

Notice that there are only 14 records in ANSWER, while there are 16 records in EMPLYEE. This occurs because several of the records in EMPLYEE have the same entry in the Last Name field and because (without knowing it) you asked Paradox to copy only unique entries to the ANSWER table. We will discuss the concept of duplicate entries in a few pages.

There's one more thing worth pointing out about this query. Notice that we didn't enter any selection conditions into the query form, but merely selected a field and pressed [Do-It!]. You don't need to use selection conditions in queries. If you don't include selection conditions in a query, Paradox will include every unique record from the table in the ANSWER table.

Figure 7-16 The ANSWER Table with One Field

```
Viewing Answer table: Record 1 of 14                           Main

EMPLYEE┬─Emp Number────┬─Last Name────┬─First Name────┬─SS Number─
       │              ╪│              │              │
       │              ╪│              │              │
       │              ╪│              │              │



ANSWER┬─Last Name─
    1 ║ Cameron
    2 ║ Emerson
    3 ║ Garrison
    4 ║ Gunn
    5 ║ Jackson
    6 ║ Jakes, Jr.
    7 ║ Jones
    8 ║ Link
    9 ║ Masters
   10 ║ Myers
   11 ║ Preston
   12 ║ Roberts
   13 ║ Robertson
   14 ║ Williams
```

Selecting More Fields

To select more than one field, place a check mark or check plus into each field you want to
select. For example, suppose you want the ANSWER table to include not only the last name,
but also the address of each employee in EMPLYEE. To do this, press [Up Image] to move
to the EMPLYEE query form. Then, move the cursor to the Address field. When the cursor
is in place, press [Check Mark] to select the field. Figure 7-17 shows the completed query.

Figure 7-17 Query Form with Two Checked Fields

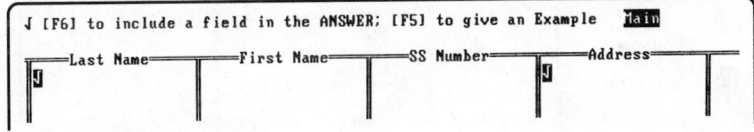

When you press [Do-It!], Paradox will create a new ANSWER table like the one shown
in Figure 7-18 on the following page. Notice that because this new table includes the
contents of both the Last Name and the Address fields of EMPLYEE, Paradox added a
second *Jones* entry.

Of course, you can use this technique to select as many of the fields in a query form as you
want. Paradox will always include all of the fields you have selected in the ANSWER table.
For example, Figure 7-19 shows a query form in which the Last Name, First Name, and
Address fields in the EMPLYEE table are selected, and also the ANSWER table that Paradox
will produce when you process that query.

Figure 7-18 Selecting Two Fields

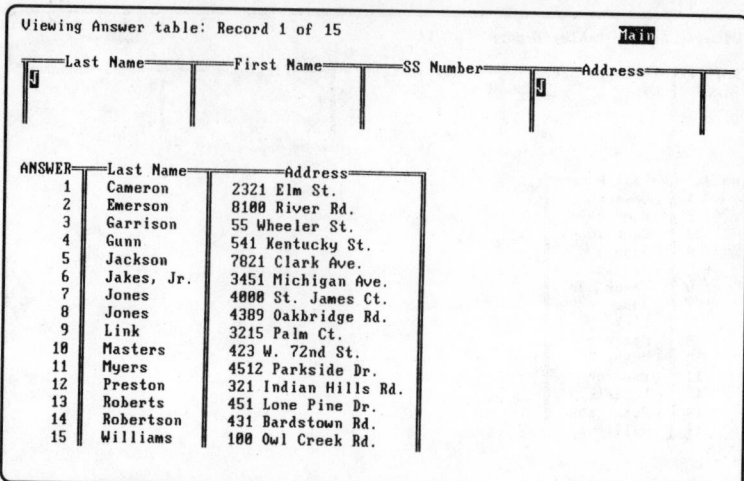

Figure 7-19 Selecting Three Fields

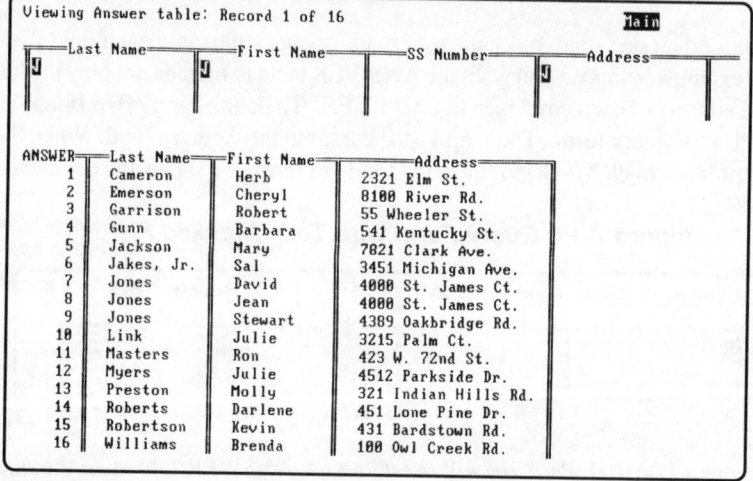

Selecting Every Field

If you want to select every field in a query form, just move the cursor to the area under the query form name and press [Check Mark]. This is the technique we used in the first example to select every field in EMPLYEE. When you do this, Paradox will place check marks in every field of the query form. When you process a query in which every field is selected, the ANSWER table will include every field that appears in the query form.

Selecting Unselected Fields

Suppose you have selected one or more fields in a form and you now want to select the remaining fields. All you need to do is move the cursor to the space under the query form name and press [Check Mark]. This action will select all of the unselected fields in the query form. As before, the result will be a query form with every field selected.

For example, suppose you had selected every field in the EMPLYEE query form except the Emp Number field. If you move the cursor to the space under the query form's name and press [Check Mark], Paradox will enter a check mark in the Emp Number field. The check marks in the other fields will not be affected by this action.

Deselecting All Fields

As you might expect, you can also use this technique to deselect all of the fields in a query form. If all of the fields in a query form are selected, then you can deselect all of the fields in one step by pressing [Check Mark] while the cursor is in the space under the query form name at the left edge of the image. If at least one field in the form is not selected, pressing [Check Mark] while the cursor is in the space under the query form name will select the field or fields that were previously unselected. You can then deselect every field simply by pressing [Check Mark] again.

Notes

As you have seen, if every field in a query form is selected, Paradox will include every field from the form in the ANSWER table. There will be times when you'll want to include all of the fields in a table in the ANSWER table when you perform a query. Usually, though, when you select every field in a query form, you'll also create selection conditions in the form that select only certain records for the ANSWER table. Otherwise, the ANSWER table will probably be an exact copy of the table you are querying. (There are two reasons why the ANSWER table might not be an identical copy. First, duplicate records, if there are any, will be excluded from ANSWER. Second, ANSWER will be sorted in order based on the first field. If you want to create an exact copy of a table, don't use a query—use the [Menu] Tools Copy Table command instead.)

You can also use the "select all" technique when you want to select most, but not all, of the fields in a form. All you need to do to select every field is press [Check Mark] while the cursor is in the space under the query name, then move through the form pressing [Check Mark] to deselect certain fields.

Determining Record Order

If you look at Figure 7-19, you'll see that the records in the ANSWER table are arranged in ascending order based on the entries in the Last Name field. If you look even closer, you'll see that the records are also sorted based on the entries in the First Name field. This multifield sort becomes apparent when you look at records 7, 8, and 9. All of these records have the same value, *Jones*, in the Last Name field. As a result, they are grouped together in the sorted ANSWER table. In addition, the three records are ordered based on their entries in the First Name field. For example, Record 7, which contains the entry *David* in the First Name field, precedes record 8, which contains the First Name entry *Jean*.

Paradox actually sorts the ANSWER table in ascending order based on every field in the table. The first field in the ANSWER table acts as the primary sort key. If two or more records in the ANSWER table have the same entry in the first field, then Paradox sorts those records on the values in the second field. If the records also have the same value in the second field, then Paradox sorts on the entries in the third field as well. As long as the records contain the same values in the sort key field, Paradox will sort on the next field. Of course, if all the fields in the query are the same, then the ANSWER table will contain only one of the records because Paradox does not place duplicate records in the ANSWER table.

If you use a version of Paradox earlier than Release 3, then the field arrangement for the ANSWER table, and therefore the sort order, depends on the field arrangement of the table on which the query is based. You can use the [Rotate] key ([Ctrl]-[R]) to move columns in the query form, but the fields in the ANSWER table will still be in the same order as in the underlying table of the query form.

For example, suppose you place the cursor in the Last Name field of the query shown in Figure 7-19 and press [Rotate]. Paradox will move the Last Name field to the end of the query form and shift all the other fields one column to the left. Figure 7-20 shows the rotated query.

Figure 7-20 The Rotated Query Form

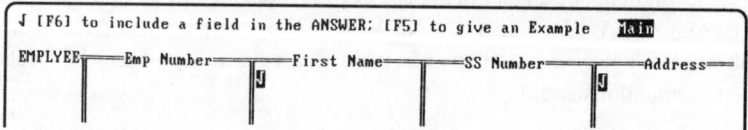

Figure 7-21 shows the ANSWER table that Paradox 1, 1.1, and 2 create when you process the rotated query. As you can see, the Last Name field is the first field in the ANSWER table, even though it is the last field in the query form. Paradox places the First Name field at the beginning of the ANSWER table because the First Name field comes before the Last Name and Address fields in the underlying EMPLYEE table.

Figure 7-21   The ANSWER Table in Paradox 1.0, 1.1, or 2

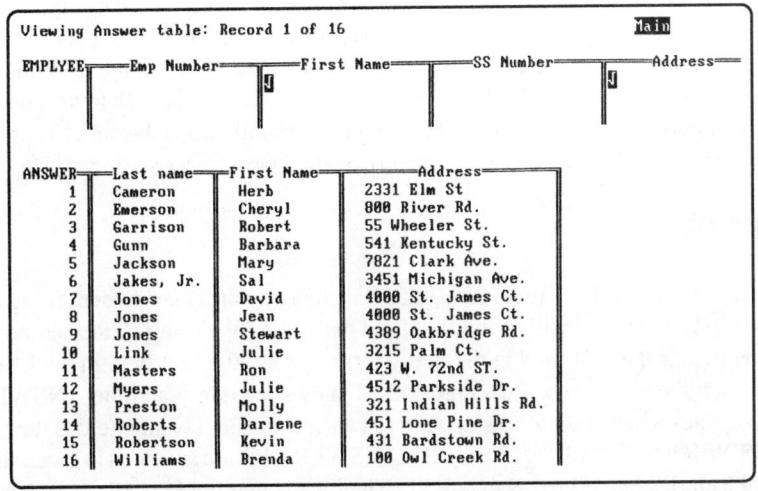

```
Viewing Answer table: Record 1 of 16                          Main

EMPLYEE        Emp Number          First Name        SS Number        Address
                                   g                                  g



ANSWER     Last name    First Name         Address
     1     Cameron      Herb      2331 Elm St
     2     Emerson      Cheryl    800 River Rd.
     3     Garrison     Robert    55 Wheeler St.
     4     Gunn         Barbara   541 Kentucky St.
     5     Jackson      Mary      7821 Clark Ave.
     6     Jakes, Jr.   Sal       3451 Michigan Ave.
     7     Jones        David     4000 St. James Ct.
     8     Jones        Jean      4000 St. James Ct.
     9     Jones        Stewart   4389 Oakbridge Rd.
    10     Link         Julie     3215 Palm Ct.
    11     Masters      Ron       423 W. 72nd ST.
    12     Myers        Julie     4512 Parkside Dr.
    13     Preston      Molly     321 Indian Hills Rd.
    14     Roberts      Darlene   451 Lone Pine Dr.
    15     Robertson    Kevin     431 Bardstown Rd.
    16     Williams     Brenda    100 Owl Creek Rd.
```

If you use Paradox 3, then you can influence the sort order of the ANSWER table in two ways. First, you can change the field arrangement of the ANSWER table, thereby changing the field that acts as the primary sort key in the ANSWER table. You can also tell Paradox to sort specified fields in the ANSWER table in descending, rather than ascending, order.

Sorting on Different Fields

The CCP for Paradox 3 lets you set Paradox to arrange the fields in the ANSWER table in either the same order as the fields in the underlying table or the same order as the fields arranged in the query form. By default, Paradox patterns the field arrangement in the ANSWER table after the field arrangement in the underlying table. If you change this default setting to arrange the ANSWER table based on the query form, then you can change the sort order of the ANSWER table by rotating the fields in the query form. Then, the first checked field in the rotated query form will serve as the primary sort key for the ANSWER table. To sort the ANSWER table on a particular field, you could use the [Rotate] key to move that field in front of the rest of the checked fields in the query form. When you press [Do-It!], Paradox will place that field at the front of the ANSWER table and sort the records in the ANSWER table in ascending order based on the entries in that field.

Changing the Default Field Order with the CCP

If you prefer ANSWER tables arranged in the same order as the fields in the query form, use the CCP to reset the field order for all ANSWER tables. First, issue the **[Menu]** Scripts **P**lay command, type **paradox3\custom** at the *Script:* prompt, and press ↵. If the CCP asks you if you are using a black-and-white monitor, answer appropriately. When the CCP presents its main menu, select **D**efaults, and then select **Q**ueryOrder from the Defaults menu. At this point, Paradox will present a menu with two selections, ImageOrder and TableOrder. The

TableOrder selection will be highlighted because it is the default setting. To make Paradox arrange the fields in ANSWER in the same order as the fields in the query form, select ImageOrder. Paradox will move back to the Defaults menu. To save the new QueryOrder setting, select Return from the Defaults menu and then DO-IT! from the CCP main menu. After you select DO-IT!, the CCP will return you to DOS. The new field arrangement for ANSWER tables will take effect the next time you load Paradox. In Chapters 13 and 17, we'll show you how to use PAL commands to override the QueryOrder setting.

An Example

If you process the query shown in Figure 7-20 after changing the QueryOrder setting to Image Order, the First Name field will be the first field in the ANSWER table. Remember that the First Name field is the first field in the query form, but not the first field in the EMPLYEE table on which the query is based. Figure 7-22 shows the query and the ANSWER table Paradox 3 creates when you process it. As you can see, the First Name field is the first field in the ANSWER table, and the records in the ANSWER table are arranged in ascending order based on the entries in the First Name field. The Last Name field, which is the last field in the rotated query form, is the last field in the ANSWER table.

Figure 7-22 Field Order Based on ImageOrder

```
Viewing Answer table: Record 1 of 16                              Main

EMPLYEE┬──Emp Number──────────First Name──────SS Number──────────Address══
       │                  │                │                 │
       │                  │                │                 │
       │                  │                │                 │

ANSWER┬─First Name────────────Address─────────Last name─────
    1 ║ Barbara      541 Kentucky St.      Gunn
    2 ║ Brenda       100 Owl Creek Rd.     Williams
    3 ║ Cheryl       800 River Rd.         Emerson
    4 ║ Darlene      451 Lone Pine Dr.     Roberts
    5 ║ David        4000 St. James Ct.    Jones
    6 ║ Herb         2331 Elm St           Cameron
    7 ║ Jean         4000 St. James Ct.    Jones
    8 ║ Julie        3215 Palm Ct.         Link
    9 ║ Julie        4512 Parkside Dr.     Myers
   10 ║ Kevin        431 Bardstown Rd.     Robertson
   11 ║ Mary         7821 Clark Ave.       Jackson
   12 ║ Molly        321 Indian Hills Rd.  Preston
   13 ║ Robert       55 Wheeler St.        Garrison
   14 ║ Ron          423 W. 72nd ST.       Masters
   15 ║ Sal          3451 Michigan Ave.    Jakes, Jr.
   16 ║ Stewart      4389 Oakbridge Rd.    Jones
```

Sorting Fields in Descending Order

Paradox 3 also lets you sort selected fields in descending, rather than ascending, order. If you press [Check Descending] ([Ctrl]-[F6]) instead of [Check Mark] to mark a field for inclusion in an ANSWER table, Paradox will sort that field in descending order. [Check Descending] is especially handy when used in conjunction with the ImageOrder QueryOrder setting.

For example, suppose you want the ANSWER table to list the names of the workers in the EMPLYEE table with the most recently hired employees at the top of the table. In other words, you want to sort the ANSWER table in descending order based on the contents of the Date of Hire field. This is possible if you have set Paradox to arrange the fields in ANSWER based on the query form. First, issue the [**Menu**] Ask command, type **EMPLYEE** at the *Table:* prompt, and press ↵ to bring a query form for the EMPLYEE table into the Paradox workspace. Since you want to sort the ANSWER table on the Date of Hire field, you need to make sure that the Date of Hire field is the first field in the query form flagged for inclusion in the ANSWER field. You can ensure this by rotating the query form until the Date of Hire field is the first field in the query. To rotate the image, press [**Rotate**] ten times. At this point, the Date of Hire field will be the first field in the empty query form.

If you marked the Date of Hire field with a check mark, then Paradox would sort the ANSWER table in ascending order based on this field. As a result, the least recent hiring dates would appear at the top of the ANSWER table. However, we want to list the most recent hiring dates at the top of the table. To sort the Date of Hire field in descending order in the ANSWER table, press [**Check Descending**] ([Ctrl]-[F6]). When you press [Check Descending], a check mark followed by a downward pointing arrow will appear in the Date of Hire field column, as shown in Figure 7-23.

Figure 7-23 A Check Descending Mark in the Query

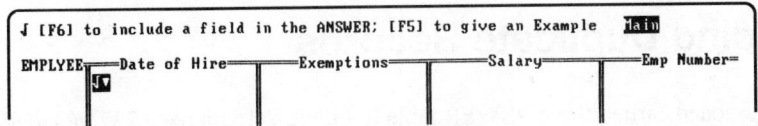

Next, press → four times to move the cursor to the Last Name field, and press [**Check Mark**] to include this field in the ANSWER table. Then, press → once to move the cursor to the First Name field, and press [**Check Mark**] again. Finally, press [**Do-It!**] to process the query. Figure 7-24 shows the completed query and the ANSWER table it produces. As you can see, the ANSWER table is arranged in descending order based on the Date of Hire field.

Figure 7-24 The Completed Query and ANSWER Table

```
Viewing Answer table: Record 1 of 16                        Main

    ═════Salary═════    ═════Emp Number═════   ════Last name════    ════First Name════
                                                            √                    √



ANSWER═╤═Date of Hire═╤═Last name═╤═First Name═
    1  │   8/15/88    │ Emerson   │ Cheryl
    2  │   6/15/88    │ Gunn      │ Barbara
    3  │   5/15/88    │ Garrison  │ Robert
    4  │   2/27/88    │ Robertson │ Kevin
    5  │   2/13/88    │ Masters   │ Ron
    6  │   2/13/88    │ Preston   │ Molly
    7  │  12/14/87    │ Jakes, Jr.│ Sal
    8  │  11/14/87    │ Jackson   │ Mary
    9  │  11/14/87    │ Link      │ Julie
   10  │   9/16/87    │ Myers     │ Julie
   11  │   8/16/87    │ Williams  │ Brenda
   12  │   7/16/87    │ Jones     │ Jean
   13  │   6/16/87    │ Roberts   │ Darlene
   14  │   2/13/87    │ Jones     │ Stewart
   15  │   1/14/87    │ Cameron   │ Herb
   16  │   1/14/87    │ Jones     │ David
```

The descending sort order caused by [Check Descending] affects only fields in which you place Check Descending marks. If two or more records have the same entry in the field that is the primary sort key and that field is flagged with a Check Descending mark, Paradox will sort any secondary sort keys flagged with a regular check mark in ascending order.

If you look at records 5 and 6 of the ANSWER table in Figure 7-24, you can see this principal of field-specific sort order demonstrated. Because both of these records contain the entry *2/13/88* in the Date of Hire field, the primary sort on the Date of Hire field places them next to one another in the ANSWER table. Because the sort on the Date of Hire field is in descending order, the records that precede records 5 and 6 all have Date of Hire entries that come after 2/13/88. However, the secondary sort key in the Last Name field arranges the two records in ascending order based on the entries in that field. As a result, the *Masters* entry in the Last Name field of record 5 places that record before record 6, which contains the entry *Preston* in the Last Name field.

A Check Descending mark does not affect Paradox's practice of including only unique records in the ANSWER table. If a query form includes any combination of check marks and Check Descending marks, Paradox will not include any duplicate records in the ANSWER table.

Including Duplicate Records

As we mentioned earlier, the ANSWER table in Figure 7-16 on page 237 includes only 14 records, while the EMPLYEE table includes 16. This difference occurs because some of the entries in the Last Name field of EMPLYEE are duplicates. When you use the [Check Mark] key to select the field or fields that you want Paradox to include in the ANSWER table, Paradox will include in the ANSWER table only one copy of any records that have the same entry in all selected fields. In the example, three records in EMPLYEE had the same entry— *Jones*—in the only field you selected—Last Name—so Paradox included only one of these three records in the ANSWER table in Figure 7-16.

What Is a Duplicate Record?

It is important to understand that, for purposes of querying, Paradox considers records to be duplicates only if they have the same entry in all of the fields you select in the query form. If two records have identical entries in the fields you have selected, Paradox will always consider them to be duplicates—even if they have different entries in the unselected fields. This means it is possible that two records that are really quite different will be considered duplicates by a query that includes only one or two fields.

For instance, the records for David Jones, Jean Jones, and Stewart Jones in the EMPLYEE table are clearly not identical in most regards. However, since the first query we created included only one field, and since these three records have the same entry in that one field, Paradox considered them to be duplicates.

On the other hand, if two records have the same entries in all but one selected field, then they will not be considered duplicates. As a general rule, the more fields you select, the less chance there is that any two records will have the same entry in all of the selected fields.

For example, look back at the query and ANSWER table shown in Figures 7-17 on page 237 and 7-18 on page 238. This query uses check marks to select both the Last Name and Address fields. Paradox included two Jones records in this ANSWER table—one with the entry *4000 St. James Ct.* in the Address field and one with the entry *4389 Oakbridge Rd.* in that field.

If you look back at the original EMPLYEE table in Figure 7-2 on page 226, you'll see why this occurred. Notice that the records for David Jones and Jean Jones have the same entries in both the Last Name and Address fields, but that the record for Stewart Jones has a different entry in the Address field. Since the records for David Jones and Jean Jones in the EMPLYEE table have the same entries in the two selected fields, only one of these two duplicate records was included in the ANSWER table. Since the record for Stewart Jones had a different entry in the Address field, it was also included in the ANSWER table.

As you might expect, selecting yet another field in the query form would cause Paradox to cease considering David Jones and Jean Jones as duplicates. For example, Figure 7-19 shows the ANSWER table that Paradox produced when you selected the First Name field in addition to the Last Name and Address fields. Notice that there are now three records in the ANSWER table that have the entry *Jones* in the Last Name field. Because all three Joneses have different first names, and because the First Name field is now selected in the query form, Paradox no longer considers these records duplicates.

Using [Check Plus]

If you want to include all instances of duplicate records in your ANSWER table, you must use the [Check Plus] key ([Alt]-[F6]) instead of the [Check Mark] key to select at least one of the fields you want to include in ANSWER. When you use [Check Plus] to select a field in a query form, Paradox will include all of the entries from the selected fields—including duplicates—in the ANSWER table.

Let's look at how this works. Suppose you want to select the Last Name field from every record in the EMPLYEE table, including duplicate records. To begin, create a new, empty EMPLYEE query form. Now, use the arrow keys to move the cursor to the Last Name field and press **[Check Plus]** ([Alt]-[F6]) to select the field. Figure 7-25 shows the completed query. Notice the check mark and plus sign in the Last Name field.

Figure 7-25 Using [Check Plus]

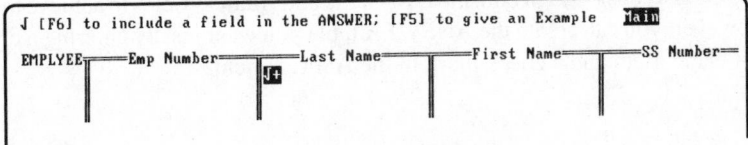

Once you have entered a check plus in the Last Name field, press **[Do-It!]** to process the query. Figure 7-26 shows the resulting ANSWER table. Notice that ANSWER now includes 16 records—the same number as EMPLYEE—and that there are three different *Jones* entries in the Last Name field of ANSWER. Because you used the [Check Plus] key rather than the [Check Mark] key to select the Last Name field, Paradox has included all of the entries from that field, including duplicates, in the ANSWER table.

Figure 7-26 The ANSWER Table with Duplicate Records

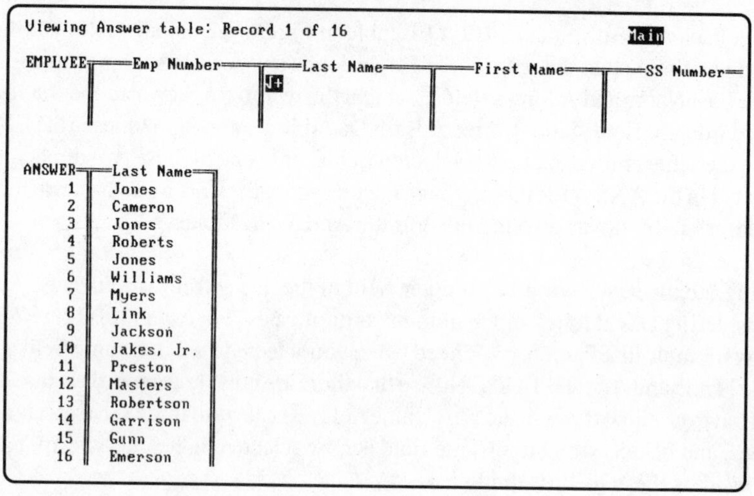

```
Viewing Answer table: Record 1 of 16                         Main

EMPLYEE    Emp Number        Last Name         First Name        SS Number
                           ↓+



ANSWER    Last Name
   1      Jones
   2      Cameron
   3      Jones
   4      Roberts
   5      Jones
   6      Williams
   7      Myers
   8      Link
   9      Jackson
  10      Jakes, Jr.
  11      Preston
  12      Masters
  13      Robertson
  14      Garrison
  15      Gunn
  16      Emerson
```

Also notice that the ANSWER table in Figure 7-26 is not sorted. Instead, the entries in ANSWER appear in the same order as the corresponding entries in EMPLYEE. Whenever you use [Check Plus] to select fields, Paradox will not sort the ANSWER table.

Check Plus and Multifield Queries

When you are defining a query in which several fields are selected and you want to include duplicate records in the ANSWER table, you need to mark only one of the fields in the query form with a check plus. The rest of the fields can be marked with simple check marks. This is true even if some of the records have the same entries in two or more of the selected fields. As long as one field in the query contains a check plus, all duplicates will be included in the ANSWER table.

For example, suppose you want to include both the Last Name and Address fields in ANSWER, and you want all three Jones records to appear in ANSWER. You might think that you need to enter a check plus in both the Last Name and Address fields to achieve the desired result. However, you can create the ANSWER table you want just by entering a check plus in the Last Name field and a check mark in the Address field.

Defining Selection Conditions

So far, we have shown you how to create query forms, how to select fields, and how to process queries. Now, we're ready to look at the next step in defining queries: defining selection conditions. In general, selection conditions tell Paradox which records you want it to include in the ANSWER table, much like check marks and check pluses tell Paradox which fields to include in ANSWER. Selection conditions are like filters, or tests, that select records based on the entries in one or more fields.

You've already seen several examples of simple selection conditions. For instance, in the first example, we entered the condition *KY* in the State field of a query form. This condition told Paradox to include in the ANSWER table only those records with the State field entry *KY*.

Selection conditions are entered in the fields of query forms. The position of the selection condition in the query form tells Paradox which field you want to test. That is, when you enter a selection condition in the Last Name field of a table, Paradox will test the entries in the Last Name field of the table against that condition.

When you process a query that contains a selection condition, Paradox will compare the entries in the indicated field of the table you are querying to the entry in that field of the query form. If the entry from the table passes the test (that is, if it satisfies the condition), then the record will be a part of the ANSWER table. Otherwise, it will not be included in ANSWER.

There are many types of selection conditions. You can create selection conditions for alpha-numeric, numeric, dollar, and date fields. These conditions will select a record that meets either of two or more tests, or the conditions will select a record only if it meets all of two or more conditions. You can even create selection conditions that will select a record that is similar to the condition.

Exact-match Conditions

Suppose you want to look at the records of all employees in EMPLYEE that have the entry *Jones* in the Last Name field. To begin, create a new, empty query form for EMPLYEE. Now, move the cursor to the space under the query form name and press [**Check Mark**] to select all the fields in the form.

Now, you are ready to define the selection condition. To do this, move the cursor to the Last Name field and type the word **Jones**. Next, press [**Do-It!**] to create the ANSWER table shown in Figure 7-27. Since there are only three records in the EMPLYEE table that have the entry *Jones* in the Last Name field, the ANSWER table includes just three records. Since you selected every field in the query form, the ANSWER table includes all the fields from EMPLYEE.

Figure 7-27 The Query for Jones

```
Viewing Answer table: Record 1 of 3                          Main
EMPLOYEE    Emp Number        Last Name       First Name      SS Number
            g                 g Jones         g               g

ANSWER    Emp Number    Last Name   First Name   SS Number         Addre
   1          1         Jones       David        414-76-3421   4000 St. Ja
   2          4         Jones       Stewart      401-32-8721   4389 Oakbri
   3          6         Jones       Jean         413-07-9123   4000 St. Ja
```

(By the way, are you surprised that Paradox copied the records for all three Joneses to the ANSWER table?   Remember that records are duplicates only if they have the same entry in all selected fields. Since the Jones entries all have different first names, employee numbers, and so on, Paradox does not consider them duplicates.)

Exact-match Condition Basics

All exact-match selection conditions work like this simple example. To select records that are exactly like a condition, just type the selection condition into that field of the query form. When you press [**Do-It!**], Paradox will compare the entries in that field of the table to the condition you entered in the query form. If the entry in the field matches the entry in the query form exactly, the entries from the appropriate fields of that record will be included in ANSWER. If not, Paradox will not include the record in ANSWER.

Perhaps the following device will help you remember the meaning of exact-match selection conditions. When you enter the selection condition in a field, imagine that there is an equal sign between the field name and the condition. For example, you could think of the condition you just created in this way: *Last Name = Jones*. As you can see, this way of thinking about alphabetic selection conditions helps to clarify the meaning of the condition. This condition says: *If the entry in the Last Name field of the table equals Jones, then the record will be selected. Otherwise, it will not be included in ANSWER.*

In fact, you can include an equal sign in your exact-match conditions if you like. For example, the selection condition you just defined could have been entered as = *Jones*, as shown in Figure 7-28. To Paradox, this condition and the one in Figure 7-27 are identical. However, since including the equal sign in the condition forces you to type one extra character, and since the equal sign is not required, we suggest that you do not use it.

Figure 7-28 Using = in a Query

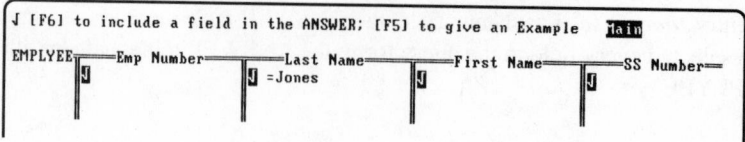

```
√ [F6] to include a field in the ANSWER; [F5] to give an Example    Main
EMPLOYEE    Emp Number        Last Name       First Name      SS Number
            g                 g =Jones        g               g
```

Exact-match conditions are literal: If an entry in the indicated field is different from the condition in any way, the record will not be selected. The entry must even agree with the condition in capitalization. For example, if one of the records in the EMPLYEE table contained the Last Name field entry *jones, JONES, or JOnes,* that record would not be selected by the selection condition *Jones.* Similarly, if you had defined the condition as *JONES,* and you queried the EMPLYEE table, none of the records would be selected.

If the selection conditions you define do not select any records, then the ANSWER table Paradox creates will be empty. For example, suppose you create the query shown in Figure 7-29. The selection condition *James* in the Last Name field of the query tells Paradox to select all records that have the entry *James* in the Last Name field. Because there are no records in EMPLYEE with the Last Name field entry *James,* Paradox will create an empty ANSWER table when you perform this query.

Figure 7-29 The Query for James

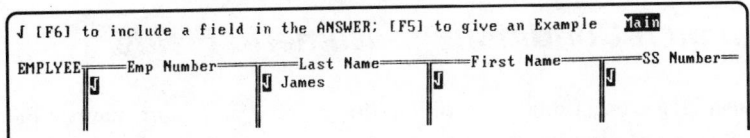

You can remove an exact-match condition from a field by moving the cursor to that field and pressing [Ctrl]-[Backspace]. For example, to remove the condition *James* from the Last Name field of the query form, move the cursor to the Last Name field and press **[Ctrl]-[Backspace]**.

Using Quotation Marks in Exact-match Conditions

Because commas have a special purpose in queries, if the exact-match condition you want to define refers to an entry that contains a comma, you'll need to enclose the condition in quotation marks. For example, suppose you want to extract the record for Sal Jakes, Jr., from EMPLYEE. To make this search, you would enter the condition **"Jakes, Jr."** (the quotation marks are required) in the Last Name field of the EMPLYEE query form. When you press **[Do-It]** to process this query, Paradox will create the ANSWER table shown in Figure 7-30.

Figure 7-30 A Query with Quotation Marks

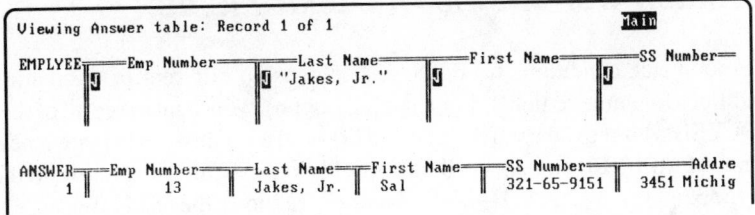

If you use a condition that includes a comma and do not enclose it in quotation marks, the query will not produce the desired result. You will learn more about the reason this happens in a few pages.

There is at least one other case in which you may need to use quotation marks in an exact-match condition. On rare occasions, you may have an entry in a table that looks to Paradox like the name of an operator. For example, you might have a record in EMPLYEE with the Last Name entry *Blank*. If you wanted to use that name as a condition, you would need to enclose it in quotation marks like this: **"Blank"**.

If an entry in a table includes quotation marks, and you want to use that entry as a selection condition, you must precede each quotation mark in the condition with a backslash (\). For example, suppose one of the entries in the Last Name field of the EMPLYEE table is *"Hot Rocks" Ford*. If you want to create an exact-match selection condition to find this entry, it will look like this: *\"Hot Rocks\" Ford*.

Exact-match Conditions in Numeric Fields

You can also create exact-match conditions for number and short number fields. For example, suppose you want to select all of the employee records that have the entry *0* in the Exemption field. To do this, first create a new, empty EMPLYEE query form and select all of the fields in the form. Next, move to the Exemptions field and type **0**. Now, press **[Do-It!]** to process the query. Figure 7-31 shows the query and the resulting ANSWER table. This table contains two records—Jean Jones and Ron Masters—both of which have the entry *0* in the Exemptions field.

Figure 7-31 Query on a Numeric Field

```
┌─────────────────────────────────────────────────────────────────────────┐
│ Viewing Answer table: Record 1 of 2                           Main        │
│ ┌─Date of Birth──┬──Date of Hire──┬──Exemptions──┬──Salary──              │
│ │                │                │    0         │                        │
│ │                │                │              │                        │
│ │                │                │              │                        │
│                                                                            │
│ ANSWER─┬─Emp Number─┬──Last Name──┬─First Name─┬─SS Number──┬──Addre      │
│   1    │     6      │   Jones     │   Jean     │ 413-87-9123│ 4000 St. Ja  │
│   2    │    15      │   Masters   │   Ron      │ 317-65-4529│ 423 W. 72nd  │
└─────────────────────────────────────────────────────────────────────────┘
```

Exact-match Conditions in Dollar Fields

Creating exact-match conditions for dollar ($) fields is no different from creating exact-match conditions for numeric fields. For example, suppose you want to see all of the records from EMPLYEE with the Salary field entry *$32,000*. To do this, first create a new, blank query form for EMPLYEE and select all of the fields in the form. Next, move to the Salary field and type **32000**. Now, press **[Do-It!]**. Figure 7-32 shows the result. Because there are only two records in the EMPLYEE table with the Salary field entry *$32,000* (the records for Julie Myers and Robert Garrison), this new ANSWER table includes only those two records.

Figure 7-32 Query on a Dollar Field

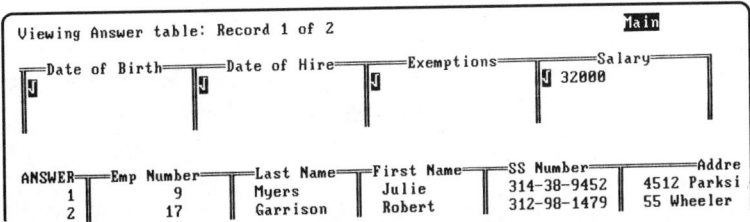

Exact-match Conditions in Date Fields

You create exact-match conditions for date fields just as you create exact-match conditions for numeric fields. For instance, suppose you want to select those records in EMPLYEE that have the Date of Hire field entry *7/01/85*. To do this, first create a new, blank EMPLYEE query form and select all of the fields in the form. Then, move to the Date of Hire field and type the date **7/01/85** or **7/1/85** (you don't need to include the zero). Now, press **[Do-It!]**. Figure 7-33 shows the query and resulting ANSWER table. As you can see, Paradox has included two records in the ANSWER table. If you look at the EMPLYEE table, you will see that these are the only two records that have the entry *7/01/85* in the Date of Hire field.

Figure 7-33 Query on a Date Field

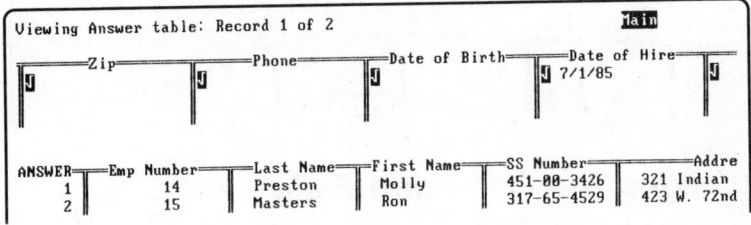

As you learned in Chapter 2, Paradox allows you to assign three different formats to dates: MM/DD/YY (the default), DD-Mon-YY, and DD.MM.YY. Paradox recognizes exact-match conditions for date fields in any of these three forms. The form of the condition does not even need to match the form of the dates in the table you are querying. For instance, in the example, you could have used the condition *1-Jul-85* instead of *7/01/85* without changing the meaning of the condition.

A Note

Although you can create exact-match criteria for number, dollar, and date fields, you are not likely to do so very often. When you are working with these types of fields, you'll more often be interested in looking at groups of records—for instance, all the records with a number greater than 60 in the Age field or all the records with a value between $30,000 and $40,000 in the Salary field. We'll cover this type of search in an upcoming section.

Selection Conditions and Selecting Fields

You don't need to select every field in the query form if you intend to use selection conditions. You can use a condition even if you select only one or two fields. For example, suppose you wanted to look at only the First Name, Last Name, and Employee Number entries that have *Jones* in the Last Name field.

To begin, create a new, empty EMPLYEE query form. Next, move to the Last Name field and type **Jones**. Now, move to the Emp Number field and press **[Check Mark]**, then move to the Last Name field and press **[Check Mark]** again. Finally, move to the First Name field and press **[Check Mark]** a third time.

When you press **[Do-It!]**, Paradox will create the ANSWER table shown in Figure 7-34. As before, the ANSWER table includes only the three records that have the entry *Jones* in the Last Name field. This time, since you selected only the Emp Number, Last Name, and First Name fields in the query form, the ANSWER table includes only those three fields.

Figure 7-34 Selecting Three Fields

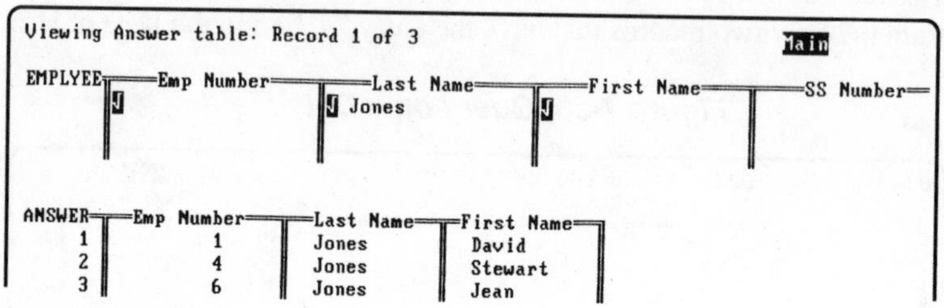

```
Viewing Answer table: Record 1 of 3                          Main

EMPLYEE┬─Emp Number─────┬──Last Name─────┬─First Name─────┬─SS Number─
       │9               │9 Jones         │9               │

ANSWER┬─Emp Number──┬──Last Name─┬─First Name─┐
    1 │      1      │  Jones     │  David     │
    2 │      4      │  Jones     │  Stewart   │
    3 │      6      │  Jones     │  Jean      │
```

Not Selecting the Condition Field

As you can see, you don't need to select every field in the query form when you use a selection condition. In fact, you don't even need to select the field that contains the selection condition. For example, suppose you want to create an ANSWER table that contains just two fields—Emp Number and First Name—and that includes only those records with the Last Name field entry *Jones*. To create this query, move the cursor back to the EMPLYEE query form and then move it into the Last Name field. Now, press **[Check Mark]** to deselect the field. Deselecting the Last Name field does not affect the condition in that field, nor does it affect check marks in any other field.

Now press **[Do-It!]** to process the query. Figure 7-35 shows the resulting ANSWER table. Notice that Paradox has included just those records that have the entry *Jones* in the Last Name field in the ANSWER table, even though the Last Name field itself was not selected and is not included in ANSWER.

Figure 7-35 Not Selecting the Condition Field

```
Viewing Answer table: Record 1 of 3                    Main

EMPLYEE┬═Emp Number═══╤═══Last Name═══╤═First Name═╤══SS Number══
       │ 9            │    Jones      │ 9          │
       │              │               │            │


ANSWER┬═Emp Number═╤═First Name═
   1  │     1      │  David
   2  │     4      │  Stewart
   3  │     6      │  Jean
```

Patterns

Like most other database programs, Paradox offers special operators, called wildcards, that can be used in place of other characters in selection conditions. Because wildcard operators match any character, you can use them when you need to create one condition to select records that are alike in some regards and different in others. In Paradox, conditions that contain wildcards are called patterns. Paradox offers two wildcard operators: .. and @.

The .. Operator

The .. operator, which is sometimes called the series wildcard operator, can be used to represent a series of any number of characters in a condition. For example, the condition *Rob..* would match any entry that began with the letters *Rob*, including *Rob, Robert, Roberts, Robertson, Roberson, Robbie,* and so on.

You can enter this operator in a condition just by typing two periods. For example, to enter the condition *Rob..* in a query form, you would type the letters *Rob* and then type two periods.

Let's use the condition *Rob..* in an EMPLYEE query. To begin, create a new, blank query form for the EMPLYEE table and select every field in the form. Next, move to the Last Name field and type **Rob...** Now, press **[Do-It!]** to process the query. Figure 7-36 shows the query and the resulting ANSWER table. Notice that this table contains two records—one for Darlene *Rob*erts, and one for Kevin *Rob*ertson—both of which begin with *Rob*.

Figure 7-36 The .. Operator

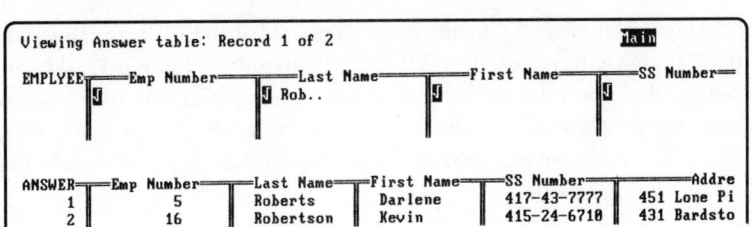

```
Viewing Answer table: Record 1 of 2                    Main

EMPLYEE┬═Emp Number══╤═══Last Name═══╤═First Name═╤══SS Number══
       │9            │9 Rob..        │9           │9


ANSWER┬═Emp Number═╤═══Last Name═══╤═First Name═╤══SS Number══╤═══════Addre
   1  │     5      │   Roberts     │  Darlene   │ 417-43-7777 │ 451 Lone Pi
   2  │    16      │   Robertson   │  Kevin     │ 415-24-6710 │ 431 Bardsto
```

You can use the .. operator at any position in a condition. For example, the condition *..n* would match any entry that ends with an *n*. If you entered the condition *..n* in the Last Name field of the EMPLYEE query form, the resulting ANSWER table would include the records for Herb Camero*n*, Mary Jackso*n*, Molly Presto*n*, Kevin Robertso*n*, Robert Garriso*n*, Barbara Gun*n,* and Cheryl Emerso*n*—all of which end with an *n*.

Similarly, the condition *G..n* will match any entry that begins with a *G* and ends with an *n*. For example, if you entered the condition *G..n* in the Last Name field of the EMPLYEE query form, the resulting ANSWER table would include the records for Robert *G*arriso*n* and Barbara *G*un*n*.

Interestingly, capitalization does not count when you use wildcards. For instance, Paradox would consider the conditions *g..n*, *G..N*, and *g..N* to be the same as *G..n*. Any of these conditions would select the same two records from EMPLYEE.

Furthermore, you can use the .. operator more than once in a single condition. For example, the condition *G..r..n* will select any record that begins with a *g*, has an *r* somewhere in the middle, and ends with an *n*. This condition would select the record for Robert *G*a*r*riso*n* from the EMPLYEE table.

The @ Operator

The second wildcard operator, @, can be used to match any single character in a condition. For example, the condition M@sters would match the entries *Masters, Misters, Mosters, Musters,* or any other entry that begins with *M*, ends with *sters*, and has one character in between. Similarly, the condition *J@@@@* matches the entries *Jones, Johns, Jakes,* or any entry that begins with the letter *J* and includes any four other characters.

It is important to understand that the condition *J@@@@* would not match the entries *Job, Jackson,* or *Jehoshaphat,* even though the condition *J..* would. Each @ operator you include in a condition can match only one character in an entry. If a condition contains four @ operators, then those four operators represent exactly four characters—no more and no less.

You can enter this operator in a condition just by typing the character @ ([Shift]-[2]). For example, to enter the condition *M@sters* in a query form, you would type the letter **M**, the symbol **@**, then the characters **sters**.

If you enter the condition *J@@@@* in the Last Name field of an EMPLYEE query form and press [Do-It!], Paradox will create the ANSWER table shown in Figure 7-37. As you can see, this table contains three records: David *J*ones, Stewart *J*ones, and Jean *J*ones—all of whose last names are made up of a *J* followed by four characters. You will notice, however, that the record for Mary Jackson is not included in ANSWER since there are more than four letters following the *J* in her last name.

Figure 7-37 The @ Operator

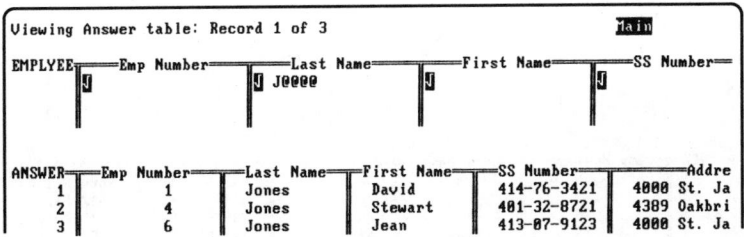

```
Viewing Answer table: Record 1 of 3                              Main

EMPLYEE──Emp Number──┬──Last Name──┬──First Name──┬──SS Number──
      │            │ J@@@@         │             │
      │                                                          │



ANSWER──Emp Number──┬──Last Name──┬──First Name──┬──SS Number──┬──Addre
   1  │     1      │   Jones     │   David      │  414-76-3421  │ 4000 St. Ja
   2  │     4      │   Jones     │   Stewart    │  401-32-8721  │ 4389 Oakbri
   3  │     6      │   Jones     │   Jean       │  413-07-9123  │ 4000 St. Ja
```

As with the .. operator, capitalization does not count when you use the @ operator. In addition, you can use the @ operator more than once in a single pattern and at any position in a pattern. You can even use the @ operator as the first or last character in a pattern.

If you need to include an @ symbol in a pattern but don't want Paradox to regard the character as a wildcard operator, you must enclose it in quotation marks. For example, suppose you have created a table with a field named Code. The Code field contains these entries:

    @13451
    #17643
    @17690
    &12340
    @14169

You want to select only the records with Code field entries that begin with an @ symbol. To do this, you would need to enter the pattern

    "@"..

in the Code field of the query form. If you did not enclose the @ symbol in quotation marks, Paradox would consider it to be a wildcard character and would select all five records.

Wildcards and Numeric Fields

Unlike most database programs, Paradox allows you to use wildcards in numeric and dollar field conditions. For example, the pattern 3.. would match the numbers 30, 35, 300, 350, 366, 3000, 3300033, and any other numbers that begin with the digit 3.

Figure 7-38 shows a query and the resulting ANSWER table Paradox created when we entered the selection condition pattern 3.. in the Salary field. The ANSWER table includes all of the records for employees with an income that begins with 3.

Figure 7-38 Wildcard in a Numeric Field

```
Viewing Answer table: Record 1 of 7                            Main

  Date of Birth      Date of Hire      Exemptions        Salary
 9                  9                 9                 9 3..




ANSWER   Emp Number      Last Name    First Name    SS Number          Addre
   1          6          Jones        Jean          413-07-9123    4000 St. Ja
   2          9          Myers        Julie         314-38-9452    4512 Parksi
   3         10          Link         Julie         345-75-1525    3215 Palm C
   4         13          Jakes, Jr.   Sal           321-65-9151    3451 Michig
   5         15          Masters      Ron           317-65-4529    423 W. 72nd
   6         16          Robertson    Kevin         415-24-6710    431 Bardsto
   7         17          Garrison     Robert        312-98-1479    55 Wheeler
```

You can also use the @ wildcard operator in numeric fields. For example, suppose you wanted to select all of the employees who have salaries that begin with a 3, followed by any four digits, a decimal, and any two digits. You could do this by entering the pattern *3@@@@.@@* in the Salary field of the EMPLYEE query form.

Wildcards and Date Fields

Paradox also allows you to use wildcards in conditions you create for date fields. For instance, the pattern *7/../85* would match the entries *7/01/85, 7/10/85, 7/14/85, 7/22/85*, and any other date entries that have 7 in the months position and 85 in the years position.

For example, suppose you enter the pattern *7/../85* in the Date of Hire field of an EMPLYEE table query form. When you process this query, Paradox will create the ANSWER table shown in Figure 7-39. This table includes the records for the three employees who were hired in July 1985: Molly Preston, Ron Masters, and Kevin Robertson. The same result would be achieved by the pattern *7/@@/85*.

Figure 7-39 Wildcard in a Date Field

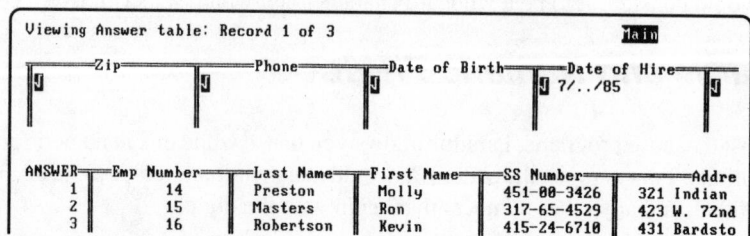

```
Viewing Answer table: Record 1 of 3                            Main

      Zip          Phone         Date of Birth     Date of Hire
 9               9              9                 9 7/../85        9




ANSWER   Emp Number      Last Name    First Name    SS Number        Addre
   1         14          Preston      Molly         451-00-3426    321 Indian
   2         15          Masters      Ron           317-65-4529    423 W. 72nd
   3         16          Robertson    Kevin         415-24-6710    431 Bardsto
```

When you use wildcard operators in date fields, the pattern you define must be in the same form as the entries in the selected field of the table. If the entries are in the MM/DD/YY form, the pattern must also be in that form. If the entries are in the DD-Mon-YY form, the pattern must be in that form too. If the pattern is in a different form from the entries, the query will not select any records. For instance, if you entered the pattern *..-Jul-85* in the Date of Hire field and pressed [Do-It!], Paradox would create an empty ANSWER table. The same thing would happen if you entered the pattern *15-J@@-85* in the query form. If the pattern has a different form from the entries, then the pattern will not match any records.

Selecting Ranges of Records

Frequently, you will want to select records that have entries that fall within a certain range. This is particularly true when you are selecting records based on the entries in numeric, dollar, or date fields. For example, you might want to locate all of the entries with a Salary entry that is greater than 30,000, or all of the records with a Date of Hire entry that is less than (before) July 1, 1985.

Paradox includes a set of operators, called range operators, that allow you to create this kind of query. Table 7-1 shows the four range operators. These operators allow you to create conditions that will match entries that are greater than, less than, greater than or equal to, or less than or equal to a stated value. Let's look at how they work.

Table 7-1 Range Operators

Operator	Meaning
>	Greater than
<	Less than
>=	Greater than or equal to
<=	Less than or equal to

Greater Than (>)

The greater than operator (>) lets you select all of the records with entries in a field that are greater than a certain value. For example, suppose you want to select all records that have an entry greater than 30,000 in the Salary field. To do this, select all of the fields in an empty EMPLYEE query form, move to the Salary field, and enter the condition **>30000**. When you press **[Do-It!]** to process the query, Paradox will create the ANSWER table shown in Figure 7-40 on the following page. This table includes every record from the EMPLYEE table that has an entry greater than 30,000 in the Salary field.

Notice, however, that the ANSWER table does not include the record for Julie Link, whose salary is exactly $30,000. When you use the greater than range operator (>) in a condition, Paradox will select only those records with entries in the indicated field that are greater than the value specified in the condition. If an entry in the indicated field is equal to the value specified by the condition, that record will not be selected.

Figure 7-40 Using Greater Than (>) in a Query

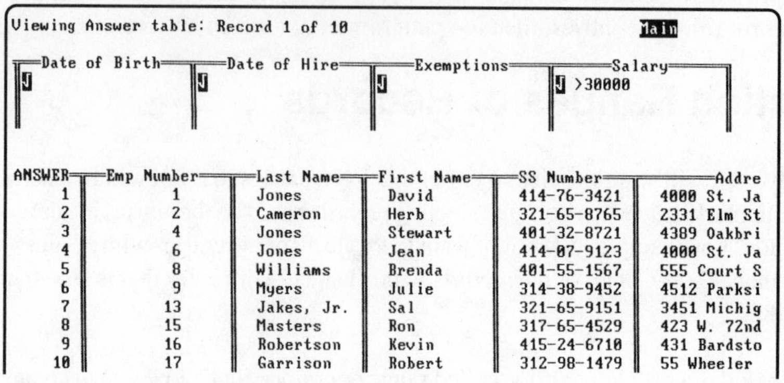

```
Viewing Answer table: Record 1 of 10                          Main
┌─Date of Birth─┐ ┌─Date of Hire─┐ ┌─Exemptions─┐ ┌─Salary─┐
│ │             │ │              │ │            │ │ >30000 │
└─┴─────────────┘ └─┴────────────┘ └─┴──────────┘ └─┴──────┘


ANSWER┬─Emp Number─┐ ┌─Last Name─┬─First Name─┐ ┌─SS Number─┐ ┌─Addre
  1   │     1      │ │ Jones     │ David      │ │414-76-3421│ │4000 St. Ja
  2   │     2      │ │ Cameron   │ Herb       │ │321-65-8765│ │2331 Elm St
  3   │     4      │ │ Jones     │ Stewart    │ │401-32-8721│ │4389 Oakbri
  4   │     6      │ │ Jones     │ Jean       │ │414-07-9123│ │4000 St. Ja
  5   │     8      │ │ Williams  │ Brenda     │ │401-55-1567│ │555 Court S
  6   │     9      │ │ Myers     │ Julie      │ │314-38-9452│ │4512 Parksi
  7   │    13      │ │ Jakes, Jr.│ Sal        │ │321-65-9151│ │3451 Michig
  8   │    15      │ │ Masters   │ Ron        │ │317-65-4529│ │423 W. 72nd
  9   │    16      │ │ Robertson │ Kevin      │ │415-24-6710│ │431 Bardsto
 10   │    17      │ │ Garrison  │ Robert     │ │312-98-1479│ │55 Wheeler
```

Greater Than or Equal To (>=)

If you want to select all of the records with entries that are greater than or equal to a stated value, you should use the greater than or equal to operator (>=). For example, Figure 7-41 shows a query on the EMPLYEE table that will select every record with a Salary entry greater than or equal to 30,000, and the ANSWER table that Paradox will create when you process this query. Notice that the record for Julie Link is included in this new ANSWER table.

Figure 7-41 Using Greater Than or Equal To (>=) in a Query

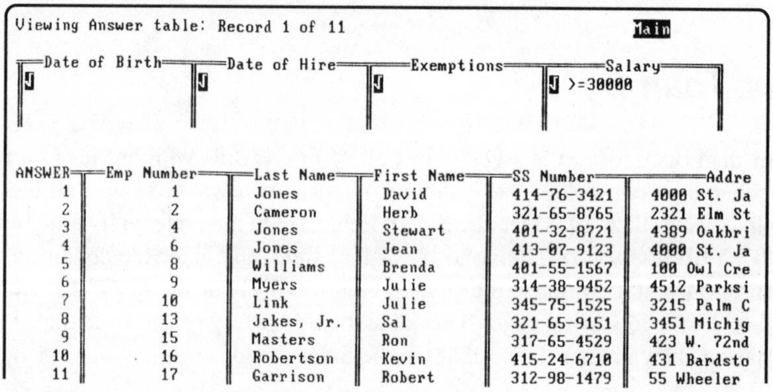

```
Viewing Answer table: Record 1 of 11                          Main
┌─Date of Birth─┐ ┌─Date of Hire─┐ ┌─Exemptions─┐ ┌─Salary──┐
│ │             │ │              │ │            │ │ >=30000 │
└─┴─────────────┘ └─┴────────────┘ └─┴──────────┘ └─┴───────┘


ANSWER┬─Emp Number─┐ ┌─Last Name─┬─First Name─┐ ┌─SS Number─┐ ┌─Addre
  1   │     1      │ │ Jones     │ David      │ │414-76-3421│ │4000 St. Ja
  2   │     2      │ │ Cameron   │ Herb       │ │321-65-8765│ │2321 Elm St
  3   │     4      │ │ Jones     │ Stewart    │ │401-32-8721│ │4389 Oakbri
  4   │     6      │ │ Jones     │ Jean       │ │413-07-9123│ │4000 St. Ja
  5   │     8      │ │ Williams  │ Brenda     │ │401-55-1567│ │100 Owl Cre
  6   │     9      │ │ Myers     │ Julie      │ │314-38-9452│ │4512 Parksi
  7   │    10      │ │ Link      │ Julie      │ │345-75-1525│ │3215 Palm C
  8   │    13      │ │ Jakes, Jr.│ Sal        │ │321-65-9151│ │3451 Michig
  9   │    15      │ │ Masters   │ Ron        │ │317-65-4529│ │423 W. 72nd
 10   │    16      │ │ Robertson │ Kevin      │ │415-24-6710│ │431 Bardsto
 11   │    17      │ │ Garrison  │ Robert     │ │312-98-1479│ │55 Wheeler
```

Less Than (<)

If you want to select all of the records with an entry that is less than a given value, you'll need to use the less than operator (<). For example, suppose you want to select all of the records that have a Salary entry of less than 50,000. To make this selection, replace the entry in the Salary field of the EMPLYEE query form with the entry *<50000.* When you press **[Do-It!]** to process this query, Paradox will create the ANSWER table shown in Figure 7-42. This table includes all of the records from EMPLYEE with a Salary entry of less than 50,000.

Figure 7-42 Using Less Than (<) in a Query

```
┌──────────────────────────────────────────────────────────────────────────────┐
│ Viewing Answer table: Record 1 of 14                          Main             │
│  ┌─Date of Birth──┬──Date of Hire──┬──Exemptions──┬──Salary──┐                 │
│  █                 █                 █              █ <50000                    │
│                                                                                │
│                                                                                │
│  ANSWER─┬─Emp Number─┬──Last Name─┬─First Name─┬─SS Number──┬───────Addre       │
│    1         4         Jones        Stewart      401-32-8721   4389 Oakbri      │
│    2         5         Roberts      Darlene      417-43-7777   451 Lone Pi      │
│    3         6         Jones        Jean         413-07-9123   4000 St. Ja      │
│    4         8         Williams     Brenda       401-55-1567   100 Owl Cre      │
│    5         9         Myers        Julie        314-38-9452   4512 Parksi      │
│    6        10         Link         Julie        345-75-1525   3215 Palm C      │
│    7        12         Jackson      Mary         424-13-7621   7821 Clark       │
│    8        13         Jakes, Jr.   Sal          321-65-9151   3451 Michig      │
│    9        14         Preston      Molly        451-00-3426   321 Indian       │
│   10        15         Masters      Ron          317-65-4529   423 W. 72nd      │
│   11        16         Robertson    Kevin        415-24-6710   431 Bardsto      │
│   12        17         Garrison     Robert       312-98-1479   55 Wheeler       │
│   13        19         Gunn         Barbara      321-97-8632   541 Kentuck      │
│   14        20         Emerson      Cheryl       404-14-1422   8100 River       │
└──────────────────────────────────────────────────────────────────────────────┘
```

Less Than or Equal To (<=)

If you want to select every record with an entry that is less than or equal to a given value, you'll need to use the less than or equal to operator (<=). For example, suppose you want to select every record that has an entry in the Salary field that is less than or equal to 50,000. Figure 7-43 shows a query that will make this selection and the ANSWER table that Paradox will produce when you process the query. As you can see, this table is similar to the ANSWER table created by the previous query, except that it includes the record for Herb Cameron, whose salary is exactly $50,000.

Figure 7-43 Using Less Than or Equal To (<=) in a Query

```
┌──────────────────────────────────────────────────────────────────────────────┐
│ Viewing Answer table: Record 1 of 15                          Main             │
│  ┌─Date of Birth──┬──Date of Hire──┬──Exemptions──┬──Salary──┐                 │
│  █                 █                 █              █ <=50000                   │
│                                                                                │
│                                                                                │
│  ANSWER─┬─Emp Number─┬──Last Name─┬─First Name─┬─SS Number──┬───────Addre       │
│    1         2         Cameron      Herb         321-65-8765   2321 Elm St      │
│    2         4         Jones        Stewart      401-32-8721   4389 Oakbri      │
│    3         5         Roberts      Darlene      417-43-7777   451 Lone Pi      │
│    4         6         Jones        Jean         413-07-9123   4000 St. Ja      │
│    5         8         Williams     Brenda       401-55-1567   100 Owl Cre      │
│    6         9         Myers        Julie        314-38-9452   4512 Parksi      │
│    7        10         Link         Julie        345-75-1525   3215 Palm C      │
│    8        12         Jackson      Mary         424-13-7621   7821 Clark       │
│    9        13         Jakes, Jr.   Sal          321-65-9151   3451 Michig      │
│   10        14         Preston      Molly        451-00-3426   321 Indian       │
│   11        15         Masters      Ron          317-65-4529   423 W. 72nd      │
│   12        16         Robertson    Kevin        415-24-6710   431 Bardsto      │
│   13        17         Garrison     Robert       312-98-1479   55 Wheeler       │
│   14        19         Gunn         Barbara      321-97-8632   541 Kentuck      │
│   15        20         Emerson      Cheryl       404-14-1422   8100 River       │
└──────────────────────────────────────────────────────────────────────────────┘
```

Using Range Operators in Date Fields

Suppose you want to select all of the records with a Date of Hire entry that is "less than" 7/1/85. To do this, enter the condition <7/1/85 in the Date of Hire field of an EMPLYEE query form. Now, when you press the [Do-It!] key to process the query, Paradox will create the ANSWER table shown in Figure 7-44. This table contains every record with a Date of Hire entry that is less than 7/1/85.

Figure 7-44 Using Range Operators in Date Fields

```
Viewing Answer table: Record 1 of 10                              Main

   ┌─Zip─┐      ┌─Phone─┐      ┌─Date of Birth─┐   ┌─Date of Hire─┐
 ▯          ▯            ▯                    ▯ <7/1/85            ▯


ANSWER──┬─Emp Number──┬──Last Name──┬──First Name──┬──SS Number──┬────────Addre
   1    │      1      │   Jones     │    David     │  414-76-3421 │  4000 St. Ja
   2    │      2      │   Cameron   │    Herb      │  321-65-8765 │  2321 Elm St
   3    │      4      │   Jones     │    Stewart   │  401-32-8721 │  4389 Oakbri
   4    │      5      │   Roberts   │    Darlene   │  417-43-7777 │  451 Lone Pi
   5    │      6      │   Jones     │    Jean      │  413-07-9123 │  4000 St. Ja
   6    │      8      │   Williams  │    Brenda    │  401-55-1567 │  100 Owl Cre
   7    │      9      │   Myers     │    Julie     │  314-38-9452 │  4512 Parksi
   8    │     10      │   Link      │    Julie     │  345-75-1525 │  3215 Palm C
   9    │     12      │   Jackson   │    Mary      │  424-13-7621 │  7821 Clark
  10    │     13      │   Jakes, Jr.│    Sal       │  321-65-9151 │  3451 Michig
```

Notice that when used in a date field, the less than operator (<) matches entries that precede the date specified by the condition. That is, the condition <1/1/85 selects dates that precede January 1, 1985. Similarly, when you use the greater than operator (>) in a date field condition, the condition matches entries that come after the specified date. For instance, the condition >1/1/85 selects dates that are after January 1, 1985.

You can also use the <= and >= operators in date fields. When you use range operators in date field conditions, you can specify the date in either the MM/DD/YY, DD.MM.YY, or the DD-Mon-YY form. For example, the conditions >7/1/85, >1.7.85, and >1-Jul-85 are all identical in Paradox. All three conditions will match all the entries in the indicated field that are greater than July 1, 1985.

Using Range Operators in Alphanumeric Fields

Paradox also allows you to use range operators in alphanumeric fields. When used in alphanumeric fields, range operators match entries whose ASCII character code is less than or greater than the code for a specified entry. In the ASCII system, numerals like 1, 2, and 3 have code values "less than" uppercase letters like A, B, and C. Lowercase letters, like a, b, and c, come after uppercase letters. The > operator selects entries that have an ASCII value that is greater than the word or phrase specified by the condition. Similarly, the < operator selects entries that have an ASCII value that is less than the specified word or phrase.

Range Operators and Patterns

You cannot use any of Paradox's range operators with patterns. In most cases, it doesn't make sense to use a range operator with a pattern. For example, what does the condition *>@Smith* mean? Since the @ wildcard can stand for any character, this condition could select any entry. Similarly, the condition *<=1..* is meaningless since the expression *1..* could represent any number from 1 to infinity. If you try to process a query that contains conditions like these, Paradox will display the message *Cannot use patterns with LIKE or range operators.*

The Like Operator

There will be times in your work with Paradox when you'll want to use a condition to select records, but you won't remember the exact spelling or capitalization of the entry you want to match. This is especially true when you are working with larger tables. As we have said, normally Paradox will not select records unless they match the selection condition exactly, so not knowing the exact form of the entry you want to match could be a real problem.

Fortunately, Paradox includes a special operator, called like, that lets you select records that are only similar to, and not exact duplicates of, the selection condition you specify. This unique tool makes it possible to find information in your tables even when you are not sure of the spelling, capitalization, or other characteristics of the entry for which you are looking.

An Example

Suppose you want to look at the record for the employee named Myers, but you can't remember whether the name is spelled *Meyers, Miers,* or *Myers.* Instead of guessing, you could create a like condition. To do this, first create a new, blank query form for EMPLYEE and select every field in the form. Next, move to the Last Name field and enter the phrase **like Meyers.** Figure 7-45 shows the completed query.

Figure 7-45 Query Form Using Like

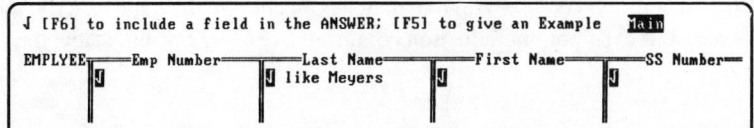

When you press **[Do-It!]**, Paradox will create the ANSWER table shown in Figure 7-46. As you can see, the table includes the record for Julie Myers. Thanks to the like operator, we were able to locate this record, even though we didn't know the exact spelling of her name.

Figure 7-46 The ANSWER Table for the Like Query

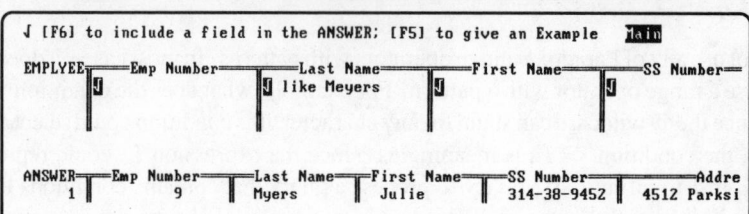

You will probably find yourself using the like operator most often when you have failed to locate a record using a conventional exact-match query. For example, suppose you have just tried to locate the record for Julie Myers using the selection condition *Meyers*. The result was an empty ANSWER table. Rather than continuing to try to match the name exactly, at this point you would be better off using a like condition to find the entry.

Like Rules

Like is a very powerful tool, but it does have a few restrictions. The condition you use with like must begin with the same letter as the entry for which you are searching. In other words, the condition *like Byers* would not select the record for Julie Myers. In addition, the condition you use with like must bear some resemblance to the entry for which you are searching. For example, the condition *like Myth* would not select the record for Julie Myers, even though the word *Myth* begins with the letters *My*.

Perhaps these two restrictions are best summarized by saying that you should use like when you can make a good, but not perfect, guess at the correct spelling of the entry for which you are looking. If you're just guessing wildly, like probably won't be much help.

The like operator ignores case. For example, the selection condition *like MEYERS* would select the entry for Julie Myers. This means that you can use like to locate entries when you are not sure if the entries are in uppercase or lowercase.

Of course, if the condition you use with like matches an entry in the table exactly, the record will be selected. For example, the selection condition *like Myers* would select the entry for Julie Myers.

The Not Operator

The not operator allows you to select entries that are not equal to some specified number or string of characters. For example, suppose you want to select every record in the EMPLYEE table except those with the entry *Jones* in the Last Name field. To make this selection, create a new, blank query form for EMPLYEE and select every field in that form. Next, enter the condition **not Jones** in the Last Name field of the EMPLYEE query form. When you press

[Do-It!] to process this query, Paradox will create the ANSWER table shown in Figure 7-47. As you can see, this table includes every record from EMPLYEE except those with the Last Name entry *Jones*.

Figure 7-47 A Query Using Not

```
Viewing Answer table: Record 1 of 13                                  Main

EMPLYEE  Emp Number      Last Name        First Name       SS Number
                         not Jones

ANSWER  Emp Number   Last Name     First Name   SS Number       Addre
   1        2        Cameron       Herb         321-65-8765     2321 Elm St
   2        5        Roberts       Darlene      417-43-7777     451 Lone Pi
   3        8        Williams      Brenda       401-55-1567     100 Owl Cre
   4        9        Myers         Julie        314-38-9452     4512 Parksi
   5       10        Link          Julie        345-75-1525     3215 Palm C
   6       12        Jackson       Mary         424-13-7621     7821 Clark
   7       13        Jakes, Jr.    Sal          321-65-9151     3451 Michig
   8       14        Preston       Molly        451-00-3426     321 Indian
   9       15        Masters       Ron          317-65-4529     423 W. 72nd
  10       16        Robertson     Kevin        415-24-6710     431 Bardsto
  11       17        Garrison      Robert       312-98-1479     55 Wheeler
  12       19        Gunn          Barbara      321-97-8632     541 Kentuck
  13       20        Emerson       Cheryl       404-14-1422     8100 River
```

You can also use the not operator with wildcard and range operators. For example, the Date of Hire field in the query form in Figure 7-48 contains the condition *not ../../84*. As you can see, when you process this query, Paradox will select all of the records that do not have a 1984 entry in the Date of Hire field. Similarly, the condition *not R..* in the Last Name field of the query in Figure 7-49 on the next page will cause Paradox to select all records that do not begin with an *R*. If you enter the condition *not >30000* in the Salary field of an EMPLYEE query form, as shown in Figure 7-50 on the following page, Paradox will select all records that have a Salary entry that is not greater than 30,000. (Of course, you could also state the condition as *<=30000*, which is probably simpler.)

Figure 7-48 Using Not with a Date Pattern

```
Viewing Answer table: Record 1 of 11                                  Main

   Zip            Phone           Date of Birth     Date of Hire
                                                    not ../../84

ANSWER  Emp Number   Last Name     First Name   SS Number       Addre
   1        8        Williams      Brenda       401-55-1567     100 Owl Cre
   2        9        Myers         Julie        314-38-9452     4512 Parksi
   3       10        Link          Julie        345-75-1525     3215 Palm C
   4       12        Jackson       Mary         424-13-7621     7821 Clark
   5       13        Jakes, Jr.    Sal          321-65-9151     3451 Michig
   6       14        Preston       Molly        451-00-3426     321 Indian
   7       15        Masters       Ron          317-65-4529     423 W. 72nd
   8       16        Robertson     Kevin        415-24-6710     431 Bardsto
   9       17        Garrison      Robert       312-98-1479     55 Wheeler
  10       19        Gunn          Barbara      321-97-8632     541 Kentuck
  11       20        Emerson       Cheryl       404-14-1422     8100 River
```

Figure 7-49 Using Not with a Pattern

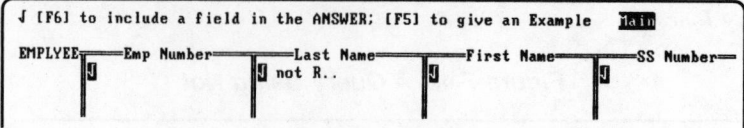

Figure 7-50 Using Not with a Range

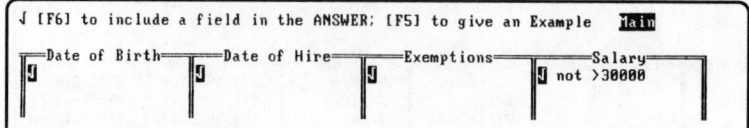

The Blank Operator

The blank operator allows you to select records that do not have entries in a specified field. This operator allows you to identify the records that are missing certain information.

To demonstrate this operator, we'll use a new table named PROJECTS. Figure 7-51 shows the structure of PROJECTS, and Figure 7-52 shows the data we've entered into the table. Notice that only some records have entries in the Actual Completion Date field. Those projects (records) with entries in this field are complete; the others are still in progress.

Figure 7-51 The Structure of the PROJECTS Table

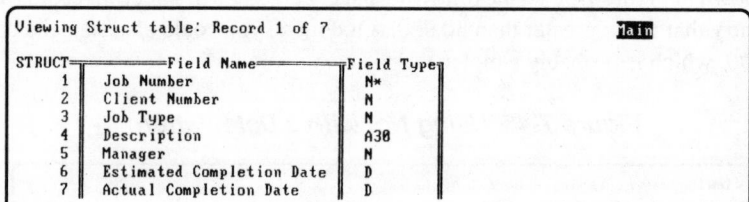

Suppose you want to look at those records that do not have an entry in the Actual Completion Date field. To make this selection, first use the **[Menu]** Ask command to create a new query form for PROJECTS, then press **[Check Mark]** while the cursor is under the query form name to select every field in the form. Next, move to the Actual Completion Date field and type the word **blank**.

Now, press **[Do-It!]** to process the query. Figure 7-53 on page 266 shows the resulting ANSWER table. Paradox has included only those records with blank Actual Completion Date fields in ANSWER.

Viewing Projects table: Record 1 of 16

PROJECTS	Job Number	Client Number	Job Type	Description	Manager	Estimated Completion Date	Actual Completion Date
1	100	1001	1	Install PC AT/Paradox/1-2-3	1	10/13/88	11/23/88
2	101	1001	3	AT/Paradox/1-2-3 Intro	1	12/13/88	
3	102	1002	2	Paradox A/R System	1	1/13/89	
4	103	1003	1	Install Compaq Plus/Symphony	1	6/15/89	
5	104	1003	2	Symphony Intro Course	4	10/05/88	9/29/88
6	105	1003	4	Recommend AR System	4	11/02/88	
7	106	1004	2	Paradox Time Accounting System	1	4/15/88	4/15/88
8	107	1004	3	1988 Compilation/Review	8	10/28/87	
9	108	1005	3	1988 Compilation/Review	8	5/29/88	5/29/88
10	109	1006	5	Tax Consultation	8	4/29/88	4/29/88
11	110	1007	2	1988 Tax Return		6/29/88	6/29/88
12	111	1008	2	1988 Tax Return	16	7/29/88	8/05/88
13	112	1009	1	1988 Audit	16	8/29/88	
14	113	1010	3	1988 Compilation/Review	1	9/29/88	
15	114	1010	6	Assist with Loan Application	4	10/27/88	
16	115	1011				5/14/88	7/14/88

Figure 7-52 The PROJECTS Table

Figure 7-53 A Query Using Blank

```
Viewing Answer table: Record 1 of 8                              Main
  ┌─────Manager─────┬──Estimated Completion Date──┬─Actual Completion Date─┐
  │                 │                             │ blank                  │
  │                 │                             │                        │
  │                 │                             │                        │


ANSWER┬─Job Number─┬─Client Number─┬─Job Type─┬──────Description══
   1  │    101     │    1001       │    3     │ AT/Paradox/1-2-3 Intro
   2  │    102     │    1002       │    2     │ Paradox A/R System
   3  │    103     │    1003       │    1     │ Install Compaq Plus/Sy
   4  │    105     │    1003       │    4     │ Recommend AR System
   5  │    107     │    1004       │    3     │ 1988 Compilation/Revie
   6  │    112     │    1009       │    2     │ 1988 Tax Return
   7  │    113     │    1010       │    1     │ 1988 Audit
   8  │    114     │    1010       │    3     │ 1988 Compilation/Revie
```

You can also use the blank operator with the not operator to select all records except those with a blank in the selected field. For example, suppose you now want to look at all of the records in PROJECTS that do contain an entry in the Actual Completion Date field (in other words, the projects that are completed). To do this, you could replace the entry in the Actual Completion Date field of the query form in Figure 7-53 with the entry *not blank*. Figure 7-54 shows the completed query and the ANSWER table Paradox will create when you press [Do-It!].

Figure 7-54 A Query Using Not Blank

```
Viewing Answer table: Record 1 of 8                              Main
  ┌─────Manager─────┬──Estimated Completion Date──┬─Actual Completion Date─┐
  │                 │                             │ not blank              │
  │                 │                             │                        │
  │                 │                             │                        │


ANSWER┬─Job Number─┬─Client Number─┬─Job Type─┬──────Description══
   1  │    100     │    1001       │    1     │ Install PC AT/Paradox/
   2  │    104     │    1003       │    2     │ Symphony Intro Course
   3  │    106     │    1004       │    2     │ Paradox Time Accountin
   4  │    108     │    1005       │    3     │ 1988 Compilation/Revie
   5  │    109     │    1006       │    3     │ 1988 Compilation/Revie
   6  │    110     │    1007       │    5     │ Tax Consultation
   7  │    111     │    1008       │    2     │ 1988 Tax Return
   8  │    115     │    1011       │    6     │ Assist with Loan Appli
```

As you might expect, you can use the blank operator in any type of field. For example, suppose you want to determine whether there are any projects in PROJECTS that have not been assigned a manager (in other words, whether there are any records with a blank in the Manager field). To make this selection, delete the condition in the Actual Completion Date field and enter the condition **blank** in the Manager field.

Be sure you understand the difference between entering the blank operator in a field of a query form and leaving that field of the query form blank. Entering the blank operator in a field tells Paradox to select only those records from the table being queried that have a blank in that field. Leaving the field blank, however, does not create a selection condition. When you leave a field in a query form blank (that is, when you do not enter a selection condition in the field), Paradox will not use that field as a basis for selecting records. In other words, leaving a field in a query form blank tells Paradox that you don't care what is in the field.

The Today Operator

The today operator allows you to enter the current date as a condition in a query form with a minimum of effort. The today operator always stands for the current date and can only be used in a date-type field. We'll use the PROJECTS table to demonstrate this function.

Suppose today is September 15, 1988. You want to look at all of the records from PROJECTS that have an Estimated Completion Date field entry that is less than today's date. In other words, you want to look at all of the projects that should be finished.

To begin, create a new, empty query form for PROJECTS and select every field in the form. Next, move to the Estimated Completion Date field and make the entry **<today**. Assuming that today is really September 15, 1988, when you process this query, Paradox will create the ANSWER table shown in Figure 7-55. This table includes only those records with estimated completion dates less than September 15, 1988. Of course, the results you get will depend upon which day you perform the query.

Figure 7-55 A Query Using Today

```
Viewing Answer table: Record 1 of 8                          Main

 ═Description═           ═Manager═          ╥Estimated Completion Date╥Actual Completi
║                      ║                    ║ <today                  ║
║                      ║                    ║                         ║


ANSWER═╥═Job Number═╥═Client Number═╥═Job Type═╥═══════════Description═
   1   ║    106     ║     1004      ║    2     ║ Paradox Time Accountin
   2   ║    107     ║     1004      ║    3     ║ 1988 Compilation/Revie
   3   ║    108     ║     1005      ║    3     ║ 1988 Compilation/Revie
   4   ║    109     ║     1006      ║    3     ║ 1988 Compilation/Revie
   5   ║    110     ║     1007      ║    5     ║ Tax Consultation
   6   ║    111     ║     1008      ║    2     ║ 1988 Tax Return
   7   ║    112     ║     1009      ║    2     ║ 1988 Tax Return
   8   ║    115     ║     1011      ║    6     ║ Assist with Loan Appli
```

Paradox derives the value of today from the system clock of your computer. If the system clock date isn't accurate, then the today operator will not be accurate. You can change the system clock date by issuing the DOS DATE command when you're at the system level.

Today can also be used as a base date in a mathematical selection condition. For example, suppose your company has a policy of placing new employees on probation for 90 days after their date of hire, and that today is September 15, 1988. Also suppose you want to select the records for all employees who are still in the probationary period.

To make this selection, first clear the PROJECTS query form, then create a new, blank query form for EMPLYEE. When the new form appears, select every field in the form, then move to the Date of Hire field and enter the condition **>today-90**. Now press **[Do-It!]** to process the query. Figure 7-56 shows the query and the resulting ANSWER table.

Figure 7-56 Using Today with a Range Operator

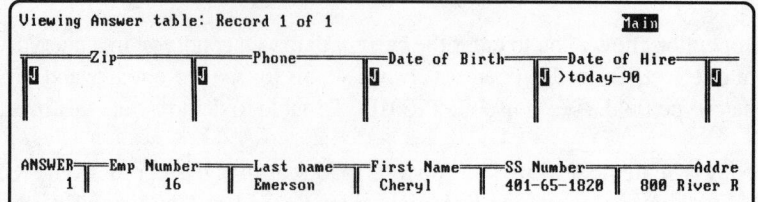

```
Viewing Answer table: Record 1 of 1                           Main
     ┌─────Zip─────┐          ┌─────Phone─────┐ ┌─Date of Birth─┐ ┌─Date of Hire─┐
   ║ │             │        ║ │               │ │               │ │ >today-90    │ ║
   ║ │             │        ║ │               │ │               │ │              │ ║


  ANSWER─┬─Emp Number──┬─Last name─┬─First Name─┬─SS Number────┬────────Addre
     1   │     16      │ Emerson   │ Cheryl     │ 401-65-1820  │ 800 River R
```

Logical ANDs and ORs

So far, we have considered only queries that select records that meet a single conditional test. In addition to these simple queries, however, Paradox also allows you to create queries that select records based on several different conditions. When you want to select records that meet all of several conditions, you should create an AND query. When you want to select records that meet one or more of several conditions, you should create an OR query.

OR Queries

In most cases, you select fields and enter selection conditions on more than one row of the query form to create an OR query. For instance, suppose you want to select the records from the EMPLYEE table that have either the entry *KY* or the entry *IN* in the State field. To do this, first create a blank query form for the EMPLYEE table. Next, press **[Check Mark]** while the cursor is in the space under the query form name EMPLYEE to select every field in the form. Then, move to the State field in this query form and type **KY**. Figure 7-57 shows the query form at this point. If you pressed **[Do-It!]** now, Paradox would select all of the records with the State field entry *KY*.

Figure 7-57 Creating an OR Query

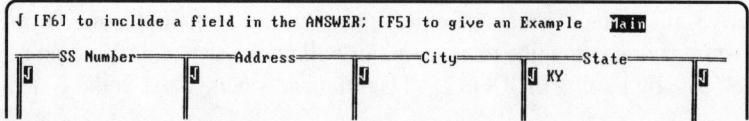

```
√ [F6] to include a field in the ANSWER; [F5] to give an Example    Main
   ┌──SS Number──┐ ┌───Address───┐ ┌────City────┐ ┌────State───┐
  ║│             │║│             │║│            │║│ KY         │║│
  ║│             │║│             │║│            │║│            │║│
```

Next, press the ↓ key to move down one row and type **IN** in the second row of the State field. Then, move to the far left of the second row, and press **[Check Mark]** to select every field in this second row of the query. Figure 7-58 shows the completed query.

Figure 7-58 The Completed OR Query

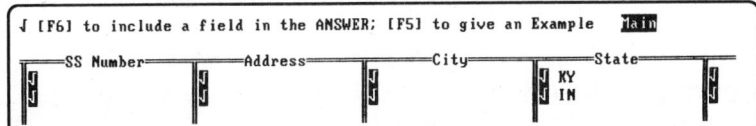

```
√ [F6] to include a field in the ANSWER; [F5] to give an Example   Main
┌─SS Number─┬─Address─┬─City─┬─State─┐
│           │         │      │ KY    │
│           │         │      │ IN    │
```

Now, press **[Do-It!]** to process the query. Figure 7-59 shows the resulting ANSWER table. Paradox has selected all of the records from the EMPLYEE table that have the entries *KY* or *IN* in the State field. In effect, Paradox has joined the two conditions with a logical OR so that the query can be translated into English like this: *Select every field of every record with the State field entry* KY *OR the State field entry* IN.

Figure 7-59 The OR Query ANSWER Table

```
Viewing Answer table: Record 1 of 12                    Main
┌─SS Number─┬─Address─┬─City─┬─State─┐
│           │         │      │ KY    │
│           │         │      │ IN    │
```

ANSWER	Emp Number	Last Name	First Name	SS Number	Addre
1	1	Jones	David	414-76-3421	4000 St. Ja
2	2	Cameron	Herb	321-65-8765	2321 Elm St
3	4	Jones	Stewart	401-32-8721	4389 Oakbri
4	5	Roberts	Darlene	417-43-7777	451 Lone Pi
5	6	Jones	Jean	413-07-9123	4000 St. Ja
6	8	Williams	Brenda	401-55-1567	100 Owl Cre
7	9	Myers	Julie	314-38-9452	4512 Parksi
8	12	Jackson	Mary	424-13-7621	7821 Clark
9	14	Preston	Molly	451-00-3426	321 Indian
10	16	Robertson	Kevin	415-24-6710	431 Bardsto
11	19	Gunn	Barbara	321-97-8632	541 Kentuck
12	20	Emerson	Cheryl	404-14-1422	8100 River

In this example, we made entries on two lines of the query form. However, you can make entries on up to 22 lines in a single query form, if you want. A query form with 22 lines would have 22 separate sets of conditions, all joined with logical ORs. In practice, however, your query forms will rarely include more than two or three lines.

Selecting Fields in OR Queries

In the example, we selected every field in both rows of the ANSWER table. As you might expect, Paradox does not require you to select every field in an OR query. You can select as many or as few fields as you want, as long as you obey two rules. First, Paradox requires that you select at least one field in each row of the query form that contains a selection condition. If you don't meet this restriction, Paradox will display the error message *One or more query rows do not contribute to the ANSWER* when you press [Do-It!].

Second, Paradox requires that you select the same fields in every row of the query form that contains a selection condition. For example, if you select just the Last Name and State fields in the first row of a query, you must select just those fields—no more and no less—

in the second and subsequent rows. If you try to process a query that breaks this rule, Paradox will display the error message *Query appears to ask two unrelated questions* when you press [Do-It!].

The Effect of Blank Rows

If you select fields in a row of the query form that does not include a selection condition, Paradox will include in the ANSWER table the selected fields from every record. Suppose you use the [Check Mark] key to select every field in the third row of the query form in Figure 7-59 so that it looks like Figure 7-60. Remember, the third row of this query does not contain a selection condition. If you press [Do-It!] to process this query, Paradox will create an ANSWER table that includes every field of every record from EMPLYEE.

Figure 7-60 A Query with a Blank Row

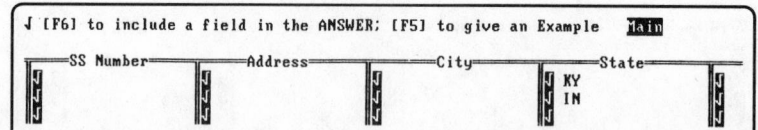

Here's why this occurs. As you saw in the first part of this chapter, a row in a query form that does not contain a selection condition will select every record from the table. It doesn't matter whether the query form has just one row, as in our earliest examples, or several rows, as in this case. If the table contains several rows, then the blank row is joined to the conditions in the other rows with a logical OR. For example, in this case, the query could be translated in this way: *Select every record with the State field entry* KY *OR the State field entry* IN *OR with any entry in any field.* Obviously, this query will select every record in the table.

The OR Operator

Paradox 3 includes an OR operator that lets you use single-row queries to test for multiple conditions that apply to the same field. To use the OR operator, list the different test conditions in the same field column, separating them with the OR operator. For example, Figure 7-61 shows a one-row query that tests for the same two conditions as the query shown in Figure 7-59. Both queries select all the records that have the State field entry *KY* or the State field entry *IN*. As you can see, both queries produce the same ANSWER table.

While the OR operator provides a great shortcut for creating OR queries that test for conditions involving only one field, there are times when you will need to use multiple-row queries even if you use Paradox 3. If you want to test for OR conditions that involve several fields, you will have to use a query with several rows, regardless of the version of Paradox you use.

Figure 7-61 The OR Operator in a Query

```
Viewing Answer table: Record 1 of 12                          Main

  Address          City            State            Zip
┌──────────┬────────────┬──────────────────┬──────────────┬─────────┐
│                        │ KY or IN │
└──────────┴────────────┴──────────────────┴──────────────┴─────────┘


ANSWER   Emp Number    Last name    First Name    SS Number         Addre
  1          1         Jones        David         414-76-3421    4000 St. Ja
  2          2         Cameron      Herb          321-65-8765    2331 Elm St
  3          4         Jones        Stewart       401-32-8721    4389 Oakbri
  4          5         Roberts      Darlene       417-43-7777    451 Lone Pi
  5          6         Jones        Jean          414-07-9123    4000 St. Ja
  6          8         Williams     Brenda        401-55-1567    100 Owl Cre
  7          9         Myers        Julie         314-38-9452    4512 Parksi
  8         12         Jackson      Mary          424-13-7621    7821 Clark
  9         14         Preston      Molly         451-00-3426    321 Indian
 10         16         Robertson    Kevin         415-24-6718    431 Bardsto
 11         19         Gunn         Barbara       321-97-8632    541 Kentuck
 12         20         Emerson      Cheryl        401-65-1820    800 River R
```

ORs on Different Fields

In the simple examples we've considered so far, we have created OR conditions within a single field. You can, however, create OR conditions that involve several fields. For example, suppose you want to select from EMPLYEE all records that have the entry *Jones* in the Last Name field or a number greater than 35,000 in the Salary field. Figure 7-62 shows a query that would make this selection. To create this query, begin with a new, empty query form for EMPLYEE. Select every field, then enter the selection condition **Jones** in the first row of the Last Name field of the query form and the condition **>35000** in the second row of the Salary field.

Figure 7-63 shows the ANSWER table that Paradox will create when you process this query. The table includes all of the records from the EMPLYEE table that have either the entry *Jones* in the Last Name field or an entry greater than 35000 in the Salary field.

Figure 7-62 Using OR on Several Fields

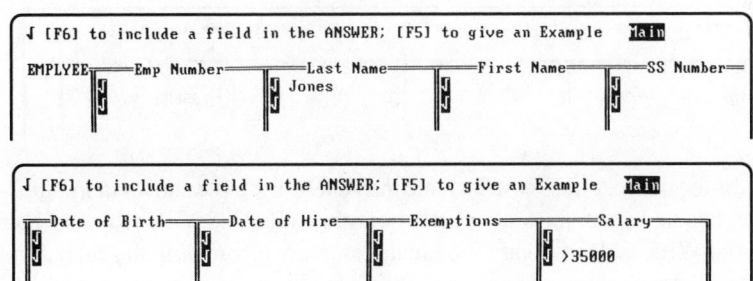

Figure 7-63 The ANSWER Table

```
Viewing Answer table: Record 2 of 7                              Main

 ┌─Date of Birth══╤══Date of Hire══╤══Exemptions══╤══Salary─┐
 │                │                │              │          │
 │                │                │              │  >35000  │


 ANSWER══╤═Emp Number══╤══Last Name══╤═First Name══╤═SS Number══╤══════Addre
    1    │      1      │   Jones     │   David     │ 414-76-3421 │ 4000 St. Ja
    2    │      2      │   Cameron   │   Herb      │ 321-65-8765 │ 2331 Elm St
    3    │      4      │   Jones     │   Stewart   │ 401-32-8721 │ 4389 Oakbri
    4    │      6      │   Jones     │   Jean      │ 414-87-9123 │ 4000 St. Ja
    5    │      8      │   Williams  │   Brenda    │ 401-55-1567 │ 555 Court S
    6    │     15      │   Masters   │   Ron       │ 317-65-4529 │ 423 W. 72nd
    7    │     16      │   Robertson │   Kevin     │ 415-24-6710 │ 431 Bardsto
```

A few records in EMPLYEE meet both of these conditions; that is, the Last Name entry is *Jones* and the Salary entry is greater than 35,000. However, notice that these records only appear in the ANSWER table once. As in this case, even though a record meets more than one condition in an OR query, the record will appear in the ANSWER table only once.

If you own Paradox 3, then you can include the OR operator in queries that combine one or more OR conditions that apply to a single field with other OR conditions that apply to multiple fields. For example, suppose you want to select from EMPLYEE all records that have either the entry *Jones* or the entry *Roberts* in the Last Name field, or a number greater than 35,000 in the Salary field. To create this query, place the cursor in the Last Name field of the query shown in Figure 7-62. Then, just after the selection condition *Jones*, type **or Roberts**. Figure 7-64 shows the completed query.

Figure 7-64 The OR Operator in a Multirow Query

```
√ [F6] to include a field in the ANSWER; [F5] to give an Example    Main

 EMPLYEE══╤═Emp Number══╤════════Last name══╤═First Name══╤══SS Num
          │             │  Jones or Roberts │             │
```

```
√ [F6] to include a field in the ANSWER; [F5] to give an Example    Main

 ┌─Date of Birth══╤══Date of Hire══╤══Exemptions══╤══Salary─┐
 │                │                │              │          │
 │                │                │              │  >35000  │
```

If you process the query, Paradox will create the ANSWER table shown in Figure 7-65. As you can see, this table contains one record more than the ANSWER table in Figure 7-63. While the ANSWER table in Figure 7-63 includes every record with the entry *Jones* in the Last Name field or a number greater than 35,000 in the Salary field, this new ANSWER table also includes any record that has the entry *Roberts* in the Last Name field. As a result, this new ANSWER table also includes the EMPLYEE record for Darlene Roberts, which is record 4 in the ANSWER table.

Figure 7-65 The ANSWER Table

```
Viewing Answer table: Record 1 of 8                                    Main

EMPLYEE┬─────Emp Number─────┬─────────Last name────────┬─────First Name────────┬────SS Num
       │                    │   Jones or Roberts        │                        │
       │                    │                           │                        │


ANSWER┬─────Emp Number─────┬────Last name────┬────First Name───┬────SS Number────┬────────Addre
  1   │        1           │  Jones          │  David          │  414-76-3421    │  4000 St. Ja
  2   │        2           │  Cameron        │  Herb           │  321-65-8765    │  2331 Elm St
  3   │        4           │  Jones          │  Stewart        │  401-32-8721    │  4309 Oakbri
  4   │        5           │  Roberts        │  Darlene        │  417-43-7777    │  451 Lone Pi
  5   │        6           │  Jones          │  Jean           │  414-07-9123    │  4000 St. Ja
  6   │        8           │  Williams       │  Brenda         │  401-55-1567    │  100 Owl Cre
  7   │       15           │  Masters        │  Ron            │  317-65-4529    │  423 W. 72nd
  8   │       16           │  Robertson      │  Kevin          │  415-24-6718    │  431 Bardsto
```

AND Queries

As you have seen, OR queries allow you to select records that meet one of several selection conditions. AND queries, on the other hand, allow you to select records that meet all of several conditions. AND conditions are created by entering more than one selection condition in a single row of a query form.

For example, suppose you want to select those records from EMPLYEE with an entry less than 10 in the Emp Number field and an entry greater than 35,000 in the Salary field. Figure 7-66 shows a completed query that will make this selection.

Figure 7-66 An AND Query

```
√ [F6] to include a field in the ANSWER; [F5] to give an Example   Main

EMPLYEE┬─────Emp Number─────┬─────Last Name────┬─────First Name────┬────Address────
       │ <10                │                  │                   │
```

```
√ [F6] to include a field in the ANSWER; [F5] to give an Example   Main

┬─────Date of Birth─────┬─────Date of Hire─────┬────Exemptions───┬────Salary────
│                       │                      │                 │ >35000
```

Notice that there are two selection conditions in the first row of this query: the formula *<10* in the Emp Number field and the entry *>35000* in the Salary field. These two conditions are joined by a logical AND, so the query could be translated into English like this: *Select every record that has an Emp Number field entry that is less than 10 AND a Salary field entry that is greater than 35000.*

Figure 7-67 shows the ANSWER table Paradox will create when you process this query. The table includes only those records that satisfy both selection conditions: David Jones, Herb Cameron, Stewart Jones, and Brenda Williams.

Figure 7-67 The ANSWER Table for an AND Query

```
Viewing Answer table: Record 1 of 4                        Main
┌─Date of Birth──┬──Date of Hire──┬──Exemptions──┬──Salary─
│                │                │              │  >35000
│                │                │              │


ANSWER┬─Emp Number─┬──Last Name─┬─First Name─┬─SS Number─┬──────Addre
   1  │     1      │   Jones    │   David    │ 414-76-3421│ 4000 St. Ja
   2  │     2      │   Cameron  │   Herb     │ 321-65-8765│ 2321 Elm St
   3  │     4      │   Jones    │   Stewart  │ 401-32-8721│ 4389 Oakbri
   4  │     8      │   Williams │   Brenda   │ 401-55-1567│ 100 Owl Cre
```

ANDs in One Field

The method shown in the previous example works fine if the selection conditions you specify apply to different fields. But what if you want to link two conditions that apply to the same field with a logical AND? For example, suppose you want to select every record from the table that has a Salary entry greater than 20,000 and less than 40,000. To do this, create a new, empty query form for EMPLYEE and select every field in the form. Then, move the cursor to the first row of the Salary field and type **>20000,<40000.**

Whenever you enter two or more conditions in a single field of a query form, Paradox joins those conditions with a logical AND. For example, this query can be translated like this: *Select every field of every record that has a Salary field entry greater than 20000 AND less than 40000.*

Figure 7-68 shows this query and the resulting ANSWER table. This table includes only those records from EMPLYEE that have a Salary entry between 20,000 and 40,000. Notice that the two conditions in the query in Figure 7-68 are separated by a comma. Whenever you enter two or more conditions into a single field of a query form, you must separate the individual conditions with commas.

Figure 7-68 A Query with More Than One AND

```
Viewing Answer table: Record 1 of 8                        Main
┌─Date of Birth──┬──Date of Hire──┬──Exemptions──┬──Salary─
│                │                │              │  >20000,<40000
│                │                │              │


ANSWER┬─Emp Number─┬──Last Name──┬─First Name─┬─SS Number─┬──────Addre
   1  │     6      │   Jones     │   Jean     │ 413-07-9123│ 4000 St. Ja
   2  │     9      │   Myers     │   Julie    │ 314-38-9452│ 4512 Parksi
   3  │    10      │   Link      │   Julie    │ 345-75-1525│ 3215 Palm C
   4  │    12      │   Jackson   │   Mary     │ 424-13-7621│ 7821 Clark
   5  │    13      │   Jakes, Jr.│   Sal      │ 321-65-9151│ 3451 Michig
   6  │    15      │   Masters   │   Ron      │ 317-65-4529│ 423 W. 72nd
   7  │    16      │   Robertson │   Kevin    │ 415-24-6710│ 431 Bardsto
   8  │    17      │   Garrison  │   Robert   │ 312-98-1479│ 55 Wheeler
```

The only limit on the number of conditions you can enter in a single field of a query form is the overall Paradox limit of 255 characters in a single entry. In most cases, this limitation will not cause you any difficulty.

Combining AND and OR Queries

So far, we've created OR queries and AND queries. As you might expect, however, you can also create combined AND/OR queries. For example, suppose you want to select those records that have a Date of Birth entry that is less than (before) January 1, 1950, and an Emp Number entry that is less than 10, or that have the entry *Jones* in the Last Name field.

Figure 7-69 shows a completed query that will do the trick. Notice that this query contains three selection conditions. The first row of the Emp Number field contains the condition *<10*. The first row of the Date of Birth field contains the condition *<1/1/50*. These two conditions combine to select only those records with a Date of Birth entry that is less than January 1, 1950, and an Emp Number entry that is less than 10. The second row of the Last Name field contains the condition *Jones*.

Figure 7-70 shows the ANSWER table that was created by processing this query. This table includes all of the records from the table that have the Last Name entry *Jones*, or a Date of Birth entry that is less than 1/1/50 and an Emp Number entry that is less than 10.

Figure 7-69 An AND and OR Query

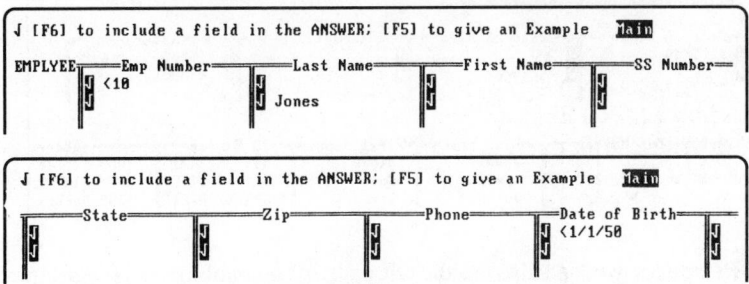

Figure 7-70 The ANSWER Table

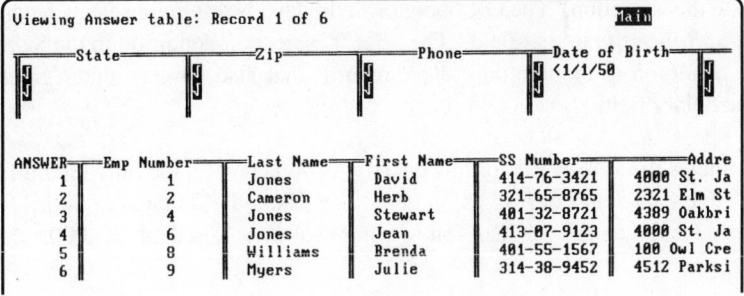

Suppose you want to select all of the records that have an entry greater than 45,000 in the Salary field and a Date of Birth entry that is less than January 1, 1940, or an entry greater than 45,000 in the Salary field and a Date of Hire entry that is less than 4/16/87. Figure 7-71 shows a completed query that will perform this selection.

Notice that there are selection conditions in two rows of this query form. The conditions in the first row (<*1/1/40* in the Date of Birth field and >*45000* in the Salary field) combine to select only those records with a Date of Birth entry that is before January 1, 1940, and a Salary entry greater than 45,000. The conditions in the second row (<*4/16/87* in the Date of Hire field and >*45000* in the Salary field) combine to select only those records with a Date of Hire entry that is before April 16, 1987, and a Salary entry greater than 45,000. When taken together, the conditions on the two rows of the form will select any record that meets the condition specified by the entries on either row. Figure 7-72 shows the ANSWER table that results from this query.

Figure 7-71 Combining ANDs and ORs in a Query

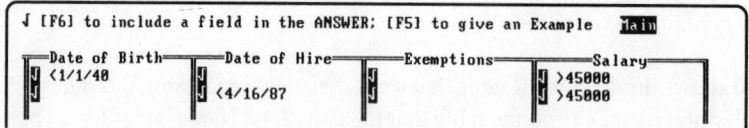

Figure 7-72 The ANSWER Table

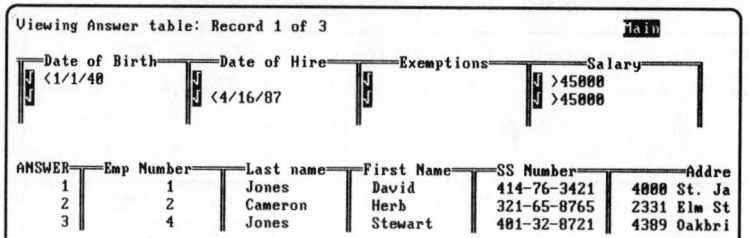

If you have Paradox 3, you can also use the OR operator in combined AND/OR queries that include more than one OR condition affecting one field. For example, suppose you want to select all the records that have the entry *Jones* or the entry *Robertson* in the Last Name field and an entry greater than 35,000 in the Salary field. Figure 7-73 shows a completed query that will make this selection. The OR operator in the Last Name field selects records with either *Jones* or *Robertson* in that field. The >*35000* selection condition in the Salary field restricts the condition to include only those records that also have an entry greater than 35,000 in the Salary field.

Figure 7-74 shows the ANSWER for this query. As you can see, the only record from the EMPLYEE table with *Jones* or *Robertson* in the Last Name field that is excluded from the ANSWER table is the record for Jean Jones, whose salary is less than $35,000.

Figure 7-73 A Query Using OR

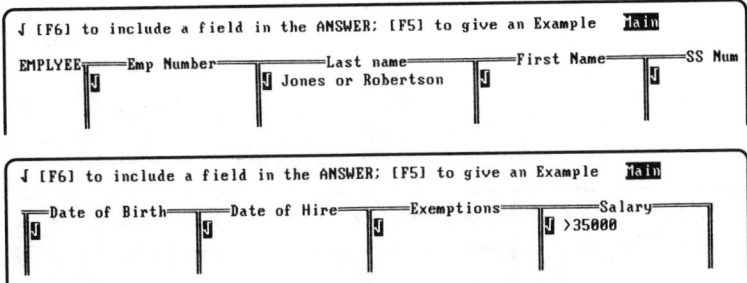

Figure 7-74 The ANSWER Table

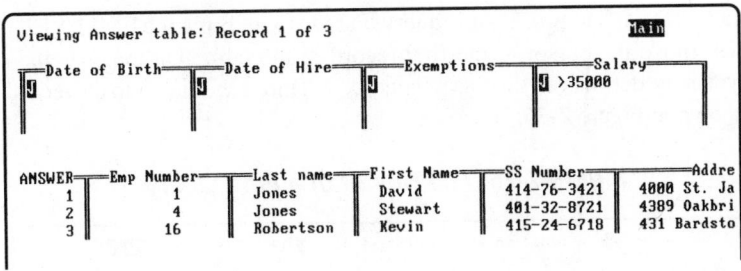

Figuring out just how to create a complex AND/OR query can take a bit of thinking. If you get confused, you might try writing the query as a sentence, complete with *ands* and *ors*, before you try to create it in Paradox.

Other Types of Queries

So far, we've worked only with conventional queries that copy the information from selected fields of selected records into an ANSWER table. However, Paradox is capable of performing several other types of queries, including queries that allow you to delete records that match selection conditions, find matching records in a table without copying them to an ANSWER table, or change entries in records that match selection conditions.

Find Queries

Find queries allow you to find the first record in a table that matches the selection conditions you specify. This type of query is useful when you need to view or edit a specific record in a table, and you don't have time to browse through the table to locate the record.

To create a find query, you first create a query form and enter the word *find* in the space under the form name at the left edge of the form. Next, you enter the appropriate selection conditions (if any) into that form. When you process a find query, Paradox will bring the table being queried into view (if it is not already on the screen) and will move the cursor to the first record that meets the conditions you have defined.

For example, suppose you need to see the record for Julie Myers, employee 9. To begin, use the **[Menu]** Ask command to create a new query form for EMPLYEE. When the new form appears on the screen, type the word **find** in the space under the query form name at the left edge of the table to signal Paradox that this is a find query. Then, move to the first row of the Emp Number field and enter the selection condition **9**. Figure 7-75 shows the results.

Figure 7-75 A Find Query

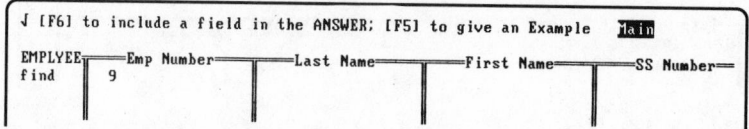

When you press **[Do-It!]** to process this query, Paradox will bring the EMPLYEE table into view and will move the cursor to the first record in the table that matches the selection conditions you have defined. In this case, Paradox will move the cursor to the record for Julie Myers, as shown in Figure 7-76.

Figure 7-76 The Result of a Find Query

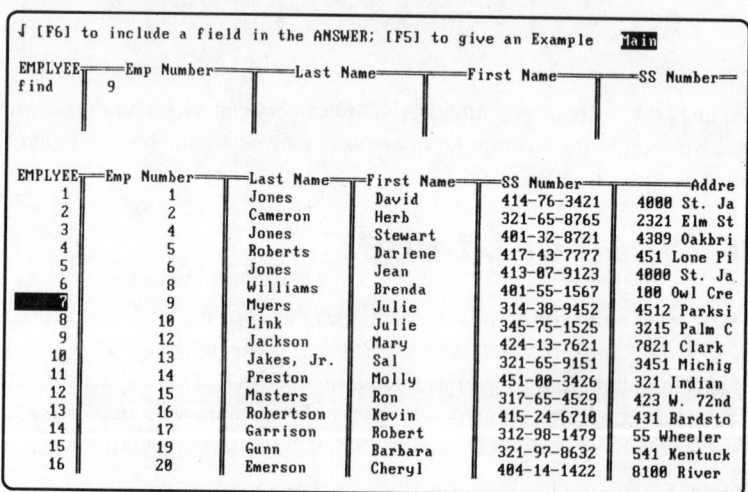

Notice that we said Paradox will bring the EMPLYEE table into view when you process this query. Whenever you perform a find query, if the table being queried is not in view, Paradox will bring it into view when you process the query. As you may recall, most conventional queries do not bring the table being queried into view.

After Paradox moves the cursor to the first matching record in the table, Paradox returns to the normal viewing mode. If you want to edit the record Paradox has located, you may press the **[Edit]** key to enter the Edit mode. If you want to review the surrounding records, you can press ↑, ↓, or any of the other movement keys.

In addition to moving the cursor to the first record that matches the defined conditions, Paradox also copies into an ANSWER table any records that match the conditions you have defined. However, this table will not appear on the screen, as it will when you process conventional queries. If you want to view the ANSWER table, just issue the View command.

The ANSWER table that is created by a find query is different from most ANSWER tables in another way. In most ANSWER tables, the records are arranged in ascending order based on the entries in the first field of the table. In find query ANSWER tables, however, the records appear in the same order as they were arranged in the queried table, as they would be if you used the [Check Plus] key.

If no records in the table being queried match the condition you have defined, Paradox will display the message *No record matches Find query*.

Notice that we didn't select any fields when we created the query in Figure 7-75. Because find queries operate on entire records, not on specified fields, there is no need to select fields in a find query. In fact, if you attempt to process a find query that includes checked fields, Paradox will display the message *Checkmark cannot be used in Find queries*.

Find Queries Versus [Zoom]

Find queries and the [Zoom] key ([Ctrl]-[Z]) perform the same task: locating a specific record in a table. The difference between the two commands is that with find queries you can have a multicolumn search, while [Zoom] allows you to search only one column. For example, to locate Stewart Jones in the EMPLYEE table, you can design a find query specifying *Jones* in the Last Name field and *Stewart* in the First Name field. When you press [Do-It!], Paradox will display the record for Stewart Jones in the ANSWER table. If you use the [Zoom] key to locate the same record, you must view the EMPLYEE table, move to the Last Name field, press the [Zoom] key, and enter *Jones* after the prompt at the top of the screen. Paradox then will move the cursor to the first occurrence of *Jones* in the table. In this case, the record will be David Jones, so you will need to press the [Zoom Next] key ([Alt]-[Z]) to locate the next Jones record, which will be Stewart, the record we are looking for. Although the find query will always find the correct record on the first try, the [Zoom] key executes faster. Therefore, you may find it quicker to use [Zoom] and [Zoom Next] to locate a specific record. (For a complete discussion of the [Zoom] key, see Chapter 2.)

Delete Queries

Delete queries allow you to delete from a table those records that match the selection conditions you specify. In addition to being deleted from the table, the deleted records are stored in a temporary table called DELETED.

To create a delete query, you first create a query form and enter the word *delete* in the space under the form name at the left edge of the form. Next, you enter the appropriate selection conditions (if any) into that form. When you process a delete query, Paradox will delete from the table the records that match the specified selection conditions. In addition, Paradox will copy the deleted records to a temporary table called DELETED.

For example, suppose Julie Link, employee 10, has resigned from her job and you want to delete her from the EMPLYEE table. Figure 7-77 shows a delete query that will do the trick.

Figure 7-77 A Delete Query

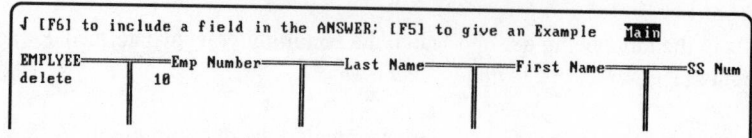

To create this query, make a new, blank query form for EMPLYEE. When the new form appears on the screen, type the word **delete** in the space under the query form name at the left edge of the table. This word signals to Paradox that this is a delete query. Now, move to the first row of the Emp Number field and type the number **10**, the Emp Number entry of the record you want to delete.

When you press [**Do-It!**] to process this query, Paradox will copy the record for Julie Link to a DELETED table and will delete her record from EMPLYEE. Figure 7-78 shows the screen as it will look after the query is processed.

Figure 7-78 A Completed Delete Query

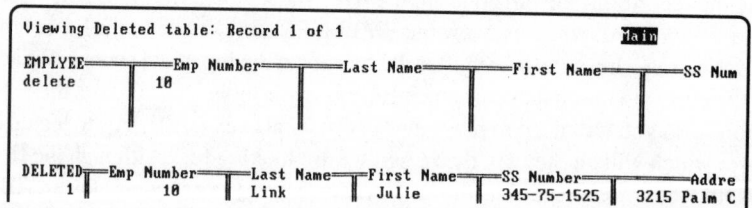

When you process a delete query, you won't see the revised table on the screen unless it was in view before you processed the query. If the table is not in view when you press [Do-It!], it will not be in view after the query is processed. The DELETED table, however, always comes into view when you process a delete query.

Like ANSWER, DELETED is a temporary table. Each time you perform a delete query, Paradox overwrites the existing DELETED table (if there is one) with the DELETED table for the new query. If you want to preserve the contents of the DELETED table, you should rename it before you perform another delete query.

Notice that we didn't select any fields when we created the delete query in Figure 7-78. Because delete queries operate on entire records, and not on specified fields, there is no need to select fields in a delete query. In fact, if you attempt to process a delete query that includes selected fields, Paradox will display the message *Insert, Delete, ChangeTo and Set rows may not be checkmarked.*

When you process a delete query, Paradox will delete those records that match the selection conditions you have defined. If you do not define any conditions before you process the query, Paradox will delete every record from the table. Be careful! Although you can restore deleted records to a table, it is easy to destroy a great deal of data by making a simple mistake with delete queries.

An Alternative Method

Of course, you can also delete records from a table with the [Del] key while editing the table. There are two major advantages to using delete queries instead of the [Del] key to delete records. First, as you have seen, when you use a delete query to delete records, the deleted records are copied to a temporary DELETED table. You can restore deleted records from the DELETED table by using the [Menu] Tools More Add command. Second, delete queries make it possible to simultaneously delete all the records that meet a given set of conditions.

Reversing a Deletion

The DELETED table provides you with a double safeguard. First, by viewing this table, you can determine whether Paradox operated on the correct records when you processed the query. Second, the DELETED table also makes it possible to reverse the effects of the delete query. If you must restore those records to the table from which they were deleted, you can use the [Menu] Tools More Add command.

For example, suppose you want to restore to EMPLYEE the record you just deleted. To do this, issue the **[Menu]** Tools More Add command, specify **DELETED** as the source table and **EMPLYEE** as the destination table. When you press ↵, Paradox will add the one record from DELETED to EMPLYEE and will bring EMPLYEE into view. Figure 7-79 on the following page shows the resulting EMPLYEE table.

Notice that the record for Julie Myers appears at the bottom of the table. If you want to restore the table to its original order, you could use the [Menu] Modify Sort command. If EMPLYEE were a keyed table, the added record would appear in order.

You can also use a special kind of query, called an insert query, to restore deleted records from DELETED. We'll show you how to create and use insert queries in Chapter 9.

Figure 7-79 Reversing a Delete Query

```
Viewing Emplyee table: Record 1 of 16                          Main ▲══

DELETED┬─Emp Number─────┬──Last Name─┬─First Name─┬─SS Number──┬────────Addre
     1 ┃       10       ┃ Link       ┃ Julie      ┃ 345-75-1525┃ 3215 Palm C


EMPLYEE┬─Emp Number─────┬──Last Name─┬─First Name─┬─SS Number──┬────────Addre
     1 ┃       1        ┃ Jones      ┃ David      ┃ 414-76-3421┃ 4000 St. Ja
     2 ┃       2        ┃ Cameron    ┃ Herb       ┃ 321-65-8765┃ 2321 Elm St
     3 ┃       4        ┃ Jones      ┃ Stewart    ┃ 401-32-8721┃ 4389 Oakbri
     4 ┃       5        ┃ Roberts    ┃ Darlene    ┃ 417-43-7777┃ 451 Lone Pi
     5 ┃       6        ┃ Jones      ┃ Jean       ┃ 413-07-9123┃ 4000 St. Ja
     6 ┃       8        ┃ Williams   ┃ Brenda     ┃ 401-55-1567┃ 100 Owl Cre
     7 ┃       9        ┃ Myers      ┃ Julie      ┃ 314-38-9452┃ 4512 Parksi
     8 ┃       12       ┃ Jackson    ┃ Mary       ┃ 424-13-7621┃ 7821 Clark
     9 ┃       13       ┃ Jakes, Jr. ┃ Sal        ┃ 321-65-9151┃ 3451 Michig
    10 ┃       14       ┃ Preston    ┃ Molly      ┃ 451-00-3426┃ 321 Indian
    11 ┃       15       ┃ Masters    ┃ Ron        ┃ 317-65-4529┃ 423 W. 72nd
    12 ┃       16       ┃ Robertson  ┃ Kevin      ┃ 415-24-6710┃ 431 Bardsto
    13 ┃       17       ┃ Garrison   ┃ Robert     ┃ 312-98-1479┃ 55 Wheeler
    14 ┃       19       ┃ Gunn       ┃ Barbara    ┃ 321-97-8632┃ 541 Kentuck
    15 ┃       20       ┃ Emerson    ┃ Cheryl     ┃ 404-14-1422┃ 8100 River
    16 ┃       10       ┃ Link       ┃ Julie      ┃ 345-75-1525┃ 3215 Palm C
```

Changeto Queries

Changeto queries allow you to change the entries in a given field for all of the records in a table that match your selection conditions. Changeto queries are similar to the search and replace capability of most word processors.

To define a changeto query, you first create a query form and enter the appropriate selection conditions (if any) into that form. Then, enter the word **changeto** into the field of the query form you want to change, followed by the new value you want to assign to the entries in that field. When you process a changeto query, Paradox will change the entries in the appropriate field of the selected records to the specified changeto value. In addition, Paradox will copy the original version of any changed records to a temporary table called CHANGED.

For example, suppose Brenda Williams, employee 8, has just changed the number of exemptions she wants to claim from 5 to 6. Let's use a changeto query to make this change. To begin, bring the EMPLYEE table into view and move to the Exemptions field. Next, create a new, blank query for EMPLYEE, then enter the selection condition **8** in the first row of the Emp Number field of the query form.

Now, you need to tell Paradox which field you want it to change and how you want it changed. To do this, move the cursor to the first row of the Exemptions field and type **changeto 6**. Figure 7-80 shows the completed query and the EMPLYEE table. Now, press **[Do-It!]** to process the query. Figure 7-81 on page 284 shows the screen as it will look after the query has been processed. Notice that the Exemptions entry for Brenda Williams, the sixth record in the table, has changed from 5 to 6, just as you requested, and that the original record for Brenda Williams has been copied into a CHANGED table.

Figure 7-80 A Changeto Query

The CHANGED Table

Whenever you process a changeto query, Paradox will copy the original versions of all the records that are changed to a CHANGED table. By viewing this table, you can determine whether Paradox operated on the correct records when you processed the query.

The CHANGED table also allows you to reverse the effects of the changeto query. To reverse a changeto query, you must delete the records that were changed incorrectly from the original table, and then use the [Menu] Tools More Add command to add the contents of CHANGED to the original table. If the original table is not keyed, then the restored records will be added to the end of the table.

Figure 7-81 The ANSWER Table

```
Viewing Changed table: Record 1 of 1                          Main ▲═

┌─Zip──┬──────Phone─────┬─Date of Birth─┬─Date of Hire─┬─Exemptions─┬─────
│ 40207│ (502) 245-6610 │  10/06/42     │   1/14/87    │     3      │ ****
│ 40208│ (502) 451-8765 │  11/24/29     │   1/14/87    │     4      │ ****
│ 40222│ (502) 452-1848 │   3/21/50     │   2/13/87    │     1      │ ****
│ 40012│ (502) 897-3215 │   9/24/60     │   6/16/87    │     3      │ ****
│ 40207│ (502) 245-6610 │   5/14/43     │   7/16/87    │     0      │ ****
│ 40223│ (502) 894-9761 │   1/12/20     │   8/16/87    │     6      │ ****
│ 40209│ (502) 454-5209 │   2/06/48     │   9/16/87    │     1      │ ****
│ 47130│ (812) 288-6754 │   8/12/56     │  11/14/87    │     3      │ ****
│ 65987│ (214) 398-1987 │   5/23/59     │  12/14/87    │     6      │ ****
│ 40208│ (502) 456-3256 │   4/17/66     │   2/13/88    │     1      │ ****
│ 10019│ (212) 276-5478 │  12/31/44     │   2/13/88    │     0      │ ****
│ 40315│ (502) 423-9823 │   3/16/25     │   2/27/88    │     1      │ ****
│ 25687│ (617) 543-4124 │   5/09/45     │   5/15/88    │     4      │ ****
│ 47132│ (812) 325-4789 │   5/18/50     │   6/15/88    │     2      │ ****
│ 40222│ (502) 896-5139 │   7/30/66     │   8/15/88    │     2      │ ****
│ 94375│ (408) 542-1948 │   6/03/33     │  11/14/87    │     2      │ ****

CHANGED─┬─Emp Number─┬──Last name─┬─First Name─┬─SS Number──┬────Addre
   1    │     8      │  Williams  │   Brenda   │ 401-55-1567│ 100 Owl Cre
```

Like ANSWER, CHANGED is a temporary table. Each time you perform a changeto query, Paradox overwrites the existing CHANGED table (if there is one) with the CHANGED table for the new query. If you want to preserve the contents of the CHANGED table, you should rename it before you process another changeto query.

There is a trap to watch out for. When your changeto query finishes and the CHANGED table appears on the screen, you'll usually want to inspect the table to see if the query worked. In the previous example, you would check to make sure that the number of exemptions had been changed to 6. Because the CHANGED table has the same structure as the EMPLYEE table, it's easy to get the two of them confused and inspect the CHANGED table by mistake (especially since Paradox leaves the cursor positioned in the CHANGED table, and the table frequently fills up the entire screen). If you check the CHANGED table, you will see that the number of exemptions is still 5 and think your query didn't work. Remember, though, that you are viewing the CHANGED table, which shows the records as they were before being changed! You should view the EMPLYEE table instead, and make your inspection there.

Changing Several Records

In the preceding example, we used changeto to change the entry in the field of one record. In most cases, you can make that kind of change just as easily by using the Edit mode. Changeto queries are most valuable when you want to change many records.

If you use a changeto operator in a query form that does not contain any selection conditions, Paradox will make the requested change to every record in the table. For example, if you created the query in Figure 7-80 but did not enter the selection condition 8 in the Emp Number field, Paradox would change the Exemptions entry for every record in the table to 6. In a more practical application, you could use this type of query to increase the salary of every employee in the table by 10 percent. (We'll show you how to do just that in the next chapter.)

If you use the changeto operator in a query form that includes selection conditions that will select several records, Paradox will change the entry in the indicated fields of all matching records. Let's use the PROJECTS table to demonstrate this concept. Suppose you want to change the Manager entry to 2 for every project with the Manager entry 4. To begin, create a new, blank query form for PROJECTS, then move to the first row of the Manager field and type **4, changeto 2**. Figure 7-82 shows the result. Paradox has changed the Manager entry to 2 for every record with the Manager entry 4 and has copied the unchanged versions of those records to a CHANGED table.

Figure 7-82 Changing More Than One Record

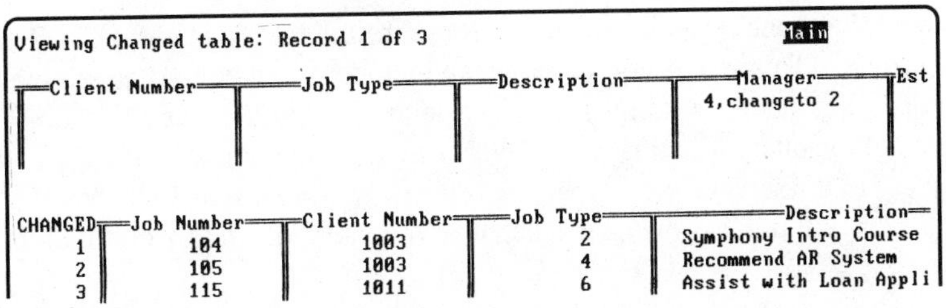

```
Viewing Changed table: Record 1 of 3                        Main

 ┌Client Number┬────Job Type─┬───Description─┬───Manager──┬─Est
 │             │             │               │   4,changeto 2
 │             │             │               │
 │             │             │               │

CHANGED┬Job Number─┬Client Number─┬Job Type─┬────Description═
   1   │   104     │   1003       │   2     │ Symphony Intro Course
   2   │   105     │   1003       │   4     │ Recommend AR System
   3   │   115     │   1011       │   6     │ Assist with Loan Appli
```

The QuerySave Command

Earlier in the chapter, we explained that queries are temporary. When you clear a query from the screen, it ceases to exist. The only way to recover the query is to recreate it from scratch. Since most of your queries will be ad hoc queries (queries that are designed to perform a particular task that is unlikely to be repeated), this characteristic usually will not be a problem.

However, there will be a few queries that you use over and over and that you would rather not recreate each time you need to use them. Fortunately, Paradox includes a command, [Menu] Scripts QuerySave, that you can use to save your queries into special script files. When you have saved a query into a script file, you can bring it back to the screen with the [Menu] Scripts Play command. Once it is on the screen, you can process it by pressing [Do-It!].

An Example

Suppose you have created the query shown in Figure 7-83 on the following page. This query selects those records that have an Estimated Date of Completion that is less than *today+90* but greater than *today*; in other words, this query will select those projects that are forecast to be completed in the next 90 days. Suppose you use this query nearly every month and you don't want to recreate it from scratch every time you need it.

To save this query, issue the **[Menu]** Scripts QuerySave command. When Paradox prompts you for a name for the saved query, choose a name that will help you remember the function of the query. For instance, in this case you might choose a name like Q90days. Once you supply the name and press ↵, Paradox will save the query into a script file. The query will not be removed from the screen, so if you want to process it after you save it, all you need to do is press [Do-It!].

Figure 7-83 A Typical Query

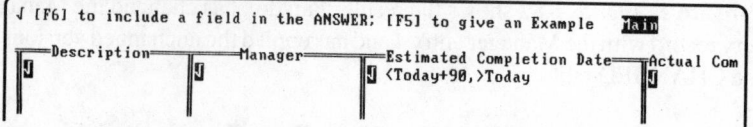

Suppose a week has gone by and you want to reuse the query. To begin, press [Clear All] to clear the screen. (This step is not required; we include it so that you can see more easily the effect of playing the query script.) Next, issue the [Menu] Scripts Play command and type the name of the query—in this case, Q90days. When you press ↵, Paradox will bring the saved query to the screen. Now, to process the query, press [Do-It!]. When you press this key, Paradox will process the query just as if you had typed it in from scratch.

Most of the queries you save will be more complex than this one. After all, if you can type in the query from scratch as easily as you can retrieve it from a script, it doesn't make much sense to save that query in a script. However, this example demonstrates all of the steps involved in saving queries.

Notes

If the active query includes several query forms (we'll see some queries like this in the next chapter), all the query forms will be saved when you issue the QuerySave command. When you play the saved query, all the forms will be retrieved to the screen.

In the example, we cleared the screen before we played the saved script Q90days. You don't need to clear the screen before you can retrieve a saved query, however. If there is a query on the screen when you play a saved query, the query you are playing will replace the existing query. If there are table images on the screen, the query being played will appear above those images at the top of the screen.

We like to name all our QuerySave scripts with names beginning with the letter *Q*. It is not necessary to do so, but it helps us to remember that these are QuerySave scripts, and distinguishes them from other kinds of Paradox scripts.

In Chapter 13, "Simple Scripts," we will explore the QuerySave command in more detail. In that chapter, we'll pay special attention to the nature of the script files that are created when you issue the QuerySave command.

Speeding Up Queries

Because the queries we have used as examples in this chapter refer to tables that contain only a few records, Paradox was able to perform them very quickly. In actual practice, however, your tables are likely to contain many more records than our sample tables. When you are querying tables that contain hundreds or thousands instead of just a dozen or so records, queries can take a great deal longer to execute.

Fortunately, Paradox offers three tools—key fields, secondary indexes, and the [Menu] Tools QuerySpeedup command—that you can use to speed up the processing of your queries. Let's look at these useful tools.

Key Fields

As you learned in Chapter 2, Paradox allows you to create key fields in your tables. These key fields have several purposes, one of which is to speed up the processing of queries.

Key Field Review

To create a key field, type an asterisk next to the field type entry in the Field Type field when you create the table. For example, Figure 7-84 shows the STRUCT table for the PROJECTS table. Notice the asterisk in the Field Type field of the Job Number record in STRUCT.

Figure 7-84 The STRUCT Table for PROJECTS

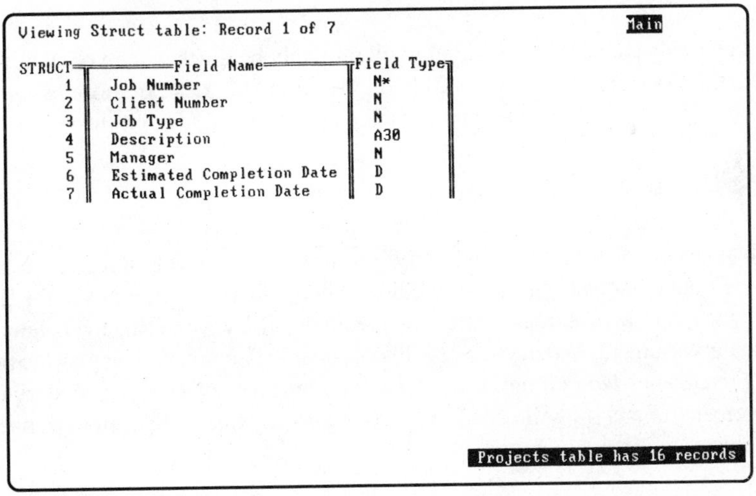

```
Viewing Struct table: Record 1 of 7                        Main

STRUCT          Field Name          Field Type
     1    Job Number                    N*
     2    Client Number                 N
     3    Job Type                      N
     4    Description                   A30
     5    Manager                       N
     6    Estimated Completion Date     D
     7    Actual Completion Date        D




                                        Projects table has 16 records
```

When you designate a key field for a table, Paradox will allow you to make only unique entries into that field. In addition, when you designate a key field, the records in the table will always be sorted according to the key field. For example, in the PROJECTS table, Job Number is a key field. When you look at the PROJECTS table, it will always be sorted on the Job Number field.

The one disadvantage of creating key fields is that they significantly reduce the capacity of each record in the table. A record in a non-keyed table has a capacity of 4,000 bytes. A record in a keyed table, on the other hand, has a capacity of only 1,350 bytes.

You can have as many key fields as you want in a Paradox table, provided that all of the key fields are adjacent and that the first key field is the first field in the table. You designate the second and subsequent key fields just as you do the first: by typing an asterisk in the Field Type column of the STRUCT table for that table as you create it. If you designate more than one key field, each key field can contain duplicate entries, just as long as no two records have the same entries in all of the key fields.

Key Fields and Queries

Another important benefit of key fields is that they speed up your queries. When you designate a key field, Paradox creates a *primary index* for that table on the key field. When you query the table and use a selection condition in the key field, Paradox will use the index to locate the matching records. If the table contains a large number of records, the query will be processed much more quickly than it would be without the key field.

The QuerySpeedup Command

Although key fields are very helpful, there will probably be times when you won't be able to make a field a key field but would still like to speed up queries. In those cases, use the [Menu] Tools QuerySpeedup command to create a secondary index on the selected field.

QuerySpeedup Basics

To take advantage of the [Menu] Tools QuerySpeedup command, you first create a query on the table you want to index. This query should include selection conditions in the fields on which you want to index the table. After you create the query, you issue the [Menu] Tools QuerySpeedup command. When you issue this command, Paradox will display the message *Processing query speedup* as it builds the secondary indexes. Once the secondary indexes have been created, Paradox will use them to speed up any query that refers to one of the indexed fields.

An Example

Suppose you frequently create queries that refer to the Salary field in EMPLYEE. To speed up these queries, you want to create a secondary index on the Salary field.

To begin, use the **[Menu]** Ask command to create a new query form for the EMPLYEE table. When the form appears, press **[Check Mark]** to select every field, then move to the Salary field and enter the selection condition **30000**. Figure 7-85 shows the completed query.

Figure 7-85 A Query Ready for QuerySpeedup

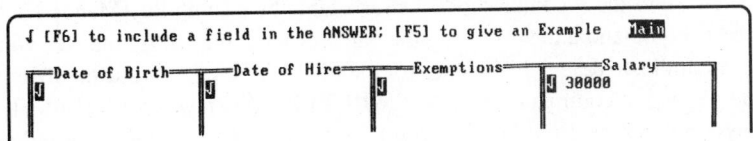

Now, issue the **[Menu]** Tools QuerySpeedup command. When you issue the command, Paradox will display the message *Processing query speedup* and will build a secondary index on the Salary field for the EMPLYEE table. The next time you issue a command that refers to this field, Paradox will use the index to speed up the operation. Once you have used the QuerySpeedup command, the indexes will remain until you delete them.

Defining the Query

Although we used the selection condition *30000* in the Salary field of the example query, we could have used any numeric condition in that field. As long as the condition you use has the correct type (dates in date fields, numbers in number fields, and so on), the actual condition you enter in the query form to create a secondary index doesn't matter to Paradox. All Paradox looks for is a selection condition. When it finds a condition—any condition—in the form, it creates an index on the field that contains the condition. If the condition you use has the wrong type, Paradox will display the message *Expression in this field has the wrong type* when you issue the [Menu] Tools QuerySpeedup command.

You must select (check-mark) at least one field in the query form you use to create indexes. If no fields in the query are selected, Paradox will display the message *Query has no checked fields* when you issue the [Menu] Tools QuerySpeedup command.

The Index Files

When you issue the **[Menu]** Tools QuerySpeedup command, Paradox creates a pair of files on disk for every field in the active query that contains a selection condition. These files have the same root name as the table to which they relate and have extensions like .X01 and .Y01, .X02 and .Y02, and .X0C and .Y0C. The amount of space consumed by these files depends on the size of the table you are indexing and the length of the indexed field.

QuerySpeedup and [Zoom]

The secondary indexes created by the QuerySpeedup command are utilized when you use the [Zoom] key ([Ctrl]-[Z]). This means the [Zoom] key operation can be enhanced (speeded up) by first creating an index on the field you are going to be searching. You create an index to be used by the [Zoom] key with the QuerySpeedup command procedure described above. If the field is a key field, then there is no need to use the QuerySpeedup command.

Deleting Indexes

You can delete all of the secondary indexes for a table by issuing the [Menu] Tools Delete QuerySpeedup command and specifying the name of the table whose indexes you want to delete. For example, to delete the indexes for the EMPLYEE table, issue the **[Menu] Tools Delete QuerySpeedup** command and type **EMPLYEE**. When you press **[Enter]**, Paradox will display the message *Deleting speedup files for EMPLYEE table* as it deletes every secondary index for EMPLYEE from the active directory.

The [Menu] Tools Delete QuerySpeedup command has no effect on key field indexes. If a table has a key field, the key field indexes will remain intact after you issue the Delete QuerySpeedup command.

You cannot delete individual indexes from within Paradox. If you want to delete one set of secondary index files, you can do so using the DOS Erase command. However, it is difficult to identify which index files relate to which field. Our suggestion is that you use the Delete QuerySpeedup command to delete all of the indexes, then recreate those you want to retain.

The "No speedup possible" Message

Sometimes when you issue the [Menu] Tools QuerySpeedup command, Paradox will display the message *No speedup possible* in the message area. You'll see this message if you try to create a secondary index on a key field or on a field for which a secondary index already exists, or if you issue the [Menu] Tools QuerySpeedup command when the active query does not contain any selection conditions.

This message also appears when you create a selection condition that contains a range operator (>, <, <=, or >=) and then use the [Menu] Tools QuerySpeedup command. No indexes will be created in the field. However, if you change the selection condition in that field into an exact-match condition, Paradox will create indexes.

Batch Mode Versus Incrementally Maintained Indexes

Paradox maintains secondary indexes in one of two ways: batch mode or incrementally. In batch mode, when the table containing an index field is updated in any way, Paradox does not immediately update the index. Instead, it makes a note to itself that the index is no longer accurate. Later, when the indexed field is about to be used, Paradox will rebuild the index from scratch before proceeding with the operation. For non-keyed tables, batch mode is the only way to maintain indexes.

When indexes are maintained incrementally, Paradox will update the index as soon as a change is made to an indexed field. Each time Paradox updates the index, it modifies only the portion of the index affected by your change.

To set up incrementally maintained indexes on keyed tables, Paradox's MaintainIndexes setting must be set to Yes. This option is set through the CCP, which we introduced in Chapter 1. When you first load Paradox on your system, the MaintainIndexes setting is automatically set to No. We believe, however, that Yes is the optimal setting since the time required to update maintained indexes while changes are made to indexed fields is minimal, and the indexes will always be up to date and ready when you need them. In batch mode, however, you may have to wait for Paradox to regenerate an index before a query can be performed.

When to Use QuerySpeedup

Secondary indexes are most useful when you need to perform a specific query that refers to non-keyed fields over and over. In those situations, the time required to create and maintain the secondary indexes is more than offset by the increased speed of your queries. On the other hand, it is probably not worthwhile to create secondary indexes for ad hoc queries or for queries you perform only once in a while.

In addition, you should keep in mind that indexes are not free. For one thing, index files consume disk space. Moreover, Paradox automatically updates every index file for a table each time you execute a command that affects a maintained indexed field on that table. To avoid wasting time and valuable disk space, you should not create unnecessary indexes on your tables.

Finally, indexes are not much help with small tables. In fact, in some cases, indexes can actually slow down queries and other commands in very small tables. If the time required to update the index, plus the time required to process the query, equals or exceeds the time required to process the query without an index, you're better off not having an index.

The pros and cons of secondary indexes are difficult to assess. The best advice we can give is that you should experiment with them in your tables. If you find that your queries work better with secondary indexes, use them; if not, get rid of them.

Key Fields Versus QuerySpeedup

One of the primary advantages of the QuerySpeedup command over key fields is that QuerySpeedup does not require that the field in which you are indexing contain only unique entries. This means you can use QuerySpeedup to create indexes on fields you refer to a great deal in queries but which are likely to contain duplicate entries. The Salary field in the EMPLYEE table is such a field. On the other hand, creating an index on a field that contains many duplicate entries will not do much to speed up queries that refer to that field.

In addition, QuerySpeedup does not require that the field in which you index be the first field in the table. This makes QuerySpeedup more flexible than key fields.

Key fields, on the other hand, are great when you have a field that logically should be the first field in a table and that will always contain unique entries. The Emp Number field in EMPLYEE and the Job Number field in PROJECTS are examples of this type of field. Remember that when you make these fields key fields, you not only speed up your queries, you also guarantee the order of the records in your table and avoid the problem of duplicate entries.

Conclusion

In this chapter, you have learned how to build and use simple queries. You have seen how to create query forms, how to select fields, and how to define selection conditions. You've also seen how to use several of Paradox's special query operators: like, find, delete, and changeto. We also showed you how to save queries in scripts and speed up queries by adding indexes to tables.

In the next chapter, we'll introduce the one remaining query topic: examples. In that chapter, you'll learn what examples are, how they are created, and how they can be used.

Chapter 8

Query by Example

In the previous chapter, you learned how to create queries in Paradox. There is still an important concept you must learn, however, before you will fully understand queries: examples. Examples are special tools that allow you to relate the entries in one field of a table to the entries in other fields of the same table, or to fields in other tables. You can use examples to link one table to another, to perform calculations, and to make selections. The power of these tools is unlimited. In fact, since examples are such a central feature to queries, database scholars refer to the Paradox query technique as "query by example."

A Simple Example

Figure 8-1 shows a query form that contains two examples. The examples are the highlighted *E*'s in the Estimated Completion Date and the Actual Completion Date fields. This query tells Paradox to select every record with an Actual Completion Date that is greater than the Estimated Completion Date for the same record. In other words, this query tells Paradox to select every project that was completed behind schedule.

Figure 8-1 Query by Example

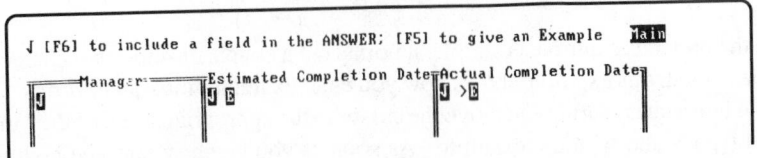

```
J [F6] to include a field in the ANSWER; [F5] to give an Example   Main
  ┌──────Manager──────┬Estimated Completion Date┬Actual Completion Date┐
  │J                  │J E                      │J >E                  │
```

To create this query, first use the [Menu] Ask command to create a new query form for PROJECTS, then use the [Check Mark] key to select every field in the form. To enter the example *E* in the Estimated Completion Date field, move to that field, press [Example] ([F5]), and type the letter E. To enter the second example, move the cursor to the Actual Completion Date field, type >, press [Example] ([F5]), and type E.

When you process this query, Paradox will create the ANSWER table shown in Figure 8-2. As you can see, this query results in only the three records from PROJECTS that have an Actual Completion Date entry greater than the Estimated Completion Date entry.

Figure 8-2 The ANSWER Table

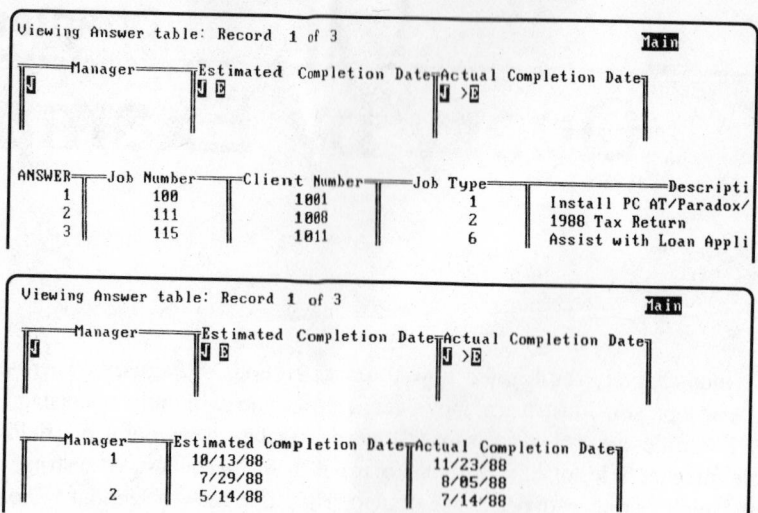

Let's consider how this query works. The example *E* in this query is a symbol, or a placeholder, for the entries in the Estimated Completion Date field of each record. This example allows you to relate the contents of the Estimated Completion Date field to the contents of other fields—in this case, to the entries in the Actual Completion Date field.

The selection condition *>E* tells Paradox to make the selection by comparing the entries in the Actual Completion Date field to the value of the example *E*. As a result of this condition, the query will select any record that has an Actual Completion Date entry that is greater than the Estimated Completion Date entry for the same record.

Example Basics

Although the previous example is simple, it points out a couple of important characteristics of examples. First, this example shows how you enter examples into query forms. To enter an example into a query form, you move the cursor to the appropriate field of the form, press [Example] ([F5]), and type the example. As soon as you begin typing, the highlight will appear around the characters you type.

Second, as in this case, examples always come in groups of at least two. You will never use just one example in a query. If you think about it for a moment, you'll realize that this makes sense. Since examples are tools that allow you to relate one field to another, there would be no point in using one example without using another.

Editing Examples

You can erase and edit examples in the same way that you erase other entries in query forms. To erase an example, move the cursor to the field that contains the example and press [Ctrl]-[Backspace]. If you want to replace the example with another example, you must press the [Example] key after you erase the old example and before you begin typing the new example. If you don't press [Example], the characters you type will be entered as a selection condition.

To erase part of an example, just move the cursor to the field that contains the example and press [Backspace]. Each time you press [Backspace], Paradox will erase one character from the example. If you want to replace the characters you erase, simply type the characters. Unless you erase every character in the old example, Paradox will include the characters you type in the example. If you use [Backspace] to erase the entire example and then want to enter another example, you must press the [Example] key before you begin typing.

You can also edit examples (although you will rarely do so). You can use the [Backspace] key to erase the characters you want to change and then replace those characters by typing the new characters. You can also use the [Field View] key ([Alt]-[F5]) to enter the field view and edit examples.

Examples Are Not Conditions

It is important that you do not confuse examples with selection conditions. When you enter the example *E* into the Estimated Completion Date field, you are not telling Paradox to select those records that have the entry *E* in the Estimated Completion Date field—it wouldn't find any, would it? Instead, you are telling Paradox to use the letter *E* as an example for the entries in the Estimated Completion Date field.

Of course, you can use examples in selection conditions. The entry *>E* is an example of a selection condition that contains an example. Even in this case, however, the role of the example is symbolic, not literal. This selection condition does not ask Paradox to select those records with an Actual Completion Date entry that is greater than the letter *E*. Instead, it asks Paradox to select those entries with an Actual Completion Date entry that is greater than the value represented by *E*, the Estimated Completion Date entry for the same record.

When it sees the condition *>E* in the Actual Completion Date field, Paradox hunts for the example *E* elsewhere in the query. It must find it; otherwise, Paradox will not be able to perform the query. If you had not typed the example *E* into the Estimated Completion Date field, Paradox would have displayed the message *Example element E has no defining occurrence* when you pressed [Do-It!]. Paradox would have understood that you wanted the Actual Completion Date entry to be greater than something—but greater than what?

Remember, examples are not literal the way conditions are. Examples are representations, or placeholders, for the contents of a given field.

Examples Can Be Any Character

It is important to understand that the actual example you use for any field is completely up to you. All that is necessary is that you use the same example in each field in the group of fields you want to relate. Although examples can contain only numbers and letters, you can use letters in number fields, numbers in alphanumeric fields, single digits, groups of digits, single letters, groups of letters, real words, or nonsense words, as long as you use the same example in all of the fields you want to relate.

For instance, you could have just as easily used the number *123* in the previous example, creating a query like the one in Figure 8-3. To define this query, just create a new, empty query for PROJECTS, select every field, move to the Estimated Completion Date field, press [**Example**], and type **123**. To enter the second example, move the cursor to the Actual Completion Date field, type >, press [**Example**], and type **123**. To Paradox, this query and the one in Figure 8-1 are identical.

Figure 8-3 Another Query by Example

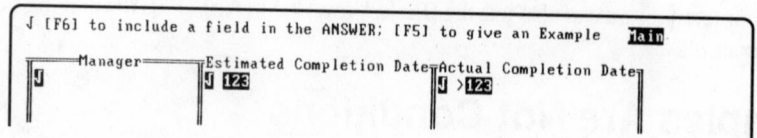

As long as you use the same example in each field you want to relate, Paradox doesn't care what type of entry you use as the example. If you use different examples in fields you want to relate, however, Paradox will be unable to process the query. (The one exception to this rule is that Paradox does not care if examples agree in case.) For example, suppose you created the query form shown in Figure 8-4. As you can see, we've entered the example *123* in the Estimated Completion Date field of this query, and the example *E* in the Actual Completion Date field. When you process this query, Paradox will display the error message *Example element E has no defining occurrence*.

Figure 8-4 An Incorrect Query by Example

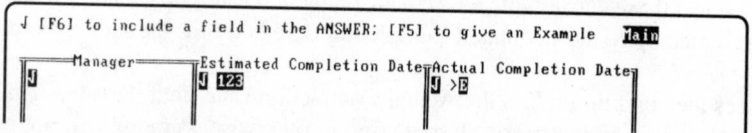

Using Examples in Single-table Queries

In the previous paragraphs, we used an example in a single-table query. Before we go on to show how examples can be used to relate different tables, let's consider several more single-table queries that use examples.

Using Examples in a Two-line Query

Suppose you want to select all records from the EMPLYEE table that have a Salary entry greater than or equal to 50 percent of the salary for David Jones. Figure 8-5 shows a query that will do the trick. To define this query, create a new query form for EMPLYEE. Next, enter the condition **Jones** in the first row of the Last Name field and the condition **David** in the first row of the First Name field. Then, move to the Salary field, press [**Example**], and enter the example **123**. Next, move the cursor to the second row of the form and select every field. Then, move to the Salary field and type

>[**Example**]123*.5

Notice that Paradox stops highlighting characters as soon as you type the asterisk. Since Paradox allows you to use only letters and numbers in examples, as soon as you type a character other than a letter or a number, Paradox assumes you are finished with the example. Remember that the characters > and *.5 are not a part of the example. The example is just the highlighted characters *123*.

Figure 8-5 Two-line Query

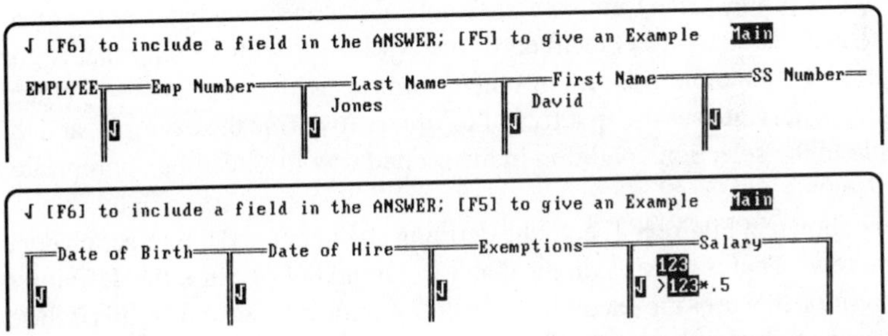

This condition says: *Select all records that have a Salary entry that is greater than 50 percent of the example salary.* When you process this query, Paradox will create the ANSWER table shown in Figure 8-6 on the following page. As you can see, this table includes every record with a Salary entry that is greater than 50 percent of David Jones' salary.

How It Works

The form of this query may be a bit confusing to you. In the last chapter, you learned that when you enter selection conditions on two rows of a query form, those conditions are joined with a logical OR. In the example query, however, the two rows are not connected in this way. In this query, the first row of the query defines the example. This line says: *Use 123 as the example for the Salary field for the record that has the entries* David *in the First Name field and* Jones *in the Last Name field.*

Figure 8-6 The ANSWER Table

```
Viewing Answer table: Record 1 of 6                              Main
┌─Date of Birth──┬─Date of Hire──┬──Exemptions──┬──Salary─┐
│               │              │             │   123    │
│ 9             │ 9            │ 9           │ 9 >123*.5│

ANSWER─┬─Emp Number──┬─Last name──┬─First Name─┬─SS Number──┬──Addre
  1    │   1         │ Jones      │ David      │414-76-3421 │4000 St. Ja
  2    │   2         │ Cameron    │ Herb       │321-65-8765 │2331 Elm St
  3    │   4         │ Jones      │ Stewart    │401-32-8721 │4389 Oakbri
  4    │   8         │ Williams   │ Brenda     │401-55-1567 │100 Owl Cre
  5    │   15        │ Masters    │ Ron        │317-65-4529 │423 W. 72nd
  6    │   16        │ Robertson  │ Kevin      │415-24-6718 │431 Bardsto
```

```
Viewing Answer table: Record 1 of 6                              Main
┌─Date of Birth──┬─Date of Hire──┬──Exemptions──┬──Salary─┐
│               │              │             │   123    │
│ 9             │ 9            │ 9           │ 9 >123*.5│

┬Date of Birth─┬Date of Hire─┬─Exemptions──┬──Salary─┐
 10/06/42      │ 1/14/87     │     3       │ 70,000.00
 11/24/29      │ 1/14/87     │     4       │ 50,000.00
 3/21/50       │ 2/13/87     │     1       │ 47,000.00
 1/12/20       │ 8/16/87     │     6       │ 40,000.00
 12/30/44      │ 2/13/88     │     0       │ 38,000.00
 3/16/25       │ 2/27/88     │     1       │ 37,000.00
```

The second row of the query form contains a selection condition that uses the example *123*. This row tells Paradox to select the records in EMPLYEE with a salary that is greater than 50 percent of the example salary—in other words, David Jones' salary. When Paradox processes this query, it uses the first row of the query to define the example, and then it uses the example in the selection condition in the second row to select the appropriate records.

In the query shown in Figure 8-1, both the defining statement and the selection condition are in the same row. That is possible in the query in Figure 8-1 because the defining statement and the condition that uses the example are in different fields. As long as this is the case, both expressions can be in the same row. If, as in the query shown in Figure 8-5, both expressions must be entered in the same field, the defining statement and the condition that uses the example must be in different rows.

Notice that we did not select any fields in the first row of this query form. If we had selected fields in that row, Paradox would have included any record that matched the conditions specified on that row in the ANSWER table. Since we don't want to use the first row to select records, but only to define the example, we didn't select any fields in that row.

The "Query may take a long time ..." Message

Did you notice the message *Query may take a long time to process,* which appeared at the bottom-right corner of the screen when you processed the query? This message is Paradox's way of telling you that the query you have defined is particularly complex and may require a long time to complete. Sometimes, as in this case, the message really doesn't mean much. In other cases, however, this message may signal that Paradox will require several minutes—or perhaps longer—to process the query.

This message can be a big help. Were it not for this message, you would have no way to know how long a query might take to process. You could end up sitting in front of your computer for several minutes waiting for the query to finish. Thanks to the message, however, you can do something else while the query is running, and come back in a few minutes to check on its progress.

A Fine Point

In the example, there was only one record in EMPLYEE that met the conditions stated in the query: *First Name equals David, Last Name equals Jones.* But suppose there had been two or more records that satisfied the condition. For example, suppose you had not entered the name *David* in the First Name field of the query form. As you recall, there are several records in EMPLYEE that satisfy the condition: *Last Name equals Jones.*

When you press [Do-It!], Paradox will create the ANSWER table shown in Figure 8-7 on the next page. If you study this table for a moment, you may notice that it contains every record from EMPLYEE that has a Salary entry greater than 50 percent of the Salary entries of any of the Jones' records. In other words, since the selection condition in the first row of the query form selected several records, the second row of the query used the Salary entry of each of those records to make the selection.

Another Two-line Query Using Examples

Suppose you want to find all of the records for people who are younger than David Jones. To make this selection, first create a new, empty query form for the EMPLYEE table and select every field in that form. Next, move to the Emp Number field and enter the selection condition **1**, David Jones' employee number. Then, move to the Date of Birth field, press **[Example]**, and type **DOB**. Now, move to the second row of the Date of Birth field and type >, press **[Example]**, and type **DOB**. Finally, move to the space under the form name in the second row and press **[Check Mark]** to select every field in this row. Figure 8-8 on the following page shows the completed query. In this query, the first row defines the condition *DOB*. Because you have entered the number 1 in the Emp Number field of this row, *DOB* is used to represent the Date of Birth for David Jones, the employee with employee number 1. The second row of the query uses the example *DOB* to select records. If the entry in the Date of Birth field for a given record is greater than the value of the example *DOB*, then that record will be included in ANSWER.

When you process this query, Paradox will create the ANSWER table shown in Figure 8-9 on page 301. As you can see, this table includes only those records with Date of Birth field entries that are greater than that of David Jones.

Figure 8-7 Two-line Query

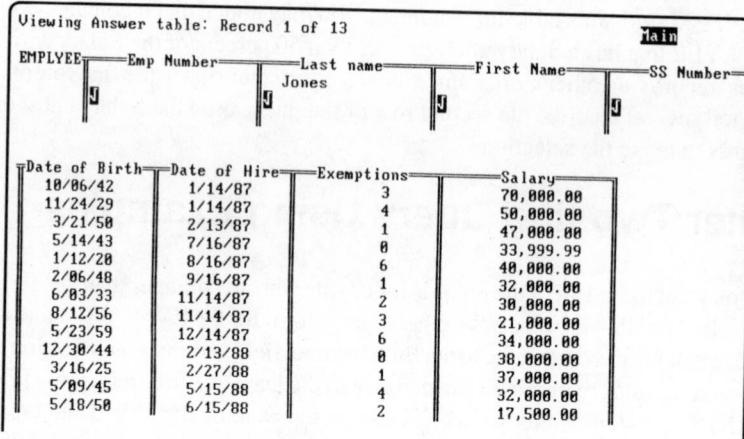

Figure 8-8 Another Two-line Query

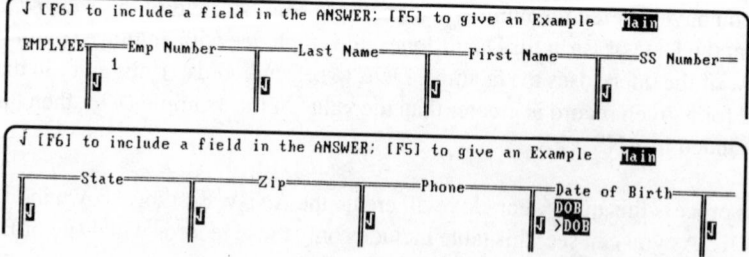

Figure 8-9 The ANSWER Table

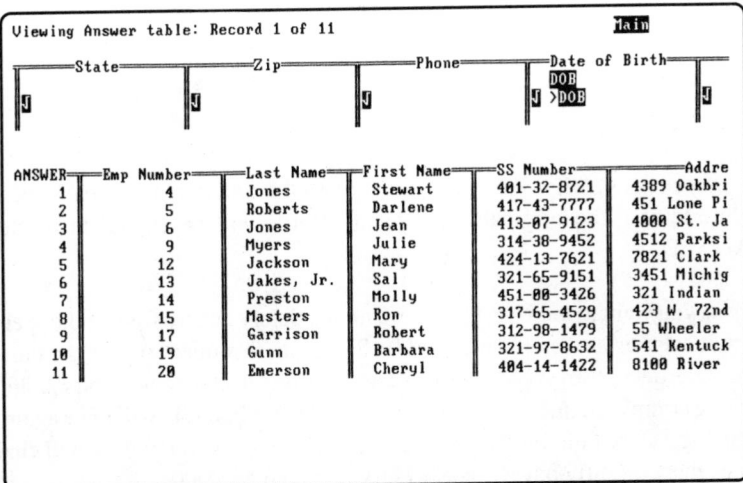

```
Viewing Answer table: Record 1 of 11                        Main
┌──────State──────┬──────Zip──────┬──────Phone──────┬──Date of Birth──┬──────┐
│                 │               │                 │     DOB          │      │
│ ▯               │ ▯             │ ▯               │ ▯  >DOB          │ ▯    │
└─────────────────┴───────────────┴─────────────────┴─────────────────┴──────┘

ANSWER─┬─Emp Number─┬─Last Name─┬─First Name─┬─SS Number──┬──────Addre
   1   │    4       │ Jones     │ Stewart    │ 401-32-8721│ 4389 Oakbri
   2   │    5       │ Roberts   │ Darlene    │ 417-43-7777│ 451 Lone Pi
   3   │    6       │ Jones     │ Jean       │ 413-07-9123│ 4000 St. Ja
   4   │    9       │ Myers     │ Julie      │ 314-38-9452│ 4512 Parksi
   5   │   12       │ Jackson   │ Mary       │ 424-13-7621│ 7821 Clark
   6   │   13       │ Jakes, Jr.│ Sal        │ 321-65-9151│ 3451 Michig
   7   │   14       │ Preston   │ Molly      │ 451-00-3426│ 321 Indian
   8   │   15       │ Masters   │ Ron        │ 317-65-4529│ 423 W. 72nd
   9   │   17       │ Garrison  │ Robert     │ 312-98-1479│ 55 Wheeler
  10   │   19       │ Gunn      │ Barbara    │ 321-97-8632│ 541 Kentuck
  11   │   20       │ Emerson   │ Cheryl     │ 404-14-1422│ 8100 River
```

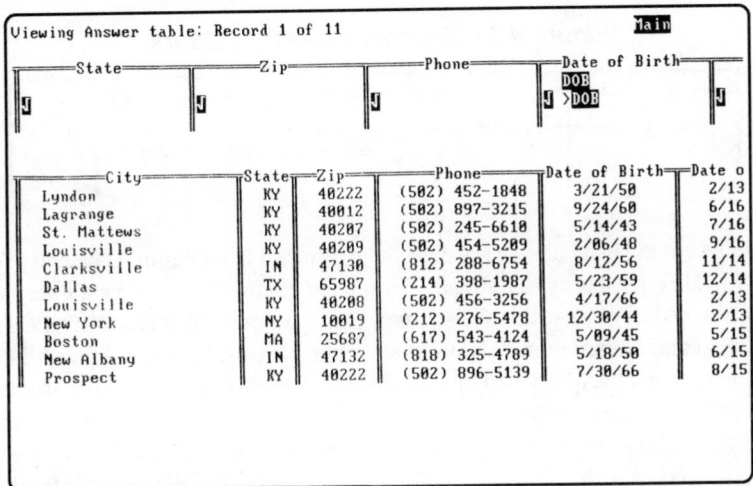

```
Viewing Answer table: Record 1 of 11                        Main
┌──────State──────┬──────Zip──────┬──────Phone──────┬──Date of Birth──┬──────┐
│                 │               │                 │     DOB          │      │
│ ▯               │ ▯             │ ▯               │ ▯  >DOB          │ ▯    │
└─────────────────┴───────────────┴─────────────────┴─────────────────┴──────┘

──────City──────┬─State─┬─Zip───┬─────Phone─────┬─Date of Birth─┬─Date o
 Lyndon         │  KY   │ 40222 │ (502) 452-1848│    3/21/50     │  2/13
 Lagrange       │  KY   │ 40012 │ (502) 897-3215│    9/24/60     │  6/16
 St. Mattews    │  KY   │ 40207 │ (502) 245-6618│    5/14/43     │  7/16
 Louisville     │  KY   │ 40209 │ (502) 454-5209│    2/06/48     │  9/16
 Clarksville    │  IN   │ 47130 │ (812) 288-6754│    8/12/56     │ 11/14
 Dallas         │  TX   │ 65987 │ (214) 398-1987│    5/23/59     │ 12/14
 Louisville     │  KY   │ 40208 │ (502) 456-3256│    4/17/66     │  2/13
 New York       │  NY   │ 10019 │ (212) 276-5478│   12/30/44     │  2/13
 Boston         │  MA   │ 25687 │ (617) 543-4124│    5/09/45     │  5/15
 New Albany     │  IN   │ 47132 │ (818) 325-4789│    5/18/50     │  6/15
 Prospect       │  KY   │ 40222 │ (502) 896-5139│    7/30/66     │  8/15
```

Using Examples in Changeto Queries

You can also use examples in changeto queries. When used in this way, examples allow you to make changes to a field based on the entries in that field or in other fields of the same record. For example, suppose you want to increase every Salary entry in EMPLYEE by 10 percent. To create a query that will make this change, first use the [Menu] Ask command to create a new query form for EMPLYEE. Then, move to the Salary field and press [Example], type **123, changeto**, press [Example], and type **123*1.1.** Figure 8-10 shows the completed query. The first part of the entry in the Salary field sets up *123* as the example for the entries in the Salary field. The second part of the entry uses the example *123* to tell Paradox to increase each entry in the Salary field by 10 percent.

Figure 8-10 A Changeto Query with Examples

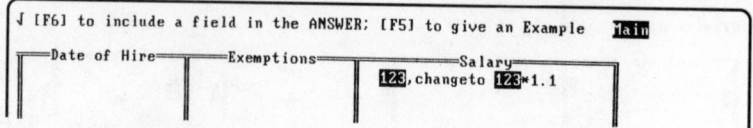

When you process this query, Paradox will increase the Salary entry in each record by 10 percent. In addition, the original, unchanged records will be copied to the temporary table CHANGED.

Now, suppose you want to increase by 10 percent the Salary entries for just those employees whose current salaries are less than $25,000. To create this query, move the cursor to the Salary field of the query form, type a comma, and type the selection condition **<25000**. Figure 8-11 shows the completed query. If you process the query, Paradox will once again increase the values in the Salary field by 10 percent. This time, however, Paradox will change only those records that currently have a Salary entry less than $25,000.

Figure 8-11 Another Changeto Query

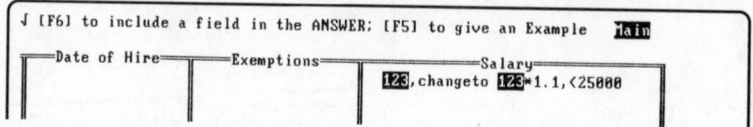

Suppose you want to push back by ten days the Estimated Completion Date entry for every project in PROJECTS that is not already complete. Figure 8-12 shows a query that will accomplish this task. To create this query, first make a new query form for PROJECTS. Next, move to the Actual Completion Date field and enter the selection condition **blank**. This condition ensures that the query will operate only on records that do not have an entry in the Actual Completion Date field (that is, those projects that are not yet complete). Now, move to the Estimated Completion Date field and press **[Example]**, type **E, changeto**, press **[Example]**, and type **E+10**. The first part of this entry sets up *E* as the example for the entries in the selected records of the Estimated Completion Date field. The second part of the entry uses the example *E* to instruct Paradox to increase the value of each Estimated Completion Date field by 10.

Figure 8-12 Another Changeto Query

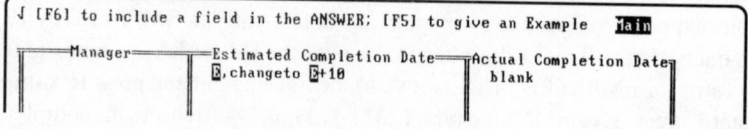

When you process this query, Paradox will add 10 to the Estimated Completion Date entry for every record with a blank in the Actual Completion Date field.

Using Examples in Other Types of Queries

Although examples are most useful in changeto queries, you can also use them with find queries and delete queries, and with the not and like operators. In general, you will use examples in this type of query in the same way you use them in other one-table queries: to make selections in one field based on entries in another field. So that you can see how useful examples are in these kinds of queries, however, we'll look at a few cases.

Using Examples with Not

Suppose you want to locate all of the entries in the EMPLYEE table that have a State entry that is different from the State entry for David Jones. Figure 8-13 shows a query that will make this selection. To define this query, first create a new, blank query form for the EMPLYEE table. Next, move to the Emp Number field and type **1**, the employee number for David Jones. Then, move to the State field, press [**Example**], and type **ST**.

Figure 8-13 A Query Using the Not Operator

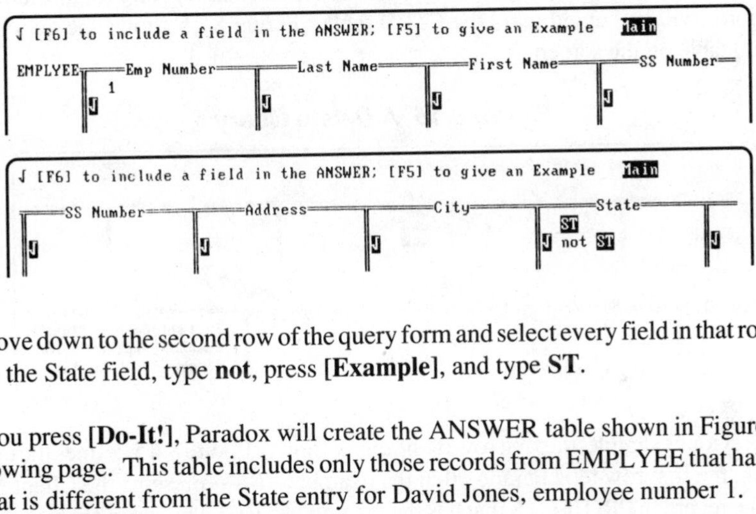

Now, move down to the second row of the query form and select every field in that row. Then, move to the State field, type **not**, press [**Example**], and type **ST**.

When you press [**Do-It!**], Paradox will create the ANSWER table shown in Figure 8-14 on the following page. This table includes only those records from EMPLYEE that have a State entry that is different from the State entry for David Jones, employee number 1.

As in the earlier examples, the first row of this query defines the example, and the second row of the query uses the example to select records. In this example, the first row tells Paradox that the example *ST* stands for the State entry for the record with the Emp Number entry 1.

A Delete Query Example

You can also use examples in delete queries. For example, suppose you want to delete from the PROJECTS table any projects that have the same Client Number entry as job number 103. To begin, create a new query form for the PROJECTS table. Next, move to the Job Number field and type **103**. Then, move to the Client Number field, press [**Example**], and type **ABC**.

Figure 8-14 The ANSWER Table

```
Viewing Answer table: Record 1 of 6                                    Main
 ┌─SS Number──┐ ┌──────Address─────┐ ┌─────City────┐ ┌──State─┐ ┌────────┐
 │■│          │■│                  │■│              │■│ ST     │■│
 │            │ │                  │ │              │ │■ not ST│ │
 └────────────┘ └──────────────────┘ └─────────────┘ └────────┘ └────────┘

 ┌─SS Number──┐ ┌──────Address─────┐ ┌─────City────┐ ┌State┐ ┌Zip─┐
 │ 345-75-1525│ │ 3215 Palm Ct.    │ │ Palo Alto   │ │ CA  │ │94375│
 │ 424-13-7621│ │ 7821 Clark Ave.  │ │ Clarksville │ │ IN  │ │47130│
 │ 321-65-9151│ │ 3451 Michigan Ave.│ │ Dallas     │ │ TX  │ │65987│
 │ 317-65-4529│ │ 423 W. 72nd St.  │ │ New York    │ │ NY  │ │10019│
 │ 312-98-1479│ │ 55 Wheeler St.   │ │ Boston      │ │ MA  │ │25687│
 │ 321-97-8632│ │ 541 Kentucky St. │ │ New Albany  │ │ IN  │ │47132│
 └────────────┘ └──────────────────┘ └─────────────┘ └─────┘ └─────┘
```

Next, move down to the second row of the query form and type the word **delete** in the space under the form name. Now, move to the Client Number field, press **[Example]**, and type **ABC**. Since this will be a delete query, you will not select any fields in any row of the form.

When you press **[Do-It!]** to process the query, Paradox will delete from PROJECTS any record whose Client Number entry is the same as the Client Number entry for job number 103. These records will be copied to a DELETED table. Figure 8-15 shows the query and the DELETED table on the screen.

Figure 8-15 A Delete Query

```
Viewing Deleted table: Record 1 of 3                                   Main
 ┌PROJECTS┐ ┌─Job Number─┐ ┌Client Number┐ ┌─Job Type─┐ ┌─Descri
 │        │ │ 103        │ │ ABC         │ │          │ │
 │ delete │ │            │ │ ABC         │ │          │ │
 └────────┘ └────────────┘ └─────────────┘ └──────────┘ └──────

 ┌DELETED┐ ┌Job Number─┐ ┌Client Number┐ ┌Job Type┐ ┌───────Description──┐
 │ 1     │ │ 103       │ │ 1003        │ │ 1      │ │ Install Compaq Plus/Sy│
 │ 2     │ │ 104       │ │ 1003        │ │ 2      │ │ Symphony Intro Course │
 │ 3     │ │ 105       │ │ 1003        │ │ 4      │ │ Recommend AR System   │
 └───────┘ └───────────┘ └─────────────┘ └────────┘ └───────────────────────┘
```

As in the previous example, the first row of the query form in Figure 8-15 defines the example. In this case, the first row tells Paradox that the example *ABC* represents the Client Number entry for the record in PROJECTS that has the job number 103. The second row of the query uses this example to delete records from the table.

Using Examples in Two-table Operations

In Chapter 2, we introduced the concept of common fields—fields that are common to two or more related tables, which contain the same type of data in all of the tables, and which can be used to relate the data stored in those tables. However, we stopped short of showing you how to use the common fields to relate these tables.

As you might have already guessed, examples are the tools you use to link two or more related tables that you want to query or join. In fact, this is probably the most common and most important use of examples. When used in this way, examples tell Paradox which fields to use to link tables. Let's look at several queries that use examples to link related tables.

Linking Two Tables

Suppose you want to create a new table that includes the Job Number and Job Type fields from PROJECTS and the Description field from a table called JOBS. The JOBS table contains the job number and description of each type of job our hypothetical company performs: system installation, application development, training, consulting, and so on. Figures 8-16 and 8-17 show the contents and structure of JOBS.

Figure 8-16 The JOBS Table

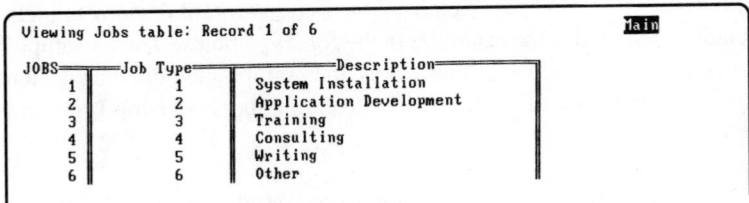

Figure 8-17 The Structure of JOBS

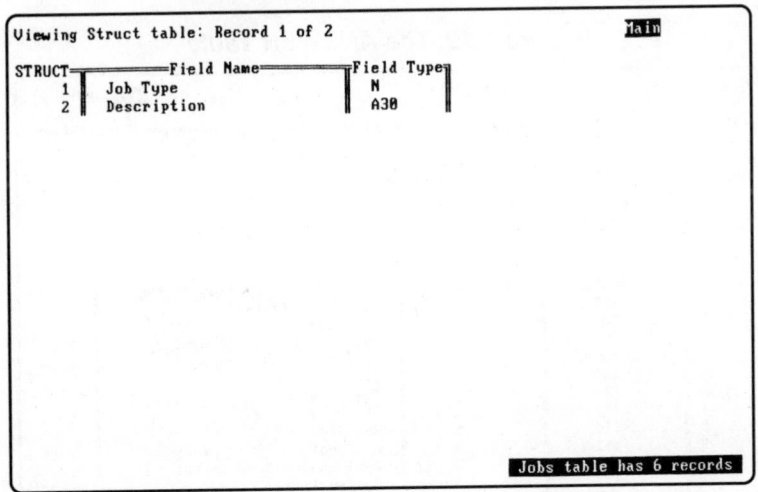

To create the new table, you'll need to define a query that uses both the PROJECTS table and the JOBS table. To begin, use the [Menu] Ask command to create a new query form for PROJECTS. Next, select the Job Number and Job Type fields in this query form. Now, with the cursor in the Job Type field, press [Example] and type 123.

Now, issue the **[Menu] A**sk command again and create a new query form for JOBS. When this query appears, move to the Description field and press **[Check Mark]**. Then, move to the Job Type field, press **[Example]**, and type **123**. Figure 8-18 shows the completed query.

Figure 8-18 A Two-table Query

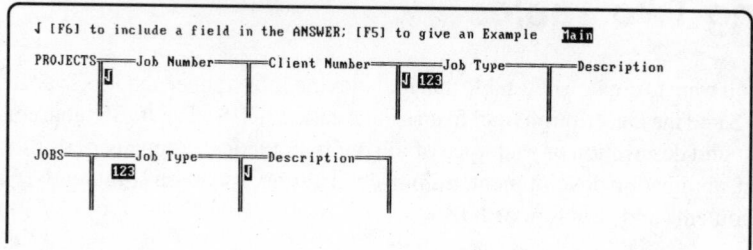

Notice that the three fields we've selected are the fields we want Paradox to include in the ANSWER table. Also notice the examples in the Job Type fields. These examples link the two tables in the Job Type field. In other words, the examples tell Paradox it should match the numbers in the Job Type field of PROJECTS to the numbers in the Job Type field of JOBS as it processes the query.

Now, press **[Do-It!]** to process the query. Figure 8-19 shows the result. As you can see, Paradox has created an ANSWER table that contains the Job Number and Job Type fields from PROJECTS and the Description field from JOBS.

Figure 8-19 The ANSWER Table

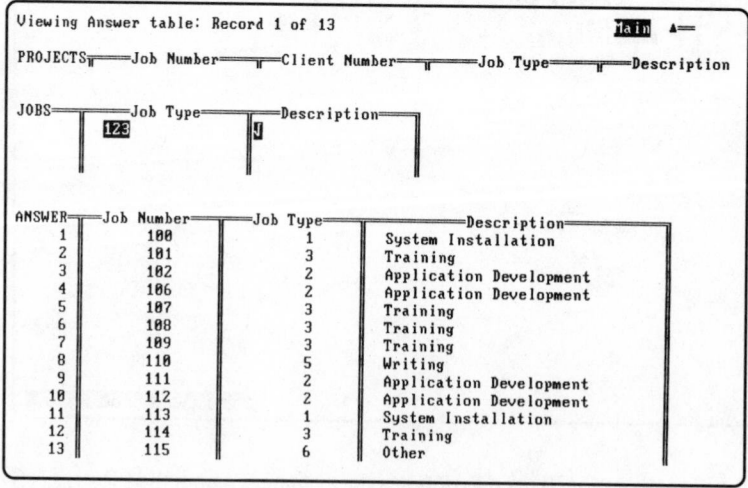

Notes

There is no absolute limit to the number of tables you can link through a query. The precise number you'll be able to relate depends on the configuration of your computer and the size of the tables you will be relating. Since most of your multitable queries will involve only two or three tables, you are unlikely to ever encounter any limit.

About Multiple Query Forms

As you have seen, a query that you use to relate two or more tables must contain one query form for each of those tables. Creating the second and subsequent query forms is like creating the first: You just issue the [Menu] Ask command and specify the name of the table for which you want to create a query form. The second and subsequent forms appear on the screen below the first form. To move from one form to another, just press [Up Image] or [Down Image].

Keep in mind that any query form that is visible is active. If there are three query forms on the screen, the conditions in all three forms will be considered by Paradox when you press **[Do-It!]**. There is no way to exclude a visible query form from being processed. If you have created a query form and do not need it any longer, you should remove it from the workspace by pressing [Clear Image] ([F8]).

Whenever there are two or more query forms in view, you must use examples to link them. Paradox must be told how the tables are related, and examples are the only way to do it. If there are two or more query forms in view when you press [Do-It!], and those forms are unrelated, Paradox will display the error message *Query appears to ask two unrelated questions.*

You might ask, "Why do I have to type in examples to link tables? Both tables, PROJECTS and JOBS, have a field named Job Type. Shouldn't Paradox be smart enough to realize that the tables should be linked on this field, even if I don't type in examples there?" Paradox doesn't make any assumptions based on field names because it's not always correct to do so. Notice that Job Type isn't the only field common to both PROJECTS and JOBS. Both tables also contain a field named Description. However, although these two fields have the same name, they do not contain the same information. If Paradox attempted to link the tables on the Description fields, it wouldn't find any matches. The designers of Paradox realized this, so they require us to use examples in multitable queries. Quite often, many of your tables will share common field names (such as Description, Name, Date, or Status) even though the fields have no relationship whatsoever among the various tables. Furthermore, the fields to be linked sometimes don't have the same name at all, as you will see in our next illustration.

The Order of ANSWER

Notice the order of the fields in the ANSWER table in Figure 8-19. Specifically, notice that the fields you selected in PROJECTS, the first query form in the query, appear in ANSWER before the field you selected in JOBS, the second query form in the query. When you create a query that operates on more than one table, the fields in the resulting ANSWER table will always be arranged in this way. All of the selected fields from the first query form in the query will appear first in ANSWER, followed by the fields from the second query form, then the third, and so on.

You'll want to keep this rule in mind when you create multitable queries. Although you can use the [Menu] Image command or the [Rotate] ([Ctrl]-[R]) key to rearrange the columns in ANSWER after you process the query, it is easier to arrange the query forms in the query so that the fields in ANSWER are in the desired order.

Normalizing Tables

It is important to understand that examples can be used to link only tables having some relationship to one another. In other words, if the PROJECTS table did not include a Job Type field, there would not be any way to link that table to the JOBS table. Only because we designed these tables to be related are we able to link them using examples.

The principle of designing tables with built-in relationships is called "normalization." We described this concept near the end of Chapter 2 in the section called "A Word about Tables," although we didn't use the term normalization there. JOBS and PROJECTS are examples of normalized tables. Rather than including the description of each job type in PROJECTS, we placed the various job descriptions in a separate table, JOBS. So that we could easily relate these two tables, we included a linking field, Job Type, in both tables. Since both tables include this field, they can be related easily using examples.

As you work with Paradox, you'll find more and more places where it makes sense to create normalized sets of tables instead of storing all the data about a particular item in one huge table. As you increase your use of this technique, you'll find yourself using examples in two-table queries more often. In the remainder of this section, we'll show other examples of normalized sets of tables, and we'll explain the use of examples in linking tables.

Another Two-table Query

Suppose you want to create a table that contains the Job Number and Description fields from the PROJECTS table and the Last Name and First Name fields from EMPLYEE. The Last Name and First Name portion of each record in this new table would be the last and first names of the project manager. This table would let you determine at a glance the manager of each project.

To begin, create a new, blank query for PROJECTS. When the query comes into view, use [Check Mark] to select the Job Number and Description fields. Then, move to the Manager field, press [Example], and type 123. Now, create a new query form for EMPLYEE. When the form appears on the screen, use the [Check Mark] key to select the Last Name and First Name fields. Then, move to the Emp Number field, press [Example], and type 123.

Figure 8-20 shows the completed query. Notice that the four fields we've selected are the four fields we want Paradox to include in the ANSWER table. Also notice the examples in the Manager and Emp Number fields. These examples link the two tables on these two fields. In other words, the examples tell Paradox that it should match the contents of the Manager field of PROJECTS to the contents of the Emp Number field of EMPLYEE as it processes the query.

Figure 8-20 Another Two-table Query

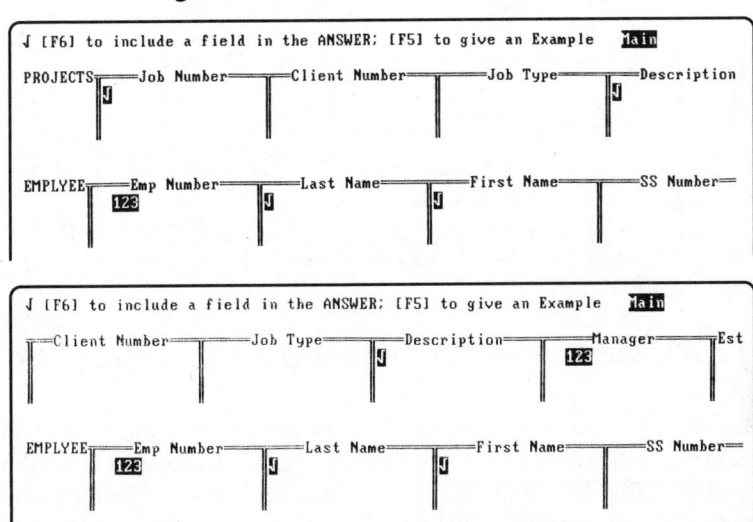

Now, press **[Do-It!]** to process the query. Figure 8-21 on the next page shows the result. Paradox has created a new ANSWER table that contains the Job Number and Description fields from PROJECTS and the First Name and Last Name fields from EMPLYEE.

Also notice that although the fields we used to relate EMPLYEE and PROJECTS have the same type and length, they do not have the same name. In some database programs, such as dBASE III and R:BASE System V, you can relate tables only on fields that have the same name. As we explained earlier, this restriction can be a real problem. In Paradox, the fields you use to relate tables should have the same type, but they do not need to have the same name.

Of course, although the fields you use to relate two tables do not need to have the same name, they should contain related data. In the example, it made sense to use the Manager and Emp Number fields to relate PROJECTS and EMPLYEE since both of these fields contain employee numbers. It would not make sense to try to relate these tables on any other fields, however, since there are no other fields in the two tables that contain related data.

Figure 8-21 The ANSWER Table

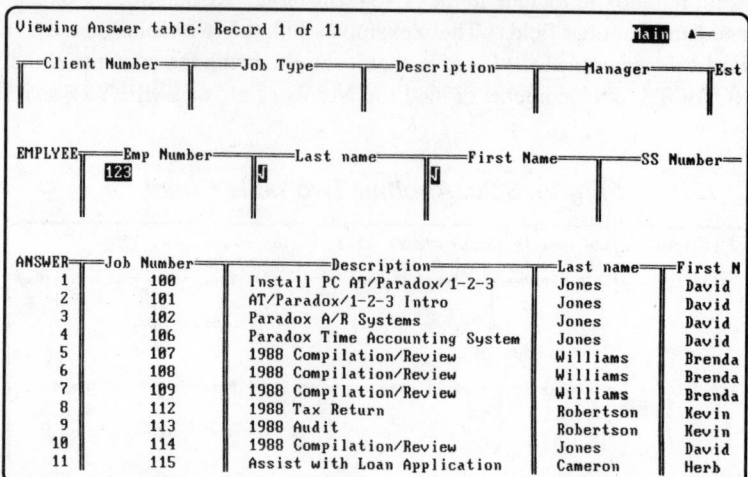

```
Viewing Answer table: Record 1 of 11                          Main  ▲══
 ┌─Client Number──────┬───Job Type───────┬────Description────────┬──Manager──────┬─Est
 │                    │                  │                       │               │
 │                    │                  │                       │               │
 │                    │                  │                       │               │

 EMPLYEE┬──Emp Number──────┬──Last name────────┬────First Name──────┬──SS Number══
        │  123             │  Y                │  Y                 │
        │                  │                   │                    │
        │                  │                   │                    │

 ANSWER┬──Job Number────────┬─────Description──────────┬──Last name──┬─First N
   1   │      100           │ Install PC AT/Paradox/1-2-3  │ Jones        │ David
   2   │      101           │ AT/Paradox/1-2-3 Intro       │ Jones        │ David
   3   │      102           │ Paradox A/R Systems          │ Jones        │ David
   4   │      106           │ Paradox Time Accounting System│ Jones       │ David
   5   │      107           │ 1988 Compilation/Review      │ Williams     │ Brenda
   6   │      108           │ 1988 Compilation/Review      │ Williams     │ Brenda
   7   │      109           │ 1988 Compilation/Review      │ Williams     │ Brenda
   8   │      112           │ 1988 Tax Return              │ Robertson    │ Kevin
   9   │      113           │ 1988 Audit                   │ Robertson    │ Kevin
  10   │      114           │ 1988 Compilation/Review      │ Jones        │ David
  11   │      115           │ Assist with Loan Application │ Cameron      │ Herb
```

Using Examples in Two-table Find Queries

Suppose you want to find the employee record for the manager of project 108. Figure 8-22 shows a query that will do the trick. To create this query, first create a new, blank query form for the EMPLYEE table. When the query form comes into view, type the word **find** into the space under the form name. Then, move to the Emp Number field, press **[Example]**, and type **123**.

Now, create a new, blank query form for the PROJECTS table. Next, move to the Job Number field and type **108**, the number of the job in which you are interested. Finally, move to the Manager field, press **[Example]**, and type **123**.

This query tells Paradox to find in EMPLYEE the record that has the same manager number as the record selected by the condition *108* in the Job Number field. The example *123* represents the manager number of the project that matches the condition you selected.

When you process this query, Paradox will bring the EMPLYEE table into view and move the cursor to the record for employee number 6. Figure 8-23 shows the screen at this point.

A More Complex Two-table Query

Let's look at a more complex two-table query. Suppose you want to see the following information about each job that was completed after its estimated completion date: the manager's employee number and name, the job number, client number, description, estimated completion date, and actual completion date. Figure 8-24 on page 312 shows a query that will make this selection.

Figure 8-22 A Two-table Find Query

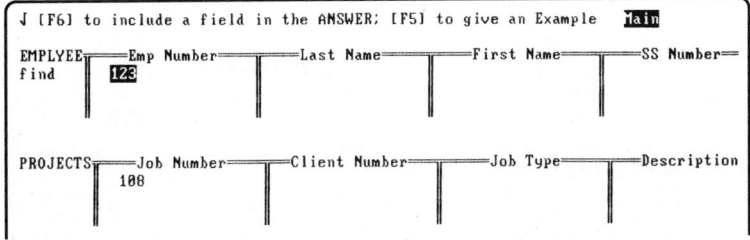

Figure 8-23 The Result —A Highlighted Record

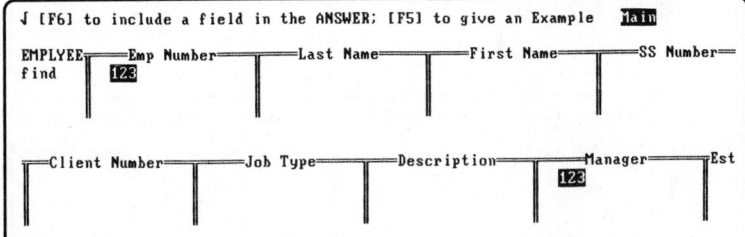

To create this query, first make new query forms for EMPLYEE and PROJECTS. Use the **[Check Mark]** key to select the Emp Number, Last Name, and First Name fields in EMPLYEE, and the Job Number, Client Number, Description, Estimated Completion Date, and Actual Completion Date fields in PROJECTS.

Once all of the fields are selected, move to the Estimated Completion Date field in the PROJ-ECTS query form, press **[Example]**, and type **E**. Then, move to the Actual Completion Date field, type >, press **[Example]**, and type **E**. These two examples work together to select only those records with an Actual Completion Date entry that is greater than the Estimated Completion Date entry. The entry in the Estimated Completion Date field defines the example, and the entry in the Actual Completion Date field uses the example in a selection condition.

Figure 8-24 A Two-table Query

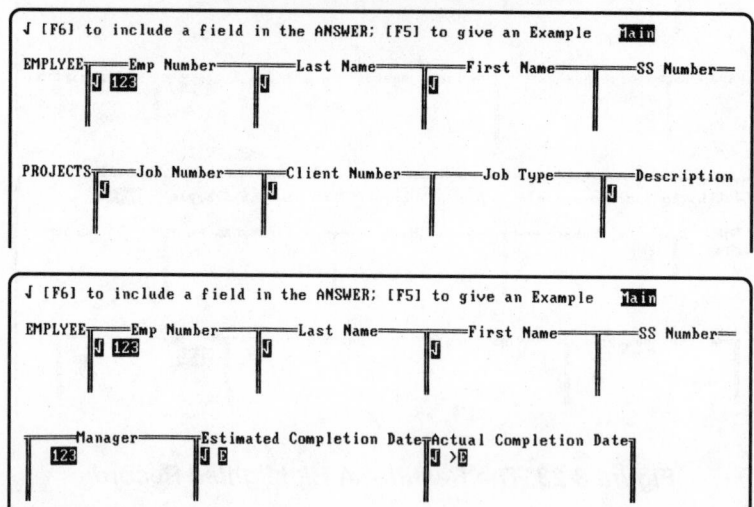

Next, move to the Manager field in PROJECTS, press **[Example]**, and type **123**. Then, move to the Emp Number field in EMPLYEE, press **[Example]**, and type **123** again. These two examples link EMPLYEE and PROJECTS on the Manager and Emp Number fields. The effect of these examples is to cause Paradox to select any record from EMPLYEE that has an Emp Number that matches the entry in the Manager field of a record selected from PROJECTS.

When you process this query, Paradox will create the ANSWER table shown in Figure 8-25. As you can see, this ANSWER table contains the selected fields from both EMPLYEE and PROJECTS, and contains only those records for which the Actual Completion Date entry is greater than the Estimated Completion Date entry.

Figure 8-25 The ANSWER Table

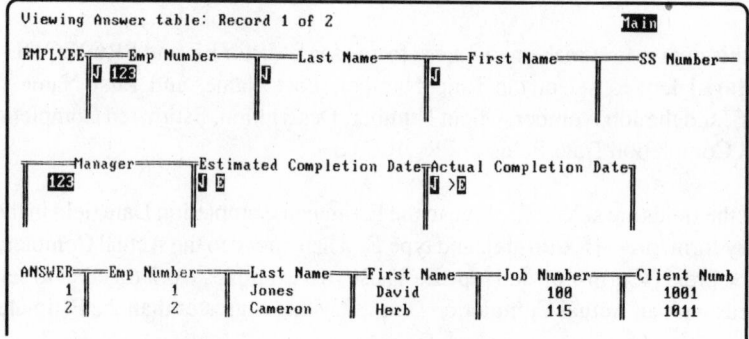

Inclusive Two-table Queries

Because queries that use examples to link two tables include only those records linked by the example in the ANSWER table, these queries can sometimes hide information in your Paradox tables. For example, if you compare the ANSWER table in Figure 8-21 to the ANSWER table in Figure 8-19, you'll see that the ANSWER table listing projects with the names of their managers (Figure 8-21) contains two fewer records than the ANSWER table listing the projects by job types (Figure 8-19). The two records missing from the ANSWER table in Figure 8-21 are the records with the Job Number entries 110 and 111. If you look at the PROJECTS table, shown in Figure 8-26 on the following page, you can see that these two records contain blank entries in the Manager field. Since the query in Figure 8-20 links the Manager field with the Emp Number field of EMPLYEE, the ANSWER table includes only those records that have matching entries in these fields. Since no record in EMPLYEE contains a blank entry in the Emp Number field, Paradox excludes the records with blank Manager entries from the ANSWER table.

When a link between two tables in a query causes the query to exclude nonmatching records from the ANSWER table, that link is called a noninclusive link. If you have a version of Paradox earlier than Release 3, then all queries that use examples to link records in two or more tables will create noninclusive links. However, if you own Paradox 3, you can create queries with inclusive links. The ANSWER tables produced by these queries can include nonmatching records from one or both of the tables in the query. A query that creates an inclusive link is called an "outer join" because it joins records linked by the examples with records from outside the set of linked records.

Defining Inclusive Links

Paradox 3 offers an inclusion operator (!), which you can use to include nonmatching records in the ANSWER table. To include data from every record of a table in the ANSWER table, simply type an inclusion operator after the example in the query form for that table.

For example, suppose you want to see a list of all the jobs in the PROJECTS table, along with the names of the managers for the records that have Manager field entries matching entries in the Emp Number field of EMPLYEE. With the query shown in Figure 8-20 on the screen, move the cursor to the Manager field in the query form for PROJECTS. Then, while the cursor is positioned just after the *123* example in that field, type !. When you press !, Paradox will automatically turn off reverse video and display the inclusion operator in regular video style. Figure 8-27 on page 315 shows the new query.

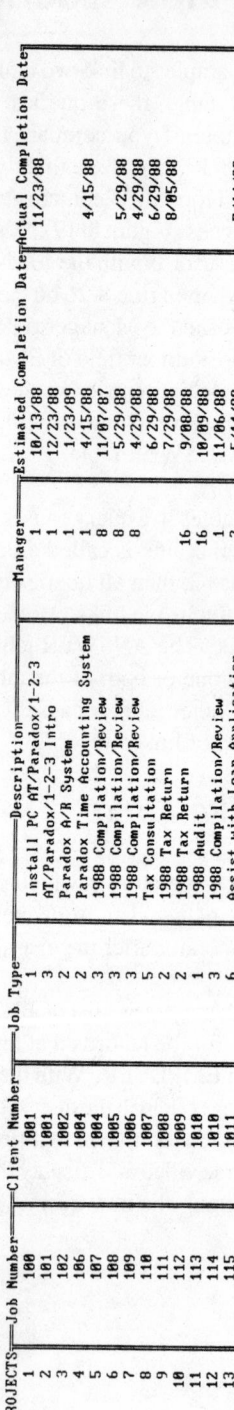

Figure 8-26 The PROJECTS Table

Viewing Projects table: Record 2 of 13

PROJECTS	Job Number	Client Number	Job Type	Description	Manager	Estimated Completion Date	Actual Completion Date
1	100	1001	1	Install PC AT/Paradox/1-2-3	1	10/13/88	11/23/88
2	101	1001	3	AT/Paradox/1-2-3 Intro	1	12/23/88	
3	102	1002	2	Paradox A/R System	1	1/23/89	
4	106	1004	2	Paradox Time Accounting System	1	4/15/88	4/15/88
5	107	1004	3	1988 Compilation/Review	8	11/07/87	
6	108	1005	3	1988 Compilation/Review	8	5/29/88	5/29/88
7	109	1006	3	1988 Compilation/Review	8	4/29/88	4/29/88
8	110	1007	5	Tax Consultation		6/29/88	6/29/88
9	111	1008	2	1988 Tax Return		7/29/88	8/05/88
10	112	1009	2	1988 Tax Return	16	9/08/88	
11	113	1010	1	1988 Audit	16	10/09/88	
12	114	1010	3	1988 Compilation/Review	1	11/06/88	
13	115	1011	6	Assist with Loan Application	2	5/14/88	7/14/88

Figure 8-27 A Query Using the Inclusion Operator

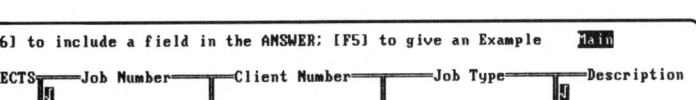

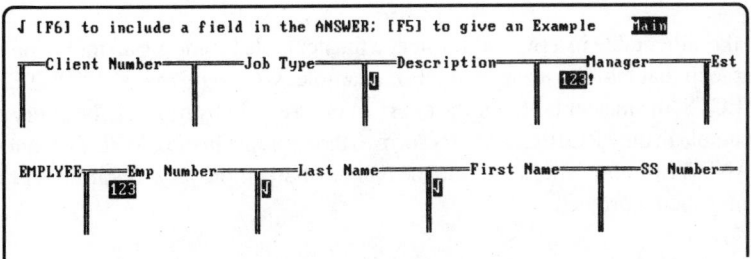

The inclusion operator in the Manager field tells Paradox to include data from every record in the PROJECTS table in the ANSWER table. Figure 8-28 shows the ANSWER table that Paradox will create if you process the query. As you can see, the ANSWER table includes information from every record in PROJECTS, including those records that have blank entries in the Manager field. Because the ANSWER table includes every record from the PROJECTS table, PROJECTS is considered a master table in the query. In regard to the query, EMPLYEE is considered a lookup table because the only records from EMPLYEE that appear in the ANSWER table are those that are referenced in the PROJECTS table.

Figure 8-28 The ANSWER Table

```
Viewing Answer table: Record 1 of 13                         Main  ▲══
╓══Client Number══╥══Job Type══╥══Description══╥══Manager══╥══Est
║                 ║            ║               ║           ║

EMPLYEE╥══Emp Number══╥══Last Name══╥══First Name══╥══SS Number══
       ║   123        ║   9         ║   9          ║

ANSWER╥══Job Number══╥════Description════╥══Last Name══╥══First N
   1  ║    100       ║ Install PC AT/Paradox/1-2-3 ║ Jones    ║ David
   2  ║    101       ║ AT/Paradox/1-2-3 Intro      ║ Jones    ║ David
   3  ║    102       ║ Paradox A/R System          ║ Jones    ║ David
   4  ║    106       ║ Paradox Time Accounting System ║ Jones ║ David
   5  ║    107       ║ 1988 Compilation/Review     ║ Williams ║ Brenda
   6  ║    108       ║ 1988 Compilation/Review     ║ Williams ║ Brenda
   7  ║    109       ║ 1988 Compilation/Review     ║ Williams ║ Brenda
   8  ║    110       ║ Tax Consultation            ║          ║
   9  ║    111       ║ 1988 Tax Return             ║          ║
  10  ║    112       ║ 1988 Tax Return             ║ Robertson ║ Kevin
  11  ║    113       ║ 1988 Audit                  ║ Robertson ║ Kevin
  12  ║    114       ║ 1988 Compilation/Review     ║ Jones    ║ David
  13  ║    115       ║ Assist with Loan Application ║ Cameron  ║ Herb
```

An ANSWER table created by an inclusive link can help you uncover information that would be lost in an ANSWER table produced by a noninclusive link. As we've already explained, the noninclusive link created by the query in Figure 8-20 did not show the PROJECTS records with the entries 110 and 111 in the Job Number field because these records contain blank entries in the Manager field. A noninclusive link would also exclude records with nonblank Manager entries that do not match one of the Emp Number entries in the EMPLYEE table. A nonmatching entry in the Manager field might occur if an employee had left the company after completing a project. However, the inclusive link shown in Figure 8-27 creates an ANSWER table that includes all the records from PROJECTS, not only those records that are linked to records in EMPLYEE.

You can make either table in a two-table query a master table by adding an inclusion operator to an example in that table's query form. For example, you could make EMPLYEE, rather than PROJECTS, the master table for the query in Figure 8-27 by moving the query operator from the example in the PROJECTS query form to the example in the EMPLYEE query form. Then, the ANSWER table would include the names of all employees, regardless of whether they have managed a project.

A query that creates an inclusive link between a master table and a detail table is called an "asymmetrical outer join" because it is inclusive on only one side of the link. However, you can also create a link that joins two master tables—that is, a link that is inclusive for both tables. This type of all-inclusive link is known as a "symmetrical outer join."

Creating a Symmetrical Outer Join

To create a symmetrical outer join, add inclusion operators to the examples in both query forms of the query. Figure 8-29 shows the PROJECTS/EMPLYEE query with inclusion operators in both the fields that contain examples. When you process this query, Paradox will produce an ANSWER table that includes data from all the records in PROJECTS and all the records in EMPLYEE. Figure 8-30 shows this ANSWER table.

As you can see, the ANSWER table includes a description of every project in the PROJECTS table and the name of every person in the EMPLYEE table, joining the information in the same records where appropriate. This type of query supplies you with several kinds of information. First, it shows you which employees have served as managers for which projects. You can see this information by looking at those records that contain entries in every field. Because an employee could manage several projects, the same entries could occur more than once in the Last Name and First Name fields of ANSWER. Second, the ANSWER table shows you which employees have not served as managers for any projects. You can see this information by looking at the records that have blank entries in the Job Number and Description fields. Third, ANSWER shows you which projects have not had managers or

have had managers who are not listed in the EMPLYEE table. You can see this information
by looking at those records that have blank entries in the Last Name and First Name fields.

Figure 8-29 A Query with Two Master Tables

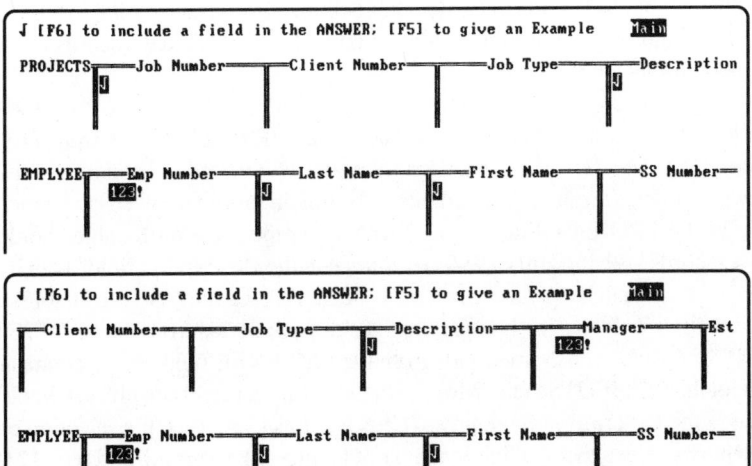

Figure 8-30 The ANSWER Table

ANSWER	Job Number	Description	Last Name	First N
1			Cheryl	Emerso
2			Garrison	Robert
3			Gunn	Barbar
4			Jackson	Mary
5			Jakes, Jr.	Sal
6			Jones	Jean
7			Jones	Stewar
8			Link	Julie
9			Masters	Ron
10			Myers	Julie
11			Preston	Molly
12			Roberts	Darlen
13	100	Install PC AT/Paradox/1-2-3	Jones	David
14	101	AT/Paradox/1-2-3 Intro	Jones	David
15	102	Paradox A/R System	Jones	David
16	106	Paradox Time Accounting System	Jones	David
17	107	1988 Compilation/Review	Williams	Brenda
18	108	1988 Compilation/Review	Williams	Brenda
19	109	1988 Compilation/Review	Williams	Brenda
20	110	Tax Consultation		
21	111	1988 Tax Return		
22	112	1988 Tax Return	Robertson	Kevin
23	113	1988 Audit	Robertson	Kevin
24	114	1988 Compilation/Review	Jones	David
25	115	Assist with Loan Application	Cameron	Herb

Viewing Answer table: Record 1 of 25   Main

Using a Selection Condition in a Master Table

If you specify a selection condition in the master table for an asymmetrical outer join, the ANSWER table will include every record from the master table that meets the condition, even those that are not linked to a record in the lookup table. However, the ANSWER table will include only those records from the lookup table that are linked to records in the master table that meet the selection condition.

For example, suppose you want to create a query that selects all records from PROJECTS with the entry *1988 Tax Return* in the Description field and includes the names of the project managers where this information is available. The link in this query needs to be inclusive of the records in the PROJECTS table. In other words, the ANSWER table should list all PROJECTS records with the entry *1988 Tax Return* in the Description field, even if some of those records are not linked to a record in EMPLYEE. To keep the ANSWER table relatively small, we'll include only the Job Number and Description fields from the PROJECTS table and the Last Name and First Name fields from the EMPLYEE field. First, create an empty query form for the PROJECTS table. Move to the Job Number field and press **[Check Mark]**. Then, move to the Description field, press **[Check Mark]**, and type the selection condition **1988 Tax Return**. Next, move to the Manager field, press **[Example]**, and type **123!**. Now, create a blank query form for the EMPLYEE table and move to the Emp Number field. Press **[Example]** and type **123**. Finally, move to the Last Name field, press **[Check Mark]**, move to the First Name field, and press **[Check Mark]** again. Figure 8-31 shows the completed query.

Figure 8-31 A Selection Condition in a Master Table

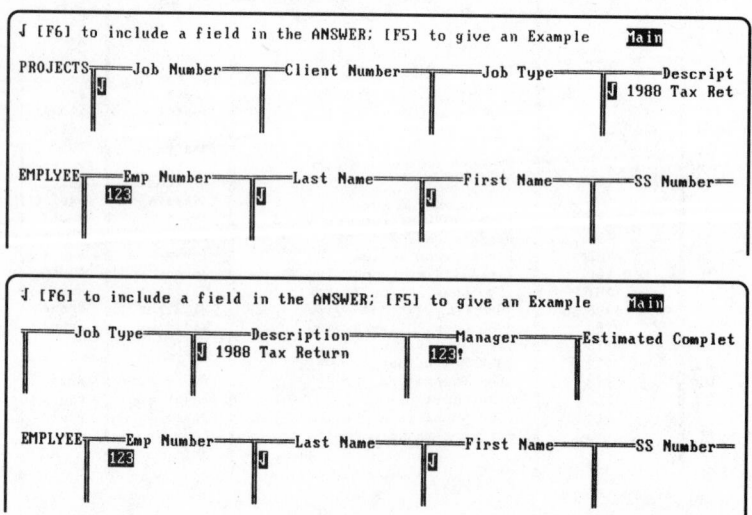

Figure 8-32 shows the ANSWER table that Paradox will create when you process the query. As you can see, the query selected both records with the entry *1988 Tax Return* in the Description field. Notice that record 1 of the ANSWER table contains blank entries in the

Last Name and First Name fields. This occurs because the PROJECTS record that supplied the Job Number and Description entries for this ANSWER record contains a blank value. This blank entry does not match any entry in the Emp Number field of the EMPLYEE table, so Paradox cannot fill the Last Name and First Name fields of the ANSWER table. A noninclusive link, that is, a link without an inclusion operator, would not include this record in the ANSWER table. Notice that record 2 of ANSWER includes entries in all fields. Paradox could fill in all the fields because the record contains data from records in PROJECTS and EMPLYEE, which the query linked on the examples in the Manager and Emp Number fields.

Figure 8-32 The ANSWER Table

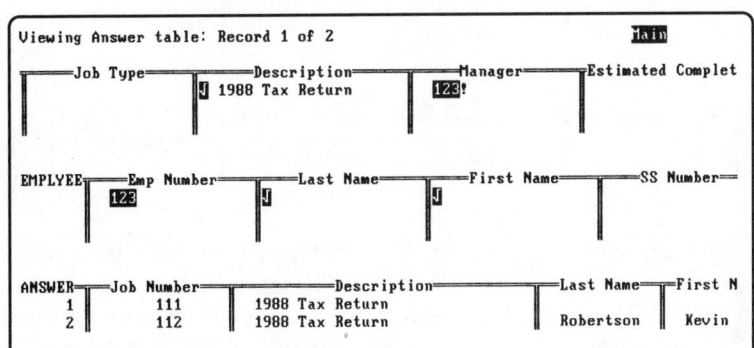

Specifying Selection Conditions in a Lookup Table

Placing a selection condition in the lookup table of an asymmetrical outer join produces an ANSWER table very different from the one produced by a query with a selection condition in the master table. A selection condition in the lookup table results in an ANSWER table that includes all records from the master table. Only those records from the lookup table that meet the selection condition and match a record in the master table will appear in ANSWER.

Suppose you want to see the numbers and names of all projects in the PROJECTS table, along with the names of any project managers who have been with the company less than one year. Figure 8-33 on the next page shows a query that will produce an ANSWER table containing this information. Let's look at the steps involved in creating this query.

To begin, create an empty query form for the PROJECTS table. Move to the Job Number field and press [**Check Mark**]. Then, move to the Description field and press [**Check Mark**] again. Next, move to the Manager field, press [**Example**], and type **123!**. Now, create a blank query form for the EMPLYEE table, move to the Emp Number field, press [**Example**], and type **123**. Next, move to the Last Name field and press [**Check Mark**], then, move to the First Name field and press [**Check Mark**] again. Finally, move to the Date of Hire field and type **>today-365**. This condition selects only those records in EMPLYEE that have Date of Hire entries that fall in the last 365 days, or those employees hired in the last year.

Figure 8-33 A Selection Condition in the Lookup Table

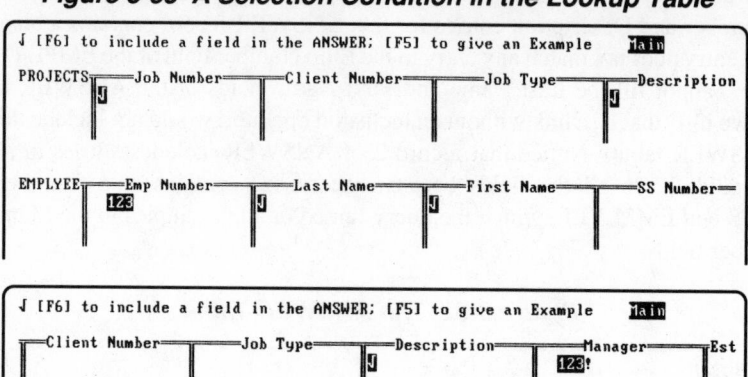

Assuming that today's date is September 15, 1988, Figure 8-34 shows the ANSWER table this query will produce. As you can see, the ANSWER table includes information from every table in the PROJECTS table, but only two records in ANSWER contain information from the EMPLYEE table. These two records both list the name of Kevin Robertson because he is the only project manager hired during the year prior to September 15, 1988.

Figure 8-34 The ANSWER Table

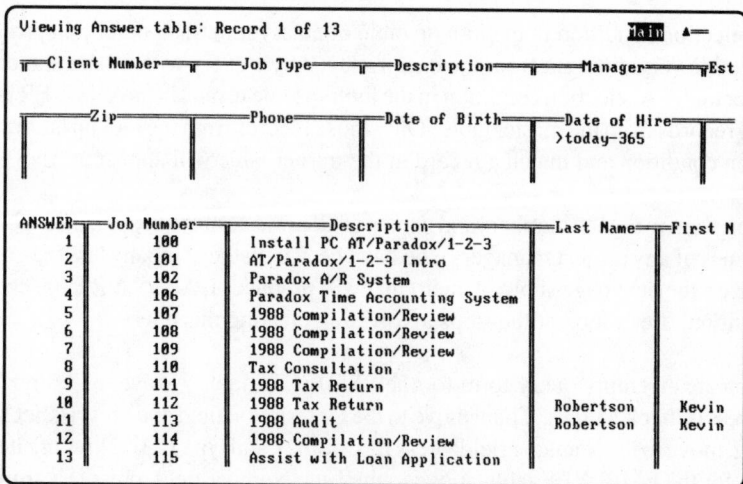

Using an Inclusion Operator in an Expression

You can also use an inclusion operator in a multitable query that includes an example from one query form in an expression in another query form. For example, suppose you want to list all the people in EMPLYEE, highlighting those who finished a project they managed less than one year after their date of hire. Of course, this query would use an example to link the Emp Number field in the EMPLYEE query form to the Manager field in the PROJECTS query form. In addition, this query would also include another example linking an expression in the Date of Hire field in the EMPLYEE table to the Actual Completion Date field in the PROJECTS table.

To begin, create a blank query form for EMPLYEE. When the blank query form appears, move to the Emp Number field, press [**Example**], then type **123!**. Then, place check marks in the Last Name and First Name fields. Move to the Date of Hire field and type **>**, press [**Example**], then type **date!-365**. Next, create a blank query form for the PROJECTS table, move to the Description field in that query form, and press [**Check Mark**]. Then, move to the Manager field, press [**Example**], and type **123**. Finally, move to the Actual Completion Date field, press [**Example**], and type **date**. Figure 8-35 shows the completed query.

Figure 8-35 An Inclusion Operator in an Expression

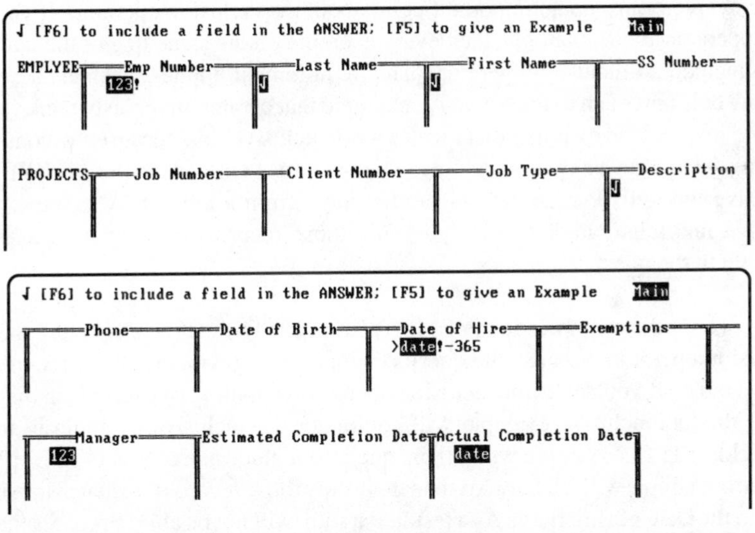

Figure 8-36 shows the ANSWER table that this query will produce. Because the examples in the EMPLYEE table have inclusion operators, the ANSWER table includes all the records from the EMPYEE table. However, the only records that appear from the PROJECTS table are those that are linked to a record in EMPLYEE by the example in the Manager field and selected by Paradox, based on the selection condition in the Date of Hire field.

Figure 8-36 The ANSWER Table

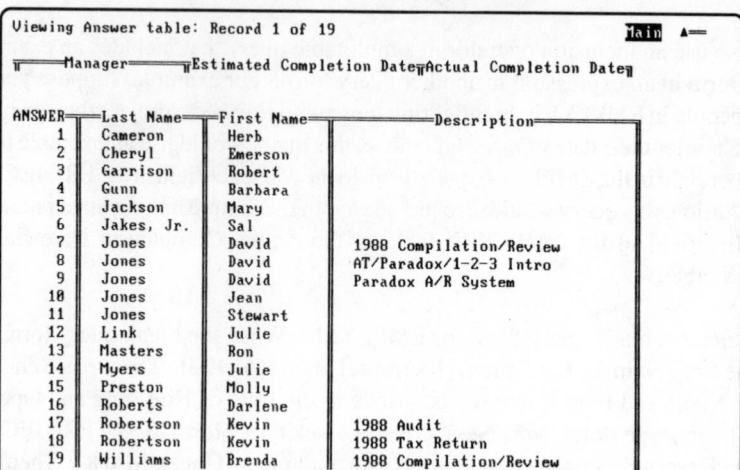

Avoiding Conflicting Examples

This last example brings up an important point about the inclusion operator. If you use an inclusion operator in one example, then every example on the same line of the query form must also include an inclusion operator. This requirement applies whether the example stands alone or is part of an expression. An example that creates an inclusive link cannot be on the same line with an example that creates a noninclusive link because the combination would confuse Paradox when it is deciding which records to include in the ANSWER table. The inclusive link tells Paradox to place all records from a table in ANSWER, while a noninclusive link tells Paradox to include only those records that match an example in another table in the query.

For instance, both the examples in the EMPLYEE query form shown in Figure 8-35 must have inclusion operators because the query is supposed to be inclusive for records in the EMPLYEE table. If you delete the inclusion operator from the *date* example in the Date of Hire field, this noninclusive example will contradict the inclusive example in the Emp Number field. The *123* example will tell the query to include all records from EMPLYEE, while the *date* example will tell Paradox to include only those records that match the selection condition in the Date of Hire field. As a result, Paradox will not be able to process the query. If you try to process a query with conflicting links, Paradox will display a message telling you that the query includes an ambiguous join.

Naming Fields in the ANSWER Table

Release 3 includes one operator not found in earlier versions of Paradox that lets you rename fields in the ANSWER table. The as operator is useful when you want to change names of fields in the ANSWER table in order to make the relationships between the fields more apparent. You can use the as operator in any query, but it is especially valuable in multitable queries that place two fields with duplicate names in the same ANSWER table. This scenario can arise when a query extracts information from two tables that contain fields with the same name. Ordinarily, Paradox simply adds numbers to the duplicate field names to distinguish them. For example, if an ANSWER table includes two fields named Address that came from two different query tables, Paradox will name the first field Address and the second field Address 1. However, by naming the fields with the as operator you can make it clear which field came from which query table.

To demonstrate the as operator, we'll use a table called CLIENTS, which lists information about the clients for the projects in the PROJECTS table. Figure 8-37 shows the structure of the CLIENTS table, and Figure 8-38 on the following page shows the data we've entered into the table. The CLIENTS and EMPLYEE tables contain several fields of the same name and type. For instance, both tables include an A10 field called First Name and an A10 field called Last Name.

Figure 8-37 The Structure of the CLIENTS Table

```
Viewing Struct table: Record 1 of 9                              Main

STRUCT          Field Name          Field Type
      1    Client Number            N*
      2    Last Name                A10
      3    First Name               A10
      4    SS Number                A11
      5    Address                  A20
      6    City                     A20
      7    State                    A2
      8    Zip                      A5
      9    Phone                    A14




                                        Clients table has 11 records
```

For our example, we'll link CLIENTS, EMPLYEE, and PROJECTS with a three-table query. This query will create an ANSWER table that lists the descriptions of the projects in the PROJECTS table, along with the last names of the client and manager for each project where this information is available.

Viewing Clients table: Record 1 of 11

CLIENTS	Client Number	Last Name	First Name	SS Number	Address	City	State	Zip	Phone
1	1001	Smith	John	345-43-2232	2378 Maple Wood Dr.	Louisville	KY	40216	(502) 448-8989
2	1002	Zoeller	Greg	401-45-8898	456 Whipps Mill Rd.	Louisville	KY	40242	(502) 422-9856
3	1003	Klausing	Fred	457-98-0432	2394 Hazelwood Ave.	Louisville	KY	40214	(502) 369-9393
4	1004	Fritz	Jules	345-67-3454	2212 Elk St.	New Albany	IN	47150	(812) 223-7472
5	1005	Gies	Helen	209-98-4628	4583 Mary Catherine	Louisville	KY	40216	(502) 773-3234
6	1006	Payne	Ann	325-23-2323	1932 Hunter Ct.	Louisville	KY	40224	(502) 233-3344
7	1007	Wooley	Paul	367-98-1244	123 Clarks Lane	Louisville	KY	40213	(502) 634-1238
8	1008	Cooley	Dwayne	417-23-2938	3237 Henry St.	Louisville	KY	40203	(502) 897-1247
9	1009	Harris	Ralph	403-42-5775	Rt. 2, Box 123-D	Floyds Knobs	IN	47119	(812) 922-7876
10	1010	Crane	John	378-24-9476	1345 18th St.	Louisville	KY	40224	(502) 247-8919
11	1011	Jones	Thiora	319-21-8219	8924 Hallmark Rd.	New Albany	IN	47150	(502) 922-8492

Figure 8-38 The CLIENTS Table

To define this query, first create a blank query form for PROJECTS. When the query form appears, move to the Client Number field, press **[Example]**, and type **123**. Then, move to the Description field and press **[Check Mark]**. Next, move to the Manager field, press **[Example]**, and type **456**. After you've finished the query form for PROJECTS, create a blank query form for EMPLYEE and move to the Emp Number field. Then, press **[Example]** and type **456**. This example links the Emp Number field to the Manager field in PROJECTS. Next, move to the Last Name field and press **[Check Mark]**. To change the name of the Last Name field in the ANSWER table, type **as Manager**. After placing the as operator, create a blank query form for CLIENTS and move to the Client Number field. Press **[Example]** and type **123**. Finally, move to the Last Name field, press **[Check Mark]**, and type **as Client**. This last as operator tells Paradox to change the name of the Last Name field to Client in the ANSWER table. Figure 8-39 shows the completed query.

Figure 8-39 A Query Using As

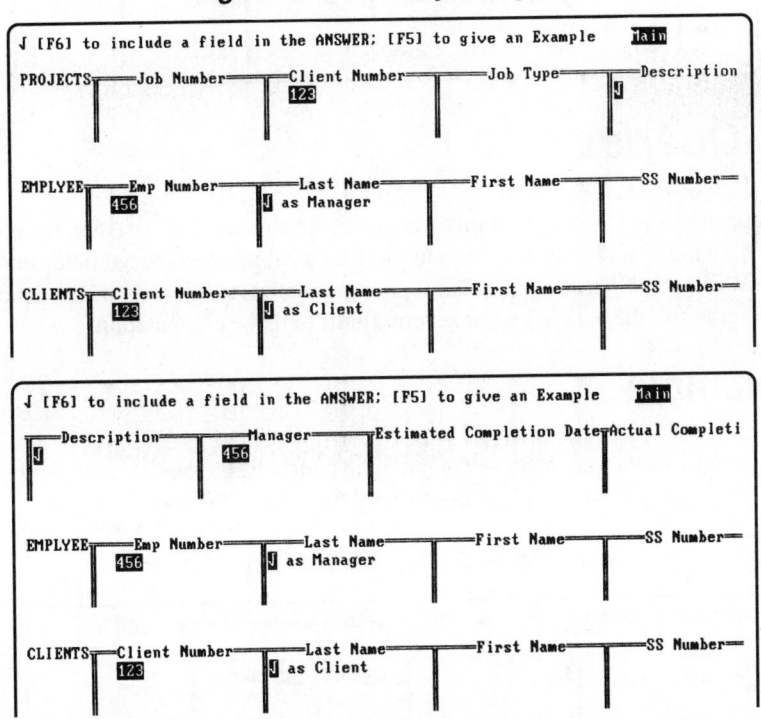

Figure 8-40 shows the ANSWER table that Paradox will create when you process the query. As you can see, Paradox has changed the names of the two Last Name fields to Manager and Client. Notice that the ANSWER table does not list job numbers 110 and 111 (records 8 and 9) from the PROJECTS table. As we explained earlier, these records do not match any records in EMPLYEE because they contain blank entries in the Manager field. As a result, the query in Figure 8-39 does not include them in ANSWER, even though the *123* example does match them with records in the CLIENTS table.

Figure 8-40 The ANSWER Table

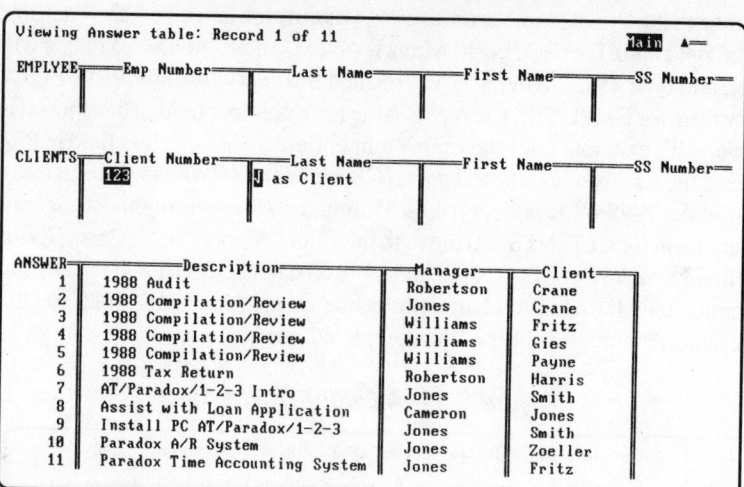

Calc Queries

The calc operator is a powerful tool that lets you make calculations based on the entries in the fields of a table. Paradox stores the results of the calculations in special fields that it adds to the ANSWER table. You can use the calc operator to compute subtotals and statistics about your tables or to use the data in one or several fields to make computations.

An Example

For example, let's use a calc query to compute the hourly wage rate for every employee in the EMPLYEE table. Figure 8-41 shows a query that makes this calculation.

Figure 8-41 A Calc Query

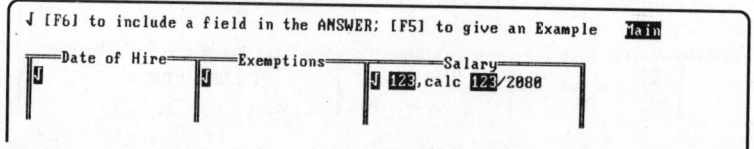

To create this query, first make a new query form for EMPLYEE. When the query form is in view, use the [**Check Mark**] key to select every field in the form. Next, move the cursor to the Salary field, press [**Example**], type **123,calc**, press [**Example**], and type **123/2080**.

This query sets *123* as the example for the contents of the Salary field and tells Paradox to divide the contents of this field for every record by 2,080. (We chose 2,080 because there are 2,080 working hours in a year.)

When you press **[Do-It!]** to perform this query, Paradox will create the ANSWER table shown in Figure 8-42. As you can see, this table includes a field, Salary / 2080, which does not exist in the EMPLYEE table. This new field contains the results of the calc query. If you check, you'll see that each entry in this field is equal to the corresponding entry in the Salary field divided by 2,080.

Figure 8-42 The ANSWER Table

```
Viewing Answer table: Record 1 of 16                            Main

 ┌─Date of Hire─────┬──────Exemptions─────┬──────────Salary────┐
 │                  │                     │  123, calc 123/2080 │
 │                  │                     │                     │


 ┌─Date of Hire─┬─Exemptions──┬──────Salary────┬─Salary / 2080─┐
 │   1/14/87    │      3      │    77,000.00   │    37.02      │
 │   1/14/87    │      4      │    55,000.00   │    26.44      │
 │   2/13/87    │      1      │    51,700.00   │    24.86      │
 │   6/16/87    │      3      │    16,940.00   │     8.14      │
 │   7/16/87    │      0      │    37,399.99   │    17.98      │
 │   8/16/87    │      6      │    44,000.00   │    21.15      │
 │   9/16/87    │      1      │    35,200.00   │    16.92      │
 │  11/14/87    │      2      │    33,000.00   │    15.87      │
 │  11/14/87    │      3      │    25,410.00   │    12.22      │
 │  12/14/87    │      6      │    37,400.00   │    17.98      │
 │   2/13/88    │      0      │    17,847.50   │     8.58      │
 │   2/13/88    │      0      │    41,800.00   │    20.10      │
 │   2/27/88    │      1      │    40,700.00   │    19.57      │
 │   5/15/88    │      4      │    35,200.00   │    16.92      │
 │   6/15/88    │      2      │    21,175.00   │    10.18      │
 │   8/15/88    │      2      │    14,520.00   │     6.98      │
```

This example illustrates one of the most important practical benefits of the calc operator. If the calc operator did not exist, you might have needed to include an Hourly Wage field in the structure of EMPLYEE. Thanks to calc, however, you don't have to store this information in your table permanently. Instead, you can simply calculate the hourly rate whenever you need it. By using calc cleverly, you may be able to eliminate certain fields from your tables, thereby saving space, reducing data entry effort, and increasing the performance of Paradox.

Another Example

Let's consider another example. Suppose you want to calculate the difference between the Actual Completion Date and the Estimated Completion Date entries for all completed projects. To begin, clear the screen, then create a new query form for PROJECTS and select every field in the first row of the form. Move to the Estimated Completion Date field, press **[Example]**, and type **E**. This entry sets E as the example for the entries in the Estimated Completion Date field.

Next, move to the Actual Completion Date field, press **[Example]**, type **A,not blank,calc**, press **[Example]**, type **A-**, press **[Example]**, and type **E**.

This entry sets A as the example for the entries in the Actual Completion Date field, tells Paradox to select only those records that do not have a blank entry in the Actual Completion

Date field, and tells Paradox to create a new, calculated field whose contents will equal *A-E*, or Actual Completion Date minus Estimated Completion Date.

When you process this query, Paradox will create the ANSWER table shown in Figure 8-43. As you can see, Paradox has created a new field, Actual Completion Date–Estimated Completion Date, in ANSWER and has stored the results of the calculation in that field. Paradox has trimmed the name of the new field to simply Actual Completion Date because a field name can be no longer than 25 characters.

Figure 8-43 Another Calc Query

```
Viewing Answer table: Record 1 of 7                              Main
   ┌──Manager──┬─Estimated Completion Date─┬──Actual Completion Date══
   │           │                           │                           
   │           │                           │ A, not blank, calc A-B
   │           │                           │                           
   │           │                           │                           


  ┌Estimated Completion Date┬Actual Completion Date┬Actual Completion Date ─┐
  │   10/13/88              │      11/23/88        │         41             │
  │    4/15/88              │       4/15/88        │          0             │
  │    5/29/88              │       5/29/88        │          0             │
  │    4/29/88              │       4/29/88        │          0             │
  │    6/29/88              │       6/29/88        │          0             │
  │    7/29/88              │       8/05/88        │          7             │
  │    5/14/88              │       7/14/88        │         61             │
```

Also notice that ANSWER includes only those records from PROJECTS that did not have a blank in the Actual Completion Date field. This example shows how easy it is to use selection conditions in calc queries.

Calc Queries on Alphanumeric Fields

You can use the calc operator to concatenate, or string together, the entries in two text fields. For example, in EMPLYEE, the first name and last name of each employee are in different fields. Suppose you want to create a new field that contains each employee's full name in normal form (as in *David Jones*).

To begin, create a new, empty query form for EMPLYEE and select every field in the form. Next, move to the Last Name field, press [**Example**], and type **L**. Now, move to the First Name field and press [**Example**], type **F, calc**, press [**Example**] again, then type **F+" "+**, press [**Example**] one more time, and type **L**.

This query sets *L* as the example for the entries in the Last Name field and *F* as the example for the entries in the First Name field. The formula *calc F+" "+L* tells Paradox to concatenate the contents of the First Name field (*F*) and the Last Name field (*L*) and to place a space between the two. The space is represented in the formula by a space enclosed in quotation marks.

Figure 8-44 shows the query and the ANSWER table that Paradox will create when you process this query. Notice the new field, First Name + Blank + Last Name, which contains the new entries Paradox has created. As you can see, this new field contains the full names of all the employees in EMPLYEE.

Figure 8-44 Using Calc with Alphanumeric Fields

```
Viewing Answer table: Record 1 of 16                          Main
┌──Emp Number──┐ ┌──Last name──┐ ┌──First Name──┐ ┌──SS Number──┐
│ 🔲            │ │ 🔲 🔲         │ │ 🔲 🔲,calc🔲+" "+🔲 │ 🔲 │              │ 🔲
│              │ │             │ │                │ │             │

┌─Date of Hire─┬──Exemptions──┬──────Salary──────┬─First Name + Blank + Last─┐
    1/14/87            3              77,000.00      David Jones
    1/14/87            4              55,000.00      Herb Cameron
    2/13/87            1              51,700.00      Stewart Jones
    6/16/87            3              16,940.00      Darlene Roberts
    7/16/87            0              37,399.99      Jean Jones
    8/16/87            6              44,000.00      Brenda Williams
    9/16/87            1              35,200.00      Julie Myers
   11/14/87            2              33,000.00      Julie Link
   11/14/87            3              25,410.00      Mary Jackson
   12/14/87            6              37,400.00      Sal Jakes, Jr.
    2/13/88            0              17,847.50      Molly Preston
    2/13/88            0              41,800.00      Ron Masters
    2/27/88            1              40,700.00      Kevin Robertson
    5/15/88            4              35,200.00      Robert Garrison
    6/15/88            2              21,175.00      Barbara Gunn
    8/15/88            2              14,520.00      Cheryl Emerson
```

In the example, we used the expression +" "+ to add a single blank space between the first name and last name. In fact, Paradox allows you to include any literal characters you want between quotation marks. For instance, look at the query and ANSWER table in Figure 8-45. The query includes the expression *calc "Dear "+F+" "+L*, which tells Paradox to concatenate the word *Dear* to each employee's full name. If you look at the resulting ANSWER table, you'll notice the word *Dear* before the names in the calculated field of this table.

Figure 8-45 Another Calc Query with Alphanumeric Fields

```
Viewing Answer table: Record 1 of 16                          Main
┌──Emp Number──┐ ┌──Last name──┐ ┌──First Name──┐ ┌──SS Numbe
│ 🔲            │ │ 🔲 🔲         │ │ 🔲 🔲,calc "Dear "+🔲+" "+🔲 │ 🔲
│              │ │             │ │                │ │

┌─Exemptions─┬──────Salary──────┬─Dear  + First Name + Blan─┐
     3              77,000.00      Dear David Jones
     4              55,000.00      Dear Herb Cameron
     1              51,700.00      Dear Stewart Jones
     3              16,940.00      Dear Darlene Roberts
     0              37,399.99      Dear Jean Jones
     6              44,000.00      Dear Brenda Williams
     1              35,200.00      Dear Julie Myers
     2              33,000.00      Dear Julie Link
     3              25,410.00      Dear Mary Jackson
     6              37,400.00      Dear Sal Jakes, Jr.
     0              17,847.50      Dear Molly Preston
     0              41,800.00      Dear Ron Masters
     1              40,700.00      Dear Kevin Robertson
     4              35,200.00      Dear Robert Garrison
     2              21,175.00      Dear Barbara Gunn
     2              14,520.00      Dear Cheryl Emerson
```

Naming Calculated Fields in ANSWER

Earlier in this chapter, we introduced the as operator, which Borland added to Paradox with Release 3, and we showed you how to use the as operator to rename fields in a two-table query. The as operator is also useful for assigning names to fields created by calc queries.

Using the as operator to name a field created by a calc query requires slightly different syntax than using that operator to rename a regular field in an ANSWER table. An as operator that renames an existing field stands alone as a separate element in the query form, set off with a comma if there are other elements in the same field. However, when you enter an as operator to name a calculated field, you enter it as part of the calc expression, without inserting a comma between the expression and the operator. Only a blank space separates the end of the expression and the as operator.

For example, suppose you want to use the query shown in Figure 8-44 to concatenate the entries in the First Name and Last Name fields, but you want to call the new field produced by the calc query Name instead of First Name + Blank + Last Name. To do this, you need to add an as operator to the First Name field of the query form. Move the cursor to the First Name field and type one blank space, then type **as Name.**

Figure 8-46 shows the modified query and the ANSWER table Paradox will present when you process the query. Instead of using the expression in the calc operator as the name for the new field, Paradox has given the field the name specified by the as operator.

Figure 8-46 The As Operator in a Calc Query

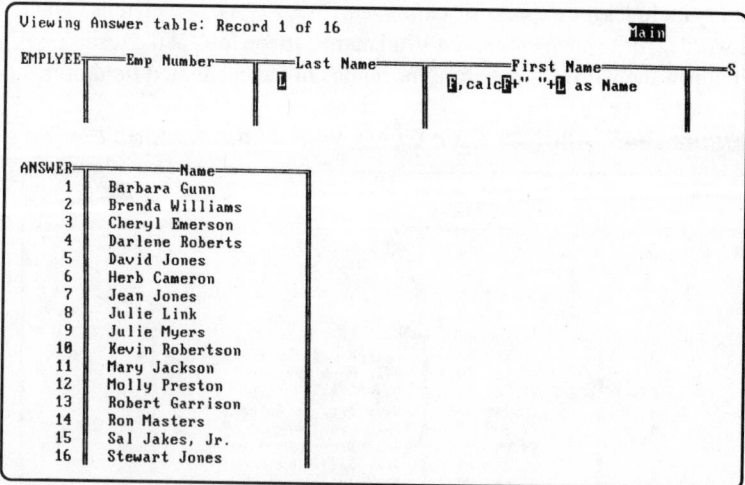

Notes

Just like other ANSWER tables, the ANSWER table that results from a calc query is a temporary table. If you want to save the contents of the new field, rename the ANSWER table. If you want the new field to be a part of the main table, you might want to assign to ANSWER the name of the table you just queried. If you want to retain the results of the calculation without including them in the main table, you should choose a different name.

Some Paradox users become confused about the difference between the calc and changeto operators. Changeto causes Paradox to change the actual values in the fields of the table being queried and doesn't create an ANSWER table at all. Calc queries, on the other hand, use the entries in the fields of the table being queried as the basis for a calculation; the result of the calculation is stored in a separate field in the ANSWER table.

For example, the query in Figure 8-47 is identical to the query in Figure 8-41 on page 326, except it uses the changeto operator instead of the calc operator. When you process this query, it will change the entries in the Salary field by dividing them by 2080. As a result, the new Salary entry for David Jones will be 37.02; the Salary entry for Julie Myers will be 16.92; and so on.

Figure 8-47 A Changeto Query

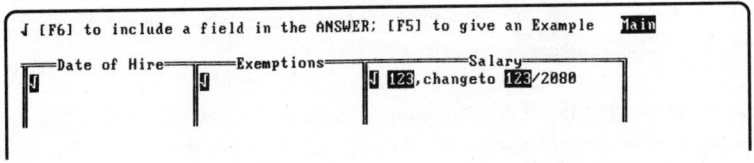

You cannot use a calc query to relate an alphanumeric field to any other type of field. For example, consider the calc query in Figure 8-48. The expression *calc DOH/S* uses the examples *DOH* and *S* to attempt to link the Date of Hire and Salary fields. If you try to process this query, Paradox will highlight the entry in the Salary field of the query form and will display the error message *Calc expression has type error*.

Figure 8-48 Field Type Mismatch

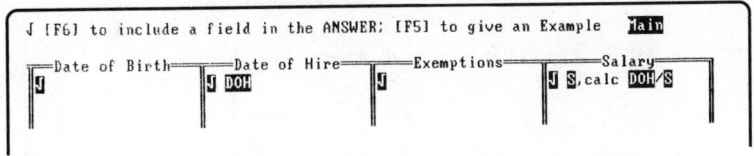

The same thing will happen if you try to use calc to link an alphanumeric field with a date field or a dollar ($) field. You can, however, use calc to link a numeric field with a dollar field or a date field. For example, the query in Figure 8-49 uses the expression *calc S/E* to link the Exemptions field in EMPLYEE to the Salary field. Although Salary has the type $ and Exemptions has the type N, this query is perfectly acceptable to Paradox.

Figure 8-49 Calc Query Combining $ and N Fields

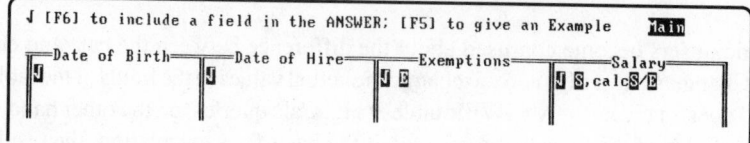

Calculating Summary Statistics

You can also use calc to calculate summary statistics on the entries in numeric and date fields. Paradox offers five special statistical operators—sum, average, max, min, and count—that you can use in conjunction with calc to compute statistics. Each of these statistical operators computes a different statistic, based upon the other entries you make in the query form. The sum operator computes the sum of the entries you specify. The max and min operators compute the maximum and minimum values of the specified entries. The average operator computes the arithmetic mean, or average, of the selected entries. The count operator counts the number of specified entries.

Let's consider a few examples of these operators. Suppose you want to know the total annual salary paid by your company (in other words, the total of the Salary field entries in EMPLYEE). To make this calculation, you'll use the sum operator in a calc query.

To begin, create a new query form for EMPLYEE. When the form appears, move to the Salary field and type **calc sum**. Now, press **[Do-It!]** to process the query and create the ANSWER table shown in Figure 8-50. As you can see, this table contains just one field—Sum of Salary—and just one record. The one entry in the table, 589,792.49, is the sum of the entries in the Salary field of EMPLYEE.

Figure 8-50 Calc Sum

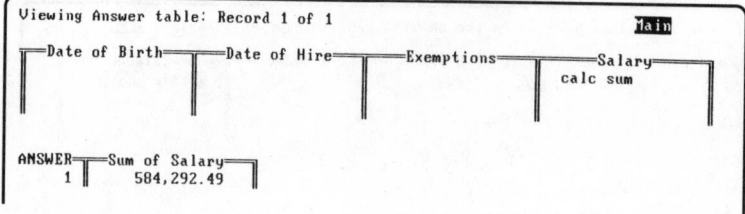

The average operator works in the same way as sum. For example, suppose you want to know the average of the Salary field entries. To calculate this statistic, just move the cursor to the Salary field of the query form, delete the word *sum* and type **average**, and press **[Do-It!]**. Figure 8-51 shows the resulting ANSWER table. The one entry in this table, 36,862.03, is the average of the Salary field entries.

Figure 8-51 Calc Average

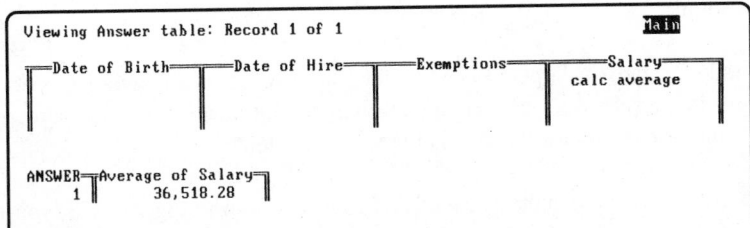

Notice that we did not select any fields in either of these queries. When you select fields in a query that uses statistical operators, Paradox will compute group statistics for the field or fields you select. Since at this point you want to compute statistics for the table as a whole, you don't need to select any fields. We'll show you how to create group summaries in a few pages.

Suppose you want to compute the total number, or count, of the entries in the Salary field. To do this, enter the expression **calc count** in the Salary field of the query form. When you process this query, Paradox will create the ANSWER table shown in Figure 8-52. As you can see, this table includes just one field, Count of Salary. The single entry in that field, 15, is the total number of entries in the Salary field.

Figure 8-52 Calc Count

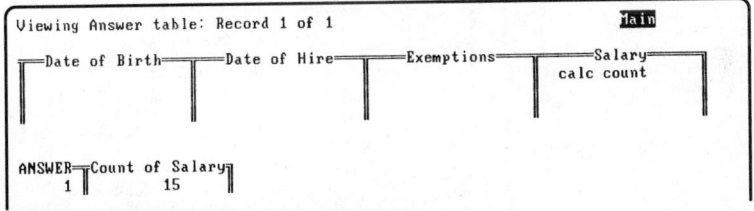

Scope and Field Compatibility

There are two concepts you must keep in mind when you use statistical operators: scope and field compatibility. The scope of an operator determines whether it will operate on all the values in a field or only on the unique ones. The field compatibility of an operator determines in which types of fields that operator can be used.

Scope of Statistical Operators

Since there are 16 records in EMPLYEE, and each of these records has a Salary field entry, you may wonder why the expression *calc count* in the previous example returned the number 15. The answer involves the concept of scope. Any time you use a statistical operator, you use one of two scopes: all or unique. The scope determines whether it will operate on all of the records in a table, or upon only those records that have a unique entry in the specified column.

Each of Paradox's statistical operators has a default scope. Sum and average operate on all of the records in the specified column, even if there are duplicate entries. Count, max, and min operate only on the unique entries in the specified field.

If you look at the Salary field in the EMPLYEE table shown in Figure 8-53, you'll notice that there are two 35,200.00 entries in this field. When Paradox evaluated the *calc count* expression, it counted only one of these two duplicate entries. The result, 15, is the number of unique entries in the Salary field. On the other hand, when Paradox computed the sum and average of the Salary field entries in the two previous examples, it evaluated both of these records. The sum and average returned by those queries include all 16 entries in the field.

Figure 8-53 The EMPLYEE Table

```
 Viewing Emplyee table: Record 1 of 16                          Main

┌Date of Birth┬─Date of Hire┬──Exemptions───────┬──Salary─────────
   10/06/42       1/14/87         3                  77,000.00
   11/24/29       1/14/87         4                  55,000.00
   3/21/50        2/13/87         1                  51,700.00
   9/24/60        6/16/87         3                  16,940.00
   5/14/43        7/16/87         0                  37,399.99
   1/12/20        8/16/87         6                  44,000.00
   2/06/48        9/16/87         1                  35,200.00
   8/12/56       11/14/87         3                  25,410.00
   5/23/59       12/14/87         6                  37,400.00
   4/17/66        2/13/88         0                  17,847.50
   12/30/44       2/13/88         0                  41,800.00
   3/16/25        2/27/88         1                  40,700.00
   5/09/45        5/15/88         4                  35,200.00
   5/18/50        6/15/88         2                  21,175.00
   7/30/66        8/15/88         2                  14,520.00
   6/03/33       11/14/87         2                  33,000.00
```

If you wish, you can override the default scope of any of Paradox's statistical operators by using the words *all* or *unique*. For example, suppose you want to compute the count of all the entries in the Salary field. To make this calculation, you would add the word **all** to the expression **calc count** in the Salary field, as shown in Figure 8-54 on the next page. When you process this query, Paradox will create the ANSWER table shown in Figure 8-55. As you can see, the result in this table, 16, includes all entries in the Salary field.

Figure 8-54 Calc Count All

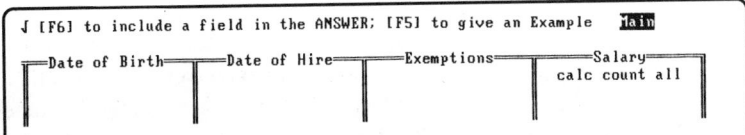

Figure 8-55 The ANSWER Table

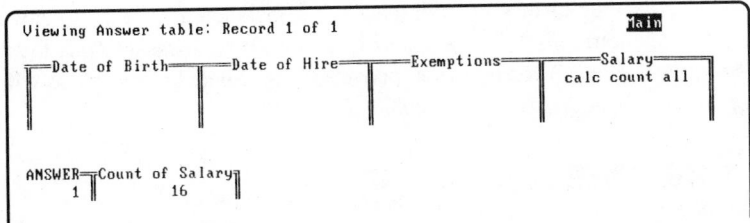

On the other hand, suppose you want to compute the sum of just the unique entries in the Salary field. To make this calculation, you would enter the expression **calc sum unique** in the Salary field of an otherwise empty EMPLYEE query form. When you process this query, Paradox will create the ANSWER table shown in Figure 8-56. Notice that the ANSWER table, which shows the sum of only the unique entries, is 35,200.00 less than the result in the earlier example. (Although this example may not seem very realistic, it demonstrates the effect of the unique operator. We'll look at a more realistic example of the unique operator in a few pages.)

Figure 8-56 Calc Sum Unique

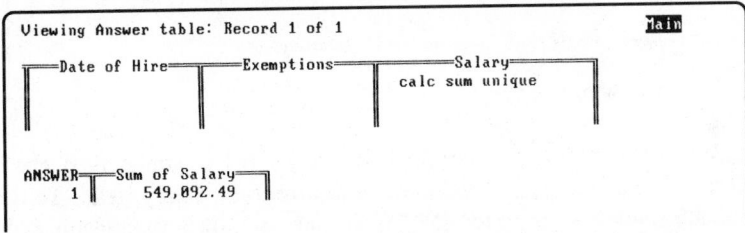

As a new Paradox user, you may find this discussion of scope to be confusing. Which one should you use? Does it really matter? It really does matter, but to keep it simple, here's the rule of thumb we follow: Use calc count all instead of calc count (or calc count unique). For any other operator, don't specify a scope at all—just rely on the Paradox defaults: calc sum, calc average, calc min, and calc max. This simple rule works for 99 percent of our queries in real applications. Occasionally, though, you'll need to use unique and all to alter the scope.

Field Compatibility

Field compatibility is another important characteristic of statistical operators. Simply put, not every operator will work in every type of field. While you can use the count, max, and min operators in all types of fields, you can only use average in number, short number, dollar, and date fields. Sum can only be used in number, short number, and dollar fields.

If you attempt to use an operator in the wrong type of field, Paradox will display an error message that describes the error you have made. For instance, if you try to calculate the average of an alphanumeric field, Paradox will display the error message *Only numeric and date fields may be averaged.* If you try to compute the sum of a date field, Paradox will display the message *Only numeric fields may be summed.*

Other Examples

You can enter statistical operators in two or more fields of a query form. Figure 8-57 shows a query form that will calculate the average salary and average number of exemptions from EMPLYEE, as well as the ANSWER table Paradox will create when you process this query. As you can see, this table includes two fields: Average of Exemptions and Average of Salary. The results in this table are the averages of the values in those two fields.

Figure 8-57 Calc Average on Two Fields

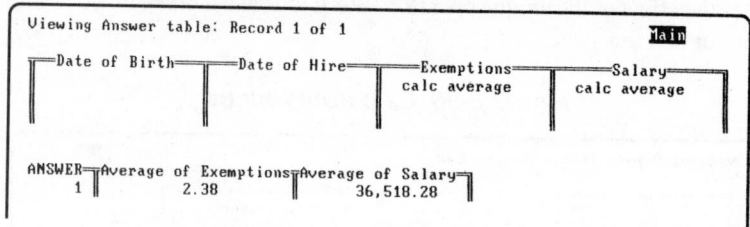

You can also enter two statistical operators in one field. For example, the query in Figure 8-58 computes the maximum and minimum values from the Salary field. To define this query, just create a new query form for EMPLYEE and type **calc max, calc min** in the Salary field. When you process this query, Paradox will create the ANSWER table shown in Figure 8-58. As you can see, this table includes two fields, Max of Salary and Min of Salary, and two entries, the maximum and minimum values from the Salary field.

In addition, you can use statistical operators in queries that include selection conditions. For example, suppose you want to know how many employees are paid more than $30,000 per year. To make this computation, you would create the query shown in Figure 8-59. Notice the selection condition *>30000* in the Salary field and the entry *calc count* in the Emp Number field. When you press [Do-It!] to process this query, Paradox will create the ANSWER table shown in Figure 8-60. As you can see, this table has just one entry, 11, which is the number of employees in EMPLYEE who earn more than $30,000.

Figure 8-58 Calc Max and Calc Min

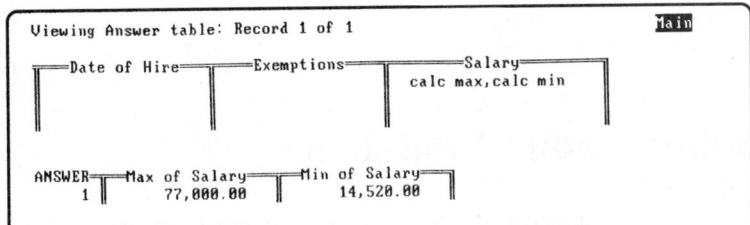

Figure 8-59 Calc Count with Selection Condition

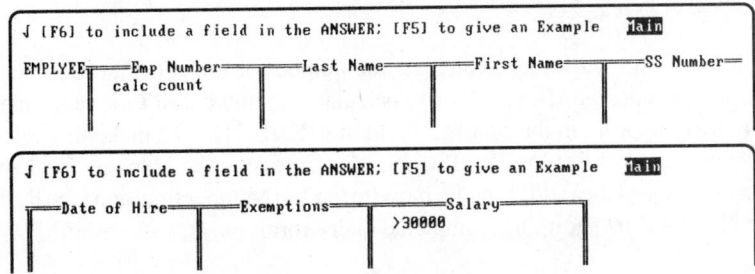

Figure 8-60 The ANSWER Table

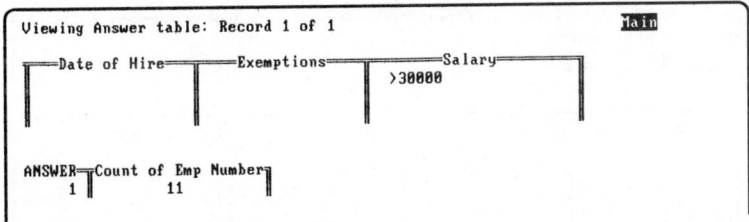

Do you wonder why we entered the formula *calc count* in the Emp Number field? We chose this field because we were sure there was a unique entry in it for each record in the table. In fact, we could have entered the function in the SS Number field and achieved essentially the same result. However, if we had entered the function in the Last Name field, as shown in Figure 8-61, the result would have been different. As you can see, the number in the table is now 9, not 11. Since there are three *Jones* entries in the Last Name field, there are only nine unique names that meet the condition.

Figure 8-61 Calc Count on a Non-unique Field

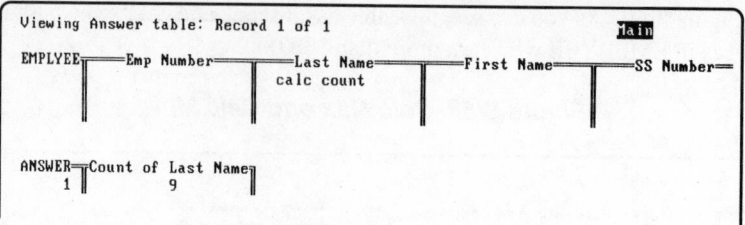

Computing Group Statistics

Paradox's statistical operators can also be used to compute group statistics. To compute a group statistic, you use [Check Mark] to select the field on which you want Paradox to group the table, and enter a statistical operator in the field or fields on which you want to compute statistics.

For example, suppose you want to calculate the number of projects that each manager is responsible for; in other words, you want to calculate the number of times each manager's employee number appears in the Manager field of PROJECTS. To make this calculation, first create a new query form for PROJECTS. Next, move to the Manager field and press [Check Mark] to select the field. Finally, move to the Job Number field and type the formula **calc count**. Figure 8-62 shows the completed query form.

Figure 8-62 Grouping with Calc Count

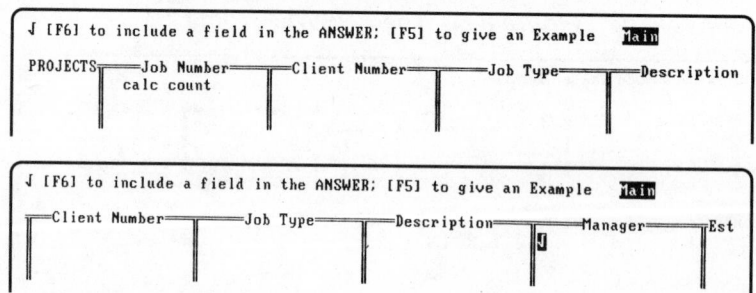

When you process this query, Paradox will create the ANSWER table shown in Figure 8-63. Notice that this table includes two fields, Manager and Count of Job Number, and five records, one for each unique employee number in the Manager field of PROJECTS. The entries in the Manager field of ANSWER are the employee numbers from the Manager field of PROJECTS. The entries in the Count of Job Number field represent the number of jobs for which each manager is responsible. In other words, the 5 in the Count of Job Number field of the second record in ANSWER means that manager number 1 is responsible for five jobs.

Figure 8-63 The ANSWER Table

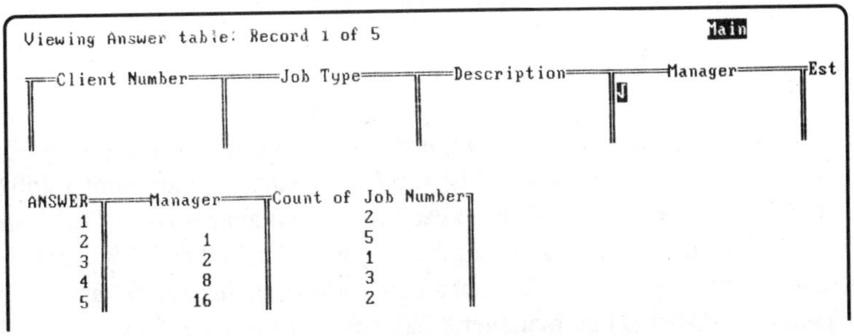

```
Viewing Answer table: Record 1 of 5                          Main
  =Client Number=        =Job Type=     =Description=       =Manager=    =Est
                                                         U

  ANSWER    =Manager=    =Count of Job Number=
    1                           2
    2          1                5
    3          2                1
    4          8                3
    5         16                2
```

Notice that the first record in ANSWER has a blank in the Manager field. This occurs because a few of the records in ANSWER do not have Manager field entries. Whenever you compute group statistics, and the field on which you're grouping has blanks, Paradox will combine all of the blanks and present them at the top of the ANSWER table.

The Location of the Formula

In the example, we entered the formula *calc count* in the Job Number field, so Paradox computed the total of different job numbers associated with each manager. If, on the other hand, we entered the formula *calc count all* in the Client Number field, Paradox would create the ANSWER table shown in Figure 8-64. The entries in the Count of Client Number field in this ANSWER table represent the number of different *clients* with which each manager is associated. As you can see, the entries in this table differ from those in the first ANSWER table.

Figure 8-64 Grouping with Calc Count All

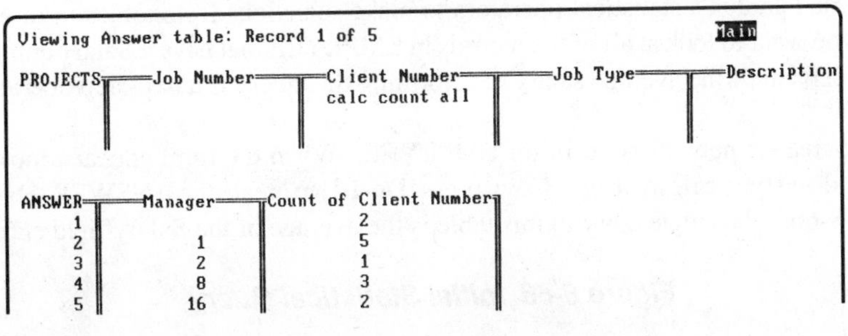

```
Viewing Answer table: Record 1 of 5                          Main
  PROJECTS   =Job Number=   =Client Number=    =Job Type=    =Description=
                             calc count all


  ANSWER    =Manager=    =Count of Client Number=
    1                           2
    2          1                5
    3          2                1
    4          8                3
    5         16                2
```

Grouping on More Than One Field

If you enter checks in more than one field of a group summary query, Paradox will compute group statistics on both fields. For example, suppose you want to know how many jobs of each type each manager is responsible for. To calculate this statistic, first create a new, empty query form for the PROJECTS table. When the form is in view, move to the Job Type field and press [**Check Mark**]. Then, move to the Manager field and press [**Check Mark**]. Finally, move to the Job Number field (again, the field that is sure to have a unique entry for every record in the table), and enter the expression **calc count**.

Now press [**Do-It!**] to process the query. Figure 8-65 shows the resulting ANSWER table. As you can see, this table includes three fields: Job Type, Manager, and Count of Job Number. Notice that there is a record in this table for each job type/manager pair. The Count of Job Number field for each record shows the number of jobs of the indicated type that belong to the indicated manager. For instance, the first record shows that manager 1 has one job of type 1. The seventh record shows that manager 8 has three jobs of type 3.

Figure 8-65 Grouping on More Than One Field

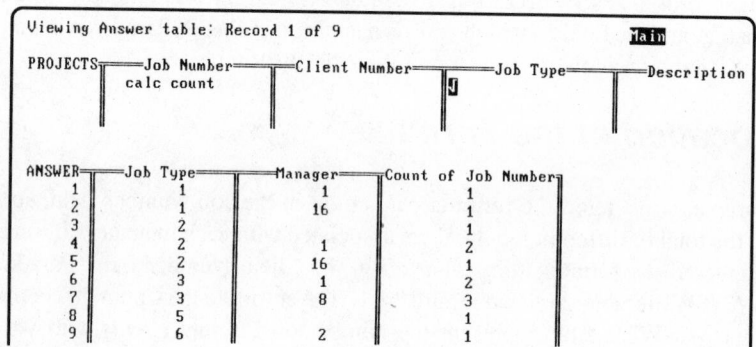

Using Computed Statistics to Make Selections

You can use Paradox's statistical operators to make selections from tables. For example, suppose you want to look at all of the records in EMPLYEE that have a Salary entry greater than 120 percent of the average salary. Performing this query is a two-step operation.

To begin, create a new query form for EMPLYEE. When the form appears, move to the Salary field and type **calc average**. Now, press [**Do-It!**] to create the ANSWER table shown in Figure 8-66. The single entry in this table is the average of the Salary field entries.

Figure 8-66 Initial Statistical Query

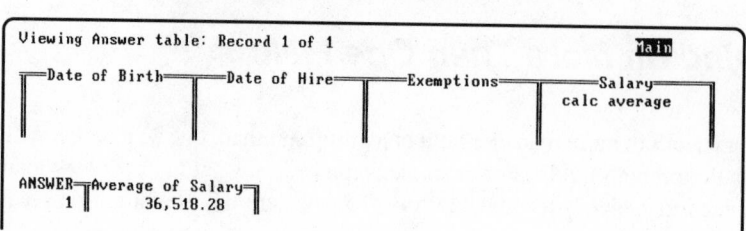

Now, press [**Up Image**] to move back to the EMPLYEE query form, press [**Clear Image**] to erase the existing form, and use the [**Menu**] **A**sk command to create two new query forms: one for EMPLYEE and one for ANSWER. Next, select every field in the EMPLYEE query form, move to the Salary field, type >, press [**Example**], and type **123*1.2**. Finally, move to the Average of Salary field in the ANSWER query form, press [**Example**], and type **123**.

Figure 8-67 shows the completed query. This query tells Paradox to select those records from EMPLYEE that have a Salary field entry greater than 120 percent of the entry in the Average of Salary field in ANSWER. The example *123* links the Average of Salary field to the Salary field.

Figure 8-67 Query Using the ANSWER table

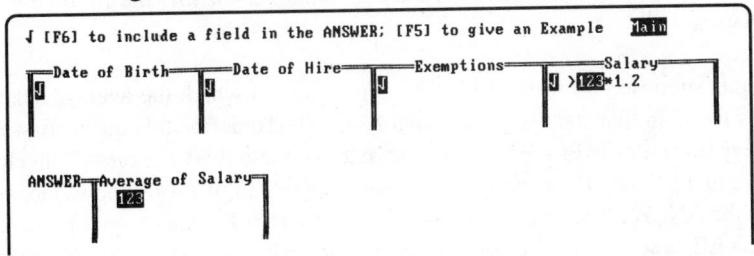

When you press [**Do-It!**] to process the query, Paradox will create the ANSWER table shown in Figure 8-68. As you can see, this table contains only the records from EMPLYEE that have a Salary field entry that is greater than 1.2 times the average salary.

Figure 8-68 The Final ANSWER Table

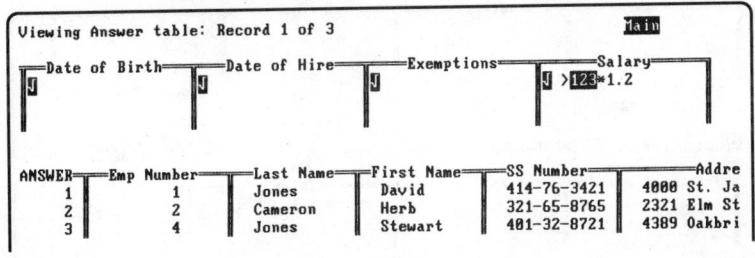

Whenever you perform a query on the ANSWER table, both the previous ANSWER table and the ANSWER query form will be erased when you press [Do-It!]. The old ANSWER table will continue to exist only as long as Paradox needs it to process the new query. If you want to preserve the first ANSWER table, rename it before you create the second query.

There are two other ways to use statistics to make selections. First, you can use the PAL calculator to compute a statistic and store the value of that statistic in a variable. Then, you can enter that variable into a query form to make your selection. We'll show you how to use the PAL calculator in this way in Chapter 14, "PAL Basics." If you have Paradox 3, you can use the set operator to define a set that includes all the records in a table, then use an expression including an example and the average operator to select records. We'll discuss this technique later in this chapter.

Identifying Groups Based on Summary Statistics

Paradox 3 also lets you use summary operators to identify groups that have specified summary statistics. The process of identifying groups based on summary statistics is essentially the opposite of calculating group statistics. When calculating group statistics, you define the fields on which Paradox should group and ask Paradox to compute statistics for each group. When you use group operators to identify groups, you define the fields on which Paradox should group, provide statistics, and ask Paradox to identify the groups described by those statistics.

For example, suppose you want to identify every state in which the average salary of the employees living in that state is greater than $33,000. To define this query, first create an empty query form for EMPLYEE. Then, move to the State field and press [**Check Mark**]. Next, move to the Salary field and type **average > 33000**. Figure 8-69 shows the completed query and the ANSWER table it produces. This query tells Paradox to group the records in the EMPLYEE table on the entries in the State field, calculate the average Salary entry for each group, and then place the State entries for those groups that have an average income greater than $33,000 in the ANSWER table.

Figure 8-69 Identifying Groups with Summary Statistics

```
√ [F6] to include a field in the ANSWER; [F5] to give an Example    Main
┌──SS Number───────┬──────Address────────┬─────City───────┬─────State──────┬──────
│                  │                     │               √│                │
│                  │                     │                │                │
│                  │                     │                │                │


Viewing Answer table: Record 1 of 4                                   Main
┌──Date of Hire───┬──────Exemptions─────┬──────Salary───────┬
│                 │                     │  average > 33000   │
│                 │                     │                    │


ANSWER─┬State┐
     1 ║ KY  ║
     2 ║ MA  ║
     3 ║ NY  ║
     4 ║ TX  ║
```

As you can see, the ANSWER table contains the State entries *KY, MA, NY,* and *TX.* This ANSWER table tells you that the average income for the employees who live in each of these four states is greater than $33,000.

If you want to identify the states in which the average salary is less than $33,000, change the summary operator in the Salary field to *average < 33000*. To select those states in which the average is exactly $33,000, use the summary operator *average = 33000*. In addition to changing the mathematical operator in the selection condition, you can also use any of the summary operators (average, count, max, min, or sum) to identify groups of records in this manner. Of course, the field in which you place a selection condition based on a summary operator must meet the field type requirements for the summary operator you are using.

The Only Operator

Paradox 3 also provides another operator that works similarly to the summary operators in identifying groups of records: the only operator. Instead of identifying groups of records that have specified summary statistics, the only operator isolates groups that have only a specified entry in a particular field. For example, suppose you want to know which employee has managed only projects involving 1988 Compilation/Reviews. This selection condition excludes employees who managed other types of projects in addition to 1988 Compilation/Reviews.

To define this query, first create a blank query form for PROJECTS. Then, move to the Description field and type **only "1988 Compilation/Review"**. Next, move to the Manager field and press **[Check Mark]**. The check mark in the Manager field tells Paradox to group the records in PROJECTS, while the only operator in the Description field tells Paradox to select just those groups that contain only the entry *1988 Compilation/Review* in the Description field. Figure 8-70 shows the completed query and the ANSWER table it will produce.

Figure 8-70 A Query Using the Only Operator

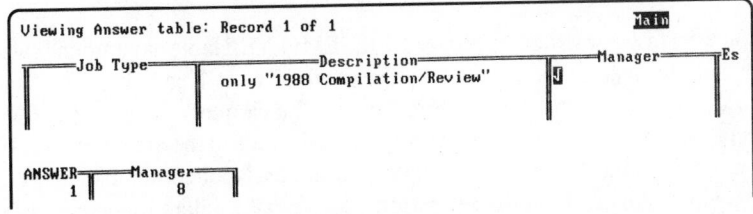

As you can see, the only record in the ANSWER table contains the entry 8 in the Manager field. If you look at the PROJECTS table, you can see that every record in which the number 8 appears in the Manager field includes the entry *1988 Compilation/Review* in the Description field. The only other PROJECTS record that contains the same Description entry is record 12, which contains the entry 1 in the Manager field. However, the ANSWER table does not include the Manager entry 1 because some PROJECTS records with this Manager entry contain Description entries other than *1988 Compilation/Review*.

Set Queries

Another query capability found only in Paradox 3 is the ability to perform operations on sets of records. With the set capabilities added to Paradox in Release 3, you can use a selection condition to define a set of records, then compare other records to that set. Once you have defined a set of records, you can determine whether records in another group match that set partially, exactly, or not at all, based on fields that you mark with examples in a query. You can also compare entries in another group of records to summary statistics based on entries in your defined set.

To define a set in a query, you type the word *set* on one or more lines of the query, then enter selection conditions on those lines to define the set. Paradox recognizes any line marked with the word *set* as a sort of query within a query. Before processing any other elements in the query, Paradox uses the set definition to isolate the records that are included in the set. Then, Paradox uses the rest of the query to compare all the records in the table to those in the defined set.

Comparisons to Summary Statistics for a Set

After you have defined a set of records in a query form, you can compare entries in other records to summary statistics derived from records in the set. To begin, we'll show you how to select groups of records that are related statistically to the records in a set. Then, we'll show you how to use the summary statistical operators to make selections based on all the records in a table.

Selections Based on the Statistics for a Set

Suppose you want to know which employees in the EMPLYEE table have annual salaries that are greater than the average salary for employees who live in Kentucky. The first step in creating this query is to define the set. First, create a blank query form for the EMPLYEE table and type **set** in the first column of the form. Then, move to the State field and type **KY**. Since you want to use the entries in the Salary field as a basis for comparison, you also need to add an example in that field of the query form. Move to the Salary field, press **[Example]** and type **123**.

Now, you are ready to enter a selection condition for the query based on the set. Press ↓ to move down to the second line of the query form. Then, place check marks in the Last Name, First Name, and State fields. Finally, move to the Salary field and type **>average**, press **[Example]**, and type **123**. Figure 8-71 shows the completed query.

Figure 8-72 shows the ANSWER table that Paradox will create when you process the query. As you can see, ANSWER includes several records that contain the entry *KY* in the State field and one record with *NY* in the State field. Because Paradox does not exclude the records that are in the defined set of a query in the ANSWER table, ANSWER includes all records that have a Salary entry greater than the average Salary entry for records with *KY* in the State field, including those that are a part of this set.

Figure 8-71 A Set Definition in a Query

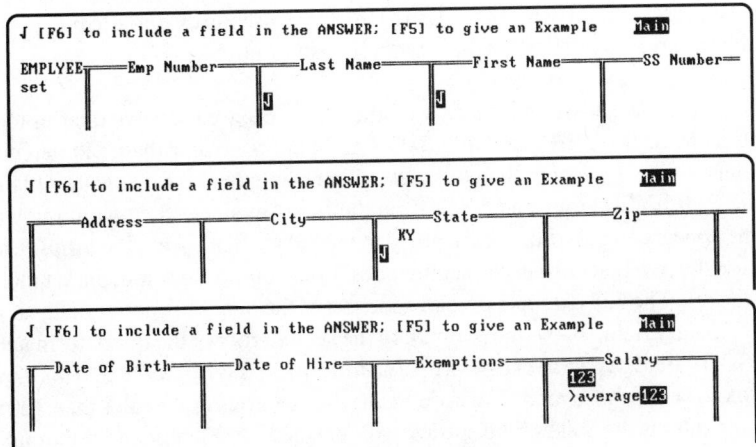

Figure 8-72 The ANSWER Table

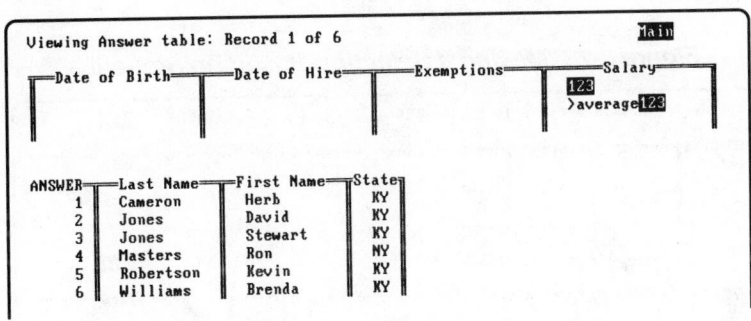

Of course, you can use any of the summary operators we discussed earlier in this chapter to ask questions about sets. For example, to find the names of employees who make more than the highest paid employee who lives in Kentucky, replace the average summary operator in Figure 8-71 with the summary operator max. This modified query will select only those records with a Salary entry that is greater than the highest Salary entry in a record with the State entry *KY*. However, if you process this new query, Paradox will create an empty ANSWER table. Because Paradox cannot find an employee with a salary higher than that of the highest paid employee in Kentucky, you know that the company's highest paid employee lives in Kentucky.

Selections Based on Statistics for a Table

Earlier in this chapter, we showed you a two-step method of selecting records based on summary statistics for a table. When used together, the enhanced summary operators and set operator of Paradox 3 let you perform this type of operation with a single query. This query defines a set that includes all of the records in a table, then uses an example to make a selection based on the summary statistics for that comprehensive set.

In our earlier example, shown in Figures 8-66 through 8-68, we used two queries to identify all the records in EMPLYEE that had a Salary field entry greater than 120 percent of the average Salary entry. To accomplish this task with a single query, first create a blank query form for the EMPLYEE table, and type **set** on the first row under the column in which the table's name appears on the form. Then, move to the Salary field, press [**Example**], and type **123**. Because the row that defines the set includes no selection condition, the set includes all records in the set. The *123* example prepares the rest of the query to operate on the collective entries in the Salary field. Next, move down to the second row of the query form and, while still in the Salary field, type **>average**, press [**Example**], and type **123*1.2**. This expression tells Paradox to select those records whose Salary field entries are greater than 120 percent of the average entry in the Salary field entries in the defined set. Finally, move the cursor back to the column under the table name and press [**Check Mark**] to select every field on the second row of the query form. Figure 8-73 shows the completed query and the ANSWER table it will produce.

Figure 8-73 Making a Selection Based on Statistics

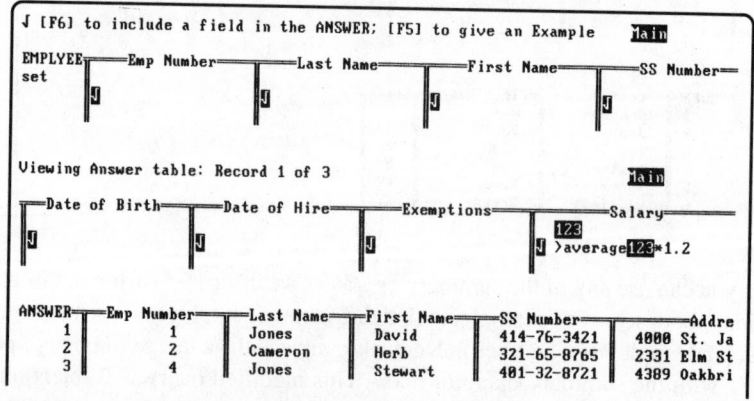

If you compare this ANSWER table to the ANSWER table shown in Figure 8-68, you will see that both tables include the same three records. Only these three records have Salary field entries that are greater than 120 percent of the average salary.

Set Operators

Set operators are tools you can use to perform several types of comparisons between sets of records. There are four set operators: only, no, every, and exactly. Combining these set operators with examples lets you identify records that are related to a defined set of records in ways that may not be readily apparent.

There are three basic elements of queries that include set operators. First, there is the set definition. The line or lines that begin with the word *set* specify which records comprise the defined set. Second, there is the example that links the defined set to the records being compared to the set. Queries that include set operators have three basic elements: the set definition, the example, and the field or fields on which the records being compared to the set are to be grouped. The line or lines that begin with the word *set* specify which records comprise the defined set. The example links the defined set to the records being compared to the set. One occurrence of the example is placed within the set definition and defines the linking field in the set. The other example defines the field that links the other records to the set. The example outside the set definition contains the set operator, which defines the type of relationship you are looking for between the set and the other records. You mark grouping fields with a check mark. When you process the query, Paradox divides the table in the query into groups of records that have common values in the check-marked field or fields. Then, Paradox compares these groups of records to the defined set of records.

A query that compares a collection of records to a defined set can involve one or several tables. We'll provide examples using each of the set operators to illustrate the types of comparisons you can make.

The Only Set Operator

The only set operator identifies groups containing only records that match records in the defined set. The only set operator selects a group only if the linking field of every record in the group matches an entry in the linking field of the set. The only set operator excludes any group that has at least one record containing a nonmatching entry in the linking field. Suppose you want to identify the types of jobs that have been managed only by employees who were hired before June 1, 1987. This selection could help you identify the types of jobs your older managers have monopolized and in which your newer managers may be lacking experience.

The first step in creating this query is defining the set on which the comparison is to be made. To do this, first create a blank query form for the EMPLYEE table and type **set** in the first column. Then, move to the Date of Hire field and type **<6/1/87**. Next, move to the Emp Number field, press **[Example]**, and type **123**. This line of the query defines a set that includes only those records with Date of Hire entries earlier than June 1, 1987. Now, we will use the example in the Emp Number field to link the records in the set to the records in the PROJECTS table. To establish this link, create a new query form for the PROJECTS table. Move to the Manager field and type **only**, press **[Example]**, and type **123**. This set operator tells Paradox to select only groups in which every record matches a record in the defined set of records in EMPLYEE. Finally, place a check mark in the Job Type field. Since Job Type is the only field in the query form that contains a check mark, the query will group on entries in Job Type, and it will be the only field in the ANSWER table. Figure 8-74 shows the completed query and the ANSWER table Paradox will create if you process the query.

Figure 8-74 A Query Using the Only Set Operator

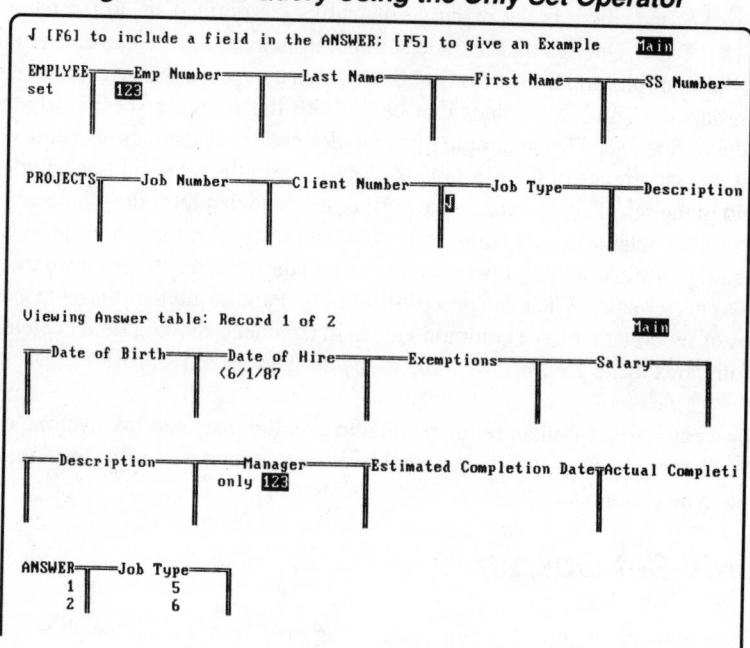

Since ANSWER includes the Job Type entries 5 and 6, you know that only employees hired before June 1, 1987, have managed projects identified by these Job Type entries. The ANSWER table does not include job types that have been managed by employees in this set or employees who do not belong to this set. If you look at the JOBS table shown on page 305, you can see that these Job Type entries refer to jobs that fall under the classifications *Writing* and *Other*.

Depending on the nature of your database system, you could use the only set operator to uncover a great deal of information that would otherwise remain hidden. For example, the only set operator could help you identify prized customers who have purchased only products priced at over $1,500 or unproductive sales representatives who deal only in accounts that bring in less than $1,000 annually.

The No Set Operator

The no set operator identifies groups containing only records that do not match records in the defined set. For example, suppose you want to identify the types of services listed in the PROJECTS table that have never been used by clients who live in Kentucky. This information could help you decide which services you should discontinue offering in your company's Kentucky office.

The first thing you need to do is define the set of clients you want to use as a basis for your comparison. To define this set, begin by creating a blank query form for the CLIENTS table. When the new query form appears, type **set** in the first column of the form. Then, move to the State field and type **KY**. Finally, move to the Client Number field, press [**Example**], and type **abc**. This line defines a set that includes all the CLIENTS records that have the State entry *KY* and sets up a link based on entries in the Client Number field.

Now, you are ready to define the comparison and specify the fields on which the compared records should be grouped. Create a blank query form for the PROJECTS table and place a check mark in the Job Type field to group on that field. Then, move to the Client Number field, type **no**, press [**Example**], and type **abc**. This set operator tells Paradox to select only those records from PROJECTS that contain Client Number entries that do not match the Client Number entries in the defined set. Since the set includes the Client Number entries for all clients that have *KY* in the State field, the ANSWER table will include only the Job Type entries that identify services never used by clients who live in Kentucky. Figure 8-75 shows the completed query and the ANSWER table Paradox will create if you process the query.

Figure 8-75 A Query Using the No Set Operator

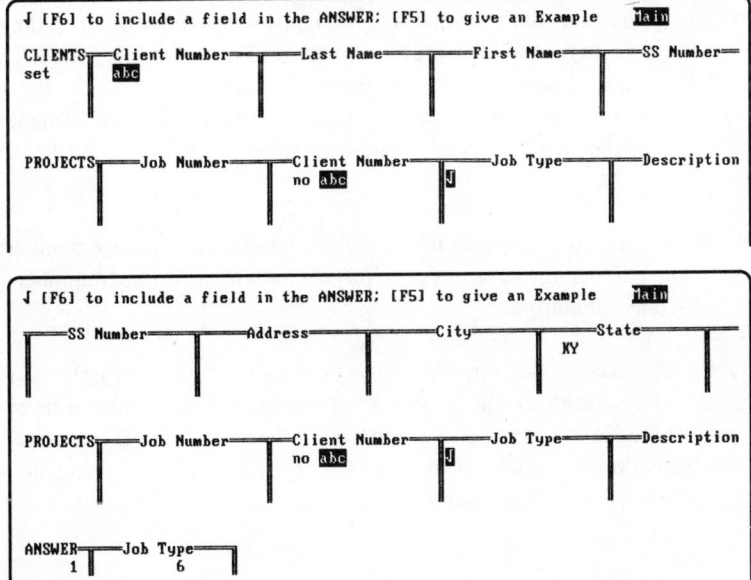

Because the ANSWER table includes only the Job Type entry 6, you can tell that clients who live in Kentucky have never hired the company for a job that fell under that classification. If you refer to the JOBS table in Figure 8-16 on page 305, you can see that Job Type entry 6 refers to a project that falls under the classification *Other*. As a result, you know that Kentucky clients have taken advantage of all the primary types of services offered by your company.

There are several questions that the no set operator could help you answer about your data. For example, you could devise a query to identify those patients who have not exhibited any symptoms associated with measles or those students who have not taken any of the classes required for graduation. As long as you can identify a set of records, then you can use the no set operator to identify groups of records that do not match any of the entries in a specified field in the set.

The Every Set Operator

The every set operator identifies those groups that contain at least one match for each record in the defined set. The every set operator will select a group only if each entry in the defined set matches a record in the group. However, the group can contain records that do not match records in the defined set. Suppose you want to identify employees who have managed every type of job for customer number 1001. This information would be useful if you were trying to decide who should be assigned to deal with this client on a continuing basis.

You can define this entire query in a query form for PROJECTS. First, create a blank query form for PROJECTS and type **set** in the first column. Then, move to the Client Number field and type **1001**. Next, move to the Job Type field, press **[Example]**, and type **123**. This line defines a set that includes all records with the Client Number entry 1001 and sets up a link based on the Job Type entries of these records. Next, press ↓ to move down to the next line of the query, then type **every**, press **[Example]**, and type **123** in the Job Type field. This every set operator tells Paradox to select only those groups that include a match for the Job Type entry in every record of the defined set. Finally, place a check mark in the Manager field to group on the entries in this field. Figure 8-76 shows the completed query and the ANSWER table it produces.

The ANSWER table includes only one record, which identifies employee number 1 as the only employee who has managed every type of project for which customer number 1001 has ever contracted with your company.

If your database system contained information on customer orders, you might use the every set operator to identify customers who have ordered every piece of a particular set of luggage so that you can let them know about a new addition to the collection. If you were working with student information, you could use the every set operator to identify students who had taken every course required for graduation.

Figure 8-76 A Query Using the Every Set Operator

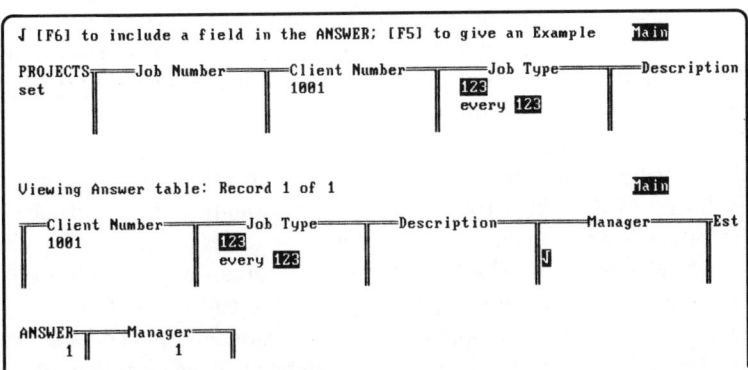

The Exactly Set Operator

The exactly set operator identifies groups containing at least one match for each record in the defined set, but no records that do not match a record in the defined set. The exactly set operator combines the selection conditions used by the only set operator and the every set operator. While every record in a group must match a record in the defined set, more than one record in the group can match the same record in the defined set.

For example, suppose you want to identify any clients who have contracted with your company for the same types of projects as client number 1010. Client number 1010 has expressed dissatisfaction with your company's services, so you want to talk to another customer who has used the same types of services, to get a second opinion. To define this query, first create a blank query form for the PROJECTS table and type **set** in the first column. Then, move to the Client Number field and type **1010**. Next, move to the Job Type field, press **[Example]**, and type **123**. This line defines a set that includes all the records that contain the entry 1010 in the Client Number field and sets up a link for these records based on the entries in the Job Type field. Next, press ↓ to move down to the next line of the query form and type **exactly**, press **[Example]**, and type **123** in the Job Type field. Finally, move to the Client Number field and press **[Check Mark]** to group on this field. This line of the query tells Paradox to select only those groups that include a match for every record in the defined set and not to include any records that do not match a record in the set. Figure 8-77 shows the completed query and the ANSWER table it will produce.

Figure 8-77 A Query Using the Exactly Set Operator

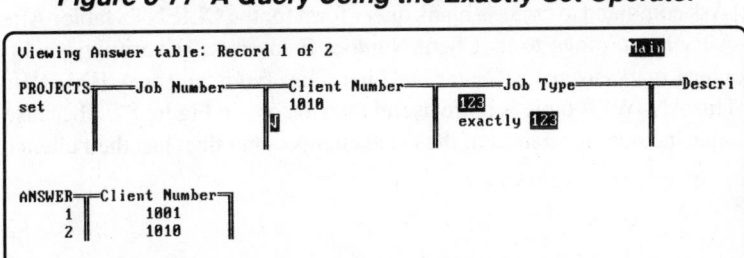

The ANSWER table includes two records, one for client number 1010 and one for 1001. ANSWER includes a record for client number 1010 because Paradox does not exclude the records in a defined set from the comparisons made by the set operator. Since the query was looking for those clients with the same Job Type entries as client number 1010, of course, client number 1010 meets this condition.

The exactly set operator can help you identify groups of records that are completely and exclusively linked to a defined set of records. For example, if your database system contained information about book orders, you could use the exactly set operator to identify customers with an intense but isolated interest in a certain area. Such a query could identify those customers who have purchased your entire collection of Wild West books, but no other books sold by your company. In a medical situation, you could use the exactly operator to identify those patients who who have exhibited all the symptoms of a particular disease but no additional symptoms.

Adding Group Information

In all of the examples we just used to demonstrate Paradox's set operators, the ANSWER tables contained only one field that identified the groups selected by the queries. For instance, the ANSWER table in our last example included only the Client Number field entries that identified clients who had contracted for the same types of jobs as client number 1010. Of course, this query would be even more useful if ANSWER listed the names of the two clients (which are stored in the CLIENTS table), along with their ID numbers. You can add information about the groups identified by set operator queries by using an example to join the group identifying fields to lookup tables that contain information about the groups.

An Example

For example, Figure 8-78 shows a modified version of the query in Figure 8-77, along with the ANSWER table this new query produces. An example in the Client Number field of the PROJECTS query form links that field to the Client Number field of the CLIENTS table. In addition to this linking example, the CLIENTS query form also includes check marks in the Last Name and First Name fields. As a result, the query includes the First Name and Last Name fields in the ANSWER table, along with the Client Number. The query fills these fields with information from CLIENTS records that correspond to Client Number field entries in the PROJECTS table. To add these new elements to the query in Figure 8-77, move the cursor to the second row in the Client Number column, press [Example], and type 456. Then, use the [Menu] Ask command to create a blank query form for the CLIENTS table. After adding this blank query form, move to its Client Number field, press [Example], and type 456. Then, place check marks in the Last Name and First Name fields, and press [Do-It!] to process the query. This ANSWER table is more useful than the one in Figure 8-77 because the new ANSWER table includes the names of the listed clients rather than just their client numbers.

Figure 8-78 Adding Group Information from a Lookup Table

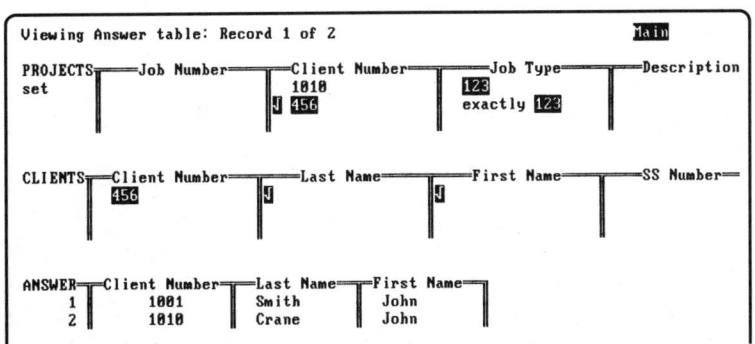

Omitting the Grouping Field

Often, the lookup information pertaining to groups identified by a set query is more useful than the field entries that actually identify the groups. For example, in our last query, you may be more interested in the names of the clients who have contracted for the same services as client number 1010 than the client numbers of those clients. Of course, if you don't want the Client Number field in the ANSWER table, you could process the query, then delete the Client Number field from the ANSWER table. However, this extra step is unnecessary because Paradox allows you to group on a field without including that field in the ANSWER table. In order to exclude a grouping field from the ANSWER table, you link the grouping field to the table that includes checked fields with the lookup information you want in ANSWER, just as we did in Figure 8-78. However, instead of using the [Check Mark] key to mark the grouping field, you press the [Group By] key ([Shift]-[F6]). Paradox identifies "Group By" fields with a reverse video *G* in the same spot where it places check, check plus, and check descending marks.

For example, suppose you wanted the set query in Figure 8-78 to group on the Client Number field in the PROJECTS table, but include only the corresponding First Name and Last Name fields from CLIENTS in the ANSWER table. To modify the query so that it does this, move the cursor to the Client Number field of the PROJECTS query form, and press **[Check Mark]** to remove the check mark that is currently in that field. Then, press **[Group By]**. At this point, a reverse video *G* will appear in front of the example in the Client Number field. After replacing the check mark with a Group By mark, press **[Do-It!]** to process the query. At this point, your screen should look like Figure 8-79 on the next page.

As you can see, the new ANSWER table contains the First Name and Last Name fields associated with clients 1001 and 1010, but not the client numbers. You could use the [Group By] key to add similar lookup information about the grouping fields in any of the examples we have discussed in this section on set operations.

Figure 8-79 Using the [Group By] Key

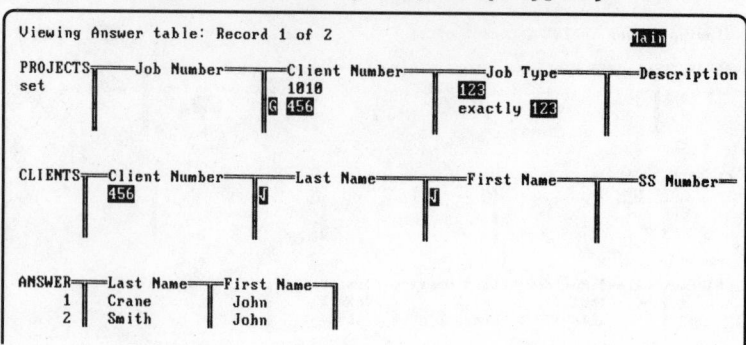

Conclusion

In this chapter, you've learned how to use examples in your queries. As you have seen, examples are extremely powerful tools that allow you to create relationships between the fields in your queries. You can use examples to make selections by comparing the entries in one field of a table to the entries in another field of that same table. You can use examples to relate the fields in two or more tables and create combined tables. You can also use examples in calc queries to make calculations on the entries in a table or set queries to compare the records in a table to a set of records in the same table or a different table.

Although you now know about the most important uses for examples, there are several other applications for these tools. Examples can be used in special queries, called insert queries, that insert the entries from the fields of one table into another table. You can also use examples with the [Menu] Modify MultiEntry Setup command to set up data entry systems for multiple tables. We'll look at these uses of examples in the next chapter.

Chapter **9**

Multitable Operations

In the previous chapters, you learned how to use queries to create new tables, and how to use examples to link related tables. In this chapter, we'll cover several commands that allow you to update one table by using the records in another table. We'll begin with a thorough discussion of the [Menu] Tools More Add command, which you've seen before. Then, we'll cover the [Menu] Tools More Subtract command, which allows you to subtract the records in one table from those in another. Next, we'll look at two related commands, [Menu] Modify MultiEntry and [Menu] Tools More MultiAdd, which allow you to divide the records in one table into two or more related tables. Finally, we'll look at Paradox's most flexible multitable tool, the insert query.

The [Menu] Tools More Add Command

The [Menu] Tools More Add command lets you add the records in one table to the records in another table with an identical structure. A primary use for the Add command is to incorporate data from several batches of tables into one master table. In addition, You can use this command to reinsert records that have been placed by the DataEntry command in a KEYVIOL table or by the Restructure command in a PROBLEMS table. You can also use the Add command to reinsert records that you have extracted with a query and then edited.

Basics

When you issue the [Menu] Tools More Add command, Paradox first prompts you for the name of the source table, which is the table that contains the records you want to add. Next, Paradox asks you to supply the name of the target table, which is the table to which you want to add records. Remember: The source and target tables must have identical structures.

What happens after you specify the source and target tables depends on the version of Paradox you are using and whether the target table is keyed. If the target table is not keyed, Paradox will immediately append the records from the source table to the target table below any records that are already in that table. If the target table is keyed, Paradox will offer you two options: NewEntries and Update. The effect of the Add command depends on which of these options you select. (Paradox 1.0 does not offer the NewEntries/Update options.)

Using Add with Non-keyed Tables

If the table to which you want to add records does not have a key field, Paradox will add the records in the source table to the target table as soon as you specify both table names and press ↵. Paradox will append the records from the source table to the target table below any records already in the target table.

For example, suppose you have created a table called TIME, which you use to maintain a record of how each employee spends his or her time. Figure 9-1 shows the structure of this table. Notice that it contains no key fields.

Figure 9-1 Structure for TIME Table

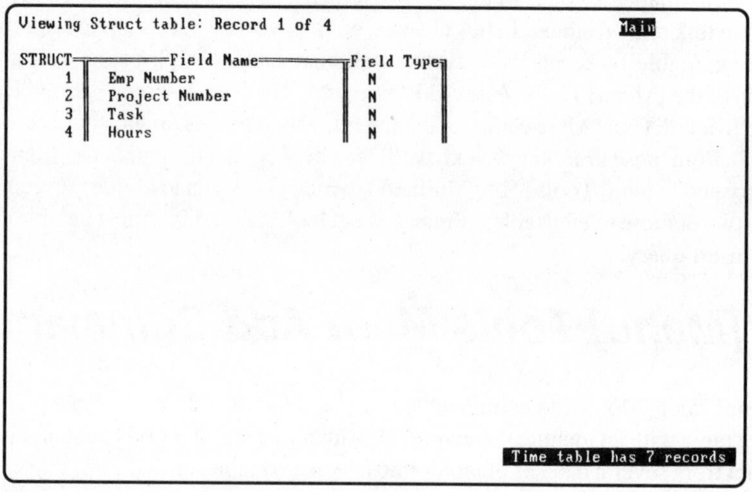

```
Viewing Struct table: Record 1 of 4                              Main

STRUCT            Field Name        Field Type
   1 ║ Emp Number              N
   2 ║ Project Number          N
   3 ║ Task                    N
   4 ║ Hours                   N




                                            Time table has 7 records
```

To simplify data entry, each employee keeps his or her own time records in a personal copy of the TIME table. At the end of each week, you consolidate the records from the individual employee tables into the TIME table. As you'll see, this is a perfect application for the Add command.

For example, suppose you want to add the contents of a table called JOHNTIME to the TIME table. Figure 9-2 shows the contents of JOHNTIME, and Figure 9-3 shows the current contents of TIME. To begin, issue the [**Menu**] **T**ools **M**ore **A**dd command. When Paradox asks for the name of the source table (the table that contains the records you want to add), type **JOHNTIME**. When Paradox asks you to identify the target table (the table to which you want to add the records), type **TIME**.

Figure 9-2 The JOHNTIME Table

```
Viewing Johntime table: Record 3 of 3                    Main

JOHNTIME═══Emp Number═══╤Project Number═══╤═══Task═══════╤═══Hours═══
   1    ║      3       ║      100        ║      8       ║      10
   2    ║      3       ║      115        ║      8       ║      20
   3    ║      3       ║      104        ║      5       ║      25
```

Figure 9-3 The TIME Table

```
Viewing Time table: Record 1 of 7                        Main

TIME═══╤═══Emp Number═══╤═══Project Number═══╤═══Task═══╤═══Hours═══
  1    ║      1         ║       100          ║    3    ║      8
  2    ║      1         ║       100          ║    5    ║     12
  3    ║      1         ║       100          ║    2    ║      6
  4    ║      1         ║       125          ║    1    ║      1
  5    ║      2         ║       100          ║    3    ║     24
  6    ║      2         ║       116          ║    5    ║      4
  7    ║      2         ║       110          ║    2    ║     40
```

When you press ↵, Paradox will display the message *Adding records from Johntime to Time*. When the records are added, Paradox will bring the TIME table (the table to which you added the records) into view. Figure 9-4 shows the TIME table with the records from JOHNTIME.

Figure 9-4 The Modified TIME Table

```
Viewing Time table: Record 1 of 10                       Main

TIME═══╤═══Emp Number═══╤Project Number═══╤═══Task═══╤═══Hours═══
  1    ║      1         ║     100         ║    3    ║      8
  2    ║      1         ║     100         ║    5    ║     12
  3    ║      1         ║     100         ║    2    ║      6
  4    ║      1         ║     125         ║    1    ║      1
  5    ║      2         ║     100         ║    3    ║     24
  6    ║      2         ║     116         ║    5    ║      4
  7    ║      2         ║     110         ║    2    ║     40
  8    ║      3         ║     100         ║    8    ║     10
  9    ║      3         ║     115         ║    8    ║     20
 10    ║      3         ║     104         ║    5    ║     25
```

Notes

The [Menu] Tools More Add command does not have any effect on the contents of the source table. The records that are in the table when you issue the command will be in the table when the command is completed. If you want to empty the source table after you have added its contents to the target table, you can use the [Menu] Tools More Empty command.

If the source and target tables do not have the same structures, Paradox will display the message *TABLENAME and TABLENAME have incompatible structures.* If you see this message, you should check the structures of the source and target tables to identify the incompatibility. For tables to have identical structures, they must have the same number of fields, and each field in the target table must be of the same type as the corresponding field in the source table. For instance, if the first field in the target table is an alphanumeric field, then the first field in the source table must be alphanumeric. If the third field in the target table is a numeric field, then the third field in the source table also must be numeric.

Although the Add command requires both tables to have the same structure, it does not care if the corresponding alphanumeric fields in the two tables have the same widths. If an alphanumeric field in the target table is shorter than the corresponding field in the source table, Paradox will trim the contents of that field as it adds the field to the target table.

Also, the Add command does not mind if the fields in the two tables have different names, as long as the two tables have the same structures. That is, as long as the source and target tables have the same types of fields, in the same order, you can add records from one to another, even if the names of the fields in the two tables are different.

The source and target tables do not need to be on the same disk or in the same directory. If one or both of the files are in a directory other than the default directory, you should indicate where the files are located when you specify the source and target table names. For example, suppose you want to add the contents of a table named MARYTIME, which is in the directory c:\paradox\data\mary to the table named TIME, which is in the default directory. When Paradox asks you to specify the name of the source table, you would type *c:\paradox\data\mary\marytime.* For another example, you would need to specify the disk drive if Mary submitted her time to you on a diskette. Insert the diskette into drive A and type *a:marytime* as the name of the source table.

Using Add with Keyed Tables

If the target table has one or more key fields, Paradox will present you with two options when you use the Add command: NewEntries and Update. The option you choose tells Paradox how to handle records from the source table with keys identical to existing records in the target table.

Remember, key field values must be unique—no two records are allowed to have the same key. If two records have the same key, you have a key violation. When you perform the [Menu] Tools More Add command, you must tell Paradox what to do about key violations. The NewEntries option tells Paradox to leave key violations out of the target table and add only source records with new keys. The Update option tells Paradox you want the source records to update target records; if there is a key violation, the source record will overwrite its counterpart.

If you are using Paradox 1.0, then you will not see these options. Instead, Paradox functions as if you selected the NewEntries option.

The NewEntries Option

If you choose the NewEntries option, Paradox will append the records in the source table to the target table below any records that are already in the target table. If key violations occur as a result of the Add command, Paradox will place those records in a KEYVIOL table. (We'll cover KEYVIOL tables and the Add command shortly.)

An Example

Suppose you have created a table called PROSPECT, which you use to collect the names and addresses of people who request information about your company's products. Figure 9-5 shows the structure of this table. Notice that the Prospect Number field is a key field.

Figure 9-5 Structure of PROSPECT

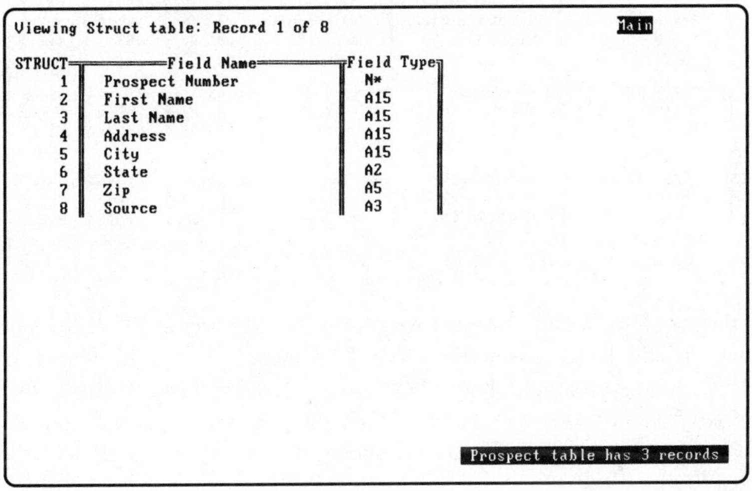

```
Viewing Struct table: Record 1 of 8                          Main

STRUCT══════════Field Name══════╦Field Type╗
    1 ║  Prospect Number         ║  N*       ║
    2 ║  First Name               ║  A15      ║
    3 ║  Last Name                ║  A15      ║
    4 ║  Address                  ║  A15      ║
    5 ║  City                     ║  A15      ║
    6 ║  State                    ║  A2       ║
    7 ║  Zip                      ║  A5       ║
    8 ║  Source                   ║  A3       ║




                              Prospect table has 3 records
```

Now, suppose that you have two employees, Mary and John, who answer the telephone and open mail. Both of these employees have their own copies of the PROSPECT table that contain the names they have collected. Mary's file is called FONEPROS and John's is called MAILPROS. Both FONEPROS and MAILPROS have the same structure as PROSPECT. (In fact, these tables could be created easily by borrowing the structure of the PROSPECT table.) At times, you must combine the records from these two files into one master PROSPECT table.

For example, PROSPECT, FONEPROS, and MAILPROS contain the records shown in Figure 9-6. You want to combine the records from FONEPROS and MAILPROS into PROSPECT. To begin, issue the **[Menu] T**ools **M**ore **A**dd command. When Paradox prompts you for the name of the source table, type **FONEPROS**. Then, when Paradox prompts you for the name of the target table, type **PROSPECT**.

Figure 9-6 Viewing PROSPECT, FONEPROS, and MAILPROS

```
Viewing Prospect table: Record 1 of 3                        Main

PROSPECT┬Prospect Number┬──First Name─┬──Last Name─┬──Address──────
   1    │      1        │ John        │ Smith      │ 111 Any Street
   2    │      2        │ Sally       │ Struthers  │ 999 Maple St.
   3    │      3        │ Mike        │ Murphy     │ 9876 Dixie Hy.


FONEPROS┬Prospect Number┬──First Name─┬──Last Name─┬──Address──────
   1    │      4        │ Jim         │ Morrison   │ 100 W. 73rd St.
   2    │      6        │ Fred        │ Foote      │ 123 Brattle St.


MAILPROS┬Prospect Number┬──First Name─┬──Last Name─┬──Address──────
   1    │      5        │ Bill        │ Johnson    │ 42 Old Rock Rd.
   2    │      7        │ Dave        │ Jones      │ 123 Yale Ct.
```

```
Viewing Prospect table: Record 1 of 3                        Main

─Last Name─┬──Address──────┬──City──────┬State┬─Zip──┬Source
 Smith     │ 111 Any Street│ Louisville │ KY  │ 40205│ WSJ
 Struthers │ 999 Maple St. │ Indianapolis│ IN │ 35001│ NYT
 Murphy    │ 9876 Dixie Hy.│ Radcliff   │ KY  │ 40322│ TEL

─Last Name─┬──Address──────┬──City──────┬State┬─Zip──┬Source
 Morrison  │ 100 W. 73rd St│ New York   │ NY  │ 10026│ NYT
 Foote     │ 123 Brattle St│ Cambridge  │ MA  │ 02165│ WSJ

─Last Name─┬──Address──────┬──City──────┬State┬─Zip──┬Source
 Johnson   │ 42 Old Rock Rd.│ Memphis   │ TN  │ 12345│ TEL
 Jones     │ 123 Yale Ct.  │ New Haven  │ CN  │ 98765│ NYT
```

When you press ↵, Paradox will present two options: New Entries and Update. Since, in this case, you want to add the records in the FONEPROS table to the records that are already in the PROSPECT table, you should choose NewEntries. Paradox then will display the message *Adding records from Fonepros to Prospect*. When the records are added, Paradox will bring the PROSPECT table into view. Figure 9-7 shows the PROSPECT table with the records from FONEPROS.

Figure 9-7 FONEPROS Records Added to PROSPECT

```
Viewing Prospect table: Record 1 of 5                        Main

PROSPECT┬Prospect Number┬──First Name─┬──Last Name─┬──Address──────
   1    │      1        │ John        │ Smith      │ 111 Any Street
   2    │      2        │ Sally       │ Struthers  │ 999 Maple St.
   3    │      3        │ Mike        │ Murphy     │ 9876 Dixie Hy.
   4    │      4        │ Jim         │ Morrison   │ 100 W. 73rd St.
   5    │      6        │ Fred        │ Foote      │ 123 Brattle St.
```

Now, to add the records from MAILPROS to PROSPECT, repeat the **[Menu] T**ools **M**ore **A**dd command, specify **MAILPROS** as the source table and **PROSPECT** as the target table. When you press ↵, Paradox will display the *Adding records...* message, add the records from MAILPROS to PROSPECT, and bring the PROSPECT table into view.

Figure 9-8 shows the PROSPECT table with the records from both FONEPROS and MAILPROS. Notice that Paradox has arranged the records in PROSPECT into ascending prospect number order. This occurs because the Prospect Number field in PROSPECT is a key field.

Figure 9-8 MAILPROS Records Added to PROSPECT

```
Viewing Prospect table: Record 1 of 7                          Main

PROSPECT┬Prospect Number┬═══First Name═══┬═══Last Name═══┬═══Address═══
    1   │       1       │     John       │    Smith      │  111 Any Street
    2   │       2       │     Sally      │    Struthers  │  999 Maple St.
    3   │       3       │     Mike       │    Murphy     │  9876 Dixie Hy.
    4   │       4       │     Jim        │    Morrison   │  100 W. 73rd St.
    5   │       5       │     Bill       │    Johnson    │  42 Old Rock Rd.
    6   │       6       │     Fred       │    Foote      │  123 Brattle St.
    7   │       7       │     Dave       │    Jones      │  123 Yale Ct.
```

Using Add to Overcome Key Violations

Another important use of the Add NewEntries command is to overcome key violation errors. For example, suppose you have used the [Menu] Modify DataEntry command to enter a few new records directly into the PROSPECT table. Figure 9-9 shows these entries in the ENTRY table. In making these entries, suppose you mistyped one prospect number. Instead of typing 10, the correct number, you typed 1, the number in the Prospect Number field of the first record in PROSPECT. Because of this typographical error, a key violation occurred when the [Menu] Entry command was executed, causing Paradox to enter one of the records from ENTRY in the KEYVIOL table shown in Figure 9-10 on the following page.

Figure 9-9 DataEntry for PROSPECT

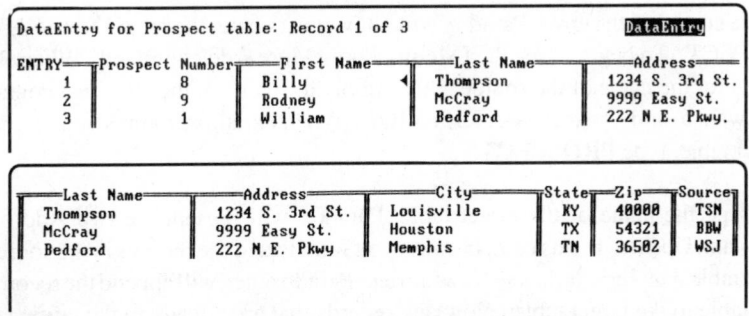

At this point, you need to edit the contents of the KEYVIOL table to eliminate the key conflict, then add the records from KEYVIOL to the target table. To correct the error in this example, bring KEYVIOL into view, press [Edit], move to the Prospect Number field, press [Backspace] to erase the erroneous entry, type 10, and press [Do-It!] [F2]. Figure 9-11 shows the corrected table.

Figure 9-10 The KEYVIOL Table

```
Viewing Keyviol table: Record 1 of 1                          Main
PROSPECT┰Prospect Number┰──First Name──┰──Last Name──┰──Address──
   1    │      1        │  John        │  Smith      │  111 Any Street
   2    │      2        │  Sally       │  Struthers  │  999 Maple St.
   3    │      3        │  Mike        │  Murphy     │  9876 Dixie Hy.
   4    │      4        │  Jim         │  Morrison   │  100 W. 73rd St.
   5    │      5        │  Bill        │  Johnson    │  42 Old Rock Rd.
   6    │      6        │  Fred        │  Foote      │  123 Brattle St.
   7    │      7        │  Dave        │  Jones      │  123 Yale Ct.
   8    │      8        │  Billy       │  Thompson   │  1234 S. 3rd St.
   9    │      9        │  Rodney      │  McCray     │  9999 Easy St.

KEYVIOL┰Prospect Number┰──First Name──┰──Last Name──┰──Address──
   1    │      1        │  William     │  Bedford    │  222 N.E. Pkwy
```

Figure 9-11 Correcting the KEYVIOL Table

```
Viewing Keyviol table: Record 1 of 1                          Main
PROSPECT┰Prospect Number┰──First Name──┰──Last Name──┰──Address──
   1    │      1        │  John        │  Smith      │  111 Any Street
   2    │      2        │  Sally       │  Struthers  │  999 Maple St.
   3    │      3        │  Mike        │  Murphy     │  9876 Dixie Hy.
   4    │      4        │  Jim         │  Morrison   │  100 W. 73rd St.
   5    │      5        │  Bill        │  Johnson    │  42 Old Rock Rd.
   6    │      6        │  Fred        │  Foote      │  123 Brattle St.
   7    │      7        │  Dave        │  Jones      │  123 Yale Ct.
   8    │      8        │  Billy       │  Thompson   │  1234 S. 3rd St.
   9    │      9        │  Rodney      │  McCray     │  9999 Easy St.

KEYVIOL┰Prospect Number┰──First Name──┰──Last Name──┰──Address──
   1    │     10        │  William     │  Bedford    │  222 N.E. Pkwy
```

Once you've corrected the error, Paradox will allow you to enter the record from KEYVIOL into PROSPECT. To begin, issue the **[Menu] T**ools **M**ore Add command. When Paradox prompts you for the name of the source table, supply the name of the table that contains the record you want to add—in this case, **KEYVIOL**. When Paradox prompts you for the name of the target table, type **PROSPECT**.

After you type the name of the target table, Paradox will present the two Add options: NewEntries and Update. In this case, because you want to add the records in the source table to the target table, you should choose NewEntries. Paradox then will append the records from the source table to the target table below any records that are already in the target table.

Figure 9-12 shows the PROSPECT table after the Add command is completed. As you can see, the single record from KEYVIOL has been added to the records in PROSPECT.

Figure 9-12 The Modified PROSPECT Table

```
Viewing Prospect table: Record 1 of 10                        Main

PROSPECT Prospect Number    First Name        Last Name        Address
      1          1          John             Smith           111 Any Street
      2          2          Sally            Struthers       999 Maple St.
      3          3          Mike             Murphy          9876 Dixie Hy.
      4          4          Jim              Morrison        100 W. 73rd St.
      5          5          Bill             Johnson         42 Old Rock Rd.
      6          6          Fred             Foote           123 Brattle St.
      7          7          Dave             Jones           123 Yale Ct.
      8          8          Billy            Thompson        1234 S. 3rd St.
      9          9          Rodney           McCray          9999 Easy St.
     10         10          William          Bedford         222 N.E. Pkwy
```

The Add NewEntries Command and Key Fields

It is possible that key violations will occur when you use the Add NewEntries command. A key violation occurs when the target table has a key field, and a record in the source table has a key field entry that is the same as a key field entry in the target table. When this occurs, Paradox will enter that record in a KEYVIOL table, but not in the target table. (Whether the source table has a key field has no effect on the command.)

For example, suppose you want to add the records from the table FONEPROS, shown in Figure 9-13, to PROSPECT. Notice that the second record in FONEPROS has a key field entry that conflicts with the key field entry for the fifth record in PROSPECT. When you use the [Menu] Tools More Add NewEntries command to add the records in FONEPROS to PROSPECT, Paradox will not add the second record, but instead will enter that record into a KEYVIOL table. Figure 9-14 on the next page shows this table. Of course, the first record from FONEPROS will be added to PROSPECT properly.

Figure 9-13 The FONEPROS Table

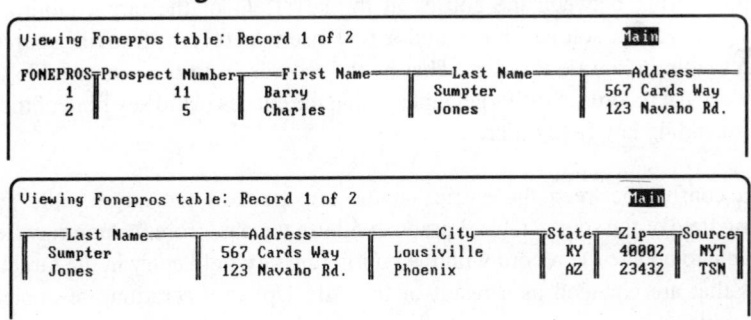

```
Viewing Fonepros table: Record 1 of 2                         Main

FONEPROS Prospect Number    First Name        Last Name        Address
      1         11          Barry            Sumpter         567 Cards Way
      2          5          Charles          Jones           123 Navaho Rd.
```

```
Viewing Fonepros table: Record 1 of 2                         Main

     Last Name        Address         City        State  Zip      Source
     Sumpter          567 Cards Way   Lousiville    KY   40002     NYT
     Jones            123 Navaho Rd.  Phoenix       AZ   23432     TSM
```

Figure 9-14 The New PROSPECT and KEYVIOL Tables

If a key violation occurs, you'll need to edit the entries in the KEYVIOL table to resolve the conflicts, then use the Add command to add the records in the KEYVIOL table to the appropriate target table. You'd have to edit the Prospect Number field of the record in KEYVIOL to remove the conflict, then use the Add command to add that record from KEYVIOL to PROSPECT.

The Update Option

If you use the [Menu] Tools More Add command to add records to a keyed table, and choose the Update option, Paradox will use the records in the source table to update the records in the target table. (Paradox 1.0 doesn't offer an Update option or a command that can duplicate its effects.) Exactly how this option works depends on whether there are records in the source table containing key field entries that conflict with key field entries in the target table.

If there is no conflict between the entries in the key field of the target table and the corresponding field of the source table, Paradox will insert the records from the source table into the target table in key field order. That is, the records from the source table will be inserted between the records in the target table so that the entries in the key field of the target table are in ascending key field order.

If there is a conflict between the entries in the key field of the target table and the corresponding field of the source table, Paradox will use the data from the non-key fields of the source table to update the record with the conflicting key field entry in the target table. Any records that are changed as a result of the Add Update operation are copied to a CHANGED table.

An Example: Using Update to Edit Tables

In Chapters 2 and 3, you learned about the [Menu] Modify Edit command, which allows you to edit the contents in your tables. In those chapters, we cautioned you that the Edit command is one of the few Paradox commands that allow you to directly affect the entries in your tables. Other commands operate on intermediate tables, which help to protect the integrity of your data. For example, the DataEntry command enters records into a table called ENTRY. Only when you press [Do-It!] are those records transferred to the permanent table.

Thanks to the Update option, you can use a similar approach to editing your tables. Instead of editing your primary table directly, you can use a query to copy all of the records in a table to an ANSWER table, edit the records in that table, and then use the Add Update command to update the original table.

For example, suppose you want to make a few changes to the PROSPECT table. Rather than editing the table directly, you decide to copy the records from PROSPECT into an ANSWER table, edit the ANSWER table, then use the [Menu] Tools More Add Update command to add the records from ANSWER back into PROSPECT.

To begin, use the [Menu] Ask command to create a query form for PROSPECT. When the form appears, press [Check Mark] to select every field. When you press [Do-It!] to process this table, Paradox will copy every record from PROSPECT into an ANSWER table. Figure 9-15 shows this table.

Figure 9-15 Creating ANSWER from PROSPECT

```
Viewing Answer table: Record 1 of 11                          Main

PROSPECT┬─Prospect Number───────First Name───────Last Name───────Address═══
        ║                    ║              ║              ║
        ║                    ║              ║              ║



ANSWER─┬Prospect Number┬──────First Name──────┬─────Last Name─────┬────Address══════
   1   ║      1          John              Smith            111 Any Street
   2   ║      2          Sally             Struthers        999 Maple St.
   3   ║      3          Mike              Murphy           9876 Dixie Hy.
   4   ║      4          Jim               Morrison         100 W. 73rd St.
   5   ║      5          Bill              Johnson          42 Old Rock Rd.
   6   ║      6          Fred              Foote            123 Brattle St.
   7   ║      7          Dave              Jones            123 Yale Ct.
   8   ║      8          Billy             Thompson         1234 S. 3rd St.
   9   ║      9          Rodney            McCray           9999 Easy St.
  10   ║     10          William           Bedford          222 N.E. Pkwy.
  11   ║     11          Barry             Sumpter          567 Cards Way
```

Once Paradox has created the ANSWER table, you can press [Edit] to enter the Edit mode and then make the following changes: (1) Change the First Name field entry for record 7 from *Dave* to **David**; (2) Change the Address field entry for record 1 from *111 Any Street* to **555 Main Street**; and (3) Add a record for **Guy Greene, 123 Park Place, Louisville, KY 40205,** source **CJT**, prospect number **12**.

When you have made these changes, press [Do-It!] to process the changes and return to the View mode. Figure 9-16 shows the edited ANSWER table.

Figure 9-16 The Edited ANSWER Table

```
Viewing Answer table: Record 1 of 12                              Main
ANSWER┬Prospect Number┬───First Name───┬───Last Name───┬───Address───
   1  │      1        │ John           │ Smith         │ 555 Main Street
   2  │      2        │ Sally          │ Struthers     │ 999 Maple St.
   3  │      3        │ Mike           │ Murphy        │ 9876 Dixie Hy.
   4  │      4        │ Jim            │ Morrison      │ 100 W. 73rd St.
   5  │      5        │ Bill           │ Johnson       │ 42 Old Rock Rd.
   6  │      6        │ Fred           │ Foote         │ 123 Brattle St.
   7  │      7        │ David          │ Jones         │ 123 Yale Ct.
   8  │      8        │ Billy          │ Thompson      │ 1234 S. 3rd St.
   9  │      9        │ Rodney         │ McCray        │ 9999 Easy St.
  10  │     10        │ William        │ Bedford       │ 222 N.E. Pkwy.
  11  │     11        │ Barry          │ Sumpter       │ 567 Cards Way
  12  │     12        │ Guy            │ Greene        │ 123 Park Place
```

To use the ANSWER table to update PROSPECT, issue the [Menu] Tools More Add command and specify ANSWER as the source table and PROSPECT as the target table. Because you want to use the records in ANSWER to update PROSPECT, you should choose Update when Paradox presents the NewEntries and Update options.

When you select Update, Paradox will use the records in ANSWER to update PROSPECT, copy any changed records from PROSPECT to a CHANGED table, and display both the CHANGED table and the new PROSPECT table. As it does these things, Paradox will display the message *Updating from Answer to Prospect* in the lower-right corner of the screen. Figure 9-17 shows the screen after Paradox completes the command.

Figure 9-17 The CHANGED Table

```
Viewing Prospect table: Record 1 of 12                           Main  =▼
PROSPECT┬Prospect Number┬───First Name───┬───Last Name───┬───Address───
    1   │      1        │ John           │ Smith         │ 555 Main Street
    2   │      2        │ Sally          │ Struthers     │ 999 Maple St.
    3   │      3        │ Mike           │ Murphy        │ 9876 Dixie Hy.
    4   │      4        │ Jim            │ Morrison      │ 100 W. 73rd St.
    5   │      5        │ Bill           │ Johnson       │ 42 Old Rock Rd.
    6   │      6        │ Fred           │ Foote         │ 123 Brattle St.
    7   │      7        │ David          │ Jones         │ 123 Yale Ct.
    8   │      8        │ Billy          │ Thompson      │ 1234 S. 3rd St.
    9   │      9        │ Rodney         │ McCray        │ 9999 Easy St.
   10   │     10        │ William        │ Bedford       │ 222 N.E. Pkwy.
   11   │     11        │ Barry          │ Sumpter       │ 567 Cards Way
   12   │     12        │ Guy            │ Greene        │ 123 Park Place

CHANGED┬Prospect Number┬───First Name───┬───Last Name───┬───Address───
    1   │      1        │ John           │ Smith         │ 111 Any Street
    2   │      2        │ Sally          │ Struthers     │ 999 Maple St.
    3   │      3        │ Mike           │ Murphy        │ 9876 Dixie Hy.
    4   │      4        │ Jim            │ Morrison      │ 100 W. 73rd St.
    5   │      5        │ Bill           │ Johnson       │ 42 Old Rock Rd.
    6   │      6        │ Fred           │ Foote         │ 123 Brattle St.
    7   │      7        │ Dave           │ Jones         │ 123 Yale Ct.
```

As you can see, the changes you made to the ANSWER table have now been brought into the PROSPECT table. For example, notice that the Address field entry for record number 1 in PROSPECT is now *555 Main Street*, not *111 Any Street*. Also notice that the First Name field entry for record number 7 is now *David*, not *Dave*.

Here's what happened: When Paradox processed the Add command, it found records in PROSPECT that had the same key field entry as the records you changed in ANSWER. Since you selected the Update option, Paradox used the entries from ANSWER to update, or change, the entries in the corresponding records in PROSPECT.

In addition, notice that Paradox has added to PROSPECT the new record you added to ANSWER. Because the entry in the Prospect Number field of this new record did not conflict with the Prospect Number field entry for any record in PROSPECT, Paradox simply added it to PROSPECT.

Although you cannot see them all in Figure 9-17, the CHANGED table includes every record from the original PROSPECT table. Because there was a record in ANSWER for every record in PROSPECT, Paradox updated every record in PROSPECT when you issued the Add Update command. Of course, since most of the records in ANSWER were identical to the corresponding records in PROSPECT, most of the records in PROSPECT were not really altered by the Add Update command. As far as Paradox is concerned, however, all the records in PROSPECT were altered, so it copied all the records to CHANGED.

Although this method of editing takes a bit more effort than just pressing the [Edit] key, it is far safer. For one thing, no changes are made to the main table until you issue the [Menu] Tools More Add Update command. This means that if you make an error in editing, you can just start over without risking your data. Even after you have used the Add Update command, the records from the main table that were changed will appear in a CHANGED table. This means that you can reverse the effects of the edit even after you use the Add command.

The [Menu] Tools More Subtract Command

The [Menu] Tools More Subtract command allows you to "subtract" one table from another table with the same structure. When you subtract one table from another, Paradox will delete from the target table all of the records that also appear in the source table. In other words, this command allows you to delete from one table all of the records it has in common with another table of identical structure. As you might expect, this command is the opposite of the [Menu] Tools More Add command.

An Example

Suppose you have created the PROSPECT table shown in the previous examples. After you do a few promotional mailings, you receive requests from people who want to remove their names from the prospect list. Therefore, you need to remove these names from PROSPECT.

To process these requests, you could create a new table, called REMOVE, that has the same structure as PROSPECT. (You could create this table easily by issuing the [Menu] Create command, specifying the name REMOVE, pressing [Menu] again, choosing the Borrow option, and specifying the name of the table whose structure you want to borrow: PROS-PECT. You could also create the table using a query.) Once you have created the table, you should enter the records shown in Figure 9-18. These are the records for the individuals who asked to be removed from your list.

Figure 9-18 The REMOVE Table

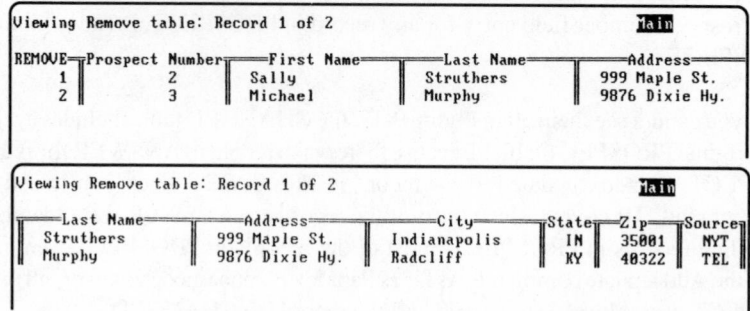

Once the records are in REMOVE, you can use the [Menu] Tools More Subtract command to remove the names from PROSPECT. When Paradox prompts you for the name of the table that contains the records you want to subtract, type **REMOVE** and press ↵. Then, when Paradox prompts you for the name of the table from which you want to remove records, type **PROSPECT**.

When you press ↵, Paradox will display the message *Subtracting Remove from Prospect* and will delete from PROSPECT every record for which there is an identical record in REMOVE. Then, Paradox will bring the revised PROSPECT table into view, as shown in Figure 9-19.

Figure 9-19 The Modified PROSPECT Table

```
Viewing Prospect table: Record 1 of 10                          Main

PROSPECT╤Prospect Number╤═══First Name══╤═══Last Name══╤═══Address═══
    1  ║       1     ║  John         ║  Smith        ║ 555 Main Street
    2  ║       4     ║  Jim          ║  Morrison     ║ 100 W. 73rd St.
    3  ║       5     ║  Bill         ║  Johnson      ║ 42 Old Rock Rd.
    4  ║       6     ║  Fred         ║  Foote        ║ 123 Brattle St.
    5  ║       7     ║  David        ║  Jones        ║ 123 Yale Ct.
    6  ║       8     ║  Billy        ║  Thompson     ║ 1234 S. 3rd St.
    7  ║       9     ║  Rodney       ║  McCray       ║ 9999 Easy St.
    8  ║      10     ║  William      ║  Bedford      ║ 222 N.E. Pkwy.
    9  ║      11     ║  Barry        ║  Sumpter      ║ 567 Cards Way
   10  ║      12     ║  Guy          ║  Greene       ║ 123 Park Place
```

Notes

If you attempt to use the Subtract command on tables that do not have the same structure, Paradox will display the message *TABLENAME and TABLENAME have incompatible struc-tures.* If you see this message, you should check the structures of the tables to identify the incompatibility. As with the Add command, for tables to have identical structures, they must have the same number of fields, and each field in the target table must be of the same type as the corresponding field in the source table. Like the Add command, Subtract does not care about the width of alphanumeric fields, nor about the names of the fields in the two tables.

The source and target tables do not need to be on the same disk or directory. If one or both of the files are in a directory other than the default directory, you should specify where the files are located when you specify the source and target table names.

Just like Tools More Add, the Tools More Subtract command functions differently depending on whether the target table is keyed. If the target table is non-keyed, the Subtract command will delete only records that are identical to records in the source table. If a record in the source table is similar but not identical to a record in the target table, that record will not be removed.

If the target table is a keyed table, however, things work a bit differently. In that event, Paradox will subtract any record in the target table with a key field entry that is the same as a key field entry of a record in the source table—even if the other fields in the two records are not identical.

For example, look at the second record in the REMOVE table in Figure 9-18. Notice that this record is identical to the third record in PROSPECT in Figure 9-17, except that the First Name field entry for this record in REMOVE is *Michael*, and the First Name field entry for the corresponding record in PROSPECT is *Mike*. When you used the Subtract command to subtract REMOVE from PROSPECT, Paradox removed the record for Mike Murphy, as shown in Figure 9-19. Because PROSPECT is a keyed table, Paradox used the record in REMOVE to delete the similar record in PROSPECT, even though these two records are not identical. Had both REMOVE and PROSPECT been non-keyed tables, however, Paradox would not have deleted the record for Mike Murphy from PROSPECT.

The [Menu] Tools More Subtract command has no effect on the contents of the source table (the table that contains the records you want to subtract). For instance, in the example, the source table REMOVE contains two records before you issue the [Menu] Tools More Subtract command. After you issue the command, this table will still contain two records.

MultiEntry and MultiAdd

Sooner or later in your work with Paradox, you will encounter an application that requires you to enter information into two tables through a single form. This will be especially true if you organize your data into groups of related normal tables. While Paradox 3 lets you create multitable forms, earlier releases attach every form to a single table. However, there is a way to enter data into two tables through a single form in most of the earlier releases. Two commands, [Menu] Modify MultiEntry and [Menu] Tools More MultiAdd, let you do this quickly and easily.

Paradox 1.0 does not offer either of these commands. If you are using Paradox 1.0, you must use insert queries to achieve this same result. (We'll show you how to use insert queries in the next section.) Paradox 3 does include the MultiEntry and MultiAdd commands, even though the multitable form capability added to Release 3 makes them all but obsolete. (We looked at multitable forms in Chapter 4.) The retention of these commands lets you use multitable applications you developed with earlier releases without modifying them to configure to Paradox 3. The MultiAdd command does have some valuable uses with Release 3, which we will discuss in this chapter.

The [Menu] Modify MultiEntry Command

The [Menu] Modify MultiEntry command makes it easy to enter data into two or more tables at one time. In fact, this command is very similar to the [Menu] Modify DataEntry command, except that it is used to enter data into more than one table at once.

The MultiEntry command offers two options: Setup and Entry. The Setup option lets you create two special tables, a source table and a map table, that enable you to enter data into two or more tables through the same form. The source table includes all of the relevant fields from the tables into which you want to make entries (we'll call these the target tables). The map table tells Paradox how to distribute the data from the source table into the target tables.

The Entry option lets you use the multitable system you've created with Setup to enter data into the target tables through the source table. When you use this command to enter data into the source table, then press [Do-It!], Paradox will distribute the data to the target tables automatically, using the relationships that are defined by the map table.

An Example

Suppose you have created the two tables whose structures are shown in Figures 9-20 and 9-21. The first table, CUSTOMER, is used to record the name, address, and so on, of your customers. Notice that the Cust Number field in this table is a key field. The second table, ORDER, records the information about what was ordered.

These two tables provide an excellent example of a normalized database. Rather than storing all the information about each order and each customer in one huge table, the data is stored in two separate, but related, tables. In this case, the tables are related on the Cust Number field. Because the tables are separate, the data is stored efficiently. Because they are related, it is easy to reconstruct the data, which facilitates many tasks, such as looking at all of the orders that relate to a particular customer.

The problem with normalized table groups like this one is that you will usually want to enter data into all of the tables in the group at once. For example, in this case, you want to enter order and customer information into the system at the same time whenever you receive an order. Without the MultiEntry command, you would need to enter the data twice, in one table at a time. Thanks to the MultiEntry command, however, you can do the whole job in one step.

Figure 9-20 Structure of CUSTOMER

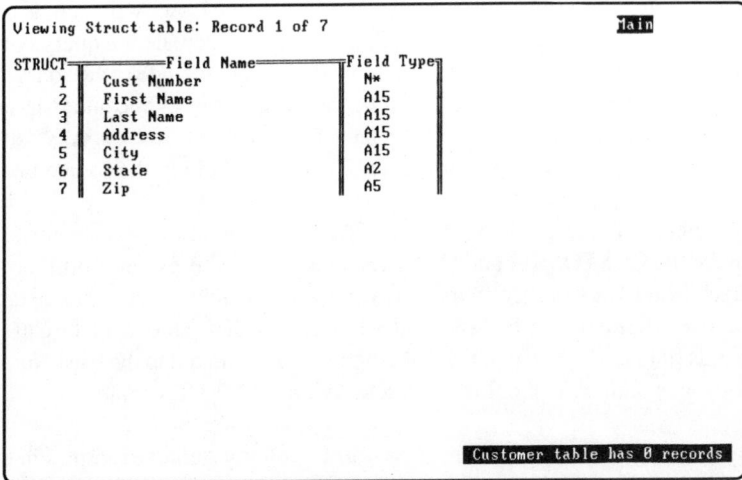

```
Viewing Struct table: Record 1 of 7                              Main
STRUCT          Field Name          Field Type
     1     Cust Number                 N*
     2     First Name                  A15
     3     Last Name                   A15
     4     Address                     A15
     5     City                        A15
     6     State                       A2
     7     Zip                         A5




                                            Customer table has 0 records
```

Figure 9-21 Structure of ORDER

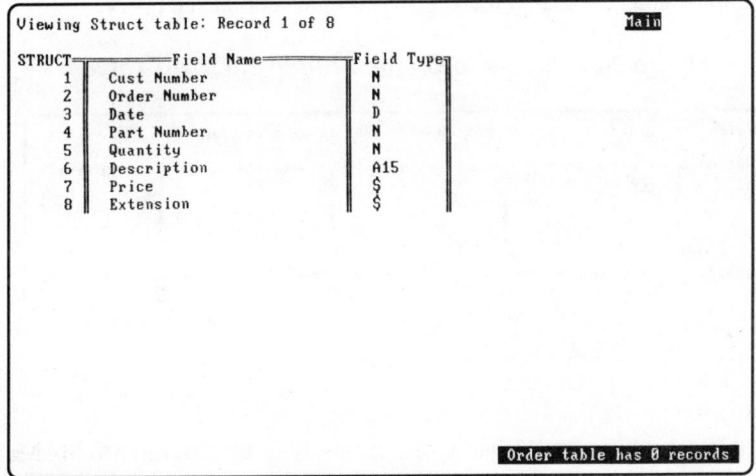

```
Viewing Struct table: Record 1 of 8                              Main
STRUCT          Field Name          Field Type
     1     Cust Number                 N
     2     Order Number                N
     3     Date                        D
     4     Part Number                 N
     5     Quantity                    N
     6     Description                 A15
     7     Price                       $
     8     Extension                   $




                                            Order table has 0 records
```

Creating the Source and Map Tables

To begin, you must create the source and map tables. First, you construct a query on the target
tables that tells Paradox which fields from each table should be included in the source table
and how the data from the source table should be divided among the target tables. Then, you
must issue the [Menu] Modify MultiEntry Setup command, inspect the query, and create the
source and map tables.

The query you use to create the source and map tables should include a query form for every table into which you want to make entries. In the example, the query will include two query forms: one for CUSTOMER and one for ORDER. Once you create the query, you should select every field in both query forms that you want Paradox to include in the source and map tables. Any field you select in the query will be included in the source and map tables. In addition, you should use examples to link the related fields in the two tables. Any pair of fields that you link with examples will be represented by a single field in the source table.

To create the query in the example, first use the [Menu] Ask command to create new, blank query forms for the CUSTOMER and ORDER tables. When these query forms are in view, use the [Check Mark] key to specify the fields you want to include in the source table. You should select every field in CUSTOMER and every field in ORDER except the Cust Number field. Since this field is selected in CUSTOMER and will be linked to the Cust Number field in ORDER by an example, it should not be selected in the ORDER table.

Once you have selected the fields in the query forms, you must enter examples in the forms that tell Paradox on which fields to relate the ORDER and CUSTOMER tables. To do this, move to the Cust Number field in CUSTOMER, press [Example], and type 123. Next, press [Down Image] to move down to the ORDER query form, move to the Cust Number field, press [Example], and type 123. Figure 9-22 shows the completed query.

Figure 9-22 Query to Create Source and Map Tables

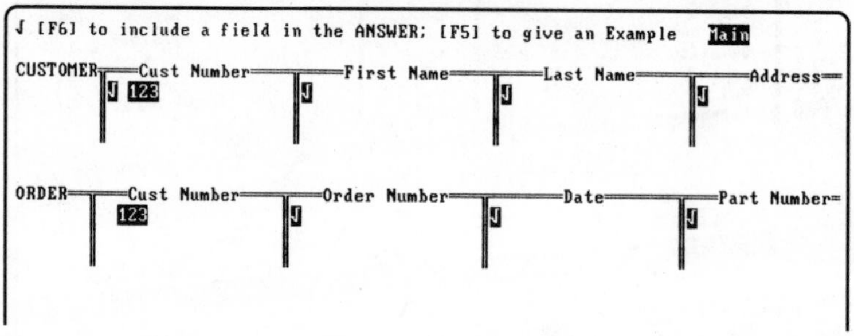

Now, you are ready to process the query. To do this, issue the [Menu] Modify MultiEntry Setup command, which will use the active query to create the source and map tables. When you issue the command, Paradox will prompt you to enter the name of the source and map tables. In the example, we'll use the name NEWORD for the source table and ORDMAP for the map table.

When you press ↵ after entering the map table name, Paradox will create the source table NEWORD and the map table ORDMAP. Figure 9-23 shows the screen after the command is completed. Figure 9-24 shows the structure of the source table NEWORD, and Figure 9-25 on page 374 shows the structure of the map table ORDMAP. Both the source table and the map table are regular, permanent Paradox tables.

Figure 9-23 The Map Table ORDMAP

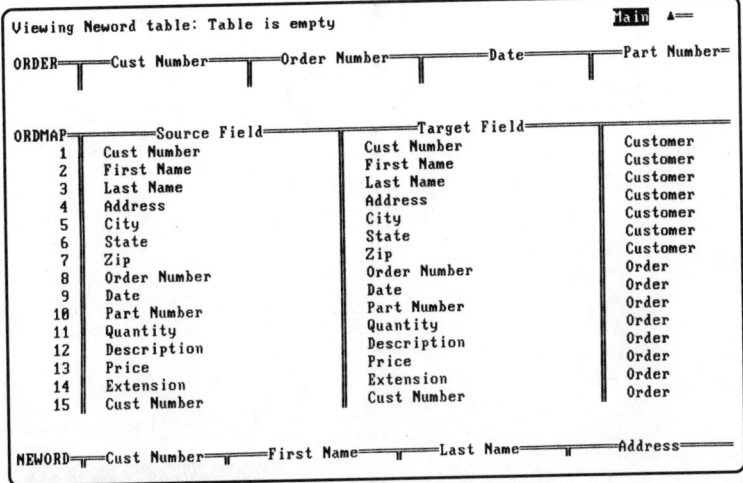

Figure 9-24 Structure of the Source Table NEWORD

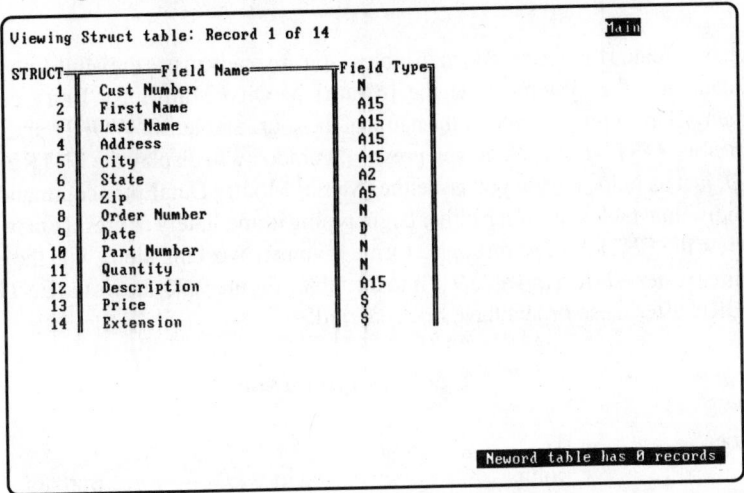

You will enter your data into the MultiEntry system through the source table. Notice that the source table includes all of the fields from the two tables ORDER and CUSTOMER. In fact, the source table has the same structure as the ANSWER table Paradox would create if you processed the query in Figure 9-22 with the [Do-It!] key.

The map table tells Paradox how to distribute entries from the source table to the target tables. You will notice that the map table ORDMAP has three fields: Source Field, Target Field, and Target Table. All map tables share this structure. Source Field lists each of the fields in the source table. Target Field and Target Table identify the target table (CUSTOMER or ORDER) and the field to which the contents of that field should be distributed.

Figure 9-25 Structure of the Map Table ORDMAP

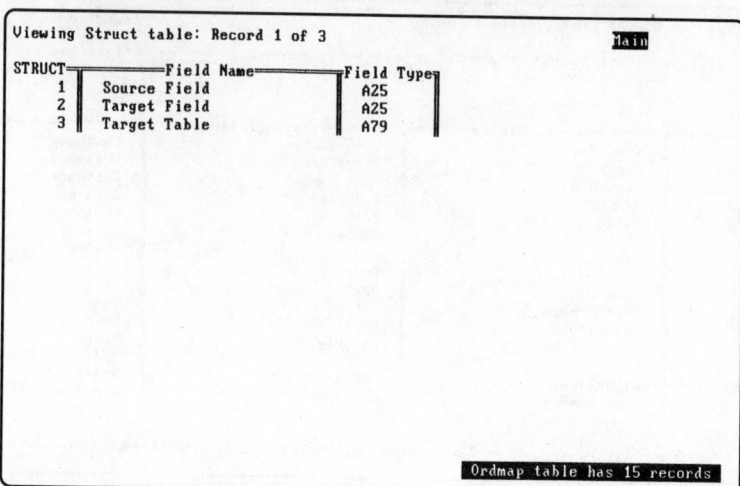

```
Viewing Struct table: Record 1 of 3                        Main

STRUCT          Field Name          Field Type
     1    Source Field                 A25
     2    Target Field                 A25
     3    Target Table                 A79




                                          Ordmap table has 15 records
```

Entering Data

Once you have created the source and map tables, you are ready to use the MultiEntry system. To enter data into the system, issue the **[Menu]** **M**odify **M**ultiEntry **E**ntry command. Paradox then will prompt you to enter the name of the source table, **NEWORD**, and the name of the map table, **ORDMAP**. When you press ↵, Paradox will display the ENTRY table for NEWORD, just as it does when you issue the [Menu] Modify DataEntry command to enter data into individual tables. You can either begin typing immediately or press **[Form Toggle]** ([F7]) to view the ENTRY table through a form. If you are working along with the example, enter the three orders shown in Table 9-1 into the table. Figure 9-26 shows the ENTRY table for NEWORD after these orders have been entered.

Table 9-1 Sample Data

Cust Number	1	2	3
First Name	John	David	Barbara
Last Name	Smith	Jones	Williams
Address	111 Main St.	1234 Elm St.	321 4th St.
City	Peru	Pikeville	New York
State	IN	KY	NY
Zip	35710	40999	10001
Order Number	100	101	102
Date	11/22/88	11/23/88	11/24/88
Part Number	1234	1000	2000
Quantity	4	1	2
Description	Red Widget	Blue Wombat	Brown Bat
Price	$100.00	$50.00	$75.00
Extension	$400.00	$50.00	$150.00

Figure 9-26 DataEntry for NEWORD

```
DataEntry for Neword table: Record 1 of 3                    DataEntry

ENTRY     Cust Number      First Name      Last Name      Address
  1          1             John            Smith          111 Main St.
  2          2             David           Jones          1234 Elm St.
  3          3             Barbara         Williams       321 4th St.
```

Distributing the Data

Once you have entered the data, press **[Do-It!]**. Paradox will automatically distribute the data to the appropriate fields in the CUSTOMER and ORDER tables. At the same time, the message *Adding records from Entry to targets in map table Ordmap* will appear at the bottom of the screen. Figure 9-27 shows the resulting tables.

Figure 9-27 The CUSTOMER and ORDER Tables

```
Viewing Order table: Record 1 of 3                          Main

CUSTOMER   Cust Number     First Name      Last Name      Address
   1          1            John            Smith          111 Main St.
   2          2            David           Jones          1234 Elm St.
   3          3            Barbara         Williams       321 4th St


ORDER     Cust Number    Order Number     Date          Part Number   Quanti
   1         1              100            11/22/88        1234          4
   2         2              101            11/23/88        1000          1
   3         3              102            11/24/88        2000          2
```

Paradox uses the map table to distribute the records from the source table to the target tables. When you press [Do-It!], Paradox will copy the entries from each field of the source table to the target tables, using the relationships defined in the map table. For instance, the map table tells Paradox that the First Name field in the source table NEWORD is related to the First Name field of the target table CUSTOMER.

Notes

There are several fine points you should keep in mind when you use the MultiEntry command. We will cover these points in this section.

Creating the Map and Source Tables

When you use the MultiEntry command to create a source table, Paradox expects that you will select only one occurrence of any field you use to relate the two tables. The fields you link with examples in the query form will receive data from a single field in the source table. In the example, we used the Cust Number field to relate the two tables. Because we entered examples in this field in both tables, Paradox expected only one occurrence to be selected. In fact, if you selected both Cust Number fields, Paradox would return the message *Only one use of 123 example element may be check-marked.*

Although only one occurrence of the Cust Number field is selected in the query, and the Cust Number field occurs only once in the source table, notice that the map table includes two Cust Number fields. The first occurrence is linked to the Cust Number field in the CUSTOMER target table, and the second is linked to the Cust Number field in the ORDER table.

In addition, the query you use to create the source and map tables can contain only check marks and examples. You cannot enter any selection conditions or special operators like delete, insert, calc, or changeto in the query.

You can use any name you want for the source and map tables. However, we suggest that you choose names that will make it easy to remember that the two tables are related. For instance, the names NEWORD and ORDMAP in the example make it easy to remember that these tables are designed to work together.

If you choose a name for either table that has already been assigned to a table, Paradox will ask whether you want to replace the existing table with the new one, or cancel the name you have selected and choose a new name.

Although you will nearly always use a query and the [Menu] Modify MultiEntry Setup command to define the source table and the map table, you don't need to. If you wish, you can create these tables with the [Menu] Modify Create command. Keep in mind that all map tables have the same three fields and include one record for each field in both target tables.

More Than Two Tables

You can use the MultiEntry command to enter data into more than two related tables. As in the two-table example, you would begin by creating a source table and a map table for the MultiEntry system. The query you use to create these tables should include query forms for all of the target tables. Each query form should include an example that tells Paradox how to relate the data in the table system.

Once you've created a source and map table, the process of using MultiEntry for a three-or-more-table system is identical to the process demonstrated in the previous example.

Reusing the MultiEntry System

After distributing the data to the target tables, Paradox empties the source table and saves it as a regular table. The map table is also saved as a regular Paradox table. You can reuse these tables as many times as you want. If you want to reuse a MultiEntry system that you have previously defined, you don't need to redefine the source and map tables. Instead, you can simply issue the [Menu] Modify MultiEntry Entry command, specify the source and map tables you want to use, and begin entering data.

It is important to note that the source and map tables are *not* part of the family of tables upon which they are based. If you restructure the target tables, the change will not be passed through to the source and map tables. If you do restructure a target table, you may also need to create a new query to redefine the source and map tables.

The Entry Menu

If you press [Menu] while you are entering records using the [Menu] Modify MultiEntry Entry command, Paradox will display the MultiEntry menu shown in Figure 9-28. This menu is identical to the menu you see when you press [Menu] while entering records using the standard [Menu] Modify DataEntry command.

Figure 9-28 The MultiEntry Menu

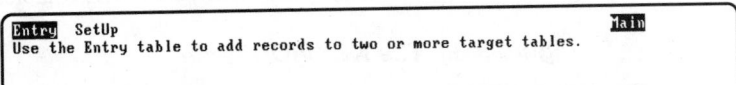

```
Entry  SetUp                                                        Main
Use the Entry table to add records to two or more target tables.
```

The MultiEntry Command and Key Fields

If one or more of the target tables have key fields, it is possible that key violation errors will occur when you use the MultiEntry command. A key violation occurs when a record that you enter through the source table has a key field entry that is the same as a key field entry in a target table, but the entries in the other fields of the source record are not identical to the entries in the corresponding fields of the target record. When this occurs, Paradox will enter that record in a KEYVIOL table instead of in a target table. This is true even if the key violation affects only one of the target tables.

For example, suppose you have issued the [Menu] Modify MultiEntry Entry command and have entered the records shown in Table 9-2 into the NEWORD table. Figure 9-29 on the next page shows these records in the ENTRY table for NEWORD. Notice that the entry in the Cust Number field for the second record in ENTRY is the same as the entry in the Cust Number field of the third record in CUSTOMER in Figure 9-27.

Table 9-2   Sample Data

Cust Number	4	3
First Name	Don	Julia
Last Name	Johnson	Baker
Address	123 Beach Road	2 River Road
City	Miami	Cincinnati
State	FL	OH
Zip	23689	23789
Order Number	103	104
Date	3/1/89	6/1/89
Part Number	1000	1000
Quantity	4	5
Description	Blue Wombat	Blue Wombat
Price	$50.00	$50.00
Extension	$200.00	$250.00

Figure 9-29 DataEntry for NEWORD

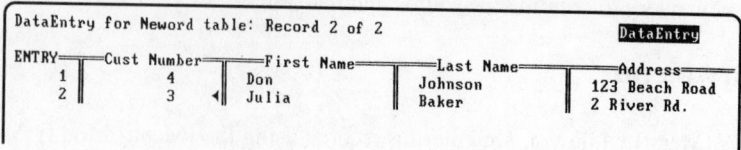

When you press [Do-It!] to process this table, Paradox will not insert any data from the second record in ENTRY into either CUSTOMER or ORDER. Instead, all of the data in that record will be entered in a KEYVIOL table. Figure 9-30 shows this table. Of course, the first record in ENTRY will be properly divided between the CUSTOMER and ORDER tables.

Figure 9-30 The KEYVIOL Table

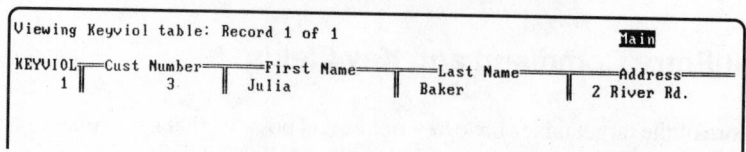

If a key violation occurs, you'll need to edit the entries in the KEYVIOL table to remove the conflict, then distribute the record to the appropriate target tables. The best way to distribute the corrected data is by using the MultiAdd command, which we'll cover shortly.

If a record you enter through the source table has a key field entry that is the same as a key field entry in a target table, and the entries in the other fields of the source record are also identical to the entries in those fields of the target table, then no key violation will occur. In that event, the new record will simply disappear. It will neither be added to the target table, placed in a KEYVIOL table, nor retained in the source table.

This rule may seem strange, but there is an important reason why MultiEntry works this way. In many cases when you use MultiEntry, there will be several records in one target table for each record in the other target table. For instance, in an order entry system, it is likely that each customer will order several different items. This means that in the CUSTOMER/ORDER table system, there are likely to be several records in ORDER for each record in CUSTOMER.

For example, suppose you've issued the [Menu] Modify MultiEntry Entry command and have entered the records shown in Table 9-3 into NEWORD. Figure 9-31 shows these entries in the ENTRY table. Notice that the CUSTOMER table field entries for the first record in ENTRY duplicate the third record in CUSTOMER in Figure 9-27, and that the second and third records in ENTRY have the same entries in all of the CUSTOMER table fields.

Table 9-3 Sample Data

Cust Number	3	6	6
First Name	Barbara	John	John
Last Name	Williams	Dawkins	Dawkins
Address	321 4th St.	123 E. St.	123 E. St.
City	New York	Washington	Washington
State	NY	DC	DC
Zip	10001	20001	20001
Order Number	105	106	107
Date	7/1/89	7/2/89	7/5/89
Part Number	1234	1000	2000
Quantity	1	3	4
Description	Red Widget	Blue Wombat	Brown Bat
Price	$100.00	$50.00	$75.00
Extension	$100.00	$150.00	$300.00

Figure 9-31 DataEntry for NEWORD

```
DataEntry for Neword table: Record 1 of 3                    DataEntry

ENTRY   Cust Number      First Name      Last Name      Address
  1          3      ◄ Barbara          Williams         321 4th St.
  2          6        John             Dawkins          123 E. St.
  3          6        John             Dawkins          123 E. St.
```

When you press [Do-It!] to process this table, Paradox will enter three records into ORDER, one for each item ordered, but will enter only the record for the new customer into CUSTOMER. Because the CUSTOMER table field entries for the first record in ENTRY duplicate the third record in CUSTOMER, Paradox will not insert the information from those fields in CUSTOMER. In addition, since the data in the CUSTOMER table fields of the second and third records in ENTRY have the same entries, Paradox will enter only one of those records in the CUSTOMER table. Figure 9-32 shows the CUSTOMER and ORDER tables at this point.

Figure 9-32 The CUSTOMER and ORDER Tables

```
Viewing Order table: Record 1 of 7                           Main

CUSTOMER  Cust Number      First Name      Last Name      Address
  1           1          John            Smith           111 Main St.
  2           2          David           Jones           1234 Elm St.
  3           3          Barbara         Williams        321 4th St
  4           4          Don             Johnson         123 Beach Road
  5           6          John            Dawkins         123 E. St.


ORDER     Cust Number     Order Number      Date       Part Number   Quanti
  1           1              100          11/22/88       1234           4
  2           2              101          11/23/88       1000           1
  3           3              102          11/24/88       2000           2
  4           4              103          3/01/89        1000           4
  5           3              105          7/01/89        1234           1
  6           6              106          7/02/89        1000           3
  7           6              107          7/05/89        2000           4
```

Keep in mind that this rule applies only if you have specified a key field in one of the target tables. If the target tables do not have key fields, Paradox will enter duplicate records into the tables. Also remember that this rule applies only when all of the fields of a record in the source table contain the same entries as the fields of a record that is already in the target table. If the two sets of entries are not identical, but the key field entries are, the record from the source table will be entered in a KEYVIOL table.

Password Protection

If you want, you can assign a password to the source table after it has been created. When you issue the [Menu] Modify MultiEntry Entry command, Paradox will prompt you for the password before it will allow you to make any entries.

If either the target table or the map table is password-protected, Paradox will not prompt you for the password when you issue the [Menu] Modify MultiEntry Entry command. Instead, it will simply deliver the message *Password not given for target table TABLENAME*, terminate the MultiEntry operation without allowing you to enter any records, and display the map table. In other words, Paradox checks the target tables for protection but does not allow you to specify a password for these tables directly.

If you want to password-protect a MultiEntry table system, you should assign the same password to every table in the system. Then, when you issue the [Menu] Modify MultiEntry Entry command and supply the password, Paradox will use the password you type to unlock both the source table and all of the target tables. Remember: If you use a different password for even one of the target tables, Paradox will not let you add records with the MultiEntry Entry command.

The [Menu] Tools More MultiAdd Command

The [Menu] Tools More MultiAdd command is closely related to the [Menu] Modify MultiEntry command and the [Menu] Tools More Add command. Like the Add command, [Menu] Tools More MultiAdd allows you to add records from one table to another. Like the MultiEntry command, MultiAdd allows you to distribute the records from a single table (the source table) into two or more target tables, using the relationships defined in a map table.

The MultiAdd command assumes that the records you want to distribute are already in the source table when you issue the command. This command does not allow you to enter records before distribution. The MultiEntry command, on the other hand, first asks you to enter records into the source table, then distributes those records to the target tables.

Like the MultiEntry command, the MultiAdd command requires that you define a source table and a map table. These tables serve precisely the same function with MultiAdd that they serve with MultiEntry. However, the MultiAdd command does not have a Setup option that allows you to define the source and map tables. You'll need to use the [Menu] Modify MultiEntry Setup command to define the source and map tables that you'll use with the MultiAdd command.

Although you probably will use the MultiAdd command less often than the MultiEntry command, MultiAdd has several important applications. One of the primary uses for the MultiAdd command is distributing records to the appropriate target tables that have been placed by the MultiEntry command in a KEYVIOL table. Another application for the MultiAdd command is distributing the records that you import from a non-normalized dBASE III or 1-2-3 database into normalized Paradox tables. MultiAdd can also be used when you want to redistribute to the original tables records that you have merged with a query and have modified.

The [Menu] Tools More MultiAdd command offers two options: NewEntries and Update. These options are similar to the NewEntries and Update options of the [Menu] Tools More Add command. The effect of the MultiAdd command depends on which of these options you select and whether the target tables include key fields.

The NewEntries Option

The NewEntries option causes the MultiAdd command to perform almost like the MultiEntry command. If you choose NewEntries, Paradox will add the records from the source table to each of the target tables. The records from the source table will be appended below any records that are already in the target tables.

An Example

Suppose you have used the [Menu] Modify MultiEntry command to enter two new records into the CUSTOMER and ORDER tables through the source table NEWORD. Figure 9-29 shows these entries in the ENTRY table. Let's suppose that in making these entries, you simply mistyped one customer number. Instead of typing 5, the correct number, you typed 3, the number of the third customer in CUSTOMER. Because of this typo, a key violation occurred when the MultiEntry command was executed, causing Paradox to enter one of the records from NEWORD in the KEYVIOL table shown in Figure 9-30.

At this point, you need to edit the contents of the KEYVIOL table to eliminate the key conflict, then distribute the entries to the appropriate target tables. To correct the error in this example, bring KEYVIOL into view, press [Edit], move to the Cust Number field, press [Backspace] to erase the error, type 5, and press [Do-It!]. Figure 9-33 shows the corrected table.

Figure 9-33 The Corrected KEYVIOL Table

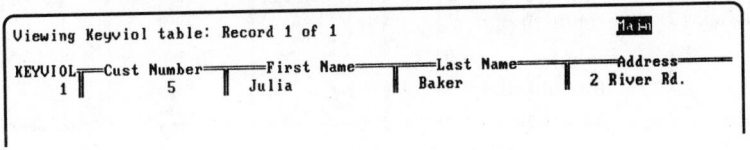

The easiest way to distribute the contents of KEYVIOL into CUSTOMER and ORDER is to use the MultiAdd NewEntries command. Before you can use this command, you have to rename the KEYVIOL table. We'll change its name to FIXED. To do this, issue the [**Menu**] **Tools Rename Table** command. When asked for the name of the table to rename, type **KEYVIOL**. When Paradox asks for a new name, type **FIXED**. Now, issue the [**Menu**] **Tools More MultiAdd** command. When Paradox prompts you for the name of the source table, you should supply the name of the table that contains the record you want to distribute—in this case, **FIXED**.

When Paradox prompts you for the name of the map table, you should supply the name of an existing map table that defines the relationship between the source table and the target tables. In this case, you already have a map table, ORDMAP, which will do the job. ORDMAP works because the FIXED table has the same structure as the source table NEWORD, which you created in the previous example. If the map table you specify in this step does not match the structure of the source table you have specified, Paradox will display an error message when you execute the command.

After you type the name of the map table, **ORDMAP**, Paradox will present the two MultiAdd options: NewEntries and Update. In this case, because you want to add the records in the source table to the target tables, you should choose NewEntries. Paradox then will add the records from the source table to each of the target tables.

Figure 9-34 shows the CUSTOMER and ORDER tables after the MultiAdd command is completed. As you can see, the single record from FIXED has been divided into two records—one for CUSTOMER and one for ORDER—each of which has been entered into the appropriate table.

Figure 9-34 Using MultiAdd

```
Viewing Order table: Record 1 of 8                          Main

FIXED======Cust Number======First Name======Last Name======Address======
   1            5           Julia            Baker          2 River Rd.


CUSTOMER===Cust Number======First Name======Last Name======Address======
   1            1           John             Smith          111 Main St.
   2            2           David            Jones          1234 Elm St.
   3            3           Barbara          Williams       321 4th St
   4            4           Don              Johnson        123 Beach Road
   5            5           Julia            Baker          2 River Rd.
   6            6           John             Dawkins        123 E. St.


ORDER======Cust Number======Order Number======Date======Part Number======Quanti
   1            1            100            11/22/88       1234           4
   2            2            101            11/23/88       1000           1
   3            3            102            11/24/88       2000           2
   4            4            103            3/01/89        1000           4
   5            3            105            7/01/89        1234           1
   6            6            106            7/02/89        1000           3
   7            6            107            7/05/89        2000           4
   8            5            104            6/01/89        1000           5
```

The MultiAdd NewEntries Command and Key Fields

If you look closely at Figure 9-34, you'll see that Paradox has added the records from KEYVIOL to CUSTOMER and ORDER differently. The portion of the record from FIXED that was added to CUSTOMER was inserted into CUSTOMER in key field order. This occurred because the Cust Number field in CUSTOMER is a key field. In general, if one or more of the target tables in a MultiAdd NewEntries operation has a key field, and there is not a conflict between the entries in the key field of the target table and the corresponding field of the source table, Paradox will insert the records from the source table into the keyed target table in key field order. That is, the records from the source table will be inserted between the records in the target table so that the entries in the key field of the resulting target table are in ascending order.

On the other hand, notice that the portion of the record from FIXED that was added to the ORDER table was appended to the end of that table. This occurred because ORDER has no key fields. In general, when you use the MultiAdd NewEntries command to add records to a non-keyed table, Paradox will append the records from the source table to the target table below any records that are already in the target table.

If one or more of the target tables have key fields, it is possible that key violations will occur when you use the MultiAdd NewEntries command. These violations are handled by MultiAdd in the same way they are handled by MultiEntry.

A key violation occurs when a record you enter through the source table has a key field entry that is the same as a key field entry in a target table, but the entries in the other fields of the source record are not the same as the entries in the corresponding fields of the target record. When this occurs, Paradox will enter that record in a KEYVIOL table. The record will not be entered in any target table. This is true even if the key violation affects only one of the target tables. If a key violation occurs, you'll need to edit the entries in the KEYVIOL table to resolve the conflict, then distribute the record to the appropriate target tables by repeating the MultiAdd command.

If a record that you enter through the source table has a key field entry that is the same as a key field entry in a target table, and if the entries in the other fields of the source record are also identical to the entries in the corresponding fields of the target record, then no key violation will occur. In that event, the new record will simply disappear. It won't be added to the target table or placed in a KEYVIOL table.

The Update Option

If you choose the Update option from the MultiAdd menu, Paradox will use the records in the source table to update the records in the target tables. Exactly how this occurs depends on whether the target tables are keyed. If a target table is not keyed, the records from the source table will be appended to the target table below any existing records, just as if you had selected the NewEntries option.

If a target table is keyed, and there is no conflict between the entries in the key field of the target table and the corresponding field of the source table, Paradox will insert the records from the source table into the target table in key field order. That is, the records from the source table will be inserted between the records in the target table so that the entries in the key field of the resulting target table are in ascending order.

If a target table is keyed, and there is a conflict between the entries in the key field of the target table and the corresponding field of the source table, Paradox will use the data from the non-key fields of the source table to update the record with the conflicting key field entry in the target table. This last case is by far the most important use of the Update option. Let's consider an example of how it works.

An Example

Suppose you receive an order from a customer who is already in your CUSTOMER table, but the customer's address has changed since he last placed an order. You have issued the MultiEntry Entry command and have entered the record shown in Table 9-4 into the NEWORD table. Figure 9-35 shows this record in place. Notice that this record has the same entry in the Cust Number field as the second entry in the CUSTOMER table shown in Figure 9-27 on page 375. Also notice that most of the other entries in the CUSTOMER table fields of ENTRY agree with the entries in the second record in CUSTOMER, but that the Address and Zip field entries are different. When you press **[Do-It!]** to execute the MultiEntry command, Paradox will detect a key violation and will place this record in a KEYVIOL table. Figure 9-36 shows this table.

Table 9-4 Sample Data

Cust Number	2
First Name	David
Last Name	Jones
Address	555 Oak St.
City	Lexington
State	KY
Zip	40555
Order Number	108
Date	8/15/89
Part Number	1234
Quantity	1
Description	Red Widget
Price	$100.00
Extension	$100.00

Figure 9-35 DataEntry for NEWORD

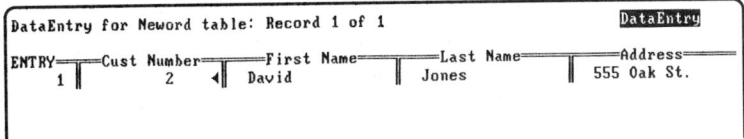

```
DataEntry for Neword table: Record 1 of 1                    DataEntry

ENTRY    Cust Number     First Name      Last Name        Address
  1            2      ◄  David           Jones            555 Oak St.
```

Figure 9-36 The KEYVIOL Table

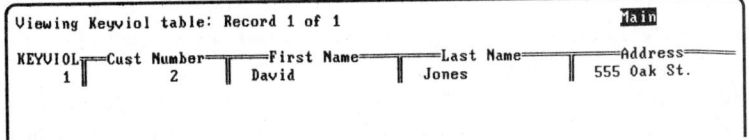

```
Viewing Keyviol table: Record 1 of 1                         Main

KEYVIOL  Cust Number     First Name      Last Name        Address
  1            2         David           Jones            555 Oak St.
```

Unlike the previous example, you don't want to add the record from KEYVIOL to CUSTOMER in this case. Instead, you want to update the record for customer number 2 in the CUSTOMER table by replacing it with the record from KEYVIOL. You can do this with the Update option of the MultiAdd command. Before you can use this command, however, you need to rename the KEYVIOL table. Let's rename it FIXED by issuing the [**Menu**] **T**ools **R**ename **T**able command. When Paradox asks for the table to rename, type **KEYVIOL**. When Paradox asks for the new name, type **FIXED**.

To update the CUSTOMER and ORDER tables, issue the [**Menu**] **T**ools **M**ore **M**ultiAdd command, then specify **FIXED** as the source table and **ORDMAP** as the map table. Next, choose the **U**pdate option. Since the entry in the key field of the second record in CUSTOMER is the same as the entry in the corresponding field of FIXED, Paradox will use the record in FIXED to update the second record in CUSTOMER. Figure 9-37 shows the CUSTOMER and ORDER tables as they will look after the MultiAdd command is finished. Notice that the Address field entry for the second record in CUSTOMER has been changed to agree with the entry from FIXED.

Figure 9-37 Modified CUSTOMER and ORDER Tables

```
Viewing Customer table: Record 1 of 6                        Main

    First Name      Last Name       Address          City         Sta
    John            Smith           111 Main St.     Peru         I
    David           Jones           555 Oak St.      Lexington    K
    Barbara         Williams        321 4th St       New York     N
    Don             Johnson         123 Beach Road   Miami        F
    Julia           Baker           2 River Rd.      Cincinnati   K
    John            Dawkins         123 E. St.       Washington   D


ORDER  Cust Number  Order Number    Date        Part Number   Quanti
  1         1          100         11/22/88       1234           4
  2         2          101         11/23/88       1000           1
  3         3          102         11/24/88       2000           2
  4         4          103         3/01/89        1000           4
  5         3          105         7/01/89        1234           1
  6         6          106         7/02/89        1000           3
  7         6          107         7/05/89        2000           4
  8         5          104         6/01/89        1000           5
  9         2          108         8/15/89        1234           1
```

Notes

The contents of the source table do not change when you use the [Menu] Tools More MultiAdd command. Whatever was in the source table before you issued the command will be in the source table after the command is completed. Whether the source table has a key field has no effect on the command.

Unlike the [Menu] Tools More Add Update command, the [Menu] Tools More MultiAdd Update command does not create a temporary CHANGED table. This means that once you execute the MultiAdd Update command, the original records in the target table will be erased.

As with the MultiEntry command, if the source table in a MultiAdd operation is password-protected, Paradox will prompt you to supply the password before it executes the command. Paradox will check the target tables and the map table for password protection, but will not allow you to specify a password for these tables directly. If you want to password-protect a MultiEntry table system, you should assign the same password to every table in the system. Then, when you issue the [Menu] Modify MultiEntry Entry command and supply the password, Paradox will use the password you type to unlock both the source table and all of the target tables.

Data Entry with a Multitable Form

In Chapters 2 and 4, we mentioned that Paradox creates several ENTRY tables when you use a multitable form in DataEntry mode. Each of these tables corresponds to one of the tables on the form. Paradox adds a number to the name of each ENTRY table that holds data for one of the detail tables displayed in an embedded form on the master form. For example, if the multitable form includes two embedded forms, Paradox will create three tables to hold the data being entered: ENTRY, ENTRY1, and ENTRY2. During the data entry session, Paradox will place data being entered into the master table on the multitable form in the ENTRY table, and data for the two detail tables on the form into the ENTRY1 and ENTRY2 tables.

While you are entering data with a multitable form, Paradox uses the prompt at the top of the screen to display the name of the table for which you are entering data, rather than the name of the ENTRY table into which the data is being stored. As a result, you will never see the names of these additional ENTRY tables unless you use the KeepEntry command to end a data entry session. If you use the KeepEntry command to end the data entry session, Paradox will save all of the ENTRY tables and create a new LIST table in which each record lists the name of one ENTRY table, along with the name of the permanent table targeted to receive the data in each ENTRY table. As we explained in Chapter 2, you might want to save the ENTRY tables if another user on your network had one of the tables to which you were entering data locked when you tried to save the new data. Or, you might simply want to save the new data in the ENTRY tables because you want to wait awhile before actually entering it into the permanent tables.

If you end the data entry session by pressing the [Do-It!] key, Paradox will automatically add all the records in each of the ENTRY tables to the appropriate permanent tables. However, if any of the records in the master ENTRY table causes a key violation in the permanent master table, Paradox will create a KEYVIOL table to hold the key-violating records from the master table, and numbered KEYVIOL tables to hold the detail records linked to the records that caused the key violations. For example, if the multitable form included two embedded forms, Paradox would store the key-violating records in KEYVIOL and the records linked to the key violators in tables named KEYVIOL1 and KEYVIOL2.

While Paradox checks for key violations in the master table, it never checks for key violations in detail tables. Instead, Paradox always treats keyed detail tables as it treats keyed tables when you press [Do-It!] to end an Edit session. If you try to add more than one record with the same key field entries to a detail table, then Paradox will add to the target table only the last record with those key field entries. The only time Paradox will create a KEYVIOL table for a detail table is when it needs to save detail records that are linked to a key-violating record in the master table. As a result, there is always the possibility that you could accidentally lose a detail record by mistakenly typing in the same key field entries for two records. To avoid losing detail records in this manner, you should be very careful to avoid entering duplicate key field entries while typing the entries in detail records.

If you do enter a record that creates a key violation in the master table, or if you use the KeepEntry command to save the ENTRY tables, you will be left with a set of temporary tables (either ENTRY tables or KEYVIOL tables) that you will eventually want to add to the tables on the multitable form. In either case, you could use the [Menu] Tools More FormAdd command to distribute the information in these temporary tables among the appropriate permanent tables. In the next section, we'll show you how to use this command.

The [Menu] Tools More FormAdd Command

The [Menu] Tools More FormAdd command lets you add records from several tables to the tables that appear on a multitable form. This command distributes records among the master and detail tables displayed on the form, maintaining the referential integrity that exists between linked records. The [Menu] Tools More FormAdd command is similar to the [Menu] Tools More MultiAdd command, but there are some very important differences. When you use the [Menu] Tools More MultiAdd command, Paradox uses a map table to distribute the information from a single table into a set of related tables. However, when you use the [Menu] Tools More FormAdd command, Paradox uses a multitable form to distribute information from several tables into a set of related tables. MultiAdd can help you complete interrupted data entry operations that you began with the [Menu] Modify MultiEntry command, a tool added to Paradox 1.1. FormAdd can help you finish interrupted data entry operations during which you were using a multitable form, a tool available only in Paradox 3.

One of the most common uses for the [Menu] Tools More FormAdd command is to add records that have been placed in KEYVIOL tables at the end of a data entry session. Another common use for the [Menu] Tools More FormAdd command is to add ENTRY tables that you saved with the KeepEntry command at the end of a data entry session. After we explain the basic steps necessary to use the [Menu] Tools More FormAdd command, we'll show you examples to illustrate how you use the command for both tasks.

FormAdd Basics

When you issue the [Menu] Tools More FormAdd command, Paradox first prompts you for the name of the master table for the form you want to use as a distribution guide. Next, Paradox displays a menu of all existing forms for that table and asks you to select the form you want to use. Then, Paradox displays a menu with two options: EntryTables and AnyTables. Selecting the EntryTables option tells Paradox that you want to use ENTRY tables that you saved when you used the KeepEntry command to end a data entry session. If you choose AnyTables, Paradox will ask you to match the names of the tables you want to add with names of tables that appear on the form. If the master table for the form is keyed (which it must be if any embedded forms are linked to the master form), Paradox will also ask you if it should try to insert all the new records into the target tables or use the new records to update the target tables.

However, if you select EntryTables, then Paradox does not need to ask you to match the names of the tables you are adding to the names of the target tables. It can determine which ENTRY tables are targeted for which tables on the form by looking at the structure of the form and the numbers on the ENTRY tables. After you pick the EntryTables option, Paradox will immediately attempt to add the ENTRY tables to the permanent tables. Paradox automatically tries to insert the records from the ENTRY tables into the target tables, as if you had pressed [Do-It!] during the data entry session.

An Example: Adding ENTRY Tables

Because it is easier, we'll demonstrate adding ENTRY tables first. For our example, we'll use a multitable form that we designed in Chapter 4. Figure 9-38 shows the structure of the CLIENTS table, and Figure 9-39 shows one of the multitable forms for CLIENTS that we created in Chapter 4. This form, which is form 1, includes an embedded form for the SALESORD table, which lists software orders placed by people listed in CLIENTS.

As we explained in Chapter 4, the CLIENTS and SALESORD tables both have Client Number fields that are key fields, but SALESORD also includes two other key fields: Date and Product Number. As a result, every record in CLIENTS has a unique Client Number entry, but several records in SALESORD can have the same Client Number entry. Because the embedded SALESORD form is linked to the CLIENTS master form on entries in the

Client Number field of both tables, the form will display only the orders placed by the client whose record is currently displayed on the form. The Client Number field does not appear on the embedded SALESORD form because linking fields appear only on the master form.

Figure 9-38 The CLIENTS Table

```
View  Ask  Report  Create  Modify  Image  Forms  Tools  Scripts  Help  Exit
View a table.
CLIENTS═Client Number═══Last Name═══First Name══SS Number════════Addre
    1       1001        Smith       John         345-43-2232   2378 Maple
    2       1003        Klausing    Fred         457-98-0432   2394 Hazelw
    3       1004        Fritz       Jules        345-67-3454   2212 Elk St
    4       1005        Gies        Helen        209-98-4628   4583 Mary C
    5       1006        Payne       Ann          325-23-2323   1932 Hunter
    6       1007        Wooley      Paul         367-98-1244   123 Clarks
    7       1008        Cooley      Dwayne       417-23-2938   3237 Henry
    8       1009        Harris      Ralph        403-42-5775   Rt. 2, Box
    9       1010        Crane       John         378-24-9476   1345 18th S
   10       1011        Jones       Thiora       319-21-8219   8924 Hallma
```

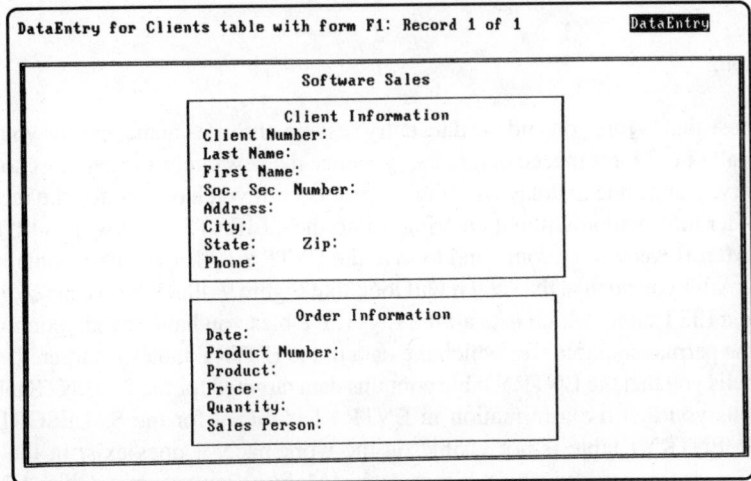

Suppose you want to use this multitable form to enter information about a new customer who has placed his first order with your company. To use the form for data entry, first issue the **[Menu]** Modify **D**ataEntry command, type **CLIENTS** when Paradox prompts you for the name of a table, and press ↵. When Paradox displays the empty ENTRY table with the same structure as CLIENTS, issue the **[Menu]** Image **P**ickForm command and select **1** from the list of existing forms for the CLIENTS table. At this point, the multitable form will appear on the screen, as shown in Figure 9-39.

Figure 9-39 A Multitable Form

```
DataEntry for Clients table with form F1: Record 1 of 1          DataEntry

                          Software Sales

                        Client Information
              Client Number:
              Last Name:
              First Name:
              Soc. Sec. Number:
              Address:
              City:
              State:      Zip:
              Phone:

                        Order Information
              Date:
              Product Number:
              Product:
              Price:
              Quantity:
              Sales Person:
```

Now, enter the data from Table 9-5 into the Client Information section of the form.

Table 9-5 Sample Data

Client Number:	1012
Last Name:	Kemp
First Name:	Ben
Soc. Sec. Number:	322-22-8923
Address:	3483 Tucker Rd.
City:	New Albany
State:	IN
Zip:	47150
Phone:	(812) 288-3637

After you have entered this data, press the **[Down Image]** key ([F3]) or the **[Up Image]** key ([F4]) to move the cursor into the Order Information area, which displays data from the SALESORD table. Then, enter two records of sales order information for the new customer with the information from Table 9-6.

Table 9-6 Sample Data

	Record 1	Record 2
Date:	2/5/88	2/5/88
Product Number:	2	3
Product:	Paradox 386	Quattro
Price:	$599.99	$149.99
Quantity:	1	2
Sales Person:	1	1

Now, suppose that before you end the data entry session, the sales manager tells you to print a report on all sales orders placed before today. Since the new client's order does not fit into that category, you decide to delay entering his orders until you have printed the report. To save the order information without entering it into the CLIENTS and SALESORD tables, issue the **[Menu] K**eepEntry command to save the ENTRY tables that now contain the information. After you do this, the screen will look like Figure 9-40. As you can see, Paradox has created a LIST table, which lists all the ENTRY tables you have saved, along with the names of the permanent tables for which the data in the ENTRY tables is targeted. Record 1 of LIST tells you that the ENTRY table contains data targeted for the CLIENTS table, and record 2 tells you that the information in ENTRY1 is meant for the SALESORD table. Though the ENTRY1 table is not visible on the workspace, it does exist in the current directory. To see the records in this table, issue the **[Menu]** View command, type **ENTRY1** at the prompt, and press ↵.

Figure 9-40 The LIST Table

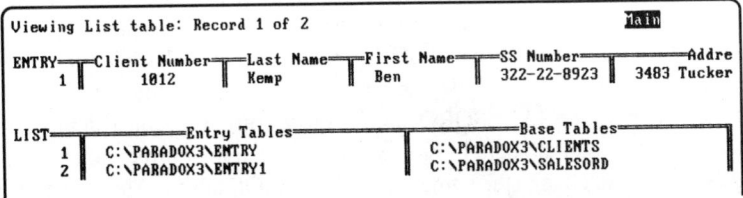

Now, suppose that you have finished printing your report and are ready to add the new information to the CLIENTS and SALESORD tables. To do this, issue the **[Menu] T**ools **More FormAdd** command. When Paradox asks you for the name of the master target table, type **CLIENTS** and press ↵. Then, select **1** from the list of forms for the CLIENTS table. Next, Paradox will present the EntryTables/AnyTables menu. Since you are adding the contents of ENTRY tables, select **E**ntryTables. After you do this, the message *Adding records from Entry to Clients (and associated 1-Many details)...* will appear briefly in the message area at the bottom of the screen. When the message disappears, you'll know that Paradox has finished adding the ENTRY tables to the permanent tables.

An Example: Overcoming a Key Violation

Now, let's look at how you can use the [Menu] Tools More FormAdd command to recover from a key violation. Suppose that while entering the data in the last example, you accidentally typed 1011 in the Client Number field instead of 1012. Also, let's assume that you pressed [Do-It!] to end the data entry session instead of issuing the [Menu] KeepEntry command. Since CLIENTS already includes a record with a Client Number entry of 1011, and Client Number is the only key field in CLIENTS, this new record will create a key violation when Paradox tries to add the ENTRY table to CLIENTS. As a result, the screen will look like Figure 9-41 after you press [Do-It!].

Figure 9-41 A Key Violation

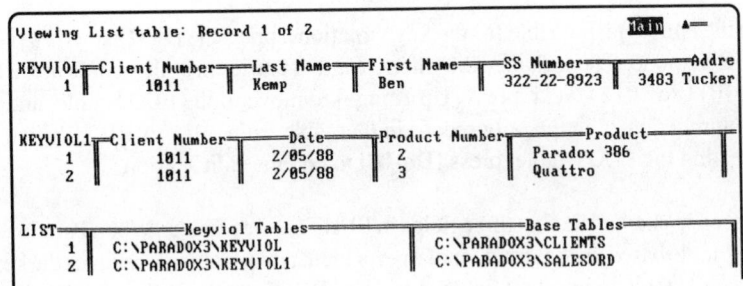

As you can see, Paradox has created two tables to hold the records involved in the key violation: KEYVIOL and KEYVIOL1. In addition to these two tables, there is also a LIST table on the workspace, which tells you for which permanent tables the information in the KEYVIOL tables was targeted. Record 1 of LIST tells you that the KEYVIOL table contains data targeted for the CLIENTS table, and record 2 tells you that the information in KEYVIOL1 is meant for the SALESORD table. Before you can use the [Menu] Tools More FormAdd command to add the data in KEYVIOL tables to the correct tables, you need to follow three steps. First, change the names of the KEYVIOL tables. Then, change the field entries that caused the key violations. Finally, restructure the KEYVIOL tables that correspond to detail tables so that they have the same key fields as their target tables. We'll explain each of these steps as we progress with our example.

Like the [Menu] Tools More Add command, [Menu] Tools More FormAdd does not allow you to add a KEYVIOL table to another table. To change the name of the KEYVIOL table, issue the **[Menu]** Tools **R**ename **T**able command, type **KEYVIOL** when Paradox prompts you for the name of a table, and press ↵. When Paradox asks you for the new name of the table, type **FIXIT** (or whatever table name you want to use) and press ↵. To change the name of KEYVIOL1, issue the **[Menu]** Tools **R**ename **T**able command, type **KEYVIOL1**, press ↵, type **FIXIT1**, and press ↵. At this point, the screen will display the LIST table and the renamed KEYVIOL tables, as shown in Figure 9-42, with the cursor in the FIXIT1 table.

Figure 9-42 The Renamed KEYVIOL Tables

```
Viewing Fixit1 table: Record 1 of 2                              Main

LIST=============Keyviol Tables==========              ======Base Tables======
     1 ║ C:\PARADOX2\ROSEMARY\KEYVIOL    ║   C:\PARADOX2\ROSEMARY\CLIENTS
     2 ║ C:\PARADOX2\ROSEMARY\KEYVIOL1   ║   C:\PARADOX2\ROSEMARY\SALESORD


FIXIT===Client Number===Last Name===First Name===SS Number=======Addre
    1 ║      1011      ║ Kemp      ║ Ben      ║ 322-22-8923 ║ 3483 Tucker

FIXIT1==Client Number======Date====Product Number=====Product====
    1 ║      1011      ║ 2/05/88   ║    2         ║ Paradox 386
    2 ║      1011      ║ 2/05/88   ║    3         ║ Quattro
```

To change the entries responsible for the key violations, press the **[Edit]** key ([F9]) to place Paradox in Edit mode. Then, change the Client Number entries in both records in the FIXIT1 table from 1011 to 1012. Next, press **[Up Image]** to move to the FIXIT table, and change the Client Number entry in the only record in that table from 1011 to 1012. When you've finish correcting the FIXIT table, press **[Do-It!]** to end the Edit session.

Now, you need to change the first three fields in FIXIT1 to key fields. When Paradox creates a KEYVIOL table based on the structure of a permanent table, it always changes the key fields in the permanent table to non-key fields in the KEYVIOL table. If Paradox left key fields in the KEYVIOL table, then the KEYVIOL table would itself not be able to hold the key violations that necessitated its creation. However, in order to direct information into a detail table on a multitable form, Paradox must refer to the key fields in the source table. As a result, you need to restore the key fields in a KEYVIOL table before you can use the [Menu] Tools More FormAdd command to add the contents of the KEYVIOL table to the detail table.

To restore the key fields to the FIXIT1 table, issue the [**Menu**] Modify **R**estructure command, type **FIXIT1** at the prompt, and press ↵. When Paradox displays the STRUCT table listing the structure of FIXIT1, type an asterisk (*) at the end of the Field Type specifications for the Client Number, Date, and Product Number fields. Figure 9-43 shows the new STRUCT table. To save the new structure for FIXIT1, press [**Do-It!**].

Figure 9-43 The Restructured FIXIT1 Table

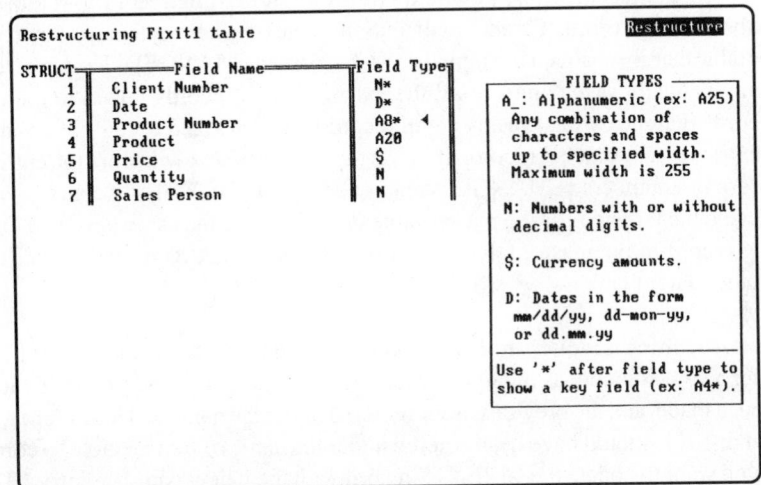

Now, you are ready to add the FIXIT and FIXIT1 tables to CLIENTS and SALESORD. To do this, issue the [**Menu**] Tools **M**ore FormAdd command. When Paradox asks you for the name of the master target table, type **CLIENTS** and press ↵. Then, select **1** from the list of forms for the CLIENTS table. Next, Paradox will present the EntryTables/AnyTables menu. Since you are not adding the contents of ENTRY tables, select **A**nyTables. When Paradox displays the NewEntries/Update menu, select NewEntries to tell Paradox that you want the records in FIXIT and FIXIT1 entered as new records, rather than as updated information for existing records.

At this point, Paradox will use the prompt shown in Figure 9-44 to ask you for the name of the source table for the CLIENTS table. When you see this prompt, type **FIXIT** and press ↵. Next, Paradox will present a similar prompt, asking you to enter the name of the source table for the SALESORD table. When you see this prompt, type **FIXIT1** and press ↵.

Figure 9-44 The Source Table Prompt

```
Source Table:                                          Main
Enter name of source for Clients Target, or press ↵ for a list of tables.
```

After you enter the names of the source tables, the message *Adding records from Fixit to Clients (and associated 1-Many tables)...* will appear at the bottom of the screen. When this message disappears, you will know that Paradox has successfully added the records in FIXIT and FIXIT1 to CLIENTS and SALESORD.

Using the Update Option

Selecting the Update option while adding records to a keyed master table will produce results similar to those encountered when you use Update with the [Menu] Forms Add command or the [Menu] Forms MultiAdd command. If you select Update, Paradox will use the data in any new record that has the same key field entries as an existing record to replace all the entries in the existing record. Paradox will also store the original contents of any records in the master table that are changed in a temporary table named CHANGED. However, Paradox will not automatically save copies of all the existing detail records linked to the changed master record. Paradox will save any detail record that is changed because it has the same key field entries as a new detail record. If this is the case, Paradox will store the entries from the old record in a numbered CHANGED table, such as CHANGED1. Of course, if a record in the source table targeted for the master table does not have the same key field entries as an existing record in the master table, Paradox will simply add that record and its detail records to their target tables.

For example, suppose that you try to enter the data for Ben Kemp as client number 1011 only to encounter a key violation, as in our last example. However, suppose you find out that an error had been made, and the previous orders entered under the name of Thiora Jones, the old client number 1011, should have been entered under the name of Ben Kemp. To correct the situation, you want to update the CLIENTS record with the Client Number entry 1011 with the information for Ben Kemp and add his new orders to the SALESORD table.

To do this, rename and restructure the KEYVIOL tables as we did in the last example. However, skip the step in which we changed the entries in the Client Number fields of the KEYVIOL tables and leave the entry 1011 in the Client Number fields of FIXIT and FIXIT1. To update the CLIENTS and SALESORD tables, issue the **[Menu] Tools More FormAdd** command. When Paradox asks you for the name of the master target table, type **CLIENTS** and press ↵. Then, select **1** from the list of forms for the CLIENTS table. Since you are not adding the contents of ENTRY tables, select AnyTables from the EntryTables/AnyTables menu. When Paradox displays the NewEntries/Update menu, select Update to specify that you want to use the records in FIXIT and FIXIT1 to update the records in CLIENTS and SALESORD rather than try to add all the new records to the target tables. When Paradox asks you for the name of the source table for CLIENTS, type **FIXIT** and press ↵. When Paradox asks you for the name of the source table for SALESORD, type **FIXIT1** and press ↵.

After you enter the names of the source tables, the message *Updating from Fixit to Clients (and associated 1-Many tables)...* will appear at the bottom of the screen. When this message disappears, Paradox will display a CHANGED table and a new LIST table, as shown in Figure 9-45. Record 1 of the LIST table tells you that the CHANGED table contains the old information from the CLIENTS records that were updated. If you look at the CHANGED table, you can see that only one CLIENTS record was changed, the record for client number 1011. The blank entry in the Changed Tables field of record 2 in LIST tells you that Paradox did not change any records in SALESORD because no records in FIXIT1 had the same key field entries as existing records in SALESORD. If you had entered a SALESORD record with the same Client Number, Date, and Product Number entries as an existing record in the table, then Paradox would have updated the existing record with information from the new record and placed the old information in a table named CHANGED1.

Figure 9-45 The CHANGED Table

```
Viewing Fixit table: Record 1 of 1                                    Main

FIXIT──┬─Client Number─┬─Last Name─┬─First Name─┬─SS Number──┬──────────Addre
   1  │      1011      │   Kemp    │    Ben     │ 322-22-8923 │ 3483 Tucker


FIXIT1─┬─Client Number─┬──────Date──────┬─Product Number─┬──────Product──────┬
   1  │      1011      │    2/05/88      │      2        │ Paradox 386       │
   2  │      1011      │    2/05/88      │      3        │ Quattro           │


CHANGED─┬Client Number─┬─Last Name─┬─First Name─┬─SS Number──┬──────────Addre
   1   │     1011      │   Jones   │   Thiora   │ 319-21-8219 │ 8924 Hallma


LIST──┬─────────Changed Tables────────┬─────────Base Tables─────────┬
   1  │ C:\PARADOX3\CHANGED           │ C:\PARADOX3\CLIENTS         │
   2  │                               │ C:\PARADOX3\SALESORD        │
```

Notes

You could use the [Menu] Tools More FormAdd command to add records from a single source table to a single target table by choosing a single table form from the list of forms for the target table. However, it is easier to simply use the [Menu] Tools More Add command when you want to add records from one single table to another.

We used a keyed master table and linked detail tables in our examples for the [Menu] Tools More FormAdd command because the command is most useful when you want to add information to linked tables. You could also use this command to add records to a set of unlinked tables that appear on the same multitable form. Since there is no referential integrity between unlinked tables, this would produce the same effect as using the [Menu] Tools More Add command several times to add records to each table on the form. Also, if you use the [Menu] Tools More FormAdd command with a form for a non-keyed table, Paradox will not present you with the NewEntries/Update option. Instead, it will automatically insert the new records at the ends of the target tables.

Insert Queries

In Chapter 7, you learned about the special query operators find and delete. There is one more special operator, insert, which allows you to insert the data from one or more tables into a different table.

Insert queries are the most flexible of Paradox's multitable tools. Although you can use the insert operator to create queries that duplicate the function of the Add, MultiAdd, and MultiEntry commands, it is more powerful than those tools. You can use insert queries to insert information into a table from another table that has a completely unrelated structure, to insert just a few fields of data from one table into another, or to insert data from several tables into one.

The importance of insert queries in your work with Paradox depends on which version of the program you are using. If you are using Release 1.0, which does not offer a MultiAdd or MultiEntry capability, you will probably need to use insert queries more often. If you are using a later version, you will probably use insert queries only when an Add, MultiAdd, or MultiEntry command will not do the job.

Insert Query Basics

To perform an insert query, you must create a query that contains a form for every table from which you want to insert records (the source tables) and a form for the table into which you want to insert records (the target table). Once the query is created, enter the word *insert* under the name of the query form for the target table. Next, use examples to link the common fields in the query forms.

When you process the query, the contents of the specified fields of the source table or tables will be added to the corresponding fields of the target table. The new data will appear in the target table below any records that are already in that table. At the same time, Paradox will copy the data from the source tables into a special temporary table called INSERTED. Paradox will bring this table into view when the query is completed.

An Example

Suppose you are about to undertake a large promotional mailing that will be sent to all the people in both your PROSPECT and CUSTOMER tables. To operate on the data more easily, you decide to add the records from CUSTOMER to PROSPECT before you begin creating mailing labels.

Instead of combining the CUSTOMER table directly into PROSPECT, we'll use a third table, MAILLIST, to receive data from both tables. Although there are several ways to create this table, the easiest is to build a simple query on the PROSPECT table. To do this, use the [Menu] Ask command to create a new query form for PROSPECT and use [Check Mark] to select the First Name, Last Name, Address, City, State, and Zip fields in the form. When you process this query, Paradox will create the ANSWER table shown in Figure 9-46. This table includes the data from the appropriate fields for all of the records in PROSPECT. You should use the [Menu] Tools Rename command to change the name of this ANSWER table to MAILLIST.

Figure 9-46 Query to Create a New Table

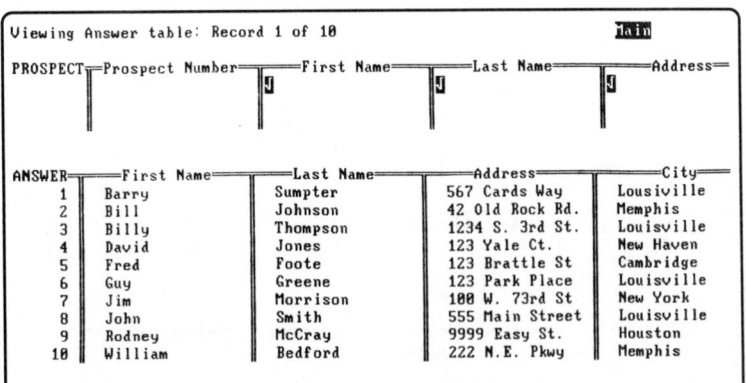

Now, you are ready to add the records from CUSTOMER to MAILLIST. Since CUSTOMER and MAILLIST have slightly different structures, you cannot use the [Menu] Tools More Add command to combine them. If you want to add these two tables, you'll need to use an insert query.

To begin, use the **[Menu] A**sk command to create new query forms for the CUSTOMER and MAILLIST tables. When these query forms come into view, move to the space under the name of the MAILLIST form (the form for the table into which you want the records inserted) and type **insert**. This entry tells Paradox that this query will insert records into the MAILLIST table.

Now, you must enter examples in the two query forms that tell Paradox how to insert the data from CUSTOMER into MAILLIST. To begin, move to the First Name field of MAILLIST, press **[Example]**, and type **FN**. Then, move to the First Name field of CUSTOMER, press **[Example]**, and type **FN**. (You can use any example to relate these fields, as long as you enter the same example in both fields. We chose FN for convenience.)

Continue entering example pairs in the corresponding fields of CUSTOMER and MAILLIST until you have entered examples in the First Name, Last Name, Address, City, State, and Zip fields of both tables. Of course, you must use a different example for each pair of fields. Figure 9-47 shows the completed query.

Figure 9-47 An Insert Query

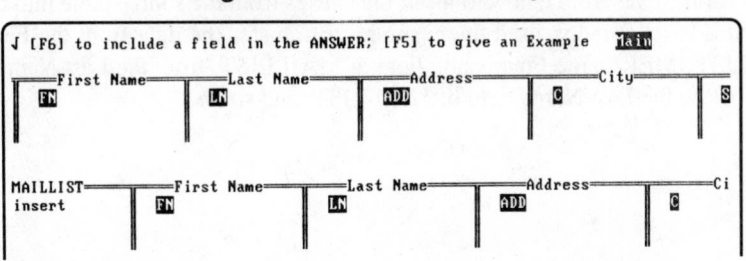

When you press [Do-It!] to process the query, Paradox will insert the data from the indicated fields of CUSTOMER into MAILLIST. In addition, the same entries will be entered in a table called INSERTED, as shown in Figure 9-48. Figure 9-49 shows the completed MAILLIST table.

Figure 9-48 The INSERTED Table

```
Viewing Inserted table: Record 1 of 6                          Main

  First Name        Last Name            Address          City
   FN                LN                  ADD                C               B


MAILLIST          First Name         Last Name            Address          Ci
insert             FN                 LN                  ADD               C


INSERTED    First Name      Last Name         Address           City
   1        John            Smith             111 Main St.      Peru
   2        David           Jones             555 Oak St.       Lexington
   3        Barbara         Williams          321 4th St.       New York
   4        Don             Johnson           123 Beach Rd.     Miami
   5        Julia           Baker             2 River Rd.       Cincinnati
   6        John            Dawkins           123 E. St.        Washington
```

Figure 9-49 The Complete MAILLIST Table

```
Viewing Maillist table: Record 1 of 16                         Main

MAILLIST    First Name      Last Name         Address           City
   1        Barry           Sumpter           567 Cards Way     Louisville
   2        Bill            Johnson           42 Old Rock Rd.   Memphis
   3        Billy           Thompson          1234 S. 3rd St.   Louisville
   4        David           Jones             123 Yale Ct.      New Haven
   5        Fred            Foote             123 Brattle St.   Cambridge
   6        Guy             Greene            123 Park Place    Louisville
   7        Jim             Morrison          100 W. 73rd St.   New York
   8        John            Smith             555 Main Street   Louisville
   9        Rodney          McCray            9999 Easy St.     Houston
  10        William         Bedford           222 N.E. Pkwy.    Memphis
  11        John            Smith             111 Main St.      Peru
  12        David           Jones             555 Oak St.       Lexington
  13        Barbara         Williams          321 4th St.       New York
  14        Don             Johnson           123 Beach Rd.     Miami
  15        Julia           Baker             2 River Rd.       Cincinnati
  16        John            Dawkins           123 E. St.        Washington
```

When you process an insert query, Paradox uses the examples you have defined in the two query forms to determine how to insert the entries from the source table into the target table. In this case, Paradox used the examples to transfer the data from the First Name field of CUSTOMER to the First Name field of MAILLIST, from the Last Name field of CUSTOMER to the Last Name field of MAILLIST, and so on.

Notes

As you have seen, insert queries allow you to transfer data from one table to another, even if the two tables have different structures. In fact, you can even use insert queries to insert data into an alphanumeric field that is shorter than the alphanumeric field in the table from which the data is inserted. If the target field is too narrow, Paradox will trim the source table entries automatically as it inserts them in the target table.

If you attempt to link two fields of different types with an example in an insert query, Paradox will highlight the second occurrence of the example and display the message *Expression in this field has the wrong type* when you try to process the query. You cannot, for example, use an insert query to insert data from an alphanumeric field in one table into a number, dollar, or date field in another table.

Insert Queries and Key Fields

If the target table of an insert query has a key field, things can become complicated. Let's consider a couple of simple examples.

Suppose you want to use an insert query to insert the records from the CUSTOMER table directly into the PROSPECT table. Remember that the Prospect Number field in the PROSPECT table is a key field. To make this insertion, you might create an insert query like the one in Figure 9-50. Note that this query includes examples that link the First Name, Last Name, Address, City, State, and Zip fields in the two tables, but that the Prospect Number and Cust Number fields are not linked.

Figure 9-50 Using a Key Field in an Insert Query

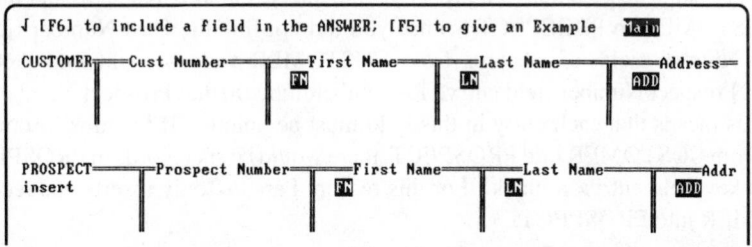

Figure 9-51 on the following page shows the screen after the query is processed. Figure 9-52, also on the next page, shows the resulting PROSPECT table. Notice that there are now 11 records in PROSPECT where there were only ten before. The trouble is that there should be 16 records in PROSPECT: the ten that were there, plus the six from CUSTOMER.

Figure 9-51 The INSERTED Table

```
Viewing Inserted table: Record 1 of 6                              Main
CUSTOMER━━Cust Number━━━━━━━First Name━━━━━━Last Name━━━━━━━━Address━━
                               FN               LN              ADD



PROSPECT━━━Prospect Number━━━━First Name━━━━━Last Name━━━━━━━Addr
insert                         FN               LN              ADD



INSERTED━Prospect Number━━━━First Name━━━━━━Last Name━━━━━━━Address━━
    1                       John            Smith           111 Main St.
    2                       David           Jones           555 Oak St.
    3                       Barbara         Williams        321 4th St.
    4                       Don             Johnson         123 Beach Road
    5                       Julia           Baker           2 River Rd.
    6                       John            Dawkins         123 E. St.
```

Figure 9-52 The PROSPECT Table

```
Viewing Prospect table: Record 1 of 11                             Main
PROSPECT━Prospect Number━━━━First Name━━━━━Last Name━━━━━━Address━━
    1                       John           Dawkins        123 E. St.
    2    1                  John           Smith          555 Main Street
    3    4                  Jim            Morrison        100 W. 73rd St
    4    5                  Bill           Johnson        42 Old Rock Rd.
    5    6                  Fred           Foote          123 Brattle St
    6    7                  David          Jones          123 Yale Ct.
    7    8                  Billy          Thompson       1234 S. 3rd St.
    8    9                  Rodney         McCray         9999 Easy St.
    9    10                 William        Bedford        222 N.E. Pkwy
   10    11                 Barry          Sumpter        567 Cards Way
   11    12                 Guy            Greene         123 Park Place
```

Here's what happened. When you processed the query, Paradox began to add the records from CUSTOMER to PROSPECT. Since you did not link the Cust Number field to the Prospect Number field, the records from CUSTOMER were brought into PROSPECT without a Prospect Number field entry. Remember, though, that Prospect Number is a key field. This means that each entry in this field must be unique. If Paradox inserted all six records from CUSTOMER into PROSPECT, there would be six records in PROSPECT with the same key field entry: a blank. For this reason, Paradox only inserts one record from CUSTOMER into PROSPECT.

The real problem is that Paradox does not give you any indication of what has happened. If you look at the INSERTED table that results from this query, you'll see that it contains all of the records from CUSTOMER, leading you to believe that the insert query was processed properly. In addition, Paradox has not placed the excluded records into a KEYVIOL table, even though a key violation has clearly occurred.

Now, let's look at an even more troublesome case. Again, suppose you want to combine CUSTOMER directly into PROSPECT, and you create the insert query shown in

Figure 9-53 to accomplish this task. This query is identical to the one in Figure 9-50 except that it includes a pair of examples that link the Prospect Number and Cust Number fields.

Figure 9-53 Using Multiple Key Fields

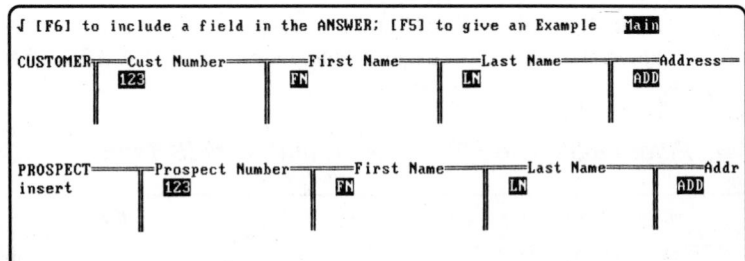

Figure 9-54 shows the PROSPECT table after this query has been processed. If you compare Figure 9-54 to Figure 9-52, you will see that Paradox has replaced the entries in PROSPECT that have Prospect Number field entries of 1, 4, 5, and 6 with the records from CUSTOMER that have those entries in the Cust Number field.

Figure 9-54 The PROSPECT Table

```
Viewing Prospect table: Record 1 of 13                          Main

PROSPECT  Prospect Number    First Name        Last Name        Address
   1                         John              Dawkins          123 E. St.
   2          1              John              Smith            111 Main St.
   3          2              David             Jones            555 Oak St.
   4          3              Barbara           Williams         321 4th St.
   5          4              Don               Johnson          123 Beach Road
   6          5              Julia             Baker            2 River Rd.
   7          6              John              Dawkins          123 E. St.
   8          7              David             Jones            123 Yale Ct.
   9          8              Billy             Thompson         1234 S. 3rd St.
  10          9              Rodney            McCray           9999 Easy St.
  11         10              William           Bedford          222 N.E. Pkwy
  12         11              Barry             Sumpter          567 Cards Way
  13         12              Guy               Greene           123 Park Place
```

Apparently, when an insert query encounters a conflict between an entry in a field of a source table and an entry in the corresponding key field of the target table, it simply replaces the target table record with the source table record. Once again, there is no indication that this has occurred. The INSERTED table shows the six records from CUSTOMER, just as it would if the query had worked correctly. And, once again, Paradox has not entered any records into a KEYVIOL table, nor has it entered the old versions of the records from PROSPECT into a CHANGED table. In other words, the old records are irretrievable.

What is the moral of all this? As with the Edit command, you should be very careful when you use insert queries to change tables that have key fields. The insert query is a very powerful tool, and you should use it with caution.

Inserting from Two Tables

You can insert records into only one table at a time. You can, however, insert data from more than one table at a time into a target table. To see how this works, let's use a simple example. Suppose you have created two tables, FIRST and LAST, that contain the first and last names of your friends. You want to insert these names into a table called NAMES. Figure 9-55 shows these tables.

Figure 9-55 The FIRST, LAST, and NAMES Tables

```
 Viewing Names table: Table is empty                          Main
 FIRST══════Number══════════First Name═══════
      1  ┃      1  ┃  John
      2  ┃      2  ┃  Steve
      3  ┃      3  ┃  Barney
      4  ┃      4  ┃  Wilma

 LAST═══════Number══════════Last Name════
      1  ┃      1  ┃  Smith
      2  ┃      2  ┃  Jobber
      3  ┃      3  ┃  Foote
      4  ┃      4  ┃  Rudolph

 NAMES══╤══Number══╤══First Name══╤══Last Name══════╗
```

To do this, first use the **[Menu] A**sk command to create three query forms: one for FIRST, one for LAST, and one for NAMES. When the query forms are in view, move to the space under the form name in the NAMES query form and type **insert**.

Next, you must enter in the fields of the three query forms examples that tell Paradox how to insert data into NAMES. To begin, enter the same example—we'll use the letter **N**—into the Number field of all three tables. Next, enter an example into the First Name field of the FIRST query form and enter the same example into the First Name field of the NAMES table. Finally, enter an example into the Last Name field of the LAST query form and into the Last Name field of the NAMES table. Figure 9-56 shows the completed query.

Figure 9-56 A Two-table Insert Query

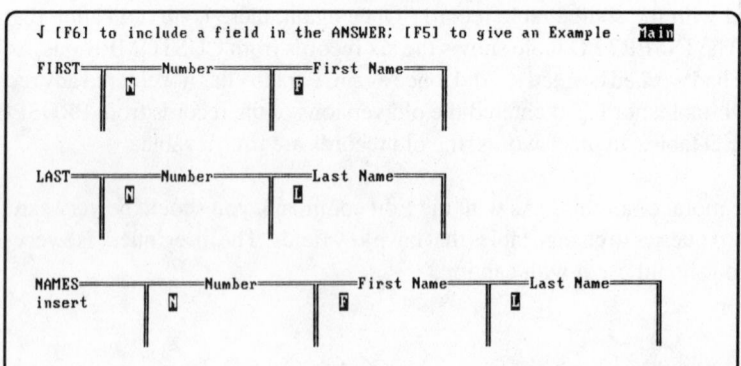

When you press [Do-It!] to process this query, Paradox will insert the entries from the First Name field of the FIRST table into the First Name field of the NAMES table and from the Last Name field of the LAST table into the Last Name field of the NAMES table. Figure 9-57 shows the NAMES table after the query is processed.

Figure 9-57 The Resulting NAMES Table

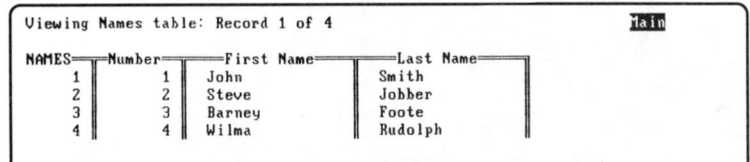

```
Viewing Names table: Record 1 of 4                              Main

NAMES═╤═Number═╤═══First Name═══╤═══Last Name═══╤
  1   │   1   │ John           │ Smith         │
  2   │   2   │ Steve          │ Jobber        │
  3   │   3   │ Barney         │ Foote         │
  4   │   4   │ Wilma          │ Rudolph       │
```

There is a fine point you must understand about multitable insert queries. As long as each source table contributes unique fields to the target table, everything will work correctly. What you cannot do with an insert query, however, is have two or more source tables, each of which contributes the same fields to the target table. For example, you could not create an insert query that would insert data from both PROSPECT and CUSTOMER into MAILLIST at once. You must use two separate queries (one for each source table) to make this insertion.

Conclusion

In this chapter, you've learned about several of Paradox's most sophisticated commands. You've seen how the Add command can be used to append the records in one table to another table, and how to update the records in one table using those in another. You've learned how to use Subtract to delete records in a source table from records in a target table. You've seen how the MultiEntry and MultiAdd commands can be used to distribute records from one table into two or more tables. In addition, you've learned how to use insert queries to perform specialized multitable operations.

This chapter concludes the second section of *Douglas Cobb's Paradox 3 Handbook*. In the next two chapters, we'll show you how to create reports from the data in your Paradox tables.

Chapter 10

Report Fundamentals

In the preceding chapters of this book, we've shown you a variety of ways to manipulate the information in a Paradox table. As you performed these manipulations, you saw the results on the screen of your computer. However, you often will want to share the information in your Paradox tables with people who don't have access to Paradox. To do this, you'll need to create printed copies of your work.

These next two chapters of *Douglas Cobb's Paradox 3 Handbook* deal with reporting. In this chapter, we'll introduce you to the basic features of the Paradox Report Generator. In Chapter 11, we'll cover more advanced topics, like summary statistics, grouping, managing reports, and using the Custom Configuration Program to customize the Report Generator.

Instant Reports

Paradox's [Instant Report] key provides the easiest way to print a hard copy of a table. When you press the [Instant Report] key ([Alt]-[F7]) while viewing a table or form, Paradox automatically sends a default report for that table to your printer. In most cases, this report will be a tabular listing of the information in the table—a "standard" report.

For example, if you want to print a copy of the information contained in the 65-record, nine-field table named LISTINGS, shown in Figure 10-1 on the following page, first issue the **[Menu]** View command, type **LISTINGS**, and press ↵ to bring LISTINGS to the workspace. Then, after making sure your printer is connected and turned on, press the **[Instant Report]** key ([Alt]-[F7]). As soon as you press this key, Paradox will display the message *Sending report to printer...* in the lower-right corner of the screen and will print the report shown in Figure 10-2 on page 407.

As you can see, the report shown in Figure 10-2 is a simple tabular listing of the information in the LISTINGS table. Each record is printed on a single line of the page, and the entries from each field are printed in their own columns. The contents of the alphanumeric fields from the table appear left aligned in the report, and the contents of the numeric fields appear right aligned, just as they do in a table. At the top of each column, Paradox has printed the name of the corresponding field in the table and has followed it with a dashed line. The order of columns in the report matches the field order in the structure of the table—but not necessarily the order of the fields in the image of that table. This is Paradox's standard report format.

Figure 10-1 The LISTINGS Table

Viewing Listings table: Record 1 of 65   Main   Viewing Listings table: Record 1 of 65   Main

LISTINGS	Address	Town	Owner	List Date	Style	Price	Sq Ft	BRs	Baths
1	123 Abby Ct.	Louisville	Kones,D	6/16/88	Ranch	32,950.00	1500	3	1
2	426 St. James Ct.	Louisville	Jones,S	6/19/88	Ranch	19,500.00	950	2	1
3	766 Baird St.	Louisville	Black,G	6/22/88	Colonial	139,950.00	2600	4	2.5
4	222 Big Ben Dr.	Louisville	Roberts,D	6/22/88	Other	53,500.00	1900	3	1.5
5	666 Montana Ave.	Louisville	Saul,H	6/23/88	Cape Cod	55,000.00	1900	4	2
6	589 Morocco Dr.	E'Town	Smith,B	6/24/88	Cape Cod	62,500.00	1875	3	1.5
7	987 Allan Dr.	Louisville	Newsome,K	6/26/88	Cape Cod	68,000.00	1900	4	2
8	549 Billtown Rd.	Louisville	Bizer,B	6/28/88	Ranch	72,500.00	2000	3	2
9	343 Market St.	Louisville	Bivins,D	6/29/88	Ranch	42,900.00	1675	3	1
10	198 Main St.	J'Town	Green,L	6/29/88	Other	27,500.00	800	3	1
11	885 Jefferson St.	J'Town	Zith,M	7/02/88	Ranch	55,000.00	1500	3	1
12	913 Whitney Dr.	North Hill	Kulp,R	7/04/88	Cape Cod	99,500.00	1000	4	2
13	363 Dower Ct.	North Fork	Culp,A	7/05/88	Cape Cod	109,000.00	2100	4	2
14	620 Windsong St.	Louisville	Pank,E	7/06/88	Colonial	250,000.00	4000	6	3.5
15	4500 Hempstead Dr.	Louisville	Pape,C	6/10/88	Colonial	150,000.00	2600	4	2.5
16	#6 Brandon Way	Louisville	Abrams,L	7/22/88	Ranch	67,000.00	2250	4	1.5
17	6610 Vermin Dr.	Louisville	Russ,J	7/24/88	Ranch	75,000.00	2100	3	1.5
18	712 Clifton Ct.	Louisville	Thomas,T	7/24/88	Ranch	30,000.00	1500	3	1
19	5432 Miller Rd.	Louisville	Young,R	7/29/88	Other	17,500.00	800	2	1
20	#12 Circle Ct.	Louisville	White,Y	8/02/88	Other	18,000.00	800	2	1
21	1222 Dee Rd.	South Fork	Smith,P	8/02/88	Ranch	22,950.00	950	3	1
22	222 Earl Ave.	J'Town	Wray,A	8/05/88	Ranch	51,900.00	1200	3	1
23	9827 Rowan St.	J'Town	Coad,B	8/10/88	Ranch	47,950.00	1100	3	1
24	3355 Bank St.	J'Town	Cobb,D	8/17/88	Ranch	37,500.00	1500	3	1
25	77 Portland Ave.	North Hill	Coe,A	8/19/88	Ranch	28,000.00	1500	3	1
26	99 Cardinal Hill Rd.	North Hill	Brand,B	8/19/88	Cape Cod	78,000.00	2000	3	1.5
27	#10 Old Mill Rd.	Louisville	Stern,M	8/21/88	Ranch	75,000.00	2150	3	1.5
28	5532 Mud Creek Dr.	Louisville	Hall,W	8/24/88	Ranch	12,000.00	950	2	1
29	4444 Normie Ln.	Louisville	James,J	8/25/88	Cape Cod	120,000.00	2400	5	2.5
30	3490 Bold Rd.	Louisville	Taft,H	8/29/88	Colonial	275,000.00	3000	5	3.5
31	#82 Rudd Rd.	Louisville	Lum,I	8/30/88	Cape Cod	88,950.00	2000	4	2
32	6712 Shelby St.	Louisville	Wood,B	8/30/88	Ranch	92,500.00	2400	4	2
33	7235 Shiloh Dr.	E'Town	Allan,J	8/31/88	Ranch	95,000.00	2750	4	2.5
34	8989 Big D Ln.	South Fork	Adkins,G	9/01/88	Ranch	17,000.00	1200	2	1
35	1001 Spring St.	North Hill	Frier,F	9/05/88	Other	45,000.00	1700	3	1.5
36	6935 Shiloh Dr.	E'Town	Grebe,C	9/08/88	Cape Cod	81,000.00	2000	3	2
37	4989 Adler Way	Louisville	Dole,V	9/13/88	Cape Cod	76,500.00	2000	3	1.5
38	5678 Beech St.	Louisville	Smith,P	9/16/88	Cape Cod	65,950.00	1800	3	1.5
39	#62 Billy Bone Ct.	Louisville	Taylor,A	9/18/88	Ranch	34,580.00	1600	3	1
40	3323 Mt. Holly Dr.	Louisville	Grizz,D	9/24/88	Ranch	22,100.00	1200	3	1
41	9909 Midway Rd.	Louisville	Maier,O	9/25/88	Ranch	61,250.00	1875	3	2
42	435 Oxted Ln.	Louisville	O'Neal,P	9/26/88	Ranch	53,790.00	1900	3	1
43	22 N. Ridge Ct.	Louisville	Munn,A	9/29/88	Colonial	200,000.00	2900	5	3
44	654 Mora Ln.	Louisville	Orwick,S	10/02/88	Cape Cod	48,000.00	1600	3	1
45	659 Ridge Rd.	Louisville	Pulley,F	10/08/88	Ranch	30,000.00	1500	3	1
46	14 Short Rd.	Louisville	Quire,I	10/13/88	Ranch	52,300.00	1600	3	1
47	721 Zabel Way	Louisville	Stich,L	10/14/88	Ranch	47,950.00	1500	3	1
48	581 Yale Dr.	Louisville	Winer,L	10/17/88	Ranch	78,000.00	2100	4	1.5
49	854 Unseld Blvd.	Louisville	Volk,H	10/19/88	Other	87,000.00	2500	4	2.5
50	#5 Ashby St.	J'Town	Wagner,H	10/22/88	Other	97,000.00	2500	4	2.5
51	1989 Eastern Pkwy.	Louisville	Klink,C	10/23/88	Ranch	26,950.00	1100	2	1
52	9819 Wilson Ave.	J'Town	Crane,B	10/23/88	Ranch	28,000.00	1200	3	1
53	956 Volar Ln.	J'Town	Lamb,M	10/25/88	Ranch	18,000.00	1200	2	1
54	5372 Tyson Pl.	Louisville	Goode,J	10/28/88	Ranch	35,000.00	1500	3	1.5
55	9849 Taylor Blvd.	J'Town	Dukes,J	10/29/88	Ranch	32,950.00	1750	3	1
56	185 Pages Ln.	J'Town	Cowan,M	11/01/88	Other	15,500.00	1000	2	1
57	3752 St. Dennis	J'Town	Levine,J	11/03/88	Cape Cod	67,950.00	2500	3	2
58	28 Seebolt Rd.	Louisville	Priest,S	11/10/88	Other	28,500.00	950	3	1
59	2216 Lacey St.	North Hill	Beat,A	11/13/88	Cape Cod	94,999.00	2700	4	2.5
60	6262 Kenwood Dr.	North Hill	Beck,D	11/17/88	Ranch	71,650.00	2000	3	1.5
61	9222 Meadow Pl.	South Fork	Baxter,H	11/22/88	Ranch	85,000.00	2100	3	2
62	6791 Lotus Ave.	South Fork	Howell,T	11/24/88	Ranch	75,000.00	2000	3	2
63	586 Ansa Way	Louisville	Noel,C	11/27/88	Colonial	69,500.00	2200	3	1.5
64	99 N. Central Blvd.	Louisville	Stevens,P	11/28/88	Ranch	49,000.00	2500	3	1.5
65	4233 Mix Ave.	Louisville	Martin,D	11/30/88	Cape Cod	49,500.00	1900	3	1.5

Paradox will always print every record from any table. In this case, for example, Paradox has printed all 65 records from the LISTINGS table. Unless you specify that the report be grouped (a topic we'll discuss in Chapter 11), Paradox will print the records in the same order as they appear in the table from which you print them.

In addition to printing the 65 records from this table in the standard report, Paradox also has printed a title line at the top of the report. This title line contains the current date, the report title (in this case, *Standard report*), and the page number.

You also will notice that this report had to be printed on four separate pages. Unless your tables are very small, the printout of those tables will occupy more than one page.

Paradox can print from only a single table at a time. It cannot draw information from more than one table into a report as a part of the reporting process. If you want to include information from two or more tables in a single report, use a query to combine information from those tables into a single table and then print from the new table.

Figure 10-2 A Standard Report

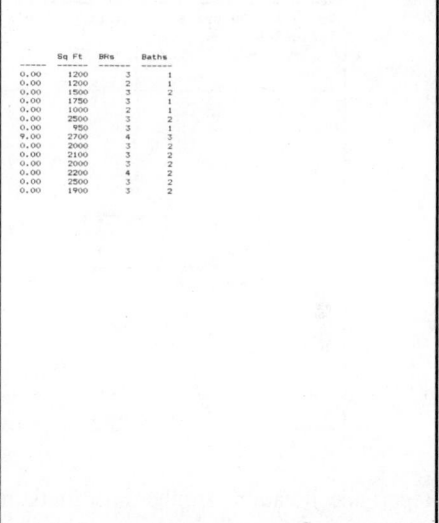

Report Specifications

When you pressed the [Instant Report] key, Paradox didn't just send an image of the current table to your printer—it added some explanatory text to the report, adjusted the spacing of the report, and so forth. The result was the standard report for the LISTINGS table. When

Paradox printed this report, it did so according to the layout defined in the standard report specification (or report spec) shown in Figure 10-3. A report spec is a template that defines the arrangement of information in a Paradox report. Paradox automatically sets up a standard report spec for any table you create.

Figure 10-3 A Standard Report Specification

```
Designing report R for Listings table                        Report    1/2
Table Band                                                            Address
....+...10....+...20....+...30....+...40....+...50....+...60....+...70....+...8*

  ─▼page─────────────────────────────────────────────────────────────────────


  mm/dd/yy                        Standard report                    Page 999

  ┌▼table──────────────────────────────────────────────────────────────────────

  Address               Town       Owner       List Date  Style       Price
  ──────────────────    ─────────  ─────────   ─────────  ─────────   ─────────
  AAAAAAAAAAAAAAAAAAAA  AAAAAAAAAA  AAAAAAAAAA  mm/dd/yy   AAAAAAAAAA  (999,999,99
  └▲table──────────────────────────────────────────────────────────────────────


  ─▲page─────────────────────────────────────────────────────────────────────
```

```
Designing report R for Listings table                        Report    2/2
Table Band                                                            Address
....+...10....+...20....+...30....+...40....+...50....+...60....+...70....+...8*




  ─────────  ┌──────┐ ┌─────┐ ┌──────┐ ─────────────────────────────────────
             │Sq Ft │ │BRs  │ │Baths │
             ─────── ─────── ───────
  9.99)     999999  999999  999999   ─────────────────────────────────────
```

Report specifications are the most fundamental element of Paradox reporting. Whenever Paradox prints information from a table, it does so according to the layout of the information in a report spec. Normally, printing a Paradox report is a two-step process. First, you design a report spec that shows Paradox how you want the report to look (you can design up to 15 report specs for any table). Then, you tell Paradox to print the table according to that spec. When you first create a table, Paradox automatically produces a standard report specification and designates it as the default report specification for that table. Whenever you press the [Instant Report] key while viewing a table, Paradox prints from the default spec for that table. Unless you have modified the standard report spec (a process we'll explain later), Paradox will print the standard report whenever you press the [Instant Report] key.

Every report spec contains the same essential components: elements, bands, and page-widths. We'll use the standard LISTINGS table report spec shown in Figure 10-3 to explain what these components are and how they work. Later, we'll tell you how to set up these components in a report spec.

Elements

If you examine the standard report shown in Figure 10-2, you'll see that it contains two types of information: entries from the fields in the source table (and from other special fields) and literal text. All Paradox reports contain one or both of these types of information, which come from two different types of elements in the report specification: field masks and literals.

Field Masks

Paradox uses special tools called field masks to represent the fields from a table in a report specification. The exact appearance of these masks depends on the type of field they represent. Masks that represent numeric fields appear as a series of the digit 9. For example, Paradox uses the mask *999999* to represent the BRs field in the report spec shown in Figure 10-3. Masks that represent alphanumeric fields appear as a series of the letter *A*. For example, Paradox uses the mask *AAAAAAAAAA* to represent the Owner field in the standard spec. Dollar ($) fields are represented with a series of 9s, like number fields, but also include parentheses, commas, and decimal points. The masks for date fields are generic representations of the form in which Paradox will display the date. For example, the mask *mm/dd/yy* instructs Paradox to print the date May 10, 1989, as *5/10/89*, while the mask *Month dd, yyyy* instructs Paradox to print the same date as *May 10, 1989*. Paradox can print a date in 11 different forms.

The length of a mask determines how much space Paradox allows each entry it prints from the field represented by that mask. If a mask is ten characters long, Paradox will devote ten spaces to the entries from the field represented by that mask when it prints the report. By default, entries from alphanumeric fields will be left aligned within their masks, while entries from numeric fields will be right aligned, although you can change this if you want.

In a standard report spec, the length of each mask is determined by the type and/or length of the field it represents, as defined in the structure (not necessarily the display image) of that field. The mask width for an alphanumeric field will equal the length designation for that field in the table's structure. Paradox will use a mask that is six characters wide for any numeric or short number field, a mask that is 16 characters wide for a dollar field, and a mask that is eight characters wide for a date field. You can adjust the length of a field mask. (We'll show you how to do this later in this chapter.)

In addition to using masks to draw information from the fields of a table, Paradox uses masks to place six kinds of special information in a report: the current date, the current time, the current page number, the current record number, the results of calculations, and summary statistics. In the standard report spec shown in Figure 10-3, the mask *mm/dd/yy* at the left edge of the spec represents the current date, and the mask *999* at the right edge of the spec represents the current page number. We'll explore time fields, calculated fields, and summary fields later in this chapter and in Chapter 11.

Literal Text

In addition to field masks, any report specification can (and usually will) contain descriptive text. Unlike masks, which draw information from the fields of a table or place other variable information into a report, any text included in a report spec will be printed literally in the report. For this reason, nonmask entries in a report spec are called literals.

Paradox has included several literals in the report specification shown in Figure 10-3. For example, it has "typed" the literal *Standard report* at the top of the report specification. Additionally, Paradox has included the name of each field as a literal immediately above the mask that represents each field. The dashed lines that appear immediately below the field names also are literals.

Bands

As you have seen, the masks and literals you include in a report specification determine what information will appear in a report. The placement of those elements within the report specification determine where they will appear in that report. Since the literal *Page* and the page number mask *999* appear to the right of the literal *Standard report* in the report spec shown in Figure 10-3, for example, the page number information will appear to the right of the title in the printed report. Additionally, since the literals *Address* and - - - - - - - - - - - - are positioned above the field mask for the Address field, Paradox will print those literals before it prints the entries from the Address field.

The position of one mask or literal relative to another mask or literal is not the only factor that determines where that element will appear in a report. The band in which that element appears also affects where it will be printed. A band is a section of a report template that is responsible for producing a certain portion of a report. A report spec's bands are defined by the horizontal lines that run across the spec. The lines that mark the beginning of a band will be marked with the symbol ▼ and the name of that band. For example, the topmost line in Figure 10-3 (the one with the legend ▼ *page*) signals the beginning of the page band. The lines that signal the end of a band will be marked with the symbol ▲ and the name of the band. For example, the line with the legend ▲ *table* signals the end of the table band.

All standard Paradox reports (and most other reports) contain three bands: the report band, the page band, and the table band. The arrangement of the bands in a report spec divides the report band and the page band into two parts: a top and a bottom, which are sometimes called a header and a footer. Each section of each band is responsible for printing a different part of the report.

The Report Header

The report header is the section of the report band that appears above the top border of the page band. Literals and masks that are situated in this section will be printed only once, at the beginning of the report. You'll want to use this section of a report spec for information you want Paradox to print only at the top of the first page of a report, such as an overall report title or the date or time of printing. In the standard report spec shown in Figure 10-3, the report header section contains only a single blank line. This causes Paradox to skip one line at the top of the first page of the report.

The Report Footer

The report footer is the section of the report band that appears below the bottom border of the page band. The masks and literals you include in this section of the report spec will be printed only once, on the last page of a report, immediately after the last record Paradox prints, but before the page footer (a band we'll discuss in a few paragraphs). You'll want to use this section for information you want Paradox to print only once, at the end of the report, such as a grand total of the entries in a column. In the standard report spec shown in Figure 10-3, the report footer consists of a single blank line. This causes Paradox to "print" a single blank line after it prints the 65th record in the LISTINGS table.

The Page Header

The table band of the standard report spec shown in Figure 10-3 divides the page band into two sections: a page header and a page footer. The page header is the section of the page band that appears above the upper border of the table band. The masks and literals you include in this section of a report specification will be printed once at the top of each page in the report. In addition to providing a place for titles, dates, and so forth at the top of each page, the page header is the only means of adding a top margin to each page.

In a standard report like the one shown in Figure 10-2, the page header occupies six lines: three blank lines, a line that contains information (a current date mask, the literal *Standard report*, the literal *Page*, and a page number mask), and then another two blank lines. This page header instructs Paradox to skip three lines at the top of each page as a top margin, print a line of information, then skip another two lines.

The Page Footer

The page footer is the section of the page band that extends below the bottom border of the table band. Paradox prints any masks or literals you place in this section at the bottom of each page of the report. You could use a summary mask in the page footer to print the total of the entries from a certain field on each page. The page footer provides the only means of specifying a bottom margin for a report. The page footer of a standard report consists of four blank lines, which causes Paradox to leave a four-line margin at the bottom of each page.

The Table Band

The central portion of any standard report is the table band. The masks and literals that you include in this section will be printed between the bottom of the page header and the top of the page footer, as many times as will fit on that page. Although the table band is not overlaid by any other band, it contains two functional sections: a header and a body. The header consists of the rows of the table band above the first mask in that band. Any information on these lines will be printed only once on the page, much like the page header, immediately below the last line of the page header. In a standard report, for example, Paradox will print a blank line, then a line of field names, then a line of dashes once on each page.

The body of the table band begins with the first row that contains a field mask and ends with the bottom of the table band. Paradox will print the information in this section of the table band once for every record in the table, in the order that those records appear in the table (unless you have grouped them—a topic we'll cover in Chapter 11). In this case, for example, Paradox will print the *123 Abby Ct.* record first, the *426 St. James Ct.* record second, the *766 Baird St.* record third, and so forth. On each "pass" through a report, the field masks in the table band refer to a different record in the table Paradox is printing.

In a standard report, the lower section of the table band consists of a single row and contains only field masks. However, the table bands of your custom reports can occupy more than one row and can contain literals as well as field masks. If you added a blank line at the end of the table band of the report spec shown in Figure 10-3, for example, Paradox would leave a blank line between each record it prints, rather than printing them one after another with no lines in between. We'll show you how to add lines, literals, and masks to a report specification later in this chapter.

Columns in the Table Band

If you look closely at the table band, you'll notice that Paradox has placed small hash marks on the lines that define the top and bottom borders of that band. These marks divide the table band into columns. As you can see, Paradox has created one column in the table band for each of the fields in the source table. Paradox has placed one field mask, one column header, and one dashed line within each column. As you will see later, because the table band is divided into columns, it is easy to rearrange the fields in the report and adjust the spacing between the columns of the report. For now, just realize that the table band of the report spec will be divided into columns.

Other Bands

The standard report that Paradox automatically creates for any table consists of only the report, page, and table bands. When we discuss grouping in Chapter 11, however, you'll see that a report spec can contain yet another type of band—a group band. Group bands allow you to separate the information in a report into groups, based on a number of factors. Any group bands in a report spec (there can be up to 16 nested within any spec) fit in layers between the page band and the table band. Later in this chapter, we'll introduce yet another type of band—the form band. A form band is the equivalent of the table band in a different type of report—a free-form report.

How Many Records Print on a Page?

Together with the Length setting (a topic we'll cover at the end of this chapter), the number of nonmask lines in a report spec determines how many records Paradox will print on each page of a report. Unless you specify otherwise, Paradox assumes that you are printing on standard 11-inch-long paper, and that your printer can print six lines per inch. Consequently, Paradox will print 66 lines per page.

Because all standard reports have the same layout, they should print the same number of records per page. Determining how many single-line records Paradox will print on a single page is a matter of subtraction. On the first page of the report, Paradox will skip one line for the report header. Next, Paradox will use six lines for the page header. The first three lines of the table band (a blank line and two lines of text) will use up three more lines on the page. The page footer uses up another four lines. Subtracting the total number of these lines (14) from the number of lines available on the first page (66) tells you that Paradox should print 52 records on that page. Paradox also should be able to print 52 records on the last page, since it will have a one-line report footer but no report header. All pages but the first and last will have neither a report header nor a report footer, so Paradox should be able to print 53 records on those pages.

Page-widths

In addition to dividing a report specification into bands, Paradox also divides it into page-widths. Paradox uses a vertical line in bright reverse video, like the ones shown in Figure 10-3, to mark the end of each page-width in the report spec. Very simply, a page-width is a graphic representation of the width of the printed pages in a report. All the page-widths in a report specification must be the same. Since most printers can print 80 characters on a line, the default page-width in a report spec is 80 characters. The horizontal position of the masks and literals in a report spec determines on which page of the report they will be printed.

When Paradox designs the standard report for a table, it includes as many 80-character page-widths as are necessary to accommodate the fields of the table. As you can see in Figure 10-3, for example, the default report spec for the LISTINGS table requires two page-widths because there is not enough room to fit all nine fields onto one page, given the default widths of their masks. Because of the system it uses to place fields in a standard report, Paradox often splits fields onto two pages. In this case, for example, the first part of the Price field appears on the first page-width, and the second part is positioned on the second page-width. As you can see in Figure 10-2, Paradox prints part of each entry from the Price column on different pages of the report. Later, we'll show you how to push a divided field onto a single page-width (and thus onto a single page of the printed report), either by adjusting the width of the column that contains the field or by adjusting the size of the page-width.

Any time a report spec contains more than a single page-width, or a table contains more records than will fit on a single page, or both, Paradox will print the table on multiple pages. In Figure 10-2, for example, the standard report for the LISTINGS table occupies four pages. Very simply, Paradox always prints the first page-width for all records in the table first, the second page-width for all the records next, and so forth. Because the page header information is contained within the first page-width of the report, Paradox prints it only on the first and second pages of the report—the ones that are printed from the first page-width.

Other Features

If you look again at Figure 10-3, you will notice a number of status messages at the top of the screen. The message at the left edge of the screen tells you the current operation: *Designing report R for Listings table*. The left edge of the second line of the screen is the band indicator. In this area, Paradox displays the band in which the cursor is positioned. The message *Table Band* on the second line of Figure 10-3 indicates that the cursor is in the table band.

At the right side of the first line of the screen, Paradox displays the word *Report* in reverse video. This message indicates that you are in the Report mode. To the right of this mode indicator, Paradox displays the message *1/2*. This page-width indicator tells you that the cursor is in the first page-width of a two-page-width report.

Paradox uses the right edge of the second line of the screen as the field mask indicator. Whenever the cursor is positioned on a mask in a report spec, Paradox displays the name of the field represented by that mask in this area. In Figure 10-3, for example, the word *Address* indicates that the cursor is positioned on the mask that represents the Address field. Because Paradox uses generic characters like *A*'s and 9s for field masks, this indicator provides the only sure way to determine which field a mask represents.

Paradox displays a stylized horizontal ruler on the third line of the report spec screen. This ruler assists you in placing and centering masks and literals on the screen. In Figure 10-3, the horizontal ruler confirms that Paradox has set page-widths of 80 characters for this standard report.

Custom Reports

The standard report spec Paradox creates for any table is useful in many reporting situations. There will be times, however, when you'll want to create custom reports that are far more complex than the simple ones produced by the standard spec. The power of the Paradox Report Generator makes it easy to create this kind of report.

Designing a custom report is a lot like creating a custom form. Paradox presents you with a "schematic diagram" of how the report will look. This is the report spec. You use commands to modify the spec by placing and reformatting fields, adding literal text, and so forth. Paradox reports can be much more complex than Paradox forms, so you have many more options during report design. After you have designed your report spec, you can save it for future use. When you print the report, Paradox uses the report spec as instructions for what to print and how to print it.

Creating a Report Specification

As we explained at the beginning of this chapter, Paradox automatically designs a standard report specification for every table it creates and makes that spec the default for the table. To create a custom report for a table, you must design a custom report specification. Including the default specification, up to 15 report specifications can be associated with any table at once.

To begin, press the [Menu] key and choose Report to reveal the Report menu shown in Figure 10-4. The Output command on this menu lets you send a report to a printer, the screen, or a file. The Design command lets you design a new report for a table. The Change command lets you make changes in an existing report. The RangeOutput command lets you send specified pages to the printer, the screen, or a file. The SetPrinter command lets you specify a setup string or printer port to be used for printer output.

Figure 10-4 The Report Menu

```
Output  Design  Change  RangeOutput  SetPrinter                    Main
Send a report to the printer, the screen, or a file.


















     Use → and ← keys to move around menu, then press ↵ to make selection.
```

Because you want to design a new report, you should choose Design from this menu. When you issue this command, Paradox will prompt you to supply the name of a table. You can do this either by typing the name and pressing ↵ or by pressing ↵ to reveal a list of names, pointing to one, and pressing ↵ again. In this case, we'll choose LISTINGS.

Once you have specified the table for which you want to create the report spec (the one whose records you want to print), Paradox will display the menu shown in Figure 10-5. As you can see, this menu contains 15 choices: the letter R and the numbers 1 to 14. Each item on this menu represents one of the 15 possible report specifications that can be associated with the table. (You may notice that this menu is very similar to the one you saw in Chapter 4 when you were creating forms.)

Figure 10-5 The Design Menu

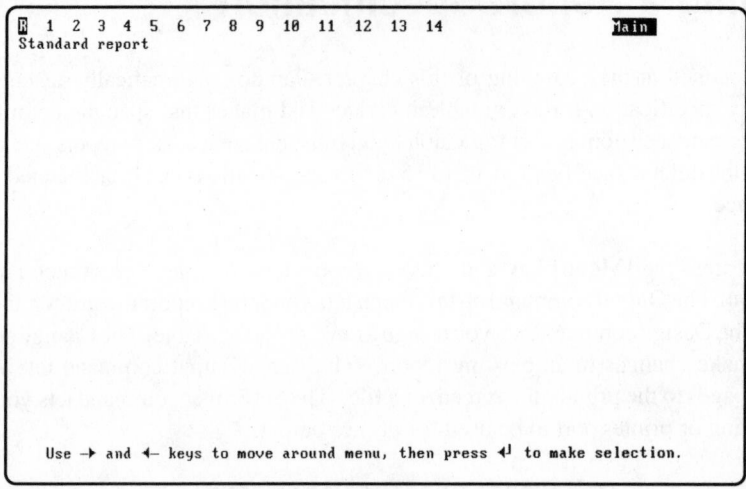

When you first create a table, Paradox designs a standard report specification for that table and stores it under the letter R. Paradox will print this report whenever you press the [Instant Report] key while you are viewing a table. The prompt *Standard report* appears below the Design menu when you highlight the R option. Unless you have previously designed a report spec for the table, no reports will be associated with the other 14 options (1-14). For that reason, the prompt *Unused report* will appear below the menu when you position the cursor on any of those choices.

When you see the Design menu, you should select the number or letter under which you want to store the report spec you are about to design. If you choose the number of any report you have designed already, Paradox will present the choices Cancel and Replace. If you choose Cancel, Paradox will return you to the Design menu and let you make another choice. If you choose Replace, Paradox will delete the old report spec to make room for the new one you create. Until you have designed 14 custom report specifications for a table, you probably will want to choose an unused number rather than overwrite an existing spec. In this case, we'll select the number **1**.

Once you have selected the number under which you want to store the report spec, Paradox will prompt you to supply a description for the report. This step is optional. If you do enter a description (which may be up to 40 characters long), it will appear on the second line of the menu when you highlight the number of the report specification. Also, Paradox will automatically place it in the page header of the report spec you are designing, just as it places the description *Standard report* in the page header of any standard report. If you choose not to enter a description, these areas will remain blank. In this case, we'll enter the description **Custom Report #1**.

After you enter a description for the report (or press ↵ to bypass this step), Paradox will display another menu that offers two options: Tabular and Free-form. Your choice from this menu determines the structure of the basic report spec Paradox will create for you. If you choose Tabular, Paradox will present a tabular report spec. Tabular report specs are well-suited for printing information in the table in a rigid columnar format. The standard report spec that Paradox automatically creates for any table is always tabular. On the other hand, free-form report specs are best suited for printing information in a less-structured format. You would use a free-form report spec to print mailing labels and form letters, for example.

If your report will be tabular (row and column), like the standard report, you should choose the Tabular option. Next, Paradox will present the report spec shown in Figure 10-6. As you can see, this specification looks like the standard report for the LISTINGS table, except that the description *Custom Report #1,* instead of *Standard report,* appears centered in the page header of the first page-width.

Figure 10-6 A New Tabular Report Spec

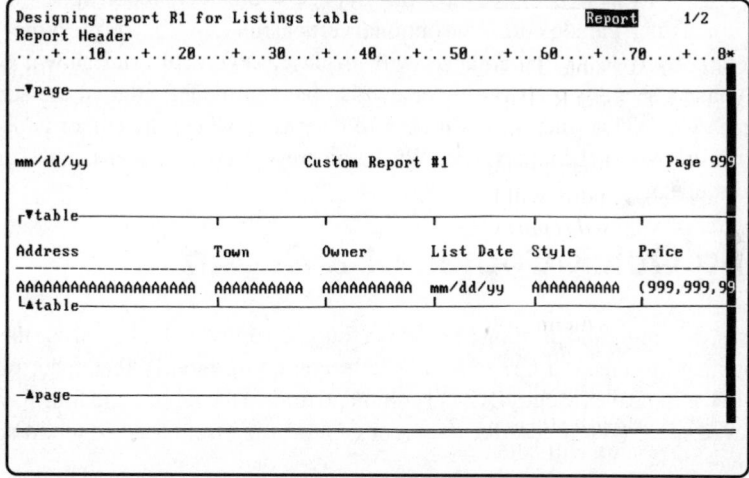

Once Paradox presents a new report spec, you can modify it in an almost unlimited number of ways. For example, you can delete, place, and move masks and literals, add and delete bands, add and delete page-widths, and so forth. Before you can do these things, however, you need to learn how to move around within a report specification.

Moving around in a Report Specification

When Paradox first displays a report specification screen, the cursor will be at the left edge of the first line of that screen. You can use the cursor keys on the numeric keypad, either by themselves or in combination with the [Ctrl] key, to move the cursor around the report specification screen.

These keys and key combinations do pretty much the same thing in the Report mode as they do in the Form mode: ➡ moves the cursor one space to the right, ⬇ moves it one row down, and so forth. Because the pages of a form are situated vertically and the pages (page-widths) of a report are situated horizontally, the actions of the [Pg Up], [Pg Dn], [Ctrl]-[➡], and [Ctrl]-[⬅] keys differ. In a report spec, the [Ctrl]-[➡] key moves the cursor a half-screen to the right or to the right edge of the rightmost page-width in the spec, whichever comes first. Similarly, the [Ctrl]-[⬅] key moves the cursor a half-screen to the left or to the left edge of the leftmost page-width in the spec. In a report spec, the [Pg Dn] key moves the cursor down one screen or to the bottom edge of the page-width, whichever comes first, and the [Pg Up] key moves the cursor up one screen or to the top of the current page-width.

The Vertical Ruler

As you can see in Figures 10-3 and 10-6, Paradox automatically displays a horizontal ruler on the third line of any report specification. This ruler lets you know where the cursor is positioned relative to the left edge of the leftmost page-width in the report spec. In addition to this horizontal ruler, Paradox offers an optional vertical ruler. When you press the [Vertical Ruler Toggle] key ([Ctrl]-[V]), Paradox will display the vertical ruler shown in Figure 10-7. As you can see, this ruler is a reverse video band at the left edge of the screen that numbers each row. This ruler makes it easy to determine where the cursor is positioned relative to the first row of the report spec. When you press [Vertical Ruler Toggle] again, the ruler will disappear.

Printing Quick Copies of a Report

In most cases, designing and printing a report is a four-step process: First, you use the Report Design command to create a new report spec; second, you modify that spec; third, you press [Do-It!] or issue the [Menu] DO-IT! command to save the report; and fourth, you print from the saved spec. (We'll describe the process of printing from a saved report spec later in this chapter.)

In some cases, you'll want to print copies of a report while designing the spec for that report. Paradox gives you a couple of ways to do this. The easiest way to print is simply to press the [Instant Report] key while you are designing the report. As you learned earlier, pressing the [Instant Report] key while you are viewing a table causes Paradox to print the default report for that table (the one stored under the letter R). If you press [Instant Report] from within the

Report Generator, however, Paradox will print a report from the report spec you are viewing. As you will see, the [Instant Report] key gives you an easy way to determine how a report will look as you are designing it.

Figure 10-7 The Vertical Ruler

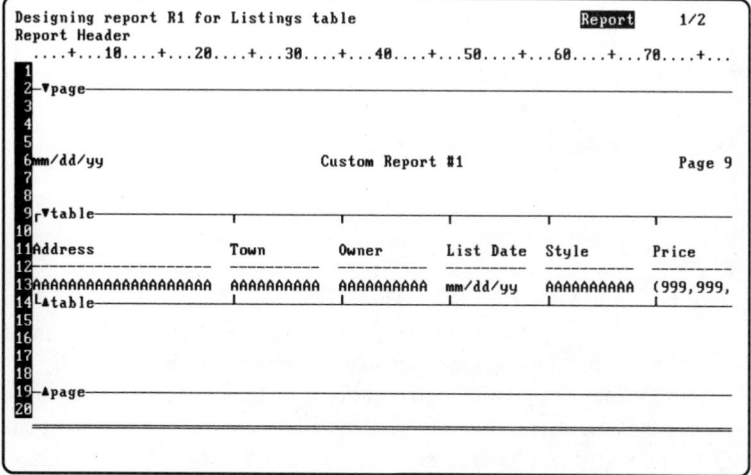

```
Designing report R1 for Listings table                    Report    1/2
Report Header
     ....+...10....+...20....+...30....+...40....+...50....+...60....+...70....+...
1
2 ─▼page────────────────────────────────────────────────────────────────
3
4
5
6 mm/dd/yy                          Custom Report #1                    Page 9
7
8
9 ┌▼table─────────────┬──────────┬──────────┬──────────┬──────────┬──────────
10
11 Address             Town       Owner      List Date  Style      Price
12 ──────────────────  ─────────  ─────────  ─────────  ─────────  ─────────
13 AAAAAAAAAAAAAAAAAAAA AAAAAAAAAA AAAAAAAAAA mm/dd/yy   AAAAAAAAAA (999,999,
14 └▲table─────────────┴──────────┴──────────┴──────────┴──────────┴──────────
15
16
17
18
19 ─▲page────────────────────────────────────────────────────────────────
20
```

The [Menu] Output command provides the second way to print a report from the spec you are editing within the Report Generator. When you issue this command, Paradox will present a menu with three options: Printer, Screen, and File. If you choose Printer, Paradox will direct the report whose spec you are viewing to your printer, as it does when you press [Instant Report]. The Screen and File options allow you to preview a report on the screen or send it to a text file, respectively. We'll discuss these options later.

Adding and Deleting Lines

Any new tabular report spec will occupy 20 lines of the screen and contain as many page-widths as are necessary to accommodate all of the fields in the source table. You can add or delete lines to make the report specification as small as one line or as large as 2,000 lines.

Deleting Lines

To delete a line from a report spec, just move the cursor to the left edge of that line and press the [Report Delete Line] key ([Ctrl]-[Y]). When you press this key, Paradox will delete the current line and squeeze the remaining lines up one row. If the line contains any field masks or literals, they will be removed from the report. For example, suppose you press [Report Delete Line] while the cursor is at the left edge of the fourth row of the page header band in the report spec shown in Figure 10-7. Figure 10-8 shows the result. This action removes the title line from the report, reducing the size of the page header by one line.

Figure 10-8 Deleting a Line from a Report Spec

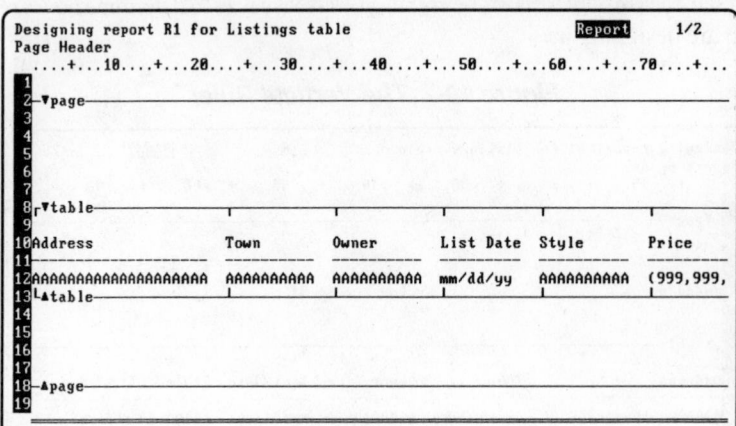

You also can use the [Report Delete Line] key to erase part of the characters on a line. When you press [Report Delete Line] while the cursor is anywhere but at the left edge of a line, Paradox will erase the character the cursor is on and all the characters to its right on the same line. Figure 10-9 shows the result of pressing [Report Delete Line] while the cursor is on the *C* in the title *Custom Report #1* on the sixth line of the report spec shown in Figure 10-7.

Figure 10-9 Deleting Part of a Line

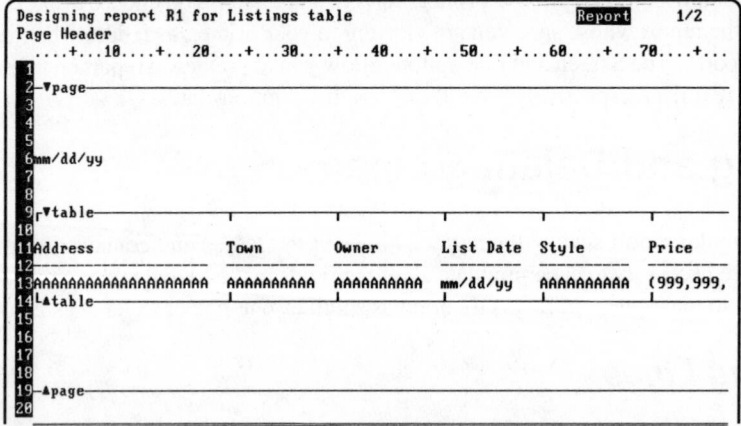

Paradox will just beep if you press the [Report Delete Line] key while the cursor is on a field mask or on a line that marks the border of a band.

Adding Lines

The ↵ key makes it possible to add new blank lines to a report spec. To add a new line at the end of a report spec, just move the cursor anywhere to the right of the rightmost character on the last line of the spec and press ↵. Unfortunately, adding a new line anywhere else in a report spec is not quite as simple. Unless the cursor is positioned to the right of the last character on the last line of the report, the action invoked by the ↵ key depends on whether Paradox is in the replace or insert mode.

The Replace and Insert Modes

Like many text editors, the Paradox Report Editor offers two editing modes: replace and insert. When you first enter the Report Editor, Paradox will be in the replace mode. While Paradox is in this mode, you cannot use the ↵ key to add new lines anywhere except at the end of a report spec. If you press ↵ while the cursor is within a line other than the border of a band, Paradox will move the cursor to the beginning of the next line. If you press ↵ while the cursor is on a line that marks the border of a band, Paradox will just beep.

To enter a blank line in the middle of a report spec, Paradox must be in the insert mode. To place Paradox in this mode, just press the [Ins] key. When you press this key, Paradox will display the mode indicator *Ins* to the right of the reverse-video report indicator in the upper-right corner of the screen.

Adding Lines in the Middle of a Spec

Once Paradox is in the insert mode, you can use the ↵ key to add new blank lines anywhere within a report spec. If you press ↵ while the cursor is positioned beyond the rightmost character in any line (except on a line that marks a border), Paradox will add a new blank line below that line and position the cursor at the beginning of that new line. Figure 10-10 on the following page shows the result of pressing ↵ while the cursor is positioned to the right of the field mask for the Baths field while Paradox is in the insert mode. As you can see, Paradox has added a new line at the end of the table band. If you printed from this report spec, Paradox would skip one line after every record.

Pressing ↵ in the insert mode when the cursor is positioned in the beginning or middle of a line produces different results. If you press ↵ while the cursor is positioned at the beginning of any line, Paradox will insert a line above that line. For example, if you press ↵ while the cursor is at the beginning of the first line in the spec shown in Figure 10-10, Paradox will add a new line at the top of the report header.

If you press the ↵ key in the insert mode while there are field masks or literals to the cursor's right, Paradox will add a new line below the current one and move the text that appears to the right of the cursor to that new line. If the cursor is in the middle of a literal, Paradox will split it onto two lines. If the cursor is on a field mask, however, Paradox will beep and will not add a new line or split the mask.

Figure 10-10 Adding a Row to the Table Band

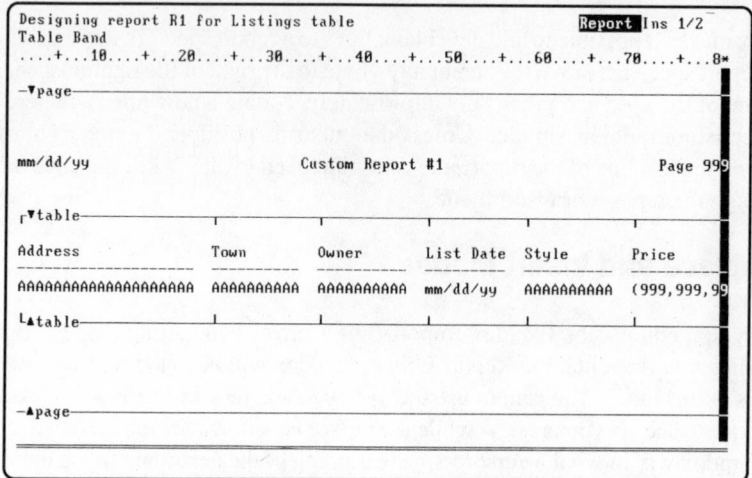

```
Designing report R1 for Listings table                    Report Ins 1/2
Table Band
....+...10....+...20....+...30....+...40....+...50....+...60....+...70....+...8*
 ▾page
 
 
mm/dd/yy                      Custom Report #1                     Page 999
 
 ▾table
 
Address              Town       Owner      List Date  Style      Price
-------------------  ---------- ---------- ---------  ---------- ---------
AAAAAAAAAAAAAAAAAAAA AAAAAAAAAA AAAAAAAAAA mm/dd/yy   AAAAAAAAAA (999,999,99
 ▴table
 
 
 ▴page
```

Paradox does not allow you to break a line of the table band onto two lines. If you press the ↵ key while the cursor is positioned anywhere in the table band other than at the beginning or end of a line, Paradox will simply move the cursor to the beginning of the next row without inserting a new row. This prevents you from accidentally destroying the columnar integrity of the tabular report. Paradox also moves the cursor to the beginning of the next row without inserting a new row if you press the ↵ key while the cursor is on a line that marks the border of a band.

Working with Page-widths

When Paradox presents you with a new report spec, that spec will consist of as many 80-character page-widths as are necessary to accommodate the fields from the source table. In the case of the LISTINGS table, Paradox creates a report spec that consists of two page-widths. However, the number of page-widths in any report spec is not fixed. Just as you can add lines to and delete lines from a report spec, you can add page-widths to and delete page-widths from a report spec. You also can adjust the size of any page-width.

Deleting a Page-width

Paradox allows you to delete the rightmost page-width from any multiple-page-width report spec. To delete a page-width, issue the [Menu] Setting PageLayout Delete command. When you issue this command, Paradox will present you with two choices: Cancel and OK. If you choose Cancel, Paradox will not delete any page-widths and will display the previous menu. If you select OK, Paradox will delete the last (rightmost) page-width in the report spec and everything on it.

Any field masks that cross the page boundary from the previous page-width will also be deleted from the report spec. Additionally, Paradox will remove from the report spec any column of the table band that crosses a boundary onto the page-width you are deleting. For example, Figure 10-11 shows the result of issuing the [Menu] Setting PageLayout Delete OK command from within the two-page-width report spec shown in Figure 10-10. As you can see, the page-width indicator now reads *1/1*, indicating that the report spec consists of a single page-width. Additionally, because the column of the table band that contains the Price field mask crosses the border between the first and second page-widths, Paradox has eliminated that column and its contents from the first page of the report. As we'll show you later, you can prevent this by altering the size of the page-widths in a report before you delete one.

Figure 10-11 Deleting a Page-width

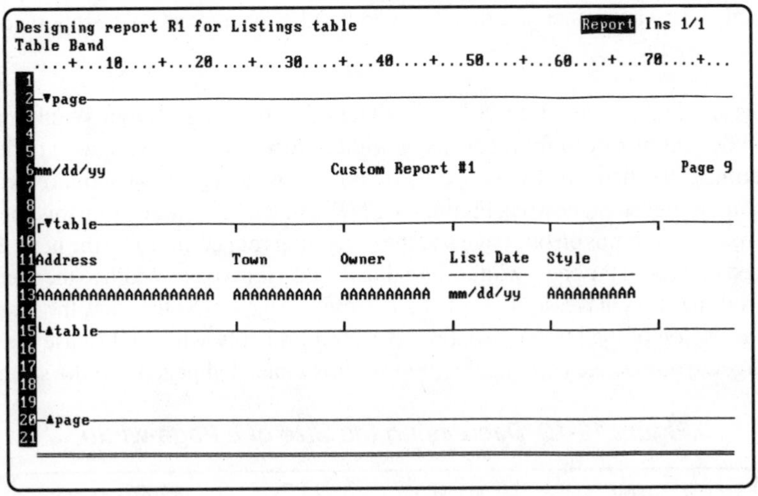

```
Designing report R1 for Listings table                    Report Ins 1/1
Table Band
   ....+...10....+...20....+...30....+...40....+...50....+...60....+...70....+...
1
2 ▼page
3
4
5
6 mm/dd/yy                    Custom Report #1                      Page 9
7
8
9 ┌▼table
10
11 Address           Town        Owner        List Date  Style
12 ─────────────      ──────────  ──────────  ─────────  ──────────
13 AAAAAAAAAAAAAAAAAAAA AAAAAAAAAA AAAAAAAAAA  mm/dd/yy   AAAAAAAAAA
14
15 └▲table
16
17
18
19
20 ▲page
21
```

(If you are following along on your computer, you should issue the **[Menu]** Cancel **Y**es command at this point to abandon the report spec, then issue the **[Menu]** **R**eport **D**esign command to bring up a new spec for the LISTINGS table.)

Adding a Page-width

The [Menu] Setting PageLayout Insert command tells Paradox to insert a new page-width to the right of the last page-width. When you issue this command, Paradox will insert a blank page-width that is the same size as the other page-widths in the report. The page-width indicator will reflect the addition of the new page. Later, we'll show you how to fill a new page-width with information by adding columns, field masks, literals, and so forth.

Resizing a Page-width

You can alter the size of the page-widths in a report. As we stated earlier, all page-widths in a new report will be 80 characters wide.

In the case of the report spec shown in Figure 10-6, the default 80-column page-width causes the sixth column of the table band to be split between the first and second pages. Therefore, Paradox prints part of the dashed-line literal and Price field entry on one page, and part on another. You can correct this problem by adjusting the page-widths in the report spec. In this case, you could reduce each page-width to 69 characters so that the first five columns of the report are printed on one page, and the remaining four columns are printed on another page. However, if you have a wide-carriage printer, or if your printer offers a compressed typeface, you probably will want to increase the page-width to 132 characters so the report consists of a single page-width.

To alter the size of the page-widths, issue the **[Menu]** **S**etting **P**ageLayout **W**idth command. When Paradox prompts you for a new page-width, press **[Ctrl]-[Backspace]** to delete the current setting (80), then type a new width. If you type **69** and press ↵, Paradox will revise the layout of the report, as shown in Figure 10-12. When Paradox prints from this spec, it will print the first five columns on one page and the remaining four columns on the next. Because you reduced the size of the page-widths, Paradox added a third page-width to the spec to hold any material that may have spilled off the narrower pages. (Notice that the page-width indicator at the top of the screen displays *1/3*.) You probably will want to use the [Menu] Setting PageLayout Delete command to remove this unneeded page from the spec.

Figure 10-12 Decreasing the Size of a Page-width

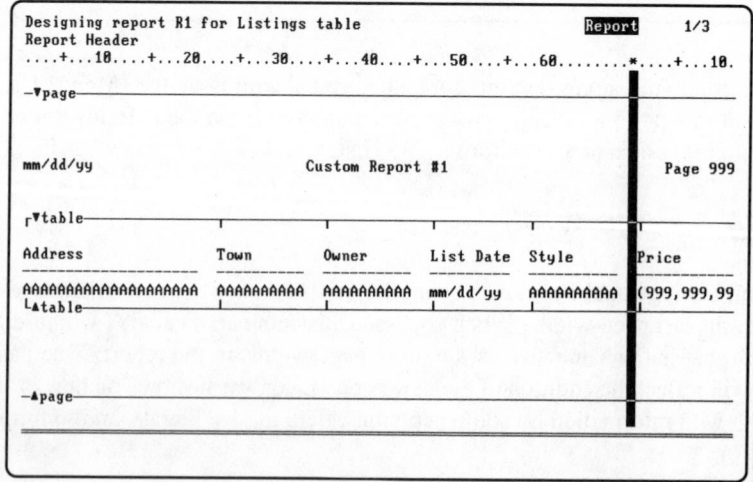

If you issue the [Menu] Setting PageLayout Width command again and specify a width of 132, Paradox will present the screen shown in Figure 10-13. When Paradox prints from this report, it will place all nine columns of the report on a single page. For this wide setting to work, you must be printing on a wide-carriage printer or be printing in compressed print. (We'll show you how to alter print styles at the end of this chapter.)

Figure 10-13 Increasing the Size of a Page-width

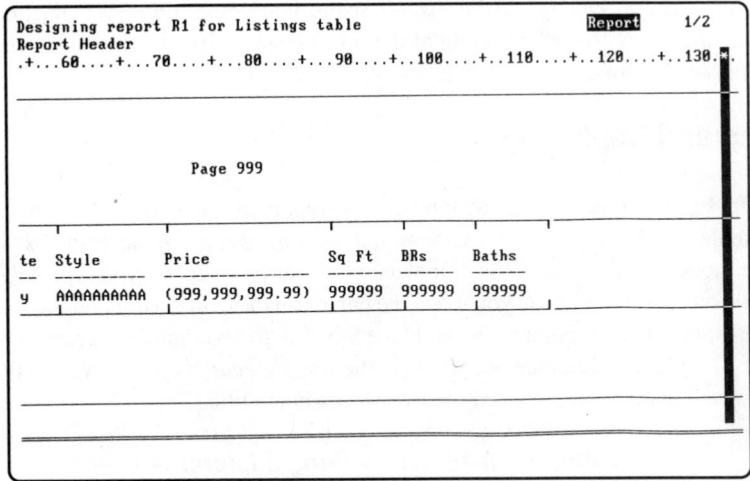

Paradox did not delete the second page-width from the report spec when you increased the page-width setting to 132. The second page-width is still in the report spec, although it contains no fields or literals. Since you don't need this page-width any longer, you probably will want to remove it from the report spec. Also, notice that Paradox did not re-center the title with respect to the expanded page-width. If you want the title to be centered, you must move it yourself using tools we'll describe in the next few paragraphs.

Working with Literals

Earlier in this chapter, you learned that report specifications can contain descriptive text that will be printed literally in reports. For example, the report spec in Figure 10-6 (and any other new tabular spec) contains a number of literals. In this case, Paradox has entered the report description *Custom Report #1* on the fourth line of the page header in the middle of the first page-width. In addition, Paradox has entered the name from one field in the LISTINGS table and dashed lines as literals in each of the columns of the table band. Once Paradox has created a spec, you can delete existing literals or add new literals.

Entering Literals

For the most part, entering a literal into a report spec is as simple as moving the cursor to where you want the literal to appear, then typing characters from the keyboard. To add the title *This Is a Tabular Report:* at the left edge of the report header for the basic LISTINGS spec shown in Figure 10-6, for example, you would move the cursor to the first character on the first (in this case, only) line of the report header section and type **This Is a Tabular Report:**. So that the line would not be printed right at the top of the page, you would add a few blank lines above it by moving the cursor to the beginning of the line, pressing **[Ins]** to enter the insert mode, and pressing ↵ once for each blank line you wanted to insert.

Inserting and Replacing

The way that Paradox places what you type into the report spec is affected by your choice of either the replace or insert mode. When you first enter the Report mode, Paradox will be in the replace mode. While Paradox is in replace mode, any characters you type will replace other literals on the same line. If you place the cursor on the *C* in *Custom* on the fourth line of the report spec shown in Figure 10-6 and type **Special**, for example, your screen will look like Figure 10-14. As you can see, the letters in the word *Special* have overwritten the letters in *Custom*, leaving no space between the two words in the title.

Figure 10-14 Overwriting a Literal

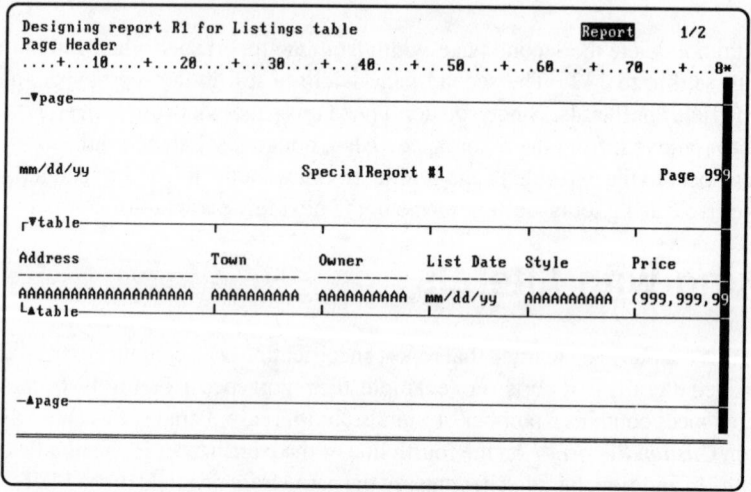

In most cases, you'll want to press the [Ins] key to place Paradox in the insert mode prior to typing literals into a report spec. The *Ins* indicator in the upper-right corner of the screen tells you when Paradox is in the insert mode. While Paradox is in the insert mode, it will push any literals or field masks that are under or to the right of the cursor, one space to the right for each character that you type. If you position the cursor on the *C* in the literal *Custom Report #1*

in the report spec shown in Figure 10-6, press the **[Ins]** key to enter the insert mode, and type **Special** and then a space, your screen will look like the one shown in Figure 10-15. As you can see, Paradox has pushed the words *Custom Report #1* to the right and has inserted the text that you typed.

Figure 10-15 Inserting a Literal

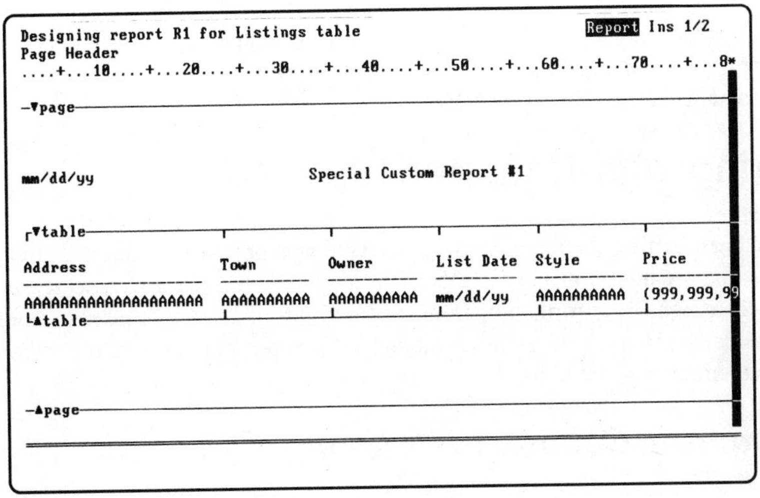

```
Designing report R1 for Listings table                     Report  Ins 1/2
Page Header
....+...10....+...20....+...30....+...40....+...50....+...60....+...70....+...8*

 —▼page————————————————————————————————————————————————————

 mm/dd/yy                        Special Custom Report #1

 ┌▼table——————————————————————————————————————————————————
 Address              Town       Owner       List Date  Style       Price
 ————————————————     —————————  —————————   —————————  —————————   —————————
 AAAAAAAAAAAAAAAAAAA  AAAAAAAAAA AAAAAAAAAA  mm/dd/yy   AAAAAAAAAA  (999,999,9
 └▲table——————————————————————————————————————————————————


 —▲page————————————————————————————————————————————————————
```

Restrictions

There are three important restrictions that prevent you from placing literals into a report spec. First, you cannot type a literal on top of a field mask. If you attempt to do this in either the overwrite or insert mode, Paradox will beep. Second, although Paradox will let you push a literal or field mask over a page-width boundary in the middle of a report, it will not let you push any element beyond the right border of the rightmost page-width in the report.

Third, when you enter a literal into the table band, Paradox will not allow you to type beyond the right edge of the column in which the literal begins, or to insert a literal so that another literal or field mask is pushed beyond the right boundary of a column. This restriction helps preserve the columnar integrity of the report.

Deleting Literals

As you might expect, you also can delete literals from a report specification. To do this, you must use the [Backspace], [Del], or [Delete Report Line] ([Ctrl]-[Y]) keys. The [Backspace] key deletes the literal character to the left of the cursor. If Paradox is in the insert mode, it will drag the characters to the right of the cursor back to the left as you delete characters with the [Backspace] key. If you press [Backspace] while Paradox is in the replace mode, however, the other characters on the line will remain in place.

The [Del] key provides the second way to delete literals from a report spec. When you press the [Del] key, Paradox will delete the literal character over which the cursor is positioned and pull the characters that are to the right of the cursor one space to the left for each character you delete. If you are in the replace mode and are using a release of Paradox prior to Release 2, the remaining characters on the line will stay in their original places as you press the [Del] key.

The [Delete Report Line] key ([Ctrl]-[Y]) provides yet another way to delete literals from a report spec. As we explained earlier, this command allows you to delete either a full or partial line that contains literals, masks, or both.

Working with Columns

As you learned earlier, the table band of any tabular report specification is divided into columns. The separation of the table band into columns makes it easy to rearrange the information in, remove information from, and add information to a tabular report. The options under the [Menu] TableBand command allow you to erase, insert, resize, move, and copy the columns in the table band.

Moving from Column to Column

As you design a tabular report, you will spend a lot of time moving the cursor from one column to another. The obvious way to do this is to use the → and ← keys. However, it takes a long time to move across a 132-character-wide report one space at a time! Luckily, there are faster ways, which are listed in Table 10-1.

Table 10-1 Cursor-movement Keys

Keystroke	Cursor Response
[Tab]	Move one column to the right
[Shift]-[Tab]	Move one column to the left
[Ctrl]-→	Move 40 spaces to the right
[Ctrl]-←	Move 40 spaces to the left
[Ctrl]-[Home]	Move to the beginning of the first column
[Ctrl]-[End]	Move to the end of the last column
[Home]	Move to the top of the report
[End]	Move to the bottom of the report

Rearranging Columns

When you use the [Menu] Report Design command to create a tabular report spec, Paradox creates one column in the table band for each field in the source table. It then places masks for those fields into the columns in the order that the fields appear in the structure of the table. However, you will not always want to print your reports in this default order. Fortunately, you can use either the [Rotate] key ([Ctrl]-[R]) or the [Menu] TableBand Move command to rearrange the columns in the table band. Rearranging the columns in the table band changes the order of the fields in the printed report.

The [Rotate] Key

You can use the [Rotate] key ([Ctrl]-[R]) to move the column you select to the right edge of the table band and shift the remaining columns to the left. For example, suppose you want to move the List Date column all the way to the right of the table band in the report spec shown in Figure 10-14. To do this, position the cursor anywhere within the List Date column (the one you want to move) and press **[Rotate]**. Instantly, Paradox will move the List Date column to the right end of the table band so that the report spec looks like the one shown in Figure 10-16. If you print from this revised specification, the List Date column will appear at the right end of the report.

Figure 10-16 Rotating Columns

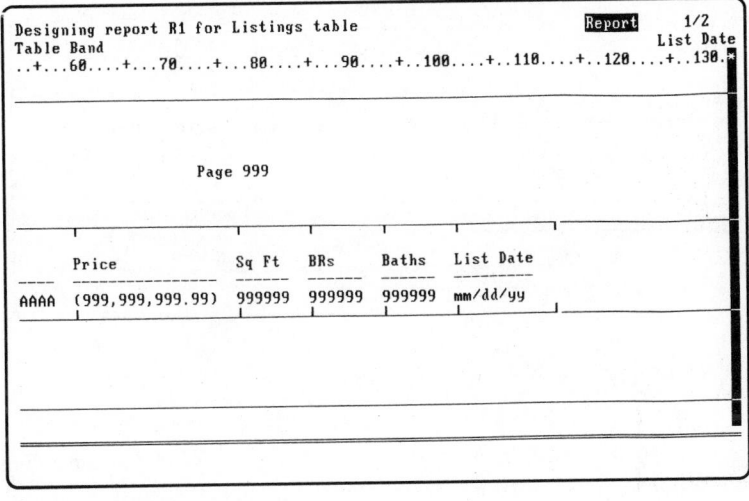

The TableBand Move Command

The TableBand Move command lets you move a column more precisely than the [Rotate] key does. Using this command, you can move a column from one place in a table band to any other position in that band in only two steps.

To demonstrate this command, suppose that you want to move the Sq Ft column in the report spec shown in Figure 10-16 to a position between the Style and Price columns. To do this, press the **[Menu]** key, select TableBand, and choose **M**ove. As soon as you issue this command, the cursor will change to a small blinking box, and Paradox will prompt you to use the arrow keys to place the cursor on the column you want to move. When you see this prompt, place the cursor anywhere in the Sq Ft column and press ↵.

After you select a column to move, Paradox will prompt you to place the cursor on the new location for the column. The position you choose depends on the direction in which you are moving the column. If you are moving it from right to left (as we are in this case), position the cursor in the column to the right of the place where you want Paradox to insert the column you are moving. (If you are moving a column to the right, position the cursor in the column to the left of the place where you want the column moved.) In this case, since you are moving a column to the right, and you want to place it between the Style and Price columns, you should position the cursor in the Price column. When you press ↵, Paradox will move the column so that the report specification looks like the one shown in Figure 10-17.

Figure 10-17 Moving a Column

```
Designing report R1 for Listings table                         Report     1/2
Table Band                                                                Sq Ft
....+...10....+...20....+...30....+...40....+...50....+...60....+...70....+...80
─▼page──────────────────────────────────────────────────────────────────────


mm/dd/yy                          Custom Report #1                    Page 999

┌▼table───────────────────────────────────────────────────────────────────────
Address              Town       Owner       Style       Sq Ft   Price
───────────────      ──────────  ──────────  ──────────  ──────  ──────────────
AAAAAAAAAAAAAAAAAAAA  AAAAAAAAAA  AAAAAAAAAA  AAAAAAAAAA  999999  (999,999,999.9
└▲table───────────────────────────────────────────────────────────────────────



─▲page──────────────────────────────────────────────────────────────────────
═══════════════════════════════════════════════════════════════════════════════
```

Erasing Columns

You can remove a column of information from a printed report by deleting the column of the table band that produces it. To delete a column from a table band, you must use the TableBand Erase command. Suppose you want to remove the Owner column from the report spec shown in Figure 10-17. To remove this column, issue the **[Menu]** TableBand Erase command. When Paradox prompts you to do so, place the cursor anywhere within the column you want to erase (in this case, Owner). When you press ↵, Paradox will remove that column from the table band. Figure 10-18 shows this result. The reports you print from this revised spec will not contain information from the Owner field of the LISTINGS table.

Inserting Columns

In addition to deleting columns from the table band, you can add columns to it. To do this, you must issue the [Menu] TableBand Insert command. Paradox will then insert a blank, 15-character-wide column into the table band at the point you choose.

For example, suppose you want to place a new column between the Town and Style columns in the table band of the report spec shown in Figure 10-18. To do this, press the **[Menu]** key and issue the **T**ableBand **I**nsert command. As soon as you issue this command, the cursor will change to a small box, and Paradox will prompt you to place the cursor in the column to the right of the place where you want the new column. In this case, you should position the cursor within the Style column. When you press ↩, Paradox will insert the new column into the table band, and your report spec will look like the one shown in Figure 10-19.

Figure 10-18 Removing a Column

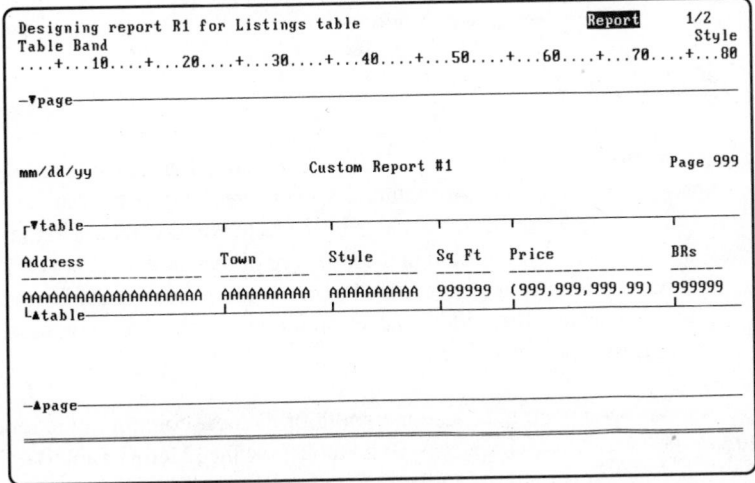

Figure 10-19 Inserting a Column

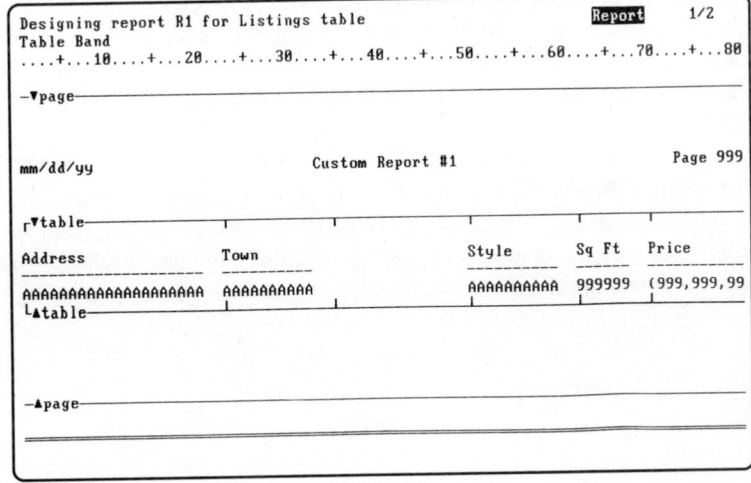

After you have inserted a new column into a report, you probably will want to enter a literal into it. You already know how to enter literals into a column. We'll show you how to place field masks in a report in a few pages. Of course, you also can use a new column purely for spacing purposes. Whenever Paradox inserts a new column into the table band, it pushes the remaining columns 15 spaces to the right.

If there are fewer than 15 empty spaces at the end of the rightmost page-width in a report spec when you attempt to insert a column, Paradox will beep and display the message *Not enough space here to insert a new column.* To insert the column, you must add another page-width, increase the width of the existing page-widths, or erase one or more columns from the spec. Alternatively, you can decrease the width of one or more columns in the table band.

Resizing Columns

When you issue the [Menu] Report Design Tabular command, Paradox creates a standard report spec whose table band has as many columns as there are fields in the source table. The width of each column is determined by the name of the field Paradox places in that column or by the width specification for that field in the structure of the table, whichever is greater. When you add a new column to a report spec, Paradox automatically sets its width at 15 spaces. If you want to change the width of any column in a table band, you must use the [Menu] TableBand Resize command.

For example, suppose you want to reduce the width of the new column in the report spec shown in Figure 10-19 to only five spaces. To do this, issue the **[Menu] T**ableBand **R**esize command. As soon as you issue the command, Paradox will prompt you to place the cursor on the column you want to resize. Although you can place the cursor anywhere within the column, you'll want to position it at the column's right edge. In this case, move the cursor to the 15th space in the new column. When you press ↵, Paradox will prompt you to use the → and ← keys to increase or decrease the width of the column. In this case, you should press the ← key ten times. Each time you press this key, Paradox will adjust the width of the column on the screen. When you press ↵, Paradox will lock in the new column width, as shown in Figure 10-20.

Paradox places two restrictions on your ability to resize a column. First, you cannot reduce the width of a column to less than the number of characters in the longest literal or field mask in that column. Second, you cannot increase the width of a column so that it pushes the remaining columns in the table band beyond the right edge of the rightmost page-width in the report spec.

Figure 10-20 Resizing a Column

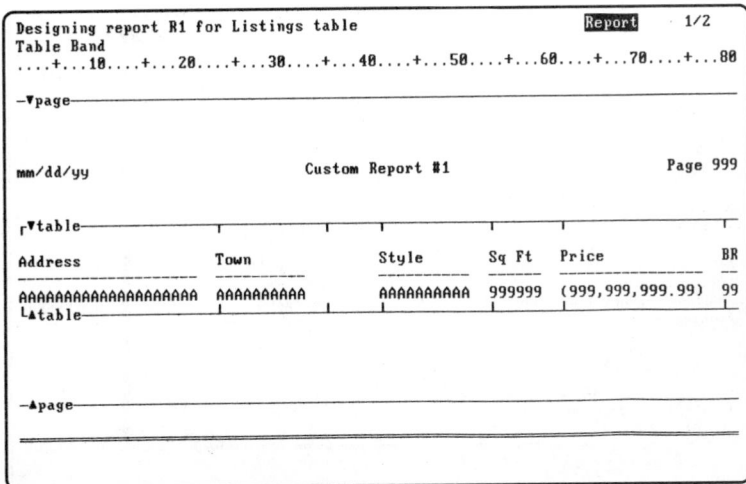

Copying Columns

The final thing you can do with a column of a table band is make a copy of it. To do this, you must use the [Menu] TableBand Copy command. This command allows you to make an exact copy of any column in a table band and place that copy elsewhere in that band. In reports that occupy more than a single page-width, you may want to place a copy of the column that identifies the individual records in each page-width. That way, the information printed on each page will make sense even if you don't glue the pages together.

For example, suppose you created a two-page-report spec like the one in Figure 10-12, and you want the Address column to appear at the left edge of both page-widths of the report spec. To do this, you must insert a copy of that column between the Style and Price columns. To copy this column, press the [**Menu**] key and issue the TableBand Copy command. As soon as you issue this command, Paradox will change the cursor to a blinking box and will prompt you to indicate the column you want to copy. In this case, you should move the cursor to any position within Address. When you press ↵, Paradox will prompt you to position the cursor in the column to the right of the place where you want to insert the copy. Now, you should move the cursor into the Price column. When you press ↵ again, Paradox will place a copy of the Address column at the left edge of the second page-width, as shown in Figure 10-21 on the following page.

As it does when you insert a column, Paradox will not allow you to copy a column unless the table band has room to accommodate the copy. If you try to copy a column within a table band that lacks sufficient space to contain the copy, the message *Not enough space here for copy* will appear in the lower-right corner of the screen. You can circumvent this problem by resizing or erasing existing columns, increasing the size of the existing page-widths, or adding an additional page-width to the report spec.

Figure 10-21 Copying a Column

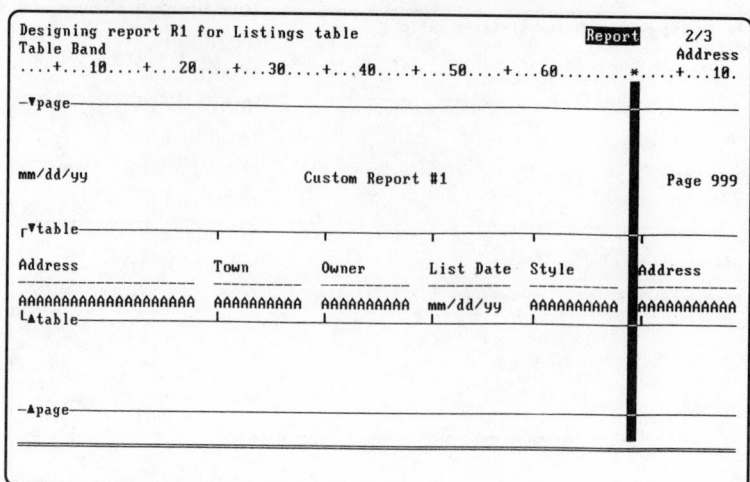

```
Designing report R1 for Listings table                    Report   2/3
Table Band                                                         Address
....+...10....+...20....+...30....+...40....+...50....+...60........*....+...10.
 ─▼page──────────────────────────────────────────────────────────


 mm/dd/yy                      Custom Report #1                    Page 999

 ┌▼table─────────────────────────────────────────────────────────

 Address               Town        Owner       List Date  Style     Address
 ────────────────────  ──────────  ──────────  ─────────  ────────  ──────────
 AAAAAAAAAAAAAAAAAAAA  AAAAAAAAAA  AAAAAAAAAA  mm/dd/yy   AAAAAAAAAA AAAAAAAAAA
 └▲table─────────────────────────────────────────────────────────



 ─▲page──────────────────────────────────────────────────────────
```

Working with Field Masks

Field masks are the means by which Paradox extracts information from the fields of a table
(as well as other special information) for use in a report. When you design a new report, like
the one shown in Figure 10-6 on page 417, Paradox will include one field mask for each
field in the source table, as well as two special masks: one for the current date and one for
the current page number. In this section, we'll show you how to insert, delete, format, and
resize field masks.

The Report Generator's [Menu] Field command controls the manipulation of field masks in
a report spec. When you select this option, Paradox will present you with six choices: Erase,
Reformat, Place, Justify, CalcEdit, and WordWrap. The Erase option allows you to delete
a field mask from a spec. The Reformat option allows you to adjust the length and other
display attributes of a field mask. The Place option allows you to add a field mask to a report
spec. The Justify option lets you specify how fields should be positioned within their masks:
left, right, or center. The CalcEdit command lets you revise a calculated field. The
WordWrap option lets you break long text fields onto multiple lines.

Erasing a Field

When you issue the [Menu] Report Design Tabular command, Paradox creates a report spec
that includes a field mask for every field in the source table, plus one for the current date and
page number. To erase a single field mask, you must use the [Menu] Field Erase command.
By removing a field mask from a report spec, you remove the information supplied by that
field from the resulting report.

For example, suppose you don't want the current date to appear at the top of each page of the report produced by the spec shown in Figure 10-6. To remove the date from the report, you must remove the current date mask from the report spec. To do this, press the **[Menu]** key and issue the Field Erase command. As soon as you issue this command, Paradox will prompt you to move the cursor to the field you want to erase. To remove the current date mask from the page header of this report, position the cursor anywhere on that mask. When you press ↵, Paradox will remove the mask from the report spec. Figure 10-22 shows this result. As you can see, Paradox has removed the current date mask from the fourth line of the report spec but has not shifted the remainder of that line to the left. Whenever you delete a field mask from a line, Paradox will leave the remainder of the line in place, whether you are in the replace or insert mode.

Figure 10-22 Erasing a Field Mask

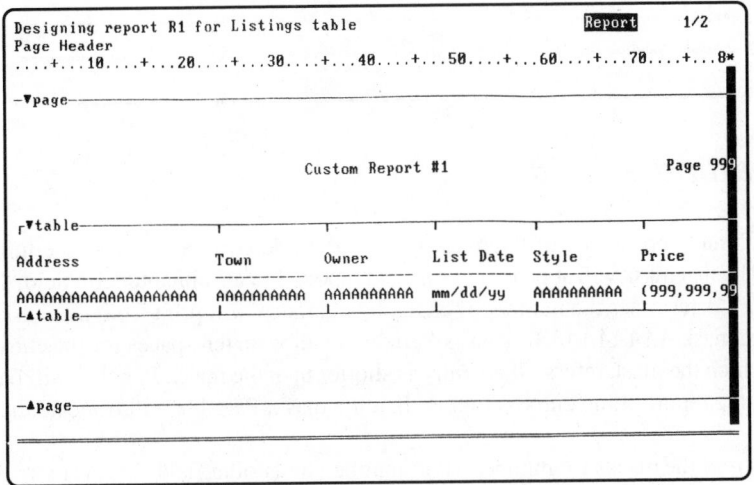

When Paradox designs a report, it places masks for each of the fields in the source table into their own columns of the table band. Because each field mask is in its own column, you can use the [Menu] TableBand Erase command to remove any field from the report. In some cases, however, you may want to erase the field mask but leave the column in place. To do this, you must use the [Menu] Field Erase command.

For example, suppose you want to erase the mask for the Owner field from the third column of the table band in the report spec shown in Figure 10-22. To do this, issue the **[Menu]** Field Erase command, position the cursor on the Owner mask, and press ↵. Figure 10-23 shows the result. As you can see, Paradox has erased the Owner mask from the third column of the table band, but has left that column (and the literals it contains) in place. At this point, you probably would want to use the [Del] or [Backspace] key to erase those literals to produce a blank column.

Figure 10-23 Erasing a Field Mask in the Table Band

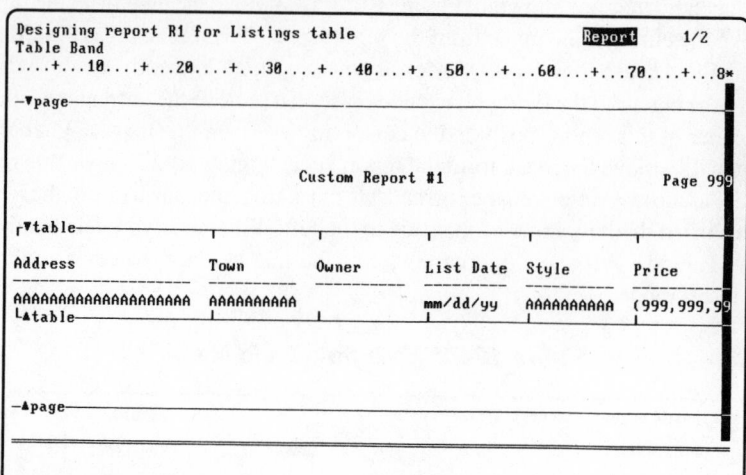

Formatting a Field

The length and appearance of the mask for any field determines the way the information extracted by that mask will appear in the printed report. For an alphanumeric field, the length of the mask determines the number of characters Paradox will print from the entries in that field. The mask *AAAAAAAAAA* causes Paradox to allocate ten spaces for the entries in the field to which the mask refers. If an entry is shorter than the mask, Paradox will pad it with spaces in the report. If an entry is longer than the mask, Paradox will truncate the entry.

The lengths of the masks for number, short number, and dollar fields have a more profound effect than just controlling the amount of space allocated to each entry. If any entry in a numeric or short number field is longer than the mask that represents it, Paradox will print that entry as a series of asterisks. Because the default mask for a number field is only six characters long, any number field entry that contains more than six digits will appear as a series of asterisks in a standard report. The masks for these fields also determine whether the printed form of the entry will contain commas or decimal points and how they will deal with signs. For example, the default mask for a dollar field specifies the use of commas, the inclusion of two digits to the right of the decimal point, and the use of parentheses for negative numbers.

The mask for a date field determines in which of 11 different forms that date will be printed. The default mask for a date field instructs Paradox to print the entries from a date field in mm/dd/yy form, even if the dates are in dd-Mon-yy form in the source table.

In many cases, the default mask Paradox uses for a field will not produce exactly the look you want when that field is printed. Paradox provides a command—Field Reformat—that lets you change the size and/or appearance of the mask for any field. Reformatting a field is a three-step process. First, issue the [Menu] Field Reformat command. Second, point to the field you want to reformat. Third, specify how you want the field to be formatted. The specifications you can make in this third step are determined by what type of field the mask represents.

Alphanumeric Fields

If the field you select is alphanumeric, the Field Reformat command will allow you to change its length. Because the default length of the field mask for an alphanumeric field is equal to the maximum number of characters the field can hold, you can't increase its length. You may want to decrease the length of an alphanumeric field mask if all of the entries in that field are shorter than the maximum, or if you don't mind having some characters "trimmed off."

For example, suppose you've created a new report spec like the one in Figure 10-6 on page 417 and you want to reduce the length of the Style mask from ten to eight characters—the maximum number of characters in any entry in that field. To do this, issue the [Menu] Field Reformat command, position the cursor anywhere within the Style mask, and press ↵. Paradox will then move the cursor to the last character in the mask and prompt you to adjust its length. Each time you press →, Paradox will add another A to the mask. Each time you press ←, Paradox will remove an A from the mask. In this case, you'll want to press ← twice to reduce the length of the mask to eight characters. When you press ↵, Paradox will lock the mask at this new length, as shown in Figure 10-24.

Figure 10-24 Reformatting an Alphanumeric Field

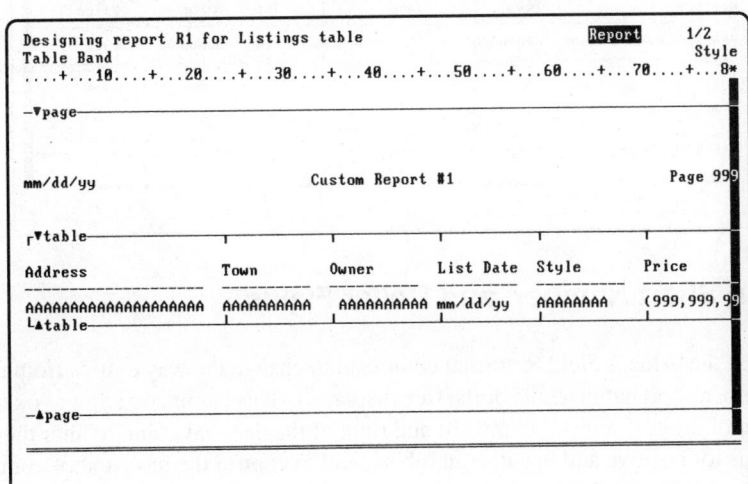

Date Fields

When Paradox places a date field in a report spec, it always uses the mask *mm/dd/yy*, which prints the dates in simple mm/dd/yy form. If you want, you can use the [Menu] Field Reformat command to select an alternative format for date fields. The 11 available formats are: mm/dd/yy; Month dd, yyyy; mm/dd; mm/yy; dd-Mon-yy; Mon yy; dd-Mon-yyyy; mm/dd/yyyy; dd.mm.yy; dd/mm/yy; and yy-mm-dd.

For example, suppose you want to convert the current date mask in the page header of the report spec shown in Figure 10-24 into Month dd, yyyy form. To do this, issue the **[Menu] Field R**eformat command and point to the current date field. When you press ↵, Paradox will display a menu that contains the 11 date formats. When you see this menu, you should choose the format in which you want the date to appear. In this case, you should choose the second format: **Month dd, yyyy**. When you press ↵, Paradox will replace the existing date mask with the new format you have chosen. Figure 10-25 shows this result. When Paradox prints from the spec, the date will appear in Month dd, yyyy form at the top of each page printed from the first page-width.

Figure 10-25 Reformatting a Date Field

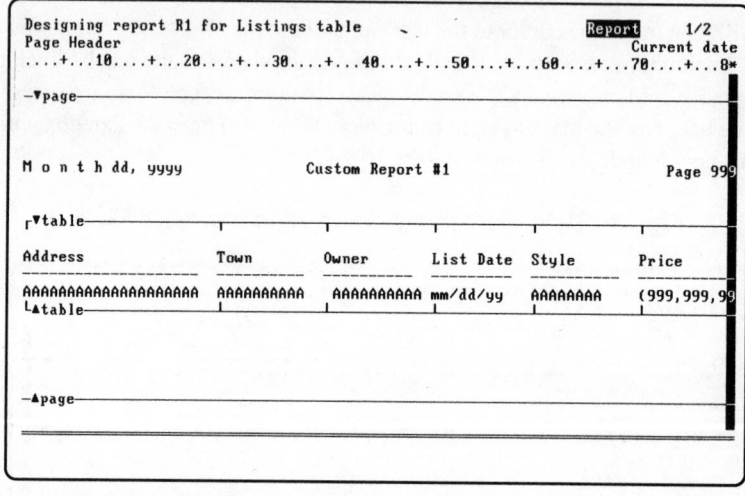

Number, Short Number, and Dollar Fields

You can use the [Menu] Field Reformat command to change the way entries from numeric fields (number, short number, and dollar) are displayed. This command allows you to adjust the number of digits displayed to the left and right of the decimal point, to alter the display conventions for positive and negative numbers, and to control the insertion of commas.

Specifying a Number of Digits

For example, suppose you want to display the entries from the Price field in the table band of the spec shown in Figure 10-25 with six digits to the left of the decimal point, and none to the right. To reformat this field, issue the **[Menu]** Field **R**eformat command and position the cursor on the Price mask. When you press ↵, Paradox will present four choices: Digits, Sign-Convention, Commas, and International. To change the number of digits, choose **D**igits. As soon as you make this choice, Paradox will move the cursor to the last character before the decimal point and prompt you to specify the number of digits you want to the left of the decimal place. To add digits, press the → key. To reduce the number of digits, press the ← key. Paradox will not allow you to increase the number of digits to more than 12, or decrease it to fewer than one. In this case, press ← three times to specify six digits to the left of the decimal point.

As soon as you press ↵ to lock in the number of digits to the left of the decimal point, Paradox will prompt you to select the number of digits you want to the right of the decimal point. You can press → to add digits or ← to reduce the number of digits. To eliminate the decimal point and the two digits to its right in the example, press ← three times, then press ↵. Figure 10-26 shows the reformatted field.

Figure 10-26 Reformatting a Dollar Field

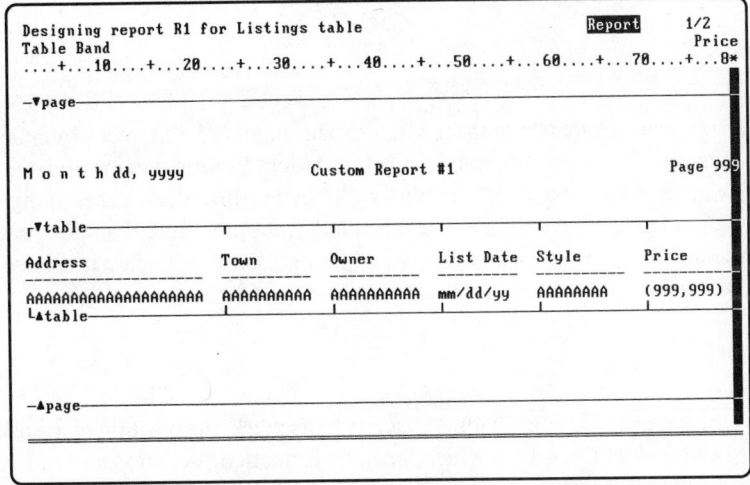

Specifying a Sign-Convention

In addition to altering the number of digits in the mask for a numeric field, you can control the use of signs. When you issue the [Menu] Field Reformat command, point to a numeric field, and select Sign-Convention, Paradox will present you with three choices: NegativeOnly, ParenNegative, and AlwaysSign. If you choose NegativeOnly (the default for number and short number fields), positive numbers will appear without a sign, but negative numbers will be prefaced with a minus sign (-). If you choose ParenNegative (the default for dollar fields), positive numbers will be printed without a sign, but negative numbers will be enclosed in parentheses. To indicate this format, Paradox will enclose the mask in parentheses. If you select AlwaysSign, Paradox will print a - sign in front of the negative numbers, print a + sign in front of the positive numbers, and display a +/- sign in front of the mask.

Specifying the Use of Commas

Paradox also lets you control the printing of commas in numeric fields. When you issue the [Menu] Field Reformat command and choose Commas, Paradox will present you with two choices: NoCommas and Commas. If you choose NoCommas (the default for number and short number fields), Paradox will print the entries from the field without commas. If you choose Commas (the default for dollar fields), Paradox will include comma separators in the printed report and in the field mask.

Paradox 2 and 3 give you two ways to display dollar fields. To choose between dollar format specifications, issue the [Menu] Field Reformat International command. Paradox will then display a menu with two choices: U.S.Convention and InternationalConvention. U.S. Convention displays numbers in dollar fields with commas after every third digit to the left of the decimal point and a period for the decimal point. InternationalConvention uses a period as the digit separator and a comma for the decimal point.

Other Fields

Paradox also lets you reformat three special fields: page number fields, record number fields, and current time fields. When you issue the [Menu] Field Reformat command and select a page number or record number field, Paradox will let you adjust the number of digits to the left of the decimal place only. When you select a current time field, Paradox will let you choose from one of two formats: hh:mm pm and hh:mm:ss. You'll learn more about these types of fields in the next section of this chapter.

A Caution

Because reformatting a field often adds characters to its mask, the position of a mask within a report spec can restrict the way in which it can be formatted. As you know, a field mask cannot extend beyond the right boundary of a column in the table band, cannot extend beyond the right border of the rightmost page-width in a spec, and cannot overlap another mask or a literal. If the format you choose causes any of these things to happen, Paradox will not reformat the mask.

Placing Fields

In addition to removing and formatting fields, you can place field masks into a spec. Paradox allows you to place four types of field masks into any report spec: regular, special, calculated, and summary. Regular fields draw information from the fields of a table. Special fields allow you to include the current date, the current time, the current page number, or the current record number in your reports. Calculated fields allow you to place the result of a calculation in a report. Summary fields command Paradox to calculate a summary statistic (such as an average, sum, or count) and place it in the report. In this section, we'll cover the first three types of fields. We'll save our discussion of summary fields for Chapter 11.

Regular Fields

Placing a regular field in a report spec allows you to draw information from a field of the table for which the report is designed. Because Paradox includes a field mask for every field in a table and places it in its own column when you first design a tabular report, you probably won't place a regular field in a tabular report very often. However, you will occasionally want to place a regular field in a group header or reinsert into the table band a field you have previously deleted from the report spec. As we'll explain later in this chapter, you'll frequently use a combination of the Field Erase and Field Place commands to move regular fields in a free-form report.

Although you can place regular fields into any band, you usually will want to place them only in the table band of a tabular report, the form band of a free-form report, or the group band of either type of report. You probably won't want to place a regular field in a page or report band of a report spec. If you place a regular field in the page header, Paradox will draw information from the first record it prints on that page. If you place a regular field in a page footer, Paradox will draw information from the last record on the current page. If you place a regular field in a report header or report footer, Paradox will draw information from the first and last records, respectively, that it prints in the report.

Every field mask in a table band must be positioned in a column. For this reason, placing a field mask into a table band usually is a two-step process: First, you add a new column to the table band; then, you place a field mask in that column. You can place a field mask into an existing column either by itself (if you have deleted the original mask from that column, for example) or in addition to another mask(s) in that column.

As an example of placing a regular field mask into a table band, suppose you want to replace the missing Owner field mask in Figure 10-23 on page 436 to restore the report spec to the form shown in Figure 10-22 on page 435. Since the column in which the mask was situated still exists, you don't need to add a column to the table band before replacing this mask.

To replace this mask, begin by issuing the [**Menu**] Field **P**lace command. From the list of field types Paradox presents, choose **R**egular. As soon as you make this choice, Paradox will display a list of the fields in the table for which you are designing the report. You should choose the field you want to place from this list. In this case, select **O**wner. After you make this selection, Paradox will prompt you to position the cursor where you want to place the field. Move the cursor to the beginning of the fourth row of the third column of the table band. When you press ↵, Paradox will place a mask for that field at the position of the cursor.

The next step of the placement process depends on what type of field the mask represents: number, dollar, short number, date, or alphanumeric. If you're placing an alphanumeric field, as we are in this case, Paradox will display the mask as a series of *A*'s. Once Paradox presents this mask, you can adjust the number of characters in the mask. In this case, we'll press ↵ to accept the default length so that the spec again will look like the one in Figure 10-22.

If you are placing a number field, Paradox will display twelve 9s and let you adjust the number of digits to the right and left of the decimal place. If you are placing a short number field, Paradox will display six 9s and let you adjust the number of digits. Unlike a number field, a short number field can have only six digits to the left of the decimal. If you are placing a dollar field, Paradox displays the mask *(999,999,999.99)* and lets you adjust the number of digits on both sides of the decimal point. If you are placing a date field, Paradox presents you with a menu of the 11 possible date formats. The form you choose is the one Paradox will place in the report spec.

Special Fields

In addition to placing regular fields in a report specification, you also can place any of four special fields: a current date field, a page number field, a current time field, and a record number field. In fact, Paradox places two of these fields—current date and page number— in the page header of every new report it creates. Like the current date and page number fields, the other two special fields—current time and record number—do not draw information from the source table. The current time field stamps your report with the time the report is printed. The record number field allows you to number the records in a report.

Current Date Fields

A current date field commands Paradox to print the current date. Although you can place this field in any part of a report, you commonly will place it in the report header, the report footer, the page header, or the page footer. To place a current date field in a report, issue the [Menu] Field Place command, select Date, and choose which of the 11 forms you want Paradox to use. When you press ↵, Paradox will place the field at the current location of the cursor.

Current Time Fields

A current time field stamps a report with the time it was printed, in much the same way a current date field stamps it with the date. Like a current date field, you probably will place a current time field only in the report or page bands. To place a current time field in a report spec, just issue the **[Menu] F**ield **P**lace command, select **T**ime, and choose from the two time forms that Paradox presents: hh:mm pm and hh:mm:ss. When you press ↵, Paradox will place the current time field in the form you select at the current position of the cursor.

Page Number Fields

If you want to number the pages in a report, you can place a page number field in either the page header or page footer. To do this, issue the **[Menu]** **F**ield **P**lace **P**age command and move the cursor to where you want to place the field. When you press ↵, Paradox will place a three-character mask into the spec and let you adjust its width between a minimum of one character and a maximum of six characters.

Record Number Fields

The fourth special field, record number, allows you to number the records Paradox prints in a report. Because this field assigns a number to each record, you'll want to use it only within the table band. In most cases, in fact, you'll want to place it in a separate column of that band.

For example, suppose you want Paradox to number the records it prints from the LISTINGS table report spec shown in Figure 10-26. To begin, use the **[Menu]** **T**ableBand **I**nsert command to add a new column at the beginning of the report. Once you have added this column, issue the **[Menu]** **F**ield **P**lace command, and choose **#Record**. When you issue this command, Paradox will present two alternatives: Overall and PerGroup. Unless you have grouped the report (a topic we'll cover in Chapter 11), your choice here makes no difference. For this example, however, select **Overall**. As soon as you make a selection, Paradox will ask you where to position the mask. In this case, you should point to the first space in the fourth row of the table band and press ↵. If you want, you can use the arrow keys to increase or decrease the width of the mask to as many as six digits or as few as one digit. In this case, just press ↵. Then, enter the literals **Record #** and - - - - - - - - so that the report spec looks like the one shown in Figure 10-27. When you print from this spec, Paradox will number the records in the report, as shown in Figure 10-28 on the following page.

Figure 10-27 A Record Number Field

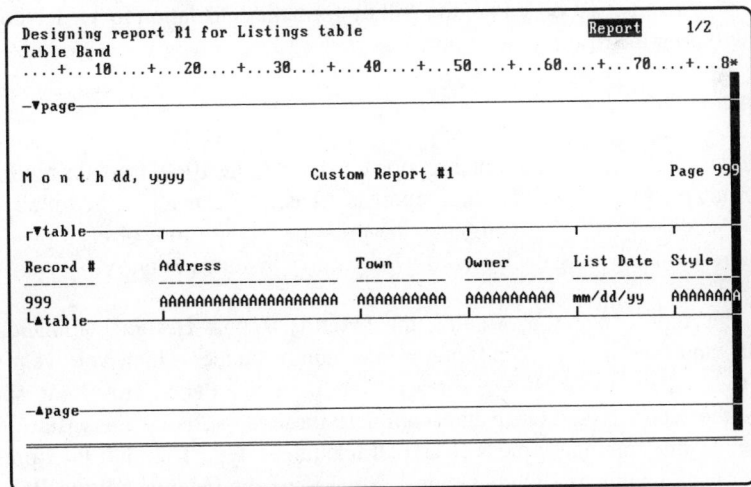

Figure 10-28 A Report with Numbered Records

Calculated Fields

Calculated fields are the third type of field you can place in a report spec. Like the calculated fields you can place in a form, the calculated fields you include in a report will be based on formulas that draw information from other fields of the table. When you include a calculated field in the table band of a report, Paradox will perform the calculation for each record in the table and will print the result in the report.

An Example

Suppose you want to print the columnar report shown in Figure 10-29 from the records in the LISTINGS table. As you can see, this report is a basic tabular report in which we have included a calculated field that computes the price per square foot of each piece of real estate—the result of dividing each record's Price entry by its Sq Ft entry.

To create this report, begin by issuing the [Menu] Report Design command, typing **LISTINGS**, and pressing ↵. Next, choose the number under which you want to store the report (we'll use number **2**), type a description like **Price Per Square Foot**, and select **T**abular as the report type. Once you complete these steps, issue the [Menu] Setting PageLayout **W**idth command, press [Ctrl]-[Backspace], type **132**, and then press ↵ to increase the page-widths to 132 characters. Now, issue the [Menu] Setting PageLayout **D**elete command to delete the second page-width from the spec. At this point, your screen will resemble Figure 10-13 on page 425.

Figure 10-29 A Report with a Calculated Field

```
9/22/88              Price Per Square Foot           Page   1

Address          Town        Owner       List Date  Style      Price        Sq Ft  BRs  Baths  Price Per Sq Ft
------------     --------    --------    ---------  ------     -------      -----  ---  -----  ---------------
123 Abby Ct.     Louisville  Kones,D      6/16/88   Ranch       32,950.00   1500    3     1      21.97
426 St. James Ct. Louisville Jones,B      6/19/88   Ranch       19,500.00    950    2     1      20.53
766 Baird St.    Louisville  Black,B      6/22/88   Colonial   139,950.00   2600    4     3      53.83
222 Big Ben Dr.  Louisville  Roberts,D    6/22/88   Other       53,500.00   1900    3     2      28.16
666 Montana Ave. Louisville  Saul,H       6/23/88   Cape Cod    55,000.00   1900    3     1      28.95
589 Morocco Dr.  E'Town      Smith,B      6/24/88   Cape Cod    62,500.00   1875    3     2      33.33
987 Allan Dr.    Louisville  Newsome,K    6/26/88   Cape Cod    60,000.00   1900    4     2      31.58
549 Billtown Rd. Louisville  Bizer,B      6/28/88   Ranch       72,500.00   2000    3     2      36.25
343 Market St.   Louisville  Bivins,D     6/29/88   Ranch       42,900.00   1675    3     1      25.61
198 Main St.     J'Town      Green,L      6/29/88   Other       27,500.00    800    3     1      34.38
885 Jefferson St. J'Town     Zith,M       7/02/88   Ranch       55,000.00   1500    3     1      36.67
913 Whitney Dr.  North Hill  Kulp,R       7/04/88   Cape Cod    99,500.00   1800    4     2      55.28
363 Dower Ct.    North Fork  Culp,A       7/05/88   Cape Cod   109,000.00   2100    4     2      51.90
620 Windsong Ct. Louisville  Pann,E       7/06/88   Colonial   250,000.00   4000    6     4      62.50
4500 Hempstead Dr. Louisville Pape,C      6/18/88   Colonial   150,000.00   2600    4     3      57.69
#6 Brandon Way   Louisville  Abrams,L     7/22/88   Ranch       67,000.00   2250    4     2      29.78
6610 Vernin Dr.  Louisville  Russ,J       7/24/88   Ranch       75,000.00   2100    3     2      35.71
712 Clifton Ct.  Louisville  Thomas,T     7/24/88   Ranch       30,000.00   1500    3     1      20.00
5432 Miller Rd.  Louisville  Young,R      7/29/88   Other       17,500.00    800    2     1      21.88
#12 Circle Ct.   Louisville  White,Y      8/02/88   Other       10,000.00    800    2     1      12.50
1222 Dee Rd.     South Fork  Smith,P      8/02/88   Ranch       22,950.00    950    3     1      24.16
222 Earl Ave.    J'Town      Wray,A       8/05/88   Ranch       51,000.00   1200    3     1      42.50
9827 Rowan St.   J'Town      Coad,B       8/10/88   Ranch       47,950.00   1100    3     1      43.59
3355 Bank St.    J'Town      Cobb,D       8/17/88   Ranch       37,500.00   1500    3     1      25.00
77 Portland Ave. Louisville  Coe,A        8/19/88   Ranch       20,000.00   1500    3     1      13.33
99 Cardinal Hill Rd. North Hill Brand,B   8/19/88   Cape Cod    70,000.00   2000    3     2      35.00
#10 Old Mill Rd. Louisville  Stern,M      8/21/88   Ranch       75,000.00   2150    3     2      34.88
5532 Mud Creek Dr. Louisville Hall,W      8/24/88   Ranch       12,000.00    950    2     1      12.63
4444 Normie Ln.  Louisville  James,J      8/25/88   Cape Cod   120,000.00   2400    5     3      50.00
3498 Bold Rd.    Louisville  Taft,H       8/29/88   Colonial   275,000.00   3800    5     4      72.37
#82 Rudd Rd.     Louisville  Lum,I        8/30/88   Cape Cod    88,950.00   2800    4     2      31.77
6712 Shelby St.  Louisville  Wood,B       8/30/88   Ranch       92,500.00   2400    4     2      38.54
7235 Shiloh Dr.  E'Town      Allan,J      8/31/88   Ranch       95,000.00   2750    4     3      34.55
8989 Big D Ln.   South Fork  Adkins,B     9/01/88   Ranch       17,000.00   1200    2     1      14.17
1001 Spring St.  North Hill  Frier,C      9/05/88   Other       45,000.00   1700    3     2      26.47
6935 Shiloh Dr.  E'Town      Grebe,C      9/08/88   Cape Cod    81,000.00   2000    3     2      40.50
4989 Adler Way   Louisville  Dole,V       9/13/88   Cape Cod    76,500.00   2000    3     2      38.25
5678 Beech St.   Louisville  Smith,P      9/16/88   Cape Cod    65,950.00   1800    3     2      36.64
#62 Billy Bone Ct. Louisville Taylor,A    9/18/88   Ranch       34,500.00   1600    3     1      21.56
3325 Mt. Holly Dr. Louisville Grizz,D     9/24/88   Ranch       22,100.00   1200    3     1      18.42
9909 Midway Rd.  Louisville  Maier,O      9/25/88   Ranch       61,250.00   1875    3     2      32.67
435 Oxted Ln.    Louisville  O'Neal,P     9/26/88   Ranch       53,790.00   1900    3     1      28.31
22 N. Ridge Ct.  Louisville  Nunn,A       9/29/88   Colonial   200,000.00   2900    5     3      68.97
654 Nora Ln.     Louisville  Orwick,B    10/02/88   Cape Cod    40,000.00   1600    3     1      25.00
659 Ridge Rd.    Louisville  Pulley,F    10/08/88   Ranch       30,000.00   1500    3     1      20.00
14 Short Rd.     Louisville  Quire,I     10/13/88   Ranch       52,300.00   1600    3     1      32.69
721 Zabel Way    Louisville  Stich,L     10/14/88   Ranch       47,950.00   1500    3     1      31.97
581 Yale Dr.     Louisville  Winer,L     10/17/88   Ranch       78,000.00   2100    4     2      37.14
654 Unseld Blvd. Louisville  Volk,H      10/19/88   Other       87,000.00   2500    3     2      34.80
#5 Ashby St.     J'Town      Wagner,H    10/22/88   Other       97,000.00   2500    4     3      38.80
1989 Eastern Pkwy. Louisville Klink,C    10/23/88   Ranch       26,950.00   1100    3     1      24.50
```

Once you have created this spec, you'll need to add a column at the end of the table band to hold the calculated field. To insert this column, issue the **[Menu]** TableBand Insert command, move the cursor beyond the last column in the table band, and press ↵. Having created this column, you probably will want to add a column header to it, just like the ones in the other columns. To do this, move the cursor to the beginning of the second row of the new column and type **Price Per Sq Ft**, then move to the beginning of the third row of that column and type a series of 15 hyphens.

You now are ready to place the calculated field into the new column. To do this, begin by issuing the **[Menu]** Field Place Calculated command. As soon as you issue this command, Paradox will prompt you to enter the expression you want it to calculate. Because you want Paradox to divide each record's entry in the Price field by its entry in the Sq Ft field, type the formula **[Price]/[Sq Ft]**, then press ↵.

After you have supplied an expression for the field, move the cursor to the location where you want Paradox to place the field (in this case, the beginning of the fourth row of the new column), and press ↵. Because one of the fields referenced by the expression is a dollar field, Paradox presents the default mask for a dollar field: *(999,999,999.99)*. At this point, Paradox will let you specify the number of characters to the left and right of the decimal place. In this case, press ← seven times, and press ↵ to specify three digits to the left of the decimal place, then press ↵ again to accept two digits to the right of the decimal. Figure 10-30 shows the result.

Figure 10-30 A Report Spec with a Calculated Field

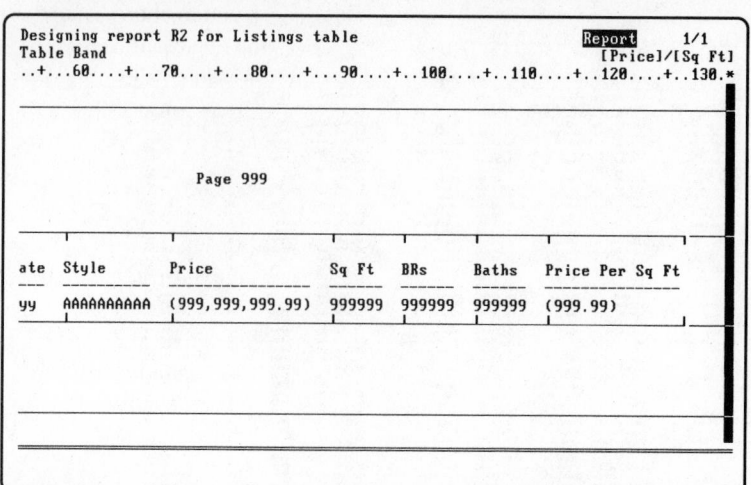

As you can see, the message *[Price]/[Sq Ft]* appears in the upper-right corner of the screen while the cursor is positioned on this new field. This message indicates that the field is a calculated field and lets you know what expression it contains.

If you press [Instant Report] at this point, Paradox will produce the report shown in Figure 10-29. As you can see, Paradox has divided each record's Price field entry by its Sq Ft field entry and printed the results in the last column of the report.

Notes

The expression you supply for any calculated field can be up to 175 characters long. It can contain field names (which must be enclosed in brackets), mathematical operators (like *, /, ( ), and +), literal strings (like *"Mr. "*), and literal numbers (like *123*). You could use an expression like *"Mr. "+[Last Name]* to concatenate the literal string *"Mr. "* to the contents of a Last Name field. Similarly, you could use an expression like *65-[Age]* to subtract each entry in an Age field from the value 65. Paradox automatically checks every expression you enter. If the expression is not valid, Paradox will beep and let you try again.

If you make a mistake while typing an expression, you can edit it by pressing the [Field View] key ([Alt]-[F5]). Pressing this key changes the cursor to a box and lets you move around within the expression and edit what you have typed. When you have made your changes, press ↵ to end the field view.

The CalcEdit Command

If you discover an error in a calculated or summary calculated field after you have placed it in the report, you can correct it by selecting the [Menu] Field CalcEdit command. Paradox will then prompt you to move the cursor to the calculated field you want to edit. You should move the cursor to that field and press ↵. When you do this, Paradox will display the expression for the field at the top of the screen and allow you to change it. You can press [Backspace] or [Ctrl]-[Backspace] to erase part or all of the expression and retype it, or you can press the [Field View] key ([Alt]-[F5]) to edit the expression. When you're done, press ↵ to complete the CalcEdit (remember to press ↵ twice if you used [Field View]).

The Justify Command

You can change the alignment of fields in reports by using the [Menu] Field Justify command. By default, alphanumeric and date fields are left justified, and numeric fields (N, $, and S) are right justified. To change the alignment of a field, select Justify from the Field menu. Paradox will then prompt you to use the arrow keys to select the field you want to realign. When the cursor is in place, press ↵. Paradox will then display a menu that asks you what type of justification you want: Left, Center, Right, or Default. Select the option you want and press ↵.

The WordWrap Command

The [Menu] Field WordWrap command allows you to print the contents of long alphanumeric fields on several lines of a narrow column. Word wrapping lets you avoid producing reports with one or two very wide columns, or reports in which the contents of one or more fields are truncated.

To use this option, first issue the [Menu] Field Reformat command to reduce the width of the field mask of the field you want to wrap so that the length of the mask equals the maximum number of characters you want Paradox to print on each line of the wrapped field. Then, issue the [Menu] Field WordWrap command. When you do this, Paradox will prompt you to move the cursor to the field you want to wrap. You should move the cursor to that field and press ↵. Next, Paradox will prompt you to specify the number of lines you want the wrapped field to include. You can specify any number of lines from 1 to 255. Once you have typed the number of lines, press ↵.

When you print a report that includes wrapped fields, Paradox will print as many characters from the wrapped fields as it can in the space you have specified. For instance, if you specify five lines of word wrap for a field mask that is ten characters long, Paradox will display up to 50 characters for that field when the report is printed. Paradox will try to break the contents of fields at spaces and hyphens. This is not possible if a word is longer than the field mask (the length of one line of the word wrap). In such a case, Paradox will break the word when it reaches the end of a line.

For example, suppose you use the [Menu] Restructure command to add a 40-character Notes field to the LISTINGS table and to enter some facts about each house into that field. (Refer to Chapter 5 for details on restructuring a table.) Figure 10-31 shows this new field with some sample data in place.

Figure 10-31 Sample Data for the Notes Field

```
Editing Listings table: Record 7 of 65                        Edit

  ══BRs══        ══Baths══        ══════════════════Notes══════════════════
       3              1           New roof, carpet, remodeled kitchen
       2              1           Lovely all brick exterior
       4              2.5         w/w carpet, built-ins
       3              1.5
       3              1           All brass plumbing
       3              1.5         Upgrades throughout
       4              2           Kitchenette alcove, new plush carpet    ◄
       3              2
       3              1           Pool
       3              1
       3              1           Security system
       4              2
       4              2
       6              3.5         Lighted tennis court
       4              2.5         Fishing pond in front yard, tennis court
       4              1.5         Lots of airport noise
       3              1.5         Two car garage in basement
       3              1
       2              1           Patio with adjoining redwood deck
       2              1
       3              1
       3              1           Hot tub built into patio
```

Now, let's create a new report for the LISTINGS table. To do this, issue the **[Menu] R**eport **D**esign command, specify LISTINGS as the table for which you want to create the report, choose report number **3**, specify the name **WordWrap Feature** for the report, and choose the **T**abular report type. When the report spec appears, be sure to use the **[Menu]** **S**etting **P**ageLayout **W**idth command to increase the page-width to 132.

To begin designing the new report, first issue the **[Menu] F**ield **R**eformat command and decrease the width of the Notes field mask to 15 characters. Now, issue the **[Menu] F**ield WordWrap command. The cursor should already be on the field mask for Notes, so you can simply press ↵ to select that field. Paradox will then ask you for the number of lines to include in the wrapped field. Press **[Backspace]** to erase the default value 1, type **4**, and press ↵ . Although the appearance of the form won't change when you issue this command, Paradox will now wrap the Notes field onto a maximum of four lines. This setting will allow up to 60 characters of output, which will be spread over four lines with 15 characters each.

Next, place the cursor at the end of the dashed line above the field mask and press **[Backspace]** to delete a few of the dashes. Then, use the **[Menu]** **T**ableBand **R**eformat command to decrease the column width of the current column so that the end-of-column marker is within the first page-width. Finally, remove the second page-width of the report by issuing the **[Menu] S**etting **P**ageLayout **D**elete **OK** command.

Figure 10-32 shows the completed report spec. If you press [Instant Report], the output will look like the report shown in Figure 10-33. As you can see, Paradox has wrapped the contents of the Notes field for each record onto a maximum of four lines.

Figure 10-32 WordWrap Feature Report Spec

```
Designing report R3 for Listings table              Report    1/1
Table Band
..+...60....+...70....+...80....+...90....+..100....+..110....+..120....+..130.

    ────────────────────────────────────────────────────────────────



        Page 999


    ────────────────────────────────────────────────────────────────


ate  Style        Price              Sq Ft    BRs     Baths    Notes
───  ──────────   ──────────────────  ──────   ──────  ──────   ────────────────
yy   AAAAAAAAAA   (999,999,999.99)   999999   999999  999999   AAAAAAAAAAAAAAAA


    ────────────────────────────────────────────────────────────────
```

Figure 10-33 Report Using WordWrap

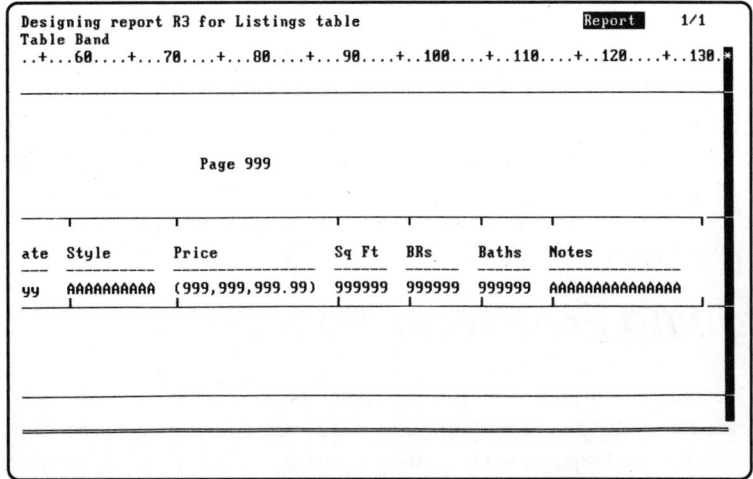

Placing Multiple Fields in a Column

In most cases, each of the columns in the table band of your tabular report specs will contain only a single field mask. This convention makes it easy to use Paradox's TableBand commands (like Move, Copy, and Erase) to modify the appearance of a tabular report. However, you can place more than one field mask in any column of a table band. For example, you could place a mask for every field of a table side by side, or stack them in a single column. In fact, you can place the same field in two or more places within the same report spec—even within the same column of a table band. To create nontabular arrangements of this sort, however, you may want to start with a free-form report format.

Designing Free-form Reports

So far, we have shown you how to design tabular reports. As you have seen, the tabular format is well-suited for creating columnar reports. However, this format is too restrictive for creating less-structured reports, such as mailing labels, form letters, and invoices. Fortunately, Paradox's free-form reporting format is ideally suited for these types of reports.

Both free-form and tabular report specs have a report band, a page band, and, optionally, one or more group bands. Additionally, you can use the same commands to add, delete, and resize page-widths, and to place, erase, and format field masks in both free-form and tabular report specs. Furthermore, you can move around both specs in the same way and can enter literals in the same way.

The principal difference between a free-form report spec and a tabular report spec is the substitution of a form band for the table band. When you print from a free-form report spec, Paradox prints the contents of the form band once for every record in the table—just as it does for the contents of the table band in a tabular report. Unlike a table band, however, a form band is not divided into columns. The noncolumnar structure of the form band provides a less-restrictive workspace for the design of nontabular reports.

A second difference between the tabular and free-form report specs is the absence of a TableBand option on the Free-form menu. Because free-form reports do not have table bands, this option would be irrelevant in the free-form environment.

One other difference between tabular and free-form reports is the presence of two special options—LineSqueeze and FieldSqueeze—on the Free-form Setting menu. These commands let Paradox close up blank lines and spaces in a report. You will understand the usefulness of these commands when we show you how to create mailing labels later in this section.

Designing a Free-form Report

Designing a free-form report is similar to designing a tabular report. For example, suppose you want to create a free-form report based on the data in the NAMES table shown in Figure 10-34. First, issue the **[Menu] R**eport **D**esign command, then select the name of the table for which you want to design the report. In this case, we'll choose **NAMES**. Now, select a number under which to store the report spec. We'll choose the number **1**. Next, enter a description for the report (in this case, **Sample Free-form Report**). Finally, instead of choosing Tabular when Paradox prompts you for the report type, choose Free-form. Figure 10-35 shows the resulting spec.

Figure 10-34 The NAMES Table

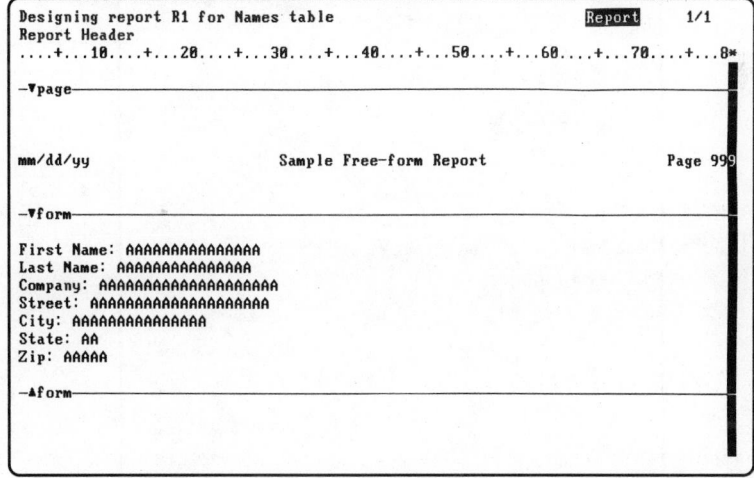

Figure 10-35   A Free-form Report Specification

Notice that this basic free-form report spec looks quite a bit like the tabular report specs we have worked with throughout this chapter, except for the substitution of a form band for the table band and the arrangement of the field masks within the form band. Although this band contains a mask for every field in the table, as well as a literal that names each field, the arrangement of this information is not the same as it is in a tabular report. Specifically, the field name literals and field masks are stacked on consecutive rows of the form band, rather than one after another across the page.

You can print a free-form report by pressing [Instant Report] while you are working within the spec. Figure 10-36 shows the first page of the report Paradox will print if you press [Instant Report] while viewing the free-form report spec in Figure 10-35. As you can see, Paradox has skipped one line at the top of the page for the report header, printed the current date, the report title, and the page number on the fifth line of the page, then skipped two more lines to reach the top of the form band. Because the first line of the form band is blank (as it always will be in a new free-form report), Paradox skips yet another line (the eighth line on the page). On the next seven lines of the page, Paradox prints the names and entries of the fields from the first record in the NAMES table. Because the last line of the form band is blank (as it always will be in a new free-form report), Paradox skips another line (the 16th line on the page). Next, Paradox makes another pass through the form band, first skipping another line (the first line of the band) and then printing the entries from the second record in the table.

Figure 10-36 A Basic Free-form Report

```
   5/17/86              Sample Free-form Report             Page   1


   First Name: Frank
   Last Name: Lang
   Company: MCC Designs
   Street: 333 Forest Way
   City: Toledo
   State: OH
   Zip: 43427


   First Name: Ruth
   Last Name: Saunders
   Company:
   Street: 123 Main Street
   City: Louisville
   State: KY
   Zip: 40205


   First Name: Curtis
   Last Name: Browning
   Company: JLR Investments
   Street: 555 Maple Street
   City: Denver
   State: CO
   Zip: 57832


   First Name: Charles
   Last Name: Kern
   Company: XYZ Engineering
   Street: 111 First Street
   City: New York
   State: NY
   Zip: 10023


   First Name: Richard
   Last Name: Franklin
   Company:
   Street: 222 Second Street
   City: Anaheim
   State: CA
   Zip: 90037
```

Paradox will continue in this fashion until it prints the last whole record it can print on the page before reaching the four-line page footer specified by the report spec. Paradox will not split records onto two pages of a report.

It is important to note that Paradox prints the single blank line from the top of the form band before each record it prints, not just once as it does for a blank line or a line of text at the top of the table band in a tabular report. Unlike table bands in tabular report specs, form bands are not divided into header and body sections. Accordingly, Paradox will print every line of a form band for each record in a table.

Mailing Labels

As a more useful example of a free-form report, suppose you want to print the names and addresses from the NAMES table on 4- by $1^1/_2$-inch continuous-feed labels, as shown in Figure 10-37 on the following page. To do this, start with the new free-form report spec shown in Figure 10-35. After bringing this spec to the screen, use the **[Delete Report Line]** key ([Ctrl]-[Y]) to delete the single line of the report header, the six lines of the page header (including the line that contains the report title and date and page number masks), the four lines of the page footer, and the single line of the report footer. After you delete these lines, all that will be left of the report spec will be the nine lines of the form band.

Once you have deleted these lines from the report spec, you are ready to design the labels. To begin, press the **[Ins]** key to enter the insert mode. Then, use the [Del] or [Backspace] keys to delete all the literals from the form band. Next, move the cursor to the left edge of the Last Name mask, press **[Backspace]** to pull the field up to the line that contains the First Name mask, and press the **[Spacebar]** once to put a space between the two field masks. Then, move the cursor to the left edge of the Zip field, press **[Backspace]** to pull that field onto the line that contains the State mask, and press the **[Spacebar]** twice to place two spaces between the two fields. Next, position the cursor at the left edge of the line that now contains the State and Zip fields, press **[Backspace]** to pull those masks onto the line that contains the City field, then type a comma and press the **[Spacebar]**. Finally, use the ↵ key to insert one blank line at the top of the form band and two blank lines at the bottom so that it contains a total of nine lines. Figure 10-38 shows the finished report specification.

Figure 10-38 The Mailing Labels Spec

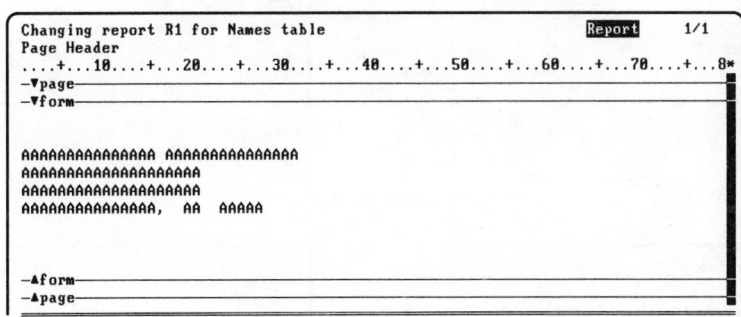

Figure 10-37
Mailing Labels

```
Frank          Lang
MCC Designs
333 Forest Way
Toledo         ,  OH  43427
```

```
Ruth           Saunders
123 Main Street
Louisville     ,  KY  40205
```

```
Curtis         Browning
JLR Investments
555 Maple Street
Denver         ,  CO  57832
```

```
Charles        Kern
XYZ Engineering
111 First Street
New York       ,  NY  10023
```

```
Richard        Franklin
222 Second Street
Anaheim        ,  CA  90037
```

```
John           Smith
SSC Computers
897 Oak Street
Phoenix        ,  AZ  85217
```

```
Nancy          Moody
LMN Medical
456 Madison Avenue
Tampa          ,  FL  33601
```

```
Patti          Irwin
DFC Publishing
246 Monroe Street
Atlanta        ,  GA  30325
```

```
Kyle           Jones
192 Hill Street
Dallas         ,  TX  45723
```

```
Thomas         Spencer
PDQ Printers
100 Lake Street
Macon          ,  GA  31024
```

Figure 10-39
Squeezed Mailing Labels

```
Frank Lang
MCC Designs
333 Forest Way
Toledo, OH  43427
```

```
Ruth Saunders
123 Main Street
Louisville, KY  40205
```

```
Curtis Browning
JLR Investments
555 Maple Street
Denver, CO  57832
```

```
Charles Kern
XYZ Engineering
111 First Street
New York, NY  10023
```

```
Richard Franklin
222 Second Street
Anaheim, CA  90037
```

```
John Smith
SSC Computers
897 Oak Street
Phoenix, AZ  85217
```

```
Nancy Moody
LMN Medical
456 Madison Avenue
Tampa, FL  33601
```

```
Patti Irwin
DFC Publishing
246 Monroe Street
Atlanta, GA  30325
```

```
Kyle Jones
192 Hill Street
Dallas, TX  45723
```

```
Thomas Spencer
PDQ Printers
100 Lake Street
Macon, GA  31024
```

Before you print labels from this spec, you should issue the **[Menu]** Setting **P**ageLayout Length command and change the page length from 66 to **C**. This setting tells Paradox to print the report continuously without page breaks. After you align the top of the first label with the print head in your printer and turn the printer on, you can press **[Instant Report]** to print the labels shown in Figure 10-37. Because you have deleted every line except the ones in the form band, Paradox does not skip any lines at the beginning or end of the report or at the beginning or end of each page. Since the top of each label is $1\frac{1}{2}$ inches from the top of the next label, and most printers print six lines to the inch, the nine-line form band ensures that the addresses will be properly spaced on the labels.

The FieldSqueeze and LineSqueeze Options

If you look at the labels displayed in Figure 10-37, you'll see a couple of problems. First, there appears to be too much space between the first and last names and between the City field and the literal comma. Second, Paradox has left a blank line in the labels for those records that have an empty Company field. To correct these problems, you can use the FieldSqueeze and LineSqueeze options.

The FieldSqueeze Option

As we explained earlier, Paradox allocates as many spaces to a field in a report as there are characters in its field mask. For example, because the mask for the First Name field in the mailing label spec is 15 characters long, Paradox always leaves 15 spaces for it at the beginning of the third line of each label. For this reason, and because we left a single space between the First Name and Last Name masks, Paradox always begins printing the Last Name entry on the 17th space of the line, regardless of the actual length of the First Name entry it prints on that line. This same principle is responsible for the gaps between the City field and the comma on the sixth line of each label.

Paradox offers a command that solves this problem: [Menu] Setting RemoveBlanks FieldSqueeze. After you issue this command, Paradox will allocate only as much space to a field as there are characters in that field—not always as many characters as there are in that field's mask. To turn off this attribute, issue the [Menu] Setting RemoveBlanks FieldSqueeze No command.

The LineSqueeze Option

The second problem with these labels is the blank line that Paradox leaves in the labels of records that have an empty Company field. The [Menu] Setting RemoveBlanks LineSqueeze command takes care of this problem. When you issue this command and choose the Yes option, Paradox gives you two choices: Fixed and Variable. Either choice will cause Paradox to squeeze out any blank lines that result from empty fields in reports. The difference between them is what happens to the lines that are removed. The Fixed option causes Paradox to add to the bottom of that band any lines it squeezes out of the form band. This preserves the proper spacing for your fixed-form reports, like mailing labels. On the other hand, the Variable option causes Paradox to throw away the lines it squeezes out of the form band, thus reducing the number of lines in the report.

Figure 10-39 on page 454 shows how the labels will print after you issue the **[Menu]** Setting **R**emoveBlanks **F**ieldSqueeze **Y**es and **[Menu]** Setting **R**emoveBlanks **L**ineSqueeze **Y**es **F**ixed commands. As you can see, Paradox has closed up the gaps between the fields on each line and has removed the blank line from the labels for the records with an empty company field without disturbing the spacing of the labels.

The Labels Command

Paradox 2 and 3 give you the option of having each page-width in a report treated as a separate form. This means you can have the same form printed two or more times horizontally across the same page. This comes in handy when you want to print two, three, or four mailing labels across a page.

For example, suppose you want to print two mailing labels across a page, as shown in Figure 10-40. To do this, create the mailing label form shown in Figure 10-38. Now, shorten the page-width to 40 columns by issuing the **[Menu]** Setting **P**ageLayout **W**idth **40** command. This leaves two page-widths, as the indicator *1/2* in the upper-right corner of the screen tells you.

At this point, issue the **[Menu]** Setting **L**abels command. When Paradox displays the No/ Yes menu, select **Y**es. Although the appearance of the form won't change when you issue this command, Paradox will now treat the form as multiple forms, not multiple page-widths. This means you should not enter any literals or masks in the form band portion of the form. When you print this report, the result will look like Figure 10-40.

There are three important things to remember in designing multiple-column mailing labels. First, you must create as many page-widths as the number of labels you want to print across. Second, the width of each page indicates the horizontal spacing between labels. Third, use the [Menu] Setting Labels Yes command to turn the feature on.

Notes

Because the fields in the NAMES table were in the order in which we wanted them to appear in the mailing labels, we were able to use the [Backspace] key to pull them into mailing label form quickly. However, you probably will not be so lucky in actual practice. In many cases, you will have to use a combination of the [Menu] Field Erase and [Menu] Field Place commands to move field masks into the proper order. The [Menu] Field Erase command allows you to remove a field mask from one place in a report spec, while the [Menu] Field Place command allows you to put it back in another location. The order in which you use these commands to move a field is not important.

Figure 10-40 Multiple Column Mailing Labels

```
Frank Lang
MCC Designs
333 Forest Way
Toledo,  OH  43427
```

```
Ruth Saunders
123 Main Street
Louisville,  KY  40205
```

```
Curtis Browning
JLR Investments
555 Maple Street
Denver,  CO  57832
```

```
Charles Kern
XYZ Engineering
111 First Street
New York,  NY  10023
```

```
Richard Franklin
222 Second Street
Anaheim,  CA  90037
```

```
John Smith
SSC Computers
897 Oak Street
Phoenix,  AZ  85217
```

```
Nancy Moody
LMN Medical
456 Madison Avenue
Tampa,  FL  33601
```

```
Patti Irwin
DFC Publishing
246 Monroe Street
Atlanta,  GA  30325
```

```
Kyle Jones
192 Hill Street
Dallas,  TX  45723
```

```
Thomas Spencer
PDQ Printers
100 Lake LStreet
Macon,  GA  31024
```

The open nature of a free-form report spec lends itself to the development of other non-columnar reports. For example, the report spec shown in Figure 10-41 on the next page shows a simple form letter based on the entries in the NAMES table. As you can see, the top portion of this report spec is identical to our mailing labels report spec. In the salutation, we reused the Last Name field. The remainder of the letter is composed of literals we typed directly into the spec. Of course, you can place fields anywhere within the body of the letter.

Cancelling and Saving Report Specs

Once you have designed a report specification, you probably will want to save it for future use. You can do this by pressing the [Do-It!] key or by issuing the [Menu] DO-IT! command while you are viewing the report spec you want to save. Paradox will then save the spec to disk in a special report file. The first part of the name of the report file will be the name of the table for which you created the report. The first character of the extension will be the letter R, and the second and third characters of the extension will be the report's number (1 to 14). The default report for any table (the one stored under the letter R) will have only the single-character extension R.

Figure 10-41 A Simple Form Letter

```
Changing report R2 for Names table                    Report  Ins 1/1
Form Band,Field Squeeze,Line Squeeze
....+...10....+...20....+...30....+...40....+...50....+...60....+...70....+...8*
─▼page─────────────────────────────────────────────────────────────────
─▼form─────────────────────────────────────────────────────────────────
M o n t h dd, yyyy

AAAAAAAAAAAAAAA AAAAAAAAAAAAAAA
AAAAAAAAAAAAAAAAAAA
AAAAAAAAAAAAAAAAAAA
AAAAAAAAAAAAAA, AA  AAAAA


Dear AAAAAAAAAAAAAA:

We are pleased to announce the grand opening of our third store at 1775
Main Street, Louisville, Kentucky 40214.

I hope you will be able to stop by on May 17, 1986 to help us celebrate.  We
will be giving away some real neat door prizes, and everything in the store
will be marked down 10%.

See you there!

Sincerely,
```

However, you do not have to save a report spec you are designing or changing. If you do not want to save the changes you have made to a spec, just press the [Menu] key from within the Report Generator and choose Cancel. If you choose Yes when Paradox presents the choices Yes and No, Paradox will return you to the Main mode without saving any changes you made to the spec. If you choose No, however, Paradox will remain within the Report Generator. You also can cancel the editing of a report spec by pressing [Ctrl]-[Break]. When you press this key, Paradox will return you to the Main mode without saving the changes you made to the spec, just as if you had issued the [Menu] Cancel Yes command.

Revising Existing Reports

In this chapter, we have outlined a three-step process for creating a report. First, you use the [Menu] Report Design command to bring a new report spec to the screen. Second, you use the editing techniques described in this chapter (adding literals, deleting masks, and rearranging columns, for example) to customize the basic spec. Finally, you issue the [Menu] DO-IT! command to save the spec.

You can change a report spec once you have designed it. To do this, you must use the [Menu] Report Change command. When you issue this command, Paradox will ask you to name the table. After you choose a table, Paradox will present a menu that lists the numbers of the existing reports for the table. If you have designed and saved reports under numbers 1 and 2 only, for example, Paradox will present the options R, 1, and 2. (The R option will always be listed since it always contains a default report spec.)

As soon as you select the report you want to change, Paradox will display the description of that report and give you the opportunity to change it. Changing the description does not change the appearance of the report. Paradox does not place the new description in the page header of the report spec. As soon as you press ↵, Paradox will present the report spec for the table. The spec will look exactly as it did when you last saved it, except that the word *Changing* will replace the word *Designing* at the top of the screen.

When you want to change an existing report, be sure to choose Change rather than Design from the Report menu. If you issue the [Menu] Report Design command and select an existing report, Paradox will present two options: Cancel and Replace. If you choose Replace, Paradox will erase the existing report stored under that number and will present you with the new basic report (either Tabular or Free-form) that you choose. Choosing Cancel spares the existing report and returns you to the previous menu.

Printing Reports

Throughout this chapter, we have presented examples of a variety of reports. In those examples, we concentrated more on the fundamentals of designing the report spec than on the process of printing the report. Now, we'll explain in detail printing a report.

Printing a Saved Report

In the previous parts of this chapter, we showed you how to use the [Instant Report] key to print a report. If you press [Instant Report] while you are viewing a table, Paradox will print a report from that table using the spec stored under the letter R. Unless you have modified this report, it will be the standard tabular report for the table. If you press [Instant Report] while you are viewing a report spec, however, Paradox will print according to the layout of that report spec. Issuing the [Menu] Output Printer command from within the Report Generator has the same effect.

Once you have saved a report spec, you can print from that spec while you are in the Main mode. To do this, issue the **[Menu] R**eport **O**utput command. When you issue this command, Paradox will prompt you for the name of the table whose records you want to print. You can press ↵ to display a list of the tables in the current directory and then choose a table from that list, or you can type the name of the table and press ↵. If the table is not in the current directory, you must specify the path to its file.

Once you have selected a table, Paradox will present a menu that lists the available reports for it. This menu will list the R report plus the numbers of any other reports you have designed and saved. If you have supplied a description for a report, Paradox will display the description of that report immediately below the menu when you highlight its number. After you select a report spec, Paradox will prompt you to specify a destination for the report: Printer, Screen, or File. If you choose Printer, Paradox will send the report to your printer. The Screen and File options allow you to preview the report on the screen and save the report in an ASCII text file, respectively. We'll discuss these alternative print destinations in a few pages.

Cancelling Printing

Once you instruct Paradox to print a report, you'll usually let it print to completion. In some cases, however, you'll want Paradox to stop before it has printed the entire report. To cancel printing in the middle of a report, press any key. When you do this, Paradox will display the message *Printing interrupted....* If you press *C*, Paradox will cancel the printing of the report and will return to what you were doing before printing. If your printer has a buffer, it may take several seconds for printing to stop once you've issued this command. If you press *R*, Paradox will continue printing the report.

Print Settings

Unless you tell it otherwise, Paradox assumes that you will print a report on $8^1/_2$- by 11-inch continuous-feed paper, and that your printer will print ten characters per inch across a page and six lines per inch down the page. However, you may want to print on different size paper, on cut sheets, in a different type style, and so forth. You can use commands on Paradox's Report Generator menu to adjust the print settings to account for these conditions while you are designing or changing a report spec. You can also change the default settings Paradox uses for new reports, as we will describe in the next chapter.

Adjusting the Width of a Page

The size of the page-widths in a report spec determines how many characters Paradox will print across each line of a page. As you have seen, Paradox sets 80-character page-widths for all new report specs. The [Menu] Setting PageLayout Width command allows you to adjust this width. If you have a wide-carriage printer, for example, you probably will want to adjust the page-widths in your reports to 132 characters, as we did to produce the spec shown in Figure 10-13 on page 425. Any elements (literals or masks) split by the border of a page-width will be printed partially on one page and partially on another. Unless you plan to glue the pages of the report together, you probably will want to adjust the placement of the information in your report so that it does not overlap a page-width boundary. Alternatively, you can adjust the size of the page-widths so that they do not divide any element in your report.

Adjusting the Length of a Page

Unless you tell it otherwise, Paradox assumes that your printer will print six lines per inch. If you plan to print a report on paper that isn't $8^1/_2$- by-11, or if your printer prints more than six lines per inch, or both, you will need to adjust the Length setting for that report. To do this, issue the **[Menu]** Setting **P**ageLayout command while you are working with the spec for the report whose settings you want to adjust. When you issue this command, Paradox will display the prompt *New page length:* at the top of the screen, followed by the current Length setting for that report (probably 66). Once you see this prompt, you should press **[Backspace]** or **[Ctrl]-[Backspace]** to erase the old setting, type in a new number, and press ↵. If you are printing on legal-size paper, for example, you might specify a length of 84.

The minimum page length Paradox will accept is two lines; the maximum is 2,000 lines. If you want Paradox to disregard page breaks entirely, you should specify a Length setting of *C*. This setting, which instructs Paradox to print continuously, is useful for printing mailing labels.

Adjusting the Left Margin

In addition to adjusting the width of a page, you can adjust the margin Paradox leaves at the left edge of each page. Unless you specify otherwise, Paradox will not leave any left margin; it will start printing at the left edge of each page. The [Menu] Setting Margin command allows you to adjust the left margin of a report. When you issue this command, Paradox will display the prompt *Margin size:* followed by the current left margin (usually 0). When you see this prompt, you should erase the old margin, type a new one, and press ↵. When you do this, Paradox will move the elements in your report spec to the right (or to the left if you decreased the margin). Figure 10-42 shows the result of adding a ten-space left margin to the report spec shown in Figure 10-11 on page 423. As you can see, Paradox has inserted ten spaces at the left edge of each row of the spec.

Figure 10-42 A Ten-character Left Margin

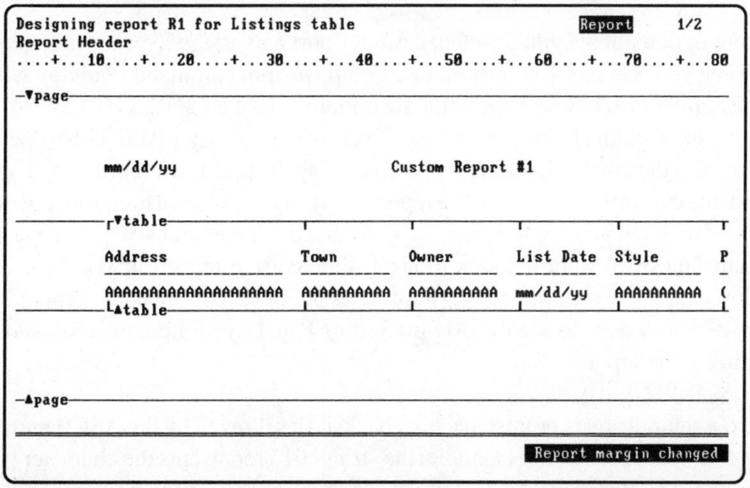

```
Designing report R1 for Listings table                    Report    1/2
Report Header
....+...10....+...20....+...30....+...40....+...50....+...60....+...70....+...80
-▼page──────────────────────────────────────────────────────────────────


        mm/dd/yy                        Custom Report #1

      ┌▼table───────┬────────────┬────────────┬───────────┬───────────┬──
        Address        Town         Owner        List Date  Style      P
        ─────────────  ──────────── ──────────── ────────── ────────── ─
        AAAAAAAAAAAAAAAAAAAAAA  AAAAAAAAAA  AAAAAAAAAA  mm/dd/yy  AAAAAAAAAA  (
      └▲table───────┴────────────┴────────────┴───────────┴───────────┴──


-▲page──────────────────────────────────────────────────────────────────

                                              Report margin changed
```

Because the [Menu] Setting Margin command acts by inserting or deleting space at the left edge of the first page-width in a report spec, it controls the left margin of only the first page-width in the report. Also, because the Margin command moves the information in a report, it can cause the information in a report to be split between two page-widths. Paradox will not insert a margin if the insertion would push any element beyond the right edge of the rightmost page-width in the spec.

Setup Strings

Most printers are able to print in a variety of type styles (such as bold, italic, compressed, expanded, and so forth). The most common way to change the style in which your printer prints is to send it a special code called a setup string. The [Menu] Setting Setup command allows you to change the style in which Paradox prints a report by instructing it to send a setup string to your printer before it begins printing that report.

To specify the style in which a report should be printed, issue the **[Menu]** Setting Setup command while you are working with the spec for that report. When you issue this command, Paradox will present two choices: Predefined and Custom. If you choose Predefined, Paradox will present a menu list of predefined setup strings for a variety of printers. (As we will explain in Chapter 11, you can use the CCP to customize this menu list to suit your printer.) Figure 10-43 shows such a list. If you choose one of these strings, Paradox will display the message *Setup string recorded* and will assign that string to the report spec. The next time you print from that spec, Paradox will use the print style you specified.

Figure 10-43 The Predefined Menu

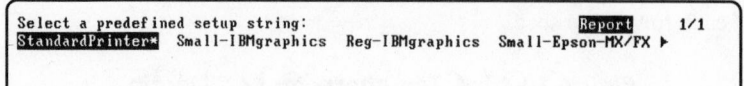

```
Select a predefined setup string:                    Report    1/1
StandardPrinter*  Small-IBMgraphics  Reg-IBMgraphics  Small-Epson-MX/FX ▶
```

The Custom option allows you to select a printer port and assign a custom setup string to a report. When you issue the **[Menu]** Setting Setup Custom command, Paradox will display the prompt *Printer Port:*. Select one of the six options—LPT1, LPT2, LPT3, COM1, COM2, or AUX—by highlighting it and pressing ↵. If you're not sure, try LPT1. If that doesn't work, experiment with the others. Paradox will then display the prompt *Setup string:*, followed by the setup string currently assigned to the report (if you have chosen a predefined string, it will show up here). When you see this prompt, you can edit the default string (if any) to specify the print attributes you want Paradox to use for the current report. If you have an Epson printer, for example, you can make it print eight lines per inch by typing \027\048. Accordingly, you'll want to use the [Menu] Setting PageLayout Length command to set the page length for the report to 88.

In Paradox, a setup string is represented as a backslash followed by the ASCII number of the character you want to send. For example, the string \015 represents the character [Ctrl]-[O], which has the ASCII code 015. If you are using an Epson or Epson-compatible printer, sending this character to your printer will cause your report to be printed in compressed print. The setup functions available, and the codes that perform them, differ from printer to printer. You should check your printer manual for the codes that will work with your printer.

The Report SetPrinter Command

The [Menu] Report SetPrinter command lets you override the printer port and setup string specified in a report spec when you print a report. When you select this command, Paradox will display the two-option menu shown in Figure 10-44. If you choose Regular, Paradox will use the printer and port stored in the report spec. If you choose Override, Paradox will display the menu shown in Figure 10-45. By selecting the PrinterPort option from this menu, you can choose a printer port from the predefined list that Paradox will display. If you select Setup, you will be prompted to specify the printer attributes you want Paradox to use. The setup string can be up to 15 characters long. The EndOf Page option lets you specify whether Paradox should send a line feed or form feed character at the end of each page.

Figure 10-44 The SetPrinter Menu

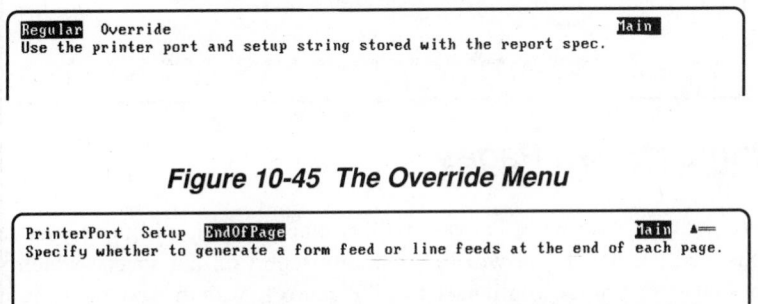

Figure 10-45 The Override Menu

The Report RangeOutput Command

If you don't need to print all the pages of a report, you can use the [Menu] Report RangeOutput Printer command to specify which pages to print. This command works just like the [Menu] Report Output command, with one exception: After you enter a destination for the report, Paradox will prompt you to specify the first page you want to print, as shown in Figure 10-46 on the next page. Paradox displays the default value 1. You can press ↵ if you want to start with page 1, or press [Backspace] to erase the default, type the page number you want to start with, and press ↵ . Paradox will then prompt you for the ending page number. If you want to print to the end of the report, press ↵. Otherwise, type the page number of the last page you want printed and press ↵. The pages you select will be sent to the device (printer, screen, or file). If your report spec has a page length setting of *C* to activate continuous-form printing, then Paradox will interpret the range of pages that you enter as the number of lines to be printed. For example, if you enter 1 as the first page of the range and 10 as the last page, Paradox will print the first ten lines of the report.

The RangeOutput command is especially valuable if the printer paper jams while a report is printing, and you lose a portion of it. You can use RangeOutput to reprint only the lost pages, rather than reprinting the entire report.

Figure 10-46 *Specifying a Beginning Page Number*

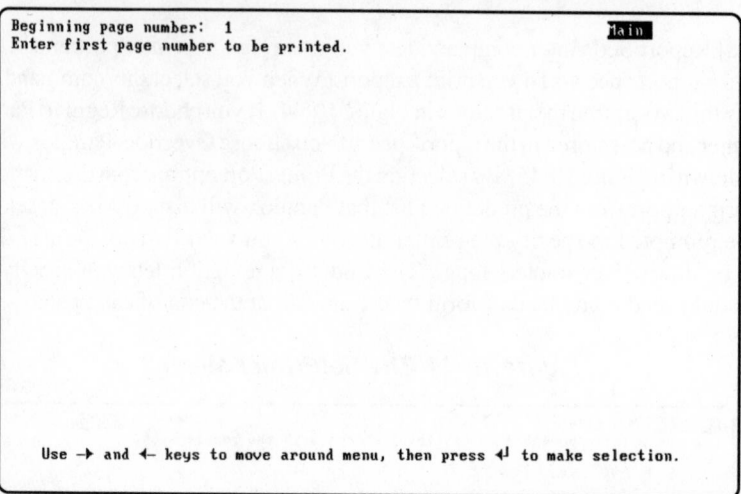

```
Beginning page number:  1                                            Main
Enter first page number to be printed.




















Use → and ← keys to move around menu, then press ↵ to make selection.
```

Waiting between Pages

Unless you indicate otherwise, Paradox will assume that you will print your reports on continuous-feed paper. If you will be printing a report on cut sheets, which you must manually feed to the printer, you'll have to tell Paradox to wait for you to insert a new sheet of paper after it prints each page. To do this, use the **[Menu]** S etting **W**ait **Y**es command. When you issue this command, Paradox will assign the Wait attribute to the report spec you currently are designing or editing. The next time you print from that spec, Paradox will stop at the end of each page and display the prompt *Insert next page in printer* and *Press any key to continue...* in the upper-left corner of the screen. As soon as you press any key (preferably after inserting a new sheet of paper), Paradox will print the next page.

Notes

When you use any one of the six commands described above, Paradox will assign the relevant attribute only to the report spec you are editing when you issue the command. The attributes you assign to one report spec do not affect the printing of any other report—not even other reports for the same table.

The settings you assign to a report spec go into effect immediately. If you change one of these settings while editing a report spec and then press the [Instant Report] key, Paradox will print using the new setting. Unless you use the [Do-It!] key or the [Menu] DO-IT! command to save the report spec, Paradox will not save those attributes with the spec. Consequently, Paradox will not use the attributes the next time it prints from that spec.

Finally, in addition to letting you change the print settings for an individual report, Paradox allows you to change the default value of these print settings. For example, if you usually want Paradox to print 88 lines per page, you could change the default Length setting from 66 to 88. We'll show you how to do this at the end of Chapter 11.

Alternative Print Destinations

Up till now, we have sent reports to a printer. Although a printer is the most common destination for a report, Paradox can send a report to two alternative devices: to the screen of your computer and to a file. Your choice between Printer, Screen, or File on the Report Output menu or the Report RangeOutput menu determines where Paradox will send a report.

Printing to the Screen

When you issue the [Menu] Report Output command, select a table, select a report spec, and choose Screen, Paradox will display the message *Sending report to screen...* and display the report on your computer screen. Paradox sends the report to the screen of your computer in the same order that it would send it to your printer: the pages of the first page-width first, the pages of the second page-width second, and so forth. Because Paradox cannot display an entire page of most reports on the screen at one time, it breaks the report into even smaller sections. Pressing any key on the keyboard brings successive sections of the report into view. As you move through the report, Paradox displays a prompt in the form *Now Viewing Page x of Page-width x* at the top of the screen to tell you what part of the report you are viewing.

For example, Figure 10-47 shows the result of issuing the [Menu] Report Output Screen command and specifying the report spec shown in Figure 10-3 on page 408. As you can see, Paradox is displaying the first part of the first page of the report on the screen. Each time you press a key, Paradox will display a new section of the report. When Paradox reaches the end of the report, it will return you to where you were before you issued the command.

Figure 10-47 Printing to the Screen

```
Now Viewing Page 1 of Page Width 1
Press any key to continue...



   2/22/89                     Standard report                    Page    1



Address                 Town         Owner         List Date  Style       Price
----------------        ----------   ----------    ---------  -------     ----------
123 Abby Ct.            Louisville   Kones,D        6/16/88   Ranch        32,95
426 St. James Ct.       Louisville   Jones,S        6/19/88   Ranch        19,50
766 Baird St.           Louisville   Black,G        6/22/88   Colonial    139,95
222 Big Ben Dr.         Louisville   Roberts,D      6/22/88   Other        53,50
666 Montana Ave.        Louisville   Saul,H         6/23/88   Cape Cod     55,00
589 Morocco Dr.         E'Town       Smith,B        6/24/88   Cape Cod     62,50
987 Allan Dr.           Louisville   Newsome,K      6/26/88   Cape Cod     60,00
549 Billtown Rd.        Louisville   Bizer,B        6/28/88   Ranch        72,50
343 Market St.          Louisville   Bivins,D       6/29/88   Ranch        42,90
198 Main St.            J'Town       Green,L        6/29/88   Other        27,50
885 Jefferson St.       J'Town       Zith,M         7/02/88   Ranch        55,00
913 Whitney Dr.         North Hill   Kulp,R         7/04/88   Cape Cod     99,50
363 Dower Ct.           North Fork   Culp,A         7/05/88   Cape Cod    109,00
```

Note that Paradox will display only the first 80 characters of any page-width on the screen when it previews a report. If you preview a report whose page-widths exceed 80 characters, you will be able to see only the left part of each page.

Printing to a File

In addition to letting you direct a report to a printer or to the screen of your computer, Paradox also lets you send a report to a disk file. This option makes it possible to transfer the information from a Paradox report into another program that can read ASCII text files, such as a word processing program. When you issue the [Menu] Report Output File command, Paradox will present you with the prompt *File name:*. In response to this prompt, you should type the name of the file in which you want to store the report. If you want to store the file in a directory other than the current one, you must preface the file name with the name of that directory. If you do not specify an extension, Paradox will add .RPT to the name.

As soon as you press ↵, Paradox will display the message *Sending report to FILENAME.RPT...* at the bottom of the screen as it writes the report into the file you named. Paradox will store the report in the file exactly as it would appear if you printed it to a printer. This means that the file will be divided into pages, just like the printed report. If you want to print a continuous stream of information, you should make the report a single large page-width and specify a Length setting of *C*.

Conclusion

In this chapter, we've demonstrated the basics of printing reports from a Paradox table. First, we showed you how to print an instant report. Next, we explained the concept of a report specification with bands, field masks, and literals. Then, we showed you how to design a custom report specification. Finally, we showed you how to print reports.

Now, it's time to look at some advanced reporting topics. In the next chapter, we'll show you how to place summary fields, how to group reports, how to create multitable reports, and how to use the CCP to change Paradox's default report settings.

Chapter 11

Other Reporting Topics

In Chapter 10, we showed you how to use Paradox's instant report capability and how to design and use custom tabular and free-form reports. In this chapter, we'll cover advanced topics, including grouping reports, using summary statistics in reports, multitable reports, and using the Custom Configuration Program (CCP) to change Paradox's default report settings. We'll also show you how to use the Tools menu commands to manage reports.

Summary Fields

Summary fields compute and display statistics on the entries in the fields in a report. For example, a summary field in a report for a table named ORDERS might display the total dollar value of the orders in the report, or the average size of the orders in the report. On the other hand, a summary field in a report for a table named CUSTOMER might display the total number of customers in the report.

To place a summary field in a report, choose the Field Place Summary command from the Report menu. When you issue this command, Paradox will display the menu shown in Figure 11-1, which has two options: Regular, which allows you to summarize a regular field, and Calculated, which allows you to summarize the results of calculations.

Figure 11-1 The Field Place Summary Menu

```
Regular  Calculated                                    Report    1/2
Summarize a regular field.
....+...10....+...20....+...30....+...40....+...50....+...60....+...70....+...8*
                                                                              ■
```

Regular Summary Fields

Selecting Regular tells Paradox you want to summarize the information from one of the regular fields in the table. When you choose Regular, Paradox will first display a list of the regular fields in the report and ask you to select the field you want to summarize.

The Type of Summary

Once you select a field, Paradox will display the menu shown in Figure 11-2. The choice you make from this menu determines what action the summary field will perform. For instance, if you select Sum, the summary field you are defining will total the entries in the specified field of the report. If you choose Average, the summary field will average the entries in that field. Choosing Count creates a summary field that counts the entries in the field. Choosing High or Low will cause the summary field to return the maximum or minimum value from the field.

Figure 11-2 The Summary Regular Menu

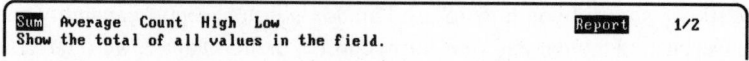

If you're summarizing a date field or an alphanumeric field, the Sum option will not be available. Average summaries are available for date, but not alphanumeric, fields.

PerGroup and Overall

After you select a type of summary field action, Paradox will display a menu that offers two options: PerGroup and Overall, as shown in Figure 11-3. Choosing PerGroup tells Paradox that the summary field should operate on only the records in the current group. (We'll tell you how to group records later in this chapter.) Choosing Overall tells Paradox to calculate a cumulative statistic. Whenever Paradox prints an Overall summary field, it will compute the selected statistic for all the records printed on the report up to that point. This option lets you include running statistics (such as running totals or moving averages) in your reports.

Figure 11-3 The PerGroup/Overall Menu

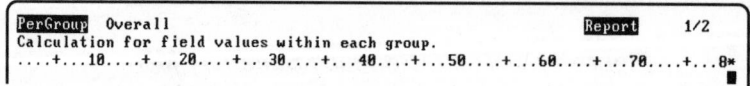

Positioning Summary Fields

Once you've made a selection from the PerGroup/Overall menu, Paradox will prompt you to set the position of the summary field. As with other types of fields, the placement of a summary field determines the position of that field on each page of your printed report. Most of the time, you will place summary fields in a footer (either a group footer, a page footer, or a report footer) below the column you want to summarize. If you place a summary field in the page footer, then the summary will be printed at the bottom of each page. Similarly, if you position the summary field in the report footer of the report spec, Paradox will print the summary statistic once at the end of the report.

If you select the PerGroup option from the PerGroup/Overall menu, you will usually place the summary field in a group footer. The summary field will then compute a statistic for the records that appear in that group.

If you choose Overall from the PerGroup/Overall menu, then the summary field will compute the requested statistic for all of the records in the report up to the position of the summary field. For instance, if you place an Overall summary field in the page footer of the report spec, then the summary field on each page of the report will display the cumulative statistic for that page and all previous pages, and will appear in the page footer section of each page.

An Example

Suppose you want to create a report for the LISTINGS table that includes the following summaries: on each page, a running total of the number of records in the report up to that point; at the end of the report, the sum and average of all entries in the Price field for the entire report.

To begin, issue the [**Menu**] **R**eport **D**esign command, type **LISTINGS**, and press ↵. When Paradox prompts you for a report number, choose **3**. Next, type **Summary Report** for the report description and select **T**abular as the report type. When the report specification screen appears, issue the [**Menu**] Setting **P**ageLayout **W**idth command, press [**Ctrl**]-[**Backspace**] to erase the current default, and type **132**. This step sets the page-width of the new report to 132 characters, eliminating problems with split fields. Next, issue the [**Menu**] Setting **P**ageLayout **D**elete command to delete the second page-width from the report. Figure 11-4 shows the report specification at this point.

Figure 11-4 A Report Specification

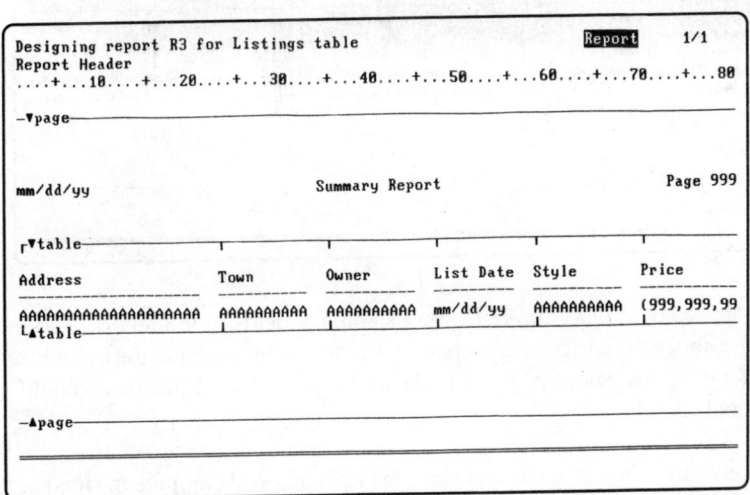

Now, you are ready to begin placing summary fields. Let's start with the summary field that computes the running total of the number of records in the report. To place this field, issue the **[Menu]** **F**ield **P**lace **S**ummary **R**egular command. After you issue this command, Paradox will prompt you to select the field you want to summarize. When you see this prompt, select the **P**rice field. Next, you'll see the menu shown in Figure 11-2. Since you want this summary field to compute a count, you should select **C**ount. Paradox will ask you whether the summary field should be an Overall or a PerGroup summary. Since this summary field will compute a running count, you should choose **O**verall.

Next, Paradox will prompt you to place the field in the report. When you see this prompt, move the cursor to the page footer, position it at column 29 (one column to the left of the column where the first summary field begins), and press ↵. After you place the field, Paradox will prompt you to adjust the number of digits to display in the field. You should press the ← key to reduce the number of digits to two, then press ↵. Paradox now will prompt you to set the number of decimal places for the field. To accept the default setting (no decimal places), just press ↵. Finally, you should move the cursor to the beginning of the line that contains the summary field and type the literal **Total Listings:**. Figure 11-5 shows the report specification screen as it will look after you've added the summary field.

Figure 11-5 Placing the Summary Field

```
Designing report R3 for Listings table                    Report    1/1
Report Footer
....+...10....+...20....+...30....+...40....+...50....+...60....+...70....+...80
 -▼page

 mm/dd/yy                        Summary Report                   Page 999

 ┌▼table
 Address                 Town        Owner        List Date  Style      Price
 ─────────────          ───────     ───────      ─────────  ───────    ───────
 AAAAAAAAAAAAAAAAAAAA    AAAAAAAAAA  AAAAAAAAAA   mm/dd/yy   AAAAAAAAAA (999,999,99
 └▲table
 Total Listings:              99

 ─▲page
```

Now, you are ready to place the remaining summary fields in the report. Before you do anything else, move the cursor to the report footer, press **[Ins]** to enter the insert mode, press ↵ to insert a new row, and then press **[Ins]** again. You'll need this row to hold your last summary field.

When the new row is in place, you can place the field that will compute the total of the Price field for every record in the report. To do this, issue the **[Menu]** **F**ield **P**lace **S**ummary **R**egular command again. When Paradox prompts you for the field you want to summarize, choose **Price**. Since you want this summary field to compute the sum of the entries in the Price field, choose **Sum** when you see the menu of summary types. Since you want this summary field to operate on every record in the report, you should select **Overall** when Paradox presents the PerGroup/Overall menu.

When Paradox prompts you to place the field in the report, move the cursor to the first row in the report footer, position it in column 71, and press ↵. By placing the summary field in the report footer, you are telling Paradox to base its value on all of the entries in the report. Next, Paradox will prompt you to set the number of digits in the field. You should press ←four times to set the number of digits to 8, and then press ↵. When Paradox prompts you to set the number of decimal places, press ← three times to remove all decimals, then press ↵. Finally, move the cursor to the left and type **Total Price of Listings:**.

Now, let's place the summary field that will compute the average price for the records in the report. To do this, issue the **[Menu]** **F**ield **P**lace **S**ummary **R**egular command and select **Price** as the field to summarize. When Paradox prompts you for the type of summary field, select **A**verage. When you see the PerGroup/Overall menu, choose **O**verall. Now, use the cursor-movement keys to move the cursor to column 74 in the second row of the report footer, and press ↵ to place the field. Then, use the ← key to set the number of digits to 6, press ↵, and press ↵ again to set the number of decimals to 2. Finally, move the cursor to the space under the letter *T* in the word *Total* and type the literal **Average Price:** into the report spec to identify the new summary field.

When you have placed all of these summary fields, your report spec will look like Figure 11-6. Now, press **[Instant Report]** to print the report. Paradox will then send the report to the printer. As you can see in the printed report in Figure 11-7 on the next page, Paradox has printed a running count of the number of records in the report at the bottom of each page. At the end of the report, Paradox has printed the total and average price of all records.

Figure 11-6 Summary Fields

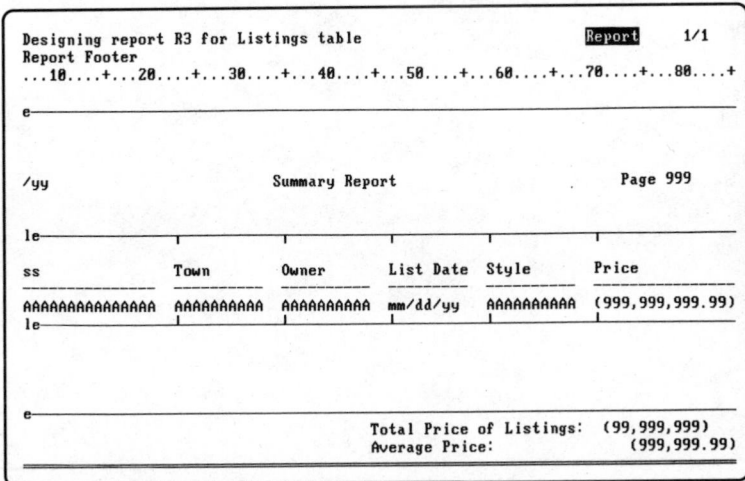

Figure 11-7 The Printed Report

11/24/88   Summary Report   Page   1

Address	Town	Owner	List Date	Style	Price	Sq Ft	BRs	Baths	Price Per Sq Ft
123 Abby Ct.	Louisville	Kones,D	6/16/88	Ranch	32,950.00	1500	3	1	21.97
426 St. James Ct.	Louisville	Jones,S	6/19/88	Ranch	19,500.00	950	2	1	20.53
766 Baird St.	Louisville	Black,B	6/22/88	Colonial	139,950.00	2600	4	3	53.83
222 Big Ben Dr.	Louisville	Roberts,D	6/22/88	Other	53,500.00	1900	3	2	28.16
666 Montana Ave.	Louisville	Saul,H	6/23/88	Cape Cod	55,000.00	1900	3	1	28.95
589 Morocco Dr.	E'Town	Smith,B	6/24/88	Cape Cod	62,500.00	1875	3	2	33.33
987 Allan Dr.	Louisville	Newsome,K	6/26/88	Cape Cod	60,000.00	1900	4	2	31.58
549 Billtown Rd.	Louisville	Bizer,B	6/28/88	Ranch	72,500.00	2000	3	2	36.25
343 Market St.	Louisville	Bivins,D	6/29/88	Ranch	42,900.00	1675	3	1	25.61
198 Main St.	J'Town	Green,L	6/29/88	Other	27,500.00	800	3	1	34.38
885 Jefferson St.	J'Town	Zith,M	7/02/88	Ranch	55,000.00	1500	3	1	36.67
913 Whitney Dr.	North Hill	Kulp,R	7/04/88	Cape Cod	99,500.00	1800	4	2	55.28
363 Dower Ct.	North Fork	Culp,A	7/05/88	Cape Cod	109,000.00	2100	4	2	51.90
620 Windsong Ct.	Louisville	Pank,E	7/06/88	Colonial	250,000.00	4000	6	4	62.50
4500 Hempstead Dr.	Louisville	Pape,C	6/18/88	Colonial	150,000.00	2600	4	3	57.69
#6 Brandon Way	Louisville	Abrams,L	7/22/88	Ranch	67,000.00	2250	4	2	29.78
6610 Vermin Dr.	Louisville	Russ,J	7/24/88	Ranch	75,000.00	2100	3	2	35.71
712 Clifton Ct.	Louisville	Thomas,T	7/24/88	Ranch	30,000.00	1500	3	1	20.00
5432 Miller Rd.	Louisville	Young,R	7/29/88	Other	17,500.00	800	2	1	21.88
#12 Circle Ct.	Louisville	White,Y	8/02/88	Other	10,000.00	800	2	1	12.50
1222 Dee Rd.	South Fork	Smith,P	8/02/88	Ranch	22,950.00	950	3	1	24.16
222 Earl Ave.	J'Town	Wray,A	8/05/88	Ranch	51,000.00	1200	3	1	42.50
9827 Rowan St.	J'Town	Coad,B	8/10/88	Ranch	47,950.00	1100	3	1	43.59
3355 Bank St.	J'Town	Cobb,D	8/17/88	Ranch	37,500.00	1500	3	1	25.00
77 Portland Ave.	North Hill	Coe,A	8/19/88	Ranch	20,000.00	1500	3	1	13.33
99 Cardinal Hill Rd.	North Hill	Brand,B	8/19/88	Cape Cod	70,000.00	2000	3	2	35.00
#10 Old Mill Rd.	Louisville	Stern,M	8/21/88	Ranch	75,000.00	2150	3	2	34.88
5532 Mud Creek Dr.	Louisville	Hall,W	8/24/88	Ranch	12,000.00	950	2	1	12.63
4444 Normie Ln.	Louisville	James,J	8/25/88	Cape Cod	120,000.00	2400	5	3	50.00
3498 Bold Rd.	Louisville	Taft,H	8/29/88	Colonial	275,000.00	3800	5	4	72.37
#82 Rudd Rd.	Louisville	Lum,I	8/30/88	Cape Cod	88,950.00	2800	4	2	31.77
6712 Shelby St.	Louisville	Wood,B	8/30/88	Ranch	92,500.00	2400	4	2	38.54
7235 Shiloh Dr.	E'Town	Allan,J	8/31/88	Ranch	95,000.00	2750	4	3	34.55
8989 Big D Ln.	South Fork	Adkins,G	9/01/88	Ranch	17,000.00	1200	2	1	14.17
1001 Spring St.	North Hill	Frier,F	9/05/88	Other	45,000.00	1700	3	2	26.47
6935 Shiloh Dr.	E'Town	Brebe,C	9/08/88	Cape Cod	81,000.00	2000	3	2	40.50
4989 Adler Way	Louisville	Dole,V	9/13/88	Cape Cod	76,500.00	2000	3	2	38.25
5678 Beech St.	Louisville	Smith,P	9/16/88	Cape Cod	65,950.00	1800	3	2	36.64
#62 Billy Bone Ct.	Louisville	Taylor,A	9/18/88	Ranch	34,500.00	1600	3	1	21.56
3323 Mt. Holly Dr.	Louisville	Grizz,D	9/24/88	Ranch	22,100.00	1200	3	1	18.42
9909 Midway Rd.	Louisville	Maier,O	9/25/88	Ranch	61,250.00	1875	3	2	32.67
435 Oxted Ln.	Louisville	O'Neal,P	9/26/88	Ranch	53,750.00	1900	3	1	28.31
22 N. Ridge Ct.	Louisville	Nunn,A	9/29/88	Colonial	200,000.00	2900	5	3	68.97
654 Nora Ln.	Louisville	Orwick,S	10/02/88	Cape Cod	40,000.00	1600	3	1	25.00
659 Ridge Rd.	Louisville	Pulley,F	10/08/88	Ranch	30,000.00	1500	3	1	20.00
14 Short Rd.	Louisville	Quire,I	10/13/88	Ranch	52,300.00	1600	3	1	32.69
721 Zabel Way	Louisville	Stich,L	10/14/88	Ranch	47,950.00	1500	3	1	31.97
581 Yale Dr.	Louisville	Winer,L	10/17/88	Ranch	78,000.00	2100	4	2	37.14
854 Unseld Blvd.	Louisville	Volk,H	10/19/88	Other	87,000.00	2500	3	2	34.80
#5 Ashby St.	J'Town	Wagner,H	10/22/88	Other	97,000.00	2500	4	3	38.80
1989 Eastern Pkwy.	Louisville	Klink,C	10/23/88	Ranch	26,950.00	1100	2	1	24.50

Total Listings: 51

11/24/88   Summary Report   Page   2

Address	Town	Owner	List Date	Style	Price	Sq Ft	BRs	Baths	Price Per Sq Ft
9819 Wilson Ave.	J'Town	Crane,B	10/23/88	Ranch	28,000.00	1200	3	1	23.33
956 Volar Ln.	J'Town	Lamb,M	10/25/88	Ranch	18,000.00	1200	2	1	15.00
5372 Tyson Pl.	Louisville	Goode,J	10/28/88	Ranch	35,000.00	1500	3	2	23.33
9849 Taylor Blvd.	J'Town	Dukes,J	10/29/88	Ranch	32,950.00	1750	3	1	18.83
185 Pages Ln.	J'Town	Cowan,M	11/01/88	Other	15,500.00	1000	2	1	15.50
3752 St. Dennis	J'Town	Levine,J	11/03/88	Cape Cod	67,950.00	2500	3	2	27.18
28 Seebolt Rt.	Louisville	Priest,S	11/10/88	Other	28,500.00	950	3	1	30.00
2216 Lacey St.	North Hill	Beat,A	11/13/88	Cape Cod	94,999.00	2700	4	3	35.18
6262 Kenwood Dr.	North Hill	Beck,U	11/17/88	Ranch	71,650.00	2000	3	2	35.83
9222 Meadow Pl.	South Fork	Baxter,H	11/22/88	Ranch	85,000.00	2100	3	2	40.48
6791 Lotus Ave.	South Fork	Howell,T	11/24/88	Ranch	75,600.00	2000	3	2	37.80
586 Ansa Way	Louisville	Noel,C	11/27/88	Colonial	69,500.00	2200	4	2	31.59
99 N. Central Blvd.	Louisville	Stevens,P	11/28/88	Ranch	49,000.00	2500	3	2	19.60
4233 Mix Ave.	Louisville	Martin,D	11/30/88	Cape Cod	49,500.00	1900	3	2	26.05

Total Price of Listings: 4,274,589
Average Price: 65,762.91

Total Listings: 65

Calculated Summary Fields

Calculated summary fields allow you to compute and display summary statistics that are based on the results of mathematical expressions. The most common use of calculated summary fields is to compute and display summary statistics for calculated fields.

When you place a calculated field in a report, you first define a formula that Paradox will evaluate once for every record in the report. The expression may include Paradox's mathematical operators, literal characters, and references to fields. If you are using the summary field to compute statistics for a calculated field, the formula you define will be identical to the formula you used to define the calculated field. After you specify the formula, you tell Paradox which summary statistic you want to compute.

For example, in Chapter 10, you created a report that includes a calculated field that computes the price per square foot of each listing in the LISTINGS table. The values in this field are computed by dividing the Price field entry for each record by the Sq Ft entry for that record, using the formula *[Price]/[Sq Ft]*.

Now, suppose you want to add a summary field to this report that computes the average price per square foot for all the records in the report. To begin, issue the [Menu] Forms Change command, specify LISTINGS as the table with which you want to work, and select the report number under which you saved the report (if you followed the example in Chapter 10, the number 2). Figure 11-8 shows the report spec on the screen.

Figure 11-8 A Calculated Field

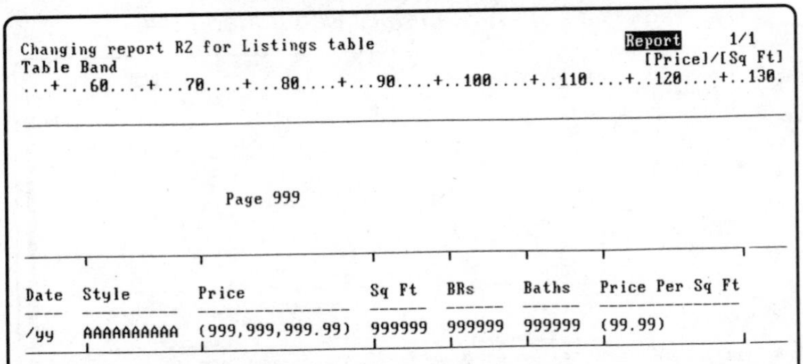

```
Changing report R2 for Listings table                    Report    1/1
Table Band                                                   [Price]/[Sq Ft]
...+...60....+...70....+...80....+...90....+..100....+..110....+..120....+..130.


                            Page 999



Date  Style      Price          Sq Ft   BRs     Baths   Price Per Sq Ft
----  --------   ---------      ------  ------  ------   ---------------
/yy   AAAAAAAAAA (999,999,999.99) 999999 999999 999999   (99.99)
```

Next, move the cursor to the calculated field and issue the [Menu] Field Place Summary Calculated command. After you issue the command, Paradox will display the prompt shown in Figure 11-9. When you see this prompt, enter an expression that tells Paradox on what to base the summary statistic you want it to compute. Since you want this summary field to compute the average of the entries in the existing field, use the same formula here that you used to define that field: [Price]/[Sq Ft]. When you have entered the expression, press ↵.

Figure 11-9 The Expression Prompt

```
Expression:
Calculation from fields in a record -- e.g. [Quan] * [Unit-Price].   Report   2/2
```

At this point, Paradox will display the same menu of summary types shown in Figure 11-2. From this menu, you should select the type of statistic you want the summary field to compute (Sum, Average, Count, High, or Low). Since you want this summary field to display the average price per square foot, you should select **A**verage.

Next, Paradox will display the familiar PerGroup/Overall menu. As before, the choice you make from this menu determines the scope of the summary field. In this case, since you want the summary to operate on every record, you should choose **O**verall.

Now, Paradox will prompt you to place the summary field. You should use the cursor-movement keys to move the cursor to the report footer, position it directly under the first character in the Price/Sq Ft field mask, and press ↵ to place the field. When Paradox prompts you to adjust the number of digits and decimal places it should display, press ← to reduce the width of the field to two digits, press ↵, then press ↵ again to accept the default number of decimal places. Finally, type the literal **Average Price Per Square Foot:** in front of the field.

After you do this, your screen will look like Figure 11-10. Now, press **[Instant Report]** to print the report shown in Figure 11-11. As you can see, the summary field we placed in the report footer displays the average value of the [Price]/[Sq Ft] calculations for every record in the report.

Figure 11-10 A Summary Calculated Field

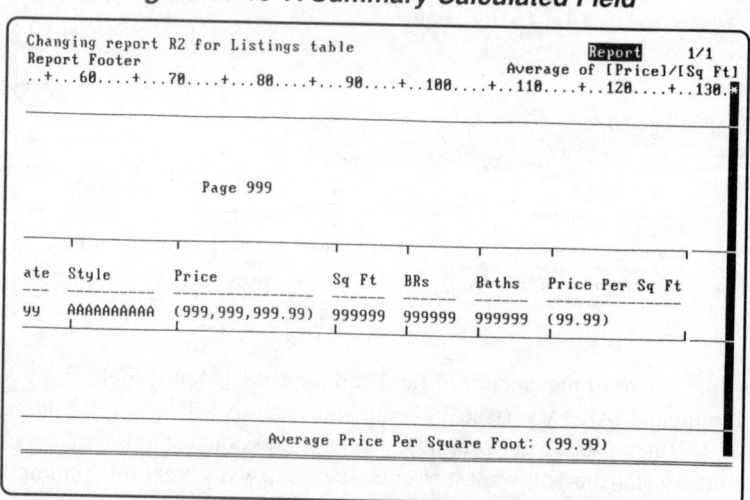

Figure 11-11 The Printed Report

```
11/24/88              Price Per Square Foot            Page   1


Address            Town         Owner        List Date  Style     Price          Sq Ft  BRs   Baths   Price Per Sq Ft
------------------ ------------ -----------  ---------  --------- -------------  -----  ----  ------  ---------------
123 Abby Ct.       Louisville   Kones,D      6/16/88    Ranch        32,950.00   1500    3      1       21.97
426 St. James Ct.  Louisville   Jones,B      6/19/88    Ranch        19,500.00    950    2      1       20.53
766 Baird St.      Louisville   Black,G      6/22/88    Colonial    139,950.00   2600    4      3       53.83
222 Big Ben Dr.    Louisville   Roberts,D    6/22/88    Other        53,500.00   1900    3      2       28.16
666 Montana Ave.   Louisville   Saul,H       6/23/88    Cape Cod     55,000.00   1900    3      1       28.95
589 Morocco Dr.    E'Town       Smith,B      6/24/88    Cape Cod     62,500.00   1875    3      2       33.33
987 Allan Dr.      Louisville   Newsome,K    6/26/88    Cape Cod     60,000.00   1900    4      2       31.58
549 Billtown Rd.   Louisville   Bizer,B      6/28/88    Ranch        72,500.00   2000    3      2       36.25
343 Market St.     Louisville   Bivins,D     6/29/88    Ranch        42,950.00   1675    3      1       25.61
198 Main St.       J'Town       Green,L      6/29/88    Other        27,500.00    800    3      1       34.38
885 Jefferson St.  J'Town       Zith,M       7/02/88    Ranch        55,000.00   1500    3      1       36.67
913 Whitney Dr.    North Hill   Kulp,R       7/04/88    Cape Cod     99,500.00   1800    4      2       55.28
363 Dower Ct.      North Fork   Culp,A       7/05/88    Cape Cod    109,000.00   2100    4      2       51.90
620 Windsong Ct.   Louisville   Pank,E       7/06/88    Colonial    250,000.00   4000    6      4       62.50
4500 Hempstead Dr. Louisville   Pape,C       6/18/88    Colonial    150,000.00   2600    4      3       57.69
#6 Brandon Way     Louisville   Abrams,L     7/22/88    Ranch        67,000.00   2250    4      2       29.78
6610 Vermin Dr.    Louisville   Russ,J       7/24/88    Ranch        75,000.00   2100    3      2       35.71
712 Clifton Ct.    Louisville   Thomas,T     7/24/88    Ranch        30,000.00   1500    3      1       20.00
5432 Miller Rd.    Louisville   Young,R      7/29/88    Ranch        17,500.00    800    2      1       21.88
#12 Circle Ct.     Louisville   White,Y      8/02/88    Other        10,000.00    800    2      1       12.50
1222 Dee Rd.       South Fork   Smith,P      8/02/88    Ranch        22,950.00    950    3      1       24.16
222 Earl Ave.      J'Town       Wray,A       8/05/88    Ranch        51,000.00   1200    3      1       42.50
9827 Rowan St.     J'Town       Coad,B       8/10/88    Ranch        47,950.00   1100    3      1       43.59
3355 Bank St.      J'Town       Cobb,D       8/17/88    Ranch        37,500.00   1500    3      1       25.00
77 Portland Ave.   North Hill   Coe,A        8/19/88    Ranch        20,000.00   1500    3      1       13.33
99 Cardinal Hill Rd. North Hill Brand,B      8/19/88    Cape Cod     70,000.00   2000    3      2       35.00
#10 Old Mill Rd.   Louisville   Stern,M      8/21/88    Ranch        75,000.00   2150    3      2       34.88
5532 Mud Creek Dr. Louisville   Hall,W       8/24/88    Ranch        12,000.00    950    2      1       12.63
4444 Normie Ln.    Louisville   James,J      8/25/88    Cape Cod    120,000.00   2400    5      3       50.00
3498 Bold Rd.      Louisville   Taft,H       8/29/88    Colonial    275,000.00   3800    5      4       72.37
#82 Rudd Rd.       Louisville   Lum,I        8/30/88    Cape Cod     88,950.00   2800    4      2       31.77
4712 Shelby St.    Louisville   Wood,B       8/30/88    Ranch        92,500.00   2400    4      2       38.54
7235 Shiloh Dr.    E'Town       Allan,J      8/31/88    Ranch        95,000.00   2750    4      3       34.55
8989 Big D Ln.     South Fork   Adkins,G     9/01/88    Ranch        17,000.00   1200    2      1       14.17
1001 Spring St.    North Hill   Frier,F      9/05/88    Other        45,000.00   1700    3      2       26.47
6935 Shiloh Dr.    E'Town       Grebe,C      9/08/88    Cape Cod     81,000.00   2000    3      2       40.50
4989 Adler Way     Louisville   Dole,V       9/13/88    Cape Cod     76,500.00   2000    3      2       38.25
5678 Beech St.     Louisville   Smith,P      9/16/88    Cape Cod     65,950.00   1800    3      2       36.64
#62 Billy Bone Ct. Louisville   Taylor,A     9/18/88    Ranch        34,500.00   1600    3      1       21.56
3323 Mt. Holly Dr. Louisville   Grizz,D      9/24/88    Ranch        22,100.00   1200    3      1       18.42
9909 Midway Rd.    Louisville   Maier,O      9/25/88    Ranch        61,250.00   1875    3      2       32.67
435 Oxted Ln.      Louisville   O'Neal,P     9/26/88    Ranch        53,790.00   1900    3      1       28.31
22 N. Ridge Ct.    Louisville   Nunn,A       9/29/88    Colonial    200,000.00   2900    5      3       68.97
654 Nora Ln.       Louisville   Orwick,S     10/02/88   Cape Cod     40,000.00   1600    3      1       25.00
659 Ridge Rd.      Louisville   Pulley,U     10/08/88   Ranch        30,000.00   1500    3      1       20.00
14 Short Rd.       Louisville   Quire,I      10/13/88   Ranch        52,500.00   1600    3      1       32.69
721 Zabel Way      Louisville   Stich,L      10/14/88   Ranch        47,950.00   1500    3      1       31.97
581 Yale Dr.       Louisville   Winer,L      10/17/88   Ranch        78,000.00   2100    4      2       37.14
854 Unseld Blvd.   Louisville   Volk,H       10/19/88   Other        87,000.00   2500    3      2       34.80
#5 Ashby St.       J'Town       Wagner,H     10/22/88   Other        97,000.00   2500    4      3       38.80
1989 Eastern Pkwy. Louisville   Klink,C      10/23/88   Ranch        26,950.00   1100    2      1       24.50
```

```
11/24/88              Price Per Square Foot            Page   2


Address            Town         Owner        List Date  Style     Price          Sq Ft  BRs   Baths   Price Per Sq Ft
------------------ ------------ -----------  ---------  --------- -------------  -----  ----  ------  ---------------
9819 Wilson Ave.   J'Town       Crane,B      10/23/88   Ranch        28,000.00   1200    3      1       23.33
956 Volar Ln.      J'Town       Lamb,M       10/25/88   Ranch        18,000.00   1200    2      1       15.00
5372 Tyson Pl.     Louisville   Goode,J      10/28/88   Ranch        35,000.00   1500    3      1       23.33
9849 Taylor Blvd.  J'Town       Dukes,J      10/29/88   Ranch        32,950.00   1750    3      1       18.83
185 Pages Ln.      J'Town       Cowan,M      11/01/88   Other        15,500.00   1000    3      1       15.50
3752 St. Dennis    J'Town       Levine,J     11/03/88   Cape Cod     67,950.00   2500    3      2       27.18
28 Seebolt Rt.     Louisville   Priest,S     11/10/88   Other        28,500.00    950    3      1       30.00
2216 Lacey St.     North Hill   Beat,A       11/13/88   Cape Cod     94,999.00   2700    4      3       35.18
6262 Kenwood Dr.   North Hill   Beck,U       11/17/88   Ranch        71,650.00   2000    3      2       35.83
9222 Meadow Pl.    South Fork   Baxter,H     11/22/88   Ranch        85,000.00   2100    3      2       40.48
6791 Lotus Ave.    South Fork   Howell,T     11/24/88   Ranch        75,600.00   2000    4      2       37.80
586 Ansa Way       Louisville   Noel,C       11/27/88   Colonial     69,500.00   2200    3      2       31.59
99 N. Central Blvd. Louisville  Stevens,P    11/28/88   Ranch        49,000.00   2500    3      2       19.60
4233 Mix Ave.      Louisville   Martin,D     11/30/88   Cape Cod     49,500.00   1900    3      2       26.05
                                                         Average Price Per Square Foot:            32.42
```

Of course, you can also create calculated summary fields that compute Sum, Count, High, and Low statistics. All you have to do is choose the appropriate option from the menu of summary types while you are defining the summary field.

While you frequently will use calculated summary fields to compute statistics for the calculated fields in your reports, you can include a calculated summary field in a report that contains no calculated fields. For example, if the report spec in Figure 11-8 did not include the calculated field Price/Sq Ft, you could still place the summary calculated field in the report spec. Even when you use a calculated summary field to summarize a calculated field, the formula that defines the summary field is independent of the formula that defines the calculated field.

Summary Operators in Calculated Fields

In addition to placing regular and calculated summary fields in your reports, there is one other way to create summary statistics: by using the summary operators Sum, Count, Average, High, and Low in calculated fields. In fact, using summary operators in calculated fields allows you to make computations that could not be made any other way. For instance, suppose you want to compute the overall price per square foot for all of the records in the LISTINGS table. The only way to make that calculation would be to use summary operators in a calculated field. You could not make the calculation with either a summary regular or a summary calculated field.

An Example

Let's walk through the process of placing a calculated field with a summary operator into report 2 for the LISTINGS table. Since that report is already in view, you're ready to place the field. (If the report were not in view, you would issue the [Menu] Report Change command, specify LISTINGS as the table with which you want to work, and select report number 2.) First, issue the **[Menu] F**ield **P**lace Calculated command. Paradox will display a prompt asking you to enter an expression. Since you want this calculated field to compute the overall price per square foot, you should type the expression **Sum([Price])/Sum([Sq Ft])** and press ↵. This expression means: *Compute the sum of the Price field divided by the sum of the Sq Ft field.*

Now, Paradox will prompt you to place the field onto the report. Use the cursor-movement keys to move the cursor to the report footer, position it directly under the first character of the Average Price Per Square Foot field mask, and press ↵ to place the field. When Paradox prompts you to adjust the number of digits and decimal places, press ← to reduce the width of the field to two digits, press ↵, then press ↵ again to accept the default number of decimal places. Finally, type the literal **Overall Price/Square Foot:** in front of the field.

At this point, your screen will look like Figure 11-12. Now, press **[Instant Report]** to print the report shown in Figure 11-13 on the following page. The summary field we placed in the report footer displays the overall value of the price per square foot below the average price per square foot.

Figure 11-12 A Calculated Summary Field

```
Changing report R2 for Listings table                    Report  Ins 1/1
Report Footer
..+...60....+...70....+...80....+...90....+..100....+..110....+..120....+..130.


                        Page 999


ate  Style       Price          Sq Ft   BRs      Baths    Price Per Sq Ft
---  ----------  -------------   ------  ------   ------   ---------------
yy   AAAAAAAAAA  (999,999,999.99)  999999  999999   999999   (99.99)



                        Average Price Per Square Foot: (99.99)
                           Overall Price/Square Foot: (99.99)
```

Notes

What's the difference between the calculated summary field and the calculated field at the bottom of this report? The calculated summary field computes the average price per square foot for all the records in the report. It adds the price per square foot for each record in the report and then divides the result by the total number of records. The result of that calculation is 32.42. The calculated field with summary operators computes the overall price per square foot for all the records in the report. It adds the price for each record in the report and the square footage for each record in the report and then divides the sum of the Price field by the sum of the Sq Ft field. The result of that calculation is 4,274,589/120125, or 35.58.

You can use any of Paradox's summary operators—Sum, Average, Count, High, Low—in calculated fields. Whenever you use a summary operator in a calculated expression, you must follow it with parentheses that contain the name of the field to summarize, as in the expression *SUM([Price])*.

You can use summary operators in calculated fields anywhere on the report. However, you usually will want to place them only in the group and footer bands, as you do with summary fields.

Figure 11-13 The Printed Report

9/22/88   Price Per Square Foot   Page   1

Address	Town	Owner	List Date	Style	Price	Sq Ft	BRs	Baths	Price Per Sq Ft
123 Abby Ct.	Louisville	Kones,D	6/16/88	Ranch	32,950.00	1500	3	1	21.97
426 St. James Ct.	Louisville	Jones,S	6/19/88	Ranch	19,500.00	950	2	1	20.53
766 Baird St.	Louisville	Black,G	6/22/88	Colonial	139,950.00	2600	4	3	53.83
222 Big Ben Dr.	Louisville	Roberts,D	6/22/88	Other	53,500.00	1900	3	2	28.16
666 Montana Ave.	Louisville	Saul,H	6/23/88	Cape Cod	55,000.00	1900	3	1	28.95
589 Morocco Dr.	E'Town	Smith,B	6/24/88	Cape Cod	62,500.00	1875	3	2	33.33
987 Allan Dr.	Louisville	Newsome,K	6/26/88	Cape Cod	60,000.00	1900	4	2	31.58
549 Billtown Rd.	Louisville	Bizer,B	6/28/88	Ranch	72,500.00	2000	3	2	36.25
343 Market St.	Louisville	Bivins,D	6/29/88	Ranch	42,900.00	1675	3	1	25.61
198 Main St.	J'Town	Green,L	6/29/88	Other	27,500.00	800	3	1	34.38
885 Jefferson St.	J'Town	Zith,M	7/02/88	Ranch	55,000.00	1500	3	1	36.67
913 Whitney Dr.	North Hill	Kulp,R	7/04/88	Cape Cod	99,500.00	1800	4	2	55.28
363 Dower Ct.	North Fork	Culp,A	7/05/88	Cape Cod	109,000.00	2100	4	2	51.90
620 Windsong Ct.	Louisville	Pank,E	7/06/88	Colonial	250,000.00	4000	6	4	62.50
4500 Hempstead Dr.	Louisville	Pape,C	6/18/88	Colonial	150,000.00	2600	4	3	57.69
#6 Brandon Way	Louisville	Abrams,L	7/22/88	Ranch	67,000.00	2250	4	2	29.78
6610 Vernin Dr.	Louisville	Russ,J	7/24/88	Ranch	75,000.00	2100	3	2	35.71
712 Clifton Ct.	Louisville	Thomas,T	7/24/88	Ranch	30,000.00	1500	3	1	20.00
5432 Miller Rd.	Louisville	Young,R	7/29/88	Other	17,500.00	800	2	1	21.88
#12 Circle Dr.	Louisville	White,Y	8/02/88	Other	10,000.00	800	2	1	12.50
1222 Dee Rd.	South Fork	Smith,P	8/02/88	Ranch	22,950.00	950	3	1	24.16
222 Earl Ave.	Louisville	Wray,A	8/05/88	Ranch	51,000.00	1200	3	1	42.50
9827 Rowan St.	J'Town	Coad,B	8/10/88	Ranch	47,950.00	1100	3	1	43.59
3355 Bank St.	J'Town	Cobb,D	8/17/88	Ranch	37,500.00	1500	3	1	25.00
77 Portland Ave.	North Hill	Coe,A	8/19/88	Ranch	20,000.00	1500	3	1	13.33
99 Cardinal Hill Rd.	North Hill	Brand,B	8/19/88	Cape Cod	70,000.00	2000	3	2	35.00
#10 Old Mill Rd.	Louisville	Stern,M	8/21/88	Ranch	75,000.00	2150	3	2	34.88
5532 Mud Creek Dr.	Louisville	Hall,W	8/24/88	Ranch	12,000.00	950	2	1	12.63
4444 Normie Ln.	Louisville	James,J	8/25/88	Cape Cod	120,000.00	2400	5	3	50.00
3498 Bold Rd.	Louisville	Taft,H	8/29/88	Colonial	275,000.00	3800	5	4	72.37
#82 Rudd Rd.	Louisville	Lum,I	8/30/88	Cape Cod	88,950.00	2800	4	2	31.77
6712 Shelby St.	Louisville	Wood,B	8/30/88	Ranch	92,500.00	2400	4	2	38.54
7235 Shiloh Dr.	E'Town	Allan,J	8/31/88	Ranch	95,000.00	2750	4	3	34.55
8989 Big D Ln.	South Fork	Adkins,B	9/01/88	Ranch	17,000.00	1200	2	1	14.17
1001 Spring St.	North Hill	Frier,F	9/05/88	Other	45,000.00	1700	3	2	26.47
6935 Shiloh Dr.	E'Town	Grebe,C	9/08/88	Cape Cod	81,000.00	2000	3	2	40.50
4989 Adler Way	Louisville	Dole,V	9/13/88	Cape Cod	76,500.00	2000	3	2	38.25
5678 Beach St.	Louisville	Smith,P	9/16/88	Cape Cod	65,950.00	1800	3	2	36.64
#62 Billy Bone Ct.	Louisville	Taylor,A	9/18/88	Ranch	34,500.00	1600	3	1	21.56
3323 Mt. Holly Dr.	Louisville	Grizz,D	9/24/88	Ranch	22,100.00	1200	3	1	18.42
9909 Midway Rd.	Louisville	Maier,O	9/25/88	Ranch	61,250.00	1875	3	2	32.67
435 Oxted Ln.	Louisville	O'Neal,P	9/26/88	Ranch	53,790.00	1900	3	1	28.31
22 N. Ridge Ct.	Louisville	Nunn,A	9/27/88	Colonial	200,000.00	2900	5	3	68.97
654 Nora Ln.	Louisville	Orwick,S	10/02/88	Cape Cod	40,000.00	1600	3	1	25.00
659 Ridge Rd.	Louisville	Pulley,F	10/08/88	Ranch	30,000.00	1500	3	1	20.00
14 Short Rd.	Louisville	Quire,I	10/13/88	Ranch	52,300.00	1600	3	1	32.69
721 Zabel Way	Louisville	Stich,L	10/14/88	Ranch	47,950.00	1500	3	1	31.97
581 Yale Dr.	Louisville	Winer,L	10/17/88	Ranch	78,000.00	2100	4	2	37.14
654 Unseld Blvd.	Louisville	Volk,H	10/19/88	Other	87,000.00	2500	3	2	34.80
#5 Ashby St.	J'Town	Wagner,H	10/22/88	Other	97,000.00	2500	4	3	38.80
1989 Eastern Pkwy.	Louisville	Klink,C	10/23/88	Ranch	26,950.00	1100	2	1	24.50

9/22/88   Price Per Square Foot   Page   2

Address	Town	Owner	List Date	Style	Price	Sq Ft	BRs	Baths	Price Per Sq Ft
9819 Wilson Ave.	J'Town	Crane,M	10/23/88	Ranch	28,000.00	1200	3	1	23.33
956 Volar Ln.	J'Town	Lamb,M	10/25/88	Ranch	18,000.00	1200	2	1	15.00
5372 Tyson Pl.	Louisville	Goode,J	10/28/88	Ranch	35,000.00	1500	3	2	23.33
9849 Taylor Blvd.	J'Town	Dukes,J	10/29/88	Ranch	32,950.00	1750	3	1	18.83
185 Pages Ln.	J'Town	Cowan,M	11/01/88	Other	15,500.00	1000	2	1	15.50
3752 St. Dennis	J'Town	Levine,J	11/03/88	Cape Cod	67,950.00	2500	3	2	27.18
28 Seebolt Rt.	Louisville	Priest,S	11/10/88	Other	28,500.00	950	3	1	30.00
226 Lacey St.	North Hill	Beat,A	11/13/88	Cape Cod	94,999.00	2700	4	3	35.18
6262 Kenwood Dr.	North Hill	Beck,U	11/17/88	Ranch	71,650.00	2000	3	2	35.83
9222 Meadow Pl.	South Fork	Baxter,H	11/22/88	Ranch	85,000.00	2100	3	2	40.48
6791 Lotus Ave.	South Fork	Howell,T	11/24/88	Ranch	75,800.00	2000	3	2	37.80
99 N. Central Blvd.	Louisville	Noel,C	11/27/88	Colonial	69,500.00	2200	4	2	31.59
586 Anna Way	Louisville	Stevens,P	11/28/88	Ranch	49,000.00	2500	3	2	19.60
4233 Mix Ave.	Louisville	Martin,D	11/30/88	Cape Cod	49,500.00	1900	3	2	26.05

Average Price Per Square Foot: 32.42
Overall Price/Square Foot: 35.58

By default, a summary operator in a calculated field computes an overall value for the expression. If you want to calculate a group summary, you must place the word *group* inside the parentheses after the field name. For example, the expression *SUM([Price],group)* will compute the sum of the Price field for the current group. Of course, the field that contains this expression should be placed in a group footer.

Grouping Your Data

The Group command on the Report menu allows you to group the information in your reports. Groups serve two major purposes: sorting and subtotaling. For example, you can use a group to specify that the records in the LISTINGS table report should be sorted by Style (one of the fields in LISTINGS). Furthermore, at the end of each group, you can print the total price of all the records in that group: a subtotal for *Cape Cod* style listings, a subtotal for *Colonial* style listings, and so forth.

When you issue the [Menu] Group command while you are designing or changing a report specification, Paradox will display the menu shown in Figure 11-14. As you can see, this menu has five commands: Insert, which allows you to insert groups in the report; Delete, which allows you to delete a group; Headings, which allows you to specify when group headings will be printed; SortDirection, which allows you to select ascending or descending sort order for a group; and Regroup, which lets you change a grouping after it has been placed in the report. We will discuss each of these commands in the sections that follow.

Figure 11-14 The Group Menu

```
Insert  Delete  Headings  SortDirection  Regroup              Report    1/2
Insert a new group based on a field, range, or number of records.
```

Inserting Groups

To place a group in a report specification, choose the Insert command from the Group menu. The next menu, which is shown in Figure 11-15, lists the types of groups you can insert. The Field command lets you insert a group based on a regular field. The Range command lets you insert a group based on a range of values. The NumberRecords command lets you create groups that contain a specific number of records. The most common choice is Field grouping.

Figure 11-15 Group Types

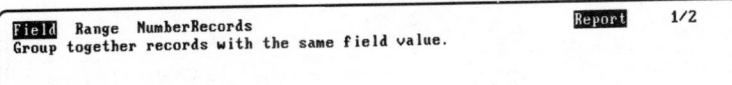

```
Field  Range  NumberRecords                                Report    1/2
Group together records with the same field value.
```

Field Groups

Field groups allow you to sort and group the records in your reports according to the entries in a particular field. When you group a report on a field, Paradox will sort the records in the report so that the entries in the grouping field are in order and will group all records with the same entry in the grouping field.

Grouping on an Alphanumeric Field

For example, suppose you want to create a report for the LISTINGS table that is grouped according to the entries in the Style field. To create this report, first issue the **[Menu] R**eport **D**esign command, type **LISTINGS**, and press ↵. Next, select a report number (we'll use **4**), enter a report description like **Listings By Style**, and select **T**abular as the report type. Then, use the **[Menu] S**etting **P**ageLayout **W**idth command to change the width of the report's page-widths to **132** characters, and then the **[Menu] S**etting **P**ageLayout **D**elete command to delete the second page-width.

When the new report specification screen comes into view, issue the **[Menu] G**roup **I**nsert command. Since you want to group the report on the entries in a field, choose the **F**ield option when you see the Group menu. Next, Paradox will display a list of the regular fields of the LISTINGS table and prompt you to select the one on which you want to group the report. When you see this list, select the **S**tyle field.

Now, Paradox will prompt you to place the group in the report. When you insert a group into a report spec, you are actually adding a new band—a group band—to the spec. You can place group bands in only two places: within the page band or within another group band. Since there are no other groups in the report yet, you must place the new group in the page band. To do this, move the cursor anywhere in the page band header or footer, and press ↵. Your screen should now look like Figure 11-16.

Figure 11-16 Inserting a Group

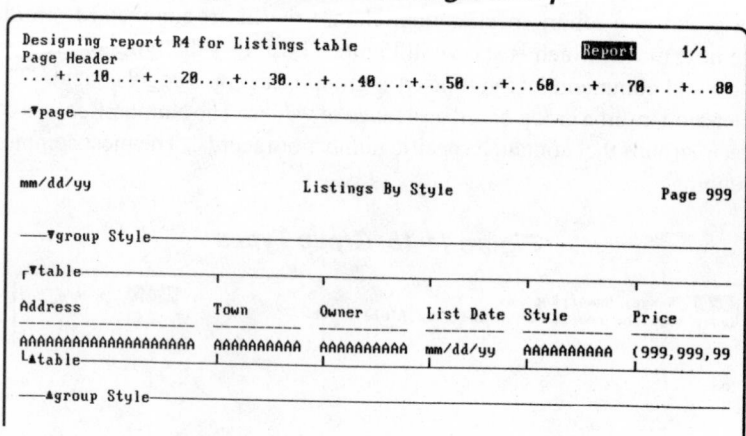

As you can see in Figure 11-16, the report spec now has a new band, *group Style*, which surrounds the Table band. Notice the blank rows at the top and bottom of the new band. These blank rows are the header and footer for the *group Style* band. As in this case, whenever you first create a new group band, the group header and group footer will be single blank lines. Later in this chapter, we will show you how to enter literals, regular fields, and summary fields into group headers and footers.

If you try to place a group anywhere other than within the page band or within another group band, the error message *Cursor must be within the Page band or a Group band to insert a new group* will appear at the bottom of the screen. If you see this message, move the cursor to the page band and press ↵ again.

To see how the addition of the group affects the printed report, press **[Instant Report]**. The printed report is shown in Figure 11-17 on the following page.

If you study this report, you'll see that the records in the report have been sorted so that the Style field entries are in alphabetical order: *Cape Cod* first, *Colonial* second, *Other* third, and *Ranch* fourth. In addition, notice that Paradox has grouped the report so that all of the records with the same Style field entry are clustered and has separated the groups with two blank lines. As you might have guessed, these blank lines are the empty group header and group footer. If you don't want the groups in your report to be separated this way, just use the [Report Delete Line] key ([Ctrl]-[Y]) to delete the blank header and footer lines from the report spec.

Grouping on Other Types of Fields

In the previous example, we grouped the report based on the Style field—an alphanumeric field. As you might expect, you can also group reports on numeric (number, short number, and dollar) fields and on date fields. Paradox places no restrictions on the type of field you may group on. The rules for sorting reports are the same as the rules for sorting tables, as explained in Chapter 6.

Range Groups

You can also group your reports according to ranges. When you group a report on a range, Paradox will group all the records in the report with grouping field entries that fall within the range you define. Exactly how you can group ranges of records, however, depends on the type of field you select as the grouping field.

Date Fields

When you issue the [Menu] Group Insert Range command and select a date field to group, Paradox will display the menu shown in Figure 11-18 on page 483.

Figure 11-17 The Printed Report

```
11/24/88              Listings By Style              Page   1


Address             Town        Owner       List Date  Style       Price                Sq Ft   BRs    Baths
-----------------   ----------  ----------  ---------  ----------  -----------------    ------  ------ ------

#82 Rudd Rd.        Louisville  Lum,I        8/30/88   Cape Cod         88,950.00        2800    4      2
2216 Lacey St.      North Hill  Beat,A      11/13/88   Cape Cod         94,999.00        2700    4      3
363 Dower Ct.       North Fork  Culp,A       7/05/88   Cape Cod        109,000.00        2100    4      2
3752 St. Dennis     J'Town      Levine,J    11/03/88   Cape Cod         67,950.00        2500    3      2
4233 Mix Ave.       Louisville  Martin,D    11/30/88   Cape Cod         49,500.00        1900    3      2
4444 Normie Ln.     Louisville  James,J      8/25/88   Cape Cod        120,000.00        2400    5      3
4989 Adler Way      Louisville  Dole,V       9/13/88   Cape Cod         76,500.00        2000    3      2
5678 Beech St.      Louisville  Smith,P      9/16/88   Cape Cod         65,950.00        1800    3      2
589 Morocco Dr.     E'Town      Smith,B      6/24/88   Cape Cod         62,500.00        1875    3      2
654 Nora Ln.        Louisville  Orwick,S    10/02/88   Cape Cod         40,000.00        1600    3      1
666 Montana Ave.    Louisville  Saul,H       6/23/88   Cape Cod         55,000.00        1900    3      1
6935 Shiloh Dr.     E'Town      Grebe,C      9/08/88   Cape Cod         81,000.00        2000    3      2
913 Whitney Dr.     North Hill  Kulp,R       7/04/88   Cape Cod         99,500.00        1800    4      2
987 Allan Dr.       Louisville  Newsome,K    6/26/88   Cape Cod         60,000.00        1900    4      2
99 Cardinal Hill Rd.North Hill  Brand,B      8/19/88   Cape Cod         70,000.00        2000    3      2


22 N. Ridge Ct.     Louisville  Nunn,A       9/29/88   Colonial        200,000.00        2900    5      3
3498 Bold Rd.       Louisville  Taft,H       8/29/88   Colonial        275,000.00        3800    5      4
4500 Hempstead Dr.  Louisville  Pape,C       6/18/88   Colonial        150,000.00        2600    4      3
586 Ansa Way        Louisville  Noel,C      11/27/88   Colonial         69,500.00        2200    4      2
620 Windsong Ct.    Louisville  Pank,E       7/06/88   Colonial        250,000.00        4000    6      4
766 Baird St.       Louisville  Black,G      6/22/88   Colonial        139,950.00        2600    4      3


#12 Circle Ct.      Louisville  White,Y      8/02/88   Other            10,000.00         800    2      1
#5 Ashby St.        J'Town      Wagner,H    10/22/88   Other            97,000.00        2500    4      3
1001 Spring St.     North Hill  Frier,F      9/05/88   Other            45,000.00        1700    3      2
105 Pages Ln.       J'Town      Cowan,M     11/01/88   Other            15,500.00        1000    2      1
198 Main St.        J'Town      Green,L      6/29/88   Other            27,500.00         800    3      1
222 Big Ben Dr.     Louisville  Roberts,D    6/22/88   Other            53,500.00        1900    3      2
28 Seebolt Rt.      Louisville  Priest,S    11/10/88   Other            28,500.00         950    3      1
5432 Miller Rd.     Louisville  Young,R      7/29/88   Other            17,500.00         800    2      1
854 Unseld Blvd.    Louisville  Volk,H      10/19/88   Other            87,000.00        2500    3      2


#10 Old Mill Rd.    Louisville  Stern,M      8/21/88   Ranch            75,000.00        2150    3      2
#6 Brandon Way      Louisville  Abrams,L     7/22/88   Ranch            67,000.00        2250    4      2
#62 Billy Bone Ct.  Louisville  Taylor,A     9/18/88   Ranch            54,500.00        1600    3      1
1222 Dee Rd.        South Fork  Smith,P      8/02/88   Ranch            22,950.00         950    3      1
123 Abby Ct.        Louisville  Kones,D      6/16/88   Ranch            32,950.00        1500    3      1
14 Short Rd.        Louisville  Quire,I     10/13/88   Ranch            52,300.00        1600    3      1
1989 Eastern Pkwy.  Louisville  Klink,C     10/23/88   Ranch            26,950.00        1100    2      1
222 Earl Ave.       J'Town      Wray,A       8/05/88   Ranch            51,000.00        1200    3      1
3323 Mt. Holly Dr.  Louisville  Grizz,D      9/24/88   Ranch            22,100.00        1200    3      1
3355 Bank St.       J'Town      Cobb,D       8/17/88   Ranch            37,500.00        1500    3      1
343 Market St.      Louisville  Bivins,D     6/29/88   Ranch            42,900.00        1675    3      1
426 St. James Ct.   Louisville  Jones,S      6/19/88   Ranch            19,500.00         950    2      1
435 Oxted Ln.       Louisville  O'Neal,P     9/26/88   Ranch            53,790.00        1900    3      1
5372 Tyson Pl.      Louisville  Goode,J     10/28/88   Ranch            35,000.00        1500    3      2
```

```
11/24/88              Listings By Style              Page   2


Address             Town        Owner       List Date  Style    Price              Sq Ft   BRs    Baths
-----------------   ----------  ----------  ---------  -------  ----------------   ------  ------ ------

549 Billtown Rd.    Louisville  Bizer,B      6/28/88   Ranch        72,500.00       2000    3      2
5532 Mud Creek Dr.  Louisville  Hall,W       8/24/88   Ranch        12,000.00        950    2      1
581 Yale Dr.        Louisville  Winer,L     10/17/88   Ranch        78,000.00       2100    4      2
6262 Kenwood Dr.    North Hill  Beck,U      11/17/88   Ranch        71,650.00       2000    3      2
659 Ridge Rd.       Louisville  Pulley,F    10/08/88   Ranch        30,000.00       1500    3      1
6610 Vermin Dr.     Louisville  Russ,J       7/24/88   Ranch        75,000.00       2100    3      2
6712 Shelby St.     Louisville  Wood,B       8/30/88   Ranch        92,500.00       2400    4      2
6791 Lotus Ave.     South Fork  Howell,T    11/24/88   Ranch        75,600.00       2000    3      2
712 Clifton Ct.     Louisville  Thomas,T     7/24/88   Ranch        30,000.00       1500    3      1
721 Zabel Way       Louisville  Stich,L     10/14/88   Ranch        47,950.00       1500    3      1
7235 Shiloh Dr.     E'Town      Allan,J      8/31/88   Ranch        95,000.00       2750    4      3
77 Portland Ave.    North Hill  Coe,A        8/19/88   Ranch        20,000.00       1500    3      1
885 Jefferson St.   J'Town      Zith,M       7/02/88   Ranch        55,000.00       1500    3      1
8989 Big D Ln.      South Fork  Adkins,G     9/01/88   Ranch        17,000.00       1200    2      1
9222 Meadow Pl.     South Fork  Baxter,H    11/22/88   Ranch        85,000.00       2100    3      2
956 Volar Ln.       J'Town      Lamb,M      10/25/88   Ranch        18,000.00       1200    2      1
9819 Wilson Ave.    J'Town      Crane,B     10/23/88   Ranch        28,000.00       1200    3      1
9827 Rowan St.      J'Town      Coad,B       8/10/88   Ranch        47,950.00       1100    3      1
9849 Taylor Blvd.   J'Town      Dukes,J     10/29/88   Ranch        32,950.00       1750    3      2
99 N. Central Blvd. Louisville  Stevens,P   11/28/88   Ranch        49,000.00       2500    3      2
9909 Midway Rd.     Louisville  Maier,D      9/25/88   Ranch        61,250.00       1875    3      2
```

Figure 11-18 The Range Menu for Date Fields

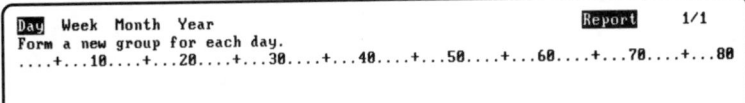

```
Day  Week  Month  Year                                    Report    1/1
Form a new group for each day.
....+...10....+...20....+...30....+...40....+...50....+...60....+...70....+...80
```

If you choose the Day option from this menu, Paradox will group all of the records in the report that have the same day value in the selected date field. If you choose Week, Paradox will group records that have the same week value. Specifying a Month range will group dates that have the same month value. Selecting Year will group records that have the same year value.

For example, suppose you want to design a report for the LISTINGS table that is grouped by month on the List Date field. To do this, first create a new report (we'll use number **9**), using the report description **Listings By Month**. When the report specification screen appears, use the **[Menu]** Setting PageLayout Width command to set the page-width at 132, and the **[Menu]** Setting PageLayout Delete command to delete the second page-width. Next, issue the **[Menu]** Insert Range command and select the List Date field.

When you see the menu in Figure 11-18, choose Month. After you do this, Paradox will prompt you to place the group in the report. As before, you should move the cursor to the page band and press ↵. Figure 11-19 shows the report specification with the new *group List Date,range=Month* band in place. Now, press **[Instant Report]**. Figure 11-20 on the next page shows the first page of the resulting report. Notice that the report is arranged so that all of the records with date field entries in the same month are grouped.

Figure 11-19 The Completed Screen

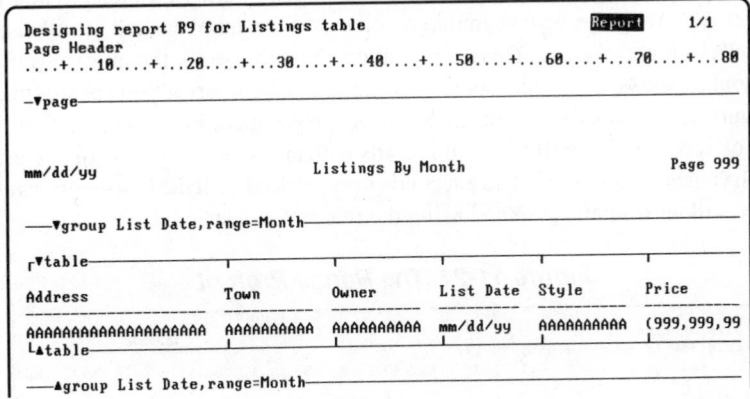

Figure 11-20 The Printed Report

```
11/24/88              Listings By Month              Page  1


Address            Town        Owner     List Date  Style     Price            Sq Ft   BRs    Baths
------------------ ----------- --------- ---------  -------   ------------      -----   ----   -----
123 Abby Ct.       Louisville  Kones,D   6/16/88    Ranch          32,950.00    1500     3       1
4500 Hempstead Dr. Louisville  Pape,C    6/18/88    Colonial      150,000.00    2600     4       3
426 St. James Ct.  Louisville  Jones,S   6/19/88    Ranch          19,500.00     950     2       1
222 Big Ben Dr.    Louisville  Roberts,D 6/22/88    Other          53,500.00    1900     3       2
766 Baird St.      Louisville  Black,B   6/22/88    Colonial      139,950.00    2600     4       3
666 Montana Ave.   Louisville  Saul,H    6/23/88    Cape Cod       55,000.00    1900     3       1
589 Morocco Dr.    E'Town      Smith,B   6/24/88    Cape Cod       62,500.00    1875     3       2
987 Allan Dr.      Louisville  Newsome,K 6/26/88    Cape Cod       60,000.00    1900     4       2
549 Billtown Rd.   Louisville  Bizer,B   6/28/88    Ranch          72,500.00    2000     3       2
198 Main St.       J'Town      Green,L   6/29/88    Other          27,500.00     800     3       1
343 Market St.     Louisville  Bivins,D  6/29/88    Ranch          42,900.00    1675     3       1

885 Jefferson St.  J'Town      Zith,M    7/02/88    Ranch          55,000.00    1500     3       1
913 Whitney Dr.    North Hill  Kulp,R    7/04/88    Cape Cod       99,500.00    1800     4       2
363 Dower Ct.      North Fork  Culp,A    7/05/88    Cape Cod      109,000.00    2100     4       2
620 Windsong Ct.   Louisville  Pank,E    7/06/88    Colonial      250,000.00    4000     6       4
#6 Brandon Way     Louisville  Abrams,L  7/22/88    Ranch          67,000.00    2250     4       2
6610 Vermin Dr.    Louisville  Russ,J    7/24/88    Ranch          75,000.00    2100     3       2
712 Clifton Ct.    Louisville  Thomas,T  7/24/88    Ranch          30,000.00    1500     3       1
5432 Miller Rd.    Louisville  Young,R   7/29/88    Other          17,500.00     800     2       1

#12 Circle Ct.     Louisville  White,Y   8/02/88    Other          10,000.00     800     2       1
1222 Dee Rd.       South Fork  Smith,P   8/02/88    Ranch          22,950.00     950     3       1
222 Earl Ave.      J'Town      Wray,A    8/05/88    Ranch          51,000.00    1200     3       1
9827 Rowan St.     J'Town      Coad,B    8/10/88    Ranch          47,950.00    1100     3       1
3355 Bank St.      J'Town      Cobb,D    8/17/88    Ranch          37,500.00    1500     3       1
77 Portland Ave.   North Hill  Coe,A     8/19/88    Ranch          20,000.00    1500     3       1
99 Cardinal Hill Rd. North Hill Brand,B  8/19/88    Cape Cod       70,000.00    2000     3       2
#10 Old Mill Rd.   Louisville  Stern,M   8/21/88    Ranch          75,000.00    2150     3       2
5532 Mud Creek Dr. Louisville  Hall,W    8/24/88    Ranch          12,000.00     950     2       1
4444 Normie Ln.    Louisville  James,J   8/25/88    Cape Cod      120,000.00    2400     5       3
3498 Bold Rd.      Louisville  Taft,H    8/29/88    Colonial      275,000.00    3800     5       4
#82 Rudd Rd.       Louisville  Lum,I     8/30/88    Cape Cod       88,950.00    2800     4       2
6712 Shelby St.    Louisville  Wood,B    8/30/88    Ranch          92,500.00    2400     4       2
7235 Shiloh Dr.    E'Town      Allan,J   8/31/88    Ranch          95,000.00    2750     4       3

8989 Big D Ln.     South Fork  Adkins,B  9/01/88    Ranch          17,000.00    1200     2       1
1001 Spring St.    North Hill  Frier,F   9/05/88    Other          45,000.00    1700     3       2
6935 Shiloh Dr.    E'Town      Grebe,C   9/08/88    Cape Cod       81,000.00    2000     3       2
4989 Adler Way     Louisville  Dole,V    9/13/88    Cape Cod       76,500.00    2000     3       2
5678 Beech St.     Louisville  Smith,P   9/16/88    Cape Cod       65,950.00    1800     3       2
#62 Billy Bone Ct. Louisville  Taylor,A  9/18/88    Ranch          34,500.00    1600     3       1
3323 Mt. Holly Dr. Louisville  Grizz,D   9/24/88    Ranch          22,100.00    1200     3       1
9909 Midway Rd.    Louisville  Maier,O   9/25/88    Ranch          61,250.00    1875     3       2
435 Oxted Ln.      Louisville  O'Neal,P  9/26/88    Ranch          53,790.00    1900     3       1
22 N. Ridge Ct.    Louisville  Nunn,A    9/29/88    Colonial      200,000.00    2900     5       3
```

Numeric Fields

You also can group a report based on ranges of entries in numeric fields. When you ask Paradox to create a range group on a number, dollar, or short number field, it will display the prompt shown in Figure 11-21. This prompt allows you to specify the interval (range) that Paradox should use to group your report. Paradox uses the interval you specify to create a series of "bins" into which the records in the report are grouped. For example, if you specify an interval of 100, Paradox will place all records with an entry of 0 to 100 in one group, all records with values from 101 to 200 in a second group, and so on. If the field contains negative values, they will be similarly grouped using the interval you specify.

Figure 11-21 The Range Prompt

```
Size of range:                                        ┌────────┐
Example: 10 produces 0-9, 10-19, etc.                 │ Report │   1/1
....+...10....+...20....+...30....+...40....+...50....+...60....+...70....+...80
─▼page─
```

Suppose you want to design a report for the LISTINGS table that is grouped by ranges on the Price field. (You want to group the records with Price field entries from 0 to 49,999, the records with Price entries between 50,000 and 99,999, and so on.) To do this, create a new report (we'll use number **7**), using the report description **Listings By Price Range**. Once again, be sure to change the page-width to 132 and delete the second page-width.

When the report specification screen appears, issue the [**Menu**] **G**roup **I**nsert **R**ange command and select **P**rice as the field to group. Paradox then will prompt you for the size of the range. When you see this prompt, type **50000** and press ↵. When Paradox prompts you to indicate where you want to insert the group, move the cursor to the page header and press ↵. After you do this, Paradox will insert the new band *group List price, range=50000* into the report spec.

Now, press [**Instant Report**]. Figure 11-22 shows the first page of the resulting report. As you can see, Paradox has grouped the records in the report using the interval you specified. Note that the first group contains all of the records with Price field entries from 0 to 49,999; the next group contains all of the records with entries from 50,000 to 99,999; and so on.

Figure 11-22 The Printed Report

```
11/24/88              Listings By Price Range              Page   1


Address           Town        Owner        List Date  Style      Price          Sq Ft   BRs    Baths
---------         ------      --------     ---------  -------    -----------     -----   ----   -----
#12 Circle Ct.    Louisville  White,Y       8/02/88   Other       10,000.00      800     2      1
5532 Mud Creek Dr. Louisville Hall,W        8/24/88   Ranch       12,000.00      950     2      1
185 Pages Ln.     J'Town      Cowan,M      11/01/88   Other       15,500.00     1000     2      1
8989 Big D Ln.    South Fork  Adkins,G      9/01/88   Ranch       17,000.00     1200     2      1
5432 Miller Rd.   Louisville  Young,R       7/29/88   Other       17,500.00      800     2      1
956 Volar Ln.     J'Town      Lamb,M       10/25/88   Ranch       18,000.00     1200     2      1
426 St. James Ct. Louisville  Jones,S       6/19/88   Ranch       19,500.00      950     2      1
77 Portland Ave.  North Hill  Coe,A         8/19/88   Ranch       20,000.00     1500     3      1
3323 Mt. Holly Dr. Louisville Grizz,D       9/24/88   Ranch       22,100.00     1200     3      1
1222 Dee Rd.      South Fork  Smith,P       8/02/88   Ranch       22,950.00      950     3      1
1989 Eastern Pkwy. Louisville Klink,C      10/23/88   Ranch       26,950.00     1100     2      1
198 Main St.      J'Town      Green,L       6/29/88   Other       27,500.00      800     3      1
9819 Wilson Ave.  J'Town      Crane,B      10/23/88   Ranch       28,000.00     1200     3      1
28 Seebolt Rt.    Louisville  Priest,S     11/10/88   Other       28,500.00      950     3      1
659 Ridge Rd.     Louisville  Pulley,F     10/08/88   Ranch       30,000.00     1500     3      1
712 Clifton Ct.   Louisville  Thomas,T      7/24/88   Ranch       30,000.00     1500     3      1
123 Abby Ct.      Louisville  Kones,D       6/16/88   Ranch       32,950.00     1500     3      1
9849 Taylor Blvd. J'Town      Dukes,J      10/29/88   Ranch       32,950.00     1750     3      1
#62 Billy Bone Ct. Louisville Taylor,A      9/18/88   Ranch       34,500.00     1600     3      1
5372 Tyson Pl.    Louisville  Goode,J      10/28/88   Ranch       35,000.00     1500     3      2
3355 Bank St.     J'Town      Cobb,D        8/17/88   Ranch       37,500.00     1500     3      1
654 Nora Ln.      Louisville  Orwick,S     10/02/88   Cape Cod    40,000.00     1600     3      1
343 Market St.    Louisville  Bivins,D      6/29/88   Ranch       42,900.00     1675     3      1
1001 Spring St.   North Hill  Frier,F       9/05/88   Other       45,000.00     1700     3      2
721 Zabel Way     Louisville  Stich,L      10/14/88   Ranch       47,950.00     1500     3      1
9827 Rowan St.    J'Town      Coad,B        8/10/88   Ranch       47,950.00     1100     3      1
99 N. Central Blvd. Louisville Stevens,P   11/28/88   Ranch       49,000.00     2500     3      2
4233 Mix Ave.     Louisville  Martin,D     11/30/88   Cape Cod    49,500.00     1900     3      2

222 Earl Ave.     J'Town      Wray,A        8/05/88   Ranch       51,000.00     1200     3      1
14 Short Rd.      Louisville  Quire,I      10/13/88   Ranch       52,300.00     1600     3      1
222 Big Ben Dr.   Louisville  Roberts,D     6/22/88   Other       53,500.00     1900     3      2
435 Oxted Ln.     Louisville  O'Neal,P      9/26/88   Ranch       53,790.00     1900     3      1
666 Montana Ave.  Louisville  Saul,H        6/23/88   Cape Cod    55,000.00     1900     3      1
885 Jefferson St. J'Town      Zith,M        7/02/88   Ranch       55,000.00     1500     3      1
987 Allan Dr.     Louisville  Newsome,K     6/26/88   Cape Cod    60,000.00     1900     4      2
9909 Midway Rd.   Louisville  Maier,O       9/25/88   Ranch       61,250.00     1875     3      2
589 Morocco Dr.   E'Town      Smith,B       6/24/88   Cape Cod    62,500.00     1875     3      2
5678 Beech St.    Louisville  Smith,P       9/16/88   Cape Cod    65,950.00     1800     3      2
#6 Brandon Way    Louisville  Abrams,L      7/22/88   Ranch       67,000.00     2250     4      2
3752 St. Dennis   J'Town      Levine,J     11/03/88   Cape Cod    67,950.00     2500     3      2
586 Ansa Way      Louisville  Noel,C       11/27/88   Colonial    69,500.00     2200     4      2
99 Cardinal Hill Rd. North Hill Brand,B     8/19/88   Cape Cod    70,000.00     2000     3      2
6262 Kenwood Dr.  North Hill  Beck,U       11/17/88   Ranch       71,650.00     2000     3      2
549 Billtown Rd.  Louisville  Bizer,B       6/28/88   Ranch       72,500.00     2000     3      2
#10 Old Mill Rd.  Louisville  Stern,M       8/21/88   Ranch       75,000.00     2150     3      2
6610 Vermin Dr.   Louisville  Russ,J        7/24/88   Ranch       75,000.00     2100     3      2
6791 Lotus Ave.   South Fork  Howell,T     11/24/88   Ranch       75,600.00     2000     3      2
4989 Adler Way    Louisville  Dole,V        9/13/88   Cape Cod    76,500.00     2000     3      2
```

Alphanumeric Fields

You can also group reports by ranges based on the entries in alphanumeric fields. When you issue the [**Menu**] **G**roup **I**nsert **R**ange command and select an alphanumeric field, Paradox will display the prompt shown in Figure 11-23. As you can see, this prompt lets you define the number of characters from each entry in the grouping field that Paradox will use to group the report. If you enter 1 in response to this prompt, Paradox will group all the entries that begin with the same first letter. If you type 2, Paradox will group all the entries that begin with the same two letters, and so on. There are several cases in which this might be useful: for example, to group by the first three digits of a zip code or the first two letters of a part number.

Figure 11-23 The Range Prompt

```
Number of initial characters in range:                        Report    1/1
Use 1 to group by first letter, 2 to group by first two letters, etc.
```

Grouping a Specific Number of Records

You can also instruct Paradox to group a specific number of records, regardless of the contents of those records. To create this type of group, you issue the [Menu] Group Insert NumberRecords command and specify the number of records you want Paradox to include in each group. When you group a report in this way, Paradox will not sort the report. Instead, it will simply create groups that contain the number of records you specify. This might help make your report more readable.

For example, suppose you want to design a report that prints the records in the LISTINGS table in groups of three. To do this, create a new report, (we'll use number **8**), using the report description **Listings By Threes**. Once again, be sure to change the page-width to 132 and delete the second page-width.

When the report spec screen appears, issue the **[Menu]** G**r**oup **I**nsert NumberRecords command. After you issue the command, Paradox will prompt you to enter the number of records to group. When you see this prompt, type **3** and press ↵. Next, Paradox will prompt you to place the group in the report spec. When it does, you should move the cursor to the page header and press ↵. Figure 11-24 shows the screen with the *group records=3* band in place.

Figure 11-24 The Report Specification Screen

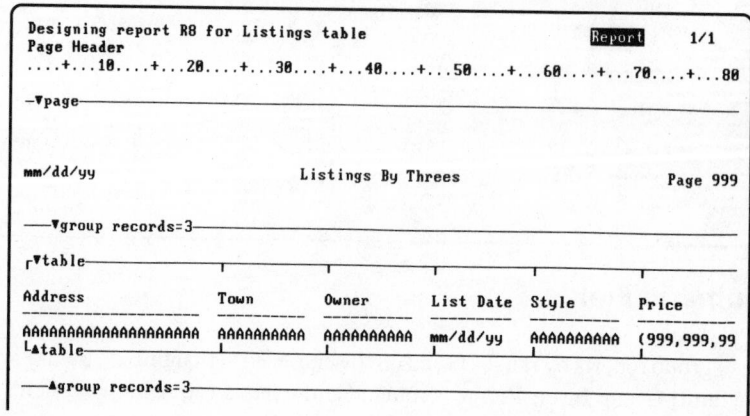

```
Designing report R8 for Listings table                        Report    1/1
Page Header
....+...10....+...20....+...30....+...40....+...50....+...60....+...70....+...80
—▼page———————————————————————————————————————————————————————————————————————


mm/dd/yy                        Listings By Threes                    Page 999

———▼group records=3———————————————————————————————————————————————————————————
┌▼table————————————————————————————————————————————————————————————————————————

Address              Town        Owner       List Date  Style       Price
————————————————————  ——————————  ——————————  ————————  ——————————  ——————————
AAAAAAAAAAAAAAAAAAAA  AAAAAAAAAA  AAAAAAAAAA  mm/dd/yy  AAAAAAAAAA  (999,999,99
└▲table————————————————————————————————————————————————————————————————————————

———▲group records=3———————————————————————————————————————————————————————————
```

Figure 11-25 shows the first page of the report that Paradox will produce when you print this report spec. As you can see, the records in this report are separated into groups of three. Notice that the report is not sorted.

Figure 11-25 The Printed Report

```
11/22/88              Listings By Threes              Page  1

                                   List Date  Style       Price          Sq Ft   BRs    Baths
Address            Town      Owner
-----------------  --------  ------ ---------  --------- -----------      -----   ----   -----
123 Abby Ct.       Louisville Kones,D  6/16/88  Ranch       32,950.00     1500    3      1
426 St. James Ct.  Louisville Jones,S  6/19/88  Ranch       19,500.00      950    2      1
766 Baird St.      Louisville Black,G  6/22/88  Colonial   139,950.00     2600    4      3

222 Big Ben Dr.    Louisville Roberts,D 6/22/88 Other       53,500.00     1900    3      2
666 Montana Ave.   Louisville Saul,H   6/23/88  Cape Cod    55,000.00     1900    3      1
589 Morocco Dr.    E'Town     Smith,B  6/24/88  Cape Cod    62,500.00     1875    3      2

987 Allan Dr.      Louisville Newsome,K 6/26/88 Cape Cod    60,000.00     1900    4      2
549 Billtown Rd.   Louisville Bizer,B  6/28/88  Ranch       72,500.00     2000    3      2
343 Market St.     Louisville Bivins,D 6/29/88  Ranch       42,900.00     1675    3      1

198 Main St.       J'Town     Green,L  6/29/88  Other       27,500.00      800    3      1
885 Jefferson St.  J'Town     Zith,M   7/02/88  Ranch       55,000.00     1500    3      1
913 Whitney Dr.    North Hill Kulp,R   7/04/88  Cape Cod    99,500.00     1800    4      2

363 Dover Ct.      North Fork Culp,A   7/05/88  Cape Cod   109,000.00     2100    4      2
620 Windsong Ct.   Louisville Pank,E   7/06/88  Colonial   250,000.00     4000    6      4
4500 Hempstead Dr. Louisville Pape,C   6/18/88  Colonial   150,000.00     2600    4      3

#6 Brandon Way     Louisville Abrams,L 7/22/88  Ranch       67,000.00     2250    4      2
6610 Vermin Dr.    Louisville Russ,J   7/24/88  Ranch       75,000.00     2100    3      2
712 Clifton Ct.    Louisville Thomas,T 7/24/88  Ranch       30,000.00     1500    3      1

5432 Miller Rd.    Louisville Young,R  7/29/88  Other       17,500.00      800    2      1
#12 Circle Ct.     Louisville White,Y  8/02/88  Other       10,000.00      800    2      1
1222 Dee Rd.       South Fork Smith,P  8/02/88  Ranch       22,950.00      950    3      1

222 Earl Ave.      J'Town     Wray,A   8/05/88  Ranch       51,000.00     1200    3      1
9827 Rowan St.     J'Town     Coad,B   8/10/88  Ranch       47,950.00     1100    3      1
3355 Bank St.      J'Town     Cobb,D   8/17/88  Ranch       37,500.00     1500    3      1

77 Portland Ave.   North Hill Coe,A    8/19/88  Ranch       20,000.00     1500    3      1
99 Cardinal Hill Rd. North Hill Brand,B 8/19/88 Cape Cod    70,000.00     2000    3      2
#10 Old Mill Rd.   Louisville Stern,M  8/21/88  Ranch       75,000.00     2150    3      2

5532 Mud Creek Dr. Louisville Hall,W   8/24/88  Ranch       12,000.00      950    2      1
4444 Normie Ln.    Louisville James,J  8/25/88  Cape Cod   120,000.00     2400    5      3
3498 Bold Rd.      Louisville Taft,H   8/29/88  Colonial   275,000.00     3800    5      4
```

Changing the Sort Order

The default sort order for grouped reports is ascending. If you want, you can use the [Menu] Group SortDirection command to change the default order of the sort to descending.

Suppose you have created the report specification shown in Figure 11-16 on page 480. As you can see, this spec instructs Paradox to group the report by the entries in the Style field. If you want to change the sort order for this report from ascending to descending, issue the **[Menu]** Group SortDirection command. After you issue the command, Paradox will prompt you to position the cursor on the group you want to change. When you see this prompt, position the cursor in the *group Style* band and press ↵. Paradox then will display a menu with two options: Ascending and Descending. To change the default setting, issue the **D**escending command. Now, press **[Instant Report]**. Figure 11-26 shows the first page of the resulting printed report. As you can see, this report is sorted in descending, rather than ascending, order.

Figure 11-26 The Printed Report

Address	Town	Owner	List Date	Style	Price	Sq Ft	BRs	Baths
11/24/88		Listings By Style				Page 1		
#10 Old Mill Rd.	Louisville	Stern,M	8/21/88	Ranch	75,000.00	2150	3	2
#6 Brandon Way	Louisville	Abrams,L	7/22/88	Ranch	67,000.00	2250	4	2
#62 Billy Bone Ct.	Louisville	Taylor,A	9/18/88	Ranch	34,500.00	1600	3	1
1222 Dee Rd.	South Fork	Smith,P	8/02/88	Ranch	22,950.00	950	3	1
123 Abby Ct.	Louisville	Kones,D	6/16/88	Ranch	32,950.00	1500	3	1
14 Short Rd.	Louisville	Quire,I	10/13/88	Ranch	52,300.00	1600	3	1
1989 Eastern Pkwy.	Louisville	Klink,C	10/23/88	Ranch	26,950.00	1100	2	1
222 Earl Ave.	J'Town	Wray,A	8/05/88	Ranch	51,000.00	1200	3	1
3323 Mt. Holly Dr.	Louisville	Grizz,D	9/24/88	Ranch	22,100.00	1200	3	1
3355 Bank St.	J'Town	Cobb,D	8/17/88	Ranch	37,500.00	1500	3	1
343 Market St.	Louisville	Bivins,D	6/29/88	Ranch	42,900.00	1675	3	1
426 St. James Ct.	Louisville	Jones,S	6/19/88	Ranch	19,500.00	950	2	1
435 Oxted Ln.	Louisville	O'Neal,P	9/26/88	Ranch	53,790.00	1900	3	1
5372 Tyson Pl.	Louisville	Goode,J	10/28/88	Ranch	35,000.00	1500	3	2
549 Billtown Rd.	Louisville	Bizer,B	6/28/88	Ranch	72,500.00	2000	3	2
5532 Mud Creek Dr.	Louisville	Hall,W	8/24/88	Ranch	12,000.00	950	2	1
581 Yale Dr.	Louisville	Winer,L	10/17/88	Ranch	78,000.00	2100	4	2
6262 Kenwood Dr.	North Hill	Beck,U	11/17/88	Ranch	71,650.00	2000	3	2
659 Ridge Rd.	Louisville	Pulley,F	10/08/88	Ranch	30,000.00	1500	3	1
6610 Vernin Dr.	Louisville	Russ,J	7/24/88	Ranch	75,000.00	2100	3	2
6712 Shelby St.	Louisville	Wood,B	8/30/88	Ranch	92,500.00	2400	4	2
6791 Lotus Ave.	South Fork	Howell,T	11/24/88	Ranch	75,600.00	2000	3	2
712 Clifton Ct.	Louisville	Thomas,T	7/24/88	Ranch	30,000.00	1500	3	1
721 Zabel Way	Louisville	Stich,L	10/14/88	Ranch	47,950.00	1500	3	1
7235 Shiloh Dr.	E'Town	Allan,J	8/31/88	Ranch	95,000.00	2750	4	3
77 Portland Ave.	North Hill	Coe,A	8/19/88	Ranch	20,000.00	1500	3	1
885 Jefferson St.	J'Town	Zith,M	7/02/88	Ranch	55,000.00	1500	3	1
8989 Big D Ln.	South Fork	Adkins,G	9/01/88	Ranch	17,000.00	1200	2	1
9222 Meadow Pl.	South Fork	Baxter,H	11/22/88	Ranch	85,000.00	2100	3	2
956 Volar Ln.	J'Town	Lamb,M	10/25/88	Ranch	18,000.00	1200	2	1
9819 Wilson Ave.	J'Town	Crane,B	10/23/88	Ranch	28,000.00	1200	3	1
9827 Rowan St.	J'Town	Coad,B	8/10/88	Ranch	47,950.00	1100	3	1
9849 Taylor Blvd.	J'Town	Dukes,J	10/29/88	Ranch	32,950.00	1750	3	1
99 N. Central Blvd.	Louisville	Stevens,P	11/28/88	Ranch	49,000.00	2500	3	2
9909 Midway Rd.	Louisville	Maier,O	9/25/88	Ranch	61,250.00	1875	3	2
#12 Circle Ct.	Louisville	White,Y	8/02/88	Other	10,000.00	800	2	1
#5 Ashby St.	J'Town	Wagner,H	10/22/88	Other	97,000.00	2500	4	3
1001 Spring St.	North Hill	Frier,F	9/05/88	Other	45,000.00	1700	3	2
185 Pages Ln.	J'Town	Cowan,M	11/01/88	Other	15,500.00	1000	2	1
198 Main St.	J'Town	Green,L	6/29/88	Other	27,500.00	800	3	1
222 Big Ben Dr.	Louisville	Roberts,D	6/22/88	Other	53,500.00	1900	3	2
28 Seebolt Rt.	Louisville	Priest,S	11/10/88	Other	28,500.00	950	3	1
5432 Miller Rd.	Louisville	Young,R	7/29/88	Other	17,500.00	800	2	1
854 Unseld Blvd.	Louisville	Volk,H	10/19/88	Other	87,000.00	2500	3	2
22 N. Ridge Ct.	Louisville	Nunn,A	9/29/88	Colonial	200,000.00	2900	5	3
3498 Bold Rd.	Louisville	Taft,H	8/29/88	Colonial	275,000.00	3800	5	4

Group Headers and Footers

Earlier in our discussion of grouping, we pointed out that Paradox automatically creates a group header and group footer for each group you place in a report. So far, we have just left the header and footer empty as we printed grouped reports. However, Paradox allows you to make entries in the group header and footer. You often will enter literals and regular fields in your group headers, and summary fields in your group footers.

Group headers are similar to page headers. Anything that you type in a group header will be printed at the top of each group. You will usually make entries in the group header that describe the entries in the group. Likewise, group footers are similar to page footers and report footers. Anything that you type in a group footer will be printed at the end of each group. The group footer is the best spot for summary fields that compute statistics about the group.

An Example

Suppose you have created a report specification like the one shown in Figure 11-16 on page 480. As you can see, this report spec instructs Paradox to group the report on the Style field. Now, suppose you want to define a group header and group footer. To begin, move the cursor to the group header and then press **[Ctrl]-[Home]** to move it to the left side of the screen.

When the cursor is in place, type **Style:**. Next, issue the **[Menu]** **F**ield **P**lace **R**egular command. When Paradox prompts you for the field to place, select the Style field, then move the cursor to a space just to the right of the literal *Style:* and press ↵ once to place the field, and again to set its length.

Now, you're ready to place a summary field in the group footer that displays the average price of the records in each group. First type **Average Price:** in the group footer for the *group Style* band. Next, issue the **[Menu]** **F**ield **P**lace **S**ummary **R**egular command and select **P**rice as the field to summarize. At the next prompt, select **A**verage as the type of summary. Since you want to compute a summary for only the records in the current group, you should choose **P**erGroup when Paradox displays the PerGroup/Overall menu. Then, place the field in the group footer next to the literal *Average Price:* and adjust the digits and decimals as you want.

Figure 11-27 shows the completed report specification. If you press **[Instant Report]** to print this report spec, Paradox will create the report shown in Figure 11-28 on the next page. Paradox has grouped the records in this report according to their Style field entries. In addition, Paradox has included a group header consisting of the literal *Style:* and the current Style field entry at the top of each field, and a footer consisting of a summary statistic at the bottom of each group. Since you selected PerGroup when you placed the summary statistic, the statistic at the foot of each group computes the average price of the records in that group.

Figure 11-27 The Group Header and Footer

```
Designing report R4 for Listings table                    Report     1/1
Group Footer for Style                          Average of Price, per group
....+...10....+...20....+...30....+...40....+...50....+...60....+...70....+...80

 —▼page————————————————————————————————————————————————————————————

 mm/dd/yy                      Listings By Style                  Page 999

 ———▼group Style——————————————————————————————————————————————————
 Style: AAAAAAAAAA
 ┌▼table———————————————————————————————————————————————————————————

 Address              Town        Owner       List Date  Style      Price
 —————————            ————        —————       —————————  —————      —————
 AAAAAAAAAAAAAAAAAAAA AAAAAAAAAA  AAAAAAAAAA  mm/dd/yy   AAAAAAAAAA (999,999,99
 └▲table———————————————————————————————————————————————————————————
 Average Price: (99,999,999.99)
 ———▲group Style——————————————————————————————————————————————————
```

Notes

Notice that there is redundant information in the report in Figure 11-28. Since Paradox is printing the appropriate Style field entry for each group in the group header, you no longer need it to print the Style field for each record. To remove these entries, you can issue the **[Menu]** **T**ableBand **E**rase command and remove the Style column from the Table band. Figure 11-29 shows the first page of the report Paradox will print from this report spec. Notice that Paradox has not printed the Style field entry for each record in this report.

Figure 11-28 The Printed Report

```
11/22/88                    Listings By Style                    Page   1


Address              Town          Owner       List Date  Style      Price           Sq Ft   BRs    Baths
------------------   ----------    --------    ---------  -----      -------------   -----   ----   -----
Style: Cape Cod
#82 Rudd Rd.                       Lum,I       8/30/88    Cape Cod       88,950.00    2800    4      2
2216 Lacey St.       Louisville    Beat,A      11/13/88   Cape Cod       94,999.00    2700    4      3
363 Dower Ct.        North Hill    Culp,A      7/05/88    Cape Cod      109,000.00    2100    4      2
3752 St. Dennis      North Fork    Levine,J    11/03/88   Cape Cod       67,950.00    2500    3      2
4233 Mix Ave.        J'Town        Martin,D    11/30/88   Cape Cod       49,500.00    1900    3      2
4444 Normie Ln.      Louisville    James,J     8/25/88    Cape Cod      120,000.00    2400    5      3
4989 Adler Way       Louisville    Dole,V      9/13/88    Cape Cod       76,500.00    2000    3      2
5678 Beech St.       Louisville    Smith,P     9/16/88    Cape Cod       65,950.00    1800    3      2
589 Morocco Dr.      E'Town        Smith,B     6/24/88    Cape Cod       62,500.00    1875    3      2
654 Nora Ln.         Louisville    Orwick,B    10/02/88   Cape Cod       40,000.00    1600    3      1
666 Montana Ave.     Louisville    Saul,H      6/23/88    Cape Cod       55,000.00    1900    3      1
6935 Shiloh Dr.      E'Town        Grebe,C     9/08/88    Cape Cod       81,000.00    2000    3      2
913 Whitney Dr.      North Hill    Kulp,R      7/04/88    Cape Cod       99,500.00    1800    4      2
987 Allan Dr.        Louisville    Newsome,K   6/26/88    Cape Cod       60,000.00    1900    4      2
99 Cardinal Hill Rd. North Hill    Brand,B     8/19/88    Cape Cod       70,000.00    2000    3      2
Average Price:  76,056.60
Style: Colonial
22 N. Ridge Ct.      Louisville    Nunn,A      9/29/88    Colonial      200,000.00    2900    5      3
3498 Bold Rd.        Louisville    Taft,H      8/29/88    Colonial      275,000.00    3800    5      4
4500 Hempstead Dr.   Louisville    Pape,C      6/18/88    Colonial      150,000.00    2600    4      3
586 Ansa Way         Louisville    Noel,C      11/27/88   Colonial       69,500.00    2200    4      2
620 Windsong Ct.     Louisville    Pank,E      7/06/88    Colonial      250,000.00    4000    6      4
766 Baird St.        Louisville    Black,G     6/22/88    Colonial      139,950.00    2600    4      3
Average Price:  180,741.67
Style: Other
#12 Circle Ct.       Louisville    White,Y     8/02/88    Other          10,000.00     800    2      1
#5 Ashby St.         J'Town        Wagner,H    10/22/88   Other          97,000.00    2500    4      3
1001 Spring St.      North Hill    Frier,F     9/05/88    Other          45,000.00    1700    3      2
185 Pages Ln.        J'Town        Cowan,M     11/01/88   Other          15,500.00    1000    2      1
198 Main St.         J'Town        Green,L     6/29/88    Other          27,500.00     800    2      1
222 Big Ben Dr.      Louisville    Roberts,D   6/22/88    Other          53,500.00    1900    3      2
28 Seebolt Rt.       Louisville    Priest,S    11/10/88   Other          28,500.00     950    3      1
5432 Miller Rd.      Louisville    Young,R     7/29/88    Other          17,500.00     800    2      1
854 Unseld Blvd.     Louisville    Volk,H      10/19/88   Other          87,000.00    2500    3      2
Average Price:  42,388.89
Style: Ranch
#10 Old Mill Rd.     Louisville    Stern,M     8/21/88    Ranch          75,000.00    2150    3      2
#6 Brandon Way       Louisville    Abrams,L    7/22/88    Ranch          67,000.00    2250    4      2
#62 Billy Bone Ct.   Louisville    Taylor,A    9/18/88    Ranch          34,500.00    1600    3      1
1222 Dee Rd.         South Fork    Smith,P     8/02/88    Ranch          22,950.00     950    3      1
123 Abby Ct.         Louisville    Kones,D     6/16/88    Ranch          32,950.00    1500    3      1
14 Short Rd.         Louisville    Quire,I     10/13/88   Ranch          52,300.00    1600    3      1
1989 Eastern Pkwy.   Louisville    Klink,C     10/23/88   Ranch          26,950.00    1100    2      1
222 Earl Ave.        J'Town        Wray,A      8/05/88    Ranch          51,000.00    1200    3      1
3323 Mt. Holly Dr.   Louisville    Grizz,D     9/24/88    Ranch          22,100.00    1200    3      1
3355 Bank St.        J'Town        Cobb,D      8/17/88    Ranch          37,500.00    1500    3      1
343 Market St.       Louisville    Bivins,D    6/29/88    Ranch          42,900.00    1675    3      1
426 St. James Ct.    Louisville    Jones,B     6/19/88    Ranch          19,500.00     950    2      1
435 Oxted Ln.        Louisville    O'Neal,P    9/26/88    Ranch          53,790.00    1900    3      1
5372 Tyson Pl.       Louisville    Goode,J     10/28/88   Ranch          35,000.00    1500    3      2
```

Figure 11-29 The Printed Report

```
11/24/88                    Listings By Style                    Page   1


Address              Town          Owner       List Date  Price           Sq Ft   BRs    Baths
------------------   ----------    --------    ---------  -------------   -----   ----   -----
Style: Cape Cod
#82 Rudd Rd.                       Lum,I       8/30/88        88,950.00    2800    4      2
2216 Lacey St.       Louisville    Beat,A      11/13/88       94,999.00    2700    4      3
363 Dower Ct.        North Hill    Culp,A      7/05/88       109,000.00    2100    4      2
3752 St. Dennis      North Fork    Levine,J    11/03/88       67,950.00    2500    3      2
4233 Mix Ave.        J'Town        Martin,D    11/30/88       49,500.00    1900    3      2
4989 Adler Way       Louisville    James,J     8/25/88       120,000.00    2400    5      3
4989 Adler Way       Louisville    Dole,V      9/13/88        76,500.00    2000    3      2
5678 Beech St.       Louisville    Smith,P     9/16/88        65,950.00    1800    3      2
589 Morocco Dr.      E'Town        Smith,B     6/24/88        62,500.00    1875    3      2
654 Nora Ln.         Louisville    Orwick,B    10/02/88       40,000.00    1600    3      1
666 Montana Ave.     Louisville    Saul,H      6/23/88        55,000.00    1900    3      1
6935 Shiloh Dr.      E'Town        Grebe,C     9/08/88        81,000.00    2000    3      2
913 Whitney Dr.      North Hill    Kulp,R      7/04/88        99,500.00    1800    4      2
987 Allan Dr.        Louisville    Newsome,K   6/26/88        60,000.00    1900    4      2
99 Cardinal Hill Rd. North Hill    Brand,B     8/19/88        70,000.00    2000    3      2
Average Price:  76,056.60
Style: Colonial
22 N. Ridge Ct.      Louisville    Nunn,A      9/29/88       200,000.00    2900    5      3
3498 Bold Rd.        Louisville    Taft,H      8/29/88       275,000.00    3800    5      4
4500 Hempstead Dr.   Louisville    Pape,C      6/18/88       150,000.00    2600    4      3
586 Ansa Way         Louisville    Noel,C      11/27/88       69,500.00    2200    4      2
620 Windsong Ct.     Louisville    Pank,E      7/06/88       250,000.00    4000    6      4
766 Baird St.        Louisville    Black,G     6/22/88       139,950.00    2600    4      3
Average Price:  180,741.67
Style: Other
#12 Circle Ct.       Louisville    White,Y     8/02/88        10,000.00     800    2      1
#5 Ashby St.         J'Town        Wagner,H    10/22/88       97,000.00    2500    4      3
1001 Spring St.      North Hill    Frier,F     9/05/88        45,000.00    1700    3      2
185 Pages Ln.        J'Town        Cowan,M     11/01/88       15,500.00    1000    2      1
198 Main St.         J'Town        Green,L     6/29/88        27,500.00     800    2      1
222 Big Ben Dr.      Louisville    Roberts,D   6/22/88        53,500.00    1900    3      2
28 Seebolt Rt.       Louisville    Priest,S    11/10/88       28,500.00     950    3      1
5432 Miller Rd.      Louisville    Young,R     7/29/88        17,500.00     800    2      1
854 Unseld Blvd.     Louisville    Volk,H      10/19/88       87,000.00    2500    3      2
Average Price:  42,388.89
Style: Ranch
#10 Old Mill Rd.     Louisville    Stern,M     8/21/88        75,000.00    2150    3      2
#6 Brandon Way       Louisville    Abrams,L    7/22/88        67,000.00    2250    4      2
#62 Billy Bone Ct.   Louisville    Taylor,A    9/18/88        34,500.00    1600    3      1
1222 Dee Rd.         South Fork    Smith,P     8/02/88        22,950.00     950    3      1
123 Abby Ct.         Louisville    Kones,D     6/16/88        32,950.00    1500    3      1
14 Short Rd.         Louisville    Quire,I     10/13/88       52,300.00    1600    3      1
1989 Eastern Pkwy.   Louisville    Klink,C     10/23/88       26,950.00    1100    2      1
222 Earl Ave.        J'Town        Wray,A      8/05/88        51,000.00    1200    3      1
3323 Mt. Holly Dr.   Louisville    Grizz,D     9/24/88        22,100.00    1200    3      1
3355 Bank St.        J'Town        Cobb,D      8/17/88        37,500.00    1500    3      1
343 Market St.       Louisville    Bivins,D    6/29/88        42,900.00    1675    3      1
426 St. James Ct.    Louisville    Jones,B     6/19/88        19,500.00     950    2      1
435 Oxted Ln.        Louisville    O'Neal,P    9/26/88        53,790.00    1900    3      1
5372 Tyson Pl.       Louisville    Goode,J     10/28/88       35,000.00    1500    3      2
```

This last example points out a very important fact about groups: You can group a report on a field that is not included in the report. In the example, we deleted the Style field from the report. As you can see, Paradox grouped the report correctly even though the Style field is no longer in the report.

Also notice that because you have defined a header and footer for the group in the report spec in Figure 11-27, Paradox no longer separates the groups in the report with blank lines. If you want to reinsert blank lines between groups, just move the cursor to the end of the group footer or group header of the report spec, press [Ins], and press ← to insert a blank row. Once you add a blank row to the group header or footer, the groups in the report will again be separated by blank lines.

You can place as many summary fields in the group footer as you want. In addition, you can use any of the five types of summaries in a group footer. For example, you could add another summary to the report spec in Figure 11-27 that computes the maximum value in the Price field for the records in each group. All you'd have to do is insert a blank row in the group footer, type a literal like *Maximum Price:* in the new row, and then use the [Menu] Field Place Summary Regular command to insert the new summary.

Group Headings

Whenever a group is split between two pages, Paradox will repeat the group header for that group at the top of the second page. By using the [Menu] Group Headings command, you can change the default setting so that the group headings will not be printed on spillover pages. After you issue the [Menu] Group Headings command, Paradox will prompt you to place the cursor on the group you want to change. When you see this prompt, move the cursor to the group header and press ←. After you do this, Paradox will display a menu with two options: Page and Group. You should select Group from this menu to change the default setting. After you do this, the band indicator line at the top of the screen will read *headings per group*. When you print the report, Paradox will not print spillover group headers.

Nesting Groups

You can have up to 16 levels of groups in a report. Adding additional groups to a report spec causes Paradox to create groups within groups in your printed reports. The highest level group serves as the primary sort key for the report. The next group serves as the secondary sort key, the third group as the tertiary sort key, and so on.

An Example

Suppose you want to create a report for the LISTINGS table that is grouped on two fields: Style and BRs. You want to use Style as the main group so that the records in the report will be arranged into Style groups. You want to use BRs as a secondary group so that the records in each Style group will be arranged in ascending order based on the entries in the BRs field. To do this, create report 10 for LISTINGS as a tabular report, and name the report **Listings By Style and Bedrooms**.

When the new report specification screen comes into view, issue the **[Menu]** Group Insert Field command. Paradox will display the regular fields of the LISTINGS table and prompt you to select the one on which you want to group the report. When you see this list, select the Style field. Next, Paradox will prompt you to place the group in the report. To place this group, move the cursor to the page header and press ↵.

Now, you are ready to insert the second group. To do this, issue the **[Menu]** Group Insert Field command again. When Paradox displays the regular fields of the LISTINGS table, select the BRs field. Next, Paradox will prompt you to place the group in the report. To place this group, move the cursor anywhere within the *group Style* band and press ↵. Your screen should now look like Figure 11-30. Notice that the new band, *group BRs*, is enclosed by, or nested in, the *group Style* band. Because the *group BRs* band is nested inside the *group Style* band, Paradox will use the Style field as the primary grouping field. Within each Style group, the records in the report will be arranged in ascending order based on the BRs field.

Figure 11-30 Nested Groups

```
Designing report R10 for Listings table                    Report     1/1
Group Header for Style
....+...10....+...20....+...30....+...40....+...50....+...60....+...70....+...80
-▼page────────────────────────────────────────────────────────────────────

mm/dd/yy                  Listings By Style And Bedrooms            Page 999

    ─▼group Style───────────────────────────────────────────────────────────
        ───▼group BRs───────────────────────────────────────────────────────
    ┌▼table──────────┬──────────┬──────────┬──────────┬──────────┬───────────
    Address           Town       Owner      List Date  Style      Price
    ────────────────  ────────── ────────── ────────── ────────── ───────────
    AAAAAAAAAAAAAAAAA AAAAAAAAAA AAAAAAAAAA mm/dd/yy   AAAAAAAAAA (999,999,99
    └▲table──────────┴──────────┴──────────┴──────────┴──────────┴───────────
        ───▲group BRs───────────────────────────────────────────────────────
    ───▲group Style───────────────────────────────────────────────────────────
```

When you have defined the report spec, press **[Instant Report]** to create the printed report whose first page is shown in Figure 11-31. As you can see, the records in this report have been grouped by their Style field entries. Within each Style field group, the records are arranged so that the BRs field entries are in ascending order.

Figure 11-31 The Printed Report

```
11/24/88              Listings By Style And Bedrooms            Page   1


Address               Town      Owner      List Date  Style     Price              Sq Ft   BRs    Baths
--------              ----      -----      ---------  -----     -----              -----   ---    -----

3752 St. Dennis       J'Town       Levine,J    11/03/88   Cape Cod   67,950.00       2500    3      2
4233 Mix Ave.         Louisville   Martin,D    11/30/88   Cape Cod   49,500.00       1900    3      2
4989 Adler Way        Louisville   Dole,V       9/13/88   Cape Cod   76,500.00       2000    3      2
5678 Beech St.        Louisville   Smith,P      9/16/88   Cape Cod   65,950.00       1800    3      2
589 Morocco Dr.       E'Town       Smith,B      6/24/88   Cape Cod   62,500.00       1875    3      2
654 Nora Ln.          Louisville   Orwick,S    10/02/88   Cape Cod   40,000.00       1600    3      1
666 Montana Ave.      Louisville   Saul,H       6/23/88   Cape Cod   55,000.00       1900    3      1
6935 Shiloh Dr.       E'Town       Grebe,C      9/08/88   Cape Cod   81,000.00       2000    3      2
99 Cardinal Hill Rd.  North Hill   Brand,B      8/19/88   Cape Cod   70,000.00       2000    3      2

#82 Rudd Rd.          Louisville   Lum,I        8/30/88   Cape Cod   88,950.00       2800    4      2
2216 Lacey St.        North Hill   Beat,A      11/13/88   Cape Cod   94,999.00       2700    4      3
363 Dower Ct.         North Fork   Culp,A       7/05/88   Cape Cod  109,000.00       2100    4      2
913 Whitney Dr.       North Hill   Kulp,R       7/04/88   Cape Cod   99,500.00       1800    4      2
987 Allan Dr.         Louisville   Newsome,K    6/26/88   Cape Cod   60,000.00       1900    4      2


4444 Normie Ln.       Louisville   James,J      8/25/88   Cape Cod  120,000.00       2400    5      3


4500 Hempstead Dr.    Louisville   Pape,C       6/18/88   Colonial  150,000.00       2600    4      3
586 Ansa Way          Louisville   Noel,C      11/27/88   Colonial   69,000.00       2200    4      2
766 Baird St.         Louisville   Black,G      6/22/88   Colonial  139,950.00       2600    4      3

22 N. Ridge Ct.       Louisville   Nunn,A       9/29/88   Colonial  200,000.00       2900    5      3
3498 Bold Rd.         Louisville   Taft,H       8/29/88   Colonial  275,000.00       3800    5      4


620 Windsong Ct.      Louisville   Pank,E       7/06/88   Colonial  250,000.00       4000    6      4


#12 Circle Ct.        Louisville   White,Y      8/02/88   Other      10,000.00        800    2      1
185 Pages Ln.         J'Town       Cowan,M     11/01/88   Other      15,500.00       1000    2      1
5432 Miller Rd.       Louisville   Young,R      7/29/88   Other      17,500.00        800    2      1

1001 Spring St.       North Hill   Frier,F      9/05/88   Other      45,000.00       1700    3      2
198 Main St.          J'Town       Green,L      6/29/88   Other      27,500.00        800    3      1
222 Big Ben Dr.       Louisville   Roberts,D    6/22/88   Other      53,500.00       1900    3      2
28 Seebolt Rt.        Louisville   Priest,S    11/10/88   Other      28,500.00        950    3      1
854 Unseld Blvd.      Louisville   Volk,H      10/19/88   Other      87,000.00       2500    3      2
```

Using Summaries in Nested Groups

If you want, you can enter summary statistics in the group footers of nested groups to create several levels of summary statistics in your reports. For example, suppose you want to compute the average of the Price field entries in each BRs subgroup and the average of the Price field entries for each Style group. To do this, first issue the [Menu] Field Place Summary Regular command, select Price as the field to summarize, and select Average from the menu of summary types. To restrict the scope of the summary to the current group, you should choose PerGroup when Paradox displays the PerGroup/Overall menu. Next, place the field in the group footer for the *group Style* band. Finally, press [Ins] and type the literal **Average Price for Style:** into the footer in front of the summary field.

Repeat the steps above to create a new Average summary field on the Price field. This time, however, when Paradox prompts you to position the field, place it in the group footer for the *group BRs* band. Finally, type the literal **Average Price:** into the band next to the summary, as shown in Figure 11-32 on the following page.

Now, press [Instant Report] to print the report whose first page is shown in Figure 11-33. As you can see, Paradox has included two levels of summaries in the report: one for each BR subgroup and one for each Style group.

Figure 11-32 Summaries in Nested Groups

```
Designing report R10 for Listings table                    Report Ins 1/1
Group Footer for Style                          Average of Price, per group
....+...10....+...20....+...30....+...40....+...50....+...60....+...70....+...80

─▼page─────────────────────────────────────────────────────────────────────


mm/dd/yy                Listings By Style And Bedrooms              Page 999


   ─▼group Style──────────────────────────────────────────────────────────

      ─▼group BRs──────────────────────────────────────────────────────────

   ┌─▼table──────┬──────────┬──────────┬──────────┬──────────┬──────────
                 │          │          │          │          │
Address          │  Town    │  Owner   │ List Date│ Style    │ Price
───────────────  ───────── ─────────  ────────── ────────── ─────────
AAAAAAAAAAAAAAAAAAAAAA  AAAAAAAAAA  AAAAAAAAAA  mm/dd/yy  AAAAAAAAAA  (999,999,99
   └─▲table──────┴──────────┴──────────┴──────────┴──────────┴──────────
Average Price: (999,999.99)
      ─▲group BRs──────────────────────────────────────────────────────────
Average Price for Style: (999,999.99)
   ─▲group Style──────────────────────────────────────────────────────────
```

Figure 11-33 The Printed Report

```
11/24/88              Listings By Style And Bedrooms            Page   1


Address            Town        Owner      List Date  Style      Price              Sq Ft  BRs    Baths
─────────────────  ─────────   ─────────  ─────────  ────────   ──────────────     ─────  ─────  ──────

3752 St. Dennis    J'Town      Levine,J   11/03/88   Cape Cod     67,950.00        2500    3      2
4233 Mix Ave.      Louisville  Martin,D   11/30/88   Cape Cod     49,500.00        1900    3      2
4989 Adler Way     Louisville  Dole,V      9/13/88   Cape Cod     76,500.00        2000    3      2
5678 Beech St.     Louisville  Smith,P     9/16/88   Cape Cod     65,950.00        1800    3      2
589 Morocco Dr.    E'Town      Smith,B     6/24/88   Cape Cod     62,500.00        1875    3      2
654 Nora Ln.       Louisville  Orwick,S   10/02/88   Cape Cod     40,000.00        1600    3      1
666 Montana Ave.   Louisville  Saul,O      6/23/88   Cape Cod     55,000.00        1900    3      1
6935 Shiloh Dr.    E'Town      Grebe,C     9/08/88   Cape Cod     81,000.00        2000    3      2
99 Cardinal Hill Rd. North Hill Brand,B    8/19/88   Cape Cod     70,000.00        2000    3      2
Average Price:  63,155.56

#82 Rudd Rd.       Louisville  Lum,I       8/30/88   Cape Cod     88,950.00        2800    4      2
2216 Lacey St.     North Hill  Beat,A     11/13/88   Cape Cod     94,999.00        2700    4      3
363 Dower Ct.      North Fork  Culp,A      7/05/88   Cape Cod    109,000.00        2100    4      2
913 Whitney Dr.    North Hill  Kulp,R      7/04/88   Cape Cod     99,500.00        1800    4      2
987 Allan Dr.      Louisville  Newsome,K   6/26/88   Cape Cod     60,000.00        1900    4      2
Average Price:  90,489.80

4444 Normie Ln.    Louisville  James,J     8/25/88   Cape Cod    120,000.00        2400    5      3
Average Price:  120,000.00
Average Price for Style:  76,056.60


4500 Hempstead Dr. Louisville  Pape,C      6/18/88   Colonial    150,000.00        2600    4      3
586 Ansa Way       Louisville  Noel,C     11/27/88   Colonial     69,500.00        2200    4      2
766 Baird St.      Louisville  Black,G     6/22/88   Colonial    139,950.00        2600    4      3
Average Price:  119,816.67

22 N. Ridge Ct.    Louisville  Nunn,A      9/29/88   Colonial    200,000.00        2900    5      3
3498 Bold Rd.      Louisville  Taft,H      8/29/88   Colonial    275,000.00        3800    5      4
Average Price:  237,500.00

620 Windsong Ct.   Louisville  Pank,E      7/06/88   Colonial    250,000.00        4000    6      4
Average Price:  250,000.00
Average Price for Style:  180,741.67

#12 Circle Ct.     Louisville  White,Y     8/02/88   Other        10,000.00         800    2      1
185 Pages Ln.      J'Town      Cowan,M    11/01/88   Other        15,500.00        1000    2      1
5432 Miller Rd.    Louisville  Young,R     7/29/88   Other        17,500.00         800    2      1
Average Price:  14,333.33

1001 Spring St.    North Hill  Frier,F     9/05/88   Other        45,000.00        1700    3      2
198 Main St.       J'Town      Green,L     6/29/88   Other        27,500.00         800    3      1
222 Big Ben Dr.    Louisville  Roberts,D   6/22/88   Other        53,500.00        1900    3      2
28 Seebolt Rt.     Louisville  Priest,S   11/10/88   Other        28,500.00         950    3      1
854 Unseld Blvd.   Louisville  Volk,H     10/19/88   Other        87,000.00        2500    3      2
Average Price:  48,300.00
```

Notes

As we mentioned previously, you can include up to 16 groups in a report spec. Inserting the third and subsequent groups is no different from inserting the second: issue the [Menu] Group Insert command, supply the appropriate information, and place the field within the appropriate group band. Each new group you insert adds a new level of grouping to the report.

In a small table such as this, secondary groupings may not make a great deal of difference in the printed report. However, when you are working with a large table, adding groups can make your report much easier to interpret.

Group Repeats

In all of the grouped reports we have created so far, Paradox has printed the entries in the grouping field for every record in the report. For example, in the report in Figure 11-28, which is grouped on the Style field, Paradox has repeated the Style field entry for every record in the report.

Sometimes, you will want Paradox to print only the first entry in the grouping field for each group. To make this change, issue the [Menu] Setting GroupRepeats command. When you do this, Paradox will display a menu with two options: Retain and Suppress. The default selection, Retain, causes Paradox to print every occurrence of the grouping field, as in Figure 11-28 on page 490. The other option, Suppress, causes Paradox to print only the first entry in the grouping field for every group.

Figure 11-34 on the following page shows the first page of a report created with GroupRepeats set to Suppress. Notice that Paradox has printed only the first entry in the grouping field for every group.

GroupsOfTables and TableOfGroups

If you look at the grouped reports we've created so far, you'll see that the literals that define the columns in the table band are printed once at the top of each page of the report. If you want, you can change the default setting so that the column titles are printed at the top of each group. To do this, issue the [Menu] Setting Format command. Paradox then will display a menu that offers two options: TableOfGroups and GroupsOfTables. The default setting, TableOfGroups, prints the literals that define the columns in the table band once at the top of each page of the report. The GroupsOfTables option causes Paradox to print the column titles one time for each group.

Figure 11-35 shows an example of a report created with the GroupsOfTables option. Notice that the literals that define the columns in the table band are now printed at the top of each group.

Figure 11-34 The Printed Report

```
11/24/88          Listings By Style And Bedrooms          Page   1


Address               Town         Owner       List Date  Style     Price          Sq Ft    BRs    Baths
--------------------  -----------  ----------  ---------  --------  -------------   ------   -----  ------
Style: Cape Cod
#82 Rudd Rd.          Louisville   Lum,I        8/30/88   Cape Cod      88,950.00   2800      4      2
2216 Lacey St.        North Hill   Beat,A      11/13/88                 94,999.00   2700      4      3
363 Dower Ct.         North Fork   Culp,A       7/05/88                109,000.00   2100      4      2
3752 St. Dennis       J'Town       Levine,J    11/03/88                 67,950.00   2500      3      2
4233 Mix Ave.         Louisville   Martin,D    11/30/88                 49,500.00   1900      3      2
4444 Normie Ln.       Louisville   James,J      8/25/88                120,000.00   2400      5      3
4989 Adler Way        Louisville   Dole,V       9/13/88                 76,500.00   2000      3      2
5678 Beech St.        Louisville   Smith,P      9/16/88                 65,950.00   1800      3      2
589 Morocco Dr.       E'Town       Smith,B      6/24/88                 62,500.00   1875      3      2
654 Nora Ln.          Louisville   Orwick,S    10/02/88                 40,000.00   1600      3      1
666 Montana Ave.      Louisville   Saul,H       6/23/88                 55,000.00   1900      3      1
6935 Shiloh Dr.       E'Town       Grebe,C      9/08/88                 81,000.00   2000      3      2
913 Whitney Dr.       North Hill   Kulp,R       7/04/88                 99,500.00   1800      4      2
987 Allan Dr.         Louisville   Newsome,K    6/26/88                 60,000.00   1900      4      2
99 Cardinal Hill Rd.  North Hill   Brand,B      8/19/88                 70,000.00   2000      3      2
Average Price:     76,056.60
Style: Colonial
22 N. Ridge Ct.       Louisville   Nunn,A       9/29/88   Colonial     200,000.00   2900      5      3
3498 Bold Rd.         Louisville   Taft,H       8/29/88                275,000.00   3800      5      4
4500 Hempstead Dr.    Louisville   Pape,C       6/18/88                150,000.00   2600      4      3
586 Ansa Way          Louisville   Noel,C      11/27/88                 69,500.00   2200      4      2
620 Windsong Ct.      Louisville   Pank,E       7/06/88                250,000.00   4000      6      4
766 Baird St.         Louisville   Black,G      6/22/88                139,950.00   2600      4      3
Average Price:    180,741.67
Style: Other
#12 Circle Ct.        Louisville   White,Y      8/02/88   Other         10,000.00    800      2      1
#5 Ashby St.          J'Town       Wagner,H    10/22/88                 97,000.00   2500      4      3
1001 Spring St.       North Hill   Frier,F      9/05/88                 45,000.00   1700      3      2
185 Pages Ln.         J'Town       Cowan,M     11/01/88                 15,500.00   1000      2      1
198 Main St.          J'Town       Green,L      6/29/88                 27,500.00    800      3      1
222 Big Ben Dr.       Louisville   Roberts,D    6/22/88                 53,500.00   1900      3      2
28 Seebolt Rt.        Louisville   Priest,S    11/10/88                 28,500.00    950      3      1
5432 Miller Rd.       Louisville   Young,R      7/29/88                 17,500.00    800      2      1
854 Unseld Blvd.      Louisville   Volk,H      10/19/88                 87,000.00   2500      3      2
Average Price:     42,388.89
Style: Ranch
#10 Old Mill Rd.      Louisville   Stern,M      8/21/88   Ranch         75,000.00   2150      3      2
#6 Brandon Way        Louisville   Abrams,L     7/22/88                 67,000.00   2250      4      2
#62 Billy Bone Ct.    Louisville   Taylor,A     9/18/88                 34,500.00   1600      3      1
1222 Dee Rd.          South Fork   Smith,P      8/02/88                 22,950.00    950      3      1
123 Abby Ct.          Louisville   Kones,D      6/16/88                 32,950.00   1500      3      1
14 Short Rd.          Louisville   Quire,I     10/13/88                 52,300.00   1600      3      1
1989 Eastern Pkwy.    Louisville   Klink,C     10/23/88                 26,950.00   1100      2      1
222 Earl Ave.         J'Town       Wray,A       8/05/88                 51,000.00   1200      3      1
3323 Mt. Holly Dr.    Louisville   Grizz,D      9/24/88                 22,100.00   1200      3      1
3355 Bank St.         J'Town       Cobb,D       8/17/88                 37,500.00   1500      3      1
343 Market St.        Louisville   Bivins,D     6/29/88                 42,900.00   1675      3      1
426 St. James Ct.     Louisville   Jones,S      6/19/88                 19,500.00    950      2      1
435 Oxted Ln.         Louisville   O'Neal,P     9/26/88                 53,790.00   1900      3      1
5372 Tyson Pl.        Louisville   Goode,J     10/28/88                 35,000.00   1500      3      1
```

Figure 11-35 The GroupsOfTables Format

```
11/22/88          Listings By Style          Page   1


Address               Town         Owner       List Date  Style     Price          Sq Ft    BRs    Baths
--------------------  -----------  ----------  ---------  --------  -------------   ------   -----  ------
#82 Rudd Rd.          Louisville   Lum,I        8/30/88   Cape Cod      88,950.00   2800      4      2
2216 Lacey St.        North Hill   Beat,A      11/13/88   Cape Cod      94,999.00   2700      4      3
363 Dower Ct.         North Fork   Culp,A       7/05/88   Cape Cod     109,000.00   2100      4      2
3752 St. Dennis       J'Town       Levine,J    11/03/88   Cape Cod      67,950.00   2500      3      2
4233 Mix Ave.         Louisville   Martin,D    11/30/88   Cape Cod      49,500.00   1900      3      2
4444 Normie Ln.       Louisville   James,J      8/25/88   Cape Cod     120,000.00   2400      5      3
4989 Adler Way        Louisville   Dole,V       9/13/88   Cape Cod      76,500.00   2000      3      2
5678 Beech St.        Louisville   Smith,P      9/16/88   Cape Cod      65,950.00   1800      3      2
589 Morocco Dr.       E'Town       Smith,B      6/24/88   Cape Cod      62,500.00   1875      3      2
654 Nora Ln.          Louisville   Orwick,S    10/02/88   Cape Cod      40,000.00   1600      3      1
666 Montana Ave.      Louisville   Saul,H       6/23/88   Cape Cod      55,000.00   1900      3      1
6935 Shiloh Dr.       E'Town       Grebe,C      9/08/88   Cape Cod      81,000.00   2000      3      2
913 Whitney Dr.       North Hill   Kulp,R       7/04/88   Cape Cod      99,500.00   1800      4      2
987 Allan Dr.         Louisville   Newsome,K    6/26/88   Cape Cod      60,000.00   1900      4      2
99 Cardinal Hill Rd.  North Hill   Brand,B      8/19/88   Cape Cod      70,000.00   2000      3      2

Address               Town         Owner       List Date  Style     Price          Sq Ft    BRs    Baths
--------------------  -----------  ----------  ---------  --------  -------------   ------   -----  ------
22 N. Ridge Ct.       Louisville   Nunn,A       9/29/88   Colonial     200,000.00   2900      5      3
3498 Bold Rd.         Louisville   Taft,H       8/29/88   Colonial     275,000.00   3800      5      4
4500 Hempstead Dr.    Louisville   Pape,C       6/18/88   Colonial     150,000.00   2600      4      3
586 Ansa Way          Louisville   Noel,C      11/27/88   Colonial      69,500.00   2200      4      2
620 Windsong Ct.      Louisville   Pank,E       7/06/88   Colonial     250,000.00   4000      6      4
766 Baird St.         Louisville   Black,G      6/22/88   Colonial     139,950.00   2600      4      3

Address               Town         Owner       List Date  Style     Price          Sq Ft    BRs    Baths
--------------------  -----------  ----------  ---------  --------  -------------   ------   -----  ------
#12 Circle Ct.        Louisville   White,Y      8/02/88   Other         10,000.00    800      2      1
#5 Ashby St.          J'Town       Wagner,H    10/22/88   Other         97,000.00   2500      4      3
1001 Spring St.       North Hill   Frier,F      9/05/88   Other         45,000.00   1700      3      2
185 Pages Ln.         J'Town       Cowan,M     11/01/88   Other         15,500.00   1000      2      1
198 Main St.          J'Town       Green,L      6/29/88   Other         27,500.00    800      3      1
222 Big Ben Dr.       Louisville   Roberts,D    6/22/88   Other         53,500.00   1900      3      2
28 Seebolt Rt.        Louisville   Priest,S    11/10/88   Other         28,500.00    950      3      1
5432 Miller Rd.       Louisville   Young,R      7/29/88   Other         17,500.00    800      2      1
854 Unseld Blvd.      Louisville   Volk,H      10/19/88   Other         87,000.00   2500      3      2

Address               Town         Owner       List Date  Style     Price          Sq Ft    BRs    Baths
--------------------  -----------  ----------  ---------  --------  -------------   ------   -----  ------
#10 Old Mill Rd.      Louisville   Stern,M      8/21/88   Ranch         75,000.00   2150      3      2
#6 Brandon Way        Louisville   Abrams,L     7/22/88   Ranch         67,000.00   2250      4      2
#62 Billy Bone Ct.    Louisville   Taylor,A     9/18/88   Ranch         34,500.00   1600      3      1
1222 Dee Rd.          South Fork   Smith,P      8/02/88   Ranch         22,950.00    950      3      1
123 Abby Ct.          Louisville   Kones,D      6/16/88   Ranch         32,950.00   1500      3      1
14 Short Rd.          Louisville   Quire,I     10/13/88   Ranch         52,300.00   1600      3      1
1989 Eastern Pkwy.    Louisville   Klink,C     10/23/88   Ranch         26,950.00   1100      2      1
222 Earl Ave.         J'Town       Wray,A       8/05/88   Ranch         51,000.00   1200      3      1
3323 Mt. Holly Dr.    Louisville   Grizz,D      9/24/88   Ranch         22,100.00   1200      3      1
3355 Bank St.         J'Town       Cobb,D       8/17/88   Ranch         37,500.00   1500      3      1
343 Market St.        Louisville   Bivins,D     6/29/88   Ranch         42,900.00   1675      3      1
426 St. James Ct.     Louisville   Jones,S      6/19/88   Ranch         19,500.00    950      3      1
```

The PAGEBREAK Keyword

In most cases, Paradox will move to the bottom of the page and print the contents of the page footer only after it has printed as many records as it can fit on a page. You can use the keyword PAGEBREAK to jump Paradox to the bottom of a page prematurely. This keyword must be typed in all capital letters at the left edge of the report spec, and it must be on a line by itself.

When Paradox encounters this keyword in a report spec, it will jump immediately to the end of the current page, where it will print the contents of the page footer (if any). It will begin printing the report at the top of the next page. If you have placed the PAGEBREAK keyword in a group footer, Paradox will begin the next page with the first record in the next group.

Groups and Record Number Fields

As you may recall from Chapter 10, when you place a record number field in a report specification, Paradox offers two options: Overall and PerGroup. The option you choose determines how the records in the report will be numbered. The Overall command tells Paradox to number the records consecutively from the beginning of the report. The PerGroup command tells Paradox to number the records within each group, starting with 1 at the beginning of each group.

If you place a record number field in a report as an Overall field, there is no way to change it to a PerGroup field. If you want to change an Overall record number field into a PerGroup record number field, you must delete and then replace the record number field.

The Regroup Command

The [Menu] Group Regroup command allows you to redefine a group you have already defined. This command allows you to change everything about a group—including its type and the field it groups—except the position of the group relative to other groups in the report. To redefine a group, you just issue the [Menu] Group Regroup command. Paradox then will prompt you to place the cursor on the group you want to regroup. When you see this prompt, move the cursor to the group header or group footer of the group band you want to change and press ↵. After you do this, Paradox will display the Group menu. From this point, redefining the group is exactly like inserting a new group.

Deleting Groups

Deleting a group from a report is as easy as issuing the [Menu] Group Delete command. After you issue the command, Paradox will prompt you to place the cursor on the group you want to delete. When you see this prompt, move the cursor to the group header or group footer of the group to be deleted and press ↵. After you select the group you want to delete, Paradox will prompt you to confirm the deletion by displaying a Cancel/OK menu. If you select Cancel from the menu, Paradox will return to the previous menu so that you can make another selection. If you select OK, Paradox will delete the group from the report.

Once you delete a group, the only way to replace it is to issue the [Menu] Group Insert command and start from scratch.

Grouping Free-form Reports

As you might expect, Paradox allows you to create groups in your free-form reports. While you will probably find more uses for groups in tabular reports, groups can also be valuable in free-form reports.

For example, you could use a group to force Paradox to print the mailing label report you created in Chapter 10 for the NAMES table in zip code order. To do this, first issue the **[Menu] R**eport Change command, specify **NAMES** as the table with which you want to work, and select the report number under which you saved the mailing label report. (If you followed the example, this report will be saved under number **1.**)

When the report spec comes into view, issue the **[Menu] G**roup Insert Field command, select the **Z**ip field, and place the group in the page band. When you have placed the group, your screen will look like Figure 11-36.

Figure 11-36 Grouping the Mailing Labels

```
Changing report R1 for Names table                    Report    1/1
Page Header
....+...10....+...20....+...30....+...40....+...50....+...60....+...70....+...8*
—▼page
———▼group Zip

—▼form

AAAAAAAAAAAAAAA AAAAAAAAAAAAAAA
AAAAAAAAAAAAAAAAAAA
AAAAAAAAAAAAAAAAAAA
AAAAAAAAAAAAAAA, AA   AAAAA


—▲form
———▲group Zip
—▲page
```

As in tabular reports, when you insert a group in a free-form report, Paradox automatically inserts a group header and a group footer around each group. Since this can affect the spacing in the printed report, you may want to eliminate these lines before you print the report. To remove the group header, just move the cursor to the blank line at the top of the group Zip band and press **[Report Delete Line]** ([Ctrl]-[Y]). Then, move the cursor to the blank group footer and press **[Report Delete Line]** again. Figure 11-37 shows the report spec without the group header and footer. When you print the report, Paradox will print the mailing labels in zip code order.

Figure 11-37 Grouping the Mailing Labels

```
Changing report R1 for Names table                    Report   1/1
Group Footer for Zip
....+...18....+...28....+...38....+...48....+...58....+...68....+...78....+...8*
-▼page────────────────────────────────────────────────────────────────────
────▼group Zip─────────────────────────────────────────────────────────────
-▼form──────────────────────────────────────────────────────────────────


AAAAAAAAAAAAAAAA AAAAAAAAAAAAAAAA
AAAAAAAAAAAAAAAAAAAAAAAA
AAAAAAAAAAAAAAAAAAAAAAAA
AAAAAAAAAAAAAAA,  AA   AAAAA



-▲form──────────────────────────────────────────────────────────────────
────▲group Zip─────────────────────────────────────────────────────────────
-▲page──────────────────────────────────────────────────────────────────
```

As with tabular reports, you can insert up to 16 groups in a free-form report. Each group you create adds another level of grouping to the report.

If you want, you can place literal text, regular fields, and summary fields in the group header and group footer of a free-form report. However, you are far more likely to use the group header and group footer this way in tabular reports.

Multitable Reports

With Release 3, Borland added a new dimension to Paradox's Report Generator—multitable reporting capabilities. The [Menu] Field Lookup command in Paradox 3 lets you link records in the table on which the report is based, the master table, to records in other tables, which serve as lookup tables. As a result, you can include data from one or more lookup tables in a report based on the master table.

In earlier releases of Paradox, you must use a query to join the data in the master and lookup tables in an ANSWER table, and then design your report spec for the ANSWER table. We discussed this query technique in Chapter 8, "Query by Example."

The Field Lookup Menu

When you issue the [Menu] Field Lookup command, Paradox displays the menu shown in Figure 11-38. As you can see, this menu has three options: Link, Unlink, and Relink. The Link option lets you establish a link between the master table and a new lookup table, and the Unlink option lets you remove an existing link. The Relink option lets you redefine an existing link between the master table and a lookup table. After discussing each of these menu options, we'll explain how to add fields from lookup tables to a report spec.

Figure 11-38 The Field Lookup Menu

```
Link  Unlink  Relink                                   Report   1/2
Link an external table to this report.
....+...18....+...28....+...38....+...48....+...58....+...68....+...78....+...8*
```

Linking Lookup Tables

If you choose the Link option on the Field Lookup menu, Paradox will prompt you for the name of the new lookup table. After you enter the name of the table, Paradox will display a menu listing all the fields in the master table and ask you to select one field to be linked to each key field in the lookup table.

After you've defined a link, you can use any field from the lookup table in a regular, calculated, or summary field anywhere in the report spec. You can even group on lookup field values and use the lookup fields in group headers and group footers. Paradox draws values for lookup fields from the record in the lookup table that has the same value(s) in its key field(s) that the current record of the master table contains in its corresponding linking field(s). If no record in the lookup table matches the linking field values in a record of the master table, Paradox will simply display nothing where lookup values for that master record should appear in the report.

An Example

To demonstrate how you can link lookup tables to a master table's report spec, we'll link the LISTINGS table to a single lookup table called SELLERS. Figure 11-39 shows the structure of the SELLERS table. As you can see, the first field in the SELLERS table, called Seller Code, is an A5 type key field. We will use the contents of the Seller Code field to link the SELLERS table to the LISTINGS table. Figure 11-40 shows the SELLERS table, which lists the names, phone numbers, and commission rates for the real estate agents selling the houses in the LISTINGS table.

Figure 11-39 The structure of SELLERS

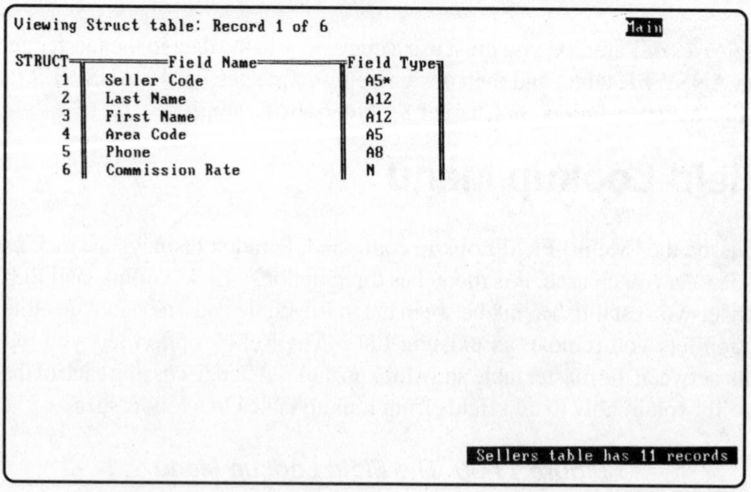

```
Viewing Struct table: Record 1 of 6                        Main

STRUCT         Field Name         Field Type
    1  │ Seller Code       │ A5*
    2  │ Last Name         │ A12
    3  │ First Name        │ A12
    4  │ Area Code         │ A5
    5  │ Phone             │ A8
    6  │ Commission Rate   │ N




                                        Sellers table has 11 records
```

Figure 11-40 The SELLERS table

Viewing Sellers table: Record 1 of 11

SELLERS	Seller Code	Last Name	First Name	Area Code	Phone	Commission Rate
1	BT01	Taylor	Barbara	(812)	233-3301	2.5
2	EB10	Brady	Edward	(502)	529-2310	2.5
3	FN89	Nelson	Frank	(812)	363-0689	3
4	HS75	Smith	Howard	(502)	233-4275	2.5
5	HW06	Walker	Henry	(502)	998-3486	3
6	JM92	McGuire	James	(502)	223-8792	3
7	MJ00	Jones	Margaret	(502)	585-2500	2.5
8	RH73	Harris	Robert	(502)	222-9173	3.5
9	SA08	Andersen	Susan	(502)	925-3608	3
10	TC56	Carpenter	Thomas	(502)	423-7756	2.5
11	WR06	Rogers	William	(502)	645-6606	3

Main

Before you can link the two tables, you need to add a field to the LISTINGS table that will match the Seller Code field of the SELLERS table. This new field will hold the code for the agent who is handling the sale of each house in the table. As we explained in Chapter 5, you can use the [Menu] Modify Restructure command to insert a field into the structure of a LISTINGS table. Since the new field corresponds to the Seller Code field in the SELLERS table, it should be the same field type (A5) as the Seller Code field. To make the relationship between the two fields more apparent, we'll also give the new field the same name as its corresponding field in the SELLERS table. Figure 11-41 shows the LISTINGS table after we inserted the Seller Code field as the fourth field in the table and entered data into the new field. As you can see, each entry in the Seller Code field of the LISTINGS table refers to one of the Seller Code entries in the SELLERS table.

Now, you're ready to design a report that links SELLERS as a lookup table for LISTINGS. First, issue the **[Menu] R**eport **D**esign command and select the LISTINGS table. When Paradox asks you to choose a report specification, select report number **11**, and type **Listings By Seller** as the title for the report. When Paradox prompts you for a report type, select **T**abular. At this point, the default report spec shown in Figure 11-42 will appear on the screen.

Figure 11-42 The Default Report Spec

```
Designing report R11 for Listings table                    Report    1/2
Report Header
....+...10....+...20....+...30....+...40....+...50....+...60....+...70....+...8*
 ─▼page──────────────────────────────────────────────────────────────────


mm/dd/yy                        Listings By Seller                    Page 999

 ┌▼table──────────────────────────────────────────────────────────────────

Address                 Town       Owner       Seller Code  List Date  Style
─────────────────       ──────     ──────      ───────────  ─────────  ─────
AAAAAAAAAAAAAAAAAAAA    AAAAAAAAAA AAAAAAAAAA  AAAAA        mm/dd/yy   AAAAAAAAAA
 └▲table──────────────────────────────────────────────────────────────────



 ─▲page──────────────────────────────────────────────────────────────────
═══════════════════════════════════════════════════════════════════════════
═══════════════════════════════════════════════════════════════════════════
```

Figure 11-41 The Modified LISTINGS Table

```
Viewing Listings table: Record 1 of 65                        Main

LISTINGS======Address======    =Town=      =Owner=    =Seller Code=List=
     1    123 Abby Ct.          Louisville  Kones,D     BT01      6/16
     2    426 St. James Ct.     Louisville  Jones,S     HS75      6/19
     3    766 Baird St.         Louisville  Black,G     JM92      6/22
     4    222 Big Ben Dr.       Louisville  Roberts,D   MJ00      6/22
     5    666 Montana Ave.      Louisville  Saul,H      TC56      6/23
     6    589 Morocco Dr.       E'Town      Smith,B     WR06      6/24
     7    987 Allan Dr.         Louisville  Newsome,K   EB10      6/26
     8    549 Billtown Rd.      Louisville  Bizer,B     WR06      6/28
     9    343 Market St.        Louisville  Bivins,D    HW86      6/29
    10    198 Main St.          J'Town      Green,L     JM92      6/29
    11    885 Jefferson St.     J'Town      Zith,M      HS75      7/02
    12    913 Whitney Dr.       North Hill  Kulp,R      EB10      7/04
    13    363 Dower Ct.         North Fork  Culp,A      MJ00      7/05
    14    620 Windsong Ct.      Louisville  Pank,E      SA08      7/06
    15    4500 Hempstead Dr.    Louisville  Pape,C      FN89      6/18
    16    #6 Brandon Way        Louisville  Abrams,L    HS75      7/22
    17    6610 Vermin Dr.       Louisville  Russ,J      WR06      7/24
    18    712 Clifton Ct.       Louisville  Thomas,T    HS75      7/24
    19    5432 Miller Rd.       Louisville  Young,R     RH73      7/29
    20    #12 Circle Ct.        Louisville  White,Y     HW86      8/02
    21    1222 Dee Rd.          South Fork  Smith,P     SA08      8/02
    22    222 Earl Ave.         J'Town      Wray,A      JM92      8/05
    23    9827 Rowan St.        J'Town      Coad,B      SA08      8/10
    24    3355 Bank St.         J'Town      Cobb,D      WR06      8/17
    25    77 Portland Ave.      North Hill  Coe,A       HS75      8/19
    26    99 Cardinal Hill Rd.  North Hill  Brand,B     EB10      8/19
    27    #10 Old Mill Rd.      Louisville  Stern,M     BT01      8/21
    28    5532 Mud Creek Dr.    Louisville  Hall,W      BT01      8/24
    29    4444 Normie Ln.       Louisville  James,J     SA08      8/25
    30    3498 Bold Rd.         Louisville  Taft,H      WR06      8/29
    31    #82 Rudd Rd.          Louisville  Lum,I       TC56      8/30
    32    6712 Shelby St.       Louisville  Wood,B      FN89      8/30
    33    7235 Shiloh Dr.       E'Town      Allan,J     SA08      8/31
    34    8989 Big D Ln.        South Fork  Adkins,G    MJ00      9/01
    35    1001 Spring St.       North Hill  Frier,F     HS75      9/05
    36    6935 Shiloh Dr.       E'Town      Grebe,C     BT01      9/08
    37    4989 Adler Way        Louisville  Dole,V      FN89      9/13
    38    5678 Beech St.        Louisville  Smith,P     HW86      9/16
    39    #62 Billy Bone Ct.    Louisville  Taylor,A    RH73      9/18
    40    3323 Mt. Holly Dr.    Louisville  Grizz,D     SA08      9/24
    41    9909 Midway Rd.       Louisville  Maier,O     EB10      9/25
    42    435 Oxted Ln.         Louisville  O'Neal,P    HS75      9/26
    43    22 N. Ridge Ct.       Louisville  Nunn,A      MJ00      9/29
    44    654 Nora Ln.          Louisville  Orwick,S    SA08     10/02
    45    659 Ridge Rd.         Louisville  Pulley,F    WR06     10/08
    46    14 Short Rd.          Louisville  Quire,I     JM92     10/13
    47    721 Zabel Way         Louisville  Stich,L     MJ00     10/14
    48    581 Yale Dr.          Louisville  Winer,L     HS75     10/17
    49    854 Unseld Blvd.      Louisville  Volk,H      MJ00     10/19
    50    #5 Ashby St.          J'Town      Wagner,H    BT01     10/22
    51    1989 Eastern Pkwy.    Louisville  Klink,C     SA08     10/23
    52    9819 Wilson Ave.      J'Town      Crane,B     TC56     10/23
    53    956 Volar Ln.         J'Town      Lamb,M      EB10     10/25
    54    5372 Tyson Pl.        Louisville  Goode,J     BT01     10/28
    55    9849 Taylor Blvd.     J'Town      Dukes,J     HW86     10/29
    56    185 Pages Ln.         J'Town      Cowan,M     SA08     11/01
    57    3752 St. Dennis       J'Town      Levine,J    FN89     11/03
    58    28 Seebolt Rt.        Louisville  Priest,S    HW86     11/10
    59    2216 Lacey St.        North Hill  Beat,A      SA08     11/13
    60    6262 Kenwood Dr.      North Hill  Beck,U      WR06     11/17
    61    9222 Meadow Pl.       South Fork  Baxter,H    EB10     11/22
    62    6791 Lotus Ave.       South Fork  Howell,T    HS75     11/24
    63    586 Ansa Way          Louisville  Noel,C      FN89     11/27
    64    99 N. Central Blvd.   Louisville  Stevens,P   RH73     11/28
    65    4233 Mix Ave.         Louisville  Martin,D    WR06     11/30
```

To link the SELLERS table as a lookup table, issue the **[Menu]** Field Lookup Link command and type **SELLERS** at the *Table:* prompt. Next, Paradox will present a menu listing all the fields in the LISTINGS table and ask you to select the field that should be linked to the Seller Code field, the only key field in the SELLERS table. Figure 11-43 shows the field name menu. To link the Seller Code field in LISTINGS to the Seller Code field in SELLERS, point to the Seller Code menu selection and press ↵.

Figure 11-43 Selecting a Linking Field

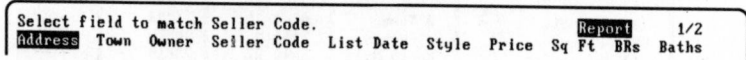

After you have linked the Seller Code field in the LISTINGS table to the Seller Code field in the SELLERS table, Paradox will link all records in the master table that have the value *BT01* in the Seller Code field to the record in the SELLERS table that contains *BT01* in its Seller Code field. Of course, only one record in the SELLERS table contains this Seller Code value because the Seller Code field is a key field.

Linking to a Table with Multiple Key Fields

As we explained in Chapter 3, tables that have more than one key field can contain duplicate values in one of the key fields but cannot include two records that have the same combination of values in all the key fields. As a result, if you're using a table with more than one key field as the lookup table in a multitable report, you must specify a linking field for each key field in the lookup table. In links based on multiple key fields, Paradox links records in the master table to a record in the lookup table based on the combination of the entries in the linking fields.

Unlinking Lookup Tables

If you choose the Unlink option from the Field Lookup menu, Paradox will present a menu of the lookup tables currently linked to the master table, asking you to select the table you want to unlink. After you choose a table, Paradox will confirm that you want to unlink that table by presenting a menu with two options: No and Yes. If you choose Yes, then Paradox will delete from the report spec all of the fields that refer to the lookup table, including calculated and summary fields. Also, Paradox will remove from the report spec any groups based on fields from the lookup table.

For example, to remove the link between the LISTINGS table and the SELLERS table that we established in the last example, you would issue the command [Menu] Field Lookup Unlink. Paradox would then present a menu like the one shown in Figure 11-44. As you can see, this menu includes only one table because the SELLERS table is the only table currently linked to the LISTINGS table. To unlink these tables, you would press ↵ to select SELLERS, then select Yes from the verification menu. After you selected Yes, Paradox would remove all fields and groups based on entries in the SELLERS table from the report spec.

Figure 11-44 Selecting a Table to Unlink

```
Select table to unlink.                          Report      1/1
[Sellers->]
```

Relinking Lookup Tables

The Relink option provides a handy way to change the linking field(s) in the master table without losing the entire report spec. If you choose the Relink option from the Field Lookup menu, Paradox will present a list of tables currently linked to the master table, asking you to select the table that you want to relink. After you choose a table, Paradox will ask you to select a field from the master table to be linked to each key field in that lookup table, just as it did when you linked the table originally.

For instance, suppose you mistakenly linked the Address field of the LISTINGS table to the Seller Code field in the SELLERS table and then designed an extensive report spec using fields from both tables. If you tried to print the report, the table band in the report would include the wrong data from the SELLERS table because the two tables would not be linked correctly. In this case, you could use the Relink option to change the linking field in the LISTINGS table from the Address field to the Seller Code field without creating an entirely new report spec.

First of all, you would issue the [Menu] Field Lookup Relink command. Paradox would then display a menu of the lookup tables that are currently linked to the master table. In this case, the menu would include only the SELLERS table, as shown in Figure 11-45. To relink the SELLERS table, you would press ↵. Next, Paradox would present a menu of the fields in the LISTINGS table like the one shown in Figure 11-43, and ask you to select a field to link to the Seller Code field of the SELLERS table. By pointing to the Seller Code field and pressing ↵, you would remove the incorrect link between the LISTINGS and SELLERS tables and set up a new link based on the entries in the Seller Code field in each table.

Figure 11-45 Selecting a Table to Relink

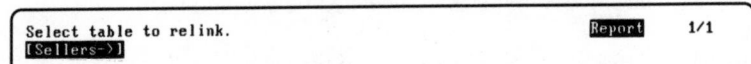

```
Select table to relink.                          Report      1/1
[Sellers->]
```

Using Lookup Fields

Using entries from a lookup table in a report spec is as easy as using entries from the master table itself. While designing the report spec, you can place a lookup field as a regular field, include a lookup field as an element in a calculated field, or use a summary field to display summary statistics based on a lookup field.

Regular Fields

When you link a lookup table in a report spec, Paradox automatically adds the name of the lookup table to the menu of field names that the Report Generator displays when you issue the [Menu] Field Place Regular command. The names of the lookup tables that are currently linked to the master table appear at the end of the menu, with each lookup table name enclosed in brackets. For example, after you have linked SELLERS as a lookup table for LISTINGS, Paradox will display a menu like the one shown in Figure 11-46 when you issue the [Menu] Field Place Regular command and press ← to highlight the last menu item. The arrow that follows the table name within the brackets indicates that this menu selection will move you into the SELLERS table. If you select the [Sellers->] option from the menu, Paradox will display another menu that lists the fields in the SELLERS table, as shown in Figure 11-47. Then, you can select one of these fields and place it just as you would place a field from the master table.

Figure 11-46 A Lookup Table on the Field Name Menu

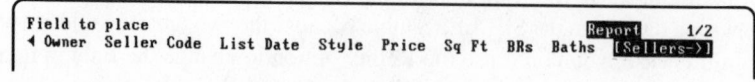

Figure 11-47 The Field Name Menu for SELLERS

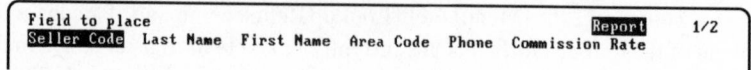

Calculated Fields

You can use a field from a lookup table as an element in a calculated field simply by including the name of the lookup table and a pointer in the field name when you type it in the expression that defines the calculated field. For example, suppose you want to add a calculated field to the *Listings By Seller* report that computes the seller's commission for each house in the LISTINGS table. The expression for this calculated field would be

[Price] *([Sellers->Commission Rate]/100)

This expression divides the value in the Commission Rate field of the SELLERS table by 100 to change the percentage to a decimal value, and then multiplies the decimal value by the entry in the Price field of the LISTINGS table. To define this calculated field, issue the **[Menu] Field Place Calculated** command, type **[Price]*([Sellers->Commission Rate]/100)** at the *Expression:* prompt, and press ↵. (After you define the expression, you will have to place the field and set the number of digits and decimals.)

Summary Fields

In addition to regular and calculated fields that display entries from a lookup table, a report spec can also include summary fields based on data in a lookup table. As we explained earlier in this chapter, summary fields compute and display statistics based on the entries in a table. These statistics can summarize the values in regular fields or the results of expressions defined in calculated fields. By adapting the procedures for placing lookup table entries in regular and calculated fields, you can also use data from lookup tables in both types of summary fields.

Regular Summary Fields

To add a regular summary field based on a lookup field, issue the [Menu] Field Place Summary Regular command, just as you would to place a summary field based on a field in the master table. When Paradox asks you to pick the field on which the summary field should be based, select the name of the lookup table from the menu. Then, select the name of the desired field from the menu of fields in the lookup table. After selecting a field name, specify the PerGroup/Overall option, place the field, and define the number of digits and decimal places Paradox should display in the field.

Calculated Summary Fields

If you want to add a calculated summary field based on data in a lookup table, issue the [Menu] Field Place Summary Calculated command. When Paradox asks you to define the expression on which the summary field should be based, use the syntax for lookup fields that we explained earlier in this section. For example, suppose you want to place a summary field that displays the average commission earned by the sellers for all of the houses in the LISTINGS table. To do this, first type **[Price]*([Sellers->Commission Rate]/100)** as the expression to be summarized. After entering this expression, select Average from the menu of summary types, choose Overall from the PerGroup/Overall menu, then place the calculated field and define the number of digits and decimal places.

Grouping on Lookup Fields

Paradox also lets you group the records in a report based on values in a lookup field. Using the Field option of the [Menu] Group Insert command, you can divide the master table into groups of records that all have the same value in a specified field in the lookup table. Using the Range option of the [Menu] Group Insert command, you can divide the master table into groups of records with entries in a specified lookup field that fall in a defined range of values. Grouping on a lookup field involves only one more step than the procedures for grouping on a regular field, which we explained earlier in this chapter. When Paradox asks you for the name of the field on which the records should be grouped, you must select the name of the lookup table from the menu of field names, then select the grouping field from the list of fields in the lookup table.

Once you have inserted a group based on a lookup table, use the options on the Group menu to manipulate the group in any of the ways that we explained earlier in this chapter. For example, you can use the [Menu] Group SortDirection command to change the order of the sort within the group, and you can use the [Menu] Group Headings command to specify whether the group heading should repeat if the group is broken between pages. You can also use the [Menu] Group Delete command to remove the group from the report spec.

Managing Reports

As you begin to design more and more reports, you will need to know how to manage those reports. For example, you will want to make copies of reports, rename reports, and delete obsolete reports. In this part of the chapter, we'll show you how to use the commands on the Tools menu to manage your reports. Since the commands you use to copy, rename, and delete reports are nearly identical to the commands you used to manage tables and forms, we'll cover them only briefly here.

Copying Reports

You can use the [Menu] Tools Copy command to make copies of your reports. Paradox 1.0, 1.1, and 2 allow you to copy reports only within the family of an individual table, but Paradox 3 lets you copy reports between families of tables that have identical structures. The ability to copy reports is most handy when you want to use a completed report as the basis for another report with a similar design.

For example, suppose you want to copy report 1 for the NAMES table to report 4 of a table called KYNAMES, which has the same structure as NAMES. To do this, issue the **[Menu] Tools Copy Report DifferentTable** command, type **NAMES** at the *Source Table:* prompt, and press ↵. When Paradox displays the menu of report numbers for the NAMES table, select **1** and press ↵. When Paradox asks you for the name of the target table, type **KYNAMES** and press ↵. When Paradox asks you to choose a report number for the copy, select **4**. After you choose the report number, Paradox will make the copy and return you to the Main menu.

If you try to copy a report to a target table that does not have the same structure as the source table, Paradox will not accept the name of the target table. Instead, Paradox will leave the *Target Table:* prompt on the screen and display the message *SOURCE and TARGET do not have the same field names or field types*, substituting the actual table names for *SOURCE* and *TARGET*.

Now, suppose you want to copy report 1 for the NAMES table to report 5 of the same table. To do this, issue the **[Menu] Tools Copy Report SameTable** command, type **NAMES**, and press ↵. When Paradox displays the menu of report numbers for the NAMES table, select **1**, and press ↵. Then, when Paradox prompts you to choose a report number for the copy, choose **5** and press ↵. After you assign a report number to the copy, Paradox will make the copy and return you to the Main menu.

You will notice that when you copy a report within the family of objects for a table, the number of the report you are copying is not on the list of available destinations. This prevents you from assigning the same number to the original and the copy.

Whether you are copying a report within the same family or to a different table, if you select a report number for the copy that is the same as an existing report, Paradox will display a Cancel/Replace menu at the top of the screen. If you select Replace, Paradox will replace the existing report with the copy. If you assign the name R to the copy and then select Replace from the Cancel/Replace menu, Paradox will replace the default report with the copy.

Renaming Reports

When you issue the [Menu] Tools Copy Report command in versions of Paradox earlier than Release 3, Paradox will not display the SameTable/DifferentTable menu. Instead, Paradox will ask you for the name of a table, the number of a source report, and the number of a target report—as if you had selected the SameTable option in Paradox 3. If you want to copy a report from one table to another in earlier releases of Paradox, you must copy the entire family of the source table by using the [Menu] Tools Copy JustFamily command that we discussed in Chapter 6, "Sorting Your Tables."

You can use the [Menu] Tools Rename Report command to rename reports. For example, suppose you design a new report for the NAMES table and assign it the number 2. Now, suppose you want to rename the report (assign it a new report number). To do this, issue the **[Menu] T**ools **R**ename **R**eport command, type **NAMES**, and press ↵. Paradox then will display a menu of the existing reports for NAMES. When you see this menu, you should select the report number you want to rename (**2**). Next, Paradox will display the Report Number menu from which you can choose a new name. When you see this menu, enter the new number for the report (we'll use **6**). After you do this, Paradox will rename the report.

If you select as the new name a report number that is already assigned to an existing report, Paradox will display a Cancel/Replace menu at the top of the screen. If you select Replace from this menu, Paradox will replace the existing report with the renamed report. If you assign the name R to the report and then select Replace from the Cancel/Replace menu, Paradox will replace the default report with the renamed report.

Deleting Reports

You can use the [Menu] Tools Delete Report command to delete reports. Suppose you design report 1 for the NAMES table, and that report subsequently becomes obsolete. To delete the report, issue the **[Menu] T**ools **D**elete **R**eport command, type **NAMES**, and press ↵. After you do this, Paradox will display a menu of the existing reports for NAMES. When you see this menu, select the report number you want to delete (in this case, **1**.) Once you select a report, Paradox will delete it and return to the main workspace.

You should exercise caution when you issue the [Menu] Tools Delete command. Once an object is deleted, there is no way to recover it.

Changing the Report Default Settings

As you have seen, Paradox has default values for many of the Report Generator settings, such as the page width and the page length. You can, of course, change the default settings from within the Report Generator for each report you design. In addition, however, Paradox allows you to change the default report settings permanently. To do this, you must use the Custom Configuration Program (CCP).

Entering the CCP

To run the CCP from within Paradox, first make sure that the script Custom is in the default directory. Then, issue the **[Menu]** Scripts **P**lay command, type **Custom**, and press ↵. After a moment, Paradox will display the CCP menu on the screen.

Making Changes

The Reports option on the CCP menu allows you to set your own report defaults. After you choose this option, Paradox will display the menu shown in Figure 11-48. As you can see, this menu has seven options: PageWidth, LengthOfPage, Margin, Wait, GroupRepeats, Setups, and Return. Each of these options (except Return) is the counterpart of a command within the Report Generator. When you issue these commands from within the Report Generator, you are setting values for the report on which you are working; when you issue them from within the CCP, the values you enter become the default values for all reports.

Figure 11-48 The CCP Reports Menu

```
PageWidth  LengthOfPage  Margin  Wait  GroupRepeats  Setups  FormFeed  Return
Change the default width of the printed report page.
```

You can use the PageWidth option to change the default width of your reports. If most of your reports are printed on a wide-carriage printer, you might want to change the default page-width from 80 to 132 characters. To do this, issue the PageWidth command from the CCP Reports menu. After you issue the command, Paradox will display the current default value and prompt you to change it. When this prompt appears on your screen, you can press [Backspace] to erase the current default value, type a new default value between 10 and 2,000 (in this case 132), and press ↵.

You can use the LengthOfPage option to change the default page length of your reports from 66 lines to any length between 2 and 2,000 lines. For example, suppose you typically print

88 lines on each page (eight lines per inch). To change the default setting to 88 lines, choose LengthOfPage from the Reports menu, press [Backspace] twice to erase the default, and then type 88. When you press ↵, the CCP will lock in your setting.

The LengthOfPage command offers another option—Continuous—which instructs Paradox to print your reports in one continuous stream without any break between pages. If you intend to print most of your reports in continuous fashion, you can select this option. However, keep in mind that setting the length to Continuous will cause Paradox to ignore the literals and fields you have placed in the page header and footer.

You can use the Margin option on the CCP Reports menu to change the default left margin on the first page-width of your reports. The standard default setting is 0; you can change the setting to any value between 0 and 255. To change this setting, choose Margin from the Reports menu, press [Backspace] to erase the current default, and type the new setting.

You can also use the CCP to change the default setting for GroupRepeats. As you may recall, the GroupRepeats setting controls whether Paradox will print every entry in the grouping field or only the first entry in each group. To change this default, choose GroupRepeats from the CCP Reports menu. Paradox then will display a menu with two options: Retain and Suppress. Retain is the default setting. To change it, you should choose the Suppress option.

The Wait option on the CCP Reports menu allows you to change the default Wait setting. The Wait setting determines whether Paradox will pause and wait for you to insert a new sheet of paper after it prints each page, or will simply begin printing the new page. When you choose Wait from the Reports menu, the CCP will present two options: No and Yes. If you choose No, Paradox will not wait after it prints each page. If you choose Yes, Paradox will wait after printing each page.

The Setups option on the CCP Reports menu allows you to customize any of Paradox's default setup strings. The default setup strings are the strings Paradox displays when you issue the [Menu] Setting Setup Predefined command from within the Report Generator. When you choose the Setups option from the Reports menu, Paradox will display a PRINTER table like the one shown in Figure 11-49. As you can see, this table contains the default setup strings for the currently supported printers.

Figure 11-49 The Default Setup Strings

```
Press [F7] for form toggle, [F2] to save your changes, or [Esc] to cancel.
To choose a default, place an asterisk at the end of name of desired string.
PRINTER          Name          Port                    Setup String
   1    StandardPrinter*        LPT1
   2    Small-IBMgraphics       LPT1    \027W\000\015
   3    Reg-IBMgraphics         LPT1    \027W\000\018
   4    Small-Epson-MX/FX       LPT1    \015
   5    Small-Oki-92/93         LPT1    \015
   6    Small-Oki-82/83         LPT1    \029
   7    Small-Oki-192           LPT1    \029
   8    HPLaserJet              LPT1    \027E
   9    HP-Landscape-Normal     LPT1    \027E\027&l10
  10    HP-Portrait-66lines     LPT1    \027E\027&l7.27C
  11    Intl-IBMcompatible      LPT1    \027\054
  12    Intl-IBMcondensed       LPT1    \027\054\015
  13
```

Once you see the PRINTER table, you can delete any setup strings that do not apply to you, or you can add new strings to the list. To delete a string, place the cursor on the row containing the string you want to delete and press [Del]. To add a new string to the table, just create a blank row in the table, then type a name for the new string in the Name column, the port it will use in the Port column, and the string itself in the Setup String column. The name you enter can be up to 20 characters long and must not include blank spaces. Acceptable port choices are LPT1, LPT2, LPT3, COM1, COM2, and AUX. The setup string you define can be up to 50 characters long. You can enter as many setup strings as you want.

Of course, you can also modify one of the existing strings (either by deleting part of it or adding to it). All you have to do is move the cursor to the appropriate record in the Setup String field and edit the entry using normal editing techniques. If you want to designate a particular string as the default, type an asterisk (*) after its name in the Name field. If you define a default setup string, Paradox will employ that string for all new reports you create (provided you do not specifically choose another string).

The FormFeed option on the CCP Reports menu lets you specify whether Paradox should send a line feed character or a form feed character after the last line on each page of a report. By default, Paradox sends a line feed character. However, if you have a laser printer, the line feed character can leave some pages in the printer. You can fix this problem by changing the FormFeed setting from No to Yes.

When you have made the changes you want to the PRINTER table, you can press [Do-It!] to return to the CCP Reports menu.

Leaving the CCP

After you have set up all the report defaults you want, issue the **Return** command from the Reports menu to return to the CCP main menu. Then, issue the **DO-IT!** command or press **[Do-It!]**. When the CCP has saved your new default settings, the DOS prompt will appear on the screen. The changes you made will take effect the next time you load Paradox.

Conclusion

In this chapter, we showed you how to use summary fields, how to group your reports, and how to design multitable reports. In addition, we showed you how to use the Tools menu commands to copy, rename, and delete reports, and how to use the CCP to change Paradox's report defaults. In the next chapter, we will examine Paradox 3's new graphing features.

Chapter 12

Graphs

In this chapter, we'll show you how to take advantage of one of Paradox's most powerful tools for analyzing the data in your Paradox tables: graphing. We'll begin by exploring the basic concepts and commands you'll use to create graphs, including some simple enhancements you'll probably want to make. Then, we'll examine each of Paradox's graph types, explaining some enhancements you can make to these individual types. Next, we'll show you how to use queries and cross tabulations to convert data from normalized tables into information that lends itself to graphing. Finally, we'll tell you how you can print graphs in Paradox.

Basics

Every graph you create in Paradox is based on data in a table. Before you can create a graph, you must be viewing the table on the Paradox workspace in Main mode. Once the table is in place, you can generate a graph by pressing the [Graph] key ([Ctrl]-[F7]) or by issuing the [Menu] Image Graph ViewGraph Screen command.

Series

A graph depicts numerical data from the table on which it is based. Paradox uses the term series to describe the fields that contain the data displayed by a graph. When you create a graph, Paradox uses the field in which the cursor is currently positioned as the first data series for the graph. As a result, the cursor must be in a numeric field (N, S, or $ type) in order for you to create a graph. If one or more fields of the same field type as the current field appear to the immediate right of the current field, Paradox also uses the data in these fields as series in the graph. Paradox graphs can display up to six series. If there are more than five series fields to the right of the current field, Paradox will graph only the data in the current field and the next five fields.

For example, you could create a graph based on a table that included ten $ type fields listing sales for ten types of products. Each field would be named after the product whose sales it listed, and each series on the graph would represent sales of one of the products. When you pressed [Graph] to graph the data in this table, Paradox would display series representing data in the current field and the five fields to its immediate right. If you positioned the cursor in a field that had fewer than five numeric fields to its right, Paradox would display a graph with series for the current field and all the fields to its right. For example, if the cursor were in the second-to-last numeric field, Paradox would create a graph with only two series. If the fields you wanted to graph did not appear next to one another at the end of the table, you could use the [Rotate] key ([Ctrl]-[R]) to rearrange the fields before you graphed the table.

When Paradox graphs the data in a table, it places the bits of information in each series into categories. For example, a graph might break the sales of several products into totals for different months or sales regions. Paradox draws these categories from the current table in one of two ways, depending on whether the table is keyed. The *Presenting Paradox Data* manual incorrectly explains one of these methods for selecting category fields. The manual says that when you create a graph based on a non-keyed table, Paradox draws the categories from the entries in the first non-numeric field of the table. Actually, Paradox draws the categories from the entries in the first field of a non-keyed table, regardless of the field type. If the table is keyed, then Paradox draws the categories from the least significant key field (the key field farthest from the top in the table's structure), as correctly stated in the manual.

Suppose that the table we described above listed monthly sales totals for the ten products. In order to hold this information, the table would need to include a field that listed the month during which the sales stored in individual records were made. Now, suppose you wanted to graph this table in order to show the sales for individual products during each month. Assuming that the table were not keyed, the month field would need to be the first field in the table in order to create this graph. If the field were not at the beginning of the table, you could use the [Rotate] key to move the field to the front of the table before you created a graph. If the table were keyed, but the month field were not the least significant key field, you would need to restructure the table, making it a non-keyed table. Then, you could use [Rotate] to move the month field to the front of the table before creating the graph.

Creating a Graph

Let's create a default graph based on the data in a Paradox table. In order to simplify this process, we'll press [Graph] to create a graph, though you could issue the [Menu] Image Graph ViewGraph Screen command instead.

The type of graph Paradox creates when you press [Graph] depends on Paradox's current graph settings. These settings also control most of the elements on the graph. However, as we've already explained, the data displayed in a graph is determined completely by the field arrangement of the current table and the position of the cursor. Because graph settings have no effect on the data displayed in the graph, you can use the same graph settings to create different graphs by moving the cursor in the current table or moving the cursor to a different table. In this section, we'll show you how to create a graph with Paradox's default settings. Later, we'll show you how you can enhance a graph by changing these default settings.

We'll base our graph on a keyed table called BALLSALE, which lists monthly unit sales for four types of basketballs. Figure 12-1 shows the structure of the BALLSALE table, and Figure 12-2 shows the data in this table.

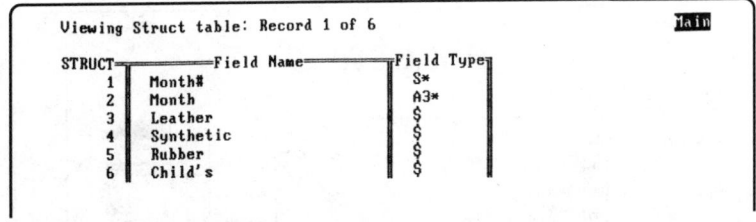

Figure 12-1 The Structure of the BALLSALE Table

Figure 12-2 The BALLSALE Table

As you can see, the first key field in BALLSALE is named Month#, and the second key field is named Month. The Month# field contains a number corresponding to a month (1 through 12), and the Month field holds a three-letter abbreviation for the same month (*Jan* through *Dec*). The rest of the fields in the table are named after one of the types of basketballs. Each record in the table lists the number sold for every type of basketball during a particular month. (This table actually contains data for a single sales region. We'll look at some national data later in this chapter.) Since you want each series of the graph to represent one type of basketball, the first thing you need to do is move the cursor to the first field that contains totals for a type of basketball. To position the cursor, use the → and ← keys to move into the Leather field. Because the least significant key field in the table is the Month field, which contains the categories into which you want to divide the series data, you are now ready to graph the table. To create the graph, press the **[Graph]** key ([Ctrl]-[F7]). After a few moments, Paradox will display the graph shown in Figure 12-3 on the following page.

Graph Elements

Let's look at the basic elements of this graph. These elements include the series, legends, x- and y-axes, tick marks, scales, and titles. This graph is called a stacked bar graph because the total number of all basketballs sold is represented by a vertical bar made up of smaller bars representing the number sold for each type of ball. Paradox uses the stacked bar as its default graph type, but you can choose from among ten types of graphs. We'll discuss all the graph types and show you how to select them later in this chapter.

Notice that Paradox uses a unique pattern on the bars of each series. The Leather series bars are solid, while the Synthetic series bars are plotted with horizontal stripes. The Rubber series bars contain a diagonal-line pattern, and the Child's field is denoted by bold diagonal lines. If you're using a color monitor, you'll also notice that Paradox displays each bar using a separate color. If you want, you can select a different color and/or pattern from the ones Paradox chooses for you. (We'll explain how to do this when we talk about Paradox's graph customizing features later in this chapter.)

Figure 12-3 A Simple Graph

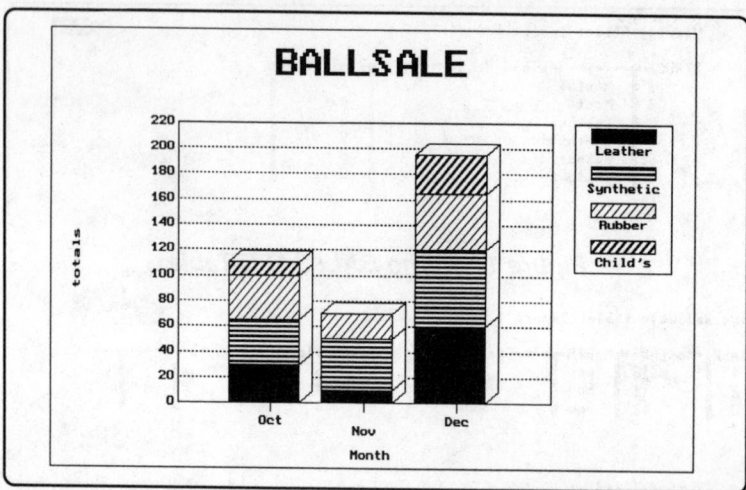

Like most graphs, this graph has horizontal and vertical axes. The horizontal axis, called the x-axis, breaks each series into the categories listed in the category field. For this reason, we'll refer to the field containing these categories as the x-axis field. We've already explained how Paradox selects the x-axis field, depending on whether the table being graphed is keyed. In our example graph, the x-axis divides the number of basketballs sold in each series into the number sold during each month.

The vertical axis, called the y-axis, generally measures the values displayed on the graph. On this graph, the y-axis measures the total number sold during each month for each type of basketball.

Along each axis, you'll notice marks, called tick marks, that divide the axis into segments. In our example graph, the x-axis includes a tick mark for each month, while the y-axis includes a tick mark for each increment of 20 balls sold. The tick marks on an axis are based on another important graph element: the scale of information shown on each axis. The scale includes the range of values shown on an axis, as well as the increments into which the axis is broken. The y-axis on our example graph has a range from 0 to 220. Each tick mark tells you the category or value represented by that tick mark. Together, all of the tick marks along an axis show the range of the scale for that axis. For example, the tick marks along the x-axis in our sample graph list the months during which the basketballs were sold (*Oct*, *Nov*, and *Dec*). For most types of graphs, Paradox arranges the x-axis field entries along the axis in the same order in which they appear in the table. (The only exception to this rule is the X-Y graph, in which Paradox distributes the field entries on a scale on the x-axis. X-axis values must be numeric on an X-Y graph.)

Each axis also includes a title that describes the type of information displayed on the axis. In our sample graph, the title *Month* under the x-axis lets you know that this axis divides the volume sales into months, while the title *totals* along the y-axis tells you that this axis shows the total number of balls sold. By default, Paradox uses the name of the category field as the x-axis title, and the literal string *totals* as the y-axis title. As you can see, there is also a title at the top of the screen, which describes the graph as a whole. By default, Paradox uses the name of the table on which the graph is based as the main title. In this case, the graph is based on data in the BALLSALE table.

Changing Graph Settings

Whether you press the [Graph] key or execute the [Menu] Image Graph ViewGraph Screen command, Paradox will apply the current graph settings to the current table on the workspace. If you haven't changed Paradox's default graph settings or loaded a saved set of graph settings, pressing [Graph] or choosing the [Menu] Image Graph ViewGraph Screen command will create a graph using Paradox's default graph settings.

You can change Paradox's default graph settings in several ways to make a graph better communicate the information in a table. Paradox's graph settings control every aspect of a graph except the data displayed. (The series and categories displayed on a graph are completely dependent on the field order of the current table and the position of the cursor in that table.) The Graph Designer is the tool that lets you change graph settings. To enter the Graph Designer, you issue the [Menu] Image Graph Modify command, which places Paradox in Graph mode. After you issue this command, you will see the Graph Type form, as shown in Figure 12-4. This form lets you change the titles on the current graph. While you are in the Graph Designer, you can see the Graph Design menu, shown in Figure 12-5 on the next page, by pressing [Menu]. You can use this menu to change all of the settings for the current graph.

Figure 12-4 The Graph Type Form

```
 Defining the type of subsequent graphs.                         Graph
 [F1] for help with defining graph types.
 ┌── Customize Graph Type ─────────────────────────────────────────────────
 │                                         Basic Graph Types:
 │    Select a basic graph type from the   (S)tacked Bar
 │    options on the right.                 (B)ar - Regular Bar Graph
 │                                         (3) 3-D Bar
 │    Graph Type: Stacked Bar         ◄    (R)otated Bar
 │                                         (L)ine
 │   ─────────────────────────────────    (M)arkers
 │                                         (C)ombined Lines & Markers
 │    Series Override Graph Type            (X) X-Y Graph
 │                                         (P)ie Graph
 │    To create a mixed graph type, select  (A)rea Graph
 │    a series override graph type for
 │    each series.
 │
 │    1st Series: Not Applicable           Series Override Types:
 │    2nd Series: Not Applicable           (L)ine
 │    3rd Series: Not Applicable           (B)ar - Regular Bar Graph
 │    4th Series: Not Applicable           (M)arkers
 │    5th Series: Not Applicable           (C)ombined Lines & Markers
 │    6th Series: Not Applicable           (N)one (for labels)
```

Figure 12-5 The Graph Design Menu

```
Type  Overall  Series  Pies  ViewGraph  Help  DO-IT!  Cancel          Graph
Change the currently specified graph type.
```

Using the Graph Designer

You can see different Graph Designer forms by pressing the [Menu] key, then issuing commands on the Graph Design menu. Each screen lists all the possible settings for the prompts on that screen. You can change most of these settings by moving the cursor to the appropriate prompt and pressing a key (usually a single letter) that corresponds to one of the possible settings for that prompt. For example, all of the possible graph types appear along the right edge of the Graph Type form. To select one of these graph types, press the letter that corresponds to the desired graph type while the cursor is positioned at the *Graph Type:* prompt.

Some Graph Designer prompts display more specialized information and require you to type the entire setting. For example, while viewing the screen that you use to customize the axes on a graph, you can specify high and low values for the scale on the y-axis. To change these settings, you must type in the actual high and low values at the appropriate prompts. You can change settings at these prompts just like the entries at other Paradox prompts. For example, you can delete the last character of these settings by pressing ← or the entire current setting by pressing [Ctrl]-[←]. You press the [Field View] key ([Alt]-[F5]) to edit characters anywhere in the current setting.

Viewing a Graph from the Graph Designer

While you are in the Graph Designer, you can view the graph produced by the current graph settings by pressing the [Graph] key or by issuing the [Menu] ViewGraph Screen command. Either way, you'll see the graph defined by the current settings. Of course, the data represented on the graph depends on the cursor position, so be sure to place the cursor in the first series field before you issue the [Menu] Image Graph Modify command to enter the Graph Designer.

Changing the Graph Type

Different types of information are best communicated with different types of graphs. For example, a line graph shows change over time better than a bar graph. To change the current graph type, all you have to do is issue the [Menu] Image Graph Modify command. After you issue this command, you will see the Graph Type form shown in Figure 12-4. Since the cursor is positioned at the *Graph Type:* prompt when you enter the Graph Designer, you can immediately select a new graph type from the list on the right side of the screen by pressing the letter that corresponds to that graph type. For example, you press 3 to select the 3-D Bar graph type, or *P* to select the Pie graph type. After making your selection, you press [Do-It!] to save the new setting. The next time you press [Graph], Paradox will transform the data in the current table into a graph of the type you have selected. We'll discuss all of Paradox's graph types later in this chapter.

Basic Graph Enhancements

While the stacked bar graph in Figure 12-3 accurately represents the data in the BALLSALE table, it does not do the best job possible of communicating what that data means. Figure 12-6 shows the same stacked bar graph with a few enhancements. These enhancements make the graph more attractive and the information easier to understand.

Figure 12-6 An Enhanced Graph

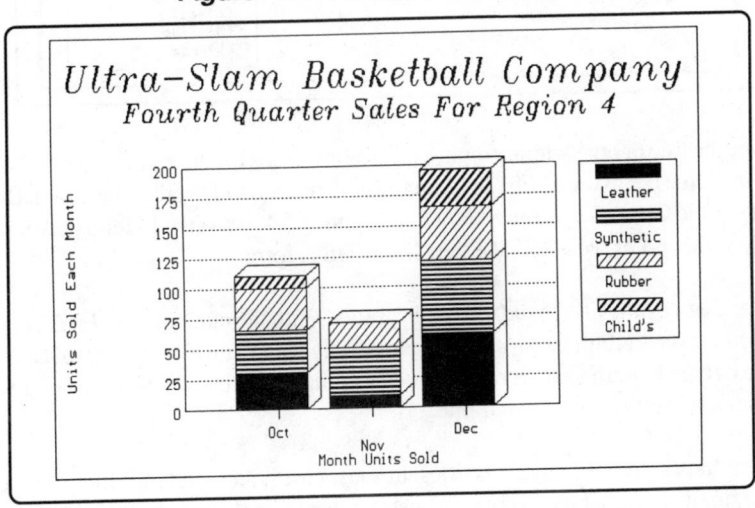

Because enhancements are such an important part of creating graphs, we'll take a moment now to examine the steps you follow to add enhancements such as custom titles and scaling. We'll explain how to make more enhancements throughout this chapter.

Adding Titles

We've already shown you how Paradox uses the name of the table being graphed as the default title for a graph, the name of the x-axis field as the x-axis title, and the literal *totals* as the y-axis title. However, you can change any of these default titles by issuing the Graph Designer's [Menu] Overall Titles command. When you issue this command, you will see the Graph Titles form shown in Figure 12-7. To change a title on the graph, you simply move the cursor to the prompt naming the title and type the title you want to use. You can define a one- or two-line main title for a graph and change the font (type style) and size for the main title. This form also lets you specify a size for the axes titles.

Figure 12-7 The Graph Titles Form

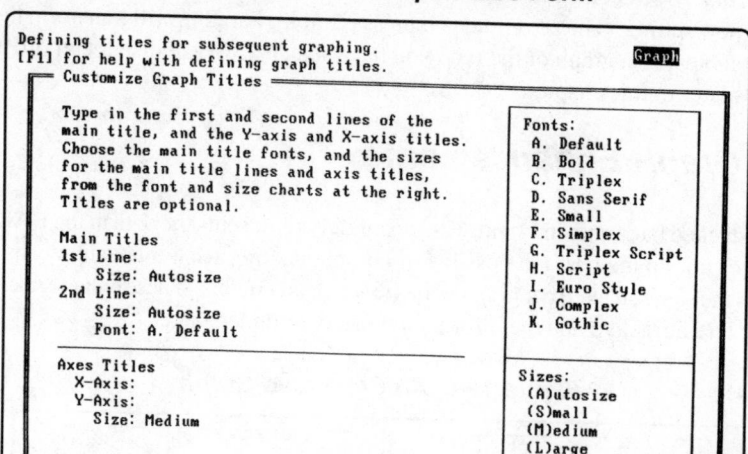

```
Defining titles for subsequent graphing.
[F1] for help with defining graph titles.                        Graph
  ┌─ Customize Graph Titles ══════════════════════════════════════
   Type in the first and second lines of the
   main title, and the Y-axis and X-axis titles.     Fonts:
   Choose the main title fonts, and the sizes          A. Default
   for the main title lines and axis titles,           B. Bold
   from the font and size charts at the right.         C. Triplex
   Titles are optional.                                D. Sans Serif
                                                       E. Small
   Main Titles                                         F. Simplex
   1st Line:                                           G. Triplex Script
       Size: Autosize                                  H. Script
   2nd Line:                                           I. Euro Style
       Size: Autosize                                  J. Complex
       Font: A. Default                                K. Gothic

   Axes Titles
     X-Axis:                                          Sizes:
     Y-Axis:                                           (A)utosize
       Size: Medium                                    (S)mall
                                                       (M)edium
                                                       (L)arge
```

Let's change the title of our sample graph, as well as the titles for the x- and y-axes. To change the titles, first issue the **[Menu]** I mage G raph M odify command to enter the Graph Designer. When you see the Graph Type form shown in Figure 12-4, issue the **[Menu]** O verall T itles command. At this point, you will see the Graph Titles form.

First, let's add a two-line title to the top of the graph. With the cursor at the *1st Line:* prompt, type **Ultra-Slam Basketball Company** and press ↵ twice to move the cursor to the *2nd Line:* prompt. Next, type **Fourth Quarter Sales For Region 4** and press ↵. Now, the cursor should be at the *Size:* prompt for the second line.

Although Paradox automatically sizes titles, in some cases, these default titles may seem too large or too small. Fortunately, you can adjust the size by replacing the *Autosize* entry at the *Size:* prompt with your own selection of Small, Medium, or Large. To change the size of the second line of our title, press **M** to select the Medium option. After you do this, Paradox will fill in the rest of the word *Medium* at the prompt. Next, press ↵ to move the cursor to the *Font:* prompt on the next line.

You can also select any of 11 fonts for the main title on a graph. Table 12-1 shows the fonts from which you can choose. To select a font for the main title, you need to enter the letter that corresponds to the desired font at the *Font:* prompt. For example, to change the main title from the default font to the Triplex Script font, press **G** while the cursor is at this prompt. After you do this, Paradox will type *G. Triplex Script* at the prompt.

Next, let's add a new x-axis title to the graph. First, press ↵ to move the cursor to the *X-Axis:* prompt in the Axes Titles area in the lower portion of the Graph Titles form. Then, type **Month Units Sold** and press ↵ to move the cursor to the *Y-Axis:* prompt. At this prompt, type **Units Sold Each Month**. Then, press ↵ again to move the cursor to the *Size:* prompt.

Table 12-1 Main Title Fonts

Paradox automatically sizes the axes titles, just as it does the main title. However, you can also override the automatic sizing by specifying a size for the axes titles at the *Size:* prompt. To select large sizing for the axes titles, press **L**. When you do this, Paradox will type the word *Large* at the prompt. The Size setting for the axes titles also determines the size that Paradox uses for the labels in the legend of the graph. If you look at Figures 12-3 and 12-6, you can see that these labels appear in the same size as the axes titles.

If you want to edit or delete the titles for the current graph, just issue the [Menu] Image Graph Modify command to enter the Graph Designer, then issue the [Menu] Overall Titles command. If you delete any of the titles specified on the Graph Titles form, Paradox will use the default titles the next time you display that graph.

Scaling

The scales of the axes in the example bar graph in Figure 12-3 were set automatically by Paradox. In other words, Paradox automatically selected the beginning and ending values that are represented on the y-axis, and the increment between the values on that axis. (As we explained earlier, Paradox uses the entries in the first field in a non-keyed table or the least significant key field for the x-axis values.) Most of the time, you will find that automatic scaling is adequate. In some cases, however, you may want to adjust the scaling of one or both axes manually. To change the scaling on a graph, you issue the Graph Designer's [Menu] Overall Axes command. When you issue this command, you will see the Graph Axes form shown in Figure 12-8.

Figure 12-8 The Graph Axes Form

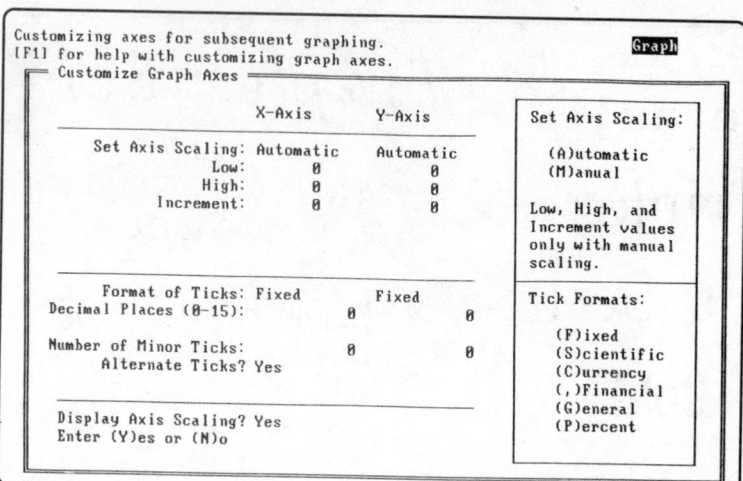

As long as the settings displayed at the *Set Axis Scaling:* prompt are set to Automatic, Paradox will create its own scaling for both axes, ensuring that the range of the y-axis scale includes both the minimum and maximum values that appear on the graph. On X-Y graphs, which include scales on the x- and y-axes, Paradox generates a scale for both axes. However, you can override Paradox's default scaling by changing the Set Axis Scaling setting for an axis to Manual, then specifying your own low, high, and increment values for the scale.

Let's change the scale of the y-axis in the example graph. To do this, issue the **[Menu]** Overall Axes command. After you do this, Paradox will present the Graph Axes form. When this form appears, the cursor will be positioned at the *Set Axis Scaling:* prompt under the X-Axis column. Since we want to change the scaling for the y-axis, begin by pressing ➡ to move the cursor to the Y-Axis column. Then, press **M** to select Manual scaling. After you select Manual scaling, you can specify Low, High, and Increment settings for the y-axis. Leave the Low setting at 0, but change the High setting to 200 and the Increment setting to 25. To do this, press ⬇ twice to move to the *High:* prompt. Then, type **200**, and press ⬇ to move to the *Increment:* prompt. Finally, type **25** at this prompt.

In addition to adjusting the scaling along the axes, you can also change the manner in which a graph displays this scaling. The settings in the bottom half of the Graph Axes form let you modify the tick marks on a graph's axes. Later in this chapter, we'll show you how to modify tick marks and set scaling for the x-axis on X-Y graphs.

Leaving the Graph Designer

After you have finished editing the graph settings in the Graph Designer, you can tell Paradox to lock in the new settings by pressing [Do-It!] or issuing the [Menu] DO-IT! command. If you decide that you do not want to use the new settings you have specified, you can leave the

Graph Designer by issuing the [Menu] Cancel command. After you issue this command, Paradox will present a menu with two choices: No and Yes. If you select No, Paradox will return you to the Graph Designer with all the settings in the same condition they were in before you issued the Cancel command. If you select Yes, Paradox will leave the Graph Designer without making any of the changes you specified for graph settings.

Since you want to use the new settings you have defined to create a new graph for the BALLSALE table, press [Do-It!]. Then, move the cursor to the Leather field of the BALLSALE table, and press [Graph]. After you do this, Paradox will display the graph shown in Figure 12-6.

Managing Graphs

As we have mentioned, the graph Paradox creates for the current table depends on Paradox's current graph settings. Fortunately, Paradox lets you save graph settings in graph files, then reload those settings whenever you want. Unlike most Paradox objects, graphs do not belong to the family of an individual table. Of course, you will probably design graphs with a particular table in mind, specifying titles and scales that are appropriate for the data in that table. However, you can use any graph with any table, as long as the table's structure makes it possible to create a graph of the data in that table.

Saving Graphs

If you want to save a graph, you can use the [Menu] Image Graph Save command. This command lets you assign a specific name to each graph you create. Once you've saved a graph, you can reset the graph settings or modify those settings to create a new graph without permanently losing the graph settings you saved. When you want to work with the saved graph settings again, you simply load the saved graph.

When you issue the [Menu] Image Graph Save command, Paradox will present a *Graph:* prompt asking you to name the graph file. To save the active graph, you should type a name for the graph, and press ↵. The name you choose must conform to the same rules that apply to any Paradox file name: It can contain any alphabetic or numeric characters, but no spaces or periods, as long as the length does not exceed eight characters. If you enter the name of a graph that already exists, Paradox will present a menu with two options: Cancel and Replace. If you choose Cancel, Paradox will return to the prompt asking for a graph name, displaying the name you just entered. If you select Replace, Paradox will save the active graph with the name you have specified and delete the graph that previously had that name.

Let's save the enhanced stacked bar graph we have been working with. To begin, make sure that you are in Main mode, then issue the [**Menu**] Image Graph **S**ave command. When Paradox prompts you for a graph name, type **Ballbar**, and press ↵. The graph settings that create the graph in Figure 12-6 are now saved.

Creating a New Graph

Once you've saved the current graph, you can create a new graph in one of two ways. You can modify the existing graph settings, or you can use the [Menu] Image Graph Reset command to reset all of the graph settings to their defaults and start over from scratch.

If you issue the [Menu] Image Graph Reset command, Paradox will present a menu with two selections: Cancel and OK. Choosing the Cancel option will cause Paradox to leave the current graph settings intact. Selecting the OK option will make Paradox reset all graph settings to their default values. You can then create your new graph from scratch. Be careful—if you issue this command before saving the current settings, those settings will be lost.

If the new graph you are creating is similar to the current graph, you can probably save time by modifying the existing settings. To do this, simply make the desired changes to the current settings (again, making sure to save the current settings if you'll need them later), then save the modified settings under a new name.

Loading a Graph

The [Menu] Graph Load command lets you activate a graph you previously saved. When you issue this command, Paradox will prompt you for the name of the graph you want to load. To activate a graph, just type its name at the prompt and press ↵. Alternatively, you can press ↵ without typing anything at the prompt to see a menu of all the graphs in the current directory, or type the name of another directory at the prompt and press ↵ to see a menu of the graphs in that directory. If you activate a menu in either of these two manners, then you can select a graph just as you select an option from any menu.

When you use the [Menu] Image Graph Load command to activate a saved graph, the settings for that graph will replace the current graph settings. Since Paradox can hold only one set of active graph settings, you can load only one graph at a time. If you have not saved the current graph, its settings will be lost. If you know that you will later want to use the current graph settings, be sure to save the current graph before loading a new graph.

Deleting Graphs

The [Menu] Tools Delete Graph command allows you to selectively erase saved graphs. When you issue this command, Paradox will prompt you for the name of the graph you want to erase. Just type the name at the prompt and press ↵. Before deleting a graph, Paradox will present a Cancel/OK menu to let you confirm the deletion.

For example, suppose you wanted to delete the graph Ballbar. To do so, you would issue the [Menu] Tools Delete Graph command, type *Ballbar* at the prompt, and press ↵. When Paradox presented the Cancel/OK menu, you would select OK. The message *Deleting Ballbar graph...* would appear in the message area at the bottom of the screen for a few moments while Paradox erased the graph from your disk.

Renaming Graphs

You can change the name of a saved graph by issuing the [Menu] Tools Rename Graph command. When you issue this command, Paradox will prompt you for the name of the graph you want to rename. To rename a graph, just type its name at the prompt and press ↵. Paradox will prompt you for the new name. After you type the new name and press ↵, Paradox will change the name of the graph.

If you try to change the name of a graph to a name already assigned to an existing graph, Paradox will present a menu with two options: Cancel and Replace. If you choose Cancel, Paradox will return to the prompt asking for a new graph name and display the name you just entered. Then, you can change the name and press ↵ to enter the new name. If you select Replace, Paradox will rename your graph with the name you specified and delete the graph that previously had that name.

Copying Graphs

Earlier in this chapter, we explained how you can create a new graph based on the current graph settings. All you have to do is save the current graph if you'll need it later, modify the current graph settings, then use the [Menu] Image Graph Save command to save the modified graph. Paradox also lets you copy all of the settings for one graph to another graph with the [Menu] Tools Copy Graph command. When you issue this command, Paradox will prompt you for the name of the graph you want to copy. After you enter the name of an existing graph, Paradox will ask you to name the new graph. After you enter this graph name, Paradox will copy all of the settings for the original graph to a new graph with the name you specified.

As we explained in Chapters 4 and 10, the [Menu] Tools Copy command is useful when you want to use an existing Paradox object, such as a form or report, as the basis for a new object of the same type. For example, to design a new report based on an existing report, all you have to do is make a copy of the existing object, then make any desired changes to the copy. However, copying a graph to create a new graph with a similar design is not an efficient technique because the process for editing graphs is very different from the processes for editing forms and reports. Both Paradox's Form Editor and Report Generator let you open an object, edit it, then save the edited object. However, the Graph Designer simply lets you edit the current graph settings, which you can then save as a new graph. As a result, if you want to base a new graph on an existing graph, it is most efficient to load the existing graph, make the changes you want, then save the new graph under a different name. There is no need to make a copy of the existing graph first.

The [Menu] Tools Copy Graph command is useful when you want to copy a graph from one directory to another, or from one disk to another. You will probably need to do this if you copy a table for which you have designed a graph into another directory or to a different disk. Unlike most Paradox objects, graphs do not belong to families of individual tables. As a result, Paradox does not automatically copy graphs you have designed for a particular table when you use the [Menu] Tools Copy command to copy the table. If you copy a table to a different disk or directory, then you will need to copy its graphs separately.

For example, suppose you have copied the BALLSALE table from the current directory (c:\paradox3) to the directory \data on a floppy disk in drive A. To copy the Ballbar graph along with the BALLSALE table, issue the [**Menu**] Tools Copy Graph command, type **Ballbar** at the first prompt, and press ↵. When Paradox asks you for the new graph name, type **a:\data\Ballbar** and press ↵. After you do this, Paradox will copy the Ballbar graph from the current directory to the \data directory of the floppy disk.

If you try to give the new graph the name of a graph that already exists, Paradox will ask you to verify the new graph name, just as it does when you try to rename a graph.

Paradox's Graph Types

As we have mentioned, Paradox can create ten types of graphs. We've already introduced a stacked bar graph, which is Paradox's default graph type. In this section, we'll create line, combined lines and markers, markers, bar, rotated bar, 3-D bar, stacked bar, area, pie, and X-Y graphs. We'll also show you enhancements you can make to some of these graph types. We'll use the BALLSALE table as the basis for our graphs. At the beginning of each example, we'll assume that Paradox's default graph settings are in place and that the BALLSALE table is in the current image, in the table view, with its original field order intact.

Line Graphs

Line graphs are probably the most commonly used business graphs. In a line graph, Paradox uses a line to connect data values in each series. For this reason, line graphs are best used to illustrate the trend of data over time. For instance, you might use a line graph to illustrate the growth (or decline) of sales for a company from one month to the next throughout a year or to illustrate the population growth of a country over several years.

To define a line graph in Paradox, you first issue the [Menu] Image Graph Modify command. When Paradox enters the Graph Designer, it will automatically place you on the Graph Type form, shown in Figure 12-4 on page 517, which lets you specify the graph type. Once you're in the Graph Type form, you should make sure the cursor is at the *Graph Type:* prompt, then press *L* to select the Line graph type.

Let's create a line graph for the BALLSALE table that represents the sales of leather basketballs over the last quarter. To begin, issue the [**Menu**] Image Graph Modify command. When Paradox displays the Graph Type form of the Graph Designer, press **L** to select the Line graph type, then press [**Do-It!**] to save that change.

Now, since you want to chart the sales of only leather basketballs, you need to rotate the fields in the BALLSALE table so that Paradox will create a graph with a single series based on data in the Leather field. Because Paradox uses the current field and all numeric fields to the right of the current field for the series in a graph, you need to make sure that Leather is the current field, and that there will be no numeric fields to its immediate right. To arrange the field order properly, move the cursor to the Leather field and press **[Rotate]**. When you do this, Paradox will move the Leather field to the end of the table and shift every other field one column to the left. After you move the cursor back to the Leather field, your screen will look like the one shown in Figure 12-9, and you will be ready to create the graph. Now, press **[Graph]** to view the graph, as shown in Figure 12-10. To clear the graph from the screen, press any key.

Figure 12-9 The Rotated BALLSALE Table

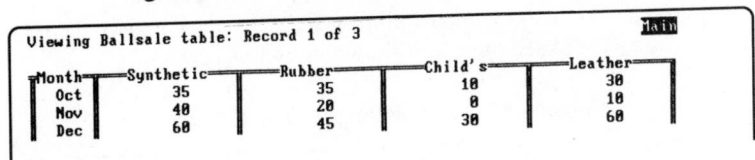

Figure 12-10 A Line Graph

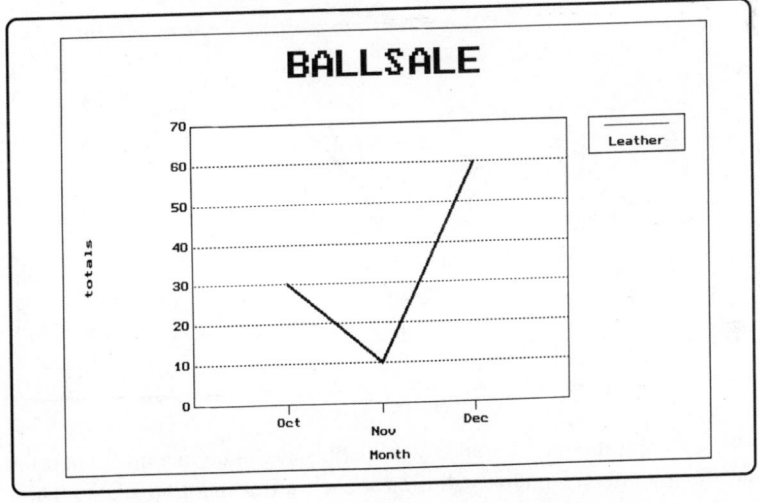

Although all of the data points in our example line graph are positive, you can also plot negative values in a line graph. In line graphs, negative values are represented by lines that dip below the graph's x-axis.

Once you've created a line graph, you can enhance it by changing titles, adding interior labels, changing the labels on the legend (or by removing the legend entirely), or by adjusting the scaling and format of the axes. We'll show you how to make changes later in this chapter.

Multiple-line Graphs

Because Paradox allows you to include up to six series in a graph, you can plot as many as six lines in one line graph, thereby creating a multiple-line graph. Multiple-line graphs are useful for comparing the trends in several different series.

If you want to create a line graph with more than one series, just arrange the fields in the table image so that the numeric fields containing data for the additional series are positioned next to one another, with the cursor in the first series field. For example, let's make the line graph in Figure 12-10 represent the sales of all four types of basketballs over the three-month period. Since we want to graph the sales of all four ball types, there is no need to rotate the fields of the BALLSALE table as you did in the last example. All you need to do is issue the [**Menu**] **I**mage **G**raph **M**odify command, change the Graph Type setting to Line, and press [**Do-It!**] to save the new setting. After changing the graph type, move the cursor to the Leather field and press the [**Graph**] key to see the graph shown in Figure 12-11.

Figure 12-11 A Multiple-line Graph

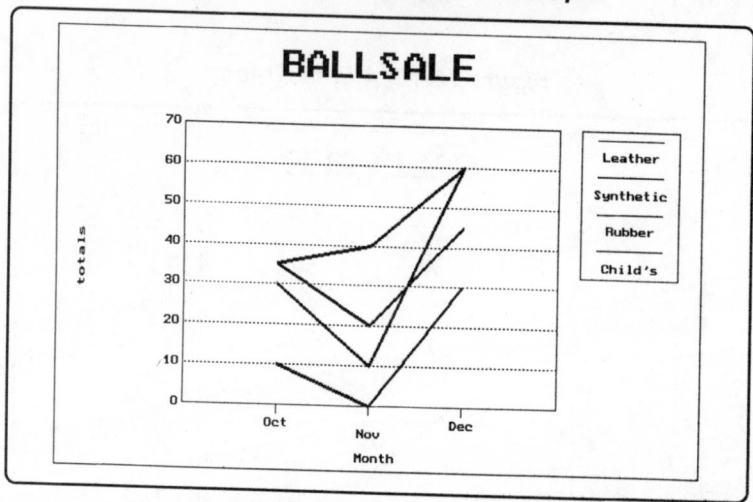

If you are using a color monitor, Paradox will display each line in a different color. Table 12-2 lists the default colors Paradox will use for each series in a line graph. These are the default colors Paradox uses for all graph types. (The actual colors that appear on your screen may vary, depending on the monitor and resolution you are using.) Of course, you can change any of these colors. If you have a monochrome monitor, it will be difficult, if not impossible, to tell one series from another. When you are designing graphs to be displayed on a monochrome monitor, you should consider using combined lines and markers graphs instead of line graphs.

Table 12-2 Paradox's Default Colors for Graphs

Series	Color	Series	Color
1st	Blue	4th	Red
2nd	Green	5th	Magenta
3rd	Cyan	6th	Brown

Combined Lines and Markers Graphs

When Paradox plots a line graph, it simply draws a line between the data points in each series—it does not use markers to define the position of each point. While this may sometimes be the result you want, at other times, you may want to include markers for the data points in your graph. Fortunately, Paradox offers a variant of the line graph type called combined lines and markers. In a combined lines and markers graph, Paradox draws a line between the data points in each series and uses markers to define the precise position of each point. Markers make it easier to identify the location of the points on the graph. If you want to make the current graph a combined lines and markers graph, you issue the [Menu] Image Graph Modify command to enter the Graph Designer, then, with the cursor positioned at the *Graph Type:* prompt, press *C*.

Let's create a combined lines and markers graph that depicts the same data as the line graph shown in Figure 12-11. To do this, issue the **[Menu]** Image Graph Modify command. When you see the Graph Type form, press **C** to select the Combined Lines & Markers graph type. When you are finished, press **[Do-It!]** to exit the Graph Designer. Then, with the cursor in the Leather field of the BALLSALE table, press the **[Graph]** key to view the graph shown in Figure 12-12 on the next page.

As you can see, Paradox has used markers to designate the data points on each line in the graph. Although the *Presenting Paradox Data* manual says that Paradox uses different markers for every series on a graph, the first available copies of Paradox 3 actually use a filled square as the marker for every series on a graph. The positions of the filled squares represent the individual values that are contained in each series. If you have a color monitor, Paradox will use the colors listed in Table 12-2 to display each line in a combined lines and markers graph.

You can enhance a combined lines and markers graph in the same ways that you can enhance line graphs. In addition to the basic enhancements we discussed earlier in this chapter, you can also use the Graph Designer to change the markers in a combined lines and markers graph.

Figure 12-12 A Combined Lines and Markers Graph

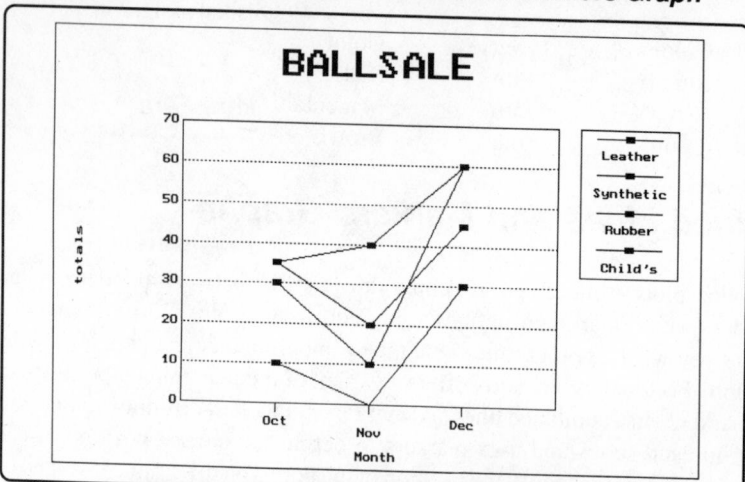

Using Different Markers

Earlier in this chapter, we suggested using combined lines and markers graphs rather than line graphs if you have a monochrome monitor. We suggested distinguishing the lines that correspond to different series on a combined lines and markers graph by using a different type of marker for each series. As we've already explained, the first available copies of Paradox 3 use the same marker for each series, but you can use the [Menu] Image Graph Modify command to change the markers for individual series. Once you are in the Graph Designer, you issue the [Menu] Series MarkersAndFills command. After you issue this command, the Graph Designer will display the Fills and Markers form shown in Figure 12-13. We'll discuss the portion of this screen that controls the fill patterns for bar and area graphs later in this chapter. For now, we want to concentrate on the bottom-left corner of the form, which lists the marker symbols for six series, the maximum number of series Paradox can display on a graph. The 13 available marker symbols are listed on the right side of the form, along with the corresponding letters you use to select them. Table 12-3 shows the symbol for each marker. To change the marker for a series, you move the cursor to the prompt for that series and press the letter that corresponds to the desired marker.

For example, to change the markers on the graph we created in the preceding example, first issue the **[Menu]** Image Graph **M**odify command. When you see the Graph Type form, issue the **[Menu]** Series MarkersAndFills command. Then, press ↓ seven times to move the cursor to the *2nd* prompt under the Series Marker Symbol heading. (We'll leave the marker for the first series as a filled square.) Next, press **B** to select the Plus selection from the list of marker symbols. After you do this, the selection after the *2nd* prompt will change from A - Filled Square to B - Plus. Use this same technique to change the marker symbol for the third series to 8 Point Star (selection **C**), and the marker symbol for the fourth series to an empty square (selection **D**). Since our graph will include only four series, there is no need to change the selections for the fifth and sixth series. After you have finished assigning marker symbols, press **[Do-It!]** to leave the Graph Designer.

Figure 12-13 The Fills and Markers Form

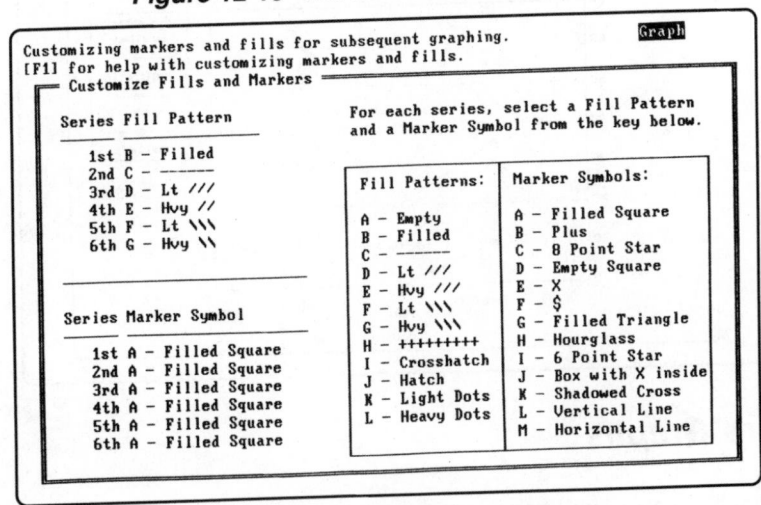

Table 12-3 Marker Symbols

Press this key...	to select this marker	
A	Filled Square	■
B	Plus	✚
C	8 Point Star	✳
D	Empty Square	□
E	X	✖
F	$	✵
G	Filled Triangle	▲
H	Hourglass	⌛
I	6 Point Star	✳
J	Box with X inside	⊠
K	Shadowed Cross	✖
L	Vertical Line	▌
M	Horizontal Line	▬

To view the new graph, move the cursor to the Leather field and press **[Graph]**. Figure 12-14 shows the combined lines and markers graph with different markers.

Figure 12-14 A Graph with Different Markers

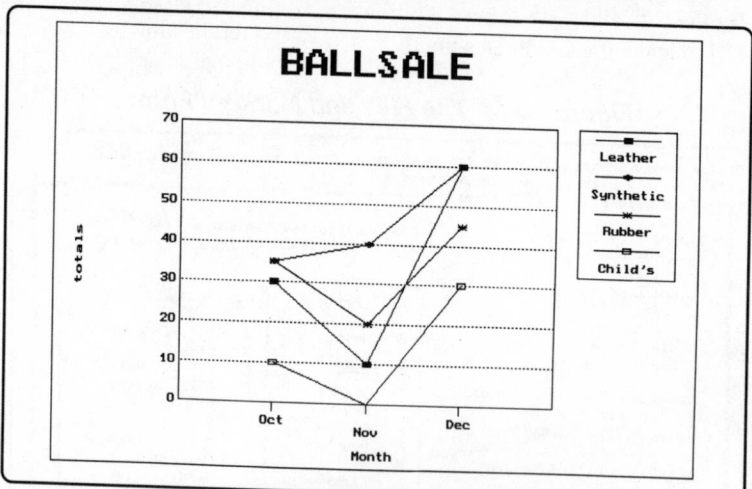

Markers Graphs

Markers graphs are very similar to line and combined lines and markers graphs. However, in markers graphs, Paradox simply uses markers to define the precise position of each point in each series. It draws no lines in the graph to connect each of the markers. Overall, the usefulness of a markers graph is limited. Of all the graph types supported by Paradox, you'll probably use markers graphs the least.

Let's create a markers graph that depicts the same data as the combined lines and markers graph shown in Figure 12-14. For this example, we'll assume that you have changed the markers for the four series, as we did in the last section. To create the markers graph, issue the **[Menu] I**mage **G**raph **M**odify command. When you see the Graph Type form, press **M** to select the Markers graph type. When you are finished, issue the **[Menu] DO**-IT! command or press **[Do-It!]** to exit the Graph Designer. Then, move the cursor to the Leather field and press the **[Graph]** key to view the graph shown in Figure 12-15.

As you can see, Paradox has used the markers you chose to mark the data points in each series in the graph. If you have a color monitor, Paradox will use the colors listed in Table 12-2 to display each set of markers in a markers graph.

You can enhance a markers graph in the same ways that you enhance combined lines and markers graphs. In addition to the basic enhancements we discussed earlier in this chapter, you can also use the Graph Designer to change the markers in a markers graph.

If you compare the graph in Figure 12-15 to the combined lines and markers graph in Figure 12-14, you will see that one point on the Child's line in Figure 12-14 is not represented by a marker in either of the graphs. This data point represents the sales of child's basketballs in November. This point falls on the x-axis because there were no child's basketballs sold in November. Due to either a bug in the program or a deficiency in its design, the first available copies of Paradox 3 do not display any marker that falls along either axis (each of which is perpendicular to the minimum tick mark of the other axis) or along the top or right edge of a graph. You can fix any graph for which this bug creates problems by using the Graph Designer's [Menu] Overall Axes command to extend the y-axis below the zero value by one increment. Then, markers hidden by the former x-axis will be visible because they will no longer appear on the x-axis.

Figure 12-15 A Markers Graph

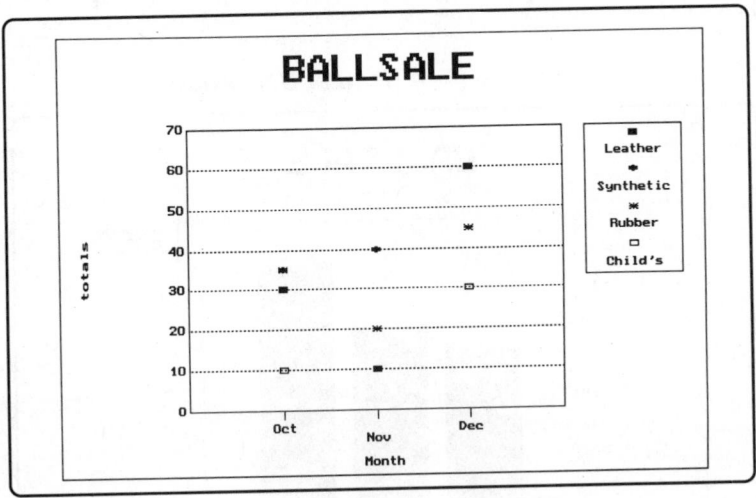

Bar Graphs

Bar graphs are the second most popular kind of business graph. In a bar graph, each series is plotted as a series of bars along the x-axis. Each data value is represented by the height of a single bar. Bar graphs are useful for making comparisons between different values. There are actually several types of bar graphs, such as regular bar graphs, stacked bar graphs, 3-D bar graphs, and rotated bar graphs. In this section, we'll discuss regular bar graphs.

If you want to define a bar graph in Paradox, you first issue the [Menu] Image Graph Modify command. Once you're in the Graph Designer, you press *B* to choose the Bar - Regular Bar Graph selection from the list of graph types.

Let's create a bar graph from the data in the BALLSALE table that compares the sales of synthetic basketballs during the last three months of 1988. To begin, issue the **[Menu]** Image Graph Modify command. When you see the Graph Type form, press **B** to select the Bar - Regular Bar Graph graph type. Then, issue the **[Menu]** DO-IT! command or press **[Do-It!]** to exit the Graph Designer.

To chart only the sales of synthetic basketballs, move the Synthetic field to the end of the BALLSALE table. To rotate the table, move the cursor to the Synthetic field and press **[Rotate]** ([Ctrl]-[R]). Figure 12-16 shows the rotated table. Next, move the cursor to the re-located Synthetic field and press the **[Graph]** key to view the graph shown in Figure 12-17.

Figure 12-16 The Rotated Table

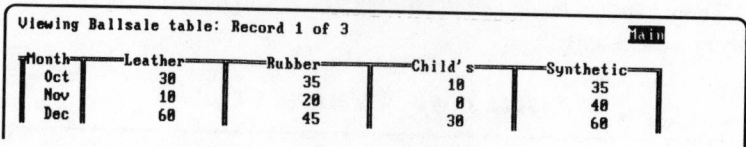

Figure 12-17 A Regular Bar Graph

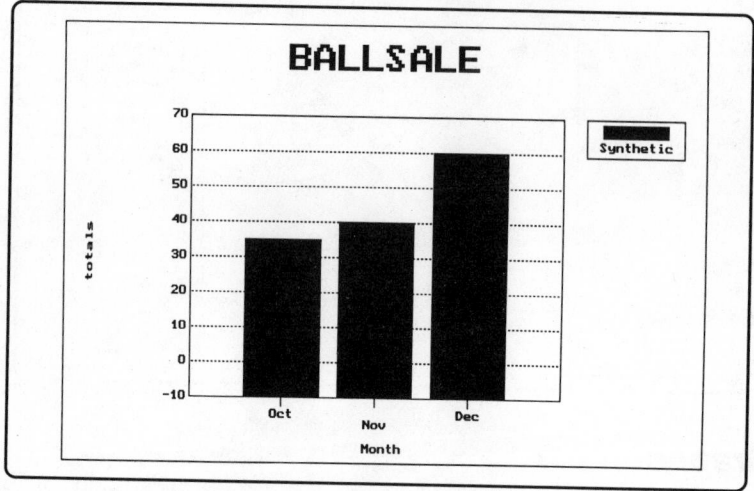

As you can see, in this graph, each bar is positioned above an x-axis tick mark. The first bar represents the sales of synthetic basketballs during October; the second, during November; and the third, during December. You can also plot negative values in bar graphs. In a bar graph, bars representing negative values descend below the x-axis.

Once you have created a bar graph, you can change titles, add labels, and make other enhancements to it. You can also format the graph's y-axis and change the fill patterns and colors in the graph.

Clustered Bar Graphs

When you plot more than one series in a bar graph, Paradox will create a clustered bar graph, in which the corresponding bars in each series are clustered. Clustered bar graphs are useful for comparing several different series in one graph.

If you want to create a bar graph with more than one series, you simply place the cursor in the first series field and arrange the table so that the rest of the series fields are immediately to the right of that field. When the fields are properly arranged, press [Graph]. For example, to chart the sales of all four types of basketballs on a clustered bar graph, use the Graph Designer to make the active graph a regular bar graph, then move the cursor to the Leather field and press **[Graph]** to see the graph shown in Figure 12-18.

Figure 12-18 A Clustered Bar Graph

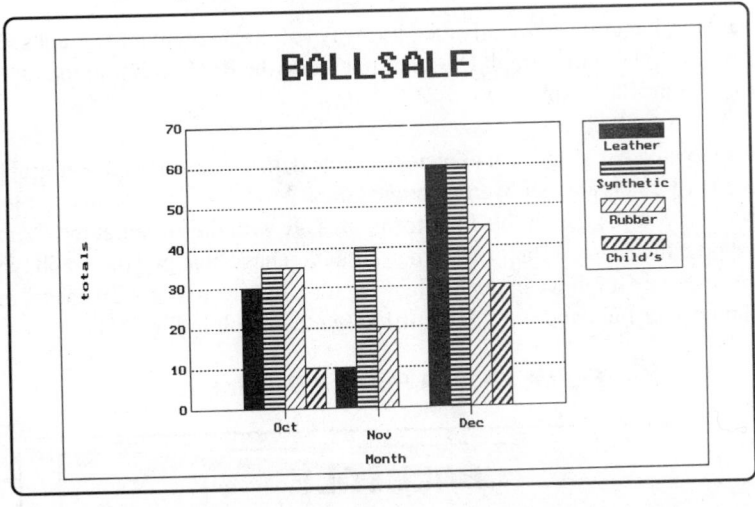

The bars in this graph are clustered around the x-axis tick marks. The first cluster illustrates the sales of the different types of basketballs during the month of October; the second cluster, sales during November; and the third, sales during December. The first bar in each cluster represents leather ball sales; the second, synthetic ball sales; the third, rubber ball sales; and the fourth, child's ball sales. Paradox always places the bar for the first series at the left of each cluster, with the bar for the second series immediately to the right, and so on.

Paradox assigns a different pattern and color to each set of bars in a clustered bar graph. If you have a monochrome monitor, Paradox will use only patterns to shade the bars in each series. Table 12-2 on page 529 shows the default colors Paradox uses for the series on a bar graph, and Table 12-4 on page 536 shows Paradox's default fill patterns. If you want, you can change the color or fill pattern for any series on a clustered bar graph. We'll show you how to change colors and fill patterns later in this chapter.

Rotated Bar Graphs

A rotated bar graph is nothing more than a regular bar graph turned on its side. In a rotated bar graph, each series is plotted as a series of bars along the graph's vertical axis. Each data value is represented by the length of a single bar. In effect, the graph's axes change places: The x-axis becomes a vertical axis and the y-axis becomes a horizontal axis.

Table 12-4 Paradox's Default Fill Patterns

Series	Fill Pattern		Series	Fill Pattern	
1st	Filled	▬▬▬	4th	Hvy ///	/////
2nd	- - - - -	≡≡≡	5th	Lt \\\	\\\\\\
3rd	Lt ///	/////	6th	Hvy \\\	\\\\\\

You create rotated bar graphs in nearly the same way you create regular bar graphs. The only difference is that you use the Graph Designer to choose the Rotated Bar graph type instead of the Bar - Regular Bar graph type.

Let's create a rotated bar graph that depicts the same data as the clustered bar graph shown in Figure 12-18. First, issue the **[Menu] I**mage **G**raph **M**odify command to enter the Graph Designer. When you see the Graph Type form, press **R** with the cursor at the *Graph Type:* prompt to choose the Rotated Bar graph type. After you have changed the graph type, press **[Do-It!]** to leave the Graph Designer. When Paradox returns to the workspace, move the cursor to the Leather field and press **[Graph]** to see the graph in Figure 12-19.

Figure 12-19 A Rotated Bar Graph

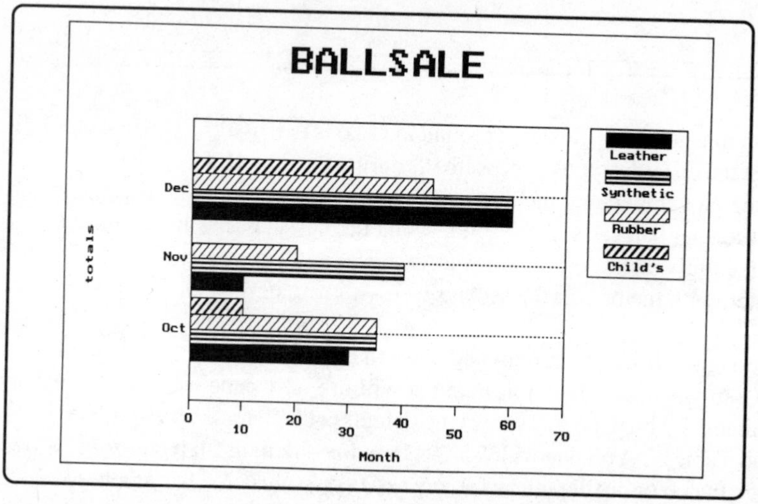

You can rotate any single series or clustered bar graph. In fact, the only difference between regular bar graphs and rotated bar graphs is their orientation. In every other way, they are identical. You can enhance a rotated bar graph in the same ways that you enhance a regular bar graph.

If you look at the rotated bar graph in Figure 12-19, you can see that Paradox has not switched the x- and y-axis titles after turning the bar graph on its side. As a result, the x-axis title (*Month*) describes the information on the y-axis, and the y-axis title (*totals*) describes information on the x-axis. To change the axes titles, issue the **[Menu]** Overall Titles command to bring up the Graph Titles form. Then, type **Totals** at the *X-Axis:* prompt and **Month** at the *Y-Axis:* prompt. Figure 12-20 shows the graph with the default titles reversed.

Figure 12-20 Reversing the Axes Titles

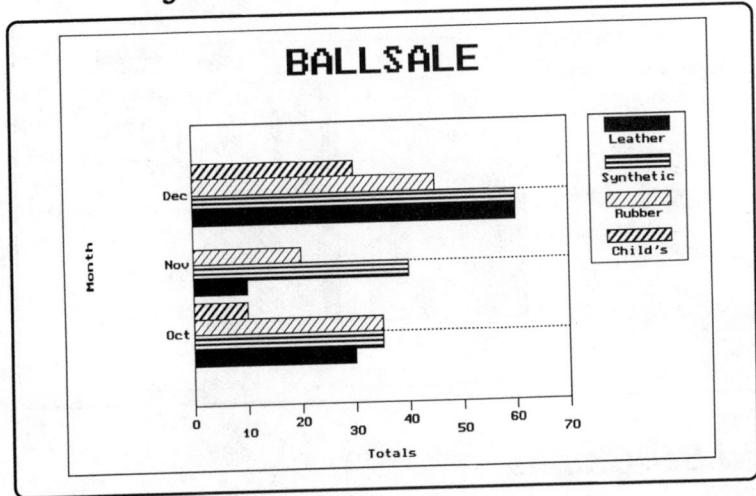

3-D Bar Graphs

Paradox offers one more variation on the regular bar graph: the 3-D bar graph. The only difference between a 3-D bar graph and a normal bar graph is cosmetic. In a 3-D Bar graph, each bar has depth in addition to having height and width.

You create 3-D bar graphs in the same way you create regular bar graphs. The only difference is that you use the Graph Designer to choose the Rotated Bar graph type instead of the Bar - Regular Bar graph type.

Let's create a 3-D bar graph that depicts the same information as the rotated bar graph shown in Figure 12-19. First, issue the **[Menu]** Image Graph Modify command to enter the Graph Designer. When you see the Graph Type form, press **3** to choose the 3-D Bar graph type, then issue the **[Menu]** DO-IT! command or press **[Do-It!]** to leave the Graph Designer. When Paradox returns to the workspace, move the cursor to the Leather field and press **[Graph]** to see the graph in Figure 12-21 on the following page.

You can create a 3-D bar graph that depicts a single series or multiple series. As you can see in Figure 12-21, however, the bars in 3-D bar graphs are positioned right next to one another. If the graph includes from two to six series, the bars will not be clustered but will be placed one after another across the graph. This can be confusing if you do not have a color monitor. The only other difference between regular bar graphs and 3-D bar graphs is the depth of the bars. You can enhance a 3-D bar graph in the same ways that you enhance a regular bar graph.

Figure 12-21 A 3-D Bar Graph

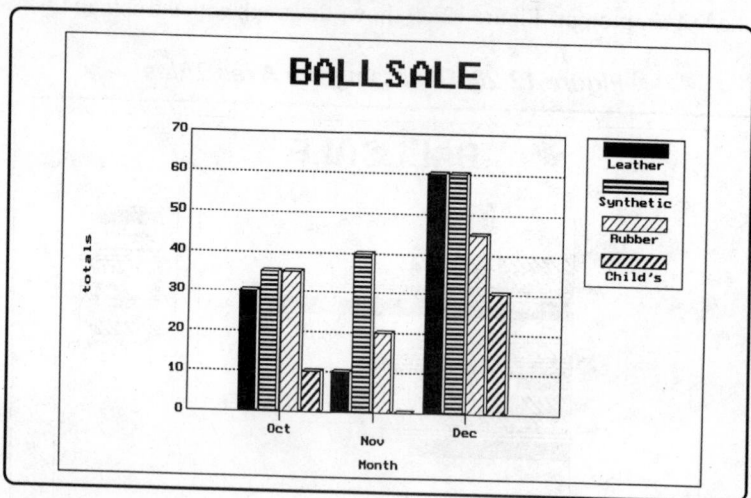

Stacked Bar Graphs

Earlier in this chapter, we introduced the stacked bar graph type, which is Paradox's default graph type. In a stacked bar graph, each bar is made up of two or more segments. Each segment represents a value from one series. The total height of each column represents the total of the values that make up that column. Stacked bar graphs are useful for showing how the components of a set of data compare to the total of the components.

If you want to create a stacked bar graph, you do not need to change the active graph type—unless you have previously changed the Graph Type setting from its default value. If you have changed the default graph type, then you can use the [Menu] Image Graph Reset command to set Paradox to its default graph settings. If you want to keep some of your non-default settings, such as titles or scaling, but change back to the Stacked Bar graph type, you should issue the [Menu] Image Graph Modify command, then choose the Stacked Bar graph type.

You can see the stacked bar effect only if you create a graph that has more than one series. If you create a stacked bar graph with a single series, the result will look like a regular bar graph. You can enhance a stacked bar graph in any of the ways that you can enhance other types of bar graphs.

Figure 12-3 on page 516 shows a stacked bar graph. Each bar in this graph represents the sales of all types of balls in one month. The segments of the bars represent the sales for an individual type of ball. In a stacked bar graph, Paradox always plots the first series at the bottom of each bar, the second series above the first, and so on.

If you have a monochrome monitor, Paradox will use only patterns to shade the bars in each series. Table 12-4 on page 536 lists the default fill patterns Paradox uses to shade the segments in a stacked bar graph. If you have a color monitor, Paradox will use both colors and patterns to distinguish the various series in a stacked bar graph. Table 12-2 on page 529 lists the default colors Paradox will use to shade the bars for each series. We'll show you how to change the default colors and fill patterns later in this chapter.

You cannot effectively plot negative values in a stacked bar graph. If you try to do so, Paradox will ignore the minus sign and plot the value as though it were a positive number, removing the fill pattern from the negative segment. The result will be confusing.

Area Graphs

Area graphs are very much like stacked bar graphs. In a stacked bar graph, each data series is represented by a series of bar segments. In an area graph, each series is represented by the area between two lines. The area between the first line and the x-axis represents the first data series; the area between the second line and the first line represents the second series; and so on. Each of the lines represents the cumulative trend of the data series below that line. The top line represents the sum of all of the data series that make up the graph. Like stacked bar graphs, area graphs are useful for depicting the relationships between the components of several data series and the totals of those components. Like line graphs, area graphs also depict the trend of the data being graphed.

If you want to create an area graph, you first issue the [Menu] Image Graph Modify command. After you're in the Graph Designer, you press A with the cursor at the *Graph Type:* prompt to select the Area graph type.

Let's use the BALLSALE table to create an area graph that shows the trend of total sales of all types of balls during the last quarter of 1988. To begin, issue the **[Menu] I**mage Graph Modify command. Once you have entered the Graph Designer, press **A** to select the Area graph type. Then, issue the **[Menu]** DO-IT! command or press **[Do-It!]** to exit from the Graph Designer. When Paradox returns to the workspace, move the cursor to the Leather field and press **[Graph]** to see the graph shown in Figure 12-22 on the next page.

As you can see, Paradox has created a graph with four lines. Each series is represented by the area between two lines. Each of the lines represents the cumulative trend of the series below that line. For example, the bottom area represents the sales of leather balls. The line above that segment shows the trend in sales of leather balls. The second area represents the sales of synthetic balls. The second line represents the trend in the cumulative sales of leather and synthetic balls. In an area graph, Paradox always plots the first series at the bottom, the second series above the first, and so on.

Figure 12-22 An Area Graph

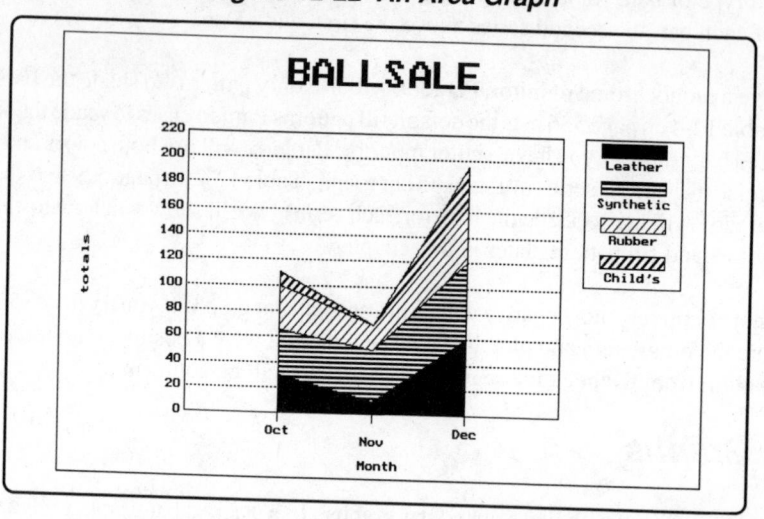

If you have a monochrome monitor, Paradox will use fill patterns to shade the areas in the graph. Table 12-4 on page 536 lists the default patterns Paradox uses to shade the areas. If you have a color monitor, Paradox will use both colors and patterns to distinguish the various series in an area graph. Table 12-2 on page 529 lists the default colors Paradox will use to shade the area for each series. We'll show you how to change colors and fill patterns later in this chapter.

Just as you cannot plot negative values in a stacked bar graph, you cannot plot negative values in an area graph. If you try to do so, Paradox will simply ignore the minus sign and will plot the value as though it were a positive number. The result will be a misleading graph.

Pie Graphs

Pie graphs may be the most familiar type of business graph. In a pie graph, each value in a series is represented by a segment (slice) of a circle (pie). The total of the values in the data series is represented by the entire pie. Pie graphs are extremely useful when you must illustrate the ratio of the components of a data set to the total of those components. Unlike other Paradox graph types, pie graphs can depict only one series at a time. There just isn't any way to plot more than one series in a pie graph.

If you want to define a pie graph in Paradox, you first issue the [Menu] Image Graph Modify command. Once you're in the Graph Designer, you press *P* to choose the Pie graph type.

Let's create a pie graph that shows the ratio of sales for synthetic basketballs during each month in relation to the total sales for that type of ball during the quarter. To begin, issue the **[Menu] I**mage **G**raph **M**odify command. Once you have entered the Graph Designer, press **P** to select the Pie graph type. After changing the graph type, issue the **[Menu] DO-IT!**

command or press [Do-It!] to exit from the Graph Designer. When Paradox returns to the workspace, move the cursor to the Synthetic field and press [Graph] to see the graph shown in Figure 12-23.

Figure 12-23 A Pie Graph

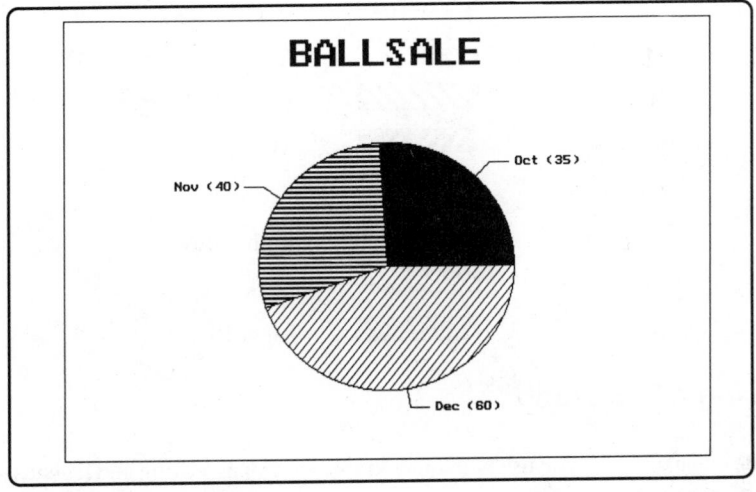

As you can see, Paradox has plotted each value in the series as a slice of the pie. The slice for the first value in the series begins at the 3 o'clock position and wraps counterclockwise toward 12 o'clock. The next slice represents the second value; the third, the third value.

Notice that the values themselves appear in parentheses beside the slices in the graph. Next to the values, you can see the month to which each value corresponds. These labels let you see the relevance of each slice compared to the other slices on the graph. For example, the label *Oct (35)* tells you that 35 synthetic basketballs were sold during the month of October. Although Paradox automatically places series values on pie graphs, it is possible to display the values as dollar values or replace the values with percentages. We'll show you how to replace the actual series values with percentages later in this section.

If you have a monochrome monitor, Paradox will use fill patterns to shade the slices in the graph. If you have a color monitor, Paradox will use both colors and patterns to distinguish the slices. Table 12-5 on the following page lists the default fill patterns and colors Paradox will use to shade the slices. We'll show you how to change the default patterns and colors later in this section.

There is no way to plot a negative value in a pie graph. If you include a negative value in a pie graph, Paradox will ignore the minus sign and graph the value as it does a positive value.

Although you can display a series with any number of elements on a pie graph, you'll probably want to keep the number of elements on a pie graph low. Pie graphs that feature a large number of slices are difficult to interpret.

Table 12-5 Default Fill Patterns and Colors for Pie Graphs

Series	Fill Pattern		Color
1st	Filled		Blue
2nd	- - - - - -		Green
3rd	Lt ///		Cyan
4th	Hvy ///		Red
5th	Lt \\\		Magenta
6th	Hvy \\\		Brown
7th	++++++		Light Grey
8th	Crosshatch		Dark Grey
9th	Hatch		Light Blue

Enhancing a Pie Graph

Many of the enhancements you use with other graphs—such as scaling and legends—do not apply to pie graphs. You can specify a main title for a graph, but you cannot use x-axis and y-axis titles. However, there are a number of enhancements you can make only to pie graphs. You can format the labels on a pie graph to display numbers as percentages or currency, or remove the labels altogether. You can also change the color or fill pattern Paradox uses to shade each segment. In addition, you can "explode" one or more segments, that is, display segments slightly removed from the rest of the pie.

The Graph Designer's [Menu] Pies command is the tool that lets you make these enhancements. When you issue this command, Paradox will display the Pie Graph form shown in Figure 12-24. We'll show you how to use this form by making some enhancements to the graph we created in our last example.

Changing the Label Format

When Paradox displays the Pie Graph form after you issue the [Menu] Pies command, the cursor will be positioned at the *Label Format:* prompt. To the right, you'll see the four valid label formats: Value, Percent, Currency, or None. To change the label format, you simply type the first letter of one of the four valid label formats at the prompt.

The Value format, which is the default label format, tells Paradox to use the actual values in the series field as pie segment labels. The pie graph in Figure 12-23 uses the Value label format to display the entries in the series field next to each slice of the pie.

Figure 12-24 The Pie Graph Form

```
Customizing pie charts for graphs.                          Graph
[F1] for help with customizing pie charts.
┌─ Customize Pie Graph ══════════════════════════════════════════

                                                            Color
       Label Format: Value              Label Formats:     Palette:
                                        (U)alue
    ─────────────────────────────       (P)ercent           A  BckGrd
           Explode                      (C)urrency           B
    Pie    Slice?    Fill      ──Colors──   (N)one           C
    Slice  (Y/N)     Pattern   Screen  Print                 D
    ─────  ─────     ───────                 Fill Patterns:  E
    1st:   Yes    B - Filled    B      B     B - Filled      F
    2nd:   No     C - ──────    C      C     C - ──────      G
    3rd:   No     D - Lt ///    D      D     D - Lt ///      H
                                             E - Hvy //      I
    4th:   No     E - Hvy //    E      E     F - Lt \\\      J
    5th:   No     F - Lt \\\    F      F     G - Hvy \\      K
    6th:   No     G - Hvy \\    G      G     H - ++++++      L
                                             I - Crosshatch  M
    7th:   No     H - +++++++   H      H     J - Hatch       N
    8th:   No     I-Crosshatch  I      I     K - Light Dots  O
    9th:   No     J - Hatch     J      J     L - Heavy Dots  P
```

The Percent format displays a percentage calculated by dividing each series field value by the sum of all entries, then multiplying the quotient by 100. If you used the Percent format for the graph shown in Figure 12-23, Paradox would replace the labels *Oct (35)*, *Nov (40)*, and *Dec (60)* with the labels *Oct (26)*, *Nov (30)*, and *Dec (44)*.

The Currency format displays the field entries as currency values. If you choose the Currency format, Paradox will round each series entry to the nearest integer and display a dollar sign ($) in front of each entry. If you selected the Percent format for the graph shown in Figure 12-23, Paradox would replace the labels *Oct (35)*, *Nov (40)*, and *Dec (60)* with the labels *Oct ($35)*, *Nov ($40)*, and *Dec ($60)*.

The None format causes Paradox to exclude series field entries from slice labels, leaving only the x-axis values in the labels. The None format would replace the labels *Oct (35)*, *Nov (40)*, and *Dec (60)* in Figure 12-23 with the labels *Oct*, *Nov*, and *Dec*.

Let's change the label format in the graph in Figure 12-23 from Value to Percent. (We are going to make several modifications to the current graph in this section. Make sure that the cursor is in the Synthetic field before entering the Graph Designer so that you can view the graph from the Graph Designer after each change.) To do this, issue the **[Menu] I**mage Graph **M**odify command. If the Graph Type form shows that the current graph type is not Pie, then press **P** to make it so. Once you are sure that the current graph is a pie graph, issue the [Menu] Pies command. After you issue this command, you will see the Pie Graph form shown in Figure 12-24, and the cursor will be positioned at the *Label Format:* prompt in the upper-left corner of the form. To change the label format from Value to Percent, press **P**. Then, press **[Graph]** to display the modified graph shown in Figure 12-25. When you are finished viewing the graph, press any key to return to the Graph Designer.

Figure 12-25 Labels Displaying Percentages

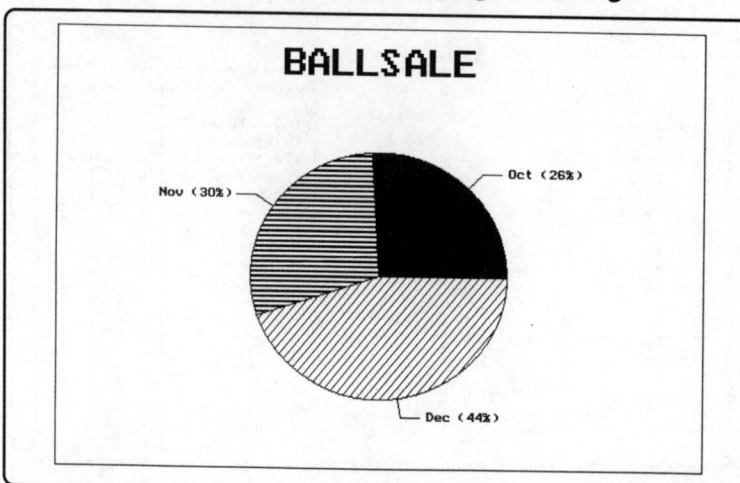

Changing Colors and Patterns for Pie Slices

If you have a color monitor, Paradox will display each slice in a pie graph in a unique color and will shade each slice with a unique fill pattern. If you have a monochrome monitor with a graphics adapter, Paradox will use a unique pattern for each slice. Unless you change the settings, Paradox will use the colors and patterns shown in Table 12-5 on page 542 to display each slice. If you create a pie graph for a data series that includes more than nine elements, Paradox will repeat the cycle of colors and patterns assigned to the first nine slices for each additional set of nine slices. For example, Paradox would display the tenth slice with the color and fill pattern assigned to the first slice, the 11th slice with the color and fill pattern assigned to the second slice, and so on.

You can see the default color setting for each pie slice under the Screen heading in the Colors column of the Pie Graph form shown in Figure 12-24. If you want to change the color Paradox assigns to a slice, you can use the →, ←, ↓, and ↑ keys to move the cursor to the screen color column for that slice, then press the letter corresponding to the color you want to choose. Table 12-6 shows all the colors you can assign to pie slices, along with the letters corresponding to each color. For other graph types, you can assign these colors to individual series, as we'll show you later in this chapter. If you have a color printer or plotter, you can change the color Paradox uses to print a series by changing the color setting in the Print column under the Colors heading. We'll show you how to print a graph later in this chapter.

For example, to change the screen color for the first slice from blue (B) to yellow (O), first move the cursor to the screen color column for the first pie slice. Then, press **O** to select yellow. If you press [Graph] to see the modified graph, Paradox will now color the first slice of the pie (the slice for the month of October) yellow instead of blue.

The default fill pattern for each series appears in the Fill Pattern column of the Pie Graph form. If you want to change the fill pattern Paradox assigns to a slice, you can use the →, ←, ↓, and ↑ keys to move the cursor to the Fill Pattern column for that slice, then press the letter corresponding to the pattern you want to choose. You can fill a pie slice with any of the fill patterns shown in Table 12-7 except the Empty pattern (A).

Table 12-6 Colors for Paradox Graphs

Press this letter…	to choose this color
A	Background color (invisible)
B	Blue
C	Green
D	Cyan
E	Red
F	Magenta
G	Brown
H	Light Grey
I	Grey
J	Light Blue
K	Light Green
L	Light Cyan
M	Light Red
N	Light Magenta
O	Yellow
P	White

Table 12-7 Possible Fill Patterns for Bar, Area, and Pie Graphs

Press this letter…	to choose this fill pattern	
A	Empty	
B	Filled	
C	- - - - - -	
D	Lt ///	
E	Hvy ///	
F	Lt \\\	
G	Hvy \\\	
H	+++++++++	
I	Crosshatch	
J	Hatch	
K	Light Dots	
L	Heavy Dots	

For example, to change the fill pattern for the first pie slice from Filled (B) to Heavy Dots (L), first move the cursor to the Fill Pattern column for the first series. Then, press **L** to select the Heavy Dots pattern. The setting will then change from B - Filled to L - Hvy Dots. If you press [Graph] to see the modified graph, Paradox will now fill the first slice of the pie (the slice for the month of October) with the Heavy Dots pattern.

Exploding Slices

The settings in the Explode Slice? column on the Pie Graph form let you explode one or more segments from a pie graph. Exploding a segment draws attention to that segment by separating it slightly from the rest of the graph. To explode a pie slice, you move the cursor to the Explode Slice? column for that slice, then press *Y* to change the setting from No to Yes.

Suppose you want to explode the slice that represents the sales of synthetic basketballs during the month of November. To do this, move the cursor to the Explode Slice? column for the second slice. (You know that the second slice represents November sales because the second record in the BALLSALE table contains data for sales in November.) Next, press **Y** to make the Explode Slice? setting Yes. After you have changed the setting, press **[Graph]** to display the modified graph shown in Figure 12-26. You might notice that the fill pattern for October is now the Heavy Dot pattern because we changed it in our last example. When you are finished viewing the graph, press any key to return to the Graph Designer.

Figure 12-26 An Exploded Pie Slice

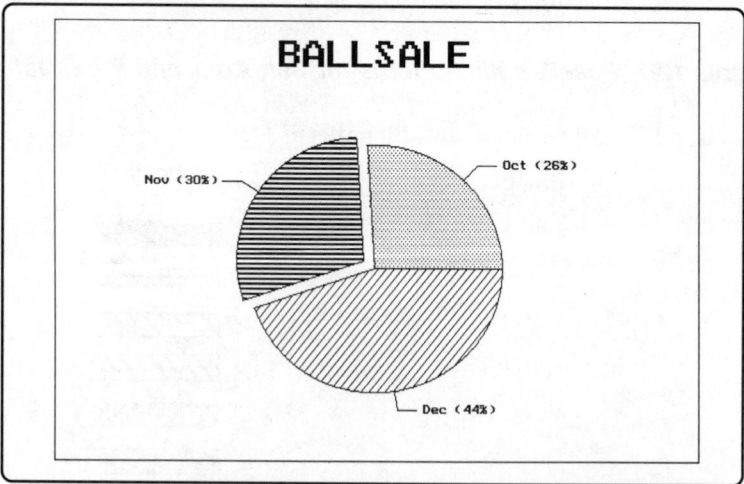

Although the series you use to define a pie graph can include more than nine entries, resulting in a pie graph with more than nine slices, only the first nine slices can be exploded. Since exploding a slice is meant to draw attention to it, you'll find that exploded pie charts are most effective when only one or two slices are exploded.

X-Y Graphs

X-Y graphs plot the relationship between two quantifiable characteristics of a set of data. They come in handy when you are using one characteristic (the independent variable) to predict another characteristic (the dependent variable) of a data set. For example, you can use an X-Y graph to plot the relationship between years of education (independent variable) and income (dependent variable), or between height (independent variable) and weight (dependent variable).

X-Y graphs—sometimes called scatter graphs—are much like line graphs and markers graphs. As a matter of fact, each X-Y graph is actually a line graph, a markers graph, or a combined lines and markers graph. However, while the x-axis values on line graphs, markers graphs and combined lines and markers graphs can be any type of value (a number, date, or string), the x-axis values for an X-Y graph must be numeric.

The *Presenting Paradox Data* manual says, incorrectly, that Paradox will extract x-axis values for an X-Y graph from the first numeric field in the table being graphed. In fact, Paradox selects the x-axis field for an X-Y graph just as it does for any other type of graph. If the current table is a keyed table, Paradox will use the least significant key field as the x-axis field. If the current table is not keyed, Paradox will use the first field in the table as the x-axis field. The x-axis field of a table on which an X-Y graph is based must be a numeric (N, S, or $ type) field. If you try to create an X-Y graph based on a table in which the first field is not a numeric field, Paradox will display the message *X axis must be numeric for X-Y graphs*. If the numeric field from which you want to draw x-axis values is not the first field in the table, then you can use the [Rotate] key ([Ctrl]-[R]) to move that field to the front of the table. Like all Paradox graph types except pie graphs, an X-Y graph can display data for up to six series. Paradox draws these data series from the entries in the current field, which must contain numeric values, and up to five numeric fields to the immediate right of the current field. To define an X-Y graph, you issue the [Menu] Image Graph Modify command, then press *X* to change the Graph Type setting to X-Y Graph.

Let's create an X-Y graph that depicts the relationship between the amount of money spent on advertising each month and the number of basketballs sold that month. Figure 12-27 on the next page shows the structure of a table called ADVERTS, which includes this information along with the sales information in the BALLSALE table. Figure 12-28, also on the following page, shows the data in this table. Notice that the ADVERTS table is non-keyed. As a result, Paradox will extract x-axis values from the first field in the table when you create a graph based on this table.

For this example, we'll want to view the graph several times as we make changes to the graph settings. Of course, this will be easiest to do if we can view the graph from the Graph Designer. To make this possible, place the ADVERTS table on the workspace, and position the cursor in the first series field (the Leather field) before entering the Graph Designer.

Figure 12-27 The Structure of the ADVERTS Table

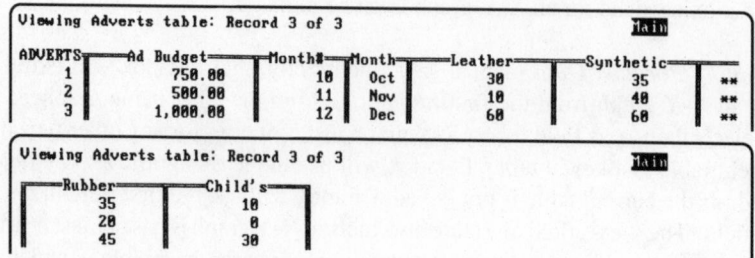

```
Restructuring Adverts table                                    Restructure

STRUCT            Field Name        Field Type
      1    Ad Budget                $
      2    Month#                   S
      3    Month                    A3    ◄              FIELD TYPES
      4    Leather                  N           A_: Alphanumeric (ex: A25)
      5    Synthetic                N           Any combination of
      6    Rubber                   N           characters and spaces
      7    Child's                  N           up to specified width.
                                                Maximum width is 255

                                                N: Numbers with or without
                                                decimal digits.

                                                $: Currency amounts.

                                                D: Dates in the form
```

Figure 12-28 The ADVERTS Table

```
Viewing Adverts table: Record 3 of 3                           Main

ADVERTS    Ad Budget        Month#    Month     Leather    Synthetic
      1       750.00          10      Oct         30          35       **
      2       500.00          11      Nov         10          40       **
      3     1,000.00          12      Dec         60          60       **

Viewing Adverts table: Record 3 of 3                           Main

      Rubber           Child's
        35               10
        20                0
        45               30
```

If you have altered Paradox's graph settings, issue the **[Menu] I**mage **G**raph **R**eset command to reset all graph settings to their default values. (Be sure to save the current settings if you want to use them later.) To make the current graph an X-Y graph, issue the **[Menu] I**mage **G**raph **M**odify command. When you see the Graph Type form, press **X** to select X-Y Graph from the list of graph types. The Graph Type setting will change from Stacked Bar to X-Y. Next, press **[Graph]** to see the graph shown in Figure 12-29.

As you can see, the graph in Figure 12-29 is a mess. By default, Paradox uses a separate line to represent each series on an X-Y graph. This line moves from one data point to the next, in the order of the point's x-axis values. The result can be confusing if the x-axis values are not arranged sequentially in the field containing these values. In this case, the second entry in the Ad Budget field ($500) is less than the first entry ($750). As a result, the series lines in Figure 12-29 begin above the 750 tick mark in the middle of the x-axis, then move backward down the x-axis scale to the 500 tick mark. From that point, the lines move to the opposite end of the scale, to the third x-axis value ($1,000) in the Ad Budget field. Instead of using a line to connect the points, you'll probably want to use markers to plot the position of the values in the graph and omit the connecting lines. The result will be a graph filled with points through which an imaginary line, which moves from left to right, can pass. To change the lines to markers on an X-Y graph, you change the Series Override Graph Type settings on the Graph Type form, shown in Figure 12-4 on page 517. (You can use the Line, Markers, or Combined Lines & Markers override types for individual series in an X-Y graph.) For example, to change the lines on the graph in Figure 12-29 into markers, first press any key to remove the graph from the screen and return to the Graph Designer. Then, press ↓ to move the cursor from the *Graph Type:* prompt to the *1st Series:* prompt under the Series Override Graph Type heading, and press **M** to select the Markers series override type. Next, go down the list of series, changing the override type for each to Markers. When you are finished, press **[Graph]** to see the graph shown in Figure 12-30.

Figure 12-29 An X-Y Graph

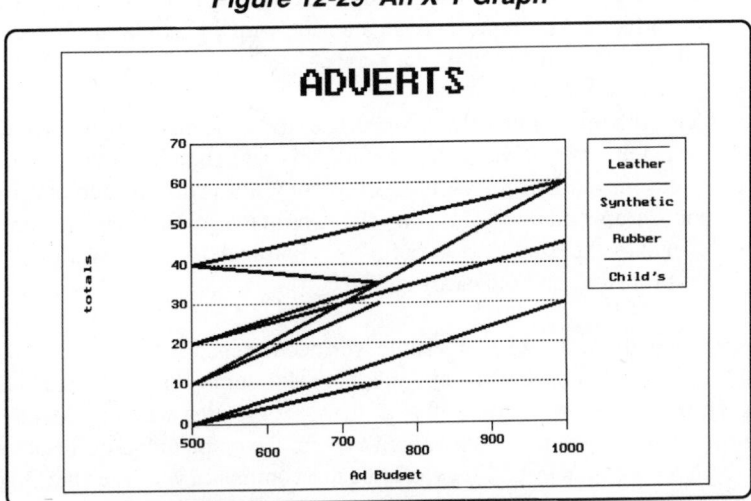

Figure 12-30 An X-Y Graph with Markers Only

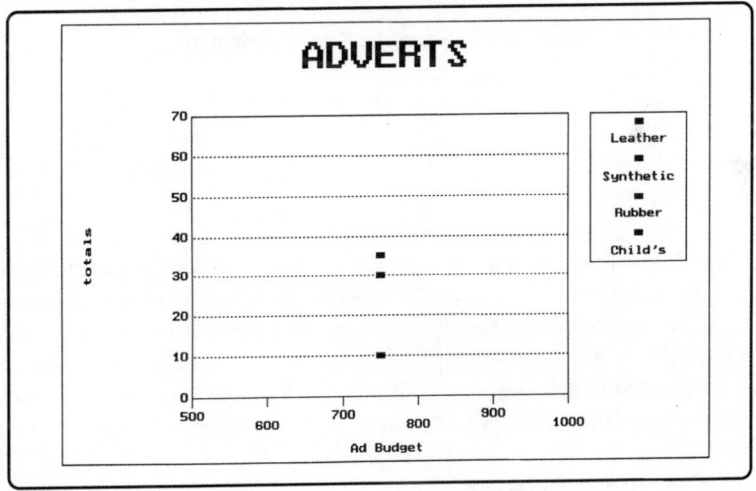

This graph has some problems of its own. First of all, many of the markers you would expect to appear on the graph are not visible. Because the ADVERTS table includes four series fields with three entires for each, the graph should display 12 markers. However, only three markers appear on the graph. Paradox does not show the missing markers because they appear either along the x- or y-axis, or along the vertical line on the right side of the graph. The markers are missing for the same reason that the single marker was missing in our earlier example of a markers graph. All of the missing markers fall on the axes or the other edges of the graph. However, the problem is compounded for X-Y graphs because Paradox uses the minimum and maximum x-axis values from the graph data to determine the range for the x-axis. As a result, markers that represent the data points with these minimum and maximum values will not appear on an X-Y graph. Also, Paradox automatically begins the scaling for the y-axis at zero. Consequently, markers representing data pairs with a y-axis value of zero will not appear on the graph because they fall on the x-axis.

The other problem with this graph is that Paradox uses the same marker symbol to represent each series on the graph. If you have a color monitor, this won't be a serious problem because Paradox will display the markers representing different series in different colors. However, if you have a monochrome monitor, or if you want to print the graph, using the same marker for every series makes the graph very confusing. Fortunately, the missing marker and duplicate marker problems are both easily solved.

To make sure that all of the markers are visible, you need to change the scaling of the x- and y-axes so that no markers appear at the minimum or maximum value on either axis. Earlier in this chapter, we showed you how to change the y-axis scaling with the [Menu] Overall Axes command. To change the scaling of both axes for the graph in Figure 12-30, issue the [Menu] Overall Axes command. After you issue this command, you'll see the Graph Axes form shown in Figure 12-8 on page 522. When you see this form, change the Set Axis scaling setting for both axes to Manual. Then, type the scale settings shown in Table 12-8 for the x-axis and y-axis:

Table 12-8 Sample Scale Settings

Setting	X-axis	Y-axis
Low:	400	70
High:	1100	-10
Increment:	100	10

Next, issue the [Menu] Series MarkersAndFills command to change the markers for the graph. When you issue this command, you'll see the Fills and Markers form shown in Figure 12-13 on page 531. Move the cursor to the *2nd:* prompt under the Marker Symbol heading, and press B to assign the Plus marker to the second series. Then, press ↓ and C to assign the 8 Point Star marker to the third series. Finally, press ↓ and D to assign an Empty Square marker to the fourth series. Now, press [Graph] to view the graph in Figure 12-31.

Mixing Graph Types

In addition to the basic graph types we've looked at so far, Paradox lets you create one more type of graph: mixed graphs. If you have created a line, markers, combined lines and markers, bar, or clustered bar graph, you can use the Graph Designer to change the type for one or more individual series in the graph. As a result, you create graphs that include combinations of bars, lines, markers, and combined lines and markers.

Figure 12-31 The Modified X-Y Graph

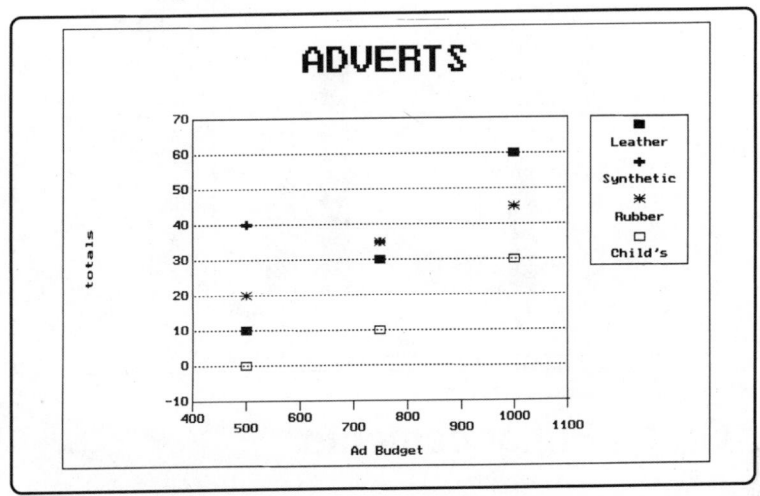

You mix graph types by changing the Series Override Graph Type settings on the Graph Type form, shown in Figure 12-4 on page 517. To override the graph type for a series, move the cursor to the prompt for that series and type the letter that corresponds to the graph type you want to use. You can select Line, Bar, Markers, Combined Lines & Markers, or None as an overriding graph type. (We'll discuss the None type later in this chapter when we show you how to place labels at data points on a graph.)

Let's use the data in the BALLSALE table to create a mixed graph. We'll use this mixed graph to draw attention to the fact that the synthetic basketball consistently outsold all other types of balls. To make this trend stand out, we'll plot the second series (based on the Leather field) as a combined lines and markers graph. To begin, issue the [**Menu**] **I**mage **G**raph **M**odify command. When you see the Graph Type form, press **B** to select the Bar - Regular Bar Graph type. Press ↓ three times to move the cursor to the *2nd Series:* prompt under the Series Override Graph Type heading. Press **C** to select the Combined Lines & Markers graph type for this series and press [**Do-It!**] to save the new settings. Then, press [**Graph**] to see the graph shown in Figure 12-32 on the following page.

Notes

You can change series override graph types only if the current graph type is Bar, Line, Markers, or Combined Lines & Markers. When you select one of these graph types, Paradox automatically changes all of the series override graph types to match the new graph type. When you choose any graph type other than these, the words *Not Applicable* appear at the prompts for the series override graph types.

Figure 12-32 A Mixed Type Graph

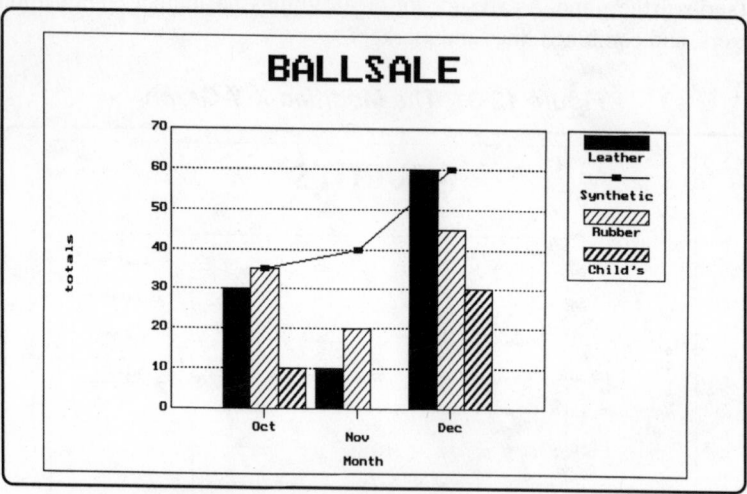

Other Graph Enhancements

So far, we've shown you how to make some basic enhancements you'll regularly use with most graph types and some enhancements you will commonly use with specific types of graphs. In this section, we'll present some other graph enhancements you may want to use in order to fine-tune your graphs even more.

Changing Colors and Fill Patterns

Paradox automatically displays the lines, markers, bars, or slices representing each series on a graph in a different color. Paradox also uses different fill patterns for each series on bar, rotated bar, 3-D bar, area, and pie graphs. We've already shown you how to change colors and fill patterns on a pie graph. In this section, we'll show you how to change these features on all other types of graphs.

Changing Series Colors

To change the screen color for a series, you must enter the Graph Designer, then issue the [Menu] Series Colors Screen command. After you issue this command, Paradox will display the Graph Colors form, shown in Figure 12-33.

You can see the default color setting for each series under the Color column. If you want to change the color that Paradox assigns to a series, you can use the ➡, ⬅, ⬇, and ⬆ keys to move the cursor to the screen color column for that series, then press the letter corresponding to the desired color. Table 12-6 on page 545 shows all the colors you can assign to series, along with the letters corresponding to each color.

Figure 12-33 The Graph Colors Form

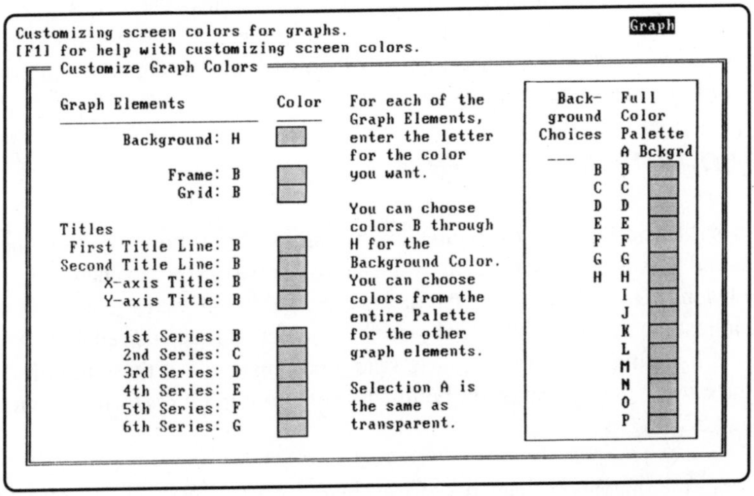

For example, to change the screen color for the first series from blue (B) to yellow (O), first move the cursor to the Color column for the first series. Then, press **O** to select the color yellow. The setting will change from *B* to *O*, and the color block next to the setting will change to match the new color setting. If you press [Graph] to view the modified graph, Paradox will color the line, bars, area, or slices representing the first series yellow instead of blue.

You can use the other prompts on the Graph Colors form to change the color Paradox uses to display the current graph's background, frame, grid, and titles. To change the color for one of these graph elements, just move the cursor to the appropriate prompt and press the letter that corresponds to the color you want to select.

Changing Fill Patterns

To change fill patterns for bar and area graphs, you enter the Graph Designer, then issue the [Menu] Series MarkersAndFills command. After you issue this command, Paradox will display the Fills and Markers form, shown in Figure 12-13 on page 531. Earlier in this chapter, we showed you how to use this form to change markers for markers graphs and combined lines and markers graphs.

The default fill pattern for each series appears in the Fill Patterns column of the Fills and Markers form. If you want to change the fill pattern Paradox assigns to a series, you use the →, ←, ↓, and ↑ keys to move the cursor to the Fill Patterns column for that series, then press the letter corresponding to the pattern you want to choose. Table 12-7 on page 545 shows all the fill patterns you can assign to series, along with the letters corresponding to each pattern.

For example, to change the fill pattern for the first series from Filled (B) to Heavy Dots (L), first move the cursor to the Fill Pattern column for the first series. Then, press *L* to select the Heavy Dots pattern. The setting will change from B - Filled to L - Hvy Dots. If you press [Graph] to view the modified graph, Paradox will now fill the bars or area representing the first series with the Heavy Dots fill pattern.

Modifying the X- and Y-axes

In the section "Basic Graph Enhancements," we showed you how to adjust the scaling along the x- and y-axes of a graph, but there are also other ways you can change the axes. By issuing the [Menu] Overall Axes command, you can also change the format of tick marks on both axes, adjust the number of decimal places in the tick marks, and remove or rearrange some tick marks to make a graph easier to read. You make all of these modifications by changing the settings that appear on the bottom half of the Graph Axes form, shown in Figure 12-8 on page 522.

To demonstrate the changes you can make to tick marks, we'll use a table called NATIONAL. The structure of the NATIONAL table is shown in Figure 12-34, and the table itself is shown in Figure 12-35. While the BALLSALE table listed monthly volume sales for a single sales region, the NATIONAL table lists monthly dollar sales for the entire nation. As a result, the figures in this new table are much larger than those in the BALLSALE table.

Figure 12-34 The Structure of the NATIONAL Table

```
Viewing Struct table: Record 1 of 6                                    Main

STRUCT            Field Name          Field Type
     1    Month#                       S*
     2    Month                        A3*
     3    Leather                      $
     4    Synthetic                    $
     5    Rubber                       $
     6    Child's                      $
```

Figure 12-35 The NATIONAL Table

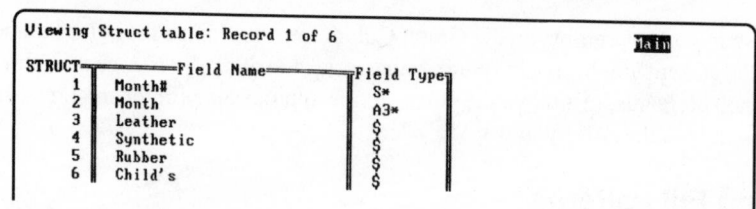

```
Viewing National table: Record 1 of 3                                  Main

NATIONAL  Month#  Month   Leather      Synthetic     Rubber       Child's
     1      10     Oct    10,920.00     8,892.00     4,340.00       840.00
     2      11     Nov     3,640.00     9,240.00     2,480.00     1,056.00
     3      12     Dec    21,840.00    13,872.00     5,580.00     2,520.00
```

Figure 12-36 shows a stacked bar graph based on the NATIONAL table. To create this graph, place the cursor in the Leather field of the NATIONAL table and press **[Graph]**.

As you can see, Paradox has automatically selected an increment of 10,000 for the y-axis and displayed values ranging from 0 to 50,000 on the scale. In other words, each tick mark as you progress up the scale represents an increase of 10,000. To make changes to the tick marks on this graph, issue the **[Menu]** I**mage** G**raph** M**odify** command to enter the Graph Designer.

Then issue the [Menu] Overall Axes command to see the Graph Axes form. We won't show the graph again until we finish making all of our changes, but you can view the graph from the Graph Designer at any time by pressing [Graph].

Figure 12-36 A Stacked Bar Graph

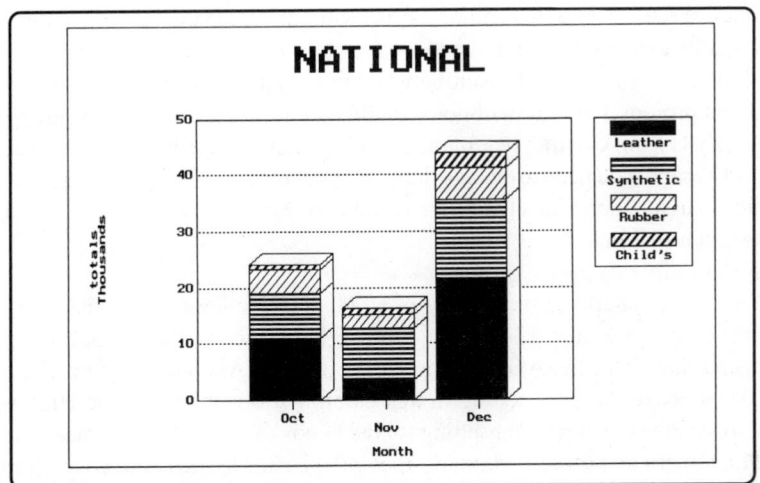

Changing Tick Mark Formats

You can select from six tick mark formats by changing the setting at the *Format of Ticks:* prompt. The six format settings are Fixed, Scientific, Currency, Financial, General, and Percent. The Fixed format, which is Paradox's default format for both axes, displays numbers with up to two decimal places. The Scientific format displays numbers in scientific notation. For example, in the Scientific format, Paradox would display the number 10 as *1E+1* (meaning 1 * 10 to the first power). The Currency format displays numbers with two decimal places and inserts a dollar sign in front of each value. The Financial format separates numbers with commas (100,000,000) and places parentheses around negative values. The Percent format simply inserts a percent sign (%) after each value. To pick one of these formats, you move the cursor to the *Format of Ticks:* prompt and press the key that corresponds to the desired format. In most cases, this letter is the first letter in the name of the format selection. There is one exception to this rule: the Financial format. To choose the Financial format, you press the comma key (,).

Let's change the tick mark format for the graph in Figure 12-36 from Fixed to Currency. To do this, move the cursor to the *Format of Ticks:* prompt under the Y-Axis column and press C. The Format of Ticks setting will change from Fixed to Currency.

You can also specify the number of decimal places Paradox should display for tick marks by changing the value at the *Decimal Places (0-15):* prompt for that axis. However, in this case, we'll leave the decimal places set to the default value of 0.

Adding Minor Ticks

There may be times when you do not want to label every tick mark on an axis. In these cases, you can tell Paradox to leave a specified number of unlabeled tick marks between labeled tick marks. These unlabeled tick marks are known as minor tick marks. You can use minor tick marks to make the scale on an axis more precise without adding clutter to the graph. To add minor tick marks to a graph, you move to the *Number of Minor Ticks:* prompt and type the number of minor tick marks you want between the regular tick marks. When you type a number at this prompt, Paradox will not actually add new tick marks to the graph but will remove the labels from existing tick marks, making them minor tick marks. To add minor tick marks to a graph, you need to change the scaling for the axes first, reducing the increment between tick marks. Then, you change the Number of Minor Ticks setting to make the new tick marks minor tick marks.

Let's add minor tick marks at increments of 5,000 between the existing tick marks on the y-axis of the graph in Figure 12-36. First, move the cursor to the top half of the Graph Axes form and change the Set Axis Scaling setting in the Y-Axis column from Automatic to Manual. Then, leave the Low setting in that column at 0 and change the High setting to 50000. Also, change the Increment setting for the y-axis to 5000. Now, to make every other tick mark on the graph a minor tick mark, move the cursor to the *Number of Minor Ticks:* prompt and type **1**.

Alternating Ticks on the X-axis

If you look at the graph in Figure 12-36, you can see that the tick mark labels along the x-axis are actually displayed on two rows on the screen, with the middle tick mark displayed one row below the other two other tick marks. By default, Paradox alternates the rows on which it displays x-axis tick mark labels. Displaying these labels on alternate rows prevents them from overlapping on graphs that have long tick mark labels and/or several tick marks. If you would rather display all x-axis tick marks on the same row, you can do this by moving the cursor to the *Alternate Ticks?* prompt on the Graph Axes form and pressing *N*. Of course, you can go back to the alternating tick marks by pressing *Y* at this prompt.

Since the x-axis tick mark labels on the graph in Figure 12-36 are neither long nor numerous, there is really no need to display them on alternate rows. To display them on the same line, move the cursor to the *Alternate Ticks?* prompt and press **N**.

Removing Axis Scaling

Because the values on the y-axis scale in Figure 12-36 are so large, Paradox scales the values by 1,000. For example, the label *50* on the y-axis actually represents the value 50,000. To make this scaling obvious, the word *Thousands* appears under the y-axis title along the left edge of the graph. Paradox automatically scales any axis that lists values equal to or greater than 10,000. As the y-axis values grow, the scaling description changes to millions, billions, and the scientific notation that represents even higher values. You can remove the scaling description from a graph by moving to the *Display Axis Scaling?* prompt and pressing *N* to change the setting from Yes to No. Since the scaling description contributes to the clarity of the graph, it is rarely advisable to change this setting. We'll leave the Display Axis Scaling? setting alone in this graph.

After you have finished modifying the tick marks, press **[Graph]** to view the graph shown in Figure 12-37. As you can see, the y-axis in this new graph includes minor tick marks between the regular tick marks, and the regular tick marks now include dollar signs because Paradox displays them in the Currency format.

Figure 12-37 The Modified Graph

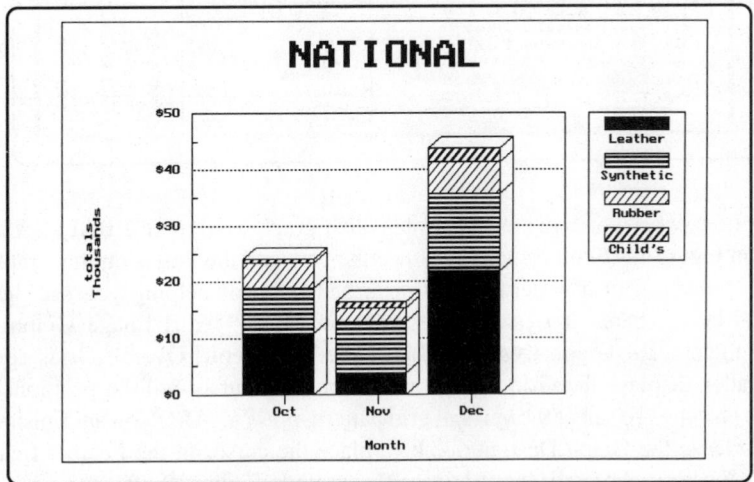

In this example, we changed the display settings for the y-axis, but as you can see in Figure 12-8 on page 522, the Graph Axes form also contains settings for the x-axis. However, you can change the appearance of the x-axis only on an X-Y graph because only X-Y graphs have scales for both the x-axis and the y-axis. You can change the x-axis tick mark settings for any graph, but unless the current graph is an X-Y graph, Paradox will ignore these settings.

Changing Grids

Each graph that we have created in this chapter, except the pie graph, has included horizontal grids that extend the y-axis tick marks across the entire graph. These grids make graphs easier to read and understand. Although the horizontal dotted line grid is Paradox's default grid style, you can change the grid for any graph by issuing the [Menu] Overall Grids command. When you issue this command, Paradox will display the Grids and Frames form shown in Figure 12-38. To change the grid for the current graph, you move the cursor to the *Grid Line:* prompt and press the number (1 through 6) that corresponds to the desired grid type. Grid types 1 through 4 are types of horizontal grid patterns, while grid type 5 is a combination of vertical and horizontal grids, and grid type 6 is a vertical pattern only.

Figure 12-38 The Grids and Frames Form

```
Setting grid lines for graphing.                              Graph
[F1] for help with setting grid lines.
┌─ Customize Grids and Frames ═══════════════════════════════════════

     Select a grid line type from    Grid Line Types:     Color
     the options at the right.                            Palette:
     Select a color from the         1. .......
     Color Palette.                  2. ─────────          A   Bckgrd
                                     3. ─ ─ ─ ─            B
     Grid Line: 1. .........         4. ── ─ ──            C
     Grid Color: P  ▢                5. + (Vertical       D
                                          and horiz.)     E
                                     6. ! (Vertical       F
                                          only)           G
                                                          H
                                                          I
                                                          J
     Decide whether or not to frame  Frame Graph:         K
     the Graph.  Select a frame                           L
     color from the Color Palette.   (Y)es                M
                                     (N)o                 N
     Frame Graph: Yes                                     O
     Frame Color: P  ▢                                    P
```

For example, suppose you had created a rotated bar graph based on the BALLSALE table, as shown in Figure 12-20 on page 537. Since the bars and the y-axis on this graph are all horizontal, a vertical grid pattern would do a better job of helping you see the values represented by the bars. To change the grid, issue the **[Menu]** Image Graph Modify command to enter the Graph Designer, then issue the **[Menu]** Overall Grids command. When Paradox displays the Grids and Frames form, the cursor will be positioned at the *Grid Line:* prompt. To select the vertical grid pattern, press **6**. After you are finished, press **[Do-It!]** to leave the Graph Designer. Then, place the cursor in the Leather field of the BALLSALE table and press **[Graph]** to see the graph in Figure 12-39.

Figure 12-39 A Vertical Grid Pattern

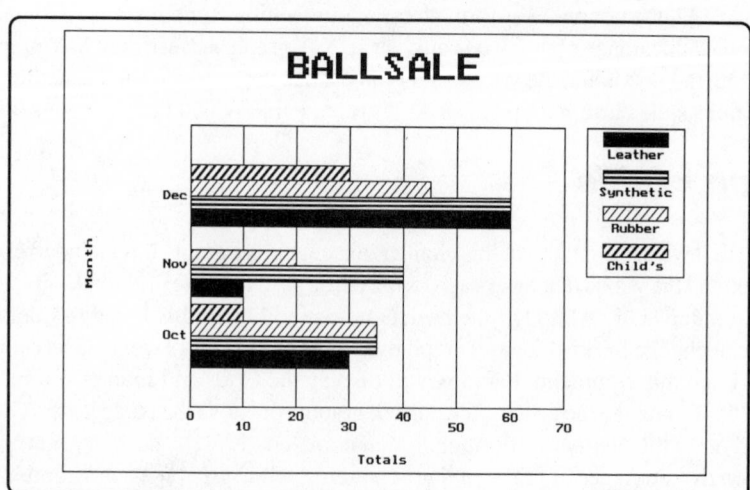

Removing the Frame

All of the graphs we have viewed in this chapter have included a single-line frame around the edge of the screen. You can remove this frame by changing the Frame Graph setting on the Grids and Frames form. To remove the frame, you move the cursor to the *Frame Graph:* prompt at the bottom of the screen and press *N*. When you do this, the setting displayed at the prompt will change from Yes to No. Of course, you can then restore the frame by pressing *Y* with the cursor at the *Frame Graph:* prompt.

Changing Frame and Grid Colors

You can also change the color of the frame or the grid from the Grids and Frames form. This form includes a list of Paradox's display colors and the letters that correspond to individual colors. (Table 12-6 on page 545 lists these colors and their corresponding letters.) To change the color for the grid, you move the cursor to the *Grid Color:* prompt and press the letter that corresponds to the desired color. To change the color for the frame, you move the cursor to the *Frame Color:* prompt and press the letter that corresponds to the color in which you want to display the frame. You can also change the colors of the grid and frame by issuing the [Menu] Overall Colors command. When you issue this command, Paradox will display the Graph Colors form shown in Figure 12-33 on 553.

Identifying Fields with Legends and Labels

By default, Paradox uses the name of the field containing the data for a series to identify that series on a graph's legend. However, there may be times when you want to specify legend labels other than the series field names. You can change the labels on a legend by issuing the [Menu] Series LegendsAndLabels command. After you issue this command, Paradox will display the Series Legends and Labels form shown in Figure 12-40 on the following page. From this form, you can change the legend label for one or more series or remove the legend from the graph completely. You can also add interior labels that display the y-axis values at each data point represented on the graph.

Removing the Legend

To remove the legend from a graph, simply move the cursor to the *Use a Legend? (Y/N)* prompt and press *N* to change this setting to No. Of course, you can then restore the legend by pressing *Y* with the cursor positioned at this prompt. Most of the time, you will want to leave the legend on the graph in order to make the graph easier to understand.

Changing a Legend Label

To replace the default legend label for a series with a new label, you move the cursor to the *Series Legend:* prompt for that series and type the new label. Paradox will let you type up to 26 characters at the prompt, but only the first ten characters will appear on the legend.

Figure 12-40 The Series Legends and Labels Form

```
Defining legends for subsequent graphing.                          Graph
[F1] for help with defining graph legends.
┌─ Customize Series Legends and Labels ═════════════════════════════════
│
│   Enter a legend for each series.  If you make no
│   entry, Paradox will use the field name.
│
│   Use a Legend?  (Y/N): Yes ◄
│     1st Series Legend:
│     2nd Series Legend:                           The interior
│     3rd Series Legend:                           label location
│     4th Series Legend:                           places the value
│     5th Series Legend:                           for each point
│     6th Series Legend:                           in the graph.
│   ──────────────────────────────────────────
│   Enter a location for each series label.        Label Placement:
│                                                    (C)enter
│     1st Series Label: None                         (A)bove
│     2nd Series Label: None                         (B)elow
│     3rd Series Label: None                         (R)ight
│     4th Series Label: None                         (L)eft
│     5th Series Label: None                         (N)one
│     6th Series Label: None                          - to reset
```

Suppose you want to clarify the type of basketball represented by the Synthetic series on the graph in Figure 12-39 by changing the legend label to *Synth Lthr*. To make this change, first issue the **[Menu]** **I**mage **G**raph **M**odify command to enter the Graph Designer. Then, issue the **[Menu]** **S**eries **L**egendsAndLabels command. When you see the Series Legends and Labels form, press ↓ twice to move the cursor to the *2nd Series Legend:* prompt, then type **Synth Lthr**. We'll view the modified graph after we change one more setting.

Adding Interior Labels

You can add interior labels for one or more series on a graph by changing the setting at the *Series Label:* prompt for that series. The *Series Label:* prompts appear in the lower portion of the Series Legends and Labels form. Interior labels display y-axis values for a data point at the position of the data point on the graph. Paradox does not automatically display interior labels because the default Series Label setting for every series is None. To display interior labels for a series, you change the Series Label setting for that series. The new setting tells Paradox where to display the labels relative to the data points for the series. The six possible Series Label settings appear along the right edge of the Series Legends and Labels form.

Sometimes, the location you choose will depend on the type of graph to which you are adding labels. For example, labels on a bar graph should be placed above data points to ensure their visibility, while labels on a rotated graph should be placed to the right of data points for the same reason. With other graph types, such as combined lines and markers graphs, the location of the data points themselves will dictate where you should place interior labels. You may want to choose different label locations for different series on the same graph in order to prevent lines or markers from obscuring the labels.

Let's place interior labels to the right of the data points on the rotated bar graph in Figure 12-39. First, move the cursor to the *1st Series Label:* prompt and press **R**. When you do this, the setting at this prompt will change from None to Right. Next, move down the list, changing the Series Label settings for the second, third, and fourth series all to Right. When you are finished, press **[Graph]** to see the graph in Figure 12-41. As you can see, this graph includes the new labels for the series based on the Synthetic field and interior labels placed to the right of each bar.

Figure 12-41 Changing Legends and Adding Interior Labels

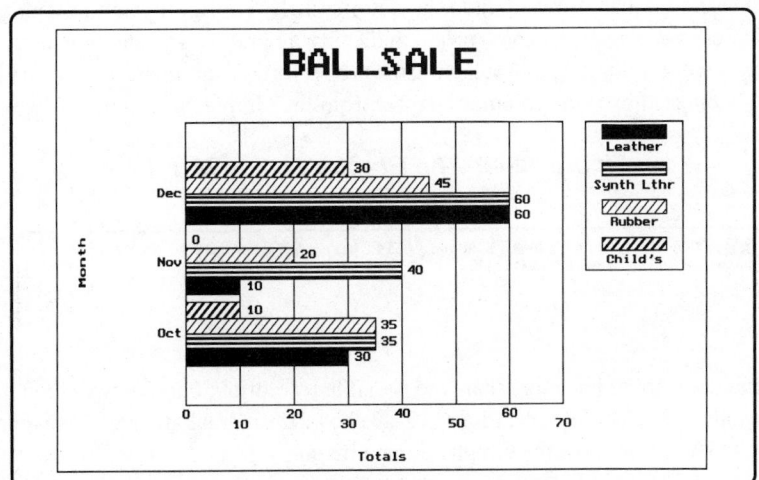

Setting the Display Period

When you view a graph on the screen, Paradox automatically displays the graph until you press any key on the keyboard. However, you can use the Graph Designer's [Menu] Overall Wait command to set a display time for an individual graph. Setting a display period is especially useful when you use a Paradox Application Language (PAL) script to display several graphs in succession.

When you issue the command, Paradox will display a menu with two options: Keystroke and Duration. The Keystroke option, which is the default selection, leaves the graph on the screen until any key is pressed. The Duration option allows you to specify how many seconds the graph should remain on the screen. If you select this option, Paradox will display the prompt *Number of seconds to wait:*. At this prompt, type in the number of seconds the graph should remain on the screen and press ↵. For example, if you enter the number 15 at this prompt, the current graph will remain on the screen for 15 seconds the next time you display it. After 15 seconds, the graph will disappear, and Paradox will return to the workspace.

Adjusting Paradox's Graphics Format

When displaying graphs on your monitor, Paradox automatically adjusts itself to take advantage of the highest possible resolution supported by your graphics adapter. However, in rare cases, Paradox may not be able to sense the graphics format best suited for your system.

If you encounter a problem because Paradox cannot detect the proper resolution for your graphics adapter, you can use the CCP to manually select a graphics format.

To do this, issue the [**Menu**] **S**cripts **P**lay command, type **\paradox3\custom**, and press ↵. When you see the CCP main menu, issue the **G**raphs **S**creen command. At this point, you will see a menu of screen display formats, as shown in Figure 12-42. The Auto selection is the default selection that allows Paradox to automatically configure itself to your graphics adapter. Unless you encounter some problem displaying graphs, you should leave the Auto selection in place. If Paradox is not selecting the proper format automatically, you can choose the format supported by your graphics adapter from the Graphs Screen menu.

Figure 12-42 The Graphs Screen Menu

```
Auto  CGA  MCGA  EGA  EGA64  EGAMono  8514  Herc  ATT  VGA  3270  T1000 ▶
Detect display type automatically.
```

If the format you choose has more than one possible resolution, Paradox will then display a menu of resolutions. For example, Figure 12-43 shows the menu Paradox will display if you choose the EGA option from the Graphs Screen menu.

Figure 12-43 The EGA Menu

```
EGALOW  EGAHI
Enhanced Graphics Adapter, 640 x 200 - 16 color.
```

After you have finished selecting a graphics format, the CCP will return to the Graphs Screen menu. To make the new format setting permanent, issue the **R**eturn command, then the **DO-IT!** command on the CCP main menu. The next time you load Paradox, graphs will appear in the graphics format you have specified.

Preparing Data for Graphing

In all the examples in this chapter, we've used tables with structures that made them easy to graph. These tables have had spreadsheet-like structures that distributed data in a grid divided into columns and rows. For example, the BALLSALE table is divided into columns associated with different types of basketballs and rows associated with different months. The rows are defined by the contents of the Month field, and the columns are defined by the names of the other fields in the table. The individual entries in the Leather, Synthetic, Rubber, and Child's fields contain information linked to the row and column that intersect at different points on the grid. When you transform a table like BALLSALE into a graph, the columns become the graph's series, the rows become the x-axis values, and the intersecting points become the y-axis values.

Of course, data is rarely stored in tables that so readily lend themselves to graphing. Usually, data is broken into small units and spread out over many records. In a normalized table system, data may also be spread out over several tables. Luckily, Paradox includes tools that help you collect and summarize the data in your Paradox tables, transforming them into new tables you can use to create meaningful graphs. Queries, PAL scripts, and cross tabulations are the three tools you will use most while preparing data for graphing. We explained queries in detail in Chapters 7 and 8, and will discuss PAL programming in Chapters 13 through 17. In this section, we'll explain cross tabulations and show you how to use them with queries and PAL scripts to prepare your data for graphing. As an example, we'll show you how to use these tools to create the BALLSALE table, which we have graphed several times in this chapter.

Cross-tabulating Tables

The [Menu] Image Graph CrossTab command and the [CrossTab] key ([Alt]-[X]) are the tools you use to transform conventionally structured tables into tables you can use to create graphs. When you cross-tabulate a table, Paradox summarizes information in the table and distributes the summary statistics in a temporary spreadsheet-like table called CROSSTAB. The CROSSTAB table always has the row and column structure that makes a table suitable for graphing. The [Menu] Image Graph CrossTab command lets you select one of four statistical operations that Paradox can use to compute the field entries for the CROSSTAB table. A cross-tabulated table can list sums of values, minimum values, maximum values, and counts of values. The [CrossTab] key automatically computes sums for groups of records in the current table. In order for you to use either of these tools, the current image must contain a table, and Paradox must be in Main mode.

The [Menu] Image Graph CrossTab Command

When you issue the [Menu] Image Graph CrossTab command, Paradox will display the menu shown in Figure 12-44. You use this menu to select the type of statistical computation Paradox should perform when producing the CROSSTAB table. Most of the time, you will probably select the 1) Sum option from this menu in order to graph summary data for a table.

Figure 12-44 The CrossTab Menu

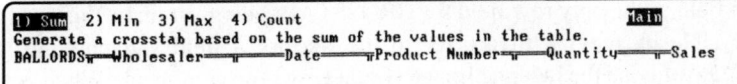

```
1) Sum   2) Min   3) Max   4) Count                              Main
Generate a crosstab based on the sum of the values in the table.
BALLORDS    Wholesaler        Date      Product Number    Quantity    Sales
```

Next, Paradox will ask you to specify which fields contain the values for the CROSSTAB row labels, column labels, and grid values. After you select these fields, Paradox will scan the row label field for unique entries and place these unique entries in the first field of the CROSSTAB table. The first field of CROSSTAB will have the same name as the row label field in the original table and will be a key field.

Next, Paradox will scan the column label field for unique entries and add one field to CROSSTAB for each unique entry. Paradox names these fields in CROSSTAB after the unique entries in the column field. Finally, Paradox scans the entries in the grid value column, grouping these entries based on common values in the row label and column label fields. Paradox performs the selected computation for each of these groups and places the results of these calculations at the intersection of the row and column labels that define the groups.

An Example

Let's look at an example cross tabulation. Figure 12-45 shows the structure of a table called PETS, which lists information about sales at a pet store. Each record includes the receipt number for a sale, the name of the salesperson, the type of animal sold, and the quantity sold. Figure 12-46 shows the data in the PETS table.

Figure 12-45 The Structure of the PETS Table

```
Viewing Struct table: Record 1 of 4                      Main

STRUCT          Field Name         Field Type
    1    Receipt #                  N*
    2    Salesperson                A10
    3    Animal                     A10
    4    Quantity                   N
```

Figure 12-46 The PETS Table

```
Viewing Pets table: Record 1 of 7                        Main

PETS      Receipt #    Salesperson    Animal    Quantity
    1        1001         Smith         Dog         1
    2        1002         Jones         Cat         2
    3        1003         Smith         Dog         1
    4        1010         Smith         Cat         2
    5        1013         Jones         Cat         1
    6        1015         Smith         Cat         2
    7        1017         Jones         Dog         1
```

Let's create a CROSSTAB table that has the types of animals as its column labels, and the names of the salespeople as its row labels. The grid values will show how many of each type of animal were sold by each salesperson. Before you begin, the PETS table must be on the workspace and Paradox must be in the Main mode. Also, since you want to use the Salesperson field as the only row field for CROSSTAB, you must make this field the first field in the table by moving the cursor to the Receipt # field and pressing **[Rotate]** ([Ctrl]-[R]). Next, issue the **[Menu]** Image Graph CrossTab command. When you see the CrossTab Menu, press ↵ to select the 1) Sum option. Paradox will display a prompt asking you to move the cursor to the field containing the row labels for CROSSTAB. When you see this prompt, move the cursor to the Salesperson field and press ↵. Paradox will display a similar prompt asking you to select the field containing the column labels. When you see this prompt, move the cursor to the Animal field and press ↵. Finally, Paradox will ask you to select the field containing the values for the CROSSTAB table. When you see this prompt, move the cursor to the Quantity field and press ↵. After you select the grid value field, Paradox will create the CROSSTAB table shown in Figure 12-47.

Figure 12-47 The CROSSTAB Table

```
Viewing Crosstab table: Record 1 of 2                    Main

PETS───Salesperson───Animal────Quantity───Receipt #──┐
   1 │  Smith        Dog           1          1001
   2 │  Jones        Cat           2          1002
   3 │  Smith        Dog           1          1003
   4 │  Smith        Cat           2          1010
   5 │  Jones        Cat           1          1013
   6 │  Smith        Cat           2          1015
   7 │  Jones        Dog           1          1017


CROSSTAB─Salesperson───Dog────Cat─┐
   1 │    Jones         1       3
   2 │    Smith         2       4
```

The [CrossTab] Key

The [CrossTab] key ([Alt]-[X]) provides a quicker method of creating a CROSSTAB table. When you press [CrossTab], Paradox assumes that the cursor is in the row label field. Also, Paradox assumes that the last field in the image contains the CROSSTAB grid values, and that the second-to-last field is the column label field. Before you can use [CrossTab], then, you must arrange your table according to these rules.

Let's use the [CrossTab] key to create the CROSSTAB table shown in Figure 12-47. First, you need to rotate the PETS table so that the Animal and Quantity fields are the last two fields in the table. Assuming that you have already rotated the Receipt # field to the end of the table, as shown in Figure 12-47, move the cursor to the Animal field and press **[Rotate]** twice. After you do this, the PETS table will have the field order shown in Figure 12-48. Now, move the cursor to the Salesperson field and press **[CrossTab]**. When you do this, Paradox will produce the same CROSSTAB table shown in Figure 12-47.

Figure 12-48 The Rotated PETS Table

```
Viewing Pets table: Record 1 of 7                       Main

PETS───Salesperson───Receipt #───Animal───Quantity─┐
   1 │  Smith         1001         Dog        1
   2 │  Jones         1002         Cat        2
   3 │  Smith         1003         Dog        1
   4 │  Smith         1010         Cat        2
   5 │  Jones         1013         Cat        1
   6 │  Smith         1015         Cat        2
   7 │  Jones         1017         Dog        1
```

Multiple Row Fields

Paradox allows you to use more than one field to label the rows on a CROSSTAB table. If the specified row field is not the first field in the table when you issue the [Menu] Image Graph CrossTab command, Paradox will use the row field and any fields that are in front of it for the row labels in the CROSSTAB table. For example, if there is one field to the left of the row field, CROSSTAB will group records that have common values in the row field, the field in front of the row field, and the column field before computing summary statistics.

Paradox will also organize the CROSSTAB table in this manner if there are one or more fields in front of the current field when you press the [CrossTab] key. Under this condition, Paradox would use each of the fields in front of the current field, as well as the current field itself, as row labels for the CROSSTAB table. As usual, Paradox would use the second-to-last field in the table as the column label field and base the summary calculations stored in the CROSSTAB table on the values in the last field in the table.

When you create a CROSSTAB table with more than one row label field, Paradox makes the row field and any fields in front of it the key fields for the CROSSTAB table. Keying CROSSTAB on these fields guarantees that no two records in CROSSTAB can contain summary information for the same group.

Using multiple row label fields can be useful when you want to sort CROSSTAB on one field but use entries in another field as the x-axis labels on the graph. For example, the BALLSALE table, which we have used throughout this chapter, is actually a CROSSTAB table whose first key field contains numeric representations of months and whose second key field contains the alphanumeric abbreviation for those months. Both fields contain the same information, but each serves a separate purpose. The first field provides the proper order for the records in the BALLSALE table because Paradox can sort the numeric values. The second key field provides information that is easier to understand on a graph. Multiple row fields are also useful for computing summary information for purposes other than graphing. For example, you can create reports based on CROSSTAB tables with multiple row fields.

An Example

Now that you are familiar with cross tabulation, let's look at an example of how you might use it, along with a query and a PAL script, to graph data from a normalized table system. For our example, we'll show you how to create our sample BALLSALE table, based on data in two different tables. Figure 12-49 shows the structure of a table called BALLORDS, which is the master table in this normalized system. BALLORDS contains information about individual sales orders placed over a three-month period for different types of basketballs. Figure 12-50 shows the data in the BALLORDS table.

As you can see, the BALLORDS table does not list the actual type of basketball ordered. Instead, the Product Number field contains a number that corresponds to one of the four types of basketballs: leather, synthetic, rubber, and child's. Figure 12-51 shows the structure of a table called BALLS, which lists the types of balls along with their product numbers and prices. Figure 12-52 shows the BALLS table. We must use the BALLS table in our example so that we can include the names of the types of balls, rather than just their product numbers, in our graphs.

Figure 12-49 The Structure of the BALLORDS Table

```
Viewing Struct table: Record 1 of 5                       Main

STRUCT          Field Name          Field Type
   1    Retailer                    N*
   2    Date                        D*
   3    Product Number              N*
   4    Quantity                    N
   5    Salesperson                 N
```

Figure 12-50 The BALLORDS Table

```
Viewing Ballords table: Record 1 of 23                    Main

BALLORDS  Retailer      Date     Product Number   Quantity   Salesp
   1         1        12/01/88        1             15         1
   2         1        12/01/88        2             15         1
   3         1        12/01/88        3             20         1
   4         1        12/01/88        4             20         1
   5         2        10/21/88        1             20         2
   6         2        10/21/88        2             25         2
   7         2        10/21/88        3             25         2
   8         3        12/07/88        1             10         1
   9         3        12/07/88        2             10         1
  10         5        10/30/88        1             10         1
  11         5        10/30/88        2             10         1
  12         5        10/30/88        3             10         1
  13         5        10/30/88        4             10         1
  14         6        11/08/88        2             25         3
  15         6        11/08/88        3             20         3
  16         7        12/04/88        1             20         3
  17         7        12/04/88        2             20         3
  18         8        11/25/88        1             10         1
  19         8        11/25/88        2             15         1
  20         9        12/03/88        1             15         2
  21         9        12/03/88        2             15         2
  22         9        12/03/88        3             25         2
  23         9        12/03/88        4             10         2
```

Figure 12-51 The Structure of the BALLS Table

```
Viewing Struct table: Record 1 of 3                       Main

STRUCT          Field Name          Field Type
   1    Product Number              N*
   2    Ball Type                   A10
   3    Price                       $
```

Figure 12-52 The BALLS Table

```
Viewing Balls table: Record 1 of 4                        Main

BALLS  Product Number   Ball Type      Price
  1          1          leather        22.75
  2          2          synthetic      14.45
  3          3          rubber          7.75
  4          4          child's         5.25
```

Using a Query to Gather Data

First, we'll use a query to gather data from the BALLORDS and BALLS tables into a single ANSWER table. The ANSWER table we want to create must include the month the order was placed, the type of ball ordered, and the number of balls ordered. Of course, the month in which the order was placed is included in the Date field of the BALLORDS table, and the number of balls ordered is in the Quantity field of that table. However, the type of ball ordered is in the Ball Type field of the BALLS table, which is referenced by entries in the Product Number field of BALLORDS. Figure 12-53 shows a query that can bring all of this information into a single table.

Figure 12-53 A Query by Example

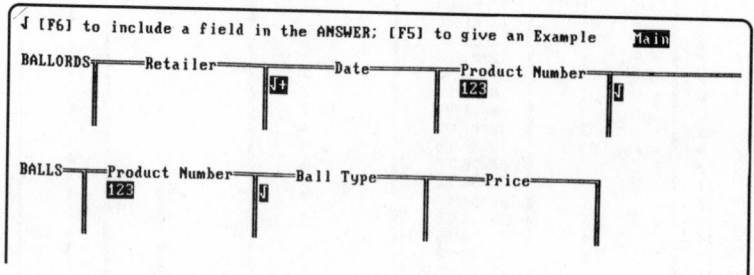

This query uses an example in the Product Number fields of both tables to link the two tables. However, neither field is marked for inclusion in the ANSWER table. Only the Date and Quantity fields from BALLORDS and the Ball Type field from BALLS are check-marked. As a result, each record in the ANSWER table will include a Date field listing the date of an order, a Quantity field listing the number of balls ordered, and a Ball Type field listing the type of ball ordered. Notice that the Date field is marked with a check plus rather than a regular check mark. The check plus tells Paradox to include duplicate records in ANSWER, ensuring that you will not lose data if any BALLORDS records contain duplicate information in checked fields. Figure 12-54 shows the ANSWER table produced by the query.

While this ANSWER table includes all the fields that contain the information we want to graph, the information is not isolated. The Date field contains the date on which all orders were placed, but we need the month the orders were placed isolated in a separate field. In cases like this, PAL provides handy and relatively easy-to-use tools for extracting elements of information in date fields.

Using a PAL Script

Before you can extract the month from each entry in the Date field, you need a place to put this information. Actually, you'll need two fields to hold this information—one to hold the numeric value representing the month (1 through 12) and another to hold the three-letter alphanumeric representation of the month (*Jan* through *Dec*). You'll need the numeric value for sorting the CROSSTAB table and the alphanumeric field for the x-axis labels when you graph the CROSSTAB table. To add these new fields to ANSWER, issue the **[Menu] M**odify **R**estructure command, type **ANSWER** at the *Table:* prompt, and press ↵. When Paradox displays the current structure of ANSWER in a STRUCT table, press **[Ins]** twice to add two new fields at the top of the ANSWER table's structure. Next, type **Month#** in the Field Name field of record 1 in the STRUCT table and **S** (for short number) in the Field Type field. Then, type **Month** in the Field Name field of record 2 and **A3** in the Field Type field. The modified STRUCT table should look like Figure 12-55. Press **[Do-It!]** to finish restructuring the table.

Figure 12-54 The ANSWER Table

```
Viewing Answer table: Record 1 of 23                          Main  ▲═

ANSWER══════════Date═══════════Quantity══════════Ball Type═══
        1      12/01/88            15            leather
        2      12/01/88            15            synthetic
        3      12/01/88            20            rubber
        4      12/01/88            20            child's
        5      10/21/88            20            leather
        6      10/21/88            25            synthetic
        7      10/21/88            25            rubber
        8      12/07/88            10            leather
        9      12/07/88            10            synthetic
       10      10/30/88            10            leather
       11      10/30/88            10            synthetic
       12      10/30/88            10            rubber
       13      10/30/88            10            child's
       14      11/08/88            25            synthetic
       15      11/08/88            20            rubber
       16      12/04/88            20            leather
       17      12/04/88            20            synthetic
       18      11/25/88            10            leather
       19      11/25/88            15            synthetic
       20      12/03/88            15            leather
       21      12/03/88            15            synthetic
       22      12/03/88            25            rubber
       23      12/03/88            10            child's
```

Figure 12-55 The New Structure for ANSWER

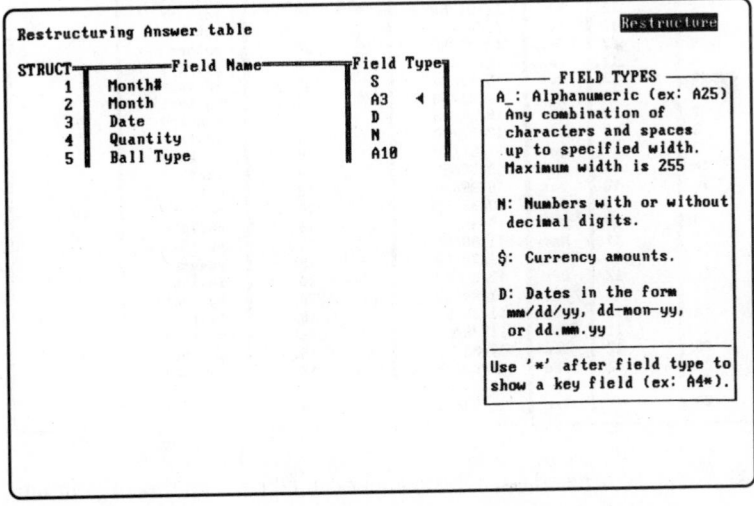

```
Restructuring Answer table                              Restructure

STRUCT═══════════Field Name═══════Field Type═
       1      Month#                 S                  ──── FIELD TYPES ────
       2      Month                  A3   ◄          A_: Alphanumeric (ex: A25)
       3      Date                   D               Any combination of
       4      Quantity               N               characters and spaces
       5      Ball Type              A10             up to specified width.
                                                     Maximum width is 255

                                                     N: Numbers with or without
                                                        decimal digits.

                                                     $: Currency amounts.

                                                     D: Dates in the form
                                                        mm/dd/yy, dd-mon-yy,
                                                        or dd.mm.yy

                                                     Use '*' after field type to
                                                     show a key field (ex: A4*).
```

Now, you need to fill the Month# and Month fields of each record in the ANSWER table. You could enter data into the Month field manually, but this would take a long time and create many opportunities for errors. However, you can fill the Month field quickly and accurately by using a script like the one shown in Figure 12-56.

Figure 12-56 The Addmonth Script

```
Changing script C:\paradox3\comprev\addmonth                    Script

....+...10....+...20....+...30....+...40....+...50....+...60....+...70....+...80
EDIT "Answer"
SCAN
  [Month#] = MONTH([Date])
  [Month] = MOY([Date])
ENDSCAN
Do_It!
```

The first line in this script uses the PAL abbreviation of the [Menu] Modify Edit command to place the ANSWER table on the Paradox workspace in Edit mode. Next, a SCAN loop processes every record in the ANSWER table. On each pass through the loop, the script uses the PAL function MONTH() to store in the Month# field the numeric value of the month in the Date field entry. The script uses the PAL function MOY() to store in the Month field the alphanumeric representation of the month in the Date field entry. After the SCAN loop has added Month# and Month entries to ANSWER, the last line of the script "presses" [Do-It!] to end the editing session. After you play this script, the ANSWER table will look like Figure 12-57. (For a more detailed explanation of how these commands and functions work, see Chapters 15 and 16.)

Figure 12-57 The New ANSWER Table

```
Viewing Answer table: Record 1 of 23                          Main  ▲▬

ANSWER┬─Month#─┬─Month─┬──Date──┬──Quantity─┬──Ball Type─┐
    1 │   12   │  Dec  │ 12/01/88 │    15     │  leather
    2 │   12   │  Dec  │ 12/01/88 │    15     │  synthetic
    3 │   12   │  Dec  │ 12/01/88 │    20     │  rubber
    4 │   12   │  Dec  │ 12/01/88 │    20     │  child's
    5 │   10   │  Oct  │ 10/21/88 │    20     │  leather
    6 │   10   │  Oct  │ 10/21/88 │    25     │  synthetic
    7 │   10   │  Oct  │ 10/21/88 │    25     │  rubber
    8 │   12   │  Dec  │ 12/07/88 │    10     │  leather
    9 │   12   │  Dec  │ 12/07/88 │    10     │  synthetic
   10 │   10   │  Oct  │ 10/30/88 │    10     │  leather
   11 │   10   │  Oct  │ 10/30/88 │    10     │  synthetic
   12 │   10   │  Oct  │ 10/30/88 │    10     │  rubber
   13 │   10   │  Oct  │ 10/30/88 │    10     │  child's
   14 │   11   │  Nov  │ 11/08/88 │    25     │  synthetic
   15 │   11   │  Nov  │ 11/08/88 │    20     │  rubber
   16 │   12   │  Dec  │ 12/04/88 │    20     │  leather
   17 │   12   │  Dec  │ 12/04/88 │    20     │  synthetic
   18 │   11   │  Nov  │ 11/25/88 │    10     │  leather
   19 │   11   │  Nov  │ 11/25/88 │    15     │  synthetic
   20 │   12   │  Dec  │ 12/03/88 │    15     │  leather
   21 │   12   │  Dec  │ 12/03/88 │    15     │  synthetic
   22 │   12   │  Dec  │ 12/03/88 │    25     │  rubber
   23 │   12   │  Dec  │ 12/03/88 │    10     │  child's
```

Using a PAL script to extract data in this manner can take a long time if your table is very large. You may find it makes more sense to extract this information during data entry. Of course, this approach would require a somewhat complex data entry script.

Cross-tabulating ANSWER

Now, you are ready to summarize the data in the ANSWER table into a new table that can be graphed. Let's use the [CrossTab] key to create a CROSSTAB table that uses the entries in the Month# and the Month fields as row labels and the entries in the Ball Type field as column labels, and summarizes data in the Quantity field as the grid values. The Month# and Month fields are already placed correctly because the row label fields need to be at the front of the table. However, the Quantity and Ball Type fields need to switch positions because the field containing the grid values must be at the end of the table in order for the [CrossTab] key to work correctly. To reverse these two fields, move the cursor to the Quantity field and press **[Rotate]**. When you do this, Paradox will move the Quantity field to the end of the table, and the Ball Type field will be on the left side of Quantity. Finally, move the cursor to the Month field and press **[CrossTab]** ([Alt]-[X]). Paradox will display the message *Creating CROSSTAB...* at the bottom of the screen for a moment, then display the CROSSTAB table shown in Figure 12-58.

Figure 12-58 The CROSSTAB Table

Viewing Crosstab table: Record 1 of 3 Main

ANSWER	Month#	Month	Date	Ball Type	Quantity
22	12	Dec	12/03/88	rubber	25
23	12	Dec	12/03/88	child's	10

CROSSTAB	Month	Month#	Leather	Synthetic	Rubber	Ch
1	Oct	10	30	35	35	****
2	Nov	11	10	40	20	****
3	Dec	12	60	60	45	****

As you can see, this CROSSTAB table is identical to the BALLSALE table we have graphed repeatedly in this chapter. To save the table permanently, you would use the [Menu] Tools Rename Table command to change the name of the CROSSTAB table to BALLSALE. Then, you could use this BALLSALE table to create any of the graphs we've shown you.

Notes

The preceding example is only one of the many approaches you could take in graphing the data in the BALLORDS table and its related table. You could add selection conditions to the query in Figure 12-53 to limit the data you would eventually graph. For example, by adding the condition *>20* to the Quantity field, you could limit your graph data to only orders for more than 20 balls. Or, instead of adding a field listing the month orders were placed, you could add a field for the day of the week each order was placed. You could use the PAL function DOW() in a script to fill this field with strings such as *Sun*, *Mon*, or *Tue*, based on the entries in the Date field. You could also rotate the Ball Type field to the front of the ANSWER table and move the Month field to the second-to-last column. Then, CROSSTAB would list the months in the column labels and the ball types in the row labels. As a result, your graphs would display the ball types on the x-axis and use the months as the series for your graph.

As you can see, Paradox gives you great flexibility in the ways you can analyze your data with graphs. Paradox can create a graph to let you view your data from almost any perspective. The more familiar you are with queries, cross tabulations, and PAL basics, the more you will be able to take advantage of Paradox's graphing capabilities.

Printing Graphs

Now that you know how to create the various types of Paradox graphs and display them on your monitor, it's time to think about printing them. In the Main mode, you can use the [Menu] Image Graph ViewGraph command to print a graph or write a graph to disk as a file. While you are working in the Graph Designer, you can use the [Menu] ViewGraph command to accomplish either of these tasks. We'll begin this section by showing you how to configure Paradox for your printer or plotter, then we'll discuss the process of printing a graph.

Getting Prepared

Before you can print a graph in Paradox, you have to configure Paradox for graph printing. You do this by playing the Custom Configuration Program (CCP). To play the CCP, issue the **[Menu]** Scripts **P**lay command, type **\paradox3\custom** at the *Script:* prompt, and press ↵. If you have a color/graphics adapter card in your computer, the CCP will ask you if you are using a black-and-white monitor. After you answer this question, you will see the CCP menu. To configure printers for graph printing, issue the **G**raphs **P**rinters command. When you issue this command, the CCP will present the menu shown in Figure 12-59. From this menu, you can configure Paradox to print graphs on up to four printers and plotters.

Figure 12-59 The Graphs GraphSettings Printers Menu

```
1stPrinter  2ndPrinter  3rdPrinter  4thPrinter  Return
Choose or make changes to Printer 1 specifications.
```

Choosing a Printer

The first step in configuring Paradox to print a graph is to select the printer you want to use. Since Paradox supports a rather large number of printers, it's almost certain that you'll be able to use your graphics printer or plotter with Paradox. To demonstrate the process of installing a graphics printer, we'll show you how to configure Paradox to use the Hewlett-Packard LaserJet Series II. You should be able to use this example as a conceptual guide when you install your own printer.

To install the first printer, choose the **1**stPrinter option from the Graphs GraphSettings Printer menu. Once you've installed the first printer, you can use the 2ndPrinter option to install a second printer, the 3rdPrinter option to install a third printer, and the 4thPrinter option to install a fourth printer. The process of installing second, third and fourth printers is identical to that of installing the first. After installing up to four printers, you select one of these printers by changing the printer settings for individual graphs.

When you choose the 1stPrinter option, the menu shown in Figure 12-60 will appear. This menu lets you tell Paradox about your printer. To tell Paradox which printer you want to use, select the TypeOfPrinter option. Then, the Printer Selection form shown in Figure 12-61 will appear. The default manufacturer, model, and mode appear in the current settings listed in the bottom-left corner of the screen. As you can see, the right half of this form lists many brands of printers: Apple, Epson, Hewlett-Packard, and so on. You can see more of the list by pressing [Pg Dn]. To change the settings for your printer, begin by moving the cursor to the name of the company that manufactured your printer. For example, to select the HP LaserJet Series II, move the cursor to the HP Printers selection and press ↵.

Figure 12-60 The 1stPrinter Menu

```
TypeOfPrinter  Settings  Return
Choose manufacturer, model and mode for printer 1.
```

Figure 12-61 The Printer Selection Form

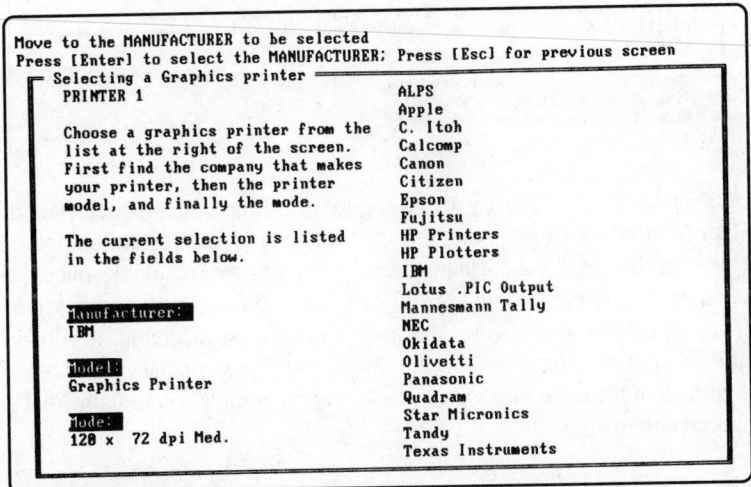

```
Move to the MANUFACTURER to be selected
Press [Enter] to select the MANUFACTURER; Press [Esc] for previous screen
 ┌─ Selecting a Graphics printer ─────────────────────────
     PRINTER 1                          ALPS
                                        Apple
   Choose a graphics printer from the   C. Itoh
   list at the right of the screen.     Calcomp
   First find the company that makes    Canon
   your printer, then the printer       Citizen
   model, and finally the mode.         Epson
                                        Fujitsu
   The current selection is listed      HP Printers
   in the fields below.                 HP Plotters
                                        IBM
                                        Lotus .PIC Output
   Manufacturer:                        Mannesmann Tally
   IBM                                  NEC
                                        Okidata
   Model:                               Olivetti
   Graphics Printer                     Panasonic
                                        Quadram
   Mode:                                Star Micronics
   120 x  72 dpi Med.                   Tandy
                                        Texas Instruments
```

Once you've chosen a type of printer, a list of printer models will appear. For example, when you choose HP Printers from the list shown in Figure 12-61, the list of printers shown in Figure 12-62 will appear. Notice that the Manufacturer setting has changed from IBM to HP Printers. When the list of models appears on your screen, you simply choose your printer from the list.

For example, when you select the HP LaserJet II (300 dpi) as your printer from the list shown in Figure 12-62, the list shown in Figure 12-63 will appear. This menu lets you define the resolution you want to use to print graphs on the selected printer.

Figure 12-62 A List of Printers

```
Move to the model to be selected
Press [Enter] to select the model; Press [Esc] for previous screen
 ┌─ Selecting a Graphics printer ═══════════════════════════════════
 │  PRINTER 1                          HP PaintJet
 │                                     HP LaserJet        (75 dpi)
 │   Choose a graphics printer from the  HP LaserJet Plus (150 dpi)
 │   list at the right of the screen.    HP LaserJet II   (300 dpi)
 │   First find the company that makes
 │   your printer, then the printer
 │   model, and finally the mode.
 │
 │   The current selection is listed
 │   in the fields below.
 │
 │  Manufacturer:
 │  HP Printers
 │
 │  Model:
 │  *
 │
 │  Mode:
```

Figure 12-63 A List of Resolutions

```
Move to the mode to be selected
Press [Enter] to select the mode; Press [Esc] for previous screen
 ┌─ Selecting a Graphics printer ═══════════════════════════════════
 │  PRINTER 1
 │                                     75  x  75 dpi
 │                                    100  x 100 dpi
 │   Choose a graphics printer from the  150  x 150 dpi
 │   list at the right of the screen.    300  x 300 dpi
 │   First find the company that makes
```

While the options on this list will vary according to the printer you have selected, this menu will generally offer high-resolution, medium-resolution, and low-resolution options. Your graphs will look best if you print them using the highest resolution available, but you may also find that the amount of time required to print a high-resolution graph is excessive. On the other hand, if you print a graph using the lowest resolution available, it will be printed relatively quickly, but you may find that the quality isn't acceptable. Your best bet is to experiment with all of the resolutions your printer supports until you find one that produces acceptable speed and quality.

Choosing a Plotter

The commands required to install a plotter are similar to those required to install a printer. Since Paradox supports only Hewlett-Packard-compatible plotters, you select the HP Plotters option from the list of manufacturers shown in Figure 12-61. Next, the CCP will display the menu shown in Figure 12-64, which lists the plotter models supported by Paradox. When you see this menu, select the particular model you want to install.

Figure 12-64 A List of Plotters

```
Move to the model to be selected
Press [Enter] to select the model; Press [Esc] for previous screen
  Selecting a Graphics printer
    PRINTER 1                          7220
                                       7470
    Choose a graphics printer from the 7475
    list at the right of the screen.   7550
    First find the company that makes  ColorPro
    your printer, then the printer     Sweet P
    model, and finally the mode.
```

After you have chosen a plotter model, a list of plotter modes will appear. For example, the list shown in Figure 12-65 will appear if you select the 7550 option from the list shown in Figure 12-64. The options on this menu tell Paradox how it should interact with the plotter. The first three plotter modes on the menu shown in Figure 12-65 are common to every plotter supported by Paradox. If you want Paradox to plot graphs using the color pens presently installed in the plotter, you should choose the Auto option. If you want the plotter to pause before changing colors, you should choose the Manual option. Finally, if you want to plot graphs using only one color, choose the Monochrome option. The last three options on the menu are specific to the models that can handle 11- by 17-inch paper and have the same effect as the first three.

Figure 12-65 A List of Plotter Modes

```
Move to the mode to be selected
Press [Enter] to select the mode; Press [Esc] for previous screen
  Selecting a Graphics printer
    PRINTER 1                          Auto
                                       Manual
    Choose a graphics printer from the Monochrome
    list at the right of the screen.   11x17 Auto
    First find the company that makes  11x17 Manual
    your printer, then the printer     11x17 Monochrome
    model, and finally the mode.
```

Paradox 3 supports only Hewlett-Packard or Hewlett-Packard-compatible plotters. If future releases of Paradox include support for other types of plotters, the basic installation process will be similar to the process we have explained.

Configuring an Output Device

After you have chosen a resolution for your printer, or a mode for your plotter, the CCP will return to the 1stPrinter menu. At this point, you need to tell Paradox which device (interface) it should use to communicate with your printer. The default device used by Paradox to communicate with a printer or plotter is Parallel1. If your printer or plotter is connected to Parallel1, you don't need to change a thing—you're ready to print. However, if your printer is attached to your computer's serial port, or if you plan to use another parallel port to communicate with your computer, you must change the default.

To select an output device, choose the Settings option from the 1stPrinter menu. When you choose this option, Paradox will display the menu shown in Figure 12-66. When you see this menu, select the Device option. The CCP will display the list of output devices shown in Figure 12-67. When this list appears on your screen, select the device your computer is using to communicate with your printer or plotter. After you select an output device, the CCP will return to the Settings menu.

Figure 12-66 The Settings Menu

```
Device  PrinterWait  Return
Choose the device for printer 1.
```

Figure 12-67 The List of Output Devices

```
Parallel1  Parallel2  Serial1  Serial2  Lpt1  Lpt2  Lpt3  Lpt4  EPT
The device is Parallel 1.
```

If you use a serial printer or plotter, you will have to configure the serial port according to the specifications recommended by the manufacturer. You can find these settings in the manual that came with your printer or plotter.

If you select any output device other than Parallel1 or Parallel2, the CCP will display the menu shown in Figure 12-68. You use this menu to configure the serial port. When you choose the Baud option, the CCP will display the menu shown in Figure 12-69. From this menu, you should select the baud rate your printer or plotter uses to communicate with your computer. If you do not want to change the baud rate setting, choose the LeaveAsIs option. Once you have made a selection, the CCP will return to the Serial Port Configuration menu.

Figure 12-68 The Serial Port Configuration Menu

```
Baud  Parity  StopBits  Return
Choose the baud for your printer 1 device.
```

Figure 12-69 The Baud Menu

```
LeaveAsIs  110  150  300  600  1200  2400  4800  9600  19200
Leave the baud rate as is.
```

When you choose the Parity option from the menu in Figure 12-68, the CCP will display a list of four options: LeaveAsIs, No, Odd, and Even. You can choose the correct parity setting for your printer or plotter from this list, or you can choose LeaveAsIs to leave the setting unchanged. After you choose a parity setting, the CCP will return to the Serial Port Configuration menu.

Finally, when you choose the StopBits option from the Serial Port Configuration menu, the CCP will display a list of three options: LeaveAsIs, 1StopBit, and 2StopBit. To change the stop bits setting, you should choose one of the settings available on this list, or choose the LeaveAsIs option to leave the setting unchanged. After you choose a stop bits setting, the CCP will return to the Serial Port Configuration menu. When you are finished configuring the serial port, press Return to return to the Settings menu.

Waiting between Pages

If you select the PrinterWait option from the Settings menu, the CCP will present a menu with two options: No and Yes. Choosing Yes tells Paradox to pause between pages for graphs printed on the printer you are configuring. The default setting of No tells Paradox not to stop between pages. Unless you must manually feed pages into your printer, you'll probably want to leave the PrinterWait option set to No.

Finishing Up

When you have finished configuring a printer, select Return from the Settings menu, then choose Return from the next menu to return to the Graphs Printers menu shown in Figure 12-58 on page 571. After you have configured all the printers you need, issue the Return command to move back to the Graphs menu. Then, issue the Return command again to move back to the CCP menu. Finally, issue the Do-It! command to save the changes you have made to the graph printer settings. After asking whether you are using a hard disk stand-alone system or a network configuration, the CCP will exit to the DOS prompt. The next time you load Paradox, the software will be ready to print graphs on the printers or plotters you have configured.

Choosing Destinations

Since Paradox allows you to install four printers or plotters, you have to tell Paradox to which printer or plotter it should send the printed graph before you actually print a graph. You can also write a file to disk in several formats, so you must specify a file format for a graph before you write it to disk. You include this information in the settings for each individual graph. To specify a printer or a field format for the current graph, issue the [Menu] Overall Device command from the Graph Designer. When you issue this command, Paradox will display a menu with two options: Printer and File.

Choosing a Printer

The Printer option lets you send the graph to one of your defined printers or plotters. If you select this option, Paradox will display the menu shown in Figure 12-70.

Figure 12-70 The Overall Device Printer Menu

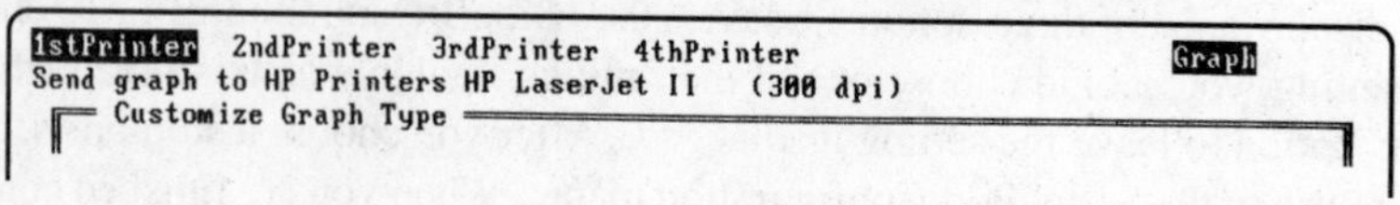

```
1stPrinter  2ndPrinter  3rdPrinter  4thPrinter                    Graph
Send graph to HP Printers HP LaserJet II   (300 dpi)
┌─ Customize Graph Type ═══════════════════════════════════════════════┐
│                                                                       │
```

If you want to send your graph to the printer or plotter you have defined as the first printer, simply select this menu's 1stPrinter option. Likewise, if you want to send graphs to the second printer, select the 2ndPrinter option. The choice you make will remain in effect until you make another choice from this menu, reset Paradox's default graph settings, or load a new graph.

Choosing a File Format

The other option available on the Overall Device menu is File. You use this option to select the format Paradox should use when printing the graph to disk. When you choose this option, Paradox will display the menu shown in Figure 12-71. This menu lets you select from three file formats.

Figure 12-71 The Overall Device File Menu

```
CurrentPrinter  EPS  PIC                                          Graph
Format file output using specs for HP Printers HP LaserJet II   (300 dpi)
┌─ Customize Graph Type ═══════════════════════════════════════════════┐
│                                                                       │
```

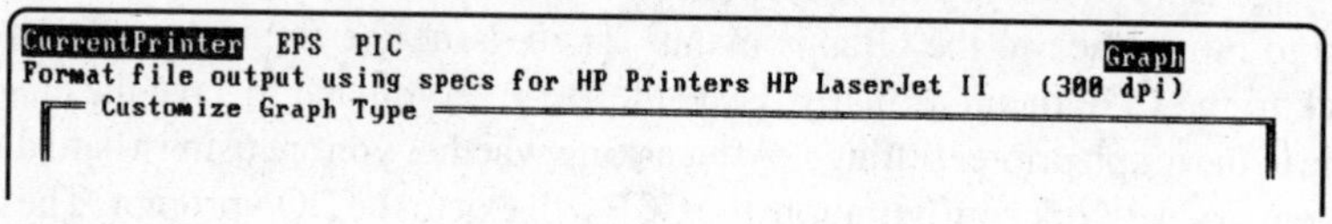

The CurrentPrinter option tells Paradox to write the graph to disk in the format used by the current printer or plotter when you issue the [Menu] ViewGraph File command from within the Graph Designer or the [Menu] Image Graph ViewGraph File command from Main mode. The formatted graph file can be sent to your printer from the DOS prompt using the DOS command COPY *filename.ext printerport* /B, or can be used by another application.

The EPS option makes it possible to write a Paradox graph to disk as an EPS (Encapsulated PostScript) file. Graphs you save in EPS format can be imported into programs that support PostScript, including Aldus PageMaker.

When you save a graph as an EPS file for use in Aldus PageMaker or some other application, all of the patterns in the graph will be converted to shades of grey. In addition, because Paradox's fonts do not match up perfectly with PostScript fonts, the fonts in your graph will be altered. Table 12-9 shows how Paradox will convert your fonts when a graph is written to disk as an EPS file.

The PIC option from the Overall Device File menu makes it possible to write a Paradox graph to disk as a Lotus-compatible PIC file. Graphs you save in PIC format can be read into and printed by Lotus 1-2-3's PrintGraph utility.

Table 12-9 Font Conversions in EPS Files

Paradox Font	PostScript Font
Default	Helvetica
Bold	Helvetica
Triplex	Helvetica-Bold
Sans Serif	Helvetica-Oblique
Small	Times-Roman
Simplex	Times-Bold
Triplex Script	Times-Italic
Script	Courier
EuroStyle	Courier-Bold
Complex	Palatino-Roman
Gothic	AvantGarde-Book

Printing a Graph

When you use the [Menu] Image Graph ViewGraph Printer command (or the [Menu] ViewGraph Printer command from the Graph Designer) to print a graph, Paradox will print the current graph based on the current table. Before you can print, then, you need to load the settings for the graph you want to print and position the cursor properly in the current table. You can use the [Menu] View command to place the table you want to graph on the workspace and the [Menu] Image Graph Load command to load the graph you want to print.

Let's print the Ballbar graph we saved earlier in this chapter. First, issue the [Menu] Image Graph Load command, type Ballbar at the *Graph:* prompt, and press ↵. Since we designed this graph for the BALLSALE table, issue the [Menu] View command, type BALLSALE at the *Table:* prompt, and press ↵ to place this table on the workspace. Next, move the cursor to the Leather field, and issue the [Menu] Image Graph ViewGraph Printer command. After you issue this command, Paradox will display the printer and resolution selected for the Ballbar graph, as shown in Figure 12-72. Figure 12-73 on the next page shows the printed Ballbar graph.

Figure 12-72 The Screen While Paradox Prints a Graph

```
Graph Printer: HP Printers - HP LaserJet II   (300 dpi)
         Mode: 150 x 150 dpi


Press <ESC> to cancel printing
```

It may take up to several minutes to print a graph. You can cancel the printing anytime by pressing [Esc]. If Paradox cannot print the graph because of some problem with the printer, Paradox will display a prompt describing the problem, along with the instructions *Press "C" to Continue, "A" to Abort:*.

Figure 12-73 A Printed Graph

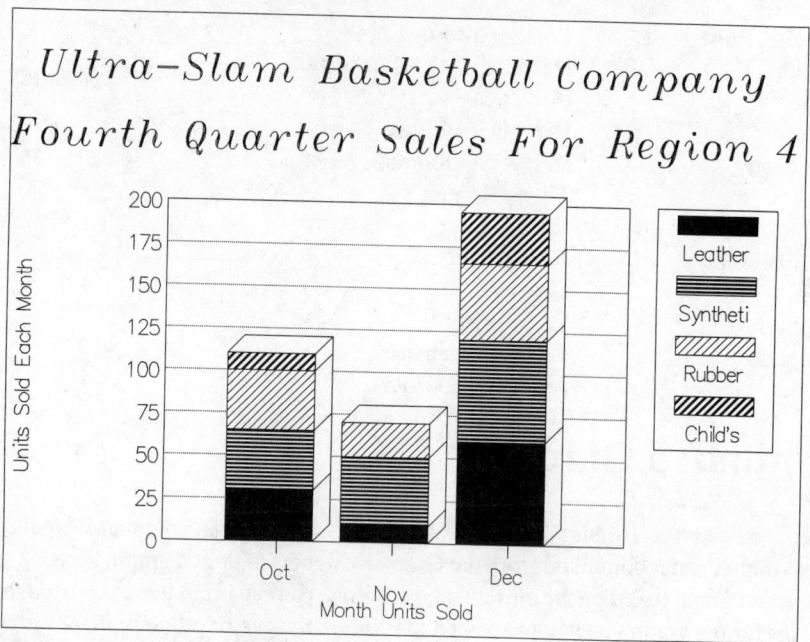

Writing a Graph to Disk

When you issue the [Menu] Image Graph ViewGraph File command, Paradox will display a *File name:* prompt asking you to name the file in which the graph is to be written. The extension Paradox will attach to this file name depends on the file format setting you have selected for the graph. If you used the Graph Designer's [Menu] Overall Device File command to select the format used by the current printer, then the graph file will have a .GRF extension. If you elected to save the graph as an Encapsulated PostScript file, Paradox will give the file an .EPS extension. If you chose the Lotus .PIC format, the file will have a .PIC extension.

Changing Page Layout

While Paradox will automatically size graphs so that they will fit on an $8^1/_2$- by 11-inch sheet of paper, on occasion you may need to adjust the size of a printed graph manually. The Graph Designer's [Menu] Overall PrinterLayout command gives you control over the dimensions of your printed graphs. When you issue this command, Paradox will display the Graph Layout for Printing form shown in Figure 12-74.

The Units setting on this form allows you to choose a unit of measure for a page. Paradox's default unit of measure is inches, but you can change the unit of measure to centimeters by moving the cursor to the *Units:* prompt and pressing *C*.

Figure 12-74 The Graph Layout for Printing Form

```
Defining the layout of the graph for printing.           Graph
[F1] for help with defining the layout of the graph printing.
  Customize Graph Layout for Printing
        Units:  Inches          Measurement Units:
                                   (I)nches
        Left Margin:   0          (C)entimeters
        Top Margin:    0

        Graph Height:  0
        Graph Width:   0          Orientation Options:
                                    (L)andscape (Horizontal)
        The margins and graph       (P)ortrait  (Vertical)
        dimensions are measured
        in inches or centimeters, Break Page Options:
        as defined above.           (Y)es - Move to the top of the next
                                           page after printing the graph.

        Orientation: Landscape    (N)o

        Break Page: No            Plotter Speed Options:
                                    0 through 9
        Plotter Speed:  0           0 uses the fastest or current speed
```

The Left Margin and Top Margin settings let you specify the number of inches or centimeters that should be used as a left and top margin when your graph is printed. By default, Paradox sets the left and top margin settings to 0. To change these settings, simply type the specified margins at the appropriate prompts, keeping in mind the unit of measure you have selected.

If you want to specify how high or wide your graph will be, use the Graph Height and Graph Width options. The default Graph Height and Graph Width settings are both 0. These default settings allow Paradox to print a graph using as much space as possible on an $8^1/_2$- by 11-inch page. For example, if you want to print a graph that is 8 inches high and 4 inches wide, you should change the Graph Height setting to 8 and the Graph Width setting to 4.

The Orientation setting allows you to specify how your graph should be printed on a page. By default, graphs are printed in Landscape orientation, which means the graph is printed on the page horizontally. If you want to print graphs vertically, move the cursor to the *Orientation:* prompt and press *P* to choose Portrait orientation.

You use the Break Page setting to specify whether you want each graph printed on a separate sheet of paper. Leave the default setting of No if you want to print graphs one after another without advancing to a new page after each graph. If you want to print only one graph on each sheet of paper, move the cursor to the *Break Page:* prompt and press *Y* to change this setting to Yes.

If you are going to print the graph on a plotter, the Plotter Speed setting lets you define the speed at which your plotter should run. The lowest plotter speed you can define is 1, while the highest possible setting is 9. Paradox's default Plotter Speed setting is zero, which allows your plotter to run at its maximum speed. You'll have to experiment to find the ideal setting for your plotter.

Defining Colors

If you are using a color printer or plotter, you can use the Graph Designer's [Menu] Overall Colors Printer command to control the colors used by Paradox to represent various components of a printed graph. When you issue this command, the Graph Colors form shown in Figure 12-75 will appear. If your printer or plotter supports color, the settings on this form allow you to define the colors you want to use in a graph.

Figure 12-75 The Graph Colors Form

```
Customizing print colors for graphs.                                    Graph
[F1] for help with customizing print colors.
┌─ Customize Graph Colors ─────────────────────────────────────────────────┐
│                                                                            │
│   Graph Elements          Color   For each of the      Back-    Full       │
│   ─────────────           ─────   Graph Elements,      ground   Color      │
│              Background: H  ▢     enter the letter     Choices  Palette     │
│                                   for the color          ───    A Bckgrd   │
│                  Frame: B   ▢     you want.               B    B           │
│                   Grid: B   ▢                            C    C           │
│                                                          D    D           │
│                                   You can choose         E    E           │
│   Titles                          colors B through       F    F           │
│     First Title Line: B   ▢       H for the              G    G           │
│    Second Title Line: B   ▢       Background Color.      H    H           │
│          X-axis Title: B  ▢       You can choose              I           │
│          Y-axis Title: B  ▢       colors from the             J           │
│                                   entire Palette              K           │
│             1st Series: B  ▢      for the other               L           │
│             2nd Series: C  ▢      graph elements.             M           │
│             3rd Series: D  ▢                                  N           │
│             4th Series: E  ▢      Selection A is              O           │
│             5th Series: F  ▢      the same as                 P           │
│             6th Series: G  ▢      transparent.                            │
└────────────────────────────────────────────────────────────────────────────┘
```

This form is exactly like the form you use to change screen colors for a graph. Only the heading on the top two lines of the screen distinguish this form from the Graph Colors form shown in Figure 12-33 on page 553.

By default, Paradox will print color graphs using the same default colors it uses to display graphs on the screen. Paradox's default printing colors are shown in Table 12-2 on page 529. The list of colors Paradox can print is shown in Table 12-6 on page 545. If the colors supported by your printer do not perfectly match those selected in your graph settings, Paradox will choose the closest approximation.

If you want to change the color of any element on a printed graph, just move the cursor to the prompt for that element and press the letter that corresponds to the color you want to select. For example, to change the color of the first series from blue (B) to yellow (O), move the cursor to the *1st Series:* prompt and press *O*.

Changing Colors for Pie Graphs

Like the color settings on the Graph Colors form for screen colors, the settings on the Graph Colors form for printer colors do not affect the colors Paradox uses for pie graphs. If you want to change printer colors for a pie graph, you'll need to issue the Graph Designer's [Menu] Pies command to change the printer color settings on the Pie Graph form, shown in Figure 12-24 on page 543.

Copying between Screen and Printer Colors

You will probably want to print a graph with the same colors you use to display the graph on the screen. You can create a set of printer color settings that duplicate a graph's screen color settings (or vice versa) without having to redefine the colors for each element on the graph. When you issue the Graph Designer's [Menu] Overall Colors Copy command, Paradox will present a graph with two options: ScreenToPrinter and PrinterToScreen. If you select the ScreenToPrinter option, Paradox will copy the graph's screen color settings to the graph's printer color settings. If you select the PrinterToScreen option, Paradox will copy the graph's printer color settings to the graph's screen color settings.

Resetting and Saving Print Settings

As we've already mentioned, all printer settings, including the destination, page layout, and color settings, are part of the overall settings for a graph. Issuing the [Menu] Image Graph Reset command to reset Paradox's default graph settings replaces the current graph printer settings with their default values. If you load a graph, then make changes to any of its printer settings, you'll need to save the graph again in order keep the new printer settings as a permanent part of the graph. If you change a graph's printer settings, then load a second graph or reset Paradox to its default graph settings without saving the first graph, you will lose the new printer settings for the first graph.

Changing Default Graph Settings

Depending on the type of data you work with or the types of presentations you often need to make, you may find yourself constantly using the same graph settings as the basis for your graphs. You could save these basic settings as a graph, then reload them every time you want to design a new graph. Alternatively, you could use the CCP to change Paradox's default graph settings so that each new graph you create conforms to your standard settings. You can use the CCP to change all of Paradox's default settings, including graph type, colors, fill patterns, and printer settings.

To change the default graph settings, repeat the steps we explained earlier to play the CCP. When you see the CCP main menu, issue the **Graphs GraphSettings** command. After you issue this command, you will see the Graph Type form with the menu shown in Figure 12-76 displayed at the top of the screen. This menu includes all of the commands on the regular Graph Designer menu except the ViewGraph and DO-IT! commands. You can change Paradox's default graph settings by issuing the commands and using the forms you use to change settings in the Graph Designer. You'll have to select the Type option from the Graphs GraphSettings menu before you can change any of the settings on the Graph Type form displayed on the screen. Once you change any of the settings on this form or any of the other Graph Designer forms, you can press the [Menu] key to see the Graphs GraphSettings menu again.

Figure 12-76 The Graphs GraphSettings Menu

```
 Type  Overall  Series  Pies  Help  Cancel  Return
Change the currently specified default graph type.
┌─ Customize Graph Type ═══════════════════════════════════
│
│   Select a basic graph type from the    │ Basic Graph Types:
│   options on the right.                  │   (S)tacked Bar
│                                          │   (B)ar - Regular Bar Graph
```

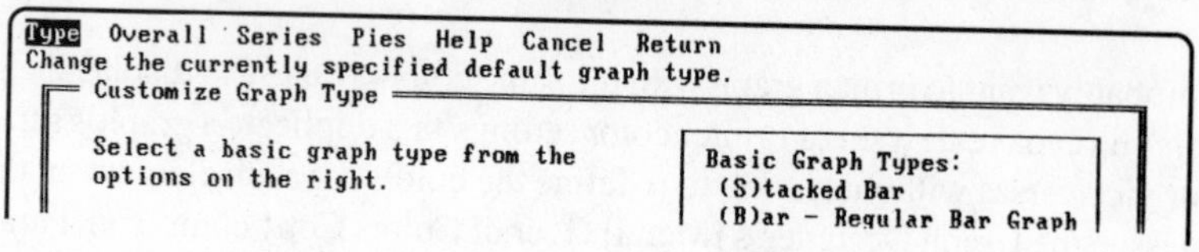

If you want to cancel the changes you have made to the default settings, issue the [Menu] Cancel command. Paradox will display a menu with No and Yes options to verify that you want to cancel the new settings you have chosen. Selecting No will return you to the Graph Designer. Selecting Yes will return you to the CCP Graphs menu. If you want to save the changes you have made to the default graph settings, issue the [Menu] Return command from the Graphs GraphSettings menu. Then, Paradox will return you to the Graphs menu. When you see this menu, issue the **Return** command to return to the CCP main menu. From this menu, issue the **Do-It!** command to save all the changes you have made during the CCP session. After asking you whether you are working with a hard disk system or on a network, Paradox will return you to the DOS prompt. The next time you start Paradox, your new default graph settings will be in place.

Conclusion

In this chapter, we have shown you how to take advantage of Paradox's graphing capabilities. We explored the basic concepts and commands you use to create and make basic enhancements to a graph. We also showed you each of Paradox's graph types. Then, we demonstrated how you might use some of Paradox's other tools, such as queries, PAL scripts, and cross tabulations, to prepare data in your Paradox tables for graphing. After showing you how to print your graphs and write them to disk as files, we concluded by explaining how you can use the CCP to change Paradox's default graph settings.

Chapter 13
Simple Scripts

In the previous chapters of this book, we have explored many of Paradox's capabilities. By now, you know how to use queries and create sophisticated forms and reports. If Paradox's capabilities stopped there, you still would have a very powerful database manager. However, Paradox does a lot more. In addition to these basic features, Paradox is also "programmable."

Paradox programs are called scripts. The simplest scripts are nothing more than recorded keystrokes stored in a text file. You can create scripts by asking Paradox to record your keystrokes as you choose commands, press function keys, or type information from the keyboard. You can also create scripts without recording them by using the PAL Script Editor.

When you play a script, Paradox "types" each keystroke you have saved in the file in much the same way that a player piano plays from a scroll of music. When Paradox plays a script, the keys on your computer's keyboard don't move, but Paradox does perform the same actions that it would if those keys actually had been pressed.

Simple scripts are most useful for recording relatively short keystroke sequences that you repeat often, or for recording complex or tedious sequences that must always be performed correctly. Scripts don't have to point and type like you do, so they can perform a task much more quickly than you can. Because Paradox never makes a typographical error while playing a script, you can use scripts to perform important tasks and know they will be performed correctly.

On a more advanced level, Paradox offers a complete programming language called PAL (Paradox Application Language). By using PAL commands and functions, you can develop scripts that use such programming devices as variables, arrays, conditional tests, loops, custom menus, and subroutines. You can use these PAL tools to develop complete turnkey applications, like an integrated accounting system, a time and billing system, or an order entry/invoicing system. You also can use PAL more casually, however, to add power to your "manual" work within Paradox.

PAL and Paradox are closely related. Any script, from a simple recording to a sophisticated PAL program, works with the tables, forms, and queries on the Paradox workspace, just as you do. In a sense, a script is a Paradox user that you control. Once you tell a script what to do, it will manipulate the objects on the Paradox workspace for you quickly, automatically, and consistently.

In this section of the book, we'll explore the ways you can program Paradox. In this chapter, we'll show you how to record keystrokes into a script, how to play a script, and how to edit a script. In Chapter 14, we'll move beyond simple recording and introduce commands, variables, and equations. In Chapter 15, we'll present another powerful PAL component: functions. Chapter 16 will explore a number of essential PAL techniques, such as displaying information on the PAL "canvas," soliciting user input, looping, and printing. Finally, in Chapter 17, we'll explore such advanced topics as arrays, macros, and procedures.

Recording Scripts

The simplest scripts are ones that duplicate actions you can perform from your keyboard. This kind of script can be used to automate tedious and repetitive tasks, thus freeing you from the chore of typing each command over and over. The easiest way to create this type of script is to record the keystrokes as you type them.

An Example

Suppose you want to record a script named Empsort that sorts the EMPLYEE table shown in Figure 13-2 into ascending order based on the entries in the Salary field. To begin recording, press the [**Menu**] key and choose Scripts to reveal the menu shown in Figure 13-1. This menu lists six items: Play, BeginRecord, QuerySave, ShowPlay, RepeatPlay, and Editor. We'll explain the purpose of each option as we move through this chapter.

Figure 13-1 The Scripts Menu

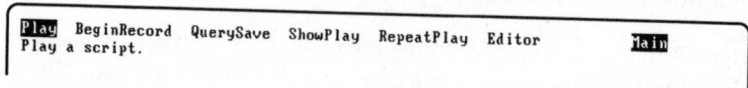

To create the script Empsort, first choose **B**eginRecord and type **Empsort** to identify the file in which you want Paradox to record your keystrokes. As soon as you press ↵ to lock in the name, Paradox will flash the message *Beginning recording of Empsort* in the message area at the lower-right corner of the screen. This message indicates that Paradox will begin recording the script with your next keystroke. During a recording session, Paradox will display the letter *R* in the upper-right corner of the screen, indicating that your keystrokes are being recorded. (The *R* is obscured when Paradox displays the Main menu.)

As soon as Paradox is ready, you should perform the task you want it to record. In this case, you should issue the **M**odify **S**ort command. (The Main menu should be visible, so you don't have to press the [Menu] key.)   After you issue the Modify Sort command, Paradox will prompt you for the name of the table you want to sort. When you see this prompt, either type the table name **EMPLYEE** or press ↵ and choose that name from the list. After you select EMPLYEE as the table to sort, choose **S**ame to command Paradox to place the sorted result back in EMPLYEE.

Figure 13-2 The EMPLYEE Table

```
Viewing Emplyee table: Record 1 of 16                          Main

EMPLYEE  Emp Number  Last Name    First Name   SS Number       Addre
   1         1       Jones        David        414-74-3421    4000 St. Ja
   2         2       Cameron      Herb         321-65-8765    2321 Elm St
   3         3       Jones        Stewart      401-32-8721    4389 Oakbri
   4         4       Roberts      Darlene      417-43-7777    451 Lone Pi
   5         5       Jones        Jean         413-07-9123    4000 St. Ja
   6         6       Williams     Brenda       401-55-1567    100 Owl Cre
   7         7       Myers        Julie        314-38-9452    4512 Parksi
   8         8       Link         Julie        345-75-1525    3215 Palm C
   9         9       Jackson      Mary         424-13-7621    7821 Clark
  10        10       Jakes, Jr.   Sal          321-65-9151    3451 Michig
  11        11       Preston      Molly        451-00-3426    321 Indian
  12        12       Masters      Ron          317-65-4529    423 W. 72nd
  13        13       Robertson    Kevin        415-24-6710    431 Bardsto
  14        14       Garrison     Robert       312-98-1479    55 Wheeler
  15        15       Gunn         Barbara      321-97-8632    541 Kentuck
  16        16       Emerson      Cheryl       404-14-1422    8100 River
```

```
Viewing Emplyee table: Record 8 of 16                          Main

Date of Birth   Date of Hire   Exemptions        Salary
  10/06/42        1/14/87          3             70,000.00
  11/24/29        1/14/87          4             50,000.00
   3/21/50        2/13/87          1             47,000.00
   9/24/60        6/16/87          3             14,000.00
   5/14/43        7/16/87          0             33,999.99
   1/12/20        8/16/87          6             40,000.00
   2/06/48        9/16/87          1             32,000.00
   6/03/33       11/14/87          2             30,000.00
   8/12/56       11/14/87          3             21,000.00
   5/23/59       12/14/87          6             34,000.00
   4/17/66        2/13/88          1             14,750.00
  12/31/44        2/13/88          0             38,000.00
   3/16/25        2/27/88          1             37,000.00
   5/09/45        5/15/88          4             32,000.00
   5/18/50        6/15/88          2             17,500.00
   7/30/66        8/15/88          2             12,000.00
```

As soon as you select Same, Paradox will present the sort specification screen for the EMPLYEE table. To specify an ascending sort on the Salary field, use the ↓ key to position the cursor beside the field name Salary, then type the number **1**. Figure 13-3 shows the resulting sort specification screen.

Figure 13-3 The Sort Specification Screen

```
Sorting Emplyee table                                    Sort    R

Number fields to set up sort order (1, 2, etc.).  If you want a field sorted
  in descending sequence, follow the number with a "D" (e.g., "2D").
       Ascending is the normal sequence and need not be indicated.


        Emp Number
        Last Name
        First Name
        SS Number
        Address
        City
        State
        Zip
        Phone
        Date of Birth
        Date of Hire
        Exemptions
    1  ◄ Salary
```

After you have specified the sort order, you can command Paradox to perform the sort in one of two ways. First, you can press the **[Do-It!]** key [F2]. Alternatively, you can issue the **[Menu]** DO-IT! command. In either case, Paradox will sort EMPLYEE into ascending order based on the values in the Salary field and will display the result on the screen. Figure 13-4 shows the sorted EMPLYEE table.

Figure 13-4 The Sorted EMPLYEE Table

```
Viewing Emplyee table: Record 1 of 16
                                                              Main        R
EMPLYEE┬═Emp Number═══════Last Name══┬═First Name══┬═SS Number═══════════Addre
    1  ║     16        Emerson      Cheryl       404-14-1422   8100 River
    2  ║      4        Roberts      Darlene      417-43-7777   451 Lone Pi
    3  ║     11        Preston      Molly        451-00-3426   321 Indian
    4  ║     15        Gunn         Barbara      321-97-8632   541 Kentuck
    5  ║      9        Jackson      Mary         424-13-7621   7821 Clark
    6  ║      8        Link         Julie        345-75-1525   3215 Palm C
    7  ║      7        Myers        Julie        314-38-9452   4512 Parksi
    8  ║     14        Garrison     Robert       312-98-1479   55 Wheeler
    9  ║      5        Jones        Jean         413-07-9123   4000 St. Ja
   10  ║     10        Jakes, Jr.   Sal          321-65-9151   3451 Michig
   11  ║     13        Robertson    Kevin        415-24-6710   431 Bardsto
   12  ║     12        Masters      Ron          317-65-4529   423 W. 72nd
   13  ║      6        Williams     Brenda       401-55-1567   100 Owl Cre
   14  ║      3        Jones        Stewart      401-32-8721   4389 Oakbri
   15  ║      2        Cameron      Herb         321-65-8765   2321 Elm St
   16  ║      1        Jones        David        414-74-3421   4000 St. Ja
```

```
Viewing Emplyee table: Record 1 of 16
                                                              Main
┬Date of Birth══┬═Date of Hire══┬═Exemptions═══════════Salary═══
   7/30/66        8/15/88           2              12,000.00
   9/24/60        6/16/87           3              14,000.00
   4/17/66        2/13/88           1              14,750.00
   5/18/50        6/15/88           2              17,500.00
   8/12/56       11/14/87           3              21,000.00
   6/03/33       11/14/87           2              30,000.00
   2/06/48        9/16/87           1              32,000.00
   5/09/45        5/15/88           4              32,000.00
   5/14/43        7/16/87           0              33,999.99
   5/23/59       12/14/87           6              34,000.00
   3/16/25        2/27/88           1              37,000.00
  12/31/44        2/13/88           0              38,000.00
   1/12/20        8/16/87           6              40,000.00
   3/21/50        2/13/87           1              47,000.00
  11/24/29        1/14/87           4              50,000.00
  10/06/42        1/14/87           3              70,000.00
```

Once you have performed the task you wanted to record, you should stop recording by issuing the **[Menu]** Scripts command again. This time, instead of displaying the six-item menu shown in Figure 13-2, Paradox will display the menu shown in Figure 13-5. This special five-item Scripts menu will appear only when you issue the [Menu] Scripts command while Paradox is recording or playing a script. The End-Record option tells Paradox to stop recording and save the keystrokes it recorded into the script file you specified. The Cancel option instructs Paradox to stop recording without saving the recorded keystrokes. The Play and RepeatPlay options allow you to play an existing script while you are recording another. As a result, you actually record yourself playing the existing script. The QuerySave option allows you to save a query into a script. We'll discuss the Play and QuerySave options later. In this case, choose End-Record to stop recording and save the script.

Figure 13-5 Five-item Script Menu

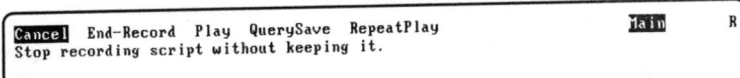

Cancel End-Record Play QuerySave RepeatPlay   Main   R
Stop recording script without keeping it.

Notes

The names of your scripts can be up to eight characters long and can contain any characters that are acceptable in DOS file names. When Paradox prompts you to specify a name, you should type only the name, not an extension. When you press ↵, Paradox will set up a file using the name you supplied and will add the extension .SC, which identifies the file as a script file. Thus, the full name of the script file we created in the preceding example will be EMPSORT.SC.

If you enter the name of an existing script file at the prompt, Paradox will present a menu with two options: Cancel and Replace. If you choose Cancel, Paradox will allow you to choose another name. If you choose Replace, Paradox will overwrite the existing script file.

Issuing Commands

While you are recording a script, you can issue commands just as you normally would: either by pointing to the command name and pressing ↵ or by typing the first letter in the name of the command. As you will see, Paradox records the commands you issue regardless of how you select them.

The same is true for selecting tables and other objects. While you are recording, you can select a table or other object either by typing its name and pressing ↵ or by pressing ↵ and selecting the table or object name from the list Paradox displays. Either way, the recorded script will look the same.

If you are in the habit of pressing the [Menu] key while the current menu already is visible at the top of the screen, you may be in for a surprise when you view your recorded scripts. Because the Paradox screen flashes briefly and then redisplays the menu in these situations, you might assume that it is recording the [Menu] key. If you view a script in which you have pressed the [Menu] key repeatedly, however, you'll see that Paradox records the keystroke as [Esc] rather than [Menu]. Although this redefinition of keys has no effect on the performance of a script, you may want to delete any unnecessary occurrences of [Esc] in your recorded scripts.

It is important to understand that while you're recording a script, all of the commands you issue affect the objects on the Paradox workspace, just as they would if you were not recording. For instance, Paradox actually sorted the EMPLYEE table as we recorded a script we'll use later to sort the table again. Always be aware that the actions you take while recording a script affect the workspace in the same way they do when you are not recording.

Recording Instant Scripts

The [Instant Script Record] key ([Alt]-[F3]) gives you an alternative way to begin recording a script. When you press this key, Paradox begins recording a script file named INSTANT.SC. The same thing will happen if you press [Menu] Scripts BeginRecord and specify Instant as the script name. The [Instant Script Record] key is a shortcut. After you have pressed this key, Paradox will record your keystrokes in the file INSTANT.SC, beginning with the next keystroke you type, in the same way any other script is recorded. To end your recording of an instant script, press the [Instant Script Record] key a second time.

If there already is a file named INSTANT.SC when you press the [Instant Script Record] key, Paradox will overwrite that file, destroying the existing script. You can prevent this from happening, of course, by using the [Menu] Tools Rename Script command to change the name of a previously recorded instant script before you press [Instant Script Record]. In general, if you want to preserve your instant script for long-term use, you'll want to rename it as soon as you've finished recording it.

In addition to allowing you to begin recording quickly, there are other benefits of using the [Instant Script Record] key. First, you can stop recording and save the script by pressing the [Instant Script Record] key again. Second, you can invoke this command at any time, no matter where you are in the Paradox menu structure. In contrast, you can issue the [Menu] Scripts BeginRecord command only when the Main menu is accessible. Third, you can play an instant script just by pressing the [Instant Script Play] key ([Alt]-[F4]).

However, there is one situation in which you should not press the [Instant Script Record] key: while the Scripts menu is in view. Usually, if you issue the [Menu] Scripts command, Paradox will display the five-item Scripts menu shown in Figure 13-1 on page 586. But, if you issue the [Menu] Scripts command during the recording or playing of a script, you will see the four-item menu shown in Figure 13-5. Only the four items on this menu should be available to you during the recording or playing of a script.

If you issue the [Menu] Scripts command to reveal the five-option Scripts menu and then press [Instant Script Record], the regular Scripts menu will still be available to you. This menu contains four commands that should not be accessible during script play or recording, but which you will continue to see: BeginRecord, QuerySave, ShowPlay, and Editor. Choosing any of these commands while you are recording a script may cause a system error, which will result in a keyboard lockup and the possible loss of data. To avoid these problems, do not press the [Instant Scripts Record] key while the Scripts menu is visible.

Viewing a Script

Now that you have recorded your first script, let's see just what Paradox has recorded. The first step in viewing (or editing) a script is to load it into a text editor. You probably will find Paradox's built-in PAL Script Editor to be the most convenient text editor to use for this task. However, you can view or edit a script in any word processor or text editor that can read an ASCII text file.

To view a script in the Script Editor, issue the **[Menu]** Scripts **E**ditor command. When you choose Editor, Paradox will present two choices: Write and Edit. The Write option allows you to compose a script from scratch, instead of recording it. We'll show you how to do that later in this chapter. In this case, we're interested in the Edit option, which allows you to view and/or edit a previously recorded (or written) script. When you choose Edit, Paradox will prompt you to specify the name of the script you want to edit. You may specify the script by typing its name or by pressing ↵ and choosing the name from a list. In this case, type the name **Empsort** and press ↵.

As soon as you select the script you want to edit, Paradox will read that script from its .SC file and display it on the screen within the Script Editor. As you can see, Figure 13-6 shows the script we recorded in the Script Editor. Within this editing environment, you can either edit or view the script. In this case, we'll just look at the script to see how Paradox has recorded each keystroke.

Figure 13-6 The Empsort Script

```
Changing script C:\paradox3\empsort                          Script
....+...10....+...20....+...30....+...40....+...50....+...60....+...70....+...80
{Modify} {Sort} {Emplyee} {Same} Down Down Down Down Down Down
Down Down Down Down Down Down "1" Do_It! Menu {Scripts} {End-Record}
```

Script Elements

A recorded script can contain three types of elements: menu selections, Special keys, and text. The script shown in Figure 13-6 contains all three.

Menu Selections

After we began recording the script, our first action was to choose Modify from the Main menu and Sort from the Modify menu. As you can see, Paradox has recorded these items as {Modify} and {Sort}, respectively—simply the names of the menu items surrounded by braces. Paradox uses the {} form to record anything you choose from a menu, including commands and the names of tables, forms, and scripts you select while issuing a command.

For example, the third item in our script is {Emplyee}. This item represents the name of the table we want Paradox to sort. We could have selected this name in any one of three ways: by typing its name, by pressing ↵ and typing the first letter of its name, or by pressing ↵ and pointing to it. No matter how it is selected, Paradox would represent it in brace form within the script.

Similarly, the last line in the script is the recorded representation of the [Menu] Scripts End-Record command. This command appears in the script as a result of choosing Scripts End-Record to end the recording of the script. This command will always be the last line of any script you record during a Paradox session. It serves no purpose in the script, but it will not cause any problem when you play the script. However, you may want to use the editing techniques we cover later in this chapter to remove this command from your scripts.

Choosing Menu Items

As we mentioned earlier, the way you choose an item from a menu doesn't affect the way Paradox records that item. (In the example, Paradox would have recorded the Modify command the same way, whether you typed *M* or pressed the ➡ key four times and then pressed ↵. Either way, Paradox would record the command as {Modify}.)

The same is true for the tables and other objects you specify while recording a script. When Paradox prompts you to supply the name of an object, such as a table, you can either type the name and press ↵ or press ↵ and choose the name from the list Paradox displays. Only the name of the object you select—and not the keystrokes you use to select it—will be recorded.

This rule has some important implications for your scripts. For one thing, it means that you cannot record a generic script, that is, a script that operates on whatever table happens to be active when you play it. To create generic scripts, either edit a recorded script or write the script from scratch. We'll show you how to create generic scripts at the end of this chapter.

Special Keys

The fifth through 16th commands in the example script are recorded representations of the ↓ key. Remember that you used this key to move the cursor to the Salary field in the sort specification. As you can see, Paradox recorded the word *Down* in the script each time you pressed the ↓ key.

Paradox always uses unquoted, unbraced words to represent any "special" key you press during the recording of a script. These special keys include the ten special function keys, the [Alt]-function key combinations, the cursor-movement keys, and keys like ↵ and [Backspace]. For example, Paradox records the [Menu] key ([F10]) as Menu, the [Do-It!] key ([F2]) as Do_It!, the [Field View] key ([Alt]-[F5]) as FieldView, the [Rotate] key ([Ctrl]-[R]) as Rotate, and the ↵ key as Enter. Table 13-1 shows a complete list of how Paradox represents these special keys in a recorded script.

Some special function keys duplicate the action of commands on the Paradox menus. In these cases, the alternative you choose affects the appearance of the script but not its outcome. Once you've filled in a sort specification, for example, you can command Paradox to perform the sort either by pressing the [Do-It!] key ([F2]) or by issuing the [Menu] DO-IT! command. If you press [Do-It!], Paradox will record the command as Do_It!. On the other hand, if you select DO-IT! from the Sort menu, Paradox will store the command as *Menu {DO-IT!}*. Although these two alternatives achieve the same result, they do so using different mechanisms. One commands Paradox to press a key, while the other commands Paradox to choose a command from a menu. Similarly, you can edit a table either by pressing the [Edit] key ([F9]) or by issuing the [Menu] Modify Edit command. If you press [Edit] during the recording of a script, the recorded script will contain the representation EditKey. If you press the [Menu] key and choose Modify Edit, the script will contain the keystroke sequence *Menu {Modify} {Edit} {filename}*.

Table 13-1 Key Representations in Scripts

Function Keys		Numeric Keypad Keys		[Ctrl] Combinations		[Alt] Combinations	
[F1]	Help	[Home]	Home	[Ctrl]-[Home]	CtrlHome	[Alt]-[K]	KeyLookup
[F2]	Do_It!	[End]	End	[Ctrl]-[End]	CtrlEnd	[Alt]-[L]	LockKey
[F3]	UpImage	[Pg Up]	PgUp	[Ctrl]-[Pg Up]	CtrlPgUp	[Alt]-[O]	DOSBig
[F4]	DownImage	[Pg Dn]	PgDn	[Ctrl]-[Pg Dn]	CtrlPgDn	[Alt]-[R]	Refresh
[F5]	Example	←	Left	[Ctrl]-←	CtrlLeft	[Alt]-[X]	CrosstabKey
[F6]	Check	→	Right	[Ctrl]-→	CtrlRight	[Alt]-[Z]	ZoomNext
[F7]	FormKey	↑	Up	[Ctrl]-[D]	Ditto		
[F8]	ClearImage	↓	Down	[Ctrl]-[F]	FieldView		
[F9]	EditKey	↵	Enter	[Ctrl]-[O]	DOS		
[F10]	Menu	[Tab]	Tab	[Ctrl]-[R]	Rotate		
[Alt]-[F3]	InstantRecord	[Ins]	Ins	[Ctrl]-[V]	VertRuler		
[Alt]-[F4]	InstantPlay	[Del]	Del	[Ctrl]-[Y]	DeleteLine		
[Alt]-[F5]	FieldView	[Esc]	Esc	[Ctrl]-[Z]	Zoom		
[Alt]-[F6]	CheckPlus	[Shift]-[Tab]	ReverseTab	[Ctrl]-[Backspace]	CtrlBackspace		
[Alt]-[F7]	InstantReport	[Backspace]	Backspace	[Ctrl]-[Break]	CtrlBreak		
[Alt]-[F9]	Coedit						
[Ctrl]-[F6]	CheckDescending						
[Ctrl]-[F7]	GraphKey						
[Shift]-[F6]	Groupby						

Literal Characters

The next item in the script, "1", is an example of text—the third type of item that can be found in a recorded script. This item corresponds to the number 1 that we typed into the sort specification form next to the field name *Salary*. Any time you type one or more characters into a table, a form, a report, a query, or a sort specification while you are recording, Paradox will enclose that character in quotation marks in the recorded script. If you had typed 1D to specify a descending sort, for example, Paradox would have recorded "1D". If you had entered the Edit mode and typed the entry *123 Main Street* into the Address field, Paradox would have included *"123 Main Street"* in the recorded script. Whenever you perform any action other than choosing a menu item or pressing a special key, Paradox will record that action as text.

Mistakes

With the exception of the way it standardizes the choices you make from menus, Paradox is quite literal in the way it records your keystrokes. For this reason, any keys you mistakenly press during the recording of a script will show up in the script. For example, suppose you move to a field of a table, then type the entry *Jones* and press ↵ without first entering the Edit mode. Although Paradox will display the message *Press Edit [F9] or Coedit [Alt][F9] if you want to make changes* and will not enter the change into the table, it will record the text *"Jones"* and the key representation *Enter* in the script. Each time you play a script that contains this kind of error, Paradox will repeat your error. To remove the mistake, you must edit the script. We'll show you how to edit a script in a few pages.

Returning to Paradox

When you're finished editing a script, you can do one of three things to return to Paradox. If you want to return to the Paradox workspace without saving any changes made to the script, issue the [Menu] Cancel command and choose the Yes option. When you issue this command, Paradox will exit from the Script Editor and return to the main Paradox workspace. If you have made any changes to the script, they will be erased. If you choose No instead of Yes after choosing Cancel, you will remain within the Script Editor.

If you have made changes to the script (we'll show you how to do this later) and you want to save them into the .SC file, you can issue the [Menu] DO-IT! command or just press the [Do-It!] key. When you do either of these things, Paradox will save the edited script and return you to the Paradox workspace. If you have not made any changes to the script, choosing either of these options has the same effect as choosing the Cancel Yes option.

Playing Scripts

The principal reason for recording a script is to enable Paradox to perform a repetitive task automatically. Once you've recorded a script, therefore, you'll probably want to play it. When you play a script, Paradox reads and executes the commands stored in that script, one at a time. Paradox doesn't actually press keys, so it can perform a task much faster than you can. Because Paradox always reads exactly what it has recorded, it never presses an incorrect key—unless you have done so during the recording of the script.

There are many ways to play a script. In most cases, you will issue the [Menu] Scripts Play command and then select the name of the script. Alternatively, you can press the [PAL Menu] key ([Alt]-[F10]) to reveal the PAL menu, choose Play, and specify the name of the script. If the script file is named INSTANT.SC (as it will be if you create it with the [Instant Script Record] key), you can play it by pressing the [Instant Script Play] key ([Alt]-[F4]). If you are viewing (or editing) a script, you can play it by pressing the [Menu] key to reveal the Script Editor menu, then selecting Go. Finally, you can play the most recently edited script by pressing the [Go] key ([Ctrl]-[G]).

Each of these methods plays a script "at top speed." Whenever you play a script in one of these ways, Paradox actually does several things. First, it appears to freeze the current image on the screen. Then, it reads the series of commands from the script file and executes them one at a time. When the script is finished, Paradox unfreezes the screen to reveal the changed Paradox workspace.

The PAL Canvas

Notice we said that Paradox *appears* to freeze the screen when you play a script. In fact, the frozen image is not the Paradox workspace, but a copy of the workspace image painted onto a new workspace called the PAL canvas. The PAL canvas is an alternative workspace that is dropped in front of the Paradox workspace whenever you begin playing a script. With few exceptions, this canvas remains in place, obscuring the main Paradox workspace, until the script is finished.

Because Paradox paints this workspace with the image that was on the Paradox workspace when you began playing the script, it appears as though you're looking at the "frozen" Paradox workspace. As we'll explain in Chapter 16, however, PAL offers commands that let you clear this canvas and display your own messages during the execution of a script. For now, just remember that you'll be seeing the PAL canvas, not the Paradox workspace, whenever you play a script.

An Example

Suppose you want to play the script shown in Figure 13-6 on page 591. To do this, issue the **[Menu]** Scripts **P**lay command and select the name of the script you want to play (in this case, Empsort). You can select the script either by typing its name and pressing ↵ or by pressing ↵ and selecting its name from the list Paradox displays. As soon as you issue this command, Paradox will drop the PAL canvas, paint it with the current image of the screen, and begin to issue the stored commands. First, Paradox will choose Modify Sort from the Main menu, select the EMPLYEE table, and specify that the results be placed in the same table. Paradox then will move down the sort specification and "type" a 1 to the left of the field name Salary. Next, Paradox will "press" the [Do-It!] key and perform the sort. Finally, Paradox will execute the [Menu] Scripts End-Record command. Because the canvas is frozen, you won't see any of this activity on your screen. When the script play ends, the sorted EMPLYEE table will appear on the screen.

Watching a Script Play

The ShowPlay option on the Scripts menu provides yet another way to play a script. Unlike the other methods, the ShowPlay command does not drop the PAL canvas prior to playing a script. As a result, it lets you watch while the script manipulates the Paradox workspace. When you issue the [Menu] Scripts ShowPlay command and specify a script, Paradox will present two choices: Fast and Slow. If you choose Fast, Paradox will execute the script relatively quickly. Because it redraws the screen after each change it makes to the workspace, however, it can take much longer than normal to play a script this way. If you choose Slow, Paradox plays the script at about the same speed you typically would issue the commands yourself. Although it sometimes can be fun to watch the execution of a script, you usually will want to take advantage of the faster execution that results when the Paradox workspace is obscured by the PAL canvas.

Playing a Script Several Times

There may be times when you want to repeat the play of a script several times. You can use the [Menu] Scripts RepeatPlay command to play a script as many times as you want or to play a script continuously.

For example, suppose you have recorded a script named Slides that uses queries and cross tabulations to generate a set of tables on which Paradox can base several graphs, then displays those graphs in a slide show. Now, suppose you want to present this slide show repeatedly for a display during a company open house. To play the slide show script 20 times, issue the [Menu] Scripts **R**epeatPlay command, type **SLIDES** at the *Script:* prompt and press ↵. After you enter the name of the script, Paradox will present the prompt *Number of times to repeat:*. Since you want the script to repeat 20 times, type **20** at the prompt and press ↵. Then, PAL will play the script 20 times without interruption.

You can make a script play continuously by typing the letter *C* at the *Number of times to repeat:* prompt. If you enter *C* at this prompt, PAL will continue playing the script until you interrupt script play by pressing [Ctrl]-[Break].

Notes

Paradox is able to execute the commands in a script quite rapidly for at least two reasons. First, even though Paradox does have to read the script from disk, it can do that significantly faster than even the fastest typist can manipulate the keyboard. Second, because the screen image doesn't change as a script is played, Paradox doesn't spend time redrawing the screen each time it issues a command. Paradox redraws the screen, showing the result of all its actions, only after it has completely executed the script.

Saving Queries

In Chapters 7 and 8, you learned how important queries are in Paradox. You also learned that Paradox does not save a query specification automatically with the other objects in a family. To save a query, you issue the [Menu] Scripts QuerySave command. To bring a query back to the workspace, you must use the [Menu] Scripts Play command and select the name of the query.

The commands for saving and retrieving queries are located on the Scripts menu because Paradox saves queries as scripts. For this reason, you can view and edit scripts in the Script Editor in the same way that you can view and edit a recorded script. In the following paragraphs, we'll show you what a recorded query looks like. In the next section of this chapter, we'll show you how to edit a query once you have saved it.

Saving a Query

Suppose you want to design and save a query that returns the entries from the Last Name and Salary fields of the records in the EMPLYEE table that have Salary field entries greater than $35,000. To design this query, first use the **[Menu] A**sk command to create a blank query for the EMPLYEE table. Then, use the **[Check Plus]** key to select the Last Name and Salary fields, and type the condition **>35000** into the Salary field. When you finish, your query will look like the one shown in Figure 13-7.

Figure 13-7 An Example Query

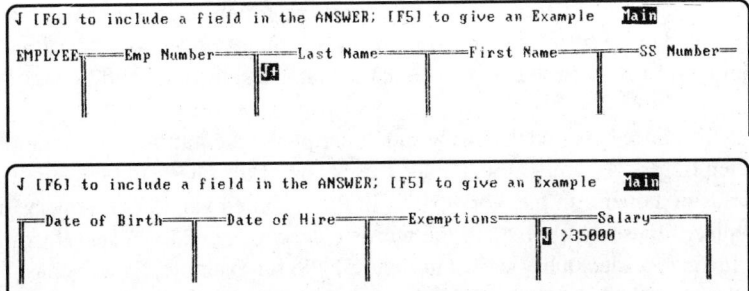

Once you have designed a query, you can execute it with the [Do-It!] key. The query will remain defined until you use the [Clear Image] or [Clear All] key to remove it from the workspace. When you clear the query from the screen, however, it will cease to exist. Unless you save a query before you remove it from the workspace, you will need to recreate it from scratch if you want to use it again.

As you learned in Chapter 7, you can save a query by issuing the [Menu] Scripts QuerySave command and specifying a name for the .SC file in which you want to save the query. To save our example query, issue the **[Menu]** Scripts QuerySave command and type the name **Highpay.** When you press ↵, PAL will save the query into the script file named HIGHPAY.SC.

Viewing the Saved Query

Because Paradox saves a query as a script, you can view or edit a saved query from within the Script Editor or any other text editor you want to use. To load our example query into the Script Editor, issue the **[Menu]** Scripts Editor Edit command, type the name of the script that contains the query, **Highpay,** and press ↵. These are the same steps you would use to view or edit any other script. Figure 13-8 shows the script form of our query.

Figure 13-8 The Query Script

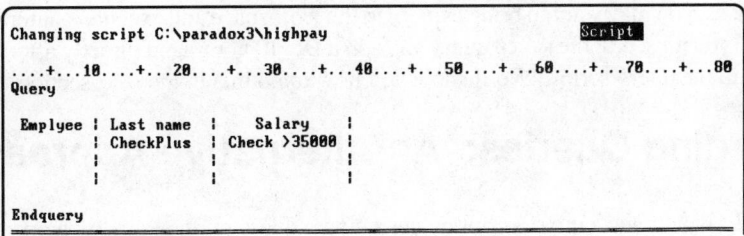

The Saved Query

As you can see, the query script shown in Figure 13-8 resembles the query in Figure 13-7, which it represents. However, there are four major differences between a query and its script representation. First, the script version of a query contains only the fields that are selected with some type of check and those fields that contain selection conditions. For example, the query represented in the script shown in Figure 13-8 contains only two fields: Last Name (a selected field) and Salary (a selected field that contains a selection condition).

The second difference between the query and its script representation is the notation used to mark selected fields. As you know, Paradox uses one of the check mark symbols to mark selected fields in a query on the workspace. In the recorded version of a query, however, Paradox replaces these symbols with the words *Check*, *CheckPlus*, *CheckDescending*, or *Groupby*. In the recorded query shown in Figure 13-8, for example, Paradox has placed the word *CheckPlus* in the Last Name field and the word *Check* in the Salary field.

The third difference between a query and its script version is the way examples are represented. On the workspace, Paradox displays examples in reverse video. In a script, however, Paradox denotes examples by preceding them with an underline. For instance, the example *zzz* would be represented as *_zzz* in a query script.

The fourth difference between the query and its script version is the presence of the words *Query* and *Endquery* at the beginning and end of the script. These two special words are PAL commands that must enclose the script version of a query. The Query command alerts Paradox that the lines that follow contain the script representation of a query. The Endquery command marks the end of that query. In Figure 13-8, you can see that a single blank line follows the Query command and another blank line precedes the Endquery command. These blank lines are essential parts of the script representation of a query.

Playing a Saved Query

Playing a saved query is similar to playing any other script. The result, however, is somewhat different. Instead of pressing keys and issuing commands, Paradox loads the query back onto the workspace in its "unabridged" form. Once the query is back on the workspace, you can process it by pressing the [Do-It!] key.

In some cases, you may want to bring a query to the workspace and execute it automatically. To do this, you must edit the saved query and add a Do_It! command directly after the word *Endquery* in the query script. We'll show you how to do this in the next section.

Recording Queries: An Alternative Approach

You usually will create a query script by designing a query on the Paradox workspace and then using the [Menu] Scripts QuerySave command to write that query into a script. Although this is the preferred method of saving a query, it is not the only way. Instead of saving a predesigned query, you can record the process of designing the query in the same way you record any other keystrokes. For example, the script

> Menu {Ask} {Emplyee} Right Right CheckPlus Right Right Right Right Right Right Right Right Right Right Check ">35000"

automates the process of designing the query shown in Figure 13-7—the same one represented by the query script shown in Figure 13-8.

Even though these two methods achieve the same result, you probably will want to save most of your queries with the QuerySave command. The graphic nature of the Query/Endquery form makes it easier for you to see and understand what the query is doing when you view and edit the script that contains the query. It also makes the query easier to edit once it is in a script.

Editing Scripts

So far, we have shown you how to record a script and save a query into a script. We also have shown you how to view a script in the Script Editor. In most cases, however, you'll want to do more than just view a script once you bring it into the Script Editor. Usually, you'll want to change it in some way. We'll refer to the process of adding to, deleting from, or replacing parts of a script as editing the script.

Loading a script into the Script Editor is a simple process. All you need to do is issue the [Menu] Scripts Editor Edit command and select the name of the script you want to edit. You can select a script by typing its name and pressing ↵. Alternatively, you can press ↵ to reveal a list of script names and then choose one of these by typing the first letter in its name or by pointing to its name and pressing ↵ again. To load the script Empsort into the Script Editor, issue the [Menu] Scripts Editor Edit command and type the script name **Empsort**. When the script is loaded into the Script Editor, your screen should look like Figure 13-6.

Moving Around in the Script Editor

Paradox uses an underline as the cursor in the Script Editor, just as it does in all other environments. This cursor always marks the point that will be affected by the next key you press. As you might expect, you can use the standard cursor-movement keys—←, →, ↑, and ↓—to move the cursor one space left, right, up, or down within the Script editor.

You can use other keys and combinations to move the cursor in increments greater than a single space or line. When you press the [Ctrl]-→ or [Ctrl]-← combinations, Paradox will move the cursor one entire screen to the right or left. The [Pg Up] and [Pg Dn] keys move the cursor up and down 12 lines at a time. The [Home] key moves the cursor to the first line of the script, while the [End] key moves it to the bottom line of the script. The [Ctrl]-[Home] and [Ctrl]-[End] combinations move the cursor to the first or last character on the current line.

The actions of these keys and combinations in the Script Editor are similar to their actions in the Report Generator. However, the nature of the two workspaces is a bit different. First, the Script Editor workspace is not divided into page-widths, as is the Report Generator workspace. Second, the width of the workspace in the Script Editor is fixed at 132 characters. Third, Paradox sets the bottom border of the Script Editor just below the last line of commands in the script you are editing.

Paradox will not allow you to move the cursor beyond the boundaries of the Script Editor workspace; nor will it allow the cursor to wrap from one edge of the Script Editor workspace to the other. If you press ➡ when the cursor is in the 132nd space on a line, or ⬅ when the cursor is in the first space, Paradox will just beep. The same thing happens if you try to move above the upper border or below the bottom border of the workspace.

The Horizontal and Vertical Rulers

If you look again at Figure 13-6 or 13-8, you'll see a row of periods, plus signs, and numbers across the third line of the Script Editor screen. This row of symbols is the horizontal ruler. Each symbol on this ruler marks one "column" in the Script Editor. The horizontal ruler is useful for determining where the cursor is positioned within the current row, relative to the left edge of the workspace. The horizontal ruler always is visible whenever you are within the Script Editor.

In addition to this horizontal ruler, the Script Editor features a vertical ruler. This ruler, shown in Figure 13-9, allows you to determine in what row of the Script Editor the cursor is positioned. Although Paradox displays the horizontal ruler whenever you are within the Script Editor, it will not display the vertical ruler unless you press [Ctrl]-[V]. To suppress the display of the vertical ruler, press [Ctrl]-[V] again. Whether you use this ruler is purely a matter of personal preference.

Figure 13-9 The Vertical Ruler

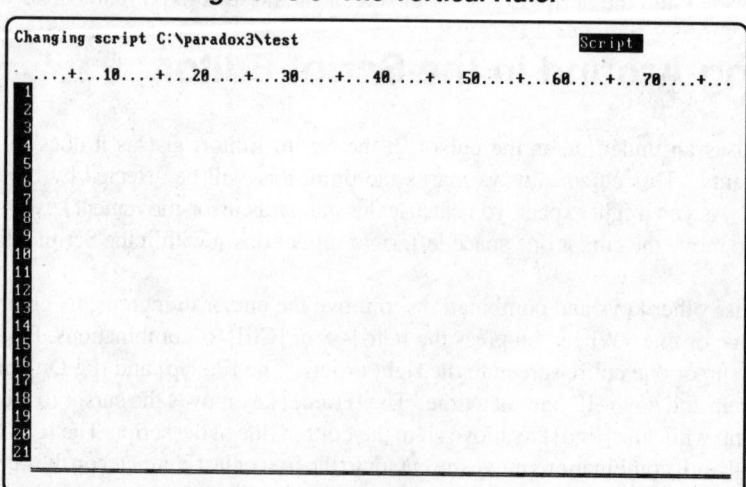

Replace Mode Versus Insert Mode

Most text editors give you a choice of two editing modes: replace and insert. The Script Editor is no exception. Your choice of mode is important when you are typing on a line that already contains characters. For example, suppose you type a character while the cursor is positioned on another character in a script. If the Script Editor is in the replace mode, it will replace the current character with the character you type. If the Script Editor is in the insert mode, however, it will place the character you type at the position of the cursor and move the remaining characters to the right. The result is an insertion, rather than a replacement, of text.

Paradox always will be in the replace mode when you first enter the Script Editor. To change to the insert mode, you must press the [Ins] key. Whenever Paradox is in the insert mode, it will display the message *Ins* in the upper-right corner of the screen. Unless this indicator is present, Paradox is in the replace mode.

Adding Lines to the Script Editor

You can add new blank lines to the workspace and thereby increase its size by pressing the ↵ key. If the cursor is positioned at the end of the last line when you press ↵, Paradox will add a new blank line to the end of the script. The result of pressing the ↵ key from other locations within a script depends on whether you are in the insert or replace mode. If the cursor is anywhere other than at the end of the last line while the Script Editor is in the replace mode, pressing ↵ will move the cursor to the beginning of the next line without inserting a new line into the script.

Pressing ↵ while the Script Editor is in the insert mode adds a new line to a script. If the cursor is positioned at or beyond the last character on any line while the Script Editor is in the insert mode, pressing ↵ adds a new blank line below that line. If the cursor is positioned in the middle of a line when you press ↵, Paradox will break the line into two lines at the point where the cursor is positioned. If the cursor is at the beginning of a line when you press ↵, the Script Editor will insert a new line above the current position of the cursor.

Deleting Characters and Lines

There are three ways to remove text from a script. First, you can position the cursor on the character you want to delete and press [Del]. Whenever you press this key, Paradox deletes the character on which the cursor is positioned and pulls the remaining text on the line one space to the left. Alternatively, you can position the cursor to the right of the character you want to delete and press [Backspace]. However, the action of the [Backspace] key is also affected by your choice of the replace or insert mode. If the Script Editor is in the replace mode, the characters to the right of the cursor remain in place as you press the [Backspace] key. The result is a gap in the line of the script. If the Script Editor is in the insert mode, Paradox pulls the characters that are to the right of the cursor one space to the left each time you press the [Backspace] key. While you are in the insert mode, then, you can combine the text from two adjacent lines by pressing [Backspace] from the beginning of the lower line.

Paradox also provides you with a way to delete whole and partial lines. When you press [Ctrl]-[Y] from within the Script Editor, Paradox will delete all characters from the position of the cursor to the right end of the line. If the cursor is on the first character of the line, this combination erases the entire line and moves the remaining lines up one row. If you press [Ctrl]-[Y] while the cursor is beyond the last character on the line, Paradox will just beep.

The Script Editor Menu

If you press the [Menu] key while editing a script, you'll see the six-item Script Editor menu shown in Figure 13-10. The first item on this menu, Read, allows you to read a copy of another script into the script you are currently editing. The ability to combine two scripts allows you to record in parts a complex series of commands and then combine the parts into the finished script. This command also allows you to reuse lines of previously recorded or written scripts in new scripts that perform similar functions.

Figure 13-10 The Script Editor Menu

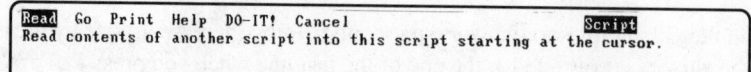

The Go command lets you save the changes you've made to the current script and play that script in one motion. The Print command sends the script to the printer, which produces a hard copy of the script. The Help command lets you obtain instructions about the Script Editor. The DO-IT! command saves the changes you've made to the current script and returns you to Paradox. The last command, Cancel, abandons any changes you've made and returns you to Paradox.

Ending the Edit

Once you have made all the changes to a script, you can stop editing in any of three ways. If you want to save the edited script and then return to the Paradox workspace, you can issue the [Menu] DO-IT! command or just press the [Do-It!] key. If you want to return to the Paradox workspace without saving the changes, you can issue the [Menu] Cancel command and choose the Yes option. When you issue this command, Paradox will not save any of the changes you have made. The script will continue to exist in its original, unedited form. If you select No instead of Yes after choosing Cancel, Paradox will return you to the edited script within the Script Editor.

If you issue the [Menu] Go command, Paradox will first save the changes you made to the script, just as it does when you choose the DO-IT! command. As soon as the changes have been saved, however, Paradox will play the revised script. If you plan to play the edited script after you save it (and you frequently will want to do this), choosing Go will save you time and keystrokes.

An Example: Modifying Our Script

Once you have loaded a script into the Script Editor, making changes to that script is as easy as moving the cursor and typing. In this case, we'll make two changes to the Empsort script. First, we'll remove the superfluous commands *Menu {Scripts} {End-Record}* from the end of the script. Then, we will change the sort order from ascending to descending.

We'll use the [Ctrl]-[Y] combination to remove the *Menu {Scripts} {End-Record}* sequence from the Empsort script. To do this, position the cursor on the *M* in Menu (or the space before it) on the second line of the script, then press [Ctrl]-[Y]. Instantly, Paradox will delete the commands *Menu {Scripts} {End-Record}* from the script.

Next, we'll make the script specify a descending sort based on the entries in the Salary field. To do this, move the cursor to the quotation marks that follow the 1 in the string *"1"*. Then, look for the *Ins* indicator in the upper-right corner of the screen to determine if the Script Editor is in the insert mode. If not, press the [Ins] key. Next, type the letter **D** (for descending) so that the string becomes *"1D"*. When you finish making these changes, your screen should look like the one in Figure 13-11. At that point, you can press [Do-It!] to end the edit and save your changes.

Figure 13-11 The Revised Empsort Script

```
Changing script C:\paradox3\empsort                    Script Ins

....+...10....+...20....+...30....+...40....+...50....+...60....+...70....+...80
{Modify} {Sort} {Employee} {Same} Down Down Down Down Down Down
Down Down Down Down Down Down "1D" Do_It!
```

Another Example

Now, let's make some changes to the query stored in the script Highpay. First, we'll change the selection condition *>35000* to *>40000*. Then, we'll add the key representation Do_It! to the end of the script so that Paradox executes the query automatically when you play the script.

To edit the Highpay script, issue the [Menu] Scripts Editor Edit command and select **Highpay**. At this point, your screen should look like the one shown in Figure 13-8. To change the selection condition from *>35000* to *>40000*, just position the cursor on the 3 and type **40**. Because Paradox will be in the replace mode when you first enter the Script Editor, this action replaces the characters 35 with the characters 40.

Now, we'll add the key representation Do_It! to the bottom of the script to make the query "self-executing." To do this, move the cursor to the right of the last character on the final line of the script. (The fastest way to do this is to press the [End] key to move to the last line, then press the [Ctrl]-[End] combination to move to the right edge of that line.) Once the cursor is in position, press ← to add a blank line at the end of the script. Then, type **Do_It!** (remember, no braces) on this line, so that the script looks like the one shown in Figure 13-12. To end the editing process, press **[Do-It!]** or issue the **[Menu]** DO-IT! command.

Figure 13-12 The Revised Highpay Script

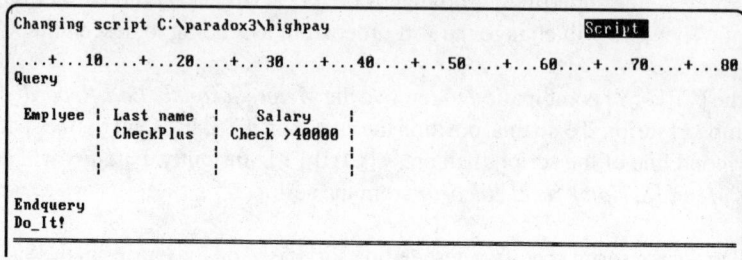

```
Changing script C:\paradox3\highpay                          Script
....+...10....+...20....+...30....+...40....+...50....+...60....+...70....+...80
Query

   Emplyee ! Last name   !   Salary   !
           ! CheckPlus   ! Check >40000 !
           !             !              !
           !             !              !

   Endquery
   Do_It!
```

Now, let's use the [Menu] Read command to combine the revised Empsort script shown in Figure 13-11 with the revised Highpay script shown in Figure 13-12. The result will be a script that first creates a two-field ANSWER table of employees whose salaries are greater than $40,000 per year, then sorts the ANSWER table into descending salary order. (To achieve this result, we will have to make a few changes once we combine the two scripts.)

The first step in this process is to read the revised Empsort script into Highpay. To begin, use the **[Menu]** Scripts Editor Edit command to load the Highpay script into the Script Editor. When the script is in view, move the cursor to the point within Highpay at which you want Paradox to insert the Empsort script. In this case, we want Paradox to place the contents of Empsort after the last command in Highpay. To do this, just place the cursor anywhere in the last line of Highpay (the line that contains only the key representation Do_It!). The position of the cursor within the line is not important. Whenever you issue the Read command, Paradox will insert the imported script immediately after the line that contains the cursor, no matter where the cursor is positioned within that line.

Once you have positioned the cursor, issue the **[Menu]** Read command and select **Empsort**, either by typing and pressing ← or by pressing ← and choosing the name from the list. As soon as you select this script, Paradox will insert it into the script you are editing, starting on the line immediately below the cursor. Figure 13-13 shows the combined script.

This combined script needs some modification before it will do what we want it to do. Currently, the commands we added into this script from Empsort direct Paradox to sort the EMPLYEE table, not the ANSWER table. Modifying these commands to sort ANSWER is a relatively easy process. First, move the cursor to the first letter of the word *Emplyee* and press **[Del]** seven times to delete it. Then, press the **[Ins]** key to enter the insert mode and type the name **Answer**.

Next, remove all but one of the Down commands from the script. Because Salary is the second of only two fields in the ANSWER table, a single Down command is all you need to move to the Salary line of the sort specification. When you finish making these changes, the script will look like the one in Figure 13-14.

Figure 13-13 The Combined Script

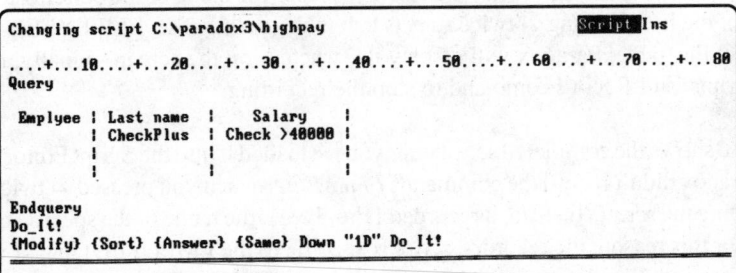

```
Changing script C:\paradox3\highpay                        Script
....+...10....+...20....+...30....+...40....+...50....+...60....+...70....+...80
Query

    Emplyee | Last name |   Salary   |
            | CheckPlus | Check >40000 |
            |           |            |
            |           |            |

Endquery
Do_It!
{Modify} {Sort} {Emplyee} {Same} Down Down Down Down Down Down
Down Down Down Down Down Down "1D" Do_It!
```

Figure 13-14 The Revised Combined Script

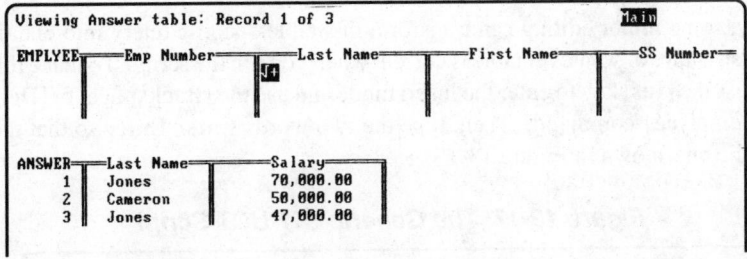

```
Changing script C:\paradox3\highpay                        Script Ins
....+...10....+...20....+...30....+...40....+...50....+...60....+...70....+...80
Query

    Emplyee | Last name |   Salary   |
            | CheckPlus | Check >40000 |
            |           |            |
            |           |            |

Endquery
Do_It!
{Modify} {Sort} {Answer} {Same} Down "1D" Do_It!
```

Once you have made these modifications to the script, you can save it, play it, or both. In this case, save and play the script all at once by pressing the [**Menu**] key and choosing **G**o. When we execute the script, Paradox will extract the Last Name and Salary entries from all records in the EMPLYEE table whose Salary entries exceed $40,000, then sort the ANSWER table into descending salary order. Figure 13-15 displays the result.

Figure 13-15 The Sorted ANSWER Table

```
Viewing Answer table: Record 1 of 3                              Main

EMPLYEE——Emp Number——      ——Last Name——      ——First Name——    ——SS Number——
                       |J4|
                       |  |            |                 |               |



ANSWER——Last Name——   ——Salary——
    1 | Jones          70,000.00
    2 | Cameron        50,000.00
    3 | Jones          47,000.00
```

Creating Generic Scripts

Because Paradox interprets the choices you make from a menu when it records your keystrokes, rather than recording the keystrokes you used to make your selection, the resulting scripts are specific to the objects you operated on during the recording. This is great for certain kinds of scripts, including saved queries and scripts not specific to any Paradox object (such as scripts that change directories). However, in many cases, you'll want to create generic scripts—scripts that perform some specific action on whatever table happens to be active. Fortunately, it is usually easy to create generic PAL scripts.

For example, suppose you want to create a script that displays the structure of whatever table is active when you play the script. To create this script, use the **[Menu]** **V**iew command to bring any table to the workspace. In this case, we'll use this command to make EMPLYEE the current table. Once the table is in view, issue the **[Menu]** **S**cripts **B**eginRecord command to begin to record the script. In this case, we'll record the script under the name **STRUCT**. Once Paradox has begun recording, issue the **[Menu]** **T**ools **I**nfo **S**tructure command and press ↵ twice: once to reveal the list of tables in the current directory and again to select the first table from that list. Because Paradox always places the name of the current table at the beginning of the list, pressing ↵ twice selects that table (in this case, EMPLYEE). As soon as you select this table, Paradox will display its structure on the screen. Finally, issue the **[Menu]** **S**cripts **E**nd-Record command to stop the recording.

Figure 13-16 shows the completed script after you've loaded it into the Script Editor. As you can see, Paradox didn't record the commands *Enter Enter* when you pressed ↵ twice as you were recording the script. Instead, it recorded {Employee}, the name of the specific table you selected. For this reason, the recorded script is specific to the EMPLYEE table. Each time you play this script, Paradox will display the structure of EMPLYEE, no matter which table you are viewing at the time.

Figure 13-16 The STRUCT Script

```
Changing script C:\paradox3\struct                          Script
....+...10....+...20....+...30....+...40....+...50....+...60....+...70....+...80
Menu {Tools} {Info} {Structure} {Emplyee} Menu {Scripts} {End-Record}
```

Fortunately, some minor editing can transform this table-specific query into one that will display the structure of whatever table is current when you run the script. To make this script generic, press the **[Ins]** key to enter the insert mode and use the **[Backspace]** or **[Del]** key to erase the {Emplyee} command. Then, type the two words **Enter Enter** so that the script looks like the one shown in Figure 13-17.

Figure 13-17 The Generic STRUCT Script

```
Changing script C:\paradox3\struct                          Script
....+...10....+...20....+...30....+...40....+...50....+...60....+...70....+...80
Menu {Tools} {Info} {Structure} Enter Enter Menu {Scripts} {End-Record}
```

When you play this revised script, Paradox will issue the [Menu] Tools Info Structure command, just like the unedited version. Instead of selecting {Emplyee}, however, this script will "press" ↵ twice, selecting the first table in the list. Since Paradox always places the name of the current table at the beginning of the list of table names, this script will display the structure of the current table. If you play the script while you are viewing the CUSTOMER table, for example, Paradox will display the structure of that table.

Writing Scripts from Scratch

Up to this point, we have shown you how to create, view, and edit a recorded script. Although recording keystrokes is not the only way to create a script, it is the preferred method for new Paradox users. This is true for one main reason: To record a script, you do not need to know how Paradox represents keystrokes in a script. As you continue recording and editing scripts, however, you will become familiar with the keystroke representations and syntax of a script. As you develop this expertise, you may prefer to write scripts from scratch rather than record them. In fact, once you begin using PAL commands in your scripts, you will usually write rather than record.

In many ways, writing a script from scratch is similar to editing a recorded script. The major difference, of course, is that you don't have a base from which to begin. To write a script from scratch, you issue the [Menu] Scripts Editor Write command, supply the name of the script you want to write, and begin typing the keystroke representation you want the script to contain. You can use any text editor to write a script.

An Example

To demonstrate the process of writing a script in the Script Editor, let's write a script that changes the current directory to c:\paradox3\examples. First, enter the Script Editor by issuing the **[Menu]** Scripts **E**ditor command, just as you did to edit a script. Instead of choosing Edit, however, choose **W**rite. When you select this option, Paradox will present the prompt *Enter name for new script:*. In response to this prompt, you should type the name under which you want Paradox to store the script you are writing. In this case, we'll use the name **CHNGDIR**. If you type the name of an existing script, Paradox will let you decide whether to replace it. If so, you should select **R**eplace. If not, you can select Cancel and choose a new name.

When you select a name for the new script, Paradox will present the screen shown in Figure 13-18. As you can see, this workspace is like the one we used earlier to edit our recorded scripts, except that it is empty and is only one line deep. This is how the Script Editor will look whenever you begin writing a new script. Once you are within this space, you can press ↵ to add new lines to it, move around with the various cursor-movement keys, and, of course, write a script.

Figure 13-18 The Empty Script

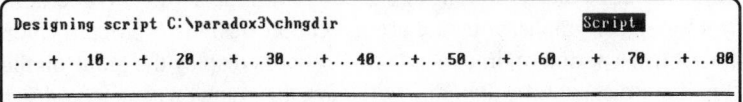

```
Designing script C:\paradox3\chngdir                          Script
....+...10....+...20....+...30....+...40....+...50....+...60....+...70....+...80
```

To change the directory from the keyboard, you would issue the [Menu] Tools More Directory command, press [Ctrl]-[Backspace] to erase the name of the current directory, type *c:\paradox3\examples*, press ↵, then choose OK. To automate this task within a script, you would write the commands

> Menu {Tools} {More} {Directory} {c:\\paradox3\\examples} {OK}

The Menu command tells Paradox to press the [Menu] key. The next three words, *{Tools} {More} {Directory}*, instruct Paradox to issue the Tools More Directory command.

The sequence *{c:\\paradox3\\examples}* tells Paradox to "type" *c:\paradox3\examples* (the name of the new directory). As you can see, we have used double backslashes in this command. In the context of a script, the backslash is a special character that commands Paradox to treat the next character literally. You will better understand the usefulness of this character as you read through the remaining PAL chapters. For now, just remember that whenever you want to include a backslash in a script, you must type two backslashes. The final command in the script, {OK}, answers the Cancel/OK prompt and commands Paradox to change the directory.

By the way, in interactive Paradox, you have to press [Ctrl]-[Backspace] to erase the old directory name before typing in the new name. You will notice that this is unnecessary in the PAL script. We could have included the CtrlBackspace command in the script after the word {Directory}, and the script would still work fine. But it is unnecessary in this context, so we have omitted it.

Once you have written a script, you can save it to disk and exit from the Script Editor by pressing the [Do-It!] key or by issuing the DO-IT! command from the Script Editor menu. If you don't want to save the script, you can issue the [Menu] Cancel command to return to the Paradox workspace. If you want to save the script and then execute it all in one step, you should select Go from the Script Editor menu.

Graph Scripts

In Chapter 12, we showed you how to create, display, and print graphs based on data in Paradox tables. We also showed you how to use queries, simple PAL scripts, and cross tabulations to prepare data for graphing. At that time, we said that you could save time by automating the steps of preparing data and creating graphs in a PAL script. In this section, we'll show you how to create a script that produces a graph based on your Paradox tables.

Before creating a slide show script, you need to design and save the graph or graphs that include the graph settings that you want to use for your slide show. While defining the settings for your graph or graphs, you may use the Graph Designer's [Menu] Overall Wait command to establish a period of time that Paradox should display the graph on the screen. (If you don't define a display time, Paradox will leave the graph on screen until you press a key.) Next, you use the [Menu] Scripts QuerySave command to save any queries needed to gather data from one or more tables for use in the graph. Then, you use the [Menu] Scripts BeginRecord command to record the keystrokes that transform the ANSWER table into the desired graph. Finally, you use the Script Editor's [Menu] Read command to combine the saved query and the recorded keystrokes into a single script that gathers the information needed for the graph and displays the graph on the screen. It is easiest to save the components of a graph script while you are actually creating the script for the first time.

Syntax and Conventions

In the example scripts we have shown you so far, we have used certain conventions involving syntax, spacing, and capitalization. Some of these conventions are necessary for the proper execution of a script, while others just make the script easier to write and understand. In either case, you'll find it easier to write scripts once you understand the following rules and conventions.

Spacing

When Paradox records a script, it leaves a single space between adjacent commands on each line. Although you'll probably want to adhere to this convention when you write a script, it is not necessary to do so in all cases. Specifically, you don't need to use a space between a menu selection and any other command. For instance, *Menu{View}* and *{Modify}{Sort}* are acceptable command sequences. Because menu selections are surrounded by braces, Paradox can tell where one command ends and the next begins.

If neither of two adjacent commands is a menu selection, you must separate them with a space. Otherwise, Paradox will not understand the command. For example, Paradox will accept the command sequence *Down Down*, but it will not understand the sequence *DownDown*.

Although Paradox sometimes cares whether you use no spaces as opposed to one space between commands, it is not particular regarding the use of multiple spaces. Paradox always allows multiple spaces where only one or none is required. For example,

Down   Down

is an acceptable sequence. However, you'll find that the use of extra spaces does nothing more than reduce the number of commands you can see on the screen at one time.

Multiple Commands on Each Line

When Paradox records a script, it usually places several commands on each line. This convention, which squeezes more commands on the screen, allows you to view a larger portion of a script at one time. At the opposite extreme, you can write each command on a different line if you want, but that practice makes a script harder to read and understand when you are viewing and editing it.

When we use PAL, we use the Script Editor to break up the command lines so that related "strings" of commands are together on the same line. This makes our scripts more readable. For example, we would reformat the script in Figure 13-10 to look like Figure 13-19.

Figure 13-19 A Formatted Script

```
Changing script C:\paradox3\empsort                              Script

....+...10....+...20....+...30....+...40....+...50....+...60....+...70....+...80
{Modify} {Sort} {Employee} {Same}
Down Down Down Down Down Down Down Down Down Down Down Down
"1D"
Do_It!
```

In the next three chapters, we will present some special PAL commands that must appear by themselves on a line and others that cannot be followed by any command on the same line. Even when these restrictions do not apply, you probably will want to use only one command per line in most situations once you start developing advanced PAL programs.

Blank Lines in Scripts

In most cases, PAL doesn't care about the presence of blank lines in a script. The exception to this rule is that certain special commands that occupy multiple lines are sometimes very sensitive to the presence of blank lines. The script representation of a query is one case in which blank lines matter. Unless you leave a blank line after the Query command and another blank line before the Endquery command, Paradox will not be able to understand the query. However, Paradox doesn't care whether you leave more than one blank line in these places.

As you read the next four chapters, you'll see other examples where blank lines are allowed or not allowed. For small scripts, a good rule of thumb is this: Unless a blank line is required, don't use one. If you do use a blank line, you'll limit the amount of the script you can see on the screen at one time. At worst, Paradox won't be able to execute the script properly.

Capitalization

When Paradox records a script, it capitalizes the first letter of each menu item and the representations of special keys, as listed in Table 13-1 on page 593. These capitalization patterns are conventions, not rules. As long as you spell each menu item and special key representation correctly, Paradox doesn't care how they are capitalized. However, these conventions make a script easier for you to read and understand.

On the other hand, capitalization does make a difference in the script representations of queries. Just as in a query on the workspace, Paradox is sensitive to the case of selection conditions in the script representation of a query.

In all other cases, including special PAL commands, functions, and references to field names and variables (subjects we'll discuss in Chapter 14), case makes no difference, except for readability. As you'll see throughout the next few chapters, however, we like to follow certain conventions when we write a script. First, the first letter of each command or object name chosen from a menu should be uppercase, but the remaining letters should be lowercase. Second, the names of all special PAL commands and functions (subjects we'll cover in Chapters 15 and 16) should be in all uppercase letters. Third, the names of variables (covered in Chapter 14) should be in lowercase form.

A Tip

Writing a script from scratch requires a high degree of familiarity with the layout of Paradox's numerous menus. If you forget a command sequence while writing a script, you'll have to save the incomplete script, work through the menus from the keyboard until you find the command you are looking for, then reload the script into the Script Editor and complete the script. If you have worked with Paradox for a while, the structure of the various menus probably will be pretty well ingrained in your mind. If you have trouble remembering the location of various commands, however, you might want to develop a written "tree" that lists the commands on each menu and keep it handy when you write your scripts.

Script Errors

Unfortunately, not all scripts run properly when you play them. Typical causes of faulty scripts include misspellings of keystroke representations and references to objects that do not exist. When Paradox encounters an error in a script that it is playing, it stops the script and presents the screen shown in Figure 13-20 on the next page. As you can see, the message *Script error – select Cancel or Debug from menu* appears in reverse video at the bottom of the screen, and a menu with the two choices, Cancel and Debug, appears at the top of the screen. If you choose Cancel from this menu, Paradox will cancel the script that is playing, "lift" the PAL canvas, and return control of the workspace to you. However, because Paradox will have executed the commands that came prior to the error, the workspace may be different from when you started.

The second option, Debug, allows you to enter the PAL Debugger. The PAL Debugger is a special environment in which you can spot and sometimes correct script-stopping errors. To understand how the Debugger works, suppose you've asked PAL to play the following script:

Menu {Tools} {More} {Drectory} {c:\\paradox3\\examples} {OK}

As you can see, the representation of the menu item Directory is misspelled in this script. When Paradox reaches this point in the script, it will stop processing the script and display the *Script error...* message. If you choose Debug at this point, Paradox will enter the PAL Debugger and present the screen shown in Figure 13-21.

Figure 13-20 The Debugger Prompt

Figure 13-21 The PAL Debugger

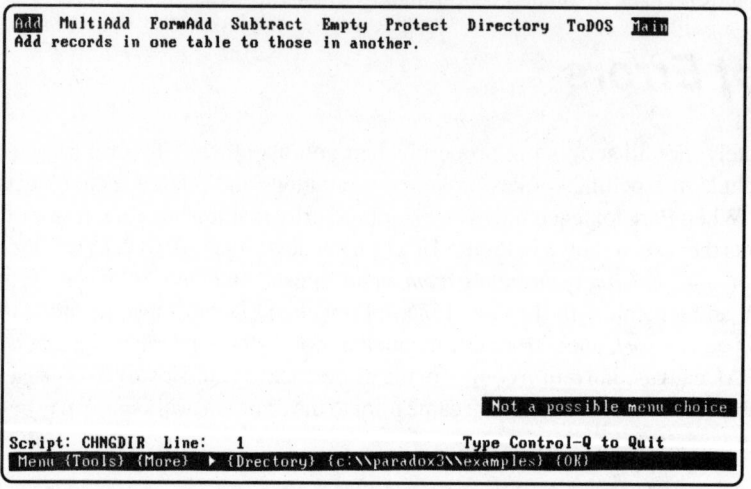

As you can see in this figure, PAL displays in reverse video at the bottom of the screen the line of the script that contains the error. (In this case, PAL displays the entire script, since it is only one line long.) The normal video message on the second line from the bottom of the screen tells you which script you are debugging and where you are within that script. In this case, the message *Script: CHNGDIR Line: 1* indicates that you are debugging the first line of the script named Chngdir. Within the line that it is debugging, PAL flashes a solid arrow to mark the error. In this case, PAL positions the arrow to the left of the menu representation {Directory}. The reverse video message on the fourth line from the bottom of the screen helps explain the error to which PAL is pointing. In this case, the message *Not a possible menu choice* points out the misspelling of the item Directory.

Once PAL has pointed out the script error, you can take a number of actions, depending on what the error is. In most cases, you will want to write down the error, leave the Debugger, edit the script to correct the error, and then play the script again. To do this, you could press [Ctrl]-[Q] to leave the Debugger, then issue the [Menu] Scripts Editor Edit command and type the name of the script that contains the error—in this case, the name *Chngdir*.

Alternatively, you can press the [PAL Menu] key ([Alt]-[F10]) while you are within the Debugger to reveal the Debugger menu, which is shown in Figure 13-22. If you choose the Editor option from the end of this menu, PAL will exit from the Debugger, clear the workspace, and present the error-containing script within the Script Editor. Once the script is in the Script Editor, Paradox will position the cursor on the line that contains the error. Pressing [Ctrl]-[E] performs this same function.

Figure 13-22 The Debugger Menu

```
Value  Step  Next  Go  MiniScript  Where?  Quit  Pop  Editor          Main
Calculate the value of an expression.
```

Once you enter the Script Editor in any of these ways, you can correct the error using the techniques we showed you earlier in this chapter. In this case, you would move the cursor to the *r* in the word *Drectory*, press **[Ins]** to enter the insert mode, and type **i**. After you have corrected the script, you can end the edit by pressing the **[Do-It!]** key (or choosing DO-IT! from the Script Editor menu). Then, you can play the corrected script by issuing the **[Menu]** Scripts **P**lay command. Alternatively, you can choose **G**o from the Script Editor menu to both save the changes and run the corrected script.

In Chapter 16, we'll explore the PAL Debugger in greater depth. In that chapter, we'll show you that there are two types of script errors: run errors and syntax errors. As you will see, it often is possible to correct run errors temporarily from within the Debugger, then continue with the execution of the script, either continuously or one command at a time. For now, you should understand that you can use the Debugger to point out the errors that Paradox encounters when executing a script.

Custom PAL Script Editors

As we mentioned earlier, the first step in editing a script is to load it into the Script Editor or another text editor. As you will see, the Script Editor is not as powerful as most stand-alone word processing programs. The Script Editor has only an extremely basic ability to move and copy parts of a script, for example, and no search-and-replace capability.

Fortunately, you aren't required to use the Script Editor. If you already use a text editor that handles unformatted ASCII text, you can substitute that editor for the Script Editor. Paradox will then access that editor instead of its own Script Editor when you issue the [Menu] Scripts Editor Edit or [Menu] Scripts Editor Write commands. To have Paradox access your favorite text editor, you need to tell Paradox how to call it. You do this through the CCP, which we discussed in Chapter 2. To run the CCP, you need to play the script called Custom from within the \paradox3 directory. When the CCP main menu appears, select the **PAL** command. This will display a menu with the choices MaintainIndexes, Editor, and Return. Select the **Editor** option. You will then be prompted to enter the command that calls your editor.

The command you type can have three parts. The first part is the DOS command you use to call your editor—for instance, WS, WP, or B. Second, if your editor accepts file names on the DOS command line, you can include an asterisk (*) after the editor name. This asterisk lets Paradox pass the name of the script you've selected to your editor. Third, if your editor can also accept line numbers on the DOS command line following the file name, you can type two more asterisks (**). This lets the Debugger pass line numbers to the editor when you choose to edit a script from the Debugger. Thus, if you call your editor with the command B and can use both a file name and line number on the command line, you would type *B * *** and press ↵.

When your text editor is used, Paradox is suspended as if you had used the [DOS] key ([Ctrl]-[O]). Therefore, you should be careful to exit back into Paradox after you finish working with a script. If you were to turn off your computer without exiting through Paradox, you could lose some data. Since using your own text editor is like using the [DOS] key, you will have the same amount of memory available for use as if you had used [DOS]. If you think you might need more memory, you can precede the Editor command with an exclamation point (!). This will give you the same amount of memory as if you pressed the [DOS Big] key ([Alt]-[O]). The command line in this case would be !B * **.

After you type in the command that will call your text editor, press ↵. If you are making no other changes in the CCP at this time, select **Return D**o-It!. When prompted, select the type of system you are using: HardDisk, or Network. Any changes you made to the CCP will take effect the next time you enter Paradox. ●

Conclusion

In this chapter, we have introduced you to the power of Paradox scripts. First, we showed you how to record your keystrokes into a simple script and showed you what a recorded script looks like. Next, we explained how Paradox represents a query in a script. After taking a look at various ways of playing a script, we showed you how to edit a script and how to write a script from scratch. We also explained the basics of debugging a script.

Simple recorded scripts like the ones presented in this chapter barely scratch the surface of the potential of PAL scripts. Although recorded scripts allow you to perform tasks quickly, they can't do anything more than you can do from the keyboard. In the next four chapters, we'll move beyond the limited realm of keystroke representations into the world of PAL.

Chapter 14

PAL Basics

As you saw in Chapter 13, scripts are powerful tools that allow you to automate any tasks you perform within Paradox. However, scripts that contain only representations of keystrokes, whether recorded or written, can accomplish no more than you can accomplish from the keyboard. The Paradox Application Language (PAL) takes you beyond the limited power of these simple scripts. PAL is a complete, structured programming language that is designed specifically to work with Paradox. PAL allows you to use variables, set up loops, develop customized menus, solicit user input, and so forth, in your scripts. These powerful features allow you to develop complex automated applications that go way beyond the scope of the simple scripts presented in Chapter 13.

Although a PAL program can do much more than a simple listing of keystrokes can, it is still a script. In fact, all PAL programs are scripts, and all scripts are PAL programs. The difference between them is one of complexity and power. The simple scripts presented in Chapter 13 are PAL programs that contain only representations of keystrokes. Because those keystroke representations are components of the Paradox Application Language, however, those simple scripts are PAL programs.

Advanced scripts use special PAL commands and functions instead of, or in addition to, keystroke representations. Because advanced PAL programs are scripts, however, you write and play them in the same way that you write and play a simple script. In this chapter, we'll assume you have a working knowledge of writing and playing scripts as we introduce the basic concepts and tools essential to PAL programming.

PAL Commands

PAL's 141 special commands are the principal tools you will use to create advanced PAL programs. These commands can be divided into six functional groups: menu-equivalent commands, input/output commands, system control commands, program control commands, workspace-manipulating commands, and variable-manipulating commands. Menu-equivalent commands provide streamlined ways to perform tasks that you can do with keystroke representations. Commands in this group include VIEW, EDIT, ADD, SORT, SETDIR, and DOS. Input/output commands allow PAL to request and receive input from a user, to display information on the screen during the execution of a script, and to send information to a printer.

Commands in this group include ACCEPT, SHOWMENU, ??, and PRINTER. System control commands allow PAL to do things like enter the Debugger, redefine the function of specific keys, and pause the execution of a script. Commands in this group include DEBUG, SETKEY, and SLEEP. Program control commands control the execution of a script based on the result of a conditional test. Commands in this group include IF, WHILE, SCAN, and SWITCH. Workspace-manipulating commands do things like move the cursor within an object, make entries into a table, and choose items from menus. Commands in this group include MOVETO, KEYPRESS, and SELECT. Variable-manipulating commands allow you to assign values to variables and arrays. Commands in this group include =, COPYTOARRAY, and RELEASE.

Command Basics

Before we begin examining individual PAL commands, let's look at the structure and syntax of commands in general. In this brief section, we'll look at the three components of a PAL command: command names, arguments, and keywords.

Command Names

A command's name is a word that identifies the command and, at least in most cases, gives you a rough idea of what that command does. For example, the CREATE command creates a table, the ACCEPT command solicits input from the keyboard, and the MESSAGE command displays a message on the screen.

Throughout the remainder of this book, we'll always present the names of PAL commands in uppercase form. This convention makes our scripts easier to read and understand, but does not have any effect on the way PAL reads and executes the commands. For example, PAL evaluates the commands *VIEW "Emplyee"*, *View "Emplyee"*, *view "Emplyee"*, and *vIeW "Emplyee"* in the same way.

Arguments

Arguments are the second component of most PAL commands. A command's arguments tell it what objects to act upon, what to display, how many times to perform the action, how long to wait, and so forth. In the command *VIEW "Emplyee"*, for example, the argument *"Emplyee"* specifies which table PAL should bring into the workspace. Similarly, in the command *SLEEP 3000*, the argument *3000* tells PAL to wait for three seconds.

Different commands require different types of arguments. Some commands, like VIEW, require string expressions as their arguments. Some commands, like SLEEP, require numeric expressions. Some commands accept date expressions as their arguments, while others accept logical expressions. By expression, we mean a literal value, a variable, a reference to a field, a formula, or a function.

A string expression is either a literal string (like *"Emplyee"*), a reference to an alphanumeric field, a variable that contains a string value, or a formula or function that returns a string value. Similarly, a numeric expression is a literal number (like 3000), a variable that contains a numeric value, a reference to a numeric field, or a formula or function that returns a numeric value. Any expression that is, contains, or returns a date value is a date expression, and any expression that is, contains, or returns a logical value is a logical expression. No matter which of these five types of expressions you use as the argument of a command, it must be of the type the command expects. You will learn more about these expressions later in this chapter and in Chapter 15.

Keywords

In addition to a command name and one or more arguments, some PAL commands contain one or more keywords. A keyword is a special word that is required for the proper execution of the command, but is not the command name itself. For example, the word ENDQUERY is a keyword that is required by the QUERY command. Similarly, in the command *IF x=y THEN x=x+1 ELSE x=x+2 ENDIF*, THEN, ELSE, and ENDIF are keywords that work in conjunction with the command name IF. Like command names, all keywords will be capitalized in the example scripts presented in this book. Although this capitalization isn't required, it does make a script easier to read.

Menu-equivalent Commands

Because menu-equivalent commands do things that you already know how to do with keystroke representations, they are a good place to begin learning PAL. Table 14-1 on the following page lists PAL's 27 menu-equivalent commands. As you can see, the names of most of these commands are spelled exactly like the menu items they represent. Some of these commands, like VIEW, PLAY, and EXIT, have the same effect as choosing the items they represent (View, Play, and Exit) from the Paradox menus. Other commands, like SORT, select the corresponding menu item and allow you to supply related information in a single step.

In almost all cases, these commands provide a more efficient way to program a task than the use of keystroke representations does. The "shorthand" nature of these commands and their ability to accept complex expressions as arguments are the two main reasons to choose them over keystroke representations. In the following pages, we'll explain each of PAL's menu-equivalent commands and give an example using each one.

Four of these commands are for use in multi-user environments: LOCK, UNLOCK, SETPRIVDIR, and SETUSERNAME. These commands are equivalent to Paradox commands found on the menu that appears when you issue the [Menu] Tools Net command. We discuss multi-user Paradox in detail in Appendix A2. If you plan to use Paradox only in single-user environments, you won't need these commands. On the other hand, if you will be requiring multi-user commands, you should read Appendix A2 before using them.

Table 14-1 Menu-equivalent Commands

PAL Command	PAL Keystroke Sequence
ADD	Menu {Tools} {More} {Add}
CANCELEDIT	Menu {Cancel} {Yes}
COEDIT	Menu {Modify} {Coedit}
COPY	Menu {Tools} {Copy} {Table} {Replace}
COPYFORM	Menu {Tools} {Copy} {Form}
COPYREPORT	Menu {Tools} {Copy} {Report}
CREATE	Menu {Create}
DELETE	Menu {Tools} {Delete} {Table} {OK}
EDIT	Menu {Modify} {Edit}
EMPTY	Menu {Tools} {More} {Empty} {OK}
EXIT	Menu {Exit} {Yes}
INDEX	Menu {Tools} {QuerySpeedup}
LOCK	Menu {Tools} {Net} {Lock}/{PreventLock}
MOVETO	Menu {Image} {Zoom}
PICKFORM	Menu {Image} {PickForm}
PLAY	Menu {Scripts} {Play}
PROTECT	Menu {Tools} {More} {Protect} {Password} {Table}
RENAME	Menu {Tools} {Rename} {Table} {Replace}
REPORT	Menu {Report} {Output} {Printer}
SETDIR	Menu {Tools} {More} {Directory} {OK}
SETPRIVDIR	Menu {Tools} {Net} {SetPrivate}
SETUSERNAME	Menu {Tools} {Net} {UserName}
SORT	Menu {Modify} {Sort}
SUBTRACT	Menu {Tools} {More} {Subtract}
UNLOCK	Menu {Tools} {Net} {Lock}/{Unlock}
UNPASSWORD	Menu {Tools} {More} {Protect} {ClearPassword}
VIEW	Menu {View}

The VIEW Command

VIEW is PAL's command equivalent to choosing View from Paradox's Main menu. The form of this command is

VIEW *tablename*

where the mandatory argument, *tablename*, is a string expression that specifies the name of a table stored in the current directory.

This command brings the specified table into view. For example, the command *VIEW "Emplyee"* will bring a table named EMPLYEE into view. This command is the equivalent of the keystroke sequence *Menu {View} {Emplyee}*.

The CREATE Command

PAL's CREATE command allows you to create a new table on the Paradox workspace. This command is the equivalent of issuing the [Menu] Create command, supplying a name for the new table, filling in the STRUCT table, and pressing [Do-It!]. The form of this command is:

> CREATE *tablename fieldname:type 1...fieldname n:type n*

The *tablename* argument supplies the name of the new table. The subsequent *fieldname:type* pairs identify the names and types of each column you want to include in the table. Since a table can have up to 255 fields, this command will accept up to 255 *fieldname:type* pairs. An asterisk to the right of a field's type designates it as a key field. Remember that key fields must be the first fields of a table. All arguments of this command must be string expressions.

For example, the command *CREATE "Test" "Birthday:D*" "Name:A25"* will create a table with two fields: Birthday and Name. Birthday will be a key field. This command is the equivalent of the keystroke sequence

> Menu {Create} {Test}
> "Birthday" Enter "D*" Enter "Name" Enter "A25" Do_It!

There is a variation of the CREATE command that lets you create a new table with the same structure as an existing table. The form of this command is:

> CREATE *tablename* LIKE *tablename*

As in the first form of the CREATE command, the first *tablename* argument supplies a name for the new table. The second *tablename* argument, which must follow the keyword LIKE, specifies the table whose structure you want to copy. This version of the command is similar to the [Menu] Borrow command on the Paradox Create menu.

The EDIT Command

The EDIT command is a substitute for the keystroke sequence *Menu {Modify} {Edit}*. The form of this command is

> EDIT *tablename*

The mandatory argument *tablename*, which must be a string expression, identifies the table you want to edit.

This command brings the specified table into view and enters the Edit mode. For example, the command *EDIT "Emplyee"* will bring the table named EMPLYEE into view and put Paradox into the Edit mode. This command is equivalent to the keystroke sequence *Menu {Modify} {Edit} {Emplyee}* and the sequence *Menu {View} {Emplyee} EditKey*.

The COEDIT Command

The COEDIT command is similar to the EDIT command. It allows one or more users to edit a table at the same time. A single user does not need to be on a network to use COEDIT. The form for this command is

COEDIT *tablename*

where *tablename* is the table to be modified. For example, *COEDIT "Emplyee"* brings the specified table into view and enters the Coedit mode. This command is equivalent to the keystroke sequence *Menu {Modify} {Coedit} {Emplyee}* and the sequence *Menu {View} {Emplyee} CoeditKey*.

The DELETE Command

The DELETE command instructs PAL to delete a table and its family of objects. The form of this command is

DELETE *tablename*

where the single argument is the name of the table you want to delete. The *tablename* argument must be a string expression.

Unlike the [Menu] Tools Delete command, the DELETE command does not allow you to delete only a form, a report, speedup files, a settings sheet, or a validity check file for a table; it always deletes the entire family associated with the table you name. For example, the command *DELETE "Emplyee"* will delete the table EMPLYEE and its family of objects. This command is equivalent to the keystroke sequence *Menu {Tools} {Delete} {Table} {Emplyee} {OK}*.

The COPY Command

The PAL COPY command is equivalent to the recorded keystrokes *Menu {Tools} {Copy} {Table}*. The form of this command is

COPY *source destination*

where *source* is the name of the table you want to copy, and *destination* is the name of the new table. Both arguments must be string expressions.

The COPY command copies a table and its family of objects into a new table whose name you provide. For example, the command *COPY "Test" "TestCopy"* performs the same action as the keystroke sequence *Menu {Tools} {Copy} {Table} {Test} {TestCopy} {Replace}*. If a table with the same name as the destination table already exists, Paradox will automatically replace the old table with a copy of the source table.

The COPYFORM Command

The COPYFORM command allows you to copy a form from one table to another, or from one form number to another within the same table's family. This command is equivalent to the recorded keystrokes *Menu {Tools} {Copy} {Form}*. The form of this command is

COPYFORM *sourcetable sourceform targettable targetform*

where *sourcetable* is the name of the table from which you want to copy a form, *sourceform* is the number of the form you want to copy, *targettable* is the name of the table to which you want to copy a form, and *targetform* is the number of the new form. All arguments must be string expressions.

If *sourcetable* and *targettable* are the same, then the COPYFORM command copies a report from one form number to another within the family of that table. Using the same table as both the source and the target causes the COPYFORM command to operate as if you had chosen the SameTable option while issuing the [Menu] Tools Copy Form command from the Paradox Main menu. For example, the command *COPYFORM "Test" "1" "Test" "2"* is equivalent to the keystroke sequence *Menu {Tools} {Copy} {Form} {SameTable} {Test} {1} {2}*.

If *sourcetable* and *targettable* are different, then the COPYFORM command copies a form from the family of one table to the family of another, as if you had chosen the DifferentTable option while issuing the [Menu] Tools Copy Form command. For example, the command *COPYFORM "Test" "1" "TestCopy" "1"* is equivalent to the keystroke sequence *Menu {Tools} {Copy} {Form} {DifferentTable} {Test} {1} {TestCopy} {1}*. In order to copy a form from one table to another, the two tables must have identical structures.

The COPYREPORT Command

The COPYREPORT command copies a report from one table to another, or from one report number to another within the same table's family. This command is the equivalent of the recorded keystrokes *Menu {Tools} {Copy} {Report}*. The form of this command is

COPYREPORT *sourcetable sourcereport targettable targetreport*

where *sourcetable* is the name of the table from which you want to copy a report, *sourcereport* is the number of the report you want to copy, *targettable* is the name of the table to which you want to copy a report, and *targetreport* is the number of the new report. All arguments must be string expressions.

If *sourcetable* and *targettable* are the same, then the COPYREPORT command copies a report from one report number to another within the family of the same table. Using the same table as both the source and the target causes the COPYREPORT command to operate as if you had chosen the SameTable option while issuing the [Menu] Tools Copy Report command from the Paradox Main menu. For example, the command *COPYREPORT "Test" "1" "Test" "2"* is equivalent to the keystroke sequence *Menu {Tools} {Copy} {Report} {SameTable} {Test} {1} {2}*.

If *sourcetable* and *targettable* are different, then the COPYREPORT command copies a report from the family of one table to the family of another table, as if you had chosen the DifferentTable option while issuing the [Menu] Tools Copy Report command. For example, the command *COPYREPORT "Test" "1" "TestCopy" "1"* is equivalent to the keystroke sequence *Menu {Tools} {Copy} {Report} {DifferentTable} {Test} {1} {TestCopy} {1}*. In order to copy a report from one table to another, the two tables must have identical structures.

The EXIT Command

The EXIT command ends the current Paradox session and returns you to DOS. The form of this command is simply EXIT; it requires and accepts no arguments. The EXIT command is equivalent to the keystroke sequence *Menu {Exit} {Yes}*.

The SORT Command

The SORT command provides an alternative way to sort a table on the basis of the entries in any number of fields. The typical form of this command is

SORT *sourcetable* ON *field 1 D, field 2 D, ...*TO *destinationtable*.

The first argument, *sourcetable*, identifies the table you want to sort. The next argument or arguments, which must follow the keyword ON, specify the fields on which you want to sort that table. The final argument, which must follow the keyword TO, specifies the table in which Paradox should store the sorted result. (If the destination table exists, it will automatically be replaced by the sorted table.) All these arguments must be string expressions.

Many of the components of this command are optional. For example, you should follow a field name with the letter *D* only if you want that field sorted in descending order. If you omit the letter *D*, the field will sort in ascending order. If you want to place the results of the sort into the same table that you sorted, you should omit the keyword TO and the *destinationtable* argument. (This portion of the command is required if the table is a keyed table.) If you leave out the keyword ON and the *field* argument(s), Paradox will sort the table into ascending order on the basis of the entries in every field, starting with the leftmost field in the table.

As you can see, this PAL command substitutes for the full process of issuing the [Menu] Modify Sort command, filling out the sort specification, and pressing the [Do-It!] key. For example, assuming that LastName and Age are the first and third fields of a table named TEST, the command *SORT "Test" ON "Age" D, "LastName" TO "Sorted"* produces the same result as the recorded keystroke sequence *Menu {Modify} {Sort} {Test} {Sorted} "2" Down Down "1D" Menu {DO-IT!}*.

The RENAME Command

The RENAME command allows you to rename a Paradox table. This command is the equivalent of the recorded keystroke sequence *Menu {Tools} {Rename}*. The form of this command is

RENAME *currentname newname*

where the first argument is the current name of the table, and the second argument is the new name. Both arguments must be string expressions.

Unlike the [Menu] Tools Rename command, PAL's RENAME command does not let you selectively rename only a report, form, or other object; it always renames a table and its entire family. For instance, the command *RENAME "Workers" "Emplyee"* changes the name of the WORKERS table and its related forms, reports, and indices to EMPLYEE, just as the keystroke sequence *Menu {Tools} {Rename} {Table} {Workers} {Emplyee} {Replace}* does. Keep in mind that if a table with the new name already exists, it will be replaced automatically.

The PICKFORM Command

The PICKFORM command is a substitute for the keystroke sequence *Menu {Image} {PickForm}*. The form of this command is

PICKFORM *formnumber*

where *formnumber* is a number from 1 through 14 or the letter F. This argument, which must be a string expression, specifies which of the current table's forms you want to view and make active. Just like the PickForm option on the Image menu, this command acts upon the current table (the one that the cursor is in when you issue this command).

This command brings the selected form into view. For example, the command *PICKFORM "2"* will bring the second form for the active table into view. This command is equivalent to the keystroke sequence *Menu {Image} {PickForm} {2}*.

The EMPTY Command

The EMPTY command clears all records from the table you specify. The form of this command is

EMPTY *tablename*

where *tablename* is a string expression that specifies the name of the table whose records you want to erase. For example, the command *EMPTY "Emplyee"* will delete every record from the EMPLYEE table. This command is equivalent to the sequence *Menu {Tools} {More} {Empty} {Emplyee} {OK}*.

The CANCELEDIT Command

The CANCELEDIT command allows you to cancel the current editing session without saving any changes. (Using this command, which accepts no arguments, is identical to pressing [Menu] during an edit and choosing Cancel Yes. In other words, it is equivalent to the keystroke sequence *Menu {Cancel} {Yes}*). Usually, you will use this command only while editing a table. However, you can use this command to end any Paradox operation that has Cancel as a menu option, such as table editing.

The INDEX Command

The INDEX command allows you to create a secondary index on any field in a table. The form of the command is

INDEX MAINTAINED *table* ON *field*

where the first argument is the name of the table you want to index, and the second argument is the name of the field on which you want to index the table. Both arguments must be string expressions. You can use the optional keyword MAINTAINED to keep keyed tables incrementally maintained. Using the MAINTAINED keyword on a non-keyed table will result in an error.

Like the [Menu] Tools QuerySpeedup command, this command creates a secondary index (which in DOS is a pair of files) for the table specified by the first argument. Unlike the QuerySpeedup command, however, which chooses the appropriate field for you, the INDEX command requires you to specify the field on which you want to index the table. Also, the query for the table you want to index does not have to be in the workspace when you issue the INDEX command, as it does when you issue the QuerySpeedup command. For example, if you wanted to create a non-maintained secondary index on the Salary field of the EMPLYEE table, you would use the command *INDEX "Emplyee" ON "Salary"*.

The ADD Command

ADD is the PAL command equivalent of the [Menu] Tools More Add command. This command allows you to append the records from one table to another table. The form of this command is

ADD *sourcetable destinationtable*

where *sourcetable* is the name of the table containing the records you are adding, and *destinationtable* is the name of the table to which you are appending the records. Both arguments must be string expressions.

For example, suppose you want to add the records in a table named MARSALES to a table named SALEHIST. You could use either the command *ADD "MarSales" "SaleHist"* or the keystroke sequence *Menu {Tools} {More} {Add} {MarSales} {SaleHist}*.

For the add to be successful, of course, the types of each pair of corresponding fields in the source and the destination tables must be identical. If the destination table is a keyed table and a key field duplication occurs, Paradox will use the source table records to update the destination table records.

The SUBTRACT Command

The action of PAL's SUBTRACT command is equivalent to that of the [Menu] Tools More Subtract command. The form of the command is

SUBTRACT *sourcetable destinationtable*

where *sourcetable* must be the name of the table containing the records to be subtracted from *destinationtable*. As with the Add command, both arguments must be string expressions.

For example, suppose you want to subtract the records in a table named EXPIRED from the records in a table named SUBSCRPT. You could do this with the command *SUBTRACT "Expired" "Subscrpt"* or the stored keystroke sequence *Menu {Tools} {More} {Subtract} {Expired} {Subscrpt}*.

The REPORT Command

REPORT is PAL's command equivalent of the [Menu] Report Output command. This command instructs PAL to print from the table you specify, using the report template you specify. The syntax of this command is

REPORT *table reportnumber*

The first argument must be the name of the table from which you want to print. The second argument, which must be a number from 1 through 14 or the letter R, identifies the report specification from which Paradox should print. The *table* argument must be a string expression. The *reportnumber* argument must be a string expression or a numeric expression.

For example, to print from report specification 2 of the table named EMPLYEE, you could use either the command *REPORT "Emplyee" "2"* or the stored keystroke sequence *Menu {Report} {Output} {Emplyee} {2} {Printer}*.

The REPORT command always sends information to a printer. You must use keystroke representations if you want to send a report to the screen or to a text file.

The SETDIR Command

SETDIR is PAL's command equivalent of the [Menu] Tools More Directory command. This command allows you to change the active drive and/or directory from within a script. The form of this command is

> SETDIR *directory*

The single argument, which must be a string expression, specifies the directory that you want to make current.

Suppose you want to change the current directory to c:\paradox3\examples. To do this, you could use the command *SETDIR "c:\\paradox3\\examples"*. Because the backslash (\) is a special character that tells PAL to treat the next character literally, two backslashes are needed to represent a single backslash.

This command is the equivalent of the recorded keystroke sequence *Menu {Tools} {More} {Directory} {c:\\paradox3\\examples} {OK}*. If the current directory were c:\paradox3, you could use the command *SETDIR "examples"* or the keystrokes *Menu {Tools} {More} {Directory} {examples} {OK}* instead.

The PLAY Command

PLAY is PAL's command equivalent of the [Menu] Scripts Play command (and the Play option on the PAL menu, which we'll discuss later). This command instructs PAL to play the script that you specify. The form of this command is simply

> PLAY *scriptname*

where the single argument, which must be a string expression, is the name of a script.

For example, to play a script named Abc, you could use either the command *PLAY "Abc"* or the keystroke sequence *Menu {Scripts} {Play} {Abc}*. In Chapter 16, we'll show you more examples using the PLAY command.

The PROTECT Command

PROTECT is PAL's command equivalent of the [Menu] Tools More Protect Password command. This command allows you to encrypt and password-protect a Paradox table. Unlike its menu equivalent, the PROTECT command can be used to protect only a table, not a script. The form of the PROTECT command is

> PROTECT *tablename password*

where the first argument is the name of the table you want to encrypt, and the second argument is the password for that table. Both arguments must be string expressions.

To assign the password *abracadabra* to the table named EMPLYEE, for example, you could use either the command *PROTECT "Emplyee" "abracadabra"* or the keystroke sequence *Menu {Tools} {More} {Protect} {Password} {Table} "Emplyee" {abracadabra} {abracadabra}*. As you can see, the PROTECT command provides a much shorter way to encrypt a table than the keystroke series. The PROTECT command will assign only a master password. There is no PAL equivalent command to assign an auxiliary password. Auxiliary passwords should be assigned while in Paradox.

The UNPASSWORD Command

You can use the UNPASSWORD command to remove any passwords that were assigned during script execution. In this way, you can ensure the safety of your tables once a user is finished running the script. UNPASSWORD works very much like the *Menu {Tools} {Protect} {ClearPassword}* keystroke sequence.

The UNPASSWORD command has the form

> UNPASSWORD *password 1, password 2, ..., password n*

where the *password 1, password 2, ..., password n* list represents the passwords you want to release. Typically, these will be passwords provided during script execution to allow the user access to the tables. After PAL executes the UNPASSWORD command, any tables associated with the removed passwords will once again be locked.

The MOVETO Command

PAL's MOVETO command allows you to navigate the cursor within the Paradox workspace. The effect of the simplest form of this command

> MOVETO RECORD *number*

is equivalent to that of the [Menu] Image Zoom Record command—it moves the cursor vertically to the record you specify within the current table. The single argument must be a number (not a string) that specifies the number of the destination record. For example, the command *MOVETO RECORD 15* moves the cursor to the 15th record of the current table, while remaining within the current field. The recorded keystroke sequence *Menu {Image} {Zoom} {Record} {15}* would do the same thing.

Another form of the MOVETO command allows you to move to a specified field within the current record. This form of the command

> MOVETO FIELD *fieldname*

is equivalent to the *Menu {Image} {Zoom} {Field}* keystroke sequence. The *fieldname* argument must be a string expression.

There are three other variations of the MOVETO command: Two forms can move the cursor from one image to another; the third form moves the cursor to a different image and field all in one step. We will describe these other variations later in this chapter.

The LOCK Command

In a network environment, the LOCK command restricts the level of access that other users have to tables you are using. The form of the command is

LOCK *table 1 locktype 1, table 2 locktype 2, ..., table n locktype n*

where *table 1* is a string expression for the first table to be locked; *table 2,* for the second; and so on. *Locktype 1* is a keyword that specifies the type of lock to place on *table 1*. *Locktype 2* is the keyword lock type that applies to *table 2*, and so on. There are four *locktype* keywords: FL (Full Lock), WL (Write Lock), PWL (Prevent Write Lock), and PFL (Prevent Full Lock).

For example, if you are working on a network, you could use the command *LOCK "Emplyee" WL, "Projects" PFL* to place a write lock on the EMPLYEE table and to prevent full locks on the PROJECTS table. Thereafter, other users could view but not edit the EMPLYEE table, and no other user could place a full lock on the PROJECTS table. The equivalent keystroke sequence for this command would be *Menu {Tools} {Net} {Lock} {WriteLock} {Emplyee} {Set} Menu {Tools} {Net} {PreventLock) {FullLock} {Projects} {Set}*.

The UNLOCK Command

The UNLOCK command allows you to unlock one or more tables. It reverses the effect of the LOCK command. The UNLOCK command has the form

UNLOCK *table 1 locktype 1, table 2 locktype 2, ..., table n locktype n*

where each *table* argument represents a table to be unlocked and the corresponding *locktype* argument represents the type of lock to be removed from the table.

Instead of unlocking tables individually, you can use the keyword *ALL* to remove all existing locks on tables currently in use. For example, *UNLOCK ALL* would remove the two locks set in the LOCK command example above. *UNLOCK ALL* would be equivalent to the keystroke sequence *Menu {Tools} {Net} {Lock} {WriteLock} {Emplyee) {Clear} Menu {Tools} {Net} {PreventLock} {FullLock} {Projects} {Clear}*.

The SETPRIVDIR Command

The SETPRIVDIR command is equivalent to the [Menu] Tools Net SetPrivate command. It can be used in a network environment to specify the private directory used to store temporary and private tables in the user's directory. The form of this command is

SETPRIVDIR *directory*

where *directory* represents the user's private directory. For example, *SETPRIVDIR* *"c:\\paradox3\\work"* will cause private and temporary tables to be stored in the subdirectory WORK. As with the SETDIR command, you must use double backslashes in the string expression of the directory path.

The *SETUSERNAME* Command

SETUSERNAME is PAL's command equivalent of the network command [Menu] Tools Net UserName. Its form is

SETUSERNAME *name*

The string expression *name* is the user name you want to use on the network.

Other Commands

PAL's other five types of commands—input/output, system control, program control, workspace-manipulating, and variable-manipulating—let you do more than just provide an alternative way to select items from the Paradox menus. Instead, they add real programming features, such as the use of variables, conditional testing, looping, user input, and so forth, to your scripts. We'll discuss most of these commands in context in Chapter 16.

For now, we'll explore the use of variables in a PAL script. In particular, we'll show you how the use of variables further distinguishes PAL's menu-equivalent commands from the keystroke sequences they represent.

Variables

Variables are a fundamental component of PAL programs. A variable is a storage place for a number, text, or date value. Once you store a value in a variable, you can use that variable, instead of the literal value, as the argument of a PAL command. For example, if you store the string *"Emplyee"* into a variable named x, you could use either the command *VIEW "Emplyee"* or the command *VIEW x* to bring the EMPLYEE table to the workspace. The use of variables, which are essential components of conditional testing, and the acceptance of user input contribute significantly to the power of a PAL program.

Assigning a Value to a Variable

PAL's = (equal sign) command lets you assign a value to a variable. The syntax of this command is

variable=expression

where *variable* is the name of the variable into which PAL will store the value of the *expression* that follows the equal sign.

A variable name can be up to 132 characters long and can contain letters, numbers, and the characters ., $, !, and _ . The name must begin with a letter. For example, *a, xyz, prodname*, and *a$B!c_123* are valid variable names, but *1abc* is not. Additionally, the name of a variable cannot contain spaces and should not be the same as any of PAL's keywords or function names. PAL makes no distinction between uppercase and lowercase letters in a variable name. For example, *ABC, Abc*, and *aBC* all refer to the same variable.

The expression to the right of the = command may take any of several forms. The simplest uses of the = command are ones in which the expression is a literal value—either a value, a string, or a date. For example, the command *x=123* stores the value 123 into the variable named *x*. The command *y="Emplyee"* stores the string *"Emplyee"* into the variable named *y*, and the command *z=11/24/58* stores the date 11/24/58 into the variable named *z*.

Although literal values are the simplest form of expression for an = command, they are not the ones you will use most often. The principal use for variables is to store values that may change each time you execute a script, such as the result of a formula or function, an entry from a table, or information supplied by the user during the execution of a program. We'll show you how to access and store information from these sources at the end of this chapter and in Chapter 16.

The Lifespan of Variables

The first time you use the = command to assign a value to a variable, PAL actually does two things: it "defines" the variable, then it stores a value in that variable. Defining a variable means bringing it into existence, a process that involves allocating a small amount of memory to that variable. Once PAL has defined a variable, that variable remains in existence until you do one of two things: end the current Paradox session or "undefine" the variable with the RELEASE VARS command.

The RELEASE VARS Command

RELEASE VARS is a PAL command that allows you to undefine variables selectively. The form of the RELEASE VARS command is

    RELEASE VARS *variable name(s)*

where the argument(s) is the name(s) of the variable(s) that you want to release. For example, the command *RELEASE VARS x* would release the variable named *x*, while the command *RELEASE VARS x,y,z* would release the variables *x, y*, and *z*.

You can also use the special argument ALL with the RELEASE VARS command, like this:

    RELEASE VARS ALL

to undefine every variable that has been defined since the beginning of the current Paradox session. Releasing a variable doesn't just erase the value that is stored in that variable—it eliminates the variable itself, freeing the memory that was allocated to it.

If you do not release a variable during the course of a program, it will remain in existence until you end the current Paradox session. Exiting to DOS temporarily by means of the ToDOS option or the DOS or RUN command has no effect on variables.

The SAVEVARS Command

PAL offers a special command, SAVEVARS, that allows you to save the current values of any or all defined variables. The form of this command is

> SAVEVARS *variable name(s)*.

Like the argument(s) of the RELEASE VARS command, the argument(s) of this command may be a single variable name, a list of names separated by commas, or the keyword ALL.

When PAL executes this command, it creates a script named Savevars. This script contains one = command for each specified variable, linking it to its current value. For example, suppose you have defined three variables during the current Paradox session: *x*, which contains the number 123; *y*, which contains the string *"testing"*; and *z*, which contains the date 11/24/58. If PAL reads the command *SAVEVARS x,y,z* or the command *SAVEVARS ALL* in a script, it will create this SAVEVARS script:

> ; Variables Saved Using Savevars Command
>
> x=123
> y="testing"
> z=11/24/58.

When PAL executes the command *SAVEVARS x*, it will store the command *x=123* into a script named Savevars. Each time PAL executes a SAVEVARS command, it replaces the former contents of the Savevars script. It does not append the new statement to the end of the existing script.

Once you've used the SAVEVARS command to save the current value of each currently defined variable into a script, you can recover those values later. You can do this within the same Paradox session or in a subsequent session simply by playing the Savevars script. For example, you could issue the [Menu] Scripts Play command and choose Savevars, or you could include the command *PLAY "Savevars"* in a script.

When you play a Savevars script, PAL will read each = command in sequence. If a variable named in the Savevars script has not yet been defined in the current Paradox session, the =

command defines it and assigns a value. If the variable already exists, the = command assigns it a new value. Consequently, you may want to edit the Savevars script before running it to remove the = command for any variables whose values you do not want to overwrite.

Assigning a New Value to a Variable

Although a variable usually will remain in existence during an entire Paradox session, it does not have to store the same value for that entire length of time. Whenever you use the name of an existing variable to the left of an = command, PAL assigns a new value to that variable, replacing the old value. For example, suppose that you had stored the string *Emplyee* in the variable *abc* early in a script. While *abc* contains the string *Emplyee*, the command *VIEW abc* would bring the table named EMPLYEE to the workspace. If PAL later executed the command *abc="Jobs"*, however, it would replace the string *Emplyee* stored in *abc* with the string *Jobs*. The next time PAL executed the command *VIEW abc*, it would display the JOBS table instead of the EMPLYEE table.

Variable Types

PAL variables can store four types of information: numbers, strings, dates, and logical values. The first three types correspond to the information that you can store in fields of a table. The fourth type, logical values (True or False), can be stored only in a variable.

The kind of information that a variable holds controls where it can be used. If a variable holds a string, it can be used in situations where PAL expects a string argument. If a variable holds a date, it can be used whenever PAL expects a date, and so forth. In this sense, PAL determines the type of the variable when it stores a value in that variable.

However, a variable's type is not permanent. Whenever you assign a new value to a variable, PAL changes that variable's type so that it is compatible with the new data. For example, suppose you store the string *Emplyee* in the variable named x when you first define that variable. While x contains this string, it is an alphanumeric variable and can be used only in situations where a string is appropriate. If PAL executes the command $x=123$ later in the script, however, it will assign the number 123 to x and change the type of the variable x from alphanumeric to numeric. While x contains this value, it can be used only when PAL expects a numeric value.

Referring to Field Values in a Table

Another fundamental PAL technique is the ability to refer to field entries in Paradox tables from within scripts. To refer to a field entry, you must use one of the following special forms:

```
[]
[fieldname]
[tablename->]
[tablename->fieldname]
```

Each of these four forms lets you refer to a field in a slightly different way. The simplest form, [], refers to the current field of the current record in the current table—in other words, the field in which the cursor is positioned when PAL processes the command. The next form, [*fieldname*], refers to the named field of the current record in the current table. When you use this form, the position of the cursor determines the table and record, but not the field from which to pull the entry. The third form, [*tablename->*], refers to the field of the record that was current the last time you viewed or edited the specified table. The hyphen (-) and greater than sign (>) must follow the name of that table. The fourth form, [*tablename->fieldname*], refers to the specified field of the record the cursor was in when you last viewed or edited the specified table. In all cases, an image of the referenced table must be on the Paradox workspace.

Typically, you will use table references in four important ways in your PAL scripts: to store an entry in a variable, to make an entry into a table, as the argument of certain PAL commands, and as the argument of certain PAL functions. In this section, we will show you how to use table references in the first three ways. We will explain how to use references as the arguments of functions in Chapter 15.

Storing a Field Value in a Variable

Storing a field value in a variable is as simple as using one of these reference forms as the argument of an = command. For example, suppose you want to store the contents of the Last Name field of the second record of the EMPLYEE table (shown in Figure 14-1 on the following page) into the variable x. To do this, you could use the script

```
VIEW "Emplyee"
Right Right Down
x=[]
```

The VIEW command brings the EMPLYEE table to the workspace, if it is not there already, and positions the cursor in the first field of the first record. The next three commands, *Right*, *Right*, and *Down*, move the cursor to the Last Name field of the second record. The final command, *x=[]*, stores the entry of the field on which the cursor is positioned into the variable x. In this case, PAL stores the string *Cameron* in the variable x.

You can assign this entry to x with any of the other three reference forms, as well. For example, you could use the script

```
VIEW "Emplyee"
Down
x=[Last Name]
```

This script brings the EMPLYEE table to the workspace, moves to the first field of the second record, and then uses the command *x=[Last Name]* to pull the value from the Last Name field of that record.

Figure 14-1 The EMPLYEE Table

```
Viewing Employee table: Record 1 of 16                    Main

EMPLYEE═╤═Emp Number════╤═Last Name═══╤═First Name══╤═SS Number═══════╤═════════Addre
    1   │      1        │  Jones      │  David      │  414-74-3421    │  4000 St. Ja
    2   │      2        │  Cameron    │  Herb       │  321-65-8765    │  2321 Elm St
    3   │      3        │  Jones      │  Stewart    │  401-32-8721    │  4389 Oakbri
    4   │      4        │  Roberts    │  Darlene    │  417-43-7777    │  451 Lone Pi
    5   │      5        │  Jones      │  Jean       │  413-07-9123    │  4000 St. Ja
    6   │      6        │  Williams   │  Brenda     │  401-55-1567    │  100 Owl Cre
    7   │      7        │  Myers      │  Julie      │  314-30-9452    │  4512 Parksi
    8   │      8        │  Link       │  Julie      │  345-75-1525    │  3215 Palm C
    9   │      9        │  Jackson    │  Mary       │  424-13-7621    │  7021 Clark
   10   │     10        │  Jakes, Jr. │  Sal        │  321-65-9151    │  3451 Michig
   11   │     11        │  Preston    │  Molly      │  451-00-3426    │  321 Indian
   12   │     12        │  Masters    │  Ron        │  317-65-4529    │  423 W. 72nd
   13   │     13        │  Robertson  │  Kevin      │  415-24-6710    │  431 Bardsto
   14   │     14        │  Garrison   │  Robert     │  312-98-1479    │  55 Wheeler
   15   │     15        │  Gunn       │  Barbara    │  321-97-8632    │  541 Kentuck
   16   │     16        │  Emerson    │  Cheryl     │  404-14-1422    │  8100 River
```

If the EMPLYEE table is anywhere on the workspace, and the cursor was in the second record when you last viewed or edited that table, the command *x=[Employee->Last Name]* also would assign the string *Cameron* to *x*. If the cursor was in the Last Name field of the second record when you last viewed EMPLYEE, and EMPLYEE was still on the workspace, the command *x=[Emplyee->]* would do the same thing.

Making an Entry into a Table

In addition to using field references to extract field values from a table, you can use them to make entries into a table. To do this, you must use a modified form of the = command. Instead of placing the table reference to the right of the = command, as you did to extract a field value, you must place the reference to the left of the command. The expression to the right of the = command tells PAL what to place in the referenced cell. To make an entry into a table in this or any other way, of course, the table must be in the Edit mode.

For example, suppose you want to change the entry in the Last Name field of the second record in EMPLYEE from *Cameron* to *Jones*. To do this, you could use the script:

```
EDIT "Emplyee"
Home CtrlHome
Right Right Down
[]="Jones"
```

This script brings the EMPLYEE table to the workspace in the Edit mode. If the table is on the workspace and the cursor is not in the upper-left corner of the table, the *Home CtrlHome* commands are needed to move it there. The *Right Right Down* commands then move the cursor to the Last Name field of the second record. Finally, the statement *[]="Jones"* enters the string *Jones* into that cell, replacing the former entry, *Cameron*. The script

```
EDIT "Emplyee"
Home CtrlHome
Down
[Last Name]="Jones"
```

uses another reference form to achieve the same effect.

Now, suppose that you want to copy the entry from the Last Name field of the second record in the EMPLYEE table to the Last Name field of the fourth record in that table. To do this, you could use the script

```
EDIT "Emplyee"
Home CtrlHome
Down
x=[Last Name]
Down Down
[Last Name]=x
```

The first three statements bring the EMPLYEE table to the workspace in the Edit mode and move the cursor to the second record. The fourth statement in this script, *x=[Last Name]*, stores that record's Last Name entry (the string *Cameron*) into the variable *x*. The two *Down* statements move the cursor to the fourth record in the table. Finally, the command *[Last Name]=x* enters the contents of *x* (the string *Cameron*) into the Last Name field of that record. You cannot perform this task without the use of a variable.

Using References as Arguments

Some PAL commands expect field references as their arguments. One form of the MOVETO command, whose basic form we discussed earlier in this chapter, is a good example. When PAL encounters a MOVETO command in the form

```
MOVETO [field reference]
```

it will move the cursor to the specified field of the current table.

For example, suppose you want to move the cursor to the Address field of the fifth record in the EMPLYEE table. To do this, you could use the script

```
VIEW "Emplyee"
MOVETO RECORD 5
MOVETO [Address]
```

The VIEW command brings the EMPLYEE table to the workspace and positions the cursor in the leftmost field of the first record. The *MOVETO RECORD 5* command moves the cursor down to the first field of the fifth record. Finally, the *MOVETO [Address]* command instructs PAL to move the cursor to the Address field within that record.

You also can use other reference forms as the argument of a MOVETO command. For example, the command *MOVETO [Jobs->]* moves the cursor to the last position it occupied in the JOBS table, and the command *MOVETO [Jobs->Description]* moves the cursor to the Description field of the record that the cursor was in when you last viewed or edited the JOBS table. For either of these commands to work, of course, an image of the referenced table (JOBS) must be in the workspace.

Formulas

PAL offers four mathematical operators: +, -, *, and /. These operators allow you to manipulate numbers, strings, and dates, whether presented in literal form or stored in a variable or a field. Any combination of values linked with operators is called a formula. In the following section, we'll explain the rules for using formulas and present some examples of their use.

Operating on Numbers

PAL's operators are most commonly used for adding, subtracting, multiplying, and dividing numbers. The simplest case of this usage is to manipulate literal numbers and store the result in a variable. When PAL reads the command $x=1+2$, for example, it adds 1 and 2 and stores the result (3) into the variable x. Likewise, the commands $x=2-1$, $x=1*2$, and $x=1/2$ subtract 1 from 2, multiply 1 by 2, and divide 1 by 2, respectively, and store the results in x.

The Precedence of Operators

As you might expect, you can use several operators in the same formula. When you do, however, PAL doesn't necessarily evaluate the formula from left to right. For example, PAL will not return the value 0 when it evaluates the formula *1+2-3*4/5*. Instead, it will perform the multiplication first, the division next, the addition third, and the subtraction last. As a result, PAL returns the value .6 when it evaluates this formula. If a formula contains multiple consecutive occurrences of the same operator, PAL evaluates them in the order in which they appear in the formula (left to right).

You can use parentheses to override PAL's default order of precedence. For example, when PAL reads the formula *1+(2-3)*4/5*, it subtracts 3 from 2 before it evaluates any other operation, and, as a result, returns the value .2. When a formula contains more than one set of unnested parentheses, it processes the operation(s) within the leftmost set of parentheses first. For example, when PAL evaluates the formula *(1-2)*(3+4)*, it performs the subtraction first, the addition next, and the multiplication last, returning the result -7. If the formula contains nested parentheses, PAL evaluates the operations in the innermost set of parentheses first, then works its way out. For example, the formula *(1-(2*3))/4*, returns the value -1.25 because PAL performs the multiplication first, the subtraction next, and the division last.

Operating on Dates

In addition to operating on numbers, PAL can operate on dates. There are only a few date operators permitted. You may add a number to a date, or a date to number, both of which result in a date. You can subtract a number from a date, which results in a date; or you can subtract a date from a date, which results in a number. Multiplication and division are not allowed in date formulas.

When you use the + operator to add a number to a date, the result is a future date. For example, the formula *11/24/58+100*, returns the date 3/04/59. When you use the - operator to subtract a number from a date, the result is an earlier date. For example, the formula *11/24/58-100*, returns the date 8/16/58. When you use the - operator to subtract one date from another, the result is the number of days that have elapsed between the two dates. When PAL evaluates the formula *11/24/58-8/16/58*, for instance, it returns the value 100.

Operating on Strings

PAL also can operate on strings, although in a much more limited way than it can operate on either numbers or dates. In fact, the only operation you can perform on strings is addition. The process of adding two strings is called concatenation. For example, when PAL evaluates the command *y="John"+" "+"Smith"*, it stores the string *John Smith* in the variable *y*. You cannot add a number or date to a string or act upon any string with the -, *, or / operators.

Variables and Field References in Formulas

In the examples of formulas we've presented so far, we've used literal numbers, dates, and strings. In your actual work with PAL, however, literal values will not be the most common component of your formulas. In most cases, you'll use variables and field entries in your formulas much more often than you'll use literal values.

You can use a variable or field reference in a formula anywhere you would use the type of information they store. Wherever you would use a number, for example, you could use a variable that stores a number or a reference to a numeric field. Wherever you would use a literal string, you could use a variable that contains a string or a reference to an alphanumeric field. Whenever you would use a date in a formula, you could use a variable that stores a date or a reference to a date field instead.

There are a variety of ways to combine literal values, variables, and field references in a formula. For example, the command *z=65-[Age]*, will store in the variable *z* the result of subtracting the contents of the Age field of the current record from 65. The command *[Full Name]=[First Name]+" "+[Last Name]* concatenates the entries from a record's First Name and Last Name fields, plus a separating space, and places the result into that record's Full Name field.

Modifying the contents of a variable is another common use for a formula. You often will use a command like *x=x+1* to increment the counter in a looping routine, for instance. Each time PAL executes this command, it will increase the value of *x* by 1. As you read through the following three chapters, you will see numerous examples of the use of formulas in PAL programs.

Conditional Testing

Conditional testing is another fundamental programming technique that is an essential component of PAL programming. In a conditional test, a value is compared to another value with any of six special operators: =, >, <, >=, <=, and <>. Conditional tests return a logical value: True or False. You typically will use conditional tests within the context of PAL commands like IF, WHILE, and SWITCH.

Simple Conditional Tests

The values on either side of these conditional operators may be literal values, variables, field references, or functions. For example, the conditional test *x<5* will be true if *x* is storing a number less than 5. If *x* stores a number greater than or equal to 5, the conditional test will be false.

Conditional tests can work on strings as well as numbers. For example, the test *x="Emplyee"* will be true whenever *x* stores the string *Emplyee*, and the test *x<>"Emplyee"* will be true when *x* stores anything but that string. You typically will use only these two operators to compare strings. If you use any of the other operators (like > and <), PAL will assign values to the strings according to alphabetical order and will compare them on the basis of those values. *A* is less than *B*, for example, and *B* is less than *C*. Lowercase letters have a higher value than uppercase letters. For instance, *a*, *b*, and *c* are all greater than *X*, *Y*, and *Z*. The value order of alphabetic characters is equivalent to the order in which Paradox arranges them in an ascending sort.

You also can use conditional operators to compare dates. For example, the conditional test *[DOB]>11/24/58* will be true if the DOB field entry of the current record contains a date more recent than November 24, 1958. You can use any conditional operator to compare two dates.

Logical Operators

In addition to these six conditional operators, PAL offers three logical operators that can act upon the outcome of conditional tests: AND, OR, and NOT. The AND and OR operators combine two conditional tests into a single test. When two conditional tests are combined with an AND operator, both tests must be true for the combined test to be true. For example, the combination *x>5 AND y<3* will be true only if the value stored in *x* is greater than 5 and the value stored in *y* is less than 3. If either or both of these conditional tests are false, the combined test will be false.

When two conditional tests are joined with the OR operator, the combined test will be true if either of the component tests is true, or if both are true. For example, the test *x>5 OR y<3* will be true in three cases: when the value stored in *x* is greater than 5, when the value stored in y is less than 3, or when both *x* is greater than 5 and *y* is less than 3. An OR combination will be false only when both components are false.

PAL's NOT operator negates a conditional test, thus reversing its result. Unlike the AND and OR operators, NOT works on a single conditional test instead of joining a pair of tests. For example, the conditional test *NOT x>5* is true when the value stored in *x* is 5 or less. This simple test is equivalent to the test *x<=5*. As another example, the test *NOT (x>5 AND y<3)* will be true when *x* is less than or equal to 5, when *y* is greater than or equal to 3, or both. The test is equivalent to the test *x<=5 OR y>=3*. The parentheses are necessary in this case to override PAL's default precedence for logical operators: NOT is evaluated first, then AND, and finally OR.

Conclusion

In this chapter, we have introduced several of the building blocks essential to the development of advanced PAL scripts. First, we introduced PAL commands by demonstrating the use of PAL's 27 menu-equivalent commands. Next, we discussed the concept of variables, showing you how to use them to store values and strings and as the arguments of PAL commands. Then, we explained how to make references to the field values in a Paradox table from within a script. Finally, we showed you how to combine literals, variables, and table references into formulas and how to develop conditional tests. In the next chapter, we'll present PAL's special functions—the last fundamental component of PAL programming.

Chapter 15

PAL Functions

In Chapter 14, you learned about the first two important elements of PAL: commands and variables. In this chapter, we'll introduce you to the third important element of PAL: functions.

Functions are special built-in tools that perform calculations and return information about PAL and Paradox. Some functions allow you to perform calculations that would be difficult or impossible to perform using conventional formulas. For example, the SQRT() function calculates the square root of a number, and the CNPV() function computes the net present value of the column entries of a table. Other functions allow you to obtain information about PAL and Paradox. For example, the DRIVESPACE() function returns the number of bytes of free disk space, and the TABLE() function returns the name of the table in which the cursor is positioned.

Although there are a number of ways to categorize PAL's functions (the *PAL User's Guide* simply lists them alphabetically), we prefer to divide them into ten groups, based on their purposes: mathematical functions, geometric functions, statistical functions, financial functions, date/time functions, string functions, informational functions, logical functions, multi-user functions, and error-trapping functions. Before we examine the functions in each group, however, let's take a moment to master a few concepts that are basic to working with PAL functions.

Function Basics

Most functions have two elements: the function name and the argument. Function names are descriptive terms, like CSUM, CNPV, and IMAGENO, that identify the task that the function performs. The argument tells PAL on what you want the function to operate. For example, in the function

ABS(-123)

ABS is the function name and *-123* is the argument. This function tells PAL to compute the absolute value of the number -123, and thus returns the value 123.

Arguments

The arguments of PAL functions must be PAL expressions. As we discussed in Chapter 14, an expression can be a literal value, a variable, a field value, a formula, or a function. Every expression is one of four types: numeric, string, date, or logical. A numeric expression is an expression that has a numeric value. A string expression is one that has a string value. A date expression is one that has a date value. A logical expression has a logical value.

Different functions require different types of arguments. For example, the ABS() function, which computes the absolute value of a number, must have a numeric expression as its argument. On the other hand, the MONTH() function, which returns the month of a date as a number, requires a date expression as its argument. No matter what kind of expression (literals, variables, field references, and so forth) you use as the argument of a function, it must be of the correct type.

Some functions require more than one argument. For example, the function FV(*amount,rate,term*), which computes the future value of a stream of cash flows at a particular rate, requires three arguments: *amount*, *rate*, and *term*. All of these arguments must be numeric expressions.

Some functions, such as PI() and RECNO(), don't take any arguments. However, you still must include a set of parentheses after the function name whenever you use those functions.

Using Functions

Like formulas, all PAL functions return one of four types of values: numbers, strings, dates, or logical values. You can use a function in any situation where you would use a literal value, a variable, a reference, or a formula that contains or returns the same type of information.

Frequently, you'll store the results of functions in variables. For example, the command

    x=ABS(-100)

stores the value 100 in the variable *x*. Once this command has stored the value 100 in *x*, additional commands in the script can use that variable as the basis for other computations.

In some cases, you will use a function in a conditional test. For example, the script

    IF x<ABS(y) THEN
       x=x+1
    ENDIF

uses an ABS() function within the conditional test of an IF command. Similarly, the script shown in Figure 15-1 uses an EOT() function as the conditional test of a WHILE command, and an ISBLANK() function as the conditional test of an IF command.

Figure 15-1 Functions in a Script

```
Changing script C:\paradox3\functns                        Script

....+...10....+...20....+...30....+...40....+...50....+...60....+...70....+...80
WHILE NOT EOT()
 IF ISBLANK([]) THEN
  []=0
 ENDIF
 SKIP
ENDWHILE
```

You can also store the result of a function directly in a table. For example, the function LN() computes the natural logarithm of a number. The command

    [NatLog]=LN([Numfield])

places the natural logarithm of the value in the Numfield field of the current record into the NatLog field of that record.

Mathematical Functions

Although PAL's mathematical functions probably are not its most useful group of functions, they're the simplest in form and, therefore, easiest to understand. These functions act upon numeric expressions and return numeric values. There are 11 functions in this group: ABS(), BLANKNUM(), EXP(), INT(), LN(), LOG(), MOD(), POW(), RAND(), ROUND(), and SQRT(). Table 15-1 on the following page shows the forms of these functions.

For the most part, the form and purpose of each function should be clear from the table. Each function performs a common mathematical task and returns a numeric value. Although we have used literal values in the arguments in the examples, you will more often use variables and field references in your scripts.

The only one of these functions that is tricky at all is BLANKNUM(). The BLANKNUM() function returns a blank numeric value. In Paradox, a blank numeric value is not the same as a value of 0. If you enter the value 0 into a numeric field, that field will contain the value 0. If you leave a record's numeric field empty, however, that field will contain a blank numeric value. (You can have Paradox treat blank numeric values like 0 in mathematical functions by setting the BLANK = ZERO option in the CCP.) The principal use of the BLANKNUM() function is for restoring a record's numeric field to its original blank state. If the cursor is positioned over a value in a numeric field, for example, the command *[]=BLANKNUM()* will replace it with a blank numeric value.

Table 15-1 Mathematical Functions

Function	Returns	Example	Returns
ABS(*value*)	Absolute value of *value*	ABS(-100)	100
		ABS(100)	100
BLANKNUM()	Blank numeric value (not 0)		
EXP(*value*)	Value *e* (2.71828) raised to the *value* power	EXP(4.605)	100
INT(*value*)	Integer portion of *value*	INT(2.765)	2
		INT(123.999)	123
		INT(-123.99)	-123
LN(*value*)	Natural logarithm of *value*	LN(100)	4.605
LOG(*value*)	Base 10 logarithm of *value*	LOG(1000)	3
MOD(*dividend,divisor*)	Remainder of *dividend* divided by *divisor*	MOD(7,2)	1
POW(*value,power*)	*Value* raised to *power*	POW(10,2)	100
RAND()	Random number between 0 and 1		
ROUND(*value,decimals*)	*Value* rounded to *decimal* places	ROUND(2.765,1)	2.8
		ROUND(100.99,0)	101
		ROUND(123.9,-1)	120
SQRT(*value*)	Square root of *value*	SQRT(100)	10

Geometric Functions

Geometric functions compute trigonometric values like the sine, cosine, and tangent of an angle. These functions are like mathematical functions in that they return numeric values and act upon numeric expressions. There are eight functions in this group: ACOS(), ASIN(), ATAN(), ATAN2(), COS(), PI(), SIN(), and TAN(). Table 15-2 shows their forms.

Table 15-2 Geometric Functions

Function	Returns	Example	Returns
ACOS(*cosine*)	Angle with cosine *cosine*	ACOS(.5)	1.047197551196
ASIN(*sine*)	Angle with sine *sine*	ASIN(.5)	.5235987755982
ATAN(*tangent*)	Angle with tangent *tangent*	ATAN(1)	.7853981633974
ATAN2(*a,b*)	Angle in a right triangle with sides *a* and *b*	ATAN2(1,1)	.7853981633974
COS(*angle*)	Cosine of *angle*	COS(2)	-.416138735681
PI()	π	PI()	3.141592653589
SIN(*angle*)	Sine of *angle*	SIN(2)	.9093048415109
TAN(*angle*)	Tangent of *angle*	TAN(3)	-.142546543074

The argument of the SIN(), COS(), and TAN() functions must be a numeric expression that specifies the measure of an angle in radians, not degrees. The result of these functions is the sine, cosine, or tangent of the specified angle.

PAL's ASIN(), ACOS(), ATAN(), and ATAN2() functions are called inverse geometric functions. The argument of the ASIN(), ACOS(), and ATAN() functions should be the sine, cosine, and tangent, respectively, of the angle you want to measure. These functions return the measure of the angle whose sine, cosine, or tangent equals the specified value. The ATAN2() function returns the measure of an angle when given both its sine and cosine. The value of the arguments for ACOS() and ASIN() in these functions must be greater than or equal to -1 or less than or equal to 1.

Statistical Functions

PAL's statistical functions compute common statistics, such as the average (mean), sum, and standard deviation. Statistical functions can be divided into three groups: simple statistical functions, columnar statistical functions, and image statistical functions. The first group, simple statistical functions, includes only two functions: MAX() and MIN(). The second group, columnar statistical functions, includes the functions CMAX(), CMIN(), CSUM(), CAVERAGE(), CCOUNT(), CSTD(), and CVAR(). The third group, image statistical functions, includes the functions IMAGECMAX(), IMAGECMIN(), IMAGECSUM(), IMAGECCOUNT(), and IMAGECAVERAGE().

MAX() and MIN()

PAL's MAX() function compares two numeric values and returns the greater of the two. Similarly, the MIN() function compares two numeric values and returns the lesser of the two. The forms of these functions are

MAX(*value 1*,*value 2*)
MIN(*value 1*,*value 2*)

The arguments *value 1* and *value 2* are the values you want to compare. These arguments can be any numeric expression. The result of the MAX() function is the greater of *value 1* or *value 2*; the result of MIN() is the lesser of the two values.

For example, the function *MAX(10,1)* returns the number 10. The function *MIN(3,2)* returns the value 2. PAL does not care which value you use as the first argument in the MAX() and MIN() functions. In other words, the function *MAX(4,6)* is identical to the function *MAX(6,4)*. Both functions return the value 6. If both arguments of either function are equal, then PAL returns that value. For example, the function *MIN(10,10)* returns the value 10.

Columnar Statistical Functions

PAL offers a group of functions that compute statistics about the entries in a specified column of a table. The functions in this group are CMAX(), CMIN(), CSUM(), CCOUNT(), CAVERAGE(), CSTD(), and CVAR().

Table 15-3 shows the form of each function. As you can see, each function takes two arguments: *table* and *field*. The *table* and *field* arguments identify the table and field that contain the values on which you want the function to operate. These arguments must be string expressions that specify the name of the table and field for which the statistic should be calculated.

Table 15-3 Columnar Statistical Functions

Function	Returns
CMAX(*table,field*)	Maximum value in *field* of *table*
CMIN(*table,field*)	Minimum value in *field* of *table*
CSUM(*table,field*)	Sum of values in *field* of *table*
CAVERAGE(*table,field*)	Average of values in *field* of *table*
CCOUNT(*table,field*)	Count of entries in *field* of *table*
CSTD(*table,field*)	Standard deviation of values in *field* of *table*
CVAR(*table,field*)	Variance of values in *field* of *table*

On a network, PAL attempts to lock the table named in a columnar statistical function before computing the statistical value. This ensures that the entries on which the statistics are based do not change while PAL is making the calculations. If another user or application already has a lock on the table, then PAL continuously tries to lock the table until the set retry period runs out. At the end of this period, columnar statistical functions cause a script error. For information on how to set the retry period, see Appendix A2, "Multi-user Paradox."

The CMAX() and CMIN() Functions

PAL's CMAX() and CMIN() functions return the maximum and minimum values from the specified numeric field of a table. For example, suppose you want to determine the maximum and minimum salaries of the people listed in the EMPLYEE table, which is shown in Figure 15-2. As you can see, the Salary field contains the annual salaries of the 16 people listed in this table. To determine the maximum salary in a script, you would use the function *CMAX("Emplyee","Salary")*, which would return the value 70000.00. To determine the minimum salary, you would use the function *CMIN("Emplyee","Salary")*, which would return the value 12000.00.

It is important to note that the CMAX() and CMIN() functions ignore blank entries. If the 16th entry in the Salary field were blank, for example, the function *CMIN("Emplyee","Salary")* would not return the value 0; it would return 14000.00—the lowest nonblank value.

Figure 15-2 The EMPLYEE Table

```
Viewing Emplyee table: Record 1 of 16                          Main
```

EMPLYEE	Emp Number	Last name	First Name	SS Number	Addre
1	1	Jones	Dave	414-76-3421	4000 St. Ja
2	2	Cameron	Herb	321-65-8765	2331 Elm St
3	3	Jones	David	401-32-8721	4389 Oakbri
4	4	Roberts	Darlene	417-43-7777	451 Lone Pi
5	5	Jones	Jean	414-07-9123	4000 St. Ja
6	6	Williams	Brenda	401-55-1567	100 Owl Cre
7	7	Myers	Julie	314-38-9452	4512 Parksi
8	8	Link	Julie	345-75-1525	3215 Palm C
9	9	Jackson	Mary	424-13-7621	7821 Clark
10	10	Jakes, Jr.	Sal	321-65-9151	3451 Michig
11	11	Preston	Molly	451-00-3426	321 Indian
12	12	Masters	Ron	317-65-4529	423 W. 72nd
13	13	Robertson	Kevin	415-24-6718	431 Bardsto
14	14	Garrison	Robert	312-98-1479	55 Wheeler
15	15	Gunn	Barbara	321-97-8632	541 Kentuck
16	16	Emerson	Cheryl	401-65-1820	800 River R

```
Viewing Emplyee table: Record 1 of 16                          Main
```

Date of Birth	Date of Hire	Exemptions	Salary
10/06/42	1/14/87	3	70,000.00
11/24/29	1/14/87	4	50,000.00
3/21/50	2/13/87	1	47,000.00
9/24/60	6/16/87	3	14,000.00
5/14/43	7/16/87	0	33,999.99
1/12/20	8/16/87	5	40,000.00
2/06/48	9/16/87	1	32,000.00
6/03/33	11/14/87	2	30,000.00
8/12/56	11/14/87	3	21,000.00
5/23/59	12/14/87	6	34,000.00
4/17/66	2/13/88	0	14,750.00
12/30/44	2/13/88	0	30,000.00
3/16/25	2/27/88	1	37,000.00
5/09/45	5/15/88	4	32,000.00
5/18/50	6/15/88	2	17,500.00
7/30/66	8/15/88	2	12,000.00

The CSUM() Function

PAL's CSUM() function totals the entries in the numeric field specified by its argument. For example, to determine the total annual salary of the people listed in the EMPLYEE table, you could use the function *CSUM("Emplyee","Salary")*, which would return 523249.99. Like the CMAX() and CMIN() functions, CSUM() ignores blank entries.

The CCOUNT() Function

PAL's CCOUNT() function returns the number of nonblank entries in a field. Unlike PAL's other columnar statistical functions, CCOUNT() can act upon the entries in any type of column. For example, the function *CCOUNT("Emplyee","Last Name")* returns the value 16 since there are 16 entries in the Last Name field of EMPLYEE. If one of the entries in this column were blank, however, this function would return the value 15.

The CAVERAGE() Function

The CAVERAGE() function calculates the mean of the values in the specified field of the specified table. For example, the function *CAVERAGE ("Emplyee","Salary")* returns the value 32703.12.

PAL does not include blanks in the count of a CAVERAGE() function. As a result, a CAVERAGE() function that acts upon a column containing blanks will return a higher average than it would if the blanks were filled with zeros. If the third record of the Salary field in the EMPLYEE table were blank, for example, the function *CAVERAGE ("Emplyee","Salary")* would return the value 31750.00. If that field contained the value 0, the function would return the value 29765.62.

The CSTD() and CVAR() Functions

PAL's CSTD() and CVAR() functions calculate the standard deviation and variance of the values in a column, respectively. For example, you would use the function *CSTD ("Emplyee","Salary")* to calculate the standard deviation of the entries in the Salary field of the EMPLYEE table, 14737.08, and the function *CVAR("Emplyee","Salary")* to calculate the variance of those entries, 217181394.86.

Image Statistical Functions

PAL also offers a group of functions that compute columnar statistics for the current column of the current image. The functions in this group are IMAGECMAX(), IMAGECMIN(), IMAGECSUM(), IMAGECCOUNT(), and IMAGECAVERAGE(). You can use these functions to compute statistical information about a numeric field in any table image, but they are especially useful for obtaining statistical information about the records on an embedded form that are linked to the current record on the master form. In our discussion of the image statistical functions, we'll demonstrate how they work with multitable forms.

Table 15-4 lists the image statistical functions, along with the values they return. Each of these functions corresponds to one of the regular columnar statistical functions. The image statistical functions do not take any arguments; instead, they compute statistics based on the current column of the current image. If the cursor is on an embedded form, these functions consider only those records that are linked to the current record of the master table while performing calculations. The cursor must be on the embedded form in order for these functions to operate in this manner.

Table 15-4 Image Statistical Functions

Function	Returns
IMAGECMAX()	Maximum entry in current column of linked records
IMAGECMIN()	Minimum entry in current column of linked records
IMAGECSUM()	Sum of values in current column of linked records
IMAGECCOUNT()	Count of values in current column of linked records
IMAGECAVERAGE()	Average of values in current column of linked records

Like the regular columnar statistical functions, in a network environment, the image statistical functions attempt to place a lock on the table for which they are computing statistics.

This precaution ensures that the entries on which the statistics are based do not change while PAL is making the calculations. If another user or application already has a lock on the table, then PAL continuously tries to lock the table until the currently set retry period runs out. At the end of this period, the image statistical functions cause a script error.

IMAGECMAX() and IMAGECMIN()

The PAL functions IMAGECMAX() and IMAGECMIN() return the maximum and minimum entries from the current field among the linked detail records. For example, suppose you want to determine the most expensive and least expensive product ordered by one of the people listed in the CLIENTS table shown in Figure 15-3. Though the CLIENTS table itself does not contain information about sales orders, form 1 for the CLIENTS table is a multitable form that includes an embedded form for the SALESORD table, which is shown in Figure 15-4. Figure 15-5 on the next page shows the multitable form from which you can view the two tables. The form links the two tables based on the entries in the Client Number field in CLIENTS and the Client Number field in SALESORD. As a result, the Client Number field does not appear on the embedded SALESORD form.

Figure 15-3 The CLIENTS Table

```
Viewing Clients table: Record 1 of 11                          Main

CLIENTS Client Number  Last Name   First Name   SS Number         Addre
   1      1001          Smith       John         345-43-2232   2378 Maple
   2      1002          Zoeller     Greg         401-45-0098   456 Whipps
   3      1003          Klausing    Fred         457-98-0432   2394 Hazelw
   4      1004          Fritz       Jules        345-67-3454   2212 Elk St
   5      1005          Gies        Helen        209-98-4628   4583 Mary C
   6      1006          Payne       Ann          325-23-2323   1932 Hunter
   7      1007          Wooley      Paul         367-98-1244   123 Clarks
   8      1008          Cooley      Dwayne       417-23-2938   3237 Henry
   9      1009          Harris      Ralph        403-42-5775   Rt. 2, Box
  10      1010          Crane       John         378-24-9476   1345 18th S
  11      1011          Jones       Thiora       319-21-8219   8924 Hallma
```

Figure 15-4 The SALESORD Table

```
Viewing Salesord table: Record 1 of 7                          Main

SALESORD Client Number   Date      Product Number   Product
   1      1001          2/01/88       1           Paradox 3.0
   2      1001          2/01/88       2           Paradox 386
   3      1001          2/01/88       5           Lotus 1-2-3
   4      1002          3/23/89       2           Paradox 386
   5      1004          12/13/88      5           Lotus 1-2-3
   6      1004          1/12/89       2           Paradox 386
   7      1010          2/01/89       6           Excel
```

Now, suppose that while viewing the record for client 1001, you press [Down Image] to move from the CLIENTS area of the master form to the embedded SALESORD form. After the cursor moves to the embedded form, only the three detail records linked to the current CLIENTS record (those detail records with a Client Number entry of 1) will appear on the embedded form. To determine the most expensive product ordered by client 1, you would move the cursor to the Price field, then use the IMAGECMAX() function, which would return the value 599.99. To determine the least expensive product ordered by client number 1, you would use the IMAGECMIN() function, which would return the value 399.99.

Figure 15-5 The Multitable Form

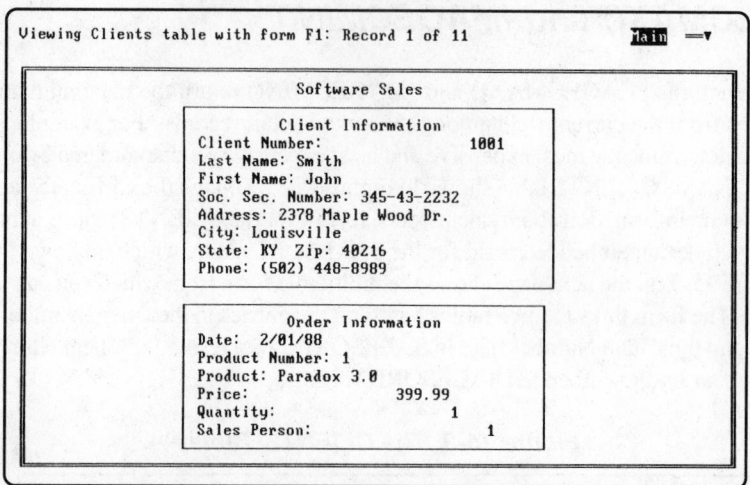

```
Viewing Clients table with form F1: Record 1 of 11                    Main  ═▼

 ┌───────────────────────────────────────────────────────────────────┐
 │                         Software Sales                              │
 │         ┌─────────────────────────────────────────────┐            │
 │         │           Client Information                 │            │
 │         │ Client Number:                    1001       │            │
 │         │ Last Name: Smith                             │            │
 │         │ First Name: John                             │            │
 │         │ Soc. Sec. Number: 345-43-2232                │            │
 │         │ Address: 2378 Maple Wood Dr.                 │            │
 │         │ City: Louisville                             │            │
 │         │ State: KY  Zip: 40216                        │            │
 │         │ Phone: (502) 448-8989                        │            │
 │         └─────────────────────────────────────────────┘            │
 │                                                                     │
 │         ┌─────────────────────────────────────────────┐            │
 │         │           Order Information                  │            │
 │         │ Date:   2/01/88                              │            │
 │         │ Product Number: 1                            │            │
 │         │ Product: Paradox 3.0                         │            │
 │         │ Price:                      399.99           │            │
 │         │ Quantity:                        1           │            │
 │         │ Sales Person:                    1           │            │
 │         └─────────────────────────────────────────────┘            │
 └───────────────────────────────────────────────────────────────────┘
```

IMAGECSUM()

PAL's IMAGECSUM() function returns the sum of the entries in the current column for the linked detail records. For example, suppose you move the cursor to the Quantity field of the SALESORD table. At this point, the IMAGECSUM() function will return the value 3, which is the sum of the Quantity entries in the linked SALESORD records. In other words, the IMAGECSUM() function will return the number of products ordered by client 1.

IMAGECCOUNT()

PAL's IMAGECCOUNT() function returns the number of nonblank entries in the current column of the linked detail records. For example, while the cursor is still in the Quantity field of the SALESORD embedded form, the IMAGECCOUNT() function will return the value 3 since all three of the linked records contain nonblank entries. If one of the entries in this column were blank, however, this function would return the value 2.

IMAGECAVERAGE()

The IMAGECAVERAGE() function calculates the mean of the entries in the current column of the linked detail records. For example, while the cursor is in the Quantity field of the SALESORD embedded form, the IMAGECAVERAGE() function will return the value 1 because adding the three entries in the Quantity field (each of which is 1), then dividing the sum by the number of entries (3), gives you an average value of 1.

Like the CAVERAGE() function, IMAGECAVERAGE() ignores blank entries in both the addition step and the division step involved in calculating an average. For example, if the Quantity field of one of the linked SALESORD records were blank, the IMAGE-CAVERAGE() function would still return a value of 1 because $(1 + 1)/2 = 1$. However, if one of the linked records contained a Quantity entry of 0, then this function would return a value of .6666666666666 because $(1 + 1 + 0)/3 = .6666666666666$.

Financial Functions

PAL offers four financial functions: PV(), FV(), PMT(), and CNPV(). These functions allow you to calculate the present and future values of an ordinary annuity, the periodic payments required to amortize a loan, and the net present value of a series of unequal cash flows, respectively.

The PV() Function

PAL's PV() function allows you to calculate the present value of a stream of periodic cash flows (also called an ordinary annuity). The form of the PV() function is

PV(*payment, rate, term*)

where *payment* is the amount of the periodic cash flow, *rate* is the rate of interest at which you want to discount the annuity, and *term* is the number of periods across which you will receive cash flows.

The result of the PV() function is the present value of the periodic payments that you will receive across the stated term, discounted at the specified rate. For instance, suppose you have an opportunity to invest in an annuity that will pay you $500 per year for the next ten years. Assuming a discount rate of 7.5 percent per year, you could use the function *PV(500,.075,10)* to compute the present value of the annuity: $3,432.04.

Importantly, PAL's PV() function assumes that the cash flows occur at the end of each period, not at the beginning. In the example above, for instance, PAL assumed that the first $500 flow occurred one year from the date of the analysis, the second flow occurred two years from the date of analysis, and so forth. This type of cash flow is termed an annuity in arrears.

The FV() Function

PAL's second financial function, FV(), calculates the future value of a stream of equal cash flows. FV() has the form

FV(*amount,rate,term*)

where *amount* is the periodic investment you plan to make, *rate* is the average rate of return you think the investment will earn, and *term* is the number of periodic investments you will make. These arguments must be numeric expressions. The result of the function is the future value of the investment.

This function is perfectly suited for analyzing a value-contribution savings plan like an IRA. Suppose you want to know how much an IRA that you start one year from today will be worth in 40 years if you contribute $2,000 to it each year, assuming a 10 percent rate of interest. You could use the function *FV(2000,.1,40)* to calculate that the IRA would be worth $855,185.10 when you retire. Like the PV() function, FV() assumes that the cash flows occur at the end of each period.

The PMT() Function

PAL's third financial function is PMT(). This function calculates the periodic payment necessary to amortize a conventional note, like an auto loan or a mortgage. The form of this function is

PMT(*principal,rate,term*)

The first argument, *principal*, is the amount borrowed. The second argument, *rate*, is the periodic rate of interest. The third argument, *term*, is the term of the loan. These arguments must be numeric expressions. The result of the function is the payment that will amortize the principal amount across the term at the stated interest rate.

For example, suppose that you want to calculate the monthly payment on a 30-year, 10.5 percent, $100,000 mortgage. You could use the function *PMT(100000,.105/12,30*12)* to calculate the monthly payment of $914.74.

The CNPV() Function

Like the PV() function, CNPV() calculates the present value of a stream of cash flows. Unlike the PV() function, however, the cash flows do not all have to be of the same amount. Also unlike the PV() function, the cash flows for the CNPV() function must be arranged in a column of a Paradox table. The form of the CNPV() function is

CNPV(*table,field,rate*)

The first two arguments, *table* and *field*, identify the table and the field of the table that contains the series of cash flows. The third argument, *rate*, specifies the rate of interest you want to use to discount the cash flows. The first two arguments must be string expressions; the third argument must be a numeric expression.

To calculate the present value of evenly spaced, unequal cash flows, you first must enter those flows into a table. Because the cash flows for this function are entries in a column of a table, you can use it to calculate a net present value—a present value calculation that takes into account cash disbursements as well as cash receipts. For example, suppose that for a cash outlay of $1,000 one year from today, you are guaranteed cash inflows of $100 two years from today, $200 three years from today, $300 four years from today, $400 five years from today, and $500 six years from today. Given a 10 percent rate of interest, what is the net present value of the investment? To perform this calculation, you would create and fill in the table shown in Figure 15-6. This table, named NPV, consists of only one field, Cashflows, and contains six records—one corresponding to each of the cash flows associated with the investment. To calculate the net present value of this cash flow stream, you could use the function *CNPV("Npv","Cashflows",.10)*, which returns the value $59.32.

Figure 15-6 The NPV Table

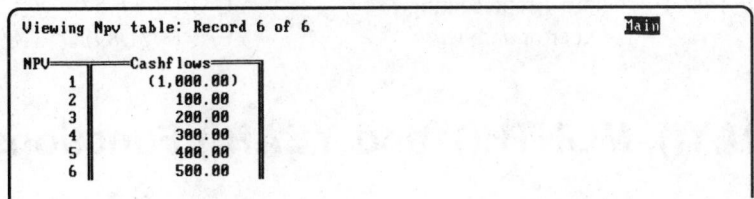

Like PAL's PV() and FV() functions, the CNPV() function assumes that the cash flows occur at the end of each period, not at the beginning.

Date/Time Functions

PAL's eight date/time functions either generate date/time values or extract information from date/time values. For example, the TODAY() function returns the date value of the current day from your computer's system clock; the TIME() function returns the current time as a string; and the YEAR() function returns the year portion of a date value.

Table 15-5 on the next page shows the form of PAL's date/time functions. Each *date value* argument must be a date expression: a literal date value (such as 11/24/58), a reference to a variable or field that contains a date value, or a formula or function that returns a date value.

The BLANKDATE() Function

The BLANKDATE() function returns a blank date value. A blank date value is the entry that Paradox stores in an empty date field. The principal use of this function is for restoring the date field of a record to its original blank state. If the cursor is positioned over a value in a date field, for example, the command *[]=BLANKDATE()* will replace that value with a blank date value.

Table 15-5 Date/Time Functions

Function	Returns	Example	Returns
BLANKDATE()	Blank *date value*	BLANKDATE()	
DAY(*date value*)	Number 1-31 representing day of *date value*	DAY(10/06/89) DAY(11/24/89)	6 24
DOW(*date value*)	String representing day of week of *date value*	DOW(10/02/89) DOW(10/03/89)	Mon Tue
MONTH(*date value*)	Number 1-12 representing month of *date value*	MONTH(10/06/89) MONTH(3/21/89)	10 3
MOY(*date value*)	String representing month of year of *date value*	MOY(10/06/89) MOY(3/21/89)	Oct Mar
TIME()	String representing current time	TIME()	
TODAY()	Today's date	TODAY()	
YEAR(*date value*)	Number representing year of *date value*	YEAR(10/06/57) YEAR(3/21/89)	57 89

The DAY(), MONTH(), and YEAR() Functions

PAL's DAY() function acts upon a date expression and returns its day portion as a value between 1 and 31. For example, the function *DAY(11/24/58)* returns the value 24. The *date value* argument can be in either MM/DD/YY or DD-Mon-YY form. For example, the function *DAY(24-Nov-58)* is identical to *DAY(11/24/58)* and also returns 24.

PAL's MONTH() function returns a value from 1 through 12 that represents the month portion of a date value. For example, the function *MONTH(11/24/58)* returns the value 11, and the function *MONTH(10/6/57)* returns the value 10.

PAL's YEAR() function returns a numeric value that identifies the year represented by a date expression. For example, the function *YEAR(11/24/58)* returns the value 1958.

The DOW() and MOY() Functions

The DOW() function returns a string that identifies a date's day of the week. The seven possible results of this function are *Mon, Tue, Wed, Thu, Fri, Sat,* and *Sun.* For example, the function *DOW(11/24/58)* returns the string *Mon,* indicating that this day was a Monday.

PAL's MOY() function returns a string that identifies the month of the year represented by a Paradox date value. The MOY() function returns one of the following 12 strings: *Jan, Feb, Mar, Apr, May, Jun, Jul, Aug, Sep, Oct, Nov,* or *Dec.* For example, the function *MOY(11/24/58)* returns the string *Nov.*

The TIME() Function

PAL's TIME() function returns the current time of day as a string in the form *hh:mm:ss*. This function draws its information from your computer's system clock, so it requires and accepts no arguments. The result returned by this function depends on the time of day at which PAL evaluates it. The TIME() function uses the 24-hour, or military, clock convention.

If PAL encounters the function TIME() in a script at exactly 10:30 a.m., the function will return the string *10:30:00*. Similarly, if PAL encounters the function TIME() in a script at 1:03:54 in the afternoon, it will return the string *13:03:54*. Note that the TIME() function does not return a time value—it returns a string that represents the current time.

The TODAY() Function

PAL's TODAY() function returns the current date in the form of a Paradox date value. Like the TIME() function, TODAY() extracts its information from your computer's system clock. For that reason, it accepts no arguments. Unlike the TIME() function, however, TODAY() returns a Paradox date value—not a string. If PAL evaluated the function TODAY() on April 15, 1989, for example, it would return the date value 4/15/89. Similarly, if PAL evaluated the equation *TODAY()-4/1/89* on April 15, 1989, it would return the value 14.

String Functions

String functions operate upon string (alphanumeric) expressions or convert other types of expressions into strings. First, we will look at a collection of simple string functions. Next, we'll look at functions that convert strings into dates or values. Finally, we'll examine PAL's complex string functions.

Simple String Functions

PAL's simple string functions allow you to do things like convert a string of uppercase letters into lowercase form or determine the length of a string. The functions in this group are ASC(), CHR(), LEN(), LOWER(), and UPPER(). Table 15-6 shows the forms of these functions.

Table 15-6 Simple String Functions

Function	Returns	Example	Returns
ASC(*character*)	ASCII code of *character*	ASC("a")	97
CHR(*ASCII code*)	Character with stated *ASCII code*	CHR(100)	d
LEN(*string*)	Length of *string*	LEN("ABC")	3
LOWER(*string*)	Converts *string* to all lowercase	LOWER("ABC")	abc
UPPER(*string*)	Converts *string* to all uppercase	UPPER("abc")	ABC

The ASC() and CHR() Functions

PAL's ASC() function returns the ASCII code that represents the character specified by its argument. The function's argument can be a single character (like *a* or *#*) or a special key representation (like *Backspace* or *F3*). Normal characters return a code from 0 to 255. For example, the function *ASC("A")* returns the value 65; the function *ASC("*")* returns the value 42; and the function *ASC("z")* returns the value 122. Special keys return negative numbers. The function *ASC("F1")* returns the value -59, for example, and the function *ASC("Up")* returns the value -72.

PAL's CHR() function is the converse of the ASC() function—it returns the character that corresponds to the ASCII code specified by its argument. The single argument of the CHR() function must be an integer value from 0 to 255. For example, the function *CHR(65)* returns the string *A*, while the function *CHR(42)* returns the string *. The argument of CHR() must be a positive number. The CHR() function will not convert negative ASCII codes to their special key representations.

The LEN() Function

The LEN() function allows PAL to determine the length of a string. The argument of this function usually will be a string expression. If you use a numeric or date expression as the argument of this function, however, PAL will convert it to a string and evaluate the function normally. The result of the function is the length of the string. For example, the function *LEN("hello")* returns the value 5, as does the function *LEN(12345)*.

The LOWER() and UPPER() Functions

PAL's LOWER() function converts the string you specify to all lowercase form. The function's argument must be a string expression. The result of the function is the same string with all letters in lowercase. For example, the function *LOWER("HELLO")* returns the string *hello*. Similarly, if the Color field of the current record contains the string *RED*, the function *LOWER([Color])* will return the string *red*.

PAL's UPPER() function converts its string argument into all uppercase form. The single argument of this function also must be a string expression. Suppose you want to convert the string entry stored in the variable *x* into all uppercase form. To do this, use the function *UPPER(x)*. If *x* contains the string *hello*, this function would return the string *HELLO*. If the argument already is in all uppercase form, the UPPER() function does not change it.

String Conversion Functions

String conversion functions either convert strings into values or dates, or convert values or dates into strings. There are three functions in this group: NUMVAL(), STRVAL(), and DATEVAL(). Table 15-7 shows the form of each function.

Table 15-7 String Conversion Functions

Function	Returns	Example	Returns
NUMVAL(*string*)	Converts *string* into a value	NUMVAL("123")	123
STRVAL(*value*)	Converts *value* into a string	STRVAL(123)	"123"
DATEVAL(*string*)	Converts *string* into a date value	DATEVAL("12/31/89")	12/31/89

The NUMVAL() Function

PAL's NUMVAL() function converts a numeric string into a value. The argument of the function must be a string expression that specifies a numeric string. For example, suppose you want to store the contents of the current record's alphanumeric Zip field as a value in the variable *x*. The command *x=NUMVAL([Zip])* would do the trick. If the current record's Zip entry is the string *12345*, this command would store the value 12345 into the variable *x*.

The STRVAL() Function

PAL's STRVAL() function is the converse of NUMVAL(). Whereas NUMVAL() converts a numeric string into a value, STRVAL() converts a value into a numeric string. The single argument of STRVAL() must be a number, a date expression, or a conditional test. For example, the function *STRVAL(123)* returns the string *123*; the function *STRVAL(11/24/58)* returns the string *11/24/58*. If the argument is a logical value, the function returns either the string *True* or *False*. For example, the function *STRVAL(10=10)* returns the string *True*.

The DATEVAL() Function

PAL's DATEVAL() function converts an alphanumeric entry into a date value. The argument of this function must be a string expression in the form MM/DD/YY, DD-Mon-YY, or DD.MM.YY. For example, if the current field contains the string *10/6/57*, the command *x=DATEVAL([])* will store the date entry 10/6/57 into the variable *x*.

Complex String Functions

The next group of string functions includes the functions SUBSTR(), FILL(), SPACES(), FORMAT(), MATCH(), and SEARCH(). These functions are more complex and powerful than those we have looked at so far.

The SUBSTR() Function

The SUBSTR() function allows PAL to extract a substring from a string, given a starting position and the number of characters to be extracted. The form of this function is

SUBSTR(*string,start position,characters*)

where *string* is the string from which you want to extract characters, *start position* specifies the position of the first character to be extracted, and *characters* specifies the number of characters to be extracted. The first argument must be a string expression. The other two arguments must be numeric expressions.

Suppose you want to extract the fifth through seventh characters from the entry in the Phone field of the current record. To do this, you could use the function *SUBSTR([Phone],5,3)*. If the current record's Phone field entry were the string *502-555-1212*, this function would extract the string *555*—the three characters beginning with the fifth character in the entry.

The FILL() Function

PAL's FILL() function allows you to generate repeating strings of a single character. The form of this function is

> FILL(*character,length*)

where *character* is the character you want to repeat and *length* is the number of times you want it to be repeated. For example, the function *FILL("=",20)* would produce the string ====================.

The SPACES() Function

PAL's SPACES() function is a special case of the FILL() function. Whereas FILL() creates a repeating string of whatever character you specify, the SPACES() function creates a repeating series of space characters. The form of this function is

> SPACES(*number*)

where the single argument specifies the number of spaces you want in the string. For example, the function *SPACES(10)* creates a series of ten spaces, as does the function *SPACES(x)*, if *x* has been assigned the value 10.

When used in conjunction with the LEN() function, SPACES() can be used to line up entries that appear on the PAL canvas (a concept we'll discuss in Chapter 16). If you want an entry to end on the 20th column of the PAL canvas, for example, you would use the command *?? SPACES(20-LEN([])),[]*. The SPACES() function in this command creates a number of spaces equal to 20 minus the length of the entry in the current field.

The FORMAT() Function

PAL's FORMAT() function allows you to convert alphanumeric, numeric, date, and logical expressions into formatted strings. For example, you can use this function to convert any value into a string of the length you specify, change the case of alphanumeric values, and convert numeric values into strings that include + and - signs, parentheses, or $ symbols. You also can use the FORMAT() function to convert date values to any of eight string forms or to convert the logical values True and False into the strings *Yes* and *No* or *On* and *Off*.

The form of the FORMAT function is

FORMAT(*format code(s),expression*)

where the *format code(s)* argument is a series of one or more format codes, and the *expression* argument is the value to be formatted. Table 15-8 on the following page lists the available format codes and the types of data to which they apply. As you can see, many of the possible format codes can be used only on numeric values; some can be used only on alphanumeric, date, or logical values, while a few can be used on all types of values.

For example, the function *FORMAT("D2",11/24/58)* converts the date value 11/24/58 into the string *November 24, 1958*. The argument *D2* in this function tells PAL to convert the second argument into a string in the Month DD, YYYY format. The function *FORMAT ("CC","testing")* would return the string *Testing*.

As another example, suppose that x=3 and y=5. While the conditional test *x=y* would return the logical value False, the function *FORMAT("LY",x=y)* would return the string *No*. In this example, the argument *LY* tells PAL to evaluate the second argument and return Yes if the argument is true and No if it is false.

Adjusting the Width

Two of the most-used format codes control the number of characters in the string result of the FORMAT() function. The code *Wx* adjusts the total number of characters in the string that the function returns. Depending on the number (x) you specify and the width of the original value, this function can either truncate the value or pad it with blank spaces. For example, the function *FORMAT("W5",123)* will return the string " *123*", which begins with two blank spaces. (The quotation marks are included in the text only to indicate the leading spaces; they are not a part of the function's result.) Similarly, the function *FORMAT("W2","hello")* returns the string *he*.

Unfortunately, this function does not do a good job of truncating numeric values. When PAL evaluates the function *FORMAT("W3",12345)*, for example, it returns the three-character string ***, rather than the strings *123* or *345*. Unless you specify a width at least one character greater than the number of characters in the original value, the FORMAT() function will return a string of asterisks.

A modification of the *Wx* code allows you to specify the number of decimal places in the string that results when the FORMAT function works on a numeric value. The form of this code is *Wx.y*, where x is the total length of the string, and y is the number of digits to include to the right of the decimal point. This special form allows you to truncate digits from, or add digits to, the right of the decimal point. For example, the function *FORMAT("W7.2",123.456)* returns the string " *123.45*". The overall width of 7 (one greater than the number of actual characters in the result) is necessary to produce a recognizable value instead of a series of asterisks. Similarly, the function *FORMAT("W7.2",123)* returns the string " *123.00*".

Table 15-8 FORMAT() Function Codes

Code	Function	Data Types
Wx	Controls display width	All
Wx.y	Controls total number of digits and number of decimal places	N
AL	Left justified	All
AR	Right justified	All
AC	Centered	All
CU	Uppercase	All
CL	Lowercase	All
CC	First letter of each word capitalized	All
E$	Print floating $ sign	N,S,$
EC	Use comma separators	N,S,$
EZ	Use leading zeros	N,S,$
EB	Substitute blanks for zeros	N,S,$
E*	Substitute *s for zeros	N,S,$
EI	Use international format	N,S,$
ES	Use scientific notation	N,S,$
S+	Use leading + or - sign	N,S,$
S-	Use - if negative	N,S,$
SP	Enclose negative numbers in ()	N,S,$
SD	Display DB for positive, CR for negative	N,S,$
SC	Display CR after negative	N,S,$
D1	MM/DD/YY	D
D2	Month DD, YYYY	D
D3	MM/DD	D
D4	MM/YY	D
D5	DD-Month	D
D6	Mon YY	D
D7	DD-Mon-YYYY	D
D8	MM/DD/YYYY	D
D9	DD.MM.YY	D
D10	DD/MM/YY	D
D11	YY-MM-DD	D
LY	Use Yes for True, No for False	L
LO	Use On for True, Off for False	L

Controlling Alignment

When you use the *Wx* code to increase the length of a numeric value, PAL usually will add extra spaces at the left of the resulting string. If you use the *Wx* code to lengthen an alphanumeric value, however, PAL adds extra spaces to the right of that string. For example, the function *FORMAT("W10","abcd")* produces the ten-character string *"abcd   "*. Because the original value was a string, PAL added the padding to the right of that string.

However, you can use three additional codes—*AL*, *AR*, and *AC*—to control placement of those extra spaces. The effect of these codes is to control the alignment of the nonspace characters in a string relative to the total width of the string. For example, the function *FORMAT("W10,AR","abcd")* produces the right-aligned string *"   abcd"*. Similarly, the function *FORMAT("W10,AL",1234)* returns the left-aligned string *"1234   "*. On the other hand, the functions *FORMAT("W10,AC","abcd")* and *FORMAT("W10,AC",1234)* return the centered strings *" abcd "* and *" 1234 "*.

Formatting Numbers

You also can use the FORMAT() function to convert numeric values into strings that include dollar signs, comma separators, + and - signs, or DB/CR notation. As you can see, the *E* codes control currency-related attributes, and the *S* codes control the use of signs. Since the attributes added by these codes increase the length of the original value, you always must use them in conjunction with a length-increasing *Wx* or *Wx.y* code. Otherwise, the function will return a string of asterisks. For example, although the function *FORMAT("W4,E$",123)* will produce the string *$123*, the function *FORMAT("E$",123)* will return the string *****.

Since the *E* codes are not mutually exclusive, you can use more than one in the same FORMAT() function. When you do this, however, you should use the letter *E* only once and follow it with one or more codes without comma separators. For example, you would use the function *FORMAT("W9.2,E$C",1234.56)* to produce the string *$1,234.56*. Since the *S* codes are mutually exclusive, however, you should use only one within each FORMAT() function. If you use more than one, the code farthest to the right will control the result.

The MATCH() Function

PAL's MATCH() function determines whether a given string matches a pattern and, if so, optionally returns the wildcard portion of that string. The first argument of this function must be the string you want to test. The second portion must be the pattern to which you want to compare the first string. The final argument or arguments, which are optional, specify the variables in which you want to store portions of the original string.

The simplest form of this function compares a string to another string—not to a pattern. If the two strings are identical in all ways (except for capitalization, which MATCH() ignores), the MATCH() function will return the logical value True. Otherwise, the function will return the value False. For example, suppose that you want to determine if the entry in the current field matches the string *abc*. To do this, you could use the function *MATCH([],"abc")*. If the current field contains the string *abc*, *Abc*, *ABc*, *ABC*, *aBc*, *abC*, *aBC*, or *AbC*, this function will return the value True. (This function differs from the equation *[]="abc"* in that it is not case-sensitive.)

However, most of your MATCH() functions will be more complex than this. Instead of comparing a string to a string, they will compare a string to a pattern. Just like the patterns you use within queries, these patterns can contain the wildcard elements .. and @. As you recall, the @ operator matches any single character, while the .. operator matches any group of adjacent characters. Suppose you want to see if the current entry begins with the letter *p* and ends with the letter *r*. To do this, you could use the function *MATCH([],"p..r")*. If the current field contained the string *Paper*, *pour*, or *paupeR*, this function would return the value True.

The most complex use of the MATCH() function involves extracting the wildcard-matching portions of the string and placing them in variables. For example, suppose you want to take the phone number entry *502-555-1212*, store the first three digits in the variable *areacode*, store the next three digits in the variable *exchange*, and store the remaining four digits in the variable *number*. To do this, you would use the function

    MATCH("502-555-1212","..-..-..",areacode,exchange,number)

When PAL evaluates this function, it matches the string *502* to the first .. operator and stores it in the first variable, *areacode*. Then, PAL matches the string *555* to the second .. operator and stores it in the second variable, *exchange*. Finally, PAL matches the string *1212* to the third .. operator and stores it in the variable *number*. In addition to assigning these strings to these variables, this function returns the value True.

The SEARCH() Function

The SEARCH() function commands PAL to look for one string within another string. The form of this function is

    SEARCH(*substring,string*)

where the *substring* argument is the string for which you want PAL to search and the *string* argument is the string in which you want it to search. If PAL finds a match for *substring* within *string*, it returns the position of the leftmost character of the match within *string*. If there is no match for the substring within the string, PAL returns the value 0. As with the MATCH() function, SEARCH() does not differentiate between uppercase and lowercase. Unlike MATCH(), however, you cannot use wildcards within the search string.

For example, suppose you want to determine if the entry in the current record's Name field contains the string *Smith*. To do this, you could use the function *SEARCH("Smith",[Name])*. If the Name field contained the entry *John Smith*, this function would return the value 6—

the starting position of the substring *Smith* within the string *John Smith*. In the same situation, the function *SEARCH("John",[Name])* would return the value 1, and the function *SEARCH("Jones",[Name])* would return the value 0.

Informational Functions

PAL's informational functions return information about the status of the workspace and the operating environment in which Paradox is running. For example, the IMAGETYPE() function returns the type of the image in which the cursor currently is positioned; the DRIVE-SPACE() function returns the number of free bytes on the disk drive you specify; and the NFIELDS() function returns the number of fields in the table you specify. We'll present these functions in alphabetical order.

The ARRAYSIZE() Function

PAL's ARRAYSIZE() function returns the number of elements that can be stored in the named array. As you will learn in Chapter 17, an array is a variable that can store more than one entry. The form of this function is

ARRAYSIZE(*arrayname*)

where *arrayname* is the name of the array you want to test. The result of the function is the number of elements in the array *arrayname*. For example, suppose you use the command *ARRAY temprec[12]* to create a 12-element array named *temprec*. In this case, the function *ARRAYSIZE(temprec)* will return the value 12.

The BANDINFO() Function

The BANDINFO() function lets PAL determine which band (section) of a report the cursor is in when you are working in the Paradox Report Generator. The function takes no arguments.

BANDINFO() returns the contents of the band indicator—the message on the second line at the upper-left corner of the Report Generator screen—as a string. If the cursor is in the report footer, for example, the function BANDINFO() will return the string *Report Footer*.

The CHECKMARKSTATUS() Function

PAL's CHECKMARKSTATUS() function lets you to determine what type of check mark, has been placed in the current field of a query form. The function takes no arguments—it returns information about the field of the query form in which the cursor is positioned.

The function returns one of five possible values. If the current field of the query form is blank, then the function returns a null string. If the current field contains a check plus, then the function returns the string *CheckPlus*. If the current field contains a check mark, then the function returns the string *Check*. The function returns the string *CheckDescending* if the field is marked with a check descending mark, or the string *Groupby* if the field is marked by a Group By mark.

The COL() Function

PAL's COL() function returns the column position of the cursor on the PAL canvas. This function takes no arguments. The possible results of this function, 0-79, correspond to the 80 columns visible on the screen. If the cursor is positioned at the left edge of the screen, the COL() function will return the value 0. If the cursor is positioned at the right edge of the screen, this function will return the value 79. The usefulness of this function will become more apparent in Chapter 16 when we show you how to create a PAL script that lets Paradox interact with the user.

The COLNO() Function

The PAL COLNO() function returns the columnar position of the cursor within the current image on the Paradox workspace. This function takes no arguments.

If the cursor is within the image of a table, this function returns the offset of the field in which the cursor is positioned, relative to the leftmost column in the table (the record number column). For example, if PAL reads the function COLNO() in a script when the cursor is anywhere in the First Name field of the EMPLYEE table, it will return the value 3. Although the record number column does not appear when you view a table through a form, PAL still counts it when it evaluates this function.

The CURSORCHAR() Function

PAL's CURSORCHAR() function returns the single character over which the cursor is positioned in the Form mode, the Report mode, or in the Script Editor. This function has no meaning in any other situation. For example, if the cursor is positioned over the first letter of the command WHILE in a script, the function CURSORCHAR() will return the string *W*.

The CURSORLINE() Function

PAL's CURSORLINE() function is similar to the CURSORCHAR() function. While the CURSORCHAR() function returns the current character in the Form mode, Report mode, or in the Script Editor, however, the CURSORLINE() function returns all the text from the present position of the cursor to the end of the line. If the cursor is positioned on the first letter of the line *VIEW "Emplyee"* in the Script Editor, for example, CURSORLINE() will return the string *VIEW "Emplyee"*. As we'll explain in Chapter 17, you can use this function in conjunction with the TYPEIN command to cut and paste text within a script, report, or form.

The DIRECTORY() Function

The DIRECTORY() function allows PAL to determine which directory Paradox currently is using. When PAL reads this function, it returns the specification of the current directory. If c:\paradox3\examples is the active directory, for example, the function DIRECTORY() will return the string *c:\paradox3 examples*.

You can use this function within an IF command to test the current directory and change it. For example, the script

```
IF DIRECTORY()<>"c:\\paradox3\\examples" THEN
  SETDIR "c:\\paradox3\\examples"
ENDIF
```

will change the current directory to c:\paradox3\examples only if that directory is not already the current one.

The DIREXISTS() Function

The DIREXISTS() function allows you to determine whether a specified directory exists. The form of this function is

DIREXISTS(*directory*)

where *directory* is the DOS path to the required directory. You can use this function to make sure a directory exists before trying to change to that directory. For example, the command *workdir = DIREXISTS(c:\\paradox3\\examples)* would store the value 0 into the variable *workdir* if the subdirectory *examples* didn't exist, or a 1 if it did. If the directory path specified is invalid, then DIREXISTS() will return the value -1.

The DRIVESPACE() Function

PAL's DRIVESPACE() function returns the amount of free space remaining on the drive you specify. The form of this function is

DRIVESPACE(*drive*)

where the argument is the single-letter designation of the drive you want to check. For example, if drive C has 2,345,678 bytes of free space, the function *DRIVESPACE("C")* will return the value 2345678. Because the case of the *drive* argument does not matter, the function *DRIVESPACE("c")* would return the same result.

The FIELD() Function

PAL's FIELD() function returns the name of the field in which the cursor currently is positioned. This function is meaningful only when the cursor is in a table, form, or query. If the cursor is positioned in the Last Name field of the EMPLYEE table, for example, the function *FIELD()* will return the string *Last Name*. If the cursor is in the leftmost field of a table (the one that contains the record numbers), the function will return the string #.

The FIELDINFO() Function

PAL's FIELDINFO() function returns the name of the field on which the cursor is currently positioned. This function works only when you are in the Form mode or Report mode. When the cursor touches a field that you have placed on a form or in a report, PAL displays the name of that field in the field indicator at the top of the screen. The FIELDINFO() function returns the contents of this field indicator area. If your screen looks like Figure 15-7, for example, FIELDINFO() will return the string *First Name*.

Figure 15-7 The FIELDINFO() Function

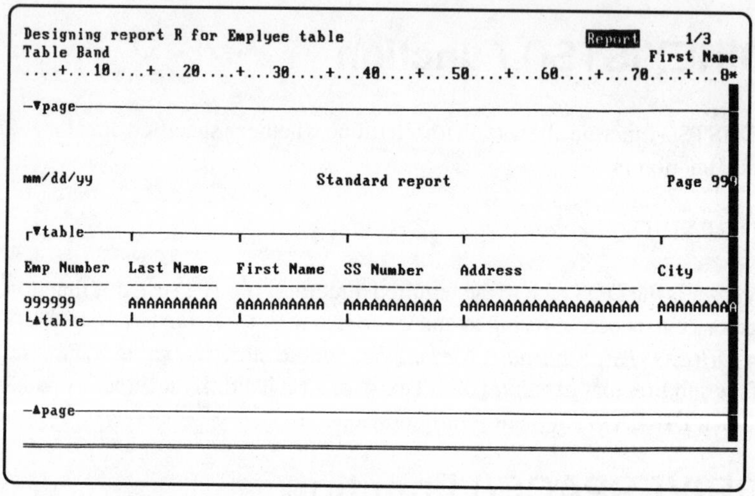

The FIELDNO() Function

PAL's FIELDNO() function returns the position of the field you specify within the structure of a designated table. Unlike the COLNO() function, which returns the position of a column in the display image of the table, the FIELDNO() function returns the absolute position of a field according to the STRUCT table for that table. The results of these two functions will be the same only if you have not rotated the order of the columns in the table's display image.

The FIELDNO() function requires two arguments expressed in the form *FIELDNO(field,table)*. The first argument must be a string or string variable that specifies the field whose position you want to check. The second argument must be a string or string variable that specifies the name of the table containing that field. Although this table may be on the workspace, it does not have to be. If it is not in the current directory, you must specify its complete path.

If c:\paradox3\examples is the current directory, for example, and contains the EMPLYEE table, you would use the function *FIELDNO("Last Name","Emplyee")* to determine the position of the Last Name field within that table. If c:\paradox3\examples is not the current directory, however, you would use the function *FIELDNO("Last Name", " c:\\paradox3\\examples\\Emplyee")*.

The FIELDSTR() Function

The FIELDSTR() function returns the contents of the current field as a string value. The FIELDSTR() function takes no arguments. FIELDSTR() works even if a field is only partially filled in. It can be used to maintain character-by-character control over data entry. For example, suppose you have the picture ###-#### as a validity check for a phone number field. When the first three numbers, 555, are entered into the field, you want to automatically fill in the last four digits, 1212. The following script would handle this situation.

```
WHILE TRUE
    ECHO Normal
    x = GETCHAR()
    KEYPRESS x
    IF FIELDSTR() = "555-" THEN
     TYPEIN "1212"
    ENDIF
    IF ISVALID() THEN
     QUITLOOP
    ENDIF
    ECHO Off
    MESSAGE "Keep on typing"
    SLEEP 1000
ENDWHILE
QUIT "All done"
```

This script will examine each keystroke as it is entered into the Phone Number field. It stores each keystroke into the variable *x* before entering it into the field. If the last character entered completes the string *"555"*, then *FIELDSTR() = "555-"* is true (remember, the picture for the phone number field will automatically put in the hyphen), and the script will enter the rest of the phone number (1212) into the field. The second IF statement determines if a valid phone number has been entered. If the phone number is valid, then the WHILE loop will end, and the message *All done* will appear in the lower-right corner of the screen. Otherwise, the message *Keep on typing* will appear, and the user must continue to enter the phone number.

We'll discuss GETCHAR() and ISVALID() later in this chapter. Other PAL functions, such as ECHO(), QUIT(), and MESSAGE(), are discussed in the other PAL chapters of this book.

The FIELDTYPE() Function

The FIELDTYPE() function can be used to determine the field type of the current field of the current table. This function takes no arguments—it returns information about the field in which the cursor is positioned. FIELDTYPE() returns the string value N if the cursor is in a number field, S if the cursor is in a short number field, $\$$ if the cursor is in a dollar field, D if the cursor is in a date field, and An if the cursor is in an alphanumeric field, where n is the length of the field. A script error will result if there is no table or query on the workspace when the FIELDTYPE() function is executed.

The FILESIZE() Function

PAL's FILESIZE() function, whose form is

FILESIZE(*filename*)

returns the number of bytes of disk space occupied by the file named by its argument, *filename*. If the file you want to inspect is not in the current directory, you must include the path and/or drive name in the argument. In all cases, you must include the file-name extension as a part of the argument. For example, you would use the function *FILESIZE("c:\\paradox3\\examples\\abc.db")* to determine the size of database file ABC, if that file is stored in the c:\paradox3\examples directory, and c:\paradox3\examples is not the current directory.

The FORM() Function

The FORM() function takes no argument and returns the name of the active form for the table in the current image. If the current table is in the form view, then this function returns a string containing the letter F or a string containing a number between 1 and 14. For example, the command *COPYFORM "Table1" FORM() "Table1" "10"* copies the form that is displaying the TABLE1 table in the current image to form 10 in that table's family.

If the current table is not in the form view, the FORM() function returns the string *None*. If the current image does not contain a table, then the FORM() function produces a script error.

The GRAPHTYPE() Function

You can use PAL's GRAPHTYPE() function to determine the current graph in Paradox's graph settings. This function takes no arguments. The GRAPHTYPE() function returns one of ten strings: *Area, Bar, Combined, Line, Marker, Pie, Rotated Bar, Stacked Bar, 3dBar*, or *XY*. For example, if the current graph settings will produce a pie graph, then the command *gtype=GRAPHTYPE()* will store the string *Pie* in the *gtype* variable.

The HELPMODE() Function

PAL's HELPMODE() function can be used to determine what type of help screen, if any, is currently being displayed. This function takes no arguments. HELPMODE() can return one of three results. If no help screen is in use when PAL executes the function, then the function will return the string *None*. If you are using the HelpAndFill option of the TableLookup command when PAL executes the function, then the function will return the string *Lookup-Help*. If you are viewing a regular help screen when PAL executes the function, then the function will return the string *Help*.

The IMAGENO() Function

The IMAGENO() function returns the position of the current image relative to the other images currently on the Paradox workspace. If the cursor is in the first image on the workspace (the one that Paradox makes current when you press the [Up Image] key until you hear a beep), this function will return the value 1. If the cursor is within the third image, this function will return the value 3, and so forth.

The IMAGETYPE() Function

The IMAGETYPE() function allows you to determine, from within a script, in what type of image the cursor currently is positioned. If the current image is a table or a form, this function returns the string *Display*. If the current image is a query, this function returns the string *Query*. If the cursor is not within an image (if the workspace is blank or Paradox is in Report mode, Form mode, or the Script Editor), this function returns the string *None*.

The LINKTYPE() Function

The LINKTYPE() function can be used to determine the type of link that exists between a master table and a detail table on a multitable form. This function takes no argument and returns one of four strings: *1-1 Group*, *1-M Group*, *Group*, or *None*.

In Chapter 4, we discussed the different types of links that can exist between a master and a detail table. The LINKTYPE() function returns the string *1-1 Group* if the cursor is in a detail table that is linked to its master table in a one-to-one relationship. This function returns the string *1-M Group* if the link between the detail and master tables creates a one-to-many relationship. If the link between the two tables creates a many-to-one or a many-to-many relationship, then the LINKTYPE() function returns the string *Group*. If the cursor is in the master table, if there is no linkage between the detail and master tables, or if there is no multitable form in the current image, this function will return the string *None*. If the current image does not display a table, or if there are no images on the workspace, the LINKTYPE() function will produce a script error.

For example, suppose the cursor is in the embedded SALESORD form of the multitable form shown in Figure 15-5 on page 650. The LINKTYPE() function will return the string *1-M Group* because each CLIENTS record is linked to many records in SALESORD, but each SALESORD record is linked to only one record in CLIENTS.

The MEMLEFT() Function

The MEMLEFT() function tells you how much RAM (random access memory) is still available for Paradox to work with. This function, which takes no arguments, comes in handy when you are working with large procedures or large numbers of variables and need to be sure that you don't run out of memory.

The MENUCHOICE() Function

PAL's MENUCHOICE() function returns the currently highlighted menu selection as a string. For example, if the cursor is highlighting the selection Report on the Paradox Main menu, when PAL reads the command *x=MENUCHOICE()*, it will store the string *Report* into the variable *x*.

The MONITOR() Function

The PAL MONITOR() function allows PAL to determine the type of monitor for which you have configured Paradox. If you have configured Paradox for use with a color monitor, the MONITOR() function will return the string *Color*. If you have configured Paradox for a black-and-white monitor for use with a graphics card, this function will return the string *B&W*. If you have configured Paradox for use with a monochrome monitor (no graphics capability), this function will return the string *Mono*.

By using this function in conjunction with PAL's IF and STYLE commands, you can direct PAL to display messages in different styles, depending on what type of monitor Paradox is using when it plays the script.

The NFIELDS() Function

PAL's NFIELDS() function allows you to determine how many fields are contained within the table that you name. The form of this function is

NFIELDS(*tablename*)

where *tablename* is a string expression that specifies the name of a table. If the table is in the current directory, the argument can simply be the name of that table. If the table you want to test is in another directory, then you must specify the complete path, remembering to use double backslashes.

For example, suppose the four-field table named JOBS is stored in c:\paradox3\examples. If c:\paradox3\examples is the current directory, then the function *NFIELDS("Jobs")* will return the value 4. If c:\paradox3\examples is not the current directory, however, you would need to use the function *NFIELDS("c:\\paradox3\\examples\\Jobs")*.

The NIMAGERECORDS() Function

You can use the NIMAGERECORDS() function to determine the number of records in the current image. If the table in the current image is a detail table linked to its master table, this function will return the number of records in the detail table that are linked to the current record in the master table. If the table in the current image is not part of a multitable form or is on a multitable form but is unlinked to other tables on the form, then this function works similarly to the NRECORDS() function. However, while the NRECORDS() function takes the name of a table as its argument, NIMAGERECORDS() takes no argument. If the current image does not display a table, or if there are no images on the workspace, the NIMAGE-RECORDS() function will produce a script error.

For example, suppose the cursor is in the embedded SALESORD form of the multitable form shown in Figure 15-5 on page 650. If record 1 of the CLIENTS table is the current record on the master form, the NIMAGERECORDS() function will return the value 3 because there are three SALESORD records linked to the first record in the CLIENTS table. These three SALESORD records are linked to record 1 of CLIENTS because they have the same entry in the Client Number field (1001) as record 1 of CLIENTS.

The NIMAGES() Function

PAL's NIMAGES() function returns the number of images (tables, forms, and queries) currently on the Paradox workspace. The NIMAGES() function counts each table on a multitable form as a separate image. If the workspace contained a multitable form with three embedded forms and two queries, for example, the NIMAGES() function would return the value 6.

The NKEYFIELDS() Function

PAL's NKEYFIELDS() function allows you to determine how many key fields a particular table contains. The form of this function is

    NKEYFIELDS(*tablename*)

where *tablename* is a string expression that specifies the name of the table whose key fields you want to count. If the table is not stored in the current directory, then you must include the path within the argument. For example, suppose that the table named ORDERS, stored in the directory c:\paradox3\examples, contains two key fields. If c:\paradox3\examples is the current directory, then the function *NKEYFIELDS("Orders")* will return the value 2.

The NPAGES() Function

The NPAGES() function allows PAL to calculate the number of pages in the current form or report. When you are viewing or editing a form, this function returns the number of pages in that form. When you are editing a report specification, this function returns the number of page-widths that the report contains. If you are viewing the EMPLYEE table through a three-page form, for example, the function NPAGES() will return the value 3.

The NRECORDS() Function

PAL's NRECORDS() function allows PAL to calculate the number of records in the table that you specify. The form of this function is

NRECORDS(*tablename*)

where *tablename* is a string expression that specifies the name of the table whose records you want to count. If the table is not in the current directory, then you must include the full path to the table within the argument of the function.

For example, suppose that the PROSPECT table, located in the directory c:\paradox3\examples, contains 1,234 records. If c:\paradox3\examples is the current directory, then the function *NRECORDS("Prospect")* will return the value 1234. If c:\paradox3\examples were not the current directory, however, this function would result in a script error. To count the records in this table, you would instead need to use the function *NRECORDS("c:\\paradox3\\examples\\Prospect")*.

The NROWS() Function

The NROWS() function returns the number of rows in the current image. Unlike NRECORDS(), the NROWS() function calculates the display size of an image, not the size of the table itself. Also unlike NRECORDS(), the NROWS() function operates upon the current image, not upon any table that you name. NROWS(), therefore, accepts no arguments.

For example, suppose that you use the [Menu] Image TableSize command to reduce the display image of the 250-record table PEOPLE so that only four records are visible at one time. If PAL reads the function NROWS() while the cursor is in the table image of PEOPLE, it will return the value 4.

The PAGENO() Function

PAL's PAGENO() function returns the number of the current page-width when you are editing a report spec and returns the number of the current page when you are designing or using a form. This function has no meaning in any other context and takes no arguments.

For example, if the cursor is within the third page of a form, the function PAGENO() will return the value 3. If the cursor is in the fourth page-width of a report spec, this function will return the value 4.

The PAGEWIDTH() Function

The PAGEWIDTH() function calculates the width, in characters, of the page-widths in the current report specification. If the cursor is in a report whose page-widths are 80 characters wide, for example, the function PAGEWIDTH() will return the value 80.

The QUERYORDER() Function

The QUERYORDER() function tells you the default field arrangement for ANSWER tables produced by queries. As we explained in Chapter 7, Paradox can arrange the fields in ANSWER tables either in the same order as the fields in the query image or in the order in which the fields are arranged in the table on which the query operates. You can set the default field order with the CCP and then use the PAL command SETQUERYORDER to change the field order for individual queries. If the current default order is based on the query image, then the QUERYORDER() function returns the string *ImageOrder*. If the default field order is based on the table structure, then this function returns the string *TableOrder*.

The RECNO() Function

The RECNO() function returns the position of the record in which the cursor is located in the current image (table or form) with respect to the first record in the table. The RECNO() function works on the current display image, so it doesn't require or accept any arguments.

As an example of this function, suppose that you use the [Menu] View command to bring a table named DATES into the workspace and make it the current image. Then, you press ↓ 50 times to position the cursor on the 51st record. If PAL reads the RECNO() function at this point, it will return the value 51.

If the cursor is in a linked detail table on a multitable form, the RECNO() function returns the position of the current record on the embedded form. For example, if the current record is the second of five linked records displayed on the embedded form, RECNO() will return the value 2, regardless of the record's position in its entire table.

The ROW() Function

PAL's ROW() function is the mate of the COL() function. While COL() returns the cursor's horizontal position on the PAL canvas, ROW() returns its vertical position on the canvas. For example, suppose you use the command *@10,20* to position the cursor at the intersection of row 10 and column 20 on the PAL canvas. If PAL reads the function ROW() while the cursor is in this position, the function will return the value 10. (We'll explain how to position the cursor on the PAL canvas in Chapter 16.)

The ROWNO() Function

PAL's ROWNO() function returns the row position of the cursor within the current image. ROWNO() is closely related to COLNO(), which returns the column position of the cursor within the current image.

For example, suppose that you issue the [Menu] View command to bring a table to the workspace. Like any default-size table, this one displays 22 records at a time. If you press the [Pg Dn] key, the cursor will be in the 22nd record, which will be displayed on the first row of the table image, as shown in Figure 15-8. If PAL evaluates the ROWNO() function at this point, it will return the value 1. Although the cursor is in the 22nd record of the table, it is in the first row of the image. If the cursor is currently in an embedded form on a multitable form, then the ROWNO() function returns the current row position on the embedded form, not the master form.

Figure 15-8 The ROWNO() Function

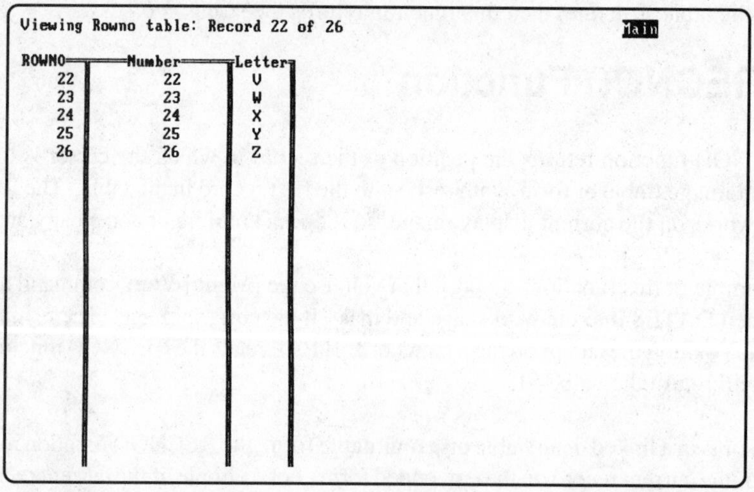

```
Viewing Rowno table: Record 22 of 26                          Main

ROWNO========Number=======Letter=
    22          22           U
    23          23           W
    24          24           X
    25          25           Y
    26          26           Z
```

The SDIR() Function

PAL's SDIR() function returns, as a string, the complete name of the directory containing the script currently being played, including the disk drive. This function takes no arguments. SDIR() is useful when you have called a script from a directory other than the one that is current. For example, suppose you issue the [Menu] Scripts Play command and type *c:\paradox3\examples\script1* while *c:\paradox3* is the current directory. If Script1 contains the function SDIR(), it will return the string *c:\paradox3\examples*—the directory from which the current script was called. In the same situation, the DIRECTORY() function will return the string *c:\\paradox3*—the default directory.

The SORTORDER() Function

The SORTORDER() function tells you which of the four possible sort orders is currently being used. The four types are ASCII, Intl (international), NorDan (Norwegian/Danish), and SwedFin (Swedish/Finish). This function takes no arguments.

The SYSMODE() Function

The SYSMODE() function allows PAL to determine which mode Paradox currently is in. Very simply, this function returns whatever message is in the mode indicator at the upper-right corner of the screen. Depending upon which mode Paradox is in when PAL evaluates this function, it will return one of 12 strings: *Coedit, Create, DataEntry, Edit, Form, Graph, Main, Password, Report, Restructure, Script,* or *Sort.* For example, if your screen looks like the one shown in Figure 15-9, the function SYSMODE() will return the string *Main.*

Figure 15-9 The SYSMODE() Function

```
Viewing Emplyee table: Record 1 of 16                           Main

EMPLYEE┬──Emp Number──┬──Last Name──┬─First Name─┬══SS Number══┬═══════Addre
    1   │      1       │   Jones      │   David     │  414-74-3421 │ 4000 St. Ja
    2   │      2       │   Cameron    │   Herb      │  321-65-8765 │ 2321 Elm St
    3   │      3       │   Jones      │   Stewart   │  401-32-8721 │ 4309 Oakbri
    4   │      4       │   Roberts    │   Darlene   │  417-43-7777 │ 451 Lone Pi
    5   │      5       │   Jones      │   Jean      │  413-07-9123 │ 4000 St. Ja
    6   │      6       │   Williams   │   Brenda    │  401-55-1567 │ 100 Owl Cre
    7   │      7       │   Myers      │   Julie     │  314-30-9452 │ 4512 Parksi
    8   │      8       │   Link       │   Julie     │  345-75-1525 │ 3215 Palm C
    9   │      9       │   Jackson    │   Mary      │  424-13-7621 │ 7821 Clark
   10   │     10       │   Jakes, Jr. │   Sal       │  321-65-9151 │ 3451 Michig
   11   │     11       │   Preston    │   Molly     │  451-00-3426 │ 321 Indian
   12   │     12       │   Masters    │   Ron       │  317-65-4529 │ 423 W. 72nd
   13   │     13       │   Robertson  │   Kevin     │  415-24-6710 │ 431 Bardsto
   14   │     14       │   Garrison   │   Robert    │  312-98-1479 │ 55 Wheeler
   15   │     15       │   Gunn       │   Barbara   │  321-97-8632 │ 541 Kentuck
   16   │     16       │   Emerson    │   Cheryl    │  404-14-1422 │ 8100 River
```

The TABLE() Function

PAL's TABLE() function returns the name of the current table image as a string. Because this function works on the current image (which must be a table, form, or query), it accepts no arguments. For example, if the cursor is within the EMPLYEE table when PAL reads the command *t=TABLE(),* PAL will store the string *Employee* in the variable *t.*

The TYPE() Function

PAL's TYPE() function returns the type of the expression used as its argument. The form of this function is

TYPE(*expression*)

where *expression* is the expression whose type you want to know. This expression can be a variable, formula, function, or field reference, or a literal value, string, or date. If the argument of the TYPE() function is a numeric expression, it will return the string *N*. If the argument is a string expression, this function will return the string *A*, followed by the number of characters in the string. If the argument is a date expression, it will return the string *D*.

You can use this function in a variety of ways. For example, when the cursor is positioned over the alphanumeric entry *Smith* in a table image, the function *TYPE([])* returns the string *A5*. Similarly, the function *TYPE(x)* returns the string *N* if *x* contains the value 1234.56, and the function *TYPE(11/24/58)* returns the string *D*.

The VERSION() Function

The VERSION() function allows PAL to determine what version of Paradox it is working in. This function accepts no arguments. If you are working in Paradox 1.0, this function will return the numeric value 1. If you are working in Release 1.1, this function will return the numeric value 1.1. If you are working in Paradox 2.0, this function will return the numeric value 2. If you are working in Paradox 3.0, this function will return the numeric value 3. As you know, some PAL commands and functions are available in later Paradox releases, but not in earlier releases. By using this function to determine what version you are working in before you play a script, you can avoid the script error that would result if Paradox 1.1 were to encounter a Paradox 2 or 3 command or function.

The WINDOW() Function

PAL's final informational function is WINDOW(). This function returns as a string the contents of the message window at the lower-right corner of the screen. Because PAL erases the text that appears in the message window as soon as you press another key, this function provides the only way to capture these messages for future use. Suppose you run the script

```
VIEW "Emplyee"
Right BackSpace
x=WINDOW()
```

Notice that this script tells Paradox to press the [Backspace] key without first entering the Edit mode. When you run this script, PAL will store in the variable *x* the error message *Press the Edit key [F9] if you want to make changes*—the result of pressing the [Backspace] key while you are not in the Edit mode.

Logical Functions

We'll conclude this chapter with the last group of PAL functions, logical functions. Unlike the functions in the seven groups we have examined so far, the functions in this group do not return numeric, string, or date values. Instead, they return one of two logical values: True or False. Because they return only these two logical results, these functions are most frequently used as the conditional tests of IF and WHILE commands.

The ATFIRST() and ATLAST() Functions

PAL's ATFIRST() and ATLAST() functions determine whether the cursor currently is positioned within the first or last record in an image. That image may contain an entire table or linked detail records on a multitable form. Because these functions operate on the image in which the cursor is positioned, they accept no arguments. The ATFIRST() function returns the logical value True if the cursor is in the first record of the current image. As a result, the function returns a True value if the cursor is in the first record of the table in a single-table image or the first record displayed in an embedded form on a multitable form. (The records on an embedded form may include just a few records from a table if the form is linked to its master form.) The ATFIRST() function returns the logical value False if the cursor is in any other record in the image. Similarly, the result of ATLAST() is True if the cursor is in the last record of an image, and False if it is anywhere else. As you will see in Chapter 16, these functions are useful when you want PAL to step through an image one record at a time, stopping at the first or last record in the image.

The BOT() and EOT() Functions

PAL's next two logical functions, BOT() and EOT(), are similar but not identical to ATFIRST() and ATLAST(). BOT(), which stands for Beginning Of Table, returns the value True when you attempt to move beyond the first record in an image with a *MOVETO RECORD* or SKIP command (not with the keystroke representation Up). Likewise, EOT(), which stands for End Of Table, returns the value True when you try to move beyond the last record in an image, using the *MOVETO RECORD* or SKIP commands (not with the keystroke representation Down). The BOT() and EOT() functions work whether the current image contains an entire table or only the linked detail records on a multitable form. You'll learn more about these functions in our discussion of the WHILE command in Chapter 16.

The CHARWAITING()/GETCHAR() Functions

If you type a character while PAL is playing a script, your computer will not pass that character on to PAL immediately. PAL will not receive the character until it reads a command or function in the script that instructs it to accept input from the user. The CHARWAITING() function allows PAL to determine whether a character is being held in your computer's keyboard buffer. The CHARWAITING() function does not accept any arguments.

You'll commonly use the CHARWAITING() function in conjunction with another PAL function: GETCHAR(). The GETCHAR() function instructs PAL to retrieve a character from the keyboard buffer, if one is waiting there, or to pause until a character is typed.

The script shown in Figure 15-10 demonstrates a simple use of the GETCHAR() and CHARWAITING() functions. The IF command on the first line of this script instructs PAL to determine if a character is waiting in the keyboard buffer. If so, the CHARWAITING() function is True, and PAL evaluates the command $x=GETCHAR()$. This command instructs PAL to retrieve the character from the buffer and store it in the variable x.

Figure 15-10 An Example of the CHARWAITING() Function

```
Changing script C:\paradox3\charwait                        Script

....+...10....+...20....+...30....+...40....+...50....+...60....+...70....+...80
IF CHARWAITING()
  x=GETCHAR()
  IF x=ASC("q") THEN
    QUIT
  ENDIF
PLAY "Subrout1"
ENDIF
```

Importantly, the GETCHAR() function returns the ASCII value (0-255) of the character it retrieves, not the character itself. The ASC() function in the command $IF\ x=ASC("q")$ converts the character q into its ASCII code, so that PAL can compare it to the number returned by GETCHAR(). If the character in the buffer were q, PAL would read the command QUIT and, therefore, exit from the script. If the character were anything but q, PAL would play the script named Subrout1.

The DRIVESTATUS() Function

PAL's next logical function, DRIVESTATUS(), determines whether the drive you name is prepared to read or write information. The form of this function is

DRIVESTATUS(*drive letter*)

where the *drive letter* argument is a string expression that specifies the disk drive you want to check.

The DRIVESTATUS() function returns the logical value True unless the drive designated in its argument does not exist or is not operational. This function will return the value False if there is no disk in the drive you name, for example, or if the door of that drive is not closed. If you have a dual-floppy system, the function *DRIVESTATUS("C")* will return the value False.

The FAMILYRIGHTS() Function

The FAMILYRIGHTS() function allows you to determine if the current user has the right to modify or create family objects for a table. The function has the form

FAMILYRIGHTS(*tablename,right*)

where *tablename* is the name of the table with which you want to work, and *right* is the one-letter abbreviation for the object you want to modify or create. The four possible strings for *right* are *F* (form), *R* (report), *S* (image setting), or *V* (validity check). You can use only one of these letters at a time—if you want to check for each type of rights, you'll have to use four separate functions. The function returns True if the current user has the specified rights to the specified table and False if the user does not.

For example, suppose you are creating an application that will allow authorized users to modify reports for a table named CUSTOMER. To make sure that only authorized users can make changes, you might want your script to include the commands

```
IF NOT FAMILYRIGHTS(CUSTOMER,R) THEN
    MESSAGE "User not authorized to change reports"
    SLEEP 5000
    QUIT
ENDIF
```

The FIELDRIGHTS() Function

The FIELDRIGHTS() function is similar to the FAMILYRIGHTS() function. It allows you to determine if the current user has the right to read or modify the contents of a specific field in a table. This function has the form

FIELDRIGHTS(*tablename, fieldname,right*)

where *tablename* is the specified table, *fieldname* is the specific field of interest, and *right* is either the string *All* or *ReadOnly*. The function returns True if the current user has the specified rights to the specified field and False if the user does not. If the *right* argument is *All*, then a True result means that the current user can read and write to the specific field. If the *right* argument is *ReadOnly*, then a True response means that the current user can read the field but will not be allowed to modify it.

The ISASSIGNED() Function

PAL's ISASSIGNED() function determines if a variable is currently defined, that is, whether the variable exists. (This function also tests for the existence of arrays and procedures—topics we'll cover in Chapter 17.) The form of this function is

ISASSIGNED(*variablename*)

where the single argument *variablename* is the name of a variable (or array or procedure). For example, if you have defined the variable *x* during the current session, the function *ISASSIGNED(x)* will return True. If you have not defined the variable, or if you have used the command *RELEASE VARS x* after defining it, this function will return the value False.

The ISBLANK() Function

PAL's ISBLANK() function checks to see if an expression contains a blank value. The form of this function is

ISBLANK(*argument*)

where *argument* is a reference to a PAL expression: a variable, field value, literal, formula, or another function. If *argument* stores or returns a blank value, the ISBLANK() function will return the value True. If *argument* stores anything other than a blank value, the ISBLANK() function will return the logical value False.

The script shown in Figure 15-11 demonstrates a simple use of the ISBLANK() function. This script begins by entering the Edit mode and moving the cursor to the Amount field of the first record in the current table. The *WHILE NOT EOF()* command tells PAL to execute the commands that come between that command and the ENDWHILE command until it reaches the end of the table (actually until it tries to move beyond the end of the table). The command *IF [ISBLANK([])* tests to see whether the current field is blank. If so, PAL enters the value 0 into it, moves down to the next row, and repeats the process. If the field contains anything other than a blank value, PAL moves down one row without replacing the entry.

The ISBLANKZERO() Function

You can use the ISBLANKZERO() function to determine whether Paradox is set to treat blank numeric field entries as zeroes in calculations. If Paradox is set to treat blank entries as zeroes, this function returns the logical value True. If Paradox is not set to treat blanks as zeroes, this function returns the logical value False.

By default, Paradox produces blank solutions for equations that involve blank field values, but you can use the CCP to tell Paradox to treat blanks as zeroes. The manner in which Paradox treats blank values can affect the results of calculated fields in reports and forms, calculations in queries (other than count calculations), and PAL calculations (other than count calculations). As a result, you may want to handle some of these calculations differently, depending on the value returned by the ISBLANKZERO() function.

Figure 15-11 An Example of ISBLANK()

```
Changing script C:\paradox3\blank                          Script
....+...10....+...20....+...30....+...40....+...50....+...60....+...70....+...80
EditKey
MOVETO [Amount]
Home
WHILE NOT EOF()
  IF ISBLANK([])
    [] = 0
  ENDIF
  SKIP 1
ENDWHILE
```

For example, suppose you are working with a table named ORDERS that includes a field for sales tax. Since the orders from some states do not require any sales tax, several records include blank entries in the Sales Tax field. To ensure that these blank entries do not produce blank solutions when a calculated field in a report or form computes the total price with tax for each order, you could use the commands

    IF NOT ISBLANKZERO() THEN
     SCAN
    IF ISBLANK([Sales Tax]) THEN
     [Sales Tax]=0
    ENDIF
     ENDSCAN
    ENDIF

to check whether Paradox treats blank values as zeroes and, if not, change blank entries in the Sales Tax field to zeroes. This technique requires the IF and SCAN commands, which we will discuss in Chapter 16.

The ISEMPTY() Function

PAL's ISEMPTY() function determines whether the table you specify is empty or whether it contains records. The form of this function is

    ISEMPTY(*tablename*)

where the single argument is the name of a table. If the table is not in the current directory, then you must include the directory and path in the argument. (Because the backslash is a special character that means *interpret the next character literally*, you must use two backslashes in the path designation wherever you normally would use only one.) If the 16-record EMPLYEE table is in the current directory, for example, the function *ISEMPTY("Emplyee")* will return the value False.

The ISENCRYPTED() Function

The ISENCRYPTED() function lets you determine if a specified table is password-protected. The ISENCRYPTED() function takes one argument: the name of the table being tested. The form of this function is

   ISENCRYPTED(*tablename*)

If the table specified by *tablename* is password-protected, then this function will return the value True. Otherwise, it will return False.

The ISFIELDVIEW() Function

PAL's ISFIELDVIEW() function determines whether Paradox is in the field view (the result of pressing the [Field View] key ([Alt]-[F5]) while Paradox is in the Main or Edit mode). If so, the function will return the logical value True. If not, the function will return the value False. Because this function refers to the current table, it does not accept any arguments.

For example, the script

   IF NOT ISFIELDVIEW() THEN
    FieldView
   ENDIF

places Paradox in the field view if it is not already in that mode.

The ISFILE() and ISTABLE() Functions

PAL's ISFILE() and ISTABLE() functions both determine whether a given file exists. PAL's ISFILE() function checks for the existence of a specified file of any type in the current directory. The form of this function is

   ISFILE(*filename*)

where the *filename* argument is the name of the file whose existence you want to verify. If the file is not in the current directory, then you must specify the directory as well as the file. (Remember to use two backslashes wherever you normally would use only one.) The *filename* argument should include the full name of the file, including any extension.

For example, if the script file MENU.SC is in the directory c:\paradox3\scripts, then the function *ISFILE("c:\\paradox3\\scripts\\menu.sc")* will return the value True. If the file does not exist, if it is in a different directory, or if you forget to include the file-name extension .SC in the function's argument, the function will return the value False.

The ISTABLE() function checks for the existence of Paradox table (.DB) files. The form of this function is

ISTABLE(*filename*)

where the *filename* argument is the name of the file whose existence you want to check. As with ISFILE(), if the file is not in the current directory, then you must specify the directory as well as the file. Because the ISTABLE() function looks for only DB files, there is no need to specify an extension.

For example, if a file named EMPLYEE.DB were in the directory c:\paradox3\data, the function *ISTABLE("c:\\paradox3\\data\\emplyee")* would return the logical value True, as would the function *ISFILE("c:\\paradox3\\data\\emplyee.db")*.

The ISFORMVIEW() Function

The ISFORMVIEW() function tests whether PAL is displaying the current table in the form view or in the table view. If the current image is a form, this function returns the logical value True. If the current image is a table, the function returns the logical value False. For example, the ISFORMVIEW() function in the script

```
VIEW "Emplyee"
PICKFORM "F"
x=ISFORMVIEW()
```

will return the logical value True.

The ISINSERTMODE() Function

PAL's ISINSERTMODE() function does pretty much what you might think—it determines whether Paradox is in the insert or the replace mode while you are editing a report, form, or script. For example, the script

```
IF NOT ISINSERTMODE() THEN
  Ins
ENDIF
```

toggles Paradox to the insert mode if it is in the replace mode.

The ISLINKLOCKED() Function

The PAL ISLINKLOCKED() function can be used to determine whether the current table is linklocked, meaning that it cannot be edited without the multitable form on which the table appeared at the beginning of the Edit session. If the current table is linklocked, the

ISLINKLOCKED() function returns the logical value True. If the table is not linklocked, this function returns the logical value False. Paradox automatically linklocks all the linked tables on a multitable form in order to prevent editing of the tables without the multitable form. Individual editing of the tables could violate the relationships based on common entries in matching fields that link the tables.

For example, suppose that while using the multitable form shown in Figure 15-5 on page 650 to edit the CLIENTS and SALESORD tables, you press [Form Toggle] to display the CLIENTS table in the table view. At this point, the ISLINKLOCKED() function will return the logical value True, indicating that the CLIENTS table is linklocked and cannot be edited without the multitable form. In a script, you could use the commands

```
IF ISLINKLOCKED() AND NOT ISFORMVIEW() THEN
  FormKey
ENDIF
```

to determine whether the CLIENTS table is linklocked and whether the table is not in the form view. Since both of these conditions are true, the commands will simulate pressing [Form Toggle] to restore the multitable form, allowing the user to edit the table. Of course, this type of test will work only if the current table is the master table on the multitable form.

The ISMULTIFORM() Function

The ISMULTIFORM() function determines whether a form includes embedded forms, meaning it is a multitable form. This function has the form

ISMULTIFORM(*tablename, formname*)

where *tablename* is the name of an existing Paradox table and *formname* is the number of a form in the table's family. The ISMULTIFORM() function returns the logical value True if the form includes an embedded form or forms, or the logical value False if it does not. For example, because the form shown in Figure 15-5 on page 650 is form 1 for the CLIENTS table, the function *ISMULTIFORM("Clients","1")* will return the logical value True.

A script error will result if the table named in the *tablename* argument or the form named in the *formname* argument does not exist. This function will also produce a script error if *formname* is not a valid form name (F or 1 to 14), or if the user cannot access the *tablename* table due to insufficient table rights or because the table is locked.

The ISMULTIREPORT() Function

The ISMULTIREPORT() function determines whether a report includes linked lookup tables, meaning it is a multitable report. This function has the form

ISMULTIREPORT(*tablename,reportname*)

where *tablename* is the name of an existing Paradox table and *reportname* is the number of a report in the table's family. The ISMULTIREPORT() function returns the logical value True if the report includes lookup tables, or the logical value False if it does not. For example, if you design report 1 for the CLIENTS table to include information about each client's sales orders from the SALESORD table, then the function *ISMULTIREPORT("Clients","1")* will return the logical value True.

A script error will result if the table named in the *tablename* argument or the report named in the *reportname* argument does not exist. This function will also produce a script error if *reportname* is not a valid report name (R or 1 to 15), or if the user cannot access the *tablename* table due to insufficient table rights or because the table is locked.

The ISRUNTIME() Function

The ISRUNTIME() function lets you determine whether your script is being played under the Runtime version of Paradox or under a regular version of Paradox. This function takes no arguments. If the script is running in Runtime Paradox, the ISRUNTIME() function returns the logical value True. Otherwise, it returns the logical value False.

The ISVALID() Function

The ISVALID() function can be used to determine if the entry in the current field is valid. A valid entry is one that has the proper type and that conforms to all of the validity checks for the field. The function returns True if the current entry is valid and False if it is not. This function is used internally by the Data Entry Toolkit. (Appendix A3 discusses the Data Entry Toolkit.)

ISVALID() comes in handy when you are allowing a user to make entries into a table from within a script. Normally, if the user makes an invalid entry into a field and then tries to move the cursor out of the field, an error will result. You can avoid this kind of error by using ISVALID() to test the entry in the field before the script allows the user to leave the current field. The script on page 667 employs the ISVALID() function to make sure a user has entered a phone number properly before he or she leaves that field.

The PRINTERSTATUS() Function

The PRINTERSTATUS() function determines whether your printer is ready to receive information from Paradox. This function accepts no arguments. If your printer is connected to the correct port, turned on, filled with paper, and in the ready mode, this function will return the value True. If any of these conditions are not met, this function will return the value False.

This command is useful within any script that prints a report. In the script shown in Figure 15-12, for example, this function tells PAL to prompt you if your printer is not ready. (In Chapter 16, we'll explain how the MESSAGE command works.)

Figure 15-12 An Example of the PRINTERSTATUS() Function

```
Changing script C:\paradox3\prtready                          Script
....+...10....+...20....+...30....+...40....+...50....+...60....+...70....+...80
IF NOT PRINTERSTATUS() THEN
 MESSAGE "Make sure printer is ready, then press any key"
 x=GETCHAR()
ENDIF
REPORT "Emplyee" "R"
```

The TABLERIGHTS() Function

The TABLERIGHTS() function is similar to the FAMILYRIGHTS() function. It allows you to determine what rights, if any, the current user has to a specified table. The function has the form

TABLERIGHTS(*tablename, right*)

where *tablename* is the table you want to use and *right* is the type of access right you are checking on. The five allowable *right* arguments are *ReadOnly*, *Update*, *Entry*, *InsDel*, and *All*. If the specified table rights exist, then TABLERIGHTS() returns the value True. Otherwise, it returns the value False.

Multi-user Functions

PAL's multi-user functions return information that may be important to your multi-user (networked) PAL applications. There are six functions in this group: LOCKSTATUS(), NETTYPE(), PRIVDIR(), RETRYPERIOD(), USERNAME(), and ISSHARED().

The LOCKSTATUS() Function

PAL's LOCKSTATUS() function lets you know if a specified type of lock has been placed on a table. The function has the form

LOCKSTATUS(*tablename, locktype*)

where *tablename* is the name of the table you want to use and *locktype* is *FL* (full lock), *WL* (write lock), *PWL* (prevent write lock), *PFL* (prevent full lock), or *All*. If the specified type of lock has not been set, the function returns the value 0. If the specified type of lock has been set, the function returns 1. If you use the string *All* as the function's *locktype* argument, the function will tell you how many locks have been set for that table. LOCKSTATUS() only considers locks that have been explicitly placed on the specified table—it disregards locks that Paradox has placed on the table as the result of some operation.

The NETTYPE() Function

PAL's NETTYPE() function returns a string that specifies the type of network system your script is running on. This function takes no arguments and returns one of the seven possible results that are listed in Table 15-9.

Table 15-9 The NETTYPE() FUNCTION

Result	Network System
Novell	Novell network
3Com	3COM 3+ network
IBM	IBM PC LAN network
Torus	Tapestry software network
AT&T Starlan	AT&T Starlan network
Other	Network type unknown
SingleUser	Not using a network

The PRIVDIR() Function

The PRIVDIR() function returns a string that represents the full DOS path of the user's private directory. (Private directories are relevant only in multi-user Paradox systems. Paradox stores a user's private and temporary tables in private directories.) This function takes no arguments. For example, if the current user's private directory is c:\paradox3\jtemp, then this function returns the string *c:\paradox3\jtemp*.

The RETRYPERIOD() Function

The RETRYPERIOD() function returns a value representing the current retry period setting. This function takes no arguments. The retry period is the period of time during which Paradox will continue trying to gain access to a locked resource. The retry period can range from 0 (the default) to 30,000 seconds. If the retry period is 0, then Paradox will not make a second attempt to access a locked resource. If the retry period is some number of seconds greater than 0, Paradox will make repeated attempts during that interval of time to gain access to a locked resource. During that time, the user (or the script) will be unable to do anything except wait.

You can use the SETRETRYPERIOD command to change the current retry period setting. We'll look at the SETRETRYPERIOD command in more detail in Chapter 17.

The USERNAME() Function

The USERNAME() function returns the user name of the current user as a string. (When Paradox is installed on a network, it keeps track of the name of each active user.) This function takes no arguments.

The ISSHARED() Function

PAL's ISSHARED() function helps you determine if a table is in a shared network directory. The form of this function is

ISSHARED(*tablename*)

where *tablename* is the table you want to work with. The function returns True if the specified table is in a shared directory and False if it is in a private directory.

Error-trapping Functions

PAL offers three functions—ERRORCODE(), ERRORMESSAGE(), and ERROR-USER()—that help you trap and diagnose errors that occur during the execution of a script. These functions are designed to be used within a special error-trapping procedure that PAL will call when an error occurs within a script. We'll explain this procedure in Chapter 17.

The ERRORCODE() Function

PAL's ERRORCODE() function returns the error number of the last error that occurred during the execution of the current script. Table 15-10 lists the possible results of the ERRORCODE() function. This function takes no arguments.

For example, if your printer is not ready when your application tries to print, the script

```
IF ERRORCODE() = 43 THEN
  QUIT "The printer is not ready at this moment"
ENDIF
```

will print an error message and stop execution. Like the functions ERRORMESSAGE() and ERRORUSER(), the ERRORCODE() function is used only in special error procedures. We'll discuss procedures and error procedures in Chapter 17.

The ERRORMESSAGE() Function

The ERRORMESSAGE() function returns the text of the last error message Paradox displayed. Like the ERRORCODE() function, ERRORMESSAGE() takes no arguments and should be used in an error-handling procedure. The possible results of the ERRORMESSAGE() function are shown in Table 15-10.

For example, the following commands use the ERRORMESSAGE() function to print an error message if there is not enough memory available for your application:

```
IF ERRORCODE() = 40 THEN
    QUIT ERRORMESSAGE()
ENDIF
```

If an error occurs, the script will display the PAL error message *Not enough memory to complete operation*.

Table 15-10 Error Codes and Messages

Code	Message	Code	Message
0	No error	26	Invalid PAL context
1	Drive not ready	27	Operation not completed
2	Directory not found	28	Too many nested closed
3	Table in use by another user		procedures
4	Full lock placed on table	30	Data type mismatch
	by another user	31	Argument out of range
5	File not found	32	Wrong number of arguments
6	File corrupted	33	Invalid argument
		34	Variable or procedure not assigned
7	Index file corrupted	35	Invalid menu selection
8	Object version mismatch	40	Not enough memory to complete
9	Record locked by another		operation
	user	41	Not enough disk space to complete
10	Directory in use by another		operation
	user	42	Not enough stack space to complete
11	Directory is private direc-		operation
	tory of another user	43	Printer not ready
12	No access to directory at	50	Record was deleted by another user
	DOS level	51	Record was changed by another user
13	Index inconsistent with sort	52	Record was inserted by another user
	order	53	Record with that key already exists
14	Multiuser access denied	54	Record or table was not locked
15	Paradox.net file conflict	55	Record is already locked by you
20	Invalid context for operation	56	Lookup key not found
21	Insufficient password rights	60	Referential integrity check
22	Table is write-protected	61	Invalid multitable form
23	Invalid field value	62	Form locked
24	Obselete procedure library	63	Link locked
25	Insufficient image rights		

The ERRORUSER() Function

PAL's ERRORUSER() function can be used in error procedures to identify the user name of the person who locked a table or record you are trying to access. This function comes in handy when one of the errors listed in Table 15-11 occurs. Each error occurs only when you have tried to access an object that is locked by another user. (Of course, you would use the ERRORCODE() function to determine which of these errors has occurred.) The function lets you determine who placed the lock on the object you are trying to access. For example, if someone with the user name DDFITZ01 has locked record 2 of the EMPLYEE table, then when your script attempts to lock that record, the ERRORUSER() function will return the string *DDFITZ01*.

Table 15-11 Run Errors That Affect ERRORUSER()

Code	Error
3	Table in use by another user
4	Full lock placed on table by another user
9	Record locked by another user
11	Directory is private directory of another user

Conclusion

In this chapter, we have explored another fundamental component of PAL programming: functions. As you have seen, functions are special tools that allow you to calculate or extract information that would be difficult or impossible to obtain with variables and field references alone. In the next two chapters of this section, we'll present a number of PAL commands in the context of essential PAL programming techniques and explore some other PAL topics, such as the use of procedures, arrays, macros, and the PAL Debugger.

Chapter 16

Fundamental
PAL Techniques

In the previous three chapters of this section, we have presented the basic building blocks you need to create PAL programs: the Script Editor, keystroke representations, commands, variables, equations, and functions. In this chapter, we'll use those building blocks as we demonstrate some fundamental PAL programming techniques. In the process, we'll present a number of the PAL commands that we didn't cover in our initial discussion of commands in Chapter 14.

Using the PAL Canvas

In Chapter 13, we introduced you to the PAL canvas. Whenever PAL begins to play a script, it obscures the Paradox workspace with the PAL canvas. When PAL "drops" the PAL canvas at the beginning of a script, it "paints" that canvas with an exact image of what is on the Paradox workspace at the time.

In many cases, the initial image will remain on the PAL canvas for the entire duration of the script play. However, this initial image does not need to stay on the PAL canvas during script play. By using various PAL commands, you can erase the initial image from the PAL canvas and replace it with the messages and prompts of your choice.

Clearing the PAL Canvas

PAL's CLEAR command allows you to erase all or part of the image displayed on the PAL canvas. The most basic form of this command is simply the word CLEAR. When PAL reads this command in a script, it immediately erases all information from the PAL canvas. For example, suppose you played the script with the single command CLEAR while the screen looks like Figure 16-1. As soon as PAL begins playing this script, it drops the PAL canvas and paints it with the image you see in Figure 16-1. Then, the CLEAR command erases that image from the PAL canvas so that your screen is completely blank.

Figure 16-1 A Sample Screen

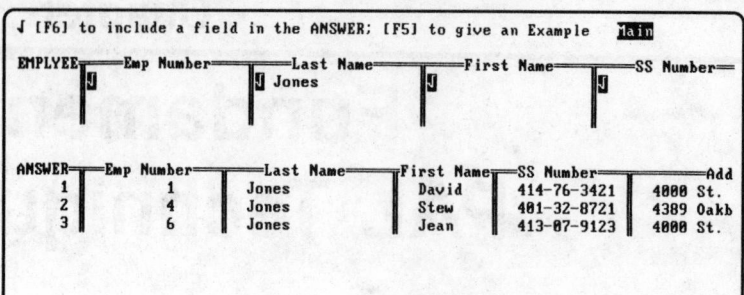

Once you have cleared the PAL canvas, it will remain empty for the entire execution of the script unless you use other PAL commands to write information onto it. (Because PAL executes this simple one-command script almost instantaneously, however, the cleared PAL canvas will be visible for only a fraction of a second before the PAL canvas is lifted to again reveal the Paradox workspace.)

Clearing Part of the PAL Canvas

Although you will most often use the CLEAR command to erase the entire PAL canvas, you can use special forms of this command to clear only selected portions. If you follow the CLEAR command with the keyword EOL (for end of line), as in CLEAR EOL, PAL will erase the current line from the cursor position all the way to the right edge of the PAL canvas. If the cursor is at the left edge of the screen, this command will erase the entire line. If the cursor is in another column, this command will erase only a partial line.

Another form of the CLEAR command allows you to clear a rectangular portion of the PAL canvas. When you follow the CLEAR command with the keyword EOS (for end of screen), PAL erases a rectangular area ranging from the current cursor position to the lower-right corner of the screen.

Positioning the Cursor on the PAL Canvas

As we have said, you can display messages, prompts, menus, and the results of calculations on the PAL canvas during the execution of a script. To write messages on the PAL canvas, you use commands like ?, ??, and TEXT, which we'll demonstrate shortly. The place on the canvas where these messages appear depends on where the cursor is when PAL reads the commands. Therefore, before we show you how to display messages, we'll show you how to position the cursor on the PAL canvas.

The @ Command

Positioning the cursor on the PAL canvas is the job of the @ command. The form of this command is

   @row,column

where *row* and *column* are numbers that specify the row and column to which you want to move the cursor. These arguments may be any PAL expression that returns a numeric value. The *row* argument can be any number from 0 to 24, where 0 is the top row on the canvas and 24 is the bottom row. The *column* argument can be any number from 0 to 79, where 0 is the first (leftmost) column and 79 is the last (rightmost) column.

When PAL encounters an @ command in a script, it moves the cursor to the indicated position on the screen. For example, the command *@11,39* moves the cursor to the intersection of row 11 and column 39 of the PAL canvas—approximately in the center of the screen.

The CURSOR Command

PAL's CURSOR command lets you decide how you want the cursor to appear on the PAL canvas (it does not affect the cursor on the Paradox workspace). There are four types of cursors to choose from. The NORMAL (default) option is the underline. The BAR option is a thicker underline. The BOX option turns the cursor into a reverse video box. The OFF option hides the cursor from view. The format of the CURSOR command is

   CURSOR *option*

where *option* is either NORMAL, BAR, BOX, or OFF. For example, when you are displaying messages on the PAL canvas, you might use the CURSOR OFF command to hide the cursor, thus displaying a "clean" message. On the other hand, when prompting the user for input, use the CURSOR BOX command to direct the user's attention to the input area on the screen.

Writing on the PAL Canvas

Three commands—?, ??, and TEXT—allow you to write information on the PAL canvas at the location you specify. Three other commands—MESSAGE, QUIT, and RETURN—write information into the message area at the lower-right corner of the screen.

The ? and ?? Commands

PAL's ? and ?? commands are the most fundamental of all the commands that display information on the PAL canvas. The forms of these functions are

> ? *argument 1, argument 2, ..., argument n*
> ?? *argument 1, argument 2, ..., argument n*

where each argument is any type of PAL expression. The ? and ?? commands can accept an unlimited number of arguments or none at all.

When PAL reads a ? command, it moves the cursor to the beginning of the next line of the PAL canvas and displays the value(s) of its argument(s) there. For example, when PAL executes the script

> CLEAR
> @10,20
> ? "This is a message"

it first clears the PAL canvas and moves the cursor to the intersection of row 10 and column 20. Then, it moves to the left edge of the next row (row 11) and displays *This is a message*.

The ?? command, on the other hand, displays the value(s) of its argument(s) at the current cursor position; it does not skip down a row before writing to the canvas. For example, when PAL executes the script

> CLEAR
> @10,20
> ?? "This is a message"

it clears the PAL canvas and moves the cursor to the intersection of row 10 and column 20, just as in the previous example. It then writes the string *This is a message* at that point instead of advancing to the beginning of the next line.

When PAL finishes executing a ? or ?? command, the cursor will be positioned on the space to the right of the last character that PAL wrote onto the canvas. For example, after PAL executes the previous script, the cursor will be positioned at the intersection of row 10 and column 37—immediately to the right of the letter *e*.

Nonstring Arguments

In the examples of the ? and ?? commands, we used literal strings as arguments. In actual use, the ? and ?? commands can accept as arguments any kind of PAL expression: literal values, literal dates, variables, references, equations, and functions. For example, the two commands *?? 5* and *?? "5"* both would produce the same result—the character *5* displayed on the PAL canvas at the current position of the cursor. Similarly, when PAL reads the command *?? 11/24/58*, it will display *11/24/58* at the current cursor position.

In some situations, you may want to use the ? and ?? commands to display the contents of variables or the entries in a table on the screen. For example, if the variable *x* contains the value 1234.56, the command *?? x* will display *1234.56* at the current position of the cursor on the PAL canvas. If *x* contains the string *This is a test*, this command will display the string *This is a test*. If *x* contains the date 11/24/58, this command will display *11/24/58* at the position of the cursor.

Displaying entries from a table on the PAL canvas is also easy. For example, if the entry in the Age column of the fifth record in your PEOPLE table contains the value 27, then the script

```
CLEAR
VIEW "People"
MOVETO RECORD 5
@10,20
?? [Age]
```

will display the number *27*, beginning at the intersection of row 10 and column 20 of the otherwise empty PAL canvas.

You also can use equations and functions as the arguments of PAL's ? and ?? commands. When you do, PAL displays not the equations or functions but rather the results of the equation or function on the PAL canvas. For example, the script

```
x=1
y=2
CLEAR
@10,20
? x+y
```

will display the result *3* at the beginning of row 11 of the PAL canvas.

Multiple Arguments

Instead of using the ? and ?? commands to display only a single label, value, or date on the screen, you can—and often will want to—join many messages together on a single line. The easiest way to do this is to include multiple arguments in the ? or ?? commands. When PAL executes a ? or ?? command that has multiple arguments, it displays those arguments (or their results) side by side on the PAL canvas with no spaces in between.

When you use more than one argument with ? or ??, you must separate them with commas. Because PAL's ? and ?? commands convert all types of expressions into strings for display purposes, the various expressions for a single command do not need to be the same type.

For example, suppose that you want PAL to calculate the sum of the values stored in the variables *x* and *y* and display the result to the right of the text *The sum of x and y is* at the intersection of row 10 and column 20. To do this, you might use the script

```
x=1
y=2
CLEAR
@10,20
?? "The sum of x and y is ",x+y,"."
```

This script clears the PAL canvas, positions the cursor at the intersection of row 10 and column 20, and writes the sentence *The sum of x and y is 3*. As you can see, this message is composed of three parts. The first argument causes PAL to type the words *The sum of x and y is* followed by a single space. Since the next argument is a formula, PAL evaluates it and displays the result, *3*, to the right of the first string. PAL then displays the final argument, a literal period, to the right of that 3.

Long Messages

Sometimes, the information that is displayed on the screen by a ? or ?? command will not fit on one line. When this happens, PAL will break the message when it reaches column 79 of the PAL canvas, then move the cursor to the beginning of the next line and continue typing there. For example, Figure 16-2 shows the result of playing the script

```
CLEAR
@1,50
?? "Now is the time for all good men to come to the aid of their country."
```

Figure 16-2 A Long Message

```
                                                  Now is the time for all good m
en to come to the aid of their country.
```

Formatting the Display

In Chapter 15, we introduced the FORMAT() function as a way to convert values into formatted strings. Another important use of this function is to alter the way the ? and ?? commands display messages on the PAL canvas. As you recall, the FORMAT() function allows you to alter the display of any type of expression: numeric, alphanumeric, date, and logical. Using this function, you can control the width and alignment of any type of value, the case of alphanumeric values, and the use of signs, parentheses, and currency notation for numeric values. You also can use the FORMAT() function to control the form in which dates are displayed and to make the logical values True/False display as either Yes/No or On/Off.

Without the use of the FORMAT() function, the ? and ?? commands display values exactly as they appear in the function or as they are stored in the variable or field. If the variable *x* holds the value 7654.321, for example, the command *?? x* will write *7654.321* onto the screen at the present position of the cursor. However, suppose you want PAL to display the value with a leading $ sign, a comma separating the thousands from the hundreds, and only two digits to the right of the decimal place, like this: $7,654.32. To display the value this way, you would use the command *?? FORMAT("W9.2,E$C",x)*. You can use the FORMAT() function as the argument of a ? or ?? command to format messages in an almost endless variety of ways. For example, while the command *? [State]* displays the contents of the current record's State field exactly as it appears in the table, the command *? FORMAT("CU",[State])* will display it in all uppercase form.

The TEXT Command

PAL's TEXT command provides yet another way to write information onto the PAL canvas. Unlike the ? and ?? commands, however, the TEXT command can write only literal text onto the screen; it cannot display the contents of variables or fields, nor the results of equations and functions. It does allow you to write multiple-line blocks of text to the screen with a single command.

The TEXT command actually is a combination of two commands: TEXT and ENDTEXT. The form of this command is

```
TEXT
one or more lines of text
ENDTEXT
```

When PAL encounters a TEXT command in a script, it writes to the screen a literal copy of the characters that come between that command and the ENDTEXT command. PAL always begins writing at the current position of the cursor. For the TEXT command to work properly, the text must begin on a line subsequent to the one that contains the TEXT command—never on that same line.

For example, consider the script

```
CLEAR
@11,0
TEXT
PAL APPLICATION #1
Press any key to continue...
ENDTEXT
```

When PAL runs the script, it will clear the screen, position the cursor in the first column of row 11, and type the message

>PAL APPLICATION #1
>Press any key to continue...

Because PAL automatically assumes that what comes between a TEXT command and an ENDTEXT command is literal text, there is no need to enclose it in quotation marks. If you do, PAL will print the quotation marks on the screen. Likewise, if you include blank lines between the TEXT and ENDTEXT commands, PAL will leave blank lines on the screen.

If the cursor is not in the first column of the screen when PAL comes to a TEXT command, it will print the first line of the text beginning at the position of the cursor. However, the second and subsequent lines will be printed beginning in column 0. For this reason, you will usually want to position the cursor in column 0 before you issue a TEXT command. If you want to position the text toward the center of the screen, you should include leading spaces on each line of text.

Because the TEXT command is not able to evaluate formulas or functions, you cannot use the FORMAT() function to customize the text that it displays.

The SETMARGIN Command

Normally, information displayed by ? commands, and all but the first line of information displayed by TEXT commands, appears flush left on the PAL canvas. (Of course, information displayed by ?? commands and the first line of information displayed by TEXT commands appear wherever the cursor is currently located.) However, you can use the SETMARGIN command to position information displayed by ? and TEXT commands in any column. The SETMARGIN command has the form

>SETMARGIN *number*

where *number* is the number of columns in the new margin on the screen. After you use this command to set the margin, PAL will indent all information in following ? and TEXT commands according to the new margin. For example, the commands

>SETMARGIN 5
>? "The margin is now set at five columns"

will set a margin of five columns for the PAL canvas, then display the string *The margin is now set at five columns* beginning at the sixth column of the next row on the screen.

The SETMARGIN OFF command deactivates any margin that has been set with a SETMARGIN command. For example, the script

> SETMARGIN 5
> ? "The margin is now set at five columns"
> SETMARGIN OFF
> ? "Now there is no margin again"

will display the same message in the same position as the example we just discussed. However, after displaying the message, this script will eliminate the margin and display the message *Now there is no margin again* flush left on the next line of the screen. Like the regular SETMARGIN command, the SETMARGIN OFF command affects only the information displayed by subsequent ? and TEXT commands. Information already displayed on the screen will remain in its original position after PAL evaluates a SETMARGIN OFF command.

The SLEEP Command

The information displayed by PAL's ?, ??, and TEXT commands disappears when PAL finishes playing the current script, when the screen is cleared, or when the information is overwritten by other information at the same location. In some cases, this means that PAL will erase the information almost as soon as it is written on the screen. You can prolong the duration of these messages on the screen, however, by using PAL's SLEEP command.

The SLEEP command allows you to pause the execution of a script for the period of time you specify. The form of this command is

> SLEEP *time in milliseconds*

where the *time in milliseconds* argument is a numeric expression with a value between 0 and 30000. Because the argument represents a number of milliseconds (1/1000 second), a value of 1000 will produce a one-second delay, a value of 15000 will produce a 15-second delay, and a value of 30000 will produce the maximum 30-second delay.

For example, suppose that you want the message *This message will last 5 seconds* to appear roughly in the middle of the screen for five seconds. To do this, you would use the script

> CLEAR
> @11,30
> ?? "This message will last for 5 seconds"
> SLEEP 5000

The CLEAR command erases the PAL canvas. The command *@11,30* moves the cursor toward the middle of the screen, where the ?? command displays the message *This message will last for 5 seconds.*

If the script ended at this point, PAL would erase this message as soon as it appeared. Because the *SLEEP 5000* command delays the end of the script for five seconds, however, this message remains for that period of time.

Hiding Changes to the PAL CANVAS

Normally, all material written by ?, ??, and TEXT commands appears on the PAL canvas immediately. However, there may be times when you want to delay displaying any of a series of changes to the PAL canvas until all the changes are complete. For example, if a script performs several time-consuming calculations between changes to the PAL canvas, the changes will appear one at a time over an extended period. In these instances, you can use the CANVAS OFF command to suppress all of the changes until the script has completed every one of them. After a script issues a CANVAS OFF command, PAL will hide any changes made to the PAL canvas until the script issues a CANVAS ON command. Then, PAL will display all the changes that the script has made to the PAL canvas.

For example, suppose you want to group the real estate properties listed in the LISTINGS table based on price ranges of $15,000, then display the number of houses in each group on the PAL canvas. Figure 16-3 shows a script that uses a FOR loop and a SCAN loop to count the number of houses with entries in the Price field that fall into each price range. The FOR loop uses a ? command to display the number of houses in each range on the next line of the PAL canvas. (We'll explain how FOR and SCAN loops work later in this chapter.) Because the script makes 15 trips through the FOR loop, it will display 15 different lines of text on the PAL canvas, pausing to perform the calculations for each pass through the loop before displaying each line. The script uses CANVAS OFF and CANVAS ON commands to hide the information until all 15 lines are ready to be displayed. Before beginning the FOR loop, the first CLEAR command in the script clears the PAL canvas. Then, the script displays the message *Now calculating...* on screen row 5, as shown in Figure 16-4. Next, the script issues a CANVAS OFF command, followed by another CLEAR command. After clearing the PAL canvas, the script displays *Breakdown of Listings According to Price* on row 5 before entering the FOR loop. Because PAL suppresses all changes to the PAL canvas after the CANVAS OFF command, neither the CLEAR command, nor the ? command that displays the heading affects the image on the screen. Also, the screen does not change while the FOR loop is displaying the number of houses in each price range. But when the FOR loop finishes, the CANVAS ON command displays the new PAL canvas, as shown in Figure 16-5. The SLEEP command at the end of the script leaves the PAL canvas on the screen for five seconds before returning to Paradox.

The MESSAGE Command

PAL's MESSAGE command provides another way to display information on the PAL canvas. Unlike the ?, ??, and TEXT commands, MESSAGE does not allow you to control where the information appears on the screen. Instead, the MESSAGE command always displays the information you specify in reverse video in the message area at the lower-right corner of the screen.

Figure 16-3 The CANVAS ON/OFF Command

```
Changing script C:\paradox3\canvas                            Script
....+...10....+...20....+...30....+...40....+...50....+...60....+...70....+...80
CLEAR
@ 5,10 ?? "Now calculating..."
CANVAS OFF
CLEAR
@ 5,15 ?? "Breakdown of Listings According to Price"
? " "
VIEW "Listings"
FOR z FROM 0 to 210000 STEP 15000
 counter = 0
 SCAN FOR [Price] > z AND [Price] < z + 14999
  counter = counter + 1
 ENDSCAN
 ? counter, " houses priced between $", z, " and $", z + 14999
ENDFOR
CANVAS ON
SLEEP 5000
```

Figure 16-4 The Original Screen

```
Now calculating...
```

Figure 16-5 The New Screen

```
            Breakdown of Listings According to Price

2 houses priced between $0 and $14999
12 houses priced between $15000 and $29999
7 houses priced between $30000 and $44999
10 houses priced between $45000 and $59999
9 houses priced between $60000 and $74999
7 houses priced between $75000 and $89999
5 houses priced between $90000 and $104999
1 houses priced between $105000 and $119999
0 houses priced between $120000 and $134999
1 houses priced between $135000 and $149999
0 houses priced between $150000 and $164999
0 houses priced between $165000 and $179999
0 houses priced between $180000 and $194999
1 houses priced between $195000 and $209999
0 houses priced between $210000 and $224999
```

Like ? and ??, the MESSAGE command can display literal values, the information stored in variables and fields of a table, or the results of formulas and functions. The form of the MESSAGE command is

MESSAGE *argument 1*, *argument 2*,..., *argument n*

Each argument (all but the first are optional) may be any valid PAL expression. When you use multiple arguments, PAL will display them side by side on the screen. PAL will not insert a space between the text from each argument unless you include a literal space in the string.

For example, suppose you want PAL to display the message *This is a test* in the message area, as shown in Figure 16-6 on the next page. To do this, you would use the command *MESSAGE "This is a test"*. If *x* contained the value 25, you could use the command *MESSAGE "The value of x is ",x* to display the message *The value of x is 25*, as shown in Figure 16-7.

Figure 16-6 A Simple Message

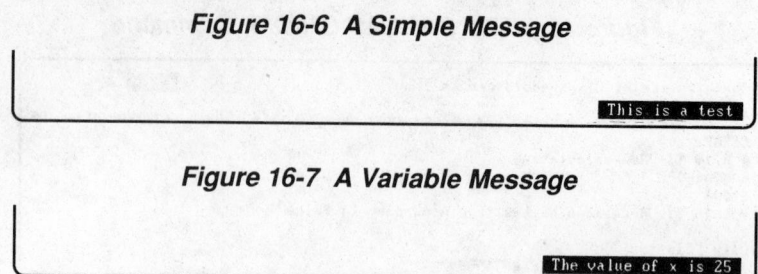

Figure 16-7 A Variable Message

As you can see, PAL makes the message area only large enough to accommodate the information it is displaying. PAL always begins the message area at the right edge of line 23 of the screen and expands it to the left as needed. In most cases, your messages will be less than 78 characters long—the maximum number that can fit on a single message line. However, PAL will accept messages of up to 255 characters. When a message exceeds 78 characters (so that it is too long to fit on one line), PAL expands the message area so that the whole message is displayed. Figure 16-8 shows how PAL displays a long message.

Figure 16-8 A Long Message

Because the MESSAGE command can display the results of functions, you can use the FORMAT() function to alter the appearance of information in the message area. For example, if the variable *x* contains the value 25, you could use the command

MESSAGE "The value of x is ",FORMAT("W6.2,E$",x)

to display the message *The value of x is $25.00*.

The QUIT and RETURN Commands

PAL provides two more commands to display information on the PAL canvas: the QUIT and RETURN commands. Although these commands do many other things, displaying information is one of their most important functions. The forms of these commands are

QUIT *expression*
RETURN *expression*

where the optional argument is a PAL expression of any type.

The QUIT command does two things. First, it terminates the execution of a script, returning you to Paradox. Second, it displays the expression, if there is one, in the lower-right corner of the screen. If the QUIT command is used, it must be on a line of its own within the script.

The QUIT command is useful in scripts that simply return the value of a variable or the result of an equation or function. For example, suppose you want to calculate the future value of investing $1,000 per year for the next 20 years at 9 percent interest. You could use the command *QUIT FV(1000,.09,20)*. Because the result of the QUIT command remains on the screen after the script has finished playing, no SLEEP command is necessary.

The effect of the RETURN command depends on the script that executes it. If the script was executed directly from Paradox, then the RETURN command is the same as QUIT—script play ends, and the expression, if any, is displayed at the bottom of the screen.

On the other hand, if the RETURN command is performed in a script or procedure that was invoked from another script or procedure, the RETURN command returns control to the calling script or procedure. In this case, the value of the expression, if any, is stored in the variable *retval* but not displayed on the screen.

The PROMPT Command

There is one more way to display messages. The PROMPT command may be used to display prompts or messages on the top two lines of the screen. However, these messages will appear only if you are using one of the ECHO commands (explained in Chapter 17), or the WAIT command (explained later in this chapter), and a Paradox menu is not being displayed.

The PROMPT command takes two arguments, both of which are alphanumeric strings. The first one will appear on the top line of the screen; the second will appear on the next line. This command has the form

        PROMPT *prompt 1,*
               prompt 2

where *prompt 1* is the first line of the prompt and *prompt 2* is the second line. In practice, you will seldom need the PROMPT command.

Styling the PAL Canvas

The STYLE and PAINTCANVAS commands provide two methods of controlling the style and color of the PAL canvas. The STYLE command lets you set the style for information printed by subsequent ?, ??, and TEXT commands, while the PAINTCANVAS command defines the style for an area or border of the area on the PAL canvas. The differences in the way the two commands work make each useful in different types of situations. The STYLE command is especially useful when you want to draw attention to individual lines of text, such as a message or a title on the screen. The PAINTCANVAS command is most useful when you want to highlight a large area of the screen or divide the screen into distinct areas.

The STYLE Command

The STYLE command allows you to change the style in which the results of the ?, ??, and TEXT commands are displayed. If you are using Paradox on a computer system with a monochrome monitor, you can use this command to display information in reverse video, intense video, blinking characters, or combinations of these three styles. If your system has a color monitor, however, you can command Paradox to display text in any of 256 background and foreground color combinations.

Because STYLE is a command, not a function, you can't use it as the argument of another command like ? or ??. Instead, you must include it in the script ahead of the command that displays the text you want to style. Once PAL reads a STYLE command, the style settings within that command remain in effect for the remainder of the script unless you subsequently include other STYLE commands that change or cancel those settings.

On a Monochrome Monitor

If you are using a monochrome monitor, you can use the STYLE command with three keywords—REVERSE, INTENSE, and BLINK—to format the messages you write to the screen with ?, ??, and TEXT commands. REVERSE causes the message to be written in reverse video. INTENSE causes the message to be written in high-intensity video. BLINK causes the message to be written in blinking characters.

For example, suppose you want PAL to display the text *This is plain video* in normal, unstyled text, starting at the intersection of row 2 and column 20 on the PAL canvas, and to display the text *This is reverse video* in reverse video two lines below it, the text *This is intense video* two lines below that, and the text *This is blinking video* two lines below that. To do this, you would use the script shown in Figure 16-9.

Figure 16-9 The STYLE Command

```
Changing script C:\paradox3\styles                              Script

....+...10....+...20....+...30....+...40....+...50....+...60....+...70....+...80
CLEAR
@2,20
?? "This is plain video."
STYLE REVERSE
@4,20
?? "This is reverse video."
STYLE INTENSE
@6,20
?? "This is intense video."
STYLE BLINK
@8,20
?? "This is blinking video."
SLEEP 10000
```

The CLEAR command that starts the script erases the PAL canvas. Then, the command *@2,20* positions the cursor at the intersection of row 2 and column 20, where PAL writes *This is plain video* without any embellishment. The command *STYLE REVERSE* that follows turns on the reverse attribute for all text that PAL subsequently writes to the canvas. The *@4,20* command positions the cursor at the intersection of row 4 and column 20. Then, the command *?? "This is reverse video"* writes *This is reverse video* on the screen. Because we turned on the reverse attribute prior to writing this text, PAL displays it in reverse video. Next, the command *@6,20* positions the cursor in row 6 and column 20.

The *STYLE INTENSE* command in the next line does two things: It cancels the previously assigned reverse attribute and it activates the intense attribute. All text that PAL writes to the screen after it reads this command will be intense, but will not be in reverse video. The ?? command writes the string *This is intense video* to the screen in intense video. Similarly, the command *STYLE BLINK* cancels the previously assigned intense attribute and activates the blink attribute. Then, the *@8,20* command positions the cursor, and the ?? command writes the string *This is blinking video* to the screen in blinking video. Figure 16-10 shows the result of this script on the screen. (Unfortunately, the blink and intense attributes cannot be represented in a figure.)

Figure 16-10 An Example of the STYLE Command

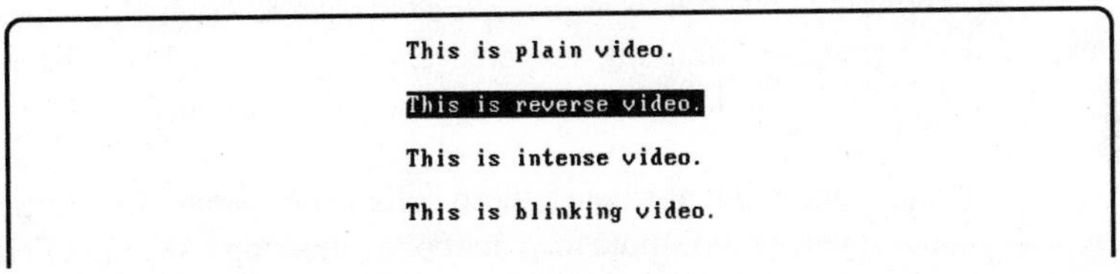

As you have seen, using a new STYLE command to select a different attribute cancels the current attribute. To cancel the current attribute and return to plain text, just use the STYLE command without an argument. For example, the script

```
STYLE
@10,20
?? "This is plain video again"
```

would turn off any active display attributes and display the line *This is plain video again* in plain video.

Although you commonly will use only one of these style attributes at a time, you can use them together to create combined effects. To do this, just follow the STYLE command with more than one keyword. For example, the command *STYLE REVERSE,BLINK* tells PAL to display reverse, blinking video. Similarly, the command *STYLE BLINK,INTENSE* instructs PAL to display bright, blinking text.

You can use the keywords REVERSE, INTENSE, and BLINK to control the display of text on a color monitor as well. On a color system, however, the characters and background colors will vary when you use the *STYLE REVERSE* command and the *STYLE INTENSE* command, depending on the default display colors.

On a Color Monitor

If you have a color monitor, PAL offers a wide variety of styles in addition to the ones available for a monochrome system. In fact, you can use any of 256 combinations of foreground and background colors. To access these styles, you must use the alternative form of the STYLE command shown below:

> STYLE ATTRIBUTE *color code*

The *color code* argument is a numeric expression between 0 and 255. The value of the expression determines what combination of background and foreground colors PAL uses. For example, the command *STYLE ATTRIBUTE 5* instructs PAL to write text in magenta characters on a black background; the command *STYLE ATTRIBUTE 73* tells PAL to display light blue characters on a red background; and the command *STYLE ATTRIBUTE 115* instructs PAL to display cyan characters on a light grey background.

Color codes from 128 to 255 use the same color combinations as their lower-level counterparts but also produce blinking text. For example, using the code 133 (which corresponds to the lower-level code 5) produces blinking magenta characters on a black background. Appendix A of the *PAL User's Guide* contains a list of the colors produced by these codes.

Unlike the reverse, intense, and blink attributes, these color codes cannot be combined in a single STYLE command. If you include more than one code following a *STYLE ATTRIBUTE* command, a script error will occur. Furthermore, you cannot use these color attributes in conjunction with the REVERSE, INTENSE, or BLINK keywords.

You can use color attributes on a monochrome monitor. Although this will not allow you to see colors, it gives you access to another display attribute: the underline. For example, the command *STYLE ATTRIBUTE 1* produces underlined text on a monochrome (nongraphics) monitor, and the command *STYLE ATTRIBUTE 9* produces high-intensity underlined text. See Appendix A in the *PAL User's Guide* for a listing of the effects of these codes on a monochrome monitor.

The PAINTCANVAS Command

When you use the PAINTCANVAS command to specify a style for a rectangular area or border on the screen, PAL uses that style for any text already displayed on the area, as well as for information placed on the area by following ?, ??, and TEXT commands. You can use the PAINTCANVAS command to apply the same styles and color combinations available with the STYLE command. The basic form for the PAINTCANVAS command is

> PAINTCANVAS
> *style/attribute*
> *row 1, column 1, row 2, column 2*

where *style/attribute* is the specified style or color attribute for the specified area, *row 1* and *column 1* are the screen coordinates of the upper-left corner of the area, and *row 2* and *column 2* are the screen coordinates of the lower-right corner of the specified area. The *style/attribute* argument can be any of the monochrome styles or color attributes we discussed while explaining the STYLE command. For example, the command

```
PAINTCANVAS
REVERSE
0,0,10,10
```

creates a reverse video box in the upper-left corner of the screen that includes the first 11 rows and the first 11 columns.

The PAINTCANVAS command also includes three optional keywords: BORDER, FILL, and BACKGROUND. By including these options, you can use the PAINTCANVAS command to draw borders on the PAL canvas. The BORDER option tells PAL to draw a border around the area specified in the PAINTCANVAS command rather than changing the style of the entire area. The FILL option defines the character that PAL should use to fill in the area specified in the command. If the PAINTCANVAS command includes the BORDER option, then the border will consist of the character defined by the FILL option. Without the BORDER option, the PAINTCANVAS command fills the entire defined area with the FILL character. The BACKGROUND option tells PAL to fill the area or border with the *string* value specified in the FILL option while leaving the style of the area or border intact. A PAINTCANVAS command that includes all of these options has the form

```
PAINTCANVAS BORDER
FILL string
style/attribute BACKGROUND
row 1, column 1, row 2, column 2
```

where *string* is a character or string of characters that make up the border.

Suppose you want to create two reverse video boxes on the screen, surrounding one box with a reverse video border of small boxes (ASCII character 254) and the other with an intense video border of the same character. Figure 16-11 shows a script that uses two PAINTCANVAS commands to create the boxes and two PAINTCANVAS commands to draw the borders. The first command in this script clears the PAL canvas. Next, the script moves the cursor to row 5 and column 10 before displaying the string *This text will appear in an intense border*. The first PAINTCANVAS command draws a reverse video box that has one corner at row 3 and column 0, and the diagonal corner at row 7 and column 57. The second PAINTCANVAS command draws a border of intense video squares around the reverse video box. Next, the script moves the cursor to row 15 and column 10 and displays the string *This text will appear in a reverse border*. The third PAINTCANVAS command in the script draws another reverse video box, this one with a corner at row 13 and column 0, and the diagonal corner at row 17 and column 57. The fourth PAINTCANVAS command draws a border of squares around the reverse video box. Because the BACKGROUND option tells PAL to leave the current style for this border intact, this border appears in the reverse video style that the script has already established for the box. The SLEEP command at the end of this script leaves the boxes on the screen for five seconds before the script concludes.

Figure 16-11 The PAINTCANVAS Command

```
Changing script C:\paradox3\paint                              Script
....+...10....+...20....+...30....+...40....+...50....+...60....+...70....+...80
CLEAR
@ 5,10 ?? "This text will appear in an intense border"
PAINTCANVAS
 REVERSE
 3,0,7,57
PAINTCANVAS BORDER
 FILL CHR(254)
 INTENSE
 3,0,7,57
@ 15,10 ?? "This text will appear in a reverse border"
PAINTCANVAS
 REVERSE
 13,0,17,57
PAINTCANVAS BORDER
 FILL CHR(254)
 BACKGROUND
 13,0,17,57
SLEEP 5000
```

Figure 16-12 shows the results of this script on the screen. Notice that PAL displays the border around the top box in intense video and the border around the bottom box in reverse video. Also, you can see that the text in both boxes appears in reverse video. PAL styles the text in the areas affected by the PAINTCANVAS command, regardless of whether the script displays the text before or after the PAINTCANVAS command.

Figure 16-12 An Example of the PAINTCANVAS Command

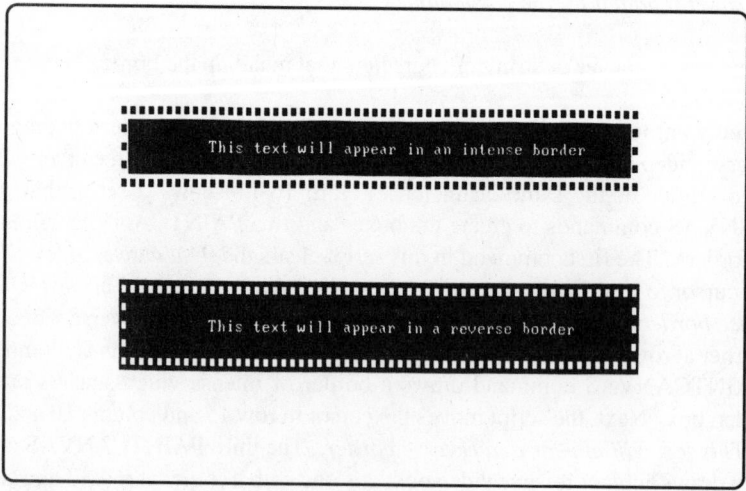

STYLE, PAINTCANVAS, and TEXT

Although we used the ? and ?? commands in our examples of STYLE and PAINTCANVAS, you can also use these commands to change the display attributes of the information presented by the TEXT command. Including a STYLE command in your script before the TEXT/ENDTEXT combination will set the style for all of the material displayed by the TEXT command. Alternatively, you can set a style for the information displayed by a TEXT command by using a PAINTCANVAS command to set the style for the region of the PAL canvas on which the information is displayed. You can also use the PAINTCANVAS command to style only part of the information displayed by a TEXT command. Of course, you can issue the PAINTCANVAS command before or after the TEXT command.

IF/THEN/ELSE

IF is PAL's most fundamental conditional testing command. This command instructs PAL to perform one of two actions, based on the result of the conditional test. Because this command is so common to PAL programming, we already have used it in several places within this and the past three chapters. So far, we have used only the basic form

        IF *conditional test* THEN
            true commands
        ENDIF

The first expression following the keyword IF must be a conditional test. As we explained in Chapter 14, a conditional test is an expression that returns one of two results: True or False. In many cases, a conditional test will consist of one expression that is compared to another expression by one of the following operators: =, >, <, >=, <=, or <>. In other cases, your conditional tests will be one of PAL's logical functions, like ISTABLE(), ATLAST(), or DRIVESTATUS(). You can even use the logical operators AND, OR, and NOT to combine different conditional tests or modify their results. (For more on conditional testing, see Chapter 14.)

The second part of any IF command must be the keyword THEN, followed by one or more commands. If the conditional test of the IF command is true, PAL will evaluate the commands that follow the keyword THEN. Once PAL has executed these commands, it will skip to the command that follows the keyword ENDIF and continue executing the script at that point. If the conditional test is false, however, PAL will not execute the THEN commands. Instead, it will exit from the IF statement and resume executing with the command that follows the keyword ENDIF.

The script shown in Figure 16-13 contains a simple use of the basic IF command. This script begins by clearing the PAL canvas, positioning the cursor at the intersection of row 10 and column 20, and displaying the prompt *Name of table to edit?* PAL then waits for you to type the name of a table, which it stores in the variable *x*. The IF command that follows tests to see whether the table you named exists. If the table does not exist, the conditional test *NOT ISTABLE(x)* will be true, and PAL will evaluate the commands that follow the keyword THEN. In this case, THEN is followed by the single command *PLAY "Maketabl"*, which calls a subroutine that lets you design the table you named. After PAL finishes with that subroutine, it returns to the command *EDIT x* that follows the ENDIF command and places that table in the Edit mode. If the table you named exists, PAL skips the subroutine and goes directly to the *EDIT x* command.

Figure 16-13 The IF Command

```
Changing script C:\paradox3\if                          Script

....+...10....+...20....+...30....+...40....+...50....+...60....+...70....+...80
CLEAR
@10,20
?? "Name of table to edit? "
ACCEPT "A8" TO x
IF NOT ISTABLE(x) THEN
 PLAY "Maketabl"
ENDIF
EDIT x
```

The ELSE Option

As you have seen, the regular form of the IF command instructs PAL to perform special actions only when the conditional test is true. It does not specify a set of commands that should be executed exclusively when the conditional test is false. However, the advanced form of the IF command allows you to do this. This advanced form is:

> IF *conditional test* THEN
> *true commands*
> ELSE
> *false commands*
> ENDIF

When PAL encounters this form of the IF command, it first evaluates the conditional test. If the conditional test is true, PAL performs the commands that follow the keyword THEN and skips to the command following the ENDIF. If the conditional test is false, PAL skips the THEN portion of the command, performs the commands that follow the keyword ELSE, and then skips to the next command in the script.

The script shown in Figure 16-14 demonstrates a basic use of this advanced form of the IF command. When PAL plays this script, it clears the screen, prompts you to type a number, and stores your response in the variable *x*. PAL then asks you to type another number and stores your response in the variable *y*. When PAL reads the IF command that follows, it first evaluates the conditional test *x>y*. If your first response is greater than your second response, this test will be true and PAL will evaluate the command that follows the keyword THEN. This MESSAGE command instructs PAL to display the message *x is greater than y* in the message area, substituting the stored values of *x* and *y* into the string. PAL then skips to the end of the IF command. Since *SLEEP 3000* is the only command that follows the keyword ENDIF, PAL displays the message for three seconds and then ends the script.

Figure 16-14 The IF Command (with ELSE Option)

```
Changing script C:\paradox3\if2                          Script

....+...10....+...20....+...30....+...40....+...50....+...60....+...70....+...80
CLEAR
@10,20
?? "Type any number: "
ACCEPT "N" TO x
@12,20
?? "Type another number: "
ACCEPT "N" TO y
IF x > y THEN
  MESSAGE x, " is greater than ", y
ELSE
  MESSAGE y, " is greater than ", x
ENDIF
SLEEP 3000
```

If your first response (*x*) is less than your second response (*y*), however, PAL follows a different course of action. Instead of evaluating the THEN portion of the IF command, PAL evaluates the command that follows the keyword ELSE. This MESSAGE command instructs PAL to display the message *y is greater than x*, again substituting the stored values of *x* and *y* into the string. PAL then proceeds to the next command (*SLEEP 3000*), waits three seconds, then returns you to the Paradox workspace.

WHILE Loops

The WHILE command instructs PAL to execute a set of commands repeatedly as long as a given condition is true. The form of this command is

> WHILE *conditional test*
>   *commands*
> ENDWHILE

The first argument of this command must be a conditional test. If the conditional test is true, PAL executes the sequence of commands that follow. These commands usually work with the objects on the Paradox workspace and alter the elements that are referred to by the conditional test. When PAL reaches the end of the command sequence, it returns to the beginning of the WHILE command and evaluates the conditional test again. As long as the conditional test is true, PAL continues with this cycle. If the conditional test becomes false, however, PAL immediately will exit from the WHILE loop, skip to the command that follows the keyword ENDWHILE, and resume the execution of the script at that point.

An Example

The script shown in Figure 16-15 shows a simple example of a WHILE loop. This script begins by bringing the 16-record EMPLYEE table to the screen and positioning the cursor in the Last Name field of the first record in that table. The WHILE loop then commands PAL to present each entry from the Last Name field in the message window for one second. The conditional test for this command, *NOT EOT()*, tests to see whether PAL has tried to move beyond the end of the table. Since the cursor begins on the first record of this table, the test is true on the first pass. As a result, PAL executes the commands *MESSAGE [ ]*, *SLEEP 1000*, and *SKIP 1*. The MESSAGE command displays the contents of the current field in the message window. The SLEEP command instructs PAL to keep the message there for one second. The SKIP command then instructs PAL to move the cursor down one row—in this case, to the Last Name field of the second record.

Figure 16-15 The WHILE Command

```
Changing script C:\paradox3\while                        Script

....+...10....+...20....+...30....+...40....+...50....+...60....+...70....+...80
VIEW "Emplyee"
Home
MOVETO [Last Name]
WHILE NOT EOT()
 MESSAGE []
 SLEEP 1000
 SKIP 1
ENDWHILE
MESSAGE "End of table"
SLEEP 3000
```

As soon as PAL finishes this first pass through the loop, it moves back to the top and re-evaluates the conditional test. Since the cursor is now in the second record of a 16-record table, the test *NOT EOT()* is still true. As a result, PAL displays the Last Name entry from the second record for one second, moves the cursor down one row, and jumps back to the top of the loop. PAL continues in this fashion, displaying the Last Name field entries from the third through 15th records. On the 16th pass through the loop, the cursor is positioned on the 16th (last) record in the table. After PAL displays the contents of the Last Name field of that record for one second, it again performs the *SKIP 1* command. Because the cursor is in the last record of the table, this command triggers an end-of-table condition. As PAL begins the 17th pass through the loop, then, the conditional test will be false. Consequently, PAL breaks from the loop and skips to the command that follows the ENDWHILE command. This MESSAGE command displays the message *End of table* in the message area.

The LOOP Command

In most cases, PAL will execute all the commands within a WHILE loop during each pass through that loop. If you want PAL to return to the top of the loop prematurely, you can use the LOOP command. When PAL encounters a LOOP command during the execution of a WHILE, SCAN, or FOR loop (we'll discuss SCAN and FOR later), it will return to the top of the loop without executing the commands that follow the LOOP command. If the conditional test is still true, PAL will make another pass through the loop.

The script shown in Figure 16-16 shows a simple use of the LOOP command. This script moves the cursor down the Quantity field of a table named ABC, replacing every blank entry with the numeric value 0. When it encounters a nonblank record, the command *IF NOT ISBLANK([])* is true. For this reason, PAL evaluates the commands *SKIP 1* and LOOP within the THEN statement. The *SKIP 1* command moves the cursor down one record. The LOOP command then returns PAL to the top of the loop, ready for another pass. Because PAL never reaches the *[]=0* command, it does not replace the entry in the current cell. PAL continues in this fashion until it reaches the end of the table, at which point it exits from the script.

Figure 16-16 The LOOP Command

```
Changing script C:\paradox3\loop                        Script

....+...10....+...20....+...30....+...40....+...50....+...60....+...70....+...80
EDIT "Abc"
Home
MOVETO [Quantity]
WHILE NOT EOT()
 IF NOT ISBLANK([]) THEN
  SKIP 1
  LOOP
 ENDIF
 [] = 0
 SKIP 1
ENDWHILE
MESSAGE "End of table"
SLEEP 3000
```

In most cases, there is a way to avoid the use of the LOOP command. In this example, for instance, you could replace the WHILE command with the one shown below:

```
WHILE NOT EOT()
    IF ISBLANK([]) THEN
       []=0
    ENDIF
    SKIP 1
ENDWHILE
```

Instead of testing for the negative condition *NOT ISBLANK([])*, the IF command within this loop tests for the positive condition *ISBLANK([])*. This allows you to use one SKIP command instead of two and eliminates the need for the LOOP command.

The QUITLOOP Command

PAL's QUITLOOP command provides an alternative way to exit from a loop. Unlike the LOOP command, which breaks only the current pass through the loop, the QUITLOOP command breaks the loop entirely. When PAL encounters a LOOP command, it returns to the top of the loop and attempts to make another pass through it. When PAL encounters a QUITLOOP command, however, it jumps to the command that follows the loop and continues executing the script there, just as if the conditional test were false.

For example, suppose you want PAL to step down through a table, one record at a time, stopping when it reaches a blank entry or the end of the table, whichever comes first. To do this, you would use the WHILE loop

```
WHILE NOT EOT()
   IF ISBLANK([]) THEN
    QUITLOOP
   ENDIF
   SKIP 1
ENDWHILE
```

The conditional test *NOT EOT()* will remain true until PAL tries to move beyond the bottom of the table. Each time PAL passes through this loop, it evaluates the conditional test defined in the command *IF ISBLANK([]) THEN QUITLOOP ENDIF*. As long as the current entry is not blank, PAL will continue to execute the loop. If PAL encounters a blank before it reaches the end of the table, however, the test *ISBLANK ([])* will be true. Consequently, PAL will evaluate the QUITLOOP command, which breaks the loop. Because no commands follow the WHILE command, PAL will end the script as well.

Infinite Loops

In some situations, you may want to create WHILE loops whose conditional tests are always true. PAL will continue to evaluate these loops until it encounters a QUITLOOP command. The easiest way to create this type of loop is to use the logical value True as the conditional test of the WHILE command. However, you also can use an unchanging true test like *1=1*, *2>1*, or *NOT FALSE*.

One common use of this technique is to lock the user within a custom menu. In most cases, after PAL has executed the commands related to a selection on a custom menu, it will continue executing the script at the command that follows the SHOWMENU command that generated the menu. If you want the same menu to reappear so that the user can make another choice, you must enclose the SHOWMENU command within a WHILE True loop. To enable the user to break from the loop, you'll want to include a selection that issues the QUITLOOP command. We'll explain this technique when we discuss SHOWMENU later in this chapter.

Another common use for WHILE True loops is to recycle a WAIT command that locks the user in the current field, record, or table. PAL exits WAIT commands after the user enters one of the keys specified in the command's UNTIL statement. If you want the script to issue certain commands based on the UNTIL key pressed by the user, then re-enter the WAIT command, you can nest the WAIT command in a WHILE True loop. We'll also demonstrate this technique later in this chapter.

FOR/ENDFOR Loops

In addition to WHILE, Paradox offers another looping command: FOR. Like the WHILE command, the FOR command instructs PAL to execute a series of commands repeatedly. The FOR command repeats the specified commands as long as the value of its built-in counter is not greater than a value you specify.

The form of the FOR command is

> FOR *counter* FROM *initial value* TO *final value* STEP *increment value*
>   *commands*
> ENDFOR

The first argument of this command, *counter*, is the name of the variable you want to use as the counter for the loop. The second argument, which must follow the keyword FROM, is a value expression that sets the initial value of the counter. The third argument, which must follow the keyword TO, specifies the value that the *counter* variable should not exceed. The fourth argument, which must follow the keyword STEP, tells PAL how much to increase (or decrease) the value of the *counter* variable after each pass through the FOR loop. PAL executes the next series of commands on each pass through the loop. The keyword ENDFOR signals the end of the loop.

The script shown in Figure 16-17 contains an example of a FOR/ENDFOR loop. This script presents the Last Name entries from the first ten records from the EMPLYEE table in the message window for one second each.

Figure 16-17 The FOR/ENDFOR Command

```
Changing script C:\paradox3\for                              Script
....+...10....+...20....+...30....+...40....+...50....+...60....+...70....+...80
VIEW "Emplyee"
Home
MOVETO [Last Name]
FOR counter FROM 1 TO 10 STEP 1
  MESSAGE [] SLEEP 1000 SKIP 1
ENDFOR
MESSAGE "End of script"
SLEEP 2000
```

The first three commands in this script bring the EMPLYEE table to the workspace and position the cursor on the Last Name field of the first record. The FOR loop that follows is responsible for displaying each of the first ten entries from that field in the message window. This loop begins by designating *counter* as the counter variable. The statement *FROM 1* assigns *counter* the initial value of 1. The *STEP 1* statement instructs PAL to add 1 to the value of *counter* after each pass through the loop. The *TO 10* statement tells PAL to stop when the value of *counter* exceeds 10.

On the first pass through the loop, counter will store the value 1. Since 1 is less than 10, PAL will execute the commands *MESSAGE []*, *SLEEP 1000*, and *SKIP 1*. These commands display the contents of the first record's Last Name field for one second, then move the cursor down one row in the table. At the end of this pass, PAL increases the value of *counter* by 1 and moves back to the top of the loop. Before the second pass, then, *counter* contains the value 2. Since 2 is less than 10, PAL makes another pass through the loop, displaying the contents of the second record's Last Name field. PAL continues in this fashion, displaying the Last Name field of the third through tenth records. During the tenth pass through the table, PAL will increase the value of *counter* to 11. Because 11 is greater than 10 (the TO value), PAL breaks from the loop and continues executing the script with the commands that follow the keyword ENDFOR. The commands *MESSAGE "End of script"* and *SLEEP 2000* instruct PAL to display the message for two seconds. Because these commands are the last ones in the script, PAL stops at this point and returns to the Paradox workspace.

Alternative Forms

Although most uses of the FOR command will include FROM, TO, and STEP statements, these terms actually are optional. If you do not include the keyword STEP and a STEP value, PAL will increment the counter by a value of 1 after each pass through the loop. In the previous example, we could have omitted the STEP statement without affecting the outcome of the script. If you do not include a FROM statement within the FOR command, you must assign an initial value to the *counter* variable from outside the loop. If this variable contains a value, PAL will use that value as the initial value of the *counter* variable. If the *counter* variable has not been assigned a value prior to the execution of a FOR command, and that FOR command does not contain a FROM statement, a script error will result.

If you omit the keyword TO and the TO value from a FOR command, PAL will continue to process the loop indefinitely. PAL's QUIT and QUITLOOP commands provide the only way to escape from such a loop. If PAL encounters a LOOP command during a pass through a FOR loop, it will break the loop but continue executing the script. If PAL encounters a QUIT command during the execution of a script, it will exit from the script entirely and return you to the Paradox workspace.

Scanning

In addition to WHILE and FOR, PAL offers one other looping command: SCAN. However, the applications for the SCAN command are much more limited than for the other two commands. Specifically, the SCAN command directs PAL to move down a field of a table one record at a time, starting at the top of the table, and to perform an action on each record. If you include an optional FOR keyword (not to be confused with the FOR command), PAL will act only upon records that meet the specified selection conditions. Although this action can be duplicated by the WHILE and FOR commands, you will find that the SCAN command provides the most convenient way to perform this type of loop.

The form of the SCAN command is

SCAN FOR *condition*
 commands
ENDSCAN

where *commands* represents the list of commands that PAL will execute for each pass through the loop, and *condition* specifies the optional selection conditions. Because PAL always begins a scan with the first record in a table, there is no need to position the cursor within the first record before the scan begins.

An Example

The script in Figure 16-18 shows an example of a SCAN loop. This script steps through the currently empty Number field of a table named XYZ, filling it with the sequential series of ascending values 1, 2, 3, and so on. This script begins by bringing XYZ to the workspace, entering the Edit mode, moving the cursor to the Number field of the first record, and assigning the value 1 to the variable *x*. Then, the SCAN loop takes control. PAL will execute the commands in this loop once for each record in the table. On the first pass, the command *[]=x* enters the value of *x* (1) into the Number field of the first record, and the command *x=x+1* increases the value of *x* to 2. When PAL completes the first pass, it moves the cursor down one row to the Number field of the second record and enters the value 2. PAL continues in this fashion until it has entered a value into the Number field of every record in the table.

Figure 16-18 The SCAN Command

```
Changing script C:\paradox3\scan                        Script
....+...10....+...20....+...30....+...40....+...50....+...60....+...70....+...80
EDIT "Xyz"
MOVETO [Number]
x = 1
SCAN
 [] = x
 x = x + 1
ENDSCAN
```

Another Example

Our first example of the SCAN command acted upon every record in the table. If your SCAN command contains a FOR keyword, however, PAL will act upon only the records that meet the specified selection conditions. Although PAL executes only the commands enclosed within the SCAN command for the selected records, it steps through every record in the table.

The script shown in Figure 16-19 demonstrates the use of a SCAN command that includes a FOR condition. This script steps through the Quantity field of a table named ABC, replacing every blank with the value 0. This script begins by bringing the ABC table to the

Paradox workspace in the Edit mode. The SCAN command that follows steps through the Quantity field, one record at a time. If the Quantity field of the current record is blank, PAL will execute the command *[Quantity]=0*, which enters the value 0 in the blank Quantity field. If the current record's Quantity field is not blank, PAL skips the *[Quantity]=0* command, moves to the next record, and tries again.

Figure 16-19 The SCAN/FOR Command

```
Changing script C:\paradox3\scan2                          Script

....+...10....+...20....+...30....+...40....+...50....+...60....+...70....+...80
EDIT "Abc"
SCAN FOR ISBLANK([Quantity])
  [Quantity] = 0
ENDSCAN
```

In this script, we have demonstrated another feature of the SCAN command—the cursor does not need to be in the field that you are acting upon or the field to which the selection conditions apply. In this case, PAL stepped through whatever field the cursor was in when the script began. Because the argument of the ISBLANK command refers to the Quantity field, however, PAL tests that field—not the one the cursor is in. Similarly, because the command *[Quantity]=0* refers to the Quantity field, PAL places the value 0 into that field—not the field in which the cursor is positioned.

Interacting with the User

The scripts we have presented so far manipulate the objects on the Paradox workspace and display information on the PAL canvas. As you become more experienced with PAL, however, you'll find situations in which you want the user to interact with the script. For example, you may want the user to supply a value, browse or edit a table, or make a selection from a custom menu. Six special PAL commands—ACCEPT, WAIT, SHOWMENU, SHOWARRAY, SHOWFILES, and SHOWTABLES—make this interaction possible.

The ACCEPT Command

The ACCEPT command instructs PAL to pause the execution of a script while you type information from the keyboard. As soon as you press ↵, PAL will store your input into a variable and continue with the script. The simplest form of this command is

        ACCEPT *type* TO *variable*

The *type* argument specifies the type of information PAL should accept. This argument may be any of the following strings: *Ax*, where *x* is a number from 1 to 255 that defines the length of the entry ACCEPT will accept; *N*; *$*; *S*; or *D*. Each type of string corresponds to one of Paradox's field types: *N* to numeric, *$* to dollar, and so on. The type that you specify limits the type of entry you can make in response to an ACCEPT statement, just as a field's type controls what you can enter into that field.

The *variable* argument, which must follow the keyword TO, must be a valid variable name. If the variable you specify has not been defined previously, PAL will create it automatically.

For example, suppose you want PAL to accept a number from the keyboard and return its square root. To do this, you could use the script shown in Figure 16-20.

Figure 16-20 The ACCEPT Command

```
Changing script C:\paradox3\accept                          Script
....+...10....+...20....+...30....+...40....+...50....+...60....+...70....+...80
CLEAR
@1,20
?? "Enter a number, please: "
ACCEPT "N" TO x
@3,20
?? "The square root of ",x," is ",SQRT(x)
SLEEP 5000
```

The first two commands in this script clear the PAL canvas and position the cursor at the intersection of row 1 and column 20. The third command displays the prompt *Enter a number, please:* at the current position of the cursor. The next command, *ACCEPT "N" TO x*, tells PAL to wait while you type a number from the keyboard. As you type an entry, the characters will appear at the current position of the cursor. Because you specified the numeric type, PAL will just beep if you attempt to type a letter. As soon as you press ↵, PAL will store your response in the variable *x* and continue with the macro. If you type 100 in response to this prompt, for example, PAL will store the numeric value 100 in *x*.

Finally, the command @3,20 moves the cursor to row 3, and the ?? command calculates the square root of the number you typed (in this case, the square root of 100, or 10) and displays the message *The square root of 100 is 10* in reverse video in the message area. Because this message will disappear as soon as PAL finishes playing the script, the SLEEP command is required to keep it visible (in this case, for five seconds).

Mandatory Input

Although the first argument of an ACCEPT command ensures that you can enter only information of the specified type, it does not require that you make an entry. If you press ↵ in response to an ACCEPT command without first typing an entry, PAL will store a blank value of the specified type in the destination variable.

Fortunately, there is a way to make sure that you make an entry in response to an ACCEPT command. If you include the keyword REQUIRED in the ACCEPT command between the *type* argument and the keyword TO, PAL will not let you press ↵ without making an entry.

For example, the command *ACCEPT "N" REQUIRED TO z* requires you to make a valid numeric entry. If you try to press ↵ in response to this command, PAL will display the message *Expecting a non-blank value* in the message area and wait for you to make a valid entry. PAL won't continue playing the script until you type a nonblank entry of the proper type.

Specifying a Default

Another optional argument of the ACCEPT command instructs PAL to present a default entry. When you specify a default, PAL will display it on the screen at the current position of the cursor. If you press ↵ while this default is visible, PAL will store that default in the specified variable. To override the default, press [Ctrl]-[Backspace] to erase it entirely and then type a new response. Alternatively, you can press the [Backspace] key to erase some characters, type more characters to add to the default, or combine the two methods.

For example, suppose that you want PAL to ask for a value but also present the value 2000 as a default. To do this, you could use the script

```
CLEAR
@10,20
?? "Amount to invest? "
ACCEPT "N"  DEFAULT 2000 TO z
```

The first three commands clear the canvas, position the cursor at the intersection of row 10 and column 20, and display the prompt *Amount to invest?* at that point. The *DEFAULT 2000* argument of the ACCEPT command then displays the characters *2000* to the right of that prompt. If you press ↵ at this point, PAL will store the value 2000 in the variable *z*. If you want to enter a different value, you should press [Ctrl]-[Backspace] to erase the default, then type the new entry.

Specifying Minimum and Maximum Values

Other optional arguments allow you to specify a minimum or maximum acceptable response to an ACCEPT command. To specify a minimum acceptable value, you must include the keyword MIN, followed by a value representing the minimum acceptable value, between the *type* argument and the keyword TO. Likewise, to specify a maximum acceptable response, use the keyword MAX, followed by a value representing the maximum acceptable value.

Suppose you want PAL to solicit a value between 0 and 4000 and store it in the variable *ira*. To do this, use the command *ACCEPT "N" MIN 0 MAX 4000 TO ira*. The *MIN 0* argument commands PAL to accept no response lower than 0, while the *MAX 4000* argument commands it to accept no value greater than 4000. If you typed the value 3500 in response to this command and pressed ↵, PAL would store that value in the variable *ira*. If you entered a value greater than 4000 or less than 0, however, PAL would display the message *Value between 0 and 4000 is expected* in the message area and would wait for you to modify your response.

Specifying a Picture

PAL also lets you specify a picture or pattern to which the response to an ACCEPT command must conform. To do this, you must include the keyword PICTURE (followed by the pattern to which the input must conform) between the *type* argument and the keyword TO.

The characters that you can use to specify the picture are the same as those you can use to specify a picture for entry of information into a field of a table. The # accepts any single digit, the ? accepts any letter, the @ accepts any character, the & accepts a letter and converts it to uppercase, and the ! accepts any character and converts letters to uppercase. A semicolon (;) tells PAL to interpret the next character literally and an asterisk (*) followed by a number tells PAL to repeat the next character. Characters enclosed in brackets ([]) are an optional part of the pattern, and characters enclosed in braces ({}) are grouped. Commas (,) are used to separate alternatives. Other characters appear literally in the string. (For a more complete discussion of pictures, see Chapter 3.)

For example, suppose that you want the user to enter a Social Security number in the form 404-74-1421 and have PAL store that entry in the variable *ss*. To do this, you would use the command *ACCEPT "A11" PICTURE "###-##-####" TO ss*. The argument A11 specifies an 11-character alphanumeric string. The argument *PICTURE "###-##-####"* tells PAL that the input must be in the form of three numbers, a hyphen, two numbers, another hyphen, then four more numbers. After you type the first three numbers, PAL will fill in the hyphen automatically, then wait for another two numbers. After you enter those numbers, PAL will insert another hyphen. As soon as you type four more numbers and press ↵, PAL will store the entry in the variable *ss*. If you press ↵ before completing the entry, or if you type any character other than a number, PAL will beep.

Using a Lookup Table

The final optional argument for the ACCEPT command allows you to use a lookup table to check the validity of an entry. To use this feature, you must include the keyword LOOKUP, followed by the name of a table between the *type* argument and the keyword TO. The first column of the table that you specify must contain the list of acceptable entries.

Suppose you want to use the ACCEPT command to solicit a valid state abbreviation from the user. To do this, you would create the table named STATES, shown in Figure 16-21, then use the command *ACCEPT "A2" LOOKUP "STATES" TO state*. When PAL evaluates this command, it will pause and wait for a two-letter response. As soon as you press ↵, PAL will check the response against the entries in the first column of the STATES table. If PAL finds an exact match for the entry within that table, it will store the entry in the variable *state*. If PAL cannot find a match, it will display the message *Not one of the possible values for this field* in the message area and wait for you to modify your response.

Figure 16-21 The STATES Table

```
Viewing States table: Record 1 of 51                      Main

STATES─┬State Abbreviation─┬───────────State Name────
     1 ┃    AL              ┃Alabama
     2 ┃    AK              ┃Alaska
     3 ┃    AZ              ┃Arizona
     4 ┃    AR              ┃Arkansas
     5 ┃    CA              ┃California
     6 ┃    CO              ┃Colorado
     7 ┃    CT              ┃Connecticut
     8 ┃    DE              ┃Delaware
     9 ┃    DC              ┃District of Columbia
    10 ┃    FL              ┃Florida
    11 ┃    GA              ┃Georgia
    12 ┃    HI              ┃Hawaii
    13 ┃    ID              ┃Idaho
    14 ┃    IL              ┃Illinois
    15 ┃    IN              ┃Indiana
    16 ┃    IA              ┃Iowa
    17 ┃    KA              ┃Kansas
    18 ┃    KY              ┃Kentucky
    19 ┃    LA              ┃Louisiana
    20 ┃    ME              ┃Maine
    21 ┃    MD              ┃Maryland
    22 ┃    MA              ┃Massachusetts
```

Using More Than One Argument

As we have seen, the ACCEPT command has six optional arguments: REQUIRED, DEFAULT, MIN, MAX, PICTURE, and LOOKUP. You may use any or all of these arguments in any combination and in any order. Here is an example of an ACCEPT command that uses all six:

> ACCEPT "A2" REQUIRED DEFAULT "CO"
> MIN "CA" MAX "CZ"
> PICTURE "!!" LOOKUP "STATES" TO *state*

This command asks the user for a two-letter state name abbreviation and stores the result in the variable *state*. User input is required and the default response is *CO*. Only states beginning with the letter *C* will be accepted. The *PICTURE "!!"* argument forces the user to enter exactly two characters and converts lowercase letters to uppercase. Finally, Paradox confirms the entry in the STATES table.

The [Esc] key and the Retval Variable

There is one more thing you need to know about the ACCEPT command: The user can press the [Esc] key in response to an ACCEPT command without making an entry. If that happens, the script will continue, but nothing will have been entered into the variable that was created to hold the user's response. This will almost certainly cause problems later in the script.

The significance of the ACCEPT command's response to the [Esc] key may not be immediately apparent, but it is a very valuable feature. It allows the user to press the [Esc] key to escape from an ACCEPT prompt, the same way [Esc] can be pressed in response to a Paradox prompt—for example, to escape from the *Table:* prompt during the [Menu] View command. This makes your PAL scripts consistent with the operation of Paradox.

Furthermore, this feature allows the user to press [Esc] even if the REQUIRED argument is used to force mandatory input. This gives the user a "way out" in case he or she doesn't know a valid response.

As the PAL script writer, you must be aware that the user may press [Esc] in response to an ACCEPT command, and you must design your script to anticipate that possibility. In most cases, this means following every ACCEPT command with an IF command that tests the value of a special system variable named *retval*. Whenever an ACCEPT command is executed, PAL sets the value of *retval* to either True or False. If the user enters a value in response to the ACCEPT command and presses ↵, then PAL sets *retval* to True. On the other hand, if the user presses the [Esc] key, PAL sets *retval* to False.

Typically, the user presses [Esc] in an effort to end the current operation. You can use an IF command to cancel the operation in response to the [Esc] key. For example, you could extend the script shown in Figure 16-20 to include the following IF command after the ACCEPT command, but before the ?? command:

```
IF NOT retval THEN
  QUIT "The user pressed [Esc] to cancel"
ENDIF
```

Now, if the user presses [Esc] instead of a value, the script will stop and the message *The user pressed [Esc] to cancel* will appear in the lower-right corner of the screen. The part of the script that would have displayed the square root of the value entered will not be executed.

The ACCEPT command is not the only place that PAL uses the *retval* variable. Quite a few commands assign a value to this variable. In fact, *retval* plays an important role in the WAIT command, which we will describe next.

The WAIT Command

In most cases, the PAL canvas obscures the Paradox workspace for the entire execution of a script. When the script is finished playing, PAL lifts the canvas to reveal the altered Paradox workspace. However, there will be many cases in which you'll want to pause during the execution of a script and permit the user to interact with an image on the Paradox workspace. PAL's WAIT command makes this possible.

The WAIT command allows you to view, edit, or perform data entry on a table, form, or query during the execution of a script. When PAL encounters a WAIT command in a script, it lifts the PAL canvas and pauses the execution of the script. Depending on the form of the WAIT command you use and whether Paradox is in the Edit or DataEntry mode, you will be able to move around in the current image, edit its entries, or make new entries.

The simplest form of the WAIT command is

> WAIT *scope*
> UNTIL *keys*

The *scope* argument must be one of three keywords: TABLE, RECORD, or FIELD. These keywords specify the user's ability to move the cursor within the current image. The WAIT TABLE command allows the user to move the cursor to any field of any record in the image. If the user presses any cursor-movement key from within a WAIT TABLE command, PAL will move the cursor just as if the user weren't within a script. The WAIT RECORD command restricts movement to the record in which the cursor was positioned when PAL lifted the canvas. If the user tries to press ↑, ↓, [Pg Up], [Pg Dn], and so forth, from within a WAIT RECORD command, PAL will beep. The WAIT FIELD command does not allow the user to move the cursor from its current location—a single field of a single record. Pressing any cursor-movement key in this situation produces a beep.

The second required part of the WAIT command is the keyword UNTIL followed by the representation of one or more keys. These key representations identify the key or keys you want to use to tell PAL to stop waiting and resume playing the script. When the user presses the specified key, PAL exits from the WAIT command, drops the PAL canvas, and continues with the execution of the script. These key representations can be in any of the following forms: an ASCII or extended IBM code (like 56 or -42), a single character as a string (like *a* or *A*), a string that names a special function key (like *F2*), or the name that Paradox assigns to a key (like *Menu* or *CtrlBackspace*).

For example, the commands *WAIT TABLE UNTIL "F2"*, *WAIT TABLE UNTIL "Do_It!"*, and *WAIT TABLE UNTIL -60* all allow you to move around an entire table until you press the [Do-It!] key ([F2]).

If you specify two or more key representations, you must separate them with commas. In addition, the cursor must be in a table, form, or query when you use the WAIT command. Otherwise, when PAL reads a WAIT command, a script error will result.

Importantly, uppercase and lowercase letters are not equivalent when you specify a single character as the UNTIL argument. For example, to end the command

> WAIT RECORD
> UNTIL "A"

you must hold down the [Shift] key and press *A*. Typing a lowercase *a* (pressing *A* without holding down the [Shift] key) will not return you to the script. If you want to use either an uppercase or lowercase *A* to return you to the script, you must use the command

> WAIT RECORD
> UNTIL "A","a"

Viewing or Editing?

What you can do to the current image while the WAIT command is in effect depends on which mode Paradox is in before PAL executes the WAIT command. If Paradox is in Edit mode before PAL reads the WAIT command, the user will be able to make or edit entries in the image on the workspace. For example, the script

```
EDIT "Emplyee"
MOVETO RECORD 5
WAIT RECORD
    UNTIL "F2"
```

allows the user to edit any entry within the fifth record of the EMPLYEE table. This is because Paradox is in the Edit mode. (The Coedit mode, invoked with the [Menu] Modify Coedit command or the [Coedit] key, is similar.) When the user presses [F2], the script will resume.

If Paradox is in the DataEntry mode when the WAIT command is issued, the user will be able to enter new records into a table. For example, the script

```
Menu {Modify} {DataEntry} {Emplyee}
WAIT TABLE
    UNTIL "F2"
Do_It!
```

allows the user to enter new records into the EMPLYEE table. When the user presses [F2], PAL will resume the script. The Do_It! command will store the records in the EMPLYEE table. Notice that we've used the *WAIT TABLE* form of the command here. This allows the user to enter any number of records.

Note, also, that we've included a Do_It! command after the WAIT command. This Do_It! is what ends the data entry session and adds the new records to the EMPLYEE table. When the user presses [F2], the key has no effect on the tables—it merely ends the WAIT.

If Paradox is not in the Edit or DataEntry modes when PAL encounters a WAIT command, the user will be able to move the cursor within the restricted range imposed by the command but will not be able to edit any of the entries in that range. For example, although the script

```
VIEW "Emplyee"
WAIT TABLE
    UNTIL "F2"
```

allows the user to move the cursor around the entire EMPLYEE table, it will not allow the user to edit any of the entries within the table.

Importantly, the user cannot enter the Edit or DataEntry modes once PAL executes the WAIT command. During the pause created by a WAIT command, PAL will lock out all special function keys. For this reason, the user cannot use either the [Edit] key ([F9]) or the [Menu] Modify Edit command to enter the Edit mode. If you want the user to be able to edit the information in an image, and not just view it, then you must make sure that Paradox is in the Edit mode before it executes the WAIT command.

Messages and Prompts

Two optional keywords, MESSAGE and PROMPT, let you display instructions on the screen during the pause created by a WAIT command. In most cases, you'll want to use at least one of these keywords to tell the user which key(s) can be used to resume playing the script.

MESSAGE

The most basic (although not most useful) of these keywords is MESSAGE. The MESSAGE keyword is always followed by an expression that defines the message you want PAL to display. When PAL reads a WAIT command that contains the optional MESSAGE keyword, it displays the value of the expression that follows the keyword MESSAGE in reverse video in the message area.

For example, the script

```
EDIT "Emplyee"
End Down
WAIT RECORD
    MESSAGE "Add a new record, then press Do-It!"
    UNTIL "F2"
```

will produce the screen shown in Figure 16-22. As you can see, the cursor is positioned in a new record at the bottom of the table, and PAL is displaying the message *Add a new record, then press Do-It!* in the message area. This message instructs the user to add a new record (the keyword RECORD restricts the user to the current record, of course) and to press the [Do-It!] key to resume execution of the script.

As you learned earlier, any information that appears in the message area will disappear as soon as the user presses a key. In this case, PAL will erase this message as soon as the user presses the → key to move to the Last Name field. Because the message does not remain on the screen during the entire editing session, the user might not remember which key to press to resume execution of the script.

PROMPT

Fortunately, the other optional argument of the WAIT command allows you to create more permanent messages. The form of this keyword is

```
PROMPT message 1,
        message 2
```

The keyword PROMPT may be followed by one or two arguments, each of which may produce a message of up to 80 characters. When PAL executes the WAIT command, it will display the first message across the top line of the screen, starting at the left edge of the screen. If there is a second message, it will appear on the second line of the screen, also flush left. Unlike the information in the message area, these prompts will remain on the screen for the duration of the WAIT command.

Figure 16-22 The MESSAGE Keyword

```
EMPLOYEE┬─Emp Number──┬──Last Name──┬─First Name──┬──────Address────┬──────
      1 │         1   │ Jones       │ David       │ 4000 St. James Ct.  │ St
      2 │         2   │ Cameron     │ Herb        │ 2321 Elm St.        │ Lo
      3 │         4   │ Jones       │ Stewart     │ 4389 Oakbridge Rd.  │ Ly
      4 │         5   │ Roberts     │ Darlene     │ 451 Lone Pine Dr.   │ La
      5 │         6   │ Jones       │ Jean        │ 4000 St. James Ct.  │ St
      6 │         8   │ Williams    │ Brenda      │ 100 Owl Creek Rd.   │ An
      7 │         9   │ Myers       │ Julie       │ 4512 Parkside Dr.   │ Lo
      8 │        10   │ Link        │ Julie       │ 3215 Palm Ct.       │ Pa
      9 │        12   │ Jackson     │ Mary        │ 7821 Clark Ave.     │ Cl
     10 │        13   │ Jakes, Jr.  │ Sal         │ 3451 Michigan Ave.  │ Da
     11 │        14   │ Preston     │ Molly       │ 321 Indian Hills Rd.│ Lo
     12 │        15   │ Masters     │ Ron         │ 423 W. 72nd St.     │ Ne
     13 │        16   │ Robertson   │ Kevin       │ 431 Bardstown Rd.   │ El
     14 │        17   │ Garrison    │ Robert      │ 55 Wheeler St.      │ Bo
     15 │        19   │ Gunn        │ Barbara     │ 541 Kentucky St.    │ Ne
     16 │        20   │ Emerson     │ Cheryl      │ 8100 River Rd.      │ Pr
     17 │          ◄  │             │             │                     │

                              ┌────────────────────────────────────────┐
                              │ Add a new record, then press Do-It!     │
                              └────────────────────────────────────────┘
```

For example, when PAL plays the script

```
EDIT "Emplyee"
End Down
WAIT RECORD
    PROMPT "Adding record number"+STRVAL(RECNO())+" to Emplyee table",
        "Press [Do-It!] when finished"
UNTIL "F2"
```

your screen will look like Figure 16-23. As you can see, the prompt *Adding record number 16 to Emplyee table* appears at the top of the screen, and the prompt *Press [Do-It!] when finished* appears just below it. This PROMPT argument uses the RECNO() function to include the number of the current record in the prompt. You can use several other PAL functions, such as TABLE(), NRECORDS(), and NIMAGERECORDS(), to add information about the current table and record to prompts displayed by WAIT commands. Note that we used the STRVAL() function to convert the numeric value returned by RECNO() into a string. Because the entire prompt must be a string, you must convert any function that returns a numeric value into a string before displaying it in a prompt.

Figure 16-23 The PROMPT Keyword

```
Adding record number 16 to Emplyee table
Press [Do-It!] when finished
EMPLYEE┬─Emp Number────┬─Last name──┬─First Name──┬─SS Number───┬────────Addre
     1 ‖      1        │ Jones      │ David       │ 414-76-3421 │ 4000 St. Ja
     2 ‖      2        │ Cameron    │ Herb        │ 321-65-8765 │ 2331 Elm St
     3 ‖      3        │ Jones      │ Stewart     │ 401-32-8721 │ 4309 Oakbri
     4 ‖      4        │ Roberts    │ Darlene     │ 417-43-7777 │ 451 Lone Pi
     5 ‖      5        │ Jones      │ Jean        │ 414-07-9123 │ 4000 St. Ja
     6 ‖      6        │ Williams   │ Brenda      │ 401-55-1567 │ 100 Owl Cre
     7 ‖      8        │ Link       │ Julie       │ 345-75-1525 │ 3215 Palm C
     8 ‖      9        │ Jackson    │ Mary        │ 424-13-7621 │ 7021 Clark
     9 ‖     10        │ Jakes, Jr. │ Sal         │ 321-65-9151 │ 3451 Michig
    10 ‖     11        │ Preston    │ Molly       │ 451-00-3426 │ 321 Indian
    11 ‖     12        │ Masters    │ Ron         │ 317-65-4529 │ 423 W. 72nd
    12 ‖     13        │ Robertson  │ Kevin       │ 415-24-6718 │ 431 Bardsto
    13 ‖     14        │ Garrison   │ Robert      │ 312-90-1479 │ 55 Wheeler
    14 ‖     15        │ Gunn       │ Barbara     │ 321-97-8632 │ 541 Kentuck
    15 ‖     16        │ Emerson    │ Cheryl      │ 404-14-1422 │ 8100 River
    16 ‖    ◄          │            │             │             │
```

Multiple UNTIL Keys

Earlier in this section, we showed you how to use more than one key to end the execution of a WAIT command. What we didn't show you is how to make PAL do different things depending on which key you press. When you press the key designated in the WAIT command, of course, PAL drops the PAL canvas and continues executing the script. PAL also saves the representation of the key you pressed within a temporary variable named *retval*, exactly as it appears in the WAIT command. For example, if you press [Do-It!] to end the command

        WAIT TABLE
          UNTIL "F2"

PAL will store the string *F2* in the variable *retval*. If you press the [Do-It!] key to end the command *WAIT TABLE UNTIL "Do_It!"*, PAL will store the string *Do_It!* in *retval*.

Using an IF/THEN/ELSE Command

By using the *retval* variable within an IF statement, you can make PAL take different actions, depending on which key the user pressed to end the WAIT command. For example, suppose you want to modify the record-entry script shown on the preceding page so that either the [Do-It!] or [Esc] keys will end the WAIT. If the user presses [Do-It!], then you want PAL to save the changes he or she has made. If the user presses [Esc], however, you want PAL to end the edit without saving the changes, then end the script.

To achieve this effect, you would use the script shown in Figure 16-24. As you can see, the UNTIL argument of the WAIT command lists two keys: [F2] and [Esc]. When the user presses either of those keys, PAL exits from the WAIT command and stores the keystroke in the variable *retval*. The IF/THEN/ELSE command directs PAL in one of two ways, depending on what is stored in *retval*. If *retval* contains the string *Esc*, PAL will issue the CANCELEDIT command, and then quit from the script. If *retval* contains the string *F2*, however, PAL will press the [Do-It!] key, thus saving the changes.

Figure 16-24 A WAIT Script

```
Changing script C:\paradox3\wait                          Script Ins
....+...10....+...20....+...30....+...40....+...50....+...60....+...70....+...80
EDIT "Emplyee"
FormKey
End PgDn
WAIT RECORD
  PROMPT "Add a new record to the table",
         "Press Do-It! when you are finished" UNTIL "F2","Esc"
  IF retval = "Esc" THEN
   CANCELEDIT
   QUIT
  ELSE
   Do_It!
ENDIF
```

Using a SWITCH Command

If you want to use more than two UNTIL keys, even an IF/THEN/ELSE command won't be enough to test *retval* for all the possible keys. In these cases, the SWITCH command lets you test for every possible key and specify commands that the script should execute for each key.

The simplest form for a SWITCH command that checks the value of *retval* is

> SWITCH
>   CASE *condition 1:*
>   *commands 1*
>   CASE *condition 2:*
>   *commands 2*
>
>   ...
>   CASE *condition n:*
>   *commands n*
> ENDSWITCH

where each condition checks *retval* for a different UNTIL key, and each set of commands tells PAL what to do if the corresponding UNTIL key was pressed. For example, *condition 1* might be *retval = "Do_It!"*, and *commands 1* might be the single command Do_It!. When PAL processes a SWITCH set, it evaluates the conditional tests in the order in which they are listed until it finds a condition that is true. When that happens, PAL will issue the commands that correspond to that condition, then exit from the SWITCH set without testing the remaining conditions.

Typically, you might nest a SWITCH command with a WAIT command in an infinite loop created by a WHILE command. As we explained earlier in this chapter, a condition of True makes a WHILE command repeat indefinitely. Placing a WAIT command and a SWITCH command inside an infinite WHILE loop gives a script the ability to interrupt the WAIT command, process a set of commands associated with an UNTIL key, then resume the WAIT command on the next pass through the WHILE loop.

Suppose you want to let the user edit the EMPLYEE table with the abilities to save the edited table, end the Edit session without saving changes, or undo the changes to the last record edited. Because the WAIT command disables all function keys, the user cannot use the [Menu] Undo command or the [Ctrl]-[U] key to undo changes. By defining [Ctrl]-[U] as an UNTIL key, you can return this ability to the user. Figure 16-25 shows a script that includes a WAIT command with three UNTIL keys: [Do-It!], [Esc], and [Ctrl]-[U] (ASCII code 21). Because the WHILE command in this script has a condition of True, the WHILE loop will repeat indefinitely. On each pass through the loop, the SWITCH set checks to see which of the three UNTIL keys ended the WAIT TABLE command. If the user presses [Do-It!] to end the WAIT TABLE command, the script will issue the Do_It! command to save the edited table, then exit the WHILE loop. If the user presses [Esc], the script will issue the CANCELEDIT command to end the Edit session, then exit the loop. If the user presses [Ctrl]-[U], the script will undo the changes made to the last record edited, loop back to the beginning of the WHILE loop, then enter the WAIT TABLE command again.

Figure 16-25 An Infinite loop with WAIT and SWITCH

```
Changing script C:\paradox3\retswich                          Script
....+...10....+...20....+...30....+...40....+...50....+...60....+...70....+...80
EDIT "Emplyee"
WHILE True
  WAIT TABLE
    PROMPT "Editing Emplyee table",
           "Press [Do-It!] to save, [Esc] to cancel, [Ctrl]-[U] to undo last"
    UNTIL "Do_It!", "Esc", 21
  SWITCH
    CASE retval = "Do_It!":
      Do_It!
      QUITLOOP
    CASE retval = "Esc":
      CANCELEDIT
      QUITLOOP
    CASE retval = 21:
      Undo
  ENDSWITCH
ENDWHILE
```

Of course, you could also nest a WAIT command and an IF\THEN\ELSE command that evaluated *retval* within a WHILE loop. In this command arrangement, either the set of commands following the THEN keyword or the commands following the ELSE keyword would loop back to the WHILE command.

Using WAIT in a Form

In the examples presented so far, we've used the WAIT command to view and/or edit the table image of a Paradox table. In many cases, however, you'll find it more useful to use the WAIT command to interact with the form image of a table, for the following reason: When you use the WAIT command to view or edit a table image, you will be able to see up to 22 records at a time, even if you have restricted the movement of the cursor to only a single record or field with the WAIT RECORD or WAIT FIELD commands. If the table is in the form view, however, you will be able to see only a single record at a time. If you've used the WAIT

TABLE command, you'll be able to press the [Pg Up] and [Pg Dn] keys to view other records through the form. If you've used the WAIT RECORD or WAIT FIELD commands, however, you will not be able to see any record other than the one you want to view or edit.

Allowing user interaction through a form is usually a three-step process. First, use the VIEW or EDIT command to bring a table to the Paradox workspace. Second, use the FORMKEY or PICKFORM command to view that table as a form. (Because PAL disables the function keys during the execution of a WAIT command, the only way to use WAIT in a form is to enter the form view of the table before PAL reads the WAIT command.) Third, if you plan to restrict movement to a single record or to a single field of that record, you'll want to move the cursor to that record or to the appropriate field within that record. Having done these three things, you are ready for PAL to execute the WAIT command. For example, the script

```
EDIT "Emplyee"
FormKey End PgDn
WAIT RECORD
    PROMPT "Add a new record to the table",
           "Press Do-It! when you are finished"
    UNTIL "F2"
```

will present the screen shown in Figure 16-26 and restrict you to adding a single record.

Figure 16-26 Using WAIT in a Form

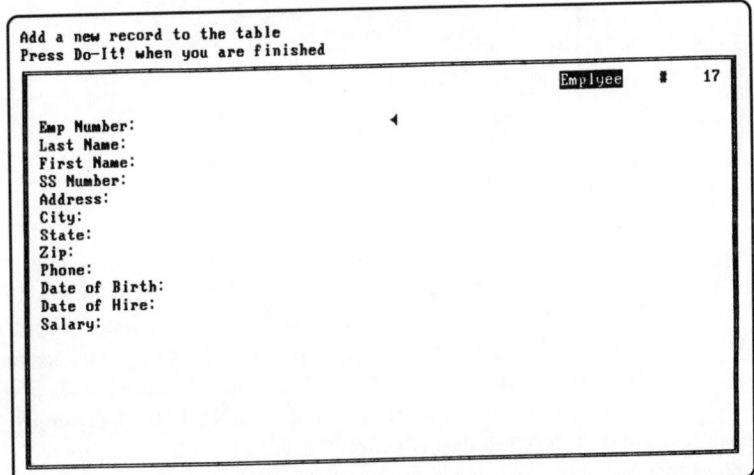

Using WAIT in a Multitable Form

Using a WAIT command with a multitable form is more complicated than using WAIT with a single-table form, because your script must move the user among the multiple images on the form. All three types of WAIT commands (WAIT TABLE, WAIT RECORD, and WAIT FIELD) hold the cursor in the current image, even if that image is one of many on the same form. To let the user move among the images on a form, you must include at least one UNTIL key that ends the current WAIT command, moves the cursor to another image, then begins a new WAIT command in that image.

The WHILE command provides a convenient means of recycling the same WAIT command for use with all the images on a multitable form. Placing the WAIT command inside a WHILE loop causes a script to repeat the WAIT command over and over, and lets you move the cursor among images between loops. Suppose you wanted to use the form shown in Figure 16-27 to edit the CLIENTS table and the SALESORD table. This form is actually a member of the CLIENTS family, but includes an embedded form for SALESORD. Figure 16-28 shows a WAIT TABLE script that would let you edit with this form.

Figure 16-27 A Multitable Form

```
Editing Clients
Press [F3] to move to among tables, [F2] to save, [Esc] to abort
┌────────────────────────────────────────────────────────┐
│                    Software Sales                        │
│         ┌──────────────────────────────────────┐         │
│         │          Client Information           │         │
│         │ Client Number:            1001      ◄ │         │
│         │ Last Name: Smith                      │         │
│         │ First Name: John                      │         │
│         │ Soc. Sec. Number: 345-43-2232         │         │
│         │ Address: 2378 Maple Wood Dr.          │         │
│         │ City: Louisville                      │         │
│         │ State: KY  Zip: 40216                 │         │
│         │ Phone: (502) 448-8989                 │         │
│         └──────────────────────────────────────┘         │
│         ┌──────────────────────────────────────┐         │
│         │          Order Information            │         │
│         │ Date:  2/01/88                        │         │
│         │ Product Number: 1                     │         │
│         │ Product: Paradox 3.0                  │         │
│         │ Price:           399.99               │         │
│         │ Quantity:           1                 │         │
│         │ Sales Person:        1                │         │
│         └──────────────────────────────────────┘         │
└────────────────────────────────────────────────────────┘
```

First, this script places the CLIENTS table on the workspace in Edit mode. Next, the script uses the PICKFORM command to place the CLIENTS table in the form view with form 1, which is the multitable form shown in Figure 16-27. The WHILE loop in this script includes a WAIT TABLE command and a SWITCH command to evaluate the key that ends the WAIT TABLE command. As we explained, a True condition in a WHILE command results in a loop that repeats indefinitely, or until a command such as QUITLOOP or QUIT explicitly ends the loop. On each trip through the loop in this script, the WAIT TABLE command locks the cursor in the current table until the user presses [Esc], [Do-It!], or [F3]. The PROMPT option of the WAIT TABLE command displays a two-line prompt, with the name of the table in the current image on the first line. For example, on the first pass through the loop, when the cursor is in the CLIENTS table, the first line of the prompt will say *Editing Clients*. The second line of the prompt always says *Press [F3] to move among tables, [F2] to save, [Esc] to abort.*

After the user presses one of the three UNTIL keys, the SWITCH command evaluates the UNTIL key that ended the WAIT TABLE command. If the user presses [Esc] to end the WAIT TABLE command, the script will end the Edit session without saving any changes, then quit the WHILE loop. If the user presses [Do-It!], the script will save changes made to both tables on the form, then quit the WHILE loop. If the user presses [F3], the script will issue an UpImage command, moving the cursor from the current image to the other image on the form. For example, if the cursor is in the CLIENTS table, pressing [F3] will move the cursor to the SALESORD table. Then, the script will loop back to the WHILE command and issue the WAIT TABLE command for the SALESORD table. On this trip through the WHILE loop, the WAIT TABLE command will display the prompt *Editing SALESORD* at the top of the screen.

Figure 16-28 A WAIT TABLE Script for a Multitable Form

```
Changing script C:\paradox3\multform                          Script

....+...10....+...20....+...30....+...40....+...50....+...60....+...70....+...80
EDIT "Clients"
PICKFORM "1"
WHILE True
  WAIT TABLE
  PROMPT "Editing " + TABLE(),
      "Press [F3] to move to among tables, [F2] to save, [Esc] to abort"
  UNTIL "Esc","F2","F3"
SWITCH
  CASE retval = "Esc":
    CANCELEDIT
    QUITLOOP
  CASE retval = "F2":
    Do_It!
    QUITLOOP
  CASE retval = "F3":
    UpImage
ENDSWITCH
ENDWHILE
```

Custom Menus

In addition to soliciting input from the user with PAL's ACCEPT and WAIT commands, you also can use PAL to design custom menus. By using PAL's SHOWMENU command in conjunction with a conditional command like IF or SWITCH, you can create custom menus that look just like standard Paradox menus. When you choose an item from a custom menu, PAL will execute the set of commands you have assigned to that item. There are four PAL menu commands: SHOWMENU, SHOWARRAY, SHOWFILES, and SHOWTABLES. The one you will use most frequently is SHOWMENU.

The SHOWMENU Command

The basic form of PAL's SHOWMENU command is

> SHOWMENU
> *choice 1 : prompt 1,*
> *choice 2 : prompt 2,*
> ...
> *choice n : prompt n*
> TO *variable*

As you can see, the keyword SHOWMENU is followed by a series of *choice/prompt* pairs. Each *choice/prompt* pair specifies a menu item that will appear on the custom menu and a prompt that PAL will display when you highlight that item in the menu. Each pair must be separated from the one that precedes it with a comma. (We find it convenient to place each pair on a separate line and to indent the pairs relative to the SHOWMENU command. However, it is not necessary to do so.) Although these choices and prompts usually will be literal strings, they can be any PAL string expression.

The list of *choice/prompt* pairs that follows a SHOWMENU command must end with the keyword TO, followed by the name of a variable. When you select an item from the custom menu, PAL stores that choice in the TO variable. If you choose a numeric value or date, PAL will store it as a string.

The number of *choice/prompt* pairs in the SHOWMENU command determines how many items will appear on the menu. Although you can include an unlimited number of choices in a menu, only about seven or eight will fit across the screen at a time, depending on their length. If you include more items than PAL can display at one time, PAL will place a solid right arrow at the right edge of the menu. As you press → to move beyond the last visible choice, a new one will scroll into view, and another one will scroll off the left edge of the screen.

Selecting an Item from a Custom Menu

You can select an item from a custom menu in the same ways you select an item from a standard Paradox menu. First, you can use the →, ←, [Home], and [End] keys to position the highlight on the item you want to choose, then press ↵. Alternatively, you can select an item by typing the first letter in its name. If only one item begins with the letter you type, PAL will select that item. If more than one choice begins with the letter you type, PAL will present a limited menu that contains only the choices that begin with that letter. To select an item from this limited menu, you must highlight it and press ↵.

When you select an item from a custom menu, PAL stores the string equivalent of that item in the TO variable. The method you use to choose that item does not affect the way it is stored. For example, suppose you choose the option Cancel from a custom menu. Whether you choose this option by pointing to it and pressing ↵ or by typing the letter *C*, PAL will store the string *Cancel* in the TO variable.

Once PAL displays a custom menu, you must either select an item from that menu or press the [Esc] key. If you press the [Esc] key, PAL will store the string *Esc* in the TO variable. If you press any key other than a cursor-movement key, the ↵ key, the [Esc] key, or the first letter of any menu choice, PAL will beep.

A Simple Example

As an example of the SHOWMENU command, suppose you want PAL to present a menu with three choices: Alpha, Beta, and Gamma. If you choose Alpha from the menu, PAL will display the message *You selected Alpha* in the message window for five seconds. If you choose Beta, PAL will display the message *You selected Beta for five seconds.* If you pick Gamma, PAL will display the message *You selected Gamma for five seconds.* To create this menu, you would use the script shown in Figure 16-29.

Figure 16-29 A Simple Menu Script

```
Changing script C:\paradox3\menu1                          Script

....+...10....+...20....+...30....+...40....+...50....+...60....+...70....+...80
CLEAR
SHOWMENU
  "Alpha"   : "Choice 1 of 3",
  "Beta"    : "Choice 2 of 3",
  "Gamma"   : "Choice 3 of 3"
TO choice
MESSAGE "You have selected "+choice
SLEEP 5000
```

The CLEAR command that begins the script erases the PAL canvas. The SHOWMENU command then displays the three choices, Alpha, Beta, and Gamma, on the first line of the screen and places the highlight on the first option. On the second line, PAL displays the prompt that corresponds to the choice that currently is highlighted. Since Alpha is highlighted, PAL displays the prompt *Choice 1 of 3.* Figure 16-30 shows this menu.

Figure 16-30 A Custom Menu

```
Alpha  Beta  Gamma
Choice 1 of 3
```

Now, suppose that you choose Beta, either by using the arrow keys to position the highlight on that option and pressing ↵ or by typing the letter *B.* Either way, PAL will store the string *Beta* in the variable *choice.* As soon as *choice* receives this string, PAL will evaluate the command *MESSAGE "You have selected "+choice.* This causes PAL to concatenate the contents of *choice* to the literal string *You have selected* and display the resulting string—*You have selected Beta*—in the message area. The final command, *SLEEP 5000*, instructs PAL to freeze the display for five seconds before it ends the script and lifts the PAL canvas.

Using the SWITCH Command

In most cases, of course, you will want PAL to do more than just store your choice in a variable and display it for you. In fact, you probably will want PAL to execute a different sequence of commands for each possible menu choice. To do this, you must use a conditional testing function like IF or SWITCH to determine which item was selected and route the execution of the script accordingly.

As we explained while discussing the WAIT command, the simplest form of the SWITCH command is

```
SWITCH
  CASE condition 1:
    commands 1
  CASE condition 2:
    commands 2
  ...
  CASE condition n:
    commands n
ENDSWITCH
```

where a series of CASE conditional tests appears between the words SWITCH and END-SWITCH. Each CASE contains a set of commands that correspond to its conditional test. When PAL executes a SWITCH command, it evaluates each conditional test, starting with the first one, until it finds one that is true. When that happens, PAL will issue the commands that correspond to that test, then exit from the SWITCH command without evaluating the remaining tests.

An Example

For example, suppose that your Paradox files are stored in three directories: c:\paradox3\ordentry, c:\paradox3\gledger, and c:\paradox3\acctspay, and you want to develop a menu-driven script that allows you to switch quickly from one directory to another. To do this, you could use a script like the one shown in Figure 16-31. As you can see, this script uses a SWITCH command to evaluate the menu choice.

Figure 16-31 A Menu Script with SWITCH

```
Changing script C:\paradox3\menu2                               Script
....+...10....+...20....+...30....+...40....+...50....+...60....+...70....+...80
CLEAR
SHOWMENU
  "Orders"   :   "Change to Order Entry subdirectory",
  "GL"       :   "Change to General Ledger subdirectory",
  "AP"       :   "Change to Accounts Payable subdirectory",
  "Cancel"   :   "Do not change directory"
  TO choice
SWITCH
  CASE choice = "Orders"  :
    SETDIR "c:\\paradox3\\ordentry\\" {OK}
  CASE choice = "GL"      :
    SETDIR "c:\\paradox3\\gledger\\" {OK}
  CASE choice = "AP"      :
    SETDIR "c\\paradox3\\acctspay\\" {OK}
ENDSWITCH
```

When PAL plays this script, it presents the four-item menu shown in Figure 16-32 and waits for you to make a choice. When you make a selection or press [Esc], PAL will store that selection or the string *Esc* in the variable *choice*. Depending on which selection you choose,

PAL will store one of four strings in the variable: *Orders, GL, AP,* or *Cancel.* As soon as you have made a selection, PAL will evaluate the SWITCH command in the following way. First, PAL will test to see if the variable *choice* contains the string *Orders.* If so, PAL will execute the command *SETDIR "c:\\paradox3\\ordentry\\ "{OK},* then exit from the SWITCH command without evaluating any of the other cases. If *choice* does not contain *Orders,* PAL will skip to the next case, *choice="GL".* If this condition is true, PAL will execute the command *SETDIR "c:\\paradox3\\gledger\\ "{OK}* and quit from the SWITCH command. If this condition is false, PAL will skip to the next case, *choice="AP".* If this condition is true, PAL will evaluate the command *SETDIR "c:\\paradox3\\acctspay\\ "{OK}* and then exit from the SWITCH command. If none of these conditions are true, PAL will exit from the SWITCH command without performing any actions.

Figure 16-32 A Custom Menu

```
Orders  GL  AP  Cancel
Change to Order Entry subdirectory
```

Although there is a fourth choice on the menu, Cancel, we have not included a CASE command to correspond to that choice. If none of the first three CASE statements are true, then you must either have selected the fourth choice, Cancel, or pressed the [Esc] key. In either case, you do not want PAL to change the directory. Because the script ends without providing instructions for either case, the current directory will remain unchanged unless you choose one of the first three items from the menu.

When PAL exits from the SWITCH command, it continues playing the script with the commands (if any) that follow the keyword ENDSWITCH. Since, in our example, the ENDSWITCH command is the last command in this script, PAL quits from the script and returns you to the Paradox workspace. If other PAL commands had followed the keyword ENDSWITCH, PAL would have executed those commands.

The OTHERWISE Option

If you have included a CASE statement for each possible menu choice, or if you do not want any action to be taken when you select an item other than the ones for which you included CASE statements, then you can use the basic form of the SWITCH command. If you want PAL to perform the same action when you select any of several choices, however, you can use the optional keyword OTHERWISE within the SWITCH command. This keyword must follow all CASE statements, but must precede the keyword ENDSWITCH.

As a modification to the example, suppose that you want PAL to display the message *Directory not changed* in the message area for three seconds if the user selects Cancel from the menu or presses [Esc]. To do this, you would add the statement

```
OTHERWISE:
  MESSAGE "Directory not changed"
  SLEEP 3000
```

to the original SWITCH statement, as shown in Figure 16-33. When you play this script, PAL will present the menu shown in Figure 16-32 and store your response in the variable *choice*. If any of the three cases specified in the SWITCH command are true, PAL will change the directory and exit from the SWITCH command, skipping the remaining cases (if any) and the OTHERWISE statement. If none of the cases are true, however, PAL will execute the commands that follow the keyword OTHERWISE. In this case, these commands instruct PAL to display the message *Directory not changed* in the message area. After three seconds, PAL will exit from the SWITCH command.

Figure 16-33 The OTHERWISE Option

```
Changing script C:\paradox3\menu2                        Script Ins

....+...10....+...20....+...30....+...40....+...50....+...60....+...70....+...80
CLEAR
SHOWMENU
  "Orders"    :    "Change to Order Entry subdirectory",
  "GL"        :    "Change to General Ledger subdirectory",
  "AP"        :    "Change to Accounts Payable subdirectory",
  "Cancel"    :    "Do not change directory"
  TO choice
SWITCH
  CASE choice = "Orders"  :
    SETDIR "c:\\paradox3\\ordentry\\" {OK}
  CASE choice = "GL"      :
    SETDIR "c:\\paradox3\\gledger\\" {OK}
  CASE choice = "AP"      :
    SETDIR "c\\paradox3\\acctspay\\" {OK}
  OTHERWISE
    MESSAGE "Directory not changed" SLEEP 3000
ENDSWITCH
```

The DEFAULT Option

When PAL executes a basic form of the SHOWMENU command, it automatically highlights the first item on the custom menu. If you press ↵ without moving the highlight, then PAL will execute the commands that relate to the first item. If you want PAL to automatically position the highlight on an item other than the first one in the list, you must include the optional DEFAULT keyword within the SHOWMENU command. The form of this keyword, which must follow the last *choice/prompt* pair, is

        DEFAULT *choice*

where the argument *choice* is one of the items on the menu.

Suppose you want PAL to automatically highlight the second option on the four-item menu shown in Figure 16-30. To do this, you should modify the script to look like Figure 16-34. The statement *DEFAULT "Beta"* in this script instructs PAL to position the cursor on the choice Beta, the second item on the menu, when it first displays that menu. Figure 16-35 shows this result.

Figure 16-34 A Menu Default Script

```
Changing script C:\paradox3\menu1                          Script
....+...10....+...20....+...30....+...40....+...50....+...60....+...70....+...80
CLEAR
SHOWMENU
  "Alpha"   : "Choice 1 of 3",
  "Beta"    : "Choice 2 of 3",
  "Gamma"   : "Choice 3 of 3"
  DEFAULT "Beta"
  TO Choice
MESSAGE "You have selected " + Choice
SLEEP 5000
```

Figure 16-35 A Simple Menu

```
Alpha Beta Gamma
Choice 2 of 3
```

The SHOWARRAY Command

Like PAL's SHOWMENU command, the SHOWARRAY command creates a Paradox-style menu with menu choices on the first line and corresponding prompts on the second line. The SHOWARRAY command has the form

> SHOWARRAY
> *array 1 array 2*
> TO *variable*

where *array 1* is the array containing the menu choices, *array 2* is the array containing the corresponding prompts, and *variable* is the name of the variable in which you want PAL to store the user's choice. *Array 1* and *array 2* are both arrays you have created with the ARRAY or COPYTOARRAY commands. These two arrays should have the same number of elements. (For more details on how to work with arrays in PAL, refer to Chapter 17.)

When PAL executes a SHOWARRAY command, it uses the elements of *array 1* and *array 2* to create a Paradox menu. It then pauses the script and waits for the user to make a choice. You make selections from an array menu in the same way you make choices from a standard Paradox menu or a menu displayed by the SHOWMENU command. When you select an item from the menu, PAL stores that choice in the variable specified by the command's *variable* argument.

Given a choice between SHOWMENU and SHOWARRAY, you will usually use SHOWMENU. However, SHOWARRAY is useful in special situations, such as when you want to display different menu choices depending on certain conditions. For example, suppose you want to display a menu that allows the user to perform various accounting procedures. On Fridays, you want this menu to include an option that lets the user back up that week's work. Figure 16-36 shows a script that would display the proper menu.

Figure 16-36 A SHOWARRAY Script

```
Changing script C:\paradox3\menu3                                   Script
....+...10....+...20....+...30....+...40....+...50....+...60....+...70....+...80
IF DOW(TODAY()) = "Fri" THEN
  ARRAY item[4]
  ARRAY prmpt[4]
  item[4] = "Backup"
  prmpt[4] = "Make backup files for all tables"
ELSE
  ARRAY item[3]
  ARRAY prmpt[3]
ENDIF
item[1] = "Orders"
item[2] = "GL"
item[3] = "AP"
prmpt[1] = "Work with customer orders"
prmpt[2] = "Work with general ledger"
prmpt[3] = "Work with accounts payable records"
SHOWARRAY
  item prmpt
  TO choice
```

The first line of this script determines whether today is Friday. If it is, the script will create two arrays—*item* and *prmpt*—with four elements in each array. Then, the script will store the string *Backup* in the fourth element of the *item* array and the string *Make backup files for all tables* in the fourth element of the *prmpt* array. If today is not Friday, then the script will create the same two arrays but place only three elements in them. Regardless of whether today is Friday, the script fills the first three elements of the arrays with the menu items and prompts for the Orders, GL, and AP menu selections. Then, the script uses a SHOWARRAY command to generate a menu based on the *item* and *prmpt* arrays. The menu will always contain the three menu choices Orders, GL, and AP. On Fridays only, the fourth option, Backup, will also appear on the menu.

The SHOWFILES Command

PAL's SHOWFILES command lets you display a group of file names (with or without extensions) in the form of a Paradox menu. This command is useful when you want to allow the user to select a table to work with, or a script to play, from within a script. The form of the SHOWFILES command is

> SHOWFILES NOEXT
> *directory*
> *prompt*
> TO *variable*

Directory is the full DOS path of the directory that contains the tables or scripts you want to include in the menu. If you want to include only files of a specified type from the designated directory in the menu, then the *directory* argument should include a file-name pattern, such as *.sc or *.db. *Prompt* is the message you want to appear on the first line, over the list of tables or scripts. Unlike the SHOWMENU and SHOWARRAY commands, the prompt line does not change as you move from choice to choice. *Variable* is the name of the variable in which you want PAL to store the user's choice. The optional keyword NOEXT may be used immediately following the command name SHOWFILES if you do not want the file extensions to be displayed in the menu.

For example, the command

>SHOWFILES NOEXT
>"c:\\paradox3\\work*.sc" "Select script and press Enter"
>TO sc

will display a menu that contains the names of all the files with the extension .sc in the directory c:\paradox3\work, along with the prompt *Select script and press Enter*. When you select an item from the menu, PAL stores that choice in the variable *sc*. If the scripts in the directory c:\paradox3\work are called Addrec, Delrec, and Modrec, the screen will look like Figure 16-37 when this command is executed.

Figure 16-37 A SHOWFILES Menu

```
Select script and press Enter
Addrec  Delrec  Modrec
```

The SHOWTABLES Command

PAL's SHOWTABLES command is very similar to the SHOWFILES command. The difference is that SHOWTABLES creates a menu that includes only the names of the Paradox tables in a specified directory. The form of the SHOWTABLES command is

>SHOWTABLES
>*directory*
>*prompt*
>TO *variable*

where *directory* is the full DOS path of the directory that contains the desired tables and *prompt* is a message to be displayed on the second line, under the list of tables. The keyword TO followed by the name of a variable is required. *Variable* is the name of the variable in which you want PAL to store the user's choice. (Because all table files have the extension .DB, there is no need for the optional keyword NOEXT.)

For example, the command

>SHOWTABLES
>"c:\\paradox3\\work"
>"Select a table to edit"
>TO choice

will display a menu that contains the names of all the tables in the directory c:\paradox3\work, along with the prompt *Select a table to edit*. When you select an item from the menu, PAL stores your selection in the variable *choice*.

Subroutine Calls and Branching

PAL's PLAY command gives you the ability to play one script from within another script. The form of this command is

> PLAY *scriptname*

where the single argument *scriptname* specifies the script you want to play. This argument may be a literal string, a reference to a variable or field that contains the name of a script, or a function or formula that returns the name of a script. For example, the command *PLAY "Script1"* commands PAL to play the script named Script1, as does the command *PLAY x* when the variable *x* contains the string *Script1*.

When PAL encounters a PLAY command, it reads the named script from disk and then executes it step by step. If the script you want to play is in the current directory, then the argument of the PLAY command can be simply the name of the script. If the script is in a different directory, you must include the directory and/or drive name in the argument. If the script named Xyz is stored in c:\paradox3\scripts, for example, and c:\paradox3\scripts is the current directory, then you can use the command *PLAY "xyz"* to play it. If c:\paradox3\scripts is" not the current directory, however, you will have to use the command *PLAY "c:\\paradox3\\scripts\\xyz"* to execute it.

A PLAY command within a script can result in either a subroutine call or a branch. To illustrate these two terms, suppose that PAL encounters the command *PLAY "ScriptB"* while playing ScriptA. When this happens, PAL pauses the execution of ScriptA and begins playing ScriptB. If PAL reads a RETURN command or comes to the end of ScriptB without encountering a QUIT command, it jumps back to ScriptA and resumes executing it at the command that follows *PLAY "ScriptB"*. In this situation, ScriptB is a subroutine that is called by ScriptA. This use of a PLAY command is a subroutine call. IF PAL encounters a QUIT command within ScriptB, however, it will exit from the script instead of passing control back to ScriptA. This one-way routing is called branching.

A Simple Subroutine Call

The script named ScriptA shown in Figure 16-38 contains a subroutine call to the script named ScriptB shown in Figure 16-39. When PAL plays ScriptA, it clears the PAL canvas and positions the cursor at the intersection of row 10 and column 30, writes the message *This is ScriptA* to the canvas, and pauses for three seconds. When PAL reads the command *PLAY "ScriptB"*, it searches the current directory for the script named ScriptB. If PAL finds that script, as it does in this case, it will clear the PAL canvas, reposition the cursor at the intersection of row 10 and column 30, then display the message *This is ScriptB* and pause for another three seconds. Because *SLEEP 3000* is the last command in ScriptB, PAL then returns to ScriptA and resumes execution with the command CLEAR—the command that immediately follows the PLAY command that called the subroutine. As soon as this statement erases the PAL canvas, PAL positions the cursor at the intersection of row 10 and column 30 again, displays the message *This is ScriptA again*, waits three seconds, then ends the script and returns to the Paradox workspace.

Figure 16-38 ScriptA

```
Designing script C:\paradox3\scripta                              Script

....+...10....+...20....+...30....+...40....+...50....+...60....+...70....+...80
CLEAR
@10,30
?? "This is ScriptA"
SLEEP 3000
PLAY "ScriptB"
CLEAR
@10,30
?? "This is ScriptA again"
SLEEP 3000
```

Figure 16-39 ScriptB

```
Designing script C:\paradox3\scriptb                              Script

....+...10....+...20....+...30....+...40....+...50....+...60....+...70....+...80
CLEAR
@10,30
?? "This is ScriptB"
SLEEP 3000
```

A Simple Branch

Very simply, a branch is a subroutine call in which control is not passed back to the calling script. This happens when PAL encounters a QUIT command somewhere within the called script. As a simple example of a branch, suppose that ScriptB looked like the script in Figure 16-40 instead of the one in Figure 16-39. When you play ScriptA, PAL will clear the canvas and display the message *This is ScriptA* starting at the intersection of row 10 and column 30. After three seconds, PAL will branch to ScriptB, clear the screen, reposition the cursor, and display the message *This is ScriptB* for three seconds.

Figure 16-40 ScriptB (Revised)

```
Changing script C:\paradox3\scriptb                              Script

....+...10....+...20....+...30....+...40....+...50....+...60....+...70....+...80
CLEAR
@10,30
?? "This is ScriptB"
SLEEP 3000
QUIT
```

If ScriptB ended at this point, PAL would return to ScriptA. However, ScriptB contains another command: QUIT. This command ends the execution of both levels of script play, returning you to the Paradox workspace. Because PAL does not pass control back to ScriptA, this PLAY command results in a branch.

Ending a Subroutine Prematurely

Reaching the end of a subroutine is only one of two ways to end the execution of a subroutine and pass control back to the calling script. The RETURN command provides the other way. In most cases, you will use this command within an IF statement to return to a calling script based on the result of a conditional test.

For example, suppose a large script named Main contains the command *PLAY "Delete"* and that Delete refers to the script shown in Figure 16-41. When PAL reads this command while playing Main, it begins playing Delete. The first two commands in Delete clear the PAL canvas and position the cursor at the intersection of row 10 and column 20. The next two commands display the prompt *Name of table to delete?* at the current position of the cursor and wait for you to type a table name. As soon as you type any combination of up to eight characters and press ↵, PAL will store that entry in the variable *name*.

Figure 16-41 The Delete Script

```
Changing script C:\paradox3\delete                              Script

....+...10....+...20....+...30....+...40....+...50....+...60....+...70....+...80
CLEAR
@10,20
?? "Name of table to delete? "
ACCEPT "A8" TO name
IF NOT ISTABLE(name) THEN
 RETURN
ENDIF
DELETE name
```

Next, the IF command tests the entry stored in *name* to see if it is a valid table name. If so, PAL will execute the *DELETE name* command, deleting the named table, then return control to the calling script (Main). If *name* does not contain a valid table name, however, PAL executes the RETURN command, passing control back to Main. This premature return prevents the execution of Delete, which would result in a script error.

Using a Menu to Call Subroutines

One of the most common situations in which you'll call or branch to another script is from within a custom menu. The script in Figure 16-42 shows an example of this use. The SHOWMENU command in this script presents the simple menu shown in Figure 16-43. When you choose an item from this menu, PAL will store your choice in the variable *choice*.

The SWITCH command that follows uses your response to route PAL to one of three other scripts: A, B, or C. If you select A from the menu so that *choice* contains the string *A*, PAL will execute the command *PLAY "A"*. If you select B, PAL will execute the command *PLAY "B"*. If you select C, PAL will execute the command *PLAY "C"*. These commands instruct PAL to pause the execution of Main and start playing the scripts A, B, or C.

Figure 16-42 A Menu Calling Subroutines

```
Changing script C:\paradox3\menu4                        Script Ins

....+...10....+...20....+...30....+...40....+...50....+...60....+...70....+...80
CLEAR
SHOWMENU
  "A"  :  "Play Script A",
  "B"  :  "Play Script B",
  "C"  :  "Play Script C"
  TO choice
SWITCH
  CASE choice = "A":
    PLAY "A"
  CASE choice = "B":
    PLAY "B"
  CASE choice = "C":
    PLAY "C"
ENDSWITCH
```

Figure 16-43 A Custom Menu

```
A  B  C
Play Script A
```

Whether these three PLAY commands call or branch to the script they name depends on whether that script contains a QUIT command. If PAL reads a QUIT command within the named script, it will exit from the script without returning to Main. If the named script does not contain a QUIT command, however, PAL will resume executing Main as soon as it reads a RETURN command or reaches the end of the subroutine script.

Printing

In addition to working with the information in tables from within scripts and interacting with the user, you often will want to print from within a script. PAL gives you three ways to do this. First, you can print from a prepared report specification. Second, you can "echo" the information that is displayed on the PAL canvas to your printer. Third, you can print specific strings to the printer, one at a time.

Printing from a Report Specification

In most cases, you will print from within a script in the same way you print manually from within Paradox—by choosing a previously designed report specification and commanding

Paradox to print from it. There are two ways to do this from within a script. First, you can use the keystroke representation

Menu {Report} {Output} {*tablename*} {*report number*} {*Printer,Screen,* or *File*}

where *tablename* is the name of the table from which you want to print, *report number* is a number from 1 to 14 or the letter R that specifies the report specification to use, and *Printer*, *Screen*, or *File* tells PAL where to print the report. If you specify *Printer*, PAL will send the report to your printer. If you specify *Screen*, PAL will preview the report on the screen. If you specify *File*, PAL will print the report to the .RPT file that you specify.

PAL's REPORT command provides an easier and more flexible way to print from a report specification within a script. As explained in Chapter 14, the form of this menu-equivalent command is

REPORT *table report*

where *table* is a string expression that is, contains, or returns the name of the table you want to print, and *report* is either a value expression that is, returns, or contains an integer from 1 to 14, or a string expression that is, contains, or returns the string *R*. The ability to use variables, field references, equations, and functions instead of literal strings is the principal advantage of this command over keystroke representations.

In most cases, you probably will manipulate the information in a table before you print that information. For example, you may wish to sort the records before printing, print only records that meet certain selection conditions, or combine information from two or more tables in the same report. This process of preparing the information for printing is an ideal task to automate in a script. For example, suppose that you want to select the SS Number and Salary fields of all the records from the EMPLYEE table with Salary field entries that exceed 30,000, arrange them into ascending order based on salary, and print them in a standard Tabular report. To do this, you could use the script shown in Figure 16-44.

Figure 16-44 A Printing Script

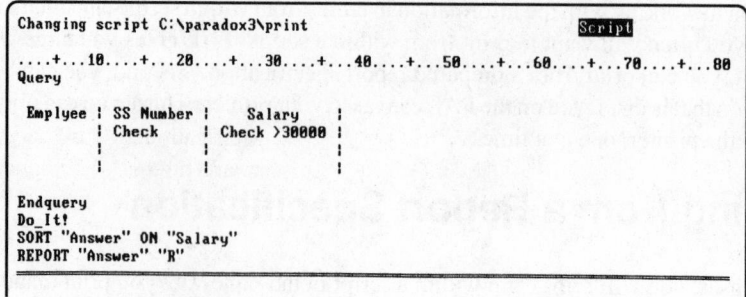

As you can see, this script begins with the script version of a query that selects the SS Number and Salary field entries for the records in the EMPLYEE table with Salary field entries that exceed 30,000. The easiest way to create this query script is to create the query in Paradox, then use the [Menu] Scripts QuerySave command to save it as a script. The Do_It! command that follows the query script instructs PAL to execute this query, placing the results into a table named ANSWER. The command *SORT "Answer" ON "Salary"* sorts the records from the ANSWER table into ascending order based on the entries in the Salary field and places the sorted results back into ANSWER. The final command, *REPORT "Answer" "R"*, instructs PAL to print a standard Tabular report of the records in the sorted ANSWER table. The second page-width of this report is shown in Figure 16-45.

Figure 16-45 The Printed Report

```
   7/22/88                          Standard Report                     Page    1


   SS Number      Salary
   -----------    -----------------
   312-98-1479        32,000.00
   314-38-9452        32,000.00
   414-07-9123        33,999.99
   321-65-9151        34,000.00
   415-24-6710        37,000.00
   317-65-4529        38,000.00
   401-55-1567        40,000.00
   401-32-8721        47,000.00
   321-65-8765        50,000.00
   414-76-3421        70,000.00
```

Instant Reports

If you want to print a standard Tabular report from within a script, you do not need to use PAL's REPORT command. Instead, you can use the special key representation Instant-Report. When PAL reads this keystroke in a script, it will print the report stored in the R selection for the current table. Unless you change the R specification from its default state, it will contain the format for a simple Tabular report. Since InstantReport prints from the current table, you must be sure that the table you want to print is on the workspace and that the cursor is within it before PAL reads this keystroke representation.

Designing a Report Specification within a Script

Although you can design a report specification from within a script, we don't recommend it. If a script contains the instructions for creating a report specification, PAL will recreate the specification each time you play that script—an unnecessary and time-consuming task. Once you design a report specification, of course, you can use PAL's REPORT command to print the report at any time.

Echoing Information to the Printer

PAL's PRINTER command provides a second way to print information from within a script. Once PAL reads a PRINTER ON command in a script, it will begin echoing to your printer all subsequent information displayed on the screen by the ?, ??, and TEXT commands. A PRINTER OFF command or the end of the script cancels this command.

For example, suppose that you want to print the records in the EMPLYEE table in the form of simple mailing labels. To do this, you would use the script shown in Figure 16-46. The PRINTER ON command that begins this script ensures that the information displayed by the following ? commands will be echoed to the printer. The SCAN command instructs PAL to execute the six ? commands that follow each record in the table, beginning with the first record. The first ? command tells PAL to skip to the beginning of a new line, both on the screen and on the printer, and print the first and last names of the current record. The next ? command skips to the beginning of the next line and displays and prints the contents of that record's Address field. The third ? command tells PAL to skip to the beginning of a new line and print the contents of the City, State, and Zip fields for that record. The final three ? commands make PAL skip three blank lines, both on the screen and on the printer. As soon as PAL finishes the first pass through this loop, it begins another, this time displaying and printing the selected fields of the second record. Once PAL has printed a label for each record in the table, it turns the printer off and exits from the script.

Figure 16-46 The PRINTER Command

```
Changing script C:\paradox3\printer                          Script

....+...10....+...20....+...30....+...40....+...50....+...60....+...70....+...80
PRINTER ON
VIEW "Emplyee"
SCAN
   ? [First Name], " ", [Last Name]
   ? [Address]
   ? [City], ", ", [State], "  ", [Zip]
   ?
   ?
   ?
ENDSCAN
PRINTER OFF
```

In almost all situations, you'll find it easier to prepare a report in the Paradox Report mode than to create it by echoing information to the printer. For example, skipping blank lines in mailing labels is a simple matter of issuing the appropriate [Menu] Settings command from within the report. Removing blank lines in an echoed report involves a complex nesting of IF commands. Overall, the principal use of the PRINTER command is to print the results or contents of variables, equations, and functions within a report. Unless you need to do this, you probably will want to use the REPORT command to output information to your printer.

The Print Command

PAL's PRINT command provides the third way to print information from within a script. This command instructs PAL to send information (literal values, the contents of variables and fields, and the results of equations and functions) directly to your printer or to a file without displaying it on the screen. The two forms of the PRINT command are

> PRINT *expression 1,expression 2,...,expression n-1,expression n*
> PRINT FILE *filename expression 1,expression 2,...,expression n-1,expression n*

The first form of this function sends information to a printer. The second form sends information to the file you name in the *filename* argument. If that file already exists, PAL appends the new information to the end of it. If the file doesn't exist, PAL creates it.

Like the PRINTER command, the PRINT command is of limited usefulness. In most cases, you'll find it easier to design a report specification than to use multiple PRINT commands to send information to a printer or to a file.

One of the best uses for the PRINT command is sending special ASCII codes to your printer. You can use a backslash followed by any of the ASCII codes 0 to 256 to send an ASCII character to your printer. This is most useful for sending print attribute codes to your printer prior to printing. The command *PRINT "\027\015"* prepares your Epson printer to print in compressed print, and the command *PRINT "\027\048"* instructs it to print eight lines per inch.

You can also use four special characters, \n, \t, \f, and \r, to send control characters to the printer. The string \n sends a line feed character; the string \t sends a tab character; the string \f sends a form feed character; and \r sends a carriage return.

Opening and Closing the Printer

If your script is going to be used on a network, then you should use the OPEN PRINTER command before issuing the PRINT or PRINTER commands. On a network, the PRINT and PRINTER commands might cause a header and footer page to be printed each time they are executed. The OPEN PRINTER command takes care of this problem. When the printing part of your script is over, you should use the CLOSE PRINTER command. Using the OPEN PRINTER and CLOSE PRINTER commands in a single user environment will not hinder a script's execution. Neither of these two commands takes an argument.

Passwords

Since most of your PAL programs will work with Paradox tables, and some of your tables will be password-protected, chances are good that you eventually will encounter a situation in which you'll need to work with a protected table in a script. There are two ways to access a password-protected table from within a script. First, you can supply the password for each table as you call it to the workspace. If the table named ORDERS is protected with the password *abracadabra*, for example, you could use the keystroke sequence

Menu {View} {Orders} {abracadabra}

within your script to bring it to the workspace. You must use a similar sequence for each password-protected table you want to access within the script.

This keystroke-representation method works well if your script calls upon only a few password-protected tables. If your script calls on several, however, you might want to take advantage of PAL's PASSWORD command. This command, which has the form

PASSWORD *password 1, password 2,...., password n*

lets you supply passwords in advance for any protected tables you'll access during the script. Once these passwords have been supplied in the context of the PASSWORD command, PAL will allow you free access to the tables to which they apply.

Suppose you want to access three password-protected tables in the course of a script: ORDERS (which has the password *abracadabra*), CUSTOMERS (which has the password *shazaam*), and PRODUCTS (which has the password *open sesame*). To ensure free access to these tables, you might include the command *PASSWORD "abracadabra","shazaam", " open sesame"* early in the script. Once PAL reads this command, you will not need to supply the passwords for these three files as you open them.

Revoking Passwords

As you learned in Chapter 6, once you supply the correct password for a file, Paradox will allow you to access that file again and again during the current Paradox session without supplying the password each time. If a script that has unprotected one or more files ends without exiting to DOS, then you will be able to access those files freely. Fortunately, PAL provides a command, UNPASSWORD, that allows you to "revoke" one or more of the passwords supplied during the play of a script. This command prevents unauthorized access to the table after the script is finished, without necessitating an exit from Paradox.

The form of the UNPASSWORD command is

UNPASSWORD *password 1, password 2,..., password n*

where the expressions that follow the command are the passwords you want to revoke. For instance, if the script in the preceding example contained the PASSWORD command, you would need to use the command *UNPASSWORD "abracadabra","shazaam","open sesame"* near the end of the script to reprotect the passwords before the end of script play. Another alternative is to remove all passwords regardless of whether your script set them, using the keystroke sequence *Menu {Tools} {More} {Protect} {ClearPasswords}*.

Password-protecting a Script

In addition to password-protecting tables, you'll probably want to password-protect any scripts that contain a PASSWORD command. Otherwise, anyone could use the [Menu] Scripts Editor Edit command to bring the script into the PAL Script Editor, view the PASSWORD command, and learn the passwords for your files. You can password-protect a script in much the same way you password-protect a table. To password-protect a script, issue the [Menu] Tools More Protect Password command. Instead of choosing Table, as you would to password-protect a table, you select Script and supply the name of the script you want to protect either by typing it and pressing ↵ or by pressing ↵ to reveal a list of scripts, highlighting the one you want to protect, and pressing ↵ again.

As soon as you supply the name of a script, PAL will prompt you to type a password. This password may be any string of up to 15 characters. As soon as you type the password and press ↵, PAL will prompt you to retype it. If you type it the same way again, PAL will accept the password and encrypt the script. If you type the password differently—even if the capitalization is not the same—PAL will reject it and will not assign the password to the script. If you want to protect the script, you must start the process again.

Password-protecting a script does a number of things. First, it prevents users from viewing the script with the Script Editor unless they know the password, or from viewing it with any other text editor. If you retrieve a password-protected script into a word processor like WordStar, the script will appear as a jumble of strange characters. If you try to bring it into the Script Editor, PAL will prompt you for the script's password. If you know the password, PAL will bring the script into the Script Editor. If you don't know the password, however, PAL will not let you see the script.

It is important to note that password-protecting a script does not prevent you from playing it. Regardless of whether a script is password-protected, PAL will play it when you issue the [Menu] Scripts Play command, choose Play from the PAL menu, or use a PLAY command from within a script.

However, password-protecting a script does prevent you from using the [Ctrl]-[Break] combination to cancel the execution of that script. If you press [Ctrl]-[Break] while PAL is playing a password-protected script, PAL will just continue playing that script.

Comments in Scripts

In addition to keystroke representations and commands, PAL programs can contain comments. Comments annotate a script, making it easier to understand what the script does when you view or edit it. Including a comment in a script is as easy as typing a semicolon and then typing the comment. The ; character signals PAL that a comment follows. When PAL encounters a semicolon in a script, it disregards all characters from the semicolon to the end of the line on which it appears.

You can place a comment on a line by itself or on a line that contains other commands. When you combine commands and comments on the same line, however, the comments must appear to the right of the commands. Otherwise, the commands will follow the semicolon, and PAL will not execute them.

Figure 16-47 shows an example of a simple annotated script. As you can see, the first line of the script is a comment that tells you the name of the script and what it does. The comment at the end of each subsequent line explains the purpose of the commands on that line.

Figure 16-47 Comments in Scripts

```
Changing script C:\paradox3\printer                        Script Ins

....+...10....+...20....+...30....+...40....+...50....+...60....+...70....+...80
;script for printing mailing labels
PRINTER ON                                 ;echos screen to printer
VIEW "Emplyee"                             ;bring EMPLYEE into view
SCAN                                       ;move through EMPLYEE record by record
   ? [First Name], " ", [Last Name]        ;prints first and last names
   ? [Address]                             ;prints address
   ? [City], ", ", [State], " ", [Zip]     ;prints city, state, zip
   ?                                       ;blank lines
   ?
   ?
ENDSCAN                                     ;loop to SCAN command
PRINTER OFF                                 ;turn off printer echo
```

Although you usually can place a comment to the right of any line of commands, you should not place comments to the right of a TEXT command, the keyword ENDTEXT, or the text that falls between them. If you include a comment to the right of a TEXT command, PAL will display the error message *Begin text on line following keyword TEXT* when you run the script. If you include a comment following the keyword ENDTEXT, PAL will display the message *ENDTEXT missing or not alone on line*. If you include a comment on a line between TEXT and ENDTEXT, PAL will display the comment on the screen as literal text.

Conclusion

In this chapter, we have explained a number of essential PAL programming techniques. First, we showed you how to display information on the PAL canvas, using the ?, ??, TEXT, and MESSAGE commands. Next, we demonstrated how to use the ACCEPT and WAIT commands to solicit input from a user within a script, and how to use the SHOWMENU command to create custom menus. Then, we used the PLAY command within one script to call and branch to other scripts, and we explored PAL's three looping commands: WHILE, FOR, and SCAN. We also showed you how to use a script to send information to your printer. Then, we explained how to supply and revoke passwords from within a script and discussed the importance of password-protecting your scripts. Finally, we showed you how to include comments in your scripts. In the next chapter, we will demonstrate some advanced PAL programming techniques, such as keyboard macros, procedures, and arrays.

Chapter 17

Other PAL Features

In the previous four chapters, we introduced you to the basics of PAL: recording, editing, and playing scripts; variables, formulas, and functions; and commonly used PAL commands. In this chapter, we'll present several other important PAL features, including the PAL Value command, miniscripts, macros, arrays, procedures, and the PAL Debugger.

The Value Command

The Value command on the PAL menu allows you to perform calculations quickly and easily. When you press the [PAL Menu] key ([Alt]-[F10]), Paradox will display the PAL menu shown in Figure 17-1. If you choose Value, the fifth item on this menu, Paradox will display the prompt and message shown in Figure 17-2. After you see this prompt, you can type any valid variable, field reference, formula, or function. When you press ↵, PAL will calculate the value of the expression you typed and display the result in the message area at the lower-right corner of the screen.

Figure 17-1 The PAL Menu

```
Play   RepeatPlay  BeginRecord  Debug  Value  MiniScript
Play a script.
```

Figure 17-2 The Value Prompt

```
Expression:                                            Main
Enter expression to calculate.
```

For example, suppose you want to know the result of multiplying 145 by 17. To make this calculation, press the [**PAL Menu**] key ([Alt]-[F10]), choose Value, and type **145*17**. When you press ↵, PAL will display the result of this formula, 2465, in the message area. Similarly, suppose you want to know the future value of investing $1,000 per year for 20 years at 10 percent interest. To make this calculation, press [**PAL Menu**], choose Value, type **FV(1000,.1,20)**, and press ↵. After a moment, PAL will display the result, 57274.99949325, in the message area.

When you use the Value command to calculate a value, PAL actually creates and plays a temporary script consisting of a single RETURN command. In the example above, for instance, PAL created and played the single-line script *RETURN 145*17*. The result of a Value command is the same as if you had written the RETURN script in the Script Editor and played it yourself.

Miniscripts

The MiniScript command on the PAL menu allows you to create and play temporary, single-line scripts that are up to 175 characters long. When you issue this command, PAL will present the prompt shown in Figure 17-3. When you type one or more PAL commands onto this line and press ↵, PAL will execute those commands as a script.

Figure 17-3 The MiniScript Prompt

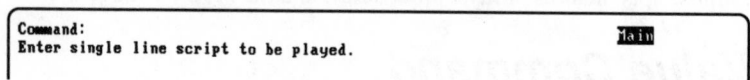

```
Command:
Enter single line script to be played.                                    Main
```

Miniscripts are useful for testing the effect of various PAL commands as you learn about PAL or for performing simple tasks that you cannot perform within Paradox, like sending a print attribute string to your printer. For instance, suppose you want Paradox to print your reports in compressed print on your Epson printer. Before you print the report, you could press [PAL Menu], choose the MiniScript command, and type *PRINT "027\015"*. As soon as you press ↵, PAL will execute the script, sending the setup string \027\015 to your printer.

As we will show you later, you also will use miniscripts to create keyboard macros and to assign values to variables while you are debugging a script.

Because a miniscript is a script, PAL automatically checks it for errors as it plays. If PAL encounters an error in the miniscript, it will display the message *Script error – select Cancel or Debug from menu* in the message area, and will present the menu choices Cancel and Debug at the top of the screen. If you choose Cancel, PAL will return you to the Paradox workspace. (We'll cover the Debug option later in this chapter.)

PAL does not save miniscripts to disk. For that reason, you must retype a miniscript each time you want to play it. If you plan to use a script more than once or twice, you should create it as a regular script.

Keyboard Macros

Up to this point, we have played scripts in three ways: by issuing the [Menu] Scripts Play command, by choosing Play from the PAL menu, or by including a PLAY command in a script. It is possible to play a script simply by pressing a single key or a combination of keys. To do this, you must use PAL's SETKEY command to link a key or key combination to a script. Once you have set up this link, you can play the script by pressing that key or combination of keys. These script/key combinations are called keyboard macros.

PAL's SETKEY command lets you create a keyboard macro. The form of this command is

SETKEY *keycode   commands*

The first argument, *keycode*, must be a keycode expression that specifies the key or combination you want to use to play the script. As you'll recall from our discussion of the WAIT command in Chapter 16, you can specify a keycode in five ways. First, you can use a single-character string, like *a*, *Z*, or *?*. Second, you can use the ASCII number for that character (a value from 0 to 255). Third, you can use a negative numeric value from -1 to -132 to represent characters from the extended IBM character set, including special function keys, arrow keys, and various [Alt] combinations (listed in Appendix B of the *PAL User's Guide*). Fourth, you can use the strings *F1*, *F2*, and so on, to represent regular function keys; *F11*, *F12*, and so on, to represent shifted function keys; *F20*, *F21*, and so on, to represent [Ctrl]-function key combinations; and *F30*, *F31*, and so on, to represent [Alt]-function key combinations. Finally, you can use the names PAL assigns to special keys, like Right, Rotate, and Check.

The second argument of this command, *commands*, is a list of one or more valid PAL commands. These can be PAL commands like SORT, WHILE, or PLAY, or keystroke representations like Menu, {Scripts}, or {View}. All the commands you want PAL to execute when you invoke the macro must be on the same line as the SETKEY command itself.

Defining a Macro

To create a macro, you must write a SETKEY script that tells PAL to assign a series of commands to a key. Then, you must play that script. When you play the SETKEY script, PAL sets up the relationship between the key and the commands specified by SETKEY.

Once you run a SETKEY script, the macro defined by that script will remain active until the end of the current Paradox session or until you undefine that macro. To return a macro-linked key to its normal function prior to the end of a Paradox session, use an abbreviated form of the SETKEY command: SETKEY *keycode*. The single argument should be the code of the key you want to return to its normal function. The absence of a set of commands following the keycode instructs PAL to "undefine" the macro and return the key to its original function.

A Simple Example

Suppose you want Paradox to display the structure of the current table whenever you press [Ctrl]-[S]. To do this, enter the PAL Script Editor and compose the simple one-line script

SETKEY 19 Menu {Tools} {Info} {Structure} Enter Enter

After writing this script, press **[Menu]** and choose **Go** from the Script Editor menu to save and play the script. Playing the script activates the macro. When you subsequently press [Ctrl]-[S], PAL will issue the [Menu] Tools Info Structure command, press ↵ once to reveal a list of table names, and press ↵ again to select the first name from the list—the name of the current table. As a result, PAL will display the structure of the current table.

A More Complex Example

As we mentioned earlier, the commands that you want to link to a key must fit entirely on the same line as the SETKEY command. For a simple macro like the one presented above, this restriction is not a problem. In many cases, however, you'll want to link a key to a script that contains more commands than can fit on a single line. In these cases, you can link the key to a PLAY command that calls the script you want PAL to execute.

For example, suppose you want PAL to play the script Newemply, which is shown in Figure 17-4, when you press [Alt]-[Q]. To link this script to the [Alt]-[Q] key, you must write and play the script

SETKEY -16 PLAY "Newemply"

Once you play this script, pressing [Alt]-[Q] will execute the command *PLAY "Newemply"*, which instructs PAL to play the script named Newemply. Because Newemply contains a query followed by a Do_It! command, PAL will bring the query to the workspace, execute it, and end the script.

Figure 17-4 The Newemply Script

```
Changing script C:\paradox3\newemply                          Script

....+...10....+...20....+...30....+...40....+...50....+...60....+...70....+...80
Query

Emplyee ! Last name !    Date of Hire      !
        ! Check     ! Check > today - 365  !
        !           !                      !
        !           !                      !

Endquery
Do_It!
```

Other Macro Notes

Instead of using the Script Editor to create a SETKEY script, you can use the MiniScript command to create and play the script. To do this, press the **[PAL Menu]** key, choose the MiniScript command, and type the SETKEY script you want to play. When you press ↵, PAL will play the script, defining the macro.

Remember, though, that PAL does not save miniscripts. If you plan to use your SETKEY scripts during future Paradox sessions, you should write them using the Script Editor. That way, all you have to do to redefine the macro in your next Paradox session is play the saved SETKEY script. If you use the MiniScript command to define these macros, you'll have to retype the SETKEY script at the start of the next Paradox session.

One useful programming technique is to combine your most used macros into one script. By playing this one script at the beginning of each Paradox session, you can activate all the macros at once for use throughout that session. If you have written your macros into separate scripts, you can use the Script Editor's READ command to combine them. To make this process even more convenient, you can designate the macro-containing script as an auto-executing script (a process we'll discuss near the end of this chapter).

One final note: Although you can link a script to any key on your computer's keyboard, you should be careful which keys you actually use. Once you link a key to a script, PAL will execute that script whenever you press that key—when you are selecting an item from a menu, when you are typing an entry into a table, when you are creating a report or script, and so forth. If you link macros to keys that have special purposes in Paradox, such as ↵, →, [End], [Edit], and so on, you'll find yourself unable to issue the commands you want to issue once a macro is in effect. Therefore, we recommend that you link your scripts to keys and combinations that Paradox does not use for any other purpose. In most cases, we prefer to use the [Alt] or [Ctrl] combinations that Paradox does not use.

Arrays

In Chapter 14, we introduced the use of variables within a PAL script. In that chapter, you learned that each variable can hold a single value. In addition to these simple variables, PAL allows the use of a special type of variable called an array.

An array is a variable that can hold more than one value at a time (up to 15,000 values, in fact). The "pockets" that store the values in an array are called elements. Each element can hold one value of any type. You can store information into and retrieve information from an array either one element at a time or all at once.

COPYTOARRAY and COPYFROMARRAY

The principal use of an array is to store a group of related values. For example, you might use an array variable to store all of the entries from a record. In fact, PAL provides two commands, COPYTOARRAY and COPYFROMARRAY, that are designed specifically for storing the contents of a record in an array and writing the contents of an array back into a table. The COPYTOARRAY command creates an array that has one more element than the number of fields in the current table, then copies the table name and every entry from the current record into that array. The form of this command is

COPYTOARRAY *arrayname*

where the single argument is the name of the array in which you want to store the record. The COPYFROMARRAY command copies the elements from an array (usually one created by the COPYTOARRAY command) back into a table. The form of this command is

COPYFROMARRAY *arrayname*

where the single argument is the name of the array whose elements you want to access.

The script shown in Figure 17-5 demonstrates a basic use of the COPYTOARRAY and COPYFROMARRAY commands. This script moves the entries from a record you choose to another row within that table. The first command in this script tests to see whether Paradox is in the Edit mode. If not, PAL places the table in the Edit mode. The WAIT TABLE command causes PAL to display the prompts *Position cursor on record you want to move* and *Then press [Enter]* at the top of the screen, and lets you move the cursor freely within the current table.

Figure 17-5 COPYTOARRAY and COPYFROMARRAY

```
Changing script C:\paradox3\arrays                          Script

....+...10....+...20....+...30....+...40....+...50....+...60....+...70....+...80
IF NOT SYSMODE() = "Edit" THEN
 EditKey
ENDIF
WAIT TABLE PROMPT "Position cursor on record you want to move",
 "Then press [Enter]"
UNTIL "Enter"
COPYTOARRAY temp
Del
WAIT TABLE PROMPT "Position cursor at destination",
 "Then press [Enter]"
UNTIL "Enter"
Ins
COPYFROMARRAY temp
```

When you position the cursor in any field of the record you want to move and press ↵, PAL will execute the command *COPYTOARRAY temp*, which creates an array named *temp* and copies the entries from the current record into it. The array that PAL creates will have one element for each field in the table, plus one to store the name of the table itself. The table name always occupies the first element in the array. The subsequent elements in the array store the entries from the fields of the record, starting with the leftmost field.

For example, if the cursor is positioned anywhere in the third record of the table shown in Figure 17-6 when you press ↵, the COPYTOARRAY command will create a four-element array. The first element would hold the name of the table—the string *Sample*. The second element would store the record's Date field entry—the date value *3/03/88*. The third element of the array would hold the entry from the third record's Number field—the numeric value *30*. The fourth element of the array would hold the entry from the third record's Name field—the string *Smith*.

After PAL has created this array and copied the entries from the third record into it, PAL reads the command *Del*, which deletes the record whose contents it just copied into the array. Next,

PAL reads another WAIT command, which instructs PAL to display the prompts *Position cursor at destination* and *Then press [Enter]*, then allows you to move the cursor freely within the table. As soon as you press ↵, PAL will read the command *Ins*, which causes it to insert a new record into the table at the current position of the cursor. Finally, PAL reads the command *COPYFROMARRAY temp*. This command instructs PAL to copy the contents of the array *temp* (the contents of the third record) back into the table in the proper fields within the record in which the cursor is positioned. Figure 17-7 shows the result of moving the third record to the beginning of the SAMPLE table.

Figure 17-6 The SAMPLE Table

```
Viewing Sample table: Record 1 of 12                          Main

SAMPLE        Date         Number          Name
    1       1/01/88          10        Jones
    2       2/02/88          20        Williams
    3       3/03/88          30        Smith
    4       4/04/88          40        Brown
    5       5/05/88          50        White
    6       6/06/88          60        Black
    7       7/07/88          70        Michaels
    8       8/08/88          80        Ford
    9       9/09/88          90        Dow
   10      10/10/88         100        Cohen
   11      11/11/88         110        Johnson
   12      12/12/88         120        Cleaver
```

Figure 17-7 The Rearranged SAMPLE Table

```
Viewing Sample table: Record 1 of 12                          Main

SAMPLE        Date         Number          Name
    1       3/03/88          30        Smith
    2       1/01/88          10        Jones
    3       2/02/88          20        Williams
    4       4/04/88          40        Brown
    5       5/05/88          50        White
    6       6/06/88          60        Black
    7       7/07/88          70        Michaels
    8       8/08/88          80        Ford
    9       9/09/88          90        Dow
   10      10/10/88         100        Cohen
   11      11/11/88         110        Johnson
   12      12/12/88         120        Cleaver
```

Importantly, the field that is assigned to an element of an array is determined by the structure of a table, not by the order of the fields in its image. If you rotate a table image after using the COPYTOARRAY command, you can still use the COPYFROMARRAY command to copy the array into another record because the underlying structure is still the same.

You also can use the COPYFROMARRAY command to place the elements from an array into a table other than the one from which they were retrieved. For this process to be successful, however, the type of each field (alphanumeric, date, number, etc.) into which PAL will place the information from the array must match the type of entry stored in the corresponding position in the array. The destination table can have more fields than there are elements in the array, as long as the types of the first fields in the table match the types of entries stored in the elements of the array.

Retrieving Individual Elements from an Array

Although you commonly will use the COPYFROMARRAY command to retrieve all the elements from an array at once, as we have in the preceding example, you also can operate on the individual elements in an array. To do this, you must use the reference form *arrayname[element]*, where *arrayname* is the name of an array and *element* is an expression that identifies which element you want to reference. If the array was created using a COPYTOARRAY command, then the *element* argument can be either a numeric expression that identifies the element you want to access, or a string that specifies the name of the field from which that element was copied. If you create an array with an ARRAY command (we'll show you how to do this shortly), you must identify the elements by number.

For example, suppose that you have created the four-element array *temp* (described previously) by issuing the COPYTOARRAY command while the cursor was in the third record of the SAMPLE table. Having stored the third record in this array, suppose you want to retrieve its individual elements into four variables: *w*, *x*, *y*, and *z*. To copy the contents of the first element in the array—the table name *Sample*—into *w*, you would use the command *w=temp[1]*. To copy the contents of the second element into *x*, you could use either the command *x=temp[2]* or the command *x=temp["Date"]*. To copy the contents of the third element into *y*, you could use either the command *y=temp[3]* or the command *y=temp["Number"]*. Similarly, you could copy the contents of the fourth element into *z* with either the command *z=temp[4]* or the command *z=temp["Name"]*. In this case, *w* would contain the string *Sample*, *x* would contain the date value *3/03/88*, *y* would contain the value *30*, and *z* would contain the string *Smith*.

Throughout the last four chapters, we have said that you can use five types of expressions— literal values, variables, field references, formulas, and functions—as the arguments of various PAL commands and functions. In fact, you also can use as arguments references to the individual elements in an array. For example, if the third element of the array named *temp* holds the value *30*, the function *SQRT(temp[3])* will return the value 6.324. Similarly, the command *MESSAGE "The third element in temp holds the value ",temp[3]* will display the message *The third element in temp holds the value 30*.

Placing Individual Elements into an Array

Just as you can retrieve the individual elements of an array, you also can store values into the elements of an array one at a time. For example, you would use the command *temp[3]=500* to place the value 500 in the third element of the array *temp* (provided that *temp* already exists). If the third element of *temp* already contains a value (as it does in this case), that value will be overwritten by the new value you assign to it. The old and new values do not have to be of the same type. For example, you could use the command *temp[3]="thirty"* to replace the value *30* with the string *thirty*. Once you do this, however, you cannot use the COPYFROMARRAY command to enter the contents of the array back into the table from which it came.

Creating an Array Manually

Although you usually will use the COPYTOARRAY command to create your arrays, you also can define an array manually. To do this, you must use PAL's ARRAY command. The form of this command is

ARRAY *arrayname*[#]

where *arrayname* is the name of the array you want to create, and # is the number of elements you want it to contain. To define a five-element array named *results*, for example, you would use the command *ARRAY results[5]*.

The ARRAY command does not automatically fill in an array when it is created. Once you have defined an array, you must use the = command to assign values to its individual elements. For example, you could use the commands *results[1]="John"*, *results[2]="Smith"*, *results[3]="123 Any Street"*, *results[4]="Indianapolis"*, and *results[5]="IN"* to store John Smith's name and address into the array *results*. The arrays you create with the ARRAY command can store any information you want to put in them. Unlike the first element of the arrays you create with the COPYTOARRAY command, the first element of a custom array does not have to hold a table name.

Undefining an Array

Once you define an array, that array remains defined until the end of the current Paradox session or until you specifically release it. As long as an array is defined, it uses memory, regardless of whether it stores any values. You can use the RELEASE command to "undefine" an array in much the same way that you can use it to release a variable. In fact, you even use the same form of the command—RELEASE VARS. To release individual arrays, you must use the form

RELEASE VARS *array 1,...,array n*

where the arguments are the names of the arrays you want to release. (You can mix array names and variable names within the same RELEASE command to release arrays and "normal" variables at the same time.) If you issue the RELEASE VARS ALL command, PAL will undefine all existing arrays and regular variables.

Procedures

Procedures are RAM-resident subroutines that you can define and use during the playing of any PAL script. A procedure can perform an action, return a value, or both. If the procedure performs an action only, then it is similar to a typical subroutine that you call with a PLAY command from within a script. As we will explain, however, a procedure gives you three advantages over a subroutine: It can accept arguments, it can execute more quickly (remember—procedures are RAM-resident), and it can use private variables. An example of this is a procedure that deletes a record from a table specified in the procedure's argument.

If a procedure returns a value result, we'll refer to the procedure as a user-defined function. Like PAL's built-in functions, user-defined functions can accept arguments and return a value result based on those arguments. This type of procedure must end with a RETURN command, which returns the value of the procedure to the calling script. A procedure that calculates the median of a column of values is an example of a user-defined function.

Defining a Procedure

To define a procedure, you must use PAL's PROC command within a script. The basic form of the PROC command is

```
PROC procedurename(arg 1, arg 2,...,arg n)
    commands
ENDPROC
```

The first argument of the PROC command must be the name you want to assign to the procedure, followed by a list of any variables that you will pass to the procedure when you call it. Like PAL's built-in functions, some procedures will require one or more arguments, and some will have none. Even if the procedure you are defining will not require any arguments, you still must include a set of parentheses following the name of the procedure in the PROC command.

Following the procedure name and argument list, you must list all of the commands you want PAL to execute when you call the procedure. The keyword ENDPROC marks the end of the PROC command.

Two Simple Examples

The script named Proc1, shown in Figure 17-8, defines a simple user-defined function. This function calculates the future value of investing a single lump sum of money today. For example, you could use this procedure to calculate the value 25 years from today of investing $100 today at a guaranteed annual rate of 10 percent. The first line of this script designates COMPVAL() (for compound value) as the name of the procedure and specifies three arguments: *amount*, *rate*, and *term*. The second line of the script calculates the formula *amount*POW(1+rate,term)* and returns the result as the value of the procedure. The ENDPROC command marks the end of the procedure.

The script named Proc2, shown in Figure 17-9, defines a script that performs an action instead of returning a value. This procedure deletes the record designated by its second argument from the table named by its first argument. The first line of this script designates DEL-REC() as the name of the procedure and specifies two arguments: *tabl* and *rec*. The second line commands PAL to bring the table named by the first argument onto the Paradox workspace in the Edit mode. The next command tells PAL to move the cursor to the record named by the second argument. The Del command tells PAL to delete that record. Then, the Do_It! command completes the edit, and the keyword ENDPROC signals the end of the procedure.

Figure 17-8 A Simple User-defined Function

```
Changing script C:\paradox3\proc1                          Script

....+...10....+...20....+...30....+...40....+...50....+...60....+...70....+...80
PROC COMPVAL(amount,rate,term)
  RETURN amount*POW(1 + rate,term)
ENDPROC
```

Figure 17-9 A Procedure That Performs an Action

```
Changing script C:\paradox3\proc2                          Script

....+...10....+...20....+...30....+...40....+...50....+...60....+...70....+...80
PROC DELREC(tabl,rec)
  EDIT tabl
  MOVETO RECORD rec
  Del
  Do_It!
ENDPROC
```

Using Procedures

Once you have written a procedure script, using the procedure in that script is a two-step process. First, you play the script that defines the procedure in order to load the procedure into memory. Then, you can call the procedure from the same script or from another one.

Loading a Procedure

Loading a procedure is a matter of playing the script that contains the PROC command. When you play a procedure script, PAL reads the commands between the command name PROC and the keyword ENDPROC and places them in RAM in a special "interpreted" form.

Unlike a macro, a procedure does not remain defined for the entire duration of a Paradox session. Instead, it remains active only during the play of the highest-level script in the script system that loaded the procedure. Once script play ends, the procedure is erased from memory. For this reason, you'll need to play a procedure script within each script system in which you will call that procedure.

Calling a Procedure

Once you have played a procedure script, you can command PAL to execute that procedure at any time during the remainder of the current script. If the procedure returns a value, then you can use it as you would a built-in PAL function or any formula. If the procedure performs an action, then you can use it in place of a series of PAL commands. In either case, you must call a procedure in the same way you would "call" a built-in function—by typing its name followed by a pair of parentheses that enclose the procedure's arguments, if any.

For example, suppose you want to use the COMPVAL() procedure shown in Figure 17-8 to calculate the value 25 years from today of investing $100 today at a guaranteed annual rate of 10 percent. To do this, you could use the simple script shown in Figure 17-10.

Figure 17-10 A Script That Calls a Procedure

```
Changing script C:\paradox3\proccall                          Script
....+...10....+...20....+...30....+...40....+...50....+...60....+...70....+...80
CLEAR
@10,20
PLAY "Proc1"
@10,20 ?? COMPVAL(100,.10,25)
SLEEP 5000
```

The first line clears the PAL canvas. The next line positions the cursor at the intersection of row 10 and column 20. The third command, *PLAY "Proc1"*, instructs PAL to play the script shown in Figure 17-8. The effect of playing this script is to load the procedure COMPVAL() into RAM in a compiled form.

As soon as COMPVAL() has been loaded, PAL can evaluate the command *??COMPVAL (100,.10,25)*. This command instructs PAL to evaluate the user-defined function COMPVAL(). When PAL evaluates this procedure, it first assigns the values of the arguments in the call to the variables in the procedure. PAL assigns the first argument in the call to the first variable in the procedure, the second argument to the second variable, and so on. In this case, PAL assigns the value 100 (the first value in the procedure call) to the variable *amount* (the first argument of the procedure definition). PAL assigns the value .10 (the second argument in the call) to the variable *rate* (the second variable in the procedure definition). Similarly, PAL assigns the value 25 to the variable *term*.

Once PAL has assigned the values from the call to the variables in the procedure definition, it evaluates the procedure's key formula: *amount*POW(1+rate,term)*. Since *amount* equals 100, *rate* equals .10, and *term* equals 25, this formula returns the value 1083.470594338. Since this procedure call is the argument of a ?? command, PAL displays this result at the current position of the cursor. The final command in the script, *SLEEP 5000*, ensures that this result will remain visible for five seconds.

In the example, we used literal values as the arguments in the call of the user-defined function COMPVAL(). However, you also can use formulas, functions, and references to variables and fields as arguments.

Efficiency Considerations

The procedure-calling script shown in Figure 17-10 takes advantage of only one of the benefits offered by procedures: the ability to pass arguments. By programming a calculation within a user-defined function, you don't have to type in a complex formula each time you want to perform that calculation. Instead, you can perform that calculation again and again simply by calling that procedure and supplying the appropriate arguments. Because the arguments of the procedure itself are generic, it will return a different value depending on what values you pass to it.

A second benefit of programming a calculation within a procedure is speed. When you play a procedure script, PAL stores the commands from that script in RAM in a compiled (or preinterpreted) form. This saves time in two ways. First, PAL does not have to read the command from disk each time it executes that command. Second, PAL does not have to interpret the commands into a form it can understand before executing them.

Unfortunately, you will not realize this increase in speed unless you call a procedure more than one time within a given script system. To call a procedure once within a script, you must do two things: play the procedure-containing script and call the procedure. When PAL plays the procedure-containing script, it reads each command in the script, interprets it, and stores it in RAM. When you call the procedure, PAL executes the commands it previously has read and interpreted.

On the second and subsequent times you call a procedure from within a script, however, PAL does not have to reread and reinterpret the commands in that procedure; it merely plays them. Consequently, PAL will execute a procedure much more rapidly the second and subsequent times it is called during a script.

The script shown in Figure 17-11 allows you to use the COMPVAL() procedure repeatedly within the same script. Because the majority of this script is enclosed in a WHILE True loop, PAL will execute it until it encounters a QUIT or QUITLOOP command—as it will when you enter n (or N) in response to the final ACCEPT statement in the script. Because the command *PLAY "Proc1"* is outside the loop, however, PAL will load the procedure COMPVAL() only once. Each time you supply a new set of values, PAL will execute the procedure without having to reread and reinterpret its commands.

Figure 17-11 Calling a Procedure More Than One Time

```
Changing script C:\paradox3\proccal2                        Script

....+...10....+...20....+...30....+...40....+...50....+...60....+...70....+...80
PLAY "Proc1"
WHILE True
  CLEAR
  @10,0
  ?? "Enter the amount to invest: "
  ACCEPT "N" TO x
  ? "Enter the annual rate of interest: "
  ACCEPT "N" TO y
  ? "Enter the number of years to hold the investment: "
  ACCEPT "N" TO z
  ? "Investing $",x," at ",y,"% will yield $",COMPVAL(x,y,z)," in ",z," years."
  ? "Calculate another? (y/n) "
  ACCEPT "A1" to answer
  IF answer <> "y"
    THEN QUITLOOP
  ENDIF
ENDWHILE
```

Public and Private Variables

The third advantage of using procedures instead of subroutine scripts is that you can use private variables with procedures. Normally, when you use the = or ACCEPT commands to define a variable, that variable remains defined for the remainder of the current Paradox session or until you use a RELEASE VARS command to undefine it. The values of these variables are accessible from any part of any script during the session and can even be saved for use in future scripts with the SAVEVARS command. For these reasons, most variables are termed "public" variables.

However, the variables you use as parameters in the PROC command that defines a procedure are private to the procedure itself. During the play of the procedure, PAL assigns values to these variables based on the order of the values in the procedure call and uses those values to calculate a result, perform an action, or both. Because PAL releases these variables after it executes a procedure, you cannot refer to an argument variable of a procedure before or after PAL has executed that procedure.

For example, the variables *amount*, *rate*, and *term* in the COMPVAL() procedure, shown in Figure 17-8, are private to that procedure because they are defined in the PROC command in the script that defines the procedure. Because they are private, you can refer to them only from within the procedure.

For example, suppose that after playing the script in Figure 17-11, which calls the COMPVAL() procedure, you press [PAL Menu], choose Value, and type *amount*. When you press ↵, Paradox will display the message *Variable amount has not been assigned a value*. This occurs because *amount* (like *rate* and *term*) is private to COMPVAL().

Importantly, the variables *x*, *y*, and *z* in the script in Figure 17-11 are public, not private. Remember—only variables that are defined within the PROC command in the script that defines a procedure are private to that procedure. Any variables that are defined in a script that calls a procedure (as are *x*, *y*, and *z*) will be public.

Because the variables used in the definition of a procedure are private to that procedure, you don't have to worry about these variables interfering with other variables in the script. This means you can use any procedure in any script without worrying about whether the variables in the procedure conflict with the variables in that script.

Other Private Variables

Although the variables defined within the PROC command in the definition of a procedure are private to that procedure, any other variables in that procedure will be public unless you tell PAL otherwise. For example, in the procedure

```
PROC ADDER(x,y)
   z=x+y
   Return z
ENDPROC
```

x and *y* are private to the procedure ADDER(), but *z* is public. Because *z* is public, you can reference it even after the procedure has been executed. In addition, the value assigned to *z* in the procedure will replace the value of any variable named *z* that you may have defined previously during the same Paradox session.

Fortunately, there is a way to make this kind of variable private. To do this, you must list the variables you want to make private after the keyword PRIVATE within the PROC command. This keyword must immediately follow the name and arguments of the procedure and must precede the commands that you want the procedure to execute. For example, the script

```
PROC ADDER(x,y)
   PRIVATE z
   z=x+y
   Return z
ENDPROC
```

makes *z* private to ADDER(). That way, the *z* used in ADDER() will not interfere with any public *z* used elsewhere in the script, and vice versa.

Closed Procedures

While the PRIVATE option lets you make variables private within a procedure, the CLOSED option lets you further isolate the environment in which a procedure operates. If you include the CLOSED keyword between the PROC command and the name of a procedure, that procedure and all procedures called within it will ignore all previously defined variables and procedures, including system variables. At the conclusion of a closed procedure, PAL forgets all procedures and variables defined within that procedure and its subordinate procedures. Closing a procedure ensures that PAL will return all memory used by the procedure to Paradox's central memory pool at the conclusion of the procedure.

Rather than playing a script to store a closed procedure in RAM, it is generally advisable to read closed procedures from the autoload library, that is, the procedure library in which PAL automatically searches for procedures that are not currently in RAM. (We'll discuss storing procedures in libraries and designating an autoload library later in this chapter.)

Though closed procedures ignore variables that are already stored in memory, there is a way to import existing variables into a closed procedure. You can use the USEVARS option to specify external variables that a closed procedure should recognize. The USEVARS option is especially useful if you want to maintain the values of system variables, such as *autolib*, which holds the name of PAL's autoloading procedure, or *errorproc*, which holds the name of the procedure PAL calls if a script encounters a run error. (We'll discuss both of these system variables in detail later in this chapter.) In order to use these system variables in a closed procedure, you must either define a value for these variables within the procedure or list them after the USEVARS option in the closed procedure's definition.

For example, this simple closed procedure

```
PROC CLOSED VIEWTABLE(tablename)
    USEVARS errorproc
    VIEW tablename
    WAIT TABLE
        PROMPT "Press [F2] when finished viewing table"
        UNTIL "F2"
ENDPROC
```

places the table named in the *tablename* argument on the workspace, then uses a WAIT TABLE command to let the user view the table until the user presses the [F2] key. Because the USEVARS command imports the value of the *errorproc* variable, PAL knows to execute the previously defined error procedure if the procedure encounters a run error. (We will also discuss the error procedures later in this chapter.) The VIEWTABLE() procedure might encounter a run error if the table named in *tablename* does not exist. Of course, you can use the USEVARS option to import any variable defined outside the closed system for use within the closed procedure and its subsystem of procedures.

Within a closed procedure, the SAVEVARS and RELEASE VARS commands affect only those variables that are defined within the closed system. As a result, there is no danger of releasing variables outside the system with the RELEASE VARS ALL command.

It is also worth noting that closed procedures are slightly slower than open procedures. It takes longer to enter and exit a closed procedure because PAL must save everything in memory before entering the procedure, then retrieve the saved variables and procedures after leaving the procedure. Closed procedures are especially useful for larger applications in which conserving memory is critical.

The Retval Variable

The variable *retval* gives you a way to access the value of a procedure call. As you know, when you end a procedure with a RETURN command followed by an expression, PAL returns the value of that expression to the calling script. In addition, PAL assigns that value to the temporary variable *retval*. When PAL plays the script shown in Figure 17-8 on page 763, for example, it assigns the value 1083.470594338 to the variable *retval*.

Once PAL has assigned a value to *retval*, that value remains in effect until PAL assigns another value to *retval* (for example, when you call another procedure), until you use the RELEASE VARS command to release it, or until you exit from Paradox. To access the value returned by the procedure later in the script, then, all you have to do is reference *retval*.

Releasing Procedures

The memory-resident nature of procedures has advantages and disadvantages. The main advantage, of course, is speed of execution. The primary disadvantage is that procedures occupy precious memory that could be used for other things. Even though PAL automatically undefines all procedures when it ends the play of a system of scripts, there may be times when you need to remove a procedure from RAM while a script is playing.

Fortunately, two special versions of PAL's RELEASE command allow you to undefine procedures in much the same way that you would undefine a variable or an array. To clear every currently defined procedure from RAM, just include the command RELEASE PROCS ALL in your script. To release only selected procedures, use the command form

        RELEASE PROCS *proc 1*, *proc 2*,...,*proc n*

where *proc 1*, *proc 2*, and so forth, are the names of the procedures you want to clear from RAM. For example, the command *RELEASE PROCS ADDER,COMPVAL* would remove the procedures ADDER() and COMPVAL() from RAM.

Procedure Libraries

As you begin to work with procedures, chances are that you'll store each procedure in its own script. That way, you can activate a specific procedure by playing the script that defines it. If you plan to use the procedure only within a single script system, you may include the PROC/ENDPROC commands directly within that system so that no PLAY command is necessary. Either way, you'll activate only one procedure at a time.

As you become more experienced with procedures, you probably will use more than one script within many of your PAL applications. In these cases, you may want to combine several PROC statements within a single script file so you can activate more than one procedure with a single PLAY command. When you issue the PLAY command, of course, PAL will read each procedure from within each PROC command one at a time, interpret it, and store it in RAM. These groupings of PROC statements are a primitive form of procedure library.

PAL offers an even more advanced form of procedure library. Through the use of PAL's WRITELIB command, you can store one or more procedures on disk in a compiled form—not as a series of PROC/ENDPROC commands. Because PAL interprets the commands before they are stored, it can execute them as soon as it reads them from disk—it does not have to interpret them first. The result is a significant timesaver for most large PAL applications.

Creating a Procedure Library

You must create a library before you can store any procedures in it. To create a procedure library, use PAL's CREATELIB command. The form of this command is

        CREATELIB *libraryname* SIZE *nprocs*

where *libraryname* is a string that specifies the name of the library you want to create. This name can be from one to eight characters long and can contain any characters that DOS allows in a file name. If the library is not in the current directory, you must include the full DOS path in the first argument. (Remember to use two backslashes wherever you normally would use only one.) When you issue the CREATELIB command, PAL creates an empty library file with the name you specify, plus the file-name extension .LIB. For example, you would use the command *CREATELIB "lib1"* to create a library named LIB1.LIB.

The *SIZE nprocs* specification in the CREATELIB command is optional. *Nprocs* is a numeric expression that tells PAL for what number of procedures to reserve space in the library. The value of *nprocs* can be between 50 and 300. If you exclude the *SIZE nprocs* specification, the library can contain up to 50 procedures.

Writing Procedures to a Library

Once you have created a procedure library, you can store one or more procedures into it. To place a procedure into a library, use PAL's WRITELIB command. The form of this command is

> WRITELIB *libraryname proc 1,...,proc n*

where *libraryname* is a string that specifies the library into which you want to store the procedures, and *proc 1,...,proc n* are the names of the procedures you want to store in that library.

A procedure must be in RAM before you can store it in a procedure library. That means that PAL has to read the PROC command that defines the procedure you want to save within the same script system that contains the WRITELIB command that saves it. If your procedures are stored in individual .SC files, then saving a procedure to a library is a simple matter of designing and playing a script that contains two commands: a PLAY command that loads the procedure-defining script, and a WRITELIB command that saves that procedure into a library.

For example, suppose you want to save the procedure named COMPVAL() defined by the script named Proc1 shown in Figure 17-8 into a library named FCNS.LIB. If FCNS.LIB did not yet exist, you would write and play the single-line script *CREATELIB "Fcns"*. (One way to do this is with a miniscript.) Once the library exists, you would write and play the script

> PLAY "Proc1" WRITELIB "Fcns" COMPVAL

Again, you probably could use a miniscript to do this. When PAL plays this script, it first will play the script Proc1, which interprets the procedure COMPVAL() and loads it into RAM. Once COMPVAL() is in RAM, the command *WRITELIB "Fcns" COMPVAL* saves a compiled copy of COMPVAL() into the procedure library FCNS.LIB.

You can use the WRITELIB command repeatedly to store additional procedures into a library. Each time you use the WRITELIB command to access a library that already contains one or more procedures, PAL will add the new procedure(s) to the library. A procedure library can hold up to 300 procedures—more than you'll likely want to put in a single library.

Reading Procedures from a Library

Once you have written one or more procedures into a library, you can use PAL's READLIB command to retrieve one or more procedures from that library into RAM. The form of the READLIB command is

READLIB *libraryname proc 1,...,proc n*

where *libraryname* is a string that specifies the library containing the procedure(s) you want to activate, and *proc 1,...,proc n* are the names of those procedures. If the library is not in the current directory, the argument must include the full path name.

Suppose you want to load the procedure named COMPVAL() from the procedure library FCNS.LIB. To do this, you would issue the command *READLIB "Fcns" COMPVAL*, either as a part of a larger script or as a miniscript. When PAL executes this command, it reads the procedure COMPVAL() from FCNS.LIB in the current directory. Because the procedures in a library are already interpreted, PAL does not have to interpret COMPVAL() as it reads it into RAM. This is more efficient than retrieving a procedure from a script file—a process that involves both reading the procedure from disk and interpreting it.

Once the procedure is in RAM, you can call it in the same way you would if you had read it from a script file. As always, the procedure will remain active until the end of the current script, or until you remove it with the RELEASE PROCS command, whichever comes first.

Taking an Inventory of a Library

PAL's INFOLIB command allows you to list the contents of a procedure library. When PAL reads this command, it will display a temporary LIST table that catalogues the procedures in the library. The LIST table that contains the procedure list includes two fields: Procedure and Size. The Procedure field lists the names of each procedure in the library. The Size field lists the number of bytes occupied by each procedure.

Removing Procedures from a Library

Although it is easy to add a procedure to a procedure library, it is next to impossible to remove a procedure from a library once it is stored. The only way to remove a procedure from a library is to use the CREATELIB command to delete and recreate the library, and then use WRITELIB commands to save into the library all but the procedures you wanted to remove.

Autoload Libraries

PARADOX.LIB is PAL's default autoload library. By autoload, we don't mean that PAL will load every procedure from PARADOX.LIB automatically whenever you run Paradox on your computer. Instead, we mean that PAL will look in that library if you call a procedure that it cannot find in RAM.

When you call a procedure, PAL first looks for that procedure in RAM. If PAL cannot find that procedure in RAM, it looks for a library named PARADOX.LIB. If that library exists, PAL will search for the procedure within it. If PAL finds the procedure in PARADOX.LIB, it will read that procedure from disk and then execute it. If PAL cannot find the PARADOX.LIB library, or if PARADOX.LIB does not contain the procedure you called, a script error will result.

Although PARADOX.LIB is the default name for the autoload library, you can command PAL to use a different library instead. To do this, you must use the = command to store the name of your autoload library in the system variable *autolib*. For example, suppose you want PAL to look in a library named JOE.LIB when it cannot find a called procedure in RAM. To do this, you would execute the command *autolib="Joe"* prior to making the procedure call. After you issue this command, PAL will look to JOE.LIB instead of PARADOX.LIB whenever you call a procedure that is not in RAM. JOE.LIB will remain the autoload library until PAL reads another command that redefines the *autolib* system variable. When you begin a new Paradox session, however, PARADOX.LIB will be the default library.

The PAL Debugger

In Chapter 14, we introduced the PAL Debugger, a useful tool that lets you test your scripts and identify errors within them. From within the PAL Debugger, you can step through a script one command at a time, viewing the results of each command as PAL executes it. In this way, you can identify errors within the script and, in some cases, correct them.

Entering the Debugger from an Error

In Chapter 14, we showed you how PAL automatically checks for errors as it plays a script. If PAL encounters an error during the execution of a script, it will pause, display the message *Script error – select Cancel or Debug from menu* in the message area, and present the two choices Cancel and Debug at the top of the screen. If you choose Cancel, PAL will cancel the execution of the script and return you to the Paradox workspace. If you choose Debug, however, PAL will take you into the PAL Debugger.

When you enter the Debugger from an error, PAL does a number of things. First, it lifts the PAL canvas to reveal the Paradox workspace. Second, it displays the script line containing the error in reverse video across the bottom of the screen. Third, it displays the name of the script, along with the number of the line it is displaying, on the second line from the bottom of the screen. Fourth, it uses a solid right arrow (the Debugger cursor) to point to the error within that line. Fifth, it presents an explanation of that error in the message area. Figure 17-12 shows an example of this basic Debugger screen.

Figure 17-12 The Basic Debugger Screen

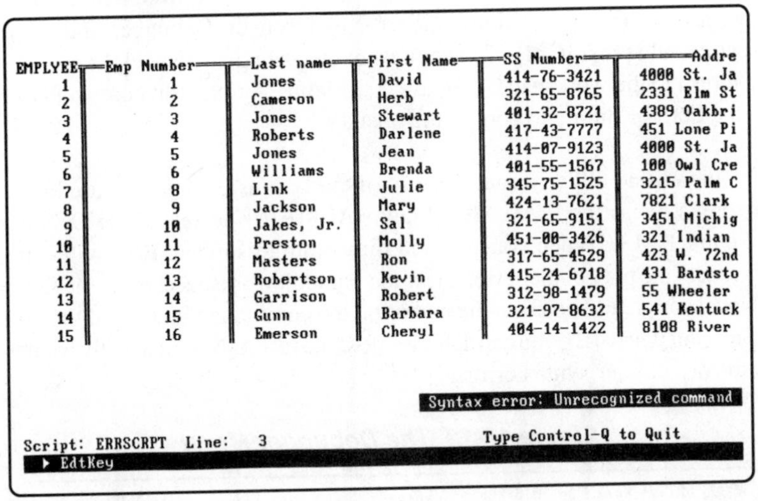

```
EMPLYEE┬─Emp Number─┬─Last name─┬─First Name─┬─SS Number─┬────────Addre
   1   │     1      ││ Jones     │ David      ││ 414-76-3421 ││ 4000 St. Ja
   2   │     2      ││ Cameron   │ Herb       ││ 321-65-8765 ││ 2331 Elm St
   3   │     3      ││ Jones     │ Stewart    ││ 401-32-8721 ││ 4389 Oakbri
   4   │     4      ││ Roberts   │ Darlene    ││ 417-43-7777 ││ 451 Lone Pi
   5   │     5      ││ Jones     │ Jean       ││ 414-87-9123 ││ 4000 St. Ja
   6   │     6      ││ Williams  │ Brenda     ││ 401-55-1567 ││ 100 Owl Cre
   7   │     8      ││ Link      │ Julie      ││ 345-75-1525 ││ 3215 Palm C
   8   │     9      ││ Jackson   │ Mary       ││ 424-13-7621 ││ 7821 Clark
   9   │    10      ││ Jakes, Jr.│ Sal        ││ 321-65-9151 ││ 3451 Michig
  10   │    11      ││ Preston   │ Molly      ││ 451-00-3426 ││ 321 Indian
  11   │    12      ││ Masters   │ Ron        ││ 317-65-4529 ││ 423 W. 72nd
  12   │    13      ││ Robertson │ Kevin      ││ 415-24-6718 ││ 431 Bardsto
  13   │    14      ││ Garrison  │ Robert     ││ 312-98-1479 ││ 55 Wheeler
  14   │    15      ││ Gunn      │ Barbara    ││ 321-97-8632 ││ 541 Kentuck
  15   │    16      ││ Emerson   │ Cheryl     ││ 404-14-1422 ││ 8100 River

                                    Syntax error: Unrecognized command

Script: ERRSCRPT  Line:    3            Type Control-Q to Quit
  ▶ EdtKey
```

Types of Errors

PAL categorizes script errors into two types: syntax errors and run errors. A syntax error results when PAL is unable to recognize a command in a script. In most cases, this happens when you misspell a command, include an incorrect number of arguments or list them in the wrong order, or omit a keyword. For example, the misspelled command EDT would cause a syntax error, as would the use of the command WHILE without the keyword ENDWHILE. Whenever PAL has entered the Debugger as the result of a syntax error, the message in the message window will begin with the words *Syntax error*.

A run error results when PAL encounters a command that has the correct syntax but is used in the wrong context. For example, the command *[]=5*, which attempts to make an entry into a table, will cause a run error if PAL is not in the Edit mode. Similarly, the command *PLAY "Abc"* will result in a run error if the file ABC.SC is not in the current directory. The message in the Debugger's message window will begin with the words *Run error* when PAL has encountered a run error.

The important difference between these types of errors is the extent to which you can recover from them within the PAL Debugger. If you encounter a syntax error, there's really nothing to do but exit from the Debugger and edit the script. If you encounter a run error, however, you generally can make a temporary correction and continue playing the script. Because syntax errors are more common and you can do less with them, we'll cover them first. Then, we'll show you how to use the Debugger to recover from a run error.

Debugging Syntax Errors

A syntax error results when PAL is unable to recognize a command within a script due to a misspelling, missing keywords, an inappropriate number of arguments, and so forth. Unfortunately, there's not much you can do about a syntax error from within the Debugger other than write down the explanation of the error, exit from the Debugger, and edit the script. To do this, you could press [Crtl]-[Q] to exit from the Debugger, cancel the execution of the script, and return to the workspace, then use the [Menu] Scripts Edit command to bring the script into the Script Editor and correct the mistake.

Fortunately, there is an easier way to perform these actions. While you are looking at the Debugger screen, press the [PAL Menu] key ([Alt]-[F10]) to reveal the Debugger menu shown in Figure 17-13. When you choose Editor from this menu, PAL will exit from the Debugger, cancel the play of the script, clear the Paradox workspace, enter the Script Editor, load the flawed script, and position the cursor on the command that caused the error. Even easier, by pressing [Ctrl]-[E], you can achieve the same result. You'll usually want to use this command to correct your syntax errors.

Figure 17-13 The Debugger Menu

```
Value Step Next Go MiniScript Where? Quit Pop Editor        Main
Calculate the value of an expression.
```

Debugging Run Errors

Fortunately, the PAL Debugger gives you more flexibility to deal with run errors than it does with syntax errors. When you enter the Debugger due to a run error, you can exit from the Debugger, edit the script, and replay it, just as you would for a syntax error. In most cases, however, you can adjust for the error from within the Debugger and continue playing the script. After the script has played to completion, you can enter the Script Editor and edit the script to remove the error.

For example, suppose that the table ABC is in the directory c:\paradox3\data, and that the current directory is c:\paradox3\info. Because ABC is not in the current directory, if you play the script in Figure 17-14, PAL will stop at the command *EDIT "Abc"*, and a run error will occur. If you choose Debug from the Script Error menu PAL displays when it encounters the error, you will see the screen shown in Figure 17-15. As you can see, PAL displays the line *EDIT "Abc"* at the bottom of the screen, points to that command, and presents the error message *Abc table not found* in the message area.

When PAL enters the Debugger, it lifts the PAL canvas to reveal the Paradox workspace and pauses the execution of the script at the point where the error occurred. For example, the prompt at the top of Figure 17-15 indicates that PAL has issued the [Menu] Modify Edit command and is waiting for the name of a table.

Figure 17-14 A Script That Causes a Run Error

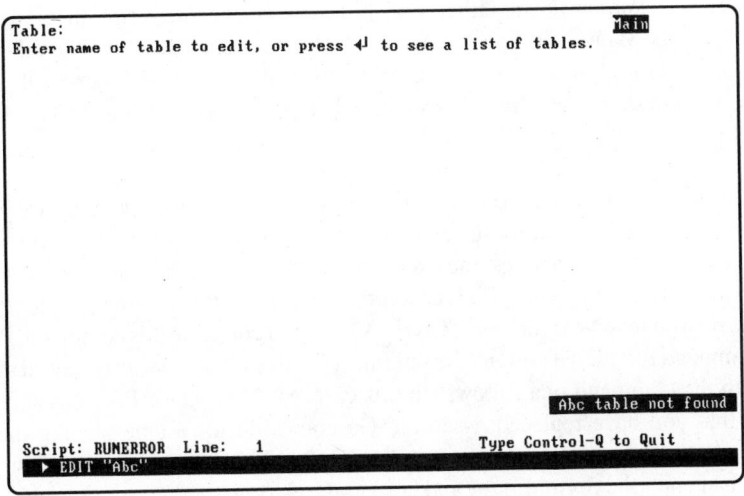

```
Changing script C:\paradox3\runerror                          Script
....+...10....+...20....+...30....+...40....+...50....+...60....+...70....+...80
EDIT "Abc"
SCAN
   FOR ISBLANK([Quantity])
   [Quantity] = 0
ENDSCAN
```

Figure 17-15 Another Debugger Screen

```
Table:                                                            Main
Enter name of table to edit, or press ◄┘ to see a list of tables.




                                                        Abc table not found

Script: RUNERROR  Line:  1                    Type Control-Q to Quit
    ▶ EDIT "Abc"
```

During this pause, you can use the Paradox menus, special keys, and even other scripts (usually miniscripts) to work with the objects on the Paradox workspace, just as if you weren't in a script at all. Once you use these techniques to adjust for the error, you can command PAL to resume the execution of the script.

Making the Command Usable: the Go Option

The error in the script in Figure 17-14 occurred because the table ABC was not in the current directory. There are two ways to deal with this problem. The first is to copy the table into the current directory. To do this, press the [Esc] key to exit from the Edit mode back to the Main menu. Then, issue the [Menu] Tools Copy Table command, specify the location and name of the table to copy (in this case, c:\paradox3\data\ABC), and specify the name for the copy, ABC. When you press ↵, Paradox will copy ABC into the current directory. (Remember—you're doing all this from within the Debugger.)

Once ABC is in the current directory, you can resume playing the script. In this case, you'll want PAL to continue by executing the command EDIT "Abc"—the one that PAL is pointing to within the Debugger. To resume playing the script with that command, just press the

[PAL Menu] key to reveal the PAL menu and select the **Go** option (or press **[Ctrl]-[G]**). Either way, this command tells PAL to resume playing the script, starting with the current command. Since you have copied ABC into the current directory, PAL will be able to execute the command *EDIT "Abc"*. As long as the script does not contain any other errors, PAL will continue to play it through to the end, just as if it never had entered the Debugger.

Replacing the Command: the Next Option

The second way to deal with this problem is to supply a replacement for the command that contains the error. You can do this either from the keyboard or with a script. In this case, press **[Esc]** to return to the Main menu, issue the Modify Edit command, type **c:\paradox\data\ABC**, and press ↵. As soon as you issue this command, PAL will bring the ABC table to the Paradox workspace in the Edit mode, which is exactly what the script command *EDIT "Abc"* was supposed to do.

Once you have made this correction, you can continue playing the script. Because you have executed a command that replaces the command that PAL is debugging, however, you will want to skip that command and resume executing the script with the command that follows it. To skip the command to which PAL is pointing, press the **[PAL Menu]** key to reveal the PAL menu, then choose Next (or press **[Ctrl]-[N]**). When you issue this command, PAL will skip the command to which it currently is pointing (in this case, the one that caused the error) and point to the command that follows (in this case, SCAN). Once PAL has skipped the command that you have replaced, issue the **Go** command to resume playing the script. Assuming that there are no more errors in the script, PAL will play it to completion. At that point, you can enter the Script Editor and correct the error within the script itself.

Using a Miniscript to Correct a Run Error

As we mentioned earlier, you can also correct a run error from within the Debugger by designing and playing a miniscript. The MiniScript option on the PAL Debugger menu makes this possible. For example, suppose you are running the script shown in Figure 17-14, and PAL has presented the Debugger screen shown in Figure 17-15. To correct the error, press the **[PAL Menu]** key to reveal the Debugger menu, choose **MiniScript**, and type the command **COPY "c:\\paradox3\\data\\ABC" "ABC"**.

When you press ↵, PAL will not play this command immediately, as it would if you had designed the miniscript outside the Debugger. Instead, it will place the miniscript in the highlighted script line at the bottom of the screen. To play the miniscript, you must press **[PAL Menu]** and issue the Go command (or press **[Ctrl]-[G]**). When you do this, PAL will play the miniscript in its entirety, copying the table ABC into the current directory. When PAL finishes playing the miniscript, it will again present the error-causing command in the Debugger's script line and await your instructions. In this case, you'll want to choose **Go** from the Debugger menu to resume playing the script. Since you have copied ABC into the current directory, PAL will be able to play the current command, *EDIT "Abc"*, and continue to execute the remainder of the script.

However, a miniscript is often the only way to correct an error. For example, suppose your script contains the command $z=x+y$, and this command causes the run error *Run error: The variable x has not been assigned a value.* There is no way to assign a value to x from the Paradox menus. You must execute a miniscript such as $x=3$ if you want to use the Go command to proceed.

Entering the Debugger Voluntarily

Although you will enter the Debugger most commonly as the result of errors in your scripts, you also can enter it if you haven't encountered an error. There are three ways to do this. First, in any situation other than during the playing or debugging of a script, you can enter the Debugger by pressing the [PAL Menu] key ([Alt]-[F10]), choosing Debug from the PAL menu, and typing the name of a script. When you enter the Debugger in this way, PAL will present a screen much like the one shown in Figure 17-15. Because you did not enter the Debugger as the result of an error, however, PAL will display the first line of the script—which may not contain an error—at the bottom of the screen. Since no error has occurred, no error message will appear in the message area.

The second way to enter the Debugger is to include the DEBUG command in a script. When PAL encounters a DEBUG command within a script, it suspends execution of that script and enters the Debugger, placing at the bottom of the screen the line that contains the command that follows the DEBUG command. The arrow will point to the command that follows the DEBUG command. Because PAL did not enter the Debugger as a result of an error, it will not display an explanation in the message area.

The third way to enter the Debugger is to press [Ctrl]-[Break] while PAL is executing a script. PAL will then pause the execution of the script and will present the options Cancel and Debug. If you choose Debug, PAL will enter the Debugger, place at the bottom of the screen the line it was executing, and point to the command it was about to execute when you interrupted the script. If you choose Cancel, PAL will return you to the main Paradox workspace. (Note that [Ctrl]-[Break] will not work during the play of a password-protected script.)

The Step Command

Now that you know how to enter the PAL Debugger outside the context of an error, you probably are asking, "Why would I want to?" The answer is: to better understand the flow of your script. By using the Debugger menu's Step command, you can execute a script one command at a time. Because the PAL canvas is lifted while PAL is in the Debugger, you can view the effect of each command on the Paradox workspace as PAL executes it. When you issue the Step command, either by pressing the [PAL Menu] key to reveal the Debugger menu and choosing Step, or by pressing [Ctrl]-[S], PAL will execute the command to which the Debugger cursor currently is pointing. After PAL executes that command, it will move the Debugger cursor to the next command and await your instructions, which might be another Step command ([Ctrl]-[S]), a Go command ([Ctrl]-[G]), or another command.

Other Debugger Commands

In addition to Go, Next, Step, MiniScript, Editor, and Quit, the Debugger menu contains three other useful commands: Value, Where?, and Pop. Although you probably will not use these three commands as often as you will the other six, they will come in handy in some programming situations.

The Value Command

The Value command on the Debugger menu does the same thing that the Value command on the PAL menu does; it lets you calculate the value of an equation or function or discern the current value of a variable. You can use the Value command from within the Debugger to determine the current value of a variable. For example, suppose you are debugging a script that uses a counter variable x. You can use the Value command to determine the current value of the counter variable from within the Debugger. To do this, issue the Value command (by choosing it from the PAL menu) and then type x. When you press ←, PAL will display the current value of x in the message area.

The Where? Command

The Where? command on the Debugger menu allows you to determine where you are within a multiple-level script. When you issue this command (either by accessing the Debugger menu and choosing Where? or by pressing [Ctrl]-[W]), PAL will present a graphic representation of the levels of the script and pinpoint the level that contains the command PAL currently is debugging.

For example, suppose that PAL is playing a script named Main. This script contains the command *PLAY "Sub1"*, which calls the script Sub1. Also suppose that the script Sub1 contains a WHILE command without a matching ENDWHILE keyword. When PAL comes to the end of Sub1, it will stop the play of the script and present the choices Cancel and Debug. If you choose Debug, PAL will present the Debugger menu. If you issue the Where? command at this point, your screen will look like the one shown in Figure 17-16. As you can see, PAL represents the levels of the script as a series of overlapping "pages." The upper level is the script Main. The second level is the script Sub1. The third level is the Debugger. The message *(You are here)* indicates that PAL currently is within the Debugger. As soon as you press any key, PAL will return you to the Debugger menu.

The Pop Command

The Pop command is another tool you can use to debug multiple-level scripts. You can issue the Pop command either by choosing it from the Debugger menu or by pressing [Ctrl]-[P]. This command causes PAL to jump out of the current subroutine and return to the command that follows the command that called the subroutine. Once you are back at the higher-level script, you can use the Go command to continue playing the script.

Figure 17-16 The Where? Command

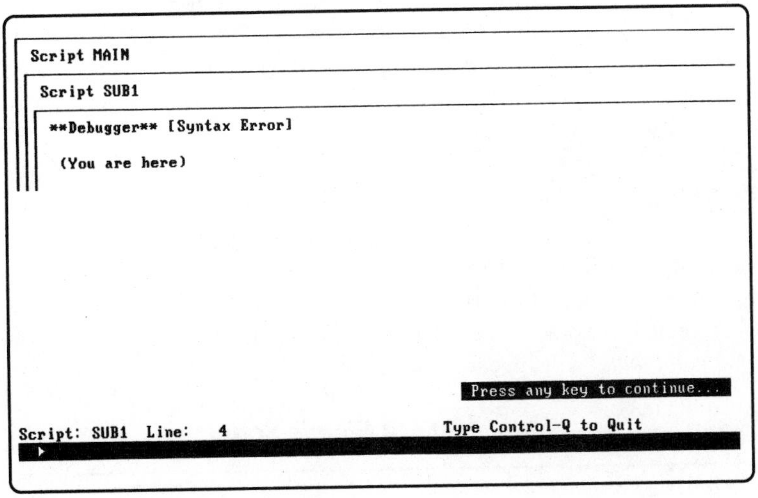

```
Script MAIN
  Script SUB1
    **Debugger** [Syntax Error]

     (You are here)




                                              Press any key to continue...
  Script: SUB1  Line:   4             Type Control-Q to Quit
    ▶
```

Errorproc

Normally, when a run error occurs during the execution of a script, the script will stop and Paradox will display the familiar Cancel/Debug menu. Fortunately, Paradox offers a way around these serious errors. PAL allows you to designate a special error-handling procedure that will be called whenever a run error occurs. This procedure analyzes the error and, if you want, corrects it—all without interrupting your script.

To create an error-handling procedure, you first design the procedure as you would any other procedure. Then, you assign the name of that procedure to the special system variable *errorproc*. For example, if you've written an error procedure named TROUBLE(), you would activate it by including the line

    errorproc = "TROUBLE"

in the main script for your application. Once you've activated an error procedure for a script, PAL will call that procedure automatically whenever a run error occurs. PAL plays the error procedure instead of displaying the familiar Cancel/Debug menu.

The procedure you write can use the error-handling functions ERRORCODE() and ERROR-MESSAGE() to help determine what error has occurred and what course of action should be taken to correct it. (See Chapter 15 for more information on these functions.)

All error procedures end with one of three RETURN commands. If the procedure ends with the command *RETURN 0*, PAL will retry the statement in the script that caused the error after it has played the error procedure. Ending the error procedure with *RETURN 0* is like pressing [Ctrl]-[S] while debugging a script. If the procedure ends with the command *RETURN 1*, PAL will skip the statement that caused the error after it has played the error procedure. Ending the error procedure with *RETURN 1* is like pressing [Ctrl]-[N] while debugging a script. Finally, you can end the error procedure with the command *RETURN 2*. A returned value of 2 tells Paradox to display the Cancel/Debug menu after it has played the error procedure. If the error procedure returns a value other than 0, 1, or 2, or if no value is returned, then the calling script will act as if 2 were returned.

An Example

Consider the simple one-line script Viewcust, shown in Figure 17-17. If you play this script when there is no table named CUSTOMER in the current directory, then a run error will occur, and PAL will display the Cancel/Debug menu. If you select Debug, the error message *Customer table not found* will appear.

Figure 17-17 A Simple Script

```
Designing script C:\paradox3\viewcust                              Script
....+...10....+...20....+...30....+...40....+...50....+...60....+...70....+...80
VIEW "Customer"
```

On the other hand, you might write an error procedure for this simple script like the one shown in Figure 17-18. This script defines a procedure named EP() and writes it into a library that is named EP.LIB. This procedure stores the result of the ERRORCODE() function—the numeric code of the error that has occurred—in the variable *ecode*. Then, the procedure stores the result of the ERRORMESSAGE() function—the error message associated with that error—in the variable *emsg*.

Figure 17-18 An Error Procedure

```
Changing script C:\paradox3\ep                                     Script
....+...10....+...20....+...30....+...40....+...50....+...60....+...70....+...80
PROC EP()
 PRIVATE ecode,emsg
 ecode = ERRORCODE()
 emsg = ERRORMESSAGE()
 SWITCH
  CASE ecode = 5:
   MESSAGE emsg + " error. Creating CUSTOMER table..."
   CREATE "Customer" "Customer #":"N", "Name":"A30", "Balance":"$"
   RETURN 0
  CASE ecode = 21 :
   MESSAGE esmg + " error. Cannot access table."
   SLEEP 5000
   RETURN 1
  OTHERWISE:
   RETURN 2
 ENDSWITCH
ENDPROC

CREATELIB "EP"
WRITELIB "EP" EP
```

Each of the CASE conditions in the SWITCH command tests the value of *ecode*. The first CASE command compares the contents of *ecode* to 5, the error code for a *File not found* error. If *ecode* contains the value 5—meaning that a *File not found* error has occurred—then the procedure will display the message *File not found error. Creating CUSTOMER table....* Notice that the procedure creates this message using the *emsg* variable, which contains the error message associated with the error that has occurred. While this message is in view, the procedure will create the CUSTOMER table. Then, the command *RETURN 0* will end the procedure, repeating the command in the script that caused the error.

Similarly, the second CASE command compares the contents of *ecode* to 21, the error code for an *Insufficient password rights* error. If *ecode* contains the value 21—meaning that an *Insufficient password rights* error has occurred—then the procedure will display for five seconds the message *Insufficient password rights error. Cannot access table.* Then, the *RETURN 1* command will end the procedure, skipping the command in the script that caused the error.

The OTHERWISE command handles any other errors that may have occurred. If *ecode* contains any value other than 5 or 21, the *RETURN 2* command will end the procedure and display the Cancel/Debug menu.

To activate the EP() procedure for the Viewcust script, you must add two lines to the Viewcust script, as shown in Figure 17-19. The command *errorproc = "EP"* defines the name of the error procedure you want PAL to call if a run error occurs (that is, if the CUSTOMER table is not in the current directory). The statement *READLIB "EP" EP* reads the EP() procedure from the EP.LIB library. From now on, if the CUSTOMER table doesn't exist, Paradox will execute the EP() procedure instead of immediately displaying the Cancel/Debug menu.

Figure 17-19 Adding Error Trapping

```
Designing script C:\paradox3\viewcust                      Script
....+...10....+...20....+...30....+...40....+...50....+...60....+...70....+...80
errorproc = "EP"
READLIB "EP" EP
VIEW "Customer"
```

Notes

You will usually want to store your error procedures in procedure libraries. Keep in mind, however, that an error procedure must be in memory before PAL needs it (that is, before an error occurs). If the procedure is stored in a library, you must read the error procedure from a library before the procedure is needed. Usually, you'll read the error procedure into memory at the same time you activate the error procedure. Interestingly, PAL cannot automatically read an error procedure from an autoload library. Even if you've stored your error procedure in an autoload library, you'll still need to read that error procedure into memory before an error occurs. Of course, PAL will be able to read any procedures that are called by an error procedure from an autoload library.

Printing Your Scripts

PAL's final debugging tool—printing a hard copy of a script—is not a part of the PAL Debugger. In fact, you cannot print a script while you are in the Debugger—you must be editing that script from within the Script Editor to print it. To print a copy of the script you are editing, issue the [Menu] Print command or press the [Instant Report] key ([Alt]-[F7]). Either way, PAL will send a copy of the script to your printer. You can use the resulting hard copy to document and debug your scripts.

Queries in Scripts

In Chapter 13, we showed you how to save queries in scripts. In addition to letting you record queries in this manner, PAL provides other tools that can make queries even more useful in scripts. The SETQUERYORDER and Query commands include options that let you control the field arrangement of ANSWER tables, and tilde variables let you use different values in a selection condition defined in a query.

Determining Field Order

As we explained in Chapter 7, you can use the Custom Configuration Program (CCP) to determine whether Paradox bases the field order for ANSWER tables on the queries that produce the ANSWER tables or the field arrangement of the tables on which the queries are based. Actually, the CCP setting determines the default field order for ANSWER tables. PAL includes a command that changes this default field order, as well as options in the basic Query commands that let you specify field orders for individual queries.

The SETQUERYORDER Command

The SETQUERYORDER command sets the default field order to correspond to either the query image or the underlying table. This command is followed by one of two keywords: IMAGEORDER or TABLEORDER.

The SETQUERYORDER IMAGEORDER command tells Paradox to display ANSWER tables with fields arranged in the same order as they appear in the query image. This setting lets you change the structure of the ANSWER table by rotating the columns in the query image—a very useful capability if you want to cross-tabulate or graph data in ANSWER. Changing the field order in the ANSWER table can also be useful if you want to sort the ANSWER table on the entries in a particular field. As we explained in Chapter 7, if you mark fields with a check mark in the query image, Paradox will sort the ANSWER table based on each field, in the order in which the fields appear in the table. As a result, you can sort an ANSWER table on a certain field by moving that field to the front of the query image and using the IMAGEORDER option.

The SETQUERYORDER TABLEORDER command tells Paradox to arrange the fields in the ANSWER table in the same order as they appear in the table that is being queried. Duplicating the structure of the original table in ANSWER ensures that you will be able to use the ADD command to add records from one table to the other or the *Menu {Tools} {Copy}* keystroke representation to copy objects from one family to the other.

Setting Field Order for a Single Query

Just as the SETQUERYORDER command overrides the CCP's default field order, a query in a script can set its own field order to override the default field order established by the CCP or the SETQUERYORDER command. To set the field order for an individual ANSWER table, add the IMAGEORDER or TABLEORDER option to the query definition in the script. For example, the scripts shown in Figures 17-20 and 17-21 contain variations of the same query on the SAMPLE table. The field order in the queries is different from that of the original table. To create the scripts, we rotated the query image, then used the [Menu] Scripts QuerySave command to save the query. Then, we edited each script, adding a field order specification (either TABLEORDER or IMAGEORDER) within the Query command, and a Do_It! command at the end of the script to process the query.

Figure 17-20 A Query with TABLEORDER

```
Changing script C:\paradox3\tableord                        Script
....+...10....+...20....+...30....+...40....+...50....+...60....+...70....+...80
Query
  TABLEORDER
  Sample :  Name   :    Date     : Number :
         : Check   : Check >6/6/88 : Check  :
         :         :              :        :
         :         :              :        :
Endquery
Do_It!
```

Figure 17-21 A Query with IMAGEORDER

```
Changing script C:\paradox3\imageord                        Script
....+...10....+...20....+...30....+...40....+...50....+...60....+...70....+...80
Query
  IMAGEORDER
  Sample :  Name   :    Date     : Number :
         : Check   : Check >6/6/88 : Check  :
         :         :              :        :
         :         :              :        :
Endquery
Do_It!
```

Because the field order option in Figure 17-20 is TABLEORDER, this script will produce an ANSWER table with fields arranged in the same order as the SAMPLE table. Figure 17-22 shows the ANSWER table produced by this script.

Figure 17-22 A TABLEORDER ANSWER Table

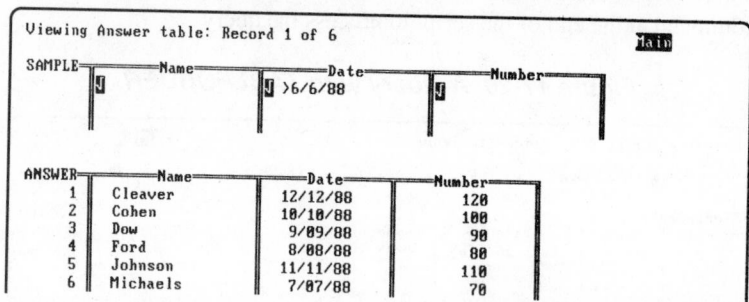

However, the query shown in Figure 17-21, which uses the IMAGEORDER option specification, will produce an ANSWER table with the same field order as the query in the script. Figure 17-23 shows the ANSWER table that this script will produce.

Figure 17-23 An IMAGEORDER ANSWER Table

```
Viewing Answer table: Record 1 of 6                        Main
SAMPLE        Name            Date           Number
              J         J >6/6/88       J

ANSWER        Name            Date          Number
   1      Cleaver          12/12/88         120
   2      Cohen            10/10/88         100
   3      Dow               9/09/88          90
   4      Ford              8/08/88          80
   5      Johnson          11/11/88         110
   6      Michaels          7/07/88          70
```

If the field arrangement of an ANSWER table is crucial in the remainder of your script, then you should include one of the field order options in the query. Otherwise, the default field order setting could cause problems by creating an inappropriately structured ANSWER table. For example, if your script requires an ANSWER table patterned after the field order of the query image in order to produce a graph, then you should be sure to add the IMAGEORDER keyword to the query in the script.

Tilde Variables

So far, we have used variables only within the context of PAL programs. However, you also can use variables within your Paradox queries to create selection conditions that are based on the results of PAL functions and formulas.

Using a variable as a selection condition within a query is as simple as prefacing that variable with a tilde (~) and entering it into the appropriate position in the query. Before you evaluate the query, of course, you should make sure that the variable contains the value you want to use as the basis of the selection condition.

Suppose you want to select from the simple PEOPLE table shown in Figure 17-24 the records with Age entries that exceed the average of all the entries in the Age field. To do this, you need to store the average of the Age field entries in a variable and design a query whose selection condition is based upon the tilde form of that variable. The order in which you perform these two tasks is not important.

Figure 17-24 The PEOPLE Table

```
Viewing People table: Record 1 of 10                        Main

PEOPLE         Name              Age
     1   Doug                     28
     2   Tom                      26
     3   Judy                     25
     4   Gena                     28
     5   Ken                      35
     6   Julie                    26
     7   Steve                    27
     8   Barbara                  36
     9   Denise                   31
    10   Pat                      21
```

In this case, we'll use a miniscript to calculate the average value of the entries in the Age field and store that result in a variable named *avg*. To do this, press the [PAL Menu] key ([Alt]-[F10]), choose MiniScript, and type **avg=CAVERAGE("People","Age")**. When you press ↵, PAL will evaluate this command and store the value 28.3 in the variable *avg*. To confirm that *avg* holds this value, issue the Value command, type **avg**, and press ↵.

After storing the average Age entry in *avg*, you can design a query that uses the tilde form of that variable to select all records with Age field entries greater than that average. To design this query, issue the [Menu] Ask command and select the PEOPLE table. Once the blank query form appears on the screen, press the [Check Mark] key while the cursor is in the record number column to select both fields of the table. Then, move the cursor to the Age column and type the selection condition **>~avg**. Figure 17-25 shows the completed query.

Figure 17-25 A Tilde-variable Query

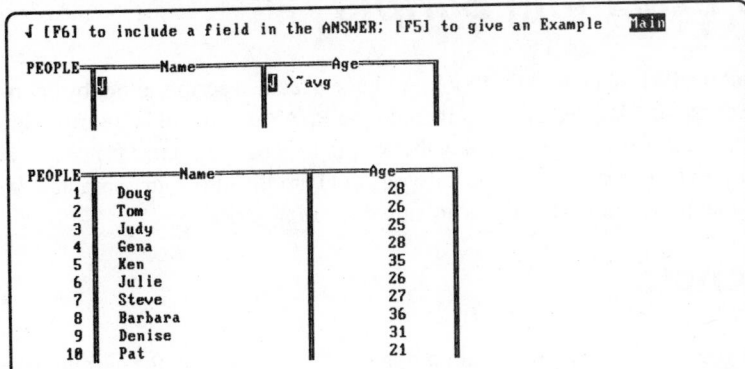

When you press [Do-It!] to execute this query, Paradox will present the ANSWER table shown in Figure 17-26. As you can see, Paradox has selected only the three records with Age field entries that exceed the value stored in *avg*: 28.3.

Figure 17-26 The ANSWER Table

```
 Viewing Answer table: Record 1 of 3                              Main

 PEOPLE             Name               Age
          █                     █ >~avg



 PEOPLE              Name               Age
      1    Doug                    28
      2    Tom                     26
      3    Judy                    25
      4    Gena                    28
      5    Ken                     35
      6    Julie                   26
      7    Steve                   27
      8    Barbara                 36
      9    Denise                  31
     10    Pat                     21


 ANSWER             Name               Age
      1    Barbara                 36
      2    Denise                  31
      3    Ken                     35
```

Because you can store the result of any PAL function or equation in a variable, and because the tilde symbol allows you to use any PAL variable within a query, you can design queries that select records based on the value returned by any PAL formula or function. Because the queries refer to variables, not literal values, they will select different sets of records each time the value of the variable changes. For example, if you add an 11th record with the Age field entry 100 to the PEOPLE table, and again use a miniscript to calculate an average Age field entry, PAL will store the value 34.8 in *avg*. When you re-execute the query shown in Figure 17-25, Paradox will select only the fifth and eighth records from PEOPLE.

Auto-executing Scripts

Throughout the PAL section of this book, we have executed scripts either by choosing Play from the Scripts or PAL menus, or by including a PLAY command in a script. Either way, we had to instruct PAL explicitly to play the script. In certain circumstances, however, PAL will play a script automatically as soon as you load Paradox into your computer. We'll refer to a script that plays automatically as an auto-executing script.

Init Scripts

Whenever you load Paradox into your computer, PAL will look in the current directory for a script named INIT.SC. If PAL finds a script with that name, it will play that script as soon as Paradox has finished loading. This feature allows you to create complete turnkey applications or to automate housekeeping tasks, such as changing the current directory.

For example, Figure 16-33 on page 738 shows a script named Menu2 that you might want to set up as an auto-executing script. When PAL plays this script, it presents you with a menu that allows you to select the directory in which you want to work.

To make this script an auto-executing script, you need only give it the name Init. If you have already created a script, you can change its name by issuing the [Menu] Tools Rename Script command. Once you have changed the name of the script to Init, PAL will run it automatically whenever you load Paradox. When PAL runs the script, it will offer four choices: Orders, General Ledger, Accounts Payable, and Cancel. If you choose any of the first three options, PAL will issue a SETDIR command to change the current directory. If you choose Cancel, PAL will exit from the script without changing the directory. When Paradox is loaded, the active directory will be the one you specified.

Running a Script from DOS

Paradox provides yet another way to execute a script automatically as it loads. Ordinarily, you will load Paradox into your computer by typing the word *paradox3* at the DOS prompt. If you follow this command with the name of a script, however, as soon as Paradox has been loaded, it will play that script. For example, if a script named Start is in the current directory when you start Paradox, you can load Paradox and play that script automatically by typing *paradox3 start* at the DOS prompt.

If the script you want to play is not in the current directory, you must preface the name of the script with its drive and/or directory. For example, if the Start script is in the directory c:\paradox3\scripts, then you would type *paradox3 c:\paradox3\scripts\start* to play the Start script.

You can use this method in place of, or in conjunction with, an Init script. If you type a script name at the DOS prompt, and the current directory contains a script named Init, PAL will play the Init script before it plays the one you specified.

If either an Init script or a script that you name at the DOS prompt ends with an EXIT command, then Paradox will return to DOS after the play of the script is over. This technique allows you to create fully automated applications that never give full control of Paradox to the user. If you often name a certain script at the DOS command line, you may want to include it in a simple .BAT file.

Other PAL Commands

In this and the previous four chapters of this book, we have presented most, but not all, of PAL's programming commands. In the final part of this chapter, we'll briefly discuss those we haven't covered.

The BEEP Command

The BEEP command instructs PAL to issue a short beep. This command, which accepts no arguments, is useful for signaling the end of a script, drawing attention to a message, and so forth. For example, the script fragment

```
@10,0
?? "Enter a number between 1 and 10: "
BEEP BEEP BEEP
ACCEPT "N" to guess
```

uses three consecutive beeps to tell the user to make an entry.

The ECHO Command

In most cases, the PAL canvas obscures the workspace during the execution of a script. PAL's ECHO command lets you lift the PAL canvas and watch the script manipulate the Paradox workspace. The form of this command is

    ECHO *speed*

where the single argument *speed* must be one of the following four keywords: NORMAL, FAST, SLOW, or OFF. The NORMAL option commands PAL to play the script at approximately the speed it would play if it were not revealing the Paradox workspace (i.e., at maximum speed). The FAST option causes PAL to play the script about as fast as you could issue commands from the keyboard. The SLOW option instructs PAL to play the script slower than normal. The OFF option tells PAL to drop the PAL canvas again. The effect of the ECHO OFF command is much like that of the [Menu] Scripts ShowPlay command.

The EDITLOG Command

While you are editing a table or tables on the workspace, Paradox keeps a transactional log of all the changes that have been made to each table. Paradox uses these transactional logs to undo the changes when you press the [Ctrl]-[U] key. The EDITLOG command lets you accept or undo groups of changes made during an Edit session, and it includes several options that have different effects on the current table.

The EDITLOG MARK command places a marker at the current point in the transactional log for the current table. There is no limit to the number of log markers a script can place during an Edit session. The EDITLOG REVERT command undoes all changes made to the current table since the last log marker in that table's transactional log. If there are no markers in the transactional log, then the EDITLOG REVERT command will undo all changes made to the table during the Edit session. If several log markers are in place, then subsequent EDITLOG REVERT commands will work backward through the log, undoing all of the changes between the markers.

The EDITLOG INDEX command updates all the primary and secondary indexes in the current table. This reindexing can take quite some time but improves the speed of LOCATE and ZOOM commands, as well as queries. However, you lose these performance gains as soon as a change to the table makes the indexes obsolete. You can continue to use the EDITLOG REVERT command to undo changes to a table after using the EDITLOG INDEX command to update its indexes.

The EDITLOG PERMANENT command makes all changes that have been made to the current table permanent and updates all indexes for that table. After a script issues this command, it cannot use the EDITLOG REVERT command or the CANCELEDIT command to undo changes to the current table. However, the script can use these commands to undo changes to other tables on the workspace, provided that the script has not issued the EDITLOG PERMANENT command for that table.

The EXECPROC Command

PAL's EXECPROC command can be used to execute (call) a procedure that has no arguments. This command has the form

EXECPROC *procedure*

where *procedure* is a variable that contains the name of the procedure you want to execute or a string that identifies the name of the procedure. The procedure called by EXECPROC may not contain any arguments. The primary advantage of EXECPROC over EXECUTE (which we'll explain in the next section) is that PAL can execute the EXECPROC command faster than the equivalent command *EXECUTE procedure + "()"*.

Suppose the variable *test* contains the procedure name REFUND(). The command

EXECPROC test

will execute the procedure REFUND().

The EXECUTE Command

PAL's EXECUTE command allows you to use string formulas to produce PAL command statements that PAL will execute just like any other PAL command. The form of this command is

EXECUTE *string*

where the argument of the command is a string (usually a formula) that returns a valid PAL command sequence.

For example, suppose you are editing a table with the structure shown in Figure 17-27. As you can see, the table contains a field for the sales amount for each month of the year.

Figure 17-27 The Structure of the SALES Table

```
Viewing Struct table: Record 1 of 13                          Main  ▲═══

STRUCT┬═══════Field Name══════┬Field Type┐
   1 │ Year                   │ A4
   2 │ Jan Sales              │ $
   3 │ Feb Sales              │ $
   4 │ Mar Sales              │ $
   5 │ Apr Sales              │ $
   6 │ May Sales              │ $
   7 │ Jun Sales              │ $
   8 │ Jul Sales              │ $
   9 │ Aug Sales              │ $
  10 │ Sep Sales              │ $
  11 │ Oct Sales              │ $
  12 │ Nov Sales              │ $
  13 │ Dec Sales              │ $
```

Suppose you want your script to add the total for today's sales, which is stored in the variable *newsales*, to the sales field for the current month, which happens to be February. The following two-line script, which uses the EXECUTE command, will do the trick:

```
m = MOY(Today())
EXECUTE "["+m+"Sales] = ["+m+"Sales]+newsales"
```

This script will work because the MOY() function returns a three-letter representation of the month for a date. If today's date is 2/15/89, for example, the MOY() function will return the string *Feb*, and PAL will evaluate the EXECUTE command as *[Feb Sales] = [Feb Sales]+newsales*.

The FIRSTSHOW Command

PAL's FIRSTSHOW command makes the current image on the workspace the first image displayed on the screen. This command is useful if your script works with several tables at once and you want to use the WAIT command to present a table in the table view. If the number of rows in the table is small, Paradox may attempt to display several tables on the screen simultaneously. The extra tables on the screen might confuse the user. However, if you issue the FIRSTSHOW command before the WAIT command, it will "push" all the images above the current one off the screen.

Unfortunately, the FIRSTSHOW command has no effect on images below the current one, if there are any. They might still appear on the screen. Therefore, the FIRSTSHOW command works best on the last image in the workspace.

The FORMTABLES Command

The FORMTABLES command provides a list of the tables embedded on a multitable form. This command stores the names of the embedded tables in an array. The form for this command is

FORMTABLES *tablename formname arrayname*

where *tablename* is the name of the master table for the multitable form, *formname* is the number of the form, and *arrayname* is the array in which the command is to store the names of the tables embedded on the form. The *formname* argument must be either one of the strings *F* or *1* to *14*, or a number between 1 and 14. PAL creates the array specified in the *arrayname* argument if it does not already exist. The FORMTABLES command sets the *retval* system variable to True if the form includes embedded forms, or False if it does not.

For example, in Chapter 4, we embedded forms for the SALESORD and PROJECTS tables on form 5 for the CLIENTS table. As a result, the command *FORMTABLES "Clients" 5 names* will store the string *Projects* in the array element *names[1]*, the string *Salesord* in the array element *names[2]*, and the logical value True in the *retval* variable.

The KEYPRESS Command

The KEYPRESS command allows PAL to type a character from within a script. The form of this command is

> KEYPRESS *keycode*

where *keycode* is the PAL keycode expression representing the key PAL should press.

When used in conjunction with the GETCHAR() function and IF command, KEYPRESS allows you to set up keyboard filters that intercept and test every character typed from the keyboard. If a character typed is among the ones you have told KEYPRESS to look for, PAL will take the action you specify. If the character is not among the ones you are looking for, PAL will pass that character on to Paradox.

The script shown in Figure 17-28 on the following page demonstrates the use of the KEYPRESS command within a simple keyboard filter that disables the use of the [Help] key. The ECHO NORMAL command ensures that you will be able to see what is happening on the Paradox workspace as you issue commands from the keyboard. The *WHILE True/ ENDWHILE* loop that encloses the remainder of the script ensures that the script will stay in effect for the duration of the current Paradox session. The command *x=GETCHAR()* tells PAL to wait for you to type a key and to store the ASCII code for that key in the variable *x*. The IF statement that follows tests to see if you pressed the [Help] key. If so, PAL beeps but does not pass the keystroke on to Paradox. If you press any key but [Help], however, PAL will execute the command *KEYPRESS x*. The effect of this command is to pass the keystroke on to Paradox, just as if it never had trapped the key at all.

The LOCATE Command

PAL's LOCATE command allows PAL to search a table for a record that matches the entries you specify in one or more fields. If PAL finds a matching record, it will move the cursor to that record. This command has two forms. The first form

> LOCATE *value*

searches for the first occurrence of its argument, *value*, among the entries in the current field of the current table, starting at the first record of the table.

Figure 17-28 The KEYPRESS Command

```
Changing script C:\paradox3\keyprssc                           Script
....+...10....+...20....+...30....+...40....+...50....+...60....+...70....+...80
ECHO NORMAL
WHILE True
  x = GETCHAR( )
  IF x = ASC("Help") THEN
    BEEP
  ELSE
    KEYPRESS x
  ENDIF
ENDWHILE
```

The second form of the LOCATE command is more complex than the first. This form

    LOCATE *value 1*,...,*value n*

searches for exact matches of its *value* arguments in the first *n* fields of the current table, starting at the first record of the table. For example, if the cursor is in a table whose first two fields are First Name and Last Name, respectively, the command *LOCATE "John","Smith"* will search the table for the first record that has the entry *John* in its First Name field and the entry *Smith* in its Last Name field. Although you can include as many *value* arguments as the table has fields, you cannot skip fields. That is, if a LOCATE command has three arguments, PAL will search the first three fields of the table for matches.

You can use the keyword NEXT with either form of LOCATE. When you use this keyword, which must come between the LOCATE command and its *value* arguments, PAL will start the search not at the top of the current table, but at the current position of the cursor within that table. For example, if the cursor is in the Last Name field of the third record of a table when PAL reads the command *LOCATE NEXT "Smith"*, PAL will search for the entry *Smith* in the Last Name field, starting with the third record. If you do not want to include the current record in your search, you must issue the command SKIP before executing the LOCATE NEXT command.

The keyword PATTERN may be used with the first form of the LOCATE command. If you use the keyword PATTERN, you can use the wildcard operators .. and @ in the value setting. The .. operator tells Paradox to allow a string of any length (including a length of zero characters), while the @ operator allows only one character. For example, the command *LOCATE PATTERN SM@TH..* would find such entries as *Smith*, *Smyth*, and *Smithson*. Also, when you use the PATTERN keyword, regardless of whether you use the wildcard operators, Paradox will ignore uppercase and lowercase specifications.

In addition to moving the cursor to a matching record, the LOCATE command assigns a value to the variable *retval*. If the LOCATE command finds a matching record, it places the logical value True in the variable *retval* and moves the cursor to that record. If the LOCATE command does not find a matching record, it stores the value False in that variable and does not move the cursor.

The REPORTTABLES Command

The REPORTTABLES command provides a list of the lookup tables that are linked to a multitable report. This command stores the names of the lookup tables in an array. The form for this command is

> REPORTTABLES *tablename reportname arrayname*

where *tablename* is the name of the master table for the multitable form, *reportname* is the number of the report, and *arrayname* is the array in which the command is to store the names of the lookup tables. The *reportname* argument must be either one of the strings *R* or *1* to *14*, or a number between 1 and 14. PAL creates the array specified in the *arrayname* argument if it does not already exist. The REPORTTABLES command sets the *retval* system variable to True if the report includes lookup tables or False if it does not.

Suppose the CLIENTS table is linked as a lookup table for report 11 of the SALESORD table. As a result, the command *REPORTTABLES "Salesord" 11 names* will store the string *Clients* in the array element *names[1]* and the logical value True in the *retval* variable.

The REQUIREDCHECK Command

PAL's REQUIREDCHECK command can be used to activate or deactivate the Required validity checks that have been assigned to a field in a table. The command REQUIRED-CHECK OFF disables the Required validity check that has been assigned to the current field and the command REQUIREDCHECK ON enables that validity check.

REQUIREDCHECK makes it possible to get the user out of a field with a Required validity check without having to make an entry into the field. This command is handy in situations where a field has both a Required validity check and a TableLookup validity check. Since the Required validity check requires the user to make an entry in the field before leaving the field, and the TableLookup validity check will accept only entries that match the entries in a lookup table, it is possible for the user to become marooned if he or she does not know any of the acceptable entries for the lookup table. In that event, your script can use the REQUIREDCHECK OFF command to deactivate the Required validity check momentarily, then it can move the cursor out of the field. The next time the cursor returns to the field, the script can use the REQUIREDCHECK ON command to restore the Required validity check.

The RESET Command

PAL's RESET command cancels any activity currently in process on the workspace (such as editing a table or designing a report), returns Paradox to the Main mode, and clears the Paradox workspace. The principal use of this command is to clear the workspace prior to executing a script. The RESET command does not alter the definitions of any procedures, variables, arrays, or macros.

The RUN Command

PAL's RUN command allows you to exit to DOS temporarily, run an external program or issue a DOS command, and then return to Paradox, all with a single command. The form of this command is

>   RUN *commandline*

where *commandline* is the name of the program you want to run. If a program is not in the current directory, specify the path to that directory (remember to use double backslashes).

For example, the command *RUN "Format A:"* tells PAL to exit from Paradox and run the DOS utility program FORMAT. When formatting is complete, PAL will return to Paradox. If more PAL commands follow, PAL will continue executing the script. If RUN is the last or only command, PAL will return you to the Paradox workspace, exactly as you left it.

The optional keyword SLEEP instructs PAL to wait for a specified period of time after exiting from the external program before it returns you to Paradox. This delay is useful when you use the RUN command to issue a DOS command, such as DIR, and want to display the results for a few seconds. This keyword must precede the *commandline* argument and must be followed by a numeric expression that specifies the number of milliseconds you want PAL to wait. For example, the command *RUN SLEEP 5000 "DIR A:"* displays a directory of the contents of drive A for five seconds, then returns to Paradox.

If you want to leave the results of the program or DOS command displayed on the screen even after PAL resumes playing your script, you can use the NORESTORE option to prevent PAL from restoring the PAL canvas. For example, the command *RUN NORESTORE "DIR A:"* will leave the contents of drive A displayed on the screen in place of the PAL canvas. The directory display will remain on the screen until the script finishes, writes additional information on the PAL canvas, or shows the workspace. If a script uses a ?, ??, or TEXT command following a RUN NORESTORE command, PAL will restore the canvas that was in place before the script issued the RUN command, then display the new information.

When you do not want the screen to change at all during a RUN command, you can use the NOREFRESH command to keep the PAL canvas in view while Paradox is suspended. This option is handy when the DOS command or program specified in the RUN command does not produce any necessary screen display. For example, the command *RUN NOREFRESH "MODE COM1:4800,E,8,1,P"* sets the asynchronous communication information for the COM1: port without disturbing the information displayed on the PAL canvas. If the DOS command in a RUN NOREFRESH command does display information on the screen, PAL will write this new information over the top of the PAL canvas.

The RUN command gives you about 200K to work with. If you need more memory than this, you can use the optional keyword BIG after the word RUN. This will suspend Paradox and give you 500K to work with. If you are using extended memory, the results of a RUN BIG command will appear to be instantaneous. Otherwise, you may notice a time delay in the execution of your program.

The SETMAXSIZE Command

By default, the maximum size of a Paradox table is 64 megabytes. If your tables are going to be larger than this, you can use the SETMAXSIZE command to allow larger tables. The command SETMAXSIZE must be followed by a number representing the allowable size of tables in megabytes. Acceptable values are 64, 128, 192, and 256. Any other number will be rounded to the nearest multiple of 64. To avoid corrupting your tables, always use the same maximum size setting every time you run Paradox.

The SETNEGCOLOR Command

The SETNEGCOLOR command lets you specify whether Paradox should display negative entries in number and dollar fields in different colors from other fields. The SET-NEGCOLOR command overrides the CCP setting that determines whether negative field entries are displayed in a different color than other field entries. (The default color for negative entries is red, but you can use the CCP to change this color.) Every SET-NEGCOLOR command includes two keywords. The first keyword must be one of three words: CURRENCY, NUMERIC, or BOTH. This keyword defines whether number fields, dollar fields, or both will be affected by the command. The second keyword, which must be either ON or OFF, determines whether the field types defined by the first keyword should be displayed in a different color. For example, the command SETNEGCOLOR CURRENCY ON tells Paradox to display all negative entries in dollar fields in a different color from other field entries. The command SETNEGCOLOR BOTH OFF tells Paradox to display negative entries in both number and dollar fields in the same color as other field entries.

The SETRECORDPOSITION Command

In applications that use multirecord forms to display information from Paradox tables, you can use the SETRECORDPOSITION command to scroll a record to a specified screen position. The form for this command is

SETRECORDPOSITION *number row*

where *number* is the number of the record you want to position and *row* is the number of the row at which you want to position the record. The *number* argument must be between 1 and the number of records in the current image, and *row* must be between 1 and the number of records displayed on the form. For example, the command *SETRECORDPOSITION RECNO() 1* scrolls the current record to the top row on the multirecord form. This command is especially useful when you want to display a specific record on a multirecord form embedded on a multitable form.

The SETRETRYPERIOD Command

If you are using Paradox on a network, there will probably be times when you try to access a table or record that has been locked by another user. When that occurs, Paradox will try repeatedly to access the locked object. The period of time during which Paradox will keep trying to access the locked object is called the retry period. The default retry period is 0, which means that Paradox will not try to access the locked object after its initial attempt is unsuccessful. If you have set the retry period to a value greater than 0, Paradox will automatically try again to gain access to the locked table or record for the specified time. If access is still denied after the specified period, a run error will occur.

PAL's SETRETRYPERIOD command can be used to specify how long Paradox should continue trying to access a locked Paradox object. The command has the form

> SETRETRYPERIOD *time*

where *time* is a value from 0 to 30,000, representing the number of seconds during which Paradox will continue to try to access the object. For example, the command *SETRETRY-PERIOD 120* changes the retry period to 120 seconds, or two minutes.

The SETSWAP Command

PAL's SETSWAP command allows you to control how much RAM Paradox will use before it starts swapping procedures in and out of memory. Normally, Paradox will begin swapping procedures when MEMLEFT falls to 0 bytes. In some cases, however, it may be advantageous to leave some memory available for images or variables. In those cases, you can use SETSWAP. The command has the form

> SETSWAP *number*

where *number* is the amount of memory (in bytes) you want to leave available for normal Paradox operations. For example, the command *SETSWAP 10000* tells Paradox to begin swapping procedures when MEMLEFT falls to 10000.

The SYNCCURSOR Command

PAL's SYNCCURSOR command moves the cursor to the same place on the PAL canvas as it is on the underlying Paradox workspace. This command takes no arguments.

The TYPEIN Command

PAL's TYPEIN command instructs PAL to "type" the value of any expression into Paradox at the current position of the cursor. The form of this command is

> TYPEIN *expression*

where the argument is the expression whose value you want PAL to type. You can use this command in any situation where you normally would type characters from the keyboard.

The TYPEIN command lets you type the value of an expression into a form, report, or script—not just into a table. Suppose the variable *z* contains the string *Sales Report for FY 1989*, and you want to use this string as the title of a report you are designing. To enter this text into the report, just position the cursor where you want the text to appear, press [**PAL Menu**], choose MiniScript, and type **TYPEIN z**. When you press ↵, PAL will type the contents of the variable *z*—the string *Sales Report for FY 1989*—at the current position of the cursor.

Conclusion

In this chapter, which concludes our discussion of PAL programming, we've explained PAL features, including miniscripts, macros, arrays, procedures, and the PAL Debugger. We also examined additional PAL commands, such as Value, RESET, and LOCATE.

Appendix **A1**

Importing and Exporting Files

If you are like many Paradox users, you probably also use other programs, such as Lotus 1-2-3, Symphony, PFS: File, or dBASE III. If so, you may need to transfer information between Paradox and another program. For example, you may want to import a file from dBASE III into Paradox or export a table from Paradox to Lotus 1-2-3. Fortunately, Paradox makes it easy to import and export data. In this appendix, we'll show you how. We'll also discuss the Custom Configuration Program's AsciiConvert command.

[Menu] Tools ExportImport

Paradox can import data from and export data to Quattro, Lotus 1-2-3 (Release 1A and Release 2.0), Symphony (Release 1.0 and Release 1.1), dBASE (II, III, and III+), PFS: File (or the IBM Filing Assistant), Reflex, VisiCalc, and ASCII text files. The command that allows you to import and export data is [Menu] Tools ExportImport. When you issue this command, you will see a menu like the one in Figure A1-1.

Figure A1-1 The ExportImport Menu

```
 Export  Import                                          Main
 Convert from Paradox format to another file format.
```

As you can see, this menu offers two choices: Export and Import. The Export command lets you export data from Paradox to a file with another format. If you choose the Export command from the menu in Figure A1-1, Paradox will display the menu shown in Figure A1-2. This menu offers options for each of the programs to which Paradox can export files. The last selection on this menu lets you export a Paradox table to an ASCII file.

Figure A1-2 The Export Menu

```
 Quattro  1-2-3  Symphony  Dbase  Pfs  Reflex  Visicalc  Ascii      Main
 Export to a .WKQ file.
```

The Import command lets you import data from another program's files into Paradox. If you choose Import from the ExportImport menu, Paradox will display the menu shown in Figure A1-3. As you can see, this menu offers the same choices as the Export menu.

Figure A1-3 The Import Menu

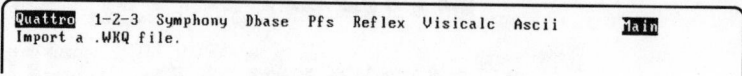

Quattro

Quattro is a full-powered, yet economically priced, spreadsheet program produced by Borland. If you use Quattro, there will probably be times when you will want to export data from Paradox into Quattro so that you can analyze that data or use it as the basis for a spreadsheet model. If you have built databases in Quattro, you might want to import the data from those databases into Paradox so that you can take advantage of Paradox's greater power.

Exporting a Table to Quattro

To export a table from Paradox to Quattro, issue the [Menu] Tools ExportImport Export command and select the Quattro option. When Paradox prompts you to enter the name of the table to export, type the name of the table you want to export and press ↵. When you do this, Paradox will prompt you to enter a name for the Quattro file it is about to create. You now should type a name for that file and press ↵. If you are exporting the table to a file on a different drive or directory, type the name of the drive or directory before you type the file name. After you do this, Paradox will write the data in the table into a Quattro file.

There are a few important rules to keep in mind about exporting tables to Quattro. As in Paradox, each column in the exported Quattro worksheet is a field, and each row is a record. The field names from the Paradox table will become the column headers in row 1 of the worksheet. The first field from the Paradox table will be in column A of the Quattro worksheet, the second field will be in column B, and so forth.

When you export a Paradox table to Quattro, Paradox uses the widths of the alphanumeric fields in the table to set the widths of the corresponding columns in the Quattro worksheet. However, since numeric fields in Paradox do not have defined widths, Paradox does not change the width of the Quattro worksheet columns that receive data from these types of fields. Long number fields are displayed in exponential notation.

Of course, Quattro's data management capabilities are not nearly as sophisticated as Paradox's. For that reason, characteristics of your Paradox tables, such as key fields, secondary indexes, and field types, will not be transferred to the Quattro worksheet. Like all Quattro worksheets, your new worksheet will have the extension .WKQ.

Importing a File from Quattro

Importing a file from Quattro is just as easy as exporting a Paradox table to Quattro. To import a file from Quattro into Paradox, issue the [Menu] Tools ExportImport Import command and select Quattro from the Import menu. Next, Paradox will prompt you to enter the name of the Quattro worksheet file you want to import. If you are uncertain about the file name, press ↵ and Paradox will display a list of the Quattro files in the current directory. When you see this list, you can choose the file you want by pointing to its name. After you select a file to import, Paradox will prompt you to enter a name for the Paradox table into which you want to import the data from the Quattro worksheet. Paradox can only import Quattro data into new tables; it cannot append imported data directly to an existing table. For that reason, when Paradox prompts you for the name of the Paradox table that will receive the imported data, you must type a new name. If the name you type conflicts with an existing name, Paradox will display a Cancel/Replace menu to alert you and give you a chance to enter a new table name.

When you press ↵, Paradox will begin the conversion process. As it converts the file, Paradox will display the message *Converting FILENAME.WKQ to TABLENAME...* at the bottom of the screen. In addition, Paradox will display in the upper-left corner of the screen a series of messages that tell you where it is in the conversion process. After a few moments, Paradox will display the new table in the workspace. Also, a message at the bottom of the screen will tell you the total number of records converted.

When Paradox imports a table from Quattro, it follows certain rules. First, Paradox requires that the Quattro worksheet contain nothing but a Quattro database and assumes that the field names for the database are in the first row of the worksheet and that the first field (column) of data is in column A. Most of your Quattro databases can be easily adjusted to conform to these rules. Paradox assumes the labels in the first row of the worksheet are the field names for the Quattro database and converts them to Paradox field names. Anything below the first row is assumed to be data. If the field names are not in the first row, Paradox will use the first row that contains text as the field names. Any rows above it will be ignored.

As you may know, fields in Quattro databases do not have field types. Of course, the fields in Paradox tables do have types, so Paradox uses a few simple rules to determine the types of fields in the imported table. The type of each field in the imported table is based on the entries in the columns of the Quattro worksheet. Any column that contains a label (text) will be converted to an alphanumeric field. A column that contains both numbers and dates will be converted to an alphanumeric field. A number column formatted as currency or with two decimal places will be converted to a dollar field. All other number columns will be converted to number fields. Columns that contain dates exclusively will be converted to date fields.

Lotus 1-2-3

Many Paradox users also use Lotus 1-2-3, the popular electronic spreadsheet. If you use 1-2-3, there will probably be times when you will want to export data from Paradox into

1-2-3 so you can analyze that data or use it as the basis for a spreadsheet model. If you have built databases in 1-2-3, you might want to import the data from those databases into Paradox so that you can take advantage of Paradox's greater power.

Exporting a Table to Lotus 1-2-3

To export a table from Paradox to Lotus 1-2-3, you should issue the [Menu] Tools ExportImport Export command and select the 1-2-3 option. When you issue this command, Paradox will display the prompt shown in Figure A1-4, which asks you which release of Lotus you are using.

Figure A1-4 The 1-2-3 Version Menu

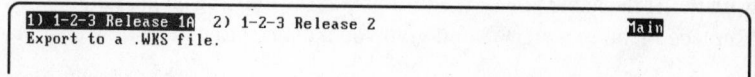

When you see this prompt, you should select the option that matches your version of Lotus. If you select the 1-2-3 Release 1A option, Paradox will export your Paradox table to a file with the extension .WKS. If you choose the 1-2-3 Release 2 option, Paradox will export the table to a .WK1 file.

Next, Paradox will prompt you to enter the name of the table to export. When the *Table:* prompt appears on your screen, you should type the name of the table you want to export and press ↵. When you do this, Paradox will prompt you to enter a name for the 1-2-3 file it is about to create. You now should type the name for that file and press ↵. If you are exporting the table to a file on a different drive or directory, type the name of the drive or directory before you type the file name. After you do this, Paradox will write the data in the table into a 1-2-3 file of the type you selected. Paradox follows the same conversion rules when exporting tables to 1-2-3 that it follows when exporting tables to Quattro.

Because of the different formats of Lotus Release 1A and 2 files, be sure to select the correct version from the 1-2-3 menu. Although 1-2-3 Release 2 will read 1-2-3 Release 1A files, 1-2-3 Release 1A will not read files that are in the 1-2-3 Release 2 format. Of course, should you export a file to the wrong format, you can start over and export it to the correct format.

Importing a File from Lotus 1-2-3

To import a file from 1-2-3 into Paradox, you issue the [Menu] Tools ExportImport Import command and select 1-2-3 from the Import menu. When Paradox displays the Version menu, choose the option that matches the version of 1-2-3 you are using. Next, Paradox will prompt you to enter the name of the 1-2-3 worksheet file you want to import. If you are uncertain about the file name, simply press ↵ and Paradox will display a list of the 1-2-3 files in the current directory. When you see this list, you can choose the file you want by pointing to its name. After you select a file to import, Paradox will prompt you to enter a name for the Paradox table into which you want the data from the 1-2-3 worksheet imported. Paradox can import 1-2-3 data only into new tables; it cannot append imported data directly to an existing table. For that reason, when Paradox prompts you for the name of the Paradox table that will receive the imported data, you must type a new name. If the name you type conflicts with an existing name, Paradox will display the Cancel/Replace menu to alert you.

When you press ↵, Paradox will begin the conversion process, which is basically the same as the process for converting a table to a Quattro file. As it converts a table to a 1-2-3 worksheet, Paradox will display the message *Converting FILENAME.WKS to TABLE-NAME...* at the bottom of the screen. In addition, Paradox will display in the upper-left corner of the screen a series of messages that tell you the status of the conversion process. After a few moments, Paradox will display the new table in the workspace, and a message at the bottom of the screen will tell you the total number of records converted.

When Paradox imports a worksheet from 1-2-3, it follows the same basic rules that it uses when importing a Quattro worksheet.

Symphony

The process of exporting tables to Symphony (Releases 1.0 and 1.1) and importing Symphony worksheets into Paradox is very similar to exporting and importing 1-2-3 files. To export a table into a Symphony file, issue the [Menu] Tools ExportImport Export command and select the Symphony option from the Export menu. Then, select the appropriate version number, 1.0 or 1.1, from the Symphony menu. When you make this choice, Paradox will prompt you first for the name of the table you want to export and then for the name of the Symphony file into which you want to export the data. After you supply both names, Paradox will write the data from the table into a Symphony file with the specified file name. The rules that Paradox follows when exporting tables to Symphony are identical to those it uses for creating 1-2-3 files. Paradox uses the same rules for setting the field types of data imported from Symphony worksheets as it uses when you import 1-2-3 worksheets.

The file-name extension that Paradox gives to the Symphony file it creates depends on which option you choose from the Version menu. If you choose the first option, Paradox will write the data into a Symphony 1.0 file with a .WRK extension. If you choose the second option, the file will be a Symphony 1.1 file with a .WR1 extension. As when exporting 1-2-3 files, you should be careful to select the correct option.

You can also import Symphony worksheets into Paradox. To import a worksheet from Symphony, issue the [Menu] Tools ExportImport Import Symphony command. Then, select the appropriate version number, 1.0 or 1.1, from the Symphony menu. Next, enter the name of the file to import, followed by a name for the new Paradox table. After you do this, Paradox will import the file.

dBASE II and III

Many Paradox users are former users of dBASE II or dBASE III. Other Paradox users work in organizations where some people use dBASE. If you fit into either category, it is likely that you will need to import data from or export data to dBASE at some point. We'll show you how to do that in this section.

Exporting Tables to dBASE II, III, or III+

Selecting Dbase from the Export menu allows you to export data from Paradox to dBASE II, dBASE III, or dBASE III+. After you issue the [Menu] Tools ExportImport Export command and choose the Dbase option, you will see the menu shown in Figure A1-5. The first option on the menu allows you to export a Paradox table to dBASE II. The second option allows you to export a table into a dBASE III or III+ file. You should choose the option that matches the version of dBASE that you are using.

Figure A1-5 The Dbase Menu

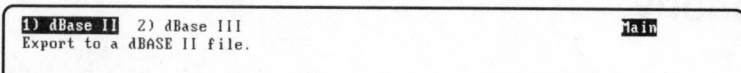

After you select the correct option, Paradox will prompt you to enter the name of the Paradox table you want to export. Then, Paradox will prompt you to enter a name for the converted file. When you enter a file name, you do not need to add an extension. Paradox will automatically assign a .DBF extension.

When you export a Paradox table to a dBASE file, the Paradox field names will become the field names for the dBASE file. However, since field names in Paradox can be up to 25 characters long, but field names in dBASE can be only ten characters long, any field names in your Paradox table that exceed ten characters will be truncated.

Since dBASE II and III both offer field types that correspond to several of the Paradox field types, most of your data will not be changed during the conversion. The only exceptions are date and short number fields. dBASE II doesn't support date fields, so any date fields will be converted to character fields when you export to dBASE II. Neither version of dBASE supports short number fields. Any short number field you export to dBASE will be treated as a numeric field. Table A1-1 summarizes the Paradox-to-dBASE field conversion rules.

Importing dBASE Files

Importing data from dBASE II, III, or III+ is just as easy as exporting tables to those programs. After you issue the [Menu] Tools ExportImport Import Dbase command, you will be prompted to select the dBASE version you are using (II, III, or III+). Then, you will be prompted to enter the name of the dBASE file you want to import. Again, you do not need to enter an extension. After you type a file name and press ↵, Paradox will prompt you to enter a name for the new Paradox table in which you want to store the imported records. As when you import data from 1-2-3 files, you must always import data from dBASE files into a new Paradox table. Once you type a table name and press ↵, the file will be converted. After a few moments, the new Paradox table will be displayed in the workspace.

Table A1-1 Paradox-to-dBASE Field Conversions

Paradox Field Type	dBASE II Field Type	dBASE III/III+ Field Type
Alphanumeric	Character	Character
Number	Numeric	Numeric
Dollar	Numeric (2 decimal places)	Numeric (2 decimal places)
Short Number	Numeric	Numeric
Date	Character	Date

Table A1-2 summarizes the rules for dBASE-to-Paradox field conversions. Paradox supports all of dBASE's field types, except logical fields and memo fields. When you import a dBASE file that contains a logical field, that field will be converted into an alphanumeric field with a width of 1. The entries in this field will be the letters *T* and *F* (for True and False) or *Y* and *N* (for Yes and No). If the file being imported contains a memo field, only the first 255 characters in that field will be imported.

Table A1-2 dBASE-to-Paradox Field Conversions

dBASE Field Type	Paradox Field Type
Character	Alphanumeric
Logical	Alphanumeric (length=1)
Number	Number
Number (2 decimal places)	Dollar
Date (dBASE III and III+ only)	Date
Memo (dBASE III and III+ only)	Alphanumeric (length=255)

PFS: File and IBM Filing Assistant

PFS: File, from Software Publishing Company, and its cousin, the IBM Filing Assistant, are two of the most popular simple database managers. Many Paradox users started out with one of these tools and graduated to Paradox when their needs outgrew the power of these programs. So that these users can move their data into Paradox, Borland has given Paradox the ability to import (and export) files from PFS: File.

To export a table to PFS: File, issue the [Menu] Tools ExportImport Export command and choose Pfs. After you issue the command, you will be prompted to enter the name of the table you wish to export, followed by a name for the exported file. Unless you enter an extension, Paradox will automatically add .PFS to the file name you specify. After you type the file name and press ↵, Paradox will export the table. After a few moments, Paradox will return to the main workspace.

PFS: File has no specific data types; therefore, it treats every field as a character string. When you export a Paradox table to PFS: File, every field in a Paradox table becomes a character string. The field names from the Paradox table are preserved in PFS: File.

To import a file from PFS into Paradox, issue the [Menu] Tools ExportImport Import Pfs command. After you do this, Paradox will prompt you to enter the name of the file you want to import (remember to include the extension .PFS). After you enter the name of the file to be imported, Paradox will prompt you to enter a name for the new Paradox table into which the data will be imported. Once you type a name and press ↵, Paradox will import the file and display the new table in the workspace. Since PFS: File has no specific data (field) types, Paradox scans the records in the file to determine how the records will be imported. Table A1-3 shows how Paradox assigns field types.

Table A1-3 PFS-to-Paradox Field Conversions

PFS Character String	Paradox Field
Non-numeric characters	Alphanumeric
Numeric characters	Number
Numeric characters (2 decimal places)	Dollar
Characters in the yy/mm/dd or mm/dd/yy format	Date
Attachment pages	Alphanumeric (length=255)

Reflex

Reflex is another database manager software package produced by Borland that is both less powerful and less expensive than Paradox. If any of your coworkers use Reflex, you might want to transfer information back and forth between Reflex databases and Paradox tables. Paradox's ExportImport facility supports two versions of Reflex, Release 1.0 and Release 1.1. The database files for both versions carry the same extension: .RXD.

Exporting Tables to Reflex

Selecting Reflex from the Export menu allows you to export data from Paradox to Reflex. After you issue the [Menu] Tools ExportImport Export command and choose the Reflex option, you will see the menu shown in Figure A1-6. The first option on the menu allows you to export a table from Paradox to Reflex Release 1.0. The second option allows you to export Paradox data into a Reflex Release 1.1 file. You should choose the option that matches the version of Reflex you are using.

Figure A1-6 The Reflex Menu

```
1) Reflex Release 1.0  2) Reflex Release 1.1                    Main
Export to a .RXD file.
```

After you select the correct option, Paradox will prompt you to enter the name of the Paradox table that you want to export. Then, Paradox will prompt you to enter a name for the converted file. When you enter a file name, you do not need to add an extension. Paradox will automatically assign an .RXD extension for you.

When you export a Paradox table to a Reflex file, the Paradox field names will become the field names for the Reflex file. Since Reflex offers field types that correspond to most of the Paradox field types, for the most part, your data will not be changed during the conversion. The only exception to this rule is the dollar field type. When Paradox exports a table to Reflex, it changes dollar fields to numeric fields formatted with two decimal places. Table A1-4 summarizes the Paradox-to-Reflex field conversion rules.

Table A1-4 Paradox-to-Reflex Field Conversions

Paradox Field Type	Reflex Field Type
Alphanumeric	Text
Number	Numeric
Dollar	Numeric (2 decimal places)
Short Number	Integer
Date	Date

Importing Reflex Files

Importing data from Reflex is just as easy as exporting tables to Reflex. After you issue the [Menu] Tools ExportImport Import Reflex command, you will be prompted to select the Reflex version you are using (1.0 or 1.1). Then, you will be prompted to enter the name of the Reflex file you want to import. Again, you do not need to enter an extension. After you type a file name and press ↵, Paradox will prompt you to enter a name for the new Paradox table in which you want to store the imported records. As when you import data from other programs, you must always import data from Reflex files into a new Paradox table. Once you type a table name and press ↵, the file will be converted. After a few moments, the new Paradox table will be displayed in the workspace.

Table A1-5 summarizes the rules for Reflex-to-Paradox field conversions. Paradox supports field types that correspond to all of Reflex's field types.

Table A1-5 Reflex-to-Paradox Field Conversions

Reflex Field Type	Paradox Field Type
Text	Alphanumeric
Repeating Text	Alphanumeric
Numeric	Number
Numeric (currency or financial format)	Dollar
Integer	Short Number
Date	Date

VisiCalc

Although VisiCalc, the "granddaddy" of spreadsheet programs, is not widely used today, Paradox does have the ability to exchange data with VisiCalc. You can export Paradox tables to VisiCalc using the Data Interchange Format (DIF). To export a table into DIF format, issue the [Menu] Tools ExportImport Export Visicalc command. After you issue this command, Paradox will prompt you to enter the name of the table you want to export, followed by the name of the DIF file to which you want to write the data. (If you do not enter an extension for the file, Paradox will automatically assign it the extension .DIF.) Once you type a file name and press ↵, Paradox will export the data in the table into the DIF file. After you have exported the table, you can exit from Paradox, load VisiCalc, and read the DIF file into VisiCalc.

When you export a Paradox table to a DIF file, Paradox field names are converted to column titles in row 1. Alphanumeric fields are converted to text columns. Number, dollar, and short number fields are converted to number columns. Date fields are converted to text in the mm/dd/yy format.

To import a file from VisiCalc (or any program that uses the DIF format), you must first use that program to create a DIF file that contains the data you want to import. Make sure that you give the name of the DIF file the extension .DIF; otherwise, the file won't be imported.

Once you have created a DIF file that contains the data to be imported, load Paradox and issue the [Menu] Tools ExportImport Import Visicalc command. After you issue the command, Paradox will prompt you to enter the name of the DIF file you want to import. Next, Paradox will prompt you to enter a name for the new Paradox table that will receive the imported data. After you type a table name and press ↵, the file will be converted and displayed in the workspace.

Paradox imports DIF files by treating each table as a record and each vector as a field. If the Label feature of DIF hasn't been used to name columns, row 1 will be imported as the field names for the table. Table A1-6 shows the conversion rules for importing DIF files.

Table A1-6 DIF-to-Paradox Field Conversions

DIF Column	Paradox Field
Text	Alphanumeric
Numbers	Number
Numbers (2 decimal places)	Dollar
Text in the mm/dd/yy format	Date

Importing and Exporting ASCII Files

In addition to being able to exchange data with the programs discussed so far, Paradox also can import and export ASCII files. ASCII files are simple files that contain only lines of text. Since many programs can create and read ASCII text files, you can use Paradox's ability to export and import these files as a way to exchange information with programs other than those on the Export/Import menus. This can be especially useful for transferring data between Paradox and a word processing program.

Exporting a Paradox Table to an ASCII File

The [Menu] Tools ExportImport Export Ascii command lets you export a Paradox table to an ASCII file. After you issue this command, Paradox will display the menu in Figure A1-7, which asks if you want to export a delimited file or a text file. If you choose Delimited, Paradox will write the table into an ASCII text file in which the fields are separated by commas and alphanumeric values are enclosed in (delimited by) quotation marks. If you choose Text, Paradox will write the data in the table into an ASCII file in which each record in the table is one line in the file. You can use the Text option only if the table you're exporting contains a single alphanumeric field.

Figure A1-7 The Export Ascii Menu

```
Delimited  Text                                                      Main
Fields separated by commas; each record on a new line.
```

You will probably use the Delimited option to export a table and then import it into a mail-merge program or a word processor. Some programs of this type may work better if you use the [Menu] Report Output command to output a report to a file, rather than export the table. The choice of this technique depends on the program to which you are exporting the data.

Importing ASCII Files

Paradox lets you import ASCII files in three ways. You can import a delimited ASCII file into either a new table or into an existing Paradox table. In addition, you can import an undelimited ASCII text file in which each line of text becomes a record in a new table.

To import an ASCII file, you first issue the [Menu] Tools ExportImport Import Ascii command. Paradox will then display the menu shown in Figure A1-8. The choices on this menu are Delimited, AppendDelimited, and Text.

Figure A1-8 The Ascii Menu

```
Delimited AppendDelimited Text                                        Main
Create a new table from an ASCII delimited text file.
```

Delimited Files

The Delimited option allows you to import a delimited ASCII file into a new Paradox table. When you choose this option, Paradox will prompt you for the name of the file you want to import, then for the name of the new table. Once you type a table name and press ↵, Paradox will convert the file and display it in the workspace.

Because the ASCII file you are importing does not include field names, Paradox provides names for each of the fields in the table. The first field becomes Field-1, the second Field-2, and so on. If you wish, you can use the [Menu] Modify Restructure command to change the names of these fields.

When Paradox imports a delimited file, it assumes that any entry enclosed in quotation marks is an alphanumeric entry. Entries not enclosed in quotation marks will become a numeric entry. Paradox also assumes that the fields in the ASCII file are separated by commas.

Later in this appendix, we'll show you how to change the delimiter and separator that Paradox uses to determine field types. This feature allows you to import any ASCII file, regardless of the way it is delimited and separated.

Importing an ASCII File into an Existing Table

The AppendDelimited option allows you to import a delimited ASCII file into an existing table. When you import an ASCII file into an existing Paradox table, Paradox does everything it can to convert the data in the ASCII file into Paradox data. However, if the file cannot be converted, the problem records will be placed into a temporary PROBLEMS table. The PROBLEMS table consists of three fields: a Line Number field, a Line field, and a Reason field. The Line Number field in the PROBLEMS table tells you the line in the ASCII file that caused the problem. The Line field shows you the first 80 characters in the line, and the Reason field gives you a brief explanation of the problem. With this information, you can edit the ASCII file and then import it. In some cases, you may find it easier to import the file into a new table, restructure that table, and then add the records to the existing table.

If you are adding records from an ASCII file to an existing table that contains a key field, Paradox will display the NewEntries/Update menu. If you select NewEntries and an imported record has a key that duplicates an existing key field, then the imported record will be put into a KEYVIOL table. Any records in the KEYVIOL table can be edited and then added to the table, as explained in Chapter 9. The Update option will cause any imported record that contains a key field value that is the same as an existing value to replace the existing record in the table. The original record will be placed into the temporary table named CHANGED. This will give you a chance to examine any conflicting records. The best way to guarantee you don't lose any data is to always make a copy of the original table before you import the file.

Importing Unseparated ASCII Files

The Text option on the ASCII menu lets you import a file in which the fields are not separated. When you issue the [Menu] Tools ExportImport Import Ascii Text command, Paradox will ask you to enter the name of the file to import, and then the name for the new table. After you do this, Paradox will convert the file and display it on the workspace.

Paradox imports unseparated ASCII files into tables with one alphanumeric field. Each line in the file is converted to one record in the table. If there are records in the file that cannot be converted, Paradox will display those records in a PROBLEMS table as described earlier.

The CCP Ascii Command

As you have learned, a delimiter is a character used to distinguish non-numeric fields in an ASCII file. A separator is the character used to separate fields in an ASCII file. When you use the [Menu] Tools More ExportImport command to exchange data between Paradox and delimited ASCII files, Paradox assumes that the default delimiter is a quotation mark and that the default separator is a comma. However, since different programs may use different delimiters and separators, Paradox allows you to change its default delimiter and separator settings. To do this, you must run the Custom Configuration Program (CCP) and issue the Ascii command from the CCP main menu. Paradox will then display the menu shown in Figure A1-9.

Figure A1-9 The CCP Ascii Menu

```
Delimiters  Separator  ZeroFill  ChooseDecimal  Return
Change default delimiter or choose fields to be delimited.
```

Changing the Delimiter

To change the default delimiters, choose the Delimiters option. When you do, Paradox will display a menu with two options: Choice and Always?. These options let you define a delimiter and decide which fields should be enclosed by the delimiter.

If you issue the Choice command, Paradox will display the default delimiter (if you have not previously made a change, the default will be a quotation mark) and prompt you to change it. To change the default delimiter, press the [Backspace] key to erase it, type a new delimiter, and press ↵.

The Always? option on the Delimiters menu allows you to define which fields should be delimited. When you issue this command, Paradox will display a menu with two options: AllFields and OnlyStrings (the default). The OnlyStrings setting tells Paradox to place delimiters around non-numeric fields only. The other option, AllFields, tells Paradox to place delimiters around all fields.

Changing the Separator

To change the default separator, choose the Separator command from the CCP Ascii menu. Paradox then will display the default separator (if you have not previously changed this setting, the default will be a comma) and prompt you to change it. To change the default, press [Backspace] to erase the current separator and type the new one.

The ZeroFill Option

The ZeroFill option on the CCP Ascii menu lets you control how blank numeric fields are exported into ASCII files. By default, Paradox exports blank numeric fields as blanks. If you wish, you can change the default to convert blank numeric fields to zeroes for export. To do this, choose the ZeroFill command from the CCP Ascii menu and select the Zeroes option.

Some programs require that numeric fields contain a value—they cannot be left blank. The Zeroes option exchanges data between Paradox and programs that have this requirement.

The ChooseDecimal Option

The ChooseDecimal option of the CCP Ascii menu gives you the option of using a period or a comma for the decimal point in numeric fields that are imported or exported. When you select the ChooseDecimal option, Paradox will display a menu with two options: Period and Comma. If you select Period, a period will be used for decimal points. If you choose Comma, a comma will be used.

Conclusion

In this appendix, we've shown you how to import data from Quattro, Lotus 1-2-3, Symphony, dBASE, PFS: File, Reflex, and VisiCalc into Paradox, and how to export data from Paradox to those programs. We've also shown you how to import and export ASCII files and how to change the default settings for ASCII files with the CCP.

Multi-user Paradox

The major enhancement to Paradox 2 was the introduction of multi-user, or network, capabilities. With Release 2.0, Paradox became a full-fledged multi-user database management system. If you install Paradox 2 or 3 on a Local Area Network, all the users on that network will be able to share data and interact with tables and other objects simultaneously. You can therefore create elaborate multi-user applications that allow several people to perform the same function at one time—for instance, entering records into a table—or that allow two or more people to perform different functions on the same table at the same time.

The best thing about multi-user Paradox is that you already know how to use it! You don't have to learn any new commands to get started. All the features of Paradox that we've covered in the other chapters of this book—queries, reports, scripts, and so on—work the same way on a Paradox network. The only important difference is that now you can share your tables and data with other Paradox users on your network. Occasionally, Paradox will prevent you from taking an action if it would interfere with what someone else is trying to do. For the most part, though, using Paradox on a network is very much like working with single-user Paradox.

This ease of use is a far cry from other multi-user database managers. With other products, you must constantly execute special commands to "lock" and "unlock" your files and records and be on the lookout for problems like the "deadly embrace." With Paradox, all this is done for you automatically, so you don't have to worry about it. (Of course, if you want, you can take direct responsibility for these functions yourself, rather than relying on Paradox.)

In this appendix, we'll provide a comprehensive tour of Paradox on a network. We'll start with a detailed example to let you see how multi-user Paradox looks. Then, we'll explain the special elements of multi-user Paradox, such as locking, Coedit, and private directories. These features will help you become a more knowledgeable network user. Finally, we will discuss multi-user PAL considerations.

A Simple Multi-user Example

Let's suppose that we have two Paradox users, Jack and Jill, working on a network on separate computers. Both want to do some work on the same Paradox table, the CUSTOMER table.

First, Jack decides to restructure the CUSTOMER table to add a new field. He issues the [Menu] Modify Restructure command, types *CUSTOMER*, and presses ↵. Paradox displays the structure for the CUSTOMER table on his screen, and Jack adds a new field named Balance Due. At this point, his screen looks like Figure A2-1.

Figure A2-1 Restructuring a Table (Jack)

```
Restructuring Customer table                                    Restructure

STRUCT══════════Field Name══════════╗Field Type╗
   1 ║ Cust Number                    ║ N          ╢        ── FIELD TYPES ──
   2 ║ Last Name                      ║ A11        ║  A_: Alphanumeric (ex: A25)
   3 ║ First name                     ║ A8         ║   Any combination of
   4 ║ Address                        ║ A15        ║   characters and spaces
   5 ║ City                           ║ A14        ║   up to specified width.
   6 ║ State                          ║ A2         ║   Maximum width is 255
   7 ║ Zip                            ║ A5         ║
   8 ║ Balance Due                    ║ $      ◄   ║  N: Numbers with or without
                                                   ║   decimal digits.
                                                   ║
                                                   ║  $: Currency amounts.
                                                   ║
                                                   ║  D: Dates in the form
                                                   ║   mm/dd/yy, dd-mon-yy,
                                                   ║   or dd.mm.yy
                                                   ║ ──────────────────────
                                                   ║ Use '*' after field type to
                                                   ║ show a key field (ex: A4*).
```

Meanwhile, Jill decides she wants to look at the customers listed in CUSTOMER. To do this, she issues the [Menu] View command, types *CUSTOMER*, and presses ↵. Instead of seeing the CUSTOMER table, however, Jill sees the message shown in Figure A2-2.

Figure A2-2 Attempt to View a Table (Jill)

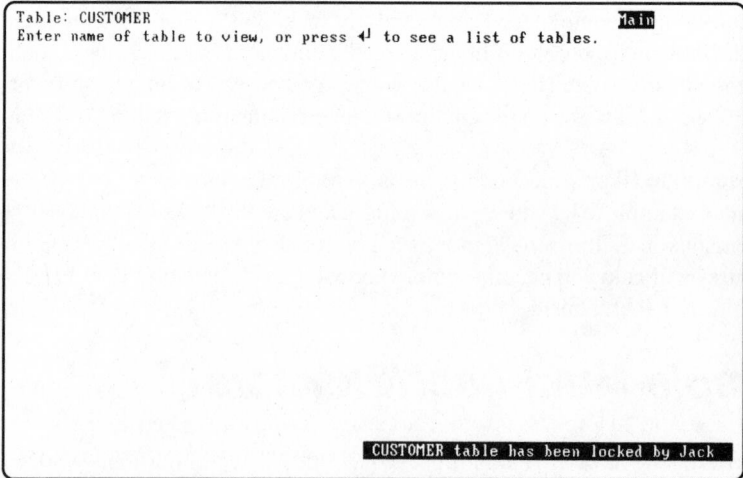

```
Table: CUSTOMER                                                      Main
Enter name of table to view, or press ↵ to see a list of tables.








                              CUSTOMER table has been locked by Jack
```

Because Jack is in the process of restructuring the table, Paradox will not let Jill view it. Because restructuring a table can result in sweeping changes to it—such as adding and deleting fields—Paradox does not let anyone else have access to it while you are restructuring it. In Paradox terminology, restructuring a table places a Full Lock on it.

By reading the message on her screen, *CUSTOMER table has been locked by Jack*, Jill knows that Jack is performing some operation that restricts her from viewing the CUSTOMER table. She will have to wait a few minutes to use the table. Meanwhile, Jack presses the [Do-It!] key to complete the restructuring. When Jill presses [Menu] View again, the CUSTOMER table will appear on her screen, as shown in Figure A2-3. (In this figure and the ones that follow, the Balance Due field appears between Last Name and Address. We'll assume that Jill and Jack have used the [Rotate] key, [Ctrl]-[R], to rearrange the columns on the screen.)

Figure A2-3 Viewing a Table (Jill)

```
Viewing Customer table: Record 1 of 20                    Main

CUSTOMER Cust Number   Last Name      Balance Due      Address
     1      1245      Priest                         123 Hill St      Loui
     2      1690      Anderson                        45 Mt. Rain      New
     3      1888      Jones                           6610 Willow      Nash
     4      1132      Smith                           Haven Drive      Loui
     5      1200      Doe                             Milltown Rd      Loui
     6      1246      Doe                             Crossbuck Dr     Loui
     7      1176      Robinson                        2323 Vane St     Jeff
     8      1509      Carson                          45 Colt St       Clar
     9      1286      Collins                         1223 Fork Ave    Jeff
    10      1751      Ross                            Apt.12 Fox St    New
    11      2376      Baxter                          # 5 Park Ave     New
    12      3726      Alda                            4077 Mash        Holl
    13      5171      Conner                          Hopewell Dr      Clar
    14      5421      Cambridge                       552 B Hill St    Loui
    15      9610      Johnson                         1000 Mob End Rd  Loui
    16      9851      Black                           P.O. Box 397     Dall
    17      1500      Thomas                          RFD 2            Goos
    18      1136      Winder                          896 Coil St      Jeff
    19      1202      Thompson                        111 River St     New
    20      3626      O'Grady                         Limrick St # 3   Pari
```

Next, Jack decides he'd like to restructure the CUSTOMER table again, to change the name of a field. He issues the [Menu] Modify Restructure command, types *CUSTOMER*, and presses ↵. This time, however, instead of seeing the table structure on his screen, Jack sees the message shown in Figure A2-4 on the following page.

Because Jill is viewing the CUSTOMER table, Paradox will not let Jack restructure it. As we have already seen, Paradox does not allow two users to view and restructure a table simultaneously. In Paradox terminology, by viewing the CUSTOMER table, Jill has "prevented Full Lock."

The message *CUSTOMER table is in use by Jill* tells Jack that Jill is doing something with the CUSTOMER table that prevents him from restructuring it. As a result, Jack decides to postpone his restructuring and, instead, enter the balance due for a few customers. He issues the [Menu] Modify Coedit command, types *CUSTOMER*, and presses ↵. The CUSTOMER table appears on his screen, as shown in Figure A2-5.

Figure A2-4 Attempt to Restructure a Table (Jack)

```
Table: CUSTOMER                                                Main
Enter name of table to restructure, or press ↵ to see a list of tables.
CUSTOMER┬Cust Number┬Last Name────┬Balance Due────┬────Address────┬
   1    │  1245     │ Priest       │               │ 123 Hill St    │ Loui
   2    │  1690     │ Anderson     │               │ 45 Mt. Rain    │ New
   3    │  1888     │ Jones        │               │ 6610 Willow    │ Nash
   4    │  1132     │ Smith        │               │ Haven Drive    │ Loui
   5    │  1200     │ Doe          │               │ Milltown Rd    │ Loui
   6    │  1246     │ Doe          │               │ Crossbuck Dr   │ Loui
   7    │  1176     │ Robinson     │               │ 2323 Vane St   │ Jeff
   8    │  1509     │ Carson       │               │ 45 Colt St     │ Clar
   9    │  1286     │ Collins      │               │ 1223 Fork Ave  │ Jeff
  10    │  1751     │ Ross         │               │ Apt.12 Fox St  │ New
  11    │  2376     │ Baxter       │               │ # 5 Park Ave   │ New
  12    │  3726     │ Alda         │               │ 4077 Nash      │ Holl
  13    │  5171     │ Conner       │               │ Hopewell Dr    │ Clar
  14    │  5421     │ Cambridge    │               │ 552 B Hill St  │ Loui
  15    │  9610     │ Johnson      │               │ 1000 Mob End Rd│ Loui
  16    │  9851     │ Black        │               │ P.O. Box 397   │ Dall
  17    │  1500     │ Thomas       │               │ RFD 2          │ Goos
  18    │  1136     │ Winder       │               │ 896 Coil St    │ Jeff
  19    │  1202     │ Thompson     │               │ 111 River St   │ New
  20    │  3626     │ O'Grady      │               │ Limrick St # 3 │ Pari

                              CUSTOMER table is in use by Jill
```

Figure A2-5 Coediting a Table (Jack)

```
Coediting Customer table: Record 1 of 20                       CoEdit

CUSTOMER┬Cust Number┬Last Name────┬Balance Due────┬────Address────┬
   1    │  1245     │ Priest       │             ◄ │ 123 Hill St    │ Loui
   2    │  1690     │ Anderson     │               │ 45 Mt. Rain    │ New
   3    │  1888     │ Jones        │               │ 6610 Willow    │ Nash
   4    │  1132     │ Smith        │               │ Haven Drive    │ Loui
   5    │  1200     │ Doe          │               │ Milltown Rd    │ Loui
   6    │  1246     │ Doe          │               │ Crossbuck Dr   │ Loui
   7    │  1176     │ Robinson     │               │ 2323 Vane St   │ Jeff
```

Jack has chosen to coedit the table, rather than simply edit it, because coediting allows him to edit the table at the same time another user is using it. In fact, if Jack had issued the [Menu] Modify Edit command, instead of the [Menu] Modify Coedit command, he would have seen the message *CUSTOMER table is in use by Jill*. Paradox allows any number of users to simultaneously view and coedit a table. However, only one user can edit a table at a time, preventing other users from viewing the table at the same time (by placing a Full Lock on the table). Coedit mode is one of the most important multi-user features in Paradox. We'll talk about it in detail later in this appendix.

Multi-user Access to Records

Now, suppose that Jack moves to the third record, William Jones, then moves to the Balance Due column. Mr. Jones owes the company $527.33. As soon as Jack starts to type in this balance by pressing **5**, his screen will look like the one shown in Figure A2-6.

Figure A2-6 Locking a Record (Jack)

```
Coediting Customer table: Record 3 of 20                        CoEdit
Record is locked
CUSTOMER┬Cust Number┬─Last Name═══┬═Balance Due═══┬═══Address═══┬═════
     1  ║   1245    ║ Priest      ║               ║ 123 Hill St ║ Loui
     2  ║   1690    ║ Anderson    ║               ║ 45 Mt. Rain ║ New
     3  ║   1888    ║ Jones       ║      5        ◄ 6610 Willow  ║ Nash
     4  ║   1132    ║ Smith       ║               ║ Haven Drive ║ Loui
     5  ║   1200    ║ Doe         ║               ║ Milltown Rd ║ Loui
     6  ║   1246    ║ Doe         ║               ║ Crossbuck Dr║ Loui
     7  ║   1176    ║ Robinson    ║               ║ 2323 Vane St║ Jeff
```

Two things have changed: The message *Record is locked* appears at the top of the screen, and the triangular edit marker to the right of the field has switched to reverse video. This indicates that Jack has exclusive rights to change the record. Until Jack finishes with the record, other users on the network can see it, but can't change it, as Jill is about to discover.

While Jill is viewing the CUSTOMER table on her computer, she notices that William Jones' address is incorrect. He lives on Spruce Street, not Willow Street. To correct the record, Jill presses the [CoEdit] key ([Alt]-[F9]), moves the cursor to the Address field in the third record, and presses the [Backspace] key to begin erasing *Willow*. As soon as she presses [Backspace], however, the error message shown in Figure A2-7 will appear on her screen.

Figure A2-7 Attempt to Lock a Record (Jill)

```
Coediting Customer table: Record 3 of 20                        CoEdit

CUSTOMER┬Cust Number┬─Last Name═══┬═Balance Due═══┬═══Address═══┬═════
     1  ║   1245    ║ Priest      ║               ║ 123 Hill St ║ Loui
     2  ║   1690    ║ Anderson    ║               ║ 45 Mt. Rain ║ New
     3  ║   1888    ║ Jones       ║               ║ 6610 Willow ◄ Nash
     4  ║   1132    ║ Smith       ║               ║ Haven Drive ║ Loui
     5  ║   1200    ║ Doe         ║               ║ Milltown Rd ║ Loui
     6  ║   1246    ║ Doe         ║               ║ Crossbuck Dr║ Loui
     7  ║   1176    ║ Robinson    ║               ║ 2323 Vane St║ Jeff
     8  ║   1509    ║ Carson      ║               ║ 45 Colt St  ║ Clar
     9  ║   1286    ║ Collins     ║               ║ 1223 Fork Ave║ Jeff
    10  ║   1751    ║ Ross        ║               ║ Apt.12 Fox St║ New
    11  ║   2376    ║ Baxter      ║               ║ # 5 Park Ave ║ New
    12  ║   3726    ║ Alda        ║               ║ 4077 Nash   ║ Holl
    13  ║   5171    ║ Conner      ║               ║ Hopewell Dr ║ Clar
    14  ║   5421    ║ Cambridge   ║               ║ 552 B Hill St║ Loui
    15  ║   9610    ║ Johnson     ║               ║ 1000 Mob End Rd║ Loui
    16  ║   9851    ║ Black       ║               ║ P.O. Box 397║ Dall
    17  ║   1500    ║ Thomas      ║               ║ RFD 2       ║ Goos
    18  ║   1136    ║ Winder      ║               ║ 896 Coil St ║ Jeff
    19  ║   1202    ║ Thompson    ║               ║ 111 River St║ New
    20  ║   3626    ║ O'Grady     ║               ║ Limrick St # 3║ Pari
                                        Record has been locked by Jack
```

Jill cannot change the record because Jack is already in the process of changing it. In Paradox terms, Jack has placed a record lock on the record, and no two users can lock the same record at the same time. Notice that Jill sees the record the way it appeared before Jack started changing it. That is, she doesn't see the 5 he has typed into the Balance Due field. Jill will not see Jack's changes until after he has finished all his work on the record.

Meanwhile, Paradox will allow Jill to make changes to any other record (provided, of course, there isn't some third user elsewhere on the network locking records, too). So Jill busies herself with other tasks while Jack works on record 3.

When Jack has finished editing Mr. Jones' record, he moves the cursor to the next record to fill in a balance due there. (Of course, he could also make other changes to Mr. Jones' record instead of moving to the next record.) As soon as Jack presses the [Down] key, he sees the message shown in Figure A2-8 on his screen.

Figure A2-8 Unlocking a Record (Jack)

```
Coediting Customer table: Record 4 of 20                       CoEdit

CUSTOMER Cust Number   Last Name       Balance Due      Address
   1        1245       Priest                           123 Hill St       Loui
   2        1690       Anderson                         45 Mt. Rain       New
   3        1888       Jones              527.33        6610 Willow       Nash
   4        1132       Smith                         ◀  Haven Drive       Loui
   5        1200       Doe                              Milltown Rd       Loui
   6        1246       Doe                              Crossbuck Dr      Loui
   7        1176       Robinson                         2323 Vane St      Jeff
   8        1509       Carson                           45 Colt St        Clar
   9        1286       Collins                          1223 Fork Ave     Jeff
  10        1751       Ross                             Apt.12 Fox St     New
  11        2376       Baxter                           # 5 Park Ave      New
  12        3726       Alda                             4077 Nash         Holl
  13        5171       Conner                           Hopewell Dr       Clar
  14        5421       Cambridge                        552 B Hill St     Loui
  15        9610       Johnson                          1000 Mob End Rd   Loui
  16        9851       Black                            P.O. Box 397      Dall
  17        1500       Thomas                           RFD 2             Goos
  18        1136       Winder                           896 Coil St       Jeff
  19        1202       Thompson                         111 River St      New
  20        3626       O'Grady                          Limrick St # 3    Pari

                                              Posted change to record 3
```

The message *Posted change to record 3* tells Jack that Paradox has made changes available to all the other users on the network. It also tells Jack that Paradox has unlocked the record for him. Notice that the message *Record is locked* has disappeared from the top of Jack's screen. Also notice that, even though Jack's cursor is now on record 4, Paradox hasn't locked record 4. Paradox only locks a record when you begin to change it.

A few seconds after Jack has moved his cursor off record 3, Jill sees a change on her screen, as shown in Figure A2-9. Paradox has automatically updated Jill's screen to show the change Jack has made: the $527.33 balance due for Mr. Jones (record 3). The message *Refreshing...* at the bottom of the screen, which appears for only a second, warns Jill that Paradox is refreshing her screen with somebody else's changes.

Now that Jack has finished with record 3, Jill can make her change to it. Of course, while Jill is changing the record, Paradox locks it for her, as shown in Figure A2-10. If Jack tries to move back and modify it at the same time, he will get the same message that Jill received earlier, as shown in Figure A2-11. Jack can, of course, change any record other than the one Jill is changing.

Figure A2-9 Refreshing the Image (Jill)

```
Coediting Customer table: Record 7 of 20                    CoEdit

CUSTOMER┬Cust Number┬─Last Name═══┬══Balance Due══┬──Address══════
    1   │   1245    │ Priest      │               │ 123 Hill St      │ Loui
    2   │   1690    │ Anderson    │               │ 45 Mt. Rain      │ New
    3   │   1888    │ Jones       │   527.33      │ 6610 Willow      │ Nash
    4   │   1132    │ Smith       │               │ Haven Drive      │ Loui
    5   │   1200    │ Doe         │               │ Milltown Rd      │ Loui
    6   │   1246    │ Doe         │               │ Crossbuck Dr     │ Loui
    7   │   1176    │ Robinson    │               │ 2323 Vane St   ◄ │ Jeff
    8   │   1509    │ Carson      │               │ 45 Colt St       │ Clar
    9   │   1286    │ Collins     │               │ 1223 Fork Ave    │ Jeff
   10   │   1751    │ Ross        │               │ Apt.12 Fox St    │ New
   11   │   2376    │ Baxter      │               │ # 5 Park Ave     │ New
   12   │   3726    │ Alda        │               │ 4077 Mash        │ Holl
   13   │   5171    │ Conner      │               │ Hopewell Dr      │ Clar
   14   │   5421    │ Cambridge   │               │ 552 B Hill St    │ Loui
   15   │   9610    │ Johnson     │               │ 1000 Mob End Rd  │ Loui
   16   │   9851    │ Black       │               │ P.O. Box 397     │ Dall
   17   │   1500    │ Thomas      │               │ RFD 2            │ Goos
   18   │   1136    │ Winder      │               │ 896 Coil St      │ Jeff
   19   │   1202    │ Thompson    │               │ 111 River St     │ New
   20   │   3626    │ O'Grady     │               │ Limrick St # 3   │ Pari

                                              Refreshing...
```

Figure A2-10 Changing a Record (Jill)

```
Coediting Customer table: Record 3 of 20                    CoEdit
Record is locked
CUSTOMER┬Cust Number┬─Last Name══┬══Balance Due══┬══Address═══════
    1   │   1245    │ Priest     │               │ 123 Hill St      │ Loui
    2   │   1690    │ Anderson   │               │ 45 Mt. Rain      │ New
    3   │   1888    │ Jones      │   527.33      │ 6610 Spruce    ◄ │ Nash
    4   │   1132    │ Smith      │               │ Haven Drive      │ Loui
    5   │   1200    │ Doe        │               │ Milltown Rd      │ Loui
    6   │   1246    │ Doe        │               │ Crossbuck Dr     │ Loui
    7   │   1176    │ Robinson   │               │ 2323 Vane St     │ Jeff
```

Figure A2-11 Attempt to Lock a Record (Jack)

```
Coediting Customer table: Record 3 of 20                    CoEdit

CUSTOMER┬Cust Number┬─Last Name══┬══Balance Due══┬──Address══════
    1   │   1245    │ Priest      │               │ 123 Hill St      │ Loui
    2   │   1690    │ Anderson    │               │ 45 Mt. Rain      │ New
    3   │   1888    │ Jones       │   527.33    ◄ │ 6610 Willow      │ Nash
    4   │   1132    │ Smith       │               │ Haven Drive      │ Loui
    5   │   1200    │ Doe         │               │ Milltown Rd      │ Loui
    6   │   1246    │ Doe         │               │ Crossbuck Dr     │ Loui
    7   │   1176    │ Robinson    │               │ 2323 Vane St     │ Jeff
    8   │   1509    │ Carson      │               │ 45 Colt St       │ Clar
    9   │   1286    │ Collins     │               │ 1223 Fork Ave    │ Jeff
   10   │   1751    │ Ross        │               │ Apt.12 Fox St    │ New
   11   │   2376    │ Baxter      │               │ # 5 Park Ave     │ New
   12   │   3726    │ Alda        │               │ 4077 Mash        │ Holl
   13   │   5171    │ Conner      │               │ Hopewell Dr      │ Clar
   14   │   5421    │ Cambridge   │               │ 552 B Hill St    │ Loui
   15   │   9610    │ Johnson     │               │ 1000 Mob End Rd  │ Loui
   16   │   9851    │ Black       │               │ P.O. Box 397     │ Dall
   17   │   1500    │ Thomas      │               │ RFD 2            │ Goos
   18   │   1136    │ Winder      │               │ 896 Coil St      │ Jeff
   19   │   1202    │ Thompson    │               │ 111 River St     │ New
   20   │   3626    │ O'Grady     │               │ Limrick St # 3   │ Pari

                                        Record has been locked by Jill
```

Jack and Jill can continue to move around the CUSTOMER table, changing various records. Whenever they both try to change the same record at the same time, one of them (the second person to try) will see the message *Record has been locked by USERNAME*. Also, from time to time, Paradox will refresh each of their screens with the changes that are being made by the other person.

What This Example Has Shown Us

This example has illustrated many of the basics of multi-user Paradox. First, notice that Jack and Jill did not have to learn anything new in order to work in multi-user Paradox. They didn't have to issue any special commands or press any special keystrokes. They just performed the same actions they would have in single-user Paradox.

Second, we saw that coediting is the preferred way to edit a table on a network. In other words, you should use the [Menu] Modify Coedit command, or press the [CoEdit] key ([Alt]-[F9]), to edit a table that you may be sharing with another user instead of using the [Menu] Modify Edit command, or the [Edit] key ([F9]).

By the way, Coedit mode is also available in single-user Paradox. In fact, coediting has some advantages over regular editing even in single-user installations. For example, Coedit gives you enhanced capabilities for dealing with key violations. Coedit is not a new feature, even though you might not have used it very often until now. However, if you're going to use Paradox on a network, you'll want to develop the habit of coediting data in shared tables.

Third, did you notice that Paradox acts as a "traffic cop," preventing multiple users from simultaneously performing different operations that might cause trouble? For example, while Jack was restructuring a table, Jill couldn't view it. While Jill was viewing a table, Jack couldn't restructure it. And although both Jack and Jill may coedit the same table at the same time, Paradox prevents them from changing the same record simultaneously.

Paradox avoids contention between users by using locks. Locking is the most important concept in understanding multi-user databases such as Paradox. Multi-user Paradox employs two types of locks: locks on tables and locks on records. Paradox sets and removes locks automatically, whenever you do anything that might affect other users on the network.

As you will see, you can also set your own locks "manually," to supplement the automatic locking that Paradox does. However, it's rarely necessary to do so. As we discuss the components of multi-user Paradox, we'll spend a great deal of time on the subject of locks.

Multi-user Basics

In this section, we'll describe the components of multi-user Paradox: installing Paradox on a network, private directories, user names, auto refresh, the Tools/Net menu, locks, Tools/Info commands, and Coedit mode versus Edit mode.

Installing Paradox on a Network

There are many brands of local area networks on the market. Each brand has its own conventions and operating instructions, and the way to install Paradox is different on each. Providing a comprehensive network installation guide would fill a whole book. The good news is that you should not have to worry about installing Paradox on a network. Your network should have one person assigned as the network administrator.

Since we don't have room in this book to cover each network in detail, we'll instead offer a few basics that apply to whatever network you have. Although far from comprehensive, the following should help you understand the process of installing Paradox on a network.

To allow multiple users on a network, you must install one copy of Paradox for every anticipated user. For example, if the maximum number of users that will be on the network at a time is 14, you'll need to install 14 copies of Paradox. On the other hand, you can purchase the Paradox NetPack, which counts as six copies. You can also mix and match NetPack copies and regular copies of Paradox in any combination. For example, two copies of the NetPack plus two copies of regular Paradox will support 14 users.

The network administrator should use the program NUPDATE, which is included on the Paradox installation disk, to set up the Paradox program files on the network. The Paradox program files themselves may reside either on the network or on the work stations' hard disks. You should experiment with various configurations to determine which way is best for you.

The file PARADOX.NET must be on the server drive. Paradox uses this file to coordinate network traffic. All users must be configured so that they use the same PARADOX.NET file.

There should be a PARADOX2.CFG file for each user or workstation. PARADOX2.CFG is created by the Custom Configuration Program (CCP). Each user must have a separate private directory, and should have a different user name. (We'll explain user names and private directories in the next few pages.) The administrator can also use the CCP to change the default auto-refresh rate for each user. Typically, each user's PARADOX2.CFG file will be in the private directory from which he or she will want to start Paradox.

For more complete instructions on installing Paradox on a network, refer to the *Network Administrator's Guide*, included with the Paradox package.

Private Directories

After you have used Paradox on a network for awhile, you might wonder how users performing queries at the same time keep their ANSWER tables from getting mixed up. After all, it makes sense for all the users to share the same version of the CUSTOMER table, but the ANSWER table must belong only to the user who creates it. Paradox can't allow Jill to replace Jack's ANSWER table before Jack has had a chance to look at it. On the other hand, Paradox shouldn't prevent Jill from performing queries of her own.

Paradox has a clever solution for this dilemma: the Private Directory. Paradox places special tables such as ANSWER into a separate directory for each user, where they don't conflict. As a result, while you are working in a network environment, you are really working in two directories at once: the regular or "public" directory, which you share with other users, and your private directory.

The public directory is typically a directory on the network server to which all Paradox users have access. You can change the public directory in which you are working by issuing the [Menu] Tools More Directory command.

The private directory must be a directory to which only you are allowed access. Often, it will be a directory on your PC's local hard disk (drive C:). However, it could also be a directory on the network server, as long as other users do not have access to it. You might decide to place your private directory on the network server, for example, if you have a diskless workstation, or if your network disk access speeds are faster than your local disk. To change your private directory, use the [Menu] Tools Net SetPrivate command.

Even though you are actually working in two directories simultaneously, Paradox gives you the illusion that you are working in only one. For example, when you issue the [Menu] View command, and press ↵ to see a list of tables, Paradox displays all the tables in both the public and private directories, intermixed. When you create a table, copy a table, or rename a table, Paradox knows into which directory to place it.

Paradox always creates and stores the following special tables in the private directory: ANSWER, CHANGED, CROSSTAB, DELETED, ENTRY, FAMILY, INSERTED, KEYVIOL, LIST, PROBLEMS, and STRUCT. In addition, Paradox will place the special scripts INSTANT.SC and INIT.SC into your private directory. If you refer to any of these tables (or scripts) while working with Paradox, Paradox will look for them in your private directory. You can use the PAL command PRIVTABLES to tell Paradox that other tables are to be created and referenced in the private directory as well.

You can always assume that tables in your private directory are for your exclusive use—just as if you have placed Full Locks on them. There is never any need for you to place locks on private directory tables. However, to be consistent, Paradox will allow you to do so.

User Names

In the examples we've looked at so far, we've seen a number of error messages such as *CUSTOMER table is locked by Jack*, and *Record has been locked by Jill*. Personalized messages like these are possible in a Paradox network because you can assign a "user name" such as *Jack* or *Jill* to each workstation.

Typically, you will set the default user name for your computer by using the CCP. The user name assigned to a workstation can be up to 15 characters long. To assign the default user name, issue the **[Menu]** Scripts **P**lay command, type **\paradox3\custom**, and press ↵. When you see the CCP menu, issue the Net UserName command. Next, Paradox will display the prompt *User Name:*. When you see this prompt, type the user name you want to use and press ↵. After you press ↵, the CCP will return to the Net menu. Select **R**eturn from this menu to return to the CCP menu. Finally, issue the **D**o-It! command to save your new user name. When you issue the Do-It! command, Paradox will ask you to describe your computer system, displaying a menu with the options HardDisk and Network. Of course, you should select Network. After you do this, Paradox will return you to the DOS prompt. Your new user name will become effective the next time you run Paradox.

You may override the default user name during a Paradox session by using the [Menu] Tools Net UserName command. When you issue this command, Paradox will display the *User Name:* prompt. After typing the new user name, press ↵ to save it.

To see a list of all the users who are currently on your Paradox network, you can issue the [Menu] Tools Info Who command. This command produces a list of active users, such as the one shown in Figure A2-12. The UserName field tells you who is currently using Paradox on the network. The Product field tells you which version of Paradox each person is using. (All versions of Paradox from 2.0 and later are network compatible. You can run different versions at different workstations in any combination.) The Product column appears only if you are using Release 2.04 or a later version of Paradox.

Figure A2-12 Tools Info Who

```
Viewing List table: Record 1 of 4                          Main

LIST        UserName          Product
    1     Jack             Paradox 2.0
    2     Jill             Paradox 2.0
    3     Hansel           Paradox OS/2
    4     Gretel           Paradox 386
```

Auto-refresh

In the example at the beginning of this appendix, we noted that as one user changes records in a table, Paradox automatically updates the screens of all users who are viewing that table. This powerful and useful feature, unique to multi-user Paradox, is known as "auto-refresh."

By default, Paradox refreshes your screen with other people's changes every three seconds. However, you can change the refresh interval to anything between one second and 3600 seconds by using the CCP, or, from within a Paradox session, by using the [Menu] Tools Net AutoRefresh command.

Typically, you'll want to leave the refresh interval setting alone. Reducing the interval speeds up refresh, but frequent refreshing slows down Paradox and might be confusing on a busy network. Increasing the interval makes it difficult to keep pace with the changes others may be making to a table you are using.

Regardless of the interval, you can force Paradox to refresh the screen any time you want by pressing the [Refresh] key, [Alt]-[R]. Furthermore, Paradox will automatically refresh a record, if necessary, whenever you lock it.

The [Menu] Tools Net Command

Many of Paradox's multi-user features are accessible through the [Menu] Tools Net command. When you issue this command, Paradox will display the menu shown in Figure A2-13. As you can see, this menu has five choices. The Lock command allows you to place or remove a lock on a table. The PreventLock command lets you prevent other people from placing locks on a table. The SetPrivate command lets you specify a private directory for placing the ANSWER table and other temporary tables. The UserName command lets you specify the name Paradox will use to identify you on the network. The AutoRefresh command allows you to tell Paradox how often to refresh your screen images with the results of other users' record changes. We will explore each of these menu options in detail.

Figure A2-13 The Tools Net Menu

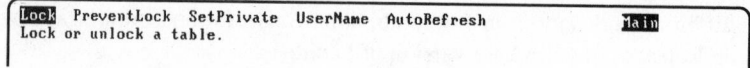

```
Lock  PreventLock  SetPrivate  UserName  AutoRefresh              Main
Lock or unlock a table.
```

Locks

As we have mentioned, Paradox uses locks to prevent two or more users on a network from performing conflicting or ambiguous actions simultaneously. In Paradox, there are two types of locks: table locks and record locks. Table locks restrict the access of other users to the tables you are using. Record locks prevent other users from changing a record at the same time you are changing it.

Locks can be placed on a table or a record manually (explicitly) or automatically by Paradox. Paradox usually applies locks to tables (or to records) automatically when there is a danger that someone's actions may conflict with something you are doing to a table. For instance, in the example at the beginning of this appendix, Paradox used a record lock to prevent Jack from changing a record Jill was editing. Likewise, Paradox used a table lock to keep Jill from viewing a table Jack was restructuring.

On the other hand, you can use the [Menu] Tools Net Lock command to apply locks to a table manually, or explicitly. You might do this to "reserve" a table that you know will be needed by a script you are about to play or to prevent someone from changing a table between two different operations you will be performing on it. (Although you set and remove table locks and record locks explicitly, most of the time it's easier to let Paradox do the locking for you automatically. The only time you'll probably consider handling locks explicitly is in a complex PAL script.)

Locking is probably the most important difference between single-user Paradox and multi-user Paradox. In this section, we'll explain this important concept.

Table Locks

Table locks control the network users' access to an entire table. They also restrict others from accessing the table you are using, preventing them from making changes and applying locks.

Types of Table Locks

There are four levels of table locks: Full Lock (*FL*), Write Lock (*WL*), Prevent Write Lock (*PWL*), and Prevent Full Lock (*PFL*). Some PAL commands require you to use the abbreviations when referring to lock levels. Even when you're not using PAL, it's convenient to use the abbreviations instead of the full names.

Full Lock (FL)

Full Lock is the most restrictive lock that can be placed on a table. When a Full Lock is placed on a table, nobody else can do anything with the table—not even view it. Paradox will not let you place an explicit or automatic Full Lock on a table if another user has placed any type of lock on it.

Table A2-1 lists the operations for which Paradox sets an automatic Full Lock. Notice, for example, that Paradox automatically places a Full Lock on a table when you use the [Menu] Modify Restructure and the [Menu] Modify Sort commands.

Table A2-1 Commands That Set an Automatic Full Lock

Action	Applies Full Lock to
Insert, ChangeTo, or Delete queries	All tables involved in the query
[Menu] Create	Table being created
[Menu] Modify Sort	Target table (may be same as source table)
[Menu] Modify Edit	Table being edited
[Menu] Modify Restructure	Table being restructured
[Menu] Report Design	Report being designed
[Menu] Report Change	Report being changed
[Menu] Image KeepSettings	Table being modified
[Menu] Tools Rename	Table being renamed
[Menu] Tools ExportImport Import	Target table
[Menu] Tools Copy	Target table
[Menu] Tools Delete	Table being deleted
[Menu] Tools More Subtract	Table being subtracted from
[Menu] Tools More Empty	Table being emptied

You can use the [Menu] Tools Net Lock command to apply a Full Lock to a table. To set a Full Lock, issue the [Menu] Tools Net Lock FullLock command, specify the table to be locked or unlocked, then select Set to lock the table or Clear to unlock it.

Remember that applying a Full Lock to a table makes it impossible for anyone else to use that table. Out of consideration to other users, therefore, you'll want to use Full Locks sparingly, and only when you are making some sweeping change to the table.

Write Lock (WL)

Write Lock prevents any user, other than yourself, from changing the contents of a table. When a Write Lock is placed on a table, other users can view and query the table—they just can't make any changes to it.

You cannot set an explicit or automatic Write Lock on a table if other users have placed a Full Lock or a Prevent Write Lock on it. However, a Write Lock may co-exist with other users' Write Locks and Prevent Full Locks.

Table A2-2 lists the cases in which Paradox will set a Write Lock on a table automatically. Note that these are operations that could run into trouble if other users were allowed to modify the source table during the process.

Table A2-2 Commands That Set an Automatic Write Lock

Action	Applies Write Lock to
[Menu] Modify Sort	Source table
[Menu] Modify MultiEntry	Source table and map table
[Menu] Tools ExportImport Export	Table being exported
[Menu] Tools Copy	Source table
[Menu] Tools Info Family	Table being analyzed and its family
[Menu] Tools More Add	Source table
[Menu] Tools More MultiAdd	Source table and map table

You can set and clear explicit Write Locks in much the same way you do Full Locks. To set a Write Lock, issue the [Menu] Tools Net Lock WriteLock command, specify the table to be locked or unlocked, then select Set to lock the table or Clear to unlock it. Explicit Write Locks are useful when you undertake an operation and must ensure that a source table remains unchanged throughout.

Prevent Write Lock (PWL)

Prevent Write Locks are defensive locks. A Prevent Write Lock does not restrict other users from reading or writing to the locked table. Instead, it simply prevents another user from setting a Write Lock on the table. Applying a Prevent Write Lock to a table tells Paradox, "I intend to make changes to this table, so I don't want anyone else to stop me."

Any number of users may place explicit or automatic Prevent Write Locks on a table simultaneously. However, you cannot place a Prevent Write Lock on a table which has been write-locked or full-locked by another user.

Table A2-3 lists the cases in which Paradox will set a Prevent Write Lock on a table automatically. These operations change the records in tables, so it's important to prevent others from write-locking the table.

Table A2-3 Commands That Set an Automatic Prevent Write Lock

Action	Applies Write Lock to
[Menu] Modify Coedit	Table being modified (while a record is locked)
[Menu] Modify DataEntry	Table being modified
[Menu] Modify MultiEntry	Target tables
[Menu] Report RangeOutput	Table for report being outputted
[Menu] Tools More Add	Target table
[Menu] Tools More MultiAdd	Target tables

You can set and clear explicit Prevent Write Locks by issuing the [Menu] Tools Net PreventLock WriteLock command, specifying the table to be locked or unlocked, then selecting Set to lock the table or Clear to unlock it.

Prevent Full Lock (PFL)

Prevent Full Locks are another defensive lock. A Prevent Full Lock prevents another user from setting a Full Lock on a table. Applying a Prevent Full Lock to a table signals your intention to read a table—to view it, report on it, or query it, for example—and ensures that the table remains available for that purpose.

Any number of users may place explicit or automatic Prevent Full Locks on a table simultaneously. Prevent Full Lock is also compatible with other users' Write Locks and Prevent Write Locks. However, you cannot place a Prevent Full Lock on a table that has been full-locked by anyone else.

Table A2-4 on the next page lists the cases in which Paradox will set a Prevent Full Lock on a table automatically. These operations read and display the contents of tables, but don't change them.

Setting Prevent Full Locks explicitly is like setting Prevent Write Locks. Just issue the [Menu] Tools Net PreventLock FullLock command, specify the table to be locked or unlocked, then select Set to lock the table or Clear to unlock it.

Table A2-4 Commands That Set an Automatic Prevent Full Lock

Action	Applies Prevent Full Lock to
View	Table being viewed (table view and form view)
Queries with check marks	Table being queried
Find queries	Table being queried
[Menu] Report	Table associated with report
[Menu] Create Borrow	Table being borrowed from
[Menu] Modify Coedit	Table being modified (when no record is locked)
[Menu] ValCheck TableLookup	Lookup table
[Menu] Forms	Table associated with form
[Menu] Tools QuerySpeedup	Table associated with query
[Menu] Tools Info Structure	Table being examined

Explicit Locks

As we have said, locks can be placed on a table or a record manually (explicitly) or automatically by Paradox. Paradox usually applies locks to tables (or to records) automatically when there is a danger that someone's actions may conflict with your work on a table.

On the other hand, you can use the [Menu] Tools Net Lock command to apply locks to a table manually, or explicitly. You might do this to "reserve" a table that you know will be needed by a script you are about to play, or to prevent someone from changing a table between two different operations you will be performing. (Although you set and remove table locks and record locks explicitly, it's usually easier to let Paradox do the locking for you automatically. The only time you'll probably consider handling locks explicitly is in a complex PAL script.)

Applying Explicit Locks

When you issue the [Menu] Tools Net Lock command, Paradox will display the menu shown in Figure A2-14. From this menu, you can place either a Full Lock or a Write Lock on a table. To apply a lock to a table, first select from this menu the type of lock you want to apply. When you do this, Paradox will prompt you for the name of the table that you want to lock. You can either type the name of the table, or press ↵ to see a menu of the tables in the current directory. Finally, Paradox will ask whether you want to set or clear the selected type of lock from the table. To set or apply the lock, choose Set.

Figure A2-14 The Tools Net Lock Menu

```
FullLock  WriteLock                                    Main
Get or release exclusive access to a table.
```

When you choose Set, Paradox will check whether other users on the network have placed on the specified table a lock that conflicts with your lock. If there is a conflict, you will see the error message *TABLENAME table is in use by USERNAME*, where *TABLENAME* is the name of the table you specified and *USERNAME* is the name of the user who has locked the table, either explicitly or automatically. Your lock will not be set. If Paradox does not see any conflicting locks, it will place your Full Lock on the table and return you to the main menu.

It is not necessary to view a table in order to place a table lock on it. In fact, you will often set explicit locks on tables before you have brought them into view.

Clearing Explicit Locks

After you have finished your work with an explicitly locked table, you must unlock the table. Don't forget to do this, or else you'll become very unpopular with your coworkers, since they may not be able to work with the table you've locked. For instance, if you have applied a Full Lock to a table and forget to remove it, no one on the network will be able to work on that table.

To remove a lock from a table, first issue the [Menu] Tools Net Lock command. When the menu shown in Figure A2-14 appears, select the type of lock you want to remove. When you do this, Paradox will prompt you for the name of the table that you want to unlock. You can either type the name of the table or press ↵ to see a menu of the tables in the current directory. Finally, Paradox will ask whether you want to set or clear the selected type of lock from the table. To clear the lock, choose Clear. This removes the lock you placed earlier, and returns you to the main menu. The table is now available to other users.

Note that explicit unlocking will only clear the explicit locks you have placed, not the automatic locks set by Paradox. Only Paradox can clear the locks that it sets automatically.

There are a number of ways to clear table locks besides explicitly unlocking them one by one. You can clear all locks by exiting from Paradox, by changing directories, by changing your user name (more on that later), or by performing a PAL RESET or UNLOCK ALL command.

An Example

To demonstrate how explicit table locking works, let's suppose that you want to restructure the CUSTOMER table to add a new field and that you then want to sort it by zip code. You don't want another user on the network to access the CUSTOMER table while you are performing this task. Therefore, you should begin by explicitly setting a Full Lock on the table.

To begin, issue the [**Menu**] Tools Net Lock command. When the menu shown in Figure A2-14 appears, choose the FullLock option. When Paradox asks what table you want to place the Full Lock on, type **CUSTOMER** and press ↵. Next, when Paradox asks whether you want to set or clear the lock, choose Set. Paradox will check whether any other user on the network has placed a lock on CUSTOMER that conflicts with your Full Lock. If so, the error message *CUSTOMER table is in use by USERNAME* will appear, and your lock will not be set. If Paradox does not see any conflicting locks, it will place your Full Lock on the CUSTOMER table, and return you to the main menu.

Once you have successfully placed the Full Lock, you will have complete and exclusive access to the CUSTOMER table. Nobody else on the network will be able to do anything with this table. They won't be able to view it, query it, report on it, set locks on it, or perform any other action on it. Anyone who tries to use the CUSTOMER table will see the message *CUSTOMER table has been locked by Yourname*.

You can now proceed with your operation, restructuring the table, then sorting it, without having to worry about any conflict. After you have completed these operations you must unlock the table. To do this, issue the [**Menu**] **T**ools **N**et **L**ock **F**ullLock command, select the **CUSTOMER** table, and choose **C**lear. This removes the lock you placed earlier, and returns you to the main menu. The table is now available to other users again. Of course, they will be able to see the changes you made to the table when you restructured and sorted it.

Explicit Locking and Automatic Locking

As we've mentioned, it usually isn't necessary to explicitly lock your tables. In most cases, it's easier to have Paradox do it for you automatically. How do you decide whether you need an explicit lock, or whether you can rely on the automatic lock?

Let's suppose that, in the previous example, you decided to perform the restructure and the sort *without* applying an explicit Full Lock to the CUSTOMER table. What would happen? When you issue the [Menu] Modify Restructure command, Paradox will automatically set the Full Lock on the CUSTOMER table. (Or tell you if it can't.) When you finish revising the table structure and press [Do-it!], Paradox clears the automatic Full Lock it placed on the CUSTOMER table. Next, you issue the [Menu] Modify Sort command. At this point, Paradox again sets a Full Lock on the CUSTOMER table automatically. After you press [Do-It!] and the sort is performed, Paradox clears the automatic lock.

Notice that, for both steps, Paradox applied and released the lock it needed automatically! If you don't need to set an explicit lock for the restructure step, and you don't need it for the sort step, why do you need it at all? The reason you need the explicit lock is because of the crucial moment between the restructure step and the sort step. At that point, Paradox has cleared its first automatic lock, but has not yet set its second lock. It may take you only a few seconds to issue the [Menu] Modify Sort command, but that might be too long. There's a "window of vulnerability" there, during which some other user can sneak in and lock the table out from under you. Then, you won't be able to proceed with the sort.

Paradox does a fine job of setting automatic locks for a single operation, but it's not able to anticipate the need for locks in a multi-step operation. Probably you will need to use explicit locks only when you are performing a multi-step operation, and even then, only when it's critical that you complete all the steps before permitting access to other users. In practice, this is rarely the case, except in complex PAL scripts.

The [Menu] Tools Info Lock command

To see a list of all the locks on a table, issue the [Menu] Tools Info Lock command. When you issue this command, Paradox will ask you for a table name. When you type the table name and press ↵, Paradox will display a list like the one in Figure A2-15. As you can see, each entry in the first field of this table contains the name of the table for which you requested lock information. Each record contains information about a different lock currently placed on that table. The entries in the UserName field list the names of the users who have placed the locks, and the LockType field shows the type of lock placed.

Figure A2-15 A List of Locks

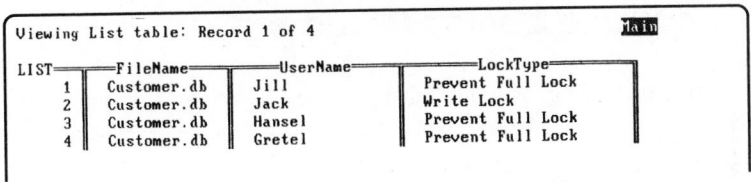

```
Viewing List table: Record 1 of 4                           Main

LIST        FileName          UserName            LockType
      1  || Customer.db  || Jill        || Prevent Full Lock
      2  || Customer.db  || Jack        || Write Lock
      3  || Customer.db  || Hansel      || Prevent Full Lock
      4  || Customer.db  || Gretel      || Prevent Full Lock
```

Notes

You can also place both automatic and explicit locks on more than one table at a time. In fact, there is no limit to the number of locks that can be placed on a table. For example, Paradox will let you place five explicit Full Locks on the CUSTOMER table. We can't see any good reason to do this, but you must be aware of this phenomenon since it can get you into trouble. If you unknowingly have placed five locks on a table, and then issue one unlock command, you'll probably think the table is unlocked. Not so—it's still locked, but now there are only four locks on it. In addition, a single table can have many locks placed on it by several users at once, as long as the locks don't conflict with each other.

Record Locking

Record locks prevent other users from changing a record at the same time you are changing it. Record locking is simpler than table locking because there is only one variety of record locking instead of four. A record is either locked or unlocked. If it's locked, only the person who locked it can modify it.

An Example

Let's look at an example to see why record locking is important in a multi-user database. Suppose Jack and Jill are both coediting the CUSTOMER table on their separate computers, and both are positioned on the record for Melinda Ross:

    Customer Name: Melinda Ross
    Balance Due: $ 1,000.00

Let's say that Jack has a $500 invoice to debit against Ms. Ross' account, while Jill has a $200 check to credit on it. If Paradox didn't allow record locking, and both Jack and Jill changed the record at approximately the same time, then trouble is likely. Jack will erase the $1,000 and replace it with $1,500. Jill will change the $1,000 to $800. Thus, Ms. Ross' closing balance will be either $1,500 or $800, instead of the correct result, $1,300.

Record locking prevents this kind of problem. Assuming Jack gets to the record first, he will lock it and change it to $1,500. Meanwhile, Jill must wait for acccess to the record. When Jack finishes his update and unlocks the record, Jill can make her change to it. But at that point, Paradox will refresh her screen, and Jill will see that the starting balance is now $1,500. So, Jill will subtract $200 from that and set the balance due to $1,300, the correct amount.

How to Lock and Unlock Records

To lock a record, you must be viewing a table in Coedit mode. You can enter Coedit mode either by using the command [Menu] Modify Coedit, or by viewing the table and pressing the [Coedit] key ([Alt]-[F9]).

The simplest way to lock a record is to begin changing it. In our initial example (Figure A2-6), as soon as Jack typed 5 into the Balance Due field of the third CUSTOMER record, Paradox locked the record for him. Paradox will always automatically lock any record you begin to change when you are coediting a table.

When you attempt to lock a record, Paradox tests to see whether the record is already locked by someone else. If it is, Paradox returns the message, *Record has been locked by USERNAME* (where *USERNAME* is the name of the user who has locked the record), and you will not be able to change the record. Otherwise, Paradox displays the message *Record is locked* at the top of the screen and changes the triangle at the right of the field into reverse video, as shown in Figure A2-6. Of course, if someone now tries to change a record you have locked, Paradox will display the message, *Record has been locked by USERNAME* (where *USERNAME* is your user name). If other users read a record that you have locked, they will see the record as it looked before you locked it. The changes you are making do not become visible to others until you unlock the record.

The simplest way to unlock a record is to move the cursor to another record. You can press ↓, ↑, [Home], [End], or any other key or combination that moves you to another record. As soon as the cursor leaves the locked record, Paradox unlocks the record and makes its new contents available to other users. This process is called "posting the record." When Paradox posts a record, it will display a message such as *Posted change to record 3*, as shown in Figure A2-8. You can also unlock a record by pressing the [Do-It!] key, or by issuing the [Menu] DO-IT! command, which switches you from Coedit mode back to Main mode.

Another way to lock and unlock a record is by pressing the [Lock Toggle] key, [Alt]-[L]. If you press [Lock Toggle] on an unlocked record, Paradox locks the record for you (unless it's locked by someone else), even though you haven't yet made any changes to it. If you press

[Lock Toggle] on a locked record, Paradox unlocks it, but leaves your cursor positioned on it. Of course, [Lock Toggle] works only when you are in Coedit mode, since you must be in Coedit to lock records.

For the most part, you can lock only one record in a table image at a time. To lock a second record, you must first unlock the first one. However, if you are viewing several tables on the workspace, you may lock one record in each. This way, you can lock related records in related tables simultaneously to ensure that they are all updated together.

When somebody else has placed a Write Lock on the table and you try to lock a record, you will get the message, *CUSTOMER table is in use by USERNAME*. If you need the constant capability to change the records in your table while you are coediting it, you should place an explicit Prevent Write Lock on the table before entering Coedit mode.

The only way you can place a record lock on more than one record at a time is if you are coediting with a multitable form that links a master table to one or more detail tables. If you lock a master record, Paradox will automatically lock all detail records linked to that master record. To ensure referential integrity based on the links between a master record and its detail records, Paradox will not lock any of the records without placing a record lock on all of them. This prevents you and another user from editing any records at the same time, which would break the links joining the records. In fact, if you press [Lock Toggle] to lock a single detail record, Paradox will lock all other linked detail records and the master record as well.

Notes

So far, we have spoken only about locks as they apply to tables. However, Paradox will also lock other sorts of objects, such as forms, reports, and scripts. These locks can only be set automatically, not explicitly. In general, they work the way you would expect. For example, while you are changing a report specification, that report is full locked, and no one else may use it or modify it until you are done. Also, when you issue the [Menu] Tools Info Family command to list all the objects in a table's family, Paradox places a Write Lock on all the objects in the family, as well as the table itself.

We have stated that there are two types of locks: record locks and table locks. In fact, there is a third type of lock, although it is used only for one special purpose: the family lock. The family lock is used to lock a table's family—that is, all reports, forms, validity checks, and settings associated with a table. You cannot explicitly set a family lock. Paradox sets and clears it automatically when you issue the [Menu] Tools Copy JustFamily command or the [Menu] Tools Copy Table command.

Queries

You may wonder how you can perform an operation, such as a query, in a multi-user environment when the data that the query is based upon might be changing even while the query is underway. For example, suppose Jack performs the query shown in Figure A2-16 on the CUSTOMER table.

Figure A2-16 A Multi-user Query

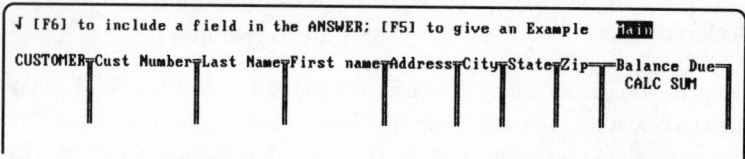

This query simply asks for the sum of the Balance Due field entries for all the records in the table. When Jack presses the [Do-It!] key to perform this query, it might take Paradox several seconds or even several minutes to process the query. What happens if Jill changes the Balance Due entries for some customers while the query is being processed? Are the new values or the old ones placed in the ANSWER table?

Paradox solves this problem by taking a "snapshot" of the table being queried immediately after the user presses [Do-It!]. That is, it makes a copy of the table (or the selected records from the table), and places that copy into the private directory. After the snapshot is made, Paradox checks to see if any user changed any records while the snapshot was being made. If so, Paradox will throw away that copy and try again until a snapshot is made without any records being changed.

Once Paradox has a successful snapshot, it can complete the query without contention, since it is working from a private copy of the table made at the moment the query was executed. The "snapshot" method guarantees data integrity in the ANSWER table, since Paradox is reporting how the data looked at one particular instant in time. If no one else is working with a table when you try to perform a query on it, Paradox skips taking the snapshot in order to reduce the time it takes to process the query.

On a busy network, the snapshot method can lead to very slow queries. If records are being changed in a table faster than Paradox can make a snapshot copy of it, Paradox might have to retry many times. In fact, it's possible the query might never finish.

If your queries seem to be taking a long time, and you believe it's because of network contention, try placing an explicit Write Lock on the table before performing the query. This will prevent other users from changing the records, and allow your query to be completed in a single attempt. Remember to clear the Write Lock once your query is finished!

Reports

Whenever you try to design, change, or edit a report based on a shared table, Paradox places a Prevent Full Lock on the table on which the report is based. If another user has already placed a Full Lock on a table, then you cannot design, change, or print a report for that table until the lock is removed.

While you are designing or changing a report, Paradox places a Full Lock on the report, in addition to the Prevent Full Lock that it places on the table. As a result, only one user can modify or print a report at one time. However, while another user is working with a report for a table, you can still work with the table itself.

Paradox handles printing, displaying, and writing a report to a file on a network in the same way it handles queries. That is, Paradox attempts to make a snapshot copy of the table if anyone else is working with it, then prints the report based on the snapshot. If another user happens to change the table while Paradox is actually taking the snapshot, Paradox will continually attempt to take the snapshot until it is successful. If Paradox is continually unable to capture a usable snapshot, you can press [Ctrl]-[Break] to halt its repeated attempts.

Graphs

Before you can graph a table, you must first be viewing it. Because, viewing a table places a Prevent Full Lock on it you cannot view or graph a table if another user has placed a Full Lock on it. However, this rarely poses a problem because most graphs are based on temporary ANSWER or CROSSTAB tables, which Paradox stores in your private directory.

When you use the [Menu] Image Graph Crosstab command or press [CrossTab] ([Alt]-[X]) to create a CROSSTAB table based on the information in a shared table, Paradox uses the snapshot approach to capture the table in its current state. Then, Paradox generates the CROSSTAB table based on the snapshot table. If no one else is using the table, or if you are cross-tabulating a private table like ANSWER, Paradox does not bother taking the snapshot.

You may realize that the information displayed on some graphs changes rapidly as a result of other users adding or changing data in the shared tables on which the graph is based. You can make Paradox automatically update a graph by recording all the steps for creating the graph in a script, then using the [Menu] Scripts RepeatPlay command to play that script over and over. As we explained in Chapter 14, you can use this command to play a script a specified number of times or to play a script continuously. Your graph script would include any queries and cross-tabulations that are needed to prepare the raw data in your tables for graphing. If you use this technique, you'll also need to use the Graph Designer's [Menu] Overall Wait command, which we explained in Chapter 12, to set a display duration for the graph you are updating. Then, as soon as the graph's display duration is complete, Paradox will play the graph script again, generating a fresh graph based on the current data in the shared tables.

Edit and Coedit

We've already stated that you should coedit tables on networks, instead of simply editing them. First, edit places a Full Lock on all the tables on the workspace. This means that while you are in Edit mode, no other user will be able to even view the tables you are using, much less change them. Second, only coediting allows for individual record locking. In addition, coediting is generally faster than regular editing and does a better job of identifying duplicate-key problems.

On the other hand, regular editing allows you to undo all the changes you've made during the editing session, using either the [Undo] key, the [Menu] Undo command, or the [Menu] Cancel command. However, in Coedit mode you may only undo the changes made to the last record you modified. This means that you have to be more careful when coediting a table.

The reason for this restriction is easy to understand. In a multi-user environment, it can be difficult, or even impossible, for Paradox to figure out how to undo all your changes. What if the records you've made changes to have been changed again by another user in the mean-time? How should Paradox undo such a record? Rather than battle with this sort of ambiguity, the designers of Paradox decided to limit Coedit mode to single record undo. In our opinion, this is a small price to pay considering all the other powers of multi-user coediting.

Multi-user PAL

In this section, we will talk about developing PAL applications in a network environment. PAL offers a variety of commands and functions that provide considerable control over the multi-user Paradox features that we've described. Tables A2-5 and A2-6 summarize these commands and functions; you'll find descriptions of them in Chapters 14, 15, and 17.

Table A2-5 Multi-user PAL Commands

PAL Command	Purpose
Lock	Sets one or more table locks
LockKey	Equivalent to [Lock Toggle] ([Alt]-[L])
LockRecord	Sets a record lock
PrivTables	Specifies private-directory tables
Refresh	Equivalent to [Alt]-[R]
SetPrivDir	Changes the private directory
SetRetryPeriod	Specifies how long to retry locking a resource
SetUserName	Changes the user name
Unlock	Clears a table lock
UnlockRecord	Clears a record lock

While the transition to multi-user Paradox is, for the most part, fairly simple, the transition from single-user PAL to multi-user PAL is a bit trickier. In fact, making the transition from single-user to multi-user PAL is more an art than a science.

To begin, you should read and understand the earlier sections of this appendix. Just as it's impossible to be a good PAL developer without understanding interactive Paradox, it's impossible to be a multi-user PAL developer without understanding the elements of multi-user Paradox, such as locks, private directories, and user names.

Table A2-6 Multi-user PAL Functions

PAL Function	Returns
ERRORUSER()	Name of the user who has locked an object
ISSHARED()	True if a file is in a shared directory, False otherwise
LOCKSTATUS()	Number of locks you have on a table
NETTYPE()	Type of network you're on
PRIVDIR()	Name of your private directory
RETRYPERIOD()	Seconds to wait to get a locked resource
USERNAME()	Your user name

One major new consideration confronts you in developing a multi-user PAL script: There are a lot more places you can go wrong. In your single-user scripts, for example, you probably follow each LOCATE command with a test to see whether the desired record was found. If you don't make tests like this, your scripts will probably fail sooner or later.

In a multi-user script, you have to make many more validity tests. For example, as you write the code for each table access and each record access, you must ask yourself, "What will happen if this table (or record or family object) is locked out by someone else?" Then, you must set up your application to deal with these possibilities: either preventing them from happening or working around them gracefully.

You'll probably want to replace your EDIT and EDITKEY commands with COEDIT and COEDITKEY. Otherwise, your scripts will lock out all other users each time someone edits a table. You'll also find it beneficial to add explicit locks and unlocks throughout your scripts. For example, at the beginning of a complex reporting script, add a LOCK command for every table to be used to guarantee that each table will be available when the script needs it.

If you don't have a network readily available, you can still do your preliminary testing on a single-user system. Include all the network commands and functions in your script as you write it. Paradox will just ignore them or return uninteresting results in a single-user environment. This allows you to test the single-user functionality of your system. When you install your application on a network, however, be sure to conduct a final round of testing.

Conclusion

In this appendix, we've discussed the elements of multi-user Paradox: network installation, private directories, user names, auto-refresh, table locking, record locking, Coedit, and multi-user PAL. We've seen that you don't have to learn very much in order to get started with Paradox on a network, since Paradox handles most of the complicated stuff for you automatically. However, as you become more advanced, Paradox offers a rich array of features you can use to develop very powerful multi-user systems.

PAL Utilities

In Chapters 13 through 17, you learned about PAL—the Paradox Application Language. In order to make PAL easier to use (and to extend its basic capabilities), Borland provides two PAL utilities with Paradox: the Paradox Personal Programmer and the Data Entry Toolkit. While complete coverage of these tools is beyond the scope of this book, we'll offer a brief overview of them in this appendix.

The Paradox Personal Programmer

The Paradox Personal Programmer is a utility that simplifies the process of creating applications in Paradox. The Personal Programmer, which is actually a complex PAL script, uses your instructions to write PAL scripts that perform many common actions. For example, you can use the Personal Programmer to create custom menus and to define the actions of the commands on those menus. These actions can include viewing and editing tables, entering data, and printing reports. The Personal Programmer also makes it possible to define customized help screens for your applications, as well as to create attractive splash screens (title pages) for your applications.

The great thing about the Personal Programmer is that it writes all (or most) of the PAL code required for your applications. The Personal Programmer can be used by almost any PAL programmer. Beginning PAL programmers can use it to build basic Paradox applications without complicated programming. Advanced programmers can use the Personal Programmer to do the easy jobs—creating menus and other basic parts of their applications—thereby avoiding hours of repetitive programming.

Basics

The Personal Programmer lets you define your applications interactively. To create an application in the Personal Programmer, you first create a subdirectory to hold all of the scripts and objects that define your application. Then, you create the tables and other objects you plan to use in the application. Next, you load the Personal Programmer and choose the Create option from its main menu, which is shown in Figure A3-1. When you do this, the Personal Programmer will ask you to supply a name for your application. Next, you specify which tables you want to use in the application. (If you did not create these tables in advance, you can create them on the fly in the Personal Programmer.) Once you have identified the tables, you design a menu for your application. Then, you define the action of each menu option, choosing from the alternatives shown on the menu definition menu: Menu, View, Report, DataEntry, Edit, Script, Help, NotDefined, and Cancel.

A3-1 The Personal Programmer Main Menu

```
Create  Modify  Summarize  Review  Play  Tools  Exit
Create a new application.
```

Most of these alternatives are self-explanatory. For example, if a menu option is defined using View, it will allow you to view all or part of one or more tables. Similarly, if you use Edit to define a menu option, that option will allow you to edit a table. The Menu option tells the Personal Programmer that the menu choice you are defining should display another menu. If you choose this option, the Personal Programmer will ask you to create another menu, and then will ask you to define each option on that menu. You can create menu systems that are up to ten levels deep. The Script option defines a menu choice to play a script that you wrote outside the Personal Programmer. The Help option tells the Personal Programmer that the menu choice you are defining should display a help screen. The NotDefined option lets you leave the action of a menu option undefined.

Many of these options ask you for more information. For instance, if you use the View option to define a menu choice, the Personal Programmer will ask you which table(s) to display, which fields to display, and which form to use. If you choose the Script option, the Personal Programmer will ask you to supply the name of the script you want to play.

When you use the View, Report, DataEntry, or Edit option to define a menu choice, and tell the Personal Programmer that you want the current operation to use more than one table, it will ask you to define a multitable view. To create this view, you fill out query forms that link the tables and specify the fields that should be included in the multitable view. This process is similar to the one you go through when using the [Menu] Modify MultiEntry SetUp command in Paradox. (Instead of using a multitable view, you can use a multitable form to view two or more tables at once.)

Once you have defined the action of each option on all of the menus in your application, the Personal Programmer will give you a chance to design a splash screen for your application. Finally, you'll see a simple Cancel/Do-It! menu. If you choose Do-It!, the Personal Programmer will write all of the scripts required to do the things you have instructed your application to do. These scripts will be saved in procedure libraries in the current directory. In addition, all of the tables, forms, reports, and queries that you have defined will be saved in the current directory.

The other options on the Personal Programmer's main menu—Modify, Summarize, Review, Play, and Tools—help you manage applications. The Modify option lets you modify an existing application. (You can also use the Script Editor to edit the scripts created by the

Personal Programmer.) The Summarize option prints several reports that document the structure and flow of your application. The Review option lets you scan an application's menu system without actually running the application. The Play option lets you play an application from within the Personal Programmer. The Tools menu includes several house-keeping tools, such as Copy, Delete, and Rename.

A Note

Although the Personal Programmer is fairly easy to learn and use, you should not expect to be able to write applications with it on the first day you work with Paradox. To use the Personal Programmer effectively, you need to have a good understanding of Paradox and of the basic building blocks of Paradox applications: tables, forms, reports, and queries. It doesn't hurt to have at least a basic understanding of PAL as well. Don't start writing your applications until you've taken the time to think your application through carefully.

The Data Entry Toolkit

The Data Entry Toolkit is a powerful utility that significantly enhances PAL's basic data entry and editing capabilities. The Toolkit gives you almost unlimited control over the process of entering data into Paradox tables. With the Toolkit, you can define automatic entries for a field as well as restrict entries based on values in other fields. In addition, you can set keys to perform special functions during data entry. You can also define special actions that will be performed automatically upon entering or exiting a field, and you can create pop-up menus that list all of the possible values for a field.

The Toolkit is a very powerful and complex tool. Before you can use it, you must have a thorough understanding of Paradox and PAL. You must understand procedures and how they work, private and global variables, and the PAL WAIT command. You'll also need a clear understanding of the difference between the PAL canvas and the Paradox workspace. Even then, mastering the Toolkit is a difficult and time-consuming process. For this reason, most PAL users will never use the Toolkit. In this appendix, we'll offer a brief overview of the Toolkit's capabilities. You can use this introduction to help you decide if you should investigate the Toolkit further.

Basics

To use the Data Entry Toolkit in an application, you replace the normal WAIT command (described in Chapter 16) with the special procedure DOWAIT(). In many ways, the DOWAIT() procedure has the same effect as the WAIT command. It lets you move through a table, making entries and changes, while the calling script is paused. However, DOWAIT() is far more powerful than WAIT because it allows you to control what happens on the workspace during the data entry process. You can think of the Toolkit as a powerful extension of Paradox's built-in validity checking, since it allows you to take almost total control over what the user does during data entry.

DOWAIT() gives you three powerful capabilities that are not readily available through regular Paradox. First, it gives you the ability to execute PAL procedures at specified times during data entry. A procedure may be called when the user enters a field or tries to move out of a field. You can also define special actions to be taken after each keystroke the user presses while in a particular field. This capability is the heart of the Toolkit. The procedures you call can do almost anything imaginable, from making automatic entries to calculating a new entry for one field based on values entered in other fields. The ability to examine each keystroke and to call procedures when the cursor enters or leaves a field lets you take complete control of the data entry process.

Second, the Toolkit lets you specify which keys a user can press and what action PAL will perform as a result of each key. You can assign each key on the keyboard to one of four categories: Regular, Illegal, Exit, or Special. The type you assign to a key tells the Toolkit how to respond to that keystroke during data entry. The Toolkit passes Regular keystrokes to Paradox in their normal form. The Toolkit will not accept Illegal keystrokes during data entry. Exit keystrokes leave the Toolkit procedures and return you to the procedure that called the Toolkit. When any key you designate as Special is pressed, a special PAL procedure you have written is called.

Third, the Toolkit lets you create pop-up menus that contain a list of selectable items that are possible entries for a field. These menus are similar to LookupHelp, but they appear in a window on the screen with the data entry table still visible underneath, rather than on a separate screen displaying just the lookup table. Toolkit procedures link pop-up menus to tables listing possible entries.

Using the Toolkit with Paradox 3

Borland substantially enhanced the Toolkit in Paradox 3. For one thing, the process of creating Toolkit applications has been overhauled. It is now more logical and easier to follow. In addition, the documentation has been vastly improved, and several new capabilities have been added, including support for multitable editing, table arrival and departure procedures, and an enhanced Form Editor utility. Unfortunately, all of these changes have resulted in some incompatibilities between the original Toolkit and the Paradox 3 Toolkit. If you have written applications using the Paradox 2 Toolkit, you'll need to make some changes before you can use them with the Paradox 3 Toolkit. If the thought of revis-ing all of your applications is more than you can bear, then you can make do by using the Paradox 2 Toolkit with Paradox 3.

Conclusion

Obviously, we have barely scratched the surface of the Personal Programmer and the Toolkit in this brief appendix. There is so much more to these utilities that it would take another complete book to do them justice! If what you have learned so far interests you, you can learn more by reading Chapter 23 of the *PAL User's Guide* and the *Guide to the Personal Programmer* you received with your copy of Paradox.

Special Versions
of Paradox

While each new release of Paradox has included enhancements to the program, Borland has also developed two special versions of Paradox designed to take advantage of the new generation of personal computers and the new OS/2 operating system. Both Paradox 386 and Paradox OS/2 feature the intuitive Paradox menu design and support multi-user network environments just like regular Paradox. However, these special versions let you reap performance benefits that would be impossible to achieve with the standard Paradox program. In this appendix, we'll briefly describe these benefits and tell you what hardware and system software you need to use these versions of Paradox.

Paradox Compatibility

Both Paradox 386 and Paradox OS/2 are completely compatible with tables and other objects, such as reports, scripts, and forms, created with regular Paradox. As a result, you can take complete applications that you designed with regular Paradox and use them with Paradox 386 or Paradox OS/2 without modifying your tables, scripts, and objects in any way.

In terms of the user interface, both of these special versions function pretty much like regular Paradox. Paradox OS/2 does include some menu commands and PAL commands that let you take advantage of the OS/2 operating system's multitasking abilities. We'll discuss these differences later in this appendix. However, if you know how to use Paradox, then you will probably have no problem using Paradox 386 or Paradox OS/2.

As *Douglas Cobb's Paradox 3 Handbook* was going to press in early 1989, Paradox 386 and Paradox OS/2 were both limited to Paradox 2 capabilities. Of course, these Paradox 2 versions wouldn't support multitable forms, multitable reports, or graphs—all features added to Paradox with Release 3.0. However, Borland representatives assured us that they plan to update both Paradox 386 and Paradox OS/2 with full Paradox 3 capabilities. These updated releases of the special versions of Paradox were expected before the end of 1989.

Paradox 386

The Paradox 386 program is coded to make optimum use of the Intel 80386 processor that drives the IBM Personal System/2 Model 80, the Compaq Deskpro 386, and other 386-based PCs. The 386 processor uses a 32-bit instruction set, compared to the 16-bit instruction set used by other PC processors. As a result, a 386-based machine running Paradox 386 can complete many Paradox operations faster than another PC running regular Paradox. In addition, Paradox 386 also picks up speed in many operations thanks to its ability to directly address the extended memory available in most 386-based machines.

Accessing Extended Memory

Extended memory is the installed regular memory above 1 megabyte. Paradox 386 can directly access up to 16 megabytes of extended memory. As a result, Paradox 386 does not have to swap its own program code, data, or your PAL code between memory and disk as much as regular Paradox. In fact, all of Paradox 386's program code is included in a single file that is loaded into memory when you run Paradox 386. Keeping program and data information in active memory speeds up several types of operations, especially those involving large tables. Some of the operations for which you can expect to see the greatest performance benefits are querying, sorting, and scrolling through large tables; developing applications with the Paradox Personal Programmer; and playing large applications that use several procedures. The more memory you have installed on your machine, the greater the performance benefits you can expect.

You can also optimize Paradox 386's memory utilization to meet your immediate needs. Usually, Paradox 386 devotes about 65 percent of available memory for the storage of data in Paradox tables. Paradox 386 uses the remaining 35 percent of memory to hold software required for Paradox activities, such as sorting and querying tables and executing PAL procedures. However, you can use the KSWAP command line option to change the percentage of memory set aside for Paradox tables. For example, suppose that you are going to work with an application that uses several procedures, but requires little room for active tables. You could set Paradox 386 to use only 40 percent of available memory for tables and save the remaining 60 percent for software by starting Paradox with this command:

        pdox386 -KSWAP 40

The *pdox386* portion of this command is the DOS command that you use to start a Paradox 386 session. The new memory allocations would remain in effect only until the end of the current Paradox 386 session.

System Requirements

To run Paradox 386, you must have a 386-based PC or network workstation. Your system must include one hard disk drive, one high-density disk drive (the software comes on high-density disks), and a minimum of 1.5 megabytes of memory, with memory above 1 megabyte configured as extended memory. As we mentioned earlier, the more memory your system has, the greater the performance benefits will be when you are working with large tables. In addition to these hardware requirements, you must also have DOS 3.0 or higher installed on your hard disk.

Paradox OS/2

Paradox was one of the first major software packages to be adapted to Microsoft's OS/2 operating system. Many PC experts expect OS/2 to replace DOS as the standard operating system because of OS/2's ability to address more than 640K of memory and its multitasking capabilities. (Paradox 386 uses special extender software to address up to 16 megabytes of RAM under DOS.) OS/2 actually lets your computer work on several tasks simultaneously, even using different software for each task, as long as your machine has enough memory to handle all of them.

The main benefits of Paradox OS/2 fall into two categories: speed and multitasking. Speed increases can be dramatic because Paradox OS/2, like Paradox 386, has the ability to address up to 16 megabytes of RAM. (Paradox OS/2 also lets you use the KSWAP command line option to control the allocation of memory.) In addition to the benefits provided by accessing extended memory, Paradox OS/2 takes full advantage of OS/2's multitasking capabilities.

Multitasking

If you start Paradox OS/2 by typing *PARADOX OS/2 -MULTI*, you can subsequently invoke additional Paradox sessions as needed. You can start another session manually through the OS/2 command line or with the new PAL SESSION command. You can also run a DOS program in the OS/2 DOS compatibility box while one or more Paradox sessions are underway. You might use this capability to toggle out of OS/2 to a spreadsheet program or to a word processor that is running concurrently.

Toggling to another OS/2 session differs from simple program swapping in that the old program continues to run in the background. If you start a long query in one Paradox OS/2 session and toggle into another session, you can do another query or report (even on the same table) while the first query is being processed. Concurrent operations can dramatically change the way you design applications. In effect, running two or more sessions concurrently is like having a network operating in your PC. Paradox OS/2 treats each MULTI session as a network user and employs all of the file-locking techniques of multi-user Paradox to protect your tables. However, because the MULTI mode maintains all the overhead of network locking, performance is slower in disk-intensive operations as opposed to Paradox OS/2 sessions that are run without the MULTI option.

The PAL command SESSION has the syntax: *SESSION [Foreground] OS/2 Command.* For example, the command *SESSION "CD \\Paradox2 & PARADOX OS/2 -MULTI Myscript"* starts another OS/2 session, changes the directory, and runs Paradox OS/2, playing a script called Myscript. The & in the command line is an OS/2 element that allows you to chain commands on a single line.

Paradox OS/2 gives you updates on the screen so you know the status of scripts that are running in background sessions during your current session. You can even write PAL code to make a script in a background session invoke another session, putting another script to work on the tasks at hand. Obviously, this technique is limited by the amount of memory available. However, when you invoke additional Paradox OS/2 sessions, they take advantage of the Paradox OS/2 program code already in memory and need memory only for data space.

System Requirements

Running Paradox OS/2 requires a 286- or 386-based PC or network workstation. Your system must include one hard disk drive, one high-density disk drive (the software comes on high-density disks), and a minimum of 3 megabytes of memory, with the memory above 640K configured as extended memory. The more memory your system has, the greater the expected performance improvements. In addition to these hardware requirements, you will also need OS/2 Standard or Extended Edition 1.0 or higher installed on your hard drive.

Conclusion

In this appendix, we introduced you to two special versions of Paradox: Paradox 386 and Paradox OS/2. From the user's viewpoint, these special versions function almost identically to regular Paradox. However, because of differences in their programming code, Paradox 386 and Paradox OS/2 let you take advantage of features found in 386-based PCs and the OS/2 operating system that you cannot access with regular Paradox. If you own a 386-based PC or have OS/2 installed on your computer, you may want to check out one of these special versions of Paradox.

Memory Management

In Chapter 1, we explained that your system must have at least 512K of RAM to run Paradox. The Paradox program files occupy much of this space while you are running the program, leaving you with substantially less memory to hold your data. However, Paradox uses a virtual memory management system (VMM) that lets you perform operations that require more memory than your computer actually has. In addition, you can speed up operations in Paradox 2 and 3 if your computer has expanded memory. In this appendix, we'll discuss how the VMM manages memory and show you a couple of ways that you can control the allocation of expanded memory if you have it on your system.

The VMM

The VMM manages available memory and disk space to make Paradox work as fast as possible. The VMM allocates memory and disk space for data in Paradox tables, the text in scripts, PAL variables and arrays, and by swapping PAL procedures into and out of memory. When any of these memory requirements need more memory than your computer has available, the VMM writes some of the data currently in memory to disk in order to make room in memory. The best thing about the VMM is that it works automatically. You never need to worry about memory management, whether you are using Paradox or playing PAL scripts.

Even though the VMM helps you get the maximum performance from your computer's available memory and disk space, there are limits to both resources. It is still possible to run out of memory if you perform certain operations involving large tables, massive scripts, or several procedures. If a situation arises in which you are approaching your memory limits, Paradox will stop the current operation and exit to DOS. To continue the operation, you may be able to provide more disk space by deleting some files from your hard drive or removing some data from memory. After taking these steps, you can return to Paradox and resume the interrupted operation by entering the EXIT command at the DOS prompt.

Expanded Memory

Paradox 2 and 3 can use the extra memory provided by two types of expanded memory boards to increase the speed of several operations. These versions of Paradox can use expanded memory to utilize RAM over the usual 640K limit imposed by DOS. Paradox supports the Expanded Memory Specification (EMS) and the Enhanced Expanded Memory Specification (EEMS). EMS is also known as the Lotus-Intel Microsoft (LIM) specification. Expanded memory boards like the Intel Above Board use this specification. (Paradox 3 supports both LIM 3 and LIM 4.0, but Paradox 2 supports only the LIM 3 specification.) EEMS is an enhanced version of the LIM specification. The AST Rampage board is an example of an EEMS board.

If you have an expanded memory board, Paradox automatically takes advantage of it. Paradox allocates all of the available expanded memory, up to 8 megabytes, in three areas: the VMM, a temporary storage area, and a disk cache.

The expanded memory that Paradox allocates to the VMM is the memory that lets Paradox break DOS's 640K barrier. Since the VMM has more memory in which to store active tables, scripts, variables, arrays, and procedures, less disk swapping is required. If you have an EMS board, then Paradox allocates the first 48K of available expanded memory to the VMM. If you have an EEMS board, then Paradox allocates the first 208K of available expanded memory to the VMM.

If there is any expanded memory left, Paradox allocates up to 192K to a temporary storage area in which it stores the program files most recently written to disk and PAL procedures most recently read from libraries. Also, when you press [DOS Big] ([Alt]-[O]), or use the PAL commands DOSBIG or RUN BIG, the suspended state of Paradox is stored in the temporary storage area. Paradox can retrieve the information in the temporary storage area much quicker than it could if the information were stored on disk. Any new information stored in the temporary storage area replaces the least recently used information currently stored in the area.

If more expanded memory is available after the temporary storage area of 192K is set up, Paradox also allocates 25 percent of the remaining memory to the temporary storage area. The other 75 percent goes to a disk cache. Paradox uses this disk cache to hold the information most recently read from or written to disk. If Paradox needs this information again, it can read it from the disk cache must faster than it could read the information from disk. However, Paradox still writes all information to disk as it would if the disk cache did not exist. This precaution ensures that no data stored in the cache will be lost in the event of a power failure or other accident.

Note that if you use the [Menu] Tools More ToDOS command, the [DOS] key ([Ctrl]-[O]), or the [DOS Big] key ([Alt]-[O]) to temporarily exit to DOS, Paradox will clear the cache to avoid interfering with other programs you might run from DOS. Also, Paradox can create a disk cache only on regular hard drives in your PC or network workstation. Paradox cannot set up a disk cache for a hard drive on a network file server, a hard disk that holds more than 32 megabytes, Bernoulli boxes, or tape backup systems.

Changing the Allocation of Expanded Memory

There are two ways that you can change the manner in which Paradox allocates expanded memory. First, you can use the command line option *emK* to limit the amount of expanded memory used by Paradox. Second, you can use the Custom Configuration Program (CCP) to change the percentage of memory allocated to the disk cache after Paradox allocates memory to the VMM and the temporary storage area.

Limiting the Amount of Expanded Memory

By default, Paradox uses all of the expanded memory available on your computer to reap the greatest performance benefits possible. However, if you are running Paradox under a system that allows two or more programs to function at the same time, you may want to limit the amount of expanded memory used by Paradox. You can do this by using the *emK* command line option when you load Paradox. The DOS command for running Paradox and limiting the amount of expanded memory used has the form

paradox(2 or 3) -emK Kused,

where *Kused* is the number of kilobytes of expanded memory that you want to use. For example, the DOS command *paradox3 -emK 1000* loads Paradox 3 and tells the program to use 1 megabyte of the available expanded memory. The command *paradox3 -emK 0* tells Paradox 3 to use no expanded memory.

Allocating Expanded Memory for the Disk Cache

You can use the CCP to change the percentages that Paradox uses when dividing this remaining expanded memory between the temporary storage area and the disk cache. Changing the distribution of expanded memory between the temporary storage area and the disk cache can lead to performance benefits, depending on the nature of your application. For example, a larger disk cache can sometimes speed up operations involving a large table. A larger temporary storage area might increase speed if your application uses a large number of procedures. Experimenting with different allocation percentages is the only way to determine the best division of expanded memory for your application.

To change the expanded memory allocations for these areas, first issue the **[Menu]** Scripts **P**lay command, type **\paradox3\Custom** at the *Script:* prompt, and press ↵. When you see the CCP main menu, issue the **Defaults EMS** command (the **More EMS** command for Paradox 2). After you do this, Paradox will present a *Percent allocated to cache:* prompt. The value that you enter at this prompt determines the percentage of remaining expanded memory that Paradox will allocate to the disk cache. For example, if you enter a value of 90, Paradox will allocate 90, rather than 75, percent of remaining expanded memory to the disk cache.

After you type the new percentage, press ↵. Next, issue the **Return** command to return to the CCP main menu.   Then, issue the **Do-It!** command and select the appropriate system configuration from the HardDisk/Network menu.   The next time you load Paradox, it will allocate expanded memory according to the percentage you specified.

Notes for Rampage Users

If you use an AST Rampage expanded memory board, you may find that pieces of hardware in your system cause memory conflicts that interfere with Paradox's use of expanded memory.   Memory conflicts can result from the use of a Rampage board with a composite color monitor, a color graphics card, an EGA card, or an IBM Token Ring Network card.

If you encounter such a memory conflict, Paradox will fail when you try to load it, and display the message *Memory conflict at....*.   You can avoid the memory conflict by changing the REMM.SYS statement in your CONFIG.SYS file, which is located in your route directory. If you have an IBM Token Ring card, your REMM.SYS statement should read either

>   DEVICE = REMM.SYS /X=CC00-CFFF

or

>   DEVICE = REMM.SYS /X=DC00-DFFF

You should consult your Token Ring card documentation to determine which statement your card requires.

If you don't have a Token Ring card, but are using a color or EGA adapter card, your REMM.SYS statement should read *DEVICE = REMM.SYS /X=B800-BFF*.

Conclusion

In this appendix, we discussed the manner in which Paradox manages memory in order to operate as quickly as possible.   After explaining how the VMM works, we showed you how Paradox allocates expanded memory.   We also showed you how to specify the manner in which Paradox allocates expanded memory.

Index

H

I